Pearson Arab World Editions—Business & Economics

The Arab world's location between three continents ensures its place at the center of an increasingly integrated global economy, as distinctive as any business culture. We think learning should be as dynamic, relevant, and engaging as the business environment. Our new Arab World Editions for Business & Economics provide this uniquely Arab perspective for students in .... d.

Each Arab World Edition integrates cases, companies, resear .... and discussions representing the diverse economic, political, ... situations across the nations that span the Arab world, whilst retaining the quality, research, and relevant global perspectives of the world's leading business thinkers.

We hope that you find this edition a valuable contribution to your teaching or business studies. We aim to set a new benchmark for contextualized learning with our adapted and new titles, and hope that they will prove a valuable contribution in the success of students and teachers along each step of their business program.

Supplementary support includes PowerPoint slides, instructor manuals, test bank generators and MyLab online tutorial and homework systems.

Titles span a range of subjects and disciplines, including:

- Management—Robbins & Coulter
- Principles of Marketing—Kotler & Armstrong
- Economics—Hubbard & O'Brien
- Statistics for Business—Benghezal
- Principles of Managerial Finance—Gitman
- Marketing Management—Kotler & Keller
- Organizational Behavior—Robbins & Judge
- Human Resource Management—Dessler
- Strategic Management—David
- Introductory Mathematical Analysis for Business, Economics, and Life and Social Sciences—Haeussler
- Marketing Research—Malhotra
- Operations Management—Heizer
- Auditing and Assurance Services—Arens

To find out more, go to www.pearson.com/middleeast/awe

PEARSON

T0342134

Marketing
Management

ARAB WORLD EDITION

PHILIP KOTLER
Northwestern University

KEVIN LANE KELLER
Dartmouth College

SALAH S. HASSAN
George Washington University

IMAD B. BAALBAKI
American University of Beirut

HAMED M. SHAMMA
American University in Cairo

Acquisitions Editor: Rasheed Roussan
Senior Development Editor: Sophie Bulbrook
Project Editors: Nicole Elliott, Bernice Luxford
    and James Benefield
Copy-editor: Nik Prowse
Proofreader: Jim Caunter
Design Manager: Sarah Fach
Permissions Editor: Rachel Thorne

Picture Researcher: Louise Edgeworth
Indexer: Indexing Specialists Ltd
Marketing Manager: Sue Mainey
Senior Manufacturing Controller: Christopher Crow
Cover Designer: Juice Creative Ltd
Typesetter: Integra
Typeface: 9.5/11.5, Minion Pro

Printed in China (GCC/01)

Pearson Education Limited
Edinburgh Gate
Harlow
Essex CM20 2JE
England

and Associated Companies throughout the world

© Pearson Education Limited 2012

First published 2012

21 20 19 18 17 16 15 14 13 12
IMP 10 9 8 7 6 5 4 3 2 1

ISBN: 978-1-4082-5273-4

PEARSON

This book is dedicated to my wife and best friend, Nancy, with love.

– PK

This book is dedicated to my wife, Punam, and my two daughters, Carolyn and Allison, with much love and thanks.

– KLK

This book is dedicated to my wife, Nesrin, and my two sons, Shareef and Ameer, with my love.

– SSH

I dedicate this work to the memory of my father, Burhan; to my self-sacrificing mother, Rabab; to my caring sisters, Thurayya, Souheir, and Salwa; to my loving wife and life partner, Annelie; and to my angels: Sarah, Roya, and Mia.

– IBB

I dedicate this book to my lovely and supportive wife, Amina, gracious parents, Shadia and Mahmoud, charming in-laws, Mona and Medhat, caring sister Rola, and dear brother Mohamed.

– HMS

About the Authors

Philip Kotler *is one of the world's leading authorities on marketing. He is the S. C. Johnson & Son Distinguished Professor of International Marketing at the Kellogg School of Management, Northwestern University. He received his master's degree at the University of Chicago and his Ph.D. at MIT, both in economics. He did postdoctoral work in mathematics at Harvard University and in behavioral science at the University of Chicago.*

*Professor Kotler is the coauthor of **Principles of Marketing** and **Marketing: An Introduction**. His **Strategic Marketing for Nonprofit Organizations**, now in its seventh edition, is the best seller in that specialized area. His other books include **Marketing Models; The New Competition; Marketing Professional Services; Strategic Marketing for Educational Institutions; Marketing for Health Care Organizations; Marketing Congregations; High Visibility; Social Marketing; Marketing Places; The Marketing of Nations; Marketing for Hospitality and Tourism; Standing Room Only: Strategies for Marketing the Performing Arts; Museum Strategy and Marketing; Marketing Moves; Kotler on Marketing; Lateral Marketing: Ten Deadly Marketing Sins;** and **Corporate Social Responsibility.***

*In addition, the Professor has published more than one hundred articles in leading journals, including the **Harvard Business Review, Sloan Management Review, Business Horizons, California Management Review, Journal of Marketing, Journal of Marketing Research, Management Science, Journal of Business Strategy,** and **Futurist.** He is the only three-time winner of the coveted Alpha Kappa Psi award for the best annual article published in the **Journal of Marketing.***

Professor Kotler was the first recipient of the American Marketing Association's (AMA) Distinguished Marketing Educator Award (1985). The European Association of Marketing Consultants and Sales Trainers awarded him their Prize for Marketing Excellence. He was chosen as the Leader in Marketing Thought by the Academic Members of the AMA in a 1975 survey. He also received the 1978 Paul Converse Award of the AMA, honoring his original contribution to marketing. In 1995, the Sales and Marketing Executives International (SMEI) named him Marketer of the Year. In 2002, Professor Kotler received the Distinguished Educator Award from the Academy of Marketing Science. He has received honorary doctoral degrees from Stockholm University, the University of Zurich, Athens University of Economics and Business, DePaul University, the Cracow School of Business and Economics, Groupe H.E.C. in Paris, the Budapest School of Economic Science and Public Administration, and the University of Economics and Business Administration in Vienna.

Professor Kotler has been a consultant to many major U.S. and foreign companies, including IBM, General Electric, AT&T, Honeywell, Bank of America, Merck, SAS Airlines, Michelin, and others in the areas of marketing strategy and planning, marketing organization, and international marketing.

He has been Chairman of the College of Marketing of the Institute of Management Sciences, a Director of the American Marketing Association, a Trustee of the Marketing Science Institute, a Director of the MAC Group, a member of the Yankelovich Advisory Board, and a member of the Copernicus Advisory Board. He was also a member of the Board of Governors of the School of the Art Institute of Chicago and a member of the Advisory Board of the Drucker Foundation. He has traveled extensively throughout Europe, Asia, and South America, advising and lecturing to many companies on global marketing opportunities.

Kevin Lane Keller *is the E. B. Osborn Professor of Marketing at the Tuck School of Business at Dartmouth College. Professor Keller has degrees from Cornell, Carnegie-Mellon, and Duke universities. At Dartmouth, he teaches MBA courses on marketing management and strategic brand management and lectures in executive programs on these topics.*

Previously, Professor Keller was on the faculty of the Graduate School of Business at Stanford University, where he also served as head of the marketing group. Additionally, he has been on the marketing faculty at the University of California at Berkeley and the University of North Carolina at Chapel Hill, been a visiting professor at Duke University and the Australian Graduate School of Management, and has two years of industry experience as Marketing Consultant for Bank of America.

*Professor Keller's general area of expertise lies in marketing strategy and planning, and branding. His specific research interest is in how understanding theories and concepts related to consumer behavior can improve marketing strategies. His research has been published in three of the major marketing journals—the **Journal of Marketing**, **Journal of Marketing Research**, and **Journal of Consumer Research**, and he has also served on the editorial review boards of these journals. With over sixty published papers, his research has been widely cited and has received numerous awards. Two of his articles, "Consumer Evaluations of Brand Extensions" and "Conceptualizing, Measuring, and Managing Customer-Based Brand Equity," were chosen by INFORMS Society for Marketing Science in March 2007 for its list of Top 20 marketing science papers written in the past 25 years that have most affected the practice of marketing science.*

Professor Keller is acknowledged as an international leader in the study of brands, branding, and strategic brand management. Actively involved with industry, he has worked on a host of different marketing projects. He has served as consultant and advisor to marketers for some of the world's most successful brands, including Accenture, American Express, Disney, Ford, Intel, Levi Strauss, Procter & Gamble, and SABMiller, and his brand consulting activities have included other top companies such as Allstate, Beiersdorf (Nivea), BlueCross BlueShield, Campbell's, Eli Lilly, ExxonMobil, General Mills, Goodyear, Kodak, Mayo Clinic, Nordstrom, Shell Oil, Starbucks, Unilever, and Young & Rubicam. He has also served as an academic trustee for the Marketing Science Institute. A popular speaker, he has conducted marketing seminars to top executives in a variety of forums.

*Professor Keller is currently conducting a variety of studies that address strategies to build, measure, and manage brand equity. His textbook on these subjects, **Strategic Brand Management**, has been adopted by top business schools and leading firms around the world and heralded as the "bible of branding."*

An avid sports, music, and film enthusiast, in his limited spare time, he has served as executive producer for one of Australia's great rock and roll treasures, The Church, as well as American power-pop legends Dwight Twilley and Tommy Keene. He is also on the Board of Directors for the Doug Flutie Jr. Foundation for Autism. Professor Keller lives in Etna, in the U.S. state of New Hampshire, with his wife, Punam (also a Tuck marketing professor), and his two daughters, Carolyn and Allison.

Dr. Salah S. Hassan *is Professor of Marketing at the George Washington University School of Business, and served as Chair of Marketing from 2005 to 2011. He received his Ph.D. in 1984 from the Ohio State University. Dr. Hassan was recognized in 2005 with the "Outstanding Marketing Teacher" award by the Academy of Marketing Science and has published well over 70 articles and papers in academic journals and trade periodicals. He was granted the "Highly Commended" award by the* **Journal of Consumer Marketing** *in 2004 for an article entitled "Understanding the New Bases for Global Market Segmentation." Dr. Hassan's research and writings have appeared in leading refereed journals such as the* **Journal of Business Research, Journal of Macromarketing, Journal of Consumer Marketing**, *and* **Journal of Travel Research**. *Dr. Hassan's opinion has been cited by leading media organizations and trade publications, such as the Chicago Tribune, REUTERS, Advertising Age, AdWEEK, Campaign, Business Monthly, Gulf Marketing Review, and Marketing News. He has published two books:* **Globalization of Consumer Markets: Structures & Strategies** *and* **Global Marketing Perspectives and Cases**.

Dr. Hassan has served on the consulting teams of several major international assignments that focused on strategic brand management, entrepreneurial marketing, economic development, destination branding, corporate branding, and CSR best-practice analysis. He has also completed numerous national and international consulting assignments and executive development programs for organizations such as: Kellogg School of Management, the World Bank, Smithsonian Institute, U.S. State Department, Ansell Healthcare Products, Raytheon International, International Institute for Tourism Studies, BlogCatalog, Winrock International, Porter/Novelli, USAID, the Fulbright Commission, International Food Institute in Australia, Saudi Arabian Airlines, the American University in Cairo, the Dubai School of Government, the American Chamber of Commerce in Egypt, and UAE National Council of Tourism & Antiquities.

In addition, Dr. Hassan has served as chairman of the board for several international conferences and as distinguished visiting professor and guest speaker for leading international universities such as King Saud University, Saudi Arabia; Dubai School of Government, UAE; State University of Management, Moscow; Kuwait University; Bahrain University; University of Puerto Rico; La-Universidad de Los Andes, Columbia; La-Universidad San Ignacio De Loyola, Peru; Griffith University, Australia; Victoria University, Australia; the American University in Cairo, Egypt; and Alexandria University, Egypt. Having lectured, consulted, and conducted research around the world, Dr. Hassan has achieved the status of an "international thought leader."

Previously, Dr. Hassan served as Chairman of the Sustainable Development Forum, a think-tank organization of experts from a variety of disciplines representing 12 countries from 5 continents, to promote a deeper understanding of global development issues. He is presently an active member of the American Marketing Association, the Academy of Marketing Science, and the International Advertising Association, and also serves on the advisory boards of several corporate and non-profit organizations as well as government agencies.

Imad B. Baalbaki

Imad B. Baalbaki *is Associate Vice President for Development at the American University of Beirut (AUB), and a Visiting Assistant Professor of Marketing at AUB's Suliman S. Olayan School of Business. He holds BBA and MBA degrees from the American University of Beirut, and a Ph.D. in Marketing and Research Methods from the Georgia Institute of Technology in Atlanta, Georgia (USA).*

Dr. Baalbaki joined the professorial ranks of the (then) Graduate School of Business and Management at AUB in 1993. Founded as the School of Commerce in 1900, the Graduate School of Business and Management is one of the largest academic units in the university. Dr. Baalbaki became Director of the School in 1997, and led the school until it became the sixth independent faculty of the American University of Beirut in academic year 2000–2001. Thereafter, Dr. Baalbaki served as Director of Development and External Affairs for the university (2001–2007), and is currently Assistant Vice President for Development at AUB.

*Dr. Baalbaki has taught courses and delivered marketing seminars in the fields of marketing and research methods in the United States, Lebanon, and the Arabian Gulf. He has researched and published in these fields in international academic journals, including leading journals such as the **Journal of the Academy of Marketing Science** and **International Marketing Review**. His article "Standardization Versus Customization in International Marketing: An Investigation Using Bridging Conjoint Analysis," published in 1995 in the **Journal of the Academy of Marketing Science**, is recognized as the first application of this technique in academia. Dr. Baalbaki's article "Patient Satisfaction with Healthcare Delivery Systems" in the **International Journal of Pharmaceutical and Healthcare Marketing** was recognized as a Highly Commended Award Winner at the Literati Network Awards for Excellence in 2009.*

Dr. Baalbaki has served as a reviewer and editorial board member for international business and marketing journals. He has participated and presented papers in numerous international and regional academic and professional business conferences in North America, Europe, the Middle East, Southeast Asia, and Australia, where he has also served as a reviewer, discussant, and session chair.

Dr. Baalbaki has contributed to the development of academic programs at universities in the Arab world, and has been consulted on higher-education development matters. He has been a member of the Arab Open University Board of Trustees since July 2010. The Arab Open University is a pan-Arab university, affiliated with the Open University in London and with branches in five Arab countries to date.

*In addition to his work on this Arab World Edition of **Marketing Management**, Dr. Baalbaki is also a coauthor, with Naresh Malhotra, of the Arab World Edition of another Pearson Publishing leading title: **Marketing Research**.*

The Office of Development at AUB is responsible for the fundraising efforts of the university and for its alumni relations. The university has two development offices, one in New York and one in Beirut. The New York Office area of responsibility extends over North America, while the Beirut Office covers the remainder of the world. Dr. Baalbaki has headed the Beirut Development Office since 2001. In 2007, the American University of Beirut successfully completed a 5-year Campaign for Excellence which had an ultimate goal of US$140 million by the date of the University's 140th anniversary. Dr. Baalbaki participated in the planning, implementation, and conclusion of what became a record-setting campaign in all aspects (total donations, number of donations, number of donors, *individual alumni participation, alumni chapter participation, and trustee participation). The campaign surpassed its goal and raised more than US$171 million, making it the largest private university fundraising campaign ever in the Arab Middle East.*

Hamed M. Shamma *is an Assistant Professor of Marketing*
at the School of Business at the American University in Cairo (AUC), Egypt. He received his Ph.D. in Marketing from the George Washington University in Washington, DC (USA). He also holds a Bachelor of Arts (BA) in Business Administration with specialization in Marketing and a Masters of Business Administration (MBA) with a double concentration in Marketing and International Business from the AUC.

Dr. Shamma's research interests are in the areas of corporate marketing, strategic brand management, and customer relationship management (CRM). He specializes in examining corporate-level issues within organizations such as corporate reputation, corporate branding, corporate image, corporate reporting, and corporate performance. As of this book's publication, he has also been working on other topics including: political marketing, marketing of e-government services, social marketing, and entrepreneurial marketing.

Dr. Shamma has over four years of corporate experience at Mobinil, a subsidiary of Orange—a leading telecommunications service provider and Egypt's leading mobile service operator. There, he was involved with corporate performance assessment, which included developing the company's balanced scorecard and corporate Key Performance Indicators (KPIs). He received several awards for his achievements at Mobinil, and was especially recognized for presenting an in-depth analysis of the prepaid market and suggesting courses of action and recommendations. His Ph.D. dissertation study—which was built on his prior experience—involved examining the corporate reputation of the major wireless operators in the U.S. as viewed by different stakeholder groups.

Dr. Shamma's papers have been published in leading journals such as the **Journal of Product and Brand Management**, **International Journal of Marketing Studies**, and **International Journal of Customer Relationship Marketing and Management**. He was invited to contribute to a book chapter with the following paper: "A Multiple Stakeholder Perspective for Measuring Corporate Brand Equity: Linking Corporate Brand Equity with Corporate Performance." He has also presented a variety of papers at leading international conferences such as the American Marketing Association Annual Conference, Academy of Marketing Science Annual Conference, Annual Macromarketing Conference, and the Society for Marketing Advances Annual Conference. He received the Best Paper Award for his paper "Customer Relationship Management in Professional Service Organizations: Factors Influencing CRM Adoption and Use in the Building Industry" presented at the Annual Society for Marketing Advances Conference in 2006.

Dr. Shamma has taught a variety of courses including marketing management, consumer behavior, marketing research, marketing strategy, and marketing of services; and has been a guest speaker for several others, including strategic brand management, advertising and promotion management, and marketing information systems. He has also conducted training and consulting for several organizations in the areas of marketing strategy, consumer perceptions analysis, and brand development and management. He has consulted and provided training to various organizations such as the Ministry of

Civil Aviation, Eva Pharma, Orange Labs, Goldman Sachs Women Entrepreneurship and Leadership, Management Center, International Advertising Association (IAA), Chartered Institute of Marketing (CIM), Future Generation Foundation, Prana for Self and Corporate Development, and Artrac, among others.

*Dr. Shamma is a reviewer for the **Journal of International Marketing**, **European Journal of Marketing**, American Marketing Association Annual Conference, and Society for Marketing Advances Annual Conference, and he is currently on the editorial board of the **International Journal of Customer Relationship Marketing & Management**. He is a member of the American Marketing Association, Academy of Marketing Science, and Society for Marketing Advances. In addition, he is a member of Global Trade Matters, a think-tank for economic and political reform policy. Dr. Shamma reviews and contributes to various leading marketing textbooks worldwide, and is also an advisor and external examiner for MBA theses. He has served as a session chair and discussant at leading academic conferences in addition to speaking and moderating at various business conferences.*

Brief Contents

Expanded Contents

PART 2   Capturing Marketing Insights   64

Feature matrix

Chapter	Chapter Title	Opening Vignette	In-Chapter Cases	Marketing Excellence
1	Defining Marketing for the Arab World	Cilantro, Egypt	Arabiata Al Shabrawy •Xerox • Emirates Airline • HSBC Bank • Mashreqbank • Carrefour • MAC Cosmetics. • KFC, Converse, Wm. Wrigley Jr. • Etisalat • Safra Defensive Driving Academy • Ben & Jerry's	Nike
2	Developing Marketing Strategies and Plans	Emirates Airline	Nike • TE Data Inc. • Brownbag • Kodak • Almarai • EgyNet • Nestlé Egypt	Intel
3	Gathering Information and Scanning the Environment	Abdul Rahman El Hallab & Sons, Lebanon	National Bank of Abu Dhabi • Information International • Toyota Prius • Agility	Google
4	Conducting Marketing Research and Forecasting Demand	Coca-Cola	InfoPro Research • TNS Global • Yahoo! Maktoob Research • Bayt.com	Maatouk 1960
5	Creating Customer Value, Satisfaction, and Loyalty	Ritz-Carlton	Hewlett-Packard Co., Dell Inc. • Abu Dhabi International Airport • Joie de Vivre • Al-Ahram Beverage Company • Commercial Bank of Qatar • Hershey Co. • Apple • Harley-Davidson • EFG-Hermes • British Broadcasting Corporation	Vodafone Egypt
6	Analyzing Consumer Markets	Mobile Communications in the Middle East	Virgin Megastore • General Motors • India's 'Gen Next' • LOHAS • Indomie Noodles • Toyota • Chipsy • Tetra Pak	Ikea
7	Analyzing Business Markets	Aramex	Cisco • RIC • Japan and Indonesia • Saudi Oger • General Motors • Karl Storz • McDonald's • Tejari • Zawya.com • Dubai Customs • Desert Diamond	GE (General Electric)
8	Identifying Market Segments and Targets	Live'ly	Stuck on You • TSC: The Sultan Center • Four Seasons • Dove • First National Bank • TNS • Starwood Hotels & Resorts • PepsiCo	HSBC
9	Creating Brand Equity	My Diamond	DHL • Allianz Group Egypt • Apple • Burger King • The Egyptian Tax Authority • Eli Lilly • Savola Group • Fawaz Alhokair and Company (JSC), Global Brands Group, and FIFA • Volvo • Harley-Davidson • Mountain Dew • Groupe Michelin, Goodyear • Bic • Armani	Procter & Gamble
10	Crafting the Brand Positioning	Isis	Crepaway • Visa versus American Express • Umpqua Bank • BMW • Roadster Diner • Aïshti • Sabek Wa Lahek • Wikipedia.org, Citizendium.org • Electrolux AB • Coca-Cola • Paper Towels	Bee
11	Dealing With Competition	Aramex	Etisalat Egypt • Ceramica Cleopatra • Gap • Air Arabia • Tarek Nour Communications • EIPICO • Al Kharafi Group • Arab Pharmaceutical Glass Co. • Sana Fashion Store	Damas

Foreword

We are extremely pleased to see the Arab World Edition of *Marketing Management*. The text was first published for the North America region, but has been enthusiastically adopted by hundreds of universities worldwide. It has become the world's leading textbook for training marketing managers. The book has been successfully adapted to meet the needs of many other countries and areas in the world including Germany, France, Italy, Canada, Australia, China, India, and Asia.

This new edition demonstrates that *Marketing Management*, in its scope and depth, effectively meets the demand of educators for a book that offers a holistic approach for developing marketing plans in various cultural and changing settings. Indeed, the text offers the most coherent treatment of marketing concepts and issues without overlooking contemporary applications and evolving business conditions.

The Arab World Edition is needed now more than ever. While maintaining the essence of the North America Edition, this Arab World version provides students with concepts, approaches, and examples relevant to the Arab culture and its business environment. We draw upon local cases and mention virtually all of the different countries in the region and their differences as well as similarities.

Professors Hassan, Baalbaki, and Shamma have done a superb job in systematically addressing strategic issues pertaining to the Arab world and in bringing the most popular marketing management text in the world to future Arab marketers.

We hope Arab educators and students alike find this edition both interesting and useful.

Philip Kotler
Kevin Lane Keller

Preface

What's New in the Arab World Edition?

As marketing techniques and organization in the Arab world have changed, so has this text. This Arab World Edition is designed not only to preserve the strengths of the *Marketing Management* text, but also to introduce new material and organization to further enhance learning about the Arab world. We retained the key theme of holistic marketing, and the recognition that 'everything matters' with marketing and that a broad, integrated perspective is often necessary. This theme is not developed so deeply, however, that it would restrict or inhibit an instructor's flexibility and teaching approach. To provide flexibility in the classroom, we have also retained the new modular structure and eight parts corresponding to the eight key marketing management tasks. This edition has been adapted to include the following:

- Many of the introductory vignettes that open each chapter have been replaced with relevant regional examples to set the stage for the chapter material to follow. By covering familiar brands or companies, the vignettes serve as great discussion starters.

- In-chapter cases have been replaced with regional cases, which are complemented by familiar global cases. Students will be able to relate to familiar companies, and will identify with the topics more, creating a more robust learning experience.

- Trends and statistics from across the region, as well as global ones, will give students a better picture of marketing management in the Arab world, and how concepts are applied in their environment, as well as globally. Regional cases are indicated by an Arab world map icon; global cases by a world map icon.

- Each chapter has one **Marketing Excellence** feature appearing at the end of each chapter to highlight innovative, insightful marketing accomplishments by leading regional and global organizations.

- Where appropriate, **Marketing Insight** and **Marketing Memo** boxes have been updated and adapted to give a regional perspective. Marketing Insight boxes delve into important marketing topics, often highlighting current research findings. Marketing Memo boxes offer practical advice and direction in dealing with various decisions at all stages of the marketing management process.

- Many in-text boxes have been adapted or replaced with regional examples, providing vivid illustrations of chapter concepts using actual companies and situations. The boxes cover a variety of products, services, and markets, and many have accompanying illustrations in the form of ads or product shots.

- Chapters are updated throughout, especially in terms of academic references.

- We have retained the **Marketing Applications**, **Marketing Debate**, and **Marketing Discussion** sections at the end of each chapter. The Marketing Applications provides two practical exercises to challenge students, and the Marketing Debate suggests opposing points of view on an important marketing topic from the chapter and asks students to take a side. Marketing Discussion identifies provocative marketing issues and allows for a personal point of view.

What is *Marketing Management: Arab World Edition* All About?

Marketing Management: An Arab World Edition is a pioneering marketing text that provides content and organization consistently reflecting current developments in marketing from an Arab world perspective. This is the first edition of *Marketing Management* that offers a focus on timely marketing concepts and case studies from the Arab world. This book offers a unique perspective on the people, markets, and culture of the Arab world. This edition is faithful to core concepts such as brand equity, customer value analysis, database marketing, e-commerce, value networks, hybrid channels, supply chain management, and integrated marketing communications. *Marketing*

Management: An Arab World Edition continues to reflect the changes in the marketing discipline over the past forty years with a perspective and focus on the Arab culture.

Firms now sell goods and services through a variety of direct and indirect channels in the Arab world. Mass advertising is not nearly as effective as it was, so marketers are exploring new forms of communication, such as experiential, viral, and entertainment marketing. Customers are telling companies what types of product or services they want and when, where, and how they want to buy them. They are increasingly reporting to other consumers what they think of specific companies and products—using e-mail, blogs, podcasts, and other digital media to do so. Company messages are becoming a smaller fraction of the total 'conversation' about products and services.

In response, companies have shifted gears from managing *product* portfolios to managing *customer* portfolios, compiling databases on individual customers so they can understand them better and construct individualized offerings and messages. They are doing less product and service standardization and more niching and customization. They are replacing monologues with customer dialogues. They are improving their methods of measuring customer profitability and customer lifetime value. They are intent on measuring the return on their marketing investment and its impact on shareholder value. They are also concerned with the ethical and social implications of their marketing decisions.

As companies change, so does their marketing organization. In the Arab world, the role of marketing is changing as major multinationals now operate in the region or consider this region as a leading growth market.

To address all these different shifts, good marketers are practicing holistic marketing. *Holistic marketing* is the development, design, and implementation of marketing programs, processes, and activities that recognize the breadth and interdependencies of today's marketing environment. Four key dimensions of holistic marketing are:

1. **Internal marketing**—ensuring everyone in the organization embraces appropriate marketing principles, especially senior management.
2. **Integrated marketing**—ensuring that multiple means of creating, delivering, and communicating value are employed and combined in the best way.
3. **Relationship marketing**—having rich, multifaceted relationships with customers, channel members, and other marketing partners.
4. **Performance marketing**—understanding returns to the business from marketing activities and programs, as well as addressing broader concerns and their legal, ethical, social, and environmental effects.

These four dimensions are woven throughout the book and at times spelled out explicitly. The text specifically addresses the following tasks that constitute modern marketing management in the 21st century:

1. Developing marketing strategies and plans
2. Capturing marketing insights and performance
3. Connecting with customers
4. Building strong brands
5. Shaping the market offerings
6. Delivering and communicating value
7. Creating successful long-term growth.

What Makes *Marketing Management* Important?

Marketing is of interest to everyone, whether they are marketing goods, services, properties, persons, places, events, information, ideas, or organizations. While maintaining its respected position among students, educators, and businesspeople, *Marketing Management* has kept up-to-date and contemporary. Students (and instructors) feel that the book is talking directly to them in terms of both content and delivery.

Marketing Management owes its marketplace success to its ability to maximize three dimensions that characterize the best marketing texts—depth, breadth, and relevance—as measured by the following criteria:

- **Depth.** Does the book have solid academic grounding? Does it contain important theoretical concepts, models, and frameworks? Does it provide conceptual guidance to solve practical problems?

- **Breadth.** Does the book cover all the right topics? Does it provide the proper amount of emphasis on those topics?

- **Relevance.** Does the book engage the reader? Is it interesting to read? Does it have lots of compelling real-life and up-to-date examples?

The thirteenth edition of Kotler and Keller's *Marketing Management*, upon which this Arab World edition is largely based, builds on the fundamental strengths of past editions that collectively distinguish it from all other marketing management texts:

- **Managerial orientation.** The book focuses on the major decisions that marketing managers and top management face in their efforts to harmonize the organization's objectives, capabilities, and resources with marketplace needs and opportunities.

- **Analytical approach.** *Marketing Management* presents conceptual tools and frameworks for analyzing recurring problems in marketing management. Cases and examples illustrate effective marketing principles, strategies, and practices.

- **Multidisciplinary perspective.** The book draws on the rich findings of various scientific disciplines—economics, behavioral science, management theory, and mathematics—for fundamental concepts and tools directly applicable to marketing challenges.

- **Universal application.** The book applies strategic thinking to the complete spectrum of marketing: products, services, persons, places, information, ideas and causes; consumer and business markets; profit and nonprofit organizations; domestic and foreign companies; small and large firms; manufacturing and intermediary businesses; and low- and high-tech industries.

- **Comprehensive and balanced coverage.** *Marketing Management* covers all the topics an informed marketing manager needs to understand in order to execute strategic, tactical, and administrative marketing.

Other features include new concepts, examples, guidelines, and developments as detailed below.

The Teaching and Learning Package

Marketing Management is an entire package of materials available to students and instructors. This edition includes a number of ancillaries designed to make the marketing management course an exciting, dynamic, interactive experience.

MyMarketingLab

MyMarketingLab gives you the opportunity to test yourself on key concepts and skills, track your progress through the course and use the personalized study plan activities—all to help you achieve success in the classroom. You can access the lab at http://middleeast.pearson.com/kotlerandkeller Features include:

- *Personalized Study Plans*—Pre- and post-tests with remediation activities directed to help you understand and apply the concepts where you need the most help.

- *Interactive Elements*—A wealth of hands-on activities and exercises let you experience and learn actively.

- *Current Events Articles*—Concise, highly relevant articles about the latest marketing-related news with thought-provoking short essay questions.

- *Critical Thinking Challenge Question*—These questions measure core critical-thinking skills through the context of marketing applications. To answer these questions, you will need to recognize assumptions, evaluate arguments, identify relevant issues, draw inferences, spot logical flaws, and recognize similarities between arguments. Knowledge of marketing content picked up through the text and the class will help you zero in on the correct issues, but you will still need to exercise critical judgment in order to get the correct answer.

Instructor's Resource Manual

The Instructor's Resource Manual includes chapter summary overviews, key teaching objectives, answers to end-of-chapter materials, Harvard Business School case suggestions, exercises, projects, and detailed lecture outlines. Also included is the feature, "Professors on the Go!" which was created with the busy professor in mind. It brings key material upfront, where an instructor who is short on time can find key points and assignments that can be incorporated into the lecture, without having to page through all the material provided for each chapter.

Test Item File

The Test Item File contains more than 3,000 multiple-choice, true–false, short-answer, and essay questions, with page references and difficulty levels provided for each question. *Please note that an entire section is dedicated to application questions.* These real-life situations take students beyond basic chapter concepts and vocabulary and ask them to apply marketing skills.

The Test Item File supports Association to Advance Collegiate Schools of Business (AACSB) International Accreditation. Each chapter of the Test Item File was prepared with the AACSB curricula standards in mind. Where appropriate, the answer line of each question* indicates a category within which the question falls. This AACSB reference helps instructors identify those test questions that support that organization's learning goals.

*Please note that not all the questions will offer an AACSB reference.

PowerPoints

This presentation includes basic outlines and key points from each chapter and has been designed for instructors who prefer to customize PowerPoints. The slides also contain advertisements and figures from the text, and discussion questions.

Marketing Management Video Gallery

Using today's popular newsmagazine format, students are taken on location and behind closed doors. Each news story profiles a well-known or up-and-coming company leading the way in its industry. A full library of video segments is available, covering key topics using leading companies. Issue-focused footage includes interviews with top executives, objective reporting by real news anchors, industry research analysts, and marketing and advertising campaign experts.

TestGen

Prentice Hall's TestGen test-generating software is available for this edition as well. This supplement is available from the *IRC Online* only (www.prenhall.com/kotler). Please note that the TestGen is NOT included on the Instructor's Resource Center on CD.

- PC/Mac compatible and preloaded with all the Test Item File questions.
- Manually or randomly view test bank questions and drag-and-drop to create a test.
- Add or modify test bank questions using the built-in Question Editor.
- Print up to 25 variations of a single test and deliver the test on a local area network using the built-in QuizMaster feature.
- Free customer support is available at media.support@pearsoned.com.

Acknowledgments

The Arab World edition bears the imprint of many people.

From Salah S. Hassan: A book of this type is unique. Although we have taken the initiative in bringing to the Arab world a pioneering adaptation of the *Marketing Management* book, it is important to acknowledge the great inspiration of Philip Kotler and Kevin Keller. Both have inspired us over the years to consider how marketing management is becoming a truly global phenomenon. While we have tried to be faithful to how they put the pieces of the marketing management map together, we would like to acknowledge the input of many reviewers who offered insightful remarks that inspired us to make this work fit within the Arab world perspective. We are very grateful to the reviewers who helped us in the selection and refinement of key marketing concepts and cases to reflect Arab culture and marketplace realities. Acknowledgment and appreciation are due to colleagues and business associates Dr. Ibrahim Hegazy, the American University in Cairo; Drs. Ahmed A. Soliman, Ahmed Al-Motawa, and Abdulrahman Al-Aali, King Saud University; Dr. Omar Ramzy, the American University in Cairo; Mr. Brendan Noonan, Emirates Airlines; Mr. Raja Trad, Leo Burnett Group; Ms. Siobhán Adams, Gulf Marketing Review; and Ms. Reina Sayegh, the George Washington University MBA Program. Also, I gratefully acknowledge the support of my colleagues and students at the Department of Marketing, GW School of Business, the George Washington University. Finally, I dedicate this book to the very special people who gave me endless emotional support and energy to complete this journey: my very caring parents Salem and Rifaat, who always inspired me to advance my career; my sisters, Thoraya and Iman; my brother, Adel; my fascinating sons, Shareef and Ameer; and my lovely wife, Nesrin, without whose endless support and inspiration a work of this magnitude would not have been possible.

From Imad B. Baalbaki: My very first word of acknowledgment has to be to my mentor Dr. Naresh K. Malhotra, my professor and Ph.D. supervisor during my doctoral studies at the Georgia Institute of Technology. Dr. Malhotra's work commitment, professional advice, meticulous attention to detail, and ethical and moral values not only guided me and my classmates at Georgia Tech through our doctoral years, but also continue to impact my academic and professional career.

I would like to acknowledge my colleagues, friends, and students at the Suliman S. Olayan School of Business at the American University of Beirut. I also recognize my colleagues at AUB's Office of Development for being my second family, and my students, past, present, and future, for enriching my experiences and my thinking. I have been blessed to be able to contribute to my community through a very noble profession—education, and at a world-class institution—the American University of Beirut.

I am indebted to several members of my immediate and extended family. My late grandparents, Afif and Samiha, my aunt Afaf, uncles Hisham and Samih, and my late uncle Addulhafiz have all embraced me with unwavering love and care, especially during my doctoral studies in the United States. A special word of thanks is also due to the Moukaddem family (Fuadi, Maya, Mashhour, and Hazem).

I owe the person I am to my parents, my late father Burhan and my mother Rabab, and my sisters Thurayya, Souheir, and Salwa. And to the one-and-only Annelie and our angels, Sarah, Roya, and Mia, I say: Thanks for being there. You are my blessing and my inspiration.

From Hamed M. Shamma: I am grateful to all my professors and colleagues who have impacted my career. They have influenced my way of thinking and provided me with timely guidance and advice. Foremost is Dr. Salah S. Hassan, my primary Ph.D. advisor at the George Washington University (GWU) and coauthor of this book. Dr. Hassan has provided me with sincere advice since the start of my Ph.D. program. His mentorship is one of a kind that I will never forget. He is a truly charismatic professor who continues to influence me. Dr. Marilyn Liebrenz-Himes, Associate Professor of Global Marketing at GWU, was very generous with her time and effort. Further, Dr. Liebrenz-Himes provided unlimited support and assistance. I am appreciative of all my respected professors at GWU, the late Dr. Salvatore Divita, Dr. Robert Dyer, Dr. Vanessa Perry, Dr. Pradeep Rau, and Dr. Lynda Maddox, who helped me in every way throughout my Ph.D.

I would like to acknowledge several faculty members of the School of Business at the American University in Cairo (AUC). Dr. Ibrahim Hegazy, Associate Professor of Marketing, was the one who initially interested me in marketing, and his outstanding marketing talents and personality encouraged me to pursue an academic career in marketing. My colleague and friend Dr. Ahmed Tolba, Assistant Professor of Marketing, was a great companion during all stages of my Ph.D. and is now as a colleague at AUC. Dr. Maha Mourad, Assistant Professor of Marketing at AUC, is always friendly and ready to cooperate at all levels. It is my pleasure to work within this amicable and collegiate marketing faculty at AUC.

I am happy to be part of the family of the AUC School of Business and to see it grow into a leading school in the region and worldwide. The Dean of the School of Business, Dr. Sherif Kamel, has helped in many ways since I joined the AUC faculty. He has always shared ideas and encouraged me to initiate and excel in my work. I always find it valuable to talk to and learn from him.

I also especially thank my research assistants, Yosra Sourour, Mona Allouba, and Manar El Batran, who helped me throughout this major work despite their busy commitments.

I owe my deepest gratitude to my family who truly encouraged me to pursue this career despite all the challenges faced throughout this journey. I am indebted for my life to you, Amina. Without your continuous support, this would not have been achieved. I greatly appreciate your understanding and unconditional support, your great personality, and your sincere encouragement to pursue this challenging task.

I owe much to my parents, Mahmoud and Shadia, who sacrificed a lot to make sure I got the best in life. I am the product of all your effort and sacrifice. The more I live, the more I feel that you were really behind all of this. You are always my source of pride and respect.

My in-laws, Medhat and Mona, are always very supportive in every aspect. Your sincerity and charm are unbeatable. I am fortunate that we are one family.

To Rola, my caring sister, and Mohamed, my brother, we await your Ph.D. completion soon. Wishing you both all the best.

The authors are indebted to the following colleagues at other universities who reviewed this new edition:

Dr. Mohammed Ibrahim Al-Habib, King Abdulaziz University, Saudi Arabia
Dr. Ahmed I. Ghoneim, Cairo University, Egypt
Michael E. Kfouri, American University of Beirut, Lebanon
Dr. Radwan Alyan Kharabsheh, the Hashemite University, Jordan
Mike Lewicki, University College Bahrain, Bahrain
Najoie I. Nasr, Haigazian University, Lebanon
Dr. Ahmed Ali Soliman, King Saud University, Saudi Arabia
Eappen Thiruvattal, University of Dubai, UAE
Philippe Vande Wiele, Bahrain Polytechnic, Bahrain

Special thanks go to Victor Sohmen for adapting the supplements (PowerPoints, Instructor's Manual and Test Bank) to accompany this Arab World Edition.

The talented staff at Pearson Publishing deserve praise for their role in the development of the Arab World Edition. We thank Rasheed Roussan, Acquisitions Editor, and Sophie Bulbrook, Senior Development Editor, for their continued support, and greatly value their constructive feedback and assistance. We also thank Project Editors Kate Sherington, Nicole Elliott, and James Benefield, and project manager Bernice Luxford. Thanks also to Fay

Gibbons and Claire Lipscomb for their work on the early stages of the project, and to Sarah Fach, Senior Designer, and Christopher Crowe, Senior Manufacturing Controller, for their contributions to this edition.

Salah S. Hassan

Professor of Marketing
School of Business
The George Washington University
Washington, D.C, USA

Imad B. Baalbaki

Associate Vice President for Development
American University of Beirut
Beirut, Lebanon

Hamed M. Shamma

Assistant Professor of Marketing
School of Business
The American University in Cairo
Cairo, Egypt

The authors would like to thank Maatouk, Karl Storz, Desert Diamond, My Diamond, the Grand Royal, Mashaweer, and Selections Antique Store for the interviews the authors conducted with them for this book.

CHAPTER 1

Cilantro, Egypt's most successful chain of modern coffee shops, utilizes careful planning and execution in formulating its marketing strategies.

In this chapter, we will address the following questions:

1. **Why is marketing important?** (pg. 3)

2. **What is the scope of marketing?** (pg. 5)

3. **What are some fundamental marketing concepts?** (pg. 12)

4. **How has marketing management changed?** (pg. 15)

5. **What are the tasks necessary for successful marketing management?** (pg. 26)

6. **How does marketing in the Arab world differ from marketing in other parts of the world?** (pg. 28)

Defining Marketing for the Arab World

Marketing is everywhere. Formally or informally, people and organizations engage in a vast number of activities that we could call marketing. Good marketing has become an increasingly vital ingredient for business success. And marketing profoundly affects our day-to-day lives. It is rooted in everything we do: from the clothes we wear, to the websites we visit, to the ads we see.

Four university students are having their lunch at Cilantro, Egypt's most successful chain of modern coffee shops, with 21 branches throughout the country. After they are all seated, they place their mobile phones, car keys, and Ray-Ban, Dolce & Gabana, and Dior sunglasses on the table. One has just bought the new iPhone and is very excited about its touch-screen display, which allows her to make calls, send text messages, check e-mail, update her Facebook status, and listen to her favorite music.

Another is excited about the new Toyota Yaris her parents have bought her, praising its practicality in the crowded streets of Cairo and its fuel efficiency. Two minutes later, they are interrupted by an Amr Diab song which turns out to be one of the students' ringtones. Another receives a call from a friend to confirm plans for dinner that night at the Studio Misr restaurant. Another checks his mobile for missed calls.

Thirty minutes later they decide to place an order for lunch. They order freshly baked breads, pastries, and vegetarian specials. But, first and foremost, they order Cilantro's Espresso Romano, Caffe Nutella, Caffe Chestnut, and cool, refreshing Eis Caffe in a tall glass with a scoop of vanilla ice cream, topped with whipped cream and a sprinkling of coffee beans.

It is important to note that these university students chose Cilantro not solely for the quality of the food, customer service, convenient location, and the savvy clientele it attracts, but also for the company's commitment to the local community, as represented in its corporate social responsibility programs and services. These students have a deep interest in being connected with their local community, as avid readers of Cilantro's own community magazine, Cilantro Central.

Good marketing is no accident, but a result of careful planning and execution. It is both an art and a science: there is constant tension between its formulated side and its creative side. It is easier to learn the formulated side, which will occupy most of our attention in this book, but we will also describe how real creativity and passion operate in many companies. In this chapter, we lay the foundation for our study by reviewing a number of important marketing concepts, tools, frameworks, and issues, paying particular attention to their application in the Arab world. ▽

The Importance of Marketing

Marketing is an activity that we do every moment as part of our lives and our life styles. People market themselves by what they wear, how they speak, and what they do. Countries market themselves as a tourist destination, as a place for investment, and as they export their products and service offerings. Companies also market their offerings in a way to differentiate them from competitors. Thus, we should all understand marketing in order to find ways to make us different and understand what customers are looking for.

Arabiata El Shabrawy   As mentioned at the beginning of the chapter, we all witness marketing in our daily lives. A perfect example that illustrates the importance of marketing is Arabiata El Shabrawy. This is a chain of oriental Egyptian restaurants which realized marvelous success followed by wide expansion. A very simple marketing strategy led El Shabrawy to flourish. Coping with environmental changes, especially the new life style of the Egyptian youth, and adapting the menu accordingly, are the main reasons for this expansion. El Shabrawy went one step further by branding itself as Arabiata El Shabrawy. To differentiate its business further, El Shabrawy provides a telephone hotline to customers and a website, which are business practices not offered by other oriental food providers in Egypt.[1]

Financial success often depends on marketing ability. Finance, operations, accounting, and other business functions will not really matter if there isn't sufficient demand for products and services so the company can make a profit. Many companies have now created a Chief Marketing Officer, or CMO, position to put marketing on a more equal footing with other senior managers such as the Chief Executive Officer (CEO) and Chief Financial Officer (CFO). Press releases from organizations of all kinds—from consumer goods makers to health care insurers and from nonprofit organizations to industrial product manufacturers—trumpet their latest marketing achievements on their websites. In the business press, countless articles are devoted to marketing strategies and tactics.

In stating their business priorities, CEOs acknowledge the importance of marketing. One survey of the top 10 challenges CEOs face around the world in 2007 revealed that among the top five were both "sustained and steady top line growth" and "customer loyalty/retention," challenges whose achievement depends heavily on marketing.[2] CEOs also recognize the importance of marketing for building brands and a loyal customer base, intangible assets that make up a large percentage of the **value** of a firm.

value the sum of the perceived tangible and intangible benefits and costs to customers.

Marketing is tricky, however, and it has been the fatal weakness of many formerly prosperous companies. Global companies such as General Motors, Kodak, Sony, and Xerox, and regional powerhouses such as Etisalat, Zain, Emirates Airline, and Aramex, have all confronted newly empowered customers and new competitors to the extent that most have had to rethink their business models.

Even market leaders such as Intel, Microsoft, and Apple recognize that they cannot afford to relax as their leadership is challenged. Jack Welch, General Electric's former CEO, repeatedly warned his company: "Change or die."

Xerox   Xerox in the Middle East changed the perception that high-quality color printing is for large businesses only. The company introduced the Phaser 6280 as its new economical color model for small businesses. By launching this cost-efficient color printer in the Middle East, Xerox successfully coped with the technological change "from black and white to colored printed material" and with new customers' needs. Xerox differentiated itself from other providers by offering a color printer at an affordable price. In the Middle East and Africa region, Xerox depends on its partners to strengthen the value that Xerox delivers to its customers.[3,4]

But making the right decisions about change isn't always easy. Marketing managers must decide what features to design into a new product, what prices to offer customers, where to sell products, and how much to spend on advertising, sales, or the internet. They must also decide on details like the exact wording or color for new packaging. The companies at greatest risk are those that fail to carefully monitor their customers and competitors and to continuously improve their value offerings. They take a short-term, sales-driven view of their business and ultimately they fail to satisfy their stockholders, employees, suppliers, and channel partners. Moreover, because of globalization, extra care should be taken in marketing, since what means something specific in one country can be translated into something totally different in another country and can negatively affect the company. For example, when Gerber started selling baby food in Africa, they used the same packaging as in the United States, with a beautiful white baby on the label. Later they learned that, in Africa, companies routinely put pictures on the label of what is inside the package, since most people can't read. Another thing to keep in mind when marketing in the Arab world is that Arabic is read from right to left, hence the need to be extremely careful in a printed commercial to make sure the message is framed correctly. Skillful marketing is a never-ending pursuit.

The Scope of Marketing

To prepare to be a marketer, you need to understand what marketing is, how it works, what is marketed, and who does the marketing.

What is Marketing?

Marketing is about identifying and meeting human and social needs. One of the shortest good definitions of marketing is "meeting needs profitably." When eBay recognized that people were unable to locate some of the items they desired most, it created an online auction clearinghouse. When IKEA noticed that people wanted good furniture at a substantially lower price, it created knock-down furniture. When the Emirate of Sharjah, the UAE, realized that expatriates wanted low-cost, affordable means of transportation for themselves and their families, it introduced Air Arabia, a no-frills airline. These firms demonstrated marketing savvy and turned a private or social need into a profitable business opportunity.

The American Marketing Association offers the following formal definition: "Marketing is the activity, set of institutions, and processes for creating, communicating, delivering, and exchanging offerings that have value for customers, clients, partners, and society at large" (American Marketing Association 2007).

Coping with these **exchange** processes calls for a considerable amount of work and skill. Marketing management takes place when at least one party to a potential exchange thinks about the means of achieving desired responses from other parties. Thus we see **marketing management** as the art and science of choosing target markets and getting, keeping, and growing customers through creating, delivering, and communicating superior customer value.

We can distinguish between a social and a managerial definition of marketing. A social definition shows the **role** marketing plays in society. In most Arab countries the social role of marketing is much appreciated, since it is closely affiliated with corporate social responsibility. This community approach is very promising and appealing due to its significant contribution to the collectivistic societies represented in the Arab world. One marketer has said that marketing's role is to "deliver a higher standard of living." Here is a social definition that serves our purpose: marketing is a societal process by which individuals and groups obtain what they need and want through creating, offering, and freely exchanging products and services of value with others.

Managers sometimes think of marketing as "the art of selling products," but many people are surprised when they hear that selling is *not* the most important part of marketing. Selling is only the tip of the marketing iceberg. Peter Drucker, a leading management theorist, puts it this way:

> There will always, one can assume, be need for some selling. But the aim of marketing is to make selling superfluous. The aim of marketing is to know and understand the customer so well that the product or service fits him and sells itself. Ideally, marketing should result in a customer who is ready to buy. All that should be needed then is to make the product or service available.[5]

When Sony designed its PlayStation 3 game system, when Apple launched its iPad tablet, and when Toyota introduced its Prius hybrid automobile, these manufacturers were swamped with orders because they had designed the 'right' product, based on doing careful marketing homework.

marketing the process of planning and executing the conception, pricing, promotion, and distribution of ideas, goods, and services to create exchanges that satisfy individual and organizational goals.

exchange the process of obtaining a desired product from someone by offering something in return.

marketing management the art and science of choosing target markets and getting, keeping, and growing customers through creating, delivering, and communicating superior customer value.

role the activities someone or something is expected to perform.

A successful new product is the result of careful marketing homework.

What is Marketed?

Marketing people market ten types of entity: goods, services, events, experiences, persons, places, properties, organizations, information, and ideas. Let's take a quick look at these categories.

GOODS Physical goods constitute the bulk of most countries' production and marketing efforts. Each year, companies around the world and the region market billions of fresh, canned, bagged, and frozen food products, and millions of cars, refrigerators, television sets, machines, and various other mainstays of a modern economy. Popular pan-Arab brands such as Americana, Juhayna, and Al Jawhara are a few examples. Not only do companies market their goods, but thanks in part to the internet, even individuals can effectively market goods. Some websites are now used to help individuals sell anything they have to anyone around the world. Notable examples are eBay and souq.com, where one can register as a user and list any item to sell, and people will bid to buy the item. Souq.com is attracting customers from the UAE, Egypt, Kuwait, Jordan, and Saudi Arabia.

SERVICES As economies advance, a growing proportion of their activities focuses on the production of services. Developed economies usually have a 70/30 services-to-goods mix. Developing countries concentrate more on selling manufactured goods to their own populations and to other developed nations.[6] Services include the work of airlines such as Emirates Airline, hotel chains like Rotana, car rental firms, barbers and beauticians such as Pace e Luce, maintenance and repair people, accountants, bankers, lawyers, engineers, contractors such as Consolidated Contractors Company (CCC), doctors, software programmers such as Murex Services, telecommunication companies such as Zain and Mobinil, television and news networks such as Al Jazeera, and management consultants. Many market offerings consist of a variable mix of goods and services. At a fast-food restaurant such as Kudu, for example, the customer consumes both a product and a service. All these examples are Arab-based companies that have acquired regional and sometimes global recognition.

Emirates Airline   After Gulf Air decided to stop its flights to and from Dubai in 1985, HH Sheikh Ahmed bin Saeed Al Maktoum identified the need for a new international airline that would satisfy travelers' need for Dubai to become a connecting hub to the rest of the world, hence the birth of Emirates Airline in 1985. Covering only three destinations at first—Bombay, Karachi, and Delhi—with two aircraft leased from Pakistan International Airlines, Emirates Airline now owns 137 aircraft and covers 100 destinations on six continents. Emirates identified opportunities and is emerging as a global icon offering customer satisfaction through high-quality service.

EVENTS Marketers promote time-based events, such as major trade shows like Dubai's Cityscape, artistic performances such as attending a Cairo Opera House performance by Smithsonian Jazz Master Works Orchestra, festivals such as the Baalbeck Festival in Lebanon or the Dubai Shopping Festival, and company anniversaries. Global and regional sporting events such as the Olympics, the World Cup, the Formula One Grand Prix, and the Gulf Cooperation

Council Football Cup are promoted aggressively to both companies and fans. For example, the addition of Bahrain and Abu Dhabi as two new circuits in the Formula One Grand Prix tour has significantly contributed to the expansion of the fan base of this sport across the region.

EXPERIENCES By coordinating several services and goods, a firm can create, stage, and market experiences. Walt Disney's Magic Kingdom theme park, part of the Walt Disney World resort in Florida, represents this kind of experiential marketing, allowing customers to visit a fairy kingdom, a pirate ship, or a haunted house. There is also a market for customized experiences, such as spending a week at Al-Ahly football camp playing with football masters such as Abu Treka, going on a Bedouin jeep safari in Dubai, or taking scuba-diving lessons in the Red Sea.

Companies such as PepsiCo use celebrity endorsement to promote their brands.

PERSONS Celebrity marketing is a major business. Artists, musicians, CEOs, physicians, high-profile lawyers and financiers, and other professionals all get help from celebrity marketers.[7] Some people have done a masterful job of marketing themselves: think of football star David Beckham, TV host Oprah Winfrey, and music legends the Rolling Stones. Some companies, like Coca-Cola and PepsiCo, use artists such as Haifa Wehbe, Wael Kfoury, Ahmed Sherif, Nancy Ajram, and others to expand their market share in the soft drinks industry. Management consultant Tom Peters, himself a master at self-branding, has advised each person to become a 'brand.'

PLACES Cities, states, regions, and whole nations compete actively to attract tourists, factories, company headquarters, and new residents.[8] Place marketers include economic development specialists, real estate agents, commercial banks, local business associations, and advertising and **public relations** agencies. Ministries of tourism all over the world, including those in Lebanon, Oman, Egypt, Jordan, and the UAE among others, work hard to promote their country and attract the largest number of tourists. Religious tourism is of special and unique importance in the Arab world. Saudi Arabia attracts more than 15 million visitors each year to perform the religious duties of *Hajj* and *Umra*. Lebanon, Syria, and Jordan also attract millions of Christians from the region and all over the world to visit religious sites.

public relations   a variety of programs designed to promote or protect a company's image or its individual products.

PROPERTIES Properties refers to intangible rights of ownership of either real property (real estate) or financial property (stocks and bonds). Properties are bought and sold, and these exchanges require marketing. Real estate developers, such as Emaar or Tameer, or real estate agents who work for property owners or sellers, buy and sell residential or commercial real estate. Investment companies and banks market securities to both institutional and individual investors.

ORGANIZATIONS Organizations actively work to build a strong, favorable, and unique image in the minds of their target publics. In the United Kingdom, Tesco's "Every Little Helps" marketing program reflects the food marketer's attention to detail in everything it does, within as well as outside the store, and in the community and the environment. The campaign has vaulted Tesco to the top of the UK supermarket chain industry. Universities such as the American University of Beirut, museums such as the Cairo Museum, cultural centers such as the El Sawy Cultural Wheel in Egypt, performing arts organizations, sporting clubs such as the Al Hilal Club in Saudi Arabia, and nonprofit organizations such as YAL (Young Arab Leaders) all use marketing to boost their public image and to compete for audiences and funds. Corporate identity campaigns are the result of intensive market research programs. This is certainly the case with HSBC Bank's "The World's Local Bank" campaign.

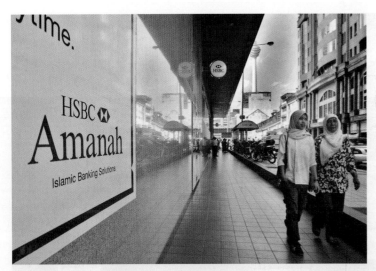

HSBC's corporate identity campaign in the Arab world recognized the demand for Islamic banking in the region.

HSBC Bank   Hong Kong and Shanghai Banking Corporation, HSBC, one of the top three banks worldwide, wanted to market themselves as a local bank in each country in which they operate. To maintain their international brand, a branch's layout is similar regardless of which country the branch operates in. The same colors, red and gray, are used all around the world; employees can also be identified by the colors of their uniform. Most of the products are used internationally as well. The Premier account, for customers with a deposit of US$100,000 or more, or the equivalent in other currencies, can be opened in any country. In addition, to make it more 'local,' a Premier customer from Lebanon, for example, can be on vacation in the United Kingdom, visit any HSBC branch, and be assisted. The local aspect is also maintained in the products. In the Arab world, HSBC identified the need and high demand for Islamic banking, and hence introduced the Sharia Mortgage and the Amanah brand. The other local aspect is the uniform, which can be tailored to the culture in which the bank is operating, for example, long skirts for the Arab world, saris for India.[9]

INFORMATION Information is essentially what books, schools, and universities produce, market, and distribute at a price to parents, students, and communities. Magazines such as *SportAuto*, *Hiteck*, *Laha*, and *Jamalouki* supply information about the car, computer, and fashion worlds, respectively. Newspapers such as the Egyptian-based *Al-Ahram*, Lebanese-based *The Daily Star*, or Saudi-based *Al-Sharq Al-Awsat* supply daily news to a wide range of readers. The production, packaging, and distribution of information is one of our society's major industries.[10] Even companies that sell physical products attempt to add value through the use of information. For example, the CEO of Siemens Medical Systems, Tom McCausland, says, "[our product] is not necessarily an X-ray or an MRI, but information. Our business is really health-care information technology, and our end product is really an electronic patient record: information on lab tests, pathology, and drugs as well as voice dictation."[11]

marketer   someone who seeks a response (attention, a purchase, a vote, a donation) from another party, called the prospect.

prospect   a third party that a marketer seeks a response—a purchase, a vote, a donation—from.

IDEAS Every market offering includes a basic idea. Products and services are platforms for delivering some idea or benefit. Social marketers are busy promoting ideas such as "*Al-baraka bil-shabab*" ("youth is a blessing"), "a mind is a terrible thing to waste," "optimize electricity consumption," or "quit smoking."

Magazines provide useful information on specialist subjects such as fashion.

Who Markets?

MARKETERS AND PROSPECTS A **marketer** is someone who seeks a response—attention, a purchase, a vote, a donation—from another party, called the **prospect.** If two parties are seeking to sell something to each other, we call them both marketers.

Marketers are indeed skilled at stimulating demand for their company's products, but that's too limited a view of the tasks they perform. Just as production and logistics professionals are responsible for supply management, marketers are responsible for demand management. Marketing managers seek to influence the level, timing, and composition of demand to meet the organization's objectives. Eight demand states are possible:

1. ***Negative demand:*** consumers dislike the product and may even pay a price to avoid it.

2. *Nonexistent demand:* consumers may be unaware of or uninterested in the product.
3. *Latent demand:* consumers may share a strong need that cannot be satisfied by an existing product.
4. *Declining demand:* consumers begin to buy the product less frequently or not at all.
5. *Irregular demand:* consumer purchases vary on a seasonal, monthly, weekly, daily, or even hourly basis.
6. *Full demand:* consumers are adequately buying all products put into the marketplace.
7. *Overfull demand:* more consumers would like to buy the product than can be satisfied.
8. *Unwholesome demand:* consumers may be attracted to products that have undesirable social consequences.

In each case, marketers must identify the underlying cause(s) of the demand state and then determine a plan of action to shift the demand to a more desired state.

MARKETS   Traditionally, a market was a physical place where buyers and sellers gathered to buy and sell goods. Economists describe a **market** as a collection of buyers and sellers who transact over a particular product or product class (such as the housing market or the grain market).

Five basic markets and their connecting flows are shown in ◭ **Figure 1.1**. Manufacturers go to resource markets (raw material markets, labor markets, money markets), buy resources and turn them into goods and services, and then sell finished products to intermediaries, who sell them to consumers. Consumers sell their labor and receive money with which they pay for goods and services. The government collects tax revenues to buy goods from resource, manufacturer, and intermediary markets and uses these goods and services to provide public services. Each nation's economy, and the global economy, consists of complex interacting sets of markets linked through exchange processes.

Marketers often use the term market to cover various groupings of customers. They view sellers as constituting the industry, and buyers as constituting the market. They talk about need markets (the diet-seeking market), product markets (the shoe market), demographic markets (the youth market), and geographic markets (the Saudi market); or they extend the concept to cover other markets. These might include voter markets, where politicians market themselves through campaigns, videos, and talk shows; labor markets, where jobseekers market themselves using their resumés and LinkedIn profiles and companies market themselves by posting jobs and positions that they need to fill; and donor markets where, in some countries, people register to be organ donors so that, in case of death, they may donate some of their organs to patients in need of a transplant.

◭ **Figure 1.2** shows the relationship between the industry and the market. Sellers and buyers are connected by four flows. The sellers send goods and services, and communications such as ads and direct mail to the market; in return they receive money and information such as customer attitudes and sales data. The inner loop shows an exchange of money for goods and services; the outer loop shows an exchange of information.

market   the set of all actual and potential buyers of a product or service.

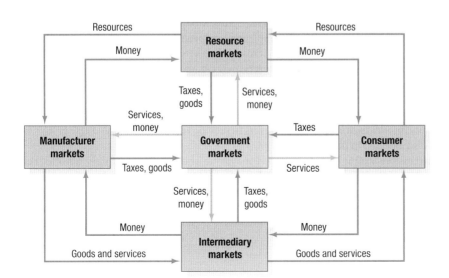

|Fig. 1.1| ◭

Structure of Flows in a Modern Exchange Economy

|Fig. 1.2| ▲

A Simple Marketing System

brand image   the perceptions and beliefs held by consumers, as reflected in the associations held in consumer memory.

KEY CUSTOMER MARKETS   Consider the following key customer markets: consumer, business, global, and nonprofit.

Consumer Markets   Companies selling mass consumer goods and services such as refreshments (Pepsi or Pampa), tea (Lipton or El-Arousa), chocolate (KitKat or Katakit) cosmetics (L'Oreal or Dali), and air travel (Air France or Qatar Airways) spend a great deal of time trying to establish a superior **brand image**. Much of a brand's strength depends on developing a superior product and packaging, ensuring its availability, and backing it with engaging communications and reliable service.

Business Markets   Companies selling business goods and services, such as raw materials used by manufacturers, often face well-trained and well-informed professional buyers who are skilled at evaluating competitive offerings. Business buyers buy goods in order to make or resell a product to others at a profit. Business marketers must demonstrate how their products will help these buyers achieve higher revenue or lower costs. Advertising can play a role, but the sales force, price, and the company's reputation for reliability and quality may play a stronger one.

Global Markets   Companies selling goods and services in the global marketplace face additional decisions and challenges. They must decide which countries to enter; how to enter each (as an exporter, licenser, joint venture partner, contract manufacturer, or solo manufacturer); how to adapt their product and service features to each country; how to price their products in different countries; and how to adapt their communications to fit different cultures. They make these decisions in the face of different requirements for buying, negotiating, owning, and disposing of property; different culture, language, and legal and political systems; and currencies that might fluctuate in value. Yet, the payoff for doing all this additional legwork can be huge.

Nonprofit and Governmental Markets   Companies selling their goods to nonprofit organizations such as churches, universities, charitable organizations, and government agencies need to price carefully, because these buyers have limited purchasing power. Lower selling prices affect the features and quality the seller can build into the offering. Most government purchasing calls for bids, and buyers often favor the lowest bid in the absence of extenuating factors.

MARKETPLACES, MARKETSPACES, AND METAMARKETS   The *marketplace* is physical, such as a store you shop in; *marketspace* is digital, as when you shop on the internet.[12]

At Northwestern University in the United States, Mohan Sawhney has proposed the concept of a *metamarket* to describe a cluster of complementary products and services that are closely related in the minds of consumers, but spread across a diverse set of industries. The automobile metamarket consists of automobile manufacturers, new car and used car dealers, financing companies, insurance companies, mechanics, spare parts dealers, service shops, auto magazines, classified auto ads in newspapers, and auto sites on the internet.

In purchasing a car, a buyer will get involved in many parts of this metamarket, and this creates an opportunity for *metamediaries* to assist buyers in moving seamlessly through these groups, although they are disconnected in physical space.

An interesting example is *Automarket* magazine and its supplementary automarket.com.lb website. The website offers car buyers or sellers of used and new cars a number of services, including valuable information about features, prices, and the technical comparison of different automobiles. The website also offers information about auto insurance and car financing, with comparison tables between various insurance and banking alternatives. The service also offers an online auto store powered by amazon.com.

Marketing in Practice

How is marketing done? Increasingly, marketing is not done only by the marketing department. Marketing needs to affect every aspect of the customer experience, meaning that marketers must properly manage all possible touch points: store layouts, package designs, product functions, employee training, and shipping and logistics methods. Marketing must also be heavily involved in key general management activities, such as product innovation and new business development.

To create a strong marketing organization, marketers must think like executives in other departments, and executives in other departments must think more like marketers.[13] Companies generally establish a marketing department to be responsible for creating and delivering customer value, but as the late David Packard of Hewlett-Packard observed, "Marketing is far too important to leave to the marketing department." Companies now know that every employee has an impact on the customer and must see the customer as the source of the company's prosperity. So they're beginning to emphasize interdepartmental teamwork to manage key processes. They're also placing more emphasis on the smooth management of core business processes, such as new-product realization, customer acquisition and retention, and order fulfillment. Moreover, all the functions in organizations are intertwined nowadays, as can be seen in the processes of Mashreq, a financial institution founded in the UAE.

Automarket.com is a metamediary website that helps prospective car buyers navigate the automobile metamarket online.

Mashreqbank

When Nabeel Malik, CMO of Mashreqbank, the UAE's sixth largest bank, was asked about recent legislative changes in the UAE, he said, "The change to land ownership rules has fundamentally changed the market and it has forced banks, including Mashreqbank, to change their approach." He said that the bank has now moved from a product-push approach to a relationship-based sales approach, reflecting the fact that as homeowners, expatriates living in the UAE—who represent a substantial number of Mashreq customers—are settling down rather than leaving after 3 or 4 years. "This has altered the business model for banking in the country; credit cards are still important, but there is now a very big opportunity in mortgages, and more fundamentally, relationship banking."[14]

In practice, marketing follows a logical process. The marketing 'planning' process consists of analyzing marketing opportunities; selecting target markets; designing marketing strategies; developing marketing programs; and managing the marketing effort. In highly competitive marketplaces, however, marketing planning is more fluid and is continually refreshed. Companies must always be moving forward with marketing programs, innovating products and services, and staying in touch with customer needs, seeking new advantages rather than relying on past strengths.

The changing new marketing environment is putting considerable demands on marketing executives. Marketers must have diverse quantitative and qualitative skills, an entrepreneurial attitude, and a keen understanding of how marketing can create value within their organization.[15] Harvard's John Quelch and Gail McGovern note that there is tremendous variability in the responsibilities and job descriptions for CMOs.[16] They offer eight ways to improve CMO success (see **Box 1.1**).

BOX 1.1   Improving CMO Success

1. **Make the mission and responsibilities clear.** Be certain that the case for having a CMO is strong and the mission is well understood by leaders in the organization, particularly the CEO, the board, and line management. Without a clear need (real or perceived), the role will be rejected by the organization.

2. **Fit the role to the marketing culture and structure.** Avoid having a CMO in a marketing-led company that has many individual brands rather than a single corporate umbrella, unless the person appointed to the position is a well-connected insider.

3. **Choose a CMO who is compatible with the CEO.** Beware of the CEO who wants to hire a CMO but doesn't want to relinquish any marketing control. Find a CEO who recognizes his or her responsibility to be the cheerleader for marketing and the brand, but realizes the need to be guided and coached by a marketing specialist.

4. **Remember that showpeople don't succeed.** The CMO should work hard to ensure the CEO is successful at being the principal cheerleader for the brand.

5. **Match the personality with the CMO type.** Be certain that the chief marketer has the right skills and personality for whichever of the three CMO models he or she might fill (VP of Marketing Services, Classic CMO, or 'Super' CMO). There is little tolerance for on-the-job training.

6. **Make line managers marketing heroes.** By stretching their marketing budgets, CMOs can improve a division's marketing productivity and help business unit leaders increase their top-line revenues.

7. **Infiltrate the line organization.** Have the CMO support the placement of marketing professionals from the corporate marketing department into divisional marketing roles. Provide input from the CMO into the annual reviews of line marketers.

8. **Require right-brain and left-brain skills.** The most successful CMO will have strong creative and technical marketing expertise, be politically savvy, and have the interpersonal skills to be a great leader and manager.

Source: "The Fall and Rise of the CMO", *strategy+business*, (Gail McGovern and John A. Quelch 2004), Winter 2004, published by Booz & Company Inc. Copyright © 2004. All rights reserved. www.strategy-business.com.

Core Marketing Concepts

To understand the marketing function, we need to understand the following core set of concepts.

Needs, Wants, and Demands

Needs are the basic human requirements. People need air, food, water, clothing, and shelter to survive. People also have strong needs for recreation, education, and entertainment. These needs become *wants* when they are directed to specific objects that might satisfy the need. Wants are shaped by our society. A consumer in Lebanon needs food, but may want *mankousheh* or a *shawarma* with laban. A person in Egypt needs food but may want a *falafel* or *taamiyya*, pickles, and tea. *Demands* are wants for specific products backed by an ability to pay. Many people want a Mercedes; only a few are willing and able to buy one. Companies must measure not only how many people want their product, but also how many would actually be willing and able to buy it.

These distinctions shed light on the frequent criticism that "marketers create needs" or "marketers get people to buy things they don't want." Marketers do not create needs: needs pre-exist marketers. Marketers, along with other societal factors, influence wants. Marketers might promote the idea that a Mercedes would satisfy a person's need for social **status**. They do not, however, create the need for social status.

Understanding customer needs and wants is not always simple. Some customers have needs of which they are not fully conscious, or they cannot articulate these needs, or they use words that require some interpretation. What does it mean when the customer asks for a "powerful" car,

status   one's position within his or her own hierarchy or culture.

a "fast" motorcycle, an "attractive" bathing suit, or a "restful" hotel? The marketer must probe further. We can distinguish among five types of need:

1. Stated needs (the customer wants an inexpensive car).
2. Real needs (the customer wants a car the operating cost of which, not initial price, is low).
3. Unstated needs (the customer expects good service from the dealer).
4. Delight needs (the customer would like the dealer to include an onboard navigation system).
5. Secret needs (the customer wants friends to see him as a savvy consumer).

Responding only to the stated need may shortchange the customer. Many consumers do not know what they want in a product. Consumers did not know much about mobile phones when they were first introduced, and Nokia and Ericsson fought to shape consumer **perceptions** of them. Simply giving customers what they want isn't enough any more: to gain an edge companies must help customers learn what they want.

> **perceptions** the process by which an individual selects, organizes, and interprets information to create a meaningful picture of the world.

Target Markets, Positioning, and Segmentation

A marketer can rarely satisfy everyone in a market. Not everyone likes the same hotel room, restaurant, automobile, college, or movie. Therefore, marketers start by dividing the market into segments. They identify and profile distinct groups of buyers who might prefer or require varying product and service mixes by examining demographic, psychographic, and behavioral differences among buyers.

Carrefour   Carrefour was introduced into several markets in the Arab world, including Egypt, the UAE, Qatar, and Saudi Arabia. Carrefour penetrated these markets to serve the needs of price-sensitive customers. Furthermore, it is seen as a place where families would spend their weekend outings. Arab families nowadays prefer shopping at giant retailers like Carrefour to meet their modern shopping preferences.

After identifying market segments, the marketer then decides which present the greatest opportunity: which are its **target markets**. For each, the firm develops a *market offering* that it *positions* in the minds of the target buyers as delivering some central benefit(s). For example, Volvo develops its cars for buyers to whom safety is a major concern. Volvo, therefore, positions its car as the safest a customer can buy. Companies do best when they choose their target market(s) carefully and prepare tailored marketing programs.

> **target market** the part of the qualified available market the company decides to pursue.
>
> **value proposition** the whole cluster of benefits the company promises to deliver.
>
> **brand** a name, term, sign, symbol, or design, or a combination of them, intended to identify the goods or services of one seller or group of sellers and to differentiate them from those of competitors.

Offerings and Brands

Companies address needs by putting forth a **value proposition**, a set of benefits they offer to customers to satisfy their needs. The intangible value proposition is made physical by an *offering*, which can be a combination of products, services, information, and experiences.

A **brand** is an offering from a known source. A brand name such as McDonald's carries many associations in people's minds, which make up the brand image: hamburgers, fun, children, fast food, convenience, and golden arches. All companies strive to build a strong, favorable, and unique brand image.

Value and Satisfaction

The offering will be successful if it delivers value and satisfaction to the target buyer. The buyer chooses between different offerings based on which she perceives to deliver the most value. *Value* reflects the sum of the perceived tangible and intangible benefits and costs to customers. It is primarily a combination of quality, service, and price (qsp), called the customer value triad. Value increases with quality and service and decreases with price, although other factors such as culture can also play an important role in our perceptions of value.

The styling of Carrefour stores is meant to appeal to shoppers who are looking for a rich shopping experience coupled with affordable prices.

satisfaction   a person's feelings of pleasure or disappointment resulting from comparing a product's perceived performance or outcome in relation to his or her expectations.

Value is a central marketing concept. We can think of marketing as the identification, creation, communication, delivery, and monitoring of customer value. **Satisfaction** reflects a person's judgments of a product's perceived performance (or outcome) in relationship to her or his expectations. If the performance falls short of expectations, the customer is dissatisfied and disappointed. If it matches expectations, the customer is satisfied. If it exceeds them, the customer is delighted.

Marketing Channels

To reach a target market, the marketer uses three kinds of marketing channels. *Communication channels* deliver and receive messages from target buyers, and include newspapers, magazines, radio, television, mail, telephone, billboards, posters, fliers, CDs, audiotapes, and the internet. Beyond these, just as we convey messages by our facial expressions and clothing, firms communicate through the look of their retail stores, the appearance of their websites, and many other media. Marketers are increasingly adding dialogue channels like social media sites such as Twitter and Facebook, e-mail, blogs, and SMS text messaging.

transaction   a trade of values between two or more parties: A gives X to B and receives Y in return.

The marketer uses *distribution channels* to display, sell, or deliver the physical product or service(s) to the buyer or user. They include distributors, wholesalers, retailers, and agents.

The marketer also uses *service channels* to carry out **transactions** with potential buyers. Service channels include warehouses, transportation companies, banks, and insurance companies that facilitate transactions. Marketers clearly face a design challenge in choosing the best mix of communication, distribution, and service channels for their offerings.

Supply Chain

supply chain   see 'value-delivery network'.

The **supply chain** is a longer channel stretching from raw materials to components to final products that are carried to final buyers. The supply chain for women's purses starts with hides and moves through tanning, cutting, manufacturing, and the marketing channels to bring products to customers. Each company captures only a certain percentage of the total value generated by the supply chain's value delivery system. When a company acquires competitors or expands, its aim is to capture a higher percent of supply chain value.

Competition

Competition includes all the actual and potential rival offerings and substitutes a buyer might consider. Suppose an automobile company is planning to buy steel for its cars. There are several possible levels of competitor. The manufacturer can buy steel from Qatar Steel in Qatar; it can buy from a foreign firm in Japan or Korea; it can buy from a mini-mill such as Nucor at a cost saving; or instead of steel, it can buy aluminum from Alcoa for certain parts to reduce the car's weight, or engineered plastics from Saudi Basic Industries Corporation (SABIC), purchasers of GE Plastics, for bumpers. Clearly, Qatar Steel would be thinking too narrowly about its competition if it thought only of other integrated steel companies. In fact, in the long run, Qatar Steel is more likely to be hurt by substitute products than by other steel companies.

Marketing Environment

The marketing environment consists of the task environment and the broad environment. The *task environment* includes the actors engaged in producing, distributing, and promoting the offering. These are the company, suppliers, distributors, dealers, and the target customers. In the supplier group are material suppliers and service suppliers, such as marketing research agencies, advertising agencies, banking and insurance companies, transportation companies, and telecommunications companies. Distributors and dealers include agents, brokers, manufacturer representatives, and others who facilitate finding and selling to customers.

The *broad environment* consists of six components: demographic environment, economic environment, physical environment, technological environment, political-legal environment, and social-cultural environment. Marketers must pay close attention to the trends and developments in these environments and make timely adjustments to their marketing strategies.

Changes in Marketing Realities

We can say with some confidence that "the marketplace isn't what it used to be." Marketers must attend and respond to a number of significant developments.

Major Societal Forces

Today the marketplace is radically different as a result of major, and sometimes interlinking, societal forces that have created new behaviors, new opportunities, and new challenges.

- *Network information technology.* The digital revolution has created an Information Age. The Industrial Age was characterized by mass production and mass consumption, stores stuffed with inventory, ads everywhere, and rampant discounting. The Information Age promises to lead to more accurate levels of production, more targeted communications, and more relevant pricing.

- *Globalization.* Technological advances in transportation, shipping, and communication have made it easier for companies to market in other countries, and easier for consumers to buy products and services from marketers in other countries.

- *Deregulation.* Many countries have deregulated industries to create greater competition and growth opportunities. Many countries' laws restricting financial services, telecommunications, and electric utilities have all been loosened in the spirit of greater competition. This has allowed for more competition from local and foreign companies.

- *Privatization.* Many countries have converted public companies to private ownership and management to increase their efficiency, such as British Airways and British Telecom in the United Kingdom, Dolphin Energy in Qatar, and Societé Anonyme de l'Industrie de Rafinage (SAMIR), Societé Cherifienne de Petrol, and Wafa Insurance in Morocco.

- *Heightened competition.* Brand manufacturers are facing intense competition from domestic and foreign brands, resulting in rising promotion costs and shrinking profit margins. They are being further buffeted by powerful retailers that command limited shelf space and are putting out their own store brands in competition with national brands. Many strong brands are extending into related product categories, creating mega-brands with much presence and reputation.

- *Industry convergence.* Industry boundaries are blurring at an incredible rate as companies are recognizing that new opportunities lie at the intersection of two or more industries. The computing and consumer electronics industries are converging as the giants of the computer world such as Dell, Gateway, and Hewlett-Packard release a stream of entertainment devices from MP3 players to plasma TVs and camcorders. The shift to digital technology is fueling this massive convergence.[17]

- *Consumer resistance.* A 2004 Yankelovich study found record levels of marketing resistance from consumers.[18] A majority of those surveyed reported negative opinions about marketing and advertising, stating that they avoid products that they feel are over-marketed.

- *Retail transformation.* Small retailers are succumbing to the growing power of giant retailers. Store-based retailers face competition from online companies such as Amazon, catalog houses; direct-mail firms; newspaper, magazine, and TV direct-to-customer ads; home-shopping TV; and e-commerce on the internet. In response, entrepreneurial retailers are building entertainment into their stores with coffee bars, lectures, demonstrations, and performances, marketing an 'experience' rather than a **product assortment**.

product assortment   the set of all products and items a particular seller offers for sale.

M·A·C Cosmetics   A division of cosmetics giant Estée Lauder, M·A·C Cosmetics is considered a significant reason for Lauder's 13 percent net makeup sales increase. Yet, M·A·C's 1,000 stores worldwide don't simply sell Small Eye Shadow, Studio Fix, Lustreglass, and Pro Longwear Lipcoulour. Instead, they rely on highly paid 'artists' to bond with each customer during a free makeup consultation and application lesson. In their three Dubai stores, services include makeup lessons and also M·A·C on location, which offers full makeup services at home or at M·A·C stores.[19] Although this strategy is hardly new in the world of retail makeup, what's unique is that M·A·C's artists are not out there to increase their commissions and load customers down with more products. Rather, they're trained to collaborate with customers so they'll leave the store with US$50 or more of M·A·C products *and* the feeling that "I can definitely do this at home." The goal, says Matthew Waitesmith, M·A·C's head of artist training and development, is for each customer to feel she's had an authentically artistic experience "that hopefully means they'll return to the place that makes them feel like an artist."[20]

- *Disintermediation.* The amazing success of early online dot-coms such as AOL, Amazon, Yahoo, eBay, E*TRADE, and dozens of others, which created *disintermediation* in the delivery of products and services by intervening between the traditional flow of goods through distribution channels, struck terror into the hearts of many established manufacturers and retailers. In response, many traditional companies engaged in *reintermediation* and became 'brick-and-click' retailers, adding online services to their existing offerings. Many brick-and-click competitors became stronger contenders than 'pure-click' firms, since they had a larger pool of resources to work with and well-established brand names.

The societal forces that spawned this Information Age have resulted in many new consumer and company capabilities.

New Consumer Capabilities

Customers today perceive fewer real product differences and show less brand loyalty, while they are becoming more price- and quality-sensitive in their search for value. Consider what consumers have today that they didn't have yesterday.

- *A substantial increase in buying power.* Buyers are only a click away from comparing competitor prices and product attributes on the internet. They can even name their price for a hotel room, airline ticket, or mortgage. Business buyers can run a *reverse auction* in which sellers compete to capture their business. They can readily join with others to combine their purchases and achieve deeper volume discounts.

- *A greater variety of available goods and services.* Amazon quickly became the world's largest bookstore but has since branched into retail sales of music and movies, clothing and accessories, consumer electronics, health and beauty aids, and home and garden products. Buyers can order goods online from anywhere in the world, bypassing limited local offerings and realizing great savings by ordering in countries with lower prices. Another example is Al Waseet, which not only lists classified ads but also lists jobs, personal ads, and others, helping small business as well as large organizations market their products.

- *A great amount of information about practically anything.* People can read almost any newspaper in any language from anywhere in the world. They can access online encyclopedias, dictionaries, medical information, movie ratings, consumer reports, and countless other information sources.

- *Greater ease in interacting and placing and receiving orders.* Today's buyers can place orders from home, office, or mobile phone 24 hours a day, 7 days a week, and quickly receive goods at their home or office.

- *An ability to compare notes on products and services.* Social networking sites bring together buyers with a common interest. At CarSpace.com, auto enthusiasts talk about chrome rims, the latest BMW model, and where to find a great mechanic in their local area. Marketers are eying the success of the site, given that 35 percent of young, first-time car buyers consider the internet their most important shopping tool.[21]

- *An amplified voice to influence peer and public opinion.* The internet fuels personal connections and user-generated content through social media such as Twitter, mySpace, Facebook, and single-use social networks such as Flickr (photos), Del.cio.us (links), Digg (news stories), Wikipedia (encyclopedia articles), and YouTube (video).[22] In January 2011, Egyptian youth interacted on Facebook and other online communities to promote their cause which helped in branding the revolution.

KFC, Converse, Wm. Wrigley Jr. While Chinese citizens are still prohibited from criticizing their government online, they have thousands of online forums for airing grievances about poor customer service, misleading ad campaigns, shoddy products, safety standards, and more. Chinese consumers are vocal and active, and when enough of them voice a complaint, companies listen. When a Chinese TV spot for Yum! Brand Inc.'s KFC Corp. depicted a hardworking student who didn't pass his exams and two carefree students who enjoyed KFC fried chicken and did, KFC received so many complaints for suggesting hard work doesn't pay that it changed the ad to show all three children doing well. Smart companies are enlisting their opinionated internet consumers to give input before a product is launched. Converse and Wm. Wrigley Jr. conducted a joint promotion encouraging Chinese consumers to come up with their own cool designs for Converse sneakers that featured Wrigley's Juicy Fruit logo.[23]

New Company Capabilities

New forces have also combined to generate a new set of capabilities for today's companies.

- Marketers can use the internet as a powerful information and sales channel, augmenting their geographical reach to inform customers and promote their businesses and products worldwide. By establishing one or more websites, they can list their products and services, history, business philosophy, job opportunities, and other information of interest to visitors. Lebanon's Wild Discovery Travel and Tourism places customer testimonials on its website as a way to attract and influence leisure travelers.

- Researchers can collect fuller and richer information about markets, customers, prospects, and competitors. They can also conduct fresh marketing research using the internet to arrange for focus groups, send out questionnaires, and gather primary data in several other ways.

- Managers can facilitate and speed internal communication among their employees by using the internet as a private intranet. Employees can query one another, seek advice, and download or upload needed information from and to the company's main computer.

- Companies can also facilitate and speed external communication among customers by creating online and offline 'buzz' through brand advocates and user communities.

- Target marketing and two-way communication have been made easier by the proliferation of special-interest magazines, TV channels, and internet newsgroups. Extranets linking suppliers and distributors let firms send and receive information, place orders, and make payments more efficiently. The company can also interact with each customer individually, to personalize messages, services, and the relationship.

- Marketers can send ads, coupons, samples, and information to customers who have requested them or have given the company permission to send them. They can now assemble information about individual customers' purchases, preferences, demographics, and profitability. For example, Carrefour offers a rewards card to its customers to encourage customer loyalty.[24]

- Companies can reach consumers on the move with mobile marketing. Using GPS technology, for instance, consumers can download company logos so they can spot brands such as Dunkin' Donuts or Baskin Robbins when they're on the road.[25] Firms can also advertise on video iPods and reach consumers on their smart phones through mobile marketing.[26] Emirates Airline knows that mobile marketing is the latest trend; to stay ahead of the market, they launched an iPhone application called iLingual, designed to translate some basic sentences from English to German, Arabic, and French.

- Firms can produce individually differentiated goods, whether they're ordered in person, on the phone, or online, thanks to advances in factory customization, computers, the internet, and database marketing software. For a price, customers can buy M&Ms with their names

More and more companies can produce individually differentiated goods, even consumer products such as these.

on them, and Heinz ketchup bottles with customized messages.[27] BMW's technology now allows buyers to design their own models from among 350 variations, with 500 options, 90 exterior colors, and 170 trims. The company claims that 80 percent of the cars bought by individuals in Europe and up to 30 percent bought in the United States are built to order.

- Managers can improve purchasing, recruiting, training, and internal and external communications. Aerospace and defense contractor Boeing has joined large, high-profile companies such as Walt Disney, General Motors, and McDonald's in embracing corporate blogging to communicate with the public, customers, and employees. External blogs allow dialogues with a marketing vice president and a glimpse into the flight testing of the new 777 model; internal blogs allow conversations on hot topics and anonymous feedback.[28] Aramex founder and CEO Fadi Ghandour uses Twitter to look after his customers and deal with their issues.[29]

- Corporate buyers can achieve substantial savings by using the internet to compare sellers' prices, and to purchase materials at auction or by posting their own terms. Companies can improve logistics and operations to reap substantial cost savings, at the same time improving accuracy and service quality.

- Firms can also recruit new employees online, and many have internet training products for download for employees, dealers, and agents.

Company Orientation Toward the Marketplace

Given these new marketing realities, what philosophy should guide a company's marketing efforts? Increasingly, marketers operate in a manner consistent with a holistic marketing concept, which will be discussed later. Let's review the evolution of earlier marketing ideas.

The Production Concept

The production concept is one of the oldest concepts in business. It holds that consumers will prefer products that are widely available and inexpensive. Managers of production-oriented businesses concentrate on achieving high production efficiency, low costs, and mass distribution. This orientation makes sense in developing countries such as China, where the largest PC manufacturer, Legend, and domestic appliances giant, Haier, take advantage of the country's huge and inexpensive labor pool to dominate the market. Marketers also use the production concept when a company wants to expand the market.[30]

The Product Concept

The product concept proposes that consumers favor products that offer the most quality, performance, or innovative features. Managers in these organizations focus on making superior products and improving them over time. However, these managers are sometimes caught up in a love affair with their products. They might commit the 'better-mousetrap' fallacy, believing that a better mousetrap will lead people to beat a path to their door. A new or improved product will not necessarily be successful unless it's priced, distributed, advertised, and sold properly.

The Selling Concept

The selling concept holds that consumers and businesses, if left alone, won't buy enough of the organization's products. The organization must, therefore, undertake an aggressive selling and promotion effort. The selling concept is expressed in the thinking of Sergio Zyman, Coca-Cola's former vice president of marketing, who said: "The purpose of marketing is to sell more stuff to more people more often for more money in order to make more profit."[31]

The selling concept is practiced most aggressively with unsought goods, goods that buyers normally do not think of buying, such as insurance, encyclopedias, and funeral plots. Most firms also practice the selling concept when they have overcapacity. Their aim is to sell what they make, rather than make what the market wants. However, marketing based on hard selling carries high risks. It assumes that customers who are coaxed into buying a product will like it, and that if they don't, they will not return or bad-mouth it, or complain to consumer organizations; and they might even buy it again.

The Marketing Concept

The marketing concept emerged in the mid-1950s.[32] Instead of a product-centered, 'make-and-sell' philosophy, business shifted to a customer-centered, 'sense-and-respond' philosophy. The job is not to find the right customers for your products, but to find the right products for your customers. Dell Computer doesn't prepare a perfect computer for its target market. Rather, it provides product platforms on which each person customizes the features he or she desires in the computer.

The marketing concept holds that the key to achieving organizational goals is being more effective than competitors in creating, delivering, and communicating superior customer value to your chosen target markets. Theodore Levitt of Harvard drew a perceptive contrast between the selling and marketing concepts:

> Selling focuses on the needs of the seller; marketing on the needs of the buyer. Selling is preoccupied with the seller's need to convert his product into cash; marketing with the idea of satisfying the needs of the customer by means of the product and the whole cluster of things associated with creating, delivering and finally consuming it.[33]

Several scholars have found that companies that embrace the marketing concept achieve superior performance.[34] This was first demonstrated by companies practicing a *reactive market orientation*: understanding and meeting customers' expressed needs. Some critics say this means companies develop only very basic innovations. Narver and his colleagues argue that more advanced, high-level innovation is possible if the focus is on customers' latent needs. Narver calls this a *proactive marketing orientation*.[35] Companies such as 3M, Hewlett Packard, and Motorola have made a practice of researching latent needs through a 'probe-and-learn' process. Companies that practice both a reactive and a proactive marketing orientation are implementing a *total market orientation* and are likely to be the most successful.

The Holistic Marketing Concept

Without question, the trends and forces defining the 21st century are leading business firms to a new set of beliefs and practices. Today's best marketers recognize the need to have a more complete, cohesive approach that goes beyond traditional applications of the marketing concept. The Marketing Memo: *Marketing Right and Wrong* suggests where companies go wrong—and how they can get it right—in their marketing.

The **holistic marketing** concept is based on the development, design, and implementation of marketing programs, processes, and activities that recognizes their breadth and interdependencies. Holistic marketing recognizes that 'everything matters' in marketing, and that a broad, integrated perspective is often necessary.

Holistic marketing is thus an approach that attempts to recognize and reconcile the scope and complexities of marketing activities. △ **Figure 1.3** provides a schematic overview of four broad components characterizing holistic marketing: relationship marketing, integrated marketing, internal marketing, and performance marketing. We'll examine these major themes throughout this book. Successful companies will be those who can keep their marketing changing with the changes in their marketplace, and marketspace.

holistic marketing a concept based on the development, design, and implementation of marketing programs, processes, and activities that recognizes their breadth and interdependencies.

Relationship Marketing

Increasingly, a key goal of marketing is to develop deep, enduring relationships with people and organizations that could directly or indirectly affect the success of the firm's marketing activities. **Relationship marketing** aims to build mutually satisfying long-term relationships with key constituents in order to earn and retain their business.[36]

relationship marketing building mutually satisfying long-term relationships with key parties, in order to earn and retain their business.

Marketing Right and Wrong

The Ten Deadly Sins of Marketing

1. The company is not sufficiently market focused and customer driven.

2. The company does not fully understand its target customers.

3. The company needs to better define and monitor its competitors.

4. The company has not properly managed its relationships with its stakeholders.

5. The company is not good at finding new opportunities.

6. The company's marketing plans and planning process are deficient.

7. The company's product and service policies need tightening.

8. The company's brand-building and communications skills are weak.

9. The company is not well organized to carry on effective and efficient marketing.

10. The company has not made maximum use of technology.

The Ten Commandments of Marketing

1. The company segments the market, chooses the best segments, and develops a strong position in each chosen segment.

2. The company maps its customers' needs, perceptions, preferences, and behavior and motivates its stakeholders to obsess about serving and satisfying the customers.

3. The company knows its major competitors and their strengths and weaknesses.

4. The company builds partners out of its stakeholders and generously rewards them.

5. The company develops systems for identifying opportunities, ranking them, and choosing the best ones.

6. The company manages a marketing planning system that leads to insightful long-term and short-term plans.

7. The company exercises strong control over its product and service mix.

8. The company builds strong brands by using the most cost-effective communication and promotion tools.

9. The company builds marketing leadership and a team spirit among its various departments.

10. The company constantly adds technology that gives it a competitive advantage in the marketplace.

Adapted source: Philip Kotler, "Ten Deadly Marketing Sins," John Wiley & Sons, Inc., 2004.

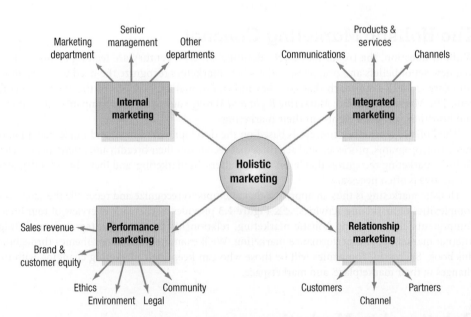

|Fig. 1.3| ▲

Holistic Marketing Dimensions

Four key factors for relationship marketing are customers, employees, marketing partners (channels, suppliers, distributors, dealers, agencies), and members of the financial community (shareholders, investors, analysts). Marketers must respect the need to create prosperity among all these constituents and develop policies and strategies to balance the returns to all key stakeholders.

To develop strong relationships with these constituents requires an understanding of their capabilities and resources, as well as their needs, goals, and desires.

The ultimate outcome of relationship marketing is a unique company asset called a marketing network. A **marketing network** consists of the company and its supporting stakeholders—customers, employees, suppliers, distributors, retailers, ad agencies, university scientists, and others—with whom it has built mutually profitable business relationships. The operating principle is simple: build an effective network of relationships with key stakeholders, and profits will follow.[37] Following this reasoning, more companies are choosing to own brands rather than physical assets. They are also increasingly subcontracting activities to outsourcing firms that can do them better and more cheaply, while retaining core activities.

> **marketing network** the company and its supporting stakeholders, with whom it has built mutually profitable business relationships.

A growing number of today's companies are also shaping separate offers, services, and messages to *individual customers*, based on information about past transactions, demographics, psychographics, and media and distribution preferences. By focusing on their most profitable customers, products, and channels, these firms hope to achieve profitable growth, capturing a larger share of each customer's expenditures by building high customer loyalty. They estimate individual customer lifetime value and design their market offerings and prices to make a profit over the customer's lifetime.

Another goal of relationship marketing is to place much more emphasis on customer retention. For example, the National Bank of Kuwait adopted a customer retention strategy through its online banking services. As the popularity of this new service grew, it became an integral part of the bank's customer retention and growth strategy.[38] Attracting a new customer may cost five times as much as doing a good enough job to retain an existing one. A bank aims to increase its share of the customer's wallet; the supermarket aims to capture a larger share of the customer's 'stomach.' Companies build customer share by offering a larger variety of goods to existing customers. They train their employees in cross-selling and up-selling.

Marketers must skillfully conduct not only customer relationship management (CRM), but partner relationship management (PRM) as well. Companies are deepening their partnering arrangements with key suppliers and distributors, thinking of these intermediaries not as customers but as partners in delivering value to final customers so that everybody benefits.

Integrated Marketing

The marketer's task is to devise marketing activities and assemble fully integrated marketing programs to create, communicate, and deliver value for consumers. Marketing activities come in all forms.[39] McCarthy classified these activities as *marketing mix* tools of four broad kinds, which he called *the four Ps* of marketing: product, price, place, and promotion.[40]

The particular marketing variables under each P are shown in △ **Figure 1.4**. Marketers make marketing-mix decisions for influencing their trade channels as well as their final consumers. Once they understand these groups, marketers make or customize an offering or solution, inform

|Fig. 1.4| △

The Four P Components of the Marketing Mix

consumers—recognizing that many other sources of information also exist—set a price that offers real value, and choose places where the offering will be accessible.

The firm can change its price, sales force size, and advertising expenditures in the short run. It can develop new products and modify its distribution channels only in the long run. Thus the firm typically makes fewer period-to-period marketing-mix changes in the short run than the number of marketing-mix decision variables might suggest.

The four Ps represent the sellers' view of the marketing tools available for influencing buyers. From a buyer's point of view, each marketing tool is designed to deliver a customer benefit. A complementary breakdown of marketing activities has been proposed that centers on customers. Its four dimensions (SIVA) and the corresponding customer questions these are designed to answer are:[41]

1.   Solution: how can I solve my problem?
2.   Information: where can I learn more about it?
3.   Value: what is my total sacrifice to get this solution?
4.   Access: where can I find it?

Winning companies satisfy customer needs and surpass their expectations economically and conveniently and with effective communication.

Two key themes of integrated marketing are that (1) many different marketing activities communicate and deliver value and (2) when coordinated, marketing activities maximize their joint effects. In other words, marketers should design and implement any one marketing activity with all other activities in mind.

For example, using an integrated communication strategy means choosing communication options that reinforce and complement each other. A marketer might selectively employ television, radio, and print advertising, public relations and events, and PR and website communications, so that each contributes on its own as well as improving the effectiveness of the others. Each communication must also deliver a consistent brand image to customers at every brand contact. Applying an integrated channel strategy ensures that direct and indirect channels, like online and retail sales, work together to maximize sales and brand equity.

Internal Marketing

Holistic marketing incorporates *internal marketing*, ensuring that everyone in the organization embraces appropriate marketing principles, especially senior management. Internal marketing is the task of hiring, training, and motivating able employees who want to serve customers well. Smart marketers recognize that marketing activities within the company can be as important as or even more important than marketing activities directed outside the company. It makes no sense to promise excellent service before the company's staff is ready to provide it.

Internal marketing must take place on two levels. At one level, the various marketing functions—sales force, advertising, customer service, product management, marketing research—must work together. Too often, the sales force thinks product managers set prices or sale quotas 'too high;' or the advertising director and a brand manager cannot agree on an advertising campaign. All these marketing functions must be coordinated from the customer's point of view. The following example highlights the coordination problem.

> The marketing vice president of a major Arab airline wants to increase the airline's traffic share. His strategy is to build up customer satisfaction by providing better food, cleaner cabins, better-trained cabin crews, and lower fares, yet he has no authority in these matters. The catering department chooses food that keeps food costs down; the maintenance department uses cleaning services that keep down cleaning costs; the human resources department hires people without regard to whether they are friendly; and the finance department sets the fares. Because these departments generally take a cost or production point of view, the vice president of marketing is hindered in his efforts to create an integrated marketing mix.

At the second level, other departments must embrace marketing; they must also 'think customer.' Marketing is not a department so much as a company orientation.[42] See ▭ **Box 1.2.**

Internal marketing thus requires vertical alignment with senior management, and horizontal alignment with other departments, so everyone understands, appreciates, and supports the marketing effort.

BOX 1.2 **Assessing Which Company Departments Are Customer-Minded**

Research and Development (R & D)

- They spend time meeting customers and listening to their problems.
- They welcome the involvement of marketing, manufacturing, and other departments to each new project.
- They benchmark competitors' products and seek 'best-of-class' solutions.
- They solicit customer reactions and suggestions as the project progresses.
- They continuously improve and refine the product on the basis of market feedback.

Purchasing

- They proactively search for the best suppliers.
- They build long-term relationships with fewer but more reliable, high-quality suppliers.
- They don't compromise quality for price savings.

Manufacturing

- They invite customers to visit and tour their plants.
- They visit customer plants.
- They willingly work overtime to meet promised delivery schedules.
- They continuously search for ways to produce goods faster and/or at lower cost.
- They continuously improve product quality, aiming for zero defects.
- They meet customer requirements for 'customization' where possible.

Marketing

- They study customer needs and wants in well-defined market segments.
- They allocate marketing effort in relation to the long-run profit potential of the targeted segments.
- They develop winning offers for each target segment.
- They measure company image and customer satisfaction on a continuous basis.
- They continuously gather and evaluate ideas for new products, product improvements, and services.
- They urge all company departments and employees to be customer-centered.

Sales

- They have specialized knowledge of the customer's industry.
- They strive to give the customer 'the best solution.'
- They make only promises that they can keep.
- They feed back customers' needs and ideas to those in charge of product development.
- They serve the same customers for a long period of time.

Logistics

- They set a high standard for service delivery time and meet this standard consistently.
- They operate a knowledgeable and friendly customer service department that can answer questions, handle complaints, and resolve problems in a satisfactory and timely manner.

Accounting

- They prepare periodic 'profitability' reports by product, market segment, geographic area (regions, sales territories), order size, channel, and individual customer.
- They prepare invoices tailored to customer needs and answer customer queries courteously and quickly.

Finance

- They understand and support marketing expenditures (e.g. image advertising) that produce long-term customer preference and loyalty.
- They tailor the financial package to the customer's financial requirements.
- They make quick decisions on customer creditworthiness.

Public Relations

- They send out favorable news about the company and 'damage control' unfavorable news.
- They act as an internal customer and public advocate for better company policies and practices.

Cammie Dunaway, executive vice president of sales and marketing for Nintendo of America, states, "You want to be connecting at the very senior levels of the organization, and you also want to be connecting in with the engineers and scientists who are doing a lot of the work on the front lines." Dunaway also emphasizes the importance of integrated marketing, comparing her former role as Yahoo! CMO to that of an orchestra conductor: "You have to figure out how to pull all those instruments together in a way that's delivering great marketing accountability and engaging marketing programs."[43]

A study conducted by the major consulting firm Booz Allen Hamilton and the Association of National Advertisers, in conjunction with *Brandweek* magazine, asked 2000 executives to describe the marketing structure within their organizations and to detail the tasks they consider integral to their missions. The researchers identified six types of marketing organizations (see ▪ Box 1.3 for a breakdown and descriptions). In the most successful type, Growth Champions, marketing heavily influenced all aspects of the organization. Growth Champions were 20 percent more likely to deliver revenue growth and profitability than the other types of marketing organization.

Performance Marketing

Holistic marketing incorporates *performance marketing* and understanding the returns to the business from marketing activities and programs, as well as addressing broader concerns and their legal, ethical, social, and environmental effects. Top management is going beyond sales revenue to examine the marketing scorecard and interpret what is happening to market share, customer loss rate, customer satisfaction, product quality, and other measures.

FINANCIAL ACCOUNTABILITY Marketers are thus being increasingly asked to justify their investments to senior management in financial and profitability terms, as well as in

---

BOX 1.3 ▪   Types of Marketing Organization

- **Growth Champions** see themselves as 'owners' of their company's key growth-support functions, whether or not these fit into conventional definitions of marketing. They lead such general-management activities as product innovation and new-business development, and even involve themselves in strategic investment decisions in areas such as new-market penetration.

- **Marketing Masters** are literally 'masters' of company-wide marketing efforts and oversee the customer-focused side of new product and service launches. They enjoy the authority to coordinate with other major business functions. They do not, however, make strategic decisions and seldom lead new-business development.

- **Senior Counselors** help guide the CEO on marketing strategy and also serve as primary advisors on marketing strategy for individual businesses. They may lead major advertising or promotional campaigns, but rarely lead product innovation and have limited decision rights over new markets or products.

- **Best Practices Advisors** work with individual business units to maximize marketing effectiveness and efficiency by bringing best practices to advertising, promotion, and PR, but are less likely to be linked with above-average growth than both the Growth Champions and the Marketing Masters.

- **Brand Builders** are efficient providers of marketing services like communications strategy, creative output, and campaign execution in support of key brands, but their leadership role and decision rights on strategy and investment are all but negligible.

- **Service Providers** have the primary role of coordinating advertising promotion and public relations at the request of the company's brand and product teams. This group is most correlated with lackluster revenue growth and lower profitability. Service Providers often work in companies that are behind their industry peers.

Source: Based on *Booz Allen Hamilton/Assn. of National Advertisers Marketing Profiles*, in conjunction with *Brandweek* from Constantine von Hoffman, "Armed with Intelligence," *Brandweek*, May 29, 2006, pp. 17–20.

terms of building the brand and growing the customer base. As a consequence, they're employing a broader variety of financial measures to assess the direct and indirect value their marketing efforts create. They're also recognizing that much of their firms' market value comes from intangible assets, particularly their brands, customer base, employees, distributor and supplier relations, and intellectual capital.

SOCIAL RESPONSIBILITY MARKETING The effects of marketing clearly extend beyond the company and the customer to society as a whole. Marketers must carefully consider their role in broader terms, and the ethical, environmental, legal, and social context of their activities. Marketing performance requires that companies determine the needs, wants, and interests of target markets to satisfy them more effectively and efficiently than competitors, but in a way that preserves or enhances customers' and society's well-being. Increasingly, consumers demand such behavior.

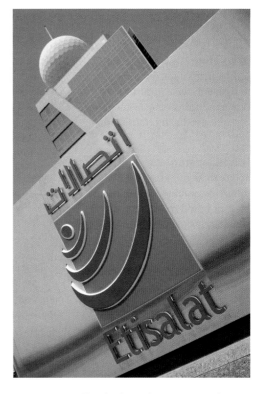

Etisalat has taken on a social responsibility role; since June 2011, they have been involved in offering innovative solutions to tackle medical challenges.

 Etisalat In June 2011 Etisalat signed a strategic memorandum of understanding with the Health Authority of Abu Dhabi to jointly develop m-health and e-health services. Having identified an existing community need for an innovative health protection project, the two organizations aim to improve the health of the residents of Abu Dhabi by launching a variety of electronic health services to all people in the Emirate. Diabetes and cardiovascular disease are the most common causes of death in Abu Dhabi, with 71 percent of the population at risk of cardiovascular disease. Consequently, the project theme is *weqaya*, or protection from illness, the aim being to deliver secure, confidential, and accurate weqaya health data to patients and Abu Dhabi residents to help them live a healthier life. Through communication and technology management, Etisalat is fulfilling its social responsibility role by offering innovative solutions to tackle these medical challenges.[44]

This realization calls for a new term that enlarges the marketing concept. We propose calling it the 'societal marketing concept.' The societal marketing concept holds that the organization's task is to determine the needs, wants, and interests of target markets, and to deliver the desired satisfactions more effectively and efficiently than competitors in a way that preserves or enhances the consumer's and society's well-being.

The societal marketing concept calls upon marketers to build social and ethical considerations into their marketing practices. They must balance and juggle the often conflicting criteria of company profits, consumer want satisfaction, and public interest.

 Safra Defensive Driving Academy The Safra Defensive Driving Academy (SDDA) represents one of the recent steps that Saudi Arabia has taken to reduce the Kingdom's road-death and injury rates, currently among the highest in the world, and to encourage a sense of social responsibility in the community.

Mrs. Olfat Kabbani, Head of the Jeddah Council for Social Responsibility at JCCI (Jeddan Chamber of Commerce and Industry), has said: "Preserving these lives is one of the most important priorities of both the public and private sectors, because road accidents are a leading cause of the high mortality rate, especially since 40 percent of those involved in accidents in Saudi Arabia are young people. Therefore, it requires all our efforts and resources available to reduce these accidents, limit them, address their causes and mitigate their impact, since protecting the lives of our sons, our mainstay, is a social responsibility upon all of us. Today we are celebrating the opening of an exemplary endeavor of social responsibility by Safra Company Limited and United Racing Company. We appreciate and value this effort and have every right to be proud of our citizens, as it reaffirms the strong principles upon which the sons of this country were raised."[45]

cause-related marketing marketing that links a firm's contributions to a designated cause to customers' direct or indirect engagement in revenue-producing transactions with the firm.

brand awareness consumers' ability to identify the brand under different conditions, as reflected by their brand recognition or recall performance.

A number of companies—including the Body Shop, Ben & Jerry's, and Patagonia—have achieved notable sales and profit gains by adopting and practicing a form of the societal marketing concept called **cause-related marketing**. Hamish Pringle, former vice chairman of marketing for Saatchi & Saatchi, a global advertising agency known for generating brand loyalty, and Marjorie Thompson, the current director of the company's Cause Connection, define this as "the activity by which a company with an image, product, or service to market builds a relationship or partnership with a 'cause,' or a number of 'causes,' for mutual benefit."[46] Companies see cause-related marketing as an opportunity to enhance their corporate reputation, raise **brand awareness**, increase customer loyalty, build sales, and increase press coverage. They believe customers will increasingly look for signs of good corporate citizenship.

Ben & Jerry's   When they founded Ben & Jerry's, Ben Cohen and Jerry Greenfield embraced the performance marketing concept by dividing the traditional financial bottom line into a 'double' bottom line, which would include a measurement of the environmental impact of their products and processes. That double bottom line later expanded into a 'triple' bottom line, to represent in objective terms the social impacts, both negative and positive, of the firm's entire range of business activities. Cohen and Greenfield informed their senior managers that they were going to be held accountable to maintain two bottom lines: "To improve the quality of life in the communities in which we operate, and to make a reasonable profit." Ben & Jerry's also recognized that just as companies require outside auditors to measure financial performance, they also require outside auditors to measure their performance along the environmental and social dimensions. As one of those outside auditors later recalled: "Measurement is a key tool to convince boards of directors and core executives that the socially responsible company is a sound business strategy. As companies make more data from their efforts available, the story becomes more compelling... To advocate transparency in business and for all of us to ascribe to that: that's the ultimate acid test."[47]

Marketing Management Tasks

With a holistic marketing philosophy as a backdrop, we can identify a specific set of tasks that make up successful marketing management and marketing leadership. We'll use the following situation to illustrate these tasks in the context of the plan of the book. The Marketing Memo: *Marketers' Frequently Asked Questions* is a good checklist for the questions marketing managers ask, all of which we examine in this book.

---

marketing
Memo

Marketers' Frequently Asked Questions

1. How can we spot and choose the right market segment(s)?
2. How can we differentiate our offerings?
3. How should we respond to customers who buy on price?
4. How can we compete against lower-cost, lower-price competitors?
5. How far can we go in customizing our offering for each customer?
6. How can we grow our business?
7. How can we build stronger brands?
8. How can we reduce the cost of customer acquisition?

9. How can we keep our customers loyal for longer?
10. How can we tell which customers are more important?
11. How can we measure the payback from advertising, sales promotion, and public relations?
12. How can we improve sales force productivity?
13. How can we establish multiple channels and yet manage channel conflict?
14. How can we get the other company departments to be more customer-oriented?

Al-Arabiyya (name disguised) is a pan-Arab conglomerate which operates in several industries, including paper and paper products, sanitary products, and furniture. The company is organized into strategic business units (SBUs). Corporate management is considering what to do with its Sedar furniture division, which produces office and home furniture. Although Sedar has a sizable market share and is producing revenue, the office furniture market itself is rapidly declining and its market share is slipping. In the faster-growing home furniture market segment, Sedar faces strong competition and has been slow to gain sales. Al-Arabiyya's corporate management wants Sedar's marketing group to produce a strong turnaround plan for the division.

Developing Marketing Strategies and Plans

The first task facing Sedar is to identify its potential long-run opportunities, given its market experience and core competencies (see Chapter 2). Sedar can manufacture furniture which is more aesthetically attractive and cheaper, but with low **durability**. Alternatively, Sedar might focus on higher-end classic designs which are sturdy and lasting, benefiting from its long expertise and core competency in the lumber business. Whichever direction it chooses, it must develop concrete marketing plans that specify future marketing strategy and tactics.

durability a measure of a product's expected operating life under natural or stressful conditions.

Capturing Marketing Insights

Sedar needs a reliable marketing information system to closely monitor its marketing environment. Its microenvironment consists of all the players that affect its ability to produce and sell furniture: suppliers, marketing intermediaries, customers, and competitors. Its macroenvironment includes demographic, economic, physical, technological, political-legal, and sociocultural forces that affect sales and profits (see Chapter 3).

Sedar also needs a dependable marketing research system. To transform marketing strategy into marketing programs, marketing managers must measure market potential, forecast demand, and make basic decisions about marketing expenditures, marketing activities, and marketing allocation.[48] To make these allocations, marketing managers may use sales-response functions that show how the amount of money spent in each application will affect sales and profits (see Chapter 4).

Connecting with Customers

Sedar must consider how to best create value for its chosen target markets and develop strong, profitable, long-term relationships with customers (see Chapter 5). To do so, it needs to understand consumer markets (see Chapter 6). Who buys furniture, and why do they buy? What are they looking for in the way of features and prices, and where do they shop? Sedar also sells furniture to business markets, including large corporations, professional firms, retailers, and government agencies (see Chapter 7), where purchasing agents or buying committees make the decisions. Sedar needs to gain a full understanding of how organizational buyers buy. It needs a sales force that is well trained in presenting product benefits.

Sedar will not want to market to all possible customers. It must divide the market into major market segments, evaluate each, and target those it can best serve (see Chapter 8).

Building Strong Brands

Sedar must understand the strengths and weaknesses of the brand as customers see it (see Chapter 9). Suppose Sedar decides to focus on the consumer market and develop a positioning strategy (see Chapter 10). Should it position itself as the 'Cadillac' brand, offering superior furniture at a premium price with excellent service and strong advertising? Should it focus, like IKEA, on low-cost modern furniture aimed at more price-conscious consumers? Or something in between?

Sedar must also pay close attention to competitors (see Chapter 11), anticipating its competitors' moves and knowing how to react quickly and decisively. It may want to initiate some surprise moves, in which case it needs to anticipate how its competitors will respond.

Shaping the Market Offerings

At the heart of the marketing program is the product: the firm's tangible offering to the market, which includes the product quality, design, features, and packaging (see Chapter 12). To gain a competitive advantage, Sedar may provide leasing, delivery, assembly, and repair as part of its product offering (see Chapter 13).

A critical marketing decision relates to price (see Chapter 14). Sedar has to decide on wholesale and retail prices, discounts, allowances, and credit terms. Its price should match well with the offer's perceived value; otherwise, buyers will turn to competitors' products.

Delivering Value

Sedar must also determine how to properly deliver to the target market the value embodied in its products and services. Channel activities include those the company undertakes to make the product accessible and available to target customers (see Chapter 15). Sedar must identify, recruit, and link various marketing facilitators to supply its products and services efficiently to the target market. It must understand the various types of retailer, wholesaler, and physical-distribution firm and how they make their decisions (see Chapter 16).

Communicating Value

sales promotion   a collection of incentive tools, mostly short term, designed to stimulate quicker or greater purchase of particular products or services by consumers or the trade.

Sedar must also adequately communicate to the target market the value embodied by its products and services. It will need an integrated marketing communication program that maximizes the individual and collective contribution of all communication activities (see Chapter 17). Sedar needs to set up mass communication programs consisting of advertising, **sales promotion**, events, and public relations (see Chapter 18). It also has to plan more personal communications, in the form of direct and interactive marketing, as well as hire, train, and motivate salespeople (see Chapter 19).

Creating Long-Term Growth

Based on its product positioning, Sedar must initiate new-product development, testing, and launching as part of its long-term view (see Chapter 20). The strategy should take into account changing global opportunities and challenges (see Chapter 21).

Finally, Sedar must build a marketing organization that's capable of implementing the marketing plan (see Chapter 22). Because surprises and disappointments can occur as marketing plans unfold, Sedar will need feedback and control to understand the efficiency and effectiveness of its marketing activities and how it can improve them.[49]

A Word about Marketing in the Arab World

We live in a global village. A company that doesn't see the international market as a potential source of clients will never survive. International companies realized decades ago that the Arab market is huge and full of diverse, profitable segments. International companies are adjusting their marketing strategies to fit the Arab world environment. Mohamed Elzubeir, Head of Mediastow, which sponsored the Click 4.0 digital marketing conference in Dubai in 2010, said, "Digital marketing is becoming increasingly common among Gulf businesses and marketers for reaching out to their stakeholders with punchy messages." He went on to say: "The tech-savvy nature of the people living in the Gulf is reflected in the fact that it has become a primary market for most multinational IT vendors. The Push and Pull digital marketing is well exploited in the region by marketers, thanks to factors like advanced ICT infrastructure, social media penetration, and a tech-savvy target audience."[50]

However, international as well as Arab companies have to keep several factors in mind when targeting the Arab audience. Values, religion, language, reading from left to right, and politics are among a few key factors to take into consideration. Liberal commercials are censored in conservative countries and can thus ruin a company's reputation, destroying any hopes of doing business in the Arab world. Although we live in a global village it would be a fatal mistake to assume that the entire globe is homogeneous. Cultural differences exist in international marketing and should be addressed carefully. These issues, together with a handful of others, will be tackled in this textbook and their implications for marketing strategy, tactics, and decisions will be highlighted and discussed.

Summary

1. From a managerial point of view, marketing is an organizational function and a set of processes for creating, communicating, and delivering value to customers and for managing customer relationships in ways that benefit the organization and its stakeholders. Marketing management is the art and science of choosing target markets and getting, keeping, and growing customers through creating, delivering, and communicating superior customer value.

2. Marketers are skilled at managing demand: they seek to influence the level, timing, and composition of demand. Marketers are involved in marketing many types of entities: goods, services, events, experiences, persons, places, properties, organizations, information, and ideas. They also operate in four different marketplaces: consumer, business, global, and nonprofit.

3. Marketing is not done only by the marketing department. Marketing needs to affect every aspect of the customer experience. To create a strong marketing organization, marketers must think like executives in other departments, and executives in other departments must think more like marketers.

4. Today's marketplace is fundamentally different as a result of major societal forces that have resulted in many new consumer and company capabilities. These forces have created new opportunities and challenges and marketing management has changed significantly in recent years as companies seek new ways to achieve marketing excellence.

5. There are five competing concepts under which organizations can choose to conduct their business: the production concept, the product concept, the selling concept, the marketing concept, and the holistic marketing concept. The first three are of limited use today.

6. The holistic marketing concept is based on the development, design, and implementation of marketing programs, processes, and activities that recognize their breadth and interdependencies. Holistic marketing recognizes that 'everything matters' with marketing and that a broad, integrated perspective is often necessary. Four components of holistic marketing are relationship marketing, integrated marketing, internal marketing, and socially responsible marketing.

7. The set of tasks necessary for successful marketing management includes developing marketing strategies and plans, capturing marketing insights, connecting with customers, building strong brands, shaping the market offerings, delivering and communicating value, and creating long-term growth.

8. The Arab world is a huge potential market for international companies. However, companies have to keep several factors in mind when targeting the Arab audience. Values, religion, language, reading from left to right, and politics are among a few key issues to take into consideration.

Applications

Marketing Debate

Does Marketing Create or Satisfy Needs?

Marketing has often been defined in terms of satisfying customers' needs and wants. Critics, however, maintain that marketing goes beyond that and creates needs and wants that did not exist before. According to these critics, marketers encourage consumers to spend more money than they should on goods and services they really do not need.

Take a position: Marketing shapes consumer needs and wants *versus* marketing merely reflects the needs and wants of consumers.

Marketing Discussion

Consider the broad shifts in marketing. Are there any themes that emerge in these shifts? Can they be related to the major societal forces? Which force has contributed to which shift?

Marketing Excellence

>>Nike

Nike hit the ground running in 1962. Originally known as Blue Ribbon Sports, the company focused on providing high-quality running shoes designed especially for athletes by athletes. Founder Philip Knight believed that high-tech shoes for runners could be manufactured at competitive prices if imported from abroad. The company's commitment to designing innovative footwear for serious athletes helped it build a cult following among its global customers.

Nike believed in a 'pyramid of influence' where product and brand choices were influenced by the preferences and behavior of a small percentage of top athletes. Therefore, from the start, Nike's marketing campaigns featured winning athletes as spokespeople.

Nike's first spokesperson, runner Steve Prefontaine, had an irreverent attitude that matched the company's spirit.

In 1985, Nike signed up Michael then-rookie basketball player Jordan as a spokesperson. Jordan was still up-and-coming, but he personified superior performance. Nike's bet paid off: the Air Jordan line of basketball shoes flew off the shelves, with revenues of over US$100 million in the first year alone.

In 1988, Nike aired the first ads in its US$20 million Just Do It ad campaign. The campaign, which ultimately featured 12 TV spots in all, subtly challenged a generation of athletic enthusiasts to chase their goals; it was a natural manifestation of Nike's attitude of self-empowerment through sports.

As Nike began expanding overseas to Europe, however, it found that its U.S.-style ads were seen as too aggressive in Europe. Nike realized it had to 'authenticate' its brand in Europe the way it had in the United States. That meant building credibility and relevance in European sports, especially football (known in the United States as soccer). Worldwide Nike began to become actively involved as a sponsor of youth leagues, local clubs, and national teams.

Worldwide, Nike is the market leader, with Adidas following second, but this is not the market situation in the Arab world. In the Middle East few people follow basketball, while people in most Arab countries are fans

Continued on next page >>

Marketing Excellence...continued

>>Nike

of different local and international football leagues. Nike is well known for its strong affiliation with basketball, as represented by Michael Jordan, but Adidas focuses on football, the most popular and beloved sport in Arab countries. For many years Adidas used the famous French football star, Zinedine Zidane, to promote its products. Unlike Nike, Adidas stores are widespread in the Arab region. This presence is managed by the Adidas Emerging Markets Head Office, which covers countries from Russia to Namibia. It is worth noting that Nike and Reebok have not given this level of attention to the Arab world.

Here is an example highlighting how Nike and Adidas are perceived in the region. "I like Adidas because they are comfortable and because I see them everywhere. Nike is more American, and I don't like New Balance because they're not sporty enough," says Fahad, a Dubai teen. "But Adidas look very good, they're very young. I bought my last pair in the Adidas shop in the City Center mall. I also like that Adidas has these huge billboards here in Dubai with Muhammad Ali," Fahad says. "He's a good symbol here—because he's a Muslim, and he represents a Muslim who succeeded in life, rather than just being somebody who's good at sports."

The Middle East market is wide and is full of potential segments for Nike, Adidas, and Reebok, but engaging in marketing programs is considered a prerequisite for success in the region.[51]

Questions

1. What are the advantages and disadvantages of hiring spokespeople to promote Nike's products?

2. Based on the information provided in the case and your own view, list six factors that may hinder marketing practices overseas.

3. Imagine that you are assigned to develop a corporate social responsibility (CSR) project for Nike. What will be the nature of your recommended project, and how could it help Nike's marketing activities?

4. As an international marketer, list five or six recommendations to boost Nike's presence in the Middle East.

Sources: 51. Justin Ewers and Tim Smart, "A Designer Swooshes In," *U.S. News & World Report*, January 26, 2004, p. 12; "Corporate Media Executive of the Year," *Delaney Report*, January 12, 2004, p. 1; "10 Top Non Traditional Campaigns," *Advertising Age*, December 22, 2003, p. 24; Chris Zook and James Allen, "Growth Outside the Core," *Harvard Business Review*, December 2003, pp. 66(8), www.ameinfo.com/42006.html.

In this chapter, we will address the following questions:

1. **How does marketing affect customer value?** (pg. 33)

2. **How is strategic planning carried out at different levels of the organization?** (pg. 48)

3. **What does a marketing plan include?** (pg. 54)

Developing Marketing Strategies and Plans

K ey ingredients of the marketing management process are insightful, creative marketing strategies and plans that can guide marketing activities. Developing the right marketing strategy over time requires a blend of discipline and flexibility. Firms must stick to a strategy but also find new ways to constantly improve it. Increasingly, marketing must also develop strategies for a range of products and services within the organization. As a highly successful airline, Emirates Airline, for instance, must continually design and implement marketing activities at many levels and for many units of the organization.

 Emirates Airline is one of the most important global airlines in the world, with over 39,000 employees, 137 aircraft, and around 100 destinations on six continents. Emirates Airline's chairman, HH Sheikh Ahmed bin Saeed Al Maktoum, sees sponsorship as vital in the airline's marketing strategy, to differentiate itself from the competition. "We believe sponsorships are one of the best ways to connect with our passengers," he said. "They allow us to share and support their interests and to build a closer relationship with them." In fact, Emirates Airline has been committed to sponsorship for more than 20 years. It is an official sponsor of FIFA, AC Milan, Paris Saint Germain, Arsenal, and other football teams. It is also a sponsor of various other sports, including rugby union, yacht racing, powerboat racing, golf, cricket, horse racing, tennis, auto racing, and many others.[1]

This chapter begins by examining some of the strategic marketing implications in creating customer value. We'll look at several perspectives on planning and describe how to draw up a formal marketing plan. ▽

Marketing and Customer Value

Marketing is about satisfying consumers' needs and wants. The task of any business is to deliver customer value at a profit. In a competitive economy with increasingly rational buyers faced with many choices, a company can win only by fine-tuning the value delivery process and choosing, providing, and communicating superior value.

The Value Delivery Process

The traditional view of marketing is that a firm makes something and then sells it. In this view, marketing takes place in the second half of the process. Companies that subscribe to this view have the best chance of succeeding in economies marked by goods shortages where consumers are not picky about quality, features, or style; for example, basic staple goods in developing markets.

This traditional view of the business process, however, will not work in economies where people face many choices. There, the 'mass market' is actually divided into several micro-markets, each with its own wants, perceptions, preferences, and buying criteria. The smart competitor must design and deliver offerings for well-defined target markets. This realization has inspired a new view of business processes that places marketing at the *beginning* of planning. Instead of emphasizing making and selling, companies now see themselves as part of a value delivery process.

The value creation and delivery sequence can be divided into three phases. The first phase, *choosing the value*, represents the 'homework' which marketing must do before any product exists. The marketing staff must segment the market, select the appropriate market target, and develop the offering's value positioning. The formula of segmentation, targeting, positioning (STP) is the core of strategic marketing. Once the business unit has chosen the value, the second phase is *providing the value*. Marketing must determine specific product features, prices, and distribution. The task in the third phase is *communicating the value* by utilizing the sales force, sales promotion, advertising, and other communication tools to announce and promote the product. Each of these value phases has cost implications. It is also the case that the value delivery process begins before there is a product and continues while it is being developed and after it becomes available.

 Nike   Critics of Nike often complain that its shoes cost almost nothing to make, yet cost the consumer so much. True, the raw materials and manufacturing costs of a sneaker are relatively cheap, but marketing the product to the consumer is expensive. Materials, labor, shipping, equipment, import duties, and suppliers' costs generally total less than US$25 a pair. Compensating the sales team, distributors, administration, and endorsers, as well as paying for advertising plus research and development, adds $15 or so to Nike's total. Nike sells its product to retailers to make a profit of $7. The retailer therefore pays roughly $47 to put a pair of Nikes on the shelf. Factoring in the retailer's overhead (typically $30 covering human resources, lease, and equipment), along with a $10 profit, the shoe costs the consumer over $80.

London Business School's Nirmalya Kumar has put forth a '3 Vs' approach to marketing: (1) define the value segment or customers (and their needs); (2) define the value proposition; and (3) define the value network that will deliver the promised service.[2] Dartmouth's Frederick Webster views marketing in terms of: (1) value-defining processes such as market research and company self-analysis; (2) value-developing processes including new-product development, sourcing strategy, and vendor selection; and (3) value-delivering processes such as advertising and managing distribution.[3]

The Value Chain

value chain the series of departments that carry out value-creating activities to design, produce, market, deliver, and support a firm's products.

Michael Porter of Harvard has proposed the **value chain** as a tool for identifying ways to create more customer value (see △ **Figure 2.1**).[4] According to this model, every firm is a synthesis of activities performed to design, produce, market, deliver, and support its product. The value chain identifies nine strategically relevant activities—five primary and four support activities—that create value and cost in a specific business.

|Fig. 2.1| △

Value Chain Analysis

Source: Michael E. Porter, Competitive Advantage: Creating and Sustaining Superior Performance (New York: Free Press, 1985).

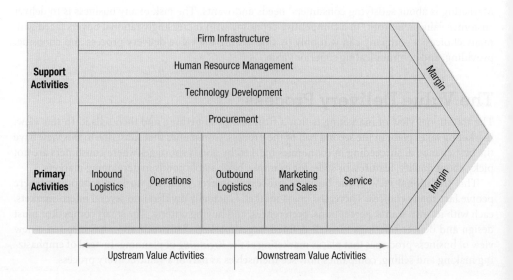

The *primary activities* are inbound logistics or bringing materials into the business; operations or converting them into final products; outbound logistics or shipping out final products; marketing them, which includes sales; and servicing them. The *support activities*—procurement, technology development, human resource management, and firm infrastructure—are handled in specialized departments. The firm's infrastructure covers the costs of general management, planning, finance, accounting, legal, and government affairs.

The firm's task is to examine its costs and performance in each value-creating activity and to look for ways to improve it. Managers should estimate their competitors' costs and performances as *benchmarks* against which to compare their own costs and performance. And they should go further and study the 'best-of-class' practices of the world's best companies.[5]

TE Data Inc.   TE Data has a national telecommunications network and is the largest IP-based data communications firm in Egypt. The company was established in late 2001 as the data communications and internet division of Telecom Egypt (the incumbent operator of Egypt). TE Data's strategy has been to tailor its products carefully to each client, so that each product is unique. It has product-based teams which use a limited number of suppliers, with the aim of building close working relationships. Suppliers are involved in the development of new products, which enables TE Data to use its partners' expertise in certain areas, thus reducing the time a product takes to reach the market, cutting costs, and improving the potential quality of each product that it makes. This, the company believes, makes for work efficiency, increased productivity, and higher profitability.[6]

The firm's success depends not only on how well each department performs its work, but also on how well the company coordinates departmental activities to conduct *core business processes.*[7] These core business processes include:

- **The market-sensing process.** All the activities in gathering market intelligence, disseminating it within the organization, and acting on the information.

- **The new-offering realization process.** All the activities in researching, developing, and launching new high-quality offerings quickly and within budget.

- **The customer-acquisition process.** All the activities in defining target markets and prospecting for new customers.

- **The customer relationship-management process.** All the activities in building deeper understanding, relationships, and offerings to individual customers.

- **The fulfillment management process.** All the activities in receiving and approving orders, shipping the goods on time, and collecting payment.

Strong companies are reengineering their work flows and building cross-functional teams to be responsible for each process.[8] At Xerox, a Customer Operations Group links sales, shipping, installation, service, and billing so these activities flow smoothly into one another. Winning companies are those that excel at managing core business processes through cross-functional teams. Aramex, DHL, UPS, and LibanPost have reorganized their employees into cross-functional teams; and cross-functional teams are also found in nonprofit and government organizations. Saudi Aramco, the largest oil corporation in the world, with the largest proven crude oil reserves and production, uses cross-functional project teams in its operations, which cover exploration, drilling, refining and distribution, shipping, and research and development. As a result, the company has received two awards from the Project Management Institute.

To be successful, a firm also needs to look for competitive advantages beyond its own operations, in the value chains of suppliers, distributors, and customers. Many companies today have partnered with specific suppliers and distributors to create a superior **value delivery network**, also called a *supply chain.*

value-delivery network a company's supply chain and how it partners with specific suppliers and distributors to make products and bring them to markets.

Saudi Aramco manages business operations through cross-functional teams.

Core Competencies

Traditionally, companies owned and controlled most of the resources that entered their businesses—labor force, materials, machines, information, and energy—but this situation is changing. Many companies today outsource less-critical resources if they can obtain better quality or lower cost. India has developed a reputation as a country that can provide ample outsourcing support.

The key, then, is to own and nurture the resources and competencies that make up the *core* of the business. Nike, for example, does not manufacture its own shoes, because certain Asian manufacturers are more competent in this task; instead Nike nurtures its superiority in shoe design and merchandising, its two core competencies. A **core competency** has three characteristics: (1) it is a source of competitive advantage in that it makes a significant contribution to perceived customer benefits; (2) it has applications in a wide variety of markets; and (3) it is difficult for competitors to imitate.[9]

core competency   attribute that (1) is a source of competitive advantage in that it makes a significant contribution to perceived customer benefits, (2) has applications in a wide variety of markets, (3) is difficult for competitors to imitate.

Competitive advantage also accrues to companies that possess distinctive capabilities. Whereas core competencies refer to areas of special technical and production expertise, *distinctive capabilities* describe excellence in broader business processes. Consider Brownbag, a delivery service based in the UAE.

Brownbag   Brownbag is an online delivery service based in Dubai. It brings high-demand products that people usually buy in stores to people's doorsteps, and promises to deliver in under an hour. With the city's expansion and the subsequent effect on traffic, it is no longer always convenient to just 'pick something up'; instead, Brownbag aims to take care of it for you instead, whether you want a DVD or something from the pharmacy. Brownbag has distinctive capabilities that are based on best practice, and on benchmarking on international business strategies and brand positioning, and it is the only business in the region that delivers the high demand products within an hour, around the clock. With its online communities of people who provide reviews and feedback, the company can identify potential fans to spread the word. Although the service they have created is unique, and there is a clear market need, other factors have to be kept in mind in order for the concept to succeed. The business needs to align itself with strategic partners to enable it to form beneficial and profitable synergies.

George Day, a professor of marketing at the Wharton School of the University of Pennsylvania, sees market-driven organizations as excelling in three distinctive capabilities: market sensing, customer linking, and channel bonding.[10] In terms of market sensing, he believes that tremendous opportunities and threats often begin as "weak signals" from the outer edges of the business.[11] He offers a systematic process for developing a wider outlook, and practical tools and strategies for building "vigilant organizations" attuned to changes in the environment, by asking questions in three categories (see ▬ **Box 2.1**).

BOX 2.1 ▬	Becoming a Vigilant Organization

- Learning from the past
  - What have been our past blind spots?
  - What instructive analogies do other industries offer?
  - Who in the industry is skilled at picking up weak signals and acting on them?

- Evaluating the present
  - What important signals are we rationalizing away?
  - What do we hear about ourselves?
  - What are our secondary customers and competitors really thinking?

- Envisioning the future
  - What future surprises could really hurt or help us?
  - What emerging technologies could change the game?
  - Is there an unthinkable scenario that might disrupt our business?

Source: George S. Day and Paul J. H. Schoemaker, *Peripheral Vision: Detecting the Weak Signals That Will Make or Break Your Company* (Boston: Harvard Business School Press, 2006).

Competitive advantage ultimately derives from how well the company has fitted its core competencies and distinctive capabilities into tightly interlocking 'activity systems.' Competitors find it hard to imitate companies such as Dell and IKEA because they are unable to copy their activity systems.

Business realignment may be necessary to maximize core competencies. It has three steps: (1) (re)defining the business concept or 'big idea'; (2) (re)shaping the business scope; and (3) (re)positioning the company's brand identity. Consider what Kodak is doing to realign its business.

 Kodak   With the advent of the digital era and consumers' new capacity to store, share, and print photos using their PCs, Kodak faces more competition than ever, both in-store and online. In 2004, after being bumped from the Dow Jones Industrial Average, where it had held a spot for more than 70 years, the company started the painful process of transformation. It started off by expanding its line of digital cameras, printers, and other equipment, and it also set out to increase market share in the profitable medical imaging business. Making changes is not without challenges, however. The company announced in the summer of 2006 that it would outsource the making of its digital cameras. Kodak eliminated almost 30,000 jobs between 2004 and 2007 and spent money acquiring a string of companies for its graphics communications unit. Not only must Kodak convince consumers to buy its digital cameras and home printers, but it must also become known as the most convenient and affordable way to process digital images. So far, the company faces sharp competition from Sony, Canon, and Hewlett-Packard.[12] Recently Kodak has been focusing on younger customers, solidifying their brand equity. In 2011, Kodak announced a film cinematography competition, recognizing talented students from around the world. The winners showed their films at the 2012 Clermont-Ferrand Short Film Festival.

A Holistic Marketing Orientation and Customer Value

A holistic marketing orientation can also help capture customer value. One view of holistic marketing sees it as "integrating the value exploration, value creation, and value delivery activities with the purpose of building long-term, mutually satisfying relationships and co-prosperity among key stakeholders."[13] According to this view, holistic marketers succeed by managing a superior value chain that delivers a high level of product quality, service, and speed. Holistic marketers achieve profitable growth by expanding customer share, building customer loyalty, and capturing customer lifetime value. △ **Figure 2.2**, a holistic marketing framework, shows how the interaction between relevant actors and value-based activities helps to create, maintain, and renew customer value.

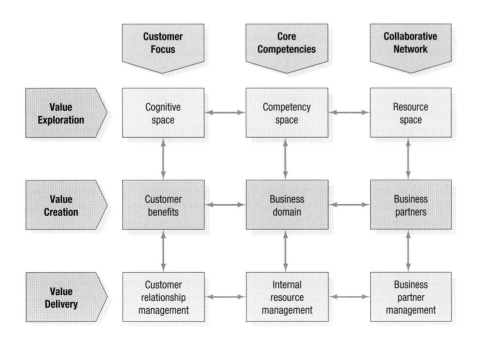

|Fig. 2.2| △

A Holistic Marketing Framework

Source: P. Kotler, D. C. Jain, and S. Maesincee, "Formulating a Market Renewal Strategy," in *Marketing Moves* (Part 1), Fig. 1-1 (Boston: Harvard Business School Press, 2002), p. 29. Copyright © 2002 by President and Fellows of Harvard College. All rights reserved.

The holistic marketing framework is designed to address three key management questions, as follows.

1. *Value exploration.* How can a company identify new value opportunities?
2. *Value creation.* How can a company efficiently create more promising new value offerings?
3. *Value delivery.* How can a company use its capabilities and infrastructure to deliver the new value offerings more efficiently?

Let's look at how marketers can answer these questions.

VALUE EXPLORATION Finding new value opportunities is a matter of understanding the relationships among three spaces: (1) the customer's cognitive space; (2) the company's competence space; and (3) the collaborator's resource space. The customer's *cognitive space* reflects existing and latent needs and includes dimensions such as the need for participation, stability, freedom, and change.[14] We can describe the company's *competency space* in terms of breadth—broad versus focused scope of business; and depth—physical versus knowledge-based capabilities. The collaborator's *resource space* includes horizontal partnerships, with partners chosen for their ability to exploit related market opportunities, and vertical partnerships, with partners who can serve the firm's value creation.

VALUE CREATION Value-creation skills for marketers include identifying new customer benefits from the customer's view; utilizing core competencies from its business domain; and selecting and managing business partners from its collaborative networks. To create new customer benefits, marketers must understand what the customer thinks about, wants, does, and worries about, and observe whom customers admire and interact with, and who influences them.

VALUE DELIVERY Delivering value often means making substantial investments in infrastructure and capabilities. The company must become proficient at customer relationship management, internal resource management, and business partnership management. *Customer relationship management* allows the company to discover who its customers are, how they behave, and what they need or want. It also enables the company to respond appropriately, coherently, and quickly to different customer opportunities. To respond effectively, the company requires *internal resource management* to integrate major business processes, such as order processing, general ledger, payroll, and production, within a single family of software modules. Finally, *business partnership management* allows the company to handle complex relationships with its trading partners to source, process, and deliver products.

The Central Role of Strategic Planning

Successful marketing thus requires companies to have capabilities such as understanding customer value, creating customer value, delivering customer value, capturing customer value, and sustaining customer value. Only a select group of companies stand out as master marketers: Procter & Gamble, Nike, Disney, Barnes & Noble, Starbucks, Walmart, Enterprise Rent-A-Car, Emirates Airline, Almarai, Sekem Group, McDonald's, Ritz-Carlton, and several Asian (Sony, Toyota, Samsung, and Canon) and European (IKEA, Med, Bang & Olufsen, Electrolux, Nokia, Lego, Tesco, and Virgin) companies.

These companies focus on the customer and are organized to respond effectively to changing customer needs. They all have well-staffed marketing departments, and all their other departments accept the concept that the customer is king.

To ensure that they select and execute the right activities, marketers must give priority to strategic planning in three key areas: managing a company's businesses as an investment portfolio, assessing each business's strength by considering the market's growth rate and the company's position and fit in that market, and establishing a strategy. For each business, the company must develop a plan for achieving its long-run objectives.

Most large companies consist of four organizational levels: the corporate level, the division level, the business unit level, and the product level. Those at corporate headquarters are responsible for designing a corporate strategic plan to guide the whole enterprise; they make decisions on the amount of resources to allocate to each division, as well as on which businesses to start or eliminate. Each division establishes a plan covering the allocation of funds to each business unit

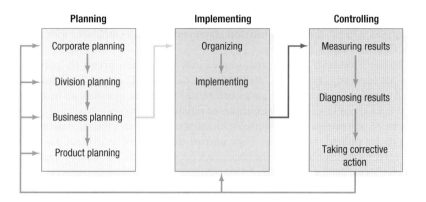

|Fig. 2.3| △

The Strategic Planning, Implementation, and Control Processes

within the division. Each business unit develops a strategic plan to carry that business unit into a profitable future. Finally, each product level (product line, brand) within a business unit develops a marketing plan for achieving its objectives in its product market.

The **marketing plan** is the central instrument for directing and coordinating the marketing effort. The marketing plan operates at two levels: strategic and tactical. The **strategic marketing plan** lays out the target markets and the value proposition the firm will offer, based on an analysis of the best market opportunities. The **tactical marketing plan** specifies the marketing tactics, including product features, promotion, merchandising, pricing, sales channels, and service.

Today, teams develop the marketing plan with inputs and sign-offs from every important function. Management then implements these plans at the appropriate levels of the organization, monitors results, and takes necessary corrective action. The complete planning, implementation, and control cycle is shown in △ **Figure 2.3**. We next consider planning at each of these four levels of the organization.

marketing plan written document that summarizes what the marketer has learned about the marketplace, indicates how the firm plans to reach its marketing objectives, and helps direct and coordinate the marketing effort.

strategic marketing plan lays out the target markets and the value proposition that will be offered, based on analysis of the best market opportunities.

tactical marketing plan marketing tactics including product features, promotion, merchandising, pricing, sales channels, and service.

Corporate and Division Strategic Planning

Some corporations give their business units a lot of freedom to set their own sales and profit goals and strategies. Others set goals for their business units but let them develop their own strategies. Still others set the goals and participate in developing individual business unit strategies.[15]

All corporate headquarters undertake four planning activities:

1. Defining the corporate mission.
2. Establishing strategic business units (SBUs).
3. Assigning resources to each SBU.
4. Assessing growth opportunities.

We'll look at each process.

Defining the Corporate Mission

An organization exists to accomplish something: to make cars, lend money, provide a night's lodging, and so on. Over time the mission may change, to take advantage of new opportunities or respond to new market conditions. Amazon.com changed its mission from being the world's largest online bookstore to aspiring to become the world's largest online store; and eBay changed its mission from running online auctions for collectors to running online auctions of all kinds of goods.

To define its mission, a company should address Peter Drucker's classic questions: What is our business? Who is the customer? What is of value to the customer? What will our business be? What should our business be?[16] These simple-sounding questions are among the most difficult a company will ever have to answer. Successful companies continually raise them and answer them thoughtfully and thoroughly.[17]

mission statement
a statement of purpose that an organization develops to share with managers, employees, and (in many cases) consumers.

Organizations develop mission statements to share with managers, employees, and (in many cases) customers. A clear, thoughtful **mission statement** provides employees with a shared sense of purpose, direction, and opportunity.

Sony's former president, Akio Morita, wanted everyone to have access to "personal portable sound," so his company created the Walkman and portable CD player. Fred Smith wanted to deliver mail anywhere in the United States before 10:30 a.m. the next day, so he created FedEx. **Box 2.2** talks about three real-life examples of mission statements.

Good mission statements have two major characteristics. First, mission statements stress the company's major policies and values. They narrow the range of individual discretion so that employees act consistently on important issues. Second, they define the major competitive spheres within which the company will operate.

- *Industry.* Some companies will operate in only one industry; some only in a set of related industries; some only in industrial goods, consumer goods, or services; and some in any industry. For example, Indevco Group Lebanon, through its different units such as Sanita and Unipak, produce consumer products, flexible packaging, and paper containers, and perform kitchen and wardrobe manufacturing, and machinery and components manufacturing.

- *Products and applications.* Firms define the range of products and applications they will supply. St. Jude Medical, based in the United States, is dedicated to developing medical technology and services that put more control in the hands of the physicians, and that advance the practice of medicine and contribute to successful outcomes for every patient.

- *Competence.* The firm identifies the range of technological and other core competencies it will master and leverage. As per an Ernst & Young study, 90 percent of companies in the Arab world are refocusing on their core competencies.[18]

- *Market segment.* The type of market or customers a company will serve is the market segment. Ghandour in Lebanon specializes in chocolates, confectionery, beverages, and other food products, while U.S. firm Gerber serves primarily the baby market.

- *Vertical.* The vertical sphere is the number of channel levels, from raw material to final product and distribution, in which a company will participate. At one extreme are companies with a large vertical scope; at one time Ford owned its own rubber plantations, sheep farms, glass manufacturing plants, and steel foundries. At the other extreme are 'hollow corporations' or 'pure marketing companies' consisting of a person with a phone, fax, computer, and desk who contracts out every service, including design, manufacture, marketing, and physical distribution.[19]

- *Geographical.* The range of regions, countries, or country groups in which a company will operate defines its geographical sphere. Some companies operate in a specific city or state. Others are multinationals such as Unilever and Caterpillar, which operate in almost every country in the world.

BOX 2.2   Mission Statements

The following is a mission statement from Orbit Company, based in Iraq.

Orbit Company aims to be the preferred local partner or service provider of international companies as it combines the trading expertise of the Middle East with the best products, technology and business practices of the West to accelerate Iraq's economic growth.

Elsewhere in the region, Mobily (Saudi Arabia) talk about exceeding expectations of employees and customers.

Elsewhere, a mission statement from eBay talks about helping people to trade 'practically anything' and aims to make the experience of lots of different types of online trading better for all.

Sources: Orbit Company website, www.orbit-iq.com; Mobily Saudi Arabia company website, www.mobily.com.sa; eBay company website, www.ebay.com.

BOX 2.3 Google's Mission Statement and Philosophy

To build total brand value by innovating to deliver customer value and customer leadership faster, better, and more completely than our competition.

We build brands and make the world a little happier by bringing our best to you.

Google Mission

To organize the world's information and make it universally accessible and useful.

Google Philosophy

1. Focus on the user and all else will follow.
2. It's best to do one thing really, really well.
3. Fast is better than slow.
4. Democracy on the web works.
5. You don't need to be at your desk to need an answer.
6. You can make money without doing evil.
7. There is always more information out there.
8. The need for information crosses all borders.
9. You can be serious without a suit.
10. Great just isn't good enough.[20]

Mission statements should be enduring; management should change the mission only when it ceases to be relevant. A good mission statement is also as short, memorable, and meaningful as possible. Marketing consultant Guy Kawasaki even advocates developing short three- to four-word corporate mantras rather than mission statements, like "peace of mind" for FedEx. In ▩ **Box 2.3**, compare the rather vague mission statements on the left with Google's mission statement and philosophy on the right.

Establishing Strategic Business Units

Companies often define their businesses in terms of products: they are in the 'auto business' or the 'clothing business.' But Harvard's famed marketing professor Ted Levitt argued that *market definitions* of a business are superior to product definitions. In other words, companies must see their business as a customer-satisfying process, not a goods-producing process. Products are transient; basic needs and customer groups endure forever. Transportation is a need: the horse and carriage, the automobile, the railroad, the airline, and the truck are products that meet that need.

Viewing businesses in terms of customer needs can suggest additional growth opportunities. IBM redefined itself from a hardware and software manufacturer to a "builder of networks." ▭ **Table 2.1** highlights the difference in having a product-oriented versus a market-oriented definition in a few companies.

TABLE 2.1 Product-Oriented versus Market-Oriented Definitions of a Business

Company	Product Definition	Market Definition
Iraqi Republic Railways Company	We run a railroad.	We are a people-and-goods mover.
Xerox	We make copying equipment.	We help improve office productivity.
Saudi Aramco	We sell gasoline.	We supply energy.
Columbia Pictures	We make movies.	We market entertainment.
Encyclopaedia Britannica	We sell encyclopedias.	We distribute information.
Zamil Air Conditioners	We make air conditioners and furnaces.	We provide climate control in the home.

A *target market definition* tends to focus on selling a product or service to a current market. PepsiCo could define its target market as everyone who drinks a cola beverage, and competitors would therefore be other cola companies. A *strategic market definition*, however, focuses also on the potential market. If PepsiCo considered everyone who might drink something to quench their thirst, their competition would also include noncola soft drinks, bottled water, fruit juices, tea, and coffee. To better compete, companies consider their offers from a customer point of view. Customers evaluate different offers as alternatives or solutions. Books, music, and video games belong to different industries but all are considered entertainment items. That's why product development and diversification strategies are employed by many firms. Increasing the range of products offered to customers is a successful strategy to occupy a place in the consumer consideration set.

A business can define itself in terms of three dimensions: customer groups, customer needs, and technology.[21] Consider a small company that defines its business as designing incandescent lighting systems for television studios. Its customer group is television studios; the customer need is lighting; and the technology is incandescent lighting. The company might want to expand. It could make lighting for other customer groups, such as homes, factories, and offices; or it could supply other services needed by television studios, such as heating, ventilation, or air conditioning. It could design other lighting technologies for television studios, such as infrared or ultraviolet lighting.

Large companies normally manage quite different businesses, each requiring its own strategy. General Electric has classified its businesses into 49 **strategic business units**, or **SBUs**. Al Hassan Group of Companies in Oman has three SBUs: Contracting, Trading, and Manufacturing. An SBU has three characteristics, as follows.

strategic business unit (SBU) a single business or collection of related businesses that can be planned separately from the rest of the company, with its own set of competitors and a manager who is responsible for strategic planning and profit performance.

1. It is a single business, or a collection of related businesses, that can be planned separately from the rest of the company.
2. It has its own set of competitors.
3. It has a manager responsible for strategic planning and profit performance, who controls most of the factors affecting profit.

The purpose of identifying the company's SBUs is to develop separate strategies and assign appropriate funding.[22]

Assigning Resources to Each SBU

Once it has defined SBUs, management must decide how to allocate corporate resources to each. The 1970s saw several portfolio-planning models introduced to provide an analytical means for making investment decisions. The GE/McKinsey Matrix classifies each SBU according to the extent of its competitive advantage and the attractiveness of its industry. Management would want to grow, 'harvest' or draw cash from, or hold on to the business. Another model, the Boston Consulting Group's Growth-Share Matrix, uses relative market share and annual rate of market growth as criteria to make investment decisions. This matrix defines four types of SBUs:

1. Stars: high-growth market, high-share product.
2. Cash cows: low-growth market, high-share product.
3. Question marks: low-share product, high-growth market.
4. Dogs: low-share product, low-growth market.

Once it has classified its SBUs, the company must determine what role each will play in the future. The company can invest more in the business unit in order to grow its share. It can invest just enough to hold the SBU's share at the current level. It can harvest the SBU, milking its short-term cash flow regardless of the long-term effect. Or it can divest the SBU by selling it or phasing it out. Problems with matrix approaches include:

- Portfolio-analysis approaches have limitations.
- They can be difficult, time-consuming, and costly to implement.
- Management may find it difficult to define SBUs and measure market share and growth.
- These approaches focus on classifying current businesses but provide little advice for future planning.

Portfolio-planning models like these have fallen out of favor as oversimplified and subjective. Because of such problems, many companies have dropped formal matrix methods in favor of more customized approaches that are better suited to their specific situations. More recent methods

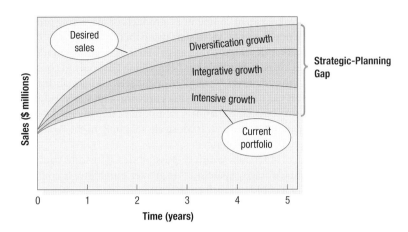

|Fig. 2.4| △

The Strategic-
Planning Gap

firms use to make internal investment decisions are based on shareholder value analysis, and whether the market value of a company is greater with an SBU or without it (whether it is sold or spun off). These value calculations assess the potential of a business based on potential growth opportunities from global expansion, repositioning or retargeting, and strategic outsourcing.

Assessing Growth Opportunities

Assessing growth opportunities includes planning new businesses, downsizing, and terminating older businesses. If there is a gap between future desired sales and projected sales, corporate management will need to develop or acquire new businesses to fill it.

△ **Figure 2.4** illustrates this strategic-planning gap for a major manufacturer of blank compact disks—CDs—called Musicale (name disguised). The lowest curve projects the expected sales over the next 5 years from the current business portfolio. The highest curve describes desired sales over the same period. Evidently, the company wants to grow much faster than its current businesses will permit. How can it fill the strategic-planning gap?

The first option is to identify opportunities to achieve further growth within current businesses (intensive opportunities). The second is to identify opportunities to build or acquire businesses that are related to current businesses (integrative opportunities). The third option is to identify opportunities to add attractive businesses unrelated to current businesses (diversification opportunities).

INTENSIVE GROWTH   Corporate management's first course of action should be a review of opportunities for improving existing businesses. One useful framework for detecting new intensive growth opportunities is called a product–market expansion grid (△ **Figure 2.5**).[23]

The company first considers whether it could gain more market share with its current products in their current markets, using a *market-penetration strategy*. Next it considers whether it can find or develop new markets for its current products, in a *market-development strategy*. Then it considers whether it can develop new products of potential interest to its current markets with a *product-development strategy*. Later the firm will also review opportunities to develop new products for new markets in a *diversification strategy*.

So, how might Musicale use these three major intensive growth strategies to increase its sales? It could try to encourage its current customers to buy more by demonstrating the benefits of using CDs for data storage in addition to music storage. Musicale could also try to attract competitors'

	Current Products	New Products
Current Markets	1. Market-penetration strategy	3. Product-development strategy
New Markets	2. Market-development strategy	(Diversification strategy)

|Fig. 2.5| △

Three Intensive Growth Strategies:
Ansoff's Product–Market Expansion Grid

Source: Adapted and reprinted by permission, *Harvard Business Review.* From "Strategies for Diversification," by Igor Ansoff, September–October 1957. Copyright © 1957 by the President and Fellows of Harvard College. All rights reserved.

customers if it noticed major weaknesses in competitors' products or marketing programs. Finally, Musicale could try to convince nonusers of CDs to start using them.

How can Musicale use a market-development strategy? First, it might try to identify potential user groups in the current sales areas. If Musicale has been selling CDs only to consumer markets, it might go after office and factory markets. Second, it might seek additional distribution channels in its present locations. If it has been selling its disks only through stereo equipment dealers, it might add mass-merchandising or online channels. Third, the company might consider selling in new locations in its home country or abroad. If Musicale sold only in the Arab world, it could consider entering the European or the U.S. market.

Management should also consider new-product possibilities. Musicale could develop new features, such as additional data-storage capabilities or greater durability. It could offer the CD at two or more quality levels, or it could research an alternative technology, such as flash drives.

By examining these intensive growth strategies, managers may discover several ways to grow. Still, that growth may not be enough. In that case, management must also look for integrative growth opportunities.

INTEGRATIVE GROWTH   A business can increase sales and profits through backward, forward, or horizontal integration within its industry. For example, drug giant Merck has gone beyond just developing and selling ethical pharmaceuticals requiring a doctor's prescription. It purchased Medco, a mail-order pharmaceutical distributor, formed a joint venture with DuPont to establish more basic research, and began another joint venture with Johnson & Johnson to bring some of its ethical products into the over-the-counter market.

How might Musicale achieve integrative growth? The company might acquire one or more of its suppliers, such as plastic material producers, to gain more control or generate more profit through backward integration. It might acquire some wholesalers or retailers, especially if they are highly profitable, in forward integration. Finally, Musicale might acquire one or more competitors, provided that the government does not bar this horizontal integration. However, these new sources may still not deliver the desired sales volume. In that case, the company must consider diversification.

DIVERSIFICATION GROWTH   Diversification growth makes sense when good opportunities exist outside the present businesses—the industry is highly attractive and the company has the right mix of business strengths to be successful. For example, from its origins as an animated film producer, Walt Disney Company has moved into licensing characters for merchandised goods, entered the broadcast industry with its own Disney Channel as well as ABC and ESPN acquisitions, and developed theme parks and vacation and resort properties.

 Almarai   In August 2005, dairy manufacturer Almarai entered into a new phase, moving from being a privately owned to a publicly listed company. The company's objective is to continue to deliver high-quality products daily to consumers and to satisfy their 125,000 new shareholders. Known for years for its fresh milk, Almarai has attempted to diversify beyond its dairy products. During the first quarter of 2007, Almarai acquired 100 percent of the shares of Western Bakeries Company Ltd and International Baking Services Company Ltd through the issuance of 9 million new shares. The share capital amounts to approximately US$290.6 million, divided into 109 million shares with a par value of approximately US$2.6. This acquisition expanded the product range of the Almarai Group to pastries, cakes, breads, and other bakery products.[24]

Almarai diversified its product range when it expanded into bakery products.

Several types of diversification are possible for Musicale. First, the company could choose a concentric strategy and seek new products that have technological or marketing synergies with existing product lines, although the new products themselves may appeal to a different group of customers. It might start a laser disk manufacturing operation, because it knows how to manufacture CDs. Second, the company might use a horizontal strategy to search for new products that could appeal to current customers, even though the new products are technologically unrelated to its current product line. Musicale might produce CD cases, for example, although they require a different manufacturing process. Finally, the company might seek new businesses that have no relationship to its current technology, products, or markets, adopting a conglomerate strategy to consider such new businesses as making application software or personal organizers.

DOWNSIZING AND DIVESTING OLDER BUSINESSES Weak businesses require a disproportionate amount of managerial attention. Companies must carefully prune, harvest, or divest tired old businesses in order to release needed resources to other uses and reduce costs.

Organization and Organizational Culture

Strategic planning happens within the context of the **organization**. A company's organization consists of its structures, policies, and **corporate culture**, all of which can become dysfunctional in a rapidly changing business environment. Whereas managers can change structures and policies (with difficulty), the company's culture is very hard to change. Yet adapting the culture is often the key to successfully implementing a new strategy.

What exactly is a corporate culture? Most businesspeople would be hard-pressed to describe this elusive concept, which some define as 'the shared experiences, stories, beliefs, and norms that characterize an organization.' Yet, walk into any company and the first thing that strikes you is the corporate culture: the way people dress, talk to one another, and greet customers.

A customer-centric culture can affect all aspects of an organization. As one expert says, "To me, being consumer-centric is more a principle—the driving value of a company—than a process. It's in a company's DNA, top to bottom. It means you recognize the diversity across the face of consumers, and that you are open to observations and opinions other than your own; this allows you to be an advocate for the consumer—whether you are a leading innovator or packing boxes in the warehouse.... The question is, do you see consumers as the driving life force of your company for as long as it exists, or do you see them as simply a hungry group of people that needs to be satisfied so your business will grow in the short term?"[25]

Sometimes corporate culture develops organically and is transmitted directly from the CEO's personality and habits to the company employees. Mike Lazaridis, president and co-CEO of Research in Motion (which created and manufactures the Blackberry wireless device), is a scientist in his own right, having won an Academy Award for technical achievement in film. He hosts a weekly, innovation-centered Vision Series at company headquarters to focus on new research and company goals. As he states, "I think we have a culture of innovation here, and [engineers] have absolute access to me. I live a life that tries to promote innovation."[26]

organization   a company's structures, policies, and corporate culture.

corporate culture   the shared experiences, stories, beliefs, and norms that characterize an organization.

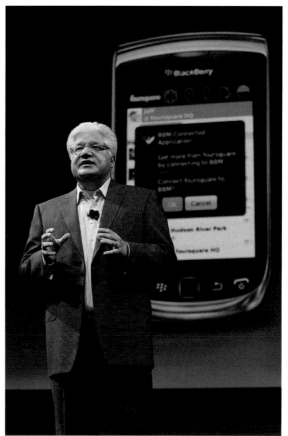

Research in Motion, the company that developed the Blackberry wireless device, fosters a culture of innovation that CEO Mike Lazaridis cultivates and values highly.

Marketing Innovation

Innovation in marketing is critical. The traditional view is that senior management hammers out the strategy and hands it down. Gary Hamel, a management expert and founder of an international management consulting firm in Chicago in the United States, and visiting professor at Harvard Business School, offers the contrasting view that imaginative ideas on strategy exist in many places within a company.[27] Senior management should identify and encourage fresh ideas from three groups that tend to be underrepresented in strategy making: employees with youthful perspectives; employees who are far removed from company headquarters;

Marketing Insight

Creating Innovative Marketing

When IBM surveyed top CEOs and government leaders about their agenda priorities, their answers about innovation were revealing. Business-model innovation and coming up with unique ways of doing things scored highly. IBM's own drive for business-model innovation led to much collaboration, both within IBM itself and externally with companies, governments, and educational institutions. CEO Samuel Palmisano noted how the breakthrough Cell processor, based on the company's Power architecture, would not have happened without collaboration with Sony and Nintendo, as well as competitors Toshiba and Microsoft.

Procter & Gamble similarly has made it a goal for 50 percent of the new company's products to come from outside P&G's labs: from inventors, scientists, and suppliers whose new product ideas can be developed in-house.

Business guru Jim Collins' research emphasizes the importance of systematic, broad-based innovation: "Always looking for the one big breakthrough, the one big idea, is contrary to what we found: to build a truly great company, it's decision upon decision, action upon action, day upon day, month upon month.... It's cumulative momentum and no one decision defines a great company." He cites the success of Walt Disney with theme parks and Walmart with retailing as examples of companies who were successful after having executed against a big idea brilliantly over such a long period of time.

Northwestern University's Mohanbir Sawhney and his colleagues outline 12 dimensions of business innovation that make up the "innovation radar" (see ▭ **Table 2.2**) and suggest that business innovation is about increasing customer *value*, not just creating new *things*; business innovation comes in many flavors and can take place on any dimension of a business system; and business innovation is systematic and requires careful consideration of all aspects of a business.

Business writer C. K. Prahalad believes much innovation in industries from financial and telecom services to health care and automobiles can come from developments in emerging markets such as India. Forced to do more with less, Indian companies and foreign competitors are finding new ways to maximize minimal resources and offer quality products and services at low prices. Consider Bangalore's Narayana Hrudayalaya

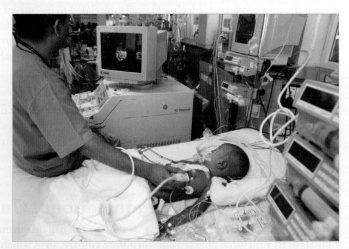

Low labor costs allow India's Narayana Hrudayalaya hospital to innovate through its pricing strategies.

hospital, which charges a flat fee of US$1,500 for heart bypass surgery that would cost 50 times that much in the United States. The low cost is a result of the hospital's low labor and operating expenses and an assembly-line view of care that has specialists focus just on their own area. The approach works: the hospital's mortality rates are half those of U.S. hospitals. Narayana also operates on hundreds of infants for free and profitably insures 2.5 million poor Indians against serious illness for 11 cents a month.

Finally, to find breakthrough ideas, some companies find ways to immerse a range of employees in solving marketing problems. Samsung's Value Innovation Program (VIP) isolates product-development teams of engineers, designers, and planners with a timetable and end date in the company's center just south of Seoul, South Korea, while 50 specialists help guide their activities. To help make tough trade-offs, team members draw 'value curves' that rank attributes such as a product's sound or picture quality on a scale from 1 to 5. To develop a new car, BMW similarly mobilizes specialists in engineering, design, production, marketing, purchasing, and finance at its Research and Innovation Center or Project House.

Sources: Steve Hamm, "Innovation: The View From the Top," *BusinessWeek*, April 3, 2006, pp. 52–53; Jena McGregor, "The World's Most Innovative Companies," *BusinessWeek*, April 24, 2006, pp. 63–74; Rich Karlgard, "Digital Rules," *Forbes*, March 13, 2006, p. 31; Jennifer Rooney and Jim Collins, "Being Great Is *Not* Just a Matter of Big Ideas," *Point*, June 2006, p. 20; Moon Ihlwan, "Camp Samsung," *BusinessWeek*, July 3, 2006, pp. 46–47; Mohanbir Sawhney, Robert C. Wolcott, and Inigo Arroniz, "The 12 Different Ways for Companies to Innovate," *MIT Sloan Management Review*, Spring 2006, pp. 75–85; Pete Engardio, "Business Prophet: How C.K. Prahalad Is Changing the Way CEO's Think," *BusinessWeek*, January 23, 2006, pp. 68–73.

and employees who are new to the industry. Each group is capable of challenging company orthodoxy and stimulating new ideas. Jump Associates, an innovative strategy firm, offers five key strategies for managing change in an organization:[28]

1. *Avoid the innovation title.* Pick a name for the innovation team that won't alienate coworkers.
2. *Use the buddy system.* Find a like-minded collaborator within the organization.

TABLE 2.2	The 12 Dimensions of Business Innovation	
Dimension	**Definition**	**Examples**
Offerings (What)	Develop innovative new products or services.	Gillette Mach3Turbo razor Apple iPod music player and iTunes music service
Platform	Use common components or building blocks to create derivative offerings.	Disney animated movies
Solutions	Create integrated and customized offerings that solve end-to-end customer problems.	UPS logistics services: Supply Chain Solutions DuPont Building Innovations for construction
Customers (Who)	Discover unmet customer needs or identify underserved customer segments.	Enterprise Rent-A-Car: focus on replacement car renters Green Mountain Energy: focus on 'green power'
Customer Experience	Redesign customer interactions across all touch points and all moments of contact.	Washington Mutual Occasio retail banking concept Cabela 'store as entertainment experience' concept
Value Capture	Redefine how the company gets paid or create innovative new revenue streams.	Google paid search Blockbuster revenue sharing with movie distributors
Processes (How)	Redesign core operating processes to improve efficiency and effectiveness.	Toyota Production System for operations General Electric Design for Six Sigma (DFSS)
Organization	Change form, function, or activity scope of the firm.	Cisco partner-centric networked virtual organization Procter & Gamble: front–back hybrid organization for customer focus
Supply Chain	Think differently about sourcing and fulfilment.	Moen ProjectNet for collaborative design with suppliers General Motors Celta use of integrated supply and online sales
Presence (Where)	Create new distribution channels or innovative points of presence, including the places where offerings can be bought or used by customers.	Starbucks music CD sales in coffee stores Diebold RemoteTeller System for banking
Networking	Create network-centric intelligent and integrated offerings.	Otis Remote Elevator Monitoring service Department of Defense Network-Centric Warfare
Brand	Leverage a brand into new domains.	Virgin Group 'branded venture capital' Yahoo! as a lifestyle brand

Source: Mohanbir Sawhney, Robert C. Wolcott, and Inigo Arroniz, "The 12 Different Ways for Companies to Innovate," *MIT Sloan Management Review*, Spring 2006, p. 78.

3. ***Set the metrics in advance.*** Establish different sets of funding, testing, and performance criteria for incremental, experimental, and potentially disruptive innovations.
4. ***Aim for quick hits first.*** Start with easily implemented ideas that will work to demonstrate that things can get done, before quickly switching to bigger initiatives.
5. ***Get data to back up your gut.*** Use testing to get feedback and improve an idea.

The Marketing Insight: *Creating Innovative Marketing* describes how some leading companies approach innovation.

Firms develop strategy by identifying and selecting among different views of the future. The Royal Dutch/Shell Group has pioneered **scenario analysis**, which consists of developing plausible representations of a firm's possible future that make different assumptions about forces driving

scenario analysis developing plausible representations of a firm's possible future that make different assumptions about forces driving the market and include different uncertainties.

the market and that include different uncertainties. Managers need to think through each scenario with the question: what will we do if it happens? They need to adopt one scenario as the most probable and watch for signposts that might confirm or disconfirm it.[29]

Business Unit Strategic Planning

The business unit strategic-planning process consists of the steps shown in △ **Figure 2.6**. We examine each step in the sections that follow.

The Business Mission

Each business unit needs to define its specific mission within the broader company mission. Thus, a company that makes lighting equipment for television studios might define its mission as "To target major television studios and become their vendor of choice for lighting technologies that represent the most advanced and reliable studio lighting arrangements." Notice that this mission does not attempt to win business from smaller television studios, win business by being lowest in price, or venture into nonlighting products.

SWOT Analysis

The overall evaluation of a company's strengths, weaknesses, opportunities, and threats is called SWOT analysis. It's a way of monitoring the external and internal marketing environment.

EXTERNAL ENVIRONMENT (OPPORTUNITY AND THREAT) ANALYSIS   A business unit must monitor key *macroenvironment forces* and significant *microenvironment factors* that affect its ability to earn profits. The business unit should set up a marketing intelligence system to track trends and important developments and any related opportunities and threats.

Good marketing is the art of finding, developing, and profiting from these opportunities.[30] A **marketing opportunity** is an area of buyer need and interest that a company has a high probability of profitably satisfying. There are three main sources of market opportunities.[31] The first is to supply something that is in short supply. This requires little marketing talent, as the need is fairly obvious. The second is to supply an existing product or service in a new or superior way. There are several ways to uncover possible product or service improvements: the *problem-detection method* asks consumers for their suggestions, the *ideal method* has them imagine an ideal version of the product or service, and the *consumption chain method* asks consumers to chart their steps in acquiring, using, and disposing of a product. This last method often leads to a totally new product or service.

marketing opportunity an area of buyer need and interest in which there is a high probability that a company can profitably satisfy that need.

|Fig. 2.6| △

The Business Unit Strategic-Planning Process

Opportunities can take many forms, and marketers need to be good at spotting them. Consider the following:

- A company may benefit from converging industry trends and introduce hybrid products or services that are new to the market. For example: mobile phone manufacturers releasing phones with digital photo capabilities.

- A company may make a buying process more convenient or efficient. Consumers can now use the internet to find more books than ever and search for the lowest price with a few clicks.

- A company can meet the need for more information and advice. Guru.com facilitates finding professional experts in a wide range of fields.

- A company can customize a product or service that was formerly offered only in a standard form. Timberland allows customers to choose colors for different sections of their boots, add initials or numbers to their boots, and choose different stitching and embroidery.

- A company can introduce a new capability. Consumers can now create and edit digital movies with the new iMac and upload them to an Apple web server or website such as YouTube to share with friends around the world.

- A company may be able to deliver a product or service faster. Aramex discovered a way to deliver mail and packages much quicker than by normal post.

- A company may be able to offer a product at a much lower price. Pharmaceutical firms have created generic versions of brand-name drugs.

To evaluate opportunities, companies can use **market opportunity analysis** (or **MOA**) to determine their attractiveness and probability of success, by asking questions like the following.

- Can we articulate the benefits convincingly to a defined target market(s)?
- Can we locate the target market(s) and reach them with cost-effective media and trade channels?
- Does our company possess or have access to the critical capabilities and resources we need to deliver the customer benefits?
- Can we deliver the benefits better than any actual or potential competitors?
- Will the financial rate of return meet or exceed our required threshold for investment?

In the opportunity matrix in △ **Figure 2.7**(a), the best marketing opportunities facing the TV-lighting-equipment company are listed in the upper-left cell (#1). The opportunities in the

market opportunity analysis (MOA)   system used to determine the attractiveness and probability of success.

(a) Opportunity Matrix

Success Probability

	High	Low
Attractiveness High	1	2
Low	3	4

1. Company develops more powerful lighting system
2. Company develops device to measure energy efficiency of any lighting system
3. Company develops device to measure illumination level
4. Company develops software program to teach lighting fundamentals to TV studio personnel

(b) Threat Matrix

Probability of Occurrence

	High	Low
Seriousness High	1	2
Low	3	4

1. Competitor develops superior lighting system
2. Major prolonged economic depression
3. Higher costs
4. Legislation to reduce number of TV studio licenses

|Fig. 2.7| △

Opportunity and Threat Matrices

lower-right cell (#4) are too minor to consider. The opportunities in the upper-right cell (#2) and lower-left cell (#3) are worth monitoring in the event that any of these improve in attractiveness and success probability.

environmental threat a challenge posed by an unfavorable trend or development that would lead to lower sales or profit.

An **environmental threat** is a challenge posed by an unfavorable trend or development that would lead, in the absence of defensive marketing action, to lower sales or profit. Figure 2.7(b) illustrates the threat matrix facing the TV-lighting-equipment company. The threats in the upper-left cell are major, because they can seriously hurt the company and they have a high probability of occurrence. To deal with them, the company needs contingency plans. The threats in the lower-right cell are very minor and can be ignored. The firm will want to carefully monitor threats in the upper-right and lower-left cells in the event they grow more serious.

INTERNAL ENVIRONMENT (STRENGTHS AND WEAKNESSES) ANALYSIS It is one thing to find attractive opportunities, and another to be able to take advantage of them. Each business needs to evaluate its internal strengths and weaknesses.

 EgyNet   The Egyptian Networks Company, EgyNet, was established in 1998 by shareholders who had previously established and operated companies in the IT and telecom sectors. EgyNet built and operated the first privately owned public data network in Egypt and the wider region. The company built a significant market share in the internet services sector, serving large corporate customers. In order to grow the company, its managers analyzed the market's strengths and weaknesses. They decided to shift the focus from a small number of large business clients to serving individual users, downsizing both the services it offered and the size of the clients it served. EgyNet started to provide internet (DSL) to individual users and various businesses. In 2001, DSL services were offered in Egypt for the first time to corporations and individuals as part of EgyNet's internet services portfolio.[32]

Businesses can evaluate their own strengths and weaknesses by using a form like the one shown in the Marketing Memo: *Checklist for Performing Strengths/Weaknesses Analysis.*

Clearly, the business doesn't have to correct *all* its weaknesses, nor should it gloat about all its strengths. The big question is whether the firm should limit itself to those opportunities for which it possesses the required strengths, or consider those that might require it to find or develop new strengths. For example, managers at Texas Instruments (TI) were split between those who wanted TI to stick to industrial electronics, where it has clear strength, and those who wanted the company to continue introducing consumer products, where it lacked some required marketing strengths.

Sometimes a business does poorly not because its people lack the required strengths, but because they don't work together as a team. In one major electronics company, engineers look down on the salespeople as 'engineers who couldn't make it,' and salespeople look down on the service people as 'salespeople who couldn't make it.' It's critical to assess interdepartmental working relationships as part of the internal environmental audit.

Goal Formulation

goal formulation the process of developing specific goals for the planning period.

Once the company has performed a SWOT analysis, it can proceed to develop specific goals for the planning period. This stage of the process is called **goal formulation**. Goals are objectives that are specific with respect to magnitude and time.

Most business units pursue a mix of objectives, including profitability, sales growth, market share improvement, risk containment, innovation, and reputation. The business unit sets these objectives and then manages by objectives (MBO). For an MBO system to work, the unit's objectives must meet four criteria:

1. *They must be arranged hierarchically, from the most to the least important.* For example, the business unit's key objective for the period may be to increase the rate of return on investment. Managers can increase profit by increasing revenue and reducing expenses. They can grow revenue, in turn, by increasing market share and prices.
2. *Objectives should be quantitative whenever possible.* The objective 'to increase the return on investment' (ROI) is better stated as the goal 'to increase ROI to 15 percent within 2 years.'

marketing Memo

Checklist for Performing Strengths/ Weaknesses Analysis

	Performance					Importance		
	Major Strength	Minor Strength	Neutral	Minor Weakness	Major Weakness	High	Med	Low
Marketing								
1. Company reputation	____	____	____	____	____	____	____	____
2. Market share	____	____	____	____	____	____	____	____
3. Customer satisfaction	____	____	____	____	____	____	____	____
4. Customer retention	____	____	____	____	____	____	____	____
5. Product quality	____	____	____	____	____	____	____	____
6. Service quality	____	____	____	____	____	____	____	____
7. Pricing effectiveness	____	____	____	____	____	____	____	____
8. Distribution effectiveness	____	____	____	____	____	____	____	____
9. Promotion effectiveness	____	____	____	____	____	____	____	____
10. Sales force effectiveness	____	____	____	____	____	____	____	____
11. Innovation effectiveness	____	____	____	____	____	____	____	____
12. Geographical coverage	____	____	____	____	____	____	____	____
Finance								
13. Cost or availability of capital	____	____	____	____	____	____	____	____
14. Cash flow	____	____	____	____	____	____	____	____
15. Financial stability	____	____	____	____	____	____	____	____
Manufacturing								
16. Facilities	____	____	____	____	____	____	____	____
17. Economies of scale	____	____	____	____	____	____	____	____
18. Capacity	____	____	____	____	____	____	____	____
19. Able, dedicated workforce	____	____	____	____	____	____	____	____
20. Ability to produce on time	____	____	____	____	____	____	____	____
21. Technical manufacturing skill	____	____	____	____	____	____	____	____
Organization								
22. Visionary, capable leadership	____	____	____	____	____	____	____	____
23. Dedicated employees	____	____	____	____	____	____	____	____
24. Entrepreneurial orientation	____	____	____	____	____	____	____	____
25. Flexible or responsive	____	____	____	____	____	____	____	____

3. **Goals should be realistic.** Goals should arise from an analysis of the business unit's opportunities and strengths, not from wishful thinking.
4. **Objectives must be consistent.** It's not possible to maximize sales and profits simultaneously.

Other important trade-offs include short-term profit versus long-term growth, deep penetration of existing markets versus developing new markets, profit goals versus nonprofit goals, and high growth versus low risk. Each choice calls for a different marketing strategy.[33]

Many believe that adopting the goal of strong market share growth may mean foregoing strong short-term profits. For years, Compaq priced aggressively in order to build its share in the computer market. Compaq later decided to pursue profitability at the expense of growth. Yet management experts Charan and Tichy believe that most businesses can be growth businesses *and* grow profitably.[34] They cite success stories such as GE Medical, Citibank, and GE Capital, which have all enjoyed profitable growth. Some so-called trade-offs may not be trade-offs at all.

Strategic Formulation

strategy   a company's game plan for achieving its goals.

Goals indicate what a business unit wants to achieve; **strategy** is a game plan for getting there. Every business must design a strategy for achieving its goals, consisting of a *marketing strategy* and a compatible *technology strategy* and *sourcing strategy*.

PORTER'S GENERIC STRATEGIES   Michael Porter has proposed three generic strategies that provide a good starting point for strategic thinking: overall cost leadership, differentiation, and focus.[35]

1. *Overall cost leadership.* Firms pursuing this strategy work hard to achieve the lowest production and distribution costs so they can price lower than their competitors and win a large market share. They need less skill in marketing. The problem with this strategy is that other firms will usually compete with still-lower costs and hurt the firm that rested its whole future on cost.
2. *Differentiation.* The business concentrates on uniquely achieving superior performance in an important customer benefit area valued by a large part of the market. Thus the firm seeking quality leadership, for example, must make products with the best components, put them together expertly, inspect them carefully, and effectively communicate their quality.
3. *Focus.* The business focuses on one or more narrow market segments. The firm gets to know these segments intimately and pursues either cost leadership or differentiation within the target segment.

Nestlé Egypt   In an example of both focus and differentiation, Nestlé has been placing greater priority on bottled water. Bottled water is very important for the consumer, and a contribution to good and balanced nutrition. The cloaked plastic cover on the top of Nestlé's water bottles makes them unique within the market. By differentiating their product in this way from the average bottle of water, which costs about US$0.21, Nestlé can charge $0.34.[36]

The online air travel industry provides a good example of these three strategies: Uflyonline is pursuing a differentiation strategy by offering the most comprehensive range of services to the traveler.

strategic group   firms producing the same strategy directed to the same target market.

According to Porter, firms pursuing the same strategy directed to the same target market constitute a **strategic group.** The firm that carries out that strategy best will make the most profits. International Harvester went out of the farm equipment business because it did not stand out in its industry as lowest in cost, highest in perceived value, or best in serving some market segment.[37]

Porter draws a distinction between operational effectiveness and strategy. Competitors can quickly copy the operationally effective company using benchmarking and other tools, thus diminishing the advantage of operational effectiveness. Porter defines strategy as "the creation of a unique and valuable position involving a different set of activities." A company can claim that it has a strategy when it "performs different activities from rivals or performs similar activities in different ways."

STRATEGIC ALLIANCES   Even giant companies—AT&T, IBM, Philips, and Nokia— often cannot achieve leadership, either nationally or globally, without forming alliances with domestic or multinational companies that complement or leverage their capabilities and resources.

Just doing business in another country may require the firm to license its product, form a joint venture with a local firm, or buy from local suppliers to meet 'domestic content' requirements. As a result, many firms are rapidly developing global strategic networks, and victory is going to those who build the best global networks. Middle East Airlines, for example, is partnering with Air France, KLM, and Qatar Airways to allow travelers to make nearly seamless connections to hundreds of destinations.

Many strategic alliances take the form of marketing alliances. These fall into four major categories.

1. **Product or service alliances.** One company licenses another to produce its product, or two companies jointly market their complementary products or a new product. The credit card industry is a complicated combination of cards jointly marketed by banks such as HSBC Bank Middle East Ltd, credit card companies such as Visa, and affinity companies such as The American University of Beirut.

2. **Promotional alliances.** One company agrees to carry a promotion for another company's product or service. McDonald's, for example, teamed up with Disney for 10 years to offer products related to current Disney films as part of its meals for children.

3. **Logistics alliances.** One company offers logistical services for another company's product. For example, Abbott Laboratories warehouses deliver 3M's medical and surgical products to hospitals across the United States.

4. **Pricing collaborations.** One or more companies join in a special pricing collaboration. Hotel and rental car companies often offer mutual price discounts.

Companies need to give creative thought to finding partners that might complement their strengths and offset their weaknesses. Well-managed alliances allow companies to obtain a greater sales impact at less cost. To keep their strategic alliances thriving, corporations have begun to develop organizational structures to support them, and many have come to view the ability to form and manage partnerships as core skills called **partner relationship management (PRM)**.[38]

partner relationship management (PRM) activities the firm undertakes to build mutually satisfying long-term relations with key partners such as suppliers, distributors, ad agencies, and marketing research suppliers.

Program Formulation and Implementation

Even a great marketing strategy can be sabotaged by poor implementation. If the unit has decided to attain technological leadership, it must plan programs to strengthen its research and development department, gather technological intelligence, develop leading-edge products, train the technical sales force, and develop ads to communicate its technological leadership.

Once they have formulated marketing programs, the marketing people must estimate their costs. Is participating in a particular trade show worth it? Will a specific sales contest pay for itself? Will hiring another salesperson contribute to the bottom line? Activity-based cost (ABC) accounting can help determine whether each marketing program is likely to produce sufficient results to justify its cost.[39]

Today's businesses are also increasingly recognizing that unless they nurture other stakeholders—customers, employees, suppliers, distributors—they may never earn sufficient profits for the stockholders. For example, a company might aim to delight its customers, perform well for its employees, and deliver a threshold level of satisfaction to its suppliers. In setting these levels, a company must be careful not to violate any stakeholder group's sense of fairness about the treatment they're receiving relative to the others.[40]

A dynamic relationship connects the stakeholder groups. A smart company creates a high level of employee satisfaction, which leads to higher effort, which leads to higher-quality products and services, which creates higher customer satisfaction, which leads to more repeat business, which leads to higher growth and profits, which leads to high stockholder satisfaction, which leads to more investment, and so on. This is the virtuous circle that spells profits and growth. The Marketing Insight: *Marketing's Contribution to Shareholder Value* highlights the increasing importance of the proper bottom-line view to marketing expenditures.

According to McKinsey & Company, strategy is only one of seven elements—all of which start with the letter 'S'—in successful business practice.[41] The first three—strategy, structure, and systems—are considered the 'hardware' of success. The next four—style, skills, staffing, and shared values—are the 'software.'

The first 'soft' element, style, means that company employees share a common way of thinking and behaving. McDonald's employees smile at the customer, and IBM employees are very professional in their customer dealings. The second element, *skills*, means employees have the skills needed to carry out the company's strategy. *Staffing* means the company has hired able people, trained them well, and assigned them to the right jobs. The fourth element, *shared values*, means employees share the same guiding values. When these elements are present, companies are usually more successful at strategy implementation.[42]

Another study of management practices found that superior performance over time depended on flawless execution, a company culture based on aiming high, a structure that is flexible and responsive, and a strategy that is clear and focused.[43]

Marketing Insight

Marketing's Contribution to Shareholder Value

Companies normally focus on profit maximization rather than on shareholder value maximization. The late Peter Doyle, in his *Value-Based Marketing*, charges that profit maximization leads to short-term planning and under-investment in marketing, promoting a focus on building sales, market share, and current profits. It also leads to cost cutting and shedding assets to produce quick improvements in earnings and erodes a company's long-term competitiveness by eliminating investment in new market opportunities.

Companies normally measure their profit performance using ROI (calculated by dividing profits by investment). This method presents two problems:

1. Profits are arbitrarily measured and subject to manipulation. Cash flow is more important. As someone observed: "Profits are a matter of opinion; cash is a fact."

2. Investment ignores the real value of the firm. More of a company's value resides in its intangible marketing assets—brands, market knowledge, customer relationships, and partner relationships—than in its balance sheet. These assets are the drivers of long-term profits.

Doyle argues that marketing will not mature as a profession until it can demonstrate the impact of marketing on shareholder value, the market value of a company minus its debt. The market value is the share price times the number of shares outstanding. The share price reflects what investors estimate is the present value of the future lifetime earnings of a company. When management is choosing a marketing strategy, Doyle wants it to apply shareholder value analysis (SVA) to see which alternative course of action will maximize shareholder value.

If we accept Doyle's arguments, instead of seeing marketing as a specific function concerned only with increasing sales or market share, senior management will see it as an integral part of the whole management process. It will judge marketing by how much it contributes to shareholder value.

Source: Based on Peter Doyle, *Value-Based Marketing: Marketing Strategies for Corporate Growth and Shareholder Value* (Chichester: John Wiley & Sons, 2000).

Feedback and Control

A company's strategic fit with the environment will inevitably erode, because the market environment changes faster than the company's seven Ss. Thus, a company might remain efficient while it loses effectiveness. Peter Drucker pointed out that it is more important to 'do the right thing'—to be effective—than 'to do things right'—to be efficient. The most successful companies excel at both.

Once an organization fails to respond to a changed environment, it becomes increasingly hard to recapture its lost position. Consider what happened to the Lotus Development Corporation. Its Lotus 1-2-3 software was once the world's leading software program, and now its market share in desktop software has slipped so low that analysts do not even bother to track it.

Organizations, especially large ones, are subject to inertia. It's difficult to change one part without adjusting everything else. Yet organizations can be changed through strong leadership, preferably in advance of a crisis. The key to organizational health is willingness to examine the changing environment and adopt new goals and behaviors.

Product Planning: The Nature and Contents of a Marketing Plan

Working within the plans set by the levels above them, product managers come up with a marketing plan for individual products, lines, brands, channels, or customer groups. Each product level, whether product line or brand, must develop a marketing plan for achieving

Marketing Plan Criteria

Here are some questions to ask in evaluating a marketing plan.

1. *Is the plan simple?* Is it easy to understand and act on? Does it communicate its content clearly and practically?

2. *Is the plan specific?* Are its objectives concrete and measurable? Does it include specific actions and activities, each with specific dates of completion, specific persons responsible, and specific budgets?

3. *Is the plan realistic?* Are the sales goals, expense budgets, and milestone dates realistic? Has a frank and honest self-critique been conducted to raise possible concerns and objections?

4. *Is the plan complete?* Does it include all the necessary elements? Does it have the right breadth and depth?

Source: Adapted from Tim Berry and Doug Wilson, *On Target: The Book on Marketing Plans* (Eugene, OR: Palo Alto Software, 2000).

---

its goals. A **marketing plan** is a written document that summarizes what the marketer has learned about the marketplace and indicates how the firm plans to reach its marketing objectives.[44] It contains tactical guidelines for the marketing programs and financial allocations over the planning period.[45] It is one of the most important outputs of the marketing process.

Marketing plans are becoming more customer- and competitor-oriented, better reasoned, and more realistic than in the past. They draw more inputs from all the functions and are developed by a team. Planning is becoming a continuous process to respond to rapidly changing market conditions.

Most marketing plans cover one year in 5 to 50 pages. The most frequently cited shortcomings of current marketing plans, according to marketing executives, are lack of realism, insufficient competitive analysis, and a short-run focus. See the Marketing Memo: *Marketing Plan Criteria* for some guideline questions to ask in developing marketing plans.

What, then, does a marketing plan look like? What does it contain?

- *Executive summary and table of contents.* The marketing plan should open with a brief summary for senior management of the main goals and recommendations. A table of contents outlines the rest of the plan and all the supporting rationale and operational detail.

- *Situation analysis.* This section presents relevant background data on sales, costs, the market, competitors, and the various forces in the macroenvironment. How do we define the market, how big is it, and how fast is it growing? What are the relevant trends? What is the product offering and what critical issues do we face? Firms will use all this information to carry out a SWOT (strengths, weaknesses, opportunities, threats) analysis.

- *Marketing strategy.* Here the product manager defines the mission, marketing and financial objectives, and groups and needs that the market offerings are intended to satisfy. The manager then establishes the product line's competitive positioning, which will inform the 'game plan' to accomplish the plan's objectives. All this requires inputs from other areas, such as purchasing, manufacturing, sales, finance, and human resources.

- *Financial projections.* Financial projections include a sales forecast, an expense forecast, and a break-even analysis. On the revenue side, the projections show the forecasted sales volume by month and product category. On the expense side, they show the expected costs of marketing, broken down into finer categories. The break-even analysis shows how many units the firm must sell monthly to offset its monthly fixed costs and average per-unit variable costs.

- *Implementation controls.* The last section of the marketing plan outlines the controls for monitoring and adjusting implementation of the plan. Typically, it spells out the goals and budget for each month or quarter, so management can review each period's results and take corrective action as needed. Firms must also take a number of different internal and external measures to assess progress and suggest possible modifications. Some organizations include contingency plans outlining the steps management would take in response to specific environmental developments, such as price wars or strikes.

marketing plan
written document that summarizes what the marketer has learned about the marketplace, indicates how the firm plans to reach its marketing objectives, and helps direct and coordinate the marketing effort.

Sample Marketing Plan | The A Hotel
www.mplans.com/sample_marketing_plans.php

1.0 Executive Summary

The A Hotel, located in Saudi Arabia, is representative of the five-star brand within the Exclusive Business Hotels of the World group. All A Hotels are boutique properties, offering between 25 and 35 exclusive rooms. The A properties are renowned for their convenient and strategic locations within major cities throughout the country. Also synonymous with the brand are the high level of personal service that guests receive, and its comprehensive range of business facilities available in luxurious settings.

The A Hotel in Riyadh has 35 exclusive rooms and targets corporate guests with a two- to three-night stay requirement. Target business segments include the energy industry; the hotel aims to capitalize on its strategic location in relation to oil refineries, gas power plants, and telecommunications. Differentiating the type of business service offered from that of the competition will assist not only in building the A brand as a whole, but will attract frequent business travelers, who require a higher level of personal service and recognition than they can receive at competitive five-star properties in Riyadh. This will provide them with an opportunity to leverage its core competencies as regards servicing the business traveler in a luxurious environment.

2.0 Situation Analysis

The Exclusive Business Hotels of the World group is the ninth largest international hotel chain in the world, with over 320 wholly owned and managed properties. The group specializes in occupying strategic, inner-city locations and serving primarily corporate clients. The properties range from three- to five-star plus categories, and include the following brands: B Inns (three star), C Houses (four star), and A Hotels (five-star plus). The group has a high instance of repeat business across all its brands, particularly the A Hotels properties, which account for 68 percent of total revenue across the group. The A Hotel in Riyadh is dependent on annually contracted clients from the petroleum and gas sectors with guaranteed room nights per year. This area of business accounts for 70 percent of the property's revenue.

2.1 Market Summary

The current market is somewhat depressed, due to the economic downturn. This threat to the critical corporate sector could be considered to be short- to medium-term, as indications of a return to business travel are observed. The A Hotel must continue to focus on delivering an exemplary business service at affordable rates, in order to develop the customer relationship beyond one stay.

Competitive room rates have been cut dramatically in order to attract contract clients over the next 10–12-month period. The hotel's survival in the current environment will be dependent on repeat corporate contract business and customer loyalty to the brand. The brand must therefore continue to deliver on its promise and values.

2.1.1 Target Market

The A Hotel is a boutique five-star plus hotel comprising 35 luxury guest rooms and specializing in servicing business and corporate clients. It serves the business community, and visiting business travelers, in the city of Riyadh, Saudi Arabia. Key clients are contracted corporate clients originating from both international and domestic markets from within the oil, gas, energy, and telecommunications segments. The strategic location of the property is key to its success in these areas. Key to business success is the level of customer loyalty and repeat business received on an annual basis. A Hotel offers its guests the most up-to-date technical business facilities, both inside the rooms and in the hotel's conference facilities. The guests feel that they can conduct their business from a less austere atmosphere than can be experienced in competitor properties, where there is less personal recognition. They appreciate being called by name when they arrive, and having staff remember their specific requirements, time and again. This service is essential in developing the relationship beyond an initial stay, and evidences its added value in relation to competitive properties in the vicinity.

2.1.2 Market Demographics

Market geographics: Riyadh is the capital of Saudi Arabia, with a population of around 7 million people.

Market behaviors: businesses in the area choose to support one another wherever possible by remaining loyal to long-standing relationships with customers and suppliers. This acts as a means of investing in and supporting the community structure, rather than shifting alliances to large 'newcomer' suppliers, despite the potential cost savings involved. This attitude supports the brand principles of the A Hotel, which has had a presence in the city for 15 years, and is well supported by local business requirements for rooms, conference facilities, and catering business functions.

Based on research carried out in 2001, more than 68 percent of the population had some awareness of the A Hotel. Awareness levels were highest among small- to medium-sized businesses with 20 or more employees, who had utilized the hotel's facilities either for visiting business guests or for their own function.

2.1.3 Market Needs

- Exemplary personal service, and level of recognition that customers have come to rely upon.

- Luxurious, relaxed environment within which to conduct business, an environment which cannot be found at our larger, more impersonal competitors.

- Guests need to know that they can develop a relationship with the hotel that will ensure efficiency, value for their money,

Source: Adapted from Tim Berry and Doug Wilson, *On Target: The Book on Marketing Plans* (Eugene, OR: Palo Alto Software, 2000).

and reliability in supplying them with the support they need, when they need it.
- The A Hotel operates in a city with a very strong sense of community, and it wants to stay an integral part of that community.

2.1.4 Market Trends

Market trends can be categorized as follows: corporate travel policies, local business trends, and economic cutbacks.
- **Corporate travel policies:** as a result of various security issues, as regards traveling in both domestic and international markets, there has been a significant drop in corporate guests visiting the city. Although the level of corporate room business appears to be increasing again, it has had a significant affect on last year's profits and consequent projections for the future.
- **Local business trends:** there has been a period of low activity in the area of conferencing and business catering with local companies electing to conduct meetings and seminars on their own premises in order to cut costs. This is changing, however, as group bookings, incoming visitors, and day use of conference facilities are on the increase.
- **Economic cutbacks:** the city has had to cancel some trade shows and conferences due to low attendance.

2.1.5 Market Growth

The growth rate of the target markets has been steady over the past 5 years. Recent world events have caused a reduction in the growth rate, but current trends indicate a return to projected growth figures within the next 3–6 months. Once restabilized, growth is anticipated to continue at a steady pace in line with the expansions in the region's drilling activities.

2.1.6 Macroenvironment

The external environmental issues that affect the A Hotel are:
- **Political:** a stable environment where little affects the hotel's ability to generate revenue.
- **Economic:** the recent recession has seen many smaller business-oriented hotel chains go into liquidation, as they do not possess the infrastructure to support under-performing properties as the larger chains do. Although recovery is beginning, it may take some time before corporate travel policy restrictions are fully lifted and business travel returns to the same levels as 3 years ago.
- **Social:** the trend towards cost-effective business travel leads hotel guests to seek more value for money, which is where the hotel's added value differentiation strategy comes into play.
- **Technological:** the installation of 'on-board' room reservation systems on certain aircraft requires integration with the hotel group's own central reservation system. This will require a high level of investment.

2.2 SWOT Summary

The following analysis highlights the internal strengths and weaknesses of the organization and the opportunities and threats facing the company in the external environment. A Hotel must work to improve on areas of weakness, while organizational strengths must be leveraged in order to capitalize on external opportunities as they arise, and contingency plans formulated in order to deal with threats presented by the environment.

2.2.1 Strengths

- **Strategy:** established differentiation strategy.
- **Structure:** flat, decentralized structure.
- **Skills:** diverse range of service skills within management and staff.
- **Style:** strong, participative culture.
- **Staff:** specialized and experienced staff who are motivated and highly skilled; a well-trained team who are proud of their hotel and respect and promote the brand values.
- **Shared values:** clear and well communicated.
- **Brand strength:** brand values well represented, engendering brand loyalty among existing and new guests.
- **Reputation:** a strong reputation within the local market and corporate and travel trade markets for reliability, exemplary service, and quality.

2.2.2 Weaknesses

- **Strategy:** differentiation strategy needs to be more clearly communicated externally, in local and national markets.
- **Systems:** formal systems result from the detail-oriented work and environment. Interdepartmental communications could be improved.
- **Staff:** seasonal turnover requires ongoing training and orientation of new staff.
- **Facilities:** certain rooms require renovation and upgrade as regards technical equipment, such as high-speed internet access and laptop links.

2.2.3 Opportunities

- **Market:** returning growth after a period of slump.
- **Competitors:** no direct competition exists at present, in terms of the five-star 'boutique business property' niche.
- **Suppliers:** strong, long-term relationships established with suppliers.
- **Guest dependency:** repeat corporate business based on personal service and quality in a small but luxurious environment.

2.2.4 Threats

- **Market entry:** potential for a competitive, global brand to enter the market with a similar product.
- **Substitutes:** fully furnished and serviced business apartments offering lower daily rates.
- **Economy:** recovery from a small dip into recession may take time.

2.2.5 Historical Results

Marketing activity in previous years has produced positive results. The areas that have produced the best results have been:

- **Service:** high-quality facilities accompanied by exemplary personal service, differentiated from competition, in line with the overall brand strategy, have proven to be a successful approach generating high levels of repeat business.
- **Price:** pricing strategy has been consistent with the differentiation objective, to provide added value for a reasonable rate as opposed to discounting and devaluing our products and services.
- **Place:** service information is provided to the guest via personal selling, direct marketing, advertising, and the internet. Delivery channels include travel agents and international reservations systems.
- **Promotion:** primary focus has been on mass communication via print ads in trade publications and on the internet, direct mail campaigns to existing and prospective clients, and personal selling in the local market. Personal selling provides the means to develop relationships within the local community and generate high levels of corporate activity through the business community. Public relations plays an important role in the marketing mix, presenting the hotel as a supportive member of the community and participating in significant local events to assist in developing ongoing cooperation, ensuring repeat business and good working relationships.

2.3 Competition

Although no direct competition exists, in terms of the five-star plus boutique-style property, other five-star hotels and serviced apartments do compete for the same corporate business sectors.

2.3.1 Direct Competition

- **Hilton:** five-star city hotel, room rates on par with A, older facilities.
- **Marriott:** five-star city hotel, room rates approximately 10 percent higher than A, facility only 4 years old.
- **Hyatt Residence:** five-star furnished apartments, daily rates 15 percent higher than A's double deluxe rates.

These properties offer similar facilities, although they are somewhat less focused on business needs, and incorporate more leisure facilities than A Hotel currently provides.

2.3.2 Indirect Competition

A's indirect competition is 'distance' meetings in the corporate world. The more companies decide to conduct meetings over the phone, using web conferencing and video phone technology, the less business people will travel and the more A Hotel will be affected. A has to keep abreast of all new distance meeting technology, and continue to reinforce with clients that there is no better way to do business than face to face.

2.4 Service Offering

High-quality facilities are accompanied by exemplary personal service, differentiated from the competition in line with the overall brand strategy. This has proven to be a successful approach generating high levels of repeat business. A Hotel offers its guests the most up-to-date technical business facilities, both inside the rooms and in the hotel's conference facilities.

2.5 Keys to Success

Key to the hotel's business success is the strategic location of the property and the level of customer loyalty and repeat business received on an annual basis.

TABLE 2.3	Historical Data		
Variable	**2008**	**2009**	**2010**
Industry Revenue	$100,000,000	$110,000,000	$115,000,000
Company Market Share	2%	2%	3%
Company Revenue	$2,000,000	$2,200,000	$3,450,000
Industry Variable Costs	$70,000,000	$80,000,000	$80,000,000
Company Variable Costs	$1,500,000	$1,700,000	$2,700,000
Industry Gross Contribution Margin	$30,000,000	$30,000,000	$35,000,000
Company Gross Contribution Margin	$500,000	$500,000	$750,000
Marketing Expenses	$300,000	$350,000	$650,000
Company Net Contribution Margin	$200,000	$150,000	$100,000

Prices in US$.

Source: http://blogoscoped.com/archive/2006-10-26-n8o.html

3.0 Marketing Strategy

The strategy is to direct the focus of hotel guests to the issues of quality and value for money, as opposed to simply the bottom-line costs associated with their stay. The marketing strategy will communicate the hotel's brand values, develop close working relationships with its customers and suppliers, and identify the needs of its guests in an effective manner. Continued differentiation and growth are two goals that have been set. Growth will take place by targeting new areas of business within both local and national communities.

3.0.1 Value Proposition

A Hotel offers the best, most personalized service for the corporate traveler. The hotel offers business essentials in every room, such as a nice desk, internet connection, and wireless access, and provides easy-to-access meeting rooms with all audiovisual and technology needs as well as catering for longer meetings.

3.0.2 Critical Issues

A Hotel has many strengths, including its differentiation strategy, flat structure, and highly skilled and well-trained staff. Its weaknesses involve the need to communicate its strategy more clearly in the external environment, and high staff turnover and training requirements due to seasonal fluctuations. Although there is a low to medium threat of a competitive brand entering the market, there are also opportunities as regards the high level of dependency of its guests on its particular service and its strong position within the community with both customers and suppliers. Critical issues for the A Hotel include:

- Continuing to differentiate from the competition and offering added value to guests.
- Retaining current levels of repeat business and developing further customer loyalty in a competitive market.
- Attracting new market sectors.
- Continuing to be perceived as a supportive member of the Riyadh community.

3.1 Mission

The A Hotel's mission is to provide guests with the highest quality of service and standards and deliver on their promise of value and quality above all else. It values its place in the community and will work to develop those relationships and to respect and protect the environment. It will continue to strive to create value for both owners and shareholders while honoring its brand values and encouraging its personnel to develop themselves in an environment of trust, loyalty, and encouragement.

3.2 Financial Objectives

- Increase overall room revenue by 10 percent on the past year.
- Accomplish growth within the given budget of US$250,000.
- Increase corporate contracted rates to reflect the return of confidence in the corporate travel market.
- Keep payroll expenses down and reduce the level of overtime within the workforce.

3.3 Marketing Objectives

- To continue to communicate its strategic objectives to its target markets effectively.
- To provide a positive hotel experience to all its guests.
- To accomplish its growth targets within the given time and budget.
- Expand its markets and identify new markets for its product and services.

3.4 Target Market Strategy

Primary targets continue to be professional visitors to the region from the following industries, where annual corporate contracts can be entered into:
- Oil.
- Energy industry.
- Telecommunication.

    Local firms will be targeted for day use of conference facilities, room nights for visiting executives, and long-stay professional guests.

3.5 Positioning

The A Hotel is positioned as a five-star plus, business traveler's hotel, strategically located and offering a high level of personal service. Its focus is on offering guests added value and differentiating itself in its levels of personal service. A Hotel provides a quality hotel experience where guests are valued and respected and their business is truly appreciated.

3.6 Strategies

3.6.1 Messaging

It is critical to the success of the A Hotel to make sure that it maintains and lives up to the high-quality branding that A properties are known for. The messaging will reflect this high standard with which it wants to be associated. Brochures will be printed with professional-quality photographs on high-quality paper. It will be important to spend a little bit extra on marketing materials to ensure that it keeps up its 'high quality' message for customers.

3.6.2 Branding

The A Hotel is representative of the five-star brand within the Exclusive Business Hotels of the World group. All A Hotels are boutique properties, offering between 25 and 35 exclusive rooms. The A properties are renowned for their convenient and strategic locations within major cities throughout the country. Also synonymous with the brand are the high level of personal service guests receive and the extensive range of comprehensive business facilities available in luxurious settings.

3.6.3 Strategy Pyramids

The A Hotel marketing strategy is to focus customers' attention on the high quality of the services offered. Within this strategy are three main points aimed at different market segments:
- Providing the best business facilities.
- Providing personalized services.
- Providing luxurious amenities.

3.7 Marketing Mix

- **Place:** product and service information is sold to the guest via personal selling, direct marketing, advertising, and the internet. Delivery channels include travel agents and international reservations systems.

- **Product marketing:** high-quality facilities accompanied by exemplary personal service, differentiated from competition quality, as the overall brand strategy has proven to be a successful approach, generating high levels of repeat business.

- **Pricing:** the pricing strategy has been consistent with the differentiation objective, to provide added value for a reasonable rate as opposed to discounting and devaluing the products and services. Room rates quoted are net of tax and service, and are per night, per room with continental breakfast included.

- **Advertizing and promotion:** the primary focus will remain on mass communication via print ads in trade publications and online. Direct mail campaigns to existing and prospective clients will increase as a cost-effective means of targeted campaigning. Personal selling in the local market will remain an important element of the mix in order to continue to build long-term relationships in the local community and generate high levels of corporate activity.

- **Public relations:** activities will continue to play an important role in the marketing mix, presenting the hotel as a supportive member of the community and participating in significant local events.

- **Direct marketing:** direct marketing will be handled by the hotel's PR agency. The hotel will select a targeted list of corporate companies and send them information about A Hotel. Understanding that the hotel staff are not experts in direct marketing, it will be important for the PR agency to handle every aspect of direct marketing for the hotel.

- **Web plan:** the hotel's website is already up and running, but needs to be revamped to give it an updated look and feel, as well as to add secure interactivity. The content is good, but needs a little refresher. It needs:
  - New home page design and navigation;
  - Online reservations capability;
  - A printable brochure;
  - Website goals.

  The website needs to be able to do the following:
  - Convey a message of high-quality, luxury business accommodation;
  - Be indexed on major travel websites so that people find the A Hotel when searching;
  - Allow users to make and change reservations online.

- **Website marketing:** the main website marketing strategy hinges on making sure all major travel sites, such as Expedia.com, uflyonline.com, and Hotels.com, list the hotel when customers search for hotels in the area.

4.0 Financials

The A Hotel's annual marketing budget is US$100,000. Sales are anticipated to achieve a revenue of US$1,172,925. Marketing expenses will equate to approximately 8.5 percent of the overall revenue.

4.1 Break-Even Analysis

Break-even-point = where line intersects with 0

|Fig. 2.8|

Break-Even Analysis

Source: Reprinted by permission of Palo Alto Software.

TABLE 2.4	Break-Even Analysis
Monthly Units Break-Even	145
Monthly Revenue Break-Even	$19,929
Assumptions	
Average Per-Unit Revenue	$137.14
Average Per-Unit Variable Cost	$13.28
Estimated Monthly Fixed Cost	$18,000
Prices in US$.	

4.2 Sales Forecast

Room revenue for this year is based on an average growth rate of 10 percent. This is based on the number of pre-contracted corporate rooms, and an anticipated return to projected business levels.

TABLE 2.5	Sales Forecast		
	FY 2013	**FY 2014**	**FY 2015**
Unit Sales			
Corporate Single	1,925	2,118	2,118
Corporate Double	3,665	4,032	4,032
Corporate Deluxe	2,695	2,965	2,965

	FY 2013	FY 2014	FY 2015
Corporate Suite	268	294	294
Total Unit Sales	8,553	9,409	9,409
Unit Prices			
Corporate Single	$95.00	$95.00	$99.00
Corporate Double	$125.00	$125.00	$135.00
Corporate Deluxe	$175.00	$175.00	$195.00
Corporate Suite	$225.00	$225.00	$240.00
Sales			
Corporate Single	$182,875	$201,210	$209,633
Corporate Double	$458,125	$504,000	$544,253
Corporate Deluxe	$471,625	$518,875	$578,175
Corporate Suite	$60,300	$66,150	$70,560
Total Sales	$1,172,925	$1,290,235	$1,402,620
Direct Unit Costs			
Corporate Single	$7.86	$11.00	$11.00
Corporate Double	$13.92	$13.50	$13.50
Corporate Deluxe	$17.50	$18.50	$18.50
Corporate Suite	$0.84	$0.00	$0.00
Direct Cost of Sales			
Corporate Single	$15,138	$23,298	$23,293
Corporate Double	$51,033	$54,432	$54,425
Corporate Deluxe	$47,163	$54,853	$54,853
Corporate Suite	$225	$0	$0
Subtotal Direct Cost of Sales	$113,558	$132,583	$132,570

Prices in US$.

TABLE 2.6	Marketing Expense Budget		
	FY 2013	FY 2014	FY 2015
Print Advertising	$10,600	$11,600	$12,826
Internet Advertising	$21,000	$23,100	$25,410
Public Relations	$ 6,000	$ 6,600	$ 7,260
Other	$21,000	$23,100	$25,410
Total Sales and Marketing Expenses	$58,600	$64,400	$70,906
Percent of Sales	5.00%	4.99%	5.06%

Prices in US$.

5.0 Controls

The marketing plan is structured to enable the A Hotel to achieve the strategic goals it has set for itself, in terms of increasing overall revenue as a result of differentiating its products and services from the competition. The marketing team will ensure that the plan is implemented to the best of its ability and with the highest levels of efficiency and accuracy.

5.1 Implementation

All figures will be monitored on an ongoing basis in relation to projections versus actuals, and the ongoing plan will be altered or manipulated as necessary in order to react to and, wherever possible, anticipate external changes to the environment.

Annual results will be evaluated at the Region General Manager's meeting where the structure of the plan for the approaching year will also be established.

5.2 Contingency Planning

Contingency plans have been made for the following unexpected developments:

- A slower recovery from the recession: this has been reflected in the moderate increase in levels of corporate business expected.
- The entry into the market of a competitively aligned hotel: differentiation would continue to be the strategic approach with the development of added value and benefits to leverage long-standing relationships and repeat business based on familiarity and personal attention to detail.

5.3 Marketing Organization

The hotel's marketing director leads the PR and marketing team of four in all advertising, promotional, and public-relations-related activities. He works closely with the members of the team to implement and monitor the effectiveness of the marketing plan and evaluate results.

4.3 Expense Forecast

Marketing expenses are projected to be approximately 8.5 percent of overall annual revenue. The breakdown of expenditures is as follows.

Summary

1. The value delivery process involves choosing (or identifying), providing (or delivering), and communicating superior value. The value chain is a tool for identifying key activities that create value and costs in a specific business.

2. Strong companies develop superior capabilities in managing core business processes such as new-product realization, inventory management, and customer acquisition and retention. Managing these core processes effectively means creating a marketing network in which the company works closely with all parties in the production and distribution chain, from suppliers of raw materials to retail distributors. Companies no longer compete: marketing networks do.

3. According to one view, holistic marketing maximizes value exploration by understanding the relationships between the customer's cognitive space, the company's competence space, and the collaborator's resource space; maximizes value creation by identifying new customer benefits from the customer's cognitive space, utilizing core competencies from its business domain, and selecting and managing business partners from its collaborative networks; and maximizes value delivery by becoming proficient at customer relationship management, internal resource management, and business partnership management.

4. Market-oriented strategic planning is the managerial process of developing and maintaining a viable fit between the organization's objectives, skills, and resources and its changing market opportunities. The aim of strategic planning is to shape the company's businesses and products so that they yield target profits and growth. Strategic planning takes place at four levels: corporate, division, business unit, and product.

5. The corporate strategy establishes the framework within which the divisions and business units prepare their strategic plans. Setting a corporate strategy entails four activities: defining the corporate mission, establishing strategic business units (SBUs), assigning resources to each SBU based on its market attractiveness and business strength, and planning new businesses and downsizing older businesses.

6. Strategic planning for individual businesses entails the following activities: defining the business mission, analyzing external opportunities and threats, analyzing internal strengths and weaknesses, formulating goals, formulating strategy, formulating supporting programs, implementing the programs, and gathering feedback and exercising control.

7. Each product level within a business unit must develop a marketing plan for achieving its goals. The marketing plan is one of the most important outputs of the marketing process.

Applications

Marketing Debate
What Good Is a Mission Statement?

Virtually all firms have mission statements to help guide and inspire employees as well as signal what is important to the firm to those outside the firm. Mission statements are often the product of much deliberation and discussion. At the same time, some critics claim that mission statements sometimes lack 'teeth' and specificity. Moreover, critics also maintain that, in many cases, mission statements do not vary much from firm to firm and make the same empty promises.

Take a position: Mission statements are critical to a successful marketing organization *versus* mission statements rarely provide useful marketing value.

Marketing Discussion

Consider Porter's value chain and the holistic marketing orientation model. What implications do they have for marketing planning? How would you structure a marketing plan to incorporate some of their concepts?

Marketing Excellence

>>Intel

Intel makes the microprocessors that are found in 80 percent of the world's personal computers. In the early days, Intel microprocessors were known simply by their engineering numbers, such as 80386 or 80486. Intel positioned its chips as the most advanced. The trouble was, as Intel soon learned, numbers can't be trademarked. Competitors came out with their own 486 chips, and Intel had no way to distinguish itself from the competition. Worse, Intel's products were hidden from consumers, buried deep inside PCs. With a hidden, untrademarked product, Intel had a hard time convincing consumers to pay more for its high-performance products.

Intel's response was a marketing campaign that made history. The company chose a trademarkable name—Pentium—and launched the 'Intel Inside' marketing campaign to build awareness of the brand and get its name outside the PC and into the minds of consumers.

Intel used an innovative cooperative scheme to extend the reach of the campaign: it would help computer makers who used Intel processors to advertise their PCs if the makers also included the Intel logo in their ads. Intel also gave computer manufacturers a co-op reimbursement on Intel processors if they agreed to place an Intel Inside sticker on the outside of their PCs and laptops.

Intel continues its integrated ingredient campaigns to this day. For example, when launching its Centrino mobile microprocessor platform, Intel began with TV ads that aired in the United States and 11 other countries. These ads include the animated logo and now familiar five-note brand signature melody. Print, online, and outdoor advertising followed shortly thereafter. Intel created eight-page inserts for major newspapers that urged the wired world to not only "Unwire," but also "Untangle. Unburden. Uncompromise. Unstress."

Intel even held a One Unwired Day event that took place in major cities such as New York, Chicago, San Francisco, and Seattle. In addition to allowing free trial wi-fi access, the company held festivals in each city that included live music, product demonstrations, and prize giveaways.

The Unwired campaign was another Intel success in marketing. The US$300 million total media effort for the Centrino mobile platform, which also included cooperative advertising with manufacturers, helped generate US$2 billion in revenue for Intel during the first 9 months of the campaign.

Going forward, Intel launched a new brand identity in 2006, supported by a US$2 billion global marketing campaign. The company introduced a new logo with a different font and updated visual look and also created a new slogan: Leap Ahead. In addition to the new logo and slogan, Intel developed a new microprocessor platform called Viiv (which rhymes with 'five') aimed at home entertainment enthusiasts. These moves were designed to create the impression of Intel as a "warm and fuzzy consumer company," with products that went beyond the PC. Intel remained one of the most valuable brands in the world, its US$32 billion brand valuation earning it fifth place in the 2006 Interbrand/*BusinessWeek* ranking of the Best Global Brands. Recently, to create awareness, Intel crowd-sourced a creative promotional campaign to promote its new family of processors that fit its ultra-thin laptops. This fresh approach led to outstanding results through its focus on users' perception rather than the conventional business orientation. The look and feel of this new product, due to user feedback, has proved a successful strategy.

Questions

1. Choose any website with high online traffic and give four marketing reasons for Intel to advertise on the site.

2. Intel operates its marketing plan at two levels: strategic and tactical. Differentiate between the two levels by providing clear examples of each.

3. Identify and discuss the exact value that Intel delivers to its customers.

4. Based on your understanding of Intel's value, draft a market-oriented mission statement for the company.

Sources: Don Clark, "Intel to Overhaul Marketing in Bid to Go beyond PCs," *Wall Street Journal*, December 30, 2005; Cliff Edwards, "Intel Everywhere?" *Business-Week*, March 8, 2004, pp. 56–62; Scott Van Camp, "ReadMe.1st," *Brandweek*, February 23, 2004, p. 17; and David Kirkpatrick, "At Intel, Speed Isn't Everything," *Fortune*, February 9, 2004, p. 34; "How to Become a Superbrand," *Marketing*, January 8, 2004, p. 15; Roger Slavens, "Pam Pollace, VP-Director, Corporate Marketing Group, Intel Corp," *B to B*, December 8, 2003, p. 19; Kenneth Hein, "Study: New Brand Names Not Making Their Mark," *Brandweek*, December 8, 2003, p. 12; Heather Clancy, "Intel Thinking Outside the Box," *Computer Reseller News*, November 24, 2003, p. 14; Cynthia L. Webb, "A Chip Off the Old Recovery?" Washingtonpost.com, October 15, 2003; "Intel Launches Second Phase of Centrino Ads," *Technology Advertising & Branding Report*, October 6, 2003. "*Intel Crowdsources Latest Ad Campaign*," http://daily crowdsource.com/2011/06/20/arts/image/intercrowdsources-latest-ad-campaign/) June 20, 2011.

PART 2 Capturing Marketing Insights

Chapter **3** | Gathering Information and Scanning the Environment
Chapter **4** | Conducting Marketing Research and Forecasting Demand

CHAPTER **3**

Family-run businesses dominate the economies of the Arab world. To grow and prosper, these family businesses have to make adjustments in the way they do business, just as Abdul Rahman Hallab & Sons had to do.

In this chapter, we will address the following questions:

1. What are the components of a modern marketing information system? (pg. 66)

2. What are useful internal records? (pg. 66)

3. What is involved in a marketing intelligence system? (pg. 70)

4. What are the key methods for tracking and identifying opportunities in the macroenvironment? (pg. 73)

5. What are some important macroenvironment developments? (pg. 77)

Gathering Information and Scanning the Environment

Developing and implementing marketing plans requires a number of decisions. Making those decisions is both an art and a science. To provide insight into and inspiration for marketing decision making, companies must possess comprehensive, up-to-date information about macro trends, as well as about micro effects particular to their business. Holistic marketers recognize the importance of proper understanding and appreciation of the marketing environment, and that the marketing environment is constantly presenting new opportunities and threats, and they understand the importance of continuously monitoring and adapting to that environment.

 The Hallab family name from the northern city of Tripoli in Lebanon has been associated with quality oriental sweets for more than 130 years. All Hallab sweets shops branch from the original founder, Rafaat al Hallab. However, when Rafaat wanted to keep the business strictly for his children under Rafaat al Hallab & Sons, three of his brothers withdrew to establish Rafaat al Hallab & Brothers. In 1980, Abdul Rahman, one of Rafaat's sons, sold his shares in the business and created his own, Abdul Rahman Hallab & Sons.

"As soon as one has sons of his own, they want to branch off and work independently. What I am trying to do now with our company is to separate family from business," said Samer el Hallab, who took over running the Abdul Rahman Hallab & Sons family business at the young age of 25. "If you want to succeed in your work you have to love it and do it to perfection. In the first few years I set about learning all I could about the business. I always tell my family that my business comes first, my family second, and I come last." Samer's objective is to run the business professionally, in order to ensure continuity. "In the past, it used to be chaotic: just because you are a Hallab, you work in the business. Now, my nephew has to go through our HR department, sit through an interview, and work as an employee in the business just like anyone else," he said.

The business has grown exponentially in the last 26 years. From a single shop in Tripoli, the company grew to include a state-of-the-art production facility, branches outside Tripoli, and a duty-free outlet at Beirut International Airport. The company's first expansion abroad was a branch in Jordan in 1987, followed by a franchise in Dubai in 2002. While both ventures ultimately closed, the expansion nonetheless helped the Hallabs learn the particulars of the franchise business. Today the company has three branches in Saudi Arabia and is opening a branch in Qatar, another in Abu Dhabi, and a third in Syria.

With so many franchises, the challenge today is maintaining a consistent quality across the whole business spectrum. "In 1980 we had only 20 employees. Today we have over 600. There is no comparison between then and now."[1]

Family businesses are not alone in making adjustments to the way they do business. Each and every business is facing up to changes in the natural environment. In this chapter, we consider how firms can develop processes to track trends. We also identify a number of important macroenvironmental trends. Chapter 4 will review how marketers can conduct more customized research that addresses specific marketing problems or issues. ▽

Components of a Modern Marketing Information System

Although every manager in an organization needs to observe the outside environment, the major responsibility for identifying significant marketplace changes falls to the company's marketers. They have two advantages: they have disciplined methods for collecting information, and they spend more time than anyone else interacting with customers and observing competition and other outside firms and groups.

Some firms have developed marketing information systems that provide management with rich detail about buyer wants, preferences, and behavior. Marketers also have extensive information about how consumption patterns vary across countries. On a per-capita basis, for example, the UAE is the largest sugar and sweetener consumer in the world, followed by the United States. The Chinese eat the most rice and eggs, Australians the most ice-cream, the Greeks eat the most cheese and vegetables, the Danes consume the most biscuits, the British consume the most chocolate, and the Turks drink the most tea.[2]

Nevertheless, many business firms are not sophisticated about gathering information. Many do not have a marketing research department. Others have a department that limits its work to routine forecasting, sales analysis, and occasional surveys. Some managers complain about not knowing how to get hold of critical information; getting too much information that they cannot use and too little that they really need; and getting important information too late. Companies with superior information enjoy a competitive advantage. They can choose their markets better, develop better offerings, and execute better marketing planning.

Every firm must organize and distribute a continuous flow of information to its marketing managers. A **marketing information system**, or **MIS,** consists of people, equipment, and procedures to gather, sort, analyze, evaluate, and distribute needed, timely, and accurate information to marketing decision makers. A marketing information system relies on internal company records, marketing intelligence activities, and marketing research. We'll discuss the first two topics here, and the third one in the next chapter.

The company's marketing information system should be a cross between what managers think they need, what they really need, and what is economically feasible. An internal MIS committee can interview a cross section of marketing managers to discover their information needs. ▪ **Box 3.1** displays some useful questions.

marketing information system (MIS) people, equipment, and procedures to gather, sort, analyze, evaluate, and distribute information to marketing decision makers.

BOX 3.1 ▪ Information Needs Probes

1. What decisions do you regularly make?
2. What information do you need to make these decisions?
3. What information do you regularly get?
4. What special studies do you periodically request?
5. What information would you want that you are not getting now?
6. What information would you want daily? Weekly? Monthly? Yearly?
7. What magazines and trade reports would you like to see on a regular basis?
8. What topics would you like to be kept informed of?
9. What data analysis programs would you want?
10. What are the four most helpful improvements that could be made in the present marketing information system?

Internal Records and Marketing Intelligence

Marketing managers rely on internal reports of orders, sales, prices, costs, inventory levels, receivables, payables, and so on. By analyzing this information, they can spot important opportunities and problems.

The Order-to-Payment Cycle

The heart of the internal records system is the order-to-payment cycle. Sales representatives, dealers, and customers send orders to the firm. The sales department prepares invoices, transmits copies to various departments, and back-orders out-of-stock items. Shipped items generate shipping and billing documents that go to various departments.

Today's companies need to perform these steps quickly and accurately, because customers favor firms that can promise timely delivery. An increasing number of companies are using the internet and extranets to improve the speed, accuracy, and efficiency of the order-to-payment cycle. Cisco Connection Online allows the computer-networking leader to connect with all its suppliers, manufacturers, customers, and resellers online. By reducing payment cycles for suppliers, eliminating paper-based purchasing, and reducing inventory levels, Cisco saved more than US$24 million in material costs and $51 million in labor costs annually in the first years of the program's operations.[3]

Sales Information Systems

Marketing managers need timely and accurate reports on current sales. Walmart, the world's largest retailer, operates a sales and inventory data warehouse that captures data on every item, for every customer, for every store, every day, and refreshes it every hour. For example, in one instance, the IT staff at headquarters tapped into the data warehouse and noticed in the United States that east coast sales of a computer-monitor holiday special were far below expectations. Marketing staff contacted stores and learned that the computers and monitors weren't being displayed together, so potential buyers couldn't see what they were getting for the posted price. Calls went out to Walmart stores across the United States to rearrange the displays. Within hours, the pace of sales could be seen picking up in the company's database.[4] Walmart also transmits nightly orders to its many suppliers for new shipments of replacement stock, even entrusting some companies such as Procter & Gamble, the world's largest consumer product manufacturer and marketers, with the management of its inventory.[5]

Companies that make good use of 'cookies,' records of website usage stored by personal browsers, are smart users of targeted marketing. Although the perception is that most people delete cookies out of concern for their privacy, the numbers tell a different story. A recent survey showed that only 8 percent of people very frequently delete cookies, down from 18 percent in 2004, and 24 percent of respondents said they never delete cookies. Not only do customers not delete cookies, but they also expect customized marketing appeals and deals once they accept cookies.

Other technological gadgets are revolutionizing sales information systems and allowing representatives to have up-to-the-second information. Companies must carefully interpret the sales data so as not to draw the wrong conclusions. For example, if there are three black mobile phones in stock, and a customer wants a white one, the person selling the phones should still be able to sell the customer a white phone. So, the white one will get sold and the factory will produce white phones. If customers want white phones but buy black ones as white is not available, marketers will draw incorrect messages from the sales data.

Databases, Data Warehousing, and Data Mining

Today, companies organize their information into databases—customer databases, product databases, salesperson databases —and then combine data from the different databases. For example, the customer database will contain every customer's name, address, past transactions, and sometimes even demographics and psychographics (activities, interests, and opinions). Instead of sending a mass mailing of a new offer to every customer in its database, a company will rank its customers according to purchase recency, frequency, and monetary value (RFM) and send the offer to only the highest-scoring customers. Besides saving on mailing expenses, this manipulation of data can often achieve a double-digit response rate.

Companies warehouse these data and make them easily accessible to decision makers. Furthermore, by hiring analysts skilled in sophisticated statistical methods, they can 'mine' the data and gather fresh insights into neglected customer segments, recent customer trends, and other useful information. Managers can cross-tabulate customer information with product and salesperson information to yield still-deeper insights. Using its own in-house technology, for example, the U.S. bank Wells Fargo has developed the ability to track and analyze every bank transaction made by its 10 million retail customers: whether at automated teller machines (ATMs), bank branches, or online. When transaction data are combined with personal information provided by customers, Wells Fargo can come up with targeted offerings to coincide with a customer's life-changing event. As a result, compared with the industry average of 2.2 products per customer, Wells Fargo sells four.[6] Aramex, the leading Arab delivery service provider, has learned a lot about its wide range of customers through these types of information systems, and is able to better serve these customers accordingly. Many other firms are also taking advantage of these rich new databases (see the Marketing Insight: *Digging for Information*).

The Marketing Intelligence System

marketing intelligence system
a set of procedures and sources managers use to obtain everyday information about developments in the marketing environment.

The internal records system supplies *results* data, but the marketing intelligence system supplies *happenings* data. A **marketing intelligence system** is a set of procedures and sources managers use to obtain everyday information about developments in the marketing environment. Marketing managers collect marketing intelligence by reading books, newspapers, and trade publications; talking to customers, suppliers, and distributors; monitoring 'social media' on the internet via online discussion groups, e-mail, lists, and blogs; and meeting with other company managers. For a specific example on this, please see *Marketing Insight: Digging for Information* below.

A company can take several steps to improve the quality of its marketing intelligence.

- ***Train and motivate the sales force to spot and report new developments.*** The company must convey clearly to its sales force their importance as intelligence gatherers. Salespeople are valuable sources of information and insight about the market actions of competitors, whether through personal observation of such actions or through their contact with distribution

Marketing Insight

Digging for Information

As companies gather more and more information, their ability to collect and analyze data to generate insights is more critical. Here is what several leading companies are doing.

Best Buy, a leading consumer electronics retailer, has assembled a 15-plus terabyte database with 7 years of data on 75 million households. The company captures information about every transaction and interaction—from phone calls and mouse clicks to delivery and rebate-check addresses—and then deploys sophisticated match-and-merge algorithms to classify over three-quarters of its customers, or more than 100 million individuals. Best Buy places its core customers into profiled categories, such as 'Buzz' (the young technology enthusiast), 'Jill' (the suburban soccer mom), 'Barry' (the wealthy professional man), and 'Ray' (the family man). The firm also applies a customer lifetime value model that measures transaction-level profitability and factors in a host of customer behaviors that either increase or decrease the value of the relationship. Knowing so much about consumers

allows Best Buy to employ precision marketing and customer-triggered incentive programs with more favorable response rates.

Some companies have applied their database knowledge to drive media purchases. To assess the effectiveness of various advertising media, a leading industry group, Interactive Advertising Bureau, conducted a series of tests over an 18-month period for 30 blue-chip companies. Analyzing customer behavior, the study concluded that Ford Motor Co. could have sold an additional US$625 million worth of trucks if it had increased its online budget from 2.5 to 6 percent. After seeing the results, Ford announced in August 2005 that it would shift up to 30 percent of its US$1 billion ad budget into media targeted to individual customers, half of it through online advertising.

Capturing online customer behavior can yield a wealth of insights. A new customer signing up with Microsoft to get a free Hotmail e-mail account is required to give the company his name, age, gender, and zip code. Microsoft can then combine these facts with information, such as observed online behavior and characteristics of the area in which the customer lives, to help advertisers better understand whether, when, and how to contact that customer. Although Microsoft must be careful to preserve consumer privacy—the company claims it won't purchase an individual's income history—it can still provide advertising clients with behavioral targeting information.

Sources: Jeff Zabin, "The Importance of Being Analytical," *Brandweek*, July 24, 2006, p. 21; Stephen Baker, "Math Will Rock Your World," *BusinessWeek*, January 23, 2006, pp. 54–62; Michelle Kessler and Byron Acohido, "Data Miners Dig a Little Deeper," *USA Today*, July 11, 2006.

channel intermediaries (wholesalers and retailers). As such, it is important for companies to motivate distributors, retailers, and other intermediaries to pass along important intelligence. Salespeople are also critical in passing on to the company feedback they receive from the ultimate consumers and business buyers with whom they are in touch.

- *Collect internal information through mystery shoppers.* Many companies hire specialists to gather marketing intelligence.[7] Service providers and retailers often send mystery shoppers to their stores to assess cleanliness of facilities, product quality, and the way employees treat customers. Mystery shoppers for McDonald's discovered that only 46 percent of its U.S. restaurants met internal speed-of-service standards, forcing the company to rethink processes and training.[8] Health care facilities that use mystery shoppers say the reports have led to a number of changes in the patient experience, including improved estimates of wait times, better explanations of medical procedures, and even less-stressful programming on the television in the waiting room.[9] In the Arab world, most full-service pan-Arab research companies (such as PARC, MRO, and Feedback Market Research), in addition to the international research companies, offer mystery shopping services.

- *Network externally.* The firm can purchase competitors' products; attend open houses and trade shows; read competitors' published reports; attend stockholders' meetings; talk to employees, dealers, distributors, suppliers, and freight agents; collect competitors' ads; and look up news stories about competitors. Sometimes one just has to go out into the field and watch the competition. Needless to say, competitive intelligence gathering must be legal and ethical.

- *Set up a customer advisory panel.* Members might include representative customers, the company's largest customers, or its most outspoken or sophisticated customers. Many business schools have advisory boards or councils made up of alumni and prominent businessmen and women who provide valuable feedback on the curriculum.

National Bank of Abu Dhabi

The National Bank of Abu Dhabi (NBAD) is the number one bank in the UAE in terms of total assets, deposits, and branch networks, and its dedication to customer service has been recognized through numerous excellence awards in the UAE, and in the wider Gulf Cooperation Council (GCC) and the Middle East and North Africa (MENA) region. In 2005, the National Bank of Abu Dhabi launched a customer research program that introduced the use of real-time mystery shopping in the UAE. The real-time mystery shopping, introduced in collaboration with Ethos Consultancy, uses the internet as its key communication and research tool to provide management with objective data about customer service levels.

"Customer service is really what sets you apart from your competitors and we believe in putting our customers first, at the heart of our business," commented Khalid Deemas, Head of the Retail Banking Group. "As a number one bank, we have always been proactive, and bringing in Ethos to set up a real-time mystery shopping program will enable us to stay ahead of our competitors by identifying key areas for enhancement and implementing the necessary changes almost instantly." Robert Keay, Managing Partner of Ethos, believes that real-time mystery shopping is a vital tool for any modern business. "Higher consumer expectations, greater regulatory requirements, and increased competition make customer service the 'difference that makes the difference.' Our program will allow the NBAD to take immediate action rather than waiting weeks or even months for feedback."[10]

National Bank of Abu Dhabi is a regional pioneer in using mystery-shopping methodology to better serve its bank customers.

Several international and pan-Arab marketing research companies provide valuable market information about the Arab markets and consumers.

- *Take advantage of available government, world, and industry secondary data resources.* Government-published information and industry association statistics are valuable sources of information about a country's key economic, demographic, social, legal, and political indicators. Such information, which is relatively easily available for free or at minimal cost, could prove to be very valuable when a company based in one country considers, say, extending its products and services into another country through export, direct investment, or partnership. Statistics from world sources such as the United Nations and the various units under its umbrella (UNESCO, ILO, WHO) are as valuable. World Bank publications and statistics are also important, especially for regions such as the MENA where some basic country indicators from governments are sometimes unavailable or unreliable.

- *Purchase information from outside suppliers.* A number of established and reputable marketing research companies exist across the Arab world. Table 4.1 in Chapter 4 lists a number of full-service and specialized-service marketing research companies that operate in countries spanning the Arab world. Some of these companies have worldwide operations covering more than 50 or 60 countries, such as Nielsen, Synovate, and Ipsos. Others have a specific Arab focus and are spread across the Arab world (Nagy Research, Marketing Research Organization, Pan Arab Research Center, and Information International). Some of these research firms gather wholesale, retail, and consumer data at a much lower cost than a company could manage on its own. Purchasing such information from these sources can be beneficial and cost effective for the company.

- *Use online customer feedback systems to collect competitive intelligence.* Online customer review boards, discussion forums, chat rooms, and blogs can distribute one customer's evaluation of a product or a supplier to a large number of other potential buyers and, of course, to marketers seeking information about the competition. Chat rooms allow users to share experiences and impressions, but their unstructured nature makes it difficult for marketers to find relevant messages. Thus some companies have adopted structured systems, such as customer discussion boards or customer reviews.

Some companies circulate marketing intelligence. The staff scan the internet and major publications, abstract relevant news, and disseminate a news bulletin to marketing managers. The competitive intelligence function works best when intelligence operations collaborate closely with key users in the decision-making process. In contrast, organizations where intelligence is seen as a distinct, separate function that only produces reports and doesn't get involved are less effective.[11]

Analyzing the Macroenvironment

Successful companies recognize and respond profitably to unmet needs and trends.

Needs and Trends

Enterprising individuals and companies manage to create new solutions to unmet needs. Aramex was created to meet the need for rapid parcel mail delivery in then war-torn Lebanon. The Toyota Prius was created to meet the need for transportation in an environmentally friendly manner. Apple created the iPhone, which provided a touch-screen user-friendly multi-purpose gadget that attended to the communication needs (phone, messaging), entertainment needs (games, music, internet), and personal needs (organizer, calendar) of the consumer. The iPhone proved to be a massive market success for Apple in an industry that was suffering from stagnant growth when Apple decided to enter it. The iPhone unit sales recorded around 11.5 million units in 2008, 20.7 million units in 2009, and reached almost 40 million in 2010. 2011 sales were expected to exceed 55 million.[12]

We distinguish among fads, trends, and megatrends. A **fad** is "unpredictable, short-lived, and without social, economic, and political significance." A company can cash in on a fad such as the frisbee or the Rubik's Cube, but getting it right is more a matter of luck and good timing than anything else.[13]

fad a craze that is unpredictable, short-lived, and without social, economic, and political significance.

A **trend** is a direction or sequence of events that has some momentum and durability. Trends are more predictable and durable than fads. A trend reveals the shape of the future and provides many opportunities. For example, the percentage of people who value physical fitness and well-being has risen steadily over the years, especially in the under-30 age group, all over the world. In a study conducted in late 2009, 85 percent of UAE consumers and 75 percent of Saudi Arabian consumers said that "maintaining or improving health" had become more important to them over the past 2 years. The study outlines how such health-driven trends influence consumer life style and product choices.[14]

trend a direction or sequence of events that has some momentum and durability.

Megatrends have been described as "large social, economic, political, and technological changes [that] are slow to form, and once in place, they influence us for some time—between seven and ten years, or longer."[15] See the Marketing Memo: *Trends Shaping the Global Business Landscape* for a look into some of the broad forces that are likely to come into play during the next decade or so.

megatrends large social, economic, political, and technological changes that are slow to form, and once in place, have an influence for seven to ten years or longer.

A new market opportunity doesn't guarantee success, even if the product is technically feasible. For example, a few years back when portable electronic books or 'e-books' started appearing on the market, some analysts questioned whether there was going to be a sufficient number of people interested in reading a book on a computer screen or willing to pay the required price. This is where market research is necessary to determine an opportunity's profit potential. Apple's approach to the development of new and innovative products is a classic case. We mentioned earlier the iPhone success story. Apple's more recent introduction of the iPad was just as successful. The iPad sold more than 300,000 units in its first day of introduction on April 3, 2010. By April 8, 450,000 units of iPads were sold, together with 3.5 million iPad applications and 600,000 iBooks being downloaded. In 28 days, iPad sales reached the landmark 1 million units, and in 60 days it surpassed 2 million units. As one industry expert pointed out, "Apple has been able to generate over US$75 million in revenue in one day on a product that 99.9 percent of purchasers haven't touched or for that matter, even seen in person."[16] The iPhone and the iPad successes would not have been possible without Apple's proper and sound market information and research, an appreciation of the market environment, and detailed understanding of their consumers.[17]

To help marketers spot cultural shifts that might bring new opportunities or threats, several firms offer sociocultural forecasts. Research firms such as Bayt.com conduct and publish annual pan-Arab research reports on issues such as jobs and salaries, the role of women in the workforce, internet usage, and consumer confidence. Information international offers a range of research services across many Arab countries.

Information International   Information International is a pan-Arab research and consultancy firm that has served the regional market since 1995. It has conducted major feasibility studies and research projects, including development and needs assessments in health, education, agriculture, and infrastructure facilities; and demographic and socioeconomic studies, including project evaluations and impact assessments. It has also established a department specialized in planning and organizing training programs, including workshops, seminars, and conferences. Over the years, Information International has expanded, with branches and representative offices in many countries including Saudi Arabia, the UAE, Jordan, Bahrain, Morocco, and Egypt, and a full operating team in each country. Its spectrum of services includes market and consumer research, policy and strategic studies, opinion polling, socioeconomic research, management consultancy, environmental studies, and training and workshops. Information International has conducted research in Algeria, Bahrain, Egypt, France, India, Iran, Iraq, Jordan, Saudi Arabia, Korea, Kuwait, Lebanon, Morocco, Oman, Palestine, Qatar, Russia, Sudan, Syria, Tunisia, the UAE, Venezuela, and Yemen.[18]

marketing Memo

Trends Shaping the Global Business Landscape

Management consulting firm McKinsey believes that macroeconomic factors, environmental and social issues, and business and industry developments will shape the business landscape profoundly in the coming years. Here are some of the main trends they have highlighted.

Macroeconomic Trends

1. *Centers of economic activity will shift profoundly, not just globally, but also regionally.* Today, Asia (excluding Japan) accounts for 26 percent of world GDP, the European Union accounts for 15 percent, and the Arab world accounts for three percent (US$1.9 trillion out of the world total of US$63 trillion).

2. *Public-sector activities will balloon, making productivity gains essential.* The unprecedented aging of populations across the developed world will call for new levels of efficiency and creativity from the public sector. Many emerging-market governments will also have to decide what level of social services to provide to citizens who increasingly demand state-provided protections such as health care and retirement security. Private-sector approaches will likely become pervasive in the provision of social services.

3. *The consumer landscape will change and expand significantly.* Almost a billion new consumers will enter the global marketplace this decade as economic growth in emerging markets pushes them beyond the threshold level of US$5,000 in annual household income, a point when people generally begin to spend on discretionary goods. Shifts within consumer segments in developed economies will also be profound.

Social and Environmental Trends

4. *Technological connectivity will transform the way people live and interact.* More transformational than technology itself is the shift in behavior that it enables. Communities and relationships are being formed in new ways. More and more people are meeting online and forming lifelong relationships thereafter. It is estimated that 17 percent of Americans who married between 2008 and 2010 met online. More than 2 billion people now use mobile phones and 9 trillion e-mails are sent a year. A billion Google searches occur every day, more than half in languages other than English. Online social networks have impacted every aspect of our lives, including the political landscape. The Arab Spring uprising of 2011 is a perfect testimony to this.

5. *The battlefield for talent will shift.* The movement to knowledge-intensive industries highlights the importance and scarcity of well-trained talent. There are 33 million university-educated young professionals in developing countries, more than double the number in developed ones. For many companies and governments, global labor and talent strategies will become as important as global sourcing and manufacturing strategies.

6. *The role and behavior of big business will come under increasingly sharp scrutiny.* The tenets of current global business ideology—for example, shareholder value, free trade, intellectual property rights, and profit repatriation—are not understood, let alone accepted, in many parts of the world. Business leaders need to argue and demonstrate more forcefully the intellectual, social, and economic case for business in society and the massive contributions business makes to social welfare.

7. *Demand for natural resources will grow, as will the strain on the environment.* Natural resources are being used at unprecedented rates. Oil demand is projected to grow by 50 percent in the next two decades, and, without large new discoveries or radical innovations, supply is unlikely to keep up. Water shortages will be the key constraint to growth in many countries. And one of our scarcest natural resources—the atmosphere—will require dramatic shifts in human behavior to escape further depletion.

Business and Industry Trends

8. *New global industry structures are emerging.* In many industries, a barbell-like structure is appearing, with a few giants on top, a narrow middle, and then a flourish of smaller, fast-moving players on the bottom. Similarly, corporate borders are becoming more blurred as interlinked 'ecosystems' of suppliers, producers, and customers emerge.

9. *Management will go from art to science.* Long gone is the day of the 'gut-instinct' management style. Today's business leaders are adopting algorithmic decision-making techniques and using highly sophisticated software to run their organizations. Scientific management is becoming the ante that gives companies the right to play the game.

10. *Worldwide open access to information is changing the economics of knowledge.* Open-source approaches to knowledge development are arising as communities, not individuals, become responsible for innovations. Knowledge production itself is growing: worldwide patent applications, for example, rose from 1990 to 2004 at a rate of 20 percent annually, and are on the rise again after a fall in 2009 due to the economic crisis.

Sources: Ian Davis and Elizabeth Stephenson, "Ten Trends to Watch in 2006," *McKinsey Quarterly*, January 2006. Used with permission from McKinsey & Company. Ellen McCarthy, "Marriage-Minded Do Better Online than at Bars, Survey Claims," *The Washington Post*, Sunday, April 25, 2010, www.washingtonpost.com/wp-dyn/content/article/2010/04/23/AR2010042300014.html; "Number of Global Patent Filings Recovers in 2010, UN Agency Reports," UN News Centre, February 9, 2011, www.un.org/apps/news/story.asp?NewsID=37498&Cr=patents&Cr1.

Identifying the Major Forces

Companies and their suppliers, marketing intermediaries, customers, competitors, and publics all operate in a macroenvironment of forces and trends, increasingly global, that shape opportunities and pose threats. These forces represent uncontrollable factors which the company must monitor and to which it must respond.

The beginning of the new century brought a series of new challenges that Arab countries and the rest of the world share: the steep decline of the stock and financial markets, which affected spending, savings, investment, and retirement funds; increasing unemployment; corporate management scandals; and growing concern over national safety and security. These dramatic events were accompanied by the continuation of existing trends that have already profoundly influenced the global landscape. Wireless technology is rapidly becoming a major mode of communication between people; the internet is emerging as a main source of information for consumers as they identify and evaluate (and sometimes even shop for) products and services that satisfy their needs; advancement in technology is bringing more innovative business and consumer solutions and at an accelerated pace; and there is consumption of our world's natural resources at an unprecedented rate. With more Arab Facebook users now than Arab newspaper readers,[19] it is not surprising that more and more companies are opening corporate Facebook accounts to better connect with their customers.

Within the rapidly changing global picture, the firm must monitor six major forces: demographic, economic, sociocultural, natural, technological, and political-legal. We'll describe these forces separately, but marketers must pay attention to their interactions, because these will lead to new opportunities and threats. For example, explosive population growth (demographic) leads to more resource depletion and pollution (natural), which leads consumers to call for more laws (political-legal), which stimulate new technological solutions and products (technological), which, if they are affordable (economic), may actually change attitudes and behavior (sociocultural). The Google case at the end of this chapter describes how that company has successfully capitalized on and even somehow shaped the new marketing environment.

The Demographic Environment

There is little excuse for being surprised by demographic developments. The Singer Company, long known in the Arab world as the 'IBM of sewing machines,' should have known for years that its sewing machine business would be hurt by smaller-size family units and more wives joining the workforce. Yet, Singer was slow in responding, which affected its market performance.

The main demographic force that marketers monitor is population, because people make up markets. Marketers are keenly interested in the size and growth rate of population in cities, regions, and nations; age and gender distribution; ethnic, religious and sectarian mix; educational levels; household patterns; and regional characteristics and movements.

Population Growth Trends

The world population is showing explosive growth: it recorded 6 billion in 1999, totaled 6.8 billion in 2010, will reach the 7 billion mark in 2012, and will exceed 7.9 billion by the year 2025.[20] Here is an interesting picture. If the world were a village of 1,000 people, it would consist of 520 females and 480 males, 330 children, 60 people over age 65, 10 college graduates, and 335 illiterate adults. The village would contain 52 North Americans, 55 Russians, 84 Latin Americans, 95 Eastern and Western Europeans, 124 Africans, and 584 Asians. Communication would be difficult because 165 people would speak Mandarin, 86 English, 83 Hindi/Urdu, 64 Spanish, 58 Russian, and 37 Arabic, and the rest would speak one of over 200 other languages. There would be 329 Christians, 178 Muslims, 132 Hindus, 62 Buddhists, 3 Jews, 167 nonreligious, 45 atheists, and 84 others.[21]

The population explosion has been a source of major concern. Moreover, population growth is highest in countries and communities that can least afford it. The less-developed regions of the world currently account for 76 percent of the world population and are growing at 2 percent per year, whereas the population in more developed countries is growing at only 0.6 percent per year. In developing countries, the death rate has been falling as a result of modern medicine, but the birth rate has remained fairly stable. Feeding, clothing, and educating children, although it can also raise the standard of living, is nearly impossible in these countries.

The Arab world has a population of nearly 330 million. Between 1950 and 1990, its population grew faster than that of any other region. Although the rate of population growth has declined from 3.4 percent in the mid-1980s to 2 percent in the last decade, the pressure remains high. The region is adding about 6 million people every year.[22]

Explosive population growth has major implications for business. A growing population does not mean growing markets unless these markets have sufficient purchasing power. Nonetheless, companies that carefully analyze their markets can find major opportunities.

Population Age and Gender Mix

In general, there is a global trend toward an aging population. By 2005, the population of people aged 60 or over surpassed the proportion of under-fives, and it is unlikely that there will ever again be more toddlers than seniors.[23] But, one has to approach such a simplistic generalization with caution. It might give a deceptive picture of the state of affairs in the Arab world, and in most of the developing world for that matter. National populations vary in their age mix. For instance, at one extreme is Saudi Arabia, a country with a very young population and rapid population growth. At the other extreme is Japan, a country with one of the world's oldest populations. Milk, diapers, toys, and educational and schools supplies will be more important products in Saudi Arabia than in Japan. The share of young adults (those aged 15–29) in the Arab population ranged between 47 and 50 percent in the 1950s to 1990s. Now, it is estimated to be around 46 percent.

The Arab world has a rather unusual and changing age structure compared to the world trend. Between 1990 and 2020 the growth of the economically active population (aged 15–64) will exceed that of the economically dependent population (aged less than 15 and more than 65) by a much greater magnitude than in any other region. The dependency ratio in the region averaged about 90 percent between 1950 and 1980, meaning that MENA had 90 dependents for every 100 adults of working age. This ratio declined to 86 percent in 1990 and to about 70 percent in 2000. It is expected to reach 50 percent in 2025. This trend promises an opportunity for accelerated economic growth in Arab countries. Yet, it also signals pressures on the labor markets. Arab policy makers are facing a new set of challenges focused around providing employment opportunities, higher education opportunities, and living standards for maturing young adults. And with this comes market opportunities for businesses that cater to this group's growing needs.[24]

In terms of gender composition, female labor force participation in the Arab world has risen consistently from about 22 percent in 1960 to 25 percent in 1980, 27 percent in the 1990s, and 32 percent in 2000. Female participation is expected to reach 43 percent in 2020. The female share of the total workforce has also risen from 18 percent in the 1950s to 27 percent in 2000, and an estimated 32 percent in 2010.[25] Several companies have attempted to cater to this growing segment of working women. For example, several GCC banks have opened dedicated branches for women.

Marketers generally divide the population into six age groups: preschool children, school-age children, teens, young adults aged 20–40, middle-aged adults aged 40–65, and older adults aged 65 and up. Some marketers like to focus on cohorts. *Cohorts* are groups of individuals who are born during the same time period and travel through life together. The 'defining moments' they experience as they become adults can stay with them for a lifetime and influence their values, principles, preferences, and also buying behaviors. In the Arab world, key political milestones came to define a series of unique environments that brought life to cohorts which shared such unique experiences. The Arab–Israeli conflict (wars of 1948, 1967, 1973, 1982, 2006), the Iraq crisis (1991, 2003), the national pan-Arab movement of the 1960s, and the changing power and governing structures in several Arab countries are examples of such environmental changes that have shaped the lives of people who lived through such times.

Several GCC banks have opened dedicated branches for women.

Ethnic, Religious, and Other Markets

Countries also vary in ethnic and racial makeup. If we look at the world, at one extreme is Japan, where almost everyone is Japanese; at the other is the United States, where people come from virtually countless national, religious, and ethnic backgrounds. The Arab world also reflects great variation in terms of inhabitant composition among its countries, although perhaps not to the extent of the Japanese/U.S. extremes.

Companies scramble to refine their products and their marketing to reach such diversified consumer groups. For example, ethnic satellite television channels are broadcast across all the pan-Arab satellite networks, particularly in the GCC countries and the Levant, with channels serving the Indian expatriate population.

Ethnic markets for expats flourish in several Arab countries.

Several food, clothing, and furniture companies direct their products and communication messages and promotions to one or more ethnic groups and cultures.[26]

Yet marketers must be careful not to overgeneralize. Within each ethnic group are consumers who are quite different from each other. People from Southeast Asia have their own very specific characteristics, speak different languages, consume different foods, practice different religions, and represent very distinct national cultures. One cannot approach the expatriate workforce from Southeast Asian countries such as Pakistan, India, Sri Lanka, Bangladesh, Nepal, or the Philippines assuming that they are all 'the same.' Even expats from one of these countries, like India, vary in ethnic and religious background.

The Arab world is the birthplace of some of the world's major religions: Judaism, Christianity, and Islam. The region is characterized by religious diversity that enriches social, cultural, and political life. By far the dominant religious belief among Arabs is Islam. Yet Iraq, Syria, Jordan, Palestine, Lebanon, and Egypt all have sizable Christian populations, in addition to Jewish minorities. The story does not end there. Within each religious grouping, there exist many sects. Take the case of Lebanon. As a country of only about 4 million citizens, it has 19 officially recognized religious sects, each with its own specific beliefs that differentiate it from the main religion from which it sprung. More importantly from a marketing perspective, each sect has its own manifestations of such beliefs (even the common ones that it shares with the mainstream religion), which translates into a certain life style and consumption pattern. That spells out diversity and complexity, but also an opportunity for marketers. Consumer purchases of food, clothing, and books are affected by their religious beliefs, creating opportunities for marketers of Halal food, conservative clothing, and religious books. Religious tourism is another. One of Saudi Arabia's primary sources of national income relates to the religious practices around Hajj and Umra. Iraq and Syria have religious shrines that attract many Shiite Muslims. Lebanon is a destination for Christian worshipers. Some travel and tourism companies specialize in and cater to these markets.

As marketers, we are more interested in the resident population (the residents in a certain country) and less interested in the national population (the citizens of a country). As mentioned before, the GCC and the Levant have a sizeable expatriate workforce, which also brings with it another spectrum of diversity. Expats from India or Sri Lanka might be Muslim, Christian, Hindu, or Buddhist. Such diversity also carries with it marketing opportunities.

Diversity goes beyond ethnic, racial, or religions markets. People with physical or learning disabilities also constitute a market force that companies have come to recognize. Some schools now specialize in catering for children with various forms of learning disability, and for children with physical and mental disabilities. Some have created niches for themselves that are much needed to serve this Arab population segment and lend a helping hand to parents and family members who must otherwise face such challenges on their own. Yet, the need is much larger than what the society supplies. Ashoka estimates that although there are 227 specialized government schools for people with disabilities in Egypt, these schools cater for much less than 10 percent of the society need.[27]

Educational Groups

The population in any society falls into five educational groups: illiterate, high-school dropout, high-school diploma, college degree, and professional degree. Over two-thirds of the world's 785 million illiterate adults are found in only eight countries (one of which, unfortunately, is an Arab country): India, China, Bangladesh, Pakistan, Nigeria, Ethiopia, Indonesia, and Egypt. Another disturbing statistic is that, of all the illiterate adults in the world, two-thirds are women.[28] The United States has one of the world's highest percentages of college-educated citizens, around 36 percent. A large number of educated people in a country spells a high demand for quality books, magazines, and travel, and a high supply of skills.

Countries in the MENA region have come a long way in having reasonably high to very high enrollment in primary education. Yet levels are not that encouraging at the secondary level, and less so at the tertiary level. This carries economic implications. A gender gap exists in education, but has been decreasing over the years. The ratio of male-to-female years of schooling fell from 2.5 in 1960 to 1.9 in 1980 and 1.4 in 2000.[29] Marketers have capitalized on this increase in the population of Arab girls attending school by offering school stationery and educational accessories with designs and features specifically targeted at schoolgirls.

Household Patterns

The 'traditional household' consists of a husband, wife, and children. In the Arab world this concept has a broader sense. People often refer to the 'extended family,' which includes grandparents, aunts and uncles, in-laws, and cousins.

In this day and age, more people are divorcing, separating, or deciding to delay getting married. Single households are also emerging, particularly around Arab expatriates working in other Arab countries. Such phenomena have their own marketing implications. Different family structures have distinctive sets of needs and buying habits. For example, people who are single need smaller apartments; inexpensive and smaller appliances, furniture, and furnishings; and smaller-size food packages. Products that target people who live alone and value convenience can be successful.[30] An Americana frozen pizza or a Chef Ramzi frozen *mulukhia* may come in handy after a long tiring day for a young Palestinian engineer working in an Aramco plant in Saudi Arabia's Eastern Province, or for a single Egyptian teacher working in a high school in Doha.

The Arab world is witnessing the global phenomenon of a delay in the age of marriage. Economic conditions are a primary reason. Both men and women are waiting to make the 'right move' until they become more professionally established and able to make a living capable of supporting a family (in both its narrow and extended sense). More women are delaying marriage until after they finish their university education and join the workforce. And more and more women have decided to continue their professional careers after marriage, and even after having children. Marketers must increasingly consider the special needs of such nontraditional households, which in some places are proliferating more rapidly than traditional ones.

Geographical Shifts in Population

This is a period of great migratory movements between and within countries. We have previously discussed issues related to the expatriate population and noted the intra-Arab world expatriate movement. We have also talked about the presence of foreign workers, which is not limited to workers from Southeast Asia, but also extends to the professional and executive workforce from Europe, North America, and Australia.

The GCC countries offer great employment opportunities for nonnationals. In 1975, nonnationals made up 39 percent of the GCC labor force. Ten years later, in 1985, the figure had jumped to 67 percent (almost 26 percent of the population). Since then, the percentage of nonnationals in the labor force has either leveled off or declined slightly, reaching about 64 percent in 2000. The percentage of nonnational workers was about 85 percent in Qatar and the UAE, about 80 percent in Kuwait, about 65 percent in Bahrain, about 60 percent in Oman, and about 55 percent in Saudi Arabia. It was estimated in 2000 that close to 10 percent of Egypt's labor force and almost 15 percent of Yemen's were employed somewhere else in the Arab world region.[31]

Another trend that the Arab world is witnessing is the migration of some of its young educated population to the United States, Canada, Europe, and Australia. Unlike intra-Arab world movement, migration to the West is usually a 'one-way ticket'. It is accompanied by immigrant status, followed by a change in nationality, and educational and work growth opportunities. Within a few years, this one-person immigrant forms a nucleus family and settles down in the host country. While this brings with it massive opportunities at a personal level for the immigrant, several economic experts and social analysts talk about the negative consequences at the national level: depriving the Arab world of some of its brightest minds and valuable talent. This phenomenon is referred to as the *brain drain*.

If we concentrate upon the inhabitants within a country, we can also note a population migration from villages and rural areas to cities and urban areas: a population shift similar to the global trend, but with much greater effects. The Arab world is one of the most urbanized regions of the world. This brings with it challenges as well as opportunities. For example, it strains urban infrastructure (to the extent that slums emerge), and deprives rural areas of working youth, negatively affecting the development of these areas and curtailing agriculture. From a social and lifestyle perspective, it is not an inaccurate generalization to say that, across the Arab world, people living in villages and rural areas lead more casual lives, have larger families, interact more with family and neighbors, and do more outdoor activities.

Other Major Macroenvironments

Other macroenvironmental forces profoundly affect the fortunes of marketers. Here we review developments in the economic, sociocultural, natural, technological, and political-legal environments.

Economic Environment

The available purchasing power in an economy depends on current income, prices, savings, debt, and credit availability. Marketers must pay careful attention to trends affecting purchasing power because these can have a strong impact on business, especially for companies whose products are geared to high-income or price-sensitive consumers.

INCOME DISTRIBUTION Some economic analysts classify the countries of the world along four types of industrial structure: *subsistence economies* like Papua New Guinea and Somalia, with few opportunities for marketers; *raw-material-exporting economies* like the Democratic Republic of Congo (copper) and Saudi Arabia (oil), with good markets for equipment, tools, supplies, and luxury goods for the rich; *industrializing economies* like India, Egypt, and the Philippines, where a new rich class and growing middle class demand new types of goods; and *industrial economies* like countries in Western Europe, which are rich markets for all sorts of goods.

Marketers often distinguish countries using five different income-distribution patterns: (1) very low incomes; (2) mostly low incomes; (3) very low, very high incomes; (4) low, medium, high incomes; and (5) mostly medium incomes. Consider the market for Lamborghinis, an automobile costing more than US$150,000. The market would be very small in countries with type (1) or (2) income patterns. One of the largest single markets for Lamborghinis turns out to be Portugal (income pattern 3), which is one of the poorer countries in Western Europe, but one with enough wealthy families to afford expensive cars.

One shared characteristic of many Arab countries is the dependence of their economies on oil and gas as their main source of national income. The economies of Algeria, Libya, Iraq, Kuwait, Saudi Arabia, the UAE, and Qatar rely primarily on oil and gas. As such, business cycles, economic opportunities, market potential and size, and national income are driven by oil prices. As worldwide demand for energy continues to escalate, and with no available efficient and cost-effective substitute for oil and its derivatives, oil prices will maintain their high levels. With this comes wealth for oil-producing countries and opportunities for business. ⌨ **Table 3.1** shows the population and GDP figures for the oil economies of the Arab world compared with their fellow Arab countries.

National and per-capita income is one thing. Income distribution is another. Over the past three decades in the world, and the Arab world too for that matter, the rich have grown richer, the middle class has shrunk, and the poor have remained poor. This has led to a two-tier market, with affluent people able to buy expensive goods and working-class people having to spend more carefully, shopping at discount stores and selecting less-expensive store brands.

TABLE 3.1	Population and GDP per Capita in Arab Countries (2008, Projections)				
Country Group	Total Population (millions)	Population Share (%)	GDP (PPP* US$ billion)	GDP Share (%)	Per-Capita GDP (PPP US$)
Group 1: Oil Economies	40.2	13.2	1,117	45.9	27,786
Group 2: Mixed Oil Economies	39.9	13.1	332	13.6	8,313
Group 3: Diversified Economies	156.4	51.5	833	34.2	5,328
Group 4: Primary Export Economies	67.1	22.1	153	6.3	2,277
Total	303.6	100	2,435	100	8,020

Group 1: Oil Economies: the GCC states (Bahrain, Kuwait, Oman, Qatar, Saudi Arabia, the UAE).
Group 2: Mixed Oil Economies: Algeria and Libya.
Group 3: Diversified Economies: Egypt, Jordan, Lebanon, Morocco, Syria, Tunisia.
Group 4: Primary Export Economies: Comoros, Djibouti, Mauritania, Sudan, Yemen.
*PPP = Purchasing Power Parity.

Source: UNDP Arab Knowledge Report, 2009.

SAVINGS, DEBT, AND CREDIT Consumer expenditures are affected by savings, debt, and credit availability. There is no doubt that the financial and banking sectors in the Arab world have developed exponentially over the past few years. Arab banks, once primarily, and perhaps exclusively, focused on the commercial business sector, have ventured into retail and consumer banking. Such ventures have not only been rewarding for the banks, but also for consumers and for a variety of sectors and industries. For instance, real estate developers, car dealerships, and universities have benefited from bank-supported housing loans, car loans, and educational loans, respectively. Insurance companies have also benefited from tagging their insurance services to these loans. For example, an insurance policy for the borrower is part of the requirements for obtaining a housing loan. Banks have also pumped money into the consumer market by placing more money in the hands and pockets of households through extending credit facilities for personal consumption through credit cards.

A number of Arab families augment their incomes through transfers they receive from relatives working and making a living in other Arab or non-Arab countries. A good number of families in Palestine, Lebanon, Egypt, Algeria, and Morocco rely on such transfers to maintain a certain standard of living. This is good business for companies and financial institutions offering money-transfer services.

FAMILY BUSINESS The opening vignette in this chapter told the story of Abdul Rahman Hallab & Sons, one of the icons of oriental sweets. Hallab is but one example of family-run businesses which dominate the private business sector in the Arab world. It is estimated that family-run businesses control 70 percent of the Middle East private business sector, reflecting the importance of this type of business enterprise to the economic development of their countries. Family businesses face unique challenges, some of which threaten their existence. The following Marketing Insight: *It's All in the Family*, sheds light upon family-run businesses in the Arab world and some of the issues they face.

In order to maintain a certain standard of living, a number of Arab families augment their incomes through transfers they receive from relatives working in other countries.

Marketing Insight

It's All in the Family

According to *Euromoney* magazine, more than 70 percent of the Middle East private sector is believed to be controlled by family-run businesses.[32] The contribution of family businesses peaks in Saudi Arabia (the largest economy in the GCC and the Levant) where it dominates around 90 percent of the private sector. As such, the participation of family-run businesses in economic life and their contribution to employment and economic growth is quite significant in the Arab world.

Experts say that family-run businesses are critical for the economic development of Arab countries as these countries attempt to drift away from reliance on the public sector and oil. The private sector, led by family businesses, will be asked to create employment opportunities for a growing Arab workforce, estimated to add an additional 80 million to its ranks by 2020 (the Arab labor force was estimated to be around 104 million workers in 2000 and 146 million in 2010, and is expected to reach 185 million by 2020).

Below is a partial sampling of families with major business interests in the MENA region:

- **Bahrain:** Fakhroo, Kanoo, Zayyani.
- **Egypt:** Fayed, Sawiris.
- **Jordan**; Darwazah, Masri, Nuqul, Saifi.
- **Kuwait:** Al-Bahr, Bahbahani, Al-Ghanem, Al-Homaidhi, Al-Kharafi, Al-Mulla, Al-Saqr, Al-Shaya.
- **Lebanon:** Audi, Frem, Ghandour, Hallab, Kassar.
- **Palestine:** Kaddumi, Khoury, Sabbagh, Abou Ghazaleh.
- **Qatar:** Darwish, Al-Fardan.
- **Saudi Arabia:** Bin Mahfouz, Gossaibi, Al-Jameel, Juffali, Olayan, Al-Rajhi, Zamil.
- **Sudan:** Haddad.
- **Syria:** Baalbaki, Haykal, Rabbat, Shallah.
- **The UAE:** Al-Futtaim, Al-Ghurair, Al-Habtoor, Al-Majed, Al-Nabouda.

Family-run businesses face a number of challenges as they attempt to defend, maintain, and sustain their existence in the face of an increasingly competitive business environment. First, there is the threat of new entrants, particularly international powerhouses looking favorably at an attractive region which was less affected by the global economic and financial crisis, and has a growing population and purchasing power.

Another critical challenge is managing the transition of their family-controlled and -run businesses to a third generation of family members. It is reported that less than 6 percent of all family businesses across the world manage to survive to the third generation. The picture is gloomier in the Arab world, where this survival rate hits a low of 2 percent.[33]

Among the reported reasons for this is a lack of sustainable growth strategies, little to no succession planning, an attachment to unprofitable businesses, poor formal governance structures, and a lack of separation between ownership and management. Family businesses have to tackle these challenges to ensure their sustainability and growth across generations and to be able to positively contribute to the development of their countries.

Sources: Euromoney, "Family Businesses and Private Equity," June 2005 Supplement, 10–11; World Bank, "Unlocking the Employment Potential in the Middle East and North Africa: Toward a New Social Contract," MENA Development Report, 2004; G. Stuart Makings, "Family Business Governance in the Middle East: The Challenges Facing Continuity of Businesses in the Middle East," Oxford University Press, 2009.

Sociocultural Environment

Society shapes the beliefs, values, and norms that largely define consumer tastes and preferences. People absorb, almost unconsciously, a world view that defines their relationships to themselves, to others, to organizations, to society, to nature, and to the universe.

- **Views of themselves.** As the economies of the Arab world grew and prospered, so did people's spending habits and life styles. Consumer leisure-time activities changed too. People bought cars and vacations, and spent more time engaged in health activities (physical exercise, sport) and doing arts and crafts. Others adopted more conservative behaviors and ambitions.

- **Views of others.** Arabs are known for their concern for the well-being of their close and extended family members and neighbors. Also, nowadays, people are showing more and more concern for the well-being of their societies and about shared social problems. At the same time, they seek out their 'own kind' for serious and long-lasting relationships, and avoid strangers. These trends mean a growing market for social-support products and services that promote direct relationships between human beings, such as health clubs, cruises, and religious activity. They also suggest a growing market for 'social surrogates' such as television, home video games, and chat rooms on the internet.

A growing appreciation of nature is among the elements of the sociocultural environment to which marketers have responded with outdoor gear and wilderness trips.

- *Views of organizations.* After a wave of company downsizings and corporate accounting scandals, there has been an overall decline in organizational loyalty.[34] Many people today see work not as a source of satisfaction, but as a required chore to earn money to enjoy their nonwork hours. Companies need to find new ways to win back consumer and employee confidence. They need to make sure they are good corporate citizens and that their consumer messages are honest.[35]

- *Views of society.* Some people defend society (preservers), some run it (makers), some take what they can from it (takers), some want to change it (changers), some are looking for something deeper (seekers), and still others want to leave it (escapers).[36] Consumption patterns often reflect social attitudes. Makers tend to be high achievers who eat, dress, and live well. Changers usually live more economically, drive smaller cars, and wear simpler clothes. Escapers and seekers are a major market for movies, music, surfing, and camping.

- *Views of nature.* People have come to realize how fragile our nature is and how limited our resources. People have grown to appreciate nature and are indulging more in exploring and experiencing it. Business has responded to the increased interest in experiencing nature by producing a variety of products and services that help people attend to such needs. The Arab world is seeing more companies, such as Wild Discovery, that provide excursions and vacations in natural resorts, and companies marketing outdoor gear and wear, such as the Baroody Group.

Other cultural characteristics of interest to marketers are the persistence of core cultural values and the existence of subcultures. Let's look at both.

HIGH PERSISTENCE OF CORE CULTURAL VALUES It is not an overgeneralization to say that people in the Arab world still believe in work, getting married, giving to charity, and being honest. *Core beliefs* and values are passed on from parents to children and reinforced by major social institutions such as schools, mosques and churches, businesses, and governments. *Secondary beliefs* and values are more open to change. Believing in the institution of marriage is a core belief; believing that people ought to get married early is a secondary belief.

core values the belief systems that underlie consumer attitudes and behavior, and that determine people's choices and desires over the long term.

Marketers have some chance of changing secondary values, but face difficulty and resistance when attempting to change **core values**. For instance, the nonprofit organization Kunhadi does not try to stop people from drinking alcohol, but it does denounce driving while drunk, and heavily emphasizes that this practice is socially unacceptable. Although core values are fairly persistent, cultural swings do take place. Major entertainers, through the assistance of mass media, have a lot of impact on young people's hairstyles, clothing, social behavior, and life goals. Today's young people are influenced by social phenomena from both within and outside the Arab society, like pop singers and bands such as Amr Diab, Nancy Ajram, U2, and Shakira; and football sensations such as Mohammad Abu Treika, Nasser Al-Kahtani, and Christiano Ronaldo. Marketers build on such identification by using such personalities in their advertising and promotion campaigns.

subculture subdivisions of a culture that provide more specific identification and socialization, such as nationalities, religions, racial groups, and geographical regions.

EXISTENCE OF SUBCULTURES Each society contains **subcultures**, groups with shared values, beliefs, preferences, and behaviors emerging from their special life experiences or circumstances. There are sometimes unexpected rewards in targeting subcultures. Marketers have always loved teenagers because they are society's trendsetters in fashion, music, entertainment, ideas, and attitudes. Marketers also know that if they attract someone as a teen, there's a good chance they will keep the person as a customer later in life. Frito-Lay, which draws 15 percent of its Lay's potato chips sales from teens, said it saw a rise in chip snacking by grown-ups. "We think it's because we brought them in as teenagers," said Frito-Lay's marketing director.[37] The teen market is of specific importance in the Arab world, given the size and growth of that segment.

Natural Environment

The deterioration of the natural environment is a major global problem. There is great concern about 'greenhouse gases' in the atmosphere due to the burning of fossil fuels (such as carbon and oil); about the depletion of the ozone layer due to certain chemicals and global warming; and about growing shortages of water. The Arab world shares those concerns with the rest of the world, although there is some variation between Arab countries (and sometimes even within an Arab country) regarding the extent of awareness and action. In Western Europe, 'green' political parties have vigorously pressed for public action to reduce industrial pollution. In the United States, experts have documented ecological deterioration, and lobby groups carry these concerns into political and social action. Greenpeace, one of the world's leading environmental activist groups, is now present and operational in several countries in the Middle East and North Africa.

New regulations have hit certain industries very hard. Steel companies and public utilities have had to invest billions of dollars in pollution-control equipment and more environmentally friendly fuels. The soap industry increased its products' biodegradability. Great opportunities await companies and marketers who can create solutions that reconcile prosperity with environmental protection. Consider how the auto industry has adjusted to environmental concerns.[38]

Toyota Prius   Some auto experts laughed at Toyota when it launched its Prius sedans with hybrid gas-and-electric engines in 2001 and predicted sales of 300,000 cars within 5 years. But by 2004 the Prius was such a huge hit that it had a 6-month waiting list. Toyota's winning formula consists of a powerful electric motor and the ability to quickly switch power sources—resulting in 23 kilometers per liter for city and highway driving—with the roominess and power of a family sedan and an eco-friendly design and look, for a little over US$20,000. The lesson? Products that consumers see as good for the environment and that are functionally successful can be enticing options. Toyota is now adding hybrids throughout its auto lineup, and other automakers have followed suit. Hybrid cars are gaining popularity in the Arab world, particularly in Jordan, which is the largest importer of fuel-efficient cars in the Levant region.

Consumers often appear conflicted about product decisions that affect the natural environment. One research study showed that although 80 percent of U.S. consumers said environmental safety influenced their decision to buy a product, only a little over half confirmed that they bought recycled or environmentally safe products.[39] Young people are generally more likely to feel that nothing they do personally makes a difference in solving environmental problems. Increasing the number of green products they buy requires consumers to break their loyalty habits, overcome skepticism about the motives behind the introduction of the products and their quality level, and change their attitudes about the role such products play in environmental protection (see Marketing Insight: *Green Marketing*).

Corporate environmentalism is the recognition of the importance of environmental issues facing the firm and the integration of these issues into the firm's strategic plans.[40] Marketers practicing corporate environmentalism need to be aware of the threats and opportunities associated with four major trends in the natural environment: the shortage of raw materials, especially water; the increased cost of energy; increased pollution levels; and the changing role of governments.

- The earth's raw materials consist of the infinite, the finite renewable, and the finite nonrenewable. *Finite nonrenewable resources*—oil, coal, platinum, zinc, silver—pose a particularly serious problem as the point of depletion approaches. Firms making products that require these increasingly scarce minerals face substantial cost increases. Firms engaged in research and development have an excellent opportunity to develop substitute materials.

- The world economy is highly dependent upon one finite nonrenewable resource: oil. As oil prices soar to record levels, companies are searching for practical means to make use of solar, nuclear, wind, and other alternative forms of energy.

- Some industrial activity will inevitably damage the natural environment. Our own consumption and life styles also contribute to this damage. A large market has been created for pollution-control solutions, such as garbage and sewage treatment plants, recycling centers, and landfill systems, and this has led to a search for alternative ways to produce and package goods.

Marketing Insight

Green Marketing

By the day, more and more people around the world, the Arab world included, are becoming more aware of and concerned about the environment. People vary in their environmental sensitivity. Environmental concerns are manifested in many behaviors, whether through trying to save electricity at home, recycle newspapers, return bottles or cans, or buy products made from or packaged in recycled materials.

A new Bank of America tower in New York designed by Cook & Fox takes sustainability to new heights. Every drop of rain that falls on its roof will be captured for use; scraps from the cafeteria will be fermented in the building to produce methane as a supplementary fuel for a generator designed to produce more than half the building's electricity; and the waste heat from the generator will both warm the offices and power a refrigeration plant to cool them.

The new headquarters of Dubiotech (the Dubai centre of excellence for biotechnology education and research) is said to comprise the world's largest green buildings. Dubiotech headquarters consist of two connected buildings oriented to maximize day-lighting and views while minimizing solar gain. It also integrates a 46,450-square-meter animal reserve for indigenous conservation and wildlife protection. Companies such as G-Building, the brainchild of Arab entrepreneur Nader El Nakib, specialize in advising on green building in the MENA and GCC regions.

Little things can add up. When Anheuser-Busch developed an aluminum can 33 percent lighter than previous cans, the reduced use of aluminum combined with an overall recycling plan saved the company US$200 million a year.

From a branding perspective, however, 'green marketing' programs have not been entirely successful. Two main problems are that (1) consumers may believe the product is of inferior quality as a result of being green and (2) they may feel the product is not really that green to begin with. Successful green products convincingly overcome both these concerns to persuade consumers they are acting in their own and society's long-term interests at the same time. Examples are organic foods that are seen as healthier, tastier, and safer, and energy-efficient appliances that cost less to run. Ottman and her colleagues refer to the tendency to overly focus on a product's greenness as "green marketing myopia." Box 3.2 displays their recommendations for avoiding myopia by following three key principles: consumer value positioning, calibration of consumer knowledge, and the credibility of product claims.

Many top companies such as McDonald's, Nike, GE, and DuPont are embracing sustainability and green marketing. UPS and FedEx have introduced alternative-fuel and hybrid electric diesel vehicles to their fleets. Aramex was one of the first companies in the Arab world (and perhaps the world) to use the Toyota Prius hybrid electric car in its operations. A few years ago Coca-Cola adopted the planting of Sedar trees in one of the mountains of Lebanon affected by deforestation.

Sources: Jerry Adler, "Going Green," *Newsweek*, July 17, 2006, pp. 43–52; Jacquelyn A. Ottman, Edwin R. Stafford, and Cathy L. Hartman, "Avoiding Green Marketing Myopia," *Environment*, June 2006, pp. 22–36; Jill Meredith Ginsberg and Paul N. Bloom, "Choosing the Right Green Marketing Strategy," *MIT Sloan Management Review*, Autumn 2004, pp. 79–84; Marc Gunther, "Tree Huggers, Soy Lovers, and Profits," *Fortune*, June 23, 2003, pp. 98–104; Roper ASW, "Green Gauge Report 2002" (New York: Roper ASW, 2002); Jacquelyn Ottman, *Green Marketing: Opportunity for Innovation*, 2nd edn (Chicago: NTC/Contemporary Publishing Company, 1998); Mahesh Basantani, "Dubiotech: New Largest Green Building in Dubai," www.inhabitat .com/2007/11/15/dubiotech-new-worlds-largest-green-building-in-dubai; www.gbldg.com.

- Governments vary in their concern for and efforts to promote a clean environment. Many poor nations are doing little about pollution, largely because they lack the funds or the political will. It is in the richer nations' interests to help the poorer nations control their pollution, but even the richer nations today lack the necessary funds.

Technological Environment

One of the most dramatic forces shaping people's lives is technology. Through the years, technology has produced wonders such as penicillin, open-heart surgery, and organ transplants, and horrors such as the atomic bomb, nerve gas, and all kinds of military weapons. It has also released mixed blessings such as mobile phones and video games.

Every new technology is a force for 'creative destruction.' Transistors hurt the vacuum-tube industry, photocopies hurt the carbon-paper business, autos hurt the railroads, and television hurt the newspapers. Instead of moving into the new technologies, many old industries fought or ignored them, and their businesses declined. Yet it is the essence of market development to be dynamic and tolerate the creative destructiveness of technology as the price of progress.

The number of major new technologies we discover affects the economy's growth rate. Unfortunately, technological discoveries do not arise evenly through time—the railroad industry

BOX 3.2	Three Keys to Avoiding Green Marketing Myopia

Consumer Value Positioning

- Design environmental products to perform as well as (or better than) alternatives.
- Promote and deliver the consumer-desired value of environmental products and target relevant consumer market segments (such as marketing health benefits among health-conscious consumers).
- Broaden mainstream appeal by bundling (or adding) consumer-desired value into environmental products (such as fixed pricing for subscribers of renewable energy).

Calibration of Consumer Knowledge

- Educate consumers with marketing messages that connect environmental product attributes with desired consumer value (for example, "pesticide-free produce is healthier"; "energy-efficiency saves money"; or "solar power is convenient").
- Frame environmental product attributes as "solutions" for consumer needs (for example, "rechargeable batteries offer longer performance").
- Create engaging and educational internet sites about environmental products' desired consumer value (for example, Tide Coldwater's interactive website allows visitors to calculate their likely annual cost savings based on their laundry habits, utility source [gas or electricity], and zip code location).

Credibility of Product Claims

- Employ environmental product and consumer benefit claims that are specific, meaningful, unpretentious, and qualified (that is, compared with comparable alternatives or likely usage scenarios).
- Procure product endorsements or eco-certifications from trustworthy third parties, and educate consumers about the meaning behind those endorsements and eco-certifications.
- Encourage consumer evangelism via consumers' social and internet communication networks with compelling, interesting, and/or entertaining information about environmental products (for example, Tide's "Coldwater Challenge" website included a map of the United States so visitors could track and watch their personal influence spread when their friends requested a free sample).

Source: Jacquelyn A. Ottman, Edwin R. Stafford, and Cathy L. Hartman, "Avoiding Green Marketing Myopia," *Environment*, June 2006, pp. 22–36.

created a lot of investment, and then investment leveled out until the auto industry emerged. In the time between major innovations, an economy can stagnate. In the meantime, minor innovations fill the gap: freeze-dried coffee, combination shampoo and conditioner, antiperspirants and deodorants, and the like. They require less risk, but they can also divert research effort away from major breakthroughs.

New technology also creates major long-run consequences that are not always foreseeable. Mobile phones, video games, and internet are not only reducing attention to traditional media, they are reducing face-to-face social interaction as people listen to music, watch a movie on their phone, and so on. Technologies also compete with each other in attending to the same underlying consumer needs. Consider the variety of means available to people to communicate and exchange information with one another: landline telephone, mobile telephone, voice-over-IP, social network sites (Facebook, Myspace, Twitter), fax, overnight courier, express courier, registered mail, traditional mail, personal delivery, etc.

The adoption of personal computers and the penetration of the internet has changed the way people acquire information and knowledge, and has had a direct impact on people's way of living. Research by Bayt.com on Arab internet users revealed that the internet provided the second (websites) and third (search engines) most cited sources of information that consumers seek before deciding on which products or services they want to buy.[41]

In most Arab countries, the number of computers per person is less than the global average. Internet usage in the Arab world has enjoyed wide proliferation in the last 5 years. However, a wide discrepancy exists in internet penetration across Arab countries, with some countries exceeding the world average of 21 percent of the population, while others are way below.[42] Internet penetration in the Arab countries in early 2011 is shown in **Table 3.2**.

TABLE 3.2	Internet Penetration in Arab countries in 2011

Country	Internet Penetration (%)
The UAE	69
Qatar	67
Bahrain	54
Palestine (West Bank)	54
Oman	49
Saudi Arabia	44
Kuwait	42
Morocco	41
Tunisia	34
Jordan	27
Lebanon	26
Egypt	25
Syria	20
Algeria	13
Yemen	10
Sudan	9
Libya	5
Djibouti	7
Iraq	1

Source: www.internetworldstats.com.

As for languages used on the internet, Arabic ranked sixth among world languages (behind English, Chinese, Spanish, Japanese, Portuguese, and German and ahead of French, Russian, and Korean). At the beginning of 2008, the number of internet users who were using Arabic approached 60 million (or 17 percent of the population). The growth rate among Arabic-speaking internet users (2064 percent in the period 2000–2008) was the highest among the top 10 languages on the internet; a positive trend.[43]

Marketers should monitor the following four trends in technology: the accelerating pace of change, the unlimited opportunities for innovation, varying research and development (R&D) budgets, and the increased regulation of technological change.

ACCELERATING PACE OF CHANGE Many of today's common products were not available 40 years ago. Electronic researchers are building smarter chips to make our cars, homes, and offices connected and more responsive to changing conditions. More ideas than ever are being developed, and the time between the appearance of new ideas and their successful implementation is diminishing. So is the time between introduction and peak production. Portfolio Research reports that it took Facebook 5 years to reach 150 million users (2004–2009), the iPod 7 years (2001–2008), mobile phones 14 years (1983–1997), TV 38 years (1928–1966), and telephone 89 years (1876–1965).[44]

UNLIMITED OPPORTUNITIES FOR INNOVATION Some of the most exciting work today is taking place in biotechnology, computers, microelectronics, telecommunications, robotics, and designer materials. The Human Genome Project for example, and the numerous fields that have arisen from it, promise to lead the biological century as biotech workers create new medical cures, new foods, and new materials. They are designing robots for firefighting, underwater exploration, and home nursing. The Dubiotech initiative (see Marketing Insight: *Green Marketing* on page 82) is another example of such innovation.

VARYING R&D BUDGETS With stakeholder pressure to produce safe and quick returns on investment in research and development, many companies are content to put their money into copying competitors' products and making minor feature and style improvements. Even basic research companies such as DuPont, Bell Laboratories, and Pfizer are proceeding cautiously, and more consortiums than single companies are directing their research efforts toward major breakthroughs. Unfortunately, the Arab world lags behind in terms of investments in R&D.

INCREASED REGULATION OF TECHNOLOGICAL CHANGE Governments have expanded their agency powers to investigate and ban potentially unsafe products. In the United States, the Federal Food and Drug Administration must approve all drugs before they can be sold. Safety and health regulations have also increased in the areas of food, automobiles, clothing, electrical appliances, and construction. Several Arab states (such as the UAE) have very strict rules and regulations relating to personal and public safety and health.

Political-Legal Environment

The political and legal environment consists of laws, government agencies, and pressure groups that influence and limit various organizations and individuals. Sometimes these laws also create new opportunities for business. For example, mandatory recycling laws have given the recycling industry a major boost and spurred the creation of dozens of new companies making new products from recycled materials. Two major trends in the political-legal environment are the increase in business legislation and the growth of special-interest groups.

INCREASE IN BUSINESS LEGISLATION Business legislation has four main purposes: to protect companies from unfair competition, to protect consumers from unfair business practices, to protect the interests of society from uncontrolled business behavior, and to charge businesses with the social costs created by their products or production processes. Although each new law may have a legitimate rationale, it may also have the unintended effect of crippling initiative and retarding economic growth.

Legislation affecting business has increased steadily over the years. The European Commission has been active in establishing a new framework of laws covering competitive behavior, product standards, product liability, and commercial transactions for the 25 member nations of the European Union. The United States has many laws on its books covering such issues as competition, product safety and liability, fair trade and credit practices, and packaging and labeling.[45] Arab countries have incorporated similar laws into their legal systems , but a lack of consistent rules and regulations across Arab countries is sometimes cited as a restriction on achieving growth potential in trade and business transactions across the Arab world.

Several countries have gone further in passing strong consumer protection legislation. Norway bans several forms of sales promotion—trading stamps, contests, premiums—as inappropriate or 'unfair' instruments for promoting products. Thailand requires food processors selling national brands to also market low-price brands, so that low-income consumers can find economy brands. In India, food companies need special approval to launch brands that duplicate what already exists on the market, such as another cola drink or brand of rice.

Companies generally establish legal review procedures and promulgate ethical standards to guide their marketing managers, and, as more business takes place in cyberspace, marketers must establish new parameters for doing electronic business ethically.

GROWTH OF SPECIAL-INTEREST GROUPS Political action committees lobby government officials and pressure business executives to pay more attention to consumers' rights, women's rights, senior citizens' rights, and minority rights.

consumerist movement
an organized movement of citizens
and government to strengthen
the rights and powers of buyers
in relation to sellers.

Many companies have established public affairs departments to deal with these groups and issues. An important force affecting business is the **consumerist movement**, an organized movement of citizens and government to strengthen the rights and powers of buyers in relation to sellers. Consumerists have advocated and won the right to know the true interest cost of a loan, the true cost per standard unit of competing brands (unit pricing), the basic ingredients in a product, the nutritional quality of food, the freshness of products, and the true benefits of a product.

With consumers increasingly willing to swap personal information for customized products from firms—as long as they can be trusted—privacy issues will continue to be a public policy issue of major concern.[46] Consumers worry that they will be robbed or cheated; that private information will be used against them; that someone will steal their identity; that they will be bombarded by solicitations; and that children will be targeted.[47] Wise companies establish consumer affairs departments to help formulate policies and resolve and respond to consumer complaints.

Clearly, new laws and growing numbers of pressure groups have put more restraints on marketers. Marketers must clear their plans with the company's legal, public relations, public affairs, and consumer affairs departments.

POLITICAL ENVIRONMENT IN THE ARAB REGION The Arab region poses another set of challenges: that of political risk. The region is one of the most active in the world in terms of political events, tensions, and developments that affect not only the region itself but the world as a whole. Needless to say, the Arab–Israeli conflict has been at the heart of world conflicts and has at times led to political tensions and confrontations between other countries in the world. This and similar conflicts and unrest influence business and marketing environments. For instance, it is considered 'risky' for some multinational companies to have a visible presence in Arab countries. Multinational companies might shy away from having their business entity in an Arab country they deem 'risky', and limit their market access to exporting and marketing their products to that country through appointed agents.

opinion leader the person
in informal, product-related
communications who offers advice
or information about a specific
product or product category.

When Coca-Cola suffered from the Arab consumer boycott of their products, Mecca Cola flourished.

Another drastic manifestation of the political issues on business potential is felt through consumer (and sometimes national) boycotting of products and brands affiliated with a country, in retaliation for that country's political stand toward their own country or a common Arab cause. The Arab League's boycott of Western companies who maintain economic relations with Israel is an example. This boycott was at its height in the 1950s, 1960s, and early 1970s. Among many other companies, Coca-Cola products were banned from a number of Arab countries for years. This left Pepsi as the sole major player in the Arab market. Pepsi did not enter the Israeli market until the 1980s with the weakening of the Arab League boycott. When the boycott began to dwindle, Coca-Cola slowly returned to the Arab market, and attempted to re-establish its presence country by country. But it still suffers the ramifications of that ban, as it struggles to gain market share in a market dominated by Pepsi. The Arab world is perhaps one of the very few regions of the world where Coca-Cola's market share is second to Pepsi's.

While the above is an example of formalized boycotts at national level, there are other less formal attempts. Activists, activist groups, and **opinion leaders** have called for and practiced economic boycotts against companies and countries of origin of brands. For instance, during the Intifada days and the Iraq wars, several boycotts of Western companies and products were implemented across the Arab world with varying success. Some caused severe economic pressure and financial loss for the companies concerned. Affected companies found themselves forced to be more proactive in defending their position through advertising and public relations.

Such a tense political environment can also be a source of opportunity. When Coca-Cola and McDonald's, considered symbols of America, suffered dearly from the consumer boycott of their products, Mecca Cola and Herfy fast food flourished. Agility capitalized on the opportunities that presented themselves after the Iraq war.

Agility   Agility, a Kuwaiti company, transformed itself into a regional logistics powerhouse through an agreement with the U.S. Army to supply food to its troops in Kuwait and Iraq. Company revenues grew from US$77 million in 2003 to $3.7 billion in 2006: increasing by almost 50 times in just 3 years. Agility sees itself as "a leading global provider of integrated logistics, bringing efficiency to business and government supply chains in some of the world's most challenging environments. [It] combines a worldwide footprint and customized capabilities to provide unmatched personal service in both developed and emerging economies." Agility has three business units: Global Integrated Logistics, which serves commercial customers in technology, retail, chemicals, and other industries; Defense and Government Services, which provides logistics services to government and military agencies, relief organizations, and international institutions; and Infrastructure, which handles the support needs of the industrial real estate, customs optimization, and airline services industries. Agility now has over 550 offices in 120 countries across the world.[48]

Agility capitalized on the opportunities that presented themselves after the Iraq war.

Summary

1. To carry out their analysis, planning, implementation, and control responsibilities, marketing managers need a marketing information system (MIS). The role of the MIS is to assess the managers' information needs, develop the needed information, and distribute that information in a timely manner.

2. An MIS has three components: (a) an internal records system, which includes information on the order-to-payment cycle and sales information systems; (b) a marketing intelligence system, a set of procedures and sources used by managers to obtain everyday information about relevant developments in the marketing environment; and (c) a marketing research system that allows for the systematic design, collection, analysis, and reporting of data and findings relevant to a specific marketing situation.

3. Marketers find many opportunities by identifying trends (directions or sequences of events that have some momentum and durability) and megatrends (major social, economic, political, and technological changes that have long-lasting influence).

4. Within the rapidly changing global and regional picture, marketers must monitor six major environmental forces: demographic, economic, sociocultural, natural, technological, and political-legal.

5. In the demographic environment, marketers must be aware of worldwide and regional population growth; changing mixes of age, ethnic composition, and educational levels; the rise of nontraditional families; and large geographic shifts in population.

6. In the economic arena, marketers need to focus on income distribution and levels of savings, debt, and credit availability.

7. In the sociocultural arena, marketers must understand people's views of themselves, others, organizations, society, nature, and the universe. They must market products that correspond to society's core and secondary values and address the needs of different subcultures within a society.

8. In the natural environment, marketers need to be aware of the public's increased concern about the health of the environment. Many marketers are now embracing sustainability and green marketing programs that provide better environmental solutions as a result.

9. In the technological arena, marketers should take account of the accelerating pace of technological change, opportunities for innovation, varying R&D budgets, and the increased governmental regulation brought about by technological change.

10. In the political-legal environment, marketers must work within the many laws regulating business practices and with various special-interest groups. The political environment might carry difficult challenges as well as promising opportunities.

Applications

Marketing Debate

Is Consumer Behavior More a Function of a Person's Age or Generation?

One of the widely debated issues in developing marketing programs that target certain age groups is how much consumers change over time. Some marketers maintain that age differences are critical and that the needs and wants of a 25-year-old in 2002 are not that different from those of a 25-year-old in 1972. Others dispute this contention and argue that cohort and generation effects are critical, and that marketing programs must therefore suit the times.

Take a position: Age differences are fundamentally more important than cohort effects *versus* cohort effects can dominate age differences.

Marketing Discussion

What brands and products do you feel successfully 'speak to you' and effectively target your age group? Why? Which ones do not? What could they do better?

Marketing Excellence

>>Google

Founded in 1998 by two Stanford University Ph.D. students, search engine Google's name is a play on the word *googol* — the number represented by a 1 followed by 100 zeros — a reference to the massive quantity of data available online, which the company helps users make sense of. Google's stated corporate mission is "to organize the world's information and make it universally accessible and useful."

The company has become the market leader for search engines through its business focus and constant innovation. As Google grew into a primary destination for web users searching for information online, it attracted a host of online advertisers. These advertisers drove Google's revenue by buying what are called 'search ads,' little text-based boxes shown alongside search results that advertisers pay for only when users click on them. Google's search ad program, called AdWords, sells space on its search pages to ads linked with specific keywords. Google auctions off the keyword ads, with the prime key words and prime page locations going to the highest bidder. The advertisers pay only if internet users click on their ads.

In addition to offering prime online 'real estate' for advertisers, Google adds value to advertisers by providing them with a variety of means to better target their ads to users and better understand the effectiveness of their marketing. Google Analytics, which Google provides free to advertisers, provides advertisers with a custom report, or dashboard, detailing how internet users found the site, what ads they saw and/or clicked on, how they behaved while at the site, and how much traffic was generated. For example, Google client Discount Tire was able to identify where visitors to the site encountered problems that led these potential customers to abandon a tire purchase midstream and exit their site without concluding the purchase. After modifying its site and updating its keyword search campaign, Discount Tire measured a 14 percent increase in sales within a week.

With its ability to deploy data that enable up-to-the-minute improvements of a web marketing program, Google supported a style of marketing where the advertising resources and budget could be constantly monitored and optimized. Google called this approach 'marketing asset management,' implying that advertising should be managed like assets in a portfolio, with management grouping certain resources at one time or place online, and others at a different time or place, depending

Continued on next page >>

Marketing Excellence...continued

>>Google

on the market conditions. Rather than follow a marketing plan that was developed months in advance, companies could use the real-time data collected on their campaigns to optimize the campaign's effectiveness by making it more responsive to the market.

Google has augmented its search capabilities with additional services and features for internet users, including Google Maps, Google Local, Google Finance, Gmail (a Google e-mail service), and Google Video (which was boosted by the US$1.65 billion acquisition of video hosting site YouTube in 2006). These new efforts all offered opportunities for Google to grow by selling the additional targeted advertising space that was created.

It is estimated that Google runs over 1 million servers in data centers around the world to support its services, and processes over 1 billion search requests on any given day. The Google homepage and interface language accommodates more than 140 languages. Needless to say, Arabic is one (www.google.com/ar). All of Google's main services are available in Arabic. Google Arabia was set up by Google as an entity responsible for localizing and developing products that serve the Arabic-speaking community. Google also introduced a dedicated online service called Ahlan Online to help and educate novice Arab users about the wide world of the internet. Ahlan Online (www.google.com/intl/ar/ahlanonline) runs small informative cartoon films on YouTube where young cartoon characters Mufid, Maher, and Basma, together with their Grandpa, Hakim, are introduced to the internet and learn how to make the best of its wealth of information through tips for effective searching.

Questions

1. What is the added value Google offers to businesses and advertisers?

2. What are the benefits Google offers to consumers?

3. Visit Google's Ahlan Online. Can you identify the different market segments that Google Arabia tries to target through these YouTube short films?

4. Why do you think Google is interested in expanding the internet knowledge of these segments?

5. What do you think is the benefit to Google of investing in initiatives such as Google Arabia and Ahlan Online?

Sources: www.google.com; Catherine P. Taylor, "Google Flex," *Adweek*, March 20, 2006, cover story; Richard Karpinski, "Keywords, Analytics Help Define User Lifetime Value," *Advertising Age*, April 24, 2006, p. S2; Danny Gorog, "Survival Guide," *Herald Sun*, March 29, 2006; Julie Schlosser, "Google," *Fortune*, October 31, 2005, pp. 168–169; Jefferson Graham, "Google's Profit Sails Past Expectations," *USA Today*, October 21, 2005; www.pandia.com/sew/481-gartner.html; www.politicalticker.blogs.cnn.com/2009/12/18/google-unveils-top-political-searches-of-2009; www.google.com/ar; www.google.com/intl/ar/ahlanonline.

Errors in marketing research can be very costly. The Coca-Cola company learned that the hard way.

In this chapter, we will address the following **questions:**

Conducting Marketing Research and Forecasting Demand

Good marketers want insights to help them interpret past performance as well as plan future activities. They need timely, accurate, and actionable information about consumers, competition, and their brands. They also need to make the best possible tactical decisions in the short run and strategic decisions in the long run. Discovering a consumer insight and understanding its marketing implications can often lead to a successful product launch or spur the growth of a brand.

 Over the years, Coca-Cola enjoyed a dominant position and a hefty market share compared to its rival competitors. But, in time, the company's comfortable position was successfully challenged by Pepsi, which slowly but surely ate into Coca-Cola's market share from the mid-1970s onward. Pepsi kept expanding its market share at Coca-Cola's expense, in spite of Coca-Cola's dominant presence over retail shelves and control of the soda fountain business. Coca-Cola attempted to counter-attack by outspending Pepsi by four to one in advertising expenditure, but was unable to defend its market share.

The Pepsi attack reached its height in the early 1980s with its Pepsi Challenge advertising and communication campaign, in which it challenged soda drinkers to take a blind test of the two colas. More people who took the challenge preferred the sweeter Pepsi taste. Coca-Cola employed a new chairman with a chemical engineering education and extensive laboratory experience, and in an effort to retaliate with a grass-roots offensive, the company engaged in a massive research study that covered the entire United States, with costs amounting to millions of dollars. The underlying assumption was that the product itself was the main cause of the market erosion: it was the taste of Coca-Cola that was to blame. Coca-Cola management believed that the 'magic formula' that Coca-Cola had so defended since its inception was being challenged.

Research was carried out in the labs (altering the chemical composition of the product) and in the market (through thousands of taste tests). The result was a new Coca-Cola product; a sweeter product, the taste of which was preferred to that of the old product and also to that of Pepsi in blind tests. In 1984, the new sweeter Coca-Cola replaced the old Coca-Cola. The decision, which Coca-Cola management thought would re-energize the brand, produced unanticipated results. Consumers did not like the change. Retaliation from loyal Coca-Cola drinkers was massive. They organized themselves, boycotted the new product, bought media space to denounce the decision, and threatened to take legal action against the company. Consumers saw Coca-Cola as 'their' brand and felt that the company had no right to take away a product that was a core part of their experience growing up and their ongoing adult lives. Realizing the value of the 'lost' asset, the company gave in and re-introduced the old product as Coca-Cola Classic, while it stood behind its decision to keep on marketing the new product as New Coke. Within a few months, sales of

Coca-Cola exceeded the figures seen prior to the introduction of New Coke. It took the company months of work and research and millions of lost dollars to realize that the problem was not the taste of the product. It was the lack of realization of the importance of its main asset: the Coca-Cola brand.[1]

In this chapter, we review the steps involved in the marketing research process. We also consider how marketers can develop effective metrics for measuring marketing productivity. Finally, we outline how marketers can develop good sales forecasts. ▽

The Marketing Research System

Marketing managers often commission formal marketing studies of specific problems and opportunities. They may request a market survey, a product-preference test, a sales forecast by region, or an advertising evaluation. It is the job of the marketing researcher to produce insight into the customer's attitudes and buying behavior. **Marketing insights** provide diagnostic information about how and why we observe certain effects in the marketplace, and what this means to marketers.[2] We define **marketing research** as the systematic design, collection, analysis, and reporting of data and findings relevant to a specific marketing situation facing the company. Spending on marketing research topped US$31.2 billion globally in 2010, according to ESOMAR, the World Association of Opinion and Market Research Professionals. The Middle East and North Africa region accounted for only two percent of world spending, at $573 million.[3]

marketing insights diagnostic information that shows how and why we observe certain effects in the marketplace.

marketing research the systematic design, collection, analysis, and reporting of data and findings relevant to a specific marketing situation facing the company.

Most large companies have their own marketing research departments, which often play crucial roles within the organization. Procter & Gamble, one of the world's largest consumer product companies with well-known brands like Ariel and Tide detergents, Crest toothpaste, and Head & Shoulders and Pert shampoo, has what it calls a Consumer & Market Knowledge (CMK) market research function with dedicated CMK groups working for P&G businesses around the world to improve both their brand strategies and program execution, as well as a relatively smaller, centralized corporate CMK group that focuses on a variety of big-picture concerns that transcend any specific line of business. Yet, marketing research is not limited to large companies with big budgets and marketing research departments. Often at much smaller companies everyone carries out marketing research, including the customers.

Companies normally budget marketing research at 1 to 2 percent of company sales. A large percentage of this is spent on the services of outside firms. Marketing research firms fall into three categories:

1. **Syndicated-service research firms.** These firms gather consumer and trade information, which they sell for a fee.
2. **Custom marketing research firms.** These firms are hired to carry out specific projects. They design the study and report the findings.
3. **Specialty-line marketing research firms.** These firms provide specialized research services. The best example is the field-service firm, which sells field interviewing services to other firms.

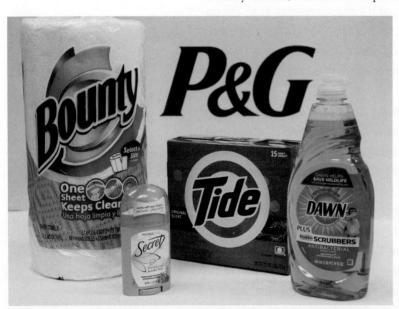

P&G has a dedicated Consumer & Market Knowledge (CMK) market research function, with groups working for P&G businesses around the world to improve their brand strategies and program execution.

▭ **Table 4.1** lists a number of marketing research firms operating in different countries of the Arab world.

Company	Website	Type of Agency	Countries of Operation
TABLE 4.1			List of Major Marketing Research Companies across the Arab World
42 Market Research	www.42mr.com	Full-Service Agency	Egypt, Saudi Arabia, the UAE
Acumen	www.acumen-sy.com	Full-Service Agency	Syria
AMRB	www.amrb-mena.com	Full-Service Agency	Algeria, Bahrain, Egypt, Iran, Jordan, Kuwait, Lebanon, Libya, Morocco, Oman, Palestinian Territories, Saudi Arabia, Sudan, Tunisia, the UAE
Ara Research & Consultancy	www.ararac.com	Full-Service Agency	Kuwait, Lebanon, Qatar, Saudi Arabia, the UAE
Arabian Echo	www.arabian-echo.com	Qualitative Agency and Consultant	Bahrain, Egypt, Jordan, Kuwait, Lebanon, Oman, Qatar, Saudi Arabia, Sudan, Syria, the UAE, Yemen
ASHARQ Research Center	www.asharqcenter.net	Full-Service Agency	Iraq
BJ Consult/BJ Marketing	www.bjgroup.ma	Full-Service Agency	Algeria, Djibouti, Egypt, Libya, Morocco, Qatar, Saudi Arabia, Syria, Tunisia, the UAE
Center for Statistical Research	www.csr.com.sa	Full-Service Agency	Algeria, Bahrain, Egypt, Jordan, Kuwait, Lebanon, Libya, Morocco, Oman, Palestinian Territories, Qatar, Saudi Arabia, Sudan, Syria, Tunisia, the UAE, Yemen
ConField-Middle East	www.confield-me.com	Fieldwork and Tabulation Research	Internationally and in the following Arab countries: Algeria, Bahrain, Egypt, Jordan, Kuwait, Lebanon, Libya, Morocco, Oman, Qatar, Saudi Arabia, Sudan, Syria, Tunisia, the UAE, Yemen
C&O Marketing	www.c-o-marketing.com	Full-Service Agency	Algeria, Egypt, Jordan, Libya, Morocco, Sudan, Tunisia
Dajani Consulting	www.dajaniconsulting.com	Full-Service Agency	Jordan
Dimensions Research	www.dimensionsintl.com	Full-Service Agency	Bahrain, Egypt, Jordan, Kuwait, Lebanon, Morocco, Oman, Qatar, Saudi Arabia, Syria, Tunisia, the UAE, Yemen
El Amouri International	www.elamouri.com	Full-Service Agency	Algeria, Libya, Tunisia
EMRHOD Consulting	www.emrhod.com	Full-Service Agency	Algeria, Egypt, Lebanon, Libya, Morocco, Tunisia
Feedback Market Research	www.feedbackme.ae, www.feedbackme.com.sa	Full-Service Agency	Algeria, Bahrain, Egypt, Jordan, Kuwait, Lebanon, Libya, Morocco, Oman, Qatar, Saudi Arabia, Sudan, Syria, Tunisia, the UAE, Yemen
Focus Marketing Consultancy Ltd	www.focuskuwait.com	Consultant Research	Kuwait
Focus Suite Co. Ltd	www.focus-suites.com	Full-Service Agency	Kuwait, Qatar, Saudi Arabia, the UAE
GfK Egypt	www.gfk.com.eg	Full-Service Agency	Internationally and in the following Arab countries: Algeria, Bahrain, Egypt, Jordan, Kuwait, Lebanon, Libya, Morocco, Oman, Qatar, Saudi Arabia, Sudan, Syria, Tunisia, the UAE, Yemen
IIACSS	www.iiacss.org	Full-Service Agency	Iraq, Jordan, Lebanon, the UAE
InCite Research & Marketing Solutions	www.incitemr.com	Full-Service Agency	Bahrain, Egypt, Jordan, Kuwait, Lebanon, Oman, Qatar, Saudi Arabia, Syria, Tunisia, the UAE, Yemen

(Continued)

TABLE 4.1 🖿 List of Major Marketing Research Companies across the Arab World (continued)

Company	Website	Type of Agency	Countries of Operation
INDICATE Marketing & Advertising Research	www.imaar.me	Full-Service Agency	Syria
Information International	www.information-international.com	Full-Service Agency	Bahrain, Egypt, Iraq, Jordan, Kuwait, Lebanon, Libya, Morocco, Saudi Arabia, Syria, the UAE
Insight Discovery	www.insight-discovery.com	Full-Service Agency	Bahrain, Kuwait, Lebanon, Oman, Qatar, Saudi Arabia, Syria, the UAE, Yemen
Integral Omnicom MediaGroup	www.integral-mena.com	Consultant Research	Algeria, Bahrain, Egypt, Iraq, Jordan, Kuwait, Lebanon, Libya, Morocco, Oman, Palestinian Territories, Qatar, Saudi Arabia, Syria, Tunisia, the UAE, Yemen
Ipsos	www.ipsos-mena.com	Full-Service Agency	Internationally and in the following Arab countries: Algeria, Bahrain, Egypt, Iraq, Jordan, Kuwait, Lebanon, Libya, Morocco, Oman, Qatar, Saudi Arabia, Sudan, Syria, Tunisia, the UAE, Yemen
KA Research Limited (KA Iraq)	www.ka.com.tr	Full-Service Agency	Iraq
Leyhausen Middle East	www.leyhausen.com	Fieldwork and Tabulation Research	Internationally and in the following Arab countries: Bahrain, Egypt, Kuwait, Lebanon, Oman, Qatar, Saudi Arabia, Syria, Tunisia, the UAE
LMS-CSA Marketing & Sondage	www.lmsmark.com	Full-Service Agency	Algeria, Morocco, Tunisia
Market Vision Research & Consulting Services	www.market-vision.com	Full-Service Agency	Bahrain, Egypt, Jordan, Kuwait, Lebanon, Oman, Saudi Arabia, Syria, the UAE
The Marketing Research Organization (MRO)	www.mrocompany.org	Full-Service Agency	Bahrain, Egypt, Jordan, Kuwait, Lebanon, Morocco, Palestinian Territories, Qatar, Saudi Arabia, Syria, the UAE, Yemen
Martpoint Marketing Research Consultants	www.martpointconsult.com	Full-Service Agency	Bahrain, Egypt, Jordan, Kuwait, Lebanon, Oman, Saudi Arabia, Sudan, Syria, the UAE, Yemen
MASMI Saudi Arabia	www.masmi.com	Full-Service Agency	Internationally and in the following Arab countries: Egypt, Lebanon, Saudi Arabia, the UAE
Mindsight Mena	www.mindsharemena.com	Full-Service Agency	Algeria, Bahrain, Egypt, Jordan, Kuwait, Lebanon, Morocco, Oman, Qatar, Saudi Arabia, Syria, Tunisia, the UAE, Yemen
Nagy Research	www.nagyresearch.com	Full-Service Agency	Algeria, Bahrain, Egypt, Iraq, Jordan, Kuwait, Lebanon, Libya, Morocco, Oman, Palestinian Territories, Qatar, Saudi Arabia, Sudan, Syria, Tunisia, the UAE, Yemen
Nielsen Company	www.nielsen.com	Full-Service Agency	Internationally and in the the following Arab countries: Algeria, Bahrain, Egypt, Jordan, Kuwait, Lebanon, Morocco, Oman, Qatar, Saudi Arabia, Tunisia, the UAE
OnTrack Marketing Research and Consultancy	www.ontrack-egypt.com	Full-Service Agency	Algeria, Bahrain, Egypt, Kuwait, Lebanon, Libya, Morocco, Oman, Qatar, Saudi Arabia, Syria, Tunisia, the UAE

(Continued)

| TABLE 4.1 | List of Major Marketing Research Companies across the Arab World (continued) | | |

Company	Website	Type of Agency	Countries of Operation
Pan Arab Research Center	www.arabresearch.com	Full-Service Agency	Bahrain, Egypt, Iraq, Jordan, Kuwait, Lebanon, Morocco, Oman, Qatar, Saudi Arabia, Syria, Tunisia, the UAE, Yemen
Prodata Insight	www.prodatainsight.com	Full-Service Agency	Egypt, Iraq, Jordan, Kuwait, Lebanon, Libya, Morocco, Oman, Qatar, Saudi Arabia, Sudan, Syria, the UAE, Yemen
RadaResearch & Public Relations Company	www.radaresearch.com	Full-Service Agency	Egypt
Real Opinions	www.real-opinions.com	Full-Service Agency	Algeria, Bahrain, Egypt, Iraq, Jordan, Kuwait, Lebanon, Libya, Morocco, Oman, Palestinian Territories, Qatar, Saudi Arabia, Syria, Tunisia, the UAE, Yemen
Realistic Management Consultancy	www.rmc11.com	Full-Service Agency	Bahrain, Kuwait, Oman, Qatar, Saudi Arabia, the UAE, Yemen
Research & Consulting House (REACH SAL)	www.reachmass.com	Full-Service Agency	Bahrain, Egypt, Jordan, Lebanon, Morocco, Oman, Saudi Arabia, Syria, the UAE
Research Now	www.researchnow.com	Consultant Research	Internationally and in the UAE
SAWT Research Field Force	www.swat.ae	Fieldwork and Tabulation Research	Algeria, Bahrain, Egypt, Iraq, Jordan, Kuwait, Lebanon, Libya, Morocco, Oman, Palestinian Territories, Qatar, Saudi Arabia, Sudan, Syria, Tunisia, the UAE, Yemen
SEREC	www.serec.ma	Fieldwork and Tabulation Research	Algeria, Morocco, Tunisia
Synovate	www.synovate.com	Full-Service Agency	Internationally and in the following Arab countries: Algeria, Bahrain, Djibouti, Egypt, Iraq, Jordan, Kuwait, Lebanon, Libya, Morocco, Oman, Palestinian Territories, Qatar, Saudi Arabia, Sudan, Syria, Tunisia, the UAE, Yemen
TNS	www.tnsglobal.com	Full-Service Agency	Internationally and in the following Arab countries: Algeria, Bahrain, Egypt, Iraq, Jordan, Kuwait, Lebanon, Libya, Morocco, Oman, Qatar, Saudi Arabia, Sudan, Syria, Tunisia, the UAE, Yemen
Unboxed Consulting, Middle East & Africa	www.un-boxed.me	Full-Service Agency	Algeria, Bahrain, Egypt, Iraq, Jordan, Kuwait, Lebanon, Libya, Morocco, Oman, Qatar, Saudi Arabia, Sudan, Syria, Tunisia, the UAE, Yemen
Ventures Middle East	www.ventures-me.com	Full-Service Agency	Bahrain, Egypt, Iraq, Jordan, Kuwait, Lebanon, Morocco, Oman, Palestinian Territories, Qatar, Saudi Arabia, Sudan, Syria, Tunisia, the UAE, Yemen
Yahoo! Middle East & Africa	www.maktoob-research.com	Full-Service Agency	Algeria, Bahrain, Egypt, Iraq, Jordan, Kuwait, Lebanon, Libya, Morocco, Oman, Palestinian Territories, Qatar, Saudi Arabia, Sudan, Syria, Tunisia, the UAE, Yemen
YouGovSiraj	www.yougovsiraj.com	Full-Service Agency	Algeria, Bahrain, Egypt, Iraq, Jordan, Kuwait, Lebanon, Libya, Morocco, Oman, Qatar, Saudi Arabia, Sudan, Syria, Tunisia, the UAE, Yemen

Source: Information from the ESOMAR Market Research Directory, http://directory.esomar.org/countries.php. The ESOMAR Directory of Research Organizations is an up-to-date, searchable resource of over 1,600 major research organizations worldwide.

Small companies can hire the services of a marketing research firm or conduct research in creative and affordable ways, such as:

- **Engaging students or professors to design and carry out projects.** Companies sometimes sponsor student competitions where university students compete in teams in developing a business solution of interest to the sponsoring company. The payoff to the students is experience and visibility; the payoff to the companies is fresh sets of eyes to solve problems at a fraction of the cost that consultants would charge.[4]

- **Using the internet.** A company can collect considerable information at very little cost by examining competitors' websites, monitoring chat rooms, and accessing published data.

- **Checking out rivals.** Many small companies routinely visit their competitors. This allows them to have first-hand exposure to their competitor's product and service, and to carry out a comparison between their offering and that of the competitor without incurring major financial burden.

Most companies use a combination of marketing research resources to study their industries, competitors, audiences, and channel strategies.

The Marketing Research Process

Effective marketing research follows the six steps shown in ▲ **Figure 4.1**. We illustrate them with the following situation:[5]

Suppose that Royal Jordanian Airlines (RJ) is considering ways to enhance its in-flight cabin services. Among the ideas the airline is reviewing is how to better cater to its first-class and business-class passengers on very long flights, mainly businesspeople whose high-priced tickets pay most of the freight. Among these ideas is the provision of internet access, with limited access to web pages and e-mail messaging. Suppose that the marketing research manager was assigned to investigate how first-class passengers would rate these services, specifically the internet connection, and how much extra they would be willing to pay for it. One source estimates revenues of US$70 billion from in-flight internet access over 10 years, if enough first-class passengers paid $25. RJ might thus recover its costs in a reasonable time. Making the connection available would cost the airline $90,000 per plane.[6]

Step 1: Define the Problem, the Decision Alternatives, and the Research Objectives

Marketing managers must be careful not to define the problem too broadly or too narrowly for the marketing researcher. A marketing manager who says, "Find out everything you can about first-class air travelers' needs," will receive a lot of unnecessary information. One who says, "Find out whether enough passengers aboard a B747 flying direct between Amman and New York would be willing to pay US$25 for an internet connection for Royal Jordanian Airlines to break even in 1 year on the cost of offering this service," is taking too narrow a view of the problem.

The marketing researcher might even ask, "Why does the internet connection have to be priced at $25 as opposed to $10, $50, or some other price? Why does RJ have to break even on the cost of the service, especially if it attracts new customers?" Another relevant question is: how important is it to be first in the market, and how long can the company sustain its lead?

The marketing manager and marketing researcher may agree to define the problem as follows: "Will offering an in-flight internet service create enough incremental preference and profit for RJ to justify its cost against other possible investments in service enhancements that RJ might make?" To help in designing the research, management should first spell out the decisions it might face and then work backward. Suppose management outlines these decisions. (1) Should RJ offer an internet connection? (2) If so, should we offer the service to first class only, or include business class, and possibly economy class? (3) What price(s) should we charge? (4) On what types of plane and lengths of trip should we offer the service?

Now management and marketing researchers are ready to set specific research objectives. (1) What types of first-class passenger would respond most to using an in-flight internet service?

Define the problem and research objectives

↓

Develop the research plan

↓

Collect the information

↓

Analyze the information

↓

Present the findings

↓

Make the decision

|Fig. 4.1| ▲

The Marketing Research Process

(2) How many first-class passengers are likely to use the internet service at different price levels? (3) How many extra first-class passengers might choose RJ because of this new service? (4) How much long-term goodwill will this service add to Royal Jordanian Airlines' image? (5) How important is internet service to first-class passengers relative to other services, such as a power plug or enhanced entertainment?

Not all research projects can be this specific. Some research is *exploratory*: its goal is to shed light on the real nature of the problem and to suggest possible solutions or new ideas. Some research is *descriptive*: it seeks to quantify demand, such as how many first-class passengers would purchase in-flight internet service at $25? Some research is *causal*: its purpose is to test a cause-and-effect relationship.

Step 2: Develop the Research Plan

The second stage of marketing research is where we develop the most efficient plan for gathering the needed information and what that will cost. Suppose the company made a prior estimate that launching an in-flight internet service would yield a long-term profit of US$50,000. If the manager believes that doing the marketing research will lead to an improved pricing and promotional plan and a long-term profit of $90,000, he should be willing to spend up to $40,000 on this research. If the research will cost more than $40,000, it's not worth doing.[7]

To design a research plan, we need to make decisions about the data sources, research approaches, research instruments, sampling plan, and contact methods.

DATA SOURCES The researcher can gather secondary data, primary data, or both. *Secondary data* are data that were collected for another purpose and already exist somewhere. *Primary data* are data freshly gathered for a specific purpose or for a specific research project.

Researchers usually start their investigation by examining some of the rich variety of low-cost and readily available secondary data, to see whether they can partly or wholly solve the problem without collecting costly primary data. For instance, if a pan-Arab bank is interested in exploring the potential of the Lebanese banking sector, it might find the BankTrak reports of InfoPro Research valuable.

 InfoPro Research   InfoPro Research offers an annual quantitative household survey on retail banking in Lebanon. The survey, BankTrak, provides insights into the attitude of consumers toward their bank and its financial products and services, and includes information on profiles, behaviors, usage, and attitudes of bank customers. Typical topics covered in the BankTrak reports include market share and banking trends and use of banking products and services. Recently, InfoPro Research added sections on Islamic banking and customer life styles. BankTrak reports would serve retail bankers in: benchmarking performance across products and services; identifying potential prospective clients across various regions of the country; developing products and services according to client preferences and behavior; and enhancing communication and advertising campaigns. InfoPro Research's BankTrak service is provided in hard copy as well as electronically in soft copy, enabling easy manipulation of the data.[8]

When the needed data don't exist or are dated, inaccurate, incomplete, or unreliable, the researcher will need to collect primary data. Most marketing research projects do include some primary-data collection.

RESEARCH APPROACHES Marketers collect primary data in five main ways: through observation, focus groups, surveys, behavioral data, and experiments.

Observational Research Researchers can gather fresh data by observing the relevant actors and settings, unobtrusively observing as they shop or as they consume products.[9] Sometimes they equip consumers with pagers and instruct them to write down what they're doing whenever prompted, or they hold informal interview sessions at a coffee shop. Photographs can also provide a wealth of detailed information.

Ethnographic Research This particular observational research approach uses concepts and tools from anthropology and other social science disciplines to provide a deep understanding of how people live and work.[10] The goal is to immerse the researcher into consumers' lives to uncover unarticulated desires that might not surface in any other form of research.[11] Firms such as IBM, Intel, and Bank of America have embraced ethnographic research to design breakthrough products.

Bank of America's ethnographic research, following women at home and while they shopped, yielded two insights. First, women tended to round up financial transactions because it was more convenient (so an invoice for US$8.85 was treated as $9). Second, those women with children found it difficult to save. Subsequent research led to the launch of Keep the Change, a debit card program whereby purchases are rounded up to the nearest dollar amount and the added difference is automatically transferred from a checking account to a savings account. Since the launch, 2.5 million customers have signed up for the program, opening 700,000 new checking accounts and 1 million new savings accounts in the process.[12]

Many other companies have benefited from ethnographic research. For example, after finding that many of their guests turned their bedrooms into work spaces, TownePlace Suites replaced a dining table with a flexible modular wall unit that could serve as either an office or a place to eat.[13] P&G also benefited from online ethnographic research methodology innovated by TNS.

TNS Global
TNS (www.tnsglobal.com) is one of the world's major suppliers of qualitative and quantitative marketing research. It is also active in several Arab countries. One innovative research solution is TNS Online Safari, which gives TNS business clients the opportunity to live with their consumers 'virtually.' Through the use of blogs, boards, e-mails, and diaries, consumers photograph or video-record their experience with the product, allowing the TNS business client to see respondents in their 'in-home' settings and real-life environments (just like a safari). It is a way to understand consumer behavior as it takes place in reality, and gives the client the opportunity to interact with the consumer virtually.

With such innovative research solutions, TNS helps global companies such as P&G explore, understand, and act upon insights into consumer perceptions, values, and motivations, as these companies attempt to cater better to the needs of their customers in a continuously evolving competitive environment.[14]

focus group a gathering of six to ten people who are carefully selected based on certain demographic, psychographic, or other considerations and brought together to discuss various topics of interest.

A focus group in session.

Several research companies conduct ethnographic research in the Arab world. Arabian Echo provides such a service in Saudi Arabia, as well as in other countries including the Gulf Cooperation Council (GCC) countries of the UAE, Kuwait, Oman, Qatar, and Bahrain, and the Levant countries of Lebanon, Jordan, and Syria, as well as Egypt and even Iran.[15]

The Royal Jordanian Airlines researchers might move around first-class and business-class lounges in airports to hear how travelers talk about the different airline carriers and their features. They might also fly on competitors' planes to observe in-flight service.

Focus-Group Research A **focus group** is a gathering of 6 to 10 people carefully selected by researchers based on certain demographic, psychographic, or other considerations, and brought together to discuss various topics of interest at length. Participants are normally paid a small sum for attending. A professional research moderator provides questions and probes based on the marketing managers' discussion guide or agenda.

Moderators try to discern consumers' real motivations and why they say and do certain things. They typically record these sessions, and marketing managers often observe from behind a two-way mirror in the next room. Focus-group research is a useful exploratory step, but researchers must avoid generalizing from focus-group participants to the whole market, because the sample size is too small and the samples are not drawn randomly.

In fact, an increasing number of marketers are relying on other means of collecting information that they believe are less artificial. Some marketers argue that it is better to 'read the signs' of consumption than ask consumers to self-consciously comment on their own consumption behavior patterns. For instance, one advertising agency insight noticed that dinner-party guests were bringing their hosts flowers instead of chocolate, in a reflection of current concerns over obesity and health. Such a finding is quite relevant to both chocolate companies and flower shops.[16]

The Marketing Insight: *Conducting Informative Focus Groups* has some practical tips to improve the quality of focus groups. In the Royal Jordanian Airlines research, the moderator might start with a broad question, such as, "How do you feel about first-class air travel?" Questions then move to how people view the different airlines, different existing services, different proposed services, and specifically, internet service.

Survey Research   Companies undertake surveys to learn about people's knowledge, beliefs, preferences, and satisfaction and to measure these magnitudes in the general population. A company such as Royal Jordanian Airlines might prepare its own survey instrument to gather the information

Marketing Insight

Conducting Informative Focus Groups

Focus groups allow marketers to observe how and why consumers accept or reject concepts, ideas, or any specific notion. The key to using focus groups successfully is to *listen and observe.* Marketers should eliminate their own biases as much as possible. Although many useful insights can emerge from thoughtfully run focus groups, questions can arise about their validity, especially in today's marketing environment.

Some researchers believe that consumers have been so bombarded with ads that they unconsciously (or perhaps cynically) parrot back what they've already heard instead of what they really think. There's always a concern that participants are just trying to maintain their self-image and public persona or have a need to identify with the other members of the group. Participants also may not be willing to admit in public—or may not even recognize—their behavior patterns and motivations. And the 'loudmouth' or 'know-it-all' problem often occurs when one highly opinionated person speaks too much and does not let the rest of the group express their opinions. It may be expensive to recruit qualified subjects who meet the sampling criteria (US$3,000 to $5,000 per group), but getting the right participants is crucial.

Even when marketers use multiple focus groups it may be difficult to generalize the results to a broader population. For example, when undertaking a pan-Arab research project, generalizing insights from a focus group conducted in Beirut or in Dubai to the wider Arab population should be done with caution. Focus-group findings often vary from one region to another, as the profiles of the focus-group participants vary.

Participants must feel as relaxed as possible and strongly motivated to be truthful. Physical surroundings can be crucial to achieving the right atmosphere. As one agency executive noted, "We wondered why people always seemed grumpy and negative: people were resistant to any idea we showed them." Finally, in one session a fight broke out between participants. The problem was the room itself: cramped, stifling, forbidding. "It was a cross between a hospital room and a police interrogation room." To fix the problem, the agency gave the room a makeover. Other firms are adapting the look of the room to fit the theme of the topic, such as designing the room to look like a playroom when speaking to children.

Many firms are substituting observational research for focus groups, but ethnographic observation can be expensive and tricky: researchers must be highly skilled and participants open and honest. Then there are lots of data to analyze. The beauty of focus groups, as one marketing executive noted, is that "it's still the most cost-effective, quickest, dirtiest way to get information in rapid time on an idea." In analyzing the pros and cons, Wharton's Americus Reed might have said it best: "A focus group is like a chainsaw. If you know what you're doing, it's very useful and effective. If you don't, you could lose a limb."

Sources: Naomi R. Henderson, "Beyond Top of Mind," *Marketing Research*, September 1, 2005; Rebecca Harris, "Do Focus Groups Have a Future?," *Marketing*, June 6, 2005, p. 17; Malcolm Gladwell, *Blink: The Power of Thinking Without Thinking* (New York: Little Brown, 2005); Linda Tischler, "Every Move You Make," *Fast Company*, April 2004, pp. 73–75; Alison Stein Wellner, "The New Science of Focus Groups," *American Demographics*, March 2003, pp. 29–33; Dennis Rook, "Out-of-Focus Groups," *Marketing Research* 15, no. 2, Summer 2003, p. 11; Dennis W. Rook, "Loss of Vision: Focus Groups Fail to Connect Theory, Current Practice," *Marketing News*, September 15, 2003, p. 40; Sarah Jeffrey Kasner, "Fistfights and Feng Shui," *Boston Globe*, July 21, 2001.

questionaires   a set of questions presented to a respondent, for the purposes of a survey or statistical study.

it needs, or it might add questions to an omnibus survey that carries the questions of several companies, at a much lower cost. It can also put the questions to an ongoing consumer panel run by itself or another company. It may do a mall intercept study by having researchers approach people in a shopping mall and ask them questions.

As we will discuss in more detail later in this chapter, many marketers are taking their surveys online where they can easily develop, administer, and collect e-mail and web-based **questionnaires**. However they conduct their surveys—online, by phone, or in person—companies must feel the information they are getting from the large volume of data makes it all worthwhile.

Of course, by putting out so many surveys each month, companies may run the risk of creating 'survey burnout' and seeing response rates fall. Keeping a survey short and simple and contacting customers no more than once a month are two keys to drawing people into the data-collection effort. Offering incentives is another way companies get consumers to respond. Companies might offer participants in such surveys coupons for discount merchandise or the chance to win a cash prize.[17]

Behavioral Data   Customers leave traces of their purchasing behavior in store scanning data, catalog purchases, and customer databases. Marketers can learn much by analyzing these data. Actual purchases reflect consumers' preferences and often are more reliable than statements they offer to market researchers. For example, grocery shopping data show that high-income people don't necessarily buy the more expensive brands, contrary to what they might state in interviews; and many low-income people buy some expensive brands. Clearly, Royal Jordanian Airlines can learn many useful things about its passengers by analyzing ticket purchase records and online behavior.

experimental research   gathering primary data by selecting matched groups of subjects, giving them different treatments, controlling related factors, and checking for differences in group responses.

Experimental Research   The most scientifically valid research is **experimental research**, designed to capture cause-and-effect relationships by eliminating competing explanations of the observed findings. If the experiment is well designed and executed, research and marketing managers can have confidence in the conclusions.

Experiments call for selecting matched groups of subjects, subjecting them to different treatments, controlling extraneous variables, and checking whether observed response differences are statistically significant. If we can eliminate or control extraneous factors, we can relate the observed effects to the variations in the treatments or stimuli. Royal Jordanian Airlines might introduce an in-flight internet service on one of its regular flights from Amman to New York and charge US$25 one week and $15 the next week. If the plane carried approximately the same number of first-class passengers each week and the particular weeks made no difference, the airline could relate any significant difference in the number of passengers using the service to the different prices charged.

RESEARCH INSTRUMENTS   Marketing researchers have a choice of three main research instruments in collecting primary data: questionnaires, qualitative measures, and technological devices.

Questionnaires   A *questionnaire* consists of a set of questions presented to respondents. Because of its flexibility, it is by far the most common instrument used to collect primary data. Researchers need to carefully develop, test, and debug questionnaires before administering them on a large scale. The form, wording, and sequence of the question can all influence the response. *Closed-end questions* specify all the possible answers and provide answers that are easier to interpret and tabulate. *Open-end questions* allow respondents to answer in their own words and often reveal more about how people think. They are especially useful in exploratory research, where the researcher is looking for insight into how people think rather than measuring how many people think a certain way. ▢ **Table 4.2** on page 101 provides examples of both types of question; also see Marketing Memo: *Questionnaire Dos and Don'ts* on page 102.

Qualitative Measures   Some marketers prefer more qualitative methods for gauging consumer opinion, because consumer actions don't always match their answers to survey questions. *Qualitative research techniques* are relatively unstructured measurement approaches that permit a range of possible responses. Their variety is limited only by the creativity of the marketing researcher.

Because of the freedom afforded both researchers in their probes and consumers in their responses, qualitative research can often be a useful first step in exploring consumers' brand and

TABLE 4.2 🔲 Types of Question

Name	Description	Example
A. Closed-End Questions		
Dichotomous	A question with two possible answers	In arranging this trip, did you personally phone Royal Jordanian Airlines? Yes No
Multiple choice	A question with three or more answers	With whom are you traveling on this flight? ☐ No one ☐ Children only ☐ Spouse ☐ Business associates/friends/relatives ☐ Spouse and children ☐ An organized tour group
Likert scale	A statement with which the respondent shows the amount of agreement/disagreement	Small airlines generally give better service than large ones. Strongly disagree Disagree Neither agree nor disagree Agree Strongly agree 1____ 2____ 3____ 4____ 5____
Semantic differential	A scale connecting two bipolar words. The respondent selects the point that represents his or her opinion	Royal Jordanian Airlines Large--Small Experienced --Inexperienced Modern--Old-fashioned
Importance scale	A scale that rates the importance of some attribute	Airline in-flight service to me is Extremely important Very important Somewhat important Not very important Not at all important 1____ 2____ 3____ 4____ 5____
Rating scale	A scale that rates some attribute from 'poor' to 'excellent'	RJ in-flight service is Excellent Very good Good Fair Poor 1____ 2____ 3____ 4____ 5____
Intention-to-buy scale	A scale that describes the respondent's intention to buy	If an in-flight telephone were available on a long flight, I would Definitely buy Probably buy Not sure Probably not buy Definitely not buy 1____ 2____ 3____ 4____ 5____
B. Open-End Questions		
Completely unstructured	A question that respondents can answer in an almost unlimited number of ways	What is your opinion of Royal Jordanian Airlines?
Word association	Words are presented, one at a time, and respondents mention the first word that comes to mind	What is the first word that comes to your mind when you hear the following? Airline-- RJ--- Travel--
Sentence completion	An incomplete sentence is presented and respondents complete the sentence	When I choose an airline, the most important consideration in my decision is--
Story completion	An incomplete story is presented and respondents are asked to complete it	"I flew RJ a few days ago. I noticed that the exterior and interior of the plane had very bright colors. This aroused in me the following thoughts and feelings…" Now complete the story.
Picture	A picture of two characters is presented, with one making a statement. Respondents are asked to identify with the other and fill in the empty balloon	WELL HERE'S THE FOOD.
Thematic apperception test (TAT)	A picture is presented and respondents are asked to make up a story about what they think is happening or may happen in the picture	

marketing
Memo

Questionnaire Dos and Don'ts

1. Ensure that questions are without bias. Don't lead the respondent into an answer.

2. Make the questions as simple as possible. Questions that include multiple ideas or two questions in one will confuse respondents.

3. Make the questions specific. Sometimes it's advisable to add memory cues. For example, be specific with time periods.

4. Avoid jargon or shorthand. Avoid trade jargon, acronyms, and initials not in everyday use.

5. Steer clear of sophisticated or uncommon words. Only use words in common speech.

6. Avoid ambiguous words. Words such as 'usually' or 'frequently' have no specific meaning.

7. Avoid questions with a negative in them. It is better to say, "Do you ever…?" than "Do you never…?"

8. Avoid hypothetical questions. It's difficult to answer questions about imaginary situations. Answers aren't necessarily reliable.

9. Do not use words that could be misheard. This is especially important when administering the interview over the telephone. "What is your opinion of sects?" could yield interesting but not necessarily relevant answers.

10. Desensitize questions by using response bands. To ask people their age or ask companies about employee turnover rates, offer a range of response bands instead of precise numbers.

11. Ensure that fixed responses do not overlap. Categories used in fixed-response questions should be distinct and not overlap.

12. Allow for 'other' in fixed-response questions. Precoded answers should always allow for a response other than those listed.

Source: Adapted from Paul Hague and Peter Jackson, *Market Research: A Guide to Planning, Methodology, and Evaluation* (London: Kogan Page, 1999). See also Hans Baumgartner and Jan-Benedict E. M. Steenkamp, "Response Styles in Marketing Research: A Cross-National Investigation," *Journal of Marketing Research*, May 2001, pp. 143–156.

Marketing Insight

Getting into Consumers' Heads with Qualitative Research

Here are some popular qualitative research approaches to getting inside consumers' minds and finding out what they think or feel about brands and products:

1. *Word associations.* Ask subjects what words come to mind when they hear the brand's name. "What does the Swatch name mean to you? Tell me what comes to mind when you think of Swatch watches." The primary purpose of free-association tasks is to identify the range of possible brand associations in consumers' minds. But they may also provide some rough indication of the relative strength, favorability, and uniqueness of brand associations.

2. *Projective techniques.* Give people an incomplete stimulus and ask them to complete it, or give them an ambiguous stimulus and ask them to make sense of it. One such approach is 'bubble exercises' in which empty bubbles, like those found in cartoons, appear in scenes of people buying or using certain products or services. Subjects fill in the bubble, indicating what they believe is happening or being said. Another technique is comparison tasks in which people compare brands to people, countries, animals, activities, fabrics, occupations, cars, magazines, vegetables, nationalities, or even other brands.

3. *Visualization.* Visualization requires people to create a collage from magazine photos or drawings to depict their perceptions. The ZMET technique asks participants in advance to select approximately 6–8 images from their own sources (magazines, catalogs, family photo albums) to represent their thoughts and feelings about the research topic. In a one-on-one interview the study administrator uses advanced interview techniques to explore the images with the participant and reveal hidden meanings. Finally, the participants use a computer program to create a collage with these images that communicates their subconscious thoughts and feelings about the topic. In one ZMET study about women's stockings, some of the respondents' pictures showed fence posts encased in plastic wrap or steel bands strangling trees, suggesting that the stockings are tight and inconvenient.

4. *Brand personification.* Ask subjects what kind of person they think of when the brand is mentioned: "If the brand were to come alive as a person, what would it be like, what would it do, where would it live, what would it wear, who would it talk to if it went to a party (and what would it talk about)?" The brand personality delivers a picture of the more human qualities of the brand.

Drawings or other pictures that express consumers' feelings about products are part of ZMET studies. This collage shows what one social media research participant of an antismoking campaign research study felt.

5. *Laddering.* A series of increasingly more specific 'why' questions can reveal consumer motivation and consumers' deeper, more abstract goals. Ask why someone wants to buy a Nokia mobile phone. "They look well built" (attribute). "Why is it important that the phone be well built?," "It suggests that the Nokia is reliable" (a functional benefit). "Why is reliability important?," "Because my colleagues or family can be sure to reach me" (an emotional benefit). "Why must you be available to them at all times?," "I can help them if they're in trouble" (brand essence). The brand makes this person feel ready to help others.

Sources: Catherine Marshall and Gretchen B. Rossman, *Designing Qualitative Research*, 4th edn (Thousand Oaks, CA: Sage Publications, 2006); Bruce L. Berg, *Qualitative Research Methods for the Social Sciences*, 6th edn (Boston: Allyn & Bacon, 2006); Norman K. Denzin and Yvonna S. Lincoln, eds., *The Sage Handbook of Qualitative Research*, 3rd edn (Thousand Oaks, CA: Sage Publications, 2005); Linda Tischler, "Every Move You Make," *Fast Company*, April 2004, pp. 73–75; Gerald Zaltman, *How Customers Think: Essential Insights into the Mind of the Market* (Boston: Harvard Business School Press, 2003).

product perceptions, but it has its drawbacks. Marketers must temper the in-depth insights that emerge with the fact that the samples are often very small and may not necessarily generalize to broader populations. And different researchers examining the same qualitative results may draw very different conclusions. The Marketing Insight: *Getting into Consumers' Heads with Qualitative Research* describes some popular approaches.

Technological Devices Technological devices are occasionally useful in marketing research. Galvanometers can measure the interest or emotions aroused by exposure to a specific ad or picture. The tachistoscope flashes an ad to a subject with an exposure interval that may range from less than one hundredth of a second to several seconds. After each exposure, the respondent describes everything he recalls. Eye cameras study respondents' eye movements to see where their eyes land first, how long they linger on a given item, and so on.

Technology has now advanced to such a degree that marketers can use devices such as skin sensors, brain-wave scanners, and full body scanners to get consumer responses.[18] One advertising technology company is studying the eye movements and brain activity of web surfers to see which ads grab their attention.[19] The Marketing Insight: *Understanding Brain Science* on page 104 provides a glimpse into some new marketing research frontiers involved with studying the brain.

Technology has replaced the diaries that participants in media surveys used to keep and in which they used to record their purchasing and consumption behavior. Audiometers attached to television sets in participating homes now record when the set is on and to which channel it is tuned. Electronic devices can record the number of radio programs a person is exposed to during the day, or, using Global Positioning System (GPS) technology, how many billboards a person may walk by or drive by during a day. Technology is also used to capture consumer reactions to programming.

SAMPLING PLAN After deciding on the research approach and instruments, the marketing researcher must design a sampling plan. This calls for three decisions:

1. *Sampling unit: who should we survey?* In the Royal Jordanian Airlines survey, should the sampling unit consist only of first-class business travelers, first-class vacation travelers, or both? Should it include travelers under age 18? Both husbands and wives? Once they have determined the sampling unit, marketers must develop a sampling frame so that everyone in the target population has an equal or known chance of being sampled.
2. *Sample size: how many people should we survey?* Large samples give more reliable results, but it's not necessary to sample the entire target population to achieve reliable results. Samples of less than 1 percent of a population can often provide good reliability, with a credible sampling procedure.

Marketing Insight

Understanding Brain Science

As an alternative to traditional consumer research, some researchers have begun to develop sophisticated techniques from neuroscience that monitor brain activity to better gauge consumer responses to marketing stimuli.

For example, a group of researchers at the University of California Los Angeles in the United States used functional magnetic resonance imaging (fMRI) to measure how consumers' brains responded to advertisements shown during the 2006 American Football championship game: the Super Bowl. The Super Bowl consistently ranks among the world's most watched TV broadcasts, and is the most expensive for advertisers. In 2010, around 80 million viewers watched the Super Bowl live. ABC television network, which carried the game, charged around US$2.6 million for a 30-second ad. It is thus important for advertisers to measure the impact of their ads.

The research demonstrated how consumers' stated preferences often contradict their inner thoughts and emotions. The fMRI showed that the "I'm going to Disney World" ad featuring members of both teams rehearsing the famous line elicited the highest levels of positive brain activity, followed by a Sierra Mist soda commercial starring an airport security screener and a traveler. Yet in a consumer poll conducted independently, a Bud Light beer ad rated highest, despite not generating significant positive reaction in the fMRI tests.

Although it can be more effective in uncovering inner emotions than conventional techniques, neurological research is costly, running to as much as US$100,000 per project. One major finding to emerge from neurological consumer research is that many purchase decisions are characterized less by the logical weighing of variables than was previously assumed and more by "a largely unconscious habitual process, as distinct from the rational, conscious, information-processing model of economists and traditional marketing textbooks." Even basic decisions, such as the purchase of gasoline, are influenced by brain activity at the subrational level.

Neurological research can be used to measure the type of emotional response that consumers exhibit when presented with marketing stimuli. A group of researchers in England used an electroencephalograph (EEG) to monitor cognitive functions related to memory recall and attentiveness for 12 different regions of the brain as subjects were exposed to advertising. Brain-wave activity in different regions indicated different emotional responses. For example, heightened activity in the left prefrontal cortex is characteristic of an 'approach' response to an ad and indicates an attraction to the stimulus. In contrast, a spike in brain activity in the right prefrontal cortex is indicative of a strong revulsion to the stimulus. In yet another part of the brain, the degree of memory formation activity correlates with purchase intent. Other research has shown that people activate different regions of the brain in assessing the personality traits of people versus brands.

The term *neuromarketing* has been used to describe brain research on the effect of marketing stimuli. By adding neurological techniques to their research arsenal, marketers are trying to move toward a more complete picture of what goes on inside consumers' heads. Given the complexity of the human brain, however, many researchers caution that neurological research should not form the sole basis for marketing decisions. These research activities have not been universally applauded though. Critics think that such a development will only lead to more marketing manipulation by companies.

Sources: Carolyn Yoon, Angela H. Gutchess, Fred Feinberg, and Thad A. Polk, "A Functional Magnetic Resonance Imaging Study of Neural Dissociations between Brand and Person Judgments," *Journal of Consumer Research,* 33, June 2006, pp. 31–40; Daryl Travis, "Tap Buyers' Emotions for Marketing Success," *Marketing News,* February 1, 2006, pp. 21–22; Deborah L. Vence, "Pick Someone's Brain," *Marketing News,* May 1, 2006, pp. 11–13; Louise Witt, "Inside Intent," *American Demographics,* March 2004, pp. 34–39; Samuel M. McClure, Jian Li, Damon Tomlin, Kim S. Cypert, Latané M. Montague, and P. Read Montague, "Neural Correlates of Behavioral Preference for Culturally Familiar Drinks," *Neuron,* 44, October 14, 2004, pp. 379–387; Melanie Wells, "In Search of the Buy Button," *Forbes,* September 1, 2003.

3. **Sampling procedure: how should we choose the respondents?** Probability sampling allows confidence limits to be calculated for sampling error and makes the sample more representative. Thus, after choosing the sample, the conclusion could be that "the interval five to seven trips per year has 95 chances in 100 of containing the true number of trips taken annually by first-class passengers flying between Amman and New York." Three types of probability sampling are described in ▭ **Table 4.3** part A. When the cost or time to use probability sampling is too high, marketing researchers will take nonprobability samples. **Table 4.3** part B describes three types.

CONTACT METHODS Now the marketing researcher must decide how to contact the subjects: by mail, by telephone, in person, or online.

Mail Questionnaire The *mail questionnaire* is the best way to reach people who would not give personal interviews or whose responses might be biased or distorted by the interviewer. Mail questionnaires require simple and clearly worded questions. Unfortunately, the response rate is usually low or slow.

TABLE 4.3	Probability and Nonprobability Samples
A. Probability Sample	
Simple random sample	Every member of the population has an equal chance of selection.
Stratified random sample	The population is divided into mutually exclusive groups (such as age groups), and random samples are drawn from each group.
Cluster (area) sample	The population is divided into mutually exclusive groups (such as city blocks), and the researcher draws a sample of the groups to interview.
B. Nonprobability Sample	
Convenience sample	The researcher selects the most accessible population members.
Judgment sample	The researcher selects population members who are good prospects for accurate information.
Quota sample	The researcher finds and interviews a prescribed number of people in each of several categories.

Telephone Interview *Telephone interviewing* is the best method for gathering information quickly; the interviewer is also able to clarify questions if respondents do not understand them. The response rate is typically higher than for mailed questionnaires, but interviews must be brief and not too personal. Telephone interviewing is getting more difficult because of consumers' growing dislike of telemarketers and their approaches.

Personal Interview In general, *personal interviewing* provides the most flexible contact method. The interviewer can ask more questions and record additional observations about the respondent, such as dress and body language. At the same time, however, personal interviewing is the most expensive method, is subject to interviewer bias, and requires more administrative planning and supervision. Personal interviewing takes two forms. In *arranged interviews*, marketers contact respondents for an appointment and often offer a small payment or incentive. In *intercept interviews*, researchers stop people at a shopping mall or busy street corner and request an interview on the spot. Intercept interviews must be quick, and they run the risk of including nonprobability samples.

Online Interview There are so many ways to use the internet to do research. A company can embed a questionnaire on its website in different ways and offer an incentive to answer it, or it can place a banner on a frequently visited site such as Yahoo! or Maktoob, inviting people to answer some questions and possibly win a prize. Marketers can also sponsor a chat room or bulletin board and introduce questions from time to time or host a real-time consumer panel or virtual focus group. The company can learn about individuals who visit its site by tracking how they *clickstream* through the website and move to other sites. It can post different prices, use different headlines, and offer different product features on different websites or at different times to learn the relative effectiveness of its offerings. Online product testing, in which companies float trial balloons for new products, is also growing and providing information much faster than traditional new-product marketing research techniques.

Online research was estimated to make up 33 percent of all survey-based research in 2006, and internet-based questionnaires also accounted for nearly one-third of U.S. spending on market research surveys in the same year.[20] Yet, as popular as online research methods are, some companies are choosing

Insights from Kraft-sponsored online communities helped the company develop its popular line of 100-calorie snacks.

Pros and Cons of Online Research

Advantages

- *Online research is inexpensive.* A typical e-mail survey can cost between 20 and 50 percent less than a conventional survey costs, and return rates can be as high as 50 percent.

- *Online research is fast.* Online surveys are fast because the survey can automatically direct respondents to applicable questions and transmit results immediately. One estimate says that 75 to 80 percent of a survey's targeted response can be generated in 48 hours using online methods, compared to a telephone survey that can take 70 days to obtain 150 interviews.

- *People tend to be honest online.* Britain's online polling company YouGov.com (which is also active in the Arab world through its collaboration with Bayt.com) surveyed 250 people via intercom in a booth and the other half online, asking questions such as "Should there be more aid to Africa?" Online answers were deemed much more honest. People may be more open about their opinions when they can respond privately and not to another person whom they feel might be judging them, especially on sensitive topics.

- *Online research is versatile.* Increased broadband penetration offers online research even more flexibility and capabilities. For instance, virtual reality software lets visitors inspect three-dimensional models of products such as cameras, cars, and medical equipment and manipulate product characteristics. Even at the basic level, online surveys can make answering a questionnaire easier and more fun than paper-and-pencil versions.

Disadvantages

- *Samples can be small and skewed.* Internet penetration varies widely across countries of the world. Some 33 percent of households are without internet access in the United States; the percentage is even higher among lower-income groups, in rural areas, and in most parts of Asia, Latin America, and Central and Eastern Europe, where socioeconomic and education levels also differ. The Arab world is no exception. Internet penetration falls from a high of 69 percent in the UAE and 67 percent in Qatar, to as low as 13 percent in Algeria and 10 percent or less in Yemen, Sudan, and Iraq. Although it's certain that more and more people will go online, online market researchers must find creative ways to reach population segments on the other side of the 'digital divide.' One option is to combine offline sources with online findings. Providing temporary internet access at locations such as malls and recreation centers is another strategy. Some research firms use statistical models to fill in the gaps in market research left by offline consumer segments.

- *Online market research is prone to technological problems and inconsistencies.* Because online research is relatively new, many market researchers have not gotten survey designs right. Others overuse technology, concentrating on the special effects and graphics while ignoring basic survey design guidelines. Problems also arise because browser software varies. The web designer's final product may look very different on the research subject's screen.

Sources: "Survey: Internet Should Remain Open to All," www.consumeraffairs.com, January 25, 2006; "Highlights from the National Consumers League's Survey on Consumers and Communications Technologies: Current and Future Use," www.nclnet.org, July 21, 2005; Catherine Arnold, "Not Done Net; New Opportunities Still Exist in Online Research," *Marketing News*, April 1, 2004, p. 17; Louella Miles, "Online, on Tap," *Marketing*, June 16, 2004, pp. 39–40; Suzy Bashford, "The Opinion Formers," *Revolution*, May 2004, pp. 42–46; Nima M. Ray and Sharon W. Tabor, "Contributing Factors; Several Issues Affect e-Research Validity," *Marketing News*, September 15, 2003, p. 50; Bob Lamons, "Eureka! Future of B-to-B Research Is Online," *Marketing News*, September 24, 2001, pp. 9–10; www.internetworldstats.com.

to use them to augment rather than replace more traditional methods. At Kraft Foods (marketers of famous Kraft cheeses, and other brands such as Oreo cookies, Milka and Toblerone chocolate, Jell-O, and Tang, and which recently acquired Cadbury), online research is a supplement to traditional research. For example, insights from Kraft-sponsored online communities helped the company develop its popular line of 100-calorie snacks.[21] This line is gaining share in some Arab markets too, given the growing consumer interest in healthier eating behavior.

The Marketing Memo: *Pros and Cons of Online Research* outlines some of the advantages and disadvantages of online research thus far. Online researchers have also begun to use instant messaging (IM) in various ways: to conduct a chat with a respondent, to probe more deeply with a member of an online focus group, or to direct respondents to a website.[22] IM is also a useful way to get teenagers to open up on topics.

Step 3: Collect the Information

The data-collection phase of marketing research is generally the most expensive and the most prone to error. Four major problems arise in surveys. Some respondents will not be at home and must be contacted again or replaced. Other respondents will refuse to cooperate. Still others will give biased or dishonest answers. Finally, some interviewers will be biased or dishonest.

Data-collection methods are rapidly improving thanks to computers and telecommunications. Some telephone research firms interview from a central location, using professional interviewers to read a set of questions from a monitor and type the respondent's answers into a computer. This procedure eliminates editing and coding, reduces errors, saves time, and produces all the required statistics. Other research firms have set up interactive terminals in shopping centers, where respondents sit at a terminal, read questions from the monitor, and type in their answers.

One of the biggest obstacles to collecting information internationally is the need to achieve consistency. Nan Martin, global accounts director for Synovate Inc., a market research firm with offices in 46 countries and which services clients in more than 60 countries, including Arab countries of the Levant, GCC, and North Africa, says: "In global research, we have to adapt culturally to how, where, and with whom we are doing the research…. A simple research study conducted globally becomes much more complicated as a result of the cultural nuances, and it's necessary for us to be sensitive to those nuances in data collection and interpretation."[23] Respondents in the Arab world may be more uncomfortable with the impersonal nature of the internet and need interactive elements in a survey, so that they feel like they're talking to a real person. On the other hand, in Asia, respondents may feel more pressure to conform and may therefore not be as forthcoming in focus groups as online.

Variations in country's economic, demographic, and technological infrastructures also have impact on the extent to which pan-Arab research methodology and data-collection procedures can be standardized. The Marketing Memo: *Pros and Cons of Online Research* illustrates variations across the Arab countries in terms of internet proliferation. ⌷ **Table 4.4** gives a snapshot of other economic, literacy, education, and telecommunication indices across the Arab world. Wide variation in internet penetration or mobile telephone penetration will affect the use of online and mobile phone research. Illiteracy might necessitate the use of personal contact method rather than mail or online.

Yahoo! Maktoob Research In a widely publicized deal that was concluded in November 2009, Yahoo! acquired the popular Arab portal Maktoob. com for a price estimated at US$100 million. Among its services, Yahoo! Maktoob Research offers an online panel covering 2 million Arabs in the Middle East and North Africa. Yahoo! Maktoob Research can target its panel members by demographics, such as age, gender and occupation among others, which makes it possible to target specific areas, a survey targeted at students, for example. Key behavioral patterns are available too. Yahoo! Maktoob Research not only provides full project support to its clients via survey programming, translations, and hosting, but also a complete research package, including consultancy. Research Portal, an online tool for real-time analysis, is also available. During any on-going research, the research data will be available 24/7. Yahoo! Maktoob Research runs an omnibus survey every month among 500 adults in the MENA region, which meets the same quality control procedures as for the customized ad-hoc studies, making this shared-cost study an effective means for gathering quick and accurate feedback.[24]

Step 4: Analyze the Information

The next step in the process is to extract findings by tabulating the data and developing frequency distributions. The researchers now compute averages and measures of dispersion for the major variables and apply some advanced statistical techniques and decision models in the hope of discovering additional findings. They may test different hypotheses and theories, applying sensitivity analysis to test assumptions and the strength of the conclusions.

Step 5: Present the Findings

The researcher presents findings relevant to the major marketing decisions facing management. Researchers increasingly are being asked to play a more proactive, consulting role in translating data and information into insights and recommendations.[25] They're also considering ways to present research findings in as understandable and compelling a fashion as possible.

TABLE 4.4   Snapshot of Indicators in the Arab World

	Qatar	Bahrain	The UAE	Saudi Arabia	Oman	Kuwait	Tunisia	Jordan	Lebanon	Morocco	Egypt	Algeria	Syria	Sudan
GNP per Capita (US$)	121,400	38,400	41,800	20,300	20,300	55,800	8,000	5,300	11,500	4,600	6,000	7,100	4,700	2,300
Internet Penetration rate (%)	52.3	55.3	60.9	26.8	13.6	37.1	26.7	23.9	23.5	32.9	15.9	12	16.4	10.2
Rate of Enrollment in Basic Education	93	98.2	90.9	84.6	72.7	88.2	95	88.6	83	88.8	95.8	95.4	94.5	50
Average Enrollment in Higher Education	15.9	32.1	22.9	30.2	25.5	17.6	30.8	39.9	39.9	11.3	34.7	24	19.4	NA
Illiteracy Rate	6.9	11.2	9.5	15	15.6	5.5	22.3	8.9	10.4	44.4	33.8	24.6	16.9	38.55
Freedom of the Press World Ranking	94	120	87	163	107	60	154	112	61	127	143	141	165	148
Number of Mobile Phones per 100 People	196.6	182.8	207.8	142.9	121.4	97.3	82.1	86.8	25.9	72.2	53.7	81.4	34.5	27.22

Source: "Mukhtarat min al-Dirasat al-Alamiyyah," *Saneou Al-Hadath* magazine, March 2010, pp. 70–71. Based on data from the World Bank, the CIA World Factbook, the World Economic Forum, Transparency International, the World Health Organization, Human Development Reports, Reporters without Borders, Internet World Stats, UNESCO, and the Global Travel & Tourism Competitiveness Report.

The main survey findings for the Royal Jordanian Airlines case could show that:

The chief reasons for using in-flight internet service are to pass the time surfing and to send and receive messages from colleagues and family. Passengers would charge the cost and their companies would pay.

At US$25, about five of 10 first-class passengers would use the internet service during a flight; about six would use it at $15. Thus, a fee of $15 would produce less revenue (6×$15=$90) than $25 (5×$25=$125). Assuming the same flight takes place 365 days a year, RJ could collect $45,625 (=$125×365) annually. Given an investment of $90,000, it would take 2 years to break even.

Offering an in-flight internet service would strengthen the public's image of Royal Jordanian Airlines as an innovative and progressive airline. RJ would gain some new passengers and customer goodwill.

Step 6: Make the Decision

The managers who commissioned the research need to weigh the evidence. If their confidence in the findings is low, they may decide against introducing the in-flight internet service. If they are predisposed to launching the service, the findings support their inclination. They may even decide to study the issues further and do more research. The decision is theirs, but rigorous research provides them with insight into the problem (see ▭ **Table 4.5**).[26]

A growing number of organizations are using a marketing decision support system to help their marketing managers make better decisions. The Massachusetts Institute of Technology's John Little defines a **marketing decision support system** (or **MDSS**) as a coordinated collection of data, systems, tools, and techniques, with supporting software and hardware, by which an organization gathers and interprets relevant information from business and the environment and turns it into a basis for marketing action.[27]

A classic MDSS example is the CALLPLAN model that helps salespeople determine the number of calls to make per period to each prospective and current client. The model takes into account travel time as well as selling time. When launched, it was tested at United Airlines with

marketing decision support system (MDSS) a coordinated collection of data, systems, tools, and techniques with supporting software and hardware by which an organization gathers and interprets relevant information from business and the environment and turns it into a basis for marketing action.

TABLE 4.5 ▭	The Seven Characteristics of Good Marketing Research
1. Scientific method	Effective marketing research uses the principles of the scientific method: careful observation, formulation of hypotheses, prediction, and testing.
2. Research creativity	At its best, marketing research develops innovative ways to solve a problem: a clothing company catering to teenagers gave several young men video cameras, then used the videos for focus groups held in restaurants and other places teens frequent.
3. Multiple methods	Marketing researchers shy away from overreliance on any one method. They also recognize the value of using two or three methods to increase confidence in the results.
4. Interdependence of models and data	Marketing researchers recognize that data are interpreted from underlying models that guide the type of information sought.
5. Value and cost of information	Marketing researchers show concern for estimating the value of information against its cost. Costs are typically easy to determine, but the value of research is harder to quantify. It depends on the reliability and validity of the findings and management's willingness to accept and act on those findings.
6. Healthy skepticism	Marketing researchers show a healthy skepticism toward glib assumptions made by managers about how a market works. They are alert to the problems caused by 'marketing myths.'
7. Ethical marketing	Marketing research benefits both the sponsoring company and its customers. The misuse of marketing research can harm or annoy consumers, increasing resentment at what consumers regard as an invasion of their privacy or a disguised sales pitch.

an experimental group that increased its sales by 8 percentage points over a matched control group.[28] Once a year, *Marketing News* (a publication of the American Marketing Association) lists hundreds of current marketing and sales software programs that assist in designing marketing research studies, segmenting markets, setting prices and advertising budgets, analyzing media, and planning sales force activity.

Overcoming Barriers to the Use of Marketing Research

In spite of the rapid growth of marketing research, many companies still fail to use it sufficiently or correctly, for several reasons:[29]

- *A narrow conception of the research.* Many managers see marketing research as a fact-finding operation. They expect the researcher to design a questionnaire, choose a sample, conduct interviews, and report results, often without their providing a careful definition of the problem. When fact-finding fails to be useful, management's idea of the limited usefulness of marketing research is reinforced.

- *Uneven caliber of researchers.* Some managers view marketing research as little more than a clerical activity and treat it as such. They hire less-competent marketing researchers, whose weak training and low creativity lead to unimpressive results. The disappointing results reinforce management's prejudice against marketing research, and low salaries perpetuate the basic problem.

- *Poor framing of the problem.* The failure of Coca-Cola's New Coke launch in the 1980s was largely due to a failure to set up the research problem correctly, from a marketing perspective. The real issue was how consumers felt about Coca-Cola as a brand, not how they felt about its taste in isolation.

- *Late and occasionally erroneous findings.* Managers want results that are accurate and conclusive. They may want the results tomorrow. Yet good marketing research takes time and money. Managers are disappointed when marketing research costs too much or takes too much time.

- *Personality and presentational differences.* Differences between the styles of line managers and marketing researchers often get in the way of productive relationships. To a manager who wants concreteness, simplicity, and certainty, a marketing researcher's report may seem abstract, complicated, and tentative. Yet in the more progressive companies, marketing researchers are being included as members of the product management team, and their influence on marketing strategy is growing.

Failure to use marketing research properly has led to numerous marketing mistakes. The New Coke case at the beginning of this chapter is a classic example.

Measuring Marketing Productivity

An important task of marketing research is to assess the efficiency and effectiveness of marketing activities.[30] Marketers increasingly are being held accountable for their investments and must be able to justify marketing expenditures to senior management.[31] One survey of top American marketers revealed that around half were not satisfied with their ability to measure the return on their marketing investments.[32] Another revealed that 63 percent of senior management were dissatisfied with their marketing performance measurement system and wanted marketing to supply prior and posterior estimates of the impact of marketing programs.[33]

Marketing research can help address this increased need for accountability. Two complementary approaches to measuring marketing productivity are: (1) *marketing metrics* to assess marketing effects and (2) *marketing-mix modeling* to estimate causal relationships and measure how marketing activity affects outcomes. *Marketing dashboards* are a structured way to disseminate the insights gleaned from these two approaches within the organization.

Marketing Metrics

Marketers employ a wide variety of measures to assess marketing effects.[34] **Marketing metrics** is the set of measures that helps them quantify, compare, and interpret their marketing performance. Marketing metrics can be used by brand managers to justify and design marketing programs and by senior management to decide on financial allocations.[35]

London Business School's Tim Ambler suggests that if firms think they are already measuring marketing performance adequately, they should ask themselves five questions.[36]

1. Do you routinely research consumer behavior (retention, acquisition, usage) and why consumers behave that way (awareness, satisfaction, perceived quality)?
2. Do you routinely report the results of this research to the board in a format integrated with financial marketing metrics?
3. In those reports, do you compare the results with the levels previously forecasted in the business plans?
4. Do you also compare them with the levels achieved by your key competitor using the same indicators?
5. Do you adjust short-term performance according to the change in your marketing-based asset(s)?

Ambler believes firms must give priority to measuring and reporting marketing performance through marketing metrics. He believes evaluation can be split into two parts: (1) short-term results and (2) changes in brand equity. Short-term results often reflect profit-and-loss concerns as shown by sales turnover, shareholder value, or some combination of the two. Brand-equity measures could include customer awareness, attitudes, and behaviors; **market share**; relative price premium; number of complaints; distribution and availability; total number of customers; perceived quality, and loyalty and retention.[37]

Companies can also monitor an extensive set of metrics internal to the company, such as innovation. For example, 3M tracks the proportion of sales resulting from its recent innovations. Ambler also recommends developing employee measures and metrics, arguing that "end users are the ultimate customers, but your own staff are your first; you need to measure the health of the internal market." **Table 4.6** summarizes a list of popular internal and external marketing metrics.[38]

marketing metrics the set of measures that helps firms to quantify, compare, and interpret their marketing performance.

market share the share of the market controlled by a particular brand, product, or company.

TABLE 4.6	Sample Marketing Metrics
External	**Internal**
Awareness	Awareness of goals
Market share (volume or value)	Commitment to goals
Relative price (market share value/volume)	Active innovation support
Number of complaints (level of dissatisfaction)	Resource adequacy
Consumer satisfaction	Staffing/skill levels
Distribution/availability	Desire to learn
Total number of customers	Willingness to change
Perceived quality/esteem	Freedom to fail
Loyalty/retention	Autonomy
Relative perceived quality	Relative employee satisfaction

Source: Tim Ambler, "What Does Marketing Success Look Like?," *Marketing Management*, Spring 2001, pp. 13–18.

Marketing-Mix Modeling

Marketing accountability also means that marketers must more precisely estimate the effects of different marketing investments. *Marketing-mix models* analyze data from a variety of sources, such as retailer scanner data, company shipment data, pricing, media, and promotion spending data, to understand more precisely the effects of specific marketing activities.[39] To deepen understanding, marketers can conduct statistical analyses, such as regression analysis, to sort through how each marketing element influences marketing outcomes such as brand sales or market share.[40]

Especially popular with packaged-goods marketers such as Procter & Gamble, Clorox, and Colgate, the findings from marketing-mix modeling help allocate or reallocate expenditures. Analyses explore which part of ad budgets are wasted, what optimal spending levels are, and what minimum investment levels should be.[41] Service providers such as hotels (Rotana or The Four Seasons) and mobile telecom operators (Zain or Vodafone) also benefit from such analysis.

Although marketing-mix modeling helps to isolate effects, it is less effective at assessing how different marketing elements work in combination. Wharton's Dave Reibstein also notes three other shortcomings:[42]

1. Marketing-mix modeling focuses on incremental growth instead of baseline sales or long-term effects.
2. Despite their importance, the integration of metrics such as customer satisfaction, awareness, and brand equity into marketing-mix modeling is limited.
3. Marketing-mix modeling generally fails to incorporate metrics related to competitors, the trade, or the sales force (the average business spends far more on the sales force and trade promotion than on advertising or consumer promotion).

Marketing Dashboards

Firms are also employing organizational processes and systems to make sure they maximize the value of all these different metrics. Management can assemble a summary set of relevant internal and external measures in a *marketing dashboard* for synthesis and interpretation. Marketing dashboards are like the instrument panel in a car or plane, visually displaying real-time indicators to ensure proper functioning. They are only as good as the information on which they're based, but sophisticated visualization tools are helping bring data alive to improve understanding and analysis.[43]

Some companies are also appointing marketing controllers to review budget items and expenses. Increasingly, these controllers are using business intelligence software to create digital versions of marketing dashboards that aggregate data from disparate internal and external sources.

As input to the marketing dashboard, companies should include two key market-based scorecards that reflect performance and provide possible early warning signals.

stakeholder-performance scorecard a measure to track the satisfaction of various constituencies who have a critical interest in and impact on the company's performance.

customer-performance scorecard how well the company is doing year after year on particular customer-based measures.

- A **customer-performance scorecard** records how well the company is doing year after year on such customer-based measures as those shown in   **Box 4.1**. Management should set norms for each measure and take action when results get out of bounds.

- A **stakeholder-performance scorecard** tracks the satisfaction of various constituencies who have a critical interest in and impact on the company's performance: employees, suppliers, banks, distributors, retailers, and stockholders. Again, management should take action when one or more groups register increased or above-norm levels of dissatisfaction.[44]

Some executives worry that they'll miss the big picture if they focus too much on a set of numbers on a dashboard. Some critics are concerned about privacy and the pressure the technique places on employees. But most experts feel the rewards offset the risks.[45] The Marketing Insight: *Marketing Dashboards to Improve Effectiveness and Efficiency* provides practical advice about the development of these marketing tools.

Marketing Consultant Pat LaPointe[46] feels a marketing dashboard can present insights from all the pathways in a graphically related view that helps management see subtle links between them.

BOX 4.1 ▨ Sample Customer-Performance Scorecard Measures

- Percentage of new customers to average number of customers
- Percentage of lost customers to average number of customers
- Percentage of win-back customers to average number of customers
- Percentage of customers falling into very dissatisfied, dissatisfied, neutral, satisfied, and very satisfied categories
- Percentage of customers who say they would repurchase the product
- Percentage of customers who say they would recommend the product to others
- Percentage of target market customers who have brand awareness or recall
- Percentage of customers who say that the company's product is the most preferred in its category
- Percentage of customers who correctly identify the brand's intended positioning and differentiation
- Average perception of company's product quality relative to chief competitor
- Average perception of company's service quality relative to chief competitor

A well-constructed dashboard can have a series of 'tabs' that allow the user to toggle easily between different 'families' of metrics organized by customer, product, experience, brand, channels, efficiency, organizational development, or macroenvironmental factors. Each tab presents the three or four most insightful metrics, with data filtered by business unit, geography, or customer segment based upon the users' needs (see ◭ **Figure 4.3** for an example).

Ideally, the number of metrics presented in the marketing dashboard would be reduced to a handful of key drivers over time. Importantly, the process of developing and refining the marketing dashboard will undoubtedly raise and resolve many key questions about the business.

Marketing Insight

Marketing Dashboards to Improve Effectiveness and Efficiency

Marketing consultant Pat LaPointe sees marketing dashboards as providing all the up-to-the-minute information necessary to run the business operations for a company, such as sales versus forecast, distribution-channel effectiveness, brand equity evolution, and human capital development. According to LaPointe, an effective dashboard will focus thinking, improve internal communications, and reveal where marketing investments are paying off and where they aren't.

LaPointe observes four common measurement 'pathways' marketers are pursuing today (see ◭ **Figure 4.2**).

1. The *customer metrics pathway* looks at how prospects become customers, from awareness to preference to trial to repeat purchase. Many companies track progression through a 'hierarchy of effects' model to follow the evolution of broad market potential to specific revenue opportunities.

2. The *unit metrics pathway* reflects what marketers know about sales of product/service units: how much is sold by product line and/or by geography; the marketing cost per unit sold as an efficiency yardstick; and where and how the margin is optimized in terms of characteristics of the product line or distribution channel.

3. The *cash-flow metrics pathway* focuses on how well marketing expenditures are achieving short-term returns. Program and campaign return-on-investment models measure the immediate impact or net present value of profits expected from a given investment.

4. The *brand metrics pathway* tracks the development of the longer-term impact of marketing through brand equity measures that assess both the perceptual health of the brand from customer and prospective customer perspectives as well as the overall financial health of the brand.

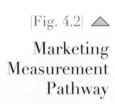

|Fig. 4.2| △

Marketing
Measurement
Pathway

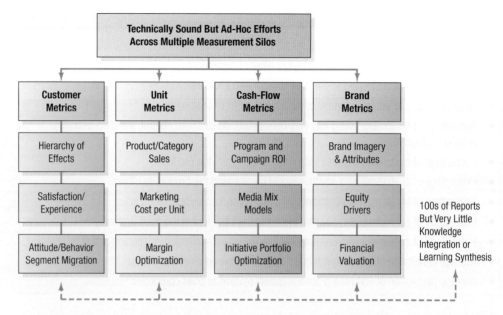

|Fig. 4.3| △

Example of a
Marketing Dashboard

Source: Adapted from Patrick LaPointe,
*Marketing by the Dashboard Light –
How to Get More Insight, Foresight,
and Accountability from Your Marketing
Investments.* © 2005, Patrick LaPointe.

Forecasting and Demand Measurement

One major reason for undertaking marketing research is to identify market opportunities. Once the research is complete, the company must measure and forecast the size, growth, and profit potential of each market opportunity. Sales forecasts are used by finance to raise the needed cash for investment and operations; by the manufacturing department to establish capacity and output levels; by purchasing to acquire the right amount of supplies; and by human resources to hire the needed number of workers. Marketing is responsible for preparing the sales forecasts. If its forecast is far off the mark, the company will face excess or inadequate inventory.

Sales forecasts are based on estimates of demand. Managers need to define what they mean by market demand. While the household brands Coke and Pepsi compete vigorously over market share of the cola-flavored carbonated soft drinks, their parent companies (Coca-Cola Company and PepsiCo) nonetheless evaluate their flagship brands much more broadly in terms of the brands' share of the refreshments market (which also includes all carbonated soft drinks, bottled juices, flavored water, and other refreshments).

The Measures of Market Demand

Companies can prepare as many as 90 different types of demand estimate for six different product levels, five space levels, and three time periods (see **Figure 4.4**). Each demand measure serves a specific purpose. A company might forecast short-run demand for a particular product for the purpose of ordering raw materials, planning production, and borrowing cash. It might forecast regional demand for its major product line to decide whether to set up regional distribution.

PepsiCo evaluates its competitive position versus close rival Coca-Cola Company in terms of its brands' share of the refreshments market, which includes carbonated drinks, juices, and other refreshments.

The size of a market hinges on the number of buyers who might exist for a particular market offer. But there are many productive ways to break down the market.

- The **potential market** is the set of consumers who profess a sufficient level of interest in a market offer. However, consumer interest is not enough to define a market for marketers unless they also have sufficient income and access to the product.

- The **available market** is the set of consumers who have interest, income, *and* access to a particular offer. For some market offers, the company or government may restrict sales to certain groups. For example, a particular country might ban motorcycle sales to anyone under 21 years of age. Eligible adults constitute the *qualified available market*: the set of consumers who have interest, income, access, and qualifications for the particular market offer.

- The *target market* is the part of the qualified available market the company decides to pursue. The company might decide to concentrate its marketing and distribution effort on one geographically defined area such as a territory within a country (e.g. Saudi Arabia Eastern

potential market the set of consumers who profess a sufficient level of interest in a market offer.

available market the set of consumers who have interest, income, and access to a particular offer.

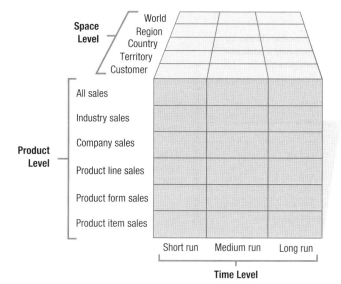

Fig. 4.4 △

Ninety Types of Demand Measurement (6 x 5 x 3)

penetrated market the set of consumers who are buying a company's product.

Province or the Emirate of Sharjah), or a country (Saudi Arabia or the UAE), or a confined region (the GCC or the Levant), or an extended region (e.g. the Arab world/Middle East and North Africa region), or even the whole world.

- The **penetrated market** is the set of consumers who are buying the company's product.

These definitions are a useful tool for market planning. If the company isn't satisfied with its current sales, it can take a number of actions. It can try to attract a larger percentage of buyers from its target market. It can lower the qualifications for potential buyers. It can expand its available market by opening distribution elsewhere or lowering its price, or it can reposition itself in the minds of its customers.

A Vocabulary for Demand Measurement

The major concepts in demand measurement are market demand and company demand. Within each, we distinguish among a demand function, a sales forecast, and a potential.

market demand the total volume of a product that would be bought by a defined customer group in a defined geographical area in a defined time period in a defined marketing environment under a defined marketing program.

MARKET DEMAND The marketer's first step in evaluating marketing opportunities is to estimate total market demand. **Market demand** for a product is the total volume that would be bought by a defined customer group in a defined geographical area in a defined time period in a defined marketing environment under a defined marketing program.

Market demand is not a fixed number, but rather a function of the stated conditions. For this reason, we can call it the *market demand function*. The dependence of total market demand on underlying conditions is illustrated in ▲ **Figure 4.5**(a). The horizontal axis shows different possible levels of industry marketing expenditure in a given time period. The vertical axis shows the resulting demand level. The curve represents the estimated market demand associated with varying levels of industry marketing expenditure.

Some base sales—called the *market minimum* and labeled Q_1 in the figure—would take place without any demand-stimulating expenditures. Higher levels of industry marketing expenditures would yield higher levels of demand, first at an increasing rate, then at a decreasing rate. Take fruit juice marketers such as Saudi Arabia's Al-Rabie, Kuwait's KDD, or Lebanon's Maccaw. Given all the indirect competition they face from other types of beverage, increased marketing expenditures would be expected to make fruit juice products stand out and increase demand and sales. Marketing expenditures beyond a certain level would not stimulate much further demand, thus suggesting an upper limit to market demand, called the **market potential** and labeled Q_2 in the figure.

market potential the upper limit to market demand whereby increased marketing expenditures would not be expected to stimulate further demand.

The distance between the market minimum and the market potential shows the overall *marketing sensitivity of demand*. We can think of two extreme types of market, the expansible and the nonexpansible. An *expansible market*, such as the market for racquetball playing, is very much affected in size by the level of industry marketing expenditures. In terms of Figure 4.5(a), the distance between Q_1 and Q_2 is relatively large. A *nonexpansible market*—for example, the market for

(a) **Marketing Demand as a Function of Industry Marketing Expenditure (assumes a particular marketing environment)**

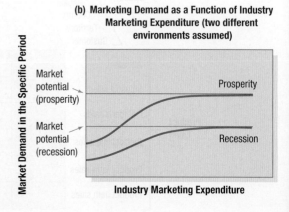

(b) **Marketing Demand as a Function of Industry Marketing Expenditure (two different environments assumed)**

|Fig. 4.5| ▲

Market Demands Functions

weekly trash or garbage removal—is not much affected by the level of marketing expenditures; the distance between Q_1 and Q_2 is relatively small. Organizations selling in a nonexpansible market must accept the market's size—the level of *primary demand* for the product class—and direct their efforts toward winning a larger *market share* for their product, that is, a higher level of selective demand for their product.

It pays to compare the current and potential levels of market demand. The result is called the **market-penetration index**. A low market-penetration index indicates substantial growth potential for all the firms. A high market-penetration index suggests it will be expensive to attract the few remaining prospects. Generally, price competition increases and margins fall when the market-penetration index is already high.

A company should also compare its current and potential market shares. The result is called the company's **share-penetration index**. A low share-penetration index indicates the company can greatly expand its share. The factors holding it back could be many: low brand awareness, low availability, benefit deficiencies, and high price. A firm should calculate the share-penetration increases that would occur if it removed each factor, to see which investments produce the greatest improvement.[47]

Remember that the market demand function is not a picture of market demand over time. Rather, the curve shows alternative current forecasts of market demand associated with possible levels of industry marketing effort.

MARKET FORECAST Only one level of industry marketing expenditure will actually occur. The market demand corresponding to this level is called the **market forecast**.

MARKET POTENTIAL The market forecast shows expected market demand, not maximum market demand. For the latter, we need to visualize the level of market demand resulting from a 'very high' level of industry marketing expenditure, where further increases in marketing effort would have little effect in stimulating further demand. *Market potential* is the limit approached by market demand as industry marketing expenditures approach infinity for a given marketing environment.

The phrase 'for a given market environment' is crucial. Consider the market potential for automobiles. It is higher during prosperity than during a recession. The dependence of market potential on the environment is illustrated in Figure 4.5(b). Market analysts distinguish between the position of the market demand function and movement along it. Companies cannot do anything about the position of the market demand function, which is determined by the marketing environment. However, they influence their particular location on the function when they decide how much to spend on marketing.

Companies interested in market potential have a special interest in the **product-penetration percentage**, which is the percentage of ownership or use of a product or service in a population. Companies assume that the lower the product-penetration percentage, the higher the market potential, although this assumes that everyone will eventually be in the market for every product.

COMPANY DEMAND **Company demand** is the company's estimated share of market demand at alternative levels of company marketing effort in a given time period. It depends on how the company's products, services, prices, and communications are perceived relative to the competitors'. If other things are equal, the company's market share will depend on the relative scale and effectiveness of its market expenditures. Marketing model builders have developed sales response functions to measure how a company's sales are affected by its marketing expenditure level, marketing mix, and marketing effectiveness.[48]

Company Sales Forecast Once marketers have estimated company demand, their next task is to choose a level of marketing effort. The **company sales forecast** is the expected level of company sales based on a chosen marketing plan and an assumed marketing environment.

We represent the company sales forecast graphically with sales on the vertical axis and marketing effort on the horizontal axis, as in **Figure 4.5**. We often hear that the company should develop its marketing plan on the basis of its sales forecast. This forecast-to-plan sequence is valid if 'forecast' means an estimate of national economic activity, or if company demand is nonexpansible. The sequence is not valid, however, where market demand is expansible or where forecast means an estimate of company sales. The company sales forecast does not establish a basis for deciding what to spend on marketing. On the contrary, the sales forecast is the result of an assumed marketing expenditure plan.

market penetration index a comparison of the current level of market demand to the potential demand level.

share penetration index a comparison of a company's current market share to its potential market share.

market forecast the market demand corresponding to the level of industry marketing expenditure.

product penetration percentage the percentage of ownership or use of a product or service in a population.

company demand the company's estimated share of market demand at alternative levels of company marketing effort in a given time period.

company sales forecast the expected level of company sales based on a chosen marketing plan and an assumed marketing environment.

sales quota   the sales goal set for a product line, company division, or sales representative.

sales budget   a conservative estimate of the expected volume of sales, used for making current purchasing, production, and cash-flow decisions.

company sales potential   sales limit approached by company demand as company marketing effort increases relative to that of competitors.

total market potential   the maximum amount of sales that might be available to all the firms in a given industry, during a given period, under a given level of industry marketing effort and environmental conditions.

Two other concepts are important here. A **sales quota** is the sales goal set for a product line, company division, or sales representative. It is primarily a managerial device for defining and stimulating sales effort. Generally, sales quotas are set slightly higher than estimated sales to stretch the sales force's effort.

A **sales budget** is a conservative estimate of the expected volume of sales, primarily for making current purchasing, production, and cash-flow decisions. It's based on the sales forecast and the need to avoid excessive risk, and is generally set slightly lower than the sales forecast.

COMPANY SALES POTENTIAL   Company sales potential is the sales limit approached by company demand as company marketing effort increases relative to that of competitors. The absolute limit of company demand is, of course, the market potential. The two would be equal if the company got 100 percent of the market. In most cases, company sales potential is less than the market potential, even when company marketing expenditures increase considerably. Each competitor has a hard core of loyal buyers who are not very responsive to other companies' efforts to woo them.

Estimating Current Demand

We are now ready to examine practical methods for estimating current market demand. Marketing executives want to estimate **total market potential**, area market potential, and total industry sales and market shares.

TOTAL MARKET POTENTIAL   *Total market potential* is the maximum amount of sales that might be available to all the firms in an industry during a given period, under a given level of industry marketing effort and environmental conditions. A common way to estimate total market potential is to multiply the potential number of buyers by the average quantity each purchases, times the price.

If, in Syria, 2 million people buy books each year, and the average book buyer buys two books a year, and the average price of a book in Syrian Pounds (SP) is 200 (around US$4), then the total market potential for books is SP800 million (2 million×2×SP200). The most difficult component to estimate is the number of buyers for the specific product or market. We can always start with the total population; to continue our example in Syria, say the population is 20 million people. Next we eliminate groups that obviously would not buy the product. Assume that illiterate people and children under 12 don't buy books and constitute 40 percent of the population. This means 60 percent of the population, or 12 million people, are in the potentials pool. We might do further research and find that people of low income and low education don't read books, and they constitute over 30 percent of the potentials pool. Eliminating them, we arrive at a prospect pool of approximately 8.4 million book buyers. We use this number of prospective buyers to calculate total market potential.

A variation on this method is the *chain-ratio method*, which multiplies a base number by several adjusting percentages. Suppose Al-Rabie is interested in estimating the market potential for a new light fruit juice mix designed to accompany food. It can make an estimate with the following calculation:

Demand for the new fruit juice mix		Average percentage of personal discretionary income per capita spent on food		Average percentage of amount spent on food that is spent on beverages		Average percentage of amount spent on beverages that is spent on fruit juices		Expected percentage of amount spent on fruit juices that will be spent on light fruit juice
	= Population ×		×		×		×	

AREA MARKET POTENTIAL   Because companies must allocate their marketing budget optimally among their best territories, they need to estimate the market potential of different cities, areas, countries, and regions. Two major methods of assessing area market potential are the market-buildup method, used primarily by business marketers, and the multiple-factor index method, used primarily by consumer marketers.

Market-Buildup Method The **market-buildup method** calls for identifying all the potential buyers in each market and estimating their potential purchases. This method produces accurate results if we have a list of all potential buyers and a good estimate of what each will buy. Unfortunately, this information is not always easy to gather.

Multiple-Factor Index Method Like business marketers, consumer companies also need to estimate area market potentials, but the customers of consumer companies are too numerous to list. The method most commonly used in consumer markets is a straightforward index method. A drug manufacturer, for example, might assume that the market potential for drugs is directly related to population size. As an example, let's consider the GCC states (comprising Bahrain, Kuwait, Oman, Qatar, Saudi Arabia, and the UAE). If Oman had 7 percent of all of the GCC countries' population, the company might assume that Oman would be a market for 7 percent of total drugs sold in the GCC.

A single factor, however, is rarely a complete indicator of sales opportunity. Regional drug sales are also influenced by per-capita income and the number of physicians per 10,000 people. Thus it makes sense to develop a multiple-factor index, with each factor assigned a specific weight. The numbers are the weights attached to each variable. For example, suppose Oman had 5 percent of the GCC disposable personal income, 4 percent of GCC retail sales, and 7 percent of the GCC population, and the respective weights were 0.5, 0.3, and 0.2. The buying-power index for Oman would then be 5.10 [0.5(5)+0.3(4)+0.2(7)]. Thus 5.1 percent of drug sales (not 7 percent) might be expected to take place in Oman.

The weights in the buying-power index are somewhat arbitrary, and companies can assign others if appropriate. A manufacturer might also want to adjust the market potential for additional factors, such as competitors' presence in that market, local promotional costs, seasonal factors, and local market idiosyncrasies.

Many companies compute other area indexes as a guide to allocating marketing resources. Suppose the drug company is reviewing its presence in the GCC area as listed in 🖳 **Table 4.7**. The first two columns show its percentage of total brand and category sales in the GCC. Column 3 shows the **brand development index** (or **BDI**), which is the index of brand sales to category sales. Bahrain, for example, has a BDI of 125 because the brand is relatively more developed than the category in Bahrain. Kuwait has a BDI of 75, which means that the brand in Kuwait is relatively underdeveloped. Normally, the lower the BDI, the higher the market opportunity, in that there is room to grow the brand. However, other marketers would argue the opposite: that marketing funds should go into the brand's *strongest* markets, where it might be important to reinforce loyalty or more easily capture additional brand share.[49]

INDUSTRY SALES AND MARKET SHARES Besides estimating total potential and area potential, a company needs to know the actual industry sales taking place in its market. This means identifying competitors and estimating their sales.

market-buildup method identifying all the potential buyers in each market and estimating their potential purchases.

brand development index (BDI) the index of brand sales to category sales.

TABLE 4.7 🖳	Calculating the Brand Development Index (BDI)		
Country	Sales: (a) Percent of GCC Brand	Sales: (b) Percent of GCC Category	BDI [(a/b)×100]
Bahrain	10	8	125
Kuwait	15	20	75
Oman	8	10	80
Qatar	12	10	120
Saudi Arabia	35	30	117
The UAE	20	22	91

The industry trade association will often collect and publish total industry sales, although it usually does not list individual company sales separately. With this information, however, each company can evaluate its own performance against the whole industry. If a company's sales are increasing by 5 percent a year, and industry sales are increasing by 10 percent, the company is losing its relative standing in the industry.

Another way to estimate sales is to buy reports from a marketing research firm that audits total sales and brand sales. Nielsen Media Research audits retail sales in various product categories in supermarkets and drugstores and sells this information to interested companies. These audits let a company compare its performance to the total industry or to any particular competitor to see whether it is gaining or losing share either overall or on a brand-by-brand basis.

Because distributors typically will not supply information about how much of competitors' products they are selling, business-goods marketers operate with less knowledge of their market share results.

Estimating Future Demand

The few products or services that lend themselves to easy forecasting generally enjoy an absolute level or a fairly constant trend and competition that is either nonexistent (public utilities) or stable (pure oligopolies). In most markets, in contrast, good forecasting is a key factor in success.

Companies commonly prepare a macroeconomic forecast first, followed by an industry forecast, followed by a company sales forecast. The macroeconomic forecast calls for projecting inflation, unemployment, interest rates, consumer spending, business investment, government expenditures, net exports, and other variables. The end result is a forecast of gross national product, which the firm uses, along with other environmental indicators, to forecast industry sales. The company derives its sales forecast by assuming that it will win a certain market share.

How do firms develop their forecasts? They may create their own or buy forecasts from outside sources such as marketing research firms, which interview customers, distributors, and other knowledgeable parties.

All forecasts are built on one of three information bases: what people say, what people do, or what people have done. Using what people say requires surveying the opinions of buyers or those close to them, such as salespeople or outside experts, with surveys of buyer's intentions, composites of sales force opinions, and expert opinion. Building a forecast on what people do means putting the product into a test market to measure buyer response. To use the final basis—what people have done—firms analyze records of past buying behavior or use time-series analysis or statistical demand analysis.

forecasting   the art of anticipating what buyers are likely to do under a given set of conditions.

purchase probability scale a scale to measure the probability of a buyer making a particular purchase.

SURVEY OF BUYERS' INTENTIONS   **Forecasting** is the art of anticipating what buyers are likely to do under a given set of conditions. For major consumer durables such as appliances, several research organizations conduct periodic surveys of consumer buying intentions and ask questions like this—for example, do you intend to buy an automobile within the next 6 months?—and put the answers on a **purchase probability scale**:

0.00	0.20	0.40	0.60	0.80	1.00
No chance	Slight possibility	Fair possibility	Good possibility	High possibility	Certain

Surveys also inquire into consumers' present and future personal finances and their expectations about the economy. They combine various bits of information into a consumer confidence measure. Bayt.com publishes a periodic Middle East Consumer Confidence Index.

Bayt.com   Bayt.com and research firm YouGov publish the Middle East Consumer Confidence Index report. The report describes consumer confidence and its importance as "a measure of the economic well-being of a country. It is a reflection of consumer satisfaction levels and expectations based on various factors in the economy—inflation, stock market performance, job opportunities/salary structures, unemployment, investment avenues/returns, business growth, state economic policies, infrastructure, cost of living, interest rates, exchange rates." It goes on to describe the effect of consumer confidence levels on the economy: "For example, if consumers are positive about the economy and have disposable income levels that are perceived as sufficient, they will tend to spend more on consumer goods. This in turn will drive business dependent on consumer spending, thereby creating further economic growth."[50]

In addition to the Consumer Confidence Index, Bayt.com also produces other market-based indices: Consumer Expectations Index, Propensity to Consumer/Spend Index, and Employee Confidence Index.

For business buying, research firms can carry out buyer-intention surveys regarding plant, equipment, and materials. Their estimates tend to fall within a 10 percent error band around the actual outcomes. Buyer-intention surveys are particularly useful in estimating demand for industrial products, consumer durables, product purchases where advanced planning is required, and new products. The value of a buyer-intention survey increases to the extent that buyers are few, the cost of reaching them is low, and they have clear intentions that they willingly disclose and implement.

COMPOSITE OF SALES FORCE OPINIONS When buyer interviewing is impractical, the company may ask its sales representatives to estimate their future sales.

Few companies use sales force estimates without making some adjustments. Sales representatives might be pessimistic or optimistic, they might not know how their company's marketing plans will influence future sales in their territory, and they might deliberately underestimate demand so the company will set a low sales quota. To encourage better estimating, the company could offer incentives or assistance, such as information about marketing plans or past forecasts compared to actual sales.

Sales force forecasts bring a number of benefits. Sales representatives might have better insight into developing trends than any other group, and forecasting might give them greater confidence in their sales quotas and more incentive to achieve them. Also, a 'grass-roots' forecasting procedure provides detailed estimates broken down by product, territory, customer, and sales representative.

EXPERT OPINION Companies can also obtain forecasts from experts, including dealers, distributors, suppliers, marketing consultants, and trade associations. Dealer estimates are subject to the same strengths and weaknesses as sales force estimates. Many companies buy economic and industry forecasts from well-known economic-forecasting firms that have more data available and more forecasting expertise.

Occasionally, companies will invite a group of experts to prepare a forecast. The experts exchange views and produce an estimate as a group (*group-discussion method*) or individually, in which case another analyst might combine them into a single estimate (*pooling of individual estimates*). Further rounds of estimating and refining follow (this is the Delphi method).[51]

PAST-SALES ANALYSIS Firms can develop sales forecasts on the basis of past sales. *Time-series analysis* breaks past time series into four components (trend, cycle, seasonal, and erratic) and projects them into the future. *Exponential smoothing* projects the next period's sales by combining an average of past sales and the most recent sales, giving more weight to the latter. *Statistical demand analysis* measures the impact of a set of causal factors (such as income, marketing expenditures, and price) on the sales level. Finally, *econometric analysis* builds sets of equations that describe a system and statistically derives the different parameters that make up the equations statistically.

MARKET-TEST METHOD When buyers don't plan their purchases carefully, or experts are unavailable or unreliable, a direct-market test can help forecast new-product sales or established product sales in a new distribution channel or territory. (We discuss market testing in detail in Chapter 20.)

Summary

1. Companies can conduct their own marketing research or hire other companies to do it for them. Good marketing research is characterized by the scientific method, creativity, multiple research methods, accurate model building, cost-benefit analysis, healthy skepticism, and an ethical focus.

2. The marketing research process consists of defining the problem, decision alternatives, and research objectives, developing the research plan, collecting the information, analyzing the information, presenting the findings to management, and making the decision.

3. In conducting research, firms must decide whether to collect their own data or use data that already exist. They must also decide which research approach (observational, focus group, survey, behavioral data, or experimental) and which research instruments (questionnaire, qualitative measures, or technological devices) to use. In addition, they must decide on a sampling plan and contact methods (by mail, by phone, in person, or online).

4. Two complementary approaches to measuring marketing productivity are: (1) marketing metrics to assess marketing effects and (2) marketing-mix modeling to estimate causal relationships and measure how marketing activity affects outcomes. Marketing dashboards are a structured way to disseminate the insights gleaned from these two approaches within the organization.

5. There are two types of demand: market demand and company demand. To estimate current demand, companies attempt to determine total market potential, area market potential, industry sales, and market share. To estimate future demand, companies survey buyers' intentions, solicit their sales force's input, gather expert opinions, analyze past sales, or engage in market testing. Mathematical models, advanced statistical techniques, and computerized data collection procedures are essential to all types of demand and sales forecasting.

Applications

Marketing Debate

What Is the Best Type of Marketing Research?

Many market researchers have their favorite research approaches or techniques, although different researchers often have different preferences. Some researchers maintain that the only way to really learn about consumers or brands is through in-depth, qualitative research. Others contend that the only legitimate and defensible form of marketing research involves quantitative measures.

Take a position: The best marketing research is quantitative in nature *versus* the best marketing research is qualitative in nature.

Marketing Discussion

When was the last time you participated in a survey? How helpful do you think was the information you provided? How could the research have been done differently to make it more effective?

Marketing Excellence

>>Maatouk 1960

Established in 1960 in downtown Beirut by Mahmoud Maatouk, an 18-year-old entrepreneur, Maatouk 1960 started as a local coffee roaster and grew to become a national coffee manufacturer whose name is synonymous with premium-quality coffee, be it Lebanese coffee, filter coffee, or espresso. Passionately attracted by the innovation and product development side of the business, the Maatouk family overlooked the importance of monitoring the competitive surroundings, market dynamics, and purchasing behavior and consumption habits of customers. With competition intensifying and competitors investing heavily in venues and product mix, Maatouk found itself struggling to maintain its sales and share despite the growth of the Lebanese coffee market locally and overseas.

To remedy this situation, management realized the need for reliable market information as a basis upon which to base their new competitive strategy. According to Marketing Manager Yusra Kanj, "A valuable decision management took which had major implications on our decision-making process was subscribing regularly to the coffee category of the A. C. Nielsen Retail Audit. The report revealed huge weaknesses in Maatouk's distribution and market coverage. It also shed light on the presence and share of each major player in the category across different geographical regions and trade channels with in-house analysis of their strengths and weaknesses."

To ensure proper coverage, Maatouk found that a huge investment in human capital, vans, and technology was required, which would not be reasonable for such a limited product portfolio. In 2010 a strategic decision was made to outsource the distribution operation to a specialized national distributor that can ensure a proper pan-Lebanon market presence for Maatouk products.

Change was not limited to the distribution strategy. Management also decided to revise all its marketing mix elements including product packaging, pricing, and communication. Kanj noted that, "The exercise was led by a team of professionals from leading regional research houses who initiated tailor-made studies of the existing market conditions and trends and techniques in packaging, pricing, and communication, and made recommendations for the launch of a re-engineered Maatouk product line." This undertaking resulted in a change to the architecture of the Maatouk brand, with color coding to emphasize heritage, and in a repositioning of the brand through innovative packaging and creative but focused communication, pricing, and distribution strategies. "The right positioning is the key to success for every brand," said Abdel Halim Jarakji, the general manager.

Management also focused on export markets. Market research reports by Euromonitor provided valuable insights into macro-country indicators as well as specific coffee market information, such as volume, value, trends, consumer habits, and competition. In addition to field visits by marketing and top management, the management used this information to identify promising regional and world markets and to decide how to penetrate these potential markets.

Maatouk's current manufacturing facility handles all the export markets, focusing on the Levant (Lebanon, Syria, Jordan, and Iraq), as well as the GCC, North Africa, Europe, and the Americas.

"Market intelligence and research can never be 100 percent accurate; yet it is highly insightful and enlightening," concludes Jawad Maatouk, owner and major shareholder of Maatouk 1960.

Questions

1. From the concepts presented in the chapter, attempt to define the problem, decision alternatives, and research objectives faced by Maatouk's management.

2. Identify the sources of secondary data that Maatouk utilized. How were these sources helpful?

3. If Maatouk was to gather primary data, which research approach would you recommend?

4. Comment on and discuss Jawad Maatouk's remark that, "Market intelligence and research can never be 100 percent accurate; yet it is highly insightful and enlightening."

Sources: www.maatouk.com; personal interviews with Maatouk management: Yusra Kanj, Marketing Manager; Jawad Maatouk, Owner; and Abdel Halim Jarakji, general manager.

CHAPTER 5

Ritz-Carlton's focus on enhancing the guest experience helped it win the prestigious Baldrige Award, among other awards in the tourism and travel industry.

In this chapter, we will address the following questions:

1. What are customer value, satisfaction, and loyalty, and how can companies deliver them? (pg. 126)

2. What is the lifetime value of customers and how can marketers maximize it? (pg. 134)

3. How can companies cultivate strong customer relationships? (pg. 137)

4. How can companies both attract and retain customers? (pg. 137)

5. What is database marketing? (pg. 147)

Creating Customer Value, Satisfaction, and Loyalty

Companies today face their toughest competition ever. Moving from a product-and-sales philosophy to a holistic marketing philosophy, however, gives them a better chance of outperforming the competition. And the cornerstone of a well-conceived marketing orientation is strong customer relationships. Marketers must connect with customers: informing, engaging, and maybe even energizing them in the process. For example, Chipsy, one of the leading Egyptian food companies, ran a large campaign in 2010 to involve people in suggesting flavors for its potato chips. This campaign engaged people in developing new flavors which made customers more emotionally attached to the brand. Another good example of a company that ensures customer satisfaction by integrating the customer centricity in its corporate culture is the Ritz-Carlton chain of hotels.

With more than 100 years of history, the Ritz-Carlton hotel chain, owned by Marriott International, is known throughout the world for its singular focus on providing guests with luxurious amenities and exceptional service. Ritz-Carlton has a presence in a few countries in the Arab world, namely Bahrain, Egypt, Oman, Qatar, and the UAE. Throughout all their locations, they apply a customer-centered approach which is expressed by the company's motto: "We are ladies and gentlemen serving ladies and gentlemen." Guests at any of the 62 Ritz-Carlton hotels in 21 countries notice the brand's famed personal touch immediately upon checking in, when they are greeted by name. To ensure guests' total experience at the hotel is of the utmost quality, Ritz-Carlton creates a daily 'Service Quality Index' (SQI) at each of its locations, so employees can continually monitor key guest service processes and swiftly address potential problem areas. At the brand's corporate headquarters in Maryland in the United States, SQIs for each hotel are displayed in a central command room, allowing instant analysis of how well a single location is performing. Other customer service initiatives include the CLASS (Customer Loyalty Anticipation Satisfaction System) database, which contains preferences and requirements of repeat Ritz-Carlton guests, and a room maintenance system known as CARE (Clean and Repair Everything), which ensures all guest rooms are free of defects every 90 days. These initiatives helped Ritz-Carlton win its second Malcolm Baldrige National Quality Award in 1999, becoming the only service company to win twice. It has also received many other awards; for example, in 2011 it received the Conde Nast Gold Award, the AAA Five & Four Diamond Award, and the Forbes Travel Guide Award.[1]

As Ritz-Carlton's experience shows, successful marketers are the ones that fully satisfy their customers profitably. In this chapter, we spell out in detail the ways companies can go about winning customers and beating competitors. The answer lies largely in doing a better job of meeting or exceeding customer expectations. It is about delighting customers at all customer touch points and not just in the final product delivered. Thus, it is important for marketers to understand the entire customer experience. ▽

LET
US
STAY
WITH
YOU.™

Let us arrange a camel ride for you on the beach.

Let us set up a bedouin tent with dinner for two.

Let us turn your weekend getaway into a weekend of laughter.

Let us be the start of fond memories that will last a lifetime.

THE RITZ-CARLTON®
DUBAI

Ritz-Carlton builds brand loyalty by personal touches, such as reception staff addressing customers by name.

Building Customer Value, Satisfaction, and Loyalty

Creating loyal customers is at the heart of every business.[2] As marketing experts Don Peppers and Martha Rogers say:[3]

"The only value your company will ever create is the value that comes from customers—the ones you have now and the ones you will have in the future. Businesses succeed by getting, keeping, and growing customers. Customers are the only reason you build factories, hire employees, schedule meetings, lay fiber-optic lines, or engage in any business activity. Without customers, you don't have a business."

Yet many companies in the Arab world are not truly customer-centric. Faisal Hammude, a business development and marketing expert, identifies three main reasons for this lack of customer focus; the first is that the focus is on the bottom line and financial indicators, so that customer service does not usually appear on performance indicators; the second is that the most popular way for measuring satisfaction is through customer surveys, which does not cover all aspects of the customer experience; the third is the lack of long-term sustainability of customer orientation philosophy over time. While most companies do this on a short-term basis, through workshops and consultants, this usually ends with these short-term activities.[4]

Managers who believe the customer is the company's only true 'profit center' consider the traditional organization chart in △ **Figure 5.1**—a pyramid with the president at the top, management in the middle, and frontline people and customers at the bottom—to be obsolete.[5]

|Fig. 5.1| △

Traditional
Organization versus
Modern Customer-
Oriented Company
Organization

(a) Traditional Organization Chart

Top management

Middle management

Frontline people

CUSTOMERS

(b) Modern Customer-Oriented Organization Chart

CUSTOMERS

Frontline people

Middle management

Top management

CUSTOMERS

CUSTOMERS

Successful marketing companies invert the chart (Figure 5.1b). At the top are customers; next in importance are frontline people who meet, serve, and satisfy customers; under them are the middle managers, whose job is to support the frontline people so they can serve customers well; and at the base is top management, whose job is to hire and support good middle managers. We have added customers along the sides of Figure 5.1 (b) to indicate that managers at every level must be personally involved in knowing, meeting, and serving customers.

Some companies have been founded with the customer-on-top business model, and customer advocacy has been their strategy—and competitive advantage—all along. With the rise of digital technologies such as the internet, today's increasingly informed consumers expect companies to do more than connect with them, more than satisfy them, and even more than delight them. They expect companies to listen to them.[6] When CompUSA permitted customer reviews on its site— which can then show up in online searches—it found that 20,000 more customers than before visited the site in a month, with a 50 percent greater propensity to buy.[7] When Ebates, an online shopping portal that offers members cash back for shopping on the web, switched to online survey software to better monitor customer responses, the site redesign and other changes that resulted from customer feedback brought increases in virtually all aspects of business performance, including sales.[8] In Dubai, the government conducted mystery shopping research to evaluate the performance of government employees with their customers, the public. In this research customers evaluated the civil servants' efficiency in terms of speed of service, reception, ease of interaction, and accuracy. The Dubai government is one of the leaders in world governments that use such tools to assess customer satisfaction. The mystery shopping method is one of the best methods to assess satisfaction and help identify the necessary steps to achieve high satisfaction levels.[9]

Customer Perceived Value

Consumers are more educated and informed than ever, and they have the tools to verify companies' claims and seek out superior alternatives.[10]

Hewlett-Packard Co., Dell Inc.
Hewlett-Packard outpaced Dell in terms of customer perceived value. Hewlett-Packard is the leader in PC shipments in the Arab world, followed by Dell.[11] Dell rode to success by offering low-priced computers, logistical efficiency, and after-sales service. Dell's focus on low costs has been a key ingredient to that business model success. When the company shifted its customer-service call centers to India and the Philippines to cut costs, the understaffing of these centers led to frequent 30-minute waits for customers. Almost half the calls required at least one transfer. To discourage customer calls, Dell even removed its free service telephone number from its website. With customer satisfaction slipping and competitors matching its product quality and prices and offering improved service, Dell's market share and stock price both declined sharply. Dell ended up hiring more North American call center employees. "The team was managing cost instead of managing service and quality," Michael Dell confesses. In contrast, Hewlett-Packard is aggressively pursuing a solutions approach based on strengthening its channel partner relationships. Don Ritchie, CEO of Sequel Data Systems, an exclusive HP partner, says he sees no threat from Dell as he continues to deliver enterprise solutions in concert with HP and says, "One of the easiest sales Sequel has is to go into an account that has been serviced by Dell."[12]

How then do customers ultimately make choices? They tend to be value maximizers, within the bounds of search costs and limited knowledge, mobility, and income. Customers estimate which offer will deliver the most perceived value and act on it (△ **Figure 5.2**). Whether the offer lives up to expectation affects customer satisfaction and the probability that the customer will purchase the product again.

Customer perceived value (CPV) is the difference between the prospective customer's evaluation of all the benefits and all the costs of an offering and the perceived alternatives. *Total customer benefit* is the perceived monetary value of the bundle of economic, functional, and psychological benefits customers expect from a given market offering because of the products, services, personnel, and image involved. **Total customer cost** is the perceived bundle of costs customers expect to

customer perceived value (CPV) the difference between the prospective customer's evaluation of all the benefits and all the costs of an offering and the perceived alternatives.

total customer cost the bundle of costs customers expect to incur in evaluating, obtaining, using, and disposing of the given market offering, including monetary, time, energy, and psychological costs.

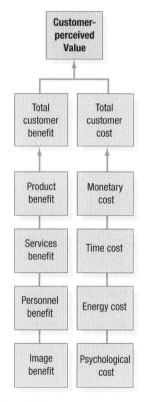

|Fig. 5.2| △

Determinants of Customer-Perceived Value

incur in evaluating, obtaining, using, and disposing of the given market offering, including monetary, time, energy, and psychological costs.

Customer-perceived value is thus based on the difference between what the customer gets and what he or she gives for different possible choices. The customer gets benefits and assumes costs. The marketer can increase the value of the customer offering by some combination of raising economic, functional, or emotional benefits and/or reducing one or more of the various types of costs. The customer choosing between two value offerings, V1 and V2, will examine the ratio V1:V2 and favor V1 if the ratio is larger than one, favor V2 if the ratio is smaller than one, and be indifferent if the ratio equals one.

APPLYING VALUE CONCEPTS Suppose the buyer for a large construction company wants to buy a tractor from Caterpillar or Komatsu. The competing salespeople carefully describe their respective offers. The buyer wants to use the tractor in residential construction work. He would like it to deliver certain levels of reliability, durability, performance, and resale value. He evaluates the tractors and decides that Caterpillar has greater product benefits based on his perceptions of those attributes. He also perceives differences in the accompanying services—delivery, training, and maintenance—and decides that Caterpillar provides better service as well as more knowledgeable and responsive personnel. Finally, he places higher value on Caterpillar's corporate image and reputation. He adds up all the economic, functional, and psychological benefits from these four sources—product, services, personnel, and image—and perceives Caterpillar as delivering greater customer benefits.

Does he buy the Caterpillar tractor? Not necessarily. He also examines his total cost of transacting with Caterpillar versus Komatsu, which consists of more than money. As Adam Smith observed over two centuries ago, "The real price of anything is the toil and trouble of acquiring it." Total customer cost also includes the buyer's time, energy, and psychological costs expended in product acquisition, usage, maintenance, ownership, and disposal. The buyer evaluates these elements together with the monetary cost to form a total customer cost. Then he considers whether Caterpillar's total customer cost is too high in relationship to the total customer benefits Caterpillar delivers. If it is, the buyer might choose Komatsu. The buyer will choose whichever source he thinks delivers the highest perceived value.

Now let's use this decision-making theory to help Caterpillar succeed in selling to this buyer. Caterpillar can improve its offer in three ways. First, it can increase total customer benefit by improving economic, functional, and psychological benefits of its product, services, personnel, and/or image. Second, it can reduce the buyer's nonmonetary costs by reducing the time, energy, and psychological costs. Third, it can reduce its product's monetary cost to the buyer.

Suppose Caterpillar concludes that the buyer sees its offer as worth US$20,000. Further, suppose Caterpillar's cost of producing the tractor is $14,000. This means Caterpillar's offer potentially generates $6,000 over the company's cost, so Caterpillar needs to charge a price between $14,000 and $20,000. If it charges less than $14,000, it won't cover its costs; if it charges more than $20,000, it will price itself out of the market.

The price Caterpillar charges will determine how much value will be delivered to the buyer and how much will flow to Caterpillar. For example, if Caterpillar charges $19,000, it is creating $1,000 of customer perceived value and keeping $5,000 for itself. The lower Caterpillar sets its price, the higher the customer perceived value and, therefore, the higher the customer's incentive to purchase. To win the sale, Caterpillar must offer more customer perceived value than Komatsu does.[13]

customer value analysis
report of the company's strengths and weaknesses relative to various competitors.

Very often, managers conduct a **customer value analysis** to reveal the company's strengths and weaknesses relative to those of various competitors. The steps in this analysis are:

1. *Identify the major attributes and benefits that customers value.* Customers are asked what attributes, benefits, and performance levels they look for in choosing a product and vendor.
2. *Assess the quantitative importance of the different attributes and benefits.* Customers are asked to rate the importance of the different attributes and benefits. If their ratings diverge too much, the marketer should cluster them into different segments.
3. *Assess the company's and competitors' performances on the different customer values against their rated importance.* Customers describe where they see the company's and competitors' performances on each attribute and benefit.
4. *Examine how customers in a specific segment rate the company's performance against a specific major competitor on an individual attribute or benefit basis.* If the company's offer

exceeds the competitor's offer on all important attributes and benefits, the company can charge a higher price (thereby earning higher profits), or it can charge the same price and gain more market share.

5. **Monitor customer values over time.** The company must periodically redo its studies of customer values and competitors' standings as the economy, technology, and features change.

CHOICES AND IMPLICATIONS Some marketers might argue that the process we have described is too rational. Suppose the customer chooses the Komatsu tractor. How can we explain this choice? Here are three possibilities.

1. **The buyer might be under orders to buy at the lowest price.** The Caterpillar salesperson's task is to convince the buyer's manager that buying on price alone will result in lower long-term profits and customer value.

2. **The buyer will retire before the company realizes that the Komatsu tractor is more expensive to operate.** The buyer will look good in the short run; he is maximizing personal benefit. The Caterpillar salesperson's task is to convince other people in the customer company that Caterpillar delivers greater customer value.

3. **The buyer enjoys a long-term friendship with the Komatsu salesperson.** In this case, Caterpillar's salesperson needs to show the buyer that the Komatsu tractor will draw complaints from the tractor operators when they discover its high fuel cost and need for frequent repairs.

The point of these examples is clear: buyers operate under various constraints and occasionally make choices that give more weight to their personal benefit than to the company's benefit.

Customer-perceived value is a useful framework that applies to many situations and yields rich insights. Here are its implications:

First, the seller must assess the total customer benefit and total customer cost associated with each competitor's offer in order to know how his or her offer rates in the buyer's mind.

Second, the seller who is at a customer-perceived-value disadvantage has two alternatives: to increase total customer benefit or to decrease total customer cost. The former calls for strengthening or augmenting the economical, functional, and psychological benefits of the offering's product, services, personnel, and image. The latter calls for reducing the buyer's costs by reducing the price or cost of ownership and maintenance, simplifying the ordering and delivery process, or absorbing some buyer risk by offering a warranty.[14]

DELIVERING HIGH CUSTOMER VALUE Consumers have varying degrees of loyalty to specific brands, stores, and companies. Oliver defines **loyalty** as "a deeply held commitment to rebuy or repatronize a preferred product or service in the future despite situational influences and marketing efforts having the potential to cause switching behavior."[15] Box 5.1 displays brands with the greatest degree of customer loyalty according to one 2010 survey.[16]

The **value proposition** consists of the whole cluster of benefits the company promises to deliver; it is more than the core positioning of the offering. For example, Volvo's core positioning has been 'safety,' but the buyer is promised more than just a safe car; other benefits include a long-lasting car, good service, and a long warranty period. The value proposition is a statement about the experience customers will gain from the company's market offering and from their relationship with the supplier. The brand must represent a promise about the total experience customers can expect. Whether the promise is kept depends on the company's ability to manage its value delivery system.[17] The **value delivery system** includes all the experiences the customer will have on the way to obtaining and using the offering. At the heart of a good value delivery system is a set of core business processes that help to deliver distinctive consumer value.[18]

Abu Dhabi's International Airport is one of the leading airports in terms of delivering customer value.

loyalty   a commitment to rebuy or re-patronize a preferred product or service.

value proposition   the whole cluster of benefits the company promises to deliver.

value-delivery system all the expectancies the customer will have on the way to obtaining and using the offering.

This volvo ad promises a rich value proposition.

BOX 5.1	Top 20 Brands in Customer Loyalty

1. Apple iPhone	11. Google
2. Samsung Wireless Handset	12. Mary Kay Cosmetics
3. Walmart	13. J. Crew Retail Store
4. Grey Goose	14. Dunkin Donuts
5. Apple Computer	15. Bing
6. Hyundai	16. Maybelline
7. Amazon.com	17. Ketel One
8. J. Crew Clothing Catalogue	18. McDonald's
9. Blackberry	19. Estee Lauder
10. Avis	20. Mary Kay Skin Moisturizer

Source: 2010 Brand Keys Customer Loyalty Leaders List, 2010, www.brandkeys.com/awards/leaders.cfm.

Abu Dhabi International Airport   Abu Dhabi

International Airport received the "Best Airport in the Middle East" award in the 2011 Business Destinations Travel Awards. The airport provides unique services to its clients, which add significant value to their travel experience. This includes top quality services in retail, food and beverage, airport lounges, airport hotel, meet-and-greet services, car parking services, and a golf club. Part of this success is due to the availability of boutiques such as Hermes, Jimmy Choo, and Burberry and also other stores such as Boots, Ibn Sina Pharmacy, and Pure Gold. James Bennett, CEO of the Abu Dhabi Airport Company, attributed this to their "continuous commitment towards promoting a culture of excellence" throughout the airport. The company tries to enhance the travel experience at all possible points, to make the experience both recognizable and unforgettable.[19]

Total Customer Satisfaction

Whether the buyer is satisfied after purchase depends on the offer's performance in relationship to the buyer's expectations, and whether the buyer interprets any deviations between the two.[20] In general, *satisfaction* is a person's feeling of pleasure or disappointment that results from comparing a product's perceived performance (or outcome) to their expectations.[21] If the performance falls short of expectations, the customer is dissatisfied. If the performance matches the expectations, the customer is satisfied. If the performance exceeds expectations, the customer is highly satisfied or delighted.[22] Customer assessments of product performance depend on many factors, especially the type of loyalty relationship the customer has with the brand.[23] Consumers often form more favorable perceptions of a product with a brand they already feel positive about.

Although the customer-centered firm seeks to create high customer satisfaction, that is not its ultimate goal. If the company increases customer satisfaction by lowering its price or increasing its services, the result may be lower profits. The company might be able to increase its profitability by means other than increased satisfaction (for example, by improving manufacturing processes or investing more in R&D). Also, the company has many stakeholders, including employees, dealers, suppliers, and stockholders. Spending more to increase customer satisfaction might divert funds from increasing the satisfaction of other 'partners.' Ultimately, the company must operate on the philosophy that it is trying to deliver

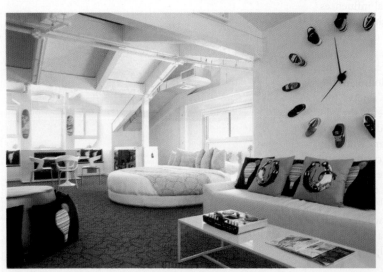

Joie de Vivre's boutique hotels offer personal touches that exceed customer expectations.

a high level of customer satisfaction subject to delivering acceptable levels of satisfaction to the other stakeholders, given its total resources.[24]

How do buyers form their expectations? Expectations result from past buying experience; friends' and associates' advice; and marketers' and competitors' information and promises. If marketers raise expectations too high, the buyer is likely to be disappointed. However, if the company sets expectations too low, it won't attract enough buyers (although it will satisfy those who do buy).[25] Some of today's most successful companies are raising expectations and delivering performances to match. Korean automaker Kia found success in the Arab world by launching low-cost, high-quality, reliable cars, which make it competitive with other brands in the same category.

A customer's decision to be loyal or to defect is the sum of many small encounters with the company. Many companies now strive to create a 'branded customer experience.' Here's how Joie de Vivre's hotel chain does this.[26]

 Joie de Vivre   Joie de Vivre Hospitality Inc. operates a chain of boutique hotels, restaurants, and resorts in the San Francisco area of the United States. Each property's unique décor, quirky amenities, and thematic style are often loosely based on popular magazines. For example, the Hotel del Sol—a converted motel bearing a yellow exterior and surrounded by palm trees wrapped with festive lights—is described as "kind of Martha Stewart Living meets Islands magazine."[27] Two Silicon Valley hotels offer guests high-speed internet connections in their rooms and by the pool.[28] The boutique concept enables the hotels to offer personal touches, such as vitamins in place of chocolates on pillows. Joie de Vivre now owns the largest number of independent hotel properties in the San Francisco Bay Area.

Monitoring Satisfaction

Many companies are systematically measuring how well they treat their customers, identifying the factors shaping satisfaction, and making changes in their operations and marketing as a result.[29] For example, organizations such as Union Bank, Chilli House, and Jordan Post in Jordan have been involved in mystery shopping research. The research has proven to be useful in providing management with gaps or problems that were unknown. It gives them all the elements they need to assess the entire customer experience and thus is very comprehensive in nature. It gives feedback on the retail store, employee's response, process, physical environment, and service level. It is becoming a more popular form to assess satisfaction than the traditional customer satisfaction cards.[30]

A company would be wise to measure customer satisfaction regularly, because one key to customer retention is customer satisfaction.[31] A highly satisfied customer generally stays loyal longer, buys more as the company introduces new products and upgrades existing products, talks favorably to others about the company and its products, pays less attention to competing brands, is less sensitive to price, offers product or service ideas to the company, and costs less to serve than new customers because transactions can become routine.[32] Greater customer satisfaction has also been linked to higher returns and lower risk in the stock market.[33]

The link between customer satisfaction and customer loyalty, however, is not proportional. Suppose customer satisfaction is rated on a scale from one to five. At a very low level of customer satisfaction (level one), customers are likely to abandon the company and even criticize it to others. At levels two to four, customers are fairly satisfied but still find it easy to switch when a better offer comes along. At level five, the customer is very likely to repurchase and even spread good word of mouth about the company. High satisfaction or delight creates an emotional bond with the brand or company, not just a rational preference. Xerox's senior management found out that its 'completely satisfied' customers were six times more likely to repurchase Xerox products over the following 18 months than its 'very satisfied' customers.[34]

When customers rate their satisfaction with an element of the company's performance—say, delivery—the company needs to recognize that customers vary in how they define good performance. Good delivery could mean early delivery, on-time delivery, order completeness, and so on.

The company must also realize that two customers can report being 'highly satisfied' for different reasons. One may be easily satisfied most of the time and the other might be hard to please but was pleased on this occasion.[35]

MEASUREMENT TECHNIQUES A number of methods exist to measure customer satisfaction. *Periodic surveys* can track customer satisfaction directly and also ask additional questions to measure repurchase intention and the respondent's likelihood or willingness to recommend the company and brand to others. Paramount attributes the success of its five theme parks to the thousands of web-based guest surveys it sends to customers who have agreed to be contacted. During a recent year, the company conducted more than 55 of these surveys and netted 100,000 individual responses that described guest satisfaction on topics including rides, dining, shopping, games, and shows.[36]

Besides conducting periodic surveys, companies can monitor their *customer loss rate* and contact customers who have stopped buying or who have switched to another supplier to find out why. Finally, companies can hire *mystery shoppers* to pose as potential buyers and report on strong and weak points experienced in buying the company's and competitors' products. Managers themselves can enter company and competitor sales situations where they are unknown and experience first hand the treatment they receive, or they can phone their own company with questions and complaints to see how employees handle the calls.

In addition to tracking customer value expectations and satisfaction for their own firms, companies need to monitor their competitors' performance in these areas. One company was pleased to find that 80 percent of its customers said they were satisfied. Then the CEO found out that its leading competitor had a 90 percent customer satisfaction score. He was further dismayed when he learned that this competitor was aiming for a 95 percent satisfaction score.

INFLUENCE OF CUSTOMER SATISFACTION For customer-centered companies, customer satisfaction is both a goal and a marketing tool. Companies need to be especially concerned today with their customer satisfaction level because the internet provides a tool for consumers to quickly spread bad word of mouth—as well as good word of mouth—to the rest of the world. Some customers even set up their own websites to air their grievances and dissatisfaction, targeting high-profile brands such as United Airlines and Mercedes-Benz.[37] Describing events and actions as being wronged by the company, these websites often attempt to increase consumer discontent and protest.

Companies that do achieve high customer satisfaction ratings make sure their target market knows it. Once they achieved number-one status on J.D. Power's customer satisfaction ratings, Countrywide home mortgage lenders, Continental airlines, and Kyocera copiers all advertised that fact. In Egypt, Le Pacha 1901, a floating boat that is one of Cairo's premier dining and entertainment venues, was awarded the 2010 Official Winner of the Best Restaurants in Egypt by the Egyptian Ministry of Tourism. They were also awarded for their superior **quality** by Superbrands Egypt. They use both awards as a tool to market their unique service to customers in their restaurants and on their website.[38]

The University of Michigan's Claes Fornell has developed the American Customer Satisfaction Index (ACSI) to measure the perceived satisfaction consumers feel with different firms, industries, economic sectors, and national economies.[39] Examples of firms that led their respective industries with high ACSI scores in 2010 were Lincoln Mercury (Ford) (89), Unilever (87), Apple (86), Dr. Pepper Snappel (85), Whirlpool (83), and Hilton (80).

CUSTOMER COMPLAINTS Some companies think they're getting a sense of customer satisfaction by tallying complaints, but studies of customer dissatisfaction show that customers are dissatisfied with their purchases about 25 percent of the time but that only about 5 percent complain. The other 95 percent either feel complaining is not worth the effort, or they do not know how or to whom to complain, and they just stop buying.[40]

Of the customers who register a complaint, between 54 and 70 percent will do business with the organization again if their complaint is resolved. The figure goes up to a staggering 95 percent if the customer feels the complaint was resolved *quickly*. Customers who have complained to an

quality the totality of features and characteristics of a product or service that bear on its ability to satisfy stated or implied needs.

organization and had their complaints satisfactorily resolved tell an average of five people about the good treatment they received.[41] The average dissatisfied customer, however, complains to 11 people. If each of them tells other people, the number of people exposed to bad word of mouth may grow exponentially.

The fact is, no matter how perfectly designed and implemented a marketing program is, mistakes will happen. The best thing a company can do is to make it easy for the customer to complain. Suggestion forms, free telephone numbers, websites, and e-mail addresses allow for quick, two-way communication. The 3M Company claims that over two-thirds of its product-improvement ideas come from listening to customer complaints.

Given the potential downside of having an unhappy customer, it's critical that marketers deal with the negative experience properly.[42] Beyond that, the following procedures can help to recover customer goodwill:[43]

1. Set up a 7-day, 24-hour free 'hotline' (by phone, fax, or e-mail) to receive and act on customer complaints.
2. Contact the complaining customer as quickly as possible. The slower the company is to respond, the more dissatisfaction may grow and lead to negative word of mouth.
3. Accept responsibility for the customer's disappointment; don't blame the customer.
4. Use customer-service people who are empathic.
5. Resolve the complaint swiftly and to the customer's satisfaction. Some complaining customers are not looking for compensation so much as a sign that the company cares.

Product and Service Quality

Satisfaction will also depend on product and service quality. What exactly is quality? Various experts have defined it as "fitness for use," "conformance to requirements," "freedom from variation," and so on. We will use the American Society for Quality Control's definition: *quality* is the totality of features and characteristics of a product or service that bear on its ability to satisfy stated or implied needs.[44] This is clearly a customer-centered definition. We can say that the seller has delivered quality whenever its product or service meets or exceeds the customers' expectations. A company that satisfies most of its customers' needs most of the time is called a quality company, but we need to distinguish between *conformance* quality and *performance* quality (or grade). A Lexus provides higher performance quality than a Hyundai: the Lexus rides smoother, goes faster, and lasts longer. Yet we can say that both a Lexus and a Hyundai deliver the same conformance quality if all the units deliver their respective promised quality.

According to General Electric's former chairman, Jack Welch Jr., "Quality is our best assurance of customer allegiance, our strongest defense against foreign competition, and the only path to sustained growth and earnings."[45] The **drive** to produce goods that are superior in world markets has led some countries—and groups of countries—to recognize or award prizes to companies that exemplify the best quality practices, such as the ISO (International Organization for Standardization) Award, Deming Prize in Japan, the Malcolm Baldrige National Quality Award in the United States, and the European Quality Award.

drive a strong internal stimulus impelling action.

IMPACT OF QUALITY Product and service quality, customer satisfaction, and company profitability are intimately connected. Higher levels of quality result in higher levels of customer satisfaction, which support higher prices and (often) lower costs. Studies have shown a high correlation between relative product quality and company profitability.[46] Companies that have lowered costs to cut corners have paid the price when the quality of the customer experience suffers:[47]

• When Home Depot—an American retailer of home improvement—decided to expand into the contractor supply business, while also cutting costs and streamlining operations in 1,816 U.S. stores, it replaced many full-time workers with part-time employees who soon made up about 40 percent of store staff. The chain's ACSI dropped to the bottom among major U.S. retailers, 11 points behind customer-friendly competitor Lowe's, and Home Depot's share price slid 24 percent during the biggest home improvement boom in history.

- Although Northwest Airlines—a domestic airline carrier in the United States—stopped offering free magazines, pillows, movies, and even minibags of pretzels on domestic flights, the carrier also raised prices and reduced its flight schedule. As one frequent flier noted, "Northwest acts low cost without *being* low cost." Not surprisingly, Northwest came in last of all top U.S. airlines in both the ACSI and J.D. Power & Associates customer satisfaction poll.

Quality is clearly the key to value creation and customer satisfaction.

TOTAL QUALITY   Total quality is everyone's job, just as marketing is everyone's job. Marketers play several roles in helping their companies define and deliver high-quality goods and services to target customers. First, they bear the major responsibility for correctly identifying the customers' needs and requirements. Second, they must communicate customer expectations properly to product designers. Third, they must make sure that customers' orders are filled correctly and on time. Fourth, they must check that customers have received proper instructions, training, and technical assistance in the use of the product. Fifth, they must stay in touch with customers after the sale to ensure that they are satisfied and remain satisfied. Sixth, they must gather customer ideas for product and service improvements and convey them to the appropriate departments. When marketers do all this, they are making substantial contributions to **total quality management (TQM)** and customer satisfaction, as well as to customer and company profitability.

total quality management (TQM)   an organization-wide approach to continuously improving the quality of all the organization's processes, products, and services.

Maximizing Customer Lifetime Value

Ultimately, marketing is the art of attracting and keeping profitable customers. Yet every company loses money on some of its customers. The well-known 20/80 rule says that the top 20 percent of the customers often generates 80 percent or more of the company's profits. In some cases the profit distribution may be more extreme: the most profitable 20 percent of customers (on a per-capita basis) may contribute as much as 150 to 300 percent of profitability. The least profitable 10 to 20 percent of customers, on the other hand, can actually reduce profits between 50 to 200 percent per account, with the middle 60 to 70 percent breaking even.[48] ▲ **Figure 5.3** displays one customer profit distribution. The implication is that a company could improve its profits by 'firing' its worst customers.

It's not always the company's largest customers who yield the most profit. The largest customers can demand considerable service and receive the deepest discounts. The smallest customers pay full price and receive minimal service, but the costs of transacting with them can reduce their profitability. The midsize customers who receive good service and pay nearly full price are often the most profitable.

|Fig. 5.3| ▲

The 150/20 Rule: "The 20% most profitable customers generate as much as 150% of the profits of a company; the 20% least profitable lose 100% of the profits."

Source: Larry Selden and Yoko S. Seldon, "Profitable Customer: The Key to Great Brands," *Point*, July–August 2006, p. 9.

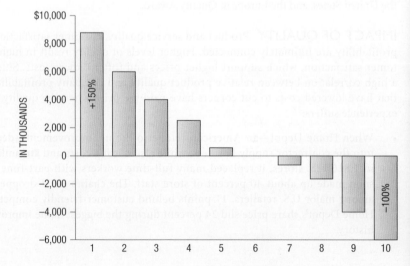

Customer Profitability

What makes a customer profitable? A **profitable customer** is a person, household, or company that over time yields a revenue stream that exceeds by an acceptable amount the company's cost stream for attracting, selling, and servicing that customer. Note that the emphasis is on the *lifetime* stream of revenue and cost, not on the profit from a particular transaction.[49] Marketers can assess customer profitability individually, by market segment, or by channel.

Although many companies measure customer satisfaction, most companies fail to measure individual customer profitability.[50] Banks claim this is a difficult task, because each customer uses different banking services and the transactions are logged in different departments. However, the number of unprofitable customers in their customer base has appalled banks that have succeeded in linking customer transactions. Some banks report losing money on over 45 percent of their retail customers.

CUSTOMER PROFITABILITY ANALYSIS A useful type of profitability analysis is shown in △ **Figure 5.4**.[51]

Customers are arrayed along the columns and products along the rows. Each cell contains a symbol representing the profitability of selling that product to that customer. Customer 1 is very profitable; he buys two profit-making products (P1 and P2). Customer 2 yields a picture of mixed profitability; he buys one profitable product (P1) and one unprofitable product (P3). Customer 3 is a losing customer because he buys one profitable product (P1) and two unprofitable products (P3 and P4).

What can the company do about customers 2 and 3? First, it can raise the price of its less profitable products or eliminate them or, second, it can try to sell customers 2 and 3 its profit-making products. Unprofitable customers who defect should not concern the company. In fact, the company should encourage these customers to switch to competitors.

Customer profitability analysis (CPA) is best conducted with the tools of an accounting technique called activity-based costing (ABC). The company estimates all revenue coming from the customer, less all costs. The costs should include not only the cost of making and distributing the products and services, but also of taking phone calls from the customer, traveling to visit the customer, paying for entertainment and gifts: all the company's resources that go into serving that customer.

When a company does this for each customer, it can classify customers into different profit tiers: *platinum customers* (most profitable), *gold customers* (profitable), *iron customers* (low profitability but desirable for volume), and *lead customers* (unprofitable and undesirable). The company can then move iron customers into the gold tier and gold customers into the platinum tier, while dropping the lead customers or making them profitable by raising their prices or lowering the cost of serving them. More generally, marketers must segment customers into those worth pursuing and those potentially less-lucrative customers that should receive less attention, if any at all.

CUSTOMER PORTFOLIOS Marketers are recognizing the need to manage customer portfolios, made up of different groups of customers[52] defined in terms of their loyalty, profitability, and other factors. One perspective is that a firm's portfolio consists of a combination

profitable customer   a person, household, or company that over time yields a revenue stream that exceeds by an acceptable amount the company's cost stream of attracting, selling, and servicing that customer.

customer profitability analysis (CPA)   a means of assessing and ranking customer profitability through accounting techniques such as Activity-Based Costing (ABC).

Products		Customers			
		C_1	C_2	C_3	
	P_1	+	+	+	Highly profitable product
	P_2	+			Profitable product
	P_3		−	−	Unprofitable product
	P_4			−	Highly unprofitable product
		High-profit customer	Mixed-bag customer	Losing customer	

|Fig. 5.4| △

Customer-Product
Profitability Analysis

of 'acquaintances,' 'friends,' and 'partners' that are constantly changing.[53] The three types of customer will differ in their product needs, their buying, selling, and servicing activities, and their acquisition costs and competitive advantages.

Another perspective compares the individuals who make up the firm's customer portfolio to the stocks that make up an investment portfolio.[54] In marketing, as in investments, it's important to calculate the beta, or risk-reward value, for each portfolio item and then diversify accordingly. From this perspective, firms should assemble portfolios of negatively correlated individuals so that the financial contributions of one offset the deficits of another to maximize the portfolio's risk-adjusted lifetime value.

Measuring Customer Lifetime Value

customer lifetime value (CLV) the net present value of the stream of future profits expected over the customer's lifetime purchases.

The case for maximizing long-term customer profitability is captured in the concept of customer lifetime value.[55] **Customer lifetime value (CLV)** describes the net present value of the stream of future profits expected over the customer's lifetime purchases. The company must subtract from its expected revenues the expected costs of attracting, selling, and servicing the account of that customer, applying the appropriate discount rate (say, between 10 and 20 percent, depending on cost of capital and risk attitudes). Lifetime value calculations for a product or service can add up to tens of thousands of dollars or even into six figures.[56]

Many methods exist to measure customer lifetime value.[57] The Marketing Memo: *Calculating Customer Lifetime Value* illustrates one. CLV calculations provide a formal quantitative framework for planning customer investment and help marketers adopt a long-term perspective. One challenge in applying CLV concepts, however, is to arrive at reliable cost and revenue

marketing Memo

Calculating Customer Lifetime Value

Researchers and practitioners have used many different approaches for modeling and estimating customer lifetime value (CLV). Columbia's Don Lehmann and Harvard's Sunil Gupta recommend the following formula to estimate the CLV for a not-yet-acquired customer:

$$CLV = \sum_{t=0}^{T} \frac{(p_t - c_t)r_t}{(1 + i)^t} - AC$$

where, p_t = price paid by a consumer at time t; c_t = direct cost of servicing the customer at time t; i = discount rate or cost of capital for the firm; r_t = probability of customer repeat buying or being 'alive' at time t; AC = acquisition cost; and T = time horizon for estimating CLV.

A key decision is what time horizon to use for estimating CLV. Typically, 3–5 years is reasonable. With this information and estimates of other variables, we can calculate CLV using spreadsheet analysis.

Gupta and Lehmann illustrate their approach by calculating the CLV of 100 customers over a 10-year period (see ▢ **Table 5.1** on page 137). In this example, the firm acquires 100 customers with an acquisition cost per customer of US$40. Therefore, in year 0, it spends $4,000. Some of these

customers defect each year. The present value of the profits from this cohort of customers over 10 years is $13,286.52. The net CLV (after deducting acquisition costs) is $9,286.52 or $92.87 per customer.

Using an infinite time horizon avoids using an arbitrary time horizon for calculating CLV. In the case of an infinite time horizon, researchers have shown that if margins (price minus cost) and retention rates stay constant over time, then the future CLV of an existing customer simplifies to the following:

$$CLV = \sum_{t=1}^{\infty} \frac{mr^t}{(1 + i)^t} - m\frac{r}{(1 + i - r)}$$

In other words, CLV simply becomes margin (m) times a margin multiple [$r/(1+i-r)$].

▢ **Table 5.2** shows the margin multiple for various combinations of r and i. This table shows a simple way to estimate the CLV of a customer. For example, when the retention rate is 80 percent and the discount rate 12 percent, the margin multiple is about 2.5. Therefore, the future CLV of an existing customer in this scenario is simply his or her annual margin multiplied by 2.5.

Sources: Sunil Gupta and Donald R. Lehmann, "Models of Customer Value," in *Handbook of Marketing Decision Models*, ed. Berend Wierenga (Berlin, Germany: Springer Science and Business Media, 2007); Sunil Gupta and Donald R. Lehmann, "Customers as Assets," *Journal of Interactive Marketing*, 17, no. 1, Winter 2006, pp. 9–24; Sunil Gupta and Donald R. Lehmann, *Managing Customers as Investments* (Upper Saddle River, NJ: Wharton School Publishing, 2005); Peter Fader, Bruce Hardie, and Ka Lee, "RFM and CLV: Using Iso-Value Curves for Customer Base Analysis," *Journal of Marketing Research*, 42, no. 4, November 2005, pp. 415–430; Sunil Gupta, Donald R. Lehmann, and Jennifer Ames Stuart, "Valuing Customers," *Journal of Marketing Research*, 41, no. 1, February 2004, pp. 7–18; Werner J. Reinartz and V. Kumar, "On the Profitability of Long-Life Customers in a Noncontractual Setting: An Empirical Investigation and Implications for Marketing," *Journal of Marketing*, 64, October 2000, pp. 17–35.

TABLE 5.I	A Hypothetical Example to Illustrate CLV Calculations										
	Year 0	Year 1	Year 2	Year 3	Year 4	Year 5	Year 6	Year 7	Year 8	Year 9	Year 10
Number of Customers	100	90	80	72	60	48	34	23	12	6	2
Revenue per Customer		100	110	120	125	130	135	140	142	143	145
Variable Cost per Customer		70	72	75	76	78	79	80	81	82	83
Margin per Customer		30	38	45	49	52	56	60	61	61	62
Acquisition Cost per Customer	40										
Total Cost or Profit	−4000	2700	3040	3240	2940	2496	1904	1380	732	366	124
Present Value	−4000	2454.55	2512.40	2434.26	2008.06	1549.82	1074.76	708.16	341.48	155.22	47.81

TABLE 5.2	Margin Multiple			
	Discount Rate			
Retention Rate	**10%**	**12%**	**14%**	**16%**
60%	1.20	1.50	1.11	1.07
70%	1.75	1.67	1.59	1.52
80%	2.67	2.50	2.35	2.22
90%	4.50	4.09	3.75	3.46

estimates. Marketers who use CLV concepts must also take into account the short-term, brand-building marketing activities that help increase customer loyalty.

Cultivating Customer Relationships

Maximizing customer value means cultivating long-term customer relationships. Companies are now moving away from wasteful mass marketing to precision marketing designed to build strong customer relationships.[58] Today's economy is supported by information businesses. Information has the advantages of being easy to differentiate, customize, personalize, and dispatch over networks at incredible speed.

But information cuts both ways. For instance, customers now have a quick and easy means of doing comparison shopping through sites such as BizRate.com, Shopping.com, and Pricegrabber.com. The internet also facilitates communication between customers. Websites such as Tripadvisor.com and Amazon.com enable customers to share information about their experiences with various products and services.

Customer empowerment has become a way of life for many companies that have had to adjust to a power shift in their customer relationships. The Marketing Insight: *Company Response to Customer Empowerment* describes some of the changes companies have made in their marketing practices as a result.

Marketing Insight

Company Response to Customer Empowerment

Often seen as the flag bearer for marketing best practices, P&G's chairman A.G. Lafley created shockwaves for marketers with his Association of National Advertiser's speech in October 2006. "The power is with the consumer," proclaimed Lafley, and "marketers and retailers are scrambling to keep up with her. Consumers are beginning in a very real sense to own our brands and participate in their creation. We need to learn to let go." In support of his contention, Lafley pointed out how a teenager had created an animated spot for Pringles snacks that was posted on YouTube; how Pantene, the hair care products company, had created a campaign that encouraged women to cut their hair and donate the clippings to make wigs for cancer patients; and how sales of Cover Girl Outlast lipstick increased 25 percent after the firm put mirrored ads in women's restrooms asking, "Is your lipstick still on?" and ran targeted five-second TV ads with the same theme.

Other marketers have begun to advocate a 'bottom-up' grassroots approach to marketing, rather than the more traditional 'top-down' approach where the marketers feel they are in control. Burger King launched edgy campaigns on consumer-friendly new media such as YouTube, MySpace, video games, and iPods. Allowing the customer to take charge just makes sense for a brand whose slogan is "Have It Your Way" and whose main rival, McDonald's, already owns the family market.

To provide a little more control, Yahoo! engages in 'participation marketing' by tapping consumers who already like a particular brand, rather than just casting a wide net. Reflecting the company philosophy, former Yahoo! CMO Cammie Dunaway noted, "Content is no longer something you push out; content is an invitation to engage with your brand."

Even the 2007 Super Bowl, the most expensive media event on the planet, had two homemade consumer commercials. To capitalize on the

Companies can benefit from using websites like YouTube or Facebook, where visitors are empowered to post comments or pictures, or encouraged to form active communities.

buzz of user-generated content, both Frito-Lay and Chevrolet created ad contests, with the winners receiving prizes and getting their ads aired during the game telecast. Perhaps the most compelling example of the new brand world comes from master marketer Nike. As part of its *Joga Bonito* (Portuguese for 'play beautiful') World Cup sponsorship, Nike spent US$100 million on a multilayered campaign. The centerpiece, however, was Joga.com, a social networking website available in 140 countries. One million members blogged, downloaded videos, created fan communities for their favorite players or teams, and expressed their passions on bulletin-board-type debates. Nike CEO Mark Parker sums up the new marketing equation well: "A strong relationship is created when someone joins a Nike community or invites Nike into their community."

Sources: Stuart Elliott, "Letting Consumers Control Marketing: Priceless," *New York Times*, October 9, 2006; Louise Story, "Super Bowl Glory for Amateurs with Video Cameras," *New York Times*, September 27, 2006; Todd Wasserman and Jim Edwards, "Marketers' New World Order," *Brandweek*, October 9, 2006, pp. 4–6; Heather Green and Robert D. Hof, "Your Attention Please," *BusinessWeek*, July 24, 2006, pp. 48–53; Brian Sternberg, "The Marketing Maze," *Wall Street Journal*, July 10, 2006.

Customer Relationship Management

customer relationship management managing detailed information about individual customers and carefully managing customer "touch points" in order to maximize customer loyalty.

Customer relationship management (CRM) is the process of carefully managing detailed information about individual customers and all customer 'touch points' to maximize customer loyalty.[59] A *customer touch point* is any occasion on which a customer encounters the brand and product: from actual experience to personal or mass communications to casual observation. For a hotel, the touch points include reservations, check-in and checkout, frequent-stay programs, room service, business services, exercise facilities, laundry service, restaurants, and bars. For instance, the Four Seasons relies on personal touches, such as a staff that always addresses guests by name, high-powered employees who understand the needs of sophisticated business travelers, and at least one best-in-region facility, such as a premier restaurant or spa.[60]

Sometimes touch points are where you least expect, such as in customer billing. Microsoft's Global CRM product manager, Karen Smith, related what happened when a telecommunications company converted to unified billing—one bill for all lines—to cut company costs. One of the customers requested a slightly modified version of unified billing to suit his expense submission purposes, but the service rep replied, "No, Sir, we can't do that. We use unified billing." The frustrated customer then switched his two business lines to another telecommunications company but lost his volume discount with the original provider, which still had his personal accounts. Even more frustrated, the customer then moved all his business to the new telecommunications company. Says Smith, "We may think that something will be great to do for our customers, but before we take action we need to really step into their shoes. Companies often focus on CRM functionality and integration, but they forget about some of the most basic touch points."[61]

Customer relationship management enables companies to provide excellent real-time customer service through the effective use of individual account information. Based on what they know about each valued customer, companies can customize market offerings, services, programs, messages, and media. CRM is important because a major driver of company profitability is the aggregate value of the company's customer base.[62] For example, the Al-Ahram Beverage Company was able to use a CRM application that reduced delivery time to customers and also reduced costs. Now, customer orders are entered into the CRM system—Microsoft Dynamics—where the system checks the availability of stock and a driver. The order is then delivered directly to the customer. In the past, customer orders were neither recorded nor tracked.[63]

Al-Ahram Beverage Company   The Al-Ahram Beverage Company (ABC), the leading beverage group in the Arab world, was the first company in Egypt to introduce a centralized call center, offering customers the opportunity to place beverage orders over the phone for delivery directly to their homes. Despite continued business success as a result of the call center's popularity, ABC's core business processes were carried out manually due to lack of integration between the call center operations and its retail outlets. ABC soon realized the need to integrate its call center operations and automate its processes in order to gain better control over its business operations. Since ABC's implementation of an integrated system using Microsoft Dynamics CRM and Microsoft Retail Management System, it has been able to introduce new control measures across the business, which has led to cost savings of up to 20 percent and cut customer delivery times by 50 percent, serving 90 percent of customers within just 45 minutes.[64]

ONE-TO-ONE MARKETING   Some of the groundwork for customer relationship management was laid by Don Peppers and Martha Rogers.[65] Peppers and Rogers outline a four-step framework for one-to-one marketing that can be adapted to CRM marketing as follows.

1. *Identify your prospects and customers.* Don't go after everyone. Build, maintain, and mine a rich customer database with information derived from all the channels and customer touch points.
2. *Differentiate customers in terms of (a) their needs and (b) their value to your company.* Spend proportionately more effort on the most valuable customers (MVCs). Apply activity-based costing and calculate customer lifetime value. Estimate net present value of all future profits coming from purchases, margin levels, and referrals, less customer-specific servicing costs.
3. *Interact with individual customers to improve your knowledge about their individual needs and to build stronger relationships.* Formulate customized offerings that you can communicate in a personalized way.
4. *Customize products, services, and messages to each customer.* Facilitate customer–company interaction through the company contact center and website.

The practice of one-to-one marketing, however, is not for every company: the required investment in information collection, hardware, and software may exceed the payout. It works best for companies that normally collect a great deal of individual customer information, carry a lot of products that can be cross-sold, carry products that need periodic replacement or upgrading, and sell products of high value.

INCREASING VALUE OF THE CUSTOMER BASE A key driver of shareholder value is the aggregate value of the customer base. Winning companies improve the value of their customer base by excelling at strategies such as the following.

- *Reducing the rate of customer defection.* Selecting and training employees to be knowledgeable and friendly increases the likelihood that the inevitable shopping questions from customers will be answered satisfactorily. Whole Foods, the world's largest retailer of natural and organic foods, woos customers with a commitment to marketing the best foods and a team concept for employees.

- *Increasing the longevity of the customer relationship.* The more involved a customer is with the company, the more likely he is to stick around. Some companies treat their customers as partners—especially in business-to-business markets—soliciting their help in the design of new products or improving their customer service. Instant Web Companies (IWCO), a U.S. direct-mail printer, launched a monthly Customer Spotlight program where guest companies provide an overview of their business and direct-mail programs and comment on IWCO practices, products, and services. IWCO's staff not only gains exposure to customers but also develops a broader perspective on customers' business and marketing objectives and how to add value and identify options that help meet its customers' goals.[66]

- *Enhancing the growth potential of each customer through 'share-of-wallet,' cross-selling, and up-selling.*[67] Increase sales from existing customers with new offerings and opportunities. Harley-Davidson sells more than motorcycles and accessories (such as gloves, leather jackets, helmets, and sunglasses). Its dealerships sell more than 3,000 items of clothing: some shops even have fitting rooms. Licensed goods sold by others range from predictable items (shot glasses, cue balls, and Zippo cigarette lighters) to the more surprising (cologne, dolls, and mobile phones).

- *Making low-profit customers more profitable or terminating them.* To avoid the direct need for termination, marketers can encourage unprofitable customers to buy more or in larger quantities, forgo certain features or services, or pay higher amounts or fees. Banks, phone companies, and travel agencies are all now charging for once-free services to ensure minimum customer revenue levels.

- *Focusing disproportionate effort on high-value customers.* The most valuable customers can be treated in a special way. Thoughtful gestures such as birthday greetings, small gifts, or invitations to special sports or arts events can send a strong positive signal to the customer.

Attracting and Retaining Customers

Companies seeking to expand their profits and sales must spend considerable time and resources searching for new customers. To generate leads, they develop ads and place them in media that will reach new prospects; send direct mail and make phone calls to possible new prospects; send their salespeople to participate in trade shows where they might find new leads; purchases names from list brokers; and so on.

Commercial Bank of Qatar   In Qatar's highly aggressive banking market, the Commercial Bank of Qatar (CBQ) distinguishes itself by offering a wide range of colored credit cards and focuses on delivering a unique customer experience at every point of usage of the cards. Local and international banks in Qatar have long used their credit cards to attract and retain customers seeking distinction, particularly as the use of point-of-sale networks in stores has increased. With the increased use of credit cards came the awareness of prestige cards and their obvious value to high-net-worth customers. For this reason, CBQ introduced a new Platinum Card to further enhance their leading market position; the new card promoted the cardholder's wealth and social stature, allowing some key VIP customers to justify having generous credit limits. As the Platinum Card focused on the prestigious class of customers of high net worth, CBQ took the further step of interlinking it with the Diners Card, which has also been recognized internationally for its distinguished clientele. It has become an additional benefit to the CBQ card, which comes with its own set of privileges: it allows access to over 100 airport lounges worldwide, continuous-charge privileges, personal liability cover up to almost US$1 million, guaranteed hotel reservations worldwide, and help in reclaiming VAT charges. This unique combination has enhanced its tangible value for customers, and positively increased card business volumes in this key segment.[68]

Table 5.3 displays one analysis of some typical acquisition costs. Different types of acquisition method can yield different types of customer with varying CLVs. One study showed that customers acquired through the offer of a 35 percent discount had about one-half the long-term value of customers acquired without any discount.[69]

REDUCING DEFECTION It is not enough, however, to attract new customers; the company must keep them and increase their business.[70] Too many companies suffer from high **customer churn** or defection. Adding customers here is like adding water to a leaking bucket. Cellular carriers and cable TV operators, for example, are plagued with 'spinners,' customers who switch carriers at least three times a year looking for the best deal. Many lose 25 percent of their subscribers each year, at an estimated cost of US$2–4 billion.

To reduce the defection rate, the company must:

1. Define and measure its retention rate. For a magazine, subscription renewal rate is a good measure of retention. For a college, it could be the first- to second-year retention rate, or the class graduation rate.
2. Distinguish the causes of customer attrition and identify those that can be managed better. Not much can be done about customers who leave the region or go out of business, but much can be done about those who leave because of poor service, shoddy products, or high prices.[71]
3. Compare the lost profit equal to the customer's lifetime value from a lost customer to the costs to reduce the defection rate. As long as the cost to discourage defection is lower than the lost profit, the company should spend the money to try to retain the customer.

RETENTION DYNAMICS △ **Figure 5.5** shows the main steps in the process of attracting and retaining customers. The starting point is everyone who might conceivably buy the product or service. These *potentials* are people or organizations who might conceivably have an interest in buying the company's product or service, but may not have the means or intention to buy. The next task is to identify which potentials are really good *prospects*—people with the motivation, ability, and opportunity to make a purchase—by interviewing them, checking on their financial standing, and so on. Marketing efforts can then concentrate on converting the prospects into *first-time customers*, and then into *repeat customers*, and then into *clients*: people to whom the company gives very special and knowledgeable treatment. The next challenge is to turn clients

customer churn high customer defection.

|Fig. 5.5| △

The Customer-Development Process

Source: See Jill Griffin, *Customer Loyalty: How to Earn It, How to Keep It* (New York: Lexington Books, 1995), p. 36. Also see Murray Raphel and Neil Raphel, *Up the Loyalty Ladder: Turning Sometimes Customers into Full-Time Advicates of Your Business* (New York: HarperBusiness, 1995).

TABLE 5.3	Customer Acquisition Costs by Marketing Activity	
Activity	**Cost per New Customer**	**Cost per Solicitation**
Personal selling	$550	$110.00
Direct mail	$130	$ 1.70
Telemarketing	$105	$ 3.75
Website, e-mail	$ 35	$ 0.07

1. Costs are based upon typical industry averages. Response rates are implied.

2. Actual costs vary from business to business depending on the complexity of the sales process. Costs are in US$.

For discussion, see Justin Zohn, "Customer Acquisition Cost—A Key Marketing Metric," *National Petroleum News*, April 2003.

into *members* by starting a membership program that offers benefits to customers who join, and then turning members into *advocates*, customers who enthusiastically recommend the company and its products and services to others. The ultimate challenge is to turn advocates into *partners*.

Unfortunately, much marketing theory and practice centers on the art of attracting new customers, rather than on retaining and cultivating existing ones. The emphasis traditionally has been on making sales rather than on building relationships; on preselling and selling rather than on caring for the customer afterward. More companies now recognize the importance of satisfying and retaining customers.

Satisfied customers constitute the company's *customer relationship capital*. If the company were to be sold, the acquiring company would pay not only for the plant and equipment and the brand name, but also for the delivered *customer base*, the number and value of the customers who would do business with the new firm. Here are some interesting facts that bear on customer retention:[72]

- The average company loses 10 percent of its customers each year.

- Acquiring new customers can cost five times more than satisfying and retaining current customers. It requires a great deal of effort to induce satisfied customers to switch away from their current suppliers.

- A 5 percent reduction in the customer defection rate can increase profits by 25 to 85 percent, depending on the industry.

- The customer profit rate tends to increase over the life of the retained customer due to increased purchases, referrals, price premiums, and reduced operating costs to service.

Building Loyalty

Creating a strong, tight connection to customers is the dream of any marketer and often the key to long-term marketing success. Companies that want to form strong customer bonds need to attend to a number of different considerations (see ▇ **Box 5.2**). One set of researchers sees retention-building activities as adding financial benefits, social benefits, or structural ties.[73] The following sections explain four important types of marketing activity that companies are using to improve loyalty and retention.

INTERACTING WITH CUSTOMERS Listening to customers is crucial to customer relationship management. Some companies have created an ongoing mechanism that keeps senior managers permanently plugged in to frontline customer feedback.

- Microsoft Egypt has an active customer feedback system that solicits customer feedback from surveys, studies, and product feedback technologies to enhance the customer experience. Customer feedback is integrated within the business processes and performance.[74]

- MBNA, the credit card giant, asks every executive to listen in on telephone conversations in the customer-service area or customer recovery units.

- Deere & Company, known for its tractors and business in construction, agriculture, and commercial sectors, has a superb record of customer loyalty: nearly 98 percent annual retention

---

BOX 5.2 ▇   Forming Strong Customer Bonds

- Create superior products, services, and experiences for the target market.
- Get cross-departmental participation in planning and managing the customer satisfaction and retention process.
- Integrate the 'voice of the customer' to capture their stated and unstated needs or requirements in all business decisions.
- Organize and make accessible a database of information on individual customer needs, preferences, contacts, purchase frequency, and satisfaction.
- Make it easy for customers to reach appropriate company personnel and express their needs, perceptions, and complaints.
- Assess the potential of frequency programs and club marketing programs.
- Run award programs recognizing outstanding employees.

in some product areas. The company has used retired employees to interview defectors and customers.[75]

- Chicken of the Sea—which sells seafood products—has 80,000 members in its Mermaid Club, a core-customer group treated to coupons and special offers. In return, club members provide valuable feedback on what the company is doing and is thinking of doing. When the company considered introducing canned whitefish, members emphatically rejected the product concept and the company chose not to introduce it.[76]

But listening is only part of the story. It is also important to be a customer advocate and, as much as possible, take the customers' side on issues, understanding their point of view.[77] USAA Insurance's legendary quality of service has led to the highest customer satisfaction in the industry. USAA subscribers will often tell stories about how the company looks out for them, even counseling them not to take out more insurance than they need. With such levels of trust, USAA enjoys high levels of customer loyalty and significant cross-selling opportunities.[78] The Marketing Memo: *Creating Customer Evangelists* describes six keys to creating customers who feel so strongly about companies and brands that they go way beyond just purchasing and consuming their products and services.

marketing Memo

Creating Customer Evangelists

Authors Ben McConnell and Jackie Huba assert that *customer evangelists* not only buy a company's products or services but believe in them so much that they are compelled to spread the word and voluntarily recruit their friends and colleagues on the company's behalf. McConnell and Huba studied brands such as Apple, Krispy Kreme, the Dallas Mavericks, Linux, Pallotta TeamWorks, SolutionPeople, and others created and sustained by customer evangelists. On their own Church of the Customer blog site (www.churchofthecustomer.com) they offer six tips for marketing evangelism:

- **Customer plus-delta.** Understand what evangelists love by continuously gathering their input. Vodafone Egypt continuously asks for customers' feedback and input on new services to offer. They allow the public to suggest ideas for new service offerings through their website. Several services offered by Vodafone Egypt are customer ideas.

- **Napsterize your knowledge.** Release your own knowledge, data, or intellectual property into a fast-moving distribution network. Sharing knowledge freely makes it more accessible, reducing your biggest threat: obscurity. It's liable to fall into the hands of people who will tell others about it. People talking about your knowledge increases its perceived and actual value.

- **Build the buzz.** Keep customer evangelists talking by providing them tools, programs, and features to demonstrate their passion. Coca-Cola in Egypt invited the public to submit short advertising videos that demonstrated their admiration for the heritage brand. The videos were reviewed and the best one was aired on TV during Ramadan, when TV viewership is at its peak. The ad had one of the highest ratings during the month of Ramadan, which helped increase the brand image and favorability of Coca-Cola.

- **Create community.** Provide like-minded customers the chance to meet. Paetec provides telecommunications services to hotels, universities, and

other companies. It has grown into a US$500 million company in 6 years, and its growth is due entirely to evangelism. Paetec's primary marketing strategy is to host informal dinners around the country for customers. Current customers and key prospects are invited to dine on Paetec's tab and meet one another. No boring PowerPoint presentations here, just customers talking about their telecommunications challenges and their unfiltered experiences of being a Paetec customer. Prospects are attracted to the company by other customers.

- **Make bite-size chunks.** Bite-size chunks of products and services reduce risk, improve sales cycles, and offer upfront value. Even if a customer doesn't purchase, he or she may spread favorable word of mouth. This is largely the marketing strategy of beverage maker Izze. The company's slightly carbonated juice drinks appear at high-profile charity events. In what surely must be confounding to some brand marketers, Izze insists that event organizers do not display Izze logos or banners anywhere at the event. The outcome is serendipity: attendees feel as if they have 'discovered' a new drink without a marketer hawking it to them. The discovery process inspires them to tell others. The result: Starbucks, Whole Foods, and Target have all sought out Izze to stock the beverages in their stores, without requiring the typical slotting fees.

- **Create a cause.** Companies that strive for a higher purpose—such as supporting 'education,' as Vodafone and Microsoft do—often find that customers, vendors, suppliers, and employees naturally support their success. Customer evangelists crave emotional connection and validation; a well-defined cause generates emotional commitment. When your brand, product, or service aspires to change the world, altruism and capitalism converge. Google launched the "voice to twitter service" in an effort to help Egyptians voice their opinions when the government shut down internet connections.

Sources: Ben McConnell and Jackie Huba, "Learning to Leverage the Lunatic Fringe," *Point*, July–August 2006, pp. 14–15; Michael Krauss, "Work to Convert Customers into Evangelists," *Marketing News*, December 15, 2006, p. 6; Ben McConnell and Jackie Huba, *Creating Customer Evangelists: How Loyal Customers Become a Loyal Sales Force* (New York: Kaplan Business, 2003); Lauren Indvik, "Google Launches Voice-to-Twitter Service to Help Protesters in Egypt," *Mashable Social Media*, January 31, 2011, http://mashable.com/2011/01/31/google-twitter-egypt-call-service/.

frequency program (FP)
program designed to provide rewards to customers who buy frequently and in substantial amounts.

DEVELOPING LOYALTY PROGRAMS Two customer loyalty programs that companies can offer are frequency programs and club marketing programs. **Frequency programs (FPs)** are designed to provide rewards to customers who buy frequently and in substantial amounts.[79] They can help build long-term loyalty with high-CLV customers, creating cross-selling opportunities in the process. Originally pioneered by the airlines, hotels, and credit card companies, FPs now exist in many other types of businesses. For example, today most clothing apparel stores offer price club cards, which provide member customers with discounts on particular items or after purchasing with a certain value.[80]

Hershey Co. In the spring of 2006, Hershey's started an unusual loyalty program in conjunction with online auction giant eBay. Consumers who collect WrapperCash points—codes printed on 1 billion single-serve Hershey products— could bank those points at the Hershey's website and then use them to outbid other players for big-ticket items in an online auction powered by eBay. That means customers may have had to eat a lot of candy to post a winning bid, but they could also win a sports car for a pretty low number of wrappers. The program successfully integrated consumers' offline and online experiences with the brand. For instance, the big-ticket items, such as the chance to be a master chocolatier for a day, spurred consumers to visit Hersheys.com to register and bank their codes.[81]

Typically, the first company to introduce an FP in an industry gains the most benefit, especially if competitors are slow to respond. After competitors respond, FPs can become a financial burden to all the offering companies, but some companies are more efficient and creative in managing FPs.

club membership programs
membership to certain clubs that can be open to everyone who purchase a product or service, or they can be limited to an affinity group or those willing to pay a fee.

Many companies have created **club membership programs**. Club membership programs can be open to everyone who purchases a product or service, or it can be limited to an affinity group or to those willing to pay a small fee. Although open clubs are good for building a database or snagging customers from competitors, limited-membership clubs are more powerful long-term loyalty builders. Fees and membership conditions prevent those with only a fleeting interest in a company's products from joining. These clubs attract and keep those customers who are responsible for the largest portion of business.

Some highly successful clubs include Apple and Harley-Davidson.

Apple Apple encourages owners of its computers to form local Apple user groups. By 2009 there were over 700, ranging in size from fewer than 25 members to over 1,000 members. The user groups provide Apple owners with opportunities to learn more about their computers, share ideas, and get product discounts. They sponsor special activities and events and perform community service. A visit to Apple's website will help a customer find a nearby user group.[82]

Harley-Davidson The world-famous motorcycle company sponsors the Harley Owners Group (H.O.G.), which now numbers 1 million members in over 1,200 chapters. The first-time buyer of a Harley-Davidson motorcycle gets a free 1-year H.O.G. membership. H.O.G. benefits include a magazine called *Hog Tales*, a touring handbook, emergency road service, a specially designed insurance program, theft reward service, discount hotel rates, and a Fly & Ride program enabling members to rent Harleys while on vacation. The company also maintains an extensive website devoted to H.O.G., which includes information on club chapters, events, and a special members-only section.[83]

PERSONALIZING MARKETING Company personnel can create strong bonds with customers by individualizing and personalizing relationships. In essence, thoughtful companies turn their customers into clients. One distinction that has been drawn:

> Customers may be nameless to the institution; clients cannot be nameless. Customers are served as part of the mass or as part of larger segments; clients are served on an individual basis. Customers are served by anyone who happens to be available; clients are served by the professional assigned to them.[84]

An increasingly essential ingredient for the best relationship marketing today is the right technology. ▭ **Table 5.4** highlights five imperatives of CRM and shows where technology fits in.

GE Plastics could not target its e-mail effectively to different customers if it were not for advances in database software. Dell Computers could not customize computer ordering for its global corporate customers without advances in web technology. Companies are using e-mail, websites, call centers, databases, and database software to foster continuous contact between company and customer. EFG-Hermes examplifies the use of technology to build customer value.

TABLE 5.4 ▭	Breaking Down Customer Relationship Management: What Customer Relationship Management Really Comprises			
CRM Imperative				
Acquiring the right customer	Crafting the right value proposition	Instituting the best processes	Motivating employees	Learning to retain customers
You Get It When…				
• You've identified your most valuable customers. • You've calculated your share of their wallet for your goods and services.	• You've studied what products or services your customers need today and will need tomorrow. • You've surveyed what products or services your competitors offer today and will offer tomorrow. • You've spotted what products or services you should be offering.	• You've researched the best way to deliver your products or services to customers, including the alliances you need to strike, the technologies you need to invest in, and the service capabilities you need to develop or acquire.	• You know what tools your employees need to foster customer relationships. • You've identified the human resources systems you need to institute in order to boost employee loyalty.	• You've learned why customers defect and how to win them back. • You've analyzed what your competitors are doing to win your high-value customers. • Your senior management monitors customer-defection metrics.
CRM Technology Can Help…				
• Analyze customer revenue and cost data to identify current and future high-value customers. • Target your direct-marketing efforts better.	• Capture relevant product and service behavior data. • Create new distribution channels. • Develop new pricing models. • Build communities.	• Process transactions faster. • Provide better information to the front line. • Manage logistics and the supply chain more efficiently. • Catalyze collaborative commerce.	• Align incentives and metrics. • Deploy knowledge management systems.	• Track customer defection and retention levels. • Track customer service satisfaction levels.

Source: Darrel K. Rigby, Frederick F. Reichheld, and Phil Schefter, "Avoid the Four Perils of CRM," *Harvard Business Review*, February 2002, p. 106.

The services EFG-Hermes provide, such as its emphasis on intercultural trading, have helped it develop a specific Arab world slant, helping it to become the top broker in the UAE in 2007.

EFG-Hermes   In 2007, EFG-Hermes was ranked top broker in the UAE and has maintained this position to the present day. It is recognized as the region's market leader in securities brokerage, asset management, investment banking, private equity, and research and is renowned for its innovation and devoted service to its clients. In 2006, EFG-Hermes launched an online trading service allowing clients to have consistent access to their portfolios and trade details without the need for a broker. They also have access to a call center for any enquiries or difficulties that customers may face. This technological growth has had outstanding effects on the brokerage service and facilitated individual and institutional trading. It will also increase intercultural trading and allow individuals in certain countries to gain support from other Arab countries.[85]

E-commerce companies looking to attract and retain customers are discovering that personalization goes beyond creating customized information.[86] For example, the Lands' End Live website offers visitors the opportunity to talk with a customer service representative. Nordstrom takes a similar approach with its website to ensure that online buyers are as satisfied with the company's customer service as the in-store visitors. Even the BBC, British archetype of an old media company, is reaping the benefits of customizing its offerings, a practice that is taking it well beyond its commercial rivals in UK broadcasting.

British Broadcasting Corporation   BBC iPlayer lets British users stream current BBC radio and TV programs up to 7 days after broadcast. Not only can viewers watch the content, they can also discuss and share it. One past project, for instance, let Britons download footage from BBC news and science shows, remix it and eventually share it online. Even more radical was the now retired http://backstage.bbc.co.uk, which provided data, resources, and support for internet developers and designers—inside and outside the BBC—to share in order to build prototypes of new concepts using BBC material. One consumer-created prototype called Sport Map allows people to find the nearest football team on the map and get its latest news, a service bound to be popular in a country full of avid football fans.[87]

At the same time, online companies need to make sure their attempts to create relationships with customers don't backfire, as when customers are bombarded by computer-generated recommendations that consistently miss the mark. Buy a baby gift on Amazon.com, and your personalized recommendations suddenly don't look so personal. E-tailers need to recognize the limitations of online personalization at the same time that they try harder to find technology and processes that really work.[88]

Companies are also recognizing the importance of the personal component to CRM and what happens once customers make actual contact. As Stanford University's business guru Jeffrey Pfeffer puts it, "the best companies build cultures in which frontline people are empowered to do what's needed to take care of the customer." He cites examples of firms such as SAS, the Scandinavian airline, which engineered a turnaround based in part on the insight that a customer's impressions of a company are formed through myriad small interactions, such as checking in, boarding the plane, and eating a meal.[89]

CREATING INSTITUTIONAL TIES   A company may supply customers with special equipment or computer links that help customers manage orders, payroll, and inventory. Customers are less inclined to switch to another supplier when this would involve high capital costs, high search costs, or the loss of loyal-customer discounts. A good example is McKesson Corporation, a leading pharmaceutical wholesaler, which invested millions of dollars in EDI capabilities to help independent pharmacies manage inventory, order-entry processes, and shelf space. Another example is Milliken & Company, which provides proprietary software programs, marketing research, sales training, and sales leads to loyal customers.

Win-Backs

Regardless of the nature of the category or how hard companies may try, some customers inevitably become inactive or drop out. The challenge is to reactivate dissatisfied customers through win-back strategies.[90] It's often easier to reattract ex-customers (because the company knows their names and histories) than to find new ones. The key is to analyze the causes of customer defection through exit interviews and lost-customer surveys and win back only those who have strong profit potential.[91]

Customer Databases and Database Marketing

Marketers must know their customers.[92] And in order to know the customer, the company must collect information and store it in a database from which to conduct database marketing. A **customer database** is an organized collection of comprehensive information about individual customers or prospects that is current, accessible, and actionable for marketing purposes such as lead generation, lead qualification, sale of a product or service, or maintenance of customer relationships. **Database marketing** is the process of building, maintaining, and using customer databases and other databases (products, suppliers, resellers) to contact, transact, and build customer relationships.

Customer Databases

Many companies confuse a customer mailing list with a customer database. A **customer mailing list** is simply a set of names, addresses, and telephone numbers. A customer database contains much more information, accumulated through customer transactions, registration information, telephone queries, cookies, and every customer contact.

Ideally, a customer database also contains the consumer's past purchases, demographics (age, income, family members, birthdays), psychographics (activities, interests, opinions), mediagraphics (preferred media), and other useful information. ReachGulfBusiness.com offers its clients a directory of information including a mobile phone database and a company database in the UAE and in the Middle East market.[93]

Ideally, a **business database** contains business customers' past purchases; past volumes, prices, and profits; buyer team member names (and ages, birthdays, hobbies, and favorite foods); status of current contracts; an estimate of the supplier's share of the customer's business; competitive suppliers; assessment of competitive strengths and weaknesses in selling and servicing the account; and relevant buying practices, patterns, and policies. For example, a Latin American unit of the Swiss pharmaceutical firm Novartis keeps data on 100,000 of Argentina's farmers, knows their crop-protection chemical purchases, groups them by value, and treats each group differently. The Marketing Excellence feature at the end of this chapter describes how Vodafone, the leading international mobile service provider, uses its database to attract and engage customers.

Data Warehouses and Datamining

Savvy companies are capturing information every time a customer comes into contact with any of their departments. Touch points include a customer purchase, a customer-requested service call, an online query, or a mail-in rebate card. Banks and credit card companies, telephone companies, catalog marketers, and many other companies have a great deal of information about their customers, including not only addresses and phone numbers, but also transactions and enhanced data on age, family size, income, and other demographic information.

These data are collected by the company's contact center and organized into a **data warehouse** where marketers can capture, query, and analyze it to draw inferences about an individual

customer database an organized collection of comprehensive information about individual customers or prospects that is current, accessible, and actionable for marketing purposes.

database marketing the process of building, maintaining, and using customer databases and other databases for the purpose of contacting, transacting, and building customer relationships.

customer mailing list a set of names, addresses, and telephone numbers.

business database complete information about business customers' past purchases; past volumes, prices, and profits.

data warehouse a collection of current data captured, organized, and stored in a company's contact center.

datamining the extracting of useful information about individuals, trends, and segments from the mass of data.

customer's needs and responses. Telemarketers can respond to customer inquiries based on a total picture of the customer relationship.

Through **datamining**, marketing statisticians can extract useful information about individuals, trends, and segments from the mass of data. Datamining uses sophisticated statistical and mathematical techniques such as cluster analysis, automatic interaction detection, predictive modeling, and neural networking.[94]

Some observers believe that a proprietary database can provide a company with a significant competitive advantage. For example, Lands' End can tell which of its 2 million customers should receive special mailings of specific clothing items that would fit their wardrobe needs (see ▦ **Box 5.3** for additional examples).

In general, companies can use their databases in five ways:

1. ***To identify prospects.*** Many companies generate sales leads by advertising their product or service. The ads generally contain a response feature, such as a business reply card or toll-free phone number, and the company builds its database from customer responses. It sorts through the database to identify the best prospects, then contacts them by mail, phone, or personal call to try to convert them into customers.

2. ***To decide which customers should receive a particular offer.*** Companies are interested in selling, up-selling, and cross-selling their products and services. Companies set up criteria describing the ideal target customer for a particular offer. Then they search their customer databases for those who most closely resemble the ideal type. By noting response rates, a company can improve its targeting precision over time. Following a sale, it can set up an automatic sequence of activities: 1 week later, send a thank-you note; 5 weeks later, send a new offer; 10 weeks later (if customer has not responded), phone the customer and offer a special discount.

3. ***To deepen customer loyalty.*** Companies can build interest and enthusiasm by remembering customer preferences and by sending appropriate gifts, discount coupons, and interesting reading material.

4. ***To reactivate customer purchases.*** Companies can install automatic mailing programs (automatic marketing) that send out birthday or anniversary cards, Ramadan shopping reminders, or off-season promotions. The database can help the company make attractive or timely offers.

BOX 5.3 ▦   Examples of Database Marketing

Qwest Twice a year Qwest sifts through its customer list looking for customers that have the potential to be more profitable. The company's database contains as many as 200 observations about each customer's calling patterns. By looking at demographic profiles, plus the mix of local versus long-distance calls or whether a consumer has voice mail, Qwest can estimate potential spending. Next, the company determines how much of the customer's likely telecom budget is already coming its way. Armed with that knowledge, Qwest sets a cutoff point for how much to spend on marketing to this customer.

Royal Caribbean Royal Caribbean uses its database to offer spur-of-the-moment cruise packages to fill all the berths on its ships. It focuses on retired people and single people because they are more able to make quick commitments. Fewer empty berths mean maximized profits for the cruise line.

Fingerhut The skillful use of database marketing and relationship building has made catalog house Fingerhut one of the nation's largest direct-mail marketers. Not only is its database full of demographic details such as age, marital status, and number of children, but it also tracks customers' hobbies, interests, and birthdays. Fingerhut tailors mail offers based on what each customer is likely to buy. Fingerhut stays in continuous touch with customers through regular and special promotions, such as annual sweepstakes, free gifts, and deferred billing. Now the company has applied its database marketing to its websites.

Mars Mars is a market leader not only in candy, but also in pet food. In Germany, Mars has compiled the names of virtually every cat-owning family by contacting veterinarians and by advertising a free booklet titled "How to Take Care of Your Cat." Those who request the booklet fill out a questionnaire, so Mars knows the cat's name, age, and birthday. Mars now sends a birthday card to each cat each year, along with a new cat-food sample or money-saving coupons for Mars brands.

American Express It is no wonder that, at its secret location in Phoenix, security guards watch over American Express's 500 billion bytes of data on how its customers have used the company's 35 million green, gold, and platinum charge cards. Amex uses the database to include precisely targeted offers in its monthly mailing of millions of customer bills.

BTM BTM stores in Egypt use the information they have about customers to continuously update them with seasonal promotions and offers. This encourages customers to accumulate points and receive discounts.

5. ***To avoid serious customer mistakes.*** A major bank confessed to a number of mistakes it had made by not using its customer database well. In one case, the bank charged a customer a penalty for late payment on his mortgage, failing to note he headed a company that was a major depositor in this bank. He quit the bank. In a second case, two different staff members of the bank phoned the same mortgage customer offering a home equity loan at different prices. Neither knew that the other had made the call. In a third case, the bank gave a premium customer only standard service in another country.

The Downside of Database Marketing and CRM

Having covered the positive aspects of database marketing, we also need to cover its limitations. Four problems can prevent a firm from effectively using CRM. The first is that building and maintaining a customer database requires a large investment in computer hardware, database software, analytical programs, communication links, and skilled personnel. It's difficult to collect the right data, especially to capture all the occasions of company interaction with individual customers. Building a customer database would not be worthwhile in the following cases: (1) when the product is a once-in-a-lifetime purchase (a grand piano); (2) when customers show little loyalty to a brand (there is lots of customer churn); (3) when the unit sale is very small (a candy bar); and (4) when the cost of gathering information is too high.

The second problem is the difficulty of getting everyone in the company to be customer-oriented and to use the available information. Employees find it far easier to carry on traditional transaction marketing than to practice customer relationship marketing. Effective database marketing requires managing and training employees as well as dealers and suppliers.

The third problem is that not all customers want a relationship with the company, and they may resent knowing that the company has collected that much personal information about them. Marketers must be concerned about customer attitudes toward privacy and security. American Express, long regarded as a leader on privacy issues, does not sell information about specific customer transactions. However, the company found itself the target of consumer outrage when it announced a partnership with KnowledgeBase Marketing Inc. that would have made data about 175 million U.S. customers available to any merchant that accepted American Express cards. American Express killed the partnership. AOL, also targeted by privacy advocates, junked a plan to sell subscribers' telephone numbers. Online companies would be smart to explain their privacy policies and to give consumers the right not to have their information stored in a database. European countries do not look favorably upon database marketing and are more protective of consumers' private information. The European Union passed a law handicapping the growth of database marketing in its member countries.

A fourth problem is that the assumptions behind CRM may not always hold true.[95] For example, it may not cost less to serve more loyal customers. High-volume customers often know their value to a company and can leverage it to extract premium service and/or price discounts. Loyal customers may expect and demand more from the firm and resent any attempt to charge full or higher prices. They may also be jealous of attention lavished on other customers. When eBay began to chase big corporate customers such as IBM, Disney, and Sears, some small shops that helped to build the brand felt abandoned.[96] Loyal customers may not necessarily be the best ambassadors for the brand. One study found that customers who scored high on behavioral loyalty and bought a lot of a company' products were less active word-of-mouth marketers than customers who scored high on attitudinal loyalty and expressed greater commitment to the firm.

Thus, the benefits of database marketing do not come without heavy costs, not only in collecting the original customer data, but also in maintaining them and mining them. When it works, a data warehouse yields more than it costs, but the data must be in good condition, and the discovered relationships must be valid.

Database marketing is most frequently used by business marketers and service providers (hotels, banks, and airlines; and insurance, credit card, and telephone companies) that normally and easily collect a lot of customer data. Other types of companies in the best position to invest in CRM are those that do a lot of cross-selling and up-selling (such as GE and Amazon.com) or whose customers have highly differentiated needs and are of highly differentiated value to the company. Packaged-goods retailers and consumer packaged-goods companies use database marketing less frequently, though some (such as Kraft, Quaker, and Nabisco) have built databases for certain brands. Businesses with low CLV, high churn, and no direct contact between the seller and ultimate buyer may not benefit as much from CRM. Some businesses cited as CRM successes include Enterprise Rent-A-Car, Fidelity Investments, Lexus, and Capital One.[97]

Deloitte Consulting found that 70 percent of firms found little or no improvement through CRM implementation. The reasons are many: the CRM system was poorly designed, it became too expensive, users didn't make much use of it or report much benefit, and collaborators ignored the system. One set of business commentators suggested the following as the four main perils of CRM:[98]

1. Implementing CRM before creating a customer strategy.
2. Rolling out CRM before changing the organization to match.
3. Assuming more CRM technology is better.
4. Stalking, not wooing, customers.

Professor George Day of the Wharton School of the University of Pennsylvania concludes that one of the reasons many CRM failures occur is that companies concentrate on customer contact processes without making corresponding changes in internal structures and systems.[99] His recommendation? Change the configuration before installing CRM: "Our survey results confirm that a superior customer-relating capability has everything to do with how a business builds and manages its organization and not much to do with the CRM tools and technologies it employs." All this points to the need for each company to determine how much (and where) to invest in building and using database marketing to conduct its customer relationships.

Summary

1. Customers are value maximizers. They form an expectation of value and act on it. Buyers will buy from the firm that they perceive offers the highest customer-delivered value, defined as the difference between total customer benefits and total customer cost.

2. A buyer's satisfaction is a function of the product's perceived performance and the buyer's expectations. Recognizing that high satisfaction leads to high customer loyalty, many companies today are aiming for TCS, or total customer satisfaction. For such companies, customer satisfaction is both a goal and a marketing tool.

3. Losing profitable customers can dramatically affect a firm's profits. The cost of attracting a new customer is estimated to be five times the cost of keeping a current customer happy. The key to retaining customers is relationship marketing.

4. Quality is the totality of features and characteristics of a product or service that bear on its ability to satisfy stated or implied needs. Marketers play a key role in achieving high levels of total quality so that firms remain solvent and profitable.

5. Marketing managers must calculate customer lifetime values of their customer base to understand their profit implications. They must also determine ways to increase the value of the customer base.

6. Companies are also becoming skilled in customer relationship management (CRM), which focuses on developing programs to attract and retain the right customers and meeting the individual needs of those valued customers.

7. Customer relationship management often requires building a customer database and doing datamining to detect trends, segments, and individual needs.

Applications

Marketing Debate
Online versus Offline Privacy

As more and more firms practice relationship marketing and develop customer databases, privacy issues are emerging as an important topic. Consumers and public interest groups are scrutinizing—and sometimes criticizing—the privacy policies of firms and raising concerns about potential theft of online credit card information or other potentially sensitive or confidential financial information. Others maintain that the online privacy fears are unfounded and that security issues are every bit as much a concern in the offline world. They argue that the opportunity to steal information exists virtually everywhere and that it's up to the consumer to protect their interests.

Take a position: Privacy is a bigger issue in the online world than the offline world *versus* privacy is no different online than offline.

Marketing Discussion

Consider the lifetime value of customers (CLV). Choose a business and show how you would go about developing a quantitative formulation that captures the concept. How would that business change if it totally embraced the customer equity concept and maximized CLV?

Marketing Excellence

>>Vodafone Egypt

The mobile service industry is an extremely competitive environment characterized by high customer turnover. Thus, Vodafone Egypt is constantly faced with the challenge of providing maximum customer satisfaction, in order not to lose market share. Since 1988, Vodafone Egypt has used the company Business Objects for reporting and business intelligence to help meet this challenge.

Business Objects software is used across business units, including finance, sales, customer operations, technology, regulatory, and strategy departments, providing Vodafone Egypt with a platform for reporting, query and analysis, and performance-management tasks. It offers a modern, service-oriented infrastructure and user-friendly tools to manage the complete business intelligence platform.[100]

Furthermore, Vodafone Egypt engaged the services of Art Technology Group (ATG), a provider of e-commerce solutions, to develop its commerce and customer service capabilities across different channels. Because customers are increasingly using a variety of channels to connect with the company, it was important for Vodafone that all the information about a customer was collated in one place, so they could provide a better service. Working with ATG, Vodafone Egypt hoped to improve their service by segmenting customers and identifying their needs, no matter what channel they were using to interact with the company.[101]

In terms of customer support, Vodafone Egypt has extensive departments, covering various services and languages, and its Customer Care center employs almost 3,000 people. "We start putting ourselves in the customer's shoes and work from there to enhance the customer experience," explains Ahmed Essam, Vodafone Egypt's Customer Care director. "The customer is always the top priority for Vodafone Egypt. We will do all it takes to make sure that our customers are happy. Our agent monitoring is 24/7. The quality assurance team looks for attitude, soft skills, and sincerity in resolving client complaints, as well as technical skills and know-how." Vodafone Egypt agents are taught to always talk in a low quiet tone, never loudly, to any customer. "This is because their principle is always to respect the customer. Further, we have systems that calculate the speed of agents' answers, their quickness in responding to the client requests and of course first-call resolution, which is a priority. Customers called could be recorded to check for commitment to service quality. When a customer calls the customer service line several times, a text message is sent to the customer to ask them about the service quality and whether their issue was solved or not. Also, there are efficiency reports generated by the system."

He adds that Vodafone Egypt's customer care is an integrated part of the business that interacts closely with other departments: the marketing department, for instance. Moreover, even within Customer Care there is technical support, communication, and reporting and analysis, so that Customer Care employees can move up the skills ladder within the department itself. In fact, for Vodafone Egypt, retaining talented, well-trained employees is as much a customer service challenge as serving the end customers themselves.[102]

Questions

1. How does Vodafone use its database software to market its business?

2. How does Vodafone deal with a customer who interacts with the company via different channels?

3. What is different about Vodafone's customer service support?

Sources: "Vodafone Egypt Standardizes on BusinessObjects XI Release 2," http://businessintelligence.com/news/2141; "Vodafone Egypt Deploys ATG Commerce Suite," http://callcenterinfo.tmcnet.com/Analysis/articles/57739-vodafone-egypt-deploys-atg-commerce-suite.htm; "Love Thy Customer," www.businesstodayegypt.com/ article.aspx?ArticleID=7824.

Mobile phones are among the latest marketing trends for wireless advertising messages.

In this chapter, we will address the following questions:

1. How do consumer characteristics influence buying behavior? (pg. 154)

2. What major psychological processes influence consumer responses to the marketing program? (pg. 162)

3. How do consumers make purchasing decisions? (pg. 167)

4. How do marketers analyze consumer decision making? (pg. 174)

Analyzing Consumer Markets

The aim of marketing is to meet and satisfy target customers' needs and wants better than competitors. Marketers are always looking for emerging customer trends that suggest new marketing opportunities. For example, the emergence of the mobile phone, especially with teens and young adults, had marketers rethinking their practices.

 With almost 6 billion mobile subscribers in the world in 2010, mobile phones represent a major opportunity for advertisers to reach consumers on the 'third screen' (after the TV and the computer). Mobile subscriptions have grown significantly in the Middle East and North Africa region, reaching 300 million subscribers. This is driven mainly by the growth of the prepaid market (bills paid by making advance payments, which enables subscribers to control their spending) and the competitive offers by the various mobile operators. Wireless carriers have a wealth of information about their customers that marketers find valuable, such as demographic data, geographic location, and content purchasing habits. Major wireless carriers had long been reluctant to allow advertising to customers via their networks, but with a shift in consumer attitudes toward mobile marketing came the introduction in 2006 of text ads, search-based ads, and even banner ads to web-enabled phones. Young people are an especially attractive target. In Saudi Arabia, about 99.2 percent of people surveyed, mostly students, military officers, and businessmen, used Bluetooth in public gatherings, which explains why major advertisers have begun embracing mobile marketing. A survey conducted by Acision, a mobile communications company providing communication solutions for over 300 network operators and service providers globally, showed that the potential for mobile advertising in the Arab world was very strong: 64 percent of respondents believed that it would mirror the success of internet advertising.

The Mobile Advertising Survey conducted at the Gulf Information Technology Exhibition (GITEX) in 2007 drew responses from almost 300 delegates across the region. Some 48 percent of them stated that they receive mobile ads at least two to four times a week. According to Nabil Y. Khalil, managing director for Acision in the Middle East and North Africa, "The survey results indicate a promising future in the region. Mobile advertising offers significant opportunities for precise targeting across all mobile data channels, along with the ability to provide users with highly personalized services. The key is keeping things lively and relevant, objectives that we at Acision work hard to achieve."[1]

Successful marketing requires that companies fully connect with their customers. Adopting a holistic marketing orientation means understanding customers: gaining a 360-degree view of both their daily lives and the changes that occur during their lifetimes so that the right products are marketed to the right customers in the right way. This chapter explores individual consumer buying dynamics; the next chapter explores the buying dynamics of business buyers. ▽

consumer behavior the study of how individuals, groups and organizations select, buy, use, and dispose of goods, services, ideas, or experiences to satisfy their needs and wants.

culture the fundamental determinant of a person's wants and behavior.

subculture subdivisions of a culture that provide more specific identification and socialization, such as nationalities, religions, racial groups, and geographical regions.

What Influences Consumer Behavior?

Consumer behavior is the study of how individuals, groups, and organizations select, buy, use, and dispose of goods, services, ideas, or experiences to satisfy their needs and wants.[2] Marketers must fully understand both the theory and reality of consumer behavior.

The Arab market is a rather heterogeneous market, with different countries exhibiting different consumer behavior patterns. For example, the Gulf Cooperation Council (GCC) countries exhibit high levels of spending as a result of their high income levels. The UAE tops the Arab nations in terms of spending on consumer goods and services, with the average person spending around US$20,000 annually on consumer goods and services.[3] Next is Qatar with around $12,500 per person, then Kuwait at $10,000, and Bahrain with around $8,000.[4] While average spending in the GCC market is quite high, countries such as Sudan and Yemen exhibit some of the lowest spending volumes in the region.

Furthermore, due to high population growth, the market is rather young. In Egypt, the most populous Arab nation with a population of 85 million, 60 percent of the population is less than 25 years old, and in the Arab world as a whole, 60 percent of people are under 30 years old. Thus there is very high demand for basic commodities and services in these markets. New schools, hospitals, and food stores are opening to keep up with the increasing demand.

A consumer's buying behavior is influenced by cultural, social, and personal factors. Cultural factors exert the broadest and deepest influence.

Cultural Factors

Culture, subculture, and social class are particularly important influences on consumer buying behavior. **Culture** is the fundamental determinant of a person's wants and behavior. Through family and other key institutions, a child growing up in the Arab region is exposed to the following values: care for the family, respect for elderly people, collectivism, and the tendency to take fewer risks than people elsewhere in the world. A child growing up in another part of the world might have a different view of himself, his relationship to others, and rituals. Marketers must pay close attention to cultural values in every country to understand how to best market their existing products and find opportunities for new products.

Each culture consists of smaller subcultures that provide more specific identification and socialization for their members. **Subcultures** include nationalities, religions, racial groups, and geographic regions. When subcultures grow large and affluent enough, companies often design specialized marketing programs to serve them.

Box 6.1 profiles Arab consumers in 2010, classifying average consumer spending on a variety of purchase decisions. The Marketing Insight on page 155: *Shopping Malls in the Arab World* and *The Arab Women's Market* shed some light on the growing phenomenon of shopping malls in the region and the relatively untapped women's market.

BOX 6.1 — Arab Consumers' Spending on Durables

The information below is based on an assessment of Arab consumers' plans to invest in durable goods.

Type of goods	Percentage
Vehicles	
Yes	28
No	57
Don't Know	15
Property	
Yes	21
No	63
Don't Know	16
Electronic Appliances	
Desktop or Laptop	30
Furniture	21
LCD or Plasma Television	17
Air Conditioner	13
Refrigerator	10
Washing Machine	10
DVD or VCD Recorder or Player	6
Vacuum Cleaner	6
Normal Color TV	6
Home Theater System	5
Cooking Range	5
Clothes Dryer	4
Normal or Digitial Camcorder	3
Video Recorder or Player	2

Source: "The Middle East Consumer Confidence Index Survey," Bayt.com, June 2010, http://img.b8cdn.com/images/uploads/article_docs/bayt_cci_june_2010_opt_8141_EN.pdf.

Marketing Insight

Shopping Malls in the Arab World

In the last decade, many Arab cities, such as Dubai and Cairo, have witnessed the creation of new shopping malls. This phenomenon has been facilitated by the increasing prosperity among certain classes and the adoption of new consumer lifestyles.

In Cairo, the shopping mall phenomenon started back in 1989, with the opening of the Al-Yamama Center in Zamalek. The number of commercial centers has steadily increased since then, with around 30 centers now competing. Despite the increasing number of people spending time in shopping malls, some managers and storekeepers complain that most visitors' sole reason for coming is just to window shop, rather than to make real purchases.

One of the greatest attractions for visitors to Dubai is its superb shopping. For example, in 2006 the Dubai Government announced the creation of the world's largest shopping area, providing 17 times more retail space than the Mall of the Emirates, currently the biggest shopping mall in Dubai. The new Bawadi Mall will aim to attract 200,000 visitors per day and 15 million visitors each year once fully developed. The project launched its first phase of development in January 2009.

Sources: "Jewel of the Nile, Cairo Offers Plentiful Property Investment Opportunities," *Global Real Estate Monitor*, 3, June/July 2010, http://nreionline.com/globalrealestate/july10_article1.html; "World's Biggest Shopping Mall Set for Dubai," *Middle East Council of Shopping Centers Newsletter*, May 2007, www.mecsc.org/newsletter/newsletter.php?mon=0507.

Marketing Insight

The Arab Women's Market

When identifying the different markets to be considered, the Arab market is definitely a crucial one. Within the Arab market, however, there are several other markets, some of which are more apparent than others. One of these is the Arab women's market, the existence and significance of which has consistently been neglected and greatly underestimated.

Women in some parts of the Middle East have a limited role in their societies. In most countries in the Arabian Gulf women do not directly interact with men; both are segregated at social events such as weddings.

- As bankers and investors have started to more closely study Gulf countries, they have gained more insight into the role of women and their entry into the business arena as well as their inheritance of significant amounts of wealth.

- Some explain the 'undercover' or 'hidden' nature of the Arab woman as being dictated by religion. Islam, however, does not call for discrimination but rather emphasizes women's rights of property ownership and control.

- Several institutions and finance groups have been providing training and offering jobs to women, thereby increasing their contribution to the community and benefiting from their untapped potential. However, these organizations are largely Western.

- Arab women are already becoming more active, holding greater amounts of capital and investment power. They have also been able to reach high positions in various jobs. The perception of women as a minority group deprived of their rights has therefore become less applicable.

- Some institutions are even exclusive to women. Critics of this type of institution point out that these can be seen as a form of segregation and increase rather than decrease discrimination. These institutions, however, are perceived as a crucial initial step towards equality.

- Because women are considered a target market segment by several companies, understanding their attitudes and lifestyles is necessary.

Source: Nawar Al-Hassan Golley, Pernille Arenfeldt, and Linzi J. Kemp, "Gender and Women's Studies in the Arab Region," *AngloHigher: The Magazine of Global English Speaking Higher Education*, 3(2), Summer 2011 (online), www.anglohigher.com/magazines/magazine_detail/107/39.

Multicultural marketing grew out of careful marketing research, which revealed that different ethnic and demographic niches did not always respond favorably to mass-market advertising.

Companies have capitalized on well-thought-out multicultural marketing strategies in recent years. As countries become more culturally diverse, however, many marketing campaigns targeting a specific cultural target can spill over and positively influence other cultural groups.[5]

social class   homogenous and enduring divisions in a society, which are hierarchically ordered and whose members share similar values, interests, and behaviors.

Virtually all human societies exhibit *social stratification*, most often in the form of **social classes**, relatively homogeneous and enduring divisions in a society, hierarchically ordered and with members who share similar values, interests, and behavior. One classic depiction of social classes in the Arab region is A class, B class, and C class.

Different countries in the Arab region have other divisions. For example, in the UAE, citizens are subdivided into four main social classes: (1) the ruling *sheikhly* families, who possess the most political power and are wealthy, (2) the *al-tujjar*, the merchant class, who were formerly pearling merchants and now trade in international goods, (3) the new middle class, those professionals who are increasing in number and have benefitted from free state education, and (4) the low-income groups represented by Bedouin nomads, former pearl divers, and oasis farmers.[6] The Marketing Insight: *Marketing to Cultural Market Segments* describes how ethnic groups in the UAE also represent unique market segments.

Social classes have several characteristics. First, those within each class tend to be more alike in dress, speech patterns, and recreational preferences than persons from two different social classes. Second, persons are perceived as occupying inferior or superior positions according to social class. Third, a *cluster* of variables—for example, occupation, income, wealth, education, and value orientation—indicates social class, rather than any single variable. Fourth, individuals can move up or down the social-class ladder during their lifetimes; how easily and how far depends on how rigid the social stratification is.

Marketing Insight

Marketing to Cultural Market Segments

Understanding the key ethnic groups present in the UAE is crucial to understanding the consumer market in that country. According to estimates from the *CIA World Factbook*, less than 20 percent of the population consists of original UAE citizens. The rest consists of South Asian tribes, which make up almost half of the population, immigrants from other Arab countries, as well as Westerners and East Asians who have made the UAE their permanent home. Understanding the varied customs and cultures is often a challenging task for marketers.

UAE Citizens

As the majority of the population is Muslim, the culture of the UAE is influenced by Islamic traditions and beliefs. However, tolerance is a liberal value that the UAE upholds. When shopping in, for example, Westernized shopping malls and foreign-brand stores, they make sure that what they buy is in line with customs and traditions.

Arab Residents

Many residents come from other Arab countries, such as Egypt, Lebanon, Syria, and Morocco, seeking a better standard of living than

in their home countries. Naturally, they bring their cultural values and norms with them. These residents constitute a large portion of the UAE population. This is why you find many Egyptian and Lebanese chain stores opening in the UAE, catering for this important target market.

South Asian Residents

These are residents that come from India, Pakistan, Sri Lanka, and other countries in South Asia, again usually seeking a better standard of living. Many of these residents live and work in the UAE alone, with their families still living in their home country. The main aim is to make money, which is transferred to the family at home. These residents often have a basic standard of living and choose to save most of their money for their families. Many of these residents share apartments.

Western Residents

Dubai and the UAE are growing in popularity as potential destinations for a fresh start. With Dubai offering employment opportunities as well as financial bonuses such as tax-free income and a rapidly booming economy, growing numbers of Westerners are moving to the UAE. Subsequently, the UAE has catered to the needs of these foreigners by developing housing compounds, Western-based educational institutions, and entertainment facilities.

Sources: "Middle East: United Arab Emirates," *The CIA World Factbook*, www.cia.gov/library/publications/the-world-factbook/geos/ae.html; "United Arab Emirates Ethnic Groups," www.mapsofworld.com/united-arab-emirates/ethnic-groups.html; Sonya A. Grier, Anne Brumbaugh, and Corliss G. Thornton, "Crossover Dreams: Consumer Responses to Ethnic-Oriented Products," *Journal of Marketing*, 70, April 2006, pp. 35–51; Countries and Their Cultures, www.everyculture.com.

Social classes show distinct product and brand preferences in many areas, including clothing, home furnishings, leisure activities, and automobiles. They also differ in media preferences, with upper-class consumers often preferring magazines and books, and lower-class consumers often preferring television. Even within a category such as TV, upper-class consumers tend to prefer news and drama, and lower-class consumers tend to prefer soap operas and sports programs. There are also language differences: advertising copy and dialogue must ring true to the targeted social class.

Social Factors

In addition to cultural factors, social factors such as reference groups, family, and social roles and statuses affect our buying behavior.

REFERENCE GROUPS A person's **reference groups** are all the groups that have a direct (face-to-face) or indirect influence on their attitudes or behavior. Groups having a direct influence are called **membership groups**. Some of these are **primary groups** with whom the person interacts fairly continuously and informally, such as family, friends, neighbors, and coworkers. People also belong to **secondary groups**, such as religious, professional, and trade-union groups, which tend to be more formal and require less continuous interaction.

Reference groups influence members in at least three ways. They expose an individual to new behaviors and life styles, they influence attitudes and self-concept, and they create pressures for conformity that may affect product and brand choices. People are also influenced by groups to which they do *not* belong. **Aspirational groups** are those a person hopes to join; **dissociative groups** are those whose values or behavior an individual rejects.

Where reference group influence is strong, marketers must determine how to reach and influence the group's opinion leaders. An **opinion leader** is the person who offers informal advice or information about a specific product or product category, such as which of several brands is best or how a particular product may be used.[7] Opinion leaders are often highly confident, socially active, and involved with the category. Marketers try to reach opinion leaders by identifying their demographic and psychographic characteristics, identifying the media they read, and directing messages at them.

Across the globe, including in the Arab world, the hottest trends in teenage music, language, and fashion often start in the inner cities. And these trends can strongly affect the Arab teenage world. Music companies such as Virgin Megastore, which hope to appeal to the youth market, have made an intensive effort to monitor and appeal to the globalization of the young opinion leaders' style and behavior.

Virgin Megastore   With 18 stores in malls in the Middle East, Virgin Megastore has been hugely successful at using alternative styles in its product offering. Not only does the chain sell CDs, it also sells DVDs, books, comics, records, mobile phones, computers, posters, T-shirts, and other paraphernalia: whether a teen is into movies, technology, or a particular genre of music, Virgin always has something to please him.[8]

In 2004, Virgin Megastore implemented a near-real-time data warehouse. Named Crescendo, the warehouse collects point-of-sale transactions and customer traffic counts and generates key performance indicator (KPI) reports in close to real time. This timely information helps the managers identify trends more quickly and react accordingly.[9] Virgin Megastore's website also encourages teens to join its online music community and talk about the music they love, the concerts they are going to, and even the artists they are still discovering, to help the company respond to customers' reactions.

FAMILY The family is the most important consumer buying organization in society, and family members constitute the most influential primary reference group.[10] There are two families in the buyer's life. The **family of orientation** consists of parents and siblings. From parents, a person acquires an orientation toward religion, politics, and economics and a sense of personal ambition, self-worth, and love.[11] Even if the buyer no longer interacts very much with their parents, their influence on behavior can be significant.

---

reference groups   all the groups that have a direct or indirect influence on a person's attitudes or behavior.

membership groups   groups having a direct influence on a person.

primary groups   groups with which a person interacts continuously and informally, such as family, friends, neighbors, and co-workers.

secondary groups   groups which tend to be more formal and require less interaction than primary groups, such as religious, professional, and trade-union groups.

aspirational groups   groups a person hopes or would like to join.

dissociative groups   those groups whose values or behavior an individual rejects.

opinion leader   the person in informal, product-related communications who offers advice or information about a specific product or product category.

family of orientation   parents and siblings.

To make Saudi women customers feel more at ease, stores that sell cosmetics recruit only Saudi female employees.

family of procreation spouse and children.

A more direct influence on everyday buying behavior is the **family of procreation**; namely, one's spouse and children. In the Arab world, husband–wife involvement in purchases has traditionally varied widely by product category. The wife has usually acted as the family's main purchasing agent, especially for food, sundries, and staple clothing items. Now traditional purchasing roles are changing, and marketers would be wise to see both men and women as possible targets.

For expensive products and services such as cars, vacations, or housing, the vast majority of husbands and wives engage in joint decision making.[12] And marketers are realizing that women actually buy more technology than men do, but consumer electronics stores have been slow to catch on to this fact. Some savvy electronics stores are starting to heed women's complaints of being ignored, patronized, or offended by salespeople. RadioShack Corp., a 7,000-store chain, began actively recruiting female store managers so that now a woman manages about one of every seven stores.[13] In Saudi Arabia, only Saudi female employees are allowed to be present at shops that sell female underwear and cosmetics. This was taken as a step to create jobs for Saudi citizens, and also to overcome the embarrassment of female customers.[14]

Nevertheless, men and women may respond differently to marketing messages.[15] One study showed that women valued connections and relationships with family and friends and placed a high priority on people. Men, on the other hand, related more to competition and placed a high priority on action. Marketers are taking more direct aim at women with products such as Activia yoghurt, Body Shop, and Victoria's Secret, which can be targeted specifically at women.

Another shift in buying patterns is an increase in the amount of money spent and the direct and indirect influence wielded by children and teens. Direct influence describes children's hints, requests, and demands: "I want to go to McDonald's." Indirect influence means that parents know the brands, product choices, and preferences of their children without hints or outright requests ("I think Ali would want to go to McDonald's").

Research has shown that teenagers are playing a more active role than before in helping parents choose a car, audio/video equipment, or a vacation spot.[16] The Gulf Ina worldwide survey showed that on average 60 percent of respondents admitted some involvement of their children in purchasing a car. In the Gulf, 79.5 percent of respondents said that they involve their children in this decision, second only to India.[17] Children in France and the United States have the least involvement.

General Motors   In August 2006, GM's Hummer division teamed up with McDonald's to put tiny toy Hummers in McDonald's Happy Meals, the first time a carmaker had directly offered toy versions of its vehicles in the meals. At the same time, GM rolled out its Hummerkids.com website with games and printable coloring pages of H3 models. Hummer's licensed goods geared to kids are also increasing in volume, from a Hummer kids' bike to a children's tent.[18]

Recognizing the power of kids, marketers are pouring money into programs targeting them. Advertising directed at children is estimated at over US$15 billion annually, about 2.5 times more than in 1992.[19] Toy firm New Boy spent approximately US$19.5 million on pan-Arab television advertising from January to September of 2005; Beyblade and Kinder were also among the top spenders.[20] Similarly, the website for children's channel Spacetoon caters to children's different interests, to help advertisers better target their consumers: content is divided into ten different 'planets,' from action and adventure to sport.[21]

Television can be powerful in reaching children, and marketers are using television to target children at younger ages than ever before. By the time children are around 2 years old they can often recognize characters, logos, and specific brands. They can distinguish between advertising and programming by about ages 6 or 7. A year or so later, they can understand the concept of persuasive intent on the part of advertisers. By 9 or 10 they can understand the discrepancies between message and product.[22] Marketers are tapping into that audience with product tie-ins, placed at a child's eye level, on just about everything including Modhesh juice and bottled water.[23]

Millions of kids under the age of 17 are also online. Marketers have jumped online with them, offering freebies in exchange for personal information. Many have come under fire for this practice and for not clearly differentiating ads from games or entertainment. Establishing ethical and legal boundaries in marketing to children online and offline continues to be a hot topic as consumer advocates decry the commercialism they believe such marketing engenders, as discussed in Chapter 8.

ROLES AND STATUS A person participates in many groups: family, clubs, organizations. Groups often are an important source of information and help to define norms for behavior. We can define a person's position in each group to which he belongs in terms of role and status. A **role** consists of the activities a person is expected to perform. Each role carries a **status**. A senior vice president of marketing has more status than a sales manager, and a sales manager has more status than an office clerk. People choose products that reflect and communicate their role and actual or desired status in society. Marketers must be aware of the status-symbol potential of products and brands.

role the activities someone or something is expected to perform.

status one's position within his or her own hierarchy or culture.

Personal Factors

A buyer's decisions are also influenced by personal characteristics. These include the buyer's age and stage in the life cycle; occupation and economic circumstances; personality and self-concept; and life style and values. Because many of these characteristics have a very direct impact on consumer behavior, it is important for marketers to follow them closely.

AGE AND STAGE IN THE LIFE CYCLE Our taste in food, clothes, furniture, and recreation is often related to our age. Consumption is also shaped by the *family life cycle* and the number, age, and gender of people in the household at any point in time. Arab households are increasingly becoming fragmented: the traditional family household of grandparents, parents, children, and grandchildren is slowly fading out of society.[24] In addition, *psychological* life-cycle stages may matter. Adults experience certain 'passages' or 'transformations' as they go through life.[25] Yet, the behavior people exhibit as they go through these passages, such as becoming a parent, is not necessarily fixed but changes with the times.

Marketers should also consider *critical life events* or *transitions*—marriage, childbirth, illness, relocation, divorce, career change, widowhood—as giving rise to new needs. These should alert service providers—banks, lawyers, and marriage, employment, and bereavement counselors—to ways they can help.[26]

OCCUPATION AND ECONOMIC CIRCUMSTANCES Occupation also influences consumption patterns. A blue-collar worker will probably buy work clothes, work shoes, and lunchboxes, while a company president is more likely to buy dress suits, air travel, and meals out at restaurants. Marketers try to identify the occupational groups that have above-average interest in their products and services, and even tailor products for certain occupational groups. Computer software companies, for example, design different products for brand managers, engineers, lawyers, and physicians.

Product choice is greatly affected by economic circumstances: spendable income (level, stability, and time pattern), savings and assets (including the percentage that is liquid), debts, borrowing power, and attitudes toward spending and saving. Luxury-goods makers such as Gucci, Prada, and Burberry can be vulnerable to an economic downturn. If economic indicators point to a recession, marketers can take steps to redesign, reposition, and reprice their products or introduce or increase the emphasis on discount brands so they can continue to offer value to target customers.

PERSONALITY AND SELF-CONCEPT Each person has personality characteristics that influence his or her buying behavior. By **personality**, we mean a set of distinguishing human psychological traits that lead to relatively consistent and enduring responses to environmental stimuli (including buying behavior). We often describe it in terms of such traits as self-confidence, dominance, autonomy, deference, sociability, defensiveness, and adaptability.[27] Personality can be a useful variable in analyzing consumer brand choices. The idea is that brands also have personalities, and consumers are likely to choose brands whose personalities match their own. We define **brand personality** as the specific mix of human traits that we can attribute to a particular brand.

personality a set of distinguishing human psychological traits that lead to relatively consistent responses to environmental stimuli.

brand personality the specific mix of human traits we can attribute to a particular brand.

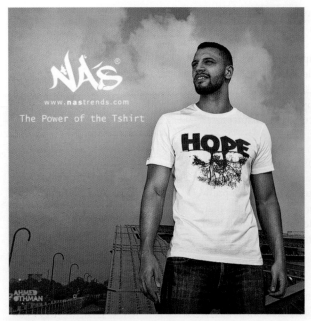

NAS Trends suggests a brand personality that is young, optimistic and proud

At Stanford University, Professor Jennifer Aaker researched brand personalities and identified the following traits:[28]

1. Sincerity (down-to-earth, honest, wholesome, and cheerful).
2. Excitement (daring, spirited, imaginative, and up-to-date).
3. Competence (reliable, intelligent, and successful).
4. Sophistication (upper-class and charming).
5. Ruggedness (outdoorsy and tough).

She analyzed some well-known brands and found that a number of them tended to be strongly linked with on one particular trait: Levi's with "ruggedness;" MTV with "excitement;" CNN with "competence;" and Campbell's with "sincerity." The implication is that these brands will attract persons who are high on the same personality traits. A brand personality may have several attributes: Levi's suggests a personality that is also youthful, rebellious, authentic, and American. The revolutions of the Arab Spring have presented Levi's with an opportunity to tap into these concepts: "We've always been about embodying the energy and events of our times and [the Go Forth campaign] is about returning to the pioneering spirit of the brand," says Robert Hanson, global president of the Levi's brand.[29]

A brand personality may have several attributes: NAS Trends suggest a personality that is young, optimistic, and proud. The revolutions of the Arab Spring have presented NAS Trends with an opportunity to tap into these personality traits. After the Arab revolutions that took place in 2011, NAS Trends took the opportunity to leverage on its brand personality and come up with new themes such as: "Hope" "Faith", and "Raise your head up, you're Egyptian."

A cross-cultural study exploring the generalizability of Aaker's scale outside the United States found that three of the five factors applied in Japan and Spain, but a "peacefulness" dimension replaced "ruggedness" both in Japan and Spain, and a "passion" dimension emerged in Spain instead of "competency."[30] Research on brand personality in Korea revealed two culture-specific factors—passive likeableness and dominance—reflecting the importance of Confucian values, specifically the nurture and development of moral perfection, in Korea's social and economic systems.[31]

Consumers often choose and use brands that have a brand personality consistent with their own *actual self-concept* (how we view ourselves), although the match may instead be based on the consumer's *ideal self-concept* (how we would like to view ourselves) or even on *others' self-concept* (how we think others see us).[32] These effects may also be more pronounced for publicly consumed products than for privately consumed goods.[33] On the other hand, consumers who are high 'self-monitors'—that is, sensitive to how others see them—are more likely to choose brands whose personalities fit the consumption situation.[34] Finally, often consumers have multiple aspects of self (serious professional, caring family member, active fun-lover) that may be evoked differently in different situations or around different types of people.

LIFE STYLE AND VALUES People from the same subculture, social class, and occupation may lead quite different life styles.

India's 'Gen Next' Within the 54 percent of India's population that is under 30, approximately 16 million, or 3 percent, are high-earning targets of youth lifestyle brands connoting high status and an affluent life style. Members of India's so-called Gen Next spend most of their money on personal clothing and accessories, food, entertainment, and consumer durables as well as on exotic holidays in India and abroad. Luxury cars and shiny motorbikes are the most sought-after status symbols among these newly prosperous young people, most of whom work in India's burgeoning IT sector. Harley-Davidson has set its sights on the Indian market, and Levi Strauss India (Pvt.) Ltd., a subsidiary of the U.S.-based clothing giant, regards India as one of the fastest-growing markets for Levi's in the world.[35]

A **life style** is a person's pattern of living in the world as expressed in activities, interests, and opinions. It portrays the 'whole person' interacting with the environment. Marketers search for relationships between their products and life style groups. For example, a computer manufacturer might find that most computer buyers are achievement-oriented and then aim the brand more clearly at the achiever life style. Here's an example of one of the latest life style trends that businesses are targeting.

 LOHAS Consumers who worry about the environment, want products to be produced in a sustainable way, and spend money to advance their personal health, development, and potential have been named LOHAS, an acronym standing for *life styles of health and sustainability.* The market for LOHAS products encompasses organic foods, energy-efficient appliances, and solar panels, as well as alternative medicine, yoga recordings, and ecotourism. Taken together, these accounted for a US$230 billion market in 2000. One estimate placed 30 percent of the adults in the United States, or 50 million people, in the LOHAS or Cultural Creatives category. We are witnessing some of these movements in the Arab world, such as the Dubiotech green buildings in Dubai (discussed in Chapter 3) ▭ **Table 6.1** breaks the LOHAS market into five segments.[36]

Life styles are shaped partly by whether consumers are *money-constrained* or *time-constrained.* Companies aiming to serve money-constrained consumers will create lower-cost products and services. By appealing to thrifty consumers, Walmart has become the largest company in the world. Its "everyday low prices" have wrung tens of billions of dollars out of the retail supply chain, passing the larger part of savings along to shoppers in the form of rock-bottom bargain prices.[37] The Marketing Excellence feature at the end of the chapter outlines IKEA's global success formula of appealing to price-conscious shoppers in the furniture market.

Consumers who experience time shortage are prone to **multitasking**, doing two or more things at the same time. They will also pay others to perform tasks because time is more important than money. Companies aiming to serve them will create convenient products and services for this group.

In some categories, notably food processing, companies targeting time-constrained consumers need to be aware that these very same people want to believe they're *not* operating within time constraints. Marketers call those who seek both convenience and some involvement in the cooking process, the "convenience involvement segment."[38]

life style a person's pattern of living in the world as expressed in activities, interests, and opinions.

multitasking doing two or more things at the same time.

TABLE 6.1 ▭ LOHAS SEGMENTATION	
LOHAS	**CONVENTIONALS**
Users of green products	Practical consumers
Socially responsible	Energy conservation efforts
Care about personal health	Recycling efforts
Care about planetary health	**UNCONCERNEDS**
NATURALITES	Little environmental responsibility
Interest in protecting the environment	No regard for social issues
Healthy	No inclination toward healthy living
Consume green products/services	
DRIFTERS	
Follow latest trends	
Price conscious	

Source: reprinted by permission of LOHAS (Lifestyles of Health and Sustainability), http://www.lohas.com/research-resources.

The "convenience involvement segment" of the food market is receptive to time-saver products such as Indomie noodles, which allow them to easily and quickly prepare a hot meal.

Indomie Noodles   Indomie Noodles is a leader in the market for instant noodles. The company originated in 1982 in Indonesia and its product has since gained worldwide popularity for its appealing taste, variety, and ease of preparation. The noodles are available in a variety of flavors, such as special chicken, shrimp, and vegetables, among others, and have become popular in many markets in the Arab world as a result of the need for a quick, easy meal. Working men and women find them particularly appealing.[39]

Consumer decisions are also influenced by core values, the belief systems that underlie attitudes and behaviors. **Core values** go much deeper than behavior or attitude and determine, at a basic level, people's choices and desires over the long term. Marketers who target consumers on the basis of their values believe that with an appeal to a person's inner self it is possible to influence the outer self, and therefore a person's purchase behavior.

core values   the belief systems that underlie consumer attitudes and behavior, and that determine people's choices and desires over the long term.

Key Psychological Processes

The starting point for understanding consumer behavior is the stimulus-response model shown in △ **Figure 6.1**. Marketing and environmental stimuli enter the consumer's consciousness, and a set of psychological processes combines with certain consumer characteristics to result in decision processes and purchase decisions. The marketer's task is to understand what happens in the consumer's consciousness between the arrival of the outside marketing stimuli and the ultimate purchase decisions. Four key psychological processes—motivation, perception, learning, and memory—fundamentally influence consumer responses.[40]

Motivation: Freud, Maslow, Herzberg

We all have many needs at any given time. Some needs are *biogenic*; they arise from physiological states of tension such as hunger, thirst, or discomfort. Other needs are *psychogenic*; they arise from psychological states of tension such as the need for recognition, esteem, or belonging. A need becomes a **motive** when it is aroused to a sufficient level of intensity to drive us to act. Motivation has both direction—we select one goal over another—and intensity—the vigor with which we pursue the goal.

Three of the best-known theories of human motivation—those of Sigmund Freud, Abraham Maslow, and Frederick Herzberg—carry quite different implications for consumer analysis and marketing strategy.

motive   a need that is sufficiently pressing to direct the person to seek satisfaction of the need.

|Fig. 6.1| △

Model of Consumer Behavior

Marketing Stimuli	Other Stimuli	Consumer Psychology	Buying Decision Process	Purchase Decision
Products & services Price Distribution Communications	Economic Technological Political Cultural	Motivation Perception Learning Memory	Problem recognition Information search Evaluation of alternatives Purchase decision Post-purchase behavior	Product choice Brand choice Dealer choice Purchase amount Purchase timing Payment method
		Consumer Characteristics		
		Cultural Social Personal		

FREUD'S THEORY Sigmund Freud assumed that the psychological forces shaping people's behavior are largely unconscious, and that a person cannot fully understand his or her own motivations. When a person examines specific brands, she will react not only to their stated capabilities, but also to other, less conscious cues such as shape, size, weight, material, color, and brand name. A technique called *laddering* lets us trace a person's motivations from the stated instrumental ones to the more terminal ones. Then the marketer can decide at what level to develop the message and appeal.[41]

Motivation researchers often collect 'in-depth interviews' with a few dozen consumers to uncover deeper motives triggered by a product. They use various *projective techniques* such as word association, sentence completion, picture interpretation, and role playing, many pioneered by Ernest Dichter, a Viennese psychologist who settled in the United States.[42]

Today motivational researchers continue the tradition of Freudian interpretation. Jan Callebaut identifies different motives a product can satisfy. For example, a mobile phone can meet the need for functional use, status, or social image. Different mobile brands need to be motivationally positioned in one of these three appeals.[43] Another motivation researcher, Clotaire Rapaille, works on breaking the 'code' behind a lot of product behavior.[44]

Toyota The market for cars in the Arab world is one that is growing at a relatively constant rate. The growth rate differs from country to another, but overall there remains a high demand for cars. While in countries such as Egypt, Algeria, and Tunisia people look for the economic values of a car, countries of the GCC such as Kuwait, the UAE, and Qatar look for the social values of a car. Saudi Arabia is a very important market for Toyota, which has a leading market share of the Saudi car market. Due to the nature of the weather, Toyota cars exported to Saudi Arabia and the GCC region are equipped to handle the extreme hot weather. The air-conditioning systems are more powerful than in cars sold elsewhere to cool the passengers when the temperature is high, often above 45 degrees. Further, reasonable price, availability of spare parts, and resale value makes Toyota attractive to many GCC customers. Due to relatively low prices of fuel, mileage is not one of the most important features that GCC customers look for in a car.

MASLOW'S THEORY Abraham Maslow sought to explain why people are driven by particular needs at particular times.[45] His answer is that human needs are arranged in a hierarchy from most to least pressing: physiological needs, safety needs, social needs, esteem needs, and self-actualization needs (see △ **Figure 6.2**). People will try to satisfy their most important needs first. When a person succeeds in satisfying an important need, he will then try to satisfy the next-most-important need. For example, a starving man (need 1) will not take an interest in the latest happenings in the art world (need 5), nor in how he is viewed by others (need 3 or 4), nor even in whether he is breathing clean air (need 2); but when he has enough food and water, the next-most-important need will become salient.

HERZBERG'S THEORY Frederick Herzberg developed a two-factor theory that distinguishes *dissatisfiers* (factors that cause dissatisfaction) from *satisfiers* (factors that cause satisfaction).[46] The absence of dissatisfiers is not enough to motivate a purchase; satisfiers must be present. For example, a computer that does not come with a warranty would be a dissatisfier. Yet the presence of a product warranty would not act as a satisfier or motivator of a purchase, because it is not a source of intrinsic satisfaction. Ease of use would be a satisfier.

Herzberg's theory has two implications. First, sellers should do their best to avoid dissatisfiers (for example, a poor training manual or a poor service policy). Although these things will not sell a product, they might easily unsell it. Second, the seller should identify the major satisfiers or motivators of purchase in the market and then supply them.

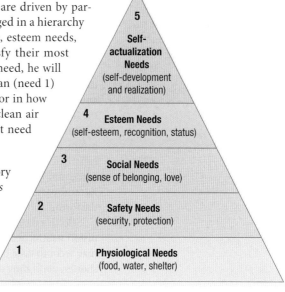

|Fig. 6.2| △

Maslow's Hierarchy of Needs

Source: A. H. Maslow, *Motivation and Personality*, 2nd edn (Upper Saddle River, NJ: Prentice Hall, 1970). Reprinted by permission of Prentice Hall Inc.

Perception

A motivated person is ready to act. *How* she acts is influenced by her view of the situation. In marketing, perceptions are more important than the reality, because it's perceptions that affect consumers' actual behavior. **Perception** is the process by which we select, organize, and interpret information inputs to create a meaningful picture of the world.[47] The key point is that it depends not only on the physical stimuli, but also on the stimuli's relationship to the surrounding field and on conditions within each of us. One person might perceive a fast-talking salesperson as aggressive and insincere; another, as intelligent and helpful. Each will respond differently to the salesperson.

In marketing, perceptions are more important than the reality, as it is perceptions that will affect consumers' actual behavior. People can emerge with different perceptions of the same object because of three perceptual processes: selective attention, selective distortion, and selective retention.

perception   the process by which an individual selects, organizes, and interprets information to create a meaningful picture of the world.

SELECTIVE ATTENTION   Attention is the notice taken of a person or an object. Voluntary attention is something purposeful; involuntary attention is grabbed by someone or something. It's estimated that the average person may be exposed to over 1,500 ads or brand communications a day. Because we cannot possibly attend to all these, we screen most stimuli out, a process called selective attention. **Selective attention** means that marketers must work hard to attract consumers' notice. The real challenge is to explain which stimuli people will notice. Here are some findings:

selective attention   the mental process of screening out certain stimuli while noticing others.

1. *People are more likely to notice stimuli that relate to a current need.* A person who is motivated to buy a computer will notice computer ads; he will be less likely to notice DVD ads.
2. *People are more likely to notice stimuli they anticipate.* You are more likely to notice computers than radios in a computer store because you don't expect the store to carry radios.
3. *People are more likely to notice stimuli whose deviations are large in relationship to the normal size of the stimuli.* You are more likely to notice an ad offering US$100 off the list price of a computer than one offering $5 off.

Though we screen out much, we are influenced by unexpected stimuli, such as sudden offers in the mail, over the phone, or from a salesperson. Marketers may attempt to promote their offers intrusively in order to bypass selective attention filters.

SELECTIVE DISTORTION   Even noticed stimuli don't always come across in the way the senders intended. **Selective distortion** is the tendency to interpret information in a way that fits our preconceptions. Consumers will often distort information to be consistent with prior brand and product beliefs and expectations.[48]

selective distortion   the tendency to interpret product information in a way that fits consumer perception.

For a stark demonstration of the power of consumer brand beliefs, consider that in 'blind' taste tests one group of consumers samples a product without knowing which brand it is, while another group knows. Invariably, the groups have different opinions, despite consuming *exactly the same product.*

When consumers report different opinions of branded and unbranded versions of identical products, it must be the case that their brand and product beliefs, created by whatever means (past experiences, marketing activity for the brand, or the like), have somehow changed their product perceptions. We can find examples with virtually every type of product.[49] When Unilever changed its toothpaste name from Signal 2 to Signal, consumers claimed the taste had changed even though the formulation had not.

Selective distortion can work to the advantage of marketers with strong brands when consumers distort neutral or ambiguous brand information to make it more positive. In other words, a soft drink may seem to taste better, a car may seem to drive more smoothly, the wait in a bank line may seem shorter, depending on the particular brands involved.

SELECTIVE RETENTION   Most of us don't remember much of the information to which we're exposed, but we do retain information that supports our attitudes and beliefs. Because of **selective retention**, we're likely to remember good points about a product we like and forget good points about competing products. Selective retention again works to the advantage of strong brands. It also explains why marketers need to use repetition: to make sure their message is not overlooked.

selective retention   the tendency to recall good points about a product that one likes and forget good points about competing products.

SUBLIMINAL PERCEPTION The selective perception mechanisms require consumers' active engagement and thought. A topic that has fascinated armchair marketers for ages is subliminal perception. They argue that marketers embed hidden, subliminal messages in ads or packaging. Consumers are not consciously aware of them, yet they affect behavior. Although it's clear that mental processes include many subtle subconscious effects,[50] no evidence supports the notion that marketers can systematically control consumers at that level, especially in terms of changing moderately important or strongly held beliefs.[51]

Learning

When we act, we learn. **Learning** induces changes in our behavior arising from experience. Most human behavior is learned, although much learning is incidental. Learning theorists believe that learning is produced through the interplay of drives, stimuli, cues, responses, and reinforcement. Two popular approaches to learning are classical conditioning and operant (instrumental) conditioning.

A **drive** is a strong internal stimulus impelling action. **Cues** are minor stimuli that determine when, where, and how a person responds. Suppose you buy a Hewlett-Packard (HP) computer. If your experience is rewarding, your response to computers and HP will be positively reinforced. Later on, when you want to buy a printer, you may assume that because HP makes good computers, HP also makes good printers. In other words, you *generalize* your response to similar stimuli. A countertendency to generalization is **discrimination**. Discrimination means we have learned to recognize differences in sets of similar stimuli and can adjust our responses accordingly.

Learning theory teaches marketers that they can build demand for a product by associating it with strong drives, using motivating cues, and providing positive reinforcement. A new company can enter the market by appealing to the same drives that competitors use and by providing similar cues, because buyers are more likely to transfer loyalty to similar brands (generalization); or the company might design its brand to appeal to a different set of drives and offer strong cue inducements to switch (discrimination).

Some researchers prefer more active, cognitive approaches when learning depends upon the inferences or interpretations consumers make about outcomes (was an unfavorable consumer experience due to a bad product or did the consumer fail to follow instructions properly?). The **hedonic bias** says people have a general tendency to attribute success to themselves and failure to external causes. Consumers are thus more likely to blame a product than themselves, putting pressure on marketers to carefully explicate product functions in well-designed packaging and labels, instructive ads, websites, and so on.

Memory

All the information and experiences we encounter as we go through life can end up in our long-term memory. Cognitive psychologists distinguish between **short-term memory (STM)**—a temporary and limited repository of information—and **long-term memory (LTM)**—a more permanent, essentially unlimited repository.

Most widely accepted views of long-term memory structure assume we form some kind of associative model.[52] For example, the **associative network memory model** views LTM as a set of nodes and links. *Nodes* are stored information connected by *links* that vary in strength. Any type of information can be stored in the memory network, including verbal, visual, abstract, and contextual. A spreading activation process from node to node determines how much we retrieve and what information we can actually recall in any given situation. When a node becomes activated because we're encoding external information (when we read or hear a word or phrase) or retrieving internal information from LTM (when we think about some concept), other nodes are also activated if they're strongly enough associated with that node.

In this model, we can think of consumer brand knowledge as a node in memory with a variety of linked associations. The strength and organization of these associations will be important determinants of the information we can recall about the brand. **Brand associations** consist of all brand-related thoughts, feelings, perceptions, images, experiences, beliefs, attitudes, and so on that become linked to the brand node.

learning changes in an individual's behavior arising from experience.

drive a strong internal stimulus impelling action.

cues stimuli that determine when, where, and how a person responds.

discrimination the process of recognizing differences in sets of similar stimuli and adjusting responses accordingly.

hedonic bias view that people have a general tendency to attribute success to themselves and failure to external causes.

short-term memory (STM) a temporary repository of information.

long-term memory (LTM) a permanent repository of information.

associative network memory model a conceptual representation that views memory as consisting of a set of nodes and interconnecting links, where nodes represent stored information or concepts and links represent the strength of association between this information or concept.

brand associations all brand-related thoughts, feelings, perceptions, images, experiences, beliefs, attitudes, and so on that become linked to a brand.

Chipsy   Chipsy has been a leader in Egypt's potato chip industry since it was first introduced in the early 1980s, and is one of many brands produced by the Chipsy Company; the Frito-Lay and PepsiCo international subsidiary also offers Lay's and Cheetos, among many others.

Chipsy has been able to create a widely recognized brand name to the extent that Egyptians now use the term "chipsy" as a generic name for all chips. With its variety of flavors, reasonable prices, and well-loved taste, Chipsy has an extremely wide consumer base. However, competitors are constantly emerging and slowly disrupting Chipsy's high and relatively stable market share. An example is Chipseco, whose recent advertisements have been focusing on its advantage with regards to the crunch, shape, and texture of its chips. The new Chipsy Max has also been emphasizing the competitive advantage of an extra "crunchy" chip, and TV as well as billboard advertisements have been successfully conveying this message using different tools. The aim is to form easier and greater associations with the brand or advertised product in the mind of the consumer.[53]

We can think of marketing as a way of making sure consumers have the right types of product and service experiences to create the right brand-knowledge structures and retain them in memory. Companies such as Procter & Gamble like to create mental maps of consumers that depict their knowledge of a particular brand in terms of the key associations that are likely to be triggered in a marketing setting, and their relative strength, favorability, and uniqueness to consumers. ▲ **Figure 6.3** displays a very simple mental map highlighting brand beliefs for a hypothetical Chipsy consumer.

MEMORY PROCESSES Memory is a very constructive process, because we don't remember information and events completely and accurately. Often we remember bits and pieces and fill in the rest based upon whatever else we know.

memory encoding how and where information gets into memory.

Memory encoding describes how and where information gets into memory. The strength of the resulting association depends on how much we process the information at the time of encoding (how much we think about it, for instance) and in what way.[54]

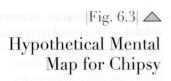

|Fig. 6.3| ▲

Hypothetical Mental
Map for Chipsy

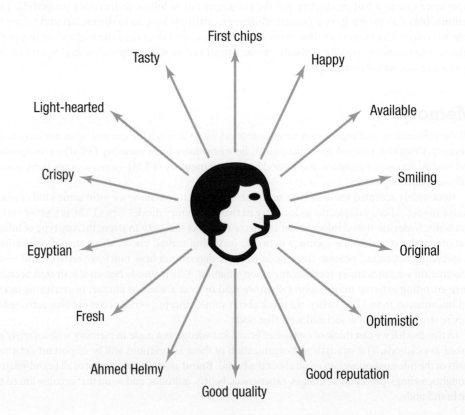

In general, the more attention we pay to the meaning of information during encoding, the stronger the resulting associations in memory will be.[55] When a consumer actively thinks about and 'elaborates' on the significance of product or service information, stronger associations are created in the memory. It's also easier for consumers to create an association with new information when extensive, relevant knowledge structures already exist in memory. One reason personal experiences create such strong brand associations is that information about the product is likely to be related to existing knowledge.

The ease with which we can integrate new information into established knowledge structures also clearly depends on its simplicity, vividness, and concreteness. Repeated exposures to information, too, provide greater opportunity for processing and thus the potential for stronger associations. Recent advertising research in a field setting, however, suggests that high levels of repetition for an uninvolving, unpersuasive ad are unlikely to have as much sales impact as lower levels of repetition for an involving, persuasive ad.[56]

MEMORY RETRIEVAL **Memory retrieval** is the way information is recalled from memory. According to the associative network memory model, a strong brand association is both more accessible and more easily recalled by 'spreading activation.' Our successful recall of brand information doesn't depend only on the initial strength of that information in memory. Three factors are particularly important.

memory retrieval how and from where information is recalled from memory.

First, the presence of *other* product information in memory can produce interference effects and cause us to either overlook or confuse new data. One marketing challenge in a category crowded with many competitors—for example, airlines, financial services, and insurance companies—is that consumers may mix up brands.

Second, the time between exposure to information and encoding matters: the longer the time delay, the weaker the association. The time elapsed since the last exposure opportunity, however, has been shown generally to produce only gradual decay. Cognitive psychologists believe memory is extremely durable, so that once information becomes stored in memory, its strength of association decays very slowly.[57]

Third, information may be *available* in memory but not be *accessible* (able to be recalled) without the proper retrieval cues or reminders. The particular associations for a brand that come to mind depend on the context in which we consider it. The more cues linked to a piece of information, however, the greater the likelihood that we can recall it. The effectiveness of retrieval cues is one reason marketing *inside* a supermarket or any retail store is so critical: the actual product packaging, the use of in-store minibillboard displays, and so on. The information they contain and the reminders they provide of advertising or other information already conveyed outside the store will be prime determinants of consumer decision making.

Memory can often be reconstructive, however, and consumers may remember an experience with a brand differently after the fact due to intervening factors or other events.[58]

The Buying-Decision Process: The Five-Stage Model

These basic psychological processes play an important role in understanding how consumers actually make their buying decisions.[59] ▭ **Box 6.2** provides a list of some key consumer behavior questions in terms of 'who, what, when, where, how, and why.'

Smart companies try to fully understand the customers' buying-decision process—all their experiences in learning, choosing, using, and even disposing of a product.[60] Bissel, a company that manufactures vacuum cleaners, developed its Steam'n Clean vacuum cleaner based on the product trial experiences of a group of local people near corporate headquarters in Grand Rapids, Michigan in the United States. The result was a name change, color-coded attachments, and an infomercial highlighting its special features.[61]

Marketing scholars have developed a 'stage model' of the buying-decision process (see ◁ **Figure 6.4** on the next page). The consumer passes through five stages: problem recognition, information search, evaluation of alternatives, purchase decision, and postpurchase behavior. Clearly, the buying process starts long before the actual purchase and has consequences long afterward.[62]

BOX 6.2   Understanding Consumer Behavior

Who buys our product or service?

Who makes the decision to buy the product?

Who influences the decision to buy the product?

How is the purchase decision made? Who assumes what role?

What does the customer buy? What needs must be satisfied?

Why do customers buy a particular brand?

Where do they go or look to buy the product or service?

When do they buy? Any seasonality factors?

How is our product perceived by customers?

What are customers' attitudes toward our product?

What social factors might influence the purchase decision?

Do customers' life styles influence their decisions?

How do personal or demographic factors influence the purchase decision?

Source: Based on list from George Belch and Michael Belch, *Advertising and Communication Management*, 6th edn (Homewood, IL: Irwin, 2003).

Consumers don't always pass through all five stages in buying a product. They may skip or reverse some. When you buy your regular brand of toothpaste, you go directly from the need for toothpaste to the purchase decision, skipping information search and evaluation. The model in Figure 6.4 provides a good frame of reference, however, because it captures the full range of considerations that arise when a consumer faces a highly involving new purchase.[63]

|Fig. 6.4|

Five-Stage Model of the Consumer Buying Process

Problem Recognition

The buying process starts when the buyer recognizes a problem or need triggered by internal or external stimuli. With an internal stimulus, one of the person's normal needs—hunger, thirst—rises to a threshold level and becomes a drive; or a need can be aroused by an external stimulus. A person may admire a neighbor's new car or see a television ad for a vacation in Indonesia which triggers thoughts about the possibility of making a purchase.

Marketers need to identify the circumstances that trigger a particular need by gathering information from a number of consumers. They can then develop marketing strategies that trigger consumer interest. Particularly for discretionary purchases such as luxury goods, vacation packages, and entertainment options, marketers may need to increase consumer motivation so that a potential purchase gets serious consideration.

Information Search

Surprisingly, consumers often search for limited amounts of information. Surveys have shown that for consumer durables, half of all consumers look at only one store, and only 30 percent look at more than one brand of appliances. We can distinguish between two levels of involvement with search. The milder search state is called *heightened attention*. At this level a person simply becomes more receptive to information about a product. At the next level, the person may enter an *active information search*: looking for reading material, phoning friends, going online, and visiting stores to learn about the product.

INFORMATION SOURCES   Major information sources to which consumers will turn fall into four groups:

1. *Personal.* Family, friends, neighbors, acquaintances.
2. *Commercial.* Advertising, websites, salespersons, dealers, packaging, displays.
3. *Public.* Mass media, consumer-rating organizations.
4. *Experiential.* Handling, examining, using the product.

The relative amount and influence of these sources vary with the product category and the buyer's characteristics. Generally speaking, the consumer receives the most information about a product from commercial—that is, marketer-dominated—sources. However, the most effective information often comes from personal sources or public sources that are independent authorities.

Each information source performs a different function in influencing the buying decision. Commercial sources normally perform an information function, whereas personal sources perform a verification or evaluation function. For example, physicians often learn of new drugs from commercial sources but turn to other doctors for evaluations.

SEARCH DYNAMICS Through gathering information, the consumer learns about competing brands and their features. The first box in △ **Figure 6.5** shows the *total set* of brands available to the consumer. The individual consumer will come to know only a subset of these brands, the *awareness set*. Some brands, the *consideration set*, will meet initial buying criteria. As the consumer gathers more information, only a few, the *choice set*, will remain strong contenders. The consumer makes a final choice from this set.[64]

Marketers need to identify the hierarchy of attributes that guide consumer decision making in order to understand different competitive forces and how these various sets get formed. This process of identifying the hierarchy is called **market partitioning**. Years ago, most car buyers first decided on the manufacturer and then on one of its car divisions (*brand-dominant hierarchy*). A buyer might favor General Motors cars and, within this set, Pontiac. Today, many buyers decide first on the nation from which they want to buy a car (*nation-dominant hierarchy*). Buyers may first decide they want to buy a Japanese car, then Toyota, and then the Corolla model of Toyota.

The hierarchy of attributes can also reveal customer segments. Buyers who first decide on price are price-dominant; those who first decide on the type of car (sports, passenger, station wagon) are type-dominant; those who first decide on the car brand are brand dominant. Type-/price-/brand-dominant consumers make up a segment; quality/service/type buyers make up another. Each segment may have distinct demographics, psychographics, and behavioristic variables in addition to different awareness, consideration, and choice sets.[65]

Figure 6.5 makes it clear that a company must strategize to get its brand into the prospect's awareness, consideration, and choice sets. If a food store owner arranges yogurt first by brand (such as Dannon and Yoplait) and then by flavor within each brand, consumers will tend to select their flavors from the same brand. However, if all the strawberry yogurts are together, then all the vanilla and so forth, consumers will probably choose which flavors they want first, and then choose the brand name they want for that particular flavor. Australian supermarkets arrange meats by the way they might be cooked, and their stores use more descriptive labels, such as "a 10-minute herbed beef roast" than U.S. stores do. The result is that Australians buy a greater variety of meats than U.S. shoppers, who choose from meats laid out by animal type: beef, chicken, and so on.[66]

The company must also identify the other brands in the consumer's choice set so that it can plan the appropriate competitive appeals. In addition, the company should identify the consumer's information sources and evaluate their relative importance. Asking consumers how

market partitioning the process of investigating the hierarchy of attributes consumers examine in choosing a brand, if they use phased decision strategies.

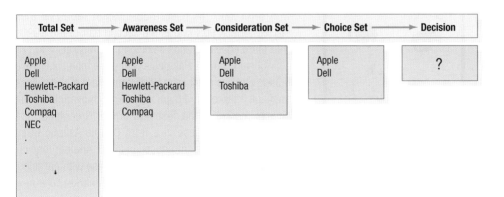

| Fig. 6.5 | △

Successive Sets Involved in Consumer Decision Making

they first heard about the brand, what information came later, and the relative importance of the different sources will help the company prepare effective communications for the target market.

Evaluation of Alternatives

How does the consumer process competitive brand information and make a final value judgment? No single process is used by all consumers, or by one consumer in all buying situations. There are several processes, and the most current models see the consumer forming judgments largely on a conscious and rational basis.

Some basic concepts will help us understand consumer evaluation processes: first, the consumer is trying to satisfy a need. Second, the consumer is looking for certain benefits from the product solution. Third, the consumer sees each product as a bundle of attributes with varying abilities for delivering the benefits sought to satisfy this need. The attributes of interest to buyers vary by product; for example:

- *Hotels*: location, cleanliness, atmosphere, price.
- *Mouthwash*: color, effectiveness, germ-killing capacity, taste/flavor, price.
- *Tires*: safety, tread life, ride quality, price.

Consumers will pay the most attention to attributes that deliver the sought-after benefits. We can often segment the market for a product according to attributes important to different consumer groups.

BELIEFS AND ATTITUDES Through experience and learning, people acquire beliefs and attitudes. These in turn influence buying behavior. A belief is a descriptive thought that a person holds about something. Just as important are attitudes, a person's enduring favorable or unfavorable evaluations, emotional feelings, and action tendencies toward some object or idea.[67] People have attitudes toward almost everything: religion, politics, clothes, music, food.

Attitudes put us into a frame of mind: liking or disliking an object, moving toward or away from it. They lead us to behave in a fairly consistent way toward similar objects. Because attitudes economize on energy and thought, they can be very difficult to change. A company is well advised to fit its product into existing attitudes rather than to try to change attitudes. Here's an example of an organization that used ad campaigns to remind consumers of their attitudes, with handsome results.

 Tetra Pak

Tetra Pak entered the cheese market in 1989 with the brand Milky Land. This was the first Feta cheese to be introduced in a carton package, in Tetra Brik Aseptic sizes 250ml and 500ml. The idea has proved successful in the Egyptian market, and in 1995, Greenland introduced its Feta cheese also in Tetra Brik Aseptic 250ml and 500ml with Tetra Pak. The cheese business in Tetra Pak then started to pick up towards the second half of the 1990s with more cheese brands coming to the market.

Currently, Tetra Pak deals with more than six cheese brands and has reached a 42 percent share of the cheese package market in Egypt. A recent innovation in the cheese market is the Tasbeera brand (Greenland), the first on-the-go cheese in a Tetra Classic Aseptic 65ml package, which was introduced in 2008. Another innovation from Greenland in 2011 is the cheese with particles, which is expected to take the cheese market to a new level.[68]

Tetra Pak changed consumers' attitudes towards dairy products with its Tasbeera snacks.

EXPECTANCY-VALUE MODEL

The consumer arrives at attitudes toward various brands through an attribute-evaluation procedure.[69] She develops a set of beliefs about where each brand stands on each attribute. The **expectancy-value model** of attitude formation posits that consumers evaluate products and services by combining their brand beliefs—the positives and negatives—according to importance.

Suppose Rola has narrowed her choice set to four laptop computers (A, B, C, D). Assume she's interested in four attributes: memory capacity, graphics capability, size and weight, and price. ▭ **Table 6.2** shows her beliefs about how each brand rates on the four attributes. If one computer dominated the others on all the criteria, we could predict that Rola would choose it. But, as is often the case, her choice set consists of brands that vary in their appeal. If Rola wants the best memory capacity, she should buy C; if she wants the best graphics capability, she should buy A; and so on.

If we knew the weights Rola attaches to the four attributes, we could more reliably predict her computer choice. Suppose she assigned 40 percent of the importance to the computer's memory capacity, 30 percent to graphics capability, 20 percent to size and weight, and 10 percent to price. To find Rola's perceived value for each computer, according to the expectancy-value model, we multiply her weights by her beliefs about each computer's attributes. This computation leads to the following perceived values:

$$\text{Computer A} = 0.4(8) + 0.3(9) + 0.2(6) + 0.1(9) = 8.0$$

$$\text{Computer B} = 0.4(7) + 0.3(7) + 0.2(7) + 0.1(7) = 7.0$$

$$\text{Computer C} = 0.4(10) + 0.3(4) + 0.2(3) + 0.1(2) = 6.0$$

$$\text{Computer D} = 0.4(5) + 0.3(3) + 0.2(8) + 0.1(5) = 5.0$$

An expectancy-model formulation predicts that Rola will favor computer A, which (at 8.0) has the highest perceived value.[70]

Suppose most computer buyers form their preferences the same way. Knowing this, the marketer of computer B, for example, could apply the following strategies to stimulate greater interest in brand B:

- **Redesign the computer.** This technique is called real repositioning.
- **Alter beliefs about the brand.** Attempting to alter beliefs about the brand is called psychological repositioning.
- **Alter beliefs about competitors' brands.** This strategy, called *competitive depositioning*, makes sense when buyers mistakenly believe a competitor's brand has more quality than it actually has.
- **Alter the importance weights.** The marketer could try to persuade buyers to attach more importance to the attributes in which the brand excels.
- **Call attention to neglected attributes.** The marketer could draw buyers' attention to neglected attributes, such as styling or processing speed.
- **Shift the buyer's ideals.** The marketer could try to persuade buyers to change their ideal levels for one or more attributes.[71]

expectancy-value model consumers evaluate products and services by combining their brand beliefs—positive and negative—according to their weighted importance.

TABLE 6.2 ▭	A Consumer's Brand Beliefs about Laptop Computers			
Laptop Computer	**Attribute**			
	Memory Capacity	Graphics Capability	Size and Weight	Price
A	8	9	6	9
B	7	7	7	7
C	10	4	3	2
D	5	3	8	5

Note: each attribute is rated from 0 to 10, where 10 represents the highest level on that attribute. Price, however, is indexed in a reverse manner, with a 10 representing the lowest price, because a consumer prefers a low price to a high price.

heuristics rules of thumb or mental shortcuts in the decision process.

noncompensatory models when consumers do not simultaneously consider all positive and negative attributes in making a decision.

conjunctive heuristic the consumer sets a minimum acceptable cutoff level for each attribute and chooses the first alternative that meets the minimum standard for all attributes.

lexicographic heuristic a consumer chooses the best brand on the basis of its perceived most important attribute.

elimination-by-aspects heuristic the consumer compares brands on an attribute selected probabilistically, and brands are eliminated if they do not meet minimum acceptable cutoff levels.

Purchase Decision

In the evaluation stage, the consumer forms preferences among the brands in the choice set. The consumer may also form an intention to buy the most preferred brand. In executing a purchase intention, the consumer may make up to five subdecisions: brand (brand A), dealer (dealer 2), quantity (one computer), timing (weekend), and payment method (credit card).

NONCOMPENSATORY MODELS OF CONSUMER CHOICE The expectancy-value model is a compensatory model, in that perceived good things about a product can help to overcome perceived bad things. But consumers often take 'mental shortcuts' using simplifying choice heuristics. **Heuristics** are rules of thumb or mental shortcuts in the decision process.

With **noncompensatory models** of consumer choice, positive and negative attribute considerations don't necessarily net out. Evaluating attributes in isolation makes decision making easier for a consumer, but it also increases the likelihood that she would have made a different choice if she had deliberated in greater detail. We highlight three such choice heuristics here.

1. With the **conjunctive heuristic**, the consumer sets a minimum acceptable cutoff level for each attribute and chooses the first alternative that meets the minimum standard for all attributes. For example, if Rola decided all attributes had to rate at least a 5, she would choose computer B.
2. With the **lexicographic heuristic**, the consumer chooses the best brand on the basis of its perceived most important attribute. With this decision rule, Rola would choose computer C.
3. With the **elimination-by-aspects heuristic**, the consumer compares brands on an attribute selected probabilistically—where the probability of choosing an attribute is positively related to its importance—and eliminates brands that do not meet minimum acceptable cutoffs.

Our brand or product knowledge, the number and similarity of brand choices and time pressure involved, and the social context (such as the need for justification to a peer or boss) may all affect whether and how we use choice heuristics.[72]

Consumers don't necessarily use only one type of choice rule. Sometimes, they adopt a phased decision strategy that combines two or more. For example, they might use a noncompensatory decision rule such as the conjunctive heuristic to reduce the number of brand choices to a more manageable number, and then evaluate the remaining brands. One reason for the runaway success of the Intel Inside campaign in the 1990s was that it made the brand the first cutoff for many consumers: they would only buy a personal computer that had an Intel microprocessor. Personal computer makers such as IBM, Dell, and Gateway had no choice but to support Intel's marketing efforts.

INTERVENING FACTORS Even if consumers form brand evaluations, two general factors can intervene between the purchase intention and the purchase decision (△ **Figure 6.6**).[73] The first is the attitudes of others. The extent to which another person's **attitude** reduces our preference for an alternative depends on two things: (1) the intensity of the other person's negative attitude toward our preferred alternative and (2) our motivation to comply with the other person's wishes.[74] The more intense the other person's negativism and the closer the other person is to us, the more we will adjust our purchase intention. The converse is also true.

Related to the attitudes of others is the role played by infomediaries who publish their evaluations. Examples include *Consumer Reports*, which provides unbiased expert reviews of all types of products and services; J.D. Power in the United States, which provides consumer-based ratings of cars, financial services, and travel products and services; professional movie, book, and music reviewers; customer reviews of products such as on Brand Power, reviews of books and music on Amazon.com; and the increasing number of chat rooms, bulletin boards, blogs, and so on where people discuss products, services, and companies. Consumers are undoubtedly influenced by these evaluations, as evidenced by the success of a small-budget movie such as *Napoleon Dynamite*, which cost only US$400,000 to make but grossed over $44 million at the box office in 2004 thanks to a slew of favorable reviews by moviegoers on many websites.

The second factor is *unanticipated situational factors* that may erupt to change the purchase intention. Rola might lose her job, some other purchase might become more urgent, or a store salesperson may turn her off. Preferences and even purchase intentions are not completely reliable predictors of purchase behavior.

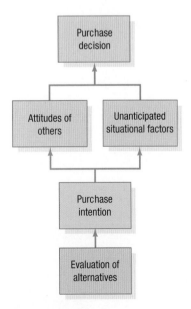

|Fig. 6.6| △

Steps Between Evaluation of Alternatives and a Purchase Decision

A consumer's decision to modify, postpone, or avoid a purchase decision is heavily influenced by *perceived risk*.[75] Consumers may perceive many types of risk in buying and consuming a product:

1. **Functional risk.** The product may not perform up to expectations.
2. **Physical risk.** The product may pose a threat to the physical well-being or health of the user or others.
3. **Financial risk.** The product may not be worth the price paid.
4. **Social risk.** The product may result in embarrassment from others.
5. **Psychological risk.** The product may affect the mental well-being of the user.
6. **Time risk.** The failure of the product may result in an opportunity cost of finding another satisfactory product.

The amount of perceived risk varies with the amount of money at stake, the amount of attribute uncertainty, and the amount of consumer self-confidence. Consumers develop routines for reducing the uncertainty and negative consequences of risk, such as decision avoidance, information gathering from friends, and preferences for national brand names and warranties. Marketers must understand the factors that provoke a feeling of risk in consumers and provide information and support to reduce perceived risk.

Postpurchase Behavior

After the purchase, the consumer might experience a difference of opinion that stems from noticing certain discomforting features or hearing favorable things about other brands and will be alert to information that supports his or her decision. Marketing communications should supply beliefs and evaluations that reinforce the consumer's choice and help him feel good about the brand.

The marketer's job therefore doesn't end with the purchase. Marketers must monitor postpurchase satisfaction, postpurchase actions, and postpurchase product usage.

POSTPURCHASE SATISFACTION Satisfaction is a function of the closeness between expectations and the product's perceived performance.[76] If performance falls short of expectations, the consumer is *disappointed*; if it meets expectations, the consumer is *satisfied*; if it exceeds expectations, the consumer is *delighted*. These feelings make a difference in whether the customer buys the product again and talks favorably or unfavorably about it to others.

The larger the gap between expectations and performance, the greater the dissatisfaction. Here the consumer's coping style comes into play. Some consumers magnify the gap when the product isn't perfect and are highly dissatisfied; others minimize it and are less dissatisfied.[77]

POSTPURCHASE ACTIONS If the consumer is satisfied, she is more likely to purchase the product again. The satisfied customer will also tend to say good things about the brand to others. On the other hand, dissatisfied consumers may abandon or return the product. They may seek information that confirms its high value. They may take public action by complaining to the company, going to a lawyer, or complaining to other groups (such as business, private, or government agencies). Private actions include deciding to stop buying the product (*exit option*) or warning friends (*voice option*).[78]

Chapter 5 described CRM programs designed to build long-term brand loyalty. Postpurchase communications to buyers have been shown to result in fewer product returns and order cancellations. Computer companies, for example, can send a letter to new owners congratulating them on having selected a fine computer. They can place ads showing satisfied brand owners. They can solicit customer suggestions for improvements and list the location of available services. They can write intelligible instruction booklets. They can send owners a magazine containing articles describing new computer applications. In addition, they can provide good channels for speedy redress of customer grievances.

POSTPURCHASE USE AND DISPOSAL Marketers should also monitor how buyers use and dispose of the product. Consumers have various options for consuming a product; this could include: using it for the original purpose, using it for a new purpose, or storing the product. Consumers also have various options for disposing of a product; this could include: getting rid of the product temporarily by renting or lending a product; or getting rid of the product permanently

attitude a person's enduring favorable or unfavorable evaluation, emotional feeling, and action tendencies toward some object or idea.

by giving it away, trading it, selling it, or throwing it away. A key driver of sales frequency is product consumption rate: the more quickly buyers consume a product, the sooner they may be back in the market to repurchase it.

One opportunity to increase frequency of product use occurs when consumers' perceptions of their usage differ from reality. Consumers may fail to replace products with relatively short life spans soon enough because they overestimate its product life.[79] One strategy to speed up replacement is to tie the act of replacing the product to a certain holiday, event, or time of year.

For example, Samsung has run TV promotions tied in with Ramadan, a month in which TV viewership increases significantly. Another strategy is to provide consumers with better information about either: (1) when they first used the product or need to replace it or (2) its current level of performance. Batteries have built-in gauges that show how much power they have left; toothbrushes have color indicators to indicate when the bristles are worn; and so on. Perhaps the simplest way to increase usage is to learn when actual usage is less than recommended and persuade customers of the merits of more regular usage.

If consumers throw the product away, the marketer needs to know how they dispose of it, especially if—like batteries, beverage containers, electronic equipment, and disposable diapers—it can damage the environment.

Other Theories of Consumer Decision Making

The consumer decision process may not always develop in a carefully planned fashion. Here are some other theories and approaches to explaining it.

Level of Consumer Involvement

The expectancy-value model assumes a high level of involvement on the part of the consumer. We can define **consumer involvement** in terms of the level of engagement and active processing the consumer undertakes in responding to a marketing stimulus.

consumer involvement the level of engagement and active processing undertaken by the consumer in responding to a marketing stimulus.

ELABORATION LIKELIHOOD MODEL Richard Petty and John Cacioppo's *elaboration likelihood model*, an influential model of attitude formation and change, describes how consumers make evaluations in both low- and high-involvement circumstances.[80] There are two means of persuasion in their model: the *central route*, where attitude formation or change stimulates much thought and is based on a diligent, rational consideration of the most important product information; and the *peripheral route*, where attitude formation or change provokes much less thought and results from the association of a brand with either positive or negative peripheral cues. *Peripheral cues* for consumers include a celebrity endorsement, a credible source, or any object that generates positive feelings.

Consumers follow the central route only if they possess sufficient motivation, ability, and opportunity. In other words, consumers must want to evaluate a brand in detail, have the necessary brand and product or service knowledge in memory, and have sufficient time and the proper setting. If any of those factors is lacking, consumers tend to follow the peripheral route and consider less central, more extrinsic factors in their decisions.

LOW-INVOLVEMENT MARKETING STRATEGIES Many products are bought under conditions of low involvement and the absence of significant brand differences. Consider salt. Consumers have little involvement in this product category. If they keep reaching for the same brand, it's out of habit, not strong brand loyalty. Evidence suggests consumers have low involvement with most low-cost, frequently purchased products.

Marketers use four techniques to try to convert a low-involvement product into one of higher involvement. First, they can link the product to some involving issue, as when Crest linked its toothpaste to avoiding cavities. Second, they can link the product to some involving personal situation; for example, fruit juice makers began to include vitamins such as calcium to fortify their drinks. Third, they might design advertising to trigger strong emotions related to personal values or ego defense, as when cereal makers began to advertise to adults the heart-healthy nature of cereals and the importance of living a long time to enjoy family life. Fourth, they might add an important feature; for example, when Samsung introduced the Android system to their mobile phones. These strategies at best raise consumer involvement from a low to a moderate level; they do not necessarily propel the consumer into highly involved buying behavior.

If, regardless of what the marketer can do, consumers have low involvement with a purchase decision, they are likely to follow the peripheral route. Marketers must pay special attention to giving consumers one or more positive cues to justify their brand choice. For instance, frequent ad repetition, visible sponsorships, and vigorous PR are all ways to enhance brand familiarity. Other peripheral cues that can tip the balance in favor of the brand include a beloved celebrity endorser, attractive packaging, and an appealing promotion.[81]

VARIETY-SEEKING BUYING BEHAVIOR Some buying situations are characterized by low involvement but significant brand differences. Here consumers often do a lot of brand switching. Think about cookies. The consumer has some beliefs about cookies, chooses a brand without much evaluation, and evaluates the product during consumption. Next time, the consumer may reach for another brand out of a wish for a different taste. Brand switching occurs for the sake of variety, rather than dissatisfaction.

The market leader and the minor brands in this product category have different marketing strategies. The market leader will try to encourage habitual buying behavior by dominating the shelf space with a variety of related but different product versions, avoiding out-of-stock conditions, and sponsoring frequent-reminder advertising. Challenger firms will encourage variety seeking by offering lower prices, deals, coupons, free samples, and advertising that tries to break the consumer's purchase-and-consumption cycle and presents reasons for trying something new.

Decision Heuristics and Biases

We've seen that consumers don't always process information or make decisions in a deliberate, rational manner. The Marketing Insight: *How Consumers Really Make Decisions* highlights some recent advances from the thriving academic study of how consumers make decisions.

Behavioral decision theorists have identified many different heuristics and biases in everyday consumer decision making. They come into play when consumers forecast the likelihood of future outcomes or events.[82]

1. The **availability heuristic**. Consumers base their predictions on the quickness and ease with which a particular example of an outcome comes to mind. If an example comes to mind too easily, consumers might overestimate the likelihood of its happening. For example, a recent product failure may lead a consumer to inflate the likelihood of a future product failure and make him more inclined to purchase a product warranty.

2. The **representativeness heuristic**. Consumers base their predictions on how representative or similar the outcome is to other examples. One reason that package appearances may be so similar for different brands in the same product category is that they want to be seen as representative of the category as a whole.

3. The **anchoring and adjustment heuristic**. Consumers arrive at an initial judgment and then adjust it based on additional information. For services marketers, it is critical to make a strong first impression to establish a favorable anchor, so that subsequent experiences are interpreted in a more favorable light.

Note that marketing managers may also use heuristics and be subject to biases in their decision making. Kaveh Kalantar proposed a number of fundamental principles that will help managers better manage people. He advised managers to:[84]

1. Make sure you hire the right people and work with people that have diverse skills.
2. Understand the needs of people and respect their values.
3. Avoid criticism in public and provide as much feedback as possible to guide employees.
4. Ask questions to employees and allow them to ask questions as well.

availability heuristic when consumers base their predictions on the quickness and ease with which a particular example of an outcome comes to mind.

representativeness heuristic when consumers base their predictions on how representative or similar an outcome is to other examples.

anchoring and adjustment heuristic when consumers arrive at an initial judgment and then make adjustments of their first impressions based on additional information.

Marketing Insight

How Consumers Really Make Decisions

One of the most active academic research areas in marketing is behavioral decision theory (BDT). Researchers have uncovered many fascinating influences and outcomes in consumer decision making, often challenging predictions from economic theory and assumptions about rationality.[83]

- Consumers are more likely to choose an alternative (a home bread bakery) after a relatively inferior option (a slightly better but significantly more expensive bakery) is added to the choice set.

- Consumers are more likely to choose an alternative that appears to be a compromise in the particular choice set under consideration.

- The choices that consumers make influence their assessment of their own tastes.

- Shifting attention to one of two considered alternatives tends to enhance the perceived attractiveness and choice probability of that alternative.

- The manner in which consumers compare products that vary in terms of price and perceived quality (features, brand name) and the way those products are displayed in the store (by brand or by model type) affect their willingness to pay more for additional features or a better-known brand.

- Consumers who think about the possibility that their purchase decisions will turn out to be wrong are more likely to choose better-known brands.

- Consumers for whom possible feelings of regret are made more relevant are more likely to choose a product that is currently on sale rather than wait for a better sale or buy a higher-priced item.

- Consumers' choices are influenced by subtle (and theoretically unimportant) changes in the way alternatives are described.

- Consumers who make purchases for later consumption appear to make systematic errors in predicting their future preferences.

- Consumer's predictions of their future tastes are not accurate: they do not really know how they will feel after consuming the same flavor of yogurt or ice cream several times.

- Consumers often overestimate the duration of their overall emotional reactions to future events (moves, financial windfalls, outcomes of sporting events).

- Consumers often overestimate their future consumption, especially if there is limited availability (which may explain why some chewing gums have higher sales when availability is limited to several months per year than when they are offered year round).

- In anticipating future consumption opportunities, consumers often assume they will want or need more variety than they actually do.

- Consumers are less likely to choose alternatives with product features or promotional premiums that have little or no value, even when these features and premiums are optional and do not reduce the actual value of the product in any way.

- Consumers are less likely to choose products selected by other consumers for reasons that they find irrelevant, even though these other reasons would not suggest anything positive or negative about the products' values.

- Consumers' interpretations and evaluations of past experiences are greatly influenced by the ending and trend of events. A positive event at the end of a service experience can color later reflections and evaluations of the experience as a whole.

What all these and other studies reinforce is that consumer behavior is very constructive and that the context of decisions really matter. Understanding how these effects show up in the marketplace can be crucial for marketers.

Sources: For an overview of some issues involved, see James R. Bettman, Mary Frances Luce, and John W. Payne, "Constructive Consumer Choice Processes," *Journal of Consumer Research*, 25, December 1998, pp. 187–217; and Itamar Simonson, "Getting Closer to Your Customers by Understanding How They Make Choices," *California Management Review*, 35, Summer 1993, pp. 68–84. For examples of classic studies in this area, see some of the following: Dan Ariely and Ziv Carmon, "Gestalt Characteristics of Experiences: The Defining Features of Summarized Events," *Journal of Behavioral Decision Making*, 13, no. 2, April 2000, pp. 191–201; Ravi Dhar and Klaus Wertenbroch, "Consumer Choice between Hedonic and Utilitarian Goods," *Journal of Marketing Research*, 37, February 2000, pp. 60–71; Itamar Simonson and Amos Tversky, "Choice in Context: Tradeoff Contrast and Extremeness Aversion," *Journal of Marketing Research*, 29, August 1992, pp. 281–295; Itamar Simonson, "The Effects of Purchase Quantity and Timing on Variety-Seeking Behavior," *Journal of Marketing Research*, 27, May 1990, pp. 150–162.

Mental Accounting

mental accounting the manner by which consumers code, categorize, and evaluate financial outcomes of choices.

Researchers have found that consumers use mental accounting when they handle their money.[85] **Mental accounting** refers to the way consumers code, categorize, and evaluate financial outcomes of choices. Formally, it is "the tendency to categorize *funds* or items of value even though there is no logical *basis* for the categorization, for example, individuals often segregate their savings into separate accounts to meet different goals even though funds from any of the accounts can be applied to any of the goals."[86]

As an example, assume you spend US$50 to buy a ticket to see a concert.[87] As you arrive at the show, you realize you've lost your ticket. You may be unsure about purchasing another ticket for $50. Assume, on the other hand, that you realize you lost $50 on the way to buy the ticket. You might be much more likely to go ahead and buy the ticket anyway. Although you lost the same amount in each case—$50—in the first case you may have mentally allocated $50 for going to a concert. Buying another ticket would exceed your mental concert budget. In the second case, the money you lost did not belong to any account, so you had not yet exceeded your mental concert budget.

According to the University of Chicago's Richard Thaler, mental accounting is based on a set of key core principles:[88]

1. Consumers tend to *segregate gains.* When a seller has a product with more than one positive dimension, it's desirable to have the consumer evaluate each dimension separately. Listing multiple benefits of a large industrial product, for example, can make the sum of the parts seem greater than the whole.
2. Consumers tend to *integrate losses.* Marketers have a distinct advantage in selling something if its cost can be added to another large purchase. House buyers are more inclined to view additional expenditures favorably given the high price of buying a house.
3. Consumers tend to *integrate smaller losses with larger gains.* The 'cancellation' principle might explain why withholding taxes from monthly paychecks is less aversive than large, lump-sum tax payments: the smaller withholdings are more likely to be absorbed by the larger pay amount.
4. Consumers tend to *segregate small gains from large losses.* The 'silver lining' principle—evaluating the gain separately from the larger loss is seen as more favorable than reducing the loss by the same amount—might explain the popularity of rebates on big-ticket purchases such as cars.

The principles of mental accounting are derived in part from prospect theory. **Prospect theory** maintains that consumers frame their decision alternatives in terms of gains and losses according to a value function. Consumers are generally loss averse. They tend to overweight very low probabilities and underweight very high probabilities.

prospect theory when consumers frame decision alternatives in terms of gains and losses according to a value function.

Profiling the Customer Buying-Decision Process

How can marketers learn about the stages in the buying process for their product? They can think about how they themselves would act, in the *introspective method.* They can interview a small number of recent purchasers, asking them to recall the events leading to their purchase, in the *retrospective method.* They can use the *prospective method* to locate consumers who plan to buy the product and ask them to think out loud about going through the buying process, or they can ask consumers to describe the ideal way to buy the product, in the *prescriptive method.* Each method yields a picture of the steps in the process.

Trying to understand the customer's behavior in connection with a product has been called mapping the customer's **consumption system**,[89] *customer activity cycle*,[90] or *customer scenario.*[91] Marketers can do this for such activity clusters as doing laundry, preparing for a wedding, or buying a car. Buying a car, for example, includes a whole cluster of activities: choosing the car, financing the purchase, buying insurance, buying accessories, and so on.

consumption system the way the user performs the tasks of getting and using products and related services.

Summary

1. Consumer behavior is influenced by three factors: cultural (culture, subculture, and social class); social (reference groups, family, and social roles and statuses); and personal (age, stage in the life cycle, occupation, economic circumstances, life style, personality, and self-concept). Research into all these factors can provide marketers with clues to reach and serve consumers more effectively.

2. Four main psychological processes affect consumer behavior: motivation, perception, learning, and memory.

3. To understand how consumers actually make buying decisions, marketers must identify who makes and has input into the buying decision; people can be initiators, influencers, deciders, buyers, or users. Different marketing campaigns might be targeted to each type of person.

4. The typical buying process consists of the following sequence of events: problem recognition, information search, evaluation of alternatives, purchase decision, and postpurchase behavior. The marketers' job is to understand the behavior at each stage. The attitudes of others, unanticipated situational factors, and perceived risk may all affect the decision to buy, as will consumers' levels of postpurchase product satisfaction, use and disposal, and actions on the part of the company.

5. Consumers are constructive decision makers and subject to many contextual influences. Consumers often exhibit low involvement in their decisions, using many heuristics as a result.

Applications

Marketing Debate

Is Target Marketing Ever Bad?

As marketers increasingly develop marketing programs tailored to certain target market segments, some critics have denounced these efforts as exploitive. For example, the prevalence of billboards advertising cigarettes and other related products in low-income urban areas is seen as taking advantage of a vulnerable market segment. Critics can be especially harsh in evaluating marketing programs that target Bedouins and other minority groups, claiming they often employ stereotypes and inappropriate depictions. Others counter that targeting and positioning is critical to marketing and that these marketing programs are an attempt to be relevant to a certain consumer group.

Take a position: Targeting minorities is exploitive *versus* targeting minorities is a sound business practice.

Marketing Discussion

What mental accounts do you have in your mind about purchasing products or services? Do you have any rules you employ in spending money? Are they different from what other people do? Do you follow Thaler's four principles in reacting to gains and losses?

Marketing Excellence

>>IKEA

IKEA was founded in 1943 by a 17-year-old Swede named Ingvar Kamprad. The company, which initially sold pens, Christmas cards, and seeds from a shed on Kamprad's family farm, eventually grew into a retail giant in home furnishings and a global cultural phenomenon, what *BusinessWeek* called a "one-stop sanctuary for coolness" and "the quintessential cult brand."

IKEA inspires remarkable levels of devotion from its customers, who visit in numbers that average 1.1 million per day. When a new location debuted in London in 2005, 6,000 people arrived before the doors opened. A contest in Atlanta crowned five winners "Ambassador of Kul" ("kul" is Swedish for 'fun') who, in order to collect their prizes, had to live in the IKEA store for 3 full days before it opened, which they gladly did.

IKEA achieved this level of success by offering a unique value proposition to consumers: leading-edge Scandinavian design at bargain prices. The company's fashionable bargains include Klippan sofas for US$249, Billy bookcases for $120, and Lack side tables for $13. In Scandinavian markets, IKEA has even sold 2,500 prefabricated homes for around $45,000, depending on local housing prices. The company is able to offer such low prices in part because most items come boxed and require complete assembly at home, meaning they are easier to transport, take up less shelf space, and seldom require delivery, which reduces costs.

IKEA's mission of providing value is predicated on founder Kamprad's statement that "People have very thin wallets. We should take care of their interests." IKEA adheres to this philosophy by reducing prices across its products by 2 to 3 percent annually. Its focus on value also benefits the bottom line: IKEA enjoys 10 percent margins, higher than competitors such as Target (7.7 percent) and Pier 1 Imports (5 percent), its main competitors in the United States.

Many of its products are sold uniformly throughout the world, but IKEA also caters to local tastes. In China, for example, it stocked 250,000 plastic placemats with Year of the Rooster themes, which quickly sold out after the holiday. When employees realized U.S. shoppers were buying vases as drinking glasses because they considered IKEA's regular glasses too small, the company developed larger glasses for the U.S. market.

IKEA managers visited European and U.S. consumers in their homes and learned that Europeans generally hang their clothes, whereas U.S. shoppers prefer to store them folded. Wardrobes for the U.S. market were designed with deeper drawers. Visits to Hispanic households in California led IKEA to add seating and dining space in its California stores, brighten the color palettes, and hang more framed picture on the walls.

IKEA evolved into a retail empire with 264 stores and revenues of US$22.2 billion in 2006, and still had excellent growth opportunities. IKEA planned to double the number of U.S. outlets by 2010. IKEA now has four stores in the Arab world region—one in Kuwait and three in Saudi Arabia—with different franchises. In the UAE, it currently has two stores under a franchise with the Al-Futtaim Group. A third opened in Abu Dhabi in 2011.

Questions

1. What is the unique value proposition that IKEA offers to its consumers?

2. How does IKEA cater to the needs of different markets?

3. How does IKEA know the different consumer needs?

Sources: Kerry Capell, "IKEA: How the Swedish Retailer Became a Global Cult Brand," *BusinessWeek*, November 14, 2005, p. 96; "Need a Home to Go with That Sofa?," *BusinessWeek*, November 14, 2005, p. 106; www.ikea.com; "IKEA Plans Middle East's Biggest Store in Abu Dhabi," *Franchiseek UAE Franchise News Kuwait*, http://www.franchiseek.com/Kuwait/NewsDetail.asp?NewsID=733.

Aramex has developed into the primary Arab company providing, among others, express, freight-forwarding, and logistics services to businesses.

In this chapter, we will address the following questions:

1. What is the business market, and how does it differ from the consumer market? (pg. 182)

2. What buying situations do organizational buyers face? (pg. 186)

3. Who participates in the business-to-business buying process? (pg. 187)

4. How do business buyers make their decisions? (pg. 190)

5. How can companies build strong relationships with business customers? (pg. 197)

6. How do institutional buyers and government agencies do their buying? (pg. 201)

Analyzing Business Markets

Business organizations do not only sell; they also buy vast quantities of raw materials, manufactured components, plant and equipment, supplies, and business services. To create and capture value, sellers need to understand these organizations' needs, resources, policies, and buying procedures.

 Started in the 1980s as a small mail courier service, Aramex has developed into the region's leading delivery company. Aramex's services now cover express mail, freight forwarding, logistics, and shopping services, with Aramex Express moving time-sensitive documents and parcels, and Aramex freight services covering land, air, and sea. Aramex has one of the largest and most advanced land freight networks, not only in the Arab world, but also in the United Kingdom and Ireland.

Aramex works closely with its business market. For example, its Supply Chain Management teams offer expert advice and service on the flow of client products from manufacturing through to retailers and end customers. Its customized solutions help business clients reduce inventory costs, increase transaction speed, and improve sales by implementing customer requirements more efficiently. But the company also works directly with consumers: its Shop & Ship service allows people in the Arab world to enjoy the benefits of shopping online from U.S. and U.K. websites, offering a personal mailing address in the United States or the United Kingdom, where customers can receive correspondence and packages. Aramex then forwards the account contents to the client at competitive rates.

Aramex's success would not have been possible without its deep understanding of the needs and requirements of both its business and consumer markets.[1]

Some of the world's and the region's most valuable brands belong to business marketers: Caterpillar, DuPont, FedEx, General Electric, Hewlett-Packard, IBM, Intel, and Siemens to name a few. Similarly, some of the Arab world's top brands also cater to businesses: Aramex (delivery and express services), SABIC (metals, chemicals, and plastic), ARAMCO (oil and gas), Promoseven (advertising), Zamil (steel and air conditioning), and Dar Al Handasah (engineering consultants). Many principles of basic marketing also apply to business marketers. They need to embrace holistic marketing principles, such as building strong relationships with their customers, just like any marketer. But they also face some unique considerations in selling to other businesses. In this chapter, we will highlight some of the crucial similarities and differences for marketing in business markets.[2] ▽

Bridgestone Tire Company exemplifies a supplier that generates good business from fewer, but larger, business buyers.

What Is Organizational Buying?

Webster and Wind define **organizational buying** as the decision-making process by which formal organizations establish the need for purchased products and services and identify, evaluate, and choose among alternative brands and suppliers.[3]

The Business Market versus the Consumer Market

The **business market** consists of all the organizations that acquire goods and services used in the production of other products or services that are sold, rented, or supplied to others. The major industries making up the business market are agriculture, forestry, and fisheries; mining; manufacturing; construction; transportation; communication; public utilities; banking, finance, and insurance; distribution; and services.

organizational buying the decision-making process by which formal organizations establish the need for purchased products and services and identify, evaluate, and choose among alternative brands and suppliers.

business market all the organizations that acquire goods and services used in the production of other products or services that are sold, rented, or supplied to others.

More money and items change hands in sales to business buyers than to consumers. Consider the process of producing and selling a simple pair of shoes. Animal skin dealers must sell them to tanners to process them into leather, who in turn sell leather to shoe manufacturers, who sell shoes to wholesalers, who sell shoes to retailers, who finally sell them to consumers. Each party in the supply chain also buys many other goods and services to support their operations.

Business marketers face many of the same challenges as consumer marketers. In particular, understanding their customers and what they value is of top importance to both.[4] Business marketers, however, have several characteristics that contrast sharply with those of consumer markets:

- *Fewer, larger buyers.* The business marketer normally deals with far fewer, much larger buyers than the consumer marketer does, particularly in such industries as aircraft engines and defense weapons. The fate of companies such as Goodyear Tire Company, Bridgestone, Michelin Tires, and other automotive part suppliers depends on getting contracts from just a handful of major automakers. It is also true, however, that as a slowing economy affects the purchases of large corporations, the small and midsize business market is offering new opportunities for suppliers.[5] See the Marketing Insight: *Big Sales to Small Business* for more on this important business-to-business (B2B) market.

- *Close supplier–customer relationship.* Because of the smaller customer base and the importance and power of the larger customers, suppliers are frequently expected to customize their offerings to individual business customer needs.

Cisco   Cisco, the network communications equipment manufacturer, leads the market in the switches and routers that direct traffic on the internet. The company sought growth by directing considerable research and marketing resources at an underserved market: small and medium-sized business (SMB) customers, which the company defined as businesses with fewer than 250 employees.[6] To better understand buyer behavior, Cisco conducted customer research that segmented the overall SMB market into four tiers by networking expenditure and purchase patterns. Tier-1 and tier-2 companies, who view networking as the core of their business, make up 30 percent of the SMB space, but account for 75 percent of total networking expenditures. Tier-3 and tier-4 companies make up 70 percent of the market, but are hesitant to invest heavily in networking technology. Based on this understanding of the market, Cisco was able to target these segments with products and services designed specifically for them. It developed a program called the Smart Business Roadmap that matched common business issues faced by SMB customer types with long-term technology solutions. One of these solutions was Linksys One, a hosted communications service offering telephone, video, data, and internet networking on one high-speed connection that debuted in 2005. Overall, Cisco raised its research and development (R&D) budget for the SMB market to US$2 billion and directed 40 percent of its total marketing expenditure toward this market. The program generated 22 percent growth in Cisco's business with SMBs.

Business buyers often select suppliers who also buy from them. A paper manufacturer might buy from a chemical company that buys a considerable amount of its paper.

- *Professional purchasing.* Business goods are often purchased by trained purchasing agents, who must follow their organizations' purchasing policies, constraints, and requirements. Many of the buying instruments—for example, requests for quotations, proposals, and purchase contracts— are not typically found in consumer buying. Professional buyers spend their careers learning how to buy better and increase their effectiveness and status. This means that business marketers must provide greater technical data about their product and its advantages over competitors' products.

- *Multiple buying influences.* More people typically influence business buying decisions. Buying committees consisting of technical experts and even senior management are common in the purchase of major goods. Business marketers need to send well-trained sales representatives and sales teams to deal with these well-trained buyers.

Marketing Insight

Big Sales to Small Business

Small and medium-size businesses are the backbone of the economic activity in any community. With technological and communication innovations and the possibilities that it offers, and with increased entrepreneurial spirit among young up-and-coming business hopefuls, more and more small-size businesses are being established by the day.

Small and medium-size businesses present enormous opportunities as well as huge challenges. The market is large and fragmented by industry, size, and number of years in operation. Small-business owners are notably averse to long-range planning and have an 'I'll buy it when I need it' decision-making style. Here are some guidelines for selling to small businesses:

- *Don't lump small and midsize businesses together.* There's a big gap between US$1 million in revenue and $50 million, or between a start-up with 10 employees and a more mature business with 100.

- *Don't waste their time.* That means no cold calls, entertaining sales shows, or sales pitches over long lavish lunches.

- *Do keep it simple.* Simplicity means one point of contact with a supplier for all service problems, or one bill for all services and products.

- *Do use the internet.* Time-strapped small-business decision makers prefer to buy, or at least research, products and services online. It would be a good idea to design a site targeted to small and midsize businesses, and pull visitors through extensive advertising, direct mail, e-mail campaigns, catalogs, and events.

- *Don't forget about direct contact.* Even if a small business owner's first point of contact is via the internet, you still need to offer phone or face contact.

- *Do provide support after the sale.* Small businesses want partners, not pitchmen. Think about building long-term business relationships, rather than concluding an immediate sales transaction.

- *Do your homework.* The realities of small or midsize business management are different from those of a large corporation. It is pertinent to know and understand the profile and challenges faced by these businesses to be able to cater to them.

Sources: Based on Barnaby J. Feder, "When Goliath Comes Knocking on David's Door," *New York Times*, May 6, 2003; Jay Greene, "Small Biz: Microsoft's Next Big Thing?," *BusinessWeek*, April 21, 2003, pp. 72–73; Jennifer Gilbert, "Small but Mighty," *Sales & Marketing Management*, January 2004, pp. 30–35; Verne Kopytoff, "Businesses Click on eBay," *San Francisco Chronicle*, July 28, 2003; Matt Krantz, "Firms Jump on the eBay Wagon," *USA Today*, May 3, 2004.

- *Multiple sales calls.* A study by McGraw-Hill found that it takes four to four-and-a-half calls to close an average industrial sale. In the case of capital equipment sales for large projects, it may take many attempts to fund a project, and the sales cycle—between quoting a job and delivering the product—is often measured in years.[7]

- *Derived demand.* The demand for business goods is ultimately derived from the demand for consumer goods. For this reason, the business marketer must closely monitor the buying patterns of ultimate consumers. For instance, automakers have driven the boom in demand for steel-bar products. Much of that demand in turn is derived from the sustained growth in sales of minivans and other light trucks, which consume far more steel than cars. Business buyers must also pay close attention to current and expected economic factors, such as the level of production, investment, consumer spending, and the interest rate. In a recession, they reduce their investment in plant, equipment, and inventories. Business marketers can do little to stimulate total demand in this environment. They can only fight harder to increase or maintain their share of the demand. The first part of the last decade was characterized by an economic boom that carried with it major business opportunities for multinational, regional, and local Arab companies, large and small alike. The construction industry in the Arab Gulf states offers a great example. Increased wealth carried with it increased demand for real estate for household use (villas, homes, and apartments), business use (offices, warehouses, and retail outlets), and public use (government buildings and infrastructure projects). That generated a major construction boom and unprecedented demand for contracting and engineering services and construction material. The trend was reversed with the severe downturn that hit the global and regional markets in the latter part of the decade.

- *Inelastic demand.* The total demand for many business goods and services is inelastic; that is, not much affected by price changes. Shoe manufacturers are not going to buy much more leather if the price of leather falls, nor will they buy much less leather if the price rises, unless they can find satisfactory substitutes. Demand is especially inelastic in the short run because producers cannot make quick changes in production methods. Demand is also inelastic for business goods that represent a small percentage of the item's total cost, such as shoelaces.

- *Fluctuating demand.* The demand for business goods and services tends to be more volatile and unpredictable than the demand for consumer goods and services. A given percentage increase in consumer demand can lead to a much larger percentage increase in the demand for plant and equipment necessary to produce the additional output. Economists refer to this as the *acceleration effect.* Sometimes a rise of only 10 percent in consumer demand can cause as much as a 200 percent rise in business demand for products in the next period; a 10 percent fall in consumer demand may cause a complete collapse in business demand. The real estate boom in Dubai in the early part of the 2000 decade, and the real estate bust as a result of the economic downturn in the latter part of the decade, are examples of such an acceleration effect.

- *Geographically concentrated buyers.* Across the Arab world, business buyers generally tend to be concentrated in capital and other major cities. Another major area of concentration is in industrial/trade zones and business parks, which gained popularity across many Arab countries as governments sought to attract foreign business investments.

The boom that the economies of the region witnessed in the early part of the last decade generated a major construction boom, and unprecedented demand for contracting and engineering services and construction materials. Real estate then suffered from the severe economic downturn at the end of the decade.

The geographical concentration of businesses helps to reduce sales-related costs. At the same time, business marketers need to monitor regional shifts in geographic concentration of certain industries.

- **Direct purchasing.** Business buyers often buy directly from manufacturers rather than through intermediaries, especially items that are technically complex or expensive, such as mainframes or aircraft.

Buying Situations

The business buyer faces many decisions in making a purchase. The number depends on the buying situation: complexity of the problem being solved, newness of the buying requirement, number of people involved, and time required. Three types of buying situations are the straight rebuy, modified rebuy, and new task.[8]

STRAIGHT REBUY In a straight rebuy, the purchasing department reorders supplies such as office supplies and bulk chemicals on a routine basis and chooses from suppliers on an approved list. The suppliers make an effort to maintain product and service quality and often propose automatic reordering systems to save time. 'Out-suppliers' attempt to offer something new or to exploit dissatisfaction with a current supplier. Their goal is to get a small order and then increase their purchase share over time.

MODIFIED REBUY In a modified rebuy, the buyer wants to modify product specifications, prices, delivery requirements, or other terms. The modified rebuy usually involves additional participants on both sides. The in-suppliers become nervous and want to protect the account. The out-suppliers see an opportunity to propose a better offer to gain some business.

NEW TASK In a new task, a purchaser buys a product or service for the first time (an office building, a new security system). The greater the cost or risk, the larger the number of participants and the greater their information gathering, and therefore the longer the time to a decision.[9]

The business buyer makes the fewest decisions in the straight rebuy situation and the most in the new-task situation. Over time, new-buy situations become straight rebuys and routine purchase behavior.

New-task buying is the marketer's greatest opportunity and challenge. The process passes through several stages: awareness, interest, evaluation, trial, and adoption.[10] Mass media can be most important during the initial awareness stage; salespeople often have their greatest impact at the interest stage; and technical sources can be most important during the evaluation stage.

In the new-task situation, the buyer must determine product specifications, price limits, delivery terms and times, service terms, payment terms, order quantities, acceptable suppliers, and the selected supplier. Different participants influence each decision, and the order in which these decisions are made varies.

Because of the complicated selling involved, many companies use a *missionary sales force* consisting of their most effective salespeople. The brand promise and the manufacturer's brand name recognition will be important in establishing trust and the customer's willingness to consider change.[11] The marketer also tries to reach as many key participants as possible and provide helpful information and assistance.

Once a customer is acquired, in-suppliers are continually seeking ways to add value to their market offer to facilitate rebuys.

RIC Rapid Impact Compaction (RIC) is an innovative ground-improvement technique that provides engineers with a more cost-effective means of dealing with poorly compacted or loose soils. RIC uses drop-weights of 5 to 12 tonnes. The drop-weight is dropped onto a special foot assembly 40 to 60 times a minute.

RIC is twice as fast and at least 40 percent cheaper than other methods of soil treatment, which is great news for engineers and contractors. In particular, Arab entrepreneurs saw an opportunity for RIC application in the Arab Gulf countries, where contractors and engineers have to deal with challenging soils. The main challenge was to create awareness among Arab contractors and engineers about RIC technology and its benefits, reports Annelie Moukaddem, board member of Rapid Impact Compaction Contracting LLC (a UAE-based company), and RIC's marketing expert. "We had to be proactive, and take initiative," says Moukaddem. "We participated in several regional engineering and contracting professional exhibits. We literally knocked on doors of the major contractors in the region, and introduced the RIC technology. We developed detailed brochures which highlighted the technical aspects of RIC, and the benefits that it offers over other conventional methods of soil treatment, not only in terms of speed and cost, but also in terms of quality assurance, improved control, and safety. We profiled some of RIC's major worldwide projects, and the feedback from contractors, site engineers, and end users with respect to their satisfaction with the RIC technology."[12] In just a little over two years the company has been quite successful in securing several multimillion dollar projects in the Gulf Cooperation Council (GCC) countries, including the Cultural Village Project in Doha, Qatar, and Palm Island in Dubai, UAE.[13]

Customers considering paying millions of dollars on one transaction for expensive goods and services want all the information they can get. One way to entice new buyers is to create a customer reference program in which satisfied existing customers act in accordance with the company's sales and marketing department by agreeing to serve as references. Technology companies such as HP, Lucent, and Unisys have all employed such programs. The Marketing Memo: *Maximizing Customer References* provides some tips for developing activities and programs with impact.

Systems Buying and Selling

Many business buyers prefer to buy a total solution to a problem from one seller. Called *systems buying*, this practice originated with government purchases of major weapons and communications systems. The government would solicit bids from *prime contractors*, who assembled the

---

marketing Memo

Maximizing Customer References

Many firms depend on the opinions and experiences of others in evaluating a new business proposal from a new company. Here is some industry wisdom as to what works and doesn't work when developing customer information and reference programs to respond to these demands.

Five Common Mistakes in Developing Customer Reference Stories

1. *Failing to state the customer's need and its implications with specificity.* Clearly state why customers had a need and how the company's products resolved it. Such detailed information can better allow salespeople to assess whether a prospect has similar needs and could obtain similar pay-offs.

2. *Failing to quantify your customer's results.* Although outside companies may seem reluctant to share too much hard data, it may just reflect the fact that they don't have the information readily accessible. Assist them in getting it.

3. *Failing to describe business benefits of any kind (quantified or not).* Don't focus on your expertise in various technologies and industries without telling how it specifically helped customers to enter or grow markets. Make an obvious cause-and-effect link between the solution provided and the claims for your product.

4. *Failing to differentiate your offerings from competition.* Make it clear why it was the case that not just any company's products or services could have led to the same solution.

5. *Failing to provide a concise, accessible summary of the story.* Make sure you package the customer reference story in a way that a prospect can easily and quickly understand. Here are seven ways to do so.

Seven Keys to Successfully Developing Customer Reference Stories

1. State the customer's needs in compelling terms.

2. Emphasize the barriers to satisfying customer needs.

3. Describe your company's solution in terms of value.

4. List quantified results, especially those that affect return on investment.

5. Differentiate your offering from those of competitors.

6. Provide a brief comprehensive summary.

7. Include numerous customer quotes.

Source: Based on Bill Lee, "Success Stories: The Top 5 Mistakes," www.lee-communications.com/.

package or system. The contractor who was awarded the contract would be responsible for bidding out and assembling the system's subcomponents from *second-tier contractors*. The prime contractor would thus provide a 'turnkey solution,' so-called because the buyer simply had to turn one key to get the job done.

Sellers have increasingly recognized that buyers like to purchase in this way, and many have adopted systems selling as a marketing tool. One variant of systems selling is *systems contracting*, where a single supplier provides the buyer with his entire requirement of maintenance, repair, and operating supplies. During the contract period, the supplier manages the customer's inventory. For example, Shell Oil manages the oil inventory of many of its business customers and knows when it requires replenishment. The customer benefits from reduced procurement and management costs and from price protection over the term of the contract. The seller benefits from lower operating costs because of a steady demand and reduced paperwork.

Systems selling is a key industrial marketing strategy in bidding to build large-scale industrial projects, such as dams, steel factories, irrigation systems, sanitation systems, pipelines, utilities, and even new towns. Project engineering firms must compete on price, quality, reliability, and other attributes to win contracts. With systems selling, customers present potential suppliers with a list of project specifications and requirements. Suppliers, however, are not just at the mercy of these customer demands. Ideally, they're involved with customers early in the process to influence the actual development of the specifications. Or they can go beyond the specifications to offer additional value in various ways, as the following examples show.

Japan and Indonesia   The Indonesian government requested bids to build a cement factory near Jakarta. A U.S. firm made a proposal that included choosing the site, designing the cement factory, hiring the construction crews, assembling the materials and equipment, and turning over the finished factory to the Indonesian government. A Japanese firm, in outlining its proposal, included all these services, plus hiring and training the workers to run the factory, exporting the cement through its trading companies, and using the cement to build roads and new office buildings in Jakarta. Although the Japanese proposal involved more money, it won the contract. Clearly, the Japanese viewed the problem not just as one of building a cement factory (the narrow view of systems selling) but as one of contributing to Indonesia's economic development. They took the broadest view of the customer's needs. This is true systems selling.

Saudi Oger   Saudi Oger Ltd is a construction company based in Riyadh, Saudi Arabia. Since being formed in 1978, it has become one of the leading construction, facilities management, and infrastructure project development companies in the Kingdom and the region, growing quickly into a multicompany, multidivisional organization. Today, its business covers construction, facilities management, real estate development, printing, telecommunication, utilities, and IT services. The company employs thousands of skilled and professional workers, whose expertise covers and supports every aspect of its business.[14]

Participants in the Business Buying Process

Who buys the trillions of dollars' worth of goods and services needed by business organizations? Purchasing agents are influential in straight-rebuy and modified-rebuy situations, whereas other department personnel are more influential in new-buy situations. Engineering personnel usually have a major influence in selecting product components, and purchasing agents dominate in selecting suppliers.[15,16]

The Buying Center

Webster and Wind call the decision-making unit of a buying organization *the buying center*. It consists of "all those individuals and groups who participate in the purchasing decision-making process, who share some common goals and the risks arising from the decisions."[17] The buying center includes all members of the organization who play any of seven roles in the purchase decision process.

1. *Initiators.* Users or others in the organization who request that something be purchased.
2. *Users.* Those who will use the product or service. In many cases, the users initiate the buying proposal and help define the product requirements.
3. *Influencers.* People who influence the buying decision, often by helping define specifications and providing information for evaluating alternatives. Technical personnel are particularly important influencers.
4. *Deciders.* People who decide on product requirements or on suppliers.
5. *Approvers.* People who authorize the proposed actions of deciders or buyers.
6. *Buyers.* People who have formal authority to select the supplier and arrange the purchase terms. Buyers may help shape product specifications, but they play their major role in selecting vendors and negotiating. In more complex purchases, buyers might include high-level managers.
7. *Gatekeepers.* People who have the power to prevent sellers or information from reaching members of the buying center. For example, purchasing agents, receptionists, and telephone operators may prevent salespersons from contacting users or deciders.

Several people can occupy a given role such as user or influencer, and one person may occupy multiple roles.[18] A purchasing manager, for example, often occupies the roles of buyer, influencer, and gatekeeper simultaneously: she can determine which sales reps can call on other people in the organization; what budget and other constraints to place on the purchase; and which firm will actually get the business, even though others (deciders) might select two or more potential vendors that can meet the company's requirements.

The typical buying center has a minimum of five or six members and often has dozens. Some may be outside the organization, such as government officials, consultants, technical advisors, and other members of the marketing channel. With increased concern over sound corporate governance, transparency, and fraud detection one can see a trend in expanding the role, size, and composition of buying centers. One study found that 3.5 more people on average were involved in making a purchase decision in 2005 than in 2001.[19]

Buying Center Influences

Buying centers usually include several participants with differing interests, authority, status, and persuasiveness and sometimes very different decision criteria. For example, engineering personnel may want to maximize the performance of the product; production personnel may want ease of use and reliability of supply; financial personnel focus on the economics of the purchase; purchasing may be concerned with operating and replacement costs; union officials may emphasize safety issues.

Business buyers also have personal motivations, perceptions, and preferences that are influenced by their age, income, education, job position, personality, attitudes toward risk, and culture. Buyers definitely exhibit different buying styles. There are 'keep-it-simple' buyers, 'own-expert' buyers, 'want-the-best' buyers, and 'want-everything-done' buyers. Some younger, highly educated buyers are computer experts who conduct rigorous analyses of competitive proposals before choosing a supplier. Other buyers are 'toughies' from the old school who get the sellers to compete against one another so that they get the best deal. One leading Arab hospital even devised a new role, 'bid nego-tiator,' whose main responsibility is to re-negotiate the terms of the bid with companies after they actually win the tender bid with a view to reducing the price. The post saved the hospital hundreds of thousands of dollars during the first year of implementation.

General Motors   Every year Bo I. Andersson, General Motors' vice president of global purchasing, is charged with cutting US$2 billion from GM's purchasing bill. A former Swedish army officer, Andersson is a hands-on individual who buys $85 billion worth of wheels, axles, seats, bolts, and other parts in a purchasing bill that ranks among the highest by a business entity in the world. Yet, he isn't focused so much on squeezing suppliers as he is on squeezing inefficiencies out of the system, such as getting GM's vehicles to share more parts. At one point in time, GM used to make 26 versions of seat frames, whereas Toyota made 2. Still, Andersson does not suffer inefficiency from suppliers. If they don't meet his standards, he will drop them even if it means forcing them into bankruptcy. In 2006, for instance, he decided to get rid of 3,200 suppliers. Perhaps that's why GM ranked last in an annual supplier satisfaction survey![20]

Webster cautions that ultimately individuals, not organizations, make purchasing decisions.[21] Individuals are motivated by their own needs and perceptions in attempting to maximize the rewards (pay, advancement, recognition, and feelings of achievement) offered by the organization. Personal needs motivate the behavior of individuals, but organizational needs justify the buying-decision process and its outcomes. People are not buying 'products.' They are buying solutions to two problems: the organization's economic and strategic problem and their own personal need for individual achievement and reward. In this sense, industrial buying decisions are both 'rational' and 'emotional,' as they serve both the organization's and the individual's needs.[22]

For example, research conducted by one industrial component manufacturer found that although top executives at small and medium-size companies stated they were comfortable in general with buying from other companies, they appeared to have subconscious insecurities about buying the manufacturer's product. Constant changes in technology had left them concerned about the internal effects within the company. Recognizing this unease, the manufacturer retooled its selling approach to emphasize more emotional appeals and how its product line actually enabled the customer's employees to improve their performance, relieving management of the complications and stress with component use.[23]

Recognizing these extrinsic, interpersonal influences, more industrial firms have put greater emphasis on strengthening their corporate brand. At one time, Emerson Electric, a global provider of power tools, compressors, electrical equipment, and engineering solutions, was a conglomerate of 60 independent—and sometimes anonymous—companies. A new Chief Marketing Officer (CMO) aligned the previously independent brands under a new global brand architecture and identity, allowing Emerson to achieve a broader presence so that it could sell locally while leveraging its global brand name. Record sales and stock price highs soon followed.[24] Similarly, SABB (formerly known as Saudi British Bank) provides a wide range of business services under a single brand, which is advertised in business magazines and in airports.

Buying Center Targeting

To target their efforts properly, business marketers need to figure out: Who are the major decision participants? What decisions do they influence? What is their level of influence? What evaluation criteria do they use? Consider the following example.

A company sells nonwoven disposable surgical gowns to hospitals. The hospital personnel who participate in this buying decision include the vice president of purchasing, the operating-room administrator, and the surgeons. The vice president of purchasing analyzes whether the hospital should buy disposable gowns or reusable gowns. If the findings favor disposable gowns, then the operating-room administrator compares various competitors' products and prices and makes a choice. This administrator considers the characteristics and quality of the gowns (such as absorbency, antiseptic quality, design) and their cost and normally buys the brand that meets the functional requirements at the lowest cost. Surgeons also influence the decision indirectly by reporting their satisfaction with the particular brand.

The business marketer is not likely to know exactly what kind of group dynamics take place during the decision process, although whatever information he can obtain about personalities and interpersonal factors is useful.

Small sellers concentrate on reaching the *key buying influencers*. Larger sellers go for *multi-level in-depth selling* to reach as many participants as possible. Their salespeople virtually 'live' with high-volume customers. Companies must rely more heavily on their communications programs to reach hidden buying influencers and keep current customers informed.[25] The example below illustrates how the German industrial group Karl Storz attempts to identify and target key buying influencers to expand its share in the Arab region.

 Karl Storz   Karl Storz is a German manufacturer of remote visual inspection (RVI) equipment, used for the nondestructive inspection of machinery and mechanical systems. RVI equipment is widely used across many industries, including civil and military aviation and aerospace, oil and gas, power generation, quality control, and security. Karl Storz's regional offices cover the Middle East and North Africa region and the United Kingdom, with offices in Lebanon, Saudi Arabia, the UAE, Egypt, Algeria, Pakistan, Turkey, and the United Kingdom. Bilal Itani, Director of Karl Storz operations in the region, uses the following marketing tools to promote their industrial line of products:

1. *Prospecting*: coordinators and sales engineers run daily searches over the net for new customers. Brochures and technical data are mailed to potential customers in the region to introduce the product and instigate interest.

2. *Attending conferences and exhibitions*: Storz staff attend international air shows, oil, gas and power exhibitions, and quality assurance and security shows.

3. *Conducting seminars*: these are arranged by invitation for potential regional clients from these industries.

4. *Demonstration visits*: the nature of Storz products requires hands-on demonstration for customers to realize the benefits and the user-friendly operation of the equipment.

Itani also stresses the importance of after-sales service. "After concluding the sale and delivery of equipment, we provide a 1–2 day office training in our training center, in our branch offices, or on the customer's site," says Itani. Storz also offers a 2-year manufacturer warranty against defects. "If any Storz product gets damaged, we provide the customer with a loaner unit to work with while we repair their equipment in our headquarters. The loaner unit is offered free of charge."[26]

Business marketers must periodically review their assumptions about buying center participants. For years, Kodak sold X-ray film to hospital lab technicians, but research indicated that professional administrators were increasingly making purchasing decisions. As a result, Kodak revised its marketing strategy and developed new advertising to reach out to these decision makers.

The Purchasing/ Procurement Process

In principle, business buyers seek to obtain the highest benefit package (economic, technical, service, and social) in relation to a market offering's costs. To make comparisons, they will try to translate all costs and benefits into monetary terms. A business buyer's incentive to purchase will be a function of the difference between perceived benefits and perceived costs.[27] The marketer's task is to construct a profitable offering that delivers superior customer value to the target buyers.

Supplier diversity is a benefit that may not have a price tag but that business buyers overlook at their risk. Large and small companies alike see having a diverse supplier base as a critical factor in securing the resources and supplies needed for their operations, and, ultimately, for their business success.

Purchasing Department Perceptions

In the past, purchasing departments occupied a low position in the management hierarchy, in spite of often managing more than half the company's costs. Recent competitive pressures have led many companies to upgrade their purchasing departments and elevate administrators to vice presidential rank. These new, more strategically oriented purchasing departments have a mission to seek the best value from fewer and better suppliers. Some multinationals have even elevated them to 'strategic supply departments' with responsibility for global sourcing and partnering. At Caterpillar, for example, purchasing, inventory control, production scheduling, and traffic have been combined into one department. Fast-food giant McDonald's also offers a good example of how business buying practices can be improved.

 McDonald's   As director of global technology supplier management for McDonald's, Joseph Youssef's mandate is to segment and measure suppliers and then manage them based on the measurements. And Youssef oversees only one aspect of McDonald's huge supplier base: its IT services and equipment. As McDonald's began to see positive results from applying its supplier relationship management methods to one of its IT suppliers, it extended the strategy to its other IT contracts, such as its network systems and its restaurant point-of-sale systems. McDonald's will now go on to apply supplier management strategies to its indirect materials suppliers.[28]

The upgrading of purchasing means that business marketers must upgrade their sales personnel to match the higher caliber of the business buyers.

Purchasing Organization and Administration

Most purchasing professionals describe their jobs as more strategic, technical, and team-oriented, and involving more responsibility than ever before. Sixty-one percent of buyers surveyed said the buying group was more involved in new-product design and development than it was 5 years ago; and more than half the buyers participate in cross-functional teams, with suppliers well represented.[29]

Some companies have started to centralize purchasing. Headquarters identifies materials purchased by several divisions and buys them centrally, gaining more purchasing power. For the business marketer, this development means dealing with fewer and higher-level buyers and using a national account sales group to deal with large corporate buyers. At the same time, companies are decentralizing some purchasing operations by empowering employees to purchase small-ticket low-priced items, such as special stationery; coffee, tea and refreshments; personal computer accessories (such as CDs, DVDs, and flash drives); or religious holiday office decorations, in cash, through corporate credit cards, or with credit line arrangements from suppliers.

Stages in the Buying Process

We're ready to describe the general stages in the business buying-decision process. Robinson and his associates identified eight stages and called them *buyphases*.[30] The model in 🖾 **Table 7.1** is the *buygrid* framework.

In modified-rebuy or straight-rebuy situations, some stages are compressed or bypassed. For example, the buyer normally has a favorite supplier or a ranked list of suppliers and can skip the search and proposal solicitation stages. Here are some important considerations in each of the eight stages.

Problem Recognition

The buying process begins when someone in the company recognizes a problem or need that can be met by acquiring a good or service. The recognition can be triggered by internal or

| TABLE 7.1 ▢ | Buygrid Framework: Major Stages (Buyphases) of the Industrial Buying Process in Relation to Major Buying Situations (Buyclasses) |

		Buyclasses		
		New Task	Modified Rebuy	Straight Rebuy
	1. Problem Recognition	Yes	Maybe	No
	2. General Need Description	Yes	Maybe	No
	3. Product Specification	Yes	Yes	Yes
Buyphases	4. Supplier Search	Yes	Maybe	No
	5. Proposal Solicitation	Yes	Maybe	No
	6. Supplier Selection	Yes	Maybe	No
	7. Order-Routine Specification	Yes	Maybe	No
	8. Performance Review	Yes	Yes	Yes

external stimuli. Internal stimuli might be that the company decides to develop a new product and needs new equipment and materials; or a machine breaks down and requires new parts; or purchased material turns out to be unsatisfactory and the company searches for another supplier; or lower prices; or better quality. Externally, the buyer may get new ideas at a trade show, see an ad, or receives a call from a sales representative who offers a better product or a lower price. Business marketers can stimulate problem recognition by direct mail, telemarketing, and calling on prospects.

General Need Description and Product Specification

Next, the buyer determines the needed item's general characteristics and required quantity. For standard items, this is simple. For complex items, the buyer will work with others—engineers, users—to define characteristics such as reliability, durability, or price. Business marketers can help by describing how their products meet or even exceed the buyer's needs.

The buying organization now develops the item's technical specifications. Often, the company will assign a product-value-analysis engineering team to the project. *Product value analysis* (PVA) is an approach to cost reduction that studies components to determine whether they can be redesigned or standardized or made by cheaper methods of production. The PVA team will identify overdesigned components, for instance, that last longer than the product itself. Tightly written specifications will allow the buyer to refuse components that are too expensive or that fail to meet specified standards. Suppliers can use product value analysis as a tool for positioning themselves to win an account.

Supplier Search

The buyer next tries to identify the most appropriate suppliers through trade directories, contacts with other companies, trade advertisements, trade shows, and the internet.[31] The move to internet purchasing has far-reaching implications for suppliers and will change the shape of purchasing for years to come.[32] Companies that purchase over the internet are utilizing electronic marketplaces in several forms.

- *Catalog sites.* Companies can order thousands of items through electronic catalogs. For example, through its paper and online catalogs, EZ Order (www.ezorder.com.lb) supplies a wide range of office stationery, office furniture, and office equipment at competitive prices and with a one-business-day delivery service.

- **Vertical markets.** Companies buying industrial products such as plastics, steel, chemicals, or services such as logistics or media can go to specialized websites (called e-hubs). For example, Plastics.com allows plastics buyers to search for the best prices among thousands of plastics sellers.

- **Auction and tender information sites.** Online marketplaces such as eBay, mazadmall.com, and salaamtrade.com could not have been realized without the internet. Business-focused websites such as METenders.com provide project intelligence and tender information in the Arab world, helping companies to locate business opportunities and market their products.

- **Spot (or exchange) markets.** On spot electronic markets, prices change by the minute. ChemConnect.com is an exchange for buyers and sellers of bulk chemicals such as benzene, and it's a B2B success in an arena littered with failed online exchanges. First to market, it is now the biggest online exchange for chemical trading, with 1 million barrels traded daily. ExpoArabia.com operates business-to-business online, providing a platform for businesses across 23 industries to participate in more than 200 trade networks.

- **Private exchanges.** Hewlett-Packard, IBM, and Walmart operate private exchanges to link with specially invited groups of suppliers and partners over the internet.

- **Barter markets.** In barter markets, participants offer to trade goods or services.

- **Buying alliances.** Some companies buying the same goods join together to form purchasing groups (called consortia) to gain deeper discounts on volume purchases.

Online business buying offers several advantages: it shaves transaction costs for both buyers and suppliers, reduces time between order and delivery, consolidates purchasing systems, and forges more direct relationships between partners and buyers. On the downside, it may help to erode supplier–buyer loyalty and create potential security problems.

E-PROCUREMENT Websites are organized around two types of e-hub: *vertical hubs* centered on industries (plastics, steel, chemicals, paper) and *functional hubs* (logistics, media buying, advertising, energy management). In addition to using these websites, companies can use e-procurement in other ways:

- **Set up direct extranet links to major suppliers.** For example, a company can set up a direct e-procurement account at the Dell computer company or the Office Depot office supplies chain, and its employees can make their purchases this way.

- **Form buying alliances.** A number of major retailers and manufacturers such as Coca-Cola, Colgate Palmolive, Johnson & Johnson, Kraft, Nestlé, Office Depot, PepsiCo, and Procter & Gamble are part of a data-sharing alliance called 1SYNC. Several auto companies (GM, Ford, DaimlerChrysler) formed Covisint for the same reason. Covisint is the leading provider of services that can integrate crucial business information and processes between partners, customers, and suppliers. The company has now also targeted health care to provide similar services.

- **Set up company buying sites.** General Electric formed the Trading Process Network (TPN), where it posts *requests for proposals* (RFPs), negotiates terms, and places orders.

Moving into e-procurement means more than acquiring software; it requires changing purchasing strategy and structure. However, the benefits are many: aggregating purchasing across multiple departments yields larger, centrally negotiated volume discounts, a smaller purchasing staff, and less buying of substandard goods from outside the approved list of suppliers. The following case study discusses Tejari, which offers an e-procurement platform used by businesses.

Tejari   Established in June 2000 by Sheikha Lubna Al-Qasimi, Tejari has become the number one B2B e-commerce hub for businesses in the Arab region. Tejari enables business buyers and sellers to share information about their goods and services via a secure internet environment. "We have brought global best practices and changed the face of how business in this region is conducted," says Tejari CEO, Suhail Al Banna. He adds that "in 2008 transactions on the Tejari marketplace crossed the US$7.7 billion mark. That's an amazing achievement in itself, but we have only just begun."

Finding new business is one of the major challenges for many organizations, particularly in the emerging economies of the Arab world. Tejari's procurement platforms provide its members with a sophisticated matchmaking service, by integrating companies into a global online marketplace and connecting them with over 200,000 potential businesses. Tejari's clients include businesses from various industries: airlines (such as Emirates Airline, Etihad Airways, Oman Air), banks (such as Kuwait's NBK, Emirates NDB, Bank Muscat), telecom companies (such as Oman Mobile, Omantel, Zain Jordan), government and public organizations (such as Dubai Government, Dubai Airports, Oman Ministry of Fisheries), and other industries. In 2009, Tejari was ranked the eighth largest electronic sourcing platform in the world by Forrester Research.[33]

LEAD GENERATION   The supplier's task is to ensure it is considered when customers are—or could be—in the market and searching for a supplier. Identifying good leads and converting them to sales requires the whole marketing and sales organizations in a company to work in a coordinated, multichannel approach in the role of trusted advisor to prospective customers. Marketing must work together with sales to define what makes a 'sales-ready' prospect and cooperate to send the right messages via sales calls, tradeshows, online activities, PR, events, direct mail, and referrals.[34]

To proactively generate leads, suppliers need to know about their customers. They can obtain background details from information service providers such as Zawya.com.

Zawya.com   Zawya is a leading Middle East business information and financial intelligence company serving the high-end business and financial professional community. Zawya has sales and support offices in the UAE, Lebanon, Kuwait, Malaysia, and Singapore, serving a global user base of over 212,000 business professionals. Zawya covers detailed information on the top 15,000 companies in the Middle East with comprehensive live news coverage through the exclusive Zawya Dow Jones newswire service. The service provides industry news, macroeconomic reports, country statistics, and stock market data as well as specialized databases such as IPO, Sukuk, and Private Equity monitors. In addition to subscription services, Zawya offers advertisers the ability to target an affluent online audience with an interest in the MENA region. Zawya's online service caters to and attracts serious professional users and decision makers with its fee paying user base. Some of Zawya's prominent clients include: the Abu Dhabi Investment Authority (ADIA), Merrill Lynch, Morgan Stanley, HSBC, Deutsche Bank, ABN Amro, Shuaa Capital, Arab Banking Corporation, Emaar, McKinsey & Co, Ernst & Young, Standard & Poor's, KPMG, Booz & Co, the U.S. Treasury, the United Nations (ESCWA), the World Bank (IFC), BMW Middle East, and American Express.[35]

Zawya is a leading business information company serving the high-end business and financial professional community.

Suppliers that lack the required production capacity or suffer from a poor reputation will be rejected. Those who qualify may be visited by the buyer's agents, who will examine the suppliers' manufacturing facilities and meet their personnel. After evaluating each company, the buyer will end up with a short list of qualified suppliers. Many professional buyers have forced suppliers to change their marketing to increase their likelihood of being considered.

Proposal Solicitation

The buyer next invites qualified suppliers to submit proposals. If the item is complex or expensive, the buyer will require a detailed written proposal from each qualified supplier. After evaluating the proposals, the buyer will invite a few suppliers to make formal presentations.

Business marketers must be skilled in researching, writing, and presenting proposals. Written proposals should be marketing documents that describe value and benefits in customer terms. Oral presentations must inspire confidence and position the company's capabilities and resources so they stand out from the competition. Proposals and selling are often team efforts.

Supplier Selection

Before selecting a supplier, the buying center will specify desired supplier attributes and indicate their relative importance. To rate and identify the most attractive suppliers, buying centers often use a supplier-evaluation model such as the one shown in 📖 **Table 7.2.**

To develop compelling value propositions, business marketers need to better understand how business buyers arrive at their valuations.[36] Researchers studying how business marketers assess customer value found eight different *customer value assessment* (CVA) methods. Companies tended to use the simpler methods, although the more sophisticated ones promise to produce a more accurate picture of customer-perceived value (see Marketing Memo: *Developing Compelling Customer Value Propositions*).

The choice and importance of different attributes varies with the type of buying situation. Delivery reliability, price, and supplier reputation are important for routine-order products. For procedural-problem products, such as a copying machine, the three most important attributes are technical service, supplier flexibility, and product reliability. For political-problem products that stir rivalries in the organization (such as the choice of a computer system), the most important attributes are price, supplier reputation, product reliability, service reliability, and supplier flexibility.

OVERCOMING PRICE PRESSURES The buying center may attempt to negotiate with preferred suppliers for better prices and terms before making the final selection. Despite moves toward strategic sourcing, partnering, and participation in cross-functional teams, buyers still spend a large chunk of their time haggling with suppliers on price. The number of price-oriented buyers can vary by country depending on customer preferences for different service configurations and characteristics of the customer's organization.[37]

Marketers can counter requests for a lower price in a number of ways. They may be able to show evidence that the total cost of ownership—that is, the 'life-cycle cost' of using their product—is lower than for competitors' products. They can cite the value of the services the buyer now receives, especially if they are superior to those offered by competitors. Research shows that service support and personal interactions, as well as a supplier's know-how and ability to improve customers' time to market, can be useful differentiators in achieving key-supplier status.[38]

Improving productivity helps reduce price pressures. Some companies even introduce a compensation bonus which is tied to improved productivity.[39]

TABLE 7.2 📖 An Example of Vendor Analysis					
Attributes	**Rating Scale**				
	Importance Weights	**Poor (1)**	**Fair (2)**	**Good (3)**	**Excellent (4)**
Price	0.30				X
Supplier Reputation	0.20			X	
Product Reliability	0.30				X
Service Reliability	0.10		X		
Supplier Flexibility	0.10			X	
Total Score: 0.30(4) + 0.20(3) + 0.30(4) + 0.10(2) + 0.10(3) = 3.5					

marketing Memo

Developing Compelling Customer Value Propositions

To command price premiums in competitive B2B markets, firms must create compelling customer value propositions. The first step is to research the customer. Here are a number of productive research methods:

1. *Internal engineering assessment.* Have company engineers use laboratory tests to estimate the product's performance characteristics. The weakness of this approach is that it ignores the fact that in different applications the product will have different economic value.

2. *Field value-in-use assessment.* Interview customers about how costs of using a new product compare to those of using the existing one. The task is to assess how much each cost element is worth to the buyer.

3. *Focus-group value assessment.* Ask customers in a focus group what value they would put on potential market offerings.

4. *Direct survey questions.* Ask customers to place a direct financial value on one or more changes in the market offering.

5. *Conjoint analysis.* Ask customers to rank their preferences for alternative market offerings or concepts. Use statistical analysis to estimate the implicit value placed on each attribute.

6. *Benchmarks.* Show customers a 'benchmark' offering and then a new-market offering. Ask how much more they would pay for the new offering or how much less they would pay if certain features were removed from the benchmark offering.

7. *Compositional approach.* Ask customers to attach a monetary value to each of three alternative levels of a given attribute. Repeat for other attributes, then add the values together for any offer configuration.

8. *Importance ratings.* Ask customers to rate the importance of different attributes and their suppliers' performance on each.

Having done this research, you can specify the customer value proposition, following a number of important principles. First, verify value claims clearly by specifying the differences between your offerings and those of competitors on the dimensions that matter most to the customer. Second, document the value delivered by creating written accounts of costs savings or added value that existing customers have actually captured by using your offerings. Finally, make sure the customer value proposition is well implemented within the company, and train and reward employees for developing a compelling one. RIC, featured earlier in the chapter, focused on the benefits that the new technology offered to its contractors and engineers through cost savings, time savings, quality assurance, improved control, and safety. They used success stories from applications of the technology in Africa, Europe, the United States, and Canada to convince prospective contractors of the benefits of the RIC technology. Finally, RIC has on-site engineers to help and assist with the installation, use, and operation of their technology.

Sources: James C. Anderson, James A. Narus, and Wouter van Rossum, "Customer Value Propositions in Business Markets," *Harvard Business Review*, March 2006, pp. 2–10; James C. Anderson and James A. Narus, "Business Marketing: Understanding What Customers Value," *Harvard Business Review*, November 1998, pp. 53–65; James C. Anderson and James A. Narus, "Capturing the Value of Supplementary Services," *Harvard Business Review*, January 1995, pp. 75–83; James C. Anderson, Dipak C. Jain, and Pradeep K. Chintagunta, "A Customer Value Assessment in Business Markets: A State-of-Practice Study," *Journal of Business-to-Business Marketing*, 1, no. 1, January 1993, pp. 3–29; www.ricsa.net; www.engineeringnews.co.za/article/new-technology-negates-traditional-soil-compaction-methods-2008-02-15.

Some firms are using technology to devise novel customer solutions. Many large printing houses can now offer professional printing services to small businesses that previously could not afford it.[40] Also, around-the-corner stationery suppliers are now able to provide professional quality printing services to small businesses. In Lebanon, Malik's Stationery, with branches next to most major universities, was able to bring professional-type printing services not only to small businesses but to university students and professors as well.

Some companies handle price-oriented buyers by setting a lower price but establishing restrictive conditions: (1) limited quantities, (2) no refunds, (3) no adjustments, and (4) no services.[41] IBM is now more of a service company aided by products than a product company aided by services. The bulk of IBM's revenues now come from offering business solutions. Once known for selling computer hardware, IBM now sells computer power on demand (like video on demand) as an alternative to selling computers.

Solution selling can also ease price pressure and comes in different forms. Examples include[42] solutions to enhance customer revenues, solutions to decrease customer risks, and solutions to reduce customer costs.

Risk and gain sharing can offset requested price reductions from customers. Consider this hypothetical example: suppose Medaid, a hospital supplier, signed an agreement with King Abdulaziz Hospital in Jeddah, promising approximately US$100,000 in savings over a year in exchange for a five-times increase in the hospitals' purchases of Medaid supplies. If Medaid achieves less than these promised savings, it will make up the difference. If Medaid achieves substantially more than promised, it gets to share part of the extra savings. To make such arrangements work, the supplier must be willing to help the customer to build a historical database, reach an agreement for measuring benefits and costs, and devise a dispute resolution mechanism.

NUMBER OF SUPPLIERS As part of the buyer selection process, buying centers must decide how many suppliers to use. Companies are increasingly reducing the number of suppliers. Ford, Motorola, and Honeywell have cut the number of suppliers by 20 to 80 percent. These companies want their chosen suppliers to be responsible for a larger component system, they want them to achieve continuous quality and performance improvement, and at the same time they want them to lower prices each year by a given percentage. These companies expect their suppliers to work closely with them during product development, and they value their suggestions. There is even a trend toward single sourcing.

Companies that use multiple sources often cite the threat of a labor strike as the biggest deterrent to single sourcing. Another reason companies may be reluctant to use a single source is that they fear they'll become too comfortable in the relationship and lose their competitive edge.

Order-Routine Specification

After selecting suppliers, the buyer negotiates the final order, listing the technical specifications, the quantity needed, the expected time of delivery, return policies, warranties, and so on. Many industrial buyers lease heavy equipment such as machinery and trucks. The 'lessee' (or the renter) gains a number of advantages: conserving capital, getting the latest products, receiving better service, and gaining some tax advantages. The 'lessor' (or the owner who is offering the equipment for rent) often ends up with a larger net income and the chance to sell to customers that could not afford outright purchase.

In the case of maintenance, repair, and operating items, buyers are moving toward blanket contracts rather than periodic purchase orders. A blanket contract establishes a long-term relationship in which the supplier promises to resupply the buyer as needed, at agreed-upon prices, over a specified period of time. Because the seller holds the stock, blanket contracts are sometimes called *stockless purchase plans*. The buyer's computer automatically sends an order to the seller when stock is needed. This system locks suppliers in tighter with the buyer and makes it difficult for out-suppliers to break in unless the buyer becomes dissatisfied with the in-supplier's prices, quality, or service.

Companies that fear a shortage of key materials are willing to buy and hold large inventories. They will sign long-term contracts with suppliers to ensure a steady flow of materials. Aramco, Toyota, and several other major companies regard long-term supply planning as a major responsibility of their purchasing managers. For example, Ford wants to buy from fewer suppliers, who must be willing to locate close to its plants and produce high-quality components. Business marketers are also setting up extranets with important customers to facilitate and lower the cost of transactions. The customers enter orders directly on the computer that are automatically transmitted to the supplier. Some companies go further and shift the ordering responsibility to their suppliers in systems called *vendor-managed inventory*. These suppliers are privy to the customer's inventory levels and take responsibility for replenishing it automatically through *continuous replenishment programs*.

Performance Review

The buyer periodically reviews the performance of the chosen supplier(s) using one of three methods. The buyer may contact the end users and ask for their evaluations; the buyer may rate the supplier on several criteria using a weighted-score method; or the buyer might aggregate the cost of poor performance to come up with adjusted costs of purchase, including price. The performance review may lead the buyer to continue, modify, or end a supplier relationship.

Many companies have set up incentive systems to reward purchasing managers for good buying performance, in much the same way that sales personnel receive bonuses for good selling performance. These systems lead purchasing managers to increase pressure on sellers for the best terms.

Ford's 'customized fleet solutions' help build long-term business relationships between the company and its business clients.

Managing Business-to-Business Customer Relationships

To improve effectiveness and efficiency, business suppliers and customers are exploring different ways to manage their relationships.[43] Closer relationships are driven in part by supply chain management, early supplier involvement, and purchasing alliances.[44] Cultivating the right relationships with business is paramount for any holistic marketing program. For example, in the UAE, Ford offers its business clients 'customized fleet solutions', whereby the business buyer can custom design certain features of Ford trucks (such as storage compartment make and finish, and installing certain special equipment) depending on their business needs and the trucks' intended use. The plan comes with a range of alternate purchase, lease, and warranty options too. Needless to say, such plans are based on a deep understanding of the client's needs, and helps build long-term business relationships. A master at business-to-business marketing is General Electric, as highlighted in the Marketing Excellence case study at the end of this chapter.

The Benefits of Vertical Coordination

Much research has supported greater vertical coordination between buying partners and sellers, so they can go beyond merely transacting and instead engage in activities that create more value for both parties.[45]

Establishing Corporate Trust and Credibility

Corporate credibility is the extent to which customers believe a firm can design and deliver products and services that satisfy their needs and wants. It reflects the supplier's reputation in the marketplace and is the foundation for a strong relationship.

Corporate credibility depends in turn on three factors:

1. **Corporate expertise**: the extent to which a company is seen as able to make and sell products or conduct services.

2. **Corporate trustworthiness**: the extent to which a company is seen as motivated to be honest, dependable, and sensitive to customer needs.

3. **Corporate likability**: the extent to which a company is seen as likable, attractive, prestigious, dynamic, and so on.

In other words, a credible firm is good at what it does, it keeps its customers' best interests in mind, and it is enjoyable to work with.

Trust is the willingness of a firm to rely on a business partner. It depends on a number of interpersonal and interorganizational factors, such as the firm's perceived competence, integrity, honesty, and goodwill. Personal interactions with employees of the firm, opinions about the company as a whole, and perceptions of trust will evolve with experience.

△ **Figure 7.1** provides a summary of some core dimensions of trust.

Building trust can be especially tricky in online settings, and firms often impose more stringent requirements on their online business partners than on others. Business buyers worry that they won't get products of the right quality delivered to the right place at the right time. Sellers worry about getting paid on time—or at all—and how much credit they should extend.

Sources: Bob Violino, "Building B2B Trust," *Computerworld*, June 17, 2002, p. 32; Richard E. Plank, David A. Reid, and Ellen Bolman Pullins, "Perceived Trust in Business-to-Business Sales: A New Measure," *Journal of Personal Selling and Sales Management*, 19, no. 3, Summer 1999, pp. 61–72; Kevin Lane Keller and David A. Aaker, "Corporate-Level Marketing: The Impact of Credibility on a Company's Brand Extensions," *Corporate Reputation Review*, 1, August 1998, pp. 356–378; Robert M. Morgan and Shelby D. Hunt, "The Commitment–Trust Theory of Relationship Marketing," *Journal of Marketing*, 58, no. 3, July 1994, pp. 20–38; Christine Moorman, Rohit Deshpande, and Gerald Zaltman, "Factors Affecting Trust in Market Research Relationships," *Journal of Marketing*, 57, January 1993, pp. 81–101.

Low		High
	Transparent	
Distorted, hidden information	⟷	Full, honest information
	Product/Service Quality	
Low product service quality fails to meet promises	⟷	Best product and service to fulfill expectations
	Incentive	
Incentives aligned for company, *not customer gains*	⟷	Incentives aligned so employees trust and meet customer need
	Partnering with Customers	
Leave customers to work out their own problems	⟶	Help customers learn and help themselves
	Cooperating Design	
Customers are sold company solutions	⟷	Customers help design products individually and through communities
	Product Comparison and Advice	
No or biased comparison and no advice	⟷	Compare to competitive products honestly and comprehensive communities
	Supply Chain	
Customer trust conflict in channel	⟷	All supply chain partners aligned to build trust
	Pervasive Advocacy	
Marketing pushes services and products	⟷	All functions work to build trust

|Fig. 7.1| △

Trust Dimensions

Source: Glen Urban, "Where Are You Positioned on the Trust Dimensions?," in *Don't Just Relate-Advocate: A Blueprint for Profit in the Era of Customer Power* (Wharton School Publishers, 2005), p. 99.

Building trust is one prerequisite for healthy long-term relationships. The Marketing Insight: *Establishing Corporate Trust and Credibility* identifies some key dimensions to such trust. Knowledge that is specific and relevant to a relationship partner is also an important factor in the strength of interfirm ties between partners.[46]

One historical study of four very different business-to-business relationships found that several factors, by affecting partner interdependence and/or environmental uncertainty, influenced the development of a relationship between business partners.[47] The relationship between advertising agencies and clients illustrates these findings:

1. *In the relationship-formation stage, one partner experienced substantial market growth.* Manufacturers capitalizing on mass-production techniques developed national brands, which increased the importance and amount of mass-media advertising.
2. *Information asymmetry between partners was such that a partnership would generate more profits than if the partner attempted to invade the other firm's area.* Advertising agencies had specialized knowledge that their clients would have had difficulty obtaining.
3. *At least one partner had high barriers to entry that would prevent the other partner from entering the business.* Advertising agencies could not easily become national manufacturers, and for years manufacturers were not eligible to receive media commissions.
4. *Dependence asymmetry existed such that one partner was more able to control or influence the other's conduct.* Advertising agencies had control over media access.
5. *One partner benefited from economies of scale related to the relationship.* Ad agencies gained by providing the same market information to multiple clients.

Research has found that buyer–supplier relationships differ according to four factors: availability of alternatives; importance of supply; complexity of supply; and supply market dynamism. Based on these four factors, they classified buyer–supplier relationships into eight different categories:[48]

1. **Basic buying and selling.** These are simple, routine exchanges with moderate levels of cooperation and information exchange.
2. **Bare bones.** These relationships require more adaptation by the seller and less cooperation and information exchange.
3. **Contractual transaction.** These exchanges are defined by formal contract and generally have low levels of trust, cooperation, and interaction.
4. **Customer supply.** In this traditional custom supply situation, competition rather than cooperation is the dominant form of governance.
5. **Cooperative systems.** The partners in cooperative systems are united in operational ways, but neither demonstrates structural commitment through legal means or adaptation.
6. **Collaborative.** In collaborative exchanges, much trust and commitment lead to true partnership.
7. **Mutually adaptive.** Buyers and sellers make many relationship-specific adaptations, but without necessarily achieving strong trust or cooperation.
8. **Customer is king.** In this close, cooperative relationship, the seller adapts to meet the customer's needs without expecting much adaptation or change in exchange.

Over time, however, the roles and nature of a relationship may shift and be activated depending on different circumstances.[49] Some needs can be satisfied with fairly basic supplier performance. Buyers then neither want nor require a close relationship with a supplier. Likewise, some suppliers may not find it worth their while to invest in customers with limited growth potential.

One study found that the closest relationships between customers and suppliers arose when the supply was important to the customer and there were procurement obstacles, such as complex purchase requirements and few alternative suppliers.[50] Another study suggested that greater vertical coordination between buyer and seller through information exchange and planning is usually necessary only when high environmental uncertainty exists and specific investments (described below) are modest.[51]

Business Relationships: Risks and Opportunities

Researchers have noted that establishing a customer–supplier relationship creates tension between safeguarding and adaptation. Vertical coordination can facilitate stronger customer–seller ties but at the same time may increase the risk to the customer's and supplier's specific investments. *Specific investments* are those expenditures tailored to a particular company and value chain partner (investments in company-specific training, equipment, and operating procedures or systems).[52] They help firms grow profits and achieve their positioning.[53] For example, Xerox has worked closely with its suppliers to develop customized processes and components that reduced its copier-manufacturing costs by 30 to 40 percent. In return, suppliers received sales and volume guarantees, an enhanced understanding of their customer needs, and a strong position with Xerox for future sales.[54]

Specific investments, however, also carry considerable risk to both customer and supplier. Transaction theory from economics maintains that because these investments are already committed, they lock the firms that make them into a particular relationship. A buyer may feel stuck in the relationship because of potentially high switching costs of moving to another supplier; while a supplier may feel defenseless toward requests of the buyer because of dedicated assets and/or sharing of technology/knowledge.

When buyers cannot easily monitor supplier performance, the supplier might avoid deadlines or commitments or not deliver the expected value. *Opportunism* is "some form of cheating or undersupply relative to an implicit or explicit contract."[55] It may entail self-interest and deliberate misrepresentation that violates contractual agreements. In creating the 1996 version of the Ford Taurus, Ford Corporation chose to outsource the whole process to one supplier, Lear Corporation. Lear committed to a contract that, for various reasons, it knew it was unable to fulfill. According to Ford, Lear missed deadlines, failed to meet weight and price objectives, and furnished parts that did not work.[56] A more passive form of opportunism might be a refusal or unwillingness to adapt to changing circumstances.

Opportunism is a concern because firms must devote resources to control and monitoring that they could otherwise allocate to more productive purposes. Contracts may become inadequate to govern supplier transactions when supplier opportunism becomes difficult to detect, when firms make specific investments in assets that they cannot use elsewhere, and when contingencies are harder to anticipate. Customers and suppliers are more likely to form a joint venture (instead of signing a simple contract) when the supplier's degree of asset specificity is high, monitoring the supplier's behavior is difficult, and the supplier has a poor reputation.[57] When a supplier has a good reputation, it is more likely to avoid opportunism to protect this valuable intangible asset.

The presence of a significant future time horizon and/or strong solidarity norms typically causes customers and suppliers to strive for joint benefits. As a result, there is a shift in specific investments from expropriation (increased opportunism on the receiver's part) to bonding (reduced opportunism).[58]

Institutional and Government Markets

Our discussion has concentrated largely on the buying behavior of profit-seeking companies. Much of what we have said also applies to the buying practices of institutional and government organizations. However, we want to highlight certain special features of these markets.

The **institutional market** consists of schools, hospitals, nursing homes, prisons, and other institutions that must provide goods and services to people in their care. Many of these organizations are characterized by low budgets and captive clienteles. For example, hospitals must decide what quality of food to buy for patients. The buying objective here is not profit, because the food is provided as part of the total service package; nor is cost minimization the sole objective, because poor food will cause patients to complain and hurt the hospital's reputation. The hospital purchasing agent must search for institutional-food vendors whose quality meets or exceeds a certain minimum standard and whose prices are low. In fact, many food vendors set up a separate division to sell to institutional buyers because of these buyers' special needs and characteristics. Indevco and Fine (paper products manufacturers that make the popular Arab brands Sanita and Fine, respectively) produce, package, and price their tissues and paper products differently to meet the requirements of hospitals and other institutional buyers such as universities, schools, and public utility companies.

In most countries, government organizations are a major buyer of goods and services. The case is perhaps even more pronounced in the Arab world, where the government and public sector share of the GNP is very high, particularly in oil-producing countries. They typically require suppliers to submit bids and often award the contract to the lowest bidder. In some cases, the government unit will make allowance for superior quality or a reputation for completing contracts on time. Governments will also buy on a negotiated contract basis, primarily in the case of complex projects involving major R&D costs and risks, and in cases where there is little competition.

A major complaint of multinational companies is that each country in which they operate shows favoritism toward its nationals despite sometimes superior offers from foreign firms. Although such practices are widely in use, several countries are attempting to remove this bias.

Governments buy goods and services valued at billions of dollars, making the government the largest and therefore most attractive potential customer in a country market. However, because their spending decisions are subject to public review, government organizations require considerable paperwork from suppliers, who often complain about bureaucracy, regulations, decision-making delays, and frequent shifts in procurement personnel (the government staff who check that the purchased goods are appropriate and as per the required standards). In some Arab countries, government departments are undertaking initiatives to deal with to these complaints. Some of these initiatives are being taken in collaboration with the private sector, including an initiative at Dubai Customs, described in the next case study.

institutional market schools, hospitals, nursing homes, prisons, and other institutions that must provide goods and services to people in their care.

Dubai Customs has worked closely with other government departments to implement an initiative to improve private to public sector trade.

Dubai Customs

Dubai Customs has been working closely with other government departments and the private sector to facilitate faster and easier processing of trade movement in Dubai. In 2010 it processed 85 percent of all declarations through electronic channels. In May 2010, Aramex joined forces with Dubai Customs and Emirates Airline to implement a new e-freight system, which would allow airlines, freight forwarders, and customs to more easily exchange electronic information and e-documents, and enhance trade movement.

Yousif Al Sahlawi, senior executive director of corporate affairs at Dubai Customs, said: "The new system to deliver e-commerce trading has been developed after an extensive examination of the country's existing mechanism for freight clearance and the tangible benefit the new system holds. In 2009, Dubai Customs cleared more than 2.5 million declarations transported by air. Industry studies have shown the potential to reduce the transportation of 62 percent of the paper volume."

Aramex Middle East and Africa CEO, Hussein Hachem, added: "The new e-freight system offers a picture of the way forward for air freight in the region, and Aramex is proud to be part of it. This initiative will also enable Aramex to reduce its carbon footprint, which is an important ongoing goal for us."[59]

Just as companies provide government agencies with guidelines about how best to purchase and use their products, governments provide would-be suppliers with detailed guidelines describing how to sell to the government. Failure to follow the guidelines or to fill out forms and contracts correctly can create a legal nightmare.[60]

Desert Diamond

Desert Diamond is the regional agent for some of the world's largest and most advanced manufacturers of fire-fighting material and equipment in several Arab countries. Governmental agencies and units (such as the army, internal security forces, civil defense, and public utility providers: airports, seaports, electricity companies, and the like) are Desert Diamond's major clients. Abdulfattah Ghali, president and CEO of Desert Diamond, asserts that the company's success and growth rests upon the ability to understand, meet, and attend to the unique characteristics and needs of the government market.[61] As noted by Ghali, "Our approach starts essentially by educating the clients about innovative cutting edge technology that caters more effectively to their developing needs, and goes all the way until assisting them in implementing the use of such technology."

Fortunately for businesses of all sizes, many governments have been trying to simplify the contracting procedure and make bidding more attractive. Some reforms place more emphasis on buying commercial off-the-shelf items instead of items built to the government's specifications; online communication with vendors to eliminate the massive paperwork; and a 'debriefing' from the appropriate government agency for vendors who lose a bid, enabling them to increase their chances of winning the next time around.[62] More purchasing is being done online via web-based forms, digital signatures, and electronic procurement cards (P-cards).[63]

In spite of these reforms, for a number of reasons many companies that sell to the government have not used a marketing orientation. Some, though, have pursued government business by establishing separate government marketing departments. Companies large and small, such as Indevco, Fine, Desert Diamond, and Aramex (all of which we have discussed in this chapter), and others such as contracting firms (Consolidated Contractors Company, Saudi Oger, Al-Habtoor, or Arabtec) or engineering design consultants (Dar Al-Handasah or Kuwait's KEO), anticipate government needs and projects, participate in the product specification phase, gather competitive intelligence, prepare bids carefully, and produce strong communications to describe and enhance their companies' reputations.

Summary

1. Organizational buying is the decision-making process by which formal organizations establish the need for purchased products and services, then identify, evaluate, and choose among alternative brands and suppliers. The business market consists of all the organizations that acquire goods and services used in the production of other products or services that are sold, rented, or supplied to others.

2. Compared to consumer markets, business markets generally have fewer and larger buyers, a closer customer–supplier relationship, and more geographically concentrated buyers. Demand in the business market is derived from demand in the consumer market and fluctuates with the business cycle. Nonetheless, the total demand for many business goods and services is quite price inelastic. Business marketers need to be aware of the role of professional purchasers and their influencers, the need for multiple sales calls, and the importance of direct purchasing, reciprocity, and leasing.

3. The buying center is the decision-making unit of a buying organization. It consists of initiators, users, influencers, deciders, approvers, buyers, and gatekeepers. To influence these parties, marketers must be aware of environmental, organizational, interpersonal, and individual factors.

4. The buying process consists of eight stages called buyphases: (1) problem recognition, (2) general need description, (3) product specification, (4) supplier search, (5) proposal solicitation, (6) supplier selection, (7) order-routine specification, and (8) performance review.

5. Business marketers must form strong bonds and relationships with their customers and provide them added value. Some customers, however, may prefer more of a transactional relationship.

6. The institutional market consists of schools, hospitals, nursing homes, prisons, and other institutions that provide goods and services to people in their care. Buyers for government organizations tend to require a great deal of paperwork from their vendors and to favor open bidding and domestic companies. Suppliers must be prepared to adapt their offers to the special needs and procedures found in institutional and government markets.

Applications

Marketing Debate
How Different Is Business-to-Business Marketing?

Many business-to-business marketing executives complain about the numerous challenges of business-to-business marketing, maintaining that many traditional marketing concepts and principles do not apply. For a number of reasons, they assert that selling products and services to a company is fundamentally different from selling to individuals. Others disagree, claiming that marketing theory is still valid and only involves some adaptation in the marketing tactics.

Take a position: Business-to-business marketing requires a special, unique set of marketing concepts and principles *versus* business-to-business marketing is really not that different and the basic marketing concepts and principles apply.

Marketing Discussion

Consider some of the consumer behavior topics from Chapter 6. How might you apply them to business-to-business settings? For example, how might noncompensatory models of choice work? Mental accounting?

Marketing Excellence

>>General Electric

General Electric, or GE, is made up of six recently reorganized major divisions that operate in areas as diverse as home appliances, jet engines, security systems, wind turbines, and financial services. The company is so large (2010 revenues of US$152 billion, and market value of $210 billion) that if each of its six business units were ranked separately, all would appear in the *Fortune* 500, the annual ranking of the top 500 U.S. corporations. If GE were a country, it would be one of the 50 largest, ahead of most Arab countries.

Founded by Thomas Edison as the Edison Electric Light Company in 1878, GE was an early pioneer in light bulbs and electrical appliances. It also served the electrical needs of various industries, such as transportation, utilities, manufacturing, and broadcasting. It became the acknowledged pioneer in business-to-business marketing in the 1950s and 1960s when its tagline was "Live Better Electrically." As the company diversified its product lines, it created new campaigns, including Progress for People and We Bring Good Things to Life.

In 2003, GE faced a new challenge: how to promote its diversified brand globally with a unified message. Its major new campaign, called Imagination at Work, highlighted its renewed focus on innovation and new technology. The award-winning campaign promoted units such as GE Aircraft Engines, GE Medical Systems, and GE Plastics, focusing on the breadth of GE's product offerings. GE spends some US$150 million on corporate advertising: a large expenditure, but one that creates efficiencies by focusing on the core GE brand. The goal was to unify these divisions under the GE brand while giving them a voice. "When you're a company like ours, with 11 different businesses, brand is really important in pulling the identity of the company together," said former CMO Beth Comstock. "Integration was important in communicating the brand across the organization and to all of our constituents."

The new integrated campaign got results. "Research indicates GE is now being associated with attributes such as being high tech, leading edge, innovative, contemporary, and creative," said Judy Hu, GE's Global Executive Director, Advertising and Brand. Just as encouraging, survey respondents still associate GE with some of its traditional attributes, such as being trustworthy and reliable.

In 2005, the company extended the campaign with its next initiative, Ecomagination, which highlighted the company's efforts to develop environmentally friendly 'green' technologies. It leveraged the Imagination tagline again with a 2006 campaign called Health Care Re-Imagined that featured innovative GE health care products for detecting, preventing, and curing diseases. GE followed that with 'Now' and 'Before' campaigns; these also attempted to reflect the imagination that inspires GE's products through imaginative advertising.

While the campaign unites all GE business units, GE's success rests on its ability to understand the business market and the business buying process, putting itself in the shoes of its business customers. Consider its approach to pricing its aircraft engines. GE is aware that purchasing an aircraft engine is a multimillion-dollar expenditure (US$21 million for each large engine). And it doesn't end with the purchase of the engine: customers (airlines) face substantial maintenance costs to meet national and international safety guidelines and ensure reliability of the engines. So in 1999, GE pioneered a new pricing option. The concept, called Power by the Hour, gives customers an opportunity to pay a fixed fee each time they run the engine. In return, GE performs all the maintenance and guarantees the engine's reliability. When demand for air travel is uncertain, GE gives its customers a lower cost of ownership.

This kind of B2B marketing savvy helped GE cement its top position in the *Financial Times'* World's Most Respected Companies survey for six consecutive years. Its understanding of the business markets, its way of doing business, and its brand marketing have kept GE's brand equity growing. Indeed, its brand equity was valued at around US$43 billion in the 2010 Interbrand/*BusinessWeek* ranking of the top 100 global brands, placing it fifth among all brands. "The GE brand is what connects us all and makes us so much better than the parts," CMO Comstock said.

Continued on next page >>

Marketing Excellence...continued

>>General Electric

Questions

1. How could GE, a company originally established in 1878, survive to the 21st century as one of the world's leading and most respected companies? What do you think lies at the core of GE's success?

2. What benefits does Power by the Hour bring to airline companies who choose to subscribe to this scheme?

3. What benefits does Power by the Hour bring to GE?

4. If you were responsible for GE's Medical Systems unit for the Middle East and North Africa region, how would you approach hospitals with your state-of-the-art medical equipment and machines? Identify who might constitute members of the buying center, and how you would approach each.

5. Would your approach differ if your potential customer was a privately owned hospital rather than a government hospital? What could differ in terms of members of the buying center, and how would your approach differ?

Sources: Geoffrey Colvin, "What Makes GE Great?," *Fortune*, March 6, 2006, pp. 90–104; Thomas A. Stewart, "Growth as a Process," *Harvard Business Review*, June 2006, pp. 60–70; Kathryn Kranhold, "The Immelt Era, Five Years Old, Transforms GE," *Wall Street Journal*, September 11, 2006; Daniel Fisher, "GE Turns Green," *Forbes*, August 15, 2005, pp. 80–85; John A. Byrne, "Jeff Immelt," *Fast Company*, July 2005, pp. 60–65; "Fortune 500: General Electric," *CNN Money*, http://money.cnn.com/magazines/fortune/fortune500/2011/snapshots/170.html.

Increasing awareness of the negative impact of obesity on health among the Arab public has prompted many to seek ways to fight their obesity. Business concepts, such as Live'ly, were designed to attend to these growing interests and concerns, and are generating good returns.

In this chapter, we will address the following questions:

1. What are the different levels of market segmentation? (pg. 208)

2. How can a company divide a market into segments? (pg. 212)

3. How should a company choose the most attractive target markets? (pg. 223)

4. What are the requirements for effective segmentation? (pg. 224)

Identifying Market Segments and Targets

Companies cannot connect with all customers in large, broad, or diverse markets. But they can divide such markets into groups of consumers or segments with distinct needs and wants. A company then needs to identify which market segments it can serve effectively. This decision requires a keen understanding of consumer behavior and careful strategic thinking. To develop the best marketing plans, managers need to understand what makes each segment unique and different.

Obesity, a major risk factor associated with serious diseases and mortality, is reaching very high levels in industrialized and developing countries, affecting both adults and children. Increased consumption of more energy-dense, nutrient-poor foods rich in simple sugars and saturated fats, combined with reduced physical activity, have caused obesity rates to rise at least three-fold since 1980 in some regions, including the Arab world.

The increased public awareness of the negative impact of obesity on health has prompted many to seek ways to fight their obesity. These attempts often fail or are only successful for a short period of time. There are many reasons for this, including a poor understanding of proven principles of healthy weight loss and the limited availability of personalized and ready-made foods to help achieve weight loss.

From this background, Live'ly was created as a concept designed to provide nutritional, educational, and catering services for people to manage their weight and live more healthily. The Live'ly project started in 2005 in Dubai, and growth into other UAE cities and other Arab countries was foreseen. Live'ly has already expanded into Abu Dhabi and Al-Ain, with plans to expand beyond the UAE to other countries such as Jordan, Saudi Arabia, and Morocco.

Live'ly is run by professional dieticians, health promoters, chefs, and a management team who work together to provide its clients with unique nutritional services and emotional and technical support. To do that in the most comprehensive way, Live'ly offers three services, and has identified corresponding market segments for each:

- *Live'ly Health and Nutrition Lounge offers nutritional assessment and health education primarily to adult men and women (aged 18–55) and adolescents; locals; Arab and Middle East expatriates of the middle and higher income groups; the health-aware; and those with special medical conditions.*
- *Live'ly Healthy Cuisine delivers healthy and appetizing meals tailored to adult men and women; working people from medium to high income groups; locals; Arab and Middle East expatriates; the health-aware; those with special medical conditions; clients of Live'ly Healthy and Nutrition Lounge and other practicing Dubai dieticians; and organizations (such as companies, schools, and clubs) that like to cater healthy and tasty food.*
- *Live'ly Gourmet and D-Lite Corner, with its light and delicious pastries, Arabic sweets, cakes, and chocolate, caters for adult men and women; locals; Arab and Middle East expatriates of the middle and higher income group; the health-aware; or those with special medical conditions such as diabetes.[1]*

To compete more effectively, many companies are now embracing market segmentation and target marketing. Instead of scattering their marketing efforts, they are focusing on those consumers whom they have the greatest chance of satisfying.

Effective target marketing requires that marketers:

1. Identify and profile distinct groups of buyers who differ in their needs and preferences (market segmentation).
2. Select one or more market segments to enter (market targeting).
3. For each target segment, establish and communicate the distinctive benefit(s) of the company's market offering (market positioning).

This chapter will focus on the first two steps. Chapters 9 and 10 discuss the third step, brand and market positioning. ▽

Levels of Market Segmentation

mass marketing mass production, mass distribution, and mass promotion of one product for all buyers.

The starting point for discussing segmentation is **mass marketing**. In mass marketing, the seller engages in the mass production, mass distribution, and mass promotion of one product for all buyers. One of the classical examples is that of Ford cars. Founder Henry Ford exemplified this strategy in the very early part of the 20th century when he offered the Model-T Ford in one design and color, black. Coca-Cola and Pepsi Cola also once practiced mass marketing when each sold only one kind of cola drink, under one brand, and in one size and bottle.

The argument for mass marketing is that it creates the largest potential market, which leads to the lowest costs, which in turn can lead to lower prices or higher margins. However, many critics point to the increasing fragmantation of the market, and the proliferation of advertising media and distribution channels, which are making it difficult and increasingly expensive to reach a mass audience. Some claim that mass marketing is dying. Most companies are turning to *micromarketing* at one of four levels: segments, niches, local areas, and individuals.

Segment Marketing

flexible market offering
(1) a naked solution containing the product and service elements that all segment members value, and (2) discretionary options that some segment members value.

A *market segment* consists of a group of customers who share a similar set of needs and wants. Rather than creating the segments, the marketer's task is to identify them and decide which one(s) to target. Segment marketing offers key benefits over mass marketing. The company can often better design, price, disclose, and deliver the product or service and also can fine-tune the marketing program and activities to better match the segment's needs.

However, even a segment is partly a fiction, in that not everyone wants exactly the same thing. Business-to-business marketing experts Anderson and Narus have urged marketers to present flexible market offerings to all members of a segment.[2] A **flexible market offering** consists of two parts: a *naked solution* containing the product and service elements that all segment members value, and *discretionary options* that some segment members value. Each option might carry an additional charge. For example, as a budget discount airline, Air Arabia offers all passengers a seat and charges

Arab discount airline Air Arabia has enjoyed tremendous growth and success, making it the world's top airline in seat efficiency. Flexible market offerings such as discretionary options have helped Air Arabia better match segment needs.

extra for beverages, snacks, and meals. Fly Dubai, another budget carrier operating from Dubai, charges for luggage too. Lately, Air Arabia and Fly Dubai added another option: seat selection for a fee, whereby a passenger can select his or her seat for an additional charge.

We can characterize market segments in different ways. One way is to identify *preference segments*. **Homogeneous preferences** exist when all consumers have roughly the same preferences; the market shows no natural segments. At the other extreme, consumers in **diffused preferences** vary greatly in their preferences. If several brands are in the market, they are likely to position themselves throughout the space and show real differences to match differences in consumer preference. Finally, **clustered preferences** result when natural market segments emerge from groups of consumers with shared preferences.

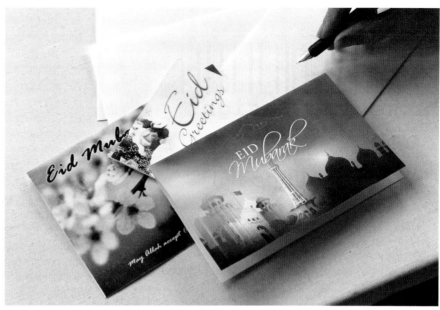

Hallmark targets several market segments including different ethnic and religious segments. Throughout the Arab world, Hallmark offers greeting cards addressing different religious occasions and holidays, and in different languages.

Niche Marketing

A niche is a more narrowly defined customer group seeking a distinctive mix of benefits. Marketers usually identify niches by dividing a segment into subsegments. To return to the airline example, mainstream airlines such as Emirates, Etihad Airways, MEA, and EgyptAir compete head-to-head for the business and leisure traveler, while Air Arabia focuses more on the expatriate market of foreign labor and their families. By attending to the different needs of this market segment, Air Arabia has enjoyed tremendous growth and success. At the other end of the spectrum is the private jet niche. International Air Charter and Qatar Executive cater exclusively to this niche.

What does an attractive niche look like? The customers have a distinct set of needs; they will pay a premium to the firm that best satisfies them; the niche is fairly small but has size, profit, and growth potential and is unlikely to attract many other competitors; and the niche marketer gains certain economies through specialization. The Live'ly example featured in the chapter opening is a good illustration.

Larger companies such as IBM have lost parts of their market to niche marketers: these confrontations have been labeled "guerrillas against gorillas."[3] This is happening in the online social networking market, where MySpace and Facebook are becoming mature service providers. In September 2011, Facebook reached 32 million users in the Arab world, and now has more subscribers than the newspapers in circulation. This surge of popularity of social media has also created new competitors for Facebook. MyArabPlace.com targets the "Arab singles community." Madina.com is a "virtual city catering to Islamic values, offering services to Muslim youth."[4]

Some large companies have even turned to niche marketing. Hallmark personal expression products can be found in hundreds of thousands of retail outlets, gift shops, and stationers around the world. Hallmark cards are available in many Arab countries through their distributor Gulf Greetings, one of the leading retailers of premium greeting cards and gift items, and the sole distributor for Hallmark cards in the region. Hallmark's success in part has been due to vigorous segmenting of its greeting card business. In addition to popular subbranded card lines such as the humorous Shoebox Greetings, Hallmark has introduced lines targeting specific market segments. For example, Fresh Ink targets 18- to 39-year-old women, while Hallmark Warm Wishes offers hundreds of 99-cent cards. Hallmark also offers cards for different ethnic and religious segments. Throughout the Arab world, Hallmark offers greeting cards addressing different religious occasions and holidays, and in different languages.

As marketing efficiency increases, niches that were seemingly too small may become more profitable.[5] The low cost of setting up shop on the internet has led to many small business start-ups aimed at niches. The recipe for internet niching success is to choose a hard-to-find product that customers don't need to see and touch. The Marketing Insight: *Chasing the Long Tail* outlines how provocative are the implications of internet niching.

homogeneous preferences
a market preference segment that occurs when all consumers have roughly the same preference and the market shows no natural segments.

diffused preferences
a market preference segment that occurs when consumer preferences vary greatly.

clustered preferences
a market preference segment that occurs when natural market segments emerge from groups of consumers with shared preferences.

Marketing Insight

Chasing the Long Tail

The advent of online commerce, made possible by technology and epitomized by Amazon.com, eBay, iTunes, and Netflix, has led to a shift in consumer buying patterns, according to Chris Anderson, editor-in-chief of *Wired* magazine and author of *The Long Tail*.

In most markets, the distribution of product sales conforms to a curve weighted heavily to one side—the "head"—where the bulk of sales are generated by a few products. The curve falls rapidly toward zero and hovers just above it far along the X-axis—the "long tail"—where the vast majority of products generate very little sales. The mass market traditionally focused on generating "hit" products that occupy the head, disdaining the low-revenue market niches comprising the tail. The Pareto principle—the "80–20" rule that 80 percent of a firm's revenue is generated by 20 percent of a firm's products—epitomizes this thinking.

Anderson asserts that as a result of consumers' enthusiastic adoption of the internet as a shopping medium, the long tail holds significantly more value than before. In fact, Anderson argues, the internet has directly contributed to the shifting of demand "down the tail, from hits to niches" in a number of product categories including music, books, clothing, and movies. According to this view, the rule that now prevails is more like "50–50," with smaller-selling products adding up to half a firm's revenue.

Anderson's long tail theory is based on three premises: (1) Lower costs of distribution make it economically easier to sell products without precise predictions of demand; (2) The more products available for sale, the greater the likelihood of tapping into latent demand for niche tastes unreachable through traditional retail channels; and (3) If enough niche tastes are aggregated, a big new market can result.

Anderson identifies two aspects of internet shopping that support these premises. First, the increased inventory and variety afforded online permit greater choice. Second, the search costs for relevant new products are lowered due to the wealth of information online, the filtering of product recommendations based on user preferences that vendors can provide, and the word-of-mouth network of internet users.

Some critics challenge the notion that old business paradigms have changed as much as Anderson suggests. Especially in entertainment, they say, the "head" where hits are concentrated is valuable also to consumers, not only to the content creators. One critique argued that "most hits are popular because they are of high quality," and another noted that the majority of products and services making up the long tail originate from a small concentration of online "long-tail aggregators."

Although some academic research supports the long tail theory, other research is more challenging, finding that poor recommendation systems render many very low-share products in the tail so obscure and hard to find that they disappear before they can be purchased frequently enough to justify their existence. For companies selling physical products, inventory, stocking, and handling costs can outweigh any financial benefits of such products.

Sources: Chris Anderson, *The Long Tail* (New York: Hyperion, 2006); "Reading the Tail," interview with Chris Anderson, *Wired*, July 8, 2006, p. 30; "Wag the Dog: What the Long Tail Will Do," *The Economist*, July 8, 2006, p. 77; Erik Brynjolfsson, Yu "Jeffrey" Hu, and Michael D. Smith, "From Niches to Riches: Anatomy of a Long Tail," *MIT Sloan Management Review*, Summer 2006, p. 67; John Cassidy, "Going Long," *New Yorker*, July 10, 2006; www.longtail.com; "Rethinking the Long Tail Theory: How to Define 'Hits' and 'Niches,'" *Knowledge@Wharton*, September 16, 2009.

Local Marketing

Target marketing is leading to marketing programs tailored to the needs and wants of local customer groups in trading areas, neighborhoods, and even individual stores. Retail and fast-food firms such as Costa Coffee, Zara, and McDonald's have all found great success emphasizing local marketing initiatives.[6] McDonald's found great success in its McArabia grilled chicken sandwich across the Arab world, and attempted to build on that success by introducing other Arab-world-based menu items such as the McArabia grilled kofta. Other types of firms are also jumping into action. Banks, such as BLOM of Lebanon, NBK of Kuwait, NCB of Saudi Arabia, or Arab Bank of Jordan provide different mixes of personal, retail, or corporate banking services in its branches, depending on location and neighborhood demographics.

Local marketing reflects a growing trend called *grass-roots marketing*. Marketing activities concentrate on getting as close and personally relevant to individual customers as possible. Much of Nike's initial success comes from engaging target consumers through grass-roots marketing such as sponsorship of local school teams, expert-conducted clinics, and provision of shoes, clothing, and equipment. When Kellogg's attempted to enter the Arab market with its cereal, it invested heavily in grass-roots marketing, going to schools and clubs and offering free samples of its cereal, and even educating their potential consumers about how to prepare and eat cornflakes and other cereal. Kellogg's success paved the way for the creation of a new industry with major Arab players in it, such as the Lebanon-based Poppins and the Saudi Wafra. The HSBC case at the end of this chapter profiles another, similar success story.

McDonald's found great success with its McArabia grilled chicken sandwich across the Arab world, and attempted to build on that by introducing other Arab-world-based menu items, such as a grilled kofta.

Marketing practitioners against local marketing argue that it drives up manufacturing and marketing costs by reducing economies of scale and magnifying logistical problems. A brand's overall image might be diluted if the product and message are different in different localities.

Individual Marketing

The ultimate level of segmentation leads to "segments of one," "customized marketing," or "one-to-one marketing."[7] Today customers are taking more individual initiative in determining what and how to buy. They log onto the internet; look up information and evaluations of product or service offers; conduct dialogue with suppliers, users, and product critics; and in many cases, design the product they want.

Wind and Rangaswamy see a movement toward "customerizing" the firm.[8] **Customerization** combines operationally driven mass customization with customized marketing in a way that empowers consumers to design the product and service offering of their choice. The firm no longer requires prior information about the customer, nor does the firm need to own manufacturing. The firm provides a platform and tools and 'rents' out to customers the means to design their own products. A company is customerized when it is able to respond to individual customers by customizing its products, services, and messages on a one-to-one basis.[9] Sportswear companies such as Nike, Adidas, and Levi's have successfully offered such a platform in some of their stores. Stuck on You also provides such a platform through the internet.

customerization the combination of operationally driven mass customization with customized marketing in a way that empowers consumers to design the product and service offering of their choice.

Stuck on You   Stuck on You is a company specialized in producing custom, personalized labels. Kids are attracted to Stuck on You labels for their designs, and mothers love them for their practicality. The labels are bright and easy to read with fun icons to choose from. The labels are of high quality and are waterproof, and dishwasher-, microwave-, and washing-machine safe. Stuck on You also has a range of shoe labels, pencil labels, and bag tags, and special occasion labels for children's birthdays and religious occasions. The company offers its services in a number of countries around the world, and has a dedicated webpage for customers in the UAE and the Gulf States.[10]

Customization is certainly not for every company.[11] It may be very difficult to implement for complex products such as automobiles. Customization can also raise the cost of goods by more than the customer is willing to pay. Some customers don't know what they want until they see actual products. They also cannot cancel the order after the company has started to work on the product. The product may be hard to repair and have little resale value. In spite of this, customization has worked well for some products.

Bases for Segmenting Consumer Markets

We use two broad groups of variables to segment consumer markets. Some researchers try to define segments by looking at descriptive characteristics: geographic, demographic, and psychographic. Then they examine whether these customer segments exhibit different needs or product responses. For example, they might examine the differing attitudes of 'young single adults,' 'newlyweds,' 'families with kids,' or 'families with teenagers,' and other groups toward, say, 'safety' as a car benefit.

Other researchers try to define segments by looking at behavioral considerations, such as consumer responses to benefits, use occasions, or brands. The researcher then sees whether different characteristics are associated with each consumer-response segment. For example, do people who want 'quality' rather than 'low price' in an automobile purchase differ in their geographic, demographic, and psychographic makeup?

Regardless of which type of segmentation scheme we use, the key is adjusting the marketing program to recognize customer differences. Examples of some of the major segmentation variables—geographic, demographic, psychographic, and behavioral segmentation— as they relate to the Arab world are summarized in ▭ **Table 8.1**.

Geographic Segmentation

Geographic segmentation calls for dividing the market into different geographical units such as regions, counties, cities, or neighborhoods. The company can operate in one or a few areas, or operate in all, but pay attention to local variations. For example, Rotana Hotels customizes rooms, lobbies, and hotel facilities according to the location of the hotel. Hotels in the heart of major cities are more cosmopolitan and address the needs of the business traveler. Hotels on beachsides and in the mountains are more resort-like, and address the touristic vacationer. Major supermarkets such as Spinneys and The Sultan Center all allow local branch managers to stock products that suit the tastes of the local communities the branch serves.

TSC: The Sultan Center   The Sultan Center is the leading supermarket chain in Kuwait. A few years ago, the company made the strategic decision to move into the Lebanese market. They did so by acquiring the stores and facilities of the then-popular Monoprix supermarket chain, and smoothly transitioned the existing stores into TSC stores.

The Sultan Center decided to differentiate the stores depending on their location and size. Regular supermarkets located in the heart of dense residential areas were known as TSC, while hypermarkets, located at the outskirts of a city, were called TSC Plus. Their most recent venture was the upscale TSC Signature, located in the lavish Solidere area in downtown Beirut. TSC, TSC Plus, and TSC Signature differ not only in terms of store name, size, and location, but also in terms of the design of the stores, the product assortment and variety they hold, and the personal in-store service.

Some approaches combine geographic data with demographic data to yield even richer descriptions of consumers and neighborhoods. Claritas Inc. has developed a geoclustering approach called PRIZM (Potential Rating Index by Zip Markets) NE (New Evolution) that classifies over half a million American residential neighborhoods into 14 distinct groups and 66 distinct life-style segments called PRIZM Clusters.[12] The groupings take into consideration 39 factors in five broad categories: (1) education and affluence, (2) family life cycle, (3) urbanization, (4) race and ethnicity, and (5) mobility. The neighborhoods are broken down by zip code (or geographic area or zone). The clusters have descriptive titles such as *Winner's Circle*, *Hometown Retired*, and *Cosmopolitan*. The inhabitants in a cluster tend to lead similar lives, drive similar cars, have similar jobs, and read similar magazines.[13]

TABLE 8.1	Examples of Major Segmentation Variables for Consumer Markets in the Arab World
Geographic Region	Middle East, North Africa, Levant, Arabian Gulf
City or Metro Size	Under 10,000, 10,000–19,999, 20,000–49,999, 50,000–99,999, 100,000–249,999, 250,000–499,999, 500,000 and over
Climate	Mediterranean, desert, mountain
Demographic Age (years)	Under 6, 6–11, 12–19, 20–34, 35–49, 50–64, 64+
Family Size	1–2, 3–4, 5+
Family Life Cycle	Young, single; young, married, no children; young, married, youngest child under 6; young, married, youngest child 6 or over; older, married, with children; older, married, no children under 18; older, single; other
Gender	Male, female
Income (in US$)	Under $5,000; $5,000–$9,999; $10,000–$14,999; $15,000–$19,999; $20,000–$29,999; $30,000–$49,999; $50,000–$99,999; $100,000 and over
Occupation	Professional and technical, managers, public workers, craftspeople, operatives, farmers, retired, students, unemployed
Education	No schooling, some high school, high school graduate, college graduate, technical school graduate
Religion	Muslim, Christian, other
Race	Arab, Armenian, Asian, European, African
Nationality	Saudi, Kuwaiti, Emirati, Bahraini, Jordanian, Syrian, Lebanese, other Arab nationalities, also nationalities of expats such as Indian, Sri Lankan, Filipino
Social Class	Lower lower, upper lower, working class, middle class, upper middle, lower upper, upper upper
Psychographic Life Style	Culture-oriented, sports-oriented, outdoor-oriented
Personality	Compulsive, gregarious, authoritarian, ambitious
Behavioral Occasions	Regular occasion, special occasion
Benefits	Quality, service, economy, speed
User Status	Nonuser, ex-user, potential user, first-time user, regular user
Usage Rate	Light user, medium user, heavy user
Loyalty Status	None, medium, strong, absolute
Readiness Stage	Unaware, aware, informed interested, desirous, intending to buy
Attitude toward Product	Enthusiastic, positive, indifferent, negative, hostile

Marketers can use PRIZM to answer questions such as: Which geographic areas or neighborhoods contain our most valuable customers? How deeply have we already penetrated these segments? Which distribution channels and promotional media work best in reaching our target clusters in each area? Geoclustering could capture the increasing diversity of the population living in a country.

Ace Hardware store has used PRIZM segmentation to help guide decisions in a number of areas: direct mail, advertising, partnerships, site selection, new concepts, and local store marketing.[14] Marketing to microsegments has become accessible even to small organizations as

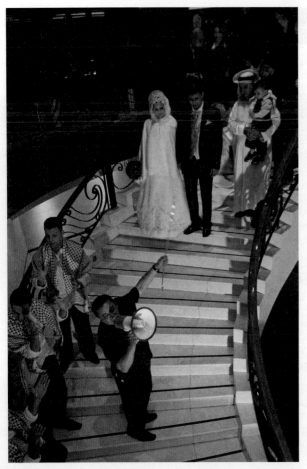

Wedding planning has become a major industry in the Arab world.

life stage   stages of life that define a person's major concern, such as going through a divorce or deciding to buy a new home.

database costs decline, PCs proliferate, software becomes easier to use, data integration increases, and the internet grows.[15]

Demographic Segmentation

In demographic segmentation, we divide the market into groups on the basis of variables such as age, family size, family life cycle, gender, income, occupation, education, religion, race, generation, nationality, and social class. One reason demographic variables are so popular with marketers is that they're often associated with consumer needs and wants. Another is that they're easy to measure. Even when we describe the target market in nondemographic terms (say, by personality type), we may need the link back to demographic characteristics in order to estimate the size of the market and the media we should use to reach it efficiently.

Here's how certain demographic variables have been used to segment markets.

AGE AND LIFE-CYCLE STAGE Consumer wants and abilities change with age. Toothpaste brands such as Crest and Colgate offer three main lines of products to target kids, adults, and older consumers. Age segmentation can be even more refined. Pampers divides its market into prenatal, new baby (0–5 months), baby (6–12 months), toddler (13–23 months), and preschooler (24 months+).

Nevertheless, age and life cycle can be tricky variables.[16] In some cases, the target market for products may be the psychologically young. For example, several car manufacturers (from the likes of Nissan to Ferrari) discovered that some of the prime customers of their sporty cars were older than their typical target segment of 30-somethings. With older men attempting to stay, feel, and look younger, the lines between age groups were getting blurred. In a similar way, Evian's campaign Live Young caters to the desire to be young again.

LIFE STAGE People in the same part of the life cycle may differ in their life stage. **Life stage** defines a person's major concern, such as going through a divorce, going into a second marriage, taking care of an older parent, deciding to buy a new home, and so on. These life stages present opportunities for marketers who can help people cope with their major concerns.

The wedding industry attracts marketers of a whole host of products and services. For instance, wedding planning has grown to be a major industry across the Arab world, especially given the age distribution of the Arab population. In Lebanon alone there are dozens of professional wedding planners, including We Plan WOW Events, Omnia Production, Mabrouk Salaf, Lili White, and Nuit de Reve, which offer full service wedding preparations not only for young Lebanese brides and grooms, but also for couples from other Arab countries who choose to have their weddings in Lebanon. Some hotels, such as the Four Seasons in Riyadh, have also added wedding planning services.

Four Seasons   The Four Seasons Hotel at the Kingdom Center in Riyadh, Saudi Arabia, not only rents out its facilities and ballrooms for wedding celebrations, but also offers wedding planning services and an on-site wedding expert specialist to help the bride and groom plan for their memorable night. A Four Seasons wedding specialist will offer expert advice on everything from theme selection to invitations, food and beverage selection, floral arrangements, wedding cake, and photography.

GENDER Men and women have different attitudes and behave differently, based partly on genetic makeup and partly on socialization.[17] For example, women tend to be more communally minded and socially oriented, while men tend to be more self-expressive and goal-directed; women tend to take in more of the data in their immediate environment, while men tend to focus on the part of the environment that helps them achieve a goal. A research study examining how men and women shop found that men often need to be invited to touch a product, whereas women are likely to pick it up without being asked to. Men often like to read product information; women may relate to a product on a more personal level.

In all societies and communities around the world, the Arab world being no exception, women's role in purchase and consumption decisions is constantly on the rise. According to studies, women in some communities control or influence over 80 percent of consumer goods and services, make 75 percent of the decisions about buying new homes, and purchase 60 percent of new cars outright. Realizing the importance of this segment, *Gulf Marketing Review* has organized an annual Marketing to Women conference across the Arabian Gulf countries.

Gender differentiation has long been applied in clothing, hairstyling, cosmetics, and magazine industries. Avon has built a US$6 billion-plus business selling beauty products to women. Other products from cars and mobile phones, to laptop computers and personal care products, have been positioned as either more masculine or more feminine.[18]

But it's not enough to label and push a product as masculine or feminine; rather, further segmentation within each gender is called for. Hypersegmentation is now occurring within both male and female personal care segments. Unilever became extremely successful in some countries by targeting women who don't look like, or aspire to look like, fashion models, with its award-winning Dove Campaign for Real Beauty.

 Dove   Dove's Campaign for Real Beauty features women of all shapes, sizes, and colors posing proudly in their underwear. The company claims that the ad series, developed by Ogilvy & Mather, was not just a vehicle to sell more soap but "aims to change the status quo and offer in its place a broader, healthier, more democratic view of beauty." The original idea was initiated as a result of a global study sponsored by Dove that researched women's attitudes toward themselves and beauty. Only 2 percent of women in the study considered themselves beautiful, so not only women, but everyone, took notice when the pictures of joyful full-figured or average-looking women began appearing. Even groups who normally are not known to approve of depictions of women in advertising have welcomed the campaign, labeling it "a step forward for the advertising industry."[19]

On the other hand, Lebanon's First National Bank innovated with a loan program targeted at women who wished to change their physical appearance.

 First National Bank   In Lebanon, First National Bank (FNB) created global hype when it introduced an innovative loan program targeted at women: the Plastic Surgery Loan. Lebanon is known as the Arab world's plastic surgery capital, with more than 200 plastic surgeons performing around 1.5 million procedures each year. In 2007, FNB introduced its Plastic Surgery Loan program. The loan ranges from US$3,000 to $5,000, to be paid over a 2–3 year period, with an interest rate of around 9% (about the same rate as a car loan). George Nasr, Director of Marketing at FNB, reflected that "now beauty is no more a luxury. Anyone can have it." FNB's Plastic Surgery Loan program was so successful that it prompted other rival banks (such as BBAC and Credit Libanaise) to follow suit with similar programs. FNB has since introduced another innovative loan program, the Fertility Loan, available to fund fertility treatment.[20]

Media have emerged to make gender targeting easier. Marketers can reach women more easily on the Fatafeet cooking channel, ART Arabic series and Arabic film channels, Rotana music and entertainment channels, and through scores of women's magazines such as *Al Hasnaa*, *Hiya*, and *Sayyidati*. Men are more likely to watch news channels such as Al Jazeera and Al Arabiya, and sports channels such as Al Jazeera Sport and Abu Dhabi Riyadiyya, and read magazines such as

Al-Iktissad wal Aamal business magazine and *Arabian Business*, and newspapers such as *Al-Sharq Al-Awsat*, *Al-Hayat*, and *Al-Ahram*.

Traditionally more male-oriented markets, such as the automobile industry, are beginning to recognize gender segmentation and are changing the way they design and sell cars.[21] Women shop differently for cars than men; they care more about interior than exterior styling, view safety in terms of features that help survive an accident rather than handling to avoid an accident, and are more interested in environmental impact.[22]

Marketing Insight

Trading Up (and Down): the New Consumer

Michael Silverstein and Neil Fiske, the authors of *Trading Up*, observed an increasing number of middle-market consumers periodically trading up to what they call "New Luxury" products and services "that possess higher levels of quality, taste, and aspiration than other goods in the category but are not so expensive as to be out of reach." For example, these consumers might trade up to high-end French restaurants, use a premium skin cream, or stay in a luxury hotel on vacation, depending on the emotional benefits gained in the trade.

Thanks to the trading-up trend, New Luxury goods sell at higher volumes than traditional luxury goods, although priced higher than conventional middle-market items. The authors identify three main types of New Luxury products:

- Accessible superpremium products, such as Victoria's Secret and Naomi Lingerie, Bateel Dates, and Zaatar w Zeit bakery, carry a significant premium over middle-market brands, yet consumers can readily trade up to them because they are relatively low-ticket items in affordable categories.

- Old Luxury brand extensions extend historically high-priced brands down-market while retaining their cachet, such as the Mercedes-Benz C-class and the American Express Blue card.

- Masstige goods, such as The Body Shop skin care and M·A·C cosmetics, are priced between average middle-market brands and superpremium Old Luxury brands. They are "always based on emotions, and consumers have a much stronger emotional engagement with them than with other goods."

To trade up to brands that offer these emotional benefits, consumers often "trade down" by shopping at discounters such as Walmart and Carrefour for staple items or goods that confer no emotional benefit but still deliver quality and functionality. As one consumer explained in

rationalizing why her kitchen boasted a Sub-Zero refrigerator, a state-of-the-art Fisher & Paykel dishwasher, and a US$900 warming drawer but a giant 12-pack of Bounty paper towels from a warehouse discounter: "When it comes to this house, I didn't give in on anything. But when it comes to food shopping or cleaning products, if it's not on sale, I won't buy it."

In a subsequent book titled *Treasure Hunt*, Silverstein notes that 82 percent of U.S. consumers trade down in five or more categories (what he calls "treasure hunting"), whereas 62 percent focus on trading up in the two categories that provide the most emotional benefits. This makes the new consumer "part martyr and part hedonist," willingly sacrificing on a number of purchases in order to experience enhanced benefits from a handful of others.

Silverstein believes successful firms will offer one of two kinds of value: New Luxury or Treasure Hunting. Brands that offer opportunities to trade up, such as Coach, Victoria's Secret, Naomi Lingerie, Four Seasons, and Bateel Dates, or to trade down, such as Quality Inn hotels, Tchibou/TCM, Daiso, Home Market, and IKEA, are optimally positioned to deliver the value modern consumers seek. The remaining firms, occupying the middle market and lacking the economic, functional, and emotional value modern consumers are searching for, will see their market share shrink as they get "trapped in the middle." Traditional grocers and department stores are already suffering, with market share declines of 30 percent and 50 percent, respectively.

Market research firm Mintel observes that consumers have also been "trading over" by switching spending from one category to another, buying a new home theater system, say, instead of a new car. In the recent economic downturn, consumers were "making substitutions that work for recession-minded lifestyles" while still preserving a desired experience. Mintel cites as examples Starbucks VIA Ready Brew coffee, a new, home-based Starbucks experience that's more affordable than coffee at one of the company's outlets, and Tide TOTALCARE, which enables users to obtain certain dry-cleaning-type results at home with prices below those of professional dry cleaners.

Sources: Michael J. Silverstein, *Treasure Hunt: Inside the Mind of the New Consumer* (New York: Portfolio, 2006); Jeff Cioletti, "Movin' on Up," *Beverage World*, June 2006, p. 20; Michael J. Silverstein and Neil Fiske, *Trading Up: The New American Luxury* (New York: Portfolio, 2003); Linda Tischler, "The Price Is Right," *Fast Company*, November 2003; Sarah Mahoney, "Top Consumer Trends: Trust, Control, Playfulness," *Marketing Daily*, September 4, 2009; David Orgel, "Quality Trumps Quantity in New Product Releases," *Supermarket News*, May 25, 2009.

INCOME Income segmentation is a long-standing practice in categories such as automobiles, clothing, cosmetics, financial services, and travel. For instance, car manufacturers introduce difference lines, models, and designs, for different income segments. However, income does not always predict the best customers for a given product. For example, when color TVs were first introduced, the working class were among the first purchasers as it was cheaper for them to buy these sets than to go to movie theaters and restaurants.

Many marketers are deliberately going after lower-income groups, in some cases discovering fewer competitive pressures or greater consumer loyalty.[23] Yet, at the same time, other marketers are finding success with premium-priced products. Increasingly, companies are finding that their markets are hourglass-shaped, as middle-market consumers move toward both discount *and* premium products.[24] Companies that miss out on this new market risk being trapped in the middle and seeing their market share steadily decline. General Motors was caught in the middle, between highly engineered German imports in the luxury market and high-value Japanese and Korean models in the economy class, and has seen its market share continually slide.[25] Eventually, the company was in such deep financial difficulty that it had to be rescued by the U.S. government. The Marketing Insight: *Trading Up (and Down): The New Consumer* describes the factors creating this trend and what it means for marketers.

GENERATION Each generation is profoundly influenced by the times in which it grows up: by the music, movies, politics, and defining events of that period. Demographers call these generational groups *cohorts*. Members share the same major cultural, political, and economic experiences and have similar outlooks and values. Marketers often advertise to a cohort by using the icons and images prominent in its experiences. The Marketing Insight: *Marketing to Generation Y* provides insight into that key age cohort.

Although we can make distinctions between them, different generational cohorts also influence each other. For instance, because so many members of Generation Y are living with their parents, parents are being influenced by the preferences and consumption habits of their Generation Y children. The same products that appeal to 21-year-olds are appealing to their parents. Examples include adult gadgets, such as mobile phones, electronic devices, and even automobiles. Also, it was noted that many adults visit Walt Disney World and other theme parks without any kids.

Marketing Insight

Marketing to Generation Y

They're called Generation Y. They grew up during economic abundance, followed by years of economic recession. They've been 'wired' almost from birth: playing computer games, using the worldwide web, downloading music, and connecting with friends via instant messaging and mobile phones. They have a sense of entitlement and abundance from growing up during the economic boom and being pampered by their parents. They are selective, confident, and impatient. They want what they want when they want it, and they often get it by using credit cards.

The influences that shaped Gen Y are incredibly important to marketers because this cohort will shape consumer and business markets for years to come. Born between 1977 and 1994, Generation Y is estimated to be three times the size of Generation X in the United States, with roughly 78 million members. Their annual spending power is estimated at US$187 billion. If you factor in career growth and household and family formation, and multiply by another 53 years of life expectancy, you're in the $10 trillion range in consumer spending over the life span of today's 21-year-olds.

It's not surprising, then, that market researchers and advertisers are racing to understand Gen Y's buying behaviour and cater to it. Because its members are often turned off by explicit branding practices and a 'hard sell,' marketers have tried many different approaches to reach and persuade them. Some of the methods adopted include: creating online buzz, recruiting student ambassadors, sponsorship of unconventional or extreme sports, and product placement in computer games, videos, and movies.

Sources: Anonymous, "Gen Y and the Future of Mall Retailing," *American Demographics*, December 2002–January 2003, pp. J1–J4; Michael J. Weiss, "To Be about to Be," *American Demographics*, September 2003, pp. 28–36; John Leo, "The Good-News Generation," *U.S. News & World Report*, November 3, 2003, p. 60; Kelly Pate, "Not 'X,' but 'Y' Marks the Spot: Young Generation a Marketing Target," *Denver Post*, August 17, 2003; Bruce Horovitz, "Gen Y: A Tough Crowd to Sell," *USA Today*, April 22, 2002; Bruce Horovitz, "Marketers Revel with Spring Breakers," *USA Today*, March 12, 2002; Martha Irvine, "Labels Don't Fit Us, Gen Y Insists," *Denver Post*, April 19, 2001; J. M. Lawrence, "Trends: X-ed Out: Gen Y Takes Over," *Boston Herald*, February 2, 1999.

Luxury goods are enjoying good returns, successfully catering to those consumers seeking 'the good life.'

psychographics the science of using psychology and demographics to better understand consumers.

Researchers have found that theme park enthusiasts return to the likes of Magic Kingdom and Euro Disney to recapture the safety and peacefulness of childhood.[26]

SOCIAL CLASS Social class has a strong influence on preferences in cars, clothing, home furnishings, leisure activities, reading habits, and retailers, and many companies design products and services for specific social classes. The tastes of social classes change with the years, however. The 1990s were about self-indulgence and show-off for the upper classes. Affluent tastes now run more conservatively, although luxury-goods makers such as Coach, Tiffany, Burberry, TAG Heuer, and Louis Vuitton still successfully sell to those seeking the good life.[27]

Psychographic Segmentation

Psychographics is the science of using psychology and demographics to better understand consumers. In *psychographic segmentation*, buyers are divided into different groups on the basis of psychological/personality traits, life style, or values. People within the same demographic group can exhibit very different psychographic profiles.

One of the most popular commercially available classification systems based on psychographic measurements is the Strategic Business Insights (SBI) VALS™ framework. VALS, signifying values and life styles, classifies U.S. adults into eight primary groups based on responses to a questionnaire featuring four demographic and 35 attitudinal questions. The VALS system is continually updated with new data from more than 80,000 surveys per year (see △ **Figure 8.1**).[28] You can find out which VALS type you are by going to SBI's website (www.strategicbusinessinsights.com).

The main dimensions of the VALS segmentation framework are consumer motivation (the horizontal dimension) and consumer resources (the vertical dimension). Consumers are inspired by one of three primary motivations: ideals, achievement, and self-expression. Those primarily motivated by ideals are guided by knowledge and principles. Those motivated by achievement look for products and services that demonstrate success to their peers. Consumers whose motivation is self-expression desire social or physical activity, variety, and risk. Personality traits such as energy, self-confidence, intellectualism, novelty seeking, innovativeness, impulsiveness, leadership, and vanity—in conjunction with key demographics—determine an individual's resources. Different levels of resources enhance or constrain a person's expression of his primary motivation.

The four groups with higher resources are:

1. **Innovators.** Successful, sophisticated, active, 'take-charge' people with high self-esteem. Purchases often reflect cultivated tastes for relatively upscale, niche-oriented products and services.
2. **Thinkers.** Mature, satisfied, and reflective people who are motivated by ideals and who value order, knowledge, and responsibility. They seek durability, functionality, and value in products.
3. **Achievers.** Successful, goal-oriented people who focus on career and family. They favor premium products that demonstrate success to their peers.
4. **Experiencers.** Young, enthusiastic, impulsive people who seek variety and excitement. They spend a comparatively high proportion of income on fashion, entertainment, and socializing.

The four groups with lower resources are:

1. **Believers.** Conservative, conventional, and traditional people with concrete beliefs. They prefer familiar products and are loyal to established brands.
2. **Strivers.** Trendy and fun-loving people who are resource-constrained. They favor stylish products that emulate the purchases of those with greater material wealth.

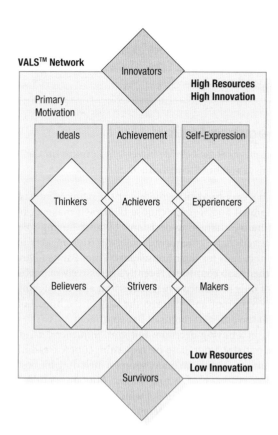

|Fig. 8.1| △

The VALS
Segmentation
System: An Eight-
Part Typology

Source: VALS™ ©, SRI Consulting
Business Intelligence. Used with
permission.

3. **Makers.** Practical, down-to-earth, self-sufficient people who like to work with their hands. They seek own-country products with a practical or functional purpose.

4. **Survivors.** Elderly, passive people who are concerned about change. They are loyal to their favorite brands.

Marketers can apply their understanding of VALS segments to marketing planning. For example, Transport Canada, the agency that operates major Canadian airports, found that Achievers, who desire to express independence and taste, made up a disproportionate percentage of air travelers. Given that segment's profile, stores such as Sharper Image (the high-end gadgets shop) and Nature Company (the high-end nature-based shop) were expected to do well in the firm's airports.

Psychographic segmentation schemes are often customized by culture. The Japanese version of VALS, Japan VALS™, divides society into 10 consumer segments on the basis of two key concepts: life orientation (traditional ways, occupations, innovation, and self-expression) and attitudes to social change (sustaining, pragmatic, adapting, and innovating).

In the Arab world, researchers from the American University of Beirut attempted to devise a psychographic-based segmentation of the Lebanese. They adopted a somewhat similar methodology to that of VALS. They utilized activities, interests, and opinions statements, coupled with demographic and resource data of respondents. While still exploratory in nature, the results revealed eight different clusters or segments which vary in terms of their psychographic and behavioral profile and patterns. It is interesting to note that the segments were highly gender-dependent, with four male-dominant segments and four female-dominant segments.[29] In a similar way, TNS attempted to identity different psychographic segments of women in Saudi Arabia.

TNS   TNS is a global marketing research company with significant presence across the Arab world. TNS conducted a detailed market study of Saudi women aged 18–45 in an attempt to answer the question, "How can your brand connect more effectively with Arab women?". The study involved more than 1,000 quantitative interviews, more than 50 qualitative interviews, and six in-depth interviews with experts. The TNS study identified 11 trends in education, health and well-being, beauty, respect, relationships, religion, a mother's role, self-identity, marital expectations, family values, and technology. The study also revealed six core personality segments: *Hayawia* (drive), *Qeyadeyah* (power), *Zakiya* (control), *Baitootyah* (reassurance), *Ijtima'eya* (belonging), and *Muntaliqa* (freedom). TNS argues that such an understanding is key to the development of effective communication strategies to reach these segments.[30]

Behavioral Segmentation

In behavioral segmentation, marketers divide buyers into groups on the basis of their knowledge of, attitude toward, use of, or response to a product.

DECISION ROLES It's easy to identify the buyer for many products. Men normally choose their own shaving equipment and women choose their own makeup; but even here marketers must be careful in making their targeting decisions, because buying roles change. For example, paint manufacturers realized that women were major decision makers in selecting a paint color (and consequently a paint brand) for their households. Tinol Paints (a household brand of paints in Lebanon and some other Arab countries) recently aggressively marketed its products and color variations to women, not only in women's magazines, but also through mass media TV channels. The TV ads had a touch of humor and featured the lady of the household selecting totally nontraditional colors to paint the different rooms of her apartment.

People play five roles in a buying decision: *initiator, influencer, decider, buyer,* and *user.* For example, assume a wife initiates a purchase by requesting a new treadmill for her birthday. The husband may then seek information from many sources, including his best friend who has a treadmill and is a key influencer in what models to consider. After presenting the alternative choices to his wife, he then purchases her preferred model which, as it turns out, ends up being used by the entire family. Different people are playing different roles, but all are crucial in the decision process and ultimate consumer satisfaction.

BEHAVIORAL VARIABLES Many marketers believe behavioral variables—occasions, benefits, user status, usage rate, buyer-readiness stage, loyalty status, and attitude—are the best starting points for constructing market segments.

Occasions Occasions can be defined in terms of the time of day, week, month, or year, or in terms of other well-defined temporal aspects of a consumer's life. We can distinguish buyers according to the occasions when they develop a need, purchase a product, or use a product. For example, air travel is triggered by occasions related to business, vacation, or family. Occasion segmentation can help expand product usage. Religious occasions are prime targets for marketers. Muslims observe fasting during the month of Ramadan, and some Christians observe a few restrictions during the 40 days of Lent. Both occasions bring unique consumption habits, particularly as it relates to food and family gatherings. For example, consumption of certain food items soar during Ramadan and Easter. Oriental sweets and *maamoul* have become staple items during the Eid holidays following these religious observances. The Hajj pilgrimage to Mecca is a multibillion-dollar industry, not only for Saudi Arabia, the host country, but also for the local economies and industries such as travel agencies, chocolate and sweets manufacturers, and decoration retailers. Other occasions such as birthdays, weddings, anniversaries, and birth extend throughout the entire year.[31]

Benefits Not everyone who buys a product wants the same benefits from it. For example, Zaatar w Zeit has created a very profitable niche for itself. At a time when competition for the traditional Lebanese breakfast menu, the *manousheh,* among bakery corner shops was bringing prices and quality down, Zaatar w Zeit opened true restaurants offering quality manousheh varieties at price premiums (sometimes reaching five times that of the local bakery). Needless to say, those willing to pay the extra cost were looking for something more than a morning breakfast. The restaurant became a round-the-clock destination and a hang-out for teenagers. The concept was a success in Lebanon, and Zaatar w Zeit has since replicated the formula in the UAE, Jordan, Kuwait, and Qatar.

User Status Every product has its nonusers, ex-users, potential users, first-time users, and regular users. Blood banks cannot rely only on regular donors to supply blood; they must also recruit new first-time donors and contact ex-donors, each with a different marketing strategy. The key to attracting potential users, or even possibly nonusers, is understanding the reasons they are not using. Do they have deeply held attitudes, beliefs, or behaviors, or just lack knowledge of the product or brand benefits and usage?

Included in the potential-user group are consumers who will become users in connection with some life stage or life event. Mothers-to-be are potential users who will turn into heavy users. Producers of infant products and services learn their names and shower them with products and ads to capture a share of their future purchases. Market share leaders tend to focus on attracting potential users because they have the most to gain. Smaller firms focus on trying to attract current users away from the market leader.

Usage Rate Markets can be segmented into light, medium, and heavy product users. Heavy users are often a small percentage of the market but account for a high percentage of total consumption. For example, for some refreshments, heavy drinkers account for 87 percent of the market by volume, almost seven times as much as light drinkers. Marketers would rather attract one heavy user than several light users. A potential problem, however, is that heavy users are often either extremely loyal to one brand or never loyal to any brand and always looking for the lowest price. They also may have less room to expand their purchase and consumption.

Buyer-Readiness Stage Some people are unaware of the product, some are aware, some are informed, some are interested, some desire the product, and some intend to buy. To help characterize how many people are at different stages and how well they have converted people from one stage to another, some marketers employ a marketing funnel. △ **Figure 8.2** displays a funnel for two hypothetical brands, A and B. Brand A performs poorly compared to Brand B at converting one-time triers to more recent triers (only 46 percent convert for Brand A as compared to 61 percent for Brand B).

The relative numbers of consumers at different stages make a big difference in designing the marketing program. Suppose a health agency wants to encourage men to have an annual test to detect diabetes, a major medical epidemic in the Arab world and particularly in the Gulf countries. At first, most men may be unaware of the urgency of the case or of the benefits of early detection. The marketing effort should go into awareness-building advertising using a simple message. Later, the advertising should dramatize the benefits of the diabetes test and the risks of not taking it. A special offer of a free health examination might motivate men to actually sign up for the test.

Loyalty Status Marketers usually envision four groups based on brand loyalty status:

1. *Hard-core loyals.* Consumers who buy only one brand all the time.
2. *Split loyals.* Consumers who are loyal to two or three brands.
3. *Shifting loyals.* Consumers who shift loyalty from one brand to another.
4. *Switchers.* Consumers who show no loyalty to any brand.[32]

A company can learn a great deal by analyzing the degrees of brand loyalty: hard-core loyals can help identify the products' strengths; split loyals can show the firm which brands are most competitive with its own; and by looking at customers who are shifting away from its brand, the company

|Fig. 8.2| △

Brand Funnel

can learn about its marketing weaknesses and attempt to correct them. One caution: what appear to be brand-loyal purchase patterns may reflect habit, indifference, a low price, a high switching cost, or the unavailability of other brands.

Attitude Five attitudes to products are: enthusiastic, positive, indifferent, negative, and hostile. Door-to-door workers in a political campaign use voter attitude to determine how much time to spend with that voter. They thank enthusiastic voters and remind them to vote; they reinforce those who are positively disposed; they try to win the votes of indifferent voters; they spend no time trying to change the attitudes of negative and hostile voters.

Combining different behavioral bases can help to provide a more comprehensive and cohesive view of a market and its segments. ▲ **Figure 8.3** depicts one possible way to break down a target market by various behavioral segmentation bases.

THE CONVERSION MODEL The Conversion Model measures the strength of consumers' psychological commitment to brands and their openness to change.[33] To determine how easily a consumer can be converted to another choice, the model assesses commitment based on factors such as consumer attitudes toward, and satisfaction with, current brand choices in a category and the importance of the decision to select a brand in the category.[34]

The model segments *users* of a brand into four groups based on strength of commitment, from low to high, as follows:

1. ***Convertible*** (most likely to defect).
2. ***Shallow*** (uncommitted to the brand and could switch; some are actively considering alternatives).
3. ***Average*** (committed to the brand they are using, but not strongly; they are unlikely to switch brands in the short term).

|Fig. 8.3| ▲

Behavioral Segmentation Breakdown

4. **Entrenched** (strongly committed to the brand they are currently using; they are highly unlikely to switch brands in the foreseeable future).

The model also classifies *nonusers* of a brand into four other groups based on their 'balance of disposition' and openness to trying the brand, from low to high, as follows:

1. **Strongly unavailable** (unlikely to switch to the brand; their preference lies strongly with their current brand).
2. **Weakly unavailable** (not available to the brand because their preference lies with their current brand, although not strongly).
3. **Ambivalent** (as attracted to the brand as they are to their current brand)
4. **Available** (most likely to be acquired in the short run).

In an application of the Conversion Model, Lloyds TSB, a major British bank, discovered that the profitability of its 'least committed' clients had fallen by 14 percent in a 12-month period, whereas for the 'most committed' it had increased by 9 percent. Those who were committed were 20 percent more likely to increase the number of products they held during the 12-month period. As a result, the bank took action to attract and retain high-value committed customers, which resulted in increased profitability.

Finally, a related method of behavioral segmentation has recently been proposed that looks more at the expectations a consumer brings to a particular kind of transaction and locates those expectations on a 'gravity of decision spectrum.' On the shallow end of the spectrum, consumers seek products and services they think will save them time, effort, and money, such as toiletries and snacks. Segmentation for these items would tend to measure consumers' price sensitivity, habits, and impulsiveness. At the other end of the spectrum, the deep end, are those decisions in which consumers' emotional investment is greatest and their core values most engaged, such as deciding on a health care facility for an aging relative or buying a new home. Here the marketer would seek to determine the core values and beliefs related to the buying decision. As the model suggests, focusing on consumer's relationships and involvement with products and product categories can often be revealing as to where and how the firm should market to consumers.[35]

Bases for Segmenting Business Markets

We can segment business markets with some of the same variables we use in consumer markets, such as geography, benefits sought, and usage rate, but business marketers also use other variables. **Box 8.1** shows one set of variables to segment the business market. The demographic variables are the most important, followed by the operating variables, down to the personal characteristics of the buyer.

The box lists major questions that business marketers should ask in determining which segments and customers to serve. A rubber-tire company, for instance, can sell tires to manufacturers of automobiles, trucks, farm tractors, forklift trucks, or aircraft. Within a chosen target industry, a company can further segment by company size. The company might set up separate operations for selling to large and small customers.

Within a given target industry and customer size, a company can segment further by purchase criteria. For example, government laboratories need low prices and service contracts for scientific equipment; university laboratories need equipment that requires little service; and industrial laboratories need equipment that is highly reliable and accurate.

Business marketers generally identify segments through a sequential process. Consider an aluminum company: the company first undertook macrosegmentation. It looked at which end-use market to serve: automobile, residential, or beverage containers. It chose the residential market, and it needed to determine the most attractive product application: semifinished material, building components, or aluminum mobile homes. Deciding to focus on building components, it considered the best customer size and chose large customers. The second stage consisted of microsegmentation. The company distinguished among customers buying on price, service, or quality. Because the aluminum company had a high-service profile, it decided to concentrate on the service-motivated segment of the market.

BOX 8.1   Major Segmentation Variables for Business Markets

Demographic

1. Industry: Which industries should we serve?
2. Company size: What size companies should we serve?
3. Location. What geographical areas should we serve?

Operating Variables

4. Technology: What customer technologies should we focus on?
5. User or nonuser status: Should we serve heavy users, medium users, light users, or nonusers?
6. Customer capabilities: Should we serve customers needing many or few services?

Purchasing Approaches

7. Purchasing-function organization: Should we serve companies with highly centralized or decentralized purchasing organization?
8. Power structure: Should we serve companies that are engineering dominated, financially dominated, and so on?
9. Nature of existing relationship: Should we serve companies with which we have a strong relationship or simply go after the most desirable companies?
10. General purchasing policies: Should we serve companies that prefer leasing? Service contracts? Systems purchases? Sealed bidding?
11. Purchasing criteria: Should we serve companies that are seeking quality? Service? Price?

Situational Factors

12. Urgency: Should we serve companies that need quick and sudden delivery or service?
13. Specific application: Should we focus on certain applications of our product rather than all applications?
14. Size or order: Should we focus on large or small orders?

Personal Characteristics

15. Buyer-seller similarity: Should we serve companies whose people and values are similar to ours?
16. Attitude toward risk: Should we serve risk-taking or risk-avoiding customers?
17. Loyalty: Should we serve companies that show high loyalty to their suppliers?

Source: Adapted from Thomas V. Bonoma and Benson P. Shapiro, *Segmenting the Industrial Market* (Lexington MA: Lexington Books, 1983).

Market Targeting

There are many methodologies for developing market segments.[36] Once the firm has identified its market-segment opportunities, it must decide how many and which ones to target. Marketers are increasingly combining several variables in an effort to identify smaller, better-defined target groups. Thus, a bank may not only identify a group of wealthy retired adults, but within that group distinguish several segments depending on current income, assets, savings, and risk preferences. This has led some market researchers to advocate a *needs-based market segmentation approach.* Roger Best proposed the seven-step approach shown in ▢ **Table 8.2**.

Effective Segmentation Criteria

Not all segmentation schemes are useful. For example, table salt buyers could be divided into short and tall customers, but height is undoubtedly irrelevant to the purchase of salt. Furthermore, if all salt buyers buy the same amount of salt each month, believe all salt is the same, and would pay only one price for salt, this market would be minimally segmentable from a marketing point of view.

TABLE 8.2	Steps in the Segmentation Process
	Description
1. Needs-Based Segmentation	Group customers into segments based on similar needs and benefits sought by customers in solving a particular consumption problem.
2. Segment Identification	For each needs-based segment, determine which demographics, life styles, and usage behaviors make the segment distinct and identifiable (actionable).
3. Segment Attractiveness	Using predetermined segment attractiveness criteria (such as market growth, competitive intensity, and market access), determine the overall attractiveness of each segment.
4. Segment Profitability	Determine segment profitability.
5. Segment Positioning	For each segment, create a 'value proposition' and product-price positioning strategy based on that segment's unique customer needs and characteristics.
6. Segment 'Acid Test'	Create a 'segment storyboard' to test the attractiveness of each segment's positioning strategy.
7. Marketing-Mix Strategy	Expand the segment positioning strategy to include all aspects of the marketing mix: product, price, promotion, and place.

Source: Adapted from Roger J. Best, *Market-Based Management*, 4th edn (Upper Saddle River, NJ: Prentice Hall, 2005).

To be useful, market segments must rate favorably on five key criteria:

- *Measurable.* The size, purchasing power, and characteristics of the segments can be measured.
- *Substantial.* The segments are large and profitable enough to serve. A segment should be the largest possible homogeneous group worth going after with a tailored marketing program. It would not pay, for example, for an automobile manufacturer to develop cars for people who are less than 1.2 meters tall.
- *Accessible.* The segments can be effectively reached and served.
- *Differentiable.* The segments are conceptually distinguishable and respond differently to different marketing-mix elements and programs. If married and unmarried women respond similarly to a sale on perfume, they do not constitute separate segments.
- *Actionable.* Effective programs can be formulated for attracting and serving the segments.

Evaluating and Selecting the Market Segments

In evaluating different market segments, the firm must look at two factors: the segment's overall attractiveness and the company's objectives and resources. How well does a potential segment score on the five criteria? Does a potential segment have characteristics that make it generally attractive, such as size, growth, profitability, scale economies, and low risk? Does investing in the segment make sense given the firm's objectives, competencies, and resources? Some attractive segments may not mesh with the company's long-run objectives, or the company may lack one or more necessary competencies to offer superior value.

After evaluating different segments, the company can consider five patterns of target market selection, shown in △ **Figure 8.4**. We describe each of them next.

SINGLE-SEGMENT CONCENTRATION Fiat and Mini Cooper concentrate on the small-car market and Porsche on the sports car market. Through concentrated marketing, the firm gains a strong knowledge of the segment's needs and achieves a strong market presence. Furthermore, the firm enjoys operating economies through specializing its production, distribution, and promotion. If it captures segment leadership, the firm can earn a high return on its investment.

supersegment a set of segments sharing some exploitable similarity.

Single-segment Concentration

M_1 M_2 M_3

P_1

P_2

P_3

Selective Specialization

M_1 M_2 M_3

P_1

P_2

P_3

Product Specialization

M_1 M_2 M_3

P_1

P_2

P_3

Market Specialization

M_1 M_2 M_3

P_1

P_2

P_3

Full Market Coverage

M_1 M_2 M_3

P_1

P_2

P_3

P = Product M = Market

|Fig. 8.4| △

Five Patterns of Target Market Selection

Source: Adapted from Derek F. Abell, *Defining the Business: The Starting Point of Strategic Planning* (Upper Saddle River, NJ: Prentice Hall, 1980), Chapter 8, pp. 192–196.

However, there are risks. A particular market segment can turn sour or a competitor may invade the segment: when digital camera technology took off, Kodak's sales from camera films fell sharply. For these reasons, many companies prefer to operate in more than one segment. If selecting more than one segment to serve, a company should pay close attention to segment interrelationships on the cost, performance, and technology side. A company carrying fixed costs (sales force, store outlets) can add products to absorb and share some costs. The sales force will sell additional products, and a fast-food outlet will offer additional menu items. Economies of scope can be just as important as economies of scale.

Companies can try to operate in supersegments rather than in isolated segments. A **supersegment** is a set of segments sharing some exploitable similarity. For example, many symphony orchestras target people who have broad cultural interests, rather than only those who regularly attend concerts.

SELECTIVE SPECIALIZATION A firm selects a number of segments, each objectively attractive and appropriate. There may be little or no synergy among the segments, but each promises to be a moneymaker. This multisegment strategy has the advantage of diversifying the firm's risk. When Procter & Gamble launched Crest Whitestrips, initial target segments included newly engaged women and brides-to-be, as well as men who care about their looks.

PRODUCT SPECIALIZATION The firm makes a certain product that it sells to several different market segments. A microscope manufacturer, for instance, sells to university, government, and commercial laboratories. The firm makes different microscopes for the different customer groups and builds a strong reputation in the specific product area. The downside risk is that the product may be supplanted by an entirely new technology.

MARKET SPECIALIZATION The firm concentrates on serving many needs of a particular customer group. For instance, a firm can sell an assortment of products only to university laboratories. The firm gains a strong reputation in serving this customer group and becomes a channel for additional products the customer group can use. The downside risk is that the customer group may suffer budget cuts or shrink in size.

FULL MARKET COVERAGE The firm attempts to serve all customer groups with all the products they might need. Only very large firms such as Microsoft (software market), Toyota (vehicle market), and Coca-Cola (beverage market) can undertake a full market coverage strategy. Large firms can cover a whole market in two broad ways: through undifferentiated marketing or differentiated marketing.

In *undifferentiated marketing*, the firm ignores segment differences and goes after the whole market with one offer. It designs a product and a marketing program that will endow the product with a superior image and appeal to the broadest number of buyers, and it relies on mass distribution and advertising. Undifferentiated marketing is "the marketing counterpart to standardization and mass production in manufacturing."[37] The narrow product line keeps down the costs of research and development, production, inventory, transportation, marketing research, advertising, and product management. The undifferentiated advertising program also reduces advertising costs. The company can turn its lower costs into lower prices to win the price-sensitive segment of the market.

In *differentiated marketing*, the firm operates in several market segments and designs different products for each. Cosmetics firm Estée Lauder markets brands that appeal to women of different tastes: the flagship brand, the original Estée Lauder, appeals to older consumers; Clinique caters to middle-aged women; M·A·C to youthful hipsters; Aveda to aromatherapy enthusiasts; and Origins to eco-conscious consumers who want cosmetics made from natural ingredients.[38]

Starwood Hotels & Resorts   In its rebranding attempt to go "beyond beds," Starwood Hotels & Resorts has differentiated its hotels along emotional, experiential lines. At upscale Westin Hotels the key definition became "renewal." Not only are guests welcomed with herbal drinks, candles, and soft music, but each room features Westin's own "Heavenly Beds." Their mainstream brand is Sheraton. Somewhat less upscale, Sheraton's core value centers on "connections." Four Points by Sheraton is a more value-oriented Sheraton chain that uses comfort as its watchword and offers free coffee and bottled water in each room. The Four Points ads talk about providing guests with "the comforts of home."[39]

Differentiated marketing typically creates more total sales than undifferentiated marketing. However, it also increases the costs of doing business. Because differentiated marketing leads to both higher sales and higher costs, nothing general can be said about the profitability of this strategy. Companies should be cautious about oversegmenting their markets. If this happens, they may want to turn to *countersegmentation* to broaden the customer base. For example, Johnson & Johnson broadened its target market for its baby shampoo to include adults. Smith Kline Beecham launched its Aquafresh toothpaste to attract three benefit segments simultaneously: those seeking fresh breath, whiter teeth, and cavity protection.

Additional Considerations

Two other considerations in evaluating and selecting segments are segment-by-segment invasion plans and ethical choice of market targets.

SEGMENT-BY-SEGMENT INVASION PLANS

A company would be wise to enter one segment at a time. Competitors must not know to what segment(s) the firm will move into next. Segment-by-segment invasion plans are illustrated in △ **Figure 8.5**. Three firms, A, B, and C, have specialized in adapting computer systems to the needs of government and public sector, universities and schools, and corporate businesses. Company A meets all the computer needs of the public sector. Company B sells large computer systems to all three sectors. Company C sells only personal computers to corporate businesses.

Where should company C move next? Arrows added to the chart show the planned sequence of segment invasions. Company C will next offer midsize computers to companies. Then, to relieve company B's concern about losing some large computer business with businesses, C's next move will be to sell personal computers to

Multisegment strategies work well for products like Crest Whitestrips that appeal equally to several attractive but separate markets.

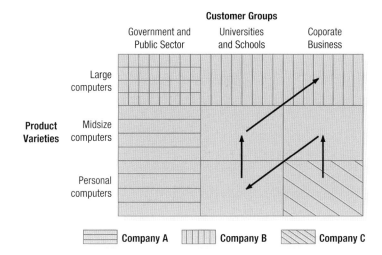

|Fig. 8.5| △

Segment-by-Segment
Invasion Plan

universities and schools. Later, C will offer midsize computers to that same segment. Finally, it may launch a full-scale attack on company B's large computer position in the corporate business segment. Of course, C's hidden planned moves are provisional, in that much depends on competitors' segment moves and responses.

Unfortunately, too many companies fail to develop a long-term invasion plan. PepsiCo is an exception. It first attacked Coca-Cola in the grocery market, then in the vending-machine market, then in the fast-food market, and so on. Japanese firms also plot their invasion sequence. They first gain a foothold in a market, then enter new segments with new products. Toyota began by introducing small cars (Tercel, Corolla), then expanded into midsize cars (Camry, Avalon), and finally into luxury cars (Lexus) and SUVs (Land Cruiser and Prado).

A company's invasion plans might not be as successful when it faces blocked markets. The invader must then figure out a way to break in, which usually calls for a megamarketing approach. **Megamarketing** is the strategic coordination of economic, psychological, political, and public relations skills, to gain the cooperation of a number of parties in order to enter or operate in a given market. Pepsi used megamarketing to enter the Indian market.

megamarketing the strategic coordination of economic, psychological, political, and public relations skills to gain the cooperation of a number of parties in order to enter or operate in a given market.

PepsiCo   After Coca-Cola left India, PepsiCo worked with an Indian business group to gain government approval for its entry over the objections of domestic soft drink companies and anti-multinational legislators. Pepsi offered to help India export some agricultural products in a volume that would more than cover the cost of importing soft-drink concentrate. PepsiCo also promised to help rural areas in their economic development. It further offered to transfer food-processing, packaging, and water-treatment technology to India. PepsiCo's bundle of benefits won the support of various Indian interest groups.

ETHICAL CHOICE OF MARKET TARGETS Marketers must target segments carefully to avoid consumer backlash. Some consumers may resist being labeled. Elderly consumers who don't feel their age may not appreciate products that identify them as 'old.'

Market targeting also can generate public controversy.[40] The public is concerned when marketers take unfair advantage of vulnerable groups (such as children) or disadvantaged groups (such as inner-city people on low incomes) or promote potentially harmful products. The cereal industry has been heavily criticized for marketing efforts directed toward children. Critics worry that high-powered appeals presented through the mouths of lovable animated characters will overwhelm children's defenses and lead them to want sugared cereals or poorly balanced breakfasts. Toy marketers have been similarly criticized. McDonald's and other chains have drawn criticism for pitching high-fat, salt-rich menu items to children and to low-income residents.

Not all attempts to target children, minorities, or other special segments draw criticism. Colgate-Palmolive's Colgate Junior toothpaste has special features designed to get children to brush longer and more often. Other companies are responding to the special needs of minority segments. Thus the issue is not who is targeted, but rather how and for what. Socially responsible marketing calls for targeting that serves not only the company's interests, but also the interests of those targeted.

Summary

1. Target marketing includes three activities: market segmentation, market targeting, and market positioning.

2. We can target markets at four levels: segments, niches, local areas, and individuals. Market segments are large, identifiable groups within a market. A niche is a more narrowly defined group. Globalization and the internet have made niche marketing more feasible to many. Marketers appeal to local markets through grass-roots marketing for trading areas, neighborhoods, and even individual stores.

3. More companies now practice individual and mass customization. The future is likely to see more self-marketing, a form of marketing in which individual consumers take the initiative in designing products and brands.

4. There are two bases for segmenting consumer markets: consumer characteristics and consumer responses. The major segmentation variables for consumer markets are geographic, demographic, psychographic, and behavioral. Marketers use them singly or in combination.

5. Business marketers use all these variables along with operating variables, purchasing approaches, and situational factors.

6. To be useful, market segments must be measurable, substantial, accessible, differentiable, and actionable.

7. A firm must evaluate the various segments and decide how many and which ones to target: a single segment, several segments, a specific product, a specific market, or the full market. If it serves the full market, it must choose between differentiated and undifferentiated marketing. Firms must also monitor segment relationships and seek economies of scope and the potential for marketing to supersegments.

8. Marketers must develop segment-by-segment invasion plans and choose target markets in a socially responsible manner at all times.

Applications

Marketing Debate

Is Mass Marketing Dead?

With marketers increasingly adopting more and more refined market segmentation schemes—fueled by the internet and other customization efforts—some critics claim that mass marketing is dead. Others counter that there will always be room for large brands that employ marketing programs targeting the mass market.

Take a position: Mass marketing is dead *versus* mass marketing is still a viable way to build a profitable brand.

Marketing Discussion

Descriptive versus Behavioral Market Segmentation Schemes

Think of various product categories. How would you classify yourself in terms of the various segmentation schemes? How would marketing be more or less effective for you depending on the segment involved? How would you contrast demographic versus behavioral segment schemes? Which ones do you think would be most effective for marketers trying to sell to you?

Marketing Excellence

>>HSBC

HSBC wants to be known as "the world's local bank." This tagline reflects HSBC's positioning as a globe-spanning financial institution with unique focus on serving local markets. Originally the Hong Kong and Shanghai Banking Corporation Limited, and once known in parts of the Arab world as the British Bank of the Middle East, HSBC was established in 1865 to finance the growing trade between China and the United Kingdom. It's now the second-largest bank in the world. HSBC serves over 100 million customers through 8,000 branches and offices in 87 countries and territories in Europe, the Asia-Pacific region, the Americas, the Middle East, and Africa. The bank has 303 offices in the Middle East and Africa alone.

In spite of this huge international network, the bank works hard to maintain a local presence and local knowledge in each area. Its fundamental operating strategy is to remain close to its customers. As former HSBC chairman Sir John Bond said, "Our position as the world's local bank enables us to approach each country uniquely, blending local knowledge with a worldwide operating platform."

HSBC was born from one small idea: a local bank serving local needs. In March 1865 HSBC opened its doors for business in Hong Kong and today it welcomes millions of customers across the globe. Ads for the World's Local Bank campaign depicted the way two different cultures interpret the same objects or events. HSBC's advertisements are well placed on TV and print media, and also found in almost 50 airports across the world. Ads for the campaign differed by region, where, according to the ad agency, "Each country has developed its own variations on the initial idea."

HSBC demonstrated its local knowledge with marketing efforts dedicated to specific locations. HSBC also targets consumer niches with unique products and services. For example, it found a little-known product area growing at 125 percent a year: pet insurance. The bank now distributes pet insurance to its depositors in the United States through its HSBC Insurance agency. In Malaysia, HSBC offered a 'smart card' and no-frills credit cards to the underserved student segment. The bank targets the high-value customer with its special HSBC Premier services. HSBC was very aggressive in marketing Premier services across the Arab world.

HSBC Amanah is the bank's global Islamic financial services division, which HSBC established to serve the particular financial needs of its Muslim customers. HSBC Amanah has the largest Islamic financial services team of any international bank. Other HSBC financial products targeted for different segments include HSBC Advance, HSBC retirement, and HSBC emerging markets. HSBC insurance offers personal, business, and corporate insurance services and advice. While all these products and services are offered all over the world, in all the countries in which HSBC operates the services are further customized by region or country whenever the need arises.

The bank pulls its worldwide businesses together under a single global brand with "the world's local bank" slogan. The aim is to link its international size with close relationships in each of the countries in which it operates. HSBC spends US$600 million annually on global marketing, which it consolidated in 2004 under the WPP group of agencies. Going forward, it will be seeking to leverage its position as "the world's local bank" to improve on its $11.5 billion brand value, which placed it 32nd in the 2010 Interbrand/*BusinessWeek* global brand rankings.

Questions

1. How did HSBC attempt to position itself as "the world's local bank"; that is, as a global bank, but a bank that also understands local cultures and needs? What benefit do you think HSBC draws from such a positioning?

Continued on next page >>

>>HSBC

2. Why would an Arab company or business choose HSBC as its banker?

3. What benefits does HSBC offer to:

   - an Arab company operating in a single Arab country?
   - a pan-Arab company?
   - a multinational company operating in the Arab world?

4. Construct a profile of a potential client who could be interested in HSBC's Amanah products. How would you target such a client?

Sources: Carrick Mollenkamp, "HSBC Stumbles in Bid to Become Global Deal Maker," *Wall Street Journal*, October 5, 2006; Kate Nicholson, "HSBC Aims to Appear Global Yet Approachable," *Campaign*, December 2, 2005, p. 15; Deborah Orr, "New Ledger," *Forbes*, March 1, 2004, pp. 72–73; "HSBC's Global Marketing Head Explains Review Decision," *Adweek*, January 19, 2004; "Now Your Customers Can Afford to Take Fido to the Vet," *Bank Marketing*, December 2003, p. 47; Kenneth Hein, "HSBC Bank Rides the Coattails of Chatty Cabbies," *Brandweek*, December 1, 2003, p. 30; Sir John Bond and Stephen Green, "HSBC Strategic Overview," presentation to investors, November 27, 2003; "Lafferty Retail Banking Awards 2003," *Retail Banker International*, November 27, 2003, pp. 4–5; "Ideas that Work," *Bank Marketing*, November 2003, p. 10; "HSBC Enters the Global Branding Big League," *Bank Marketing International*, August 2003, pp. 1–2; Normandy Madden, "HSBC Rolls out Post-SARS Effort," *Advertising Age*, June 16, 2003, p. 12; www.hsbc.com.

CHAPTER 9

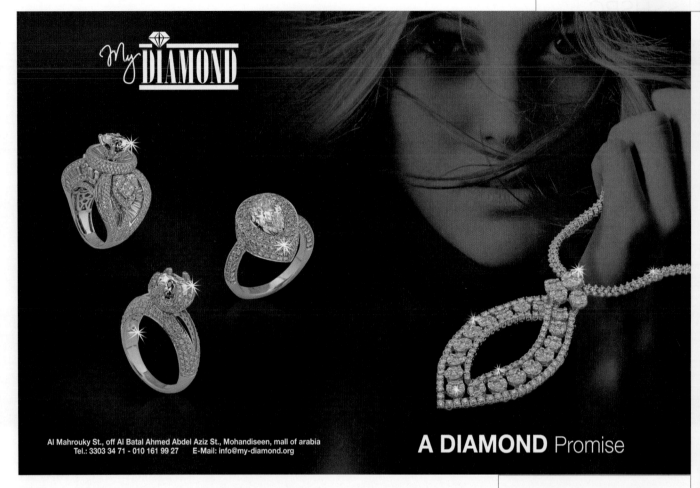

My Diamond conducts situational analysis continuously. This strategic-thinking approach led the company to rebrand its products and to cope with political moves and all other competitive tactics.

In this chapter, we will address the following questions:

1. **What is a brand and how does branding work?** (pg. 249)

2. **What is brand equity?** (pg. 234)

3. **How is brand equity built, measured, and managed?** (pg. 242)

4. **What are the important decisions in developing a branding strategy?** (pg. 252)

Creating Brand Equity

At the heart of a successful brand is a great product or service, backed by careful planning, a great deal of long-term commitment, and creatively designed and executed marketing. A strong brand commands intense consumer loyalty.

My Diamond is a stylist jewelry chain which started its business in Egypt in 2005 with capital of US$500,000. My Diamond is progressively expanding in the Egyptian market by applying a competitive market strategy, which has led the chain to triple its investment in 6 years. The My Diamond management has the ability to be flexible, as can be seen in their prompt responses to environmental changes. The first store opened by My Diamond is located in Cairo's El-Mohandseen area, followed by another store in the Mall of Arabia, the largest mall in the Middle East, and a third branch in El-Korba Square in Cairo's Heliopolis area. Tarek Saied says that My Diamond's expansion was financed entirely from the net profit gains generated from the original El-Mohandseen branch. This success is based on a marketing strategy which has three main dimensions: positive word of mouth and customer relationship management; buzz marketing; and selling unique and stylish models at competitive prices.

My Diamond is a family business which obtains some of its luxury products from its own jewelry factory. Other sophisticated models are very expensive to produce locally and can be imported at a lower cost from abroad. Mr. Saied[1] says, "In this business category, the main competitors are neighborhood jewelry stores. Most of these stores obtain part of their merchandise from the My Diamond factory and import the rest. When our management realized that our direct competitors depended mainly on My Diamond factory supplies to build their customer base, a swift decision was taken to supply only My Diamond stores with our factory's products." The timing of this strategic decision made good economic sense not only from a competititive perspective but also from economic and political ones. The decision was taken after the Egyptian revolution in January 2011, which was followed by an economic downturn and market slowdown, especially in luxury products, due to the uncertainty associated with the political changes. Limiting the supply of the factory's products to My Diamond outlets reduced the factory's overheads during the economic recession. From a marketing perspective the decision allowed My Diamond to cope with the economic, political, and competitive environment. Mr. Saied goes on to explain the validity of the decision, saying, "We realized that My Diamond products are somehow considered anchors to generate traffic at our competitors' stores. Then it is obvious to capitalize on our unique stylish products in My Diamond stores only. We figured that My Diamond jewelry is well recognized in our customers' minds as stylish modern models and we felt that a competitive branding strategy should take place from our side to position My Diamond as it is supposed to be perceived in the market." This strategy is a positive step towards building My Diamond as a standalone brand and reaching its potential equity.

strategic brand management the design and implementation of marketing activities and programs to build, measure, and manage brands to maximize their value.

To build the My Diamond brand personality, management decided to engage with buzz marketers, specifically loyal, elegant women. These 'buzz ladies' have the same personality as My Diamond brands, and can share their insights and emotions easily with others. My Diamond managed to attract some celebrities—actresses and opinion leaders—to wear their products at public events and during TV and press interviews. This anchored the image of My Diamond as an elite, high-class jewelry store. Another competitive strategy which distinguishes My Diamond is providing free diamond consultations to loyal customers. Mr. Saied says "Some customers are friends who love to come to the store to seek my opinion regarding stone grading, pricing, and models. These customers are evangelists of My Diamond products who enjoy being involved in the diamond circle while sipping a cup of Turkish coffee."

Marketers of successful 21st-century brands must excel at the strategic brand management process. **Strategic brand management** combines the design and implementation of marketing activities and programs to build, measure, and manage brands to maximize their value. The strategic brand management process has four main steps:

- Identifying and establishing brand positioning.
- Planning and implementing brand marketing.
- Measuring and interpreting brand performance.
- Growing and sustaining brand value.

Chapter 10 deals with brand positioning, while the remaining topics are discussed in this chapter. Chapter 11 reviews important concepts dealing with competition. ▽

What Is Brand Equity?

Perhaps the most distinctive skill of professional marketers is their ability to create, maintain, enhance, and protect brands.[2] Starbucks, Sony, Emirates Airline, Almarai, Afia, and Nike brands command a price premium and elicit deep customer loyalty. Newer brands such as Google and Red Bull capture the imagination of consumers and the financial community alike.

brand a name, term, sign, symbol, or design, or a combination of them, intended to identify the goods or services of one seller or group of sellers and to differentiate them from those of competitors.

The American Marketing Association defines a **brand** as "a name, term, sign, symbol, or design, or a combination of them, intended to identify the goods or services of one seller or group of sellers and to differentiate them from those of competitors." A brand is thus a product or service whose dimensions differentiate it in some way from other products or services designed to satisfy the same need. These differences may be functional, rational, or tangible: related to product performance of the brand. They may also be more symbolic, emotional, or intangible: related to what the brand represents.

Branding has been around for centuries as a means to distinguish the goods of one producer from those of another.[3] The earliest signs of branding in Europe were the medieval guilds' requirement that craftspeople put trademarks on their products to protect themselves and their customers against inferior quality. In the fine arts, branding began with artists signing their works. Brands today play a number of important roles that improve consumers' lives and enhance the financial value of firms.

Almarai do command a premium price, but this helps to produce strong customer loyalty.

The Role of Brands

Brands identify the source or maker of a product and allow consumers—either individuals or organizations—to assign responsibility for its performance to a particular manufacturer or distributor. Consumers may evaluate the identical product differently depending on how it is branded. They learn about brands through past experiences with the product and its marketing program, finding out which brands satisfy their needs and which do not. As consumers' lives become more complicated, rushed, and time starved, the ability of a brand to simplify decision making and reduce risk is invaluable.[4]

Brands also perform valuable functions for firms.[5] First, they simplify product handling or tracing. Brands help to organize inventory and accounting records. A brand also offers the firm legal protection for unique features or aspects of the product.[6] The brand name can be protected through registered trademarks; manufacturing processes can be protected through patents; and packaging can be protected through copyrights and proprietary designs. These intellectual property rights ensure that the firm can safely invest in the brand and reap the benefits of a valuable asset.

Brands signal a certain level of quality so that satisfied buyers can easily choose the product again.[7] Brand loyalty provides predictability and security of demand for the firm, and it creates barriers to entry that make it difficult for other firms to enter the market. Loyalty can also translate into customer willingness to pay a higher price: often 20 to 25 percent more than competing brands.[8] Although competitors may duplicate manufacturing processes and product designs, they cannot easily match lasting impressions left in the minds of individuals and organizations by years of product experience and marketing activity. In this sense, branding can be a powerful means to secure a competitive advantage.[9] **Table 9.1** shows *Forbes* magazine's Top 40 Arab Brands in 2006.

TABLE 9.1	Top 40 Arab Brands	
Rank	**Brand**	**Country**
1	Al Jazeera	Qatar
2	Emirates Group	UAE
3	Almarai	KSA
4	Al Arabia	KSA
5	Afia	KSA
6	Americana	Kuwait
7	Burj el Arab (UAE)	UAE
8	Fine (Jordan)	Jordan
9	Jarir Bookstore	KSA
10	Emaar	UAE
11	Qatar Airways	Qatar
12	Gulf Air	Bahrain
13	Aramex	Jordan
14	LBC	Lebanon
15	Patchi	Lebanon
16	Rotana	KSA
17	Future Television	Lebanon
18	Etihad Airways	UAE
19	Kudu	KSA
20	Rotana Hotels	UAE
21	Gandour (Lebanon)	Lebanon
22	Thuraya	UAE
23	Ajmal	UAE

(continued)

TABLE 9.1	continued	
Rank	**Brand**	**Country**
24	Al-Islami	UAE
25	Kassatly Chtaura	Lebanon
26	Gulfa	UAE
27	Air Arabia	UAE
28	Wataniya Telecom	Kuwait
29	Mikyajy	KSA
30	Nakheel	UAE
31	Mecca Cola	UAE
32	Milco	UAE
33	Melody	Egypt
34	Al Tazaj	KSA
35	Fayrouz	Egypt
36	Splash (UAE)	UAE
37	Jashanmal	Bahrain
38	Al Nakhla Tobacco	Egypt
39	Rawabi	UAE
40	Orascom Construction Industries	Egypt

Source: "The Top 40 Arab Brands," www.forbes.com/2006/10/17/top-arab-brands-biz_cz_fas_1018toparabbrands.html.

Sometimes marketers don't see the real importance of brand loyalty until they change a crucial element of the brand and that creates uproar among loyal customers who decide to switch to another brand. Others are more aware of this risk and prefer to keep a popular and strong brand name, such as DHL.

 DHL   In 2002, after a series of mergers and acquisitions, Deutsche Post (DP), the world's largest airfreight carrier, purchased DHL. To consolidate its image worldwide, DP did not only mandate its yellow and red color combination to DHL but also had to restructure after a year of extensive market research so as to unify their operations, create more synergies, and have a strong and efficient company. "One of the challenges of rebranding activities is that you are rebranding from a very strong brand," says Aly Thabet, DHL country marketing manager for Egypt. "The old DHL was a very strong brand, with the highest brand equity in Asia, Europe, and Africa, so migrating to a new logo meant you need to convey the old brand's attributes, plus the new reason for the change."[10]

 Allianz Group Egypt   The Allianz Group has been active on the Egyptian market for over 25 years. After acquiring 80 percent ownership of Arab International Insurance in 2000, it soon launched a sister company, Arab International

Life, in 2001, but it was not until 2004 that both companies began operations under the Allianz Egypt name to harness some global brand equity. Mostafa Salama, marketing director for Allianz Egypt, says, "The rebranding was a natural step. We are a subsidiary of a big giant, the Allianz Group, and although Arab International, our former name, is a local name that has been in the country for around 27 years, the Allianz Group is an older name that has more history and background." All subsidiaries of the Allianz Group took the company's identity and logo in an effort to unify the brand. "We had a choice either to invest in Arab International as a brand name and keep it living or rebrand to the Allianz Group. We find that the Allianz brand adds to our credibility and it gives the right image in the minds of our prospective customers, such as high service standards, flexible products, and the know-how from outside." The company implemented its new identity from the inside out: any piece of communication, from leaflets to brochures, had to follow the Allianz brand's layout. There was also a great deal of emphasis on internal communication throughout the process.[11]

To firms, brands represent enormously valuable pieces of legal property that can influence consumer behavior, be bought and sold, and provide the security of sustained future revenues to their owner. Companies have paid large earning multiples for brands in mergers or acquisitions, often justifying the price premium on the basis of the extra profits to be extracted and sustained from the brands, as well as the tremendous difficulty and expense of creating similar brands from scratch. The U.S. Stock Exchange on Wall Street in New York believes strong brands result in better earnings and profit performance for firms, which, in turn, create greater value for shareholders.[12] One of the master marketers of creating brands is Procter & Gamble, as described in the Marketing Excellence case at the end of this chapter.

The Scope of Branding

How do you 'brand' a product? Although firms provide brand creation through marketing programs and other activities, ultimately a brand resides in the minds of consumers. It is a perceptual entity rooted in reality but reflecting the perceptions and idiosyncrasies of consumers.

Branding is endowing products and services with the power of a brand. It's all about creating differences between products. Marketers need to teach consumers 'who' the product is—by giving it a name and other brand elements to identify it—as well as what the product does and why consumers should care. Branding creates mental structures that help consumers organize their knowledge about products and services in a way that clarifies their decision making and, in the process, provides value to the firm.

branding endowing products and services with the power of a brand.

For branding strategies to be successful and brand value to be created, consumers must be convinced there are meaningful differences among brands in the product or service category. Brand differences are often related to attributes or benefits of the product itself. Gillette, Merck, 3M, Gandour, Afia, Patchi and others have been leaders in their product categories for decades, due, in part, to continual innovation. Other brands create competitive advantages through non-product-related means. Gucci, Chanel, Louis Vuitton, and others have become leaders in their product categories by understanding consumer motivations and desires and creating relevant and appealing images around their products.

Marketers can apply branding virtually anywhere a consumer has a choice. It's possible to brand a physical good (Pantene shampoo, Mercedes automobiles, or Lipitor cholesterol medication), a service (Qatar Airlines, National Bank of Kuwait, or Aramex), a store (ABC department store in Lebanon, Enoteca specialty store, or Panda supermarket), a person (Sheikh Ahmed bin Saeed Al Maktoum or Andre Agassi), a place (Alexandria, Egypt, or Dubai), an organization (UNICEF or Youth Association for Social Awareness, known as 'YASA' in Lebanon), or an idea (free trade or freedom of speech).[13]

Defining Brand Equity

Brand equity is the added value endowed on products and services. It may be reflected in the way consumers think, feel, and act with respect to the brand, as well as in the prices, market share, and profitability the brand commands for the firm.

brand equity the added value endowed to products and services.

Marketers and researchers use various perspectives to study brand equity.[14] Customer-based approaches view it from the perspective of the consumer, either an individual or an organization.[15]

customer-based brand equity   the differential effect that brand knowledge has on a consumer response to the marketing of that brand.

brand knowledge   all the thoughts, feelings, images, experiences, beliefs, and so on that become associated with the brand.

The premise of customer-based brand equity models is that the power of a brand lies in what customers have seen, read, heard, learned, experienced, thought, and felt about the brand over time.[16]

Customer-based brand equity is the differential effect that brand knowledge has on consumer response to the marketing of that brand.[17] A brand has *positive* customer-based brand equity when consumers react more favourably to a product and the way it is marketed when the brand is *identified* than when it is not identified. A brand has negative customer-based brand equity if consumers react less favourably to marketing activity for the brand under the same circumstances. There are three key ingredients of customer-based brand equity.

First, brand equity arises from differences in consumer response. If no differences occur, then the brand name product is essentially a commodity or generic version of the product.[18] Competition will probably be based on price.

Second, differences in response are a result of consumers' knowledge about the brand. **Brand knowledge** consists of all the thoughts, feelings, images, experiences, beliefs, and so on that become associated with the brand. In particular, brands must create strong, favorable, and unique brand associations with customers, as have Volvo (safety), BMW (performance), and Harley-Davidson (adventure).

Third, the differential response by consumers that makes up brand equity is reflected in perceptions, preferences, and behavior related to all aspects of the marketing of a brand. Stronger brands lead to greater revenue.[19] ▬ **Box 9.1** summarizes some of these key benefits of brand equity.

The challenge for marketers in building a strong brand is therefore ensuring that customers have the right type of experiences with products, services, and their marketing programs to create the desired brand knowledge.

 Apple   Apple is a master at building a strong brand that resonates with customers across generations and national boundaries. It achieves incredible brand loyalty largely by delivering on its mission, as defined by the company's late founder, Steve Jobs: "To create great things that change people's lives." The company has created an army of Apple evangelists, not just because it produces great advertising but also because it focuses on the consumer in everything it does. Apple's innovative products combine superior design functionality and style, and many cite the wildly successful iPod music player as a prime example. Apple has also created retail stores worldwide to fuel excitement for the brand. The rationale behind the move to retail was that the more people could see and touch Apple products—and see what Apple could do for them—the more likely Apple was to increase its market share.[20]

Consumer knowledge is what drives the differences that manifest themselves in brand equity. In an abstract sense, we can think of brand equity as providing marketers with a vital strategic 'bridge' from their past to their future.[21]

BOX 9.1 ▬	Marketing Advantages of Strong Brands

Improved perceptions of product performance

Greater loyalty

Less vulnerability to competitive marketing actions

Less vulnerability to marketing crises

Larger margins

More inelastic consumer response to price increases

More elastic consumer response to price decreases

Greater trade cooperation and support

Increased marketing communications effectiveness

Possible licensing opportunities

Additional brand extension opportunities

Brand Equity as a Bridge

From the perspective of brand equity, marketers should think of all the marketing dollars spent on products and services each year as investments in consumer brand knowledge. The *quality* of the investment in brand building is the critical factor, not necessarily the *quantity*, beyond some minimal threshold amount. It's actually possible to overspend on brand building, if money is not spent wisely. 7Up saw sales decline in the 1990s despite sizable marketing support, arguably because of poorly targeted and delivered marketing campaigns.

At the same time, the brand knowledge created by marketing investments dictates appropriate future directions for the brand. Consumers will decide, based on what they think and feel about the brand, where (and how) they believe the brand should go and grant permission (or not) to any marketing action or program. New products such as Crystal Pepsi, Levi's Tailored Classic suits, Fruit of the Loom laundry detergent, and Cracker Jack cereal failed because consumers found them inappropriate extensions for the brand.

A **brand promise** is the marketer's vision of what the brand must be and do for consumers. The true value and future prospects of a brand rest with consumers, their knowledge about the brand, and their likely response to marketing activity as a result of this knowledge. Understanding consumer brand knowledge—all the different things that become linked to the brand in the minds of consumers—is thus of paramount importance because it is the foundation of brand equity.

Oxford University's Douglas Holt believes for companies to build iconic, leadership brands, they must assemble cultural knowledge, strategize according to cultural branding principles, and hire and train cultural experts.[22] Even Procter & Gamble, a company that has long controlled how shoppers perceive its products, has started on what its chief executive, A. G. Lafley, calls "a learning journey" with the consumer. "Consumers are beginning in a very real sense to own our brands and participate in their creation," he said. "We need to learn to begin to let go." One company that has let go is Burger King.

> **brand promise** the marketer's vision of what the brand must be and do for consumers.

 Burger King   "If you have a global brand promise, 'Have It Your Way'," says Russ Klein, Burger King's president for global marketing, strategy, and innovation, "it's about putting the customer in charge," even if they say "bad things" about the brand. In competing against McDonald's, with its family-friendly image, "it's more important for us to be provocative than pleasant," adds Klein, especially when appealing to a market of mainly teenage boys. Burger King's brash ad campaigns—featuring its creepy bobble-head king and talking chicken—appear on social networking sites such as You Tube and MySpace, so that the company can take advantage of what Klein calls "social connectivity" as consumers react to the ads. Burger King encourages customers to build online communities around their favorite company icons and products. Previously, Burger King used the mascot as an icon to engage wih customers. In August 2011, they announced that they will begin phasing this out, focusing on burger quality instead.[23]

Brand Equity Models

Although marketers agree about basic branding principles, a number of models of brand equity offer some different perspectives. Here we highlight four of the more-established ones.

BRAND ASSET VALUATOR Advertising agency Young and Rubicam (Y&R) developed a model of brand equity called brand asset valuator (BAV). Based on research with almost 500,000 consumers in 44 countries, BAV provides comparative measures of the brand equity of thousands of brands across hundreds of different categories. There are five key components—or pillars—of brand equity, according to BAV:

- *Differentiation* measures the degree to which a brand is seen as different from others.
- *Energy* measures the brand's sense of momentum.
- *Relevance* measures the breadth of a brand's appeal.
- *Esteem* measures how well the brand is regarded and respected.
- *Knowledge* measures how familiar and intimate consumers are with the brand.

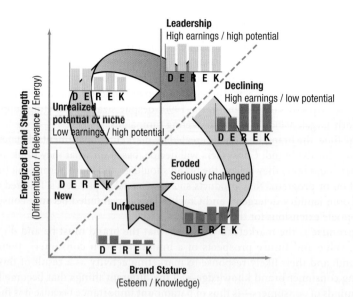

|Fig. 9.1| △

BAV Power Grid

Differentiation, energy, and relevance combine to determine *energized brand strength*. these three pillars point to the brand's future value. Esteem and knowledge together create *brand stature*, which is more of a 'report card' on past performance.

The relationships among these dimensions—a brand's 'pillar pattern'—reveal much about a brand's current and future status. Energized brand strength and brand stature combined form the *power grid*, depicting the stages in the cycle of brand development—each with characteristic pillar patterns—in successive quadrants (see △ **Figure 9.1**). Strong new brands show higher levels of differentiation and energy than relevance, whereas both esteem and knowledge are lower still. leadership brands show high levels on all pillars. Finally, declining brands show high knowledge—evidence of past performance—a lower level of esteem, and even lower relevance, energy, and differentiation.

BRANDZ Marketing research consultants Millward Brown and WPP have developed the BRANDZ model of brand strength, at the heart of which is the BrandDynamics pyramid. According to this model, brand building follows a sequential series of steps, each contingent upon successfully accomplishing the preceding one (see △ **Figure 9.2**).

'Bonded' consumers, those at the top of the pyramid, build stronger relationships with the brand and spend more on it than those at lower levels. More consumers, however, will be found at the lower levels. The challenge for marketers is to develop activities and programs that help consumers move up the pyramid.

AAKER MODEL Former marketing professor at University of California Berkeley, David Aaker, views brand equity as the brand awareness, brand loyalty, and brand associations that combine to add to or subtract from the value provided by a product or service.[24] According

|Fig. 9.2| △

BrandDynamics™
Pyramid

Source: BrandDynamics™ Pyramid.
Reprinted by permission of MillwardBrown
Optimor

to Aaker, brand management starts with developing a *brand identity*: the unique set of brand associations that represent what the brand stands for and promises to customers, an aspirational brand image.[25] Brand identity is typically 8 to 12 elements that represent concepts such as product scope, product attributes, quality/value, uses, users, country of origin, organizational attributes, brand personality, and symbols. The most important of these, which will drive brand-building programs, are the *core identity elements*. The others, *extended identity elements*, add texture and guidance. In addition, a *brand essence* can communicate the brand identity in a compact and inspiring way.

For example, according to Aaker, Ajax, a large industrial service company, has a brand essence of "Commitment to Excellence—Anytime, Anywhere, Whatever It Takes;" a core identity of "Spirit of Excellence," "Team Solutions," and "Technology That Fits;" and an extended identity of "Worldly But Informal," "Confident and Competent," "Open Communicator," "Global Network of Local Experts," and a "Supporter of World Health." The "Team Solutions" core identity was aspirational for a firm that consisted of several autonomous divisions, but necessary to support its strategy going forward.

Aaker maintains that the identity should be differentiating on some dimensions, suggest parity on others, resonate with customers, drive brand-building programs, reflect the culture and strategy of the business, and be credible. Credibility can be based on proof points, current assets or programs or strategic initiatives, or investments in new or revitalized assets or programs.

BRAND RESONANCE MODEL The brand resonance model also views brand building as an ascending series of steps, from bottom to top: (1) ensuring identification of the brand with customers and an association of the brand in customers' minds with a specific product class or customer need; (2) firmly establishing the totality of brand meaning in the minds of customers by strategically linking a host of tangible and intangible brand associations; (3) eliciting the proper customer responses in terms of brand-related judgment and feelings; and (4) converting brand response to create an intense, active loyalty relationship between customers and the brand.

According to this model, enacting the four steps means establishing a pyramid of six 'brand building blocks' with customers, as illustrated in △ **Figure 9.3**. The model emphasizes the duality of brands; the rational route to brand building is the left-hand side of the pyramid, whereas the emotional route is the right-hand side.[26]

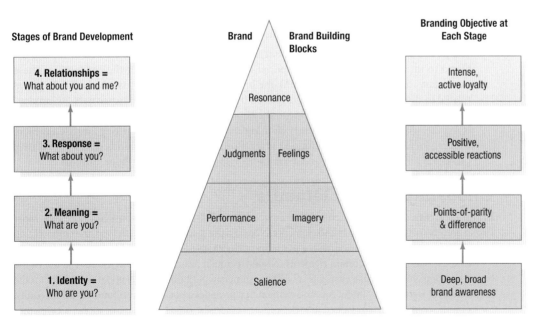

|Fig. 9.3| △

Brand Resonance Pyramid

MasterCard is an example of a brand with duality, because it emphasizes both the rational advantages of the credit card—its acceptance at establishments worldwide, as well as the emotional advantages—expressed in the award-winning Priceless advertising campaign, which shows people buying items to reach a certain goal. The goal itself—a feeling, an accomplishment, or other intangible—is "priceless" ("There are some things money can't buy; for everything else, there's MasterCard.").

The creation of significant brand equity requires reaching the top or pinnacle of the brand pyramid, which occurs only if the right building blocks are put into place.

- **Brand salience** is how often and how easily customers think of the brand under various purchase or consumption situations.
- **Brand performance** is how well the product or service meets customers' functional needs.
- **Brand imagery** describes the extrinsic properties of the product or service, including the ways in which the brand attempts to meet customers' psychological or social needs.
- **Brand judgments** focus on customers' own personal opinions and evaluations.
- **Brand feelings** are customers' emotional responses and reactions with respect to the brand.
- **Brand resonance** refers to the nature of the relationship customers have with the brand and the extent to which they feel they're 'in sync' with it.

Resonance is the intensity or depth of the psychological bond customers have with the brand, as well as the level of activity engendered by this loyalty.[27] Brands with high resonance include Harley-Davidson, Mercedes, Porsche, Diwan Bookstore, Apple, and eBay.[28]

Building Brand Equity

Marketers build brand equity by creating the right brand knowledge structures with the right consumers. This process depends on *all* brand-related contacts: whether marketer-initiated or not. From a marketing management perspective, however, there are three main sets of *brand equity drivers*:

- ***The initial choices for the brand elements or identities making up the brand.*** Brand names, URLs, logos, symbols, characters, spokespeople, slogans, jingles, packages, and signage.
- ***The integration of all accompanying marketing activities and supporting marketing programs.*** Brands are built around customer experiences. Customers come to know a brand through a range of contacts and touch points like personal observation and use, word of mouth, interactions with company personnel, online or telephone experiences, and payment transactions. The company must put strong focus on integrating marketing efforts and managing customer experiences.[29]
- ***The power of leveraging Secondary Associations.*** Brand equity can be created by linking the brand to information that conveys special meanings in the mind of the consumers. These 'secondary' brand associations can link the brand to key people that use the brand, to places related to the brand, or to the company itself by making reference to its partners, its employees, or other resources that add value to the equity of the brand. Aïshti's fastest-growing label is Aizone, whose edgy, contemporary clothing and accessories have a strong lifestyle appeal to women, men, and children. Positioned as an affordable luxury, the brand creates its exclusive cachet via limited distribution and a somewhat risqué name and rebellious attitude.

Choosing Brand Elements

brand elements those trademarkable devices that serve to identify and differentiate the brand such as a brand name, logo, or character.

Brand elements are those trademarkable devices that identify and differentiate the brand. Most strong brands employ multiple brand elements. Nike has the distinctive swoosh logo, the empowering Just Do It slogan, and the Nike name based on the ancient Greeks' winged goddess of victory.

Marketers should choose brand elements to build as much brand equity as possible. The test of the brand-building ability of these elements is what consumers would think or feel about the product *if* the brand element were all they knew. A brand element that provides a positive contribution to brand equity, for example, conveys certain valued associations or responses. Based on its name alone, a consumer might expect ColorStay lipsticks to be long-lasting and SnackWell to be healthful snack foods.

BRAND ELEMENT CHOICE CRITERIA There are six main criteria for choosing brand elements. The first three—memorable, meaningful, and likable—are 'brand building.' The latter three—transferable, adaptable, and protectable—are 'defensive' and deal with how to leverage and preserve the equity in a brand element in the face of opportunities and constraints.

- **Memorable.** How easily is the brand element recalled and recognized? Is this true at both purchase and consumption? Short names such as Tatra, Pampa, and Crest are memorable brand elements.

- **Meaningful.** Is the brand element credible and suggestive of the corresponding category? Does it suggest something about a product ingredient or the type of person who might use the brand? Consider the inherent meaning in names such as Almarai dairy produce, Bekhero milk, and Fawry for electronic payment.

- **Likable.** How aesthetically appealing is the brand element? Is it likable visually, verbally, and in other ways? Brand names such as Ocean Blue Hotel and Resort, Dream City, and Madinat residential areas evoke much imagery.

- **Transferable.** Can the brand element be used to introduce new products in the same or different categories? Does it add to brand equity across geographic boundaries and market segments? Although initially an online book seller, Amazon.com was smart enough not to call itself Books 'R' Us. The Amazon is famous as the world's biggest river, and the name suggests the wide variety of goods that could be shipped, an important descriptor of the diverse range of products the company now sells.

- **Adaptable.** How adaptable and updatable is the brand element?

- **Protectible.** How legally protectible is the brand element? How competitively protectible? Names that become synonymous with product categories—such as Chipsy, Kleenex, Jell-O, Scotch Tape, Xerox, and Fiberglass—should retain their trademark rights and not become generic.

DEVELOPING BRAND ELEMENTS Brand elements can play a number of brand-building roles.[30] If consumers don't examine much information in making their product decisions, brand elements should be easy to recognize and recall and inherently descriptive and persuasive. The likability and appeal of brand elements may also play a critical role in awareness and associations leading to brand equity.[31]

Of course, brand names aren't the only important brand element. Often, the less concrete brand benefits are, the more important it is that brand elements capture intangible characteristics.

Like brand names, slogans are an extremely efficient means to build brand equity. They can function as useful 'hooks' or 'handles' to help consumers grasp what the brand is and what makes it special, summarizing and translating the intent of a marketing program. Think of the inherent brand meaning in slogans such as "Fly Emirates," "World's 5-star Airline" (Qatar Airways), and "From Abu Dhabi to the World" (Etihad Airways).

The Egyptian Tax Authority   The Egyptian Tax Authority adopted a new tax law which reduced income tax to 20 percent but relied heavily on voluntary tax filing rather than coercive tax collection. It needed a very strong marketing campaign to convey this idea to the Egyptian taxpayers, amid a culture of tax evasion and mistrust. The Egyptian Tax Authority used Tarek Nour's advertising agency to undertake this pioneering awareness campaign. The agency addressed this very controversial issue with a very successful series of comic yet informative advertisements with the constant slogan Tax is Your Benefit, using a pun with the word *Maslahtek*, which means your benefit and your agency at the same time. The main character featured in this campaign, Ahmed Shoman, was a new face on TV. The success of this campaign has many facets: (1) increasing tax revenue, (2) the slogan Tax is Your Benefit has engaged with adults and children, and (3) last, but not least, the actor in the campaign became a popular movie star.[32]

But choosing a name with inherent meaning creates less flexibility, making it harder to add a different meaning or update the positioning.[33]

Designing Holistic Marketing Activities

Brands are not built by advertising alone. Customers come to know a brand through a range of contacts and touch points: personal observation and use, word of mouth, interactions with company personnel, online or telephone experiences, and payment transactions. A **brand contact** is any information-bearing experience, whether positive or negative, a customer or

brand contact any information-bearing experience a customer or prospect has with the brand, the product category, or the market that relates to the marketer's product or service.

prospect has with the brand, the product category, or the market that relates to the marketer's product or service.[34] The company must put as much effort into managing these experiences as into producing its ads.[35]

The strategy and tactics behind marketing programs have changed dramatically in recent years.[36] Marketers are creating brand contacts and building brand equity through many avenues, such as clubs and consumer communities, trade shows, event marketing, sponsorship, factory visits, public relations and press releases, and social cause marketing.

Regardless of the particular tools or approaches they choose, holistic marketers emphasize three important new themes in designing brand-building marketing programs: personalization, integration, and internalization.

PERSONALIZATION   The rapid expansion of the internet has created opportunities to personalize marketing.[37] Marketers are increasingly abandoning the mass-market practices that built brand powerhouses in the 1950s, 1960s, and 1970s for new approaches that are in fact a throwback to marketing practices from a century ago, when merchants literally knew their customers by name. *Personalizing marketing* is about making sure the brand and its marketing are as relevant as possible to as many customers as possible: this is a challenge given that no two customers are identical.

To adapt to the increased consumer desire for personalization, marketers have embraced concepts such as experiential marketing, one-to-one marketing, and permission marketing. From a branding point of view, these different concepts are about getting consumers more actively involved with a brand.

Permission marketing, the practice of marketing to consumers only after gaining their express permission, is based on the premise that marketers can no longer use 'interruption marketing' via mass-media campaigns. According to Seth Godin, a pioneer in the technique, marketers can develop stronger consumer relationships by respecting consumers' wishes and sending messages only when they express a willingness to become more involved with the brand.[38] Godin believes permission marketing works because it is "anticipated, personal, and relevant."

Permission marketing, like other personalization concepts, does presume consumers know what they want. But in many cases consumers have undefined, ambiguous, or conflicting preferences. 'Participatory marketing' may be a more appropriate concept than permission marketing, because marketers and consumers need to work together to find out how the firm can best satisfy consumers.

INTEGRATION   The traditional 'marketing-mix' concept and the notion of the 'four Ps' (see Chapter 1) do not adequately describe modern marketing programs. Integration marketing is about mixing and matching marketing activities to maximize their individual and collective effects.[39] To achieve it, marketers need a variety of different marketing activities that reinforce the brand promise.

brand image the set of beliefs, ideas, and impressions a person holds regarding a company or product.

In this regard, we should distinguish between brand identity and image. *Brand identity* is the way a company aims to identify or position itself or its product. **Brand image** is the way the public actually perceives them. For the right brand image to be established in the minds of consumers, the marketer must convey brand identity through every available communication vehicle and brand contact. Identity should be diffused in ads, annual reports, brochures, catalogs, packaging, company stationery, and business cards. If "IBM means service," this message must be expressed in symbols, colors and slogans, atmosphere, events, and employee behavior. Although it's fast becoming an economic powerhouse, China is late in the game when it comes to developing these aspects of branding—both image and identity—but some Chinese companies are learning fast.

Different marketing activities have different strengths and can accomplish different objectives. Marketers should therefore engage in a mixture of activities, each of which plays a specific role in building or maintaining brand equity. Although Michelin may invest in R&D and engage in advertising, promotions, and other communications to reinforce its 'safety' brand association, it may also choose to sponsor events to make sure it is seen as contemporary and up-to-date. Marketing programs should be put together synergistically so that the whole is greater than the sum of the parts. In other words, the effects of any one option should be enhanced or complemented by the presence of the other options.

INTERNALIZATION Marketers must now 'walk the walk' to deliver the brand promise. They must adopt an *internal* perspective to be sure employees and marketing partners appreciate and understand basic branding notions and how they can help—or hurt—brand equity.[40] **Internal branding** is activities and processes that help to inform and inspire employees.[41] It is critical for service companies and retailers that all employees have an up-to-date, deep understanding of the brand and its promise. Holistic marketers must go even further and train and encourage distributors and dealers to serve their customers well. Poorly trained dealers can ruin the best efforts to build a strong brand image.

Brand bonding occurs when customers experience the company as delivering on its brand promise. All the customers' contacts with company employees and company communications must be positive.[42] *The brand promise will not be delivered unless everyone in the company lives the brand.* Disney is so successful at internal branding and having employees support its brand that it holds seminars on the 'Disney Style' for employees from other companies.

internal branding activities and processes that help to inform and inspire employees.

Eli Lilly In 2000, Eli Lilly launched a new brand-building initiative with the slogan Answers That Matter. The aim was to establish Eli Lilly as a pharmaceutical firm that could give doctors, patients, hospitals, insurance companies, and governments trustworthy answers to questions of concern to them. To make sure everyone at Eli Lilly could deliver the right answers, the company developed a comprehensive Brand-to-Action training program. These sessions educated and engaged employees in the role of the corporate brand, Lilly's intended positioning, and how employees' behavior affected the customer experience and key touch points. Lilly also set up a brand governance structure, began to measure their corporate brand image, and developed a communications plan for the corporate branding effort.[43]

When employees care about and believe in the brand, they're motivated to work harder and feel greater loyalty to the firm. Some important principles for internal branding are:[44]

1. *Choose the right moment.* Turning points are ideal opportunities to capture employees' attention and imagination.
2. *Link internal and external marketing.* Internal and external messages must match.
3. *Bring the brand alive for employees.* A professional branding campaign should be based on marketing research and supervised by the marketing department. Internal communications should be informative and energizing.

Savola Group The Savola Group, a Saudi group of consumer food companies, strongly believes that core values and a balanced way of conducting business is key to the success and survival of any company. Savola's values are derived from Islamic ethical and moral principles. The strong vision that Savola Group has identified is easily adapted and accepted by its employees. This has led to the development of a successful company with motivated staff.

Leveraging Secondary Associations

The third and final way to build brand equity is, in effect, to 'borrow' it. That is, create brand equity by linking the brand to other information in memory that conveys meaning to consumers (see △ **Figure 9.4**).

These 'secondary' brand associations can link the brand to sources, such as the company itself (through branding strategies), to countries or other geographical regions (through identification

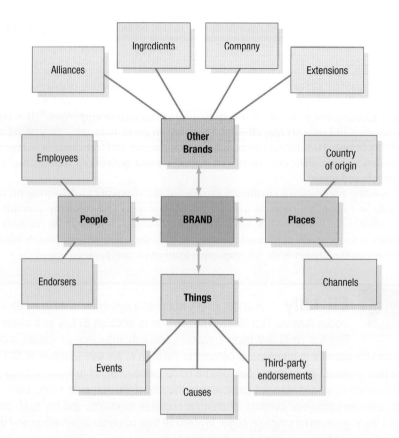

|Fig. 9.4| ◢

Secondary Sources of
Brand Knowledge

of product origin), and to channels of distribution (through channel strategy); as well as to other brands (through ingredient or co-branding), characters (through licensing), spokespeople (through endorsements), sporting or cultural events (through sponsorship), or some other third-party sources (through awards or reviews).

Fawaz Alhokair and Company (JSC), Global Brands Group, and FIFA   Fawaz Alhokair and Company (JSC)

linked itself with Global Brands Group, the exclusive worldwide Master Licensee of FIFA, by signing a four-year deal, starting in 2010, to open 14 FIFA Official Stores in key regions in the Middle East and North Africa and the Gulf Cooperation Council (GCC). In addition, a number of 2010 FIFA World Cup Official Event 'Shop in Shops' were opened across the Middle East during the 2010 World Cup tournament. The shops are large retail spaces set in prime retail locations. The first was opened in Riyadh, Saudi Arabia. FIFA Official Flagship Stores aim to connect football fans with FIFA's heritage, and stock Official FIFA Collections, event merchandise, and products from FIFA Commercial Affiliates. The stores sell football lifestyle apparel and accessories that link football, fashion, and culture. One of the partners in this deal, Fawaz Alhokair and Company (JSC), owns around 70 international fashion brands in the Middle East and employs over 4,000 people. The arrangement is beneficial to all parties concerned: Fawaz Alhokair and Company, Global Brands Group, and FIFA. Simon Hawkins, senior vice president and general manager for the FIFA & Football Business Unit of Global Brands Group said: "It's a very exciting time for us. Since we signed our agreement with FIFA, we have been working closely with them and are delighted to confirm Fawaz Alhokair and Company as our partner for this phase of our retail programme roll-out. It is a testament to the power of the FIFA brand that we have signed a deal with a retail partner of such magnitude." In addition, Thierry Weil, FIFA director Marketing Division, said: "We are pleased about the conclusion of the agreement between Fawaz Alhokair and Company (JSC) and Global Brands Group, which will develop the FIFA Brand retail business within the Middle East region. This assignment is important for the development of the FIFA Brand and ensures that FIFA merchandise reaches as wide an audience as possible."[45]

Measuring Brand Equity

Given that the power of a brand resides in the minds of consumers and the way it changes their response to marketing, there are two basic approaches to measuring brand equity. An *indirect* approach assesses potential sources of brand equity by identifying and tracking consumer brand knowledge structures.[46] A *direct* approach assesses the actual impact of brand knowledge on consumer response to different aspects of the marketing. The Marketing Insight: *The Brand Value Chain* shows how to link the two approaches.[47]

The two general approaches are complementary, and marketers can employ both. In other words, for brand equity to perform a useful strategic function and guide marketing decisions, marketers need to fully understand (1) the sources of brand equity and how they affect outcomes of interest, as well as (2) how these sources and outcomes change, if at all, over time. Brand audits are important for the former; brand tracking for the latter.

A **brand audit** is a consumer-focused series of procedures to assess the health of the brand, uncover its sources of brand equity, and suggest ways to improve and leverage its equity. Marketers should conduct a brand audit whenever they're considering important shifts in strategic direction. Conducting brand audits on a regular basis, such as annually, allows marketers to keep their fingers on the pulse of their brands so they can manage them more proactively and responsively. Audits are particularly useful background for managers as they set up their marketing plans.

Brand-tracking studies collect quantitative data from consumers on a routine basis over time to provide marketers with consistent, baseline information about how their brands and marketing programs are performing on key dimensions. Tracking studies are a means of understanding where, how much, and in what ways brand value is being created, to facilitate day-to-day decision making.

brand audit a consumer-focused exercise that involves a series of procedures to assess the health of the brand, uncover its sources of brand equity, and suggest ways to improve and leverage its equity.

brand-tracking studies studies that collect quantitative data from consumers on a routine basis over time to provide marketers with consistent, baseline information about how their brands and marketing programs are performing on key dimensions.

Marketing Insight

The Brand Value Chain

The brand value chain is a structured approach to assessing the sources and outcomes of brand equity and the manner in which marketing activities create brand value (see △ **Figure 9.5**). It is based on several premises.

First, the brand value creation process is assumed to begin when the firm invests in a marketing program targeting actual or potential customers. Any marketing program investment that can be attributed to brand value development, intentional or not, falls into this category: product research, development, and design; trade or intermediary support; and marketing communications.

Next, customers' mindsets are assumed to change as a result of the marketing program. The question is how. This change, in turn, is assumed to affect the way the brand performs in the marketplace through the collective impact of individual customers deciding how much to purchase and when, how much they pay, and so on. Finally, the investment community considers market performance and other factors such as replacement cost and purchase price in acquisitions to arrive at an assessment of shareholder value in general and the value of a brand in particular.

The model also assumes that a number of linking factors intervene between these stages and determine the extent to which value created at one stage transfers to the next stage. Three sets of multipliers moderate the transfer between the marketing program and the subsequent three value stages: the program multiplier, the customer multiplier, and the market multiplier.

The *program multiplier* determines the marketing program's ability to affect the customer mind-set and is a function of the quality of the program investment. The *customer multiplier* determines the extent to which value created in the minds of customers affects market performance. This result depends on contextual factors external to the customer.

Three such factors are:

- ***Competitive superiority.*** How effective the quantity and quality of the marketing investment of other competing brands are.

- ***Channel and other intermediary support.*** How much brand reinforcement and selling effort various marketing partners are putting forth.

- ***Customer size and profile.*** How many and what types of customers, profitable or not, are attracted to the brand.

- The *market multiplier* determines the extent to which the value shown by the market performance of a brand is manifested in shareholder value. It depends, in part, on the actions of financial analysts and investors.

Sources: Kevin Lane Keller and Don Lehmann, "How Do Brands Create Value," *Marketing Management*, May–June 2003, pp. 27–31. See also Marc J. Epstein and Robert A. Westbrook, "Linking Actions to Profits in Strategic Decision Making," *MIT Sloan Management Review*, Spring 2001, pp. 39–49; and Rajendra K. Srivastava, Tasadduq A. Shervani, and Liam Fahey, "Market-Based Assets and Shareholder Value," *Journal of Marketing*, 62, no. 1, January 1998, pp. 2–18.

Source: Kevin Lane Keller, *Strategic Brand Management*, 3rd edn (Upper Saddle River, NJ: Prentice Hall, 2008). Reproduced by permission of Pearson Education, Inc., Upper Saddle River, NJ.

|Fig. 9.5|

Brand Value Chain

Brand Valuation

brand valuation an estimate of the total financial value of the brand.

Marketers should distinguish brand equity from **brand valuation**, which is the job of estimating the total financial value of the brand. ⬜ **Table 9.2** displays the world's most valuable brands in 2010 according to one ranking.[48] In these well-known companies, brand value is typically over half the total company market capitalization. John Stuart, cofounder of Quaker Oats, said: "If this business were split up, I would give you the land and bricks and mortar, and I would take the brands and trademarks, and I would fare better than you." U.S. companies do not list brand equity on their balance sheets because of the arbitrariness of the estimate. However, brand equity is given a value by some companies in the United Kingdom, Hong Kong, and Australia. The Marketing Insight: *What Is a Brand Worth?* reviews one popular valuation approach.

TABLE 9.2 ⬜	The World's 10 Most Valuable Brands in 2010	
Rank	**Brand**	**2010 Brand Value (billions of US$)**
1	Apple	$57.4
2	Microsoft	$56.6
3	Coca-Cola	$55.4
4	IBM	$43.0
5	Google	$39.7
6	McDonald's	$35.9
7	General Electric	$33.7
8	Marlboro	$29.1
9	Intel	$28.6
10	Nokia	$27.4

Source: Kurt Badenhausen, "The World's Most Valuable Brands," *Forbes* online, July 28, 2010.[49]

What is a Brand Worth?

Top brand management firm Interbrand has developed a model to formally estimate the dollar value of a brand. Interbrand defines brand value as the net present value of the earnings a brand is expected to generate in the future and believes both marketing and financial analyses are equally important in determining the value of a brand. Its process follows five steps (see △ **Figure 9.6** for a schematic overview).

1. **Market segmentation.** The first step in the brand valuation process is to divide the market(s) in which the brand is sold into mutually exclusive segments of customers that help to determine the variances in the brand's economic value.

2. **Financial analysis.** Interbrand assesses purchase price, volume, and frequency to help calculate accurate forecasts of future brand sales and revenues. Specifically, Interbrand performs a detailed review of the brand's equities, industry and customer trends, and historic financial performance across each segment. Once it has established branded revenues, it deducts all associated operating costs to derive earnings before interest and tax (EBIT). It also deducts the appropriate taxes and a charge for the capital employed to operate the underlying business, leaving intangible earnings; that is, the earnings attributed to the intangible assets of the business.

3. **Role of branding.** Interbrand next attributes a proportion of intangible earnings to the brand in each market segment, by first identifying the various drivers of demand, then determining the degree to which the brand directly influences each. The role of branding assessment is based on market research, client workshops, and interviews, and represents the percentage of intangible earnings the brand generates. Multiplying the role of branding by intangible earnings yields brand earnings.

4. **Brand strength.** Interbrand then assesses the brand's strength profile to determine the likelihood that the brand will realize forecast earnings. This step relies on competitive benchmarking and a structured evaluation of the brand's market, stability, leadership position, growth trend, support, geographic footprint, and ability to be legally protected. For each segment, Interbrand applies industry and brand equity metrics to determine a risk premium for the brand. The company's analysts derive the overall brand discount rate by adding a brand-risk premium to the risk-free rate, represented by the yield on government bonds. The brand discount rate, applied to the brand earnings forecast, yields the net present value of the brand earnings. The stronger the brand, the lower the discount rate, and vice versa.

5. **Brand value calculation.** Brand value is the net present value (NPV) of the forecast brand earnings, discounted by the brand discount rate. The NPV calculation comprises both the forecast period and the period beyond, reflecting the ability of brands to continue generating future earnings.

Increasingly, Interbrand uses brand value assessments as a dynamic, strategic tool to identify and maximize return on brand investment across a whole host of areas.

Source: Interbrand, the Interbrand Brand Glossary, and Jeff Swystun.

Managing Brand Equity

Effective brand management requires a long-term view of marketing actions. Because consumer responses to marketing activity depend on what they know and remember about a brand, short-term marketing actions, by changing brand knowledge, necessarily increase or decrease the long-term success of future marketing actions.

Brand Reinforcement

As a company's major enduring asset, a brand needs to be carefully managed so that its value does not depreciate.[49] Many brand leaders of 70 years ago remain brand leaders today—Coca-Cola, Heinz, Abdul Rahman Al Hallab, and others—but only by constantly striving to improve their products, services, and marketing.

Brand equity is reinforced by marketing actions that consistently convey the meaning of the brand in terms of (1) what products the brand represents, what core benefits it supplies, and what needs it satisfies, as well as (2) how the brand makes products superior, and which strong, favorable, and unique brand associations should exist in the minds of consumers.[50] Nivea, one of Europe's strongest brands, has expanded its scope from a skin cream brand to a skin care and

Market Segments

↓   ↓   ↓

(Financial
Analysis)   (Demand
Drivers)   (Competitive
Benchmarking)

(Intangible
Earnings)   (Role of
Branding)   (Brand
Strength)

(Brand
Earnings)   (Brand
Discount
Rate)

Brand Value
(net present value of future brand earnings)

|Fig. 9.6| △

Interbrand Brand Valuation Method

personal care brand through carefully designed and implemented brand extensions reinforcing the Nivea brand promises of "mild," "gentle," and "caring" in a broader arena.

Reinforcing brand equity requires innovation and relevance throughout the marketing program. The brand must always be moving forward, but moving forward in the right direction, with new and compelling offerings and ways to market them. Brands that fail to move forward—such as Kmart, Levi Strauss, Montgomery Ward, Oldsmobile, and Polaroid—find that their market leadership dwindles or even disappears.

An important part of reinforcing brands is providing marketing support that's consistent in amount and kind. Consistency doesn't mean uniformity without change; many tactical changes may be necessary to maintain the strategic thrust and direction of the brand. Unless there is some change in the marketing environment, however, there is little need to deviate from a successful positioning. When change *is* necessary, marketers should vigorously preserve and defend sources of brand equity.

Volvo   In an attempt to woo a different audience, Volvo drifted away from its heritage of safety in the late 1990s to push driving fun, speed, and performance. Purchased by Ford in 1999, the company dropped its ReVOLVOlution-themed ad campaign for the brand and went back to its roots in an attempt to revive sagging sales. Volvo's positioning was updated, however, to convey "active safety" to transcend the brand's boxy, sturdy "passive safety" image. With product introductions that maximized safety but still encompassed style, performance, and luxury, Volvo's sales set records in 2003.[51]

In managing brand equity, marketers must recognize the trade-offs between activities that fortify the brand and reinforce its meaning, such as a well-received new product improvement or a creatively designed ad campaign, and those that leverage or borrow from existing brand equity to reap some financial benefit, such as a short-term promotional discount that just emphasizes the lower price.[52] At some point, failure to reinforce the brand will diminish brand awareness and weaken brand image.

Brand Revitalization

Changes in consumer tastes and preferences, the emergence of new competitors or new technology, or any new development in the marketing environment can affect the fortunes of a brand. In virtually every product category, once-prominent and admired brands have fallen on hard times or even disappeared.[53] Nevertheless, a number of brands have managed to make impressive comebacks in recent years, as marketers have breathed new life into their customer franchises. Volkswagen, Dr. Scholl's, and Rotana Hotels have all seen their brand fortunes successfully turned around to varying degrees in recent years.

Often, the first thing to do in revitalizing a brand is to understand what the sources of brand equity were to begin with. Are positive associations losing their strength or uniqueness? Have negative associations become linked to the brand? Then decide whether to retain the same positioning or create a new one, and if so, which new one. Sometimes the actual marketing program is the source of the problem, because it fails to deliver on the brand promise. Then a 'back-to-basics' strategy may make sense, as it did for Harley-Davidson.

Harley recovered from a brush with bankruptcy and revitalized its brand with a renewed commitment to quality and to grass-roots marketing efforts that appeal to its image-conscious customers.

Harley-Davidson Founded in 1903 in Milwaukee, Wisconsin, in the United States, Harley-Davidson has twice narrowly escaped bankruptcy but is today one of the most recognized motor vehicle brands in the world. In dire financial straits in the 1980s, Harley desperately licensed its name for ill-advised ventures such as cigarettes. Although consumers loved the brand, sales were depressed by product-quality problems, so Harley began its return to greatness by improving manufacturing processes. It also developed a strong brand community in the form of an owners' club, called the Harley Owners Group (H.O.G.), which sponsors bike rallies, charity rides, and other motorcycle events. Harley-Davidson has continued to promote its brand with grass-roots marketing efforts and now finds itself in the enviable position of demand exceeding supply.[54]

In other cases, however, the old positioning is just no longer viable and a 'reinvention' strategy is necessary. Mountain Dew completely overhauled its brand image to become a soft-drink powerhouse. As its history reveals, it is often easier to revive a brand that is alive but has been more or less forgotten.

Mountain Dew Pepsi initially introduced Mountain Dew in 1969 and marketed it with the countrified tagline "Yahoo Mountain Dew! It'll Tickle Your Innards." By the 1990s, the brand was languishing on store shelves despite an attempt to evolve the image with outdoor action scenes. To turn the brand around, Mountain Dew updated the packaging and launched ads featuring a group of anonymous young males—the "Dew Dudes"—participating in extreme sports such as bungee jumping, skydiving, and snowboarding while consuming Mountain Dew. The brand slogan became "Do the Dew." The brand's successful pursuit of young soda drinkers led to Mountain Dew's passing Diet Pepsi and challenging Diet Coke to become the number-four selling soft drink in terms of market share by 2005.

There is obviously a continuum of revitalization strategies, with pure 'back to basics' at one end, pure 'reinvention' at the other, and many combinations in between. Brand revitalizations of almost any kind start with the product.[55]

Devising a Branding Strategy

branding strategy   the number and nature of common and distinctive brand elements applied to the different products sold by the firm.

A firm's **branding strategy** reflects the number and nature of both common and distinctive brand elements it applies to the products it sells. Deciding how to brand new products is especially critical. When a firm introduces a new product, it has three main choices:

- It can develop new brand elements for the new product.
- It can apply some of its existing brand elements.
- It can use a combination of new and existing brand elements.

brand extension   a company's use of an established brand to introduce a new product.

sub-brand   a new brand combined with an existing brand.

parent brand   an existing brand that gives birth to a brand extension.

family brand   a parent brand that is already associated with multiple products through brand extensions.

line extension   the parent brand is used to brand a new product that targets a new market segment within a product category currently served by the parent brand.

category extension   using the parent brand to brand a new product outside the product category currently served by the parent brand.

brand line   all products, original as well as line and category extensions, sold under a particular brand name.

brand mix   the set of all brand lines that a particular seller makes available to buyers.

branded variants   specific brand lines uniquely supplied to different retailers or distribution channels.

licensed product   one whose brand name has been licensed to other manufacturers who actually make the product.

When a firm uses an established brand to introduce a new product, the product is called a **brand extension**. When marketers combine a new brand with an existing brand, the brand extension can also be called a **sub-brand**. The existing brand that gives birth to a brand extension or sub-brand is the **parent brand**. If the parent brand is already associated with multiple products through brand extensions, it can also be called a **family brand**.

Brand extensions fall into two general categories:[56] in a **line extension**, the parent brand covers a new product within a product category it currently serves, such as with new flavors, forms, colors, ingredients, and package sizes. Dannon has introduced several types of Dannon yogurt line extensions through the years: Fruit on the Bottom, All Natural Flavors, and Fruit Blends. In a **category extension**, the parent brand is used to enter a different product category from the one it currently serves, such as Swiss Army watches. Honda has used its company name to cover such different products as automobiles, motorcycles, snowblowers, lawn-mowers, marine engines, and snowmobiles. This allows Honda to advertise that it can fit "six Hondas in a two-car garage."

A **brand line** consists of all products—original as well as line and category extensions—sold under a particular brand. A **brand mix** (or brand assortment) is the set of all brand lines that a particular seller makes available to buyers. Many companies are now introducing **branded variants**, which are specific brand lines supplied to specific retailers or distribution channels. They result from the pressure retailers put on manufacturers to provide distinctive offerings. A camera company may supply its low-end cameras to mass merchandisers while limiting its higher-priced items to specialty camera shops. Elie Saab may design and supply different lines of suits and jackets to different department stores.[57]

A **licensed product** is one whose brand name has been licensed to other manufacturers that actually make the product. Corporations have seized on licensing to push their company name and image across a wide range of products—from bedding to shoes—making licensing a US$35 billion business.[58] Jeep's licensing program, which now has 600 products and 150 licensees, includes every-thing from strollers (built for a father's longer arms) to apparel (with teflon in the denim), as long they fit the brand's positioning of "Life without Limits." Licensing revenue rose by 20 percent from 2004 to 2006.[59]

Branding Decisions

How to develop brand name strategy for products and services is becoming a major decision facing firms. Firms most often use one or a combination of the following four general strategies when branding products and services:

- *Individual names.* Indevco uses individual names, such as Sanita, Charm, Club, Dreams, Gipsy, Select, Happies, Medica, and others. A major advantage of an individual-names strategy is that the company does not tie its reputation to the product. If the product fails or appears to have low quality, the company's name or image is not hurt. Companies often use different brand names for different quality lines within the same product class. Flydubai is an example of using a different brand for lower budget flying within the same region that will not hurt the image of the master brand. Although it's not part of the Emirates Group, its founder is Sheikh Ahmed bin Saeed Al Maktoum, the Chairman of the Emirates Airlines, and Emirates have supported Flydubai to get started.

- *Blanket family names.* Many firms, such as Heinz and General Electric, use their corporate brand across their range of products.[60] Development costs are lower with blanket names because there's no need to run 'name' research or spend heavily on advertising to create recognition. Campbell's introduces new soups under its brand name with extreme simplicity and achieves instant recognition. Sales of the new product are likely to be strong if the manufacturer's name is good. Corporate-image associations of innovativeness, expertise, and trustworthiness have been shown to directly influence consumer evaluations.[61] Finally, a corporate branding strategy can lead to greater intangible value for the firm.[62]

- *Separate family names for all products.* Debbane Group (DESCO Holding) currently owns 23 companies in different industries, comprising Exotica Flowers, PESCO International, ENOTECA, IMC, SODAMCO, EVER GULF, and others. If a company produces quite different products like these, one blanket name is often not desirable.

- *Corporate name combined with individual product names.* Kellogg's combines corporate and individual names in Kellogg's Rice Krispies, Kellogg's Raisin Bran, and Kellogg's Corn Flakes, as do Honda, Sony, Americana, Panda, and Hewlett-Packard for their products. The company name legitimizes, and the individual name individualizes, the new product.

Individual names and blanket family names are sometimes referred to as a 'house of brands' and a 'branded house,' respectively, and they represent two ends of a brand relationship continuum. Separate family names come in between the two, and corporate-plus-individual names combine them. Not every company follows one strategy. For instance, when Aramex International acquired the UAE's primary express delivery service provider, Memo Express Service LLC, the branding decision was trickier. Fadi Ghandour, CEO of Aramex, and Kurt Springis, general manager for Memo Express Services LLC, decided to keep the two companies as separate brands, but to fully integrate the companies' staff, systems, and technological capabilities.[63]

So, although firms rarely adopt a pure example of any of the four strategies, deciding which general strategy to emphasize depends on several factors, such as whether the parent brand adds associations, credibility, visibility, and communication efficiencies; or whether a separate brand creates its own association, represents something new, whether it can retain or capture a customer/brand bond, and whether it can deal with channel conflict.[64]

Two key components of virtually any branding strategy are brand extensions and brand portfolios.

HYBRID BRANDING DECISIONS: Although firms rarely adopt a pure example of any of the four strategy decision options presented above, some firms go with a hybrid approach to branding decisions that will achieve one or both of the following strategic objectives:

1. To integrate the family brand in a way that contributes to the offering by adding associations and credibility that enhance core value propositions such as in the case of the Jumeirah Group's branding strategy (see in-chapter case below). This strategic option is often referred to as a "Branded House" strategy. The Jumeirah Group, as a luxury hospitality company, developed a strategy to integrate its portfolio of top hotels in Dubai that includes the Jumeirah Emirates Towers, the MadinatJumeirah, the Jumeirah Beach Hotel, the JumeirahZabeelSaray, and the JumeirahCreekside Hotel, as well as hotels around the world including the Jumeirah Frankfurt; the Jumeirah Himalayas Hotel, Shanghai; the Jumeirah Grand Hotel Via Veneto, Rome; and the JumeirahMessilah Beach Hotel & Spa in Kuwait. For Alice Royton, the Director of Branding for the Jumeirah Group, the challenge was how to create brand synergy whilst expanding the portfolio of Jumeirah hotels, all in an increasingly competitive international marketplace.

3. To separate the family brand from new or existing service and product brands in order to represent new or different offerings with unique associations, which aims to capture and connect with different customers. This strategy was adopted by the Jumeirah Group when it identified a compelling need to create experiential brands that include water parks, spas, and a restaurant division. While the Jumeirah Group's main brand offering is managing luxury hotels and resorts, the group also manages Talise Spa, a global spa brand; The Taste Department, a restaurant division; and the Wild Wadi water park. With all this, the Jumeirah Group implements what is commonly referred to as a "House of Brands" that plays a supporting role to Jumeirah as a master brand. Also, this "House of Brands" by the Jumeirah Group includes the Burj Al Arab, the world's most luxurious hotel that maintains its own association with customers in the super-rich segment of the hospitality market.

Jumeirah: How to Stay Different   The Dubai-based Jumeirah Group was founded in 1997 as a luxury hospitality company, with the ambition of becoming a global brand leader in the hospitality industry. As a member of Dubai Holding, the corporate brand portfolio of Jumeirah Group was reorganized in January 2008 to create two subsidiaries – Jumeirah Group LLC (management activity) and Jumeirah Assets LLC (ownership). This corporate brand reorganization was intended to separate the management and operation of hotels from the ownership of assets in order to allow the Jumeirah Group to re-focus and to excel in operating hotels, resorts and associated hospitality businesses. Jumeirah now focuses its expansion strategy on management agreements to operate establishments on behalf of hotel owners for negotiated and agreed fees.

This brand strategy allowed a high rate of growth over a short period of time. Now, the ambition of achieving global brand leadership has been realized. The Jumeirah brand name is now synonymous with luxury, dedicated service in all aspects of hotel management, with a strong emphasis on personalized relationships. The brand's vision and guiding principles are based on the commitment to STAY DIFFERENT™. The CEO, Guy Crawford, has commented that their driving force is a commitment to the STAY DIFFERENT™ philosophy which motivates everyone in the group. He hopes it builds rewarding relationships "through creative thinking and innovative strategy." He hopes his guests also share similar values – people looking for something different who want a unique luxury hotel experience "with striking architecture and design." The promise of STAY DIFFERENT™ is summarised as the offer of imaginative and exhilarating experiences in culturally connected environments delivered with thoughtful and generous service.

While focusing on the management of luxury hotels and resorts, Jumeirah Group also manages Jumeirah Living, a luxury brand of serviced residences; Talise Spa, their global spa brand; Jumeirah Restaurants, their restaurant division; the thrilling Wild Wadi water park; and The Emirates Academy of Hospitality Management and a tertiary level management school. The Jumeirah brand portfolio includes over 5,000 luxury suites, rooms, and apartments within 17 luxury hotels, resorts, and serviced residences.

A result of recent growth in the Dubai tourism market, Jumeirah's beachfront resorts, which include Madinat Jumeirah, Jumeirah Beach Hotel, and Jumeirah Zabeel Saray, experienced a surge in average occupancy reaching a 90% rate during the 2011 – 2012 festive season. Also, the revenue per available room (RevPAR), the hospitality industry standard for measuring hotel performance, stood at AED 2,600 (US $ 712) during this period. While Burj Al Arab, which aims to be the world's most luxurious hotel, recorded average occupancy of 80.7% during this period and RevPAR of AED 7,284 (US $ 1,983). This surely makes the company one of the leading luxury hospitality brands in the world and also suggests that the Middle East, including Dubai, continues to be increasingly popular with tourists. [65]

Brand Extensions

Many firms have decided to leverage their most valuable asset by introducing a host of new products under their strongest brand names. Most new products are in fact line extensions, typically 80 to 90 percent in any one year. Moreover, many of the most successful new products, as rated by various sources, are extensions. Among the most successful new products in 2009 were Campbell's Select Harvest, Bud Light Lime, Green Giant Valley Fresh Steamers, Gatorade Tiger, Tide Total Care, and others. Nevertheless, many new products are introduced each year as new brands.

ADVANTAGES OF BRAND EXTENSIONS   Two main advantages of brand extensions are that they can facilitate new-product acceptance and provide positive feedback to the parent brand and company.

Improved Odds of New-Product Success   Consumers can make inferences and form expectations about the composition and performance of a new product based on what they already know about the parent brand and the extent to which they feel this information is relevant to the new product.[66] For example, when Sony introduced a new personal computer tailored for multimedia applications, the VAIO, consumers may have felt comfortable with its anticipated performance because of their experience with and knowledge of other Sony products.

By setting up positive expectations, extensions reduce risk.[67] It may also be easier to convince retailers to stock and promote a brand extension because of increased customer demand. From a marketing communications perspective, an introductory campaign for an extension doesn't need to create awareness of both the brand *and* the new product, but instead it can concentrate on the new product itself.[68]

Extensions can thus reduce costs of the introductory launch campaign, important given that establishing a new brand name in the U.S. marketplace for a mass-consumer-packaged good can cost US$100 million! Extensions also can avoid the difficulty—and expense—of coming up with a new name and allow for packaging and labeling efficiencies. Similar or identical packages and labels can result in lower production costs for extensions and, if coordinated properly, more prominence in the retail store via a 'billboard' effect. With a portfolio of brand variants within a product category, consumers who need a change—because of boredom, satiation, or whatever—can switch to a different product type without having to leave the brand family. Business-to-business companies are even finding that brand extensions are a powerful way to enter consumer markets, as these two name brand rubber companies discovered.

 Groupe Michelin, Goodyear   Both Groupe Michelin and Goodyear, known primarily for their rubber tires, have launched a number of brand extensions in recent years. Although Michelin's extensions have mainly been in the auto accessories area—from inflation- and pressure-monitoring goods to automotive floor mats—its sports and leisure category now has the potential to overtake the auto accessories line. So far, its brand extensions fall into three categories: (1) automotive and cycle-related products, (2) footwear, apparel, accessories, and equipment for work, sports, and leisure, and (3) personal accessories, gifts, and collectibles promoting Michelin culture and heritage featuring Bibendum, the trademark "Michelin Man." Like Michelin, Goodyear has a category of products closely aligned to the automotive industry, such as jack stands and auto repair tools, but it, too, has branched out into consumer areas. The company is selling its own line of cleaning wipes for windows and upholstery, mechanic's gloves, and garden hose nozzles, among other products, at Home Depot stores.[69]

Positive Feedback Effects   Besides facilitating acceptance of new products, brand extensions can also provide feedback benefits.[70] They can help to clarify the meaning of a brand and its core brand values or improve consumer loyalty and perceptions of the credibility of the company behind the extension.[71] Thus, through brand extensions, Crayola means "colorful crafts for kids," Aunt Jemima means "breakfast foods," and Weight Watchers means "weight loss and maintenance." Juhayna has extended its yogurt product line by launching Zabado, a healthy yogurt for snacking or with meals.

Line extensions can renew interest and liking for the brand and benefit the parent brand by expanding market coverage.[72] When Mobinil, the wireless network provider, chose "Mobile in Every Hand" as a slogan, it did not take into consideration the diversified Egyptian segments. In 2011, Mobinil managed to introduce very aggressive subscription plans with different brand names such as Alo, Star, and Business. This brand extension strategy, with its different subscription fees, enabled Mobinil to extend its subscription base and to position itself as a patriotic company appealing to the majority.

One benefit of a successful extension is that it may also serve as the basis for subsequent extensions.[73]

DISADVANTAGES OF BRAND EXTENSIONS   On the downside, line extensions may cause the brand name to be less strongly identified with any one product.[74] Ries and Trout, marketing gurus who came up with the term "positioning," call this the "line-extension trap."[75] By linking its brand to mainstream food products such as mashed potatoes, powdered milk, soups, and beverages, Cadbury ran the risk of losing its more specific meaning as a chocolates and candy brand.[76] **Brand dilution** occurs when consumers no longer associate a brand with a specific product or highly similar products, and start thinking less highly of the brand.

brand dilution   when consumers no longer associate a brand with a specific product or highly similar products, and start thinking less favorably about the brand.

If a firm launches extensions consumers deem inappropriate, they may question the integrity of the brand or become confused and perhaps even frustrated: which version of the product is the 'right one' for them? Retailers reject many new products and brands because they don't have the shelf or display space for them. And the firm itself may become overwhelmed. When Lego decided to become a lifestyle brand and launch its own lines of clothes, watches, and video games, as well as design programs to attract more girls into the brand franchise, it neglected its core market of five- to nine-year-old boys. When plunging profits led to layoffs of almost half its employees in 2004, the firm streamlined its brand portfolio to emphasize its core businesses.[77]

The worst possible scenario is for an extension not only to fail, but also to harm the parent brand image in the process. Fortunately, such events are rare. 'Marketing failures,' where insufficient consumers were attracted to a brand, are typically much less damaging than 'product failures,' where the brand fundamentally fails to live up to its promise. Even then, product failures dilute brand equity only when the extension is seen as very similar to the parent brand. The Audi 5000 car suffered from a tidal wave of negative publicity and word of mouth in the mid-1980s when it was alleged to have a 'sudden acceleration' problem. The adverse publicity also spilled over to the 4000 model. But the Quattro was relatively insulated from negative repercussions, because it was distanced from the 5000 by its more distinct branding and advertising strategy.[78]

Even if sales of a brand extension are high and meet targets, the revenue may be coming from consumers switching to the extension from existing parent-brand offerings, in effect *cannibalizing* the parent brand. Intrabrand shifts in sales may not necessarily be undesirable if they're a form of *preemptive cannibalization*. In other words, consumers might have switched to a competing brand instead of the line extension if the extension hadn't been introduced. Tide laundry detergent maintains the same market share it had 50 years ago because of the sales contributions of its various line extensions: scented and unscented powder, tablet, liquid, and other forms.

One easily overlooked disadvantage of brand extensions is that the firm forgoes the chance to create a new brand with its own unique image and equity.

SUCCESS CHARACTERISTICS
Marketers must judge each potential brand extension by how effectively it leverages existing brand equity from the parent brand, as well as how effectively, in turn, it contributes to the parent brand's equity.[79] Crest White Strips leveraged the strong reputation of Crest and dental care to provide reassurance in the teeth-whitening arena, while also reinforcing its dental authority image. The most important consideration with extensions is that there should be a 'fit' in the mind of the consumer, based on common physical attributes, usage situations, or user types.

Box 9.2 lists a number of academic research findings on brand extensions.[80] One major mistake in evaluating extension opportunities is failing to take *all* consumers' brand knowledge structures into account and focusing instead on one or perhaps a few brand associations as a potential basis of fit.

 Bic   The French company Société Bic, by emphasizing inexpensive, disposable products, was able to create markets for nonrefillable ballpoint pens in the late 1950s; disposable cigarette lighters in the early 1970s; and disposable razors in the early 1980s. It unsuccessfully tried the same strategy in marketing Bic perfumes in the United States and Europe in 1989. The perfumes—two for women (Nuit and Jour) and two for men (Bic for Men and Bic Sport for Men)—were packaged in quarter-ounce glass spray bottles that looked like fat cigarette lighters and sold for US$5 each. The products were displayed on racks at checkout counters throughout Bic's extensive distribution channels. At the time, a Bic spokeswoman described the new products as extensions of the Bic heritage: "high quality at affordable prices, convenient to purchase, and convenient to use." The brand extension was launched with a US$20 million advertising and promotion campaign containing images of stylish people enjoying themselves with the perfume and using the tagline "Paris in Your Pocket." Nevertheless, Bic was unable to overcome its lack of cachet and negative image associations, and the extension was a failure.[81]

BOX 9.2	Research Insights on Brand Extensions

Academics have studied brand extensions closely. Here is a summary of some of their key research findings.

- Successful brand extensions occur when the parent brand is seen as having favorable associations and there is a perception of fit between the parent brand and the extension product.

- There are many bases of fit: product-related attributes and benefits, as well as nonproduct-related attributes and benefits related to common usage situations or user types.

- Depending on consumer knowledge of the categories, perceptions of fit may be based on technical or manufacturing commonalties or more surface considerations such as necessary or situational complementarity.

- High-quality brands stretch farther than average-quality brands, although both types of brands have boundaries.

- A brand that is seen as prototypical of a product category can be difficult to extend outside the category.

- Concrete attribute associations tend to be more difficult to extend than abstract benefit associations.

- Consumers may transfer associations that are positive in the original product class but become negative in the extension context.

- Consumers may infer negative associations about an extension, perhaps even based on other inferred positive associations.

- It can be difficult to extend into a product class that is seen as easy to make.

- A successful extension can not only contribute to the parent brand image but also enable a brand to be extended even farther.

- An unsuccessful extension hurts the parent brand only when there is a strong basis of fit between the two.

- An unsuccessful extension does not prevent a firm from 'backtracking' and introducing a more-similar extension.

- Vertical extensions can be difficult and often require subbranding strategies.

- The most effective advertising strategy for an extension emphasizes information about the extension (rather than reminders about the parent brand).

Source: Kevin Lane Keller, *Strategic Brand Management*, 3rd edn (Upper Saddle River, NJ: Prentice Hall, 2008). Reproduced by permission of Pearson Education, Inc., Upper Saddle River, NJ.

Brand Portfolios

All brands have boundaries: a brand can only be stretched so far, and all the segments the firm would like to target may not view the same brand equally favorably. Marketers often need multiple brands in order to pursue these multiple segments. Some other reasons for introducing multiple brands in a category include:[82]

- increasing shelf presence and retailer dependence in the store;

- attracting consumers seeking variety who may otherwise have switched to another brand;

- increasing internal competition within the firm;

Armani's line of luxury clothing is differentiated to appeal to three distinct price tiers, each with different styles and levels of luxury and customization.

brand portfolio   the set of all brands and brand lines a particular firm offers for sale to buyers in a particular category.

- yielding economies of scale in advertising, sales, merchandising, and physical distribution.

The **brand portfolio** is the set of all brands and brand lines a particular firm offers for sale in a particular category or market segment.

Armani   Armani has set out to create a product line differentiated by style, luxury, customization, and price to compete in three distinct price tiers. In the most expensive Tier I, it sells Giorgio Armani and Giorgio Armani Privé, which are custom-made runway couture products that sell for thousands of dollars. In the more moderately priced Tier II, it offers Emporio Armani, young and modern with more affordable prices, as well as the informal Armani jeans that focus on technology and ecology. In the lower-priced Tier III, the firm sells the more youthful and street-savvy translation of Armani style, AlX Armani Exchange, at retail locations in cities and suburban malls.

The hallmark of an optimal brand portfolio is the ability of each brand in it to maximize equity in combination with all the other brands in it. Marketers generally need to trade off market coverage with costs and profitability. If they can increase profits by dropping brands, a portfolio is too big; if they can increase profits by *adding* brands, it's not big enough. The basic principle in designing a brand portfolio is to *maximize market coverage*, so that no potential customers are being ignored, but to *minimize brand overlap*, so brands are not competing for customer approval. Each brand should be clearly differentiated and appealing to a sizable enough marketing segment to justify its marketing and production costs.[83]

Marketers carefully monitor brand portfolios over time to identify weak brands and kill unprofitable ones.[84] Brand lines with poorly differentiated brands are likely to be characterized by much cannibalization and require pruning.[85] One brand of cereal can come in several flavors. Investors can choose among thousands of mutual funds. Students can choose among hundreds of business schools. For the seller, this spells hypercompetition. For the buyer, it may mean too much choice. Brands can also play a number of specific roles as part of a portfolio.

FLANKERS   Flanker or 'fighter' brands are positioned with respect to competitors' brands so that more important (and more profitable) *flagship brands* can retain their desired positioning. Procter & Gamble markets Luvs diapers in a way that flanks the more premium Pampers. Marketers walk a fine line in designing fighter brands, which must not be so attractive that they take sales away from their higher-priced comparison brands. At the same time, if fighter brands are seen as connected to other brands in the portfolio in any way—say, by virtue of a common branding strategy—then they also can't be designed so cheaply that they reflect poorly on these other brands.

CASH COWS   Some brands may be kept around despite declining sales because they still manage to hold on to enough customers and maintain their profitability with virtually no marketing support. Companies can effectively 'milk' these 'cash cow' brands by capitalizing on their reservoir of existing brand equity. For example, despite the fact that technological advances have moved much of its market to the newer Mach III and Fusion brands of razors, Gillette still sells the older Trac II, Atra, and Sensor brands. Because withdrawing them may not necessarily move customers to another Gillette brand, it may be more profitable for Gillette to keep them in its brand portfolio for razor blades.

LOW-END ENTRY LEVEL   The role of a relatively low-priced brand in the portfolio often may be to attract customers to the brand franchise. Retailers like to feature these 'traffic builders' because they are able to 'trade up' customers to a higher-priced brand. For example, BMW introduced certain models into its 3-series automobiles in part as a means of bringing new customers into the brand franchise, with the hope of later 'moving them up' to higher-priced models when they decided to trade in their cars.

HIGH-END PRESTIGE The role of a relatively high-priced brand often is to add prestige and credibility to the entire portfolio. For example, Elie Saab's designs are considered among the most luxurious and modern of brands. His designs have been worn by several local and international celebrities such as Christina Aguilera, Catherine Zeta-Jones, Beyoncé, Halle Berry, Queen Rania of Jordan, Angelina Jolie, Nawal Al Zoghbi, Rihanna, and many others.

Customer Equity

Brand equity should be a top priority for any organization. The Marketing Memo: *Twenty-First-Century Branding* offers some contemporary perspectives on enduring brand leadership.

Finally, we can relate brand equity to one other important marketing concept, **customer equity**. The aim of customer relationship management (CRM) is to produce high customer equity.[86] Although we can calculate it in different ways, one definition of customer equity is "the sum of lifetime values of all customers."[87] As Chapter 5 reviewed, customer lifetime value is affected by revenue and cost considerations related to customer acquisition, retention, and cross-selling.[88]

> **customer equity** the total combined customer lifetime values of all of the company's customers.

- *Acquisition* is affected by the number of prospects, the acquisition probability of a prospect, and acquisition spending per prospect.
- *Retention* is influenced by the retention rate and retention spending level.
- *Add-on spending* is a function of the efficiency of add-on selling, the number of add-on selling offers given to existing customers, and the response rate to new offers.

The brand equity and customer equity perspectives certainly share many common themes.[89] Both emphasize the importance of customer loyalty and the notion that value is created by having as many customers as possible pay as high a price as possible.

As they've been put into practice, however, the two perspectives emphasize different things. The customer equity perspective focuses on bottom-line financial value. Its clear benefit is its quantifiable measures of financial performance. But it offers limited guidance for go-to-market strategies. It largely ignores some of the important advantages of creating a strong brand, such as the ability to attract higher-quality employees; to elicit stronger support from channel and supply chain partners; and to create growth opportunities through line and category extensions and licensing. The customer equity approach can overlook the 'option value' of brands and their potential to affect future revenues and costs. It does not always fully account for competitive moves and countermoves, or for social network effects, word-of-mouth, and customer-to-customer recommendations.

Brand equity, on the other hand, tends to emphasize strategic issues in managing brands and creating and leveraging brand awareness and image with customers. It provides much practical guidance for specific marketing activities. With a focus on brands, however, managers don't always develop detailed customer analyses in terms of the brand equity they achieve or the resulting long-term profitability they create.[90] Brand equity approaches could benefit from sharper segmentation schemes afforded by customer-level analyses and more consideration of how to develop personalized, customized marketing programs for individual customers: whether individuals or organizations such as retailers. There are generally fewer financial considerations put into play with brand equity than with customer equity.

Nevertheless, both brand equity and customer equity matter. There are no brands without customers and no customers without brands. Brands serve as the 'bait' that retailers and other channel intermediaries use to attract customers from whom they extract value. Customers serve as the tangible profit engine for brands to monetize their brand value.

Summary

1. A brand is a name, term, sign, symbol, design, or some combination of these elements, intended to identify the goods and services of one seller or group of sellers and to differentiate them from those of competitors. The different components of a brand—brand names, logos, symbols, package designs, and so on—are brand elements.

2. Brands offer a number of benefits to customers and firms. Brands are valuable intangible assets that need to be managed carefully. The key to branding is that consumers perceive differences among brands in a product category.

3. Brand equity should be defined in terms of marketing effects uniquely attributable to a brand. That is, brand equity relates to the fact that different outcomes result in the marketing of a product or service because of its brand, as compared to the results if that same product or service was not identified by that brand.

4. Building brand equity depends on three main factors: (1) the initial choices for the brand elements or identities making up the brand; (2) the way the brand is integrated into the supporting marketing program; and (3) the associations indirectly transferred to the brand by linking the brand to some other entity (e.g. the company, country of origin, channel of distribution, or another brand).

5. Brand equity needs to be measured in order to be managed well. Brand audits measure 'where the brand has been,' and tracking studies measure 'where the brand is now' and whether marketing programs are having the intended effects.

6. A branding strategy for a firm identifies which brand elements a firm chooses to apply across the various products it sells. In a brand extension, a firm uses an established brand name to introduce a new product. Potential extensions must be judged by how effectively they leverage existing brand equity to a new product, as well as how effectively the extension, in turn, contributes to the equity of the existing parent brand.

7. Brands can play a number of different roles within the brand portfolio. Brands may expand coverage, provide protection, extend an image, or fulfill a variety of other roles for the firm. Each brand name product must have a well-defined positioning. In that way, brands can maximize coverage and minimize overlap and thus optimize the portfolio.

8. Customer equity is a complementary concept to brand equity that reflects the sum of lifetime values of all customers for a brand.

Applications

Marketing Debate
Are Brand Extensions Good or Bad?

Some critics vigorously denounce the practice of brand extensions, as they feel that too often companies lose focus and consumers become confused. Other experts maintain that brand extensions are a critical growth strategy and source of revenue for the firm.

Take a position: Brand extensions can endanger brands *versus* brand extensions are an important brand-growth strategy.

Marketing Discussion

How can you relate the different models of brand equity presented in this chapter? How are they similar? How are they different? Can you construct a brand-equity model that incorporates the best aspects of each model?

Marketing Excellence

>>Procter & Gamble

Procter & Gamble (P&G) is one of the most skilful marketers of consumer packaged goods. The company's scope and accomplishments are staggering. It employs people in more than 80 countries; is a global leader in the majority of the different product categories in which it competes; has 24 billion-dollar global brands; spends more than US$5 million a day on R&D; and its 2011 sales were US$82.6 billion. Its sustained market leadership rests on a number of different capabilities and philosophies:

- *Customer knowledge:* P&G studies its customers—both end consumers and trade partners—through continuous marketing research and intelligence gathering. It spends more than US$100 million annually on more than 10,000 formal consumer research projects every year and generates more than 3 million consumer contacts via its e-mail and phone center.

- *Long-term outlook:* P&G takes the time to analyze each opportunity carefully and prepare the best product, and then commits itself to making this product a success. It struggled with Pringles potato chips for almost a decade before achieving market success.

- *Product innovation:* P&G is an active product innovator, devoting US$1.8 billion (3.5 percent of sales) to research and development, an impressively high amount for a packaged-goods company. It employs more science Ph.D.s than Harvard, Berkeley, and the Massachusetts Institute of Technology combined, and applies for roughly 3,000 patents each year. Part of its innovation process is developing brands that offer new consumer benefits. Recent examples include Febreze, an odor-eliminating fabric spray; Swiffer, a new cleaning system that more effectively removes dust, dirt, and hair from floors and other

hard surfaces; and Mr. Clean Magic Eraser, an innovative cleaning sponge that contains a special chemical compound developed by BASF.

- *Quality strategy:* P&G designs products of above-average quality and continuously improves them. When P&G says "new and improved," it means it. Recent examples include Pantene Ice Shine shampoo, conditioner, and styling gel, and Pampers BabyDry with Caterpillar Flex, a diaper designed to prevent leaks when babies' stomachs shrink at night.

- *Brand extension strategy:* P&G produces its brands in several sizes and forms. This strategy gains more shelf space and prevents competitors from moving in to satisfy unmet market needs. P&G also uses its strong brand names to launch new products with instant recognition and much less advertising outlay. The Mr. Clean brand has been extended from household cleaner to bathroom cleaner, and even to a carwash system. Old Spice was successfully extended from men's fragrances to deodorant.

- *Multibrand strategy:* P&G markets several brands in the same product category, such as Luvs and Pampers diapers and Oral-B and Crest toothbrushes. Each brand meets a different consumer want and competes against specific competitors' brands. At the same time, P&G has become careful not to sell too many brands and has reduced its vast array of products, sizes, flavors, and varieties in recent years to assemble a stronger brand portfolio.

- *Communication pioneer:* With its acquisition of Gillette, P&G became the nation's largest advertiser, spending over $5 billion a year on advertising. A pioneer in using the power of television to create strong consumer awareness and preference, P&G is now taking a leading role in building its brands on the internet. It's also infusing stronger emotional appeals into its communications to create deeper consumer connections. P&G promoted Ariel as a sociably responsible brand that contributes positively to Egyptian society. Now Ariel is perceived in Egypt as an honest and dedicated brand.

- *Manufacturing efficiency and cost cutting:* P&G's reputation as a great marketing company is matched by its excellence as a manufacturing company. P&G spends large sums developing and improving production operations to keep its costs among the lowest in the industry, allowing it to reduce the premium prices at which some of its goods sell.

Continued on next page >>

Marketing Excellence...continued

>>Procter & Gamble

- **Brand-management system:** P&G originated the brand-management system, in which one executive is responsible for each brand. The system has been copied by many competitors but not often with P&G's success. Recently, P&G modified its general management structure so that each brand category is now run by a category manager with volume and profit responsibility. Although this new organization does not replace the brand-management system, it helps to sharpen strategic focus on key consumer needs and competition in the category.

It's easy to see that P&G's success is based not on doing one thing well, but on successfully orchestrating the myriad factors that contribute to market leadership.

Questions

1. Identify P&G's core competency. Provide valid justification for your argument.

2. Choose one of P&G's brands and discuss its emotional and functional aspects.

3. What is the main disadvantage of brand extension strategy? How could the company avoid this drawback?

4. Branding is an integrated mechanism to reflect the desired brand personality. How do you relate this statement to P&G's effort to build strong brands?

Sources: Robert Berner, "Detergent Can Be So Much More," *BusinessWeek*, May 1, 2006, pp. 66–68; "A Post-Modern Proctoid," *The Economist*, April 15, 2006, p. 68; *P&G Fact Sheet*, December 2006; John Galvin, "The World on a String," *Point*, February 2005, pp. 13–24; Jack Neff, "P&G Kisses Up to the Boss: Consumers," *Advertising Age*, May 2, 2005, p. 18; www.pg.com.

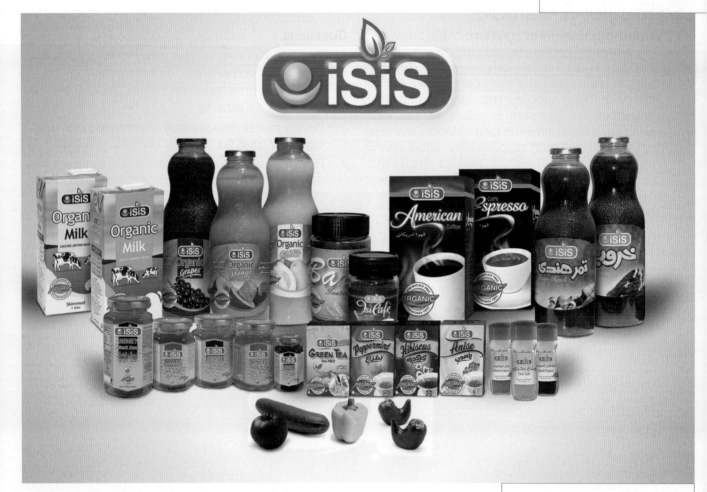

Isis is addressing the extended marketing concept by focusing on the consumer's long-term welfare.

In this chapter, we will address the following questions:

1. How can a firm choose and communicate an effective positioning in the market? (pg. 266)

2. How are brands differentiated? (pg. 273)

3. What marketing strategies are appropriate at each stage of the product life cycle? (pg. 274)

4. What are the implications of market evolution for marketing strategies? (pg. 283)

Crafting the Brand Positioning

No company can win if its products and services resemble every other product and offering. As part of the strategic brand management process, each offering must represent a compelling, distinctive big idea in the mind of the target market.

 In September 2010, the organic food industry received a blow when a newspaper featured an article indicating that the industry was non-existent in Egypt, saying that organic food producers in Egypt didn't adopt any production measures or standards. At that time, Isis, the largest organic food producer in Egypt, was working with the relevant authorities to initiate Egyptian organic production standards. And even then, adopting organic production standards was not a new concept for Isis; the company had followed European organic production standards since its establishment in 1995. This belief came from Isis' commitment to customers' welfare, embedded in the company mission statement: "Isis is marketing natural biodynamic food products in both local and global markets aiming to satisfy its customer's needs for better human health, while also maintaining a balanced environment."

Isis has its own agricultural plants in Belbes, Egypt, and deals with around 200 organic agricultural farmers in Egypt. This huge production capacity enabled Isis to produce 250 stock-keeping units (SKUs) in nine production lines or categories, including juice, milk, jam, cheese, ketchup, and many others. Generally, the organic processed food industry is supported by improved health awareness and customers' desire to achieve personal well-being. The impact of animal disease crises such as H1N1 avian influenza, along with food safety standards and other environmental and animal concerns, has given a positive impetus to producers of organic food. On the other hand, the organic industry is facing many challenges that hinder consumer and market growth. From the consumer point of view, higher prices and a limited number of varieties are the most common barriers. Lack of governmental and retailer support are considered the major obstacles for growth of the organic market. However, Isis capitalized on some top-priority trends in designing its promotional campaigns. Isis communicates with ageing, health-oriented, anxious, and ethical consumers. Isis has managed to differentiate its brand and to be positioned on the basis of long-term customer welfare.

Young, educated people are another recipient segment for products made by Isis in the Gulf region (5 percent of total exports), particularly in Saudi Arabia. To reflect Isis's caring personality, a simple slogan—"Yes, we care"—was used in multiple communication vehicles. All Isis organic brands were positioned based on the 'new golden triangle' concept: health, convenience, and pleasure. Mamdouh Abu El-Aish, general manager of Isis, said, "This triangle represents our internal quality assurance guidelines which we are always referring to." Dr. Abu El-Aish said, "we never use TV advertisements because our target market is so limited and can be reached in more efficient ways. Promotion through direct marketing with in-store consumer activities such as tasting, and advertisements in selected magazines such as Sport and Fitness, What Women Want, Kol Elnas, *and* Kalam Elnas *with advertorial educational campaigns create the optimal desired awareness." Lately, Isis has introduced a new marketing campaign:* Go Organic: Chemical Free, Pesticide Free.

During the holy month of Ramadan, Isis fresh dates are served on all EgyptAir trips to blend Iftar *with Isis' natural brand. The company is always adapting its brand to cope with market dynamics and to ensure that the preferred branding identity is recognized in the market. It is true that organic food products are more expensive in developing countries than in developed ones, but this picture will change in the future. It is estimated that the global organic food market will be worth US$518 billion by the year 2020.*[1]

As the success of Isis demonstrates, a company can reap the benefits of carving out a unique position in the marketplace. But circumstances often dictate that companies reformulate their marketing strategies and offerings several times. Economic conditions change, competitors launch new assaults, and products pass through new stages of buyer interest and requirements. Marketers must develop strategies for each stage in the product's life cycle. This chapter explores specific ways a company can effectively position and differentiate its offerings to achieve a competitive advantage throughout the entire life cycle of a product or an offering. ▽

Developing and Communicating a Positioning Strategy

positioning   arranging for a product to occupy a clear, distinctive, and desirable place relative to competing products in the minds of target consumers.

points-of-parity (POPs) associations that are not necessarily unique to the brand but may in fact be shared with other brands.

points-of-difference (PODs) attributes or benefits consumers strongly associate with a brand, positively evaluate, and believe they could not find to the same extent with a competitive brand.

All marketing strategy is built on STP: segmentation, targeting, and **positioning**. A company discovers different needs and groups in the marketplace, targets those it can satisfy in a superior way, and then positions its offering so the target market recognizes the company's distinctive offering and image. If a company does a poor job of positioning, the market will be confused.

Positioning is the act of designing the company's offering and image to occupy a distinctive place in the minds of the target market.[2] The goal is to locate the brand in the minds of consumers to maximize the potential benefit to the firm. A good brand positioning helps guide marketing strategy by clarifying the brand's essence, what goals it helps the consumer achieve, and how it does so in a unique way. Everyone in the organization should understand the brand positioning and use it as context for making decisions.

The result of positioning is the successful creation of a *customer-focused value proposition*, a strong reason why the target market should buy the product. ▭ **Table 10.1** shows how three companies—Perdue, Volvo, and Domino's—have defined their value proposition given their target customers, benefits, and prices.

Positioning requires that similarities and differences between brands be defined and communicated. Specifically, deciding on a positioning requires determining a frame of reference by identifying the target market and the competition and identifying the ideal **points-of-parity** and **points-of-difference** brand associations.

TABLE 10.1 ▭ Examples of Value Propositions				
Company and Product	**Target Customers**	**Benefits**	**Price**	**Value Proposition**
Perdue (chicken)	Quality-conscious consumers of chicken	Tenderness	10% premium	More tender golden chicken at a moderate premium price
Volvo (station wagon)	Safety-conscious 'upscale' families	Durability and safety	20% premium	The safest, most durable wagon in which your family can ride
Domino's (pizza)	Convenience-minded pizza lovers	Delivery speed and good quality	15% premium	A good, hot pizza, delivered promptly to your door, at a moderate price

Competitive Frame of Reference

A starting point in defining a competitive frame of reference for a brand positioning is to determine **category membership**: the products or sets of products with which a brand competes and which function as close substitutes. As we will discuss in Chapter 11, competitive analysis will consider a whole host of factors—including the resources, capabilities, and likely intentions of various other firms—in choosing those markets where consumers can be profitably served.

Deciding to target a certain type of consumer, in particular, can define the nature of competition, because certain firms have decided to target that segment in the past (or plan to do so in the future), or because consumers in that segment may already look to certain products or brands in their purchase decisions. To determine the proper competitive frame of reference, marketers need to understand consumer behavior and the consideration sets consumers use in making brand choices. In Lebanon, Crepaway is known as a pioneer in the dining and restaurant industry.

category membership the products or sets of products with which a brand competes and which function as close substitutes.

Crepaway   Crepaway started in 1984, with a young boy making crepes in a small kiosk and selling them to the public after learning the recipe from his mother. In 1985, Crepaway was founded as a limited liability company and then continued to expand, becoming a joint stock company in 2003. Currently, Crepaway owns 13 branches around Lebanon and even in Saudi Arabia, Qatar, and Egypt. What differentiated Crepaway from other stores was the good quality, good value, good customer service, and reasonable prices. This strategy allowed it to grow continuously, while maintaining a good reputation and loyal customers.[3]

Points-of-Difference and Points-of-Parity

Once marketers have fixed the competitive frame of reference for positioning by defining the customer target market and the nature of the competition, they can define the appropriate points-of-difference and points-of-parity associations.[4]

POINTS-OF-DIFFERENCE Points-of-difference (PODs) are attributes or benefits consumers strongly associate with a brand, positively evaluate, and believe they could not find to the same extent with a competitive brand. Associations that make up points-of-difference may be based on virtually any type of attribute or benefit. Examples are Apple (*design*), Nike (*performance*), and Lexus (*quality*). Creating strong, favorable, and unique associations is a real challenge, but essential in terms of competitive brand positioning.

POINTS-OF-PARITY Points-of-parity (POPs), on the other hand, are associations that are not necessarily unique to the brand but may in fact be shared with other brands.[5] These types of associations come in two basic forms: category and competitive.

Category points-of-parity are associations consumers view as essential to a legitimate and credible offering within a certain product or service category. In other words, they represent necessary—but not sufficient—conditions for brand choice. Consumers might not consider a travel agency truly a travel agency unless it is able to make air and hotel reservations, provide advice about leisure packages, and offer various ticket payment and delivery options. Category points-of-parity may change over time due to technological advances, legal developments, or consumer trends, but they are the 'greens fees' necessary to play the marketing game.

Competitive points-of-parity are associations designed to negate *competitors*' points-of-difference. If, in the eyes of consumers, a brand

Crepaway has continuously grown, while maintaining a good reputation and loyal customers.

can 'break even' in those areas where the competitors are trying to find an advantage *and* achieve advantages in other areas, the brand should be in a strong—and perhaps unbeatable—competitive position.

POINTS-OF-PARITY VERSUS POINTS-OF-DIFFERENCE For an offering to achieve a POP on a particular attribute or benefit, a sufficient number of consumers must believe the brand is 'good enough' on that dimension. There is a zone or range of tolerance or acceptance with points-of-parity. The brand does not literally need to be seen as equal to competitors, but consumers must feel that the brand does well enough on that particular attribute or benefit. If they do, they may be willing to base their evaluations and decisions on other factors potentially more favorable to the brand. A fat-free chocolate presumably would never taste as good as a regular chocolate, but it would need to taste close enough to be able to effectively compete.

With PODs, however, the brand must demonstrate clear superiority. Consumers must be convinced that Louis Vuitton has the most stylish handbags, Energizer is the longest-lasting battery, and that Emirates NBD offers the best financial advice and planning.

Often, the key to positioning is not so much achieving a point-of-difference as achieving points-of-parity!

 Visa versus American Express   Visa's POD in the credit card category is that it is the most widely available card, which underscores the category's main benefit of convenience. American Express, on the other hand, has built the equity of its brand by highlighting the prestige associated with the use of its card. Having established their PODs, Visa and American Express now compete by attempting to blunt each others' advantage to create POPs. Visa offers gold and platinum cards to enhance the prestige of its brand and advertises "It's Everywhere You Want to Be" in settings that reinforce exclusivity and acceptability. American Express has substantially increased the number of merchants that accept its cards and created other value enhancements.

Establishing Category Membership

Target customers are aware that Maybelline is a leading brand of cosmetics, Kellogg's is a leading brand of cereal, Qatar Airways is a leading airline firm, and so on. Often, however, marketers must inform consumers of a brand's category membership. Perhaps the most obvious situation is the introduction of new products, especially when category identification itself is not clear.

There are also situations where consumers know a brand's category membership, but may not be convinced that the brand is a valid member of the category. For example, consumers may be aware that Hewlett-Packard produces digital cameras, but they may not be certain whether Hewlett-Packard cameras are in the same class as Sony, Olympus, Kodak, and Nikon. In this instance, HP might find it useful to reinforce category membership.

Brands are sometimes affiliated with categories in which they do *not* hold membership. This approach is one way to highlight a brand's point-of-difference, providing that consumers know the brand's actual membership.

 Umpqua Bank   Most consumers would never describe a bank transaction as soul satisfying, but Oregon-based Umpqua Bank isn't your average bank. Umpqua has become affiliated with the café/retail categories in order to establish points-of-difference between itself and other banks. Umpqua's 'stores' were designed to stimulate cozy connections between customers and feature a computer café with wi-fi access and branded merchandise, including Umpqua's own blend of coffee (a must in the coffee-obsessed Northwest of the United States). Like Starbucks, Umpqua has also made music a part of its product mix. Working with Portland's Rumblefish, it created something called Discover Local Music. Listening stations with headphones allow bank customers to browse and sample songs and even purchase customized CDs. After-hours activities such as movies, knitting, and yoga classes are encouraged just as much as financial events. However, creating the cool, inviting environment is just half the equation. Umpqua also fosters what it calls 'extreme service.' Every new employee receives guest service education through the Ritz-Carlton Hotel training group, well known for its award-winning service. Not only has Umpqua managed to go from US$140 million in assets in 1994 to $7 billion in 2006, but the company was also heralded in *BusinessWeek*'s "Best Ideas of 2005," in an article that said, "…customers aren't just paying for a cup of coffee at Starbucks or, say, simply doing transactions at Umpqua Bank. They're paying admission to a club—one that delivers something to satisfy the soul."[6]

Umpqua Bank competes in the U.S. Pacific Northwest by turning the idea of brand categories upside down. Its 'stores' offer music, coffee, wi-fi access, and, of course, banking services.

With this approach, however, it's important not to be trapped between categories. Consumers should understand what the brand stands for, and not just what it's not. The Konica e-mini M digital camera and MP3 player was marketed as the "four-in-one entertainment solution," but it suffered from functional deficiencies in each of its product applications and languished in the marketplace.

The typical approach to positioning is to inform consumers of a brand's membership before stating its point-of-difference. Presumably, consumers need to know what a product is and what function it serves before deciding whether it dominates the brands against which it competes. For new products, initial advertising often concentrates on creating brand awareness, and subsequent advertising attempts to craft the brand image.

STRADDLE POSITIONING Occasionally, a company will try to include two frames of reference.

BMW   When BMW first made a strong competitive push into the U.S. market in the early 1980s, it positioned the brand as the only automobile that offered both luxury *and* performance. At that time, consumers saw American luxury cars as lacking performance, and American performance cars as lacking luxury. By relying on the design of its cars, its German heritage, and other aspects of a well-conceived marketing program, BMW was able to simultaneously achieve (1) a point-of-difference on luxury and a point-of-parity on performance with respect to performance cars and (2) a point-of-difference on performance and a point-of-parity on luxury with respect to luxury cars. The clever slogan "The Ultimate Driving Machine" effectively captured the newly created umbrella category: luxury/performance cars.

Although a straddle positioning often is attractive as a means of reconciling potentially conflicting consumer goals and creating a 'best-of-both-worlds' solution, it also carries an extra burden. If the points-of-parity and points-of-difference with respect to both categories are not credible, the brand may not be viewed as a legitimate player in either category and may end up in 'no-man's-land.' Many early personal digital assistants (PDAs) that unsuccessfully tried to straddle categories ranging from pagers to laptop computers provide a vivid illustration of this risk.

COMMUNICATING CATEGORY MEMBERSHIP   There are three main ways to convey a brand's category membership:

1. *Announcing category benefits.* To reassure consumers that a brand will deliver on the fundamental reason for using a category, marketers frequently use benefits to announce category membership. Thus, industrial tools might claim to have durability and antacids might announce their efficacy. A brownie mix might attain membership in the baked desserts category by claiming the benefit of great taste and support this claim by including high-quality ingredients (performance) or by showing users delighting in its consumption (imagery).

2. *Comparing to exemplars.* Well-known, noteworthy brands in a category can also help a brand specify its category membership. Dubai Media City, a member of TECOM Investments, was established in January 2001 as a hub for media in the Arab world. Over a short period of time, Dubai Media City has grown to become a globally, as well as regionally, recognized media cluster by hosting leading advertising, communication, and media brands such as CNN, Forbes, Leo Burnett, MBC, and CCTV. Their main brand value proposition is based on offering an environment for media companies to operate with collective synergy and freedom while enjoying free zone benefits including 100 percent business ownership and tax-free income. There are also value added services such as networking opportunities, venue management services, and government services. Additionally, Dubai Media City links its brand with world-class universities such as the George Washington University, who are invited annually as part of an international residency for the MBA students and faculty members. Jamal Al Sharif, Managing Director of Dubai Media City and Dubai Studio City, said, "Such collaborations with academic institutions promote innovation and a platform for sharing industry insights that eventually help to meet the needs of the global marketplace." These brand associations link Dubai Media City with leading globally recognized brands.[7]

3. *Relying on the product descriptor.* The product descriptor that follows the brand name is often a concise means of conveying category origin. Ford Motor Co. invested more than US$1 billion on a radical 2004 model called the X-Trainer, which combined the attributes of an SUV, a minivan, and a station wagon. To communicate its unique position and to avoid association with its Explorer and Country Squire models, the vehicle is designated a "sports wagon."[8]

Choosing POPs and PODs

Points-of-parity are driven by the needs of category membership (to create category POPs) and the necessity of negating competitors' PODs (to create competitive POPs). In addition to distinctiveness, two other important considerations in choosing points-of-difference are that consumers find the POD desirable and that the firm has the capabilities to deliver on it. As ▭ **Table 10.2** shows, three criteria can judge both desirability and deliverability.

Marketers must decide at which level(s) to anchor the brand's points-of-difference. At the lowest level are the *brand attributes*; at the next level are the *brand benefits*; and at the top are the *brand values*. Thus marketers of Dove soap can talk about its attribute of one-quarter cleansing cream; or its benefit of softer skin; or its value of being more attractive. Attributes are typically the least desirable level to position. First, the buyer is more interested in benefits. Second, competitors can easily copy attributes. Third, current attributes may become less desirable over time.

Research has shown, however, that brands can sometimes be successfully differentiated on seemingly irrelevant attributes, *if* consumers infer the proper benefit.[9] Procter & Gamble differentiates its Folger's instant coffee by its "flaked coffee crystals," created through a "unique patented process." In reality, the shape of the coffee particles is irrelevant because the crystals immediately dissolve in the hot water. Saying that a brand of coffee is "mountain grown" is irrelevant because most coffee is mountain grown. The Marketing Memo: *Writing a Positioning Statement* outlines how marketers can express positioning formally.

Creating POPs and PODs

One common difficulty in creating a strong, competitive brand positioning is that many of the attributes or benefits that make up the points-of-parity and points-of-difference are negatively correlated. For example, it might be difficult to position a brand as 'inexpensive' and at the same time assert that it is 'of the highest quality.' ▭ **Box 10.1** (on page 272) displays some other examples of negatively correlated attributes and benefits. Moreover, individual attributes and benefits often have positive *and* negative aspects. For example, consider a long-lived brand such as Gandour. The brand's heritage could suggest experience, wisdom, and expertise. On the other hand, it could also imply being old-fashioned and out of date.[10]

TABLE 10.2 Judging Desirability and Deliverability for Points-of-Difference

Desirability Criteria	Deliverability Criteria
Relevance Target consumers must find the POD personally relevant and important. • The Westin Stamford hotel in Singapore advertised that it was the world's tallest hotel, but a hotel's height is not important to many tourists.	**Feasibility** The product design and marketing offering must support the desired association. Does communicating the desired association require real changes to the product itself, or just perceptual shifts in the way the consumer thinks of the product or brand? The latter is typically easier. • General Motors has had to work to overcome public perceptions that Cadillac is not a youthful, contemporary brand.
Distinctiveness Target consumers must find the POD distinctive and superior. • Splenda sugar substitute overtook Equal and Sweet'N'Low to become the leader in its category in 2003 by differentiating itself on its authenticity as a product derived from sugar, without any of the associated drawbacks.[11]	**Communicability** Consumers must be given a compelling reason and understandable rationale as to why the brand can deliver the desired benefit. What factual, verifiable evidence or 'proof points' can ensure consumers will actually believe in the brand and its desired associations? • Substantiators often come in the form of patented, branded ingredients, such as Nivea Wrinkle Control Crème with Q10 co-enzyme or Herbal Essences hair conditioner with Hawafena.
Believability Target consumers must find the POD believable and credible. A brand must offer a compelling reason for choosing it over the other options. • Mountain Dew may argue that it is more energizing than other soft drinks and support this claim by noting that it has a higher level of caffeine. • Chanel No. 5 perfume may claim to be the quintessential elegant French perfume and support this claim by noting the long association between Chanel and haute couture.	**Sustainability** The firm must be sufficiently committed and willing to devote enough resources to create an enduring positioning. Is the positioning preemptive, defensible, and difficult to attack? Can the favorability of a brand association be reinforced and strengthened over time? • It is generally easier for market leaders such as ADM, Visa, and SAP, whose positioning is based in part on demonstrable product or service performance, to sustain their positioning than for market leaders such as Fendi, Prada, and Hermes, whose positioning is based on fashion and is thus subject to the whims of a more fickle market.

marketing Memo

Writing a Positioning Statement

To communicate a company or brand positioning, marketing plans often include a *positioning statement.* The statement should follow the form: To *(target group and need),* our *(brand)* is *(the concept)* that *(what the point-of-difference is or does).* For example: "To *busy professionals who need to stay organized, Palm Pilot is an electronic organizer that allows you to back up files on your PC more easily and reliably than competitive products.*" Sometimes the positioning statement is more detailed:

Mountain Dew: To young, active soft-drink consumers who have little time for sleep, Mountain Dew is the soft drink that gives you more energy than any other brand because it has the highest level of caffeine. With Mountain Dew, you can stay alert and keep going even when you haven't been able to get a good night's sleep.

Note that the positioning first states the product's membership in a category (Mountain Dew is a soft drink) and then shows its point-of-difference from other members of the group (it has more caffeine). The product's membership in the category suggests the points-of-parity that it might have with other products in the category, but the case for the product rests on its points-of-difference. Sometimes the marketer will put the product in a surprisingly different category before indicating the points of difference.

Sources: Bobby J. Calder and Steven J. Reagan, "Brand Design," in *Kellogg on Marketing*, ed. Dawn Iacobucci (New York: John Wiley & Sons, 2001), p. 61; Alice M. Tybout and Brian Sternthal, "Brand Positioning," in *Kellogg on Marketing*, ed. Dawn Iacobucci (New York: John Wiley & Sons, 2001), p. 54.

BOX 10.1	Examples of Negatively Correlated Attributes and Benefits
Low price—High quality	Powerful—Safe
Taste—Low calories	Strong—Refined
Nutritious—Good tasting	Ubiquitous—Exclusive
Efficacious—Mild	Varied—Simple

Roadster Diner   In 1998, Roadster diner was founded in Achrafieh, Lebanon, and over the last decade its popularity has expanded tremendously. The concept was to create a diner with American food and the "swingingest, homiest, most authentic diner experience the city had ever seen."[12] With its unique décor from the 1960s and a diverse menu including everything from breakfast to burgers, Roadster has overcome the challenge of promoting itself as an American diner but also serving healthy food. Roadster can satisfy all its customers, from the younger crowd looking for a good time with oldies and classic music and delicious food, to more mature audiences looking for a healthy meal. Currently, Roadster is the only diner chain in the Middle East to receive ISO 22000 certification in 2008 for its food safety management systems.

After opening and operating 10 branches in Lebanon, Roadster recently opened its second branch in the UAE after entering into a partnership with Cravia. Cravia CEO, Walid Hajj, says that the speed with which Roadster diner is being implemented throughout the UAE is testament to the brand's popularity. "Roadster diner was already one of the most popular dining experiences in its home country of Lebanon and people from there have been waiting a long time for the brand to make its way here," said Hajj. "It is their discerning taste in both food and atmosphere that has put Roadster diner on the map…"[13]

Unfortunately, consumers typically want to maximize *both* the negatively correlated attributes or benefits. Much of the art and science of marketing is dealing with trade-offs, and positioning is no different. The best approach, clearly, is to develop a product or service that performs well on both dimensions. BMW was able to establish its 'luxury and performance' straddle positioning due in large part to product design, and the fact that the car was in fact seen as both luxurious and high performance. Roadster diner was able to establish its straddle positioning through affordability and uniqueness of experience.

Some marketers have adopted other approaches to address attribute or benefit trade-offs: launching two different marketing campaigns, each one devoted to a different brand attribute or benefit; linking themselves to any kind of entity that possesses the right kind of equity to establish an attribute or benefit as a POP or POD; and even attempting to convince consumers that the negative relationship between attributes and benefits is in fact positive.

To deal with negative associations, marketers might adopt one of the following strategies.

1. **Presenting attributes or benefits separately.** Some marketers launch two different marketing campaigns, each one devoted to a different brand attribute or benefit.
2. **Leveraging equity of another entity.** Marketers can link brands to any kind of entity (person, place, or thing) that possesses the right kind of equity as a means to establish an attribute or benefit as a POP or POD, such as linking the brand to a well-known celebrity.
3. **Redefining the relationship.** A marketer may attempt to convince consumers that the negative relationship between attributes and benefits, if they consider it differently, is in fact positive.

Roadster diner's unique 60s theme, with guaranteed cleanliness and food quality, provides a unique dining experience for its brand-loyal customers.

Differentiation Strategies

To avoid the commodity trap, marketers must start with the belief that you can differenti-ate anything (see Marketing Memo: *How to Derive Fresh Consumer Insights to Differentiate Products and Services*). Differentiation creates a competitive advantage to the firm. A **com-petitive advantage** is a company's ability to perform in one or more ways that competitors cannot or will not match. Michael Porter urged companies to build a sustainable competitive advantage.[14] But few competitive advantages are sustainable. At best, they may be leverageable. A *leverageable advantage* is one that a company can use as a springboard to new advantages, much as Microsoft has leveraged its operating system to Microsoft Office and then to net-working applications. In general, a company that hopes to endure must be in the business of continuously inventing new advantages.

Customers must see any competitive advantage as a *customer advantage*. For example, if a com-pany delivers faster than its competitors, it won't be a customer advantage if customers don't value speed. Therefore, companies must focus on building customer advantages.[15] Then they will deliver high customer value and satisfaction, which leads to high repeat purchases and ultimately to high company profitability.

Marketers can differentiate brands on the basis of many variables. Aïshti is a good example.

> **competitive advantage** a company's ability to perform in one or more ways that competitors cannot or will not match.

 Aïshti   In 1989, Tony Salame identified a niche market and subse-quently started clothing chain Aïshti, now a synonym for luxury. Aïshti differenti-ates itself by focusing on an elegant life style, suited to the new millennium. Since its inception, Aïshti moved from being a single high-end clothing store to a globally known chain. Aïshti stores stock prominent luxury fashion brands, including Prada, YSL, Dolce & Gabbana, Dior, Sergio Rossi, Burberry, Fendi, Chloe, and many others. Moreover, Aïshti also operates a fur-niture and home accessories store, known as the Aïshti Seaside Store; along with Aizone, a full spa and hair salon which targets the younger consumer; a fashion magazine; three restaurants; and a café.

The obvious means of differentiation, and often most compelling ones to consumers, relate to aspects of the product and service (reviewed in Chapters 12 and 13). Swatch offers

---

marketing Memo

How to Derive Fresh Consumer Insights to Differentiate Products and Services

In the article "Discovering New Points of Differentiation," Ian C. MacMillan and Rita Gunther McGrath argue that if companies examine customers' entire experience with a product or service—the consumption chain—they can uncover opportunities to position their offerings in ways that neither they nor their competitors thought possible. MacMillan and McGrath list a set of questions marketers can use to help them identify new, consumer-based points of differentiation.

- How do people become aware of their need for your product and service?
- How do consumers find your offering?
- How do consumers make their final selection?
- How do consumers order and purchase your product or service?

- What happens when your product or service is delivered?
- How is your product installed?
- How is your product or service paid for?
- How is your product stored?
- How is your product moved around?
- What is the consumer really using your product for?
- What do consumers need help with when they use your product?
- What about returns or exchanges?
- How is your product repaired or serviced?
- What happens when your product is disposed of or no longer used?

Source: Ian C. MacMillan and Rita Gunther McGrath, "Discovering New Points of Differentiation," *Harvard Business Review,* July–August 1997, pp. 133–145.

colorful, fashionable watches. Subway differentiates itself in terms of healthy sandwiches as an alternative to fast food. In competitive markets, however, firms may need to go beyond these. Consider these other dimensions, among the many that a company can use to differentiate its market offerings:

- **Personnel differentiation.** Companies can have better-trained employees. Emirates Airline is well regarded in large part because of the quality service provided by its flight attendants.
- **Channel differentiation.** Companies can more effectively and efficiently design their distribution channels' coverage, expertise, and performance.
- **Image differentiation.** Companies can craft powerful, compelling images. The primary explanation for Marlboro's extraordinary worldwide market share (around 30 percent) is that Marlboro's 'macho cowboy' image has struck a responsive chord with much of the cigarette-smoking public.

Product Life-Cycle Marketing Strategies

A company's positioning and differentiation strategy must change as the product, market, and competitors change over the *product life cycle* (PLC). To say that a product has a life cycle is to assert four things:

1. Products have a limited life.
2. Product sales pass through distinct stages, each posing different challenges, opportunities, and problems to the seller.
3. Profits rise and fall at different stages of the product life cycle.
4. Products require different marketing, financial, manufacturing, purchasing, and human resource strategies in each life-cycle stage.

Product Life Cycles

Most product life-cycle curves are portrayed as bell-shaped (see ▲ **Figure 10.1**). This curve is typically divided into four stages: introduction, growth, maturity, and decline.[16]

1. **Introduction.** A period of slow sales growth as the product is introduced in the market. Profits are nonexistent because of the heavy expenses of product introduction.
2. **Growth.** A period of rapid market acceptance and substantial profit improvement.
3. **Maturity.** A slowdown in sales growth because the product has achieved acceptance by most potential buyers. Profits stabilize or decline because of increased competition.
4. **Decline.** Sales show a downward drift and profits erode.

|Fig. 10.1| ▲

Sales and Profit
Life Cycles

(a) Growth-Slump-Maturity Pattern

(b) Cycle-Recycle Pattern

(c) Scalloped Pattern

|Fig. 10.2| △

Common Product Life-Cycle Patterns

We can use the PLC concept to analyze a product category (food), a product form (sweets), a product (chocolate), or a brand (Patchi). Not all products exhibit a bell-shaped PLC.[17] Three common alternate patterns are shown in △ **Figure 10.2**.

Figure 10.2 (a) shows a *growth-slump-maturity pattern*, often characteristic of small kitchen appliances such as handheld mixers and bread makers. Sales grow rapidly when the product is first introduced and then fall to a 'petrified' level that is sustained by late adopters buying the product for the first time and early adopters replacing it.

The *cycle-recycle pattern* in Figure 10.2 (b) often describes the sales of new drugs. The pharmaceutical company aggressively promotes its new drug, and this produces the first cycle. Later, sales start declining and the company gives the drug another promotion push, which produces a second cycle (usually of smaller magnitude and duration).[18]

Another common pattern is the *scalloped PLC* in Figure 10.2 (c). Here sales pass through a succession of life cycles based on the discovery of new-product characteristics, uses, or users. The sales of nylon, for example, show a scalloped pattern because of the many new uses—parachutes, hosiery, shirts, carpeting, boat sails, automobile tires—that continue to be discovered over time.[19]

Style, Fashion, and Fad Life Cycles

We need to distinguish three special categories of product life cycles: styles, fashions, and fads (△ **Figure 10.3**). A *style* is a basic and distinctive mode of expression appearing in a field of human endeavor. Styles appear in homes (modern, classic); clothing (formal, casual, funky); and art (realistic, surrealistic). A style can last for generations and go in and out of vogue. A *fashion* is a currently accepted or popular style in a given field. Fashions pass through four stages: distinctiveness, emulation, mass fashion, and decline.[20]

The length of a fashion cycle is hard to predict. One point of view is that fashions end because they represent a purchase compromise, and consumers start looking for the missing attributes.[21] For example, as automobiles become smaller, they become less comfortable, and then a growing number of buyers start wanting larger cars. Another explanation is that too many consumers

Style

Fashion

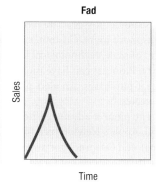

Fad

|Fig. 10.3| △

Style, Fashion, and Fad Life Cycles

adopt the fashion, thus turning others away. Still another is that the length of a particular fashion cycle depends on the extent to which the fashion meets a genuine need, is consistent with other trends in the society, satisfies societal norms and values, and keeps within technological limits as it develops.[22]

fad a craze that is unpredictable, short-lived, and without social, economic and political significance.

Fads are fashions that come quickly into public view, are adopted with great zeal, peak early, and decline very fast. Their acceptance cycle is short, and they tend to attract only a limited following who are searching for excitement or want to distinguish themselves from others. Fads fail to survive because they don't normally satisfy a strong need. The marketing winners are those who recognize fads early and leverage them into products with staying power.

Sabek Wa Lahek *Sabek Wa Lahek* was a 1990s children's television program which appealed to most kids in the Arab world. The program focused on car races using stimulating music and images. To capture the maximum benefits possible from the program's success, the company launched *Sabek Wa Lahek* racing cars in the toy market. At first, there was an unexpected demand for *Sabek Wa Lahek* cars, which quickly went out of stock in all toy stores. Then, after 3 or 4 months, the demand curve slowed down tremendously.

Marketing Strategies: Introduction Stage and the Pioneer Advantage

Because it takes time to roll out a new product, work out the technical problems, fill dealer pipelines, and gain consumer acceptance, sales growth tends to be slow in the introduction stage.[23] Profits are negative or low, and promotional expenditures are at their highest ratio to sales because of the need to (1) inform potential consumers, (2) induce product trial, and (3) secure distribution in retail outlets.[24] Firms focus on those buyers who are the most ready to buy, usually in higher-income groups. Prices tend to be high because costs are high.

Companies that plan to introduce a new product must decide when to enter the market. To be first can be rewarding, but risky and expensive. To come in later makes sense if the firm can bring superior technology, quality, or brand strength.

Speeding up innovation time is essential in an age of shortening product life cycles. Being early—a pioneer—has been shown to pay. One prior study found that products that came out 6 months late—but on budget—earned an average of 33 percent less profit in their first 5 years; products that came out on time but 50 percent over budget cut their profits by only 4 percent.[25] Most studies indicate that the market pioneer gains the greatest advantage.[26] Companies such as Campbell, Coca-Cola, Hallmark, and Amazon.com developed sustained market dominance. Carpenter and Nakamoto found that 19 out of the 25 companies that were market leaders in 1923 were still the market leaders in 1983, 60 years later.[27] Robinson and Min found that in a sample of industrial-goods businesses, 66 percent of pioneers survived at least 10 years, compared with 48 percent of the early followers.[28]

What are the sources of the pioneer's advantage?[29] Early users will recall the pioneer's brand name if the product satisfies them. The pioneer's brand also establishes the attributes the product class should possess. The pioneer's brand normally aims at the middle of the market and so captures more users. Customer inertia also plays a role; and there are producer advantages: economies of scale, technological leadership, patents, ownership of scarce assets, and other barriers to entry. Pioneers can have more effective marketing spending and enjoy higher rates of consumer repeat purchases. An alert pioneer can maintain its leadership indefinitely by pursuing various strategies.[30]

The pioneer advantage, however, is not inevitable.[31] Look at the fate of Bowmar (hand calculators), Apple's Newton (personal digital assistant), Netscape (internet browser), Reynolds (ballpoint pens), and Osborne (portable computers), market pioneers overtaken by later entrants. First movers also have to watch out for what some have called the 'second mover' advantage.

Wikipedia.org, Citizendium.org

Launched in January 2001, the collaborative internet encyclopedia Wikipedia has ridden its pioneer advantage to become as familiar as eBay and Google. Its 5 million pages of content are created entirely by volunteers and are available, free, to users in 250 languages. It might seem that no other internet encyclopedia could hope to eclipse Wikipedia's reach and brand equity at this point. Yet, who better than Wikipedia's cofounder, Larry Sanger, to try? Sanger believes his other site, Citizendium, enjoys certain 'second mover' advantages that might help it overtake his old site. First, second movers avoid heavy investment in R&D by replicating the first mover's approach. Citizendium will open up as an exact copy of Wikipedia, saving 5 years of development time. Next, second movers enjoy the advantage of positioning. Because Sanger knows exactly how Wikipedia is perceived, he can use that data to aim Citizendium at what

Wikipedia, the web's first and most popular reader-created encyclopedia, may soon face competition from second-in-the-market Citizendium, a similar site created by Wikipedia's founder.

he calls "different social niches." Finally, second movers learn from the pioneer's mistakes. Citizendium is introducing site sponsorship and an editorial team of experts who can prove their expertise in their respective subjects. Wikipedia, watch your back![32]

Steven Schnaars studied 28 industries where the imitators surpassed the innovators.[33] He found several weaknesses among the failing pioneers, including new products that were too crude, were improperly positioned, or appeared before there was strong demand; product-development costs that exhausted the innovator's resources; a lack of resources to compete against entering larger firms; and managerial incompetence or unhealthy complacency. Successful imitators thrived by offering lower prices, improving the product more continuously, or using brute market power to overtake the pioneer. None of the companies that now dominate in the manufacture of personal computers—including Dell, Gateway, and Compaq—were first movers.[34]

Golder and Tellis raise further doubts about the pioneer advantage.[35] They distinguish between an *inventor*, first to develop patents in a new-product category, a *product pioneer*, first to develop a working model, and a *market pioneer*, first to sell in the new-product category. They also include nonsurviving pioneers in their sample. They conclude that although pioneers may still have an advantage, a larger number of market pioneers fail than has been reported, and a larger number of early market leaders (though not pioneers) succeed. Examples of later entrants overtaking market pioneers are IBM over Sperry in mainframe computers and maybe Etihad Airways in the future.

In a more recent study, Tellis and Golder identify the following five factors as underpinning long-term market leadership: vision of a mass market, persistence, relentless innovation, financial commitment, and asset leverage.[36] Other research has highlighted the importance of the novelty of the product innovation.[37] When a pioneer starts a market with a really new product, survival can be very challenging. In contrast, when the market is started by an incremental innovation, as was the case with MP3 players with video capabilities, pioneers' survival rates are much higher.

The pioneer should visualize the various product markets it could initially enter, knowing it cannot enter all of them at once. Suppose market-segmentation analysis reveals the product market segments shown in ▲ **Figure 10.4**. The pioneer should analyze the profit potential of each product market singly and in combination and decide on a market expansion path. Thus the pioneer in Figure 10.4 plans first to enter product market P_1M_1, then move the product into a second market (P_1M_2), then surprise the competition by developing a second

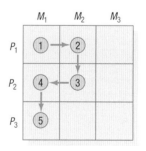

|Fig. 10.4| △

Long-Range Product Market Expansion Strategy (P_i = product i; M_j = market j)

product for the second market (P_2M_2), then take the second product back into the first market (P_2M_1), and then launch a third product for the first market (P_3M_1). If this game plan works, the pioneer firm will own a good part of the first two segments and serve them with two or three products.

Marketing Strategies: Growth Stage

The growth stage is marked by a rapid climb in sales. Early adopters like the product, and additional consumers start buying it. New competitors enter, attracted by the opportunities. They introduce new product features and expand distribution.

Prices remain where they are or fall slightly, depending on how fast demand increases. Companies maintain their promotional expenditures at the same or at a slightly increased level to meet competition and to continue to educate the market. Sales rise much faster than promotional expenditures, causing a welcome decline in the promotion/sales ratio. Profits increase during this stage as promotion costs are spread over a larger volume and unit manufacturing costs fall faster than price declines, owing to the producer learning effect. Firms must watch for a change from an accelerating to a decelerating rate of growth in order to prepare new strategies.

During the growth stage, a firm can use several strategies to sustain rapid market growth:

- Improve product quality and add new product features and improved styling.
- Add new models and flanker products (i.e. products of different sizes, flavors, and so forth that protect the main product).
- Enter new market segments.
- Increase its distribution coverage and enter new distribution channels.
- Shift from product-awareness advertising to product-preference advertising.
- Lower prices to attract the next layer of price-sensitive buyers.

These market-expansion strategies strengthen the firm's competitive position.

A firm in the growth stage faces a trade-off between high market share and high current profit. By spending money on product improvement, promotion, and distribution, it can capture a dominant position. It forgoes maximum current profit in the hope of making even greater profits in the next stage.

Marketing Strategies: Maturity Stage

At some point, the rate of sales growth will slow, and the product will enter a stage of relative maturity. This stage normally lasts longer than the previous stages and poses big challenges to marketing management. Most products are in the maturity stage of the life cycle.

The maturity stage divides into three phases: growth, stable, and decaying maturity. In the first phase, the sales growth rate starts to decline. There are no new distribution channels to fill. New competitive forces emerge (see the Marketing Insight: *Competitive Category Dynamics*). In the second phase, sales flatten on a per-capita basis because of market saturation. Most potential consumers have tried the product, and future sales are governed by population growth and replacement demand. In the third phase, decaying maturity, the absolute level of sales starts to decline, and customers begin switching to other products.

The third phase of maturity poses the most challenges. The sales slowdown creates overcapacity in the industry, which leads to intensified competition. Competitors scramble to find niches. They engage in frequent markdowns. They increase advertising and trade and consumer promotion. They increase R&D budgets to develop product improvements and line extensions. They make deals to supply private brands. A shakeout begins, and weaker competitors withdraw. The industry eventually consists of well-entrenched competitors whose basic drive is to gain or maintain market share.

Dominating the industry are a few giant firms—perhaps a quality leader, a service leader, and a cost leader—that serve the whole market and make their profits mainly through high volume and lower costs. Surrounding these dominant firms is a multitude of market nichers, including market specialists, product specialists, and customizing firms. The issue facing a firm in a mature market is

Competitive Category Dynamics

One of marketing's most astute observers, former University of California Berkeley professor David Aaker, notes that because new categories can represent strategically important threats or opportunities, marketers must be very attentive to the forces that drive their emergence. He cites seven such dynamics that result in new categories.

1. *A new product or service dimension expands the boundaries of an existing category.* Almaza in Lebanon decided to come up with Almaza 0 percent alcohol, a non-alcoholic beer, to tap the specific audience that doesn't drink alcohol.

2. *A new product or set of products carves out a fresh niche in an existing category.* Lebanon's Roadster diner decided to start another restaurant called Deek Duke, which originally just offered chicken.

3. *A new competitor devises a way to bundle existing categories into a supercategory.* In the late 1990s, Siebel created internet-based customer relationship management software by pulling together a host of applications, including customer loyalty programs, customer acquisition, call centers, customer service, customer contact, and sales force automation. In doing so, Siebel rendered irrelevant, for some customers, the more specialized application programs of competitors.

4. *A new competitor repositions existing products or services to create an original category.* In the UAE, Etihad Airways positioned itself as a business and first-class air travel provider, suitable for busy executives.

5. *Customer needs propel a new product category or subcategory.* Dual trends—wellness and the use of herbs and natural supplements—have supported a huge new beverage category: healthy refreshment beverages. It now contains a host of subcategories, including enhanced teas, fruit drinks, soy-based drinks, and specialty waters. Zein El Atat is one of the main pioneers in that industry.

6. *A new technology leads the development of a product category or subcategory.* Bee provides payment solutions for countries who use cash only (cash economies). Bee payment solutions in Egypt are now covering Mobinil, Etsalat, LINK DSL and have recently contracted with Vodafone, Telecom Egypt, and TE Data. Bee works as a payment intermediary between Information, Communication, and Technology providers and their subscribers. The core value of Bee centers around providing multiple cash payment venues through its wide network of contracted retailers. The idea behind choosing cash economies as the target market rests on the culture of full resistance to e-payment transactions. Bee services provide cash payment as an alternative payment method to e-payment.

7. *A company exploits changing technologies to invent a new category.* TiVo Inc. created a new category for home television viewing by combining the personal video player, a computer hard drive, and an electronic program guide, changing the way people watch television. Any new entrant must define itself with respect to TiVo.

Sources: "The Innovator's Prescription: The Relevance of Brand Relevance", *strategy+business*, 35, pp.1–10 (David A. Aaker), Summer 2004, published by Booz & Company Inc. Copyright © 2004. All rights reserved. www.strategy-business.com

whether to struggle to become one of the 'big three' and achieve profits through high volume and low cost, or to pursue a niching strategy and achieve profits through low volume and a high margin. Sometimes, however, the market will become polarized between low- and high-end segments, and the firms in the middle see their market share steadily erode. Here's how Swedish appliance manufacturer, Electrolux, has coped with this situation.

 Electrolux AB In 2002, Electrolux began facing a rapidly polarizing appliance market. At one end, low-cost Asian companies such as Haier, LG, and Samsung were applying downward price pressure. At the other end, premium competitors such as Bosch, Sub-Zero, and Viking were continuing to grow at the expense of the middle-of-the-road brands. Electrolux's new CEO, Hans Stråberg, who took over the reins just as the middle was dropping out of the market, decided to escape the middle by rethinking Electrolux's customers' wants and needs. For instance, rather than accept the stratification between low and high, Stråberg segmented the market according to the life style and purchasing patterns of about 20 different types of consumer: "20 product positions" as he called them. Electrolux now successfully markets its steam ovens to health-oriented consumers, for example, and its compact dishwashers, originally developed for smaller kitchens, to a broader consumer segment interested in washing dishes more often. To companies finding themselves stuck in the middle of a mature market, Stråberg offers these words of advice: "Start with consumers and understand what their latent needs are and what problems they experience . . . then put the puzzle together yourself to discover what people really want to have. Henry Ford is supposed to have said, 'If I had asked people what they really wanted, I would have made faster horses' or something like that. You need to figure out what people really want, although they can't express it."[38]

Some companies abandon weaker products to concentrate on more-profitable and new products. Yet they may be ignoring the high potential many mature markets and old products still have. Industries widely thought to be mature—autos, motorcycles, television, watches, cameras—were proved otherwise by the innovations of Japanese companies, who found ways to offer new value to customers. Seemingly declining brands such as Jell-O have achieved sales revivals through the exercise of marketing imagination.

Three potentially useful ways to change the course for a brand are market, product, and marketing program modifications.

MARKET MODIFICATION   A company might try to expand the market for its mature brand by working with the two factors that make up sales volume, as in ▅ **Box 10.2**:

$$\text{Volume} = \text{number of brand users} \times \text{usage rate per user}$$

PRODUCT MODIFICATION   Managers also try to stimulate sales by modifying the product's characteristics through quality improvement, feature improvement, or style improvement.

Quality improvement aims at increasing the product's functional performance. A manufacturer can often overtake its competition by launching a 'new and improved' product. Grocery manufacturers call this a 'plus launch' and promote a new additive or advertise something as 'stronger,' 'bigger,' or 'better.' This strategy is effective to the extent that the quality is improved, buyers accept the claim, and a sufficient number will pay for it. In the case of the canned coffee industry, manufacturers are using 'freshness' to better position their brands in the face of fierce competition from premium rivals, such as store brands that let customers grind their own beans in the store. Kraft's Maxwell House touts coffee sold in its new Fresh Seal packaging and P&G's Folger's ads show how its AromaSeal canisters—plastic, peel-top, resealable, and easy-grip packages—keep its ground beans fresher.[39]

BOX 10.2 ▅	Alternative Ways to Increase Sales Volume
Expand the Number of Brand Users	**Increase the Usage Rates Among Users**
• *Convert nonusers.* The key to the growth of air freight service is the constant search for new users to whom air carriers can demonstrate the benefits of using air freight rather than ground transportation.	• *Have consumers use the product on more occasions.* Serve Campbell's soup for a snack. Use Heinz vinegar to clean windows. Take Kodak pictures of your pets.
• *Enter new market segments.* When Goodyear decided to sell its tires via Walmart, Sears, and Discount Tire, it boosted market share from 14 to 16 percent in the first year.[40]	• *Have consumers use more of the product on each occasion.* Drink a larger glass of orange juice.
• *Attract competitors' customers.* Marketers of Puffs facial tissues are always wooing Kleenex customers.	• *Have consumers use the product in new ways.* Use Tums antacid as a calcium supplement.[41]

Feature improvement aims at adding new features such as size, weight, materials, additives, and accessories that expand the product's performance, versatility, safety, or convenience. This strategy has several advantages. New features build the company's image as an innovator and win the loyalty of market segments that value these features. They provide an opportunity for free publicity and they generate sales force and distributor enthusiasm. The chief disadvantage is that feature improvements are easily imitated; unless the marketer realizes a permanent gain from being first, the feature improvement might not pay off in the long run.[42]

Style improvement aims at increasing the product's aesthetic appeal. The periodic introduction of new car models is largely about style competition, as is the introduction of new packaging for consumer products. A style strategy might give the product a unique market identity. Yet style competition has problems. First, it's difficult to predict whether people—and which people—will like a new style. Second, a style change usually requires discontinuing the old style, and the company risks losing customers.

Regardless of the type of improvement, marketers must beware of a possible backlash. Customers are not always willing to accept an 'improved' product, as the now-classic tale of New Coke illustrates.

 Coca-Cola   Battered by competition from the sweeter Pepsi Cola, Coca-Cola decided in 1985 to replace its old formula with a sweeter variation, named New Coke. Coca-Cola spent US$4 million on market research. Blind taste tests showed that Coke drinkers preferred the new, sweeter formula, but the launch of New Coke provoked an uproar. Market researchers had measured the taste but had failed to measure the emotional attachment consumers had to Coca-Cola. There were angry letters, formal protests, and even lawsuit threats to force the retention of 'The Real Thing.' Ten weeks later, the company withdrew New Coke and reintroduced its century-old formula as Coca-Cola Classic.

MARKETING PROGRAM MODIFICATION   Product managers might also try to stimulate sales by modifying other marketing program elements and using the appropriate marketing mix. They should ask the following questions:

- *Prices.* Would a price cut attract new buyers? If so, should we lower the list price or lower prices through price specials, volume or early-purchase discounts, freight cost absorption, or easier credit terms? Or would it be better to *raise* the price, to signal higher quality?

- *Distribution.* Can the company obtain more product support and display in existing outlets? Can it penetrate more outlets? Can the company introduce the product into new distribution channels?

- *Advertising.* Should we increase advertising expenditures? Change the message or ad copy? The media mix? What about the timing, frequency, or size of ads?

- *Sales promotion.* Should the company step up sales promotion: trade deals, cents-off coupons, rebates, warranties, gifts, and contests?

- *Personal selling.* Should we increase the number or quality of salespeople? Should we change the basis for sales force specialization? Revise sales territories or sales force incentives? Can we improve sales-call planning?

- *Services.* Can the company speed up delivery? Can we extend more technical assistance to customers? More credit?

Marketing Strategies: Decline Stage

Sales decline for a number of reasons, including technological advances, shifts in consumer tastes, and increased domestic and foreign competition. All can lead to overcapacity, increased price cutting, and profit erosion. The decline might be slow, as in the case of sewing machines, or rapid, as in the case of 5.25-inch floppy disks. Sales may plunge to zero, or they may petrify at a low level.

As sales and profits decline, some firms withdraw from the market. Those remaining may reduce the number of products they offer. They may withdraw from smaller market segments and weaker trade channels, and they may cut their promotion budgets and reduce prices further. Unfortunately, most companies have not developed a policy for handling aging products.

Unless strong reasons for retention exist, carrying a weak product is very costly to the firm, and not just by the amount of uncovered overhead and profit: there are many hidden costs. Weak products often consume a disproportionate amount of management's time; require frequent price and inventory adjustments; incur expensive setup for short production runs; draw both advertising and sales force attention that might be better used to make healthy products more profitable; and cast a shadow on the company's image. The biggest cost might well lie in the future. Failing to eliminate weak products delays the aggressive search for replacement products. The weak products create a lopsided product mix, long on yesterday's breadwinners and short on tomorrow's.

In handling aging products, a company faces a number of tasks and decisions. The first task is to establish a system for identifying weak products. Many companies appoint a product-review committee with representatives from marketing, R&D, manufacturing, and finance who, based on all available information, makes a recommendation for each product: leave it alone, modify its marketing strategy, or drop it.[43]

Some firms abandon declining markets earlier than others. Much depends on the height of exit barriers in the industry.[44] The lower the exit barriers, the easier it is for firms to leave the industry, and the more tempting it is for the remaining firms to stay and attract the withdrawing firms' customers. For example, Procter & Gamble stayed in the declining liquid-soap business and improved its profits as others withdrew.

The appropriate strategy also depends on the industry's relative attractiveness and the company's competitive strength in that industry. A company that is in an unattractive industry but possesses competitive strength should consider shrinking selectively. A company that is in an attractive industry but has competitive strength should consider strengthening its investment. Companies that successfully restage or rejuvenate a mature product often do so by adding value to the original offering.

If the company were choosing between harvesting and divesting, its strategies would be quite different. *Harvesting* calls for gradually reducing a product or business's costs while trying to maintain sales. The first step is to cut R&D costs and plant and equipment investment. The company might also reduce product quality, sales force size, marginal services, and advertising expenditures. It would try to cut these costs without letting customers, competitors, and employees know what is happening. Harvesting is difficult to execute. Yet many mature products warrant this strategy. It can substantially increase the company's current cash flow.[45]

When a company decides to drop a product, it faces further decisions. If the product has strong distribution and residual goodwill, the company can probably sell it to another firm. If the company can't find any buyers, it must decide whether to liquidate the brand quickly or slowly. It must also decide on how much inventory and service to maintain for past customers.

Evidence on the Product Life-Cycle Concept

Based on the above discussion, Table 10.3 summarizes the characteristics, marketing objectives, and marketing strategies of the four stages of the PLC. The PLC concept helps marketers interpret product and market dynamics, conduct planning and control, and do forecasting.

One recent study of 30 product categories uncovered a number of interesting findings concerning the PLC.[46] New consumer durables showed a distinct takeoff, after which sales increased by roughly 45 percent a year, but also showed a distinct slowdown, when sales declined by roughly 15 percent a year. Slowdown occurred at 34 percent penetration on average, well before the majority of households owned a new product. The growth stage lasted a little over 8 years and did not seem to shorten over time. Informational cascades existed, meaning that people were more likely to adopt over time if others already did, instead of making careful product evaluations. One implication, however, is that product categories with large sales increases at takeoff tend to have larger sales decline at slowdown.

Critique of the Product Life-Cycle Concept

The PLC theory has its share of critics. They claim that life-cycle patterns are too variable in shape and duration to be generalized, and that marketers can seldom tell what stage their product is in. A product may appear to be mature when actually it has reached a plateau prior to another

TABLE 10.3 ▱ Summary of Product Life-Cycle Characteristics, Objectives, and Strategies				
	Introduction	**Growth**	**Maturity**	**Decline**
Characteristics				
Sales	Low sales	Rapidly rising sales	Peak sales	Declining sales
Costs	High cost per customer	Average cost per customer	Low cost per customer	Low cost per customer
Profits	Negative	Rising profits	High profits	Declining profits
Customers	Innovators	Early adopters	Middle majority	Laggards
Competitors	Few	Growing number	Stable number beginning to decline	Declining number
Marketing Objectives				
	Create product awareness and trial	Maximize market share	Maximize profit while defending market share	Reduce expenditure and milk the brand
Strategies				
Product	Offer a basic product	Offer product extensions, service, warranty	Diversify brands, items and models	Phase out weak products
Price	Charge cost-plus	Price to penetrate market	Price to match or beat competitors	Cut price
Distribution	Build selective distribution	Build intensive distribution	Build more intensive distribution	Go selective: phase out unprofitable outlets
Advertising	Build product awareness among early adopters and dealers	Build awareness and interest in the mass market	Stress brand differences and benefits	Reduce to level needed to retain hard-core loyals
Sales Promotion	Use heavy sales promotion to entice trial	Reduce to take advantage of heavy consumer demand	Increase to encourage brand switching	Reduce to minimal level

Sources: Chester R. Wasson, *Dynamic Competitive Strategy and Product Life Cycles* (Austin, TX: Austin Press, 1978); John A. Weber, "Planning Corporate Growth with Inverted Product Life Cycles," *Long Range Planning*, October 1976, pp. 12–29; Peter Doyle, "The Realities of the Product Life Cycle," *Quarterly Review of Marketing*, Summer 1976.

upsurge. Critics also charge that, rather than an inevitable course that sales must follow, the PLC pattern is the self-fulfilling result of marketing strategies and that skillful marketing can in fact lead to continued growth.[47] The Marketing Memo: *How to Build a Breakaway Brand* provides 10 rules for long-term marketing success.

Market Evolution

Because the PLC focuses on what's happening to a particular product or brand rather than on what's happening to the overall market, it yields a product-oriented picture rather than a market-oriented picture. Firms also need to visualize a *market's* evolutionary path as it is affected by new needs, competitors, technology, channels, and other developments.[48] In the course of a product's or brand's existence, its positioning must change to keep pace with market developments. Like products, markets evolve through four stages: emergence, growth, maturity, and decline.

EMERGENCE Before a market materializes, it exists as a latent market. For example, for centuries people have wanted faster means of calculation. The market satisfied this need with abacuses, slide rules, and large adding machines. Suppose an entrepreneur recognizes this need and imagines a technological solution in the form of a small, handheld electronic calculator. He now must determine

marketing Memo

How to Build a Breakaway Brand

Arnold Worldwide marketing experts Francis Kelly and Barry Silverstein define a *breakaway brand* as one that stands out, not just in its own product category but from all other brands, and that achieves significant results in the marketplace. Here is a summary of their 10 tips for building a breakaway brand:

1. *Make a commitment.* Your entire organization, from the top down, needs to make a commitment to build and support a breakaway brand. Get your company behind developing new products that have breakaway attributes.

2. *Get a 'chief' behind it.* Few breakaway branding initiatives have a chance of success without the enthusiastic support of your CEO (Chief Executive Officer), COO (Chief Operations Officer), or CMO (Chief Marketing Officer). A senior executive at your company must play the role of brand visionary, brand champion, and brand architect.

3. *Find your brand truth.* Ultimately, the DNA of your breakaway brand is its brand truth. It is what defines and differentiates every breakaway brand. It is the single most important weapon a brand will ever have in the battle for increased awareness, profitability, market share, and even share price.

4. *Target a winning mind-set.* The winning mind-set is the potent, aspirational, shared 'view of life' among all core audience segments. It becomes the filter through which all of your advertising and promotional activities should flow.

5. *Create a category of one.* To be a breakaway brand, your brand needs not only to stand apart from others in its own category but also to transcend categories and open a defining gap between itself and its competitors. Then it becomes a category of one.

6. *Demand a great campaign.* Great campaigns are a team sport: they require a partnership between you and your agency to create a campaign that breaks away. Never compromise on a campaign, because without a great campaign, your breakaway brand can fizzle.

7. *Tirelessly integrate.* Integration is the name of the game. Depending on the audience you're trying to reach, your campaign might integrate both network and cable TV, print and online advertising, direct mail, e-mail, radio, and nontraditional media: from street marketing to publicity stunts to contests.

8. *Take risks.* Today, 80 percent of brands are merely treading water in a sea of gray. Only 20 percent are making waves. You can't afford to have your product sink in the sea, and that may mean taking a calculated risk or two—or three—to ensure your brand rises above the others.

9. *Accelerate new-product development.* Nothing is more important than differentiating a product in the marketplace, but the only way to rise above me-too branding is to innovate and do something different and unique with the product. It may mean throwing away an old product brand and reinventing it. Or it may mean starting from scratch.

10. *Invest as if your brand depends on it.* Building a breakaway brand is serious business, so it takes a serious business investment. Invest in the product, of course, but also in the packaging and a smart integrated marketing campaign. Invest wisely . . . as if your brand depends on it.

Source: adapted from Francis J. Kelly III and Barry Silverstein, *The Breakaway Brand* (New York: McGraw-Hill, 2005).

the product attributes, including physical size and number of mathematical functions. Because he is market-oriented, he interviews potential buyers and finds that target customers vary greatly in their preferences. Some want a four-function calculator (adding, subtracting, multiplying, and dividing) and others want more functions (calculating percentages, square roots, and logarithms). Some want a small hand calculator and others want a large one. This type of market, in which buyer preferences scatter evenly, is called a *diffused-preference market*. The entrepreneur's problem is to design an optimal product for this market. There are three options:

1. Design the new product to meet the preferences of one of the corners of the market: *a single-niche strategy.*
2. Launch two or more products simultaneously to capture two or more parts of the market: *a multiple-niche strategy.*
3. Design the new product for the middle of the market: *a mass-market strategy.*

A small firm doesn't have the resources for capturing and holding the mass market, so a single-niche market strategy makes the most sense. A large firm might go after the mass market by designing a product that's medium in size and in its number of functions. Assume our pioneer firm is large and designs its product for the mass market. Once it has launched the product, the *emergence* stage begins.[49]

GROWTH If the new product sells well, new firms will enter the market, ushering in a *market-growth stage*. Where will a second firm enter the market, assuming the first firm established itself in the center? If the second firm is small, it's likely to avoid head-on competition with the pioneer and to launch its brand in one of the market corners. If the second firm is large, it might launch its brand in the center against the pioneer. The two firms can easily end up sharing the mass market. Or a large second firm can implement a multiple-niche strategy and surround and box in the pioneer.

MATURITY Eventually, the competitors cover and serve all the major segments and the market enters the *maturity stage*. In fact, the competitors go further and invade each others' segments, reducing everyone's profits in the process. As market growth slows down, the market splits into finer segments and high *market fragmentation* occurs. This situation is illustrated in △ **Figure 10.5** (a) where the letters represent different companies supplying various segments. Note that two segments are unserved because they're too small to yield a profit.

Market fragmentation is often followed by *market consolidation*, caused by the emergence of a new attribute that has strong appeal. This situation is illustrated in Figure 10.5 (b) and the expansive size of the X territory. However, even a consolidated market condition will not last. Other companies will copy a successful brand, and the market will eventually splinter again. Mature markets swing between fragmentation brought about by competition and consolidation brought about by innovation. Consider the evolution of the paper towel market.

(a) Market-Fragmentation Stage

(b) Market-Consolidation Stage

Fig. 10.5 △

Market-Fragmentation and Market-Consolidation Strategies

Paper Towels   Originally, homemakers used cotton and linen dishcloths and towels in their kitchens. A paper company, looking for new markets, developed paper towels. This development crystallized a latent market, and other manufacturers entered. The number of brands grew and created market fragmentation. Industry overcapacity led manufacturers to search for new features. One manufacturer, hearing consumers complain that paper towels were not absorbent, introduced 'absorbent' towels and increased its market share. This market consolidation didn't last long because competitors came out with their own versions of absorbent paper towels. The market fragmented again. Then another manufacturer introduced a 'superstrength' towel. It was soon copied. Another manufacturer introduced a 'lint-free' paper towel, which was subsequently copied. Thus, paper towels evolved from a single product to one with various absorbencies, strengths, and applications. Market evolution was driven by the forces of innovation and competition.

DECLINE Eventually, demand for the current products will begin to decrease, and the market will enter the *decline stage*. Either society's total need level declines, or a new technology replaces the old. For example, shifts in tradition and a trend toward cremation have caused casket makers and funeral homes to reconsider how to conduct their business.[50]

Summary

1. Deciding on positioning requires the determination of a frame of reference—by identifying the target market and the nature of the competition—and the ideal points-of-parity and points-of-difference brand associations. To determine the proper competitive frame of reference, one must understand consumer behavior and the considerations consumers use in making brand choices.

2. Points-of-difference are those associations unique to the brand that are also strongly held and favorably

evaluated by consumers. Points-of-parity are those associations not necessarily unique to the brand but perhaps shared with other brands. Category point-of-parity associations are associations consumers view as being necessary to a legitimate and credible product offering within a certain category. Competitive point-of-parity associations are those associations designed to negate competitors' points-of-difference.

3. The key to competitive advantage is relevant brand differentiation: consumers must find something

unique and meaningful about a market offering. These differences may be based directly on the product or service itself or on other considerations related to factors such as personnel, channels, or image.

4. Because economic conditions change and competitive activity varies, companies normally find it necessary to reformulate their marketing strategy several times during a product's life cycle. Technologies, product forms, and brands also exhibit life cycles with distinct stages. The general sequence of stages in any life cycle is introduction, growth, maturity, and decline. The majority of products today are in the maturity stage.

5. Each stage of the product life cycle calls for different marketing strategies. The introduction stage is marked by slow growth and minimal profits. If successful, the product enters a growth stage marked by rapid sales growth and increasing profits. There follows a maturity stage in which sales growth slows and profits stabilize. Finally, the product enters a decline stage. The company's task is to identify the truly weak products; develop a strategy for each one; and phase them out in a way that minimizes the hardship to company profits, employees, and customers.

6. Like products, markets evolve through four stages: emergence, growth, maturity, and decline.

Applications

Marketing Debate

Do Brands Have Finite Lives?

Often, after a brand begins to slip in the marketplace or disappears altogether, commentators observe, 'all brands have their day.' Their rationale is that all brands, in some sense, have a finite life and cannot be expected to be leaders forever. Other experts contend, however, that brands can live forever, and their long-term success depends on the skill and insight of the marketers involved.

Take a position: Brands cannot be expected to last forever *versus* there is no reason for a brand to ever become obsolete.

Marketing Discussion

Identify other negatively correlated attributes and benefits not included in 🖳 **Table 10.3** on page 183. What strategies do firms use to try to position themselves on the basis of pairs of attributes and benefits?

Marketing Excellence

>>Bee

TBE Egypt is a subsidiary of Technobiz which is a Singapore-based company, established in 2005, with operations currently in five countries. Cash economies are the main target market for Technobiz products. Technobiz had opened its Egyptian subsidiary in 2009 under the brand Bee with a capitalisation of US$20 million. Based on the company's global leadership and Egyptian market awareness, Bee smart payment solutions now cover Mobinil, Etsalat, and LINK DSL, and have lately contracted with Vodafone and TE Data. Bee works as a payment intermediary between information and communication technology providers and their subscribers. The core value of Bee centers around providing multiple cash payment venues through its wide network of contracted retailers. The idea behind choosing cash economies as the target market rests on the culture of high resistance to e-payment transactions. Bee services provide cash payment as an alternative in lieu of e-payment. Another attractive advantage for Bee business in developing countries is the convenience of the places used for payment, such as kiosks and other small independent retailers that are extensively distributed throughout rural and other isolated neighborhoods. Common traits among residents of these districts are: lack of trust, security concerns, and technological illiteracy. As a result, Bee services are very well accepted and welcomed. Bee is currently expanding in the Egyptian market.

To continue expanding in Egypt, the company needs to launch its services in the provinces which are not yet covered. A prerequisite for future progress is high market awareness and superiority. There are three other players that offer payment solutions in Egypt: Fawry, Masary, and Khadamat. Fawry is the market leader and has twice as many retailers as Bee. Fawry has operated in Egypt since March 2010, while Bee activated its services in July 2011. Bee conducted modest marketing research to identify Fawry's areas of weakness. Based on the research results, Bee customized its advertising campaign so as to highlight these weaknesses as areas of strength for Bee's products. The research sample incorporated 20 retailers who deal with Fawry besides 50 of Fawry's final customers. Mystery shoppers were used at retailers to acquire the full transaction experience as ultimate customers, and ethnographic researchers interviewed Fawry's real customers in front of the outlets. One striking finding was that Fawry charges its final customers/users additional fees for transactions on cellphones, landlines, and internet payments, with varying amounts for each. To capitalize on this major finding, Fawry's customers were asked about their perception regarding these additional charges. Customers rejected the extra charges in principle and wondered why they were being charged, especially when Fawry's bill issuers or providers were also charged. The retailing research also indicated that Fawry collects insurance in the form of deposits for providing payment equipment to conventional independent retailers, while Bee never loads its retailers with any charges.

The only providers who don't pay charges to payment solution companies are Telecom Egypt and its affiliated company TE Data. Fawry is passing on these charges to its ultimate customers. However, Bee had neither Telecom Egypt nor TE Data as its providers. Thus Bee had the flexibility to turn the disadvantage of not covering Telecom Egypt and TE Data into an advantage by presenting a new value proposition. Bee automatically launched an aggressive marketing campaign highlighting its free charging services to customers. The campaign theme was focusing on "For Free" (or Bebelash). Bee allocated US$250,000 to the Bebelash marketing campaign applied to multiple communication instruments such as radio stations, outdoor and cab billboards, posters and flyers at retailing outlets, and Facebook. The campaign lasted two months and fully achieved its objectives by doubling Bee's daily transactions. It also achieved an immediate activation contract with Vodafone and TE Data. Mohamed Abu Khadra, senior marketing manager, said, "The marketing research led Bee to identifying an opportunity and conducting the Bebelash campaign. If this venture didn't exist, there would have been for sure another value to discover and to build upon Bee's value proposition." Before the market research was conducted, Bee had only 1500 retailers carrying its services. This number jumped to 3000 retailers thanks to the marketing campaign. To maximize the acquired benefits, Bee aims to continue introducing its full portfolio of services in Egypt. Abu Khadra said, "Our objective is to reach 10,000 retailers by the end of 2011."

Questions

1. Identify Bee's positioning. How do you perceive Bee's position against Fawry?

2. Do you think Bee conveyed a clear positioning message to its target market? How and why?

3. Access Bee and Fawry's websites and then write two paragraphs detailing differences between the brands.

4. Imagine you are Bee's marketing manager. Based on the text here, outline the company's competitive marketing strategy for the next year.

5. Self-knowledge is the ability to identify the product attributes that are important to you. From the case, determine and discuss your e-payment self-knowledge. Do you think companies have the ability to raise consumers' self-knowledge. How and why?

Sources: Reem Abdellatif, "Bee offers payment solutions to Egypt customers," *Daily News Egypt*, July 20, 2011, http://www.thedailynewsegypt.com/economy/bee-offers-payment-solutions-to-egypt-customers.html; Bee company profile (2011).

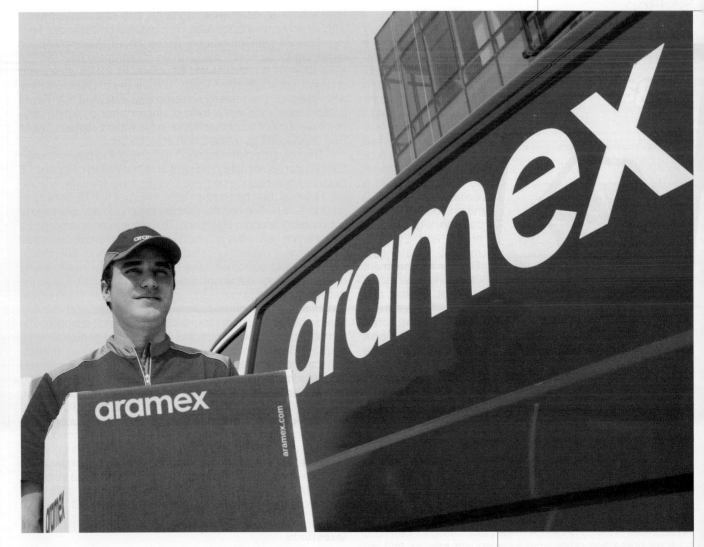

In this chapter, we will address the following questions:

1. How do marketers identify primary competitors? (pg. 290)

2. How should we analyze competitors' strategies, objectives, strengths, and weaknesses? (pg. 293)

3. How can market leaders expand the total market and defend market share? (pg. 297)

4. How should market challengers attack market leaders? (pg. 303)

5. How can market followers or nichers compete effectively? (pg. 305)

Dealing With Competition

Building strong brands requires a keen understanding of competitors, and competition grows more intense every year. New competition is coming from all directions: from global competitors eager to grow sales in new markets; from online competitors seeking cost-efficient ways to expand distribution; from private-label and store brands designed to provide low-price alternatives; and from brand extensions of megabrands leveraging their strengths to move into new categories. One good way to start to deal with competition is through creatively designed and well-executed marketing programs.

 Starting out as a business-to-business express delivery wholesaler to North America competing with key players like FedEx, Purolator, Burlington Northern, Emery, and Airborne Express, Aramex has grown to be one of the major global transportation and logistics services companies. With corporate headquarters in Amman, Jordan, Aramex has created a unique place for itself within the international express market. A consistently high standard of service to its customers and constant innovation and improvement in technology have been major factors in its ability to compete with major global companies such as DHL in the region.

Today, Aramex provides a wide range of services from express, logistics, freight forwarding, and domestic distribution to mail-order catalog and mail forwarding services. The real success of this company lies in its strategic objectives to provide high-quality service to its customers complemented by time-framed solutions to meet their expectations.

Aramex achieved a strong competitive advantage by offering value-added services to support its standard express services and by tailoring these to fulfill the varying needs of their different customers. These services range from facilitating payment methods, schedules, and fees, to business solutions, and managing and delivering mail between business branches on a regular basis to customer requirements. Furthermore, Aramex provides mass mail solutions, distributing regular mass mail including customers' monthly invoices, marketing and promotional materials, and event invitations; as well as financial and telecom solutions such as handling the secure distribution of credit cards, and the delivery of high-value SIM cards and mobile phones on behalf of telecom operators. Aramex's ever-increasing annual net profits are solid proof of the company's strategy: differentiating itself from other express companies by tailoring its services to its customers' needs, yielding superior benefits, and establishing a leading position in the global marketplace.[1]

To effectively devise and implement the best possible brand-positioning strategies, companies must pay keen attention to their competitors. Markets have become too competitive to focus on the consumer alone. This chapter examines the role competition plays and how marketers can best manage their brands, depending on their market position.[2] ▽

Competitive Forces

Michael Porter has identified five forces that determine the intrinsic long-run attractiveness of a market or market segment: industry competitors, potential entrants, substitutes, buyers, and suppliers. The threats these forces pose are as follows:

1. *Threat of intense segment rivalry.* A segment is unattractive if it already contains numerous, strong, or aggressive competitors. It's even more unattractive if it's stable or declining, if plant capacity must be added in large increments, if fixed costs or exit barriers are high, or if competitors have high stakes in staying in the segment. These conditions will lead to frequent price wars, advertising battles, and new-product introductions and will make it expensive to compete. The mobile phone market has seen fierce competition due to segment rivalry.

2. *Threat of new entrants.* The most attractive segment is one in which entry barriers are high and exit barriers are low.[3] Few new firms can enter the industry, and poorly performing firms can easily exit. When both entry and exit barriers are high, profit potential is also high, but firms face more risk because poorer-performing firms stay in and fight it out. When both entry and exit barriers are low, firms enter and leave the industry easily, and the returns are stable and low. The worst case is when entry barriers are low and exit barriers are high: here firms enter during good times but find it hard to leave during bad times. The result is frequent overcapacity and depressed earnings for all. The airline industry has low entry barriers but high exit barriers, leaving all carriers struggling during economic downturns.

3. *Threat of substitute products.* A segment is unattractive when there are actual or potential substitutes for the product. Substitutes place a limit on prices and on profits. If technology advances or competition increases in these substitute industries, prices and profits are likely to fall. Telecom Egypt and other fixed-line telecommunication companies have seen their profitability threatened by the rise of mobile service operators such as Vodafone and Etisalat.

4. *Threat of buyers' growing bargaining power.* A segment is unattractive if buyers possess strong or growing bargaining power. The rise of retail giants such as Carrefour has led some analysts to conclude that the potential profitability of packaged-goods companies will become curtailed. Buyers' bargaining power grows when they become more concentrated or organized, when the product represents a significant fraction of the buyers' costs, when the product is undifferentiated, when buyers' switching costs are low, when buyers are price sensitive because of low profits, or when they can integrate upstream. To protect themselves, sellers might select buyers who have the least power to negotiate or switch suppliers. A better defense consists of developing superior offers that strong buyers cannot refuse.

5. *Threat of suppliers' growing bargaining power.* A segment is unattractive if the company's suppliers are able to raise prices or reduce quantity supplied. Oil companies such as ExxonMobil, Shell, and BP are at the mercy of the limited amount of oil reserves and the actions of oil-supplying cartels such as the Organization of Petroleum Exporting Countries (OPEC). Suppliers tend to be powerful when they are concentrated or organized, when there are few substitutes, when the supplied product is an important input, when the costs of switching suppliers are high, and when the suppliers can integrate downstream. The best defenses are to build win–win relationships with suppliers or use multiple supply sources.

Identifying Competitors

It would seem a simple task for a company to identify its competitors. PepsiCo knows that Coca-Cola's Dasani is the major bottled-water competitor for its Aquafina brand; Dell knows that Apple is a major competitor in the computer market; and Henkel which sells Persil detergents knows that their major competitor is Proctor & Gamble's Ariel and Tide detergents.

However, the range of a company's actual and potential competitors can be much broader than the obvious. And a company is more likely to be hurt by emerging competitors or new technologies than by current competitors.

In recent years, for instance, a number of new 'emerging giants' have arisen from developing countries, and these nimble competitors are not only competing with multinationals on their home turf but also becoming global forces in their own right. They have gained competitive advantage by exploiting their knowledge about local factors of production—capital and talent—and supply chains in order to build world-class businesses.

Etisalat Egypt   Founded in 1976, and headquartered in Abu Dhabi, Etisalat is one of the largest telecommunications companies in the world and the leading operator in the region, serving over 100 million customers. Launched in 2006, Etisalat Egypt is one of 19 subsidiaries of Etisalat. When Etisalat Egypt decided to penetrate the Egyptian market it faced fierce competition from the two existing mobile operators, Mobinil and Vodafone, but was able to compete by introducing new services to the Egyptian market. Etisalat introduced the first 3.5G network, bringing rich multimedia content, mobile television, high-speed internet access, and video calling to Egypt for the first time, and acquiring almost 1 million subscribers in the first 50 days. This success story was the result of the company's ability to customize its latest technology to best serve the Egyptian culture. With changing value propositions, from "It's time for it," during its initial launch, to the later "There is more to life," Etisalat has shown its ability to adapt to local market needs. Today, it has more than 14 million active subscribers out of almost 70 million mobile customers in Egypt.[4]

Ceramica Cleopatra   Founded by Egyptian entrepreneur Mohamed Abou El Enein, Ceramica Cleopatra is a good example of a company that highly utilizes local resources, and is successful enough to compete in the local and international markets. From the early 1980s to the early 1990s, Ceramica Cleopatra was dependent on imported tiles to meet its local and international market requirements. However, after opening the first factory for porcelain and granite tiles in the region, Ceramica Cleopatra was able to satisfy the market's needs. The quality of its products, as well as the 50 percent lower cost of producing tiles in Egypt compared with importing Italian ones, allowed Ceramica Cleopatra to penetrate strong markets such as Japan, Saudi Arabia, and the UAE. The availability of rich Egyptian resources and the skilled labor force needed to produce porcelain and granite have resulted in the establishment of four large factories to meet the demand. Further, it has allowed Ceramica Cleopatra to reach the top of the industry, producing 90 million square meters of tiling annually, and exporting to more than 100 countries.[5]

We can examine competition from both an industry and a market point of view.[6] An **industry** is a group of firms that offer a product or class of products that are close substitutes for one another. Marketers classify industries according to the number of sellers; degree of product differentiation; presence or absence of entry, mobility, and exit barriers; cost structure; degree of **vertical integration**; and degree of globalization.

Using the market approach, we define *competitors* as companies that satisfy the same customer need. For example, a customer who buys a word-processing package really wants 'writing ability:' a need that can also be satisfied by pencils, pens, or typewriters. Marketers must overcome 'marketing myopia' and stop defining competition in traditional category and industry terms.[7] Coca-Cola, focused on its soft-drink business, missed seeing the market for coffee shops and fresh-fruit-juice shops, which eventually penetrated the soft-drink business.

The market concept of competition reveals a broader set of actual and potential competitors than competition defined in just product category terms. Professors Rayport and Jaworski suggest profiling a company's direct and indirect competitors by mapping the buyer's steps

industry   a group of firms that offer a product or class of products that are close substitutes for one another.

vertical integration   situation in which manufactures try to control or own their suppliers, distributors, or other intermediaries.

in obtaining and using the product. This type of analysis highlights both the opportunities and the challenges a company faces.[8] The Marketing Insight: *High Growth Through Value Innovation* describes how firms can tap into new markets that minimize competition from others.

Marketing Insight

High Growth Through Value Innovation

Professors W. Chan Kim and Renée Mauborgne of the INSEAD Business School believe that too many firms engage in 'red-ocean thinking:' seeking bloody, head-to-head battles with competitors based largely on incremental improvements in cost, quality, or both. They advocate engaging instead in 'blue-ocean thinking' by creating products and services for which there are no direct competitors. Their belief is that instead of searching within the conventional boundaries of industry competition, managers should look beyond those boundaries to find unoccupied market positions that represent real value innovation.

The authors cite as one example Bert Claeys, a Belgian movie theater operator, and its introduction of the 25-screen, 7,600-seat Kinepolis megaplex. Despite an industry slump, Kineopolis has thrived on a unique combination of features, such as ample, safe, and free parking; large screens and state-of-the-art sound and projection equipment; and roomy, comfortable, oversized seats with unobstructed views. Through smart planning and economies of scale, Bert Claeys creates Kinepolis's unique cinema experience at a lower cost.

This is classic blue-ocean thinking: designing creative business ventures to positively affect both a company's cost structure and its value proposition to consumers. Cost savings result from eliminating and reducing the factors affecting traditional industry competition; value to consumers comes from introducing factors the industry has never before offered. Over time, costs drop even more as superior value leads to higher sales volume, and that generates economies of scale.

Other examples of marketers that exhibit unconventional, blue-ocean thinking are listed below.

- Jazeera Airways offers a convenient service at low cost.

- Callaway Golf designed Big Bertha, a golf club with a large head and expanded sweet spot that helped golfers frustrated by the difficulty of hitting a golf ball squarely.

- NetJets figured out how to offer private jet service to a larger group of customers through fractional ownership.

The Belgian Kinepolis movie megaplex exemplifies 'blue-ocean' thinking, a competitive strategy that focuses on finding unoccupied market positions. Here is an exterior shot of the Kinepolis in Antwerp, Belgium.

- Cirque du Soleil reinvented circus as a higher form of entertainment by eliminating high-cost elements such as animals and enhancing the theatrical experience instead.

Kim and Mauborgne propose four crucial questions for marketers to ask themselves in guiding blue-ocean thinking and creating value innovation:

- Which of the factors that our industry takes for granted should we eliminate?

- Which factors should we reduce well *below* the industry's standard?

- Which factors should we raise well *above* the industry's standard?

- Which factors should we create that the industry has never offered?

They maintain that the most successful blue-ocean thinkers take advantage of all three platforms on which value innovation can take place: *physical product*; *service* including maintenance, customer service, warranties, and training for distributors and retailers; and *delivery*, meaning channels and logistics. **Box 11.1** summarizes key principles driving the successful formulation and execution of blue-ocean strategy.

Sources: W. Chan Kim and Renée Mauborgne, *Blue-Ocean Strategy: How to Create Uncontested Market Space and Make the Competition Irrelevant* (Cambridge, MA: Harvard Business School Press, 2005); W. Chan Kim and Renée Mauborgne, "Creating New Market Space," *Harvard Business Review*, January–February 1999; W. Chan Kim and Renée Mauborgne, "Value Innovation: The Strategic Logic of High Growth," *Harvard Business Review*, January–February 1997.

BOX 11.1 ■ Key Principles of Blue-Ocean Strategy

FORMULATION PRINCIPLES

a. Reconstruct market boundaries
   - Look across alternative industries
   - Look across strategic groups within industries
   - Look across the chain of buyers
   - Look across complementary product and service offerings
   - Look across functional or emotional appeal to buyers
   - Look across time

b. Focus on the big picture not the numbers

c. Reach beyond existing demand

d. Get the strategic sequence right

   - Is there buyer utility?
   - Is the price acceptable?
   - Can we attain target cost?
   - What are the adoption challenges?

EXECUTION PRINCIPLES

a. Overcome key organizational hurdles
   - Cognitive hurdle
   - Resource hurdle
   - Motivational hurdle
   - Political hurdle

b. Build execution into strategy

Source: W. Chan Kim and Renée Mauborgne, *Blue-Ocean Strategy: How to Create Uncontested Market Space and Make the Competition Irrelevant* (Cambridge, MA: Harvard Business School Press, 2005). Copyright © 2005 by the Harvard Business School Publishing Corporation; all rights reserved.

Analyzing Competitors

Once a company identifies its primary competitors, it must ascertain their strategies, objectives, and strengths and weaknesses.[9]

Strategies

A group of firms following the same strategy in a given target market is a **strategic group**.[10] Suppose a company wants to enter the major-appliance industry. What is its strategic group?

The company develops the chart shown in △ **Figure 11.1** on page 294 and discovers four strategic groups based on product quality and level of vertical integration. Group A has one competitor (Samsung); group B has three (General Electric, White Westing House, and Toshiba); group C has four; and group D has two. Important insights emerge from this exercise. First, the height of entry barriers differs for each group. Second, if the company successfully enters a group, the members of that group become its key competitors.

strategic group firms pursuing the same strategy directed to the same target market.

Objectives

Once a company has identified its main competitors and their strategies, it must ask: what is each competitor seeking in the marketplace? What drives each competitor's behavior? Many factors shape a competitor's objectives, including size, history, current management, and financial

High

Group A
• Narrow line
• Lower mfg. cost
• Very high service
• High price

Group C
• Moderate line
• Medium mfg. cost
• Medium service
• Medium price

Quality

Group B
• Full line
• Low mfg. cost
• Good service
• Medium price

Low

Group D
• Broad line
• Medium mfg. cost
• Low service
• Low price

High   Low

Vertical Integration

|Fig. 11.1| △

Strategic Groups in the Major-Appliance Industry

situation. If the competitor is a division of a larger company, it's important to know whether the parent company is running it for growth or profits, or milking it.

It's useful to assume that competitors strive to maximize profits. However, companies differ in the relative emphasis they put on short-term and long-term profits. Many firms in the Arab world strive to maximize sales and profits in the short-term. While this is a fair goal for any organization, the true benefits start to be realized *after* a large number of consumers trust the brand and the service offered, and this is when a large volume of sales will be realized in terms of profits. Internationally, many U.S. firms have been criticized for operating on a short-run model, largely because current performance is judged by stockholders who might lose confidence, sell their stock, and cause the company's cost of capital to rise. Japanese firms operate largely on a market-share-maximization model. They receive much of their funds from banks at a lower interest rate and in the past have readily accepted lower profits. So another reliable assumption is that each competitor pursues some mix of objectives: current profitability, market share growth, cash flow, technological leadership, and service leadership.[11]

Finally, a company must monitor competitors' expansion plans. △ **Figure 11.2** shows a product-market battlefield map for the personal computer industry. Dell, which started out as a strong force in the sale of personal computers to individual users, is now a major force in the commercial and industrial market. Other incumbents may try to set up mobility barriers to Dell's further expansion.

Strengths and Weaknesses

A company needs to gather information about each competitor's strengths and weaknesses. ▢ **Table 11.1** on page 295 shows the results of a company survey that asked customers to rate its three competitors, A, B, and C, on five attributes. Competitor A turns out to be well known and respected for producing high-quality products sold by a good sales force, but is poor at providing product availability and technical assistance. Competitor B is good across the board and excellent in product availability and sales force. Competitor C rates poor to fair on most attributes. This result suggests that the company could attack Competitor A on product availability and technical assistance and Competitor C on almost anything, but should not attack B, which has no glaring weaknesses.

In general, a company should monitor three variables when analyzing competitors:

1. ***Share of market***: the competitor's share of the target market.
2. ***Share of mind***: the percentage of customers who named the competitor in responding to the statement, "Name the first company that comes to mind in this industry."
3. ***Share of heart***: the percentage of customers who named the competitor in responding to the statement, "Name the company from which you would prefer to buy the product."

There's an interesting relationship among these three measures. ▢ **Table 11.2** shows them as recorded for the three competitors listed in ▢ **Table 11.1**. Competitor A enjoys the highest market share but is slipping. Its mind share and heart share are also slipping, probably because it's not providing good product availability and technical assistance. Competitor B is steadily gaining

|Fig. 11.2| △

A Competitor's Expansion Plans

	Individual Users	Commercial and Industrial	Educational
Personal Computers	DELL →		
Hardware Accessories	↓		
Software			

TABLE 11.1	Customers' Ratings of Competitors on Key Success Factors				
	Customer Awareness	**Product Quality**	**Product Availability**	**Technical Assistance**	**Selling Staff**
Competitor A	E	E	P	P	G
Competitor B	G	G	E	G	E
Competitor C	F	P	G	F	F

Note: E = excellent, G = good, F = fair, P = poor.

TABLE 11.2	Market Share, Mind Share, and Heart Share								
	Market Share			**Mind Share**			**Heart Share**		
	2009	**2010**	**2011**	**2009**	**2010**	**2011**	**2009**	**2010**	**2011**
Competitor A	50%	47%	44%	60%	58%	54%	45%	42%	39%
Competitor B	30	34	37	30	31	35	44	47	53
Competitor C	20	19	19	10	11	11	11	11	8

market share, probably due to strategies that are increasing its mind share and heart share. Competitor C seems to be stuck at a low level of market share, mind share, and heart share, probably because of its poor product and marketing attributes. We could generalize as follows: *companies that make steady gains in mind share and heart share will inevitably make gains in market share and profitability.* Firms such as Starbucks, Timberland, Dell, Swatch, and Toyota are all reaping the financial benefits of providing emotional, experiential, social, and financial value to satisfy customers and all their constituents.[12]

To improve market share, many companies benchmark their most successful competitors, as well as other world-class performers.[13] This technique and its benefits are described in the Marketing Memo: *Benchmarking to Improve Competitive Performance* on page 296.

Selecting Competitors

After the company has conducted customer value analysis and examined its competitors carefully, it can focus its attack on one of the following classes of competitors: strong versus weak, close versus distant, and 'good' versus 'bad.'

- **Strong versus weak.** Most companies aim their shots at weak competitors, because this requires fewer resources per share point gained. Yet, the firm should also compete with strong competitors to keep up with the best. Even strong competitors have some weaknesses.

- **Close versus distant.** Most companies compete with the competitors that resemble them the most. Chevrolet competes with Ford, not with Ferrari. Yet companies should also identify distant competitors. Coca-Cola recognizes that its number-one competitor is tap water, not Pepsi.

- **'Good' versus 'bad.'** Every industry contains 'good' and 'bad' competitors.[14] Good competitors play by the industry's rules; they set prices in reasonable relationship to costs; and they favor a healthy industry. Bad competitors try to buy share rather than earn it;

Benchmarking to Improve Competitive Performance

Benchmarking is the art of learning from companies that perform certain tasks better than other companies. There can be as much as a tenfold difference between the quality, speed, and cost performance of a world-class company and that of an average company. The aim of benchmarking is to copy or improve on 'best practices,' either within an industry or across industries. Benchmarking has seven steps:

1. Determine which functions or processes to benchmark.
2. Identify the key performance variables to measure.
3. Identify the best-in-class companies.
4. Measure the performance of best-in-class companies.
5. Measure the company's performance.
6. Specify programs and actions to close the gap.
7. Implement and monitor results.

How can companies identify best-practice companies? A good starting point is consulting customers, suppliers, distributors, financial analysts, trade associations, and magazines to see whom they rate as doing the best job. Even the best companies can benchmark to improve their performance. To aid its corporate goal to be more innovative, GE has benchmarked against P&G as well as developing its own new best practices.

Sources: www.benchmarking.org; Patricia O'Connell, "Bringing Innovation to the Home of Six Sigma," *BusinessWeek*, August 1, 2005; John E. Prescott, Stephen H. Miller, and The Society of Competitive Intelligence Professionals, *Proven Strategies in Competitive Intelligence: Lessons from the Trenches* (New York: John Wiley & Sons, 2001); Robert Hiebeler, Thomas B. Kelly, and Charles Ketteman, *Best Practices: Building Your Business with Customer-Focused Solutions* (New York: Arthur Andersen/Simon & Schuster, 1998); Michael Hope, "Contrast and Compare," *Marketing*, August 28, 1997, pp. 11–13.

they take large risks; they invest in overcapacity; and they upset industrial equilibrium. A company may find it necessary to attack its bad competitors to reduce or end their dysfunctional practices.

Selecting Customers

As part of the competitive analysis, a firm must evaluate its customer base and think about which customers it is willing to lose and which it wants to retain. One way to divide up the customer base is in terms of whether a customer is valuable and vulnerable, creating a grid of four segments as a result; see ▥ **Table 11.3**. Each segment suggests different competitive activities.[15]

Most mobile operators in the Arab region conducted segmentation analysis and developed premium packages designed to retain the Valuable/Vulnerables but without losing the margin realized on the Valuable/Not Vulnerables. These premium packages had a subscription fee but offered significant net savings. Because Valuable/Vulnerables were highly involved with the category, they were able to see how they could benefit from such packages, but the Valuable/Not Vulnerables regarded the plans as unnecessary. As a result, the packages usually achieved the desired goals.[16]

TABLE 11.3 ▥ Customer Selection Grid		
	Vulnerable	**Not Vulnerable**
Valuable	These customers are profitable but not completely happy with the company. Find out and address their sources of vulnerability to *retain them*.	These customers are loyal and profitable. Don't take them for granted but *maintain margins* and reap the benefits of their satisfaction.
Not Valuable	These customers are likely to defect. Let them go or even *encourage their departure*.	These unprofitable customers are happy. Try to *make them valuable or vulnerable*.

Source: John H. Roberts, "Defensive Marketing: How a Strong Incumbent Can Protect Its Position," *Harvard Business Review*, November 2005, p. 156. Copyright © 2005 by the Harvard Business School Publishing Corporation; all rights reserved.

Competitive Strategies for Market Leaders

We can gain further insight by classifying firms by the roles they play in the target market: leader, challenger, follower, or nicher. Suppose a market is occupied by the firms shown in △ **Figure 11.3**. Forty percent of the market is in the hands of a *market leader*; another 30 percent is in the hands of a *market challenger*; another 20 percent is in the hands of a *market follower*, a firm that is willing to maintain its market share and not rock the boat. The remaining 10 percent is in the hands of *market nichers*, firms that serve small market segments not being served by larger firms.

Many industries contain one firm that is the acknowledged market leader. This firm has the largest market share in the relevant product market and usually leads the other firms in price changes, new-product introductions, distribution coverage, and promotional intensity. Some historical market leaders are Microsoft (computer software), Gatorade (sports drinks), Best Buy (retail electronics), McDonald's (fast food), Alico (health insurance), and Visa (credit cards).

Although marketers assume well-known brands are distinctive in consumers' minds, unless a dominant firm enjoys a legal monopoly, it must maintain constant attention. A product innovation may come along and hurt the leader; a competitor might unexpectedly find a fresh new marketing angle or commit to a major marketing investment; or the leader might find its cost structure spiraling upward. One well-known brand and market leader that lost its way is Gap.

40%	Market leader
30%	Market challenger
20%	Market follower
10%	Market nichers

|Fig. 11.3| △

Hypothetical Market Structure

Gap   Nowadays when people think about Gap, they don't think of hip, contemporary clothes. They think quite literally, of a 'gap:' what's missing from the company's 1,295 stores. Young people will be quick to tell you that the missing ingredient is a unique style. In an era when small niche fashion brands—Zara, Mango—have risen to success in retailing, Gap has continued to push timeless, simple, and some would say bland, casual clothing. The main problem is that Gap doesn't have a target customer but tries to appeal to everyone, from newborn babies to teenagers to senior citizens. "If you stand for everything in fashion today, you stand for nothing," says Paul R. Charron, the former chief executive of Liz Claiborne, who revitalized that ailing clothing company by buying Juicy Couture and Lucky Brand. By not being vigilant about responding to (or better, yet, envisioning) the changing retailing scene, Gap has seen sales fall dramatically; sales at stores open at least a year have experienced a 4 percent decline, on top of a 1 percent comparative store decline in September 2010.[17] Still, the former leading brand is planning a number of strategies to get it out of the doldrums. Among them are selling other-branded merchandise inside its stores (as it used to sell Levi's and now sells Converse), shrinking the number of stores to cut back on overexposure, and focusing on a narrower group of consumers with clothing tailored to meet their needs.[18]

In the Arab world, Gap has plans to penetrate several markets including Egypt and Morocco, and to add to the already existing stores in countries such as Kuwait, Saudi Arabia, and the UAE. The decline in growth in the U.S. market has been offset by growth in the Arab region, as a decline in tariffs on imported goods results in lower prices.[19]

In many industries, a discount competitor has entered and undercut the leader's prices. The Marketing Insight: *When Your Competitor Delivers More for Less* describes how leaders can respond to an aggressive competitive price discounter.

Staying the number-one firm calls for action on three fronts. First, the firm must find ways to expand total market demand. Second, the firm must protect its current market share through good defensive and offensive actions. Third, the firm can try to increase its market share, even if market size remains constant. Let's look at each strategy.

Gap is expanding in the Arab world, in contrast to its performance in the United States.

Marketing Insight

When your Competitor Delivers More for Less

Companies offering the powerful combination of low prices and high quality are capturing the hearts and wallets of consumers all over the world. In the United States, more than half the population now shops weekly at mass merchants such as Walmart and Target, up from 25 percent in 1996. In Egypt, fast food restaurants such as McDonald's and Hardee's are scrambling to meet intensifying price—and quality—competition from Burger King and local fast food restaurants such as Mo'men and Cook Door.

These and similar value players, such as Carrefour, Dell, Barclays, and Air Arabia, are transforming the way consumers of nearly every age and income purchase groceries, computers, financial services, and airline tickets. As value-driven companies in a growing number of industries change the way they compete, traditional players are right to feel threatened. The formula these upstart firms often rely on includes focusing on one or a few consumer segments; providing better delivery of the basic product or one additional benefit; and matching low prices with highly efficient operations to keep costs down.

To compete with value-based rivals, mainstream companies must reconsider the perennial routes to business success: keeping costs in line, finding sources of differentiation, and managing prices effectively. To succeed in value-based markets, companies need to infuse these timeless strategies with greater intensity and focus, and then execute them flawlessly. Differentiation, for example, becomes less about the abstract goal of rising above competitive clutter and more about identifying opportunities left open by the value players' business models. Effective pricing means waging a transaction-by-transaction perception battle to win over those consumers who are predisposed to believe that value-oriented competitors are always cheaper.

Competitive outcomes will be determined, as always, on the ground: in product aisles, on merchandising displays, in reconfigured processes, and on pricing stickers. When it comes to value-based competition, traditional players can't afford to drop a stitch. Value-driven competitors have changed consumer expectations about the trade-off between quality and price. This shift is gathering momentum, placing a new premium on—and adding new twists to—the old imperatives of differentiation and execution.

Differentiation

To counter value-based players, marketers will need to focus on areas where their business models give other companies room to maneuver. Successful differentiation calls for marshalling multiple tactics to provide superior delivery of a highly desired consumer benefit. Instead of trying to compete with Carrefour and other value retailers on price, for example, Metro in Egypt emphasizes quality and convenience across all elements of its business. It has expanded rapidly to make its stores ubiquitous, meanwhile ensuring that most are on corner locations with easy parking. Metro stores are easily accessible as they are located within the heart of major cities such as Cairo and Alexandria. Carrefour, on the other hand, locates its stores on major highways, requiring more travel time for customers, and they are not easily accessible by public transportation. Metro has also implemented a delivery system, by which customers can order their purchases on the phone and get them delivered to their homes or work. These differentiators have helped Metro strive in a market that is heavily dominated by large hypermarkets.

Execution

Value-based markets also place a premium on execution, particularly in prices and costs. Kmart's disastrous experience in trying to compete head-on with Walmart highlights the difficulty of challenging value leaders on their own terms. Matching or even beating a value player's prices—as Kmart briefly did—won't necessarily win the battle of consumer perceptions against companies with reputations for the lowest prices. To effectively compete against value-based players, firms may need to downplay or even abandon some target market segments. To compete with Air Arabia and Jazeera Airlines, Emirates Airline has put more emphasis on its long-haul routes, where value-based players are not evident, and less on the highly competitive short-haul routes where low-cost carriers thrive.

Major airlines have also tried another competitive response, introducing their own low-cost airlines, such as Egypt Air Express. But Continental's Lite, KLM's Buzz, SAS's Snowflake, and United's Shuttle have all been unsuccessful. One school of thought is that companies should set up low-cost operations only if: (1) the firm's existing businesses will be made more competitive as a result and (2) the new business will derive some advantages it would not have gained by being independent. The success of low-cost operations set up by HSBC, ING, Merrill Lynch, and Royal Bank of Scotland—First Direct, ING Direct, ML Direct, and Direct Line Insurance, respectively—is due in part to synergies between the old and new lines of business. Thus, success dictates that the low-cost operation must be designed and launched to be a moneymaker in its own right, not just as a defensive play.

Sources: Adapted from two insightful articles: Nirmalya Kumar, "Strategies to Fight Low-Cost Rivals," *Harvard Business Review*, December 2006, pp. 104–112; and Robert J. Frank, Jeffrey P. George, and Laxman Narasimhan, "When Your Competitor Delivers More for Less," *McKinsey Quarterly*, Winter 2004, pp. 48–59; additional information from www.metro-markets.com and www.egyptair.com websites.

Expanding the Total Market

When the total market expands, the dominant firm usually gains the most. If Saudi consumers increase their consumption of milk, Almarai stands to gain the most because it sells the most milk in Saudi Arabia. If it can convince more people to drink more milk, or to use milk with food, Almarai will benefit considerably. In general, the market leader should search for new customers or more usage from existing customers.

NEW CUSTOMERS Every product class has the potential to attract buyers who are unaware of the product or who are resisting it because of price or lack of certain features. As Chapter 2 suggested, a company can search for new users among three groups: those who might use it but do not (*market-penetration strategy*), those who have never used it (*new-market segment strategy*), or those who live elsewhere (*geographical-expansion strategy*).

Starbucks Coffee is one of the best-known brands in the world. Starbucks is able to sell a cup of coffee for US\$3 while the store next door can only get \$1. In July 2011, Starbucks had 17,018 locations throughout the world, and its annual revenue for 2010 topped \$10.7 billion. The coffee experience is a new concept for many people living in the Arab world. People in many countries such as Egypt are used to drinking tea, and other countries like Saudi Arabia and Kuwait have their own coffee, which uses cardamom. Thus, it was necessary for Starbucks to introduce coffee as an alternative to existing drinks. Information at its corporate website (www.starbucks.com) gives a more detailed peek into its multipronged approach to growth and the many product lines it sells.[20]

MORE USAGE Marketers can try to increase the amount, level, or frequency of consumption.

The *amount* of consumption can sometimes be increased through packaging or product redesign. Larger package sizes have been shown to increase the amount of product that consumers use at one time.[21] The usage of impulse consumption products such as soft drinks and snacks also increases when the product is made more available.

Increasing *frequency* of consumption, on the other hand, requires either (1) identifying additional opportunities to use the brand in the same basic way or (2) identifying completely new and different ways to use the brand. Consumers may see the product as useful only in certain places and at certain times, especially if it has strong associations to particular usage situations or user types.

To generate additional opportunities to use the brand in the same basic way, a marketing program can communicate the appropriateness and advantages of using the brand more frequently in new or existing situations or remind consumers to actually use the brand as close as possible to those situations. Clorox has run ads stressing the many benefits of its bleach, such as how it eliminates kitchen odors. Another opportunity arises when consumers' perceptions of their usage differs from the reality. Consumers may fail to replace a short-lived product when they should, because they overestimate how long it stays fresh.[22]

One strategy to speed up product replacement is to tie the act of replacing the product to a holiday, event, or time of year. Another might be to provide consumers with better information about either (1) when they first used the product or need to replace it or (2) the current level of product performance. Gillette razor cartridges feature colored stripes that slowly fade with repeated use, signaling the user to move on to the next cartridge.

The second approach to increasing frequency of consumption is to identify completely new and different applications. For example, food product companies have long advertised recipes that use their branded products in entirely different ways. After discovering that consumers used the Arm & Hammer baking soda brand as a refrigerator deodorant, the company launched a heavy promotion campaign focusing on this single use. After succeeding in getting half the homes in the United States to place an open box of baking soda in the refrigerator,

Starbucks' expansion efforts have included new lines of smoothies (Vivanno™), premium teas (Tazo™), and ready-to-drink iced beverages.

the company expanded the brand into a variety of new product categories, such as toothpaste, antiperspirant, and laundry detergent.

Product development can also spur new uses. Chewing gum manufacturers such as Cadbury Schweppes, maker of Trident, are producing 'nutraceutical' products to strengthen or whiten teeth. Aquafresh has successfully launched dental chewing gums with health and cosmetic benefits.[23]

Defending Market Share

While trying to expand total market size, the dominant firm must continuously and actively defend its current business: Boeing against Airbus; Toyota against Nissan; and Google against Yahoo! and Microsoft.[24] The success of online social network sites Twitter and Facebook has brought challenges from upstarts such as the LinkedIn personal business network, Eons and Vox for sharing photos and videos, and blog posts for older consumers.[25]

What can the market leader do to defend its terrain? The most constructive response is *continuous innovation*. The leader should lead the industry in developing new products and customer services, distribution effectiveness, and cost cutting. It keeps increasing its competitive strength and value to customers by providing comprehensive solutions.

 Air Arabia   With the value proposition "Pay less, fly more," Air Arabia is a good example of the marketing concept of Less = More. Headquartered in the UAE, Air Arabia is the Middle East and North Africa's first and largest low-cost carrier with over 65 destinations across the Middle East, North Africa, Asia, and Europe, flying from its hubs in the UAE, Morocco, and Egypt. In the second quarter of 2010, the airline served 1,108,310 passengers, an 11 percent increase on the same period in the previous year.

With a commitment to providing affordable, comfortable, and reliable air travel, Air Arabia is constantly coming up with innovative ways to compete with first-class airlines such as Qatar Airways, Emirates Airline, and Saudi Airlines. Its Less = More strategies include using a single passenger class and single aircraft type in order to save on training, maintenance, and multicabin costs, and the use of optional, paid for in-flight food and beverages to cut catering costs. It flies to secondary, less congested airports, reducing major airport charges and avoiding rush hours. And customers purchase their tickets online, which lowers distribution costs.

The varying offerings also provide Air Arabia with a unique selling appeal, pushing its profits from US$125 million in 2009 to $132 million in the same period of 2010. Air Arabia's airline success is in no small part due to its ability to creatively spot and select new market opportunities, think of the best options on behalf of its customers, and provide them with premium services and benefits for less.[26]

Air Arabia is a competitive airline carrier catering to price-sensitive customers in the Arab region.

In satisfying customer needs, we can draw a distinction between responsive marketing, anticipative marketing, and creative marketing. A *responsive* marketer finds a stated need and fills it. An *anticipative* marketer looks ahead into what needs customers may have in the near future. A *creative* marketer discovers and produces solutions customers did not ask for but to which they enthusiastically respond. Creative marketers are *market-driving firms*, not just market-driven. Tarek Nour Communications, a major advertising agency in Egypt, is one such firm.

 Tarek Nour Communications
Nowadays, TNC is a comprehensive communications group, but the company has been a pioneer in advertising since its inception as the first Egyptian private advertising agency in 1978. Through three decades of listening to local consumers, nobody has developed a deeper

understanding of regional and local markets. For this reason, TNC has become a trademark for leading advertising campaigns. TNC is a success not just by coming up with the latest advertising methodologies, but also through speaking the language of the people, and reflecting the real meaning of the culture each company represents. TNC's strong production facilities, media buying, experienced planners, as well as its long record of creativity are what have allowed it to outdo its competitors in Egypt and the region, earning the trust of major local and international companies and institutions such as LG, GB Auto, UNDP, Vodafone, ExxonMobil, and the Universal group.[27]

Market-driving firms become market leaders through superior value delivery of unmet—and maybe even unknown—consumer needs. Think of Sony. In the late 1970s, Akio Morita, the Sony founder, was working on a pet project that would revolutionize the way people listened to music: a portable cassette player he called the Walkman. Engineers at the company insisted there was little demand for such a product, but Morita refused to part with his vision. By the 20th anniversary of the Walkman, Sony had sold over 250 million in nearly 100 different models.[28]

Even when it does not launch offensives, the market leader must not leave any major flanks exposed. It must consider carefully which terrains are important to defend, even at a loss, and which can be surrendered. The aim of defensive strategy is to reduce the probability of attack, divert attacks to less-threatening areas, and lessen their intensity. The defender's speed of response can make an important difference in the profit consequences. A dominant firm can use the six defense strategies, summarized in △ **Figure 11.4**.[29]

POSITION DEFENSE Position defense means occupying the most desirable market space in consumers' minds, making the brand almost impregnable, as Procter & Gamble has done with Tide detergent for cleaning, Crest toothpaste for cavity prevention, and Pampers diapers for dryness.

FLANK DEFENSE Although position defense is important, the market leader should also erect outposts to protect a weak front or possibly serve as an invasion base for counterattack. When Toyota Corolla was attacked by low-priced competitors such as Hyundai and Kia, Toyota increased the car size and options, which raised its price. At the same time, Toyota introduced another brand, Yaris, to compete with Hyundai and Kia. This strategy effectively bracketed the Korean players and protected Toyota's market share.

PREEMPTIVE DEFENSE A more aggressive maneuver is to attack before the enemy starts its offense. A company can launch a preemptive defense in several ways. It can wage guerrilla action across the market—hitting one competitor here, another there—and keep everyone off balance; or it can try to achieve a grand market envelopment. The National Bank of Kuwait's network of automated teller machines (ATMs) and retail branches nationwide create steep competition for local and regional banks. In this way the firm can send out market signals to dissuade competitors from attacking.[30]

Marketers can introduce a stream of new products, making sure to precede them with *pre-announcements*: deliberate communications regarding future actions.[31] Preannouncements can signal to competitors that they will need to fight to gain market share.[32] If Microsoft announces plans for a new-product development, smaller firms may choose to concentrate their development

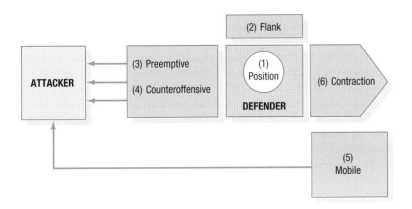

|Fig. 11.4| △

Six Types of Defense Strategies

efforts in other directions to avoid head-to-head competition. Some high-tech firms have even been accused of engaging in selling "vaporware:" preannouncing products that miss delivery dates or are never introduced.[33]

COUNTEROFFENSIVE DEFENSE   When attacked, most market leaders will respond with a counterattack. In a *counteroffensive*, the leader can meet the attacker frontally or hit its flank or launch a pincer movement. An effective counterattack is to invade the attacker's main territory so that it will pull back to defend it. After FedEx watched UPS successfully invade its airborne delivery system, FedEx invested heavily in ground delivery service through a series of acquisitions to challenge UPS on its home turf.[34]

Another common form of counteroffensive is the exercise of economic or political clout. The leader may try to crush a competitor by subsidizing lower prices for the vulnerable product with revenue from its more profitable products, or the leader may prematurely announce that a product upgrade will be available, to prevent customers from buying the competitor's product. Or the leader may lobby legislators to take political action to inhibit the competition.

MOBILE DEFENSE   In mobile defense, the leader stretches its domain over new territories that can serve as future centers for defense and offense through market broadening and market diversification. *Market broadening* shifts focus from the current product to the underlying generic need. The company gets involved in R&D across the whole range of technology associated with that need. Thus 'petroleum' companies such as BP sought to recast themselves as 'energy' companies. Implicitly, this change demanded that they dip their research fingers into the oil, coal, nuclear, hydroelectric, and chemical industries.

Market diversification shifts into unrelated industries. When U.S. tobacco companies such as Reynolds and Philip Morris acknowledged growing restrictions on cigarette smoking, they were not content with position defense or even with looking for cigarette substitutes. Instead they moved quickly into new industries, such as soft drinks and frozen foods.

CONTRACTION DEFENSE   Large companies sometimes must recognize that they can no longer defend all their territory. The best course of action then appears to be *planned contraction* (also called *strategic withdrawal*): giving up weaker territories and reassigning resources to stronger territories. Honda withdrew its Honda trucks, so it could concentrate on its well-known cars, such as the Civic and Accord.

Expanding Market Share

In many markets, one share point is worth tens of millions of dollars. No wonder competition has turned fierce in so many markets. Gaining increased share in the served market, however, does not automatically produce higher profits, especially for labor-intensive service companies that may not experience many economies of scale. Much depends on the company's strategy.[35]

Because the cost of buying higher market share may far exceed its revenue value, a company should consider four factors before pursuing increased share:

1. *The possibility of provoking antitrust action.* Jealous competitors are likely to cry 'monopoly' if a dominant firm makes further inroads. This rise in risk would diminish the attractiveness of pushing market share gains too far. Microsoft and Intel are examples of companies that have faced great scrutiny for their market leadership and practices.

2. *Economic cost.* **Figure 11.5** shows that profitability might fall with further market share gains after some level. In the illustration, the firm's *optimal market share* is 50 percent. The cost of gaining further market share might exceed the value. The 'holdout' customers may dislike the company, be loyal to competitive suppliers, have unique needs, or prefer dealing with smaller suppliers. And the costs of legal work, public relations, and lobbying rise with market share. Pushing for higher share is less justified when there are few economies of scale or experience, unattractive market segments exist, buyers want multiple sources of supply, and exit barriers are high. Some market leaders have even increased profitability by selectively *decreasing* market share in weaker areas.[36]

3. *Pursuing the wrong marketing activities.* Companies successfully gaining share typically outperform competitors in three areas: new-product activity, relative product quality, and marketing expenditures.[37] On the other hand, companies that attempt to increase market share by cutting

|Fig. 11.5| △

The Concept of
Optimal Market Share

prices more deeply than competitors typically don't achieve significant gains, because enough rivals meet the price cuts and others offer other values so buyers don't switch. Competitive rivalry and price cutting have been shown to be most intense in industries with high fixed costs, high inventory costs, and stagnant primary demand, such as steel, auto, paper, and chemicals.[38]

4. **The effect of increased market share on actual and perceived quality.**[39] Too many customers can put a strain on the firm's resources, hurting product value and service delivery. Consumers may also infer that 'bigger is not better' and assume that growth will lead to a deterioration of quality. If 'exclusivity' is a key brand benefit, existing customers may resent additional new customers.

Other Competitive Strategies

Firms that occupy second, third, and lower ranks in an industry are often called runner-up or trailing firms. Some, such as PepsiCo, Ford, Avis, and General Electric are quite large in their own right. These firms can adopt one of two postures. They can attack the leader and other competitors in an aggressive bid for further market share as *market challengers*, or they can play ball and not 'rock the boat' as *market followers*.

Market-Challenger Strategies

Many market challengers have gained ground or even overtaken the leader. Toyota today produces more cars than General Motors and AMD has been chipping away at Intel's market share.[40] Challengers set high aspirations, leveraging their resources while the market leader often runs the business as usual. Now let's examine the competitive attack strategies available to market challengers.[41]

DEFINING THE STRATEGIC OBJECTIVE AND OPPONENT(S) A market challenger must first define its strategic objective. Most aim to increase market share. The challenger must decide whom to attack:

- **It can attack the market leader.** This is a high-risk but potentially high-payoff strategy and makes good sense if the leader is not serving the market well. It often has the added benefit of distancing the firm from other challengers. An alternative strategy is to out-innovate the leader across the whole segment. Xerox wrested the copy market from 3M by developing a better copying process. Later, Canon grabbed a large chunk of Xerox's market by introducing desk copiers.

- **It can attack firms of its own size that are not doing the job and are underfinanced.** These firms have aging products, are charging excessive prices, or are not satisfying customers in other ways.

- **It can attack small local and regional firms.** Several major banks grew to their present size by gobbling up smaller regional banks, or 'guppies.'

CHOOSING A GENERAL ATTACK STRATEGY Given clear opponents and objectives, what attack options are available? We can distinguish among five attack strategies: frontal, flank, encirclement, bypass, and guerilla attacks.

Frontal Attack In a pure *frontal attack*, the attacker matches its opponent's product, advertising, price, and distribution. The principle of force says that the side with the greater resources will win. A modified frontal attack, such as cutting price, can work if the market leader doesn't retaliate, and if the competitor convinces the market that its product is equal to the leader's. Samsung is a master at convincing the market that its brands are equal in quality but better value than higher-priced brands.

Flank Attack An enemy's weak spots are natural targets. A *flank attack* can be directed along two strategic dimensions: geographic and segmental. In a geographic attack, the challenger spots areas where the opponent is underperforming. Although the internet has siphoned newspaper readers and advertisers away in many markets, Independent News & Media, a more than 100-year-old Irish media company, sells the majority of its newspaper and magazine titles in cities where the economy is strong but the internet is still relatively weak: countries such as Ireland, South Africa, Australia, New Zealand, and India.[47] The other flanking strategy is to serve uncovered market needs. Ariat's cowboy boots have challenged long-time market leaders Justin Boots and Tony Lama by making boots that were every bit as ranch-ready, but ergonomically designed to feel as comfortable as a running shoe: a totally new benefit in the category.[43]

A flanking strategy is another name for identifying shifts in market segments that are causing gaps to develop, then rushing in to fill the gaps and develop them into strong segments. Flanking is in the best tradition of modern marketing, which holds that the purpose of marketing is to discover needs and satisfy them. It's particularly attractive to a challenger with fewer resources than its opponent and much more likely to be successful than frontal attacks.

Encirclement Attack The *encirclement* maneuver is an attempt to capture a wide slice of the enemy's territory through a blitz. It means launching a grand offensive on several fronts. Encirclement makes sense when the challenger commands superior resources and believes a swift encirclement will break the opponent's will. In making a stand against archrival Microsoft, Sun Microsystems licensed its Java software to hundreds of companies and millions of software developers for all sorts of consumer devices. As consumer electronics products began to go digital, Java started appearing in a wide range of gadgets.

Bypass Attack The most indirect assault strategy is *bypassing* the enemy altogether and attacking easier markets to broaden the firm's resource base. This strategy offers three lines of approach: diversifying into unrelated products, diversifying into new geographical markets, and leapfrogging into new technologies to supplant existing products. In the past, Pepsi has used bypass strategies against Coke by: (1) aggressively rolling out Aquafina bottled water nationally in 1997 before Coke launched its Dasani brand; (2) purchasing orange juice giant Tropicana for US$3.3 billion in 1998, which owned almost twice the market share of Coca-Cola's Minute Maid; and (3) purchasing The Quaker Oats Company, owner of market leader Gatorade sports drink, for $14 billion in 2000.[44]

Technological leapfrogging is a bypass strategy practiced in high-tech industries. The challenger patiently researches and develops the next technology and launches an attack, shifting the battleground to its own territory where it has an advantage. Nintendo's successful attack in the video-game market was precisely about wresting market share by introducing a superior technology and redefining the "competitive space." Then Sega/Genesis did the same with more advanced technology, and now Sony's PlayStation and Microsoft's Xbox have grabbed the technological lead to gain almost half the video-game market.[45] Challenger Google used technological leapfrogging to overtake Yahoo! and become the market leader in online search engines.

Guerrilla Warfare Guerrilla warfare consists of waging small, intermittent attacks to harass and demoralize the opponent and eventually secure permanent footholds. The guerrilla challenger uses both conventional and unconventional means of attack. These include selective price cuts, intense promotional blitzes, and occasional legal action. Princeton Review successfully challenged Kaplan Educational Centers, the largest test-preparation business in the United States, through e-mail horror stories about Kaplan and brash ads—"Stanley's a wimp," or "Friends don't let friends take Kaplan"—while always touting the Princeton Review's smaller, livelier classes.

A guerrilla campaign can be expensive, although less so than a frontal, encirclement, or flank attack. Guerrilla warfare is more a preparation for war than a war itself. Ultimately, it must be backed by a stronger attack if the challenger hopes to beat the opponent. Guerrilla marketing must, however, not cross lines of legality or morality. On January 31, 2007, several guerrilla-marketing magnetic light displays in and around the U.S. city of Boston, Massachusetts, were mistaken for possible explosive devices. Subway stations, bridges, and a portion of Interstate 93 were closed as police examined, removed, and in some cases, destroyed the devices. The suspicious objects were revealed to be ads depicting characters from the Cartoon Network's animated television series *Aqua Teen Hunger Force*, resulting in a fine for network owner's Turner Broadcasting System and a wave of negative publicity.[46]

CHOOSING A SPECIFIC ATTACK STRATEGY
The challenger must go beyond the five broad strategies and develop more specific strategies. Any aspect of the marketing program can serve as the basis for attack, such as lower-priced or discounted products, new or improved products and services, a wider variety of offerings, and innovative distribution strategies. A challenger's success depends on combining several strategies to improve its position over time. The Marketing Memo: *Making Smaller Better* provides some additional tips for challenger brands.

marketing
Memo

Making Smaller Better

Adam Morgan offers eight suggestions on how small brands can better compete:

- **Break with your immediate past.** Don't be afraid to ask 'dumb' questions to challenge convention and view your brand differently.

- **Build a 'lighthouse identity.'** Establish values and communicate who you are and why. Apple excels at this task.

- **Assume thought leadership of the category.** Break convention in terms of what you say about yourself, where you say it, and what you do beyond talk.

- **Create symbols of reevaluation.** A rocket uses half its fuel in the first mile to break loose from Earth's gravitational pull: you may need to polarize people to get them to rethink your brand.

- **Sacrifice.** Focus your target, message, reach and frequency, distribution, and line extensions, and recognize that less can be more.

- **Overcommit.** Although you may do fewer things, do 'big' things when you do them.

- **Use publicity and advertising to enter popular culture.** Unconventional communications can get people talking.

- **Be idea centered, not consumer centered.** Sustain challenger momentum by not losing sight of what the brand is about and can be, and redefine marketing support as the center of the company to reflect this vision.

Sources: Adam Morgan, *Eating the Big Fish: How Challenger Brands Can Compete against Brand Leaders* (New York: John Wiley & Sons, 1999). See also Adam Morgan, *The Pirate Inside: Building a Challenger Brand Culture within Yourself and Your Organization* (West Sussex, England: John Wiley & Sons, 2004). Reprinted by permission of John Wiley & Sons, Inc.

Market-Follower Strategies

Some years ago, Theodore Levitt wrote an article entitled "Innovative Imitation," in which he argued that a strategy of *product imitation* might be as profitable as a strategy of *product innovation*.[47] The innovator bears the expense of developing the new product, getting it into distribution, and informing and educating the market. The reward for all this work and risk is normally market leadership. However, another firm can come along and copy or improve on the new product. Although it probably will not overtake the leader, the follower can achieve high profits because it did not bear any of the innovation expense.

EIPICO   The pharmaceutical industry in Egypt experiences high demand, given the low prices of locally produced Egyptian medicine compared to foreign counterparts. EIPICO was established as a private investment company in 1980, specializing in pharmaceuticals. It has become the largest local producer in Egypt and a major drug exporter in the Arab world with exports also to Africa, Asia, and Eastern Europe. Combining optimized prices with quality, EIPICO applies Good Manufacturing Practice regulations throughout its operational departments to ensure supreme medical quality that can compete with international products. The company's main goal is to replace imported drugs through continual product enhancement, achieved by applying the newest technology in the pharmaceutical industry and cutting-edge research. It also uses mutual cooperation between Egyptian experts and researchers at EIPICO, and those of the foreign international pharmaceutical companies through license agreements, to cover the increasing demand and to acquire foreign expertise.[48]

Many companies prefer to follow rather than challenge the market leader. Patterns of 'conscious parallelism' are common in capital-intensive, homogeneous-product industries, such as steel, fertilizers, and chemicals. The opportunities for product differentiation and image differentiation are low; service quality is often comparable; and price sensitivity runs high. The mood in these industries is against short-run grabs for market share because that strategy only provokes retaliation. Most firms decide against stealing one another's customers. Instead, they present similar offers to buyers, usually by copying the leader. Market shares show high stability.

That's not to say that market followers lack strategies. A market follower must know how to hold current customers and win a fair share of new ones. Each follower tries to bring distinctive advantages to its target market: location, services, financing. Because the follower is often a major target of attack by challengers, it must keep its manufacturing costs low and its product quality and services high. It must also enter new markets as they open up. The follower must define a growth path, but one that doesn't invite competitive retaliation. We distinguish four broad strategies:

1. *Counterfeiter.* The counterfeiter duplicates the leader's product and packages and sells it on the black market or through disreputable dealers. Music firms, Apple, and Rolex have been plagued by the counterfeiter problem. This occurs in many countries in the Arab world and Asia.
2. *Cloner.* The cloner emulates the leader's products, name, and packaging, with slight variations. For example, Ralcorp Holding Inc. sells imitations of name-brand cereals in look-alike boxes. Its Tasteeos, Fruit Rings, and Corn Flakes sell for nearly US$1 less per box than the leading name brands.
3. *Imitator.* The imitator copies some things from the leader but maintains differentiation in terms of packaging, advertising, pricing, or location. The leader doesn't mind the imitator as long as the imitator doesn't attack the leader aggressively. Fernandez Pujals grew up in Fort Lauderdale, Florida in the United States, and took Domino's home delivery idea to Spain, where he borrowed US$80,000 to open his first store in Madrid. His TelePizza chain now operates almost 1,000 stores in Europe and Latin America.
4. *Adapter.* The adapter takes the leader's products and adapts or improves them. The adapter may choose to sell to different markets, but often it grows into the future challenger, as many Japanese firms have done after improving products developed elsewhere.

What does a follower earn? Normally, less than the leader. For example, a study of food-processing companies showed the largest firm averaging a 16 percent return on investment; the number-two firm, 6 percent; the number-three firm, minus 1 percent, and the number-four firm, minus 6 percent. In this case, only the top two firms have profits. No wonder Jack Welch, former CEO of GE, told his business units that each must reach the number-one or -two position in its market or else! Followership is often not a rewarding path.

Market-Nicher Strategies

An alternative to being a follower in a large market is to be a leader in a small market, or niche, as we introduced in Chapter 8. Smaller firms normally avoid competing with larger firms by targeting small markets of little or no interest to the larger firms. But even large, profitable firms may choose to use niching strategies for some of their business units or companies.

 Al Kharafi Group   Pioneering the construction industry for more than 50 years with firm roots in civil engineering, the Al Kharafi Group has begun to diversify its activities, growing new offshoots into food production and processing, printing and aviation, and hotel and tourism real estate development. Mohammed Abdulmohsen Al-Kharafi & Sons Company (MAK Group) is a private Kuwaiti-based group, established as a trading company more than 100 years ago that has since developed into a large multinational company. At an international level, MAK has evolved many diversified specialties, including cakes, car brakes, and extruded aluminum in Egypt and Saudi Arabia. In Iraq, MAK holds interests in telecoms and finance through the family's 30 percent stake in Atheer Telecom. Al Kharafi's breakaway leadership in the construction industry, as well as its other various specializations have proven to be a successful strategy, maintaining a balance between its diversified activities while remaining loyal to its core operations. Its expansion into different product categories also acts as a shield against economic downturns in the construction sector, providing MAK with a defense against the uncertainty affecting the Middle East's property market.[49]

Firms with low shares of the total market can become highly profitable through smart niching. Such companies tend to offer high value, charge a premium price, achieve lower manufacturing costs, and shape a strong corporate culture and vision. Family-run Tire Rack sells 2 million specialty tires a year through the internet and by telephone and mail from its South Bend, Indiana, location in the United States.[50] Houston-based VAALCO Energy decided that its odds of striking it rich were better in foreign territory than at home where they faced hundreds of competitors. Drilling in an oil field off the coast of Gabon in West Central Africa, it met with a lot less competition. The company's revenues rose so much it was deemed *BusinessWeek*'s number-one hot growth company in 2006.[51]

In a study of hundreds of business units, the Strategic Planning Institute found that the return on investment averaged 27 percent in smaller markets, but only 11 percent in larger markets.[52] Why is niching so profitable? The main reason is that the market nicher ends up knowing the target customers so well, it meets their needs better than other firms selling to this niche casually. As a result, the nicher can charge a substantial price over costs. The nicher achieves *high margin*, whereas the mass marketer achieves *high volume.*

Nichers have three tasks: creating niches, expanding niches, and protecting niches. Niching carries a major risk in that the market niche might dry up or be attacked. The company is then stuck with highly specialized resources that may not have high-value alternative uses.

Arab Pharmaceutical Glass Co.

The Arab Pharmaceutical Glass Company is an Egyptian company with more than 30 years of experience in glass production. It is the largest manufacturer of pharmaceutical glass in the Arab world and its customers are spread throughout the region. Initially the company produced standardized bottles for its pharmaceutical clients. However, it soon realized that this was not enough to meet the needs of its quality-conscious customers; it had to customize. Currently, it produces a variety of different forms of glass packaging products including jars, syrup bottles, juice bottles, and foodstuff jars to cater to the needs of different companies. This has enabled APG to be more customer-driven, making sure that its products meet the changing needs of its pharmaceutical clients.[53]

Because niches can weaken, the firm must continually create new ones. The Marketing Memo: *Niche Specialist Roles* on page 308 outlines some options. The firm should 'stick to its niching' but not necessarily to its niche. That is why *multiple niching* is preferable to *single niching.* By developing strength in two or more niches, the company increases its chances for survival.

Firms entering a market should initially aim at a niche rather than the whole market. The apparel industry has experienced phenomenal growth but is now facing fierce competition in almost all countries in the Arab region. Sana Fashion Store has successfully tapped into the market for those who are very sensitive to price, but aspire to buy well-known branded clothes.

Sana Fashion Store

In countries such as Qatar and the UAE people are often attracted by international fashion brands such as Gant, Gap, Marks & Spencer, Dolce & Gabana, Zara, and Gucci. In the high-income Gulf countries, consumers' high purchasing power allows them to acquire such brands. However, such countries are occupied by a wide working-class segment coming from South Asian countries, whose finances are more limited. The UAE-headquartered fashion store Sana targets this specific segment of consumers, delivering the best value through very low prices. Sana Fashion is renowned for branded clothing at bargain basement prices, as most of its products are seconds and overruns from factories in the UAE and India. In fact, it is not uncommon to find Gap-wear starting from US$4. Sana Fashion Store aims to serve the working-class consumer segment found in Gulf countries by delivering good-quality apparel with supreme value.[54]

Niche Specialist Roles

The key idea in successful nichemanship is specialization. Here are some possible niche roles:

- **End-user specialist:** the firm specializes in serving one type of end-use customer. For example, a *value-added reseller* (VAR) customizes the computer hardware and software for specific customer segments and earns a price premium in the process.

- **Vertical-level specialist:** the firm specializes at some vertical level of the production-distribution value chain. A copper firm may concentrate on producing raw copper, copper components, or finished copper products.

- **Customer-size specialist:** the firm concentrates on selling to either small, medium-sized, or large customers. Many nichers specialize in serving small customers neglected by the majors.

- **Specific-customer specialist:** the firm limits its selling to one or a few customers. Many firms sell their entire output to a single company, such as Bloomingdale's or General Motors.

- **Geographic specialist:** the firm sells only in a certain locality, region, or area of the world.

- **Product or product-line specialist:** the firm carries or produces only one product line or product. A manufacturer may produce only lenses for microscopes. A retailer may carry only ties.

- **Product-feature specialist:** the firm specializes in producing a certain type of product or product feature.

- **Job-shop specialist:** the firm customizes its products for individual customers.

- **Quality-price specialist:** the firm operates at the low- or high-quality ends of the market. Hewlett-Packard specializes in the high-quality, high-price end of the handheld calculator market.

- **Service specialist:** the firm offers one or more services not available from other firms. A bank might take loan requests over the phone and hand-deliver the money to the customer.

- **Channel specialist:** the firm specializes in serving only one channel of distribution. For example, a soft-drink company decides to make a very large-sized serving available only at gas stations.

Balancing Customer and Competitor Orientations

We've stressed the importance of a company's positioning itself competitively as a market leader, challenger, follower, or nicher. Yet a company must not spend *all* its time focusing on competitors.

Competitor-Centered Companies

A *competitor-centered company* sets its course as follows:

Observed situation

- Competitor W is going all-out to crush us in Riyadh.
- Competitor X is improving its distribution coverage in Beirut and hurting our sales.
- Competitor Y has cut its price in Cairo, and we lost three share points.
- Competitor Z has introduced a new service feature in Manama, and we are losing sales.

Reactions

- We will withdraw from the Riyadh market because we cannot afford to fight this battle.
- We will increase our advertising expenditure in Beirut.
- We will meet competitor Y's price cut in Cairo.
- We will increase our sales promotion budget in Manama.

This kind of planning has some pluses and minuses. On the positive side, the company develops a fighter orientation. It trains its marketers to be on constant alert, to watch for weaknesses in its competitors' and its own position. On the negative side, the company is too reactive. Rather than formulating and executing a consistent, *customer-oriented* strategy, it determines its moves based on its competitors' moves. It does not move toward its own goals. It does not know where it will end up, because so much depends on what its competitors do.

Customer-Centered Companies

A *customer-centered company* focuses more on customer developments in formulating its strategies.

Observed situation

- The total market is growing at 4 percent annually.
- The quality-sensitive segment is growing at 8 percent annually.
- The deal-prone customer segment is also growing fast, but these customers do not stay with any supplier very long.
- A growing number of customers have expressed an interest in a 24-hour hotline, which no one in the industry offers.

Reactions

- We will focus more effort on reaching and satisfying the quality segment of the market. We will buy better components, improve quality control, and shift our advertising theme to quality.
- We will avoid cutting prices and making deals because we do not want the kind of customer that buys this way.
- We will install a 24-hour hotline if it looks promising.

Clearly, the customer-centered company is in a better position to identify new opportunities and set a course that promises to deliver long-run profits. By monitoring customer needs, it can decide which customer groups and emerging needs are the most important to serve, given its resources and objectives. Jeff Bezos, founder of Amazon.com, strongly favors a customer-centered orientation: "Amazon.com's mantra has been that we were going to obsess over our customers and not our competitors. We watch our competitors, learn from them, see the things that they [are doing for customers] and copy those things as much as we can. But we were never going to obsess over them."[55]

Summary

1. To prepare an effective marketing strategy, a company must study competitors as well as actual and potential customers. Marketers need to identify competitors' strategies, objectives, strengths, and weaknesses.

2. A company's closest competitors are those seeking to satisfy the same customers and needs and making similar offers. A company should also pay attention to latent competitors, who may offer new or other ways to satisfy the same needs. A company should identify competitors by using both industry- and market-based analyses.

3. A market leader has the largest market share in the relevant product market. To remain dominant, the leader looks for ways to expand total market demand, attempts to protect its current market share, and perhaps tries to increase its market share.

4. A market challenger attacks the market leader and other competitors in an aggressive bid for more market share. Challengers can choose from five types of general attack; challengers must also choose specific attack strategies.

5. A market follower is a runner-up firm willing to maintain its market share and not rock the boat. A follower can play the role of counterfeiter, cloner, imitator, or adapter.

6. A market nicher serves small market segments not being served by larger firms. The key to nichemanship is specialization. Nichers develop offerings to fully meet a certain group of customers' needs, commanding a premium price in the process.

7. As important as a competitive orientation is in today's global markets, companies should not overdo the emphasis on competitors. They should maintain a good balance of consumer and competitor monitoring.

Applications

Marketing Debate

How Do You Attack a Category Leader?

Attacking a leader is always difficult. Some strategists recommend attacking a leader 'head on' by targeting its strengths. Other strategists disagree and recommend flanking and attempting to avoid the leader's strengths.

Take a position: The best way to challenge a leader is to attack its strengths *versus* the best way to attack a leader is to avoid a head-on assault and to adopt a flanking strategy.

Marketing Discussion

Pick an industry. Classify firms according to the four different roles they might play: leader, challenger, follower, and nicher. How would you characterize the nature of competition? Do the firms follow the principles described in this chapter?

Marketing Excellence

>>Damas

Damas is a jewelry retailer that operates in the Middle East, North Africa, Europe, and India. Damas-Egypt was established in 1999 as a subsidiary of the Damas Group. In Egypt the subsidiary expanded, with 18 branches in Cairo, Alexandria, Mansoura, and Marina. The Egyptian retail jewelry market is extremely fragmented. Market share is dominated by small jewelry retailers and the presence of giant chains is insignificant. Even the very few well-established jewelry chains are operated by family members as independent stores.

Damas's target market is composed of 25 percent B class, 50 percent A class, and 25 percent upper A class, and the firm's mix is tailored to suit these three segments. Items considered conventional commodities are directed by Damas to serve the B segment only. The Farfasha brand of accessories is targeted at the stylish and educated B segment. This brand is affordable to the B class, which is represented by young adult girls and teenagers. The Farfasha brand is being promoted in the Middle East by Nancy Ajram, a famous and cheerful young Lebanese diva. Other international diamond brands attract the attention of the A and upper A segments. The international brands Damas retails are well known and are brought in mainly from Italy and the Far East. Cost reduction and differentiated models are two competing constraints for Damas when ordering international brands. Damas customizes some of its fashionable branded items by reducing the weight of the diamonds, thus enabling it to sell trendy, fashionable, and appealing jewellery at affordable prices. The core competencies and competitive edge of Damas are based on the following:

1. Offering affordable, stylish, competitive gold and diamonds.
2. Providing excellent customer service.
3. Utilizing the Damas brand name as a respectable and trustworthy jewelry chain.
4. Upgrading production quality standards using new technology.

Lazurde is one of the largest gold and jewelry producers and wholesalers in the world. This Saudi group has wholesaling offices in major Saudi cities, the UAE, and Egypt, in addition to showrooms across the region. Lazurde is applying the wholesaling concept to the Egyptian market by offering comparable undifferentiated

Continued on next page >>

Marketing Excellence...continued

>>Damas

gold and jewelry items. The celebrity Elissa, a well-known Lebanese singer, has endorsed Lazurde products.

Other small independent retailers have imitated Damas products. Dr Mohamed Omar, the owner of the Damas Egyptian subsidiary, said, "We are not concerned about similar competitive practices because Damas is permanently changing and newcomers are merely following our practices." He continued, "We are making diamonds and gold affordable to middle income segments by reducing diamond weight and offering stylish models. Unique models are shaped according to the regional Oriental culture with embedded artistic touches from Kuwait, Bahrain, and India." "This deep cultural understanding will always position Damas ahead of competition," Dr. Omar added.

The trendy image and culturally modern products at affordable prices will always differentiate Damas from other providers. Offering occasional gifts such as those made by local brand Fulla for newborn babies is another of Damas's competitive tactics. In a fragmented market composed of small jewelry stores, staff are motivated to sell goods at higher prices to please store owners. The habit of offering gifts is nonexistent in the local market, where the focus is on maximizing profit from the customer by maximizing the price.

Geographical and cultural understanding creates further competitive advantages for Damas. For Damas-Emirates, the variety and assortment of products are wider and deeper than in Egypt due to the diversified nature of Emirate residents. This is not the case in Oman and Kuwait, where Damas sells appealing products that fit local preferences. Small local Egyptian jewelry stores do not use these competition concepts to their advantage and consider that imitating the market leader is the only way to do business. Damas's policy is standardized around the globe. The only differentiating factor is the merchandise mix, which differs from one geographical location to another.

Damas carries regular conventional unbranded models to cover its running expenses. Dr. Omar said, "We are facing tremendous daily expenses that cannot be offset only by selling international branded products which are neither highly perceived nor fully understood by Egyptians." Damas monitors the competition through ongoing marketing intelligence activities. Damas operates in Egypt by serving its customers through valid customer relationship management (CRM) approaches, not by practicing aggressive selling techniques. Damas has managed to expand the size of the jewelry market, enabling new entrants to enter while managing to differentiate itself by selling stylish, trendy types of jewelry.

Questions

1. In your opinion how would fragmented and concentrated competitive strategies differ? Why?

2. Suppose you are hired as a marketing consultant to one of the independent small jewelry stores in Egypt. Discuss your recommended competitive strategy against Damas.

3. List and analyze Damas's points of strength.

4. Damas managed to create generic need recognition by stimulating primary demand and expanding the size of the total diamond market, a strategy that allowed the participation of new competitors. Explain the competitive strategy that Damas implemented after expansion of the market. How do you view the rationale behind this competitive strategy? Why?

Sources: www.damasjewel.com/index.aspx#; www.damasjewellery.com/promotion.aspx?id=132; www.tradeegypt.com/lazurdegypt/?company=y.

CHAPTER 12

www.**rayashop**.com

Raya offers a series of auxiliary services, including a warranty, customer service, a trade-in option for old mobile phones, and free delivery, all of which are part of Raya's successful product strategy.

In this chapter, we will address the following questions:

1. What are the characteristics of products, and how do marketers classify products? (pg. 313)

2. How can companies differentiate products? (pg. 317)

3. How can a company build and manage its product mix and product lines? (pg. 322)

4. How can companies combine products to create strong co-brands or ingredient brands? (pg. 331)

5. How can companies use packaging, labeling, warranties, and guarantees as marketing tools? (pg. 334)

Setting Product Strategy

A t the heart of a great product is the overall value received from a product. Market leaders generally offer products and services of superior quality that provide unsurpassed customer value. The intangible value-added services are what most customers look for when comparing products. These service differentiators are a key element in the market offering.

 *Raya operates in distribution, retail, and maintenance of consumer electronics. Raya's range of consumer electronics spans mobile phones and accessories, laptops, cameras, flat-panel TVs, and white goods. Raya has become a leading firm by maximizing **total customer value** in the retail electronics industry, despite challenges from a number of competitors, including Mobile Shop and Mansour Group.*

Raya offers various service differentiators that attract its customers. First, Raya offers the Raya Warranty, which is a key point of differentiation. Raya is known for its reliable customer maintenance service, with a maintenance tracking service, which is known to be one of the best in the Arab region. Second, it offers online and telephone-based customer service to answer customers' enquiries. At Raya stores you can get lifetime insurance for mobile phones. You can also trade in your old mobile phone and buy a new one. Customers have the option to buy cheaper refurbished products. Further, customers can order their products, get them delivered for free, and pay upon delivery. The sum of the intangible benefits that customers get along with the product is what makes Raya's products worth much more than the core product itself.[1]

Marketing planning begins with formulating an offering to meet target customers' needs or wants. The customer will judge the offering by three basic elements: product features and quality, services mix and quality, and price (see △ **Figure 12.1**). In this chapter we examine product; in Chapter 13, services; and in Chapter 14, price. All three elements must be meshed into a competitively attractive offering. ▽

Product Characteristics and Classifications

Many people think a **product** is a tangible offering, but it can be more than that. Broadly, a product is anything that can be offered to a market to satisfy a want or need, including physical goods, services, experiences, events, persons, places, properties, organizations, information, and ideas.

Product Levels: The Customer-Value Hierarchy

In planning its market offering, the marketer needs to address five product levels (see △ **Figure 12.2**).[2] Each level adds more customer value, and the five constitute a **customer-value hierarchy**.

|Fig. 12.1| △

Components of the Market Offering

|Fig. 12.2| ▲

Five Product Levels

Potential product
Augmented product
Expected product
Basic product
Core benefit

product　anything that can be offered to a market for attention, acquisition, use, or consumption that might satisfy a want or need.

customer-value hierarchy　five product levels that must be addressed by marketers in planning a market offering.

core benefit　the service or benefit the customer is really buying.

basic product　what specifically the actual product is.

expected product　a set of attributes and conditions buyers normally expect when they purchase this product.

- The fundamental level is the **core benefit**: the service or benefit the customer is really buying. A hotel guest is buying rest and sleep. The purchaser of a drill is buying 'holes.' Marketers must see themselves as benefit providers.

- At the second level, the marketer must turn the core benefit into a **basic product**. Thus a hotel room includes a bed, bathroom, towels, desk, dresser, and closet.

- At the third level, the marketer prepares an **expected product**, a set of attributes and conditions buyers normally expect when they purchase this product. Hotel guests expect a clean bed, fresh towels, working lamps, and a relative degree of quiet.

- At the fourth level, the marketer prepares an **augmented product** that exceeds customer expectations. In developed countries, brand positioning and competition take place at this level. In developing and emerging markets such as India, Brazil, and Egypt, however, competition takes place mostly at the expected product level.

- At the fifth level stands the **potential product**, which encompasses all the possible augmentations and transformations the product or offering might undergo in the future. For more on this, see the Marketing Insight: *Metamarkets and Metamediaries*. Here is where companies search for new ways to satisfy customers and distinguish their offering.

Marketing Insight

Metamarkets and Metamediaries

There are some products whose purchase necessitates other purchases. The new-automobile market is a good example of a 'metamarket.' The consumer chooses an automobile but also must buy insurance from an insurance company and often must get a loan from a bank. A smart auto company or auto dealer would make all three purchases easy for the buyer by partnering with an insurance company and a bank. Such an auto dealer is performing as a 'metamediary.'

The wedding market is also a metamarket. The bride and groom need a bridal gown and tuxedo respectively, a hotel for the wedding, a caterer, and possibly a wedding planner. Here the wedding dress seller or the wedding planner might perform as a wedding metamediary.

Metamarkets are the result of marketers observing the total consumption system and 'packaging' a system that simplifies carrying out these related product/service activities. Professor Mohan Sawhney defines a metamarket as "a set of products and services that consumers need to perform a *cognitively related* set of activities." Other metamarkets that are organized around major assets or major life events include:

- Buying a home.
- Giving birth to a child.
- Getting a divorce.
- Planning a vacation.

Source: Adapted from Mohan Sawhney, "Rethinking Marketing and Mediation in the Networked Economy," Winning Strategies for E-Commerce Lecture at the Kellogg School of Management, April 7–10, 1999.

Differentiation arises and competition increasingly occurs on the basis of product augmentation, which also leads the marketer to look at the user's total **consumption system:** the way the user performs the tasks of getting and using products and related services.[3] Each augmentation adds cost, however, and augmented benefits soon become expected benefits and necessary points-of-parity. Today's hotel guests expect cable or satellite television with a remote control and high-speed internet access or two phone lines. This means competitors must search for still other features and benefits.

As some companies raise the price of their augmented product, others offer a 'stripped-down' version at a much lower price. Thus, alongside the growth of fine hotels such as Four Seasons and Ritz-Carlton, we see the emergence of lower-cost hotels and motels such as Holiday Inn and Comfort Inn, which cater to clients who simply want the basic product.

augmented product   a product that includes features that go beyond consumer expectations and differentiate the product from competitors.

potential product   all the possible augmentations and transformations the product or offering might undergo in the future.

consumption system   the way the user performs the tasks of getting and using products and related services.

Saudi Paper Manufacturing Company   The Saudi

Paper Manufacturing Company (SPMC), a Saudi Arabia-based company, differentiates itself from its competitors in the tissue paper industry in several ways. First, SPMC became committed to developing its activities and to operating at the various levels in the tissue paper industry. It specialized in waste paper collection to help achieve the strategic objectives of growth and supply-chain integration, so it grouped its operations under waste paper collection, recycling, manufacturing and converting, and marketing and distribution processes. Secondly, SPMC offers a wide range of products and brands of tissue paper products, including facial and toilet tissues, kitchen and industrial towels, napkins, pocket tissues, and tissue for diapers. The company's brand names include Manadeel, Excellence, Mouchoir, Zaman, City, Pure, and Weekend. Thirdly, SPMC has a strong reputation for being environmentally friendly. One of its primary activities, as mentioned, is the collection of waste paper, which has a positive impact on the environment and society as a whole. It continuously aims to increase its reliance on waste paper as a major production factor in its manufacturing operations. This is done by investing in paper de-inking technology and waste paper collection centers throughout the Arab world.[4]

Product Classifications

Marketers have traditionally classified products on the basis of durability, tangibility, and use (consumer or industrial). Each product type has an appropriate marketing-mix strategy.[5]

DURABILITY AND TANGIBILITY   Marketers classify products into three groups according to durability and tangibility:

1. *Nondurable goods* are tangible goods normally consumed in one or a few uses, such as tea and soap. Because these goods are purchased frequently, the appropriate strategy is to make them available in many locations, charge only a small markup, and advertise heavily to encourage consumers to try the product and to build preference.
2. *Durable goods* are tangible goods that normally survive many uses: refrigerators, machine tools, and clothing. Durable products normally require more personal selling and service, command a higher margin, and require more seller guarantees.
3. *Services* are intangible, inseparable, variable, and perishable products. As a result, they normally require more quality control, supplier credibility, and adaptability. Examples include haircuts, legal advice, and appliance repairs.

Marketers rely on well-trained salespeople to help customers compare the quality and features of shopping goods, such as mobile phones.

CONSUMER-GOODS CLASSIFICATION

We classify the vast array of goods consumers buy on the basis of shopping habits. We distinguish among convenience, shopping, specialty, and unsought goods.

convenience goods goods the consumer purchases frequently, immediately, and with a minimum of effort.

The consumer usually purchases **convenience goods** frequently, immediately, and with a minimum of effort. Examples include soft drinks, soaps, and newspapers. Convenience goods can be further divided. *Staples* are goods consumers purchase on a regular basis. A buyer might routinely purchase Signal toothpaste, Regina spaghetti, and Nice biscuits. *Impulse goods* are purchased without any planning or search effort. Chocolate bars and magazines can be impulse goods. *Emergency goods* are purchased when a need is urgent—like a car emergency service when a car breaks down on the road. Manufacturers of impulse and emergency goods will place them in those outlets where consumers are likely to experience an urge or compelling need to make a purchase.

shopping goods goods that the consumer, in the process of selection and purchase, characteristically compares on such bases as suitability, quality, price, and style.

Shopping goods are goods that the consumer characteristically compares on such bases as suitability, quality, price, and style. Examples include furniture, clothing, used cars, and major appliances. We further divide this category. *Homogeneous shopping goods* are similar in quality but different enough in price to justify shopping comparisons. *Heterogeneous shopping goods* differ in product features and services that may be more important than price. The seller of heterogeneous shopping goods carries a wide assortment to satisfy individual tastes and must have well-trained salespeople to inform and advise customers.

specialty goods goods that have unique characteristics or brand identification for which a sufficient number of buyers are willing to make a special purchasing effort.

Specialty goods have unique characteristics or brand identification for which a sufficient number of buyers are willing to make a special purchasing effort. Examples include cars, stereo components, photographic equipment, and men's suits. A Mercedes is a specialty good because interested buyers will travel far to buy one. Specialty goods don't require comparisons; buyers invest time only to reach dealers carrying the wanted products. Dealers don't need convenient locations, although they must let prospective buyers know their locations.

unsought goods those the consumer does not know about or does not normally think of buying, like smoke detectors.

Unsought goods are those the consumer does not know about or does not normally think of buying, such as smoke detectors. The classic examples of known but unsought goods are life insurance, cemetery plots, gravestones, and encyclopedias. Unsought goods require advertising and personal-selling support.

INDUSTRIAL-GOODS CLASSIFICATION

Industrial goods can be classified in terms of their relative cost and how they enter the production process: materials and parts, capital items, and supplies and business services.

materials and parts goods that enter the manufacturer's product completely.

Materials and parts are goods that enter the manufacturer's product completely. They fall into two classes: raw materials, and manufactured materials and parts. *Raw materials* fall into two major groups: *farm products* (wheat, cotton, livestock, fruits, and vegetables) and *natural products* (fish, lumber, crude petroleum, iron ore). Farm products are supplied by many producers, who turn them over to marketing intermediaries, who provide assembly, grading, storage, transportation, and selling services. Their perishable and seasonal nature gives rise to special marketing practices, whereas their commodity character results in relatively little advertising and promotional activity, with some exceptions. At times, commodity groups will launch campaigns to promote their product, such as potatoes, cheese, and beef. Some producers brand their products, for example Isis cucumbers and Chiquita bananas.

Natural products are limited in supply. They usually have great bulk and low unit value and must be moved from producer to user. Fewer and larger producers often market them directly to industrial users. Because users depend on these materials, long-term supply contracts are common. The homogeneity of natural materials limits the amount of demand-creation activity. Price and delivery reliability are the major factors influencing the selection of suppliers.

Manufactured materials and parts fall into two categories: component materials (iron, yarn, cement, wires) and component parts (small motors, tires, castings). *Component materials* are usually fabricated further: pig iron is made into steel, and yarn is woven into cloth. The standardized nature of component materials usually means that price and supplier reliability are key purchase factors. *Component parts* enter the finished product with no further change in form, as when small motors are put into vacuum cleaners, and tires are put on automobiles. Most manufactured materials and parts are sold directly to industrial users. Price and service are major marketing considerations, and branding and advertising tend to be less important.

capital items long-lasting goods that facilitate developing or managing the finished product.

Capital items are long-lasting goods that facilitate developing or managing the finished product. They include two groups: installations and equipment. Installations consist of buildings (factories, offices) and heavy equipment (generators, drill presses, mainframe computers, elevators). Installations are major purchases. They are usually bought directly from the producer, whose sales force includes technical personnel, and a long negotiation period precedes the typical sale. Producers must be willing to design to specification and to supply postsale services. Advertising is much less important than personal selling.

Equipment includes portable factory equipment and tools (hand tools, lift trucks) and office equipment (personal computers, desks). These types of equipment don't become part of a finished product. They have a shorter life than installations but a longer life than operating supplies. Although some equipment manufacturers sell direct, more often they use intermediaries, because the market is geographically dispersed, the buyers are numerous, and the orders are small. Quality, features, price, and service are major considerations. The sales force tends to be more important than advertising, although advertising can be used effectively.

Supplies and business services are short-term goods and services that facilitate developing or managing the finished product. Supplies are of two kinds: maintenance and repair items (paint, nails, brooms) and *operating supplies* (lubricants, coal, writing paper, pencils). Together, they go under the name of MRO goods. Supplies are the equivalent of convenience goods; they are usually purchased with minimum effort on a straight-rebuy basis. They are normally marketed through intermediaries because of their low unit value and the great number and geographic dispersion of customers. Price and service are important considerations, because suppliers are standardized and brand preference is not high.

> **supplies and business services** short-term goods and services that facilitate developing or managing the finished product.

Business services include *maintenance and repair services* (window cleaning, copier repair) and *business advisory services* (legal, management consulting, advertising). Maintenance and repair services are usually supplied under contract by small producers or are available from the manufacturers of the original equipment. Business advisory services are usually purchased on the basis of the supplier's reputation and staff.

Differentiation

To be branded, products must be differentiated. Physical products vary in their potential for differentiation. At one extreme, we find products that allow little variation: chicken, aspirin, and steel. Yet even here, some differentiation is possible: Sadia chickens, Panadol aspirin, and India's Tata Steel have carved out distinct identities in their categories. Procter & Gamble makes Tide, Ariel, and Oxi laundry detergents, each with a separate brand identity. At the other extreme are products capable of high differentiation, such as automobiles, commercial buildings, and furniture. Here the seller faces an abundance of differentiation possibilities, including form, features, customization, performance quality, conformance quality, durability, reliability, repairability, and style.[6] Design has become an increasingly important means of differentiation and we will discuss it separately.

Product Differentiation

FORM Many products can be differentiated in **form**: the size, shape, or physical structure of a product. Consider the many possible forms taken by products such as aspirin. Although aspirin is essentially a commodity, it can be differentiated by dosage size, shape, color, coating, or action time.

> **form** the size, shape, or physical structure of a product.

FEATURES Most products can be offered with varying **features** that supplement their basic function. A company can identify and select appropriate new features by surveying recent buyers and then calculating *customer value* versus *company cost* for each potential feature. The company should also consider how many people want each feature, how long it would take to introduce it, and whether competitors could easily copy it. To avoid 'feature fatigue,' the company also must be careful to prioritize those features that are included and find unobtrusive ways to provide information about how consumers can use and benefit from the feature.[7] Companies must also think in terms of feature bundles or packages. Auto companies often manufacture cars at several 'trim levels.' This lowers manufacturing and inventory costs. Each company must decide whether to offer feature customization at a higher cost or a few standard packages at a lower cost.

> **features** things that enhance the basic function of a product.

CUSTOMIZATION Marketers can differentiate products by making them customized to an individual. As companies have grown capable at gathering information about individual customers and business partners (suppliers, distributors, retailers), and as their factories are being designed

mass customization   the ability of a company to meet each customer's requirements and to prepare on a mass basis individually designed products, services, programs, and communications.

design   the totality of features that affect how a product looks, feels, and functions in terms of customer requirements.

more flexibly, they have increased their ability to individualize market offerings, messages, and media. **Mass customization** is the ability of a company to meet each customer's requirements: to prepare on a mass basis individually designed products, services, programs, and communications.[8]

Although Levi's and Lands' End were among the first clothing manufacturers to introduce custom jeans, other players have introduced mass customization into other markets. Arab Group Architects is able to **design** different skyscrapers according to the needs of its clients. Lego has embraced mass customization from the start.

 Lego   Lego has always focused on the mass customization strategy. Every child who has ever had a set of the most basic Legos has built his or her own unique and amazing creations, brick by plastic brick. However, in 2005, Lego set up the Lego Factory, which, as it says on the company website, "lets you design, share, and build your very own custom Lego products." Using Lego's freely downloadable Digital Designer software, customers were able to create any structure. The creations can exist—and be shared with other enthusiasts—solely online or, if customers want to build it, the software tabulates the pieces required and sends an order to Lego. The employees put all the pieces into a box and send it off. Not only do Lego Factory customers have the pride of building their own creations, but they can also earn royalties if Lego decides the design is good enough to put in its own catalog. And in 2006, the Lego Factory initiated a design competition in which eight contestants competed to be profiled on the Lego Factory website along with their creations.[9]

performance quality   the level at which the product's primary characteristics operate.

PERFORMANCE QUALITY Most products are established at one of four performance levels: low, average, high, or superior. **Performance quality** is the level at which the product's primary characteristics operate. Quality is becoming an increasingly important dimension for differentiation as companies adopt a value model and provide higher quality for less money. Firms, however, should not necessarily design the highest performance level possible. The manufacturer must design a performance level appropriate to the target market and competitors' performance levels. A company must also manage performance quality through time. Continuously improving the product can produce high returns and market share; failing to do so can have negative consequences.

conformance quality   the degree to which all the produced units are identical and meet the promised specifications.

 Mercedes-Benz   From 2003 to 2006, Mercedes-Benz endured one of its most painful stretches in its 127-year history, as its stellar quality reputation took a beating in major global rankings and surveys, and BMW surpassed it in global sales. As a consequence, DaimlerChrysler Chief Executive Dieter Zetsche and his new management team initiated a major restructuring, organizing the company around functional elements of the car—motors, chassis, and electronic systems—instead of by model lines. To improve quality, the company also made a number of changes in product development. Engineers begin testing electronic systems a year earlier than in the past. Lab workers put each new model's electronic system through a battery of 10,000 tests that ran 24 hours a day for 3 weeks. Trying to uncover even the most unlikely event, Mercedes searched out more than 1,000 errors in the new S-Class. Mercedes now also uses three times as many prototypes of new designs, allowing engineers to drive a new model 4.8 million kilometers before it goes into production. As a result of these and other changes, the number of flaws in a car has dropped 72 percent from its peak in 2002 and warranty costs have decreased by 25 percent as well.[10]

Performance quality is such a critical part of Mercedes-Benz's product strategy that the company recently undertook a series of sweeping changes in its quality-control processes to reduce errors and flaws when its quality ratings fell.

CONFORMANCE QUALITY Buyers expect products to have a high **conformance quality**, which is the degree to which all the produced units are identical and meet the promised specifications. Suppose a Porsche 911 is designed to accelerate to 95 kilometers per hour within 10 seconds. If every Porsche 911 coming off the assembly line does this, the model is said to have high conformance quality. The problem with low conformance quality is that the product will disappoint some buyers.

DURABILITY **Durability**, a measure of the product's expected operating life under natural or stressful conditions, is a valued attribute for certain products. Buyers will generally pay more for vehicles and kitchen appliances that have a reputation for being long lasting. However, this rule is subject to some qualifications. The extra price must not be excessive. Furthermore, the product must not be subject to rapid technological obsolescence, as are personal computers and video cameras.

durability   a measure of a product's expected operating life under natural or stressful conditions.

RELIABILITY Buyers normally will pay a premium for more reliable products. **Reliability** is a measure of the probability that a product will not malfunction or fail within a specified time period. General Electric, which manufactures major home appliances, has an outstanding reputation for creating reliable appliances. The Marketing Excellence on Toyota at the end of this chapter describes how that company has excelled at making and selling high-quality, dependable automobiles.

reliability   a measure of the probability that a product will not malfunction or fail within a specified time period.

REPAIRABILITY **Repairability** is a measure of the ease of fixing a product when it malfunctions or fails. Ideal repairability would exist if users could fix the product themselves with little cost in money or time. Some products include a diagnostic feature that allows service people to correct a problem over the telephone or advise the user how to correct it. Many computer hardware and software companies offer technical support over the phone, by fax or e-mail, or by real-time 'chat' online.

repairability   a measure of the ease of fixing a product when it malfunctions or fails.

STYLE **Style** describes the product's look and feel to the buyer. Car buyers pay a premium for Jaguars because of their extraordinary looks. Aesthetics play a key role in such brands as Apple computers, Montblanc pens, Godiva chocolate, and Harley-Davidson motorcycles.[11] Style has the advantage of creating distinctiveness that is difficult to copy. On the negative side, strong style does not always mean high performance. A car may look sensational but spend a lot of time in the car repair shop.

style   a product's look and feel to the buyer.

Design

As competition intensifies, design offers a compelling way to differentiate and position a company's products and services.[12] In increasingly fast-paced markets, price and technology are not enough. Design is the factor that will often give a company its competitive edge. Design is the totality of features that affect how a product looks, feels, and functions in terms of customer requirements.

Design is particularly important in making and marketing retail services, apparel, packaged goods, and durable equipment. The designer must figure out how much to invest in form, feature development, performance, conformance, durability, reliability, repairability, and style. To the company, a well-designed product is one that is easy to manufacture and distribute. To the customer, a well-designed product is one that is pleasant to look at and easy to open, install, use, repair, and dispose of. The designer must take all these factors into account.

The arguments for good design are particularly compelling for smaller consumer-products companies and start-ups that don't have big advertising dollars. A case in point is NoDust.

NoDust   House dust is found in the cleanest of homes. An average-sized apartment can collect up to 18 kilograms of dust every year. NoDust Egypt was established in 1998 in Cairo; they have now grown to currently employ over 75 service staff and a fleet of 40 delivery vehicles. NoDust products are designed professionally and treated with a special formula that attracts 90 percent of dust from floors, furniture, and equipment. The company's client list comprises over 25,000 individuals and 1,000 businesses including hotels such as the Four Seasons, Movenpick, Le Meridien, sports clubs, hospitals, and universities. The NoDust customer service center assists people to choose the right products for their needs, offering specially designed mops, mitts, mats, dusters, and other products which are easy to use, cost effective, and eco-friendly for household and business use. Its philosophy is "Keep it clean and simple;" an extensive and reliable pick-up and delivery service does just that, ensuring that clean, treated products are "Always new" and freshly delivered on a regular basis, avoiding expensive purchase and maintenance costs.[13]

Boeing 777 airplanes are designed to appear roomier and be more comfortable than before. They continue to be a flagship of top airlines with Emirates recently receiving the 1000th 777 ever built.

Certain countries and companies are winning on design: Italian design in apparel and furniture; and Scandinavian design for functionality, aesthetics, and environmental consciousness. Finland's Nokia was the first to introduce user-changeable covers for mobile phones, the first to have oval-shaped, soft, and friendly forms, and the first with big screens, all contributing to its remarkable rise. Braun, a German division of Gillette, has elevated design to a high art in its electric shavers, coffeemakers, hair dryers, and food processors. The company's design department enjoys equal status with engineering and manufacturing.

Manufacturers, service providers, and retailers seek new designs to create differentiation and establish a more complete connection with consumers. Holistic marketers recognize the emotional power of design and the importance to consumers of how things look and feel. THIS is a brand that aims to promote the *miswak*—a tooth cleaning twig used in the Middle East, Pakistan, and India—as an organic, portable, biodegradable, and viable substitute for toothbrush and toothpaste. In order to make it appealing for the American audience, THIS was designed in a cigar-cutter-like cap to show its natural bristles. It also protects the stick from germs and other contaminants.[14]

In an increasingly visually oriented culture, translating brand meaning and positioning through design is critical. "In a crowded marketplace," writes Virginia Postrel in *The Substance of Style*, "aesthetics is often the only way to make a product stand out." Design can shift consumer perceptions to make brand experiences more rewarding. Consider the lengths Boeing went to in making its 777 airplane seem roomier and more comfortable. Raised center bins, side luggage bins, divider panels, gently arched ceilings, and raised seats make the aircraft interior seem bigger. As one design engineer noted, "If we do our jobs, people don't realize what we have done. They just say they feel more comfortable."

A bad design can also ruin a product's prospects. Sony's e-Villa internet appliance was intended to allow consumers to access the internet using a device in their kitchens. But at nearly 14 kilograms and 41 centimeters, the mammoth product was so awkward and heavy that the owner's manual recommended customers bend their legs, not their back, to pick it up. The product was withdrawn after 3 months.

Services Differentiation

When the physical product cannot easily be differentiated, the key to competitive success may lie in adding valued services and improving their quality. Rolls Royce PLC has ensured its aircraft engines are in high demand by continuously monitoring the health of its 3,000 engines for 45 airlines through live satellite feeds. Under its TotalCare program, airlines pay Rolls Royce a fee for every hour an engine is in flight, and Rolls Royce assumes the risks and costs of downtime and repairs in return.[15]

The main service differentiators are ordering ease, delivery, installation, customer training, customer consulting, and maintenance and repair.

ordering ease how easy it is for the customer to place an order with the company.

ORDERING EASE **Ordering ease** refers to how easy it is for the customer to place an order with the company. Otlob.com—which is available in Egypt, the UAE, Saudi Arabia, Bahrain, and Sudan—has eased the ordering process for fast food restaurants by offering customers its menu online and making online orders. Customers then pay their orders upon delivery. Many financial service institutions in the Arab region offer secure online sites to help customers get information and do transactions more efficiently.

delivery how well the product or service is delivered to the customer.

DELIVERY **Delivery** refers to how well the product or service is brought to the customer. It includes speed, accuracy, and care throughout the process. Today's customers have grown to expect delivery speed: pizza delivered in one-half hour, film developed in 1 hour, eyeglasses made in 1 hour, cars lubricated in 15 minutes. Levi Strauss, Benetton, and The Limited have adopted computerized *quick response systems* (QRS) that link the information systems of their suppliers, manufacturing plants, distribution centers, and retailing outlets. LaFarge, a giant cement company based in Mexico, has transformed the cement business by promising to deliver concrete faster than pizza. LaFarge equips every truck with a *global positioning system* (GPS) so that its real-time location is known and full information is available to drivers and dispatchers. LaFarge is able to promise that if your load is more than 10 minutes late you get a 20 percent discount.[16]

INSTALLATION **Installation** refers to the work done to make a product operational in its planned location. Buyers of heavy equipment expect good installation service. Differentiating at this point in the consumption chain is particularly important for companies with complex products. Ease of installation becomes a true selling point, especially when the target market is technology novices.

installation the work done to make a product operational in its planned location.

CUSTOMER TRAINING **Customer training** refers to training the customer's employees to use the vendor's equipment properly and efficiently. General Electric not only sells and installs expensive X-ray equipment in hospitals, it also gives extensive training to users of this equipment. McDonald's implements the Hamburger University training courses in Dubai, the UAE, for McDonald's franchises located in the Arab region. The training offers employees the skills needed to deal with their customers.

customer training training the customer's employees to use the vendor's equipment properly and efficiently.

CUSTOMER CONSULTING **Customer consulting** refers to data, information systems, and advice services that the seller offers to buyers.

customer consulting data, information systems, and advice services that the seller offers to buyers.

Hydra Properties Hydra Properties, the Abu Dhabi-based master planner and developer, recently launched an in-house call center. This call center aims to handle all customer queries, with the target of fulfilling 80 percent of customer enquiries during the first contact. While most companies nowadays prefer to outsource their call center service, Hydra Properties believes that it is important for its customers to have direct access to the organization and its people. As a result of its commitment to delivering the highest quality of service to its customers, Hydra Properties recruited a team of bilingual call centre agents to provide customer advice in both Arabic and English. Each agent on the team goes through intensive training of 40 hours in customer service and product knowledge.[17]

MAINTENANCE AND REPAIR **Maintenance and repair** describes the service program for helping customers keep purchased products in good working order. Hewlett-Packard offers online technical support, or 'e-support,' for its customers. In the event of a service problem, customers can use various online tools to find a solution. Those aware of the specific problem can search an online database for fixes; those unaware can use diagnostic software that finds the problem and searches the online database for an automatic fix. Customers can also seek online help from a technician.[18]

maintenance and repair the service program for helping customers keep purchased products in good working order.

Acer As a PC vendor, Acer ranks second in the world, behind only HP. It employs 5,300 people supporting dealers and distributors in more than 100 countries and reported total revenue for 2010 of almost US$20 billion. For Acer to live up to its reputation in the Arab world, besides providing its customers with the latest technologies and competitive pricing, the company focused on offering a top notch after-sales service in the Middle East and Africa (MEA) according to an investigation by a leading regional IT magazine. It provided a 'pick and drop' scheme, the only one of its kind in the region. The scheme was established in the UAE and Saudi Arabia, and allowed notebooks and LCD monitors to be picked up, repaired, and delivered back to the customer's door. Acer's MEA operation also won an internal award for best customer satisfaction for the second year running. "Acer products are extremely popular across the region and a world-class after sales service is needed to maintain consumer confidence in the Acer brand," said Kelvyn D'souza, regional customer service manager at Acer MEA. "Our regional service center staff is trained to handle all customer queries and provide customers with a support system that is reliable and reassuring," added D'souza.[19]

RETURNS   Although product returns are undoubtedly a nuisance to customers, manufacturers, retailers, and distributors alike, they are also an unavoidable reality of doing business, especially with online purchases. Although the average return rate for online sales is roughly 5 percent, return and exchange policies are estimated to serve as a deterrent for one-third to one-half of online buyers. The cost of processing a return can be two to three times that of an outbound shipment, totaling an average of US$30–35 for items bought on the internet.

Costco Wholesale Corp.   Costco is the largest membership warehouse club chain in the United States. Costco is different from other major hypermarkets such as Walmart, in that customers have to be members in order to buy from Costco. Costco's ultragenerous return policy was perhaps the most flexible in the retail electronics business. Until recently, a customer could buy an expensive plasma TV, use it indefinitely, and take it back at any time. Then he or she could use the refund to buy a newer model, often at a cheaper price. However, what was the customer's gain was Costco's loss. The membership warehouse chain ended up losing "tens of millions of dollars" annually with this policy. In early 2007, Costco cut its return policy for electronics to (a still generous) 90 days within the state of California which was then extended to all other states. Some customers, who had come to rely on the trust and generosity embodied in Costco's return policy, vowed to shop for electronics elsewhere. Yet, most realized the good times had to come to a halt. To Costco's credit, it is now offering more technical support for installing and operating the electronics it sells; the company had discovered that most returns were due not to problems with the items so much as to customers' inability to set up today's very complicated electronic devices. And with the exception of electronics and computers—which now must be returned within 6 months—all other Costco items can still be returned for any reason at any time.[20]

We can think of product returns in two ways:[21]

- *Controllable returns* result from problems, difficulties, or errors of the seller or customer and can mostly be eliminated with proper strategies and programs by the company or its supply chain partners. Improved handling or storage, better **packaging**, and improved transportation and forward logistics can eliminate problems before they happen.

- *Uncontrollable returns* can't be eliminated by the company in the short-run through any of these means.

One basic returns strategy that companies can adopt is to attempt to eliminate the root causes of controllable returns while at the same time developing processes for handling uncontrollable product returns. The goal of a product return strategy is to have fewer products returned and a higher percentage of returns that can go back into the distribution pipeline to be sold again.

The customer return policy is a rather new policy that has been implemented in the Arab markets during the past decade. Before that, most shops used to display the sign, "Sold products cannot be returned or exchanged." However, with the introduction of consumer protection agencies, most shops are required by law to exchange or refund purchased products that are in the original condition and have a receipt. This has encouraged customers to buy more, as they do not feel 'stuck' in case they need to return a product or exchange it.

packaging   the activities of designing and producing the container or wrapper for a product.

Product and Brand Relationships

Each product can be related to other products to ensure that a firm is offering and marketing the optimal set of products.

The Product Hierarchy

The product hierarchy stretches from basic needs to particular items that satisfy those needs. We can identify six levels of the product hierarchy, using life insurance as an example:

1. *Need family.* The core need that underlies the existence of a product family. Example: financial security.
2. *Product family.* All the product classes that can satisfy a core need with reasonable effectiveness. Example: savings and income.

3. **Product class.** A group of products within the product family recognized as having a certain functional coherence. Also known as a product category. Example: financial instruments.
4. **Product line.** A group of products within a product class that are closely related because they perform a similar function, are sold to the same customer groups, are marketed through the same outlets or channels, or fall within given price ranges. A product line may consist of different brands, a single family brand, or an individual brand that has been line extended. Example: life insurance.
5. **Product type.** A group of items within a product line that share one of several possible forms of the product. Example: term life insurance.
6. **Item (also called *stockkeeping unit* or *product variant*).** A distinct unit within a brand or product line distinguishable by size, price, appearance, or some other attribute. Example: Prudential renewable term life insurance.

Product Systems and Mixes

A **product system** is a group of diverse but related items that function in a compatible manner. For example, the PalmOne handheld and smartphone product lines come with attachable products including headsets, cameras, keyboards, presentation projectors, e-books, MP3 players, and voice recorders. A product mix (also called a product assortment) is the set of all products and items a particular seller offers for sale.

A **product mix** (also called a **product assortment**) consists of various product lines. Seagate now makes 29 kinds of drive that are essential to servers, PCs, and consumer electronic products such as video games, DVRs, and cameras. In General Electric's Consumer Appliance Division, there are product-line managers for refrigerators, stoves, and washing machines. NEC's (Japan) product mix consists of communication products and computer products. Michelin has three product lines: tires, maps, and restaurant-rating services. At the American University in Cairo, there are separate academic deans for the different schools, such as the business school, sciences and engineering school, humanities and social sciences school, and graduate school.

A company's product mix has a certain width, length, depth, and consistency. These concepts are illustrated in 🖫 **Table 12.1** for selected Procter & Gamble consumer products.

- The *width* of a product mix refers to how many different product lines the company carries. Table 12.1 shows a product-mix width of five lines. (In fact, P&G produces many additional lines.)

product system a group of diverse but related items that function in a compatible manner.

product mix see product assortment.

product assortment the set of all products and items a particular seller offers for sale.

TABLE 12.1 🖫	Product-Mix Width and Product-Line Length for Procter & Gamble Products (including Dates of Introduction)				
	Product-Mix Width				
	Detergents	**Toothpaste**	**Bar Soap**	**Disposable Diapers**	**Paper Products**
	Ivory Snow (1930)	Gleem (1952)	Ivory (1879)	Pampers (1961)	Charmin (1928)
	Dreft (1933)	Crest (1955)	Camay (1926)	Luvs (1976)	Puffs (1960)
	Tide (1946)		Zest (1952)		Bounty (1965)
Product Line Length	Cheer (1950)		Safeguard (1963)		
	Dash (1954)		Oil of Olay (1993)		
	Bold (1965)				
	Gain (1966)				
	Era (1972)				

- The *length* of a product mix refers to the total number of items in the mix. In Table 12.1, it is 20. We can also talk about the average length of a line. We obtain this by dividing the total length (here 20) by the number of lines (here 5), for an average product-line length of 4.

- The *depth* of a product mix refers to how many variants are offered of each product in the line. If Tide comes in two scents (Mountain Spring and Regular), two formulations (liquid and powder), and two additives (with or without bleach), Tide has a depth of eight because there are eight distinct variants. We can calculate the average depth of P&G's product mix by averaging the number of variants within the brand groups.

- The *consistency* of the product mix refers to how closely related the various product lines are in end use, production requirements, distribution channels, or some other way. P&G's product lines are consistent as long as they are consumer goods that go through the same distribution channels. The lines are less consistent insofar as they perform different functions for the buyers.

These four product-mix dimensions permit the company to expand its business in four ways. It can add new product lines, thus widening its product mix. It can lengthen each product line. It can add more product variants to each product and deepen its product mix. Finally, a company can pursue more product-line consistency. To make these product and brand decisions, it is useful to conduct product-line analysis.

Product-Line Analysis

In offering a product line, companies normally develop a basic platform and modules that can be added to meet different customer requirements. Car manufacturers build their cars around a basic platform. Homebuilders show a model home to which buyers can add additional features. This modular approach enables the company to offer variety and to lower production costs.

Product-line managers need to know the sales and profits of each item in their line in order to determine which items to build, maintain, harvest, or divest.[22] They also need to understand each product line's market profile.

SALES AND PROFITS △ **Figure 12.3** shows a sales and profit report for a five-item product line. The first item accounts for 50 percent of total sales and 30 percent of total profits. The first two items account for 80 percent of total sales and 60 percent of total profits. If these two items were suddenly hurt by a competitor, the line's sales and profitability could collapse. These items must be carefully monitored and protected. At the other end, the last item delivers only 5 percent of the product line's sales and profits. The product-line manager may consider dropping this item unless it has strong growth potential.

Every company's product portfolio contains products with different margins. Supermarkets make almost no margin on bread and milk; reasonable margins on canned and frozen foods; and even better margins on flowers, ethnic food lines, and freshly baked goods. A local telephone company makes different margins on its core telephone service, call waiting, caller ID, and voicemail.

A company can classify its products into four types that yield different gross margins, depending on sales volume and promotion. To illustrate with laptop computers:

- **Core products.** Basic laptop computers that produce high sales volume and are heavily promoted but with low margins because they are viewed as undifferentiated commodities.

|Fig. 12.3| △

Product-Item
Contributions to a
Product Line's Total
Sales and Profits

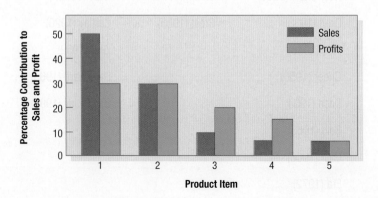

- *Staples.* Items with lower sales volume and no promotion, such as faster CPUs or bigger memories. These yield a somewhat higher margin.

- *Specialties.* Items with lower sales volume but that might be highly promoted, such as digital moviemaking equipment; or might generate income for services, such as personal delivery, installation, or on-site training.

- *Convenience items.* Peripheral items that sell in high volume but receive less promotion, such as carrying cases and accessories, upscale video or sound cards, and software. Consumers tend to buy them where they buy the original equipment because it is more convenient than making further shopping trips. These items can carry higher margins.

The main point is that companies should recognize that these items differ in their potential for being priced higher or advertised more as ways to increase their sales, their margins, or both.[23]

MARKET PROFILE The product-line manager must review how the line is positioned against competitors' lines. Consider paper company X with a paperboard product line.[24] Two paperboard attributes are weight and finish quality. Paper is usually offered at standard levels of 90, 120, 150, and 180 weight. Finish quality is offered at low, medium, and high levels. △ **Figure 12.4** shows the location of the various product-line items of company X and four competitors, A, B, C, and D. Competitor A sells two product items in the extra-high weight class ranging from medium to low finish quality. Competitor B sells four items that vary in weight and finish quality. Competitor C sells three items in which the greater the weight, the greater the finish quality. Competitor D sells three items, all lightweight but varying in finish quality. Company X offers three items that vary in weight and finish quality.

The *product map* shows which competitors' items are competing against company X's items. For example, company X's low-weight, medium-quality paper competes against competitor D's and B's papers, but its high-weight, medium-quality paper has no direct competitor. The map also reveals possible locations for new items. No manufacturer offers a high-weight, low-quality paper. If company X estimates a strong unmet demand and can produce and price this paper at low cost, it could consider adding this item to its line.

Another benefit of product mapping is that it identifies market segments. Figure 12.4 shows the types of paper, by weight and quality, preferred by the general printing industry, the point-of-purchase display industry, and the office supply industry. The map shows that company X is well positioned to serve the needs of the general printing industry but is less effective in serving the other two industries.

Product-line analysis provides information for two key decision areas: product-line length and **product-mix pricing**.

product-mix pricing price-setting when a product is part of a product mix.

Product-Line Length

Company objectives influence product-line length. One objective is to create a product line to induce upselling: thus General Motors would like to move customers up from the Chevrolet to the Buick to the Cadillac. A different objective is to create a product line that facilitates

|Fig. 12.4| △

Product Map for a Paper-Product Line

Source: Benson P. Shapiro, *Industrial Product Policy: Managing the Existing Product Line* (Cambridge, MA: Marketing Science Institute Report No. 77–110). Copyright © 2003. Reprinted by permission of Marketing Science Institute and Benson P. Shapiro.

cross-selling: Hewlett-Packard sells printers as well as computers. Still another objective is to create a product line that protects against economic ups and downs; Electrolux offers white goods such as refrigerators, dishwashers, and vacuum cleaners under different brand names in the discount, middle-market, and premium segments, in part in case the economy moves up or down.[25] Companies seeking high market share and market growth will generally carry longer product lines. Companies that emphasize high profitability will carry shorter lines consisting of carefully chosen items.

Product lines tend to lengthen over time. Excess manufacturing capacity puts pressure on the product-line manager to develop new items. The sales force and distributors also pressure the company for a more complete product line to satisfy customers. But as items are added, costs rise: design and engineering costs, inventory-carrying costs, manufacturing-changeover costs, order-processing costs, transportation costs, and new-item promotional costs. Eventually, someone calls a halt: top management may stop development because of insufficient funds or manufacturing capacity. The controller may call for a study of money-losing items. A pattern of product-line growth followed by massive pruning may repeat itself many times. Increasingly, consumers are growing weary of dense product lines, over-extended brands, and feature-laden products (see the Marketing Insight: *When Less Is More*).

A company lengthens its product line in two ways: line stretching and line filling.

line stretching a company lengthens its product line beyond its current range.

LINE STRETCHING Every company's product line covers a certain part of the total possible range. For example, Mercedes automobiles are located in the upper price range of the automobile market. **Line stretching** occurs when a company lengthens its product line beyond its current range. The company can stretch its line down-market, up-market, or both ways.

Down-Market Stretch A company positioned in the middle market may want to introduce a lower-priced line for any of three reasons:

1. The company may notice strong growth opportunities as mass retailers such as Carrefour, Spinneys, and others attract a growing number of shoppers who want value-priced goods.
2. The company may wish to tie up lower-end competitors who might otherwise try to move up-market. If the company has been attacked by a low-end competitor, it often decides to counterattack by entering the low end of the market.
3. The company may find that the middle market is stagnating or declining.

A company faces a number of naming choices in deciding to move a brand down-market:

1. Use the parent brand name on all its offerings. Sony has used its name on products in a variety of price tiers.
2. Introduce lower-priced offerings using a sub-brand name, such as: Intercontinental Hotel Group's Holiday Inn and Juhayna's Bekhiro milk.
3. Introduce the lower-priced offerings under a different name, such as Gap's Old Navy brand. This strategy is expensive to implement, and consumers may not accept a new brand that lacks the equity of the parent brand name.

Moving down-market carries risks. Thus, it is important to make sure that moving down the market does not hurt the image of other products or result in cannibalization. A success story is that of Al Wifaq. The company developed as a sub-brand for the Union National Bank, one of the leading banks in the UAE. The objective was to have more visibility and presence in the streets. Al Wifaq partnered with Emirates Post to position its mini branches within existing post offices. This resulted in an increase in the bank's market penetration and added 40 branches to its existing network.[26]

Up-Market Stretch Companies may wish to enter the high end of the market to achieve more growth, to realize higher margins, or simply to position themselves as full-line manufacturers. Many markets have generated surprising upscale segments: Starbucks in coffee, Häagen-Dazs in ice cream, and Evian in bottled water. The leading Japanese auto companies have each introduced an upscale automobile: Toyota's Lexus; Nissan's Infiniti; and Honda's Acura. Note that they invented entirely new names rather than using or including their own names, because consumers may not have given the brand 'permission' to stretch upward at the time when these different lines were first introduced.

Other companies have included their own name in moving up-market. General Electric introduced the GE Profile brand for its large appliance offerings in the upscale market.[27] Some brands

Marketing Insight

When Less is More

Although many consumers find the notion of having more choices appealing, the reality is that consumers can sometimes be overwhelmed by the choices involved. With thousands of new products introduced each year, consumers find it harder and harder to successfully navigate through store aisles. One study found that the average shopper spent 40 seconds or more in the supermarket soda aisle, compared to 25 seconds 6 or 7 years ago. Another research study showed that although consumers expressed greater interest in shopping with a larger assortment of 24 different flavored jams than a smaller assortment of six, they were 10 times more likely to actually make a selection with the smaller assortment.

Although consumers with well-defined preferences may benefit from more differentiated products that offer specific benefits to better suit their needs, too much product choice may be a source of frustration, confusion, and regret for other consumers. Extensive product choice has another downside. Exposing the customer to constant product changes and introductions may nudge them into reconsidering their choices, resulting in their switching to a competitor's product as a result.

And not all the new choices may be winners anyway, as Nestlé found out with its KitKat bars, among the best-selling candy bars in the United Kingdom since they were invented there in the 1930s. To increase sales in 2004, the company rolled out a vast array of new flavors. The summer saw the launch of strawberries and cream, passion fruit and mango, and red berry versions; with winter came Christmas pudding and low-carb versions. The new flavors were a disaster—the tastes were too sweet and unusual for many—and even worse, some consumers couldn't find the classic KitKat bars among all the new varieties. An ill-timed switch from the classic slogan, Have a Break, Have a KitKat, didn't help, and sales dropped 18 percent as a result. The new flavors were then discontinued.

Smart marketers are also realizing that it's not just the product lines that are making consumer heads spin: many products themselves are

Marketers are learning through sometimes painful experience that product lines can get too long, or products can become just too complicated.

just too complicated for the average consumer. Royal Philips Electronics learned its lesson when the company asked 100 top managers to take various Philips electronic products home one weekend and see whether they could make them work. The number of executives who returned frustrated and angry spoke volumes about the challenges the ordinary consumer faced. A Yankee Group research study in 2004 reinforces this fact: almost a third of all home-networking products sold that year were returned because the consumer couldn't get them to work; almost half of potential digital camera buyers were delaying their purchase because they thought the products were too complicated; and about a quarter of consumers thought they already owned an HDTV (they didn't). Philips launched an initiative in September 2004 with a goal to make technology simpler, backed by a US$100 million ad campaign, Sense and Simplicity.

Sources: Deborah Ball, "Flavor Experiment for KitKat Leaves Nestlé with a Bad Taste," *Wall Street Journal*, July 6, 2006; Barry Schwartz, *The Paradox of Choice: Why More Is Less* (New York: Harper Collins Ecco, 2004); Frisco Endt, "It Is Rocket Science," *Newsweek*, October 18, 2004, p. E8; Alexander Chernev, "When More Is Less and Less Is More: The Role of Ideal Point Availability and Assortment in Choice," *Journal of Consumer Research*, 30, September 2003, pp. 170–183; Sheena S. Iyengar and Mark R. Lepper, "When Choice Is Demotivating: Can One Desire Too Much of a Good Thing?" *Journal of Personality and Social Psychology*, 79, no. 6, December 2000, pp. 995–1006; Ravi Dhar, "Consumer Preference for a No-Choice Option," *Journal of Consumer Research*, 27, September 1997, pp. 233–248.

have used modifiers to signal a noticeable, although presumably not dramatic, quality improvement, such as Ultra Dry Pampers or Panadol Extra.

Two-Way Stretch Companies serving the middle market might decide to stretch their line in both directions. Consider how Purina Dog Food has stretched up and down to create a product line differentiated by benefits to dogs, breadth of varieties, ingredients, and price:

- Pro Plan (US$22.49/9 kg bag): helps dogs live long and healthy lives with high-quality ingredients (real meat, fish, and poultry).

- Purina ONE ($17.99/9 kg bag): meets dog's changing and unique nutritional needs and provides superpremium nutrition for good health.

- Purina Dog Chow ($11.49/10 kg bag): provides dogs complete nutrition to build, replenish, and repair at each life stage.
- Alpo by Purina ($8.99/8 kg bag): offers beef, liver, and cheese flavor combinations and three meaty varieties.

Rotana Hotel   Rotana performed a very successful two-way stretch of its hotel product line by breaking its hotels down into nine distinct chains, catering for nine different target market segments. The chains are: Rotana Rewards, Centro, Meeting Plus, Zen, Arjaan, Rayhaan, Bodylines, Rotana Club, and the traditional Rotana Hotel. Centro, which is Rotana's budget hotel brand, represents the low end of the two-way stretch; it meets the demands of budget-conscious consumers who seek finesse and functionality at reasonable rates. On the high end of the two-way stretch lies the Arjaan, which offers spacious, luxurious suites that are fully equipped with up-to-date technology and decorated in a stylishly modern manner. The remaining Rotana Hotel chains are designed to meet various other unique needs. For example, Zen offers its health-oriented customers exquisitely designed relaxation areas and treatment rooms that include professional therapists from around the world, while Meeting Plus offers a business environment, with many value-added service facilities including specially designed 12-hour meeting chairs, working wall meeting rooms, and the latest in high technology communication platforms. By developing this wide array of hotel chains targeting distinct customer segments, Rotana Hotel has successfully managed to prevent overlap between its different brands.[28]

The relative position of a brand and its competitor context will also affect consumer acceptance. Research has shown that a high-end model of a low-end brand is favored over a low-end model of a high-end brand, even when information about competing categories is made available.[29]

LINE FILLING   A firm can also lengthen its product line by adding more items within the present range. There are several motives for *line filling*: reaching for additional profits, trying to satisfy dealers who complain about lost sales because of missing items in the line, trying to utilize excess capacity, trying to be the leading full-line company, and trying to plug holes to keep out competitors.

Hamil Al Musk   Hamil Al Musk is a well-known company that makes products for the salon industry. Established in Saudi Arabia in 1990, and with branches in Dubai, Abu Dhabi, and Sharjah, the company manufactures oriental nonalcoholic perfumes, natural soaps, toiletries, home fragrances, and personal grooming products. Not only has Hamil Al Musk managed to expand its perfume product line downward with body lotions priced between US$5 and $10, but it has also built it upward with decanted loose perfumes in a price range from US$100 to $200. In order to fill the gap between these two different categories, it introduced new spray perfumes that are affordable to a very large target market segment. Hamil Al Musk's line-filling strategy opened the door to a massive number of new customers who are contributing to the company's generation of incremental profits.[30]

Line filling is overdone if it results in self-cannibalization and customer confusion. The company needs to differentiate each item in the consumer's mind with a *just-noticeable difference*. According to Weber's law, customers are more attuned to relative than to absolute difference.[31] They will perceive the difference between boards 2 and 3 meters long and boards 10 and 15 meters long, but not between boards 14 and 15 meters long. The company should also check that the proposed item meets a market need and is not being added simply to satisfy an internal need. The infamous Edsel automobile, on which Ford lost US$350 million in the late 1950s, met Ford's internal positioning needs for a car between its Ford and Lincoln lines, but not the market's needs.

LINE MODERNIZATION, FEATURING, AND PRUNING

Product lines need to be modernized. The issue is whether to overhaul the line gradually or all at once. A gradual approach allows the company to see how customers and dealers take to the new style. It is also less draining on the company's cash flow, but it allows competitors to see changes and to start redesigning their own lines.

In rapidly changing product markets, modernization is continuous. Companies plan improvements to encourage customer migration to higher-valued, higher-priced items. Microprocessor companies such as Intel and AMD, and software companies such as Microsoft and Oracle, continually introduce more-advanced versions of their products. A major issue is timing improvements so they do not appear too early (damaging sales of the current line) or too late (after the competition has established a strong reputation for more-advanced equipment).

The product-line manager typically selects one or a few items in the line to feature. Sears will announce a special low-priced washing machine to attract customers. At other times, managers will feature a high-end item to lend prestige to the product line.

Pruning slow-selling brands in product lines often benefits the brands that are left, such as Good Morning soap in Egypt.

Sometimes a company finds one end of its line selling well and the other end selling poorly. The company may try to boost demand for the slower sellers, especially if they are produced in a factory that is inactive from lack of demand; but it could be counterargued that the company should promote items that sell well rather than try to prop up weak items. Nike's Air Force 1 basketball shoe, introduced in the 1980s, is a billion-dollar brand that is still a consumer and retailer favorite and moneymaker for the company due to collectable designs and tight supplies.[32]

Product-line managers must periodically review the line for dead wood that is depressing profits.[33] The weak items can be identified through sales and cost analysis. One study found that for a big Dutch retailer, a major assortment reduction led to a short-term drop in category sales, caused mainly by fewer category purchases by former buyers, but it also attracted new category buyers at the same time. These new buyers partially offset the sales losses among former buyers of the delisted items.[34]

In 1999, Unilever announced its Path to Growth program designed to get the most value from its brand portfolio by eliminating three-quarters of its 1,600 distinct brands by 2003.[35] More than 90 percent of its profits came from just 400 brands, prompting Unilever cochairman Niall FitzGerald to liken the brand reduction to weeding a garden, so "the light and air get in to the blooms which are likely to grow the best." The company retained global brands such as Lipton, as well as regional brands and 'local jewels' such as Good Morning soap, the number one soap in the Egyptian market.[36]

Multibrand companies all over the world are attempting to optimize their brand portfolios. In many cases, this has led to a greater focus on core brand growth and to concentrating energy and resources on the biggest and most established brands. Hasbro has designated a set of core toy brands, including GI Joe, Transformers, and My Little Pony, to emphasize in its marketing. Procter & Gamble's 'back-to-basics strategy' concentrated on its brands with over US$1 billion in revenue, such as Tide, Crest, Pampers, and Pringles. Every product in a product line must play a role, as must any brand in the brand portfolio.

Volkswagen

Volkswagen has four different brands to manage in its European portfolio. Initially, Audi and Seat had a sporty image and VW and Skoda had a family-car image. Audi and VW were in a higher price-quality tier than their respective counterparts. Skoda and Seat with their basic simple interiors and utilitarian engine performance were clearly differentiated. With the goal of reducing costs, streamlining part/systems designs, and eliminating redundancies, Volkswagen upgraded the Seat and Skoda brands. Once viewed as below-average products by European consumers, Skoda and Seat have captured market share with attractive interiors, a full array of safety systems, and reliable powertrains borrowed from

Volkswagen. The danger, of course, is that by borrowing from its higher value Audi and Volkswagen products, Volkswagen may have diluted their status. Economical European automotive consumers may convince themselves that a Seat or Skoda is almost identical to its VW sister, at several thousand euros less.[37]

Product-Mix Pricing

Chapter 14 describes pricing concepts in detail, but let's quickly consider some basic product-mix pricing issues here. Marketers must modify their price-setting logic when the product is part of a product mix. In product-mix pricing, the firm searches for a set of prices that maximizes profits on the total mix. Pricing is difficult because the various products have demand and cost interrelationships and are subject to different degrees of competition. We can distinguish six situations calling for product-mix pricing: product-line pricing, optional-feature pricing, captive-product pricing, two-part pricing, by-product pricing, and product-bundling pricing.

PRODUCT-LINE PRICING Companies normally develop product lines rather than single products and introduce price steps. In many lines of trade, sellers use well-established price points for the products in their line. A men's clothing store might carry men's suits at three price levels: US$200, $400, and $600. Customers will associate low-, average-, and high-quality suits with the three price points. The seller's task is to establish perceived quality differences that justify the price differences.

OPTIONAL-FEATURE PRICING Many companies offer optional products, features, and services along with their main product. The automobile buyer can order power window controls, remote adjustable mirrors, a sunroof, and theft protection. Pricing is a sticky problem, because companies must decide which items to include in the standard price and which to offer as options. For example, car showrooms in the Arab world often advertise cars 'with special prices' to pull people into showrooms, but the cars are stripped of so many features that many buyers leave the showroom spending thousands more than the special price advertised.

Restaurants face a similar pricing problem. Many price the drinks and beverages high and their food low. The food revenue covers costs, and the drinks and beverages produce the profit. This explains why servers often press hard to get customers to order drinks.

CAPTIVE-PRODUCT PRICING Some products require the use of ancillary products, or **captive products**. Manufacturers of razors, digital phones, and cameras often price them low and set high markups on razor blades and film. Zain may give a mobile phone free if the person commits to buying two years of phone service.

captive products products that are necessary to the use of other products, such as razor blades or film.

 Vodafone Qatar QSC   Vodafone Qatar was launched in March 2009 and since then has been successfully delivering great value to its customers through its state-of-the-art products and distinguished services. Its vision is "to be the most admired brand in Qatar within three years."[38]

By applying captive-product pricing, Vodafone Qatar has managed to attract numerous customers and hence increase its sales. Its strategy was to introduce a new Vodafone-brand mobile to the market, which was cheaper than other brands it offered. The Vodafone mobiles range in complexity from very primitive to somewhat sophisticated phones to cater for the different needs of Vodafone's extensive target market. The introduction of this new brand enabled the company to guarantee customer loyalty, as Vodafone mobiles can only function if a Vodafone chip/SIM card is inserted in them. So the customer who buys this cheap mobile brand will have to subscribe to Vodafone to be able to use it and so, based on the payment plan that suits her best, she will end up spending more money on the service in the long run. By offering this new mobile brand, Vodafone Qatar has not only managed to expand its target market and increase its profit margins but also to maintain a significant number of Vodafone-loyal customers.[39]

There is a danger in pricing the captive product too high in the aftermarket, however. If parts and service are too expensive, counterfeiting and substitutions can erode sales. Consumers can now buy mobile phones from cheaper mobile stores in the market and save around 20 percent or more of what it would cost them to buy directly from the mobile service providers such as Vodafone.

TWO-PART PRICING Service firms engage in **two-part pricing**, consisting of a fixed fee plus a variable usage fee. Telephone users pay a minimum monthly fee plus charges for calls beyond a certain area. Amusement parks charge an admission fee plus fees for rides over a certain minimum. The service firm faces a problem similar to captive-product pricing; namely, how much to charge for the basic service and how much for the variable usage. The fixed fee should be low enough to induce purchase of the service; the profit can then come from the usage fees.

two-part pricing a fixed fee plus a variable usage fee.

BY-PRODUCT PRICING The production of certain goods—meats, petroleum products, and other chemicals—often results in by-products. If the by-products have value to a customer group, they should be priced on their value. Any income earned on the by-products will make it easier for the company to charge a lower price on its main product if competition forces it to do so. Formed in 1855, Australia's CSR was originally named the Colonial Sugar Refining Company, and its early reputation was forged as a sugar company. The company began to sell by-products of its sugar cane: waste sugar cane fiber was used to manufacture wallboard. Today, through product development and acquisition, the renamed CSR had become one of the top 10 companies in Australia, selling building and construction materials.

PRODUCT-BUNDLING PRICING Sellers often bundle products and features. **Pure bundling** occurs when a firm offers its products only as a bundle. OSN sells its subscription-based satellite channels together with a receiver, satellite dish, and its related appliances. This is a form of *tied-in sales*. In **mixed bundling**, the seller offers goods both individually and in bundles. When offering a mixed bundle, the seller normally charges less for the bundle than if the items were purchased separately. An auto manufacturer might offer an option package at less than the cost of buying all the options separately. A theater will price a season subscription at less than the cost of buying all the performances separately. Customers may not have planned to buy all the components, so the savings on the price bundle must be substantial enough to induce them to buy it.[40]

pure bundling a firm only offers its products as a bundle.

mixed bundling the seller offers goods both individually and in bundles.

Some customers will want less than the whole bundle. Suppose a medical-equipment supplier's offer includes free delivery and training. A particular customer might ask to forgo the free delivery and training in exchange for a lower price. The customer is asking the seller to 'unbundle' or 'rebundle' its offer. If a supplier saves US$100 by not supplying delivery and reduces the customer's price by $80, the supplier has kept the customer happy while increasing its profit by $20.

Studies have shown that as promotional activity increases on individual items in the bundle, buyers perceive fewer savings on the bundle and are less apt to pay for it. This research suggests the following guidelines for correctly implementing a bundling strategy:[41]

- Don't promote individual products in a package as frequently and cheaply as the bundle. The bundle price should be much lower than the sum of individual products or the consumer will not perceive its attractiveness.
- Limit promotions to a single item in the mix if you still want to promote individual products. Another option is alternate promotions, one after another, in order to avoid running conflicting promotions.
- If you decide to offer large rebates on individual products, make them the absolute exception and do it with discretion. Otherwise, the consumer uses the price of individual products as an external reference for the bundle, which then loses value.

Co-Branding and Ingredient Branding

CO-BRANDING Marketers often combine their products with products from other companies in various ways. In **co-branding**—also called dual branding or brand bundling—two or more well-known brands are combined into a joint product or marketed together in some fashion.[42] One form of co-branding is *same-company co-branding*, as when Unilever advertises Mazola-Knor products. Still another form is *joint-venture co-branding*, such as General Electric and Hitachi lightbulbs in Japan, and the Citibank AAdvantage credit card. There is also *multiple-sponsor co-branding*, such as Taligent, a one-time technological alliance of Apple, IBM, and Motorola.[43] Finally, there is *retail co-branding*, where two retail establishments use the same location as a way to optimize both space and profits, such as jointly owned Pizza Hut, KFC, and Taco Bell fast-food restaurants.

co-branding when two or more well-known brands are combined into a joint product or marketed together in some fashion.

The main advantage of co-branding is that a product may be convincingly positioned by virtue of the multiple brands. Co-branding can generate greater sales from the existing target market as well as opening additional opportunities for new consumers and channels. It can also reduce the cost of product introduction, because it combines two well-known images and speeds adoption. And co-branding may be a valuable means to learn about consumers and how other companies approach them. Companies within the automotive industry have harvested all these benefits of co-branding.

The potential disadvantages of co-branding are the risks and lack of control in becoming aligned with another brand in the minds of consumers. Consumer expectations about the level of involvement and commitment with co-brands are likely to be high, so unsatisfactory performance could have negative repercussions for both brands. If the other brand has entered into a number of co-branding arrangements, overexposure may dilute the transfer of any association. It may also result in a lack of focus on existing brands.

For co-branding to succeed, the two brands must separately have brand equity: adequate brand awareness and a sufficiently positive brand image. The most important requirement is a logical fit between the two brands, such that the combined brand or marketing activity maximizes the advantages of each while minimizing their disadvantages. Research studies show that consumers are more apt to perceive co-brands favorably if the two brands are complementary rather than similar.[44]

Besides remembering these strategic considerations, managers must enter into co-branding ventures carefully. There must be the right kind of fit in values, capabilities, and goals, in addition to an appropriate balance of brand equity. There must be detailed plans to legalize contracts, make financial arrangements, and coordinate marketing programs. As one executive at Nabisco put it, "Giving away your brand is a lot like giving away your child—you want to make sure everything is perfect." The financial arrangement between brands may vary, although one common approach is for the brand more deeply involved in the production process to pay a licensing fee and royalty.

Brand alliances require a number of decisions.[45] What capabilities do you not have? What resource constraints are you faced with (people, time, money, etc.)? What are your growth goals or revenue needs? In assessing a joint branding opportunity, ask whether it's a profitable business venture. How does it help maintain or strengthen brand equity? Is there any risk of dilution of brand equity? Does the opportunity offer any extrinsic advantages such as learning opportunities?

ingredient branding a special case of co-branding that involves creating brand equity for materials, components, or parts that are necessarily contained within other branded products.

INGREDIENT BRANDING **Ingredient branding** is a special case of co-branding. It creates brand equity for materials, components, or parts that are necessarily contained within other branded products. Some successful ingredient brands include Intel processors and Splenda sweetener. Some popular ingredient-branded products are Lunchables lunch combinations with Subway's sandwiches and Chipsy's potato chips. Ingredient branding is taking off in an area known as 'nutraceuticals:' food products that have health-increasing properties. For example, there's Dannon's Activia yogurt that advertises its trademarked probiotic Bacillus Regularis, promoting healthy digestion, or Heinz Ketchup's bottles touting the inclusion of lycopene, a "powerful antioxidant that gives tomatoes their red color."

Moroccanoil's ingredient brand, Argan Oil, opened up opportunities for other products in the beauty industry, too.

Moroccanoil

Moroccanoil's high-profile ingredient brand—Argan Oil—is the key factor behind the company's success. Argan Oil is a powerful antioxidant and UV protector, rich in vitamins and natural elements that protect and fortify the hair. Due to increasing consumer awareness about the benefits of the ingredient, numerous companies in the salon industry have started to add Argan Oil to their products to attract more customers. Famous brands such as diCesare, Kiehl's, and Josie Maran have realized that Argan Oil has become the point-of-entry to their products and so advertise their inclusion of this legendary ingredient. Surprisingly enough, the discovery of this ingredient has opened the gate to success for various companies, influencing their consumers' preferences, and convincing them that Argan Oil is one of the most essential ingredients in cosmetics and beauty products.[46]

An interesting take on ingredient branding is 'self-branding' in which companies advertise and even trademark their own branded ingredients. For instance, Westin Hotels advertises its Heavenly Bed and Heavenly Shower. The Heavenly Bed has been so successful that Westin now sells the bed, pillows, sheets, and blankets via an online catalog, along with other Heavenly gifts and bath items. If it can be done well, it makes much more sense for companies to use self-brand ingredients because they have more control and can develop the ingredient to suit their purposes.[47]

Ingredient brands try to create enough awareness and preference for their product so consumers will not buy a 'host' product that doesn't contain the ingredient. DuPont has achieved success in marketing its products as ingredient brands.

DuPont   Over the years, DuPont has introduced a number of innovative products, such as Corian® solid-surface material, for use in markets ranging from apparel to aerospace. Many of DuPont's products, such as Lycra® and Stainmaster® fabrics, Teflon® coating, and Kevlar® fiber, became household names as ingredient brands in consumer products manufactured by other companies. Several recent ingredient brands include Supro® isolated soy proteins used in food products and RiboPrinter® genetic fingerprinting technology.[48]

Many manufacturers make components or materials that enter into final branded products but lose their individual identity. One of the few component branders that has succeeded in building a separate identity is Intel. Intel's consumer-directed brand campaign convinced many personal computer buyers to buy only computer brands with Intel Inside. As a result, major PC manufacturers—IBM, Dell, Compaq—purchase their chips from Intel at a premium price rather than buy equivalent chips from an unknown supplier. Most component manufacturers, however, would find it difficult to create a successful ingredient brand. The Marketing Memo: *Making Ingredient Branding Work* outlines the characteristics of successful ingredient branding.

Making Ingredient Branding Work

What are the requirements for success in ingredient branding?

1. Consumers must perceive that the ingredient matters to the performance and success of the end product. Ideally, this essential value is easily seen or experienced.

2. Consumers must be convinced that not all ingredient brands are the same and that the ingredient is superior.

3. A distinctive symbol or logo must clearly signal to consumers that the host product contains the ingredient. Ideally, the symbol or logo would function like a 'seal' and would be simple and versatile and credibly communicate quality and confidence.

4. A coordinated 'pull' and 'push' program must help consumers understand the importance and advantages of the branded ingredient. Channel members must offer full support. Often this will require consumer advertising and promotions and—sometimes in collaboration with manufacturers—retail merchandising and promotion programs.

Sources: Kevin Lane Keller, *Strategic Brand Management*, 3rd edn (Upper Saddle River, NJ: Prentice Hall, 2008); Philip Kotler and Waldemar Pfoertsch, *B2B Brand Management* (New York: Springer, 2006); Paul F. Nunes, Stephen F. Dull, and Patrick D. Lynch, "When Two Brands Are Better Than One," *Outlook*, January 2003, pp. 14–23.

Packaging, Labeling, Warranties, and Guarantees

Most physical products must be packaged and labeled. Some packages—such as the Coke bottle—are world famous. Many marketers have called packaging a fifth P, along with price, product, place, and promotion. Most marketers, however, treat packaging and labeling as an element of product strategy. **Warranties** and guarantees can also be an important part of the product strategy, and often appear on the package.

warranties   formal statements of expected product performance by the manufacturer.

Packaging

We define *packaging* as all the activities of designing and producing the container for a product. Packages might include up to three levels of material. Cool Water cologne comes in a bottle (*primary package*) in a cardboard box (*secondary package*) inside a corrugated box (*shipping package*) containing six dozen boxes.

Well-designed packages can build brand equity and drive sales. The package is the buyer's first encounter with the product and is capable of turning the buyer on or off. Packaging also affects consumers' later product experiences. Various factors have contributed to the growing use of packaging as a marketing tool:

- *Self-service.* An increasing number of products are sold on a self-service basis. In an average supermarket, which stocks 15,000 items, the typical shopper passes by some 300 items per minute. Given that 50 to 70 percent of all purchases are made in the store, the effective package must perform many of the sales tasks: attract attention, describe the product's features, create consumer confidence, and make a favorable overall impression.

- *Consumer affluence.* Rising consumer affluence means consumers are willing to pay a little more for the convenience, appearance, dependability, and prestige of better packages.

- *Company and brand image.* Packages contribute to instant recognition of the company or brand. In the store, packages for a brand can create a visible billboard effect, such as Garnier Fructis and their bright green packaging in the hair care aisle.

- *Innovation opportunity.* Innovative packaging can bring large benefits to consumers and profits to producers. Companies are incorporating unique materials and features such as resealable spouts and openings. Heinz's unique, colorful EZ Squirt ketchup and upside-down bottle have helped to revitalize the brand's sales.[49]

From the perspective of both the firm and consumers, packaging must achieve a number of objectives:[50]

1. Identify the brand.
2. Convey descriptive and persuasive information.
3. Facilitate product transportation and protection.
4. Assist at-home storage.
5. Aid product consumption.

To achieve the marketing objectives for the brand and satisfy the desires of consumers, marketers must choose the aesthetic and functional components of packaging correctly. Aesthetic considerations relate to a package's size and shape, material, color, text, and graphics. Blue is cool and serene, red is active and lively, yellow is medicinal and weak, pastel colors are feminine, and dark colors are masculine. Functionally, structural design is crucial. For example, innovations with food products over the years have resulted in packages that are resealable, tamperproof, and more convenient to use (easy to hold, easy to open, or squeezable). The packaging elements must harmonize with each other and with pricing, advertising, and other parts of the marketing program.

Packaging changes can have immediate impact on sales. A good example is the book publishing industry, where customers often quite literally choose a book by its cover: The number-one classics publisher, Penguin Books Ltd, repackaged most of its titles and spent US$500,000 to promote them under the banner Classic Books, Fresh Looks. Sales increased 400 percent for Dorothy Parker's *Complete Stories*, 50 percent for a new translation of *Don Quixote*, and 43 percent for *Pride and*

Prejudice.[51] Packaging changes can come in all forms. Kleenex tissues' seasonally themed oval-shaped boxes, Domino sugar's easy-to-store plastic canister, and Crest toothpaste's beauty-product-inspired Vivid White packaging all led to sales increases.[52] Fine Tissues adapted its packaging as Egyptians become more patriotic and want to be more involved in building their nation.

After the company designs its packaging, it must test it. *Engineering tests* ensure that the package stands up under normal conditions; *visual tests*, that the script is legible and the colors harmonious; *dealer tests*, that dealers find the packages attractive and easy to handle; and *consumer tests*, that buyers will respond favorably. Eye tracking by hidden cameras can assess how much consumers notice and examine packages. For Comtrex cold medicine, tracking research was able to confirm that only 50 percent of consumers considered the old package on the shelf, versus 62 percent for a newly redesigned package.[53]

Although developing effective packaging may cost several hundred thousand dollars and take several months to complete, companies must pay attention to growing environmental and safety concerns to reduce packaging. Fortunately, many companies have gone 'green' and are finding new ways to develop their packaging.

Labeling

The label may be a simple tag attached to the product or an elaborately designed graphic that is part of the package. It might carry only the brand name, or a great deal of information. Even if the seller prefers a simple label, the law may require more.

Labels perform several functions. First, the label *identifies* the product or brand—for instance, the name Sunkist stamped on oranges. The label might also *grade* the product: canned peaches are grade-labeled A, B, and C. The label might *describe* the product: who made it, where it was made, when it was made, what it contains, how it is to be used, and how to use it safely. Finally, the label might *promote* the product through attractive graphics. New technology allows for 360-degree shrink-wrapped labels to surround containers with bright graphics and accommodate more on-pack product information, replacing paper labels glued onto cans and bottles.[54]

Labels eventually become old-fashioned and need freshening up. The label on Ivory soap has been redone at least 18 times since the 1890s, with gradual changes in the size and design of the letters. Companies with labels that have become icons need to be very careful when initiating a redesign.

 Kazouza   Kazouza, a fruity sparkling drink that comes in a traditionally shaped bottle, is a new Lebanese brand launched by FDC (Food & Drug Corporation) and Sedar's Premium. What is interesting about this new beverage is the name on the label: Kazouza 1941. That is because in 1941 the first bottled soft drink, kazouza, was launched in Lebanon under the name Najem. People in Lebanon loved the new product so much that they started to refer to all carbonated beverages as 'kazouza' from then onwards. By naming their new product Kazouza 1941, the FDC and Sedar's Premium conveyed to Lebanese customers that the drink was an authentic Lebanese product, taking them back in time; they wanted adults to have their childhoods flash before their eyes when they saw Kazouza 1941 on the supermarket shelves. At the same time, adolescents are attracted to the new brand because of its unique bottle shape and innovative flavors, such as strawberry melon and pink lemonade, which differentiate it from other products on the market.[55]

There is a long history of legal concerns surrounding labels and packaging. In 1914, the U.S. Federal Trade Commission Act held that false, misleading, or deceptive labels or packages constitute unfair competition. The Fair Packaging and Labeling Act, passed by U.S. Congress in 1967, set mandatory labeling requirements, encouraged voluntary industry packaging standards, and allowed federal agencies to set packaging regulations in specific industries. Such laws also exist in many parts of the Arab world. In Saudi Arabia for example, products offered for sale in Saudi Arabia have to be sealed in packaging with Arabic details, which applies also to imported products. Information such as production and expiration dates must be presented in such a way that they cannot be erased, scratched, or altered. This is in addition to other information such as name and address of the manufacturer, country of origin, ingredients, storage instructions, and net weight.[56]

The Food and Drug Administration (FDA) in the United States has required processed-food producers to include nutritional labeling that clearly states the amounts of protein, fat, and carbohydrate, and the number of calories contained in products, as well as their vitamin and mineral content as a percentage of the recommended daily allowance.[57] The FDA has also taken action against the potentially misleading use of such descriptions as 'light,' 'high fiber,' and 'low fat.' Such agencies are also available in the Arab world to ensure safety standards for food and drugs, such as the Jordanian Food and Drug Administration and the Saudi Food and Drug Authority.

Warranties and Guarantees

All sellers are legally responsible for fulfilling a buyer's normal or reasonable expectations. *Warranties* are formal statements of expected product performance by the manufacturer. Products under warranty can be returned to the manufacturer or designated repair center for repair, replacement, or refund. Whether expressed or implied, warranties are legally enforceable.

Toshiba El Araby
Toshiba is an international icon of electronics. Mahmoud El Araby, one of Egypt's most prominent businessmen and founder and chairman of El Araby Group, has taken what was essentially an import business, and turned it around into a Toshiba-licensed manufacturing company, even expanding it to produce his own brand of electronic appliances. In his first year of production, El Araby focused on building enough facilities to enable his company to produce fans. The real challenge he faced was to build consumer confidence in his own Egyptian-made product. In order to reach his goal, El Araby offered a 5-year warranty instead of the usual 1-year warranty on his Egyptian-made Toshiba fans. The objective of the 4-year-longer warranty was to prove to consumers that the company had high confidence in the reliability and quality of its Egyptian fans. As hoped, this strategy encouraged consumers to buy the Egyptian fans rather than the imported ones. In order to entice consumers even more, El Araby provided full-service maintenance, equipping each truck with a generator so that if the power was out at a customer's home, professional engineers could still fix the fans in the truck. El Araby has proven that a warranty can be a useful and effective marketing strategy, because now consumers favor all Toshiba El Araby products over imported ones.[58]

Sometimes a warranty can be an incredibly smart marketing strategy. Extended warranties can be extremely lucrative for manufacturers and retailers. Retail stores such as Raya are known in the Egyptian market for their guarantee. The slogan Raya and Relax made products purchased from Raya valued in the market. This prompted other retail competitors such as Carrefour and Spinneys to offer warranties on electronics to better compete.

Many sellers offer either general guarantees or specific guarantees.[59] A company such as Procter & Gamble promises general or complete satisfaction without being more specific: "If you are not satisfied for any reason, return for replacement, exchange, or refund." Other companies offer specific and in some cases extraordinary guarantees:

- A. T. Cross guarantees its Cross pens and pencils for life. The customer mails the pen to A. T. Cross (mailing envelopes are provided at stores selling Cross writing instruments), and the pen is repaired or replaced at no charge.

- In the Middle East and North Africa, the Jaguar XF, XK, and XJ models have a mandatory 2 years' extended warranty on top of the original 3 year warranty. The warranty covers complete operational failure, or internal damage caused by the sudden and unexpected failure of any manufacturer's fitted component other than those specifically excluded.[60]

- "Bugs" Burger Bugs Killers (BBBK), a pest extermination company serving the U.S. hospitality industry, offers the following guarantee: (1) no payment until all pests are eradicated; (2) if the effort fails, the customer receives a full refund to pay the next exterminator; (3) if guests on the client's premises spot a pest, BBBK will pay for the guest's room and send an apology letter; and (4) if the client's facility is closed down, BBBK will pay all fines, lost profits, and US$5,000.

Guarantees reduce the buyer's perceived risk. They suggest that the product is of high quality and that the company and its service performance are dependable. They can be especially helpful when the company or product is not that well known or when the product's quality is superior to competitors.

Providing guarantees to customers is starting to become a source of differentiation for many brands in the Arab world. As new markets open up, competion increases, and agencies for consumer protection are introduced, sellers are obliged to offer guarantees to customers. The first ever recall of cars in Egypt took place in 2010. This was for a Toyota car which had a problem with the accelerator, and also applied to all of these cars sold in the Middle East. The customer filed a complaint with the Consumer Protection Agency which then required Toyota to replace the car or repay the full amount of the vehicle. This created a culture where consumers knew their rights and sellers had to meet their expectations.[61]

Summary

1. Product is the first and most important element of the marketing mix. Product strategy calls for making coordinated decisions on product mixes, product lines, brands, and packaging and labeling.

2. In planning its market offering, the marketer needs to think through the five levels of the product: the core benefit, the basic product, the expected product, the augmented product, and the potential product, which encompasses all the augmentations and transformations the product might ultimately undergo.

3. Products can be classified in several ways. In terms of durability and reliability, products can be nondurable goods, durable goods, or services. In the consumer-goods category, products are convenience goods (staples, impulse goods, emergency goods), shopping goods (homogeneous and heterogeneous), specialty goods, or unsought goods. In the industrial-goods category, products fall into one of three categories: materials and parts (raw materials and manufactured materials and parts), capital items (installations and equipment), or supplies and business services (operating supplies, maintenance and repair items, maintenance and repair services, and business advisory services).

4. Brands can be differentiated on the basis of a number of different product or service dimensions: product form, features, performance, conformance, durability, reliability, repairability, style, and design, as well as such service dimensions as ordering ease, delivery, installation,

customer training, customer consulting, and maintenance and repair.

5. Most companies sell more than one product. A product mix can be classified according to width, length, depth, and consistency. These four dimensions are the tools for developing the company's marketing strategy and deciding which product lines to grow, maintain, harvest, and divest. To analyze a product line and decide how many resources should be invested in that line, product-line managers need to look at sales and profits and market profile.

6. A company can change the product component of its marketing mix by lengthening its product line via line stretching (down-market, up-market, or both) or line filling; by modernizing its products; by featuring certain products; and by pruning its products to eliminate the least profitable.

7. Brands are often sold or marketed jointly with other brands. Ingredient brands and co-brands can add value, assuming they have equity and are perceived as fitting appropriately.

8. Physical products must be packaged and labeled. Well-designed packages can create convenience value for customers and promotional value for producers. In effect, they can act as '5-second commercials' for the product. Warranties and guarantees can offer further assurance to consumers.

Applications

Marketing Debate

With Products, Is It Form or Function?

The 'form versus function' debate applies in many arenas, including marketing. Some marketers believe that product performance is most important. Other marketers maintain that the looks, feel, and other design elements of products are what really make the difference.

Take a position: Product functionality is the key to brand success *versus* product design is the key to brand success.

Marketing Discussion

Consider the different means of differentiating products and services. Which ones have the most impact on your choices? Why? Can you think of certain brands that excel on a number of these different means of differentiation?

Marketing Excellence

>>Toyota

Toyota may have started doing business in the automobile market by being a fast follower, but it is now the innovator. In 1936, Toyota admitted following Chrysler's landmark Airflow and patterning its engine after a 1933 Chevrolet engine. But by 2000, when it introduced the first hybrid electric-gasoline car, the Prius, Toyota was the leader. In 2002, when the second-generation Prius hit showrooms, dealers received 10,000 orders before the car was even available; GM followed with an announcement that it would enter the hybrid market with models of its own.

Toyota offers a variety of cars for the Arab market, from family sedans to sport utility vehicles, trucks to minivans. Toyota also has products for different price points, from the lower-cost Yaris to mid-priced Camrys to the luxury Lexus. Designing these different products means listening to different customers, building the cars they want, and then crafting the marketing to reinforce each make's image. Toyota realized that many customers were looking to own a Toyota, but could not afford to buy a Corolla or a Camry. To meet that preference, Toyota designed the Toyota Yaris, positioned as a small economy car with very basic options. The car had a contemporary look and shape, which is what customers were looking for, and gave the car a 'young feel.' It is a popular car for university students and those who aspire to own a higher-priced Toyota. In order to avoid cannibalization with Corolla, Toyota increased the body size of the Corolla and added more features and options in order to create a difference between both brands. The Toyota Yaris was a success in many markets in the Arab world.

In contrast, Toyota's marketing strategy for the Lexus line focuses on perfection. The tagline for the global strategy is "Passionate Pursuit of Perfection". Dealerships offer white-glove treatment. Toyota markets Lexus globally and understands that each country defines perfection differently. In the Arab world, for example, luxury means high social class image. In the United States, perfection and luxury mean comfort, size, and dependability. In Europe, luxury means attention to detail and brand heritage. Therefore, although the core of Lexus marketing is similar (a consistent Lexus visual vocabulary, logo, font, and overall communication), the advertising varies by country.

A big reason behind Toyota's success is its manufacturing. Toyota's combination of manufacturing speed and flexibility is world class. It is the master of lean manufacturing and continuous improvement. Its plants can make as many as eight different models at the same time, which brings Toyota huge increases in productivity and market responsiveness. And it persistently innovates. A typical Toyota assembly line makes thousands of operational changes

Continued on next page >>

Marketing Excellence...continued

>>Toyota

in the course of a single year. Toyota employees see their purpose as threefold: making cars, making cars better, and teaching everyone how to make cars better. The company encourages problem solving, always looking to improve the process by which it improves all other processes.

Toyota is integrating its assembly plants around the world into a single giant network. The plants will customize cars for local markets and be able to shift production quickly to satisfy any surges in demand from markets worldwide. With a manufacturing network, Toyota can build a wide variety of models much more inexpensively. That means Toyota will be able to fill market niches as they emerge without building whole new assembly operations. "If there's a market or market segment where they aren't present, they go there," said Tatsuo Yoshida, auto analyst at Deutsche Securities Ltd. And with consumers being increasingly indecisive about what they want in a car, such market agility gives Toyota a huge competitive edge.

In 2010, Toyota earned over US$4 billion. Most of its cars are produced outside Japan, including plants in the United States and South Africa. In June 2011, Toyota witnessed a decline in sales over the same period of 2010.

This is mainly as a result of the earthquake and nuclear disaster that hit Japan in January 2011, which brought many automakers and their suppliers to a halt.

Questions

1. How does Toyota manage to market its different car product?

2. How does Toyota differentiate between its different cars?

3. What are the reasons behind Toyota's success as a leading automobile manufacturer?

4. How does Toyota's manufacturing strategy enable it to fulfil the needs of its different local markets?

Sources: Martin Zimmerman, "Toyota's First Quarter Global Sales Beat GM's Preliminary Numbers," *Los Angeles Times*, April 24, 2007; Charles Fishman, "No Satisfaction at Toyota," *Fast Company*, December 2006–January 2007, pp. 82–90; Stuart F. Brown, "Toyota's Global Body Shop," *Fortune*, February 9, 2004, p. 120; James B. Treece, "Ford Down; Toyota Aims for No. 1," *Automotive News*, February 2, 2004, p. 1; Brian Bemner and Chester Dawson, "Can Anything Stop Toyota?," *BusinessWeek*, November 17, 2003, pp. 114–122; and www.toyota.com; Mashfique Hussain Chowdhury, "2006 Toyota Yaris Sedan," www.drivearabia.com/toyota/toyotayaris.html; yaris.toyotaegypt.com.eg/offer.aspx.

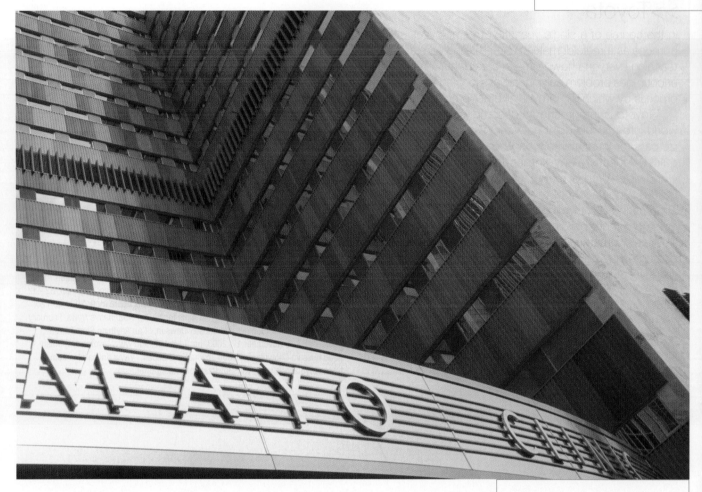

The Mayo Clinic's approach to patient care and service has set new standards in the health care industry.

In this chapter, we will address the following questions:

1. How do we define and classify services, and how do they differ from goods? (pg. 341)

2. How do we market services? (pg. 348)

3. How can we improve service quality? (pg. 353)

4. How do services marketers create strong brands? (pg. 362)

5. How can goods marketers improve customer-support services? (pg. 364)

Designing and Managing Services

As product companies find it harder and harder to differentiate their physical products, they turn to service differentiation. Many in fact find significant profitability in delivering superior service,[1] whether that means on-time delivery, better and faster answering of inquiries, or quicker resolution of complaints. Service providers know these advantages well. The Mayo Clinic has set new standards in the health care industry by considering all aspects of the patient experience.

 The Mayo Clinic is the first and largest integrated not-for-profit medical group practice in the world. It has built one of the most powerful services brands on its firmly held brand beliefs and its relentless focus on the patient experience. Two interrelated core values that trace back to the clinic's founders, William and Charles Mayo, over a century ago are at the heart of all the organization does: placing the patient's interests above all others, and practicing teamwork. Every aspect of the patient experience is considered. From public exam rooms to laboratories, Mayo facilities have been designed so that, in the words of the architect of one of the buildings, "patients feel a little better before they see their doctors." The 20-story Gonda Building in Rochester, Minnesota, in the United States, has spectacular wide-open spaces, and the lobby of the Mayo Clinic hospital in Scottsdale, Arizona, has an indoor waterfall and a wall of windows overlooking mountains. In pediatric exam rooms, resuscitation equipment is hidden behind a large cheery picture. Hospital rooms feature microwave ovens and chairs that really do convert to beds because, as one staff member explained, "People don't come to the hospital alone."[2]

Because it is critical to understand the special nature of services and what that means to marketers, in this chapter we systematically analyze services and how to market them most effectively. ▽

The Nature of Services

The service-related economy is the employment driver of most economies in the Arab world. This is mainly driven by growth in the financial services, transportation, and tourism sectors. Employment in manufacturing-based sectors is expected to decline. With the opportunities available in the service-related companies, entrepreneurs are paying more attention to the marketing of services. Thus, there is a growing interest in the special problems of marketing services.

Service Industries Are Everywhere

The *government sector*, with its courts, employment services, hospitals, loan agencies, military services, police and fire departments, postal service, regulatory agencies, and schools, is in the service business. The *private nonprofit sector*, with its museums, charities, mosques, churches, colleges, foundations, and hospitals, is in the service business. A good part of the *business sector*, with its airlines, banks, hotels, insurance companies, law firms, management consulting firms, medical practices, motion picture companies, plumbing repair companies, and real estate firms, is in the service business. Many workers in the *manufacturing sector*, such as computer operators, accountants, and legal staff, are really service providers. In fact, they make up a 'service factory' providing services to the 'goods factory.' And those in the *retail sector*, such as cashiers, clerks, salespeople, and customer-service representatives, are also providing a service.

We define a service as follows: a **service** is any act or performance one party can offer to another that is essentially intangible and does not result in the ownership of anything. Its production may or may not be tied to a physical product. Increasingly, however, manufacturers, distributors, and retailers are providing value-added services, or simply excellent customer service, to differentiate themselves.

service any act or performance that one party can offer to another that is essentially intangible and does not result in the ownership of anything.

Luxury Automobiles   To operate effectively in the lucrative but highly competitive U.S. luxury automobile market, Lexus, Cadillac, and Porsche all are committed to making sure their customers have another car at their disposal if theirs happens to be in service. The Al-Futtaim Group, agent for several auto brands in the Arab region, including Lexus, offers its customers "Lexus Customer Service." The quality of Lexus service is evidenced in various examples: when Lexus had to recall the RX330 in 2006, it gave its inconvenienced customers a free iPod Nano. When customers refused the price and inconvenience of early scheduled maintenance, Lexus implemented a new system that cut the average appointment time in half. For Cadillac, General Motors has put an early warning system for mechanical problems into its OnStar telematics system, standard in all models. OnStar service helps customers with related tasks including emergency services dispatch, stolen vehicle location, roadside assistance, remote diagnostics, and route support. Although the first year of OnStar is free to GM car owners, it now claims renewal rates as high as 80 percent at annual subscription fees ranging from US$200 to more than $600.[3]

Many services, though, include no physical products and many pure service firms are now using the internet to reach customers.

Some service firms are even purely online. Monster.com, which provides services across the world, including to Arab countries including Bahrain, Jordan, Lebanon, and Qatar, has won a Webby award for its website to support its online career advice and employment recruiting efforts.[4] Done correctly, improvements in customer service can have a big payoff.   **Box 13.1** summarizes some high-impact customer-service projects.

Categories of Service Mix

The service component can be a minor or a major part of the total offering. We distinguish five categories of offerings:

* **Pure tangible good.** The offering consists primarily of a tangible good such as soap, toothpaste, or salt. No services accompany the product.

* **Tangible good with accompanying services.** The offering consists of a tangible good accompanied by one or more services. Typically, the more technologically advanced the product, the greater the need for a broad range of high-quality supporting services. Services are often crucial for cars, computers, and mobile phones.

* **Hybrid.** The offering consists of equal parts goods and services. For example, people patronize restaurants for both the food and its preparation.

* **Major service with accompanying minor goods and services.** The offering consists of a major service along with additional services or supporting goods. For example, though the trip includes a few tangibles such as snacks and drinks, what airline passengers buy is transportation. This service requires a capital-intensive good—an airplane—for its realization, but the primary item is a service.

* **Pure service.** The offering consists primarily of a service. Examples include babysitting, psychotherapy, and massage.

BOX 13.1	High-Impact Online Customer-Service Projects	
	Project	**Payoff**
Oman Arab Bank	Oman Arab Bank has simplified online shopping and bill payments using Vasco's DIGIPASS technology.	Customers of Oman Arab Bank do not need to supply their credit card details. To complete the transaction, customers enter their account number followed by the OTP-generated DIGIPASS. It's a simpler system.
	Customers can withdraw cash or settle cash payments without the use of a credit or debit card: "Card-Less ATM Banking."	Customers are able to use their DIGIPASS for ATM banking, which reduces costs for the bank and is convenient for consumers.
Qatarlyst	Enables businesses to link directly and securely to in-house systems.	Combines the flexibility of the web with the stability of high-cost internal systems and architectures.
Zipcar	Zaps busy signals by linking the car-sharing service's phone reservation system to its website and client databases. Customers are automatically recognized when they call and their requests are routed efficiently.	Cut in half the number of calls that need operator assistance and improved service, contributing US$3.5 million to 2005's estimated $15 million in sales.
Continental Airlines	Analyzes data on the fly to improve customer care. One online system alerts the company when planes arrive late and assesses passengers' needs, delaying departures of other flights or sending carts to make connections easier.	After ranking last in the industry for customer satisfaction in the 1990s, Continental climbed into the top tier – ahead of American, United, and US Air.
Museum of Modern Art in New York City	As part of its US$425 million rebuilding project, the museum's management pumped up the use of technology to cater better to visitors.	New services include podcast audio tours, on-demand printing of tickets, and a 35-foot flat-panel display featuring art and informational updates on shows and lectures.
Enel Telgestore	Installs meters for the customers of one of Italy's major electricity utilities and remotely monitors them.	Reaped nearly US$600 million annually in savings and benefits by recommending shifts in usage from peak to nonpeak hours and slashing field service costs.
BT Group	Entirely revamped its self-service web portal used by customers to manage telecom accounts and linked it to the system used by the company's customer-support staff to improve consistency.	Customer-support transactions done via the web tripled from 2003 to 2006, and half of all new orders for broadband services were made online. Saved tens of millions annually in costs, and boosted customer satisfaction 40%.
Whirlpool	Signed up for Rearden Commerce, an online hub that provides employees at 10 companies with a one-stop shop for services from 13,000 suppliers, including booking travel, shipping packages, and restaurant reservations.	During the first phase of the rollout of the shipping service over a 2-month period, employees saved 10% and cut the time spent arranging for shipping by 52%.

Sources: Catherine Yang, *BusinessWeek*, November 21, 2005, pp. 84–85; "Oman Arab Bank provides customers secure e-banking services with DIGIPASS technology to prevent identity theft and fraud," Vasco website – case studies, www.vasco.com/Images/Oman_Arab_Bank_ENG.pdf; "How It Works," Qatarlyst website, www.qatarlyst.com/about-qatarlyst/how-it-works/.

The range of service offerings makes it difficult to generalize without a few further distinctions.

- Services vary as to whether they are *equipment-based* (automated car washes, vending machines) or *people-based* (window washing, accounting services). People-based services vary by whether unskilled, skilled, or professional workers provide them.

- Service companies can choose among different *processes* to deliver their service. Restaurants have developed cafeteria-style, fast-food, buffet, and candlelight service formats.

- Some services need the *client's presence*. Brain surgery requires the client's presence, a car repair does not. If the client must be present, the service provider must be considerate of his or her needs. Thus beauty salon operators will invest in décor, play background music, and engage in light conversation with the client.

- Services may meet a *personal need* (personal services) or a *business need* (business services). Service providers typically develop different marketing programs for personal and business markets.

- Service providers differ in their *objectives* (profit or nonprofit) and *ownership* (private or public). These two characteristics, when crossed, produce four quite different types of organization. The marketing programs of a private investor hospital will differ from those of a private charity hospital or a public or army hospital.[5]

Customers cannot judge the technical quality of some services even after they have received them. Different products and services differ in their ease of evaluation. On the one hand, there are goods that are high in *search qualities*: characteristics the buyer can evaluate before purchase. Examples of such goods include clothing, furniture, and automobiles. There are also goods and services that are high in *experience qualities*, characteristics the buyer can evaluate after purchase, such as food in a restaurant or holidays. Other goods and services such as legal services or medical treatment are high in *credence qualities*: characteristics the buyer finds hard to evaluate, even after consumption.[7]

Because services are generally high in experience and credence qualities, there is more risk in purchase. This factor has several consequences. First, service consumers generally rely on word of mouth rather than advertising. Second, they rely heavily on price, personnel, and physical cues to judge quality. Third, they are highly loyal to service providers who satisfy them. Fourth, because switching costs are high, consumer inertia can make it challenging to entice a customer away from a competitor.

Distinctive Characteristics of Services

Services have four distinctive characteristics that greatly affect the design of marketing programs: *intangibility*, *inseparability*, *variability*, and *perishability*.[8]

INTANGIBILITY Unlike physical products, services cannot be seen, tasted, felt, heard, or smelled before they are bought. A person getting cosmetic surgery cannot see the results before the purchase, and the patient in the psychiatrist's office cannot know the exact outcome of treatment. To reduce uncertainty, buyers will look for evidence of quality by drawing inferences from the place, people, equipment, communication material, symbols, and price. Therefore, the service provider's task is to "manage the evidence," to "tangibilize the intangible."[9]

Service companies can try to demonstrate their service quality through *physical evidence* and *presentation*.[10] A hotel will develop a look and a style of dealing with customers that realizes its intended customer-value proposition, whether it's cleanliness, speed, or some other benefit. Suppose a bank wants to position itself as the 'fast' bank. It could make this positioning strategy tangible through any number of marketing tools:

- **Place.** The exterior and interior should have clean lines. The layout of the desks and the traffic flow should be planned carefully. Waiting lines should not get overly long.

- **People.** Personnel should be busy, but there should be a sufficient number of employees to manage the workload.

- **Equipment.** Computers, copying machines, and desks should be and look 'state of the art.'

- **Communication material.** Printed materials—text and photos—should suggest efficiency and speed.

- **Symbols.** The name and symbol could suggest fast service.

- **Price.** The bank could advertise that it will deposit US$5 in the account of any customer who waits in line for more than 5 minutes.

Service marketers must be able to transform intangible services into concrete benefits and a well-defined experience.[11] The Disney Company is a master at "tangibilizing the intangible" and creating magical fantasies in its theme parks. Grand Royal, a hotel that opened in July 2010 in Alexandria, Egypt, has been highly successful using its careful design to convey the classical and historical Roman personality of the hotel.

Grand Royal

Walk into the Grand Royal hotel, located in the old town area in Alexandria, and you will immediately notice the unique style and personality of the hotel. You are greeted by a bellman dressed in classical style, and offered traditional tea. The hotel style is classically Roman, which used to be the design of Alexandrian architecture in the 19th century; the brand mantra of the hotel is "We offer business in style." The hotel is located strategically close to many historical places, such as the Alexandria Library, Sultan Qait Bay Fort, the Pompeii Pillar, and many other attractions.

The rooms are designed to give a feel of the old Roman style, and overlook the old town to offer a unique view. The Grand Roof located on the roof of the hotel also gives a panaromic view of the old town, Sultan Qait Bay Fort, and the Mediterranean Sea. The King, Queen, and Prince ballrooms and meeting rooms match the elegance of the historical design.

The Grand Royal is able to attract foreign tourists who are looking for the historical feel of Alexandria, together with state-of-the-art customer service. Most tourists are over 40 years old and are interested more in historical styles than the modern style.[12]

The Grand Royal gives you the sense and feel of the classic and historical styles of Alexandria from the moment you enter the hotel.

INSEPARABILITY Whereas physical goods are manufactured, put into inventory, distributed through multiple resellers, and consumed later, services are typically produced and consumed simultaneously. A barber can't give a haircut without being present. If a person renders the service, then the provider is part of the service. Because the client is also often present as the service is produced, provider–client interaction is a special feature of services marketing.

In the case of entertainment and professional services, buyers are very interested in the specific provider. It's not the same concert if Amr Diab is indisposed and replaced by Ragheb Alama. When clients have strong provider preferences, the provider can raise its price to ration its limited time.

Several strategies exist for getting around the limitations of inseparability. The service provider can learn to work with larger groups. Psychotherapists have moved from one-on-one therapy to small-group therapy to groups of over 300 people in a large hotel ballroom. The service provider can learn to work faster: the psychotherapist can spend 30 more-efficient minutes with each patient instead of 50 less-structured minutes and can see more patients. The service organization can train more service providers and build up client confidence. Mashaweer has also developed techniques to overcome the limits of inseparability.

Mashaweer

Mashaweer started out as the first service company in Alexandria committed to running customers' errands around the coastal city. It is not just about the service they provide, but also the way they provide it. "The life blood of our company is good customer service … our strategy is simple and straightforward—your comfort," says Ahmed Kordy, a business partner. Errands are run with high efficiency; and in a way that positions them as a service with the values of being trust worthy, reachable, personal, and effective. For example, delivery cars are equipped with GPS devices to ensure accurate tracking, along with a safe box to secure money and expensive objects. Mashaweer offers a 24/7 hotline to meet any customers' request.

The demand for their services is uneven throughout the year: they are faced with a higher number of calls during the summer months, mainly July and August. In order to match this above-normal number of calls, Mashaweer hires part-time employees to meet the high level of demand. Many of them are students who are on holiday during the summer. This helps them to meet their commitments all year round. Since its establishment in April 2010, Mashaweer has proven to be a success, appealing to the modern sense that time is increasingly valuable.[13] The service has also recently been launched in Cairo, meaning more possibilities for the future.

Mashaweer is a convenient service for customers in Alexandria and Cairo, running errands to save them valuable time.

VARIABILITY Because the quality of services depends on who provides them, when and where, and to whom, services are highly variable. Some doctors have an excellent bedside manner; others are less empathic.

Service buyers are aware of this variability and often talk to others before selecting a service provider. To reassure customers, some firms offer *service guarantees* that may reduce consumer perceptions of risk.[14] Here are three steps service firms can take to increase quality control.

1. ***Invest in good hiring and training procedures.*** Recruiting the right employees and providing them with excellent training is crucial, regardless of whether employees are highly skilled professionals or low-skilled workers. Better-trained personnel exhibit six characteristics: *competence*: they possess the required skill and knowledge; *courtesy*: they are friendly, respectful, and considerate; *credibility*: they are trustworthy; *reliability*: they perform the service consistently and accurately; *responsiveness*: they respond quickly to customers' requests and problems; and *communication*: they make an effort to understand the customer and communicate clearly.[15] Starbucks worldwide invests a lot of time and money in recruiting their employees, which they refer to as partners or baristas. Starbucks customers are usually regular customers who look for the consistently high level of the "Starbucks experience."

2. ***Standardize the service-performance process throughout the organization.*** A *service blueprint* can simultaneously map out the service process, the points of customer contact, and the evidence of service from the customer's point of view.[16] ▲ **Figure 13.1** on page 347 shows a service blueprint for a guest spending a night at a hotel.[17] The guest's experience includes a series of steps he or she must enact before even getting to sleep. Behind the scenes, the hotel must skillfully help the guest move from one step to the next. Service blueprints can be helpful in developing a new service, supporting a 'zero defects' culture, and devising service recovery strategies.

3. ***Monitor customer satisfaction.*** Employ suggestion and complaint systems, customer surveys, and comparison shopping. Many restaurants ask their customers to rate their service before they leave the restaurant. Vodafone Egypt occasionally sends text messages to its customers after they have called the customer-service support line, to assess the service quality. General Electric sends out 700,000 response cards a year asking households to rate its service people's performance. Citibank checks continuously on measures of ART (accuracy, responsiveness, and timeliness). Recognizing how customer needs may vary in different geographical areas can allow firms to develop region-specific programs to improve total customer satisfaction.[18] Firms can also develop customer information databases and systems to permit more personalized, customized service, especially online.[19]

PERISHABILITY Services cannot be stored, so their perishability can be a problem when demand fluctuates. For example, public transportation companies must own much more equipment because of rush-hour demand than if demand were even throughout the day. Some doctors charge patients for missed appointments because the service value (the doctor's availability) exists only at the time of the appointment.

Demand or yield management is critical: the right services must be available to the right customers at the right places at the right times and right prices to maximize profitability.

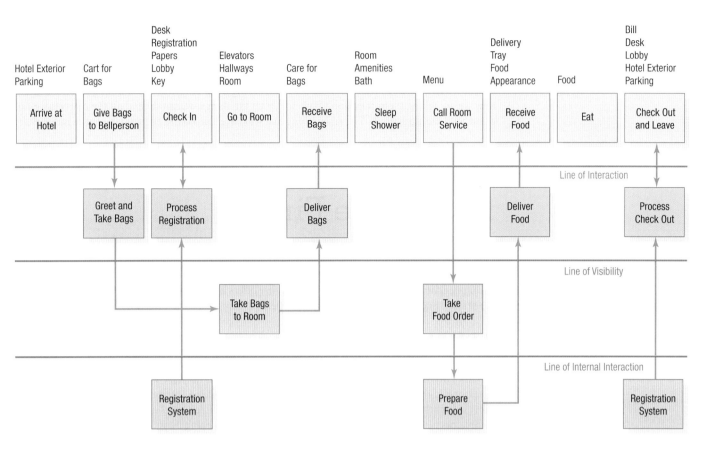

|Fig. 13.1| △

Blueprint for Overnight Hotel Stay

Source: Valarie Zeithaml, Mary Jo Bitner, and Dwayne D. Gremler, *Services Marketing: Integrating Customer Focus across the Firm*, 4th edn (New York: McGraw-Hill, 2006).

Several strategies can produce a better match between demand and supply in a service business.[20] On the demand side:

- **Differential pricing** will shift some demand from peak to off-peak periods. Examples include low early-evening movie prices and weekend discounts for car rentals.[21]
- **Nonpeak demand** can be cultivated. McDonald's pushes breakfast service, and hotels promote minivacation weekends.
- **Complementary services** can provide alternatives to waiting customers, such as cocktail lounges in restaurants and automated teller machines (ATMs) in banks.
- **Reservation systems** are a way to manage the demand level. Airlines, hotels, and physicians employ them extensively.

On the supply side:

- **Part-time employees** can serve peak demand. Colleges add part-time teachers when enrollment goes up, stores hire extra clerks during holiday periods, and restaurants call in part-time servers when needed.
- **Peak-time efficiency** routines can allow employees to perform only essential tasks during peak periods. Paramedics assist physicians during busy periods.
- **Increased consumer participation** can be encouraged. Consumers fill out their own medical records or bag their own groceries.
- **Shared services** can improve offerings. Several hospitals can share medical-equipment purchases.
- **Facilities for future expansion** can be a good investment. An amusement park buys surrounding land for later development.

Many airlines, hotels, and resorts send e-mail alerts to self-selected segments of their customer base that offer special short-term discounts and promotions. After 40 years of making people stand in line at its theme parks, Disney instituted Fastpass, which allows visitors to reserve a spot in line and eliminate the wait. When visitors were polled, it turned out that 95 percent liked the change. Disney's Dale Stafford told a reporter, "We have been teaching people how to stand in line since 1955, and now we are telling them they don't have to. Of all the things we can do and all the marvels we can create with the attractions, this is something that will have a profound effect on the entire industry."[22]

Marketing Strategies for Service Firms

At one time, service firms lagged behind manufacturing firms in their use of marketing because they were small, or they were professional businesses that did not use marketing, or they faced large demand or little competition. This has certainly changed. The Marketing Memo: *Recommendations for Improving Service Quality* offers a comprehensive set of guidelines to which top service-marketing organizations can adhere.

A Shifting Customer Relationship

Not all companies, however, have invested in providing superior service, at least not to all customers. In many service industries, such as airlines, banks and hotels, customer satisfaction has actually dropped in recent years.[23] Customers complain about inaccurate information; unresponsive, rude, or poorly trained personnel; and long wait times. Even worse, many customers find their complaints never actually successfully reach a live human being because of slow or faulty phone or online customer service. Such incidents are common in many places in the Arab market:

- Salespeople not paying attention to customers when they enter their shops, and salespeople lacking the sufficient knowledge about products sold.
- Salespeople "pressurizing" customers to buy their products.
- Appointments for maintaining appliances such as air conditioning units not being respected, and being delayed by 24–48 hours.
- Enquiries sent to companies by e-mail sometimes not being taken care of.

It doesn't have to be that way. Raya, one of the leading distributors of mobile phones, appliances, and electronics in the region, is able to handle the increase in number of phone calls to its five-digit short number, especially during sales promotions, because customer-service representatives are well-trained and briefed about the products that are sold after going through specialized training courses. Raya also has a special team for technical issues, in case a customer has a more specific technical question.[24]

Hewlett-Packard tries to respond to every e-mail query within an hour, and usually answers within 10 minutes. The firm monitors its e-mail centers minute by minute to ensure it meets its service-quality standards. Because of its successful e-mail service centers, HP received 25 percent fewer calls to its call center between 2005 and 2006. E-mail volume rose, which improved profits because an e-mail response costs HP 60 percent less than a phone call.

E-mail response must be implemented properly to be effective.[25] One expert believes companies should (1) send an automated reply to tell customers when a more complete answer will arrive (ideally within 24 hours); (2) ensure the subject line always contains the company name; (3) make the message easy to scan for relevant information; and (4) give customers an easy way to respond with follow-up questions.[26]

PROFIT TIERS Firms have decided to raise fees and lower service to those customers who barely pay their way and to coddle big spenders to retain their patronage as long as possible. Customers in high-profit tiers get special discounts, promotional offers, and lots of special service; customers in lower-profit tiers may get more fees, stripped-down service, and voice messages to process their inquiries.

Mobinil's high-value customers have a dedicated customer service line, where they receive faster and more comprehensive customer-service support. High-value customers at Commercial

Recommendations for Improving Service Quality

Pioneers in conducting academic service research, Berry, Parasuraman, and Zeithaml offer 10 lessons that they maintain are essential for improving service quality across service industries.

1. **Listening.** Understand what customers really want through continuous learning about the expectations and perceptions of customers and noncustomers (for instance, by means of a service-quality information system).

2. **Reliability.** Reliability is the single most important dimension of service quality and must be a service priority.

3. **Basic service.** Service companies must deliver the basics and do what they are supposed to do: keep promises, use common sense, listen to customers, keep customers informed, and be determined to deliver value to customers.

4. **Service design.** Develop a holistic view of the service while managing its many details.

5. **Recovery.** To satisfy customers who encounter a service problem, service companies should encourage customers to complain (and make it easy for them to do so), respond quickly and personally, and develop a problem-resolution system.

6. **Surprising customers.** Although reliability is the most important dimension in *meeting* customers' service expectations, process dimensions such as assurance, responsiveness, and empathy are most important in *exceeding* customer expectations, for example, by surprising them with uncommon swiftness, grace, courtesy, competence, commitment, and understanding.

7. **Fair play.** Service companies must make special efforts to *be* fair, and to *demonstrate* fairness, to customers and employees.

8. **Teamwork.** Teamwork is what enables large organizations to deliver service with care and attentiveness by improving employee motivation and capabilities.

9. **Employee research.** Marketers should conduct research with employees to reveal why service problems occur and what companies must do to solve problems.

10. **Servant leadership.** Quality service comes from inspired leadership throughout the organization; from excellent service-system design; from the effective use of information and technology; and from a slow-to-change, invisible, all-powerful, internal force called corporate culture.

Sources: Leonard L. Berry, A. Parasuraman, and Valarie A. Zeithaml, "Ten Lessons for Improving Service Quality," *MSI Reports Working Paper Series, No.03-001* (Cambridge, MA: Marketing Science Institute, 2003), pp. 61–82. See also Leonard L. Berry's books, *On Great Service: A Framework for Action* (New York: Free Press, 2006) and *Discovering the Soul of Service* (New York: Free Press, 1999), as well as his articles, Leonard L. Berry, Venkatesh Shankar, Janet Parish, Susan Cadwallader, and Thomas Dotzel, "Creating New Markets through Service Innovation," *Sloan Management Review*, Winter 2006, pp. 56–63; Leonard L. Berry, Stephan H. Haeckel, and Lewis P. Carbone, "How to Lead the Customer Experience," *Marketing Management*, January–February 2003, pp. 18–23; and Leonard L. Berry, Kathleen Seiders, and Dhruv Grewal, "Understanding Service Convenience," *Journal of Marketing*, July 2002, pp. 1–17.

International Bank (CIB) receive a special account manager to advise them, in addition to special customer-service treatment.[27] Companies that provide differentiated levels of service, however, must be careful about claiming superior service: the customers who receive poor treatment will bad-mouth the company and injure its reputation. Delivering services that maximize both customer satisfaction and company profitability can be challenging.

CUSTOMER EMPOWERMENT Customers are becoming more sophisticated about buying product-support services and are pressing for 'services unbundling.' They may want separate prices for each service element and the right to select the elements they want. Customers also increasingly dislike having to deal with a multitude of service providers handling different types of equipment. Some third-party service organizations now service a greater range of equipment.

Most important, the internet has empowered customers by letting them vent their rage about bad service—or reward good service—and have their comments beamed around the world with a mouse click.[28] Ninety percent of angry customers reported that they shared their story with a friend. Now, they can share their stories with strangers via the internet, or "word of mouth on steroids" as some say. With a few clicks on the Planetfeedback.com website, shoppers can send an e-mail complaint, compliment, suggestion, or question directly to a company with the option to post comments publicly at the site as well. Most companies respond quickly, some within an hour.

More important than simply responding to a disgruntled customer, however, is preventing dissatisfaction from occurring in the future. That may mean simply taking the time to nurture customer relationships and give customers attention from a real person. Vodafone Egypt invested in expanding its customer-service support, especially with the increase in demand for data lines as opposed to voice lines. A dedicated customer-service line was provided for those who need to ask about technical issues related to installing, operating, and paying for data lines.[29]

JetBlue   JetBlue is one of the most recently established domestic airline carriers in the United States. Former CEO David Neeleman set the bar high for responding to enraged customers after the company's drastic Valentine's Day failure in 2007. During storms in New York City, JetBlue left hundreds of passengers stranded aboard grounded aircraft—some for longer than 9 hours—and cancelled more than 1,000 flights. JetBlue had built its reputation on being a more responsive, humane company in an era of minimal services and maximal delays for airline passengers. Hence, Neeleman knew he had to act fast to stem another kind of storm: a whirlwind of customer defections. Within 24 hours, Neeleman had placed full-page ads in newspapers nationwide in which he personally responded to JetBlue's debacle. "We are sorry and embarrassed," the ads declared, "But most of all we are deeply sorry." Along with the heartfelt apology, JetBlue gave concrete reparations to passengers. Neeleman announced a new "customer bill of rights" that promises passengers travel credits for excessive waits. For instance, passengers who are unable to disembark from an arriving flight for 3 hours or more will receive vouchers worth the full value of their round-trip ticket. Waiting for as little as 30 minutes will bring smaller amounts. JetBlue will also hand out vouchers for the full amount of passengers' round trips if a flight is cancelled within 12 hours of a scheduled departure. The apology, backed by concrete benefits for the angry and inconvenienced passengers, netted kudos for the company from both the business press and JetBlue's own true blue customers. Neeleman eventually stepped down as CEO though, as new management was brought in to address some of the growth challenges the airline faced.[30]

COPRODUCTION   The reality is that customers do not merely purchase and use services, they play an active role in the delivery of that service every step of the way.[31] Their words and actions affect the quality of their service experiences and those of others, and the productivity of frontline employees. One study estimated that one-third of all service problems are caused by the customer.[32] With an increasing shift to self-service technologies, this percentage can be expected to rise.

Preventing service failures from ever happening to begin with is crucial, as service recovery is always challenging. One of the biggest problems is attribution—customers will often feel that the firm is at fault or, even if not, that it is still responsible for righting any wrongs. Unfortunately, although many firms have well-designed and executed procedures to deal with their own failures, they find that managing customer failures is much more difficult.

△ **Figure 13.2** displays the four broad categories of root causes for customer failures, although there often are multiple causes at work. Solutions come in all forms, as illustrated by some of the following examples.[33]

|Fig. 13.2| △

Root Causes of Customer Failure

Source: Stephen Tax, Mark Colgate, and David Bowen, *MIT Sloan Management Review*, Spring 2006, pp. 30–38.

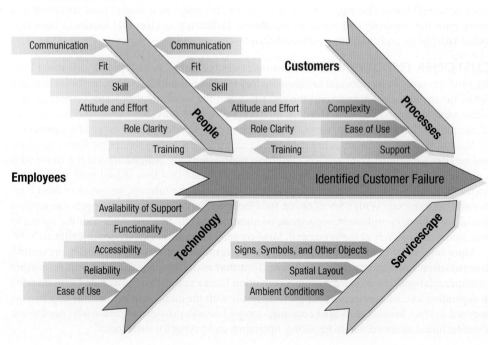

1. **Redesign processes and redefine customer roles to simplify service encounters.** One of the reasons why many customers like to go to Carnivore, an African restaurant, is the flat fee each customers pays, which allows customers to eat as much of the different varieties of meats they like, gives customers greater flexibility, and allows them to know what they will pay up front.

2. **Incorporate the right technology to aid employees and customers.** Circuit City keeps a virtual copy of purchase information in case customers are unable to produce a receipt needed for a return.

3. **Create high-performance customers by enhancing their role clarity, motivation, and ability.** Mobinil reminds its customers to temporarily suspend their lines when they are not using them, for example when travelling abroad for a while. This is useful for many Egyptians who work in the Arabian Gulf and come to Egypt only during the summer vacation.

4. **Encourage 'customer citizenship' where customers help customers.** At golf courses, players can not only follow the rules by playing and behaving appropriately, they can encourage others to do so.

Holistic Marketing for Services

The service outcome, and whether people will remain loyal to a service provider, is influenced by a host of variables. One study identified more than 800 critical behaviors that cause customers to switch services.[34] These behaviors fall into eight categories (see ▦ **Box 13.2**).

Holistic marketing for services requires external, internal, and interactive marketing (see △ **Figure 13.3**).[35] *External marketing* describes the normal work of preparing, pricing, distributing, and promoting the service to customers. *Internal marketing* describes training

---

BOX 13.2 ▦	Factors Leading to Customer Switching Behavior

Pricing

- High price
- Price increases
- Unfair pricing
- Deceptive pricing

Inconvenience

- Location/hours
- Wait for appointment
- Wait for service

Core Service Failure

- Service mistakes
- Billing errors
- Service catastrophe

Service Encounter Failures

- Uncaring
- Impolite
- Unresponsive
- Unknowledgeable

Response to Service Failure

- Negative response
- No response
- Reluctant response

Competition

- Found better service

Ethical Problems

- Cheat
- Hard sell
- Unsafe
- Conflict of interest

Involuntary Switching

- Customer moved
- Provider closed

Source: Susan M. Keaveney, "Customer Switching Behavior in Service Industries: An Exploratory Study," *Journal of Marketing*, April 1995, pp. 71–82. Copyright © 1995 American Marketing Association. Used with permission.

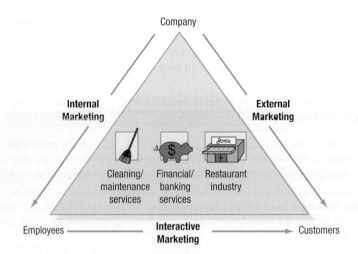

|Fig. 13.3| △

Three Types of Marketing in Service Industries

and motivating employees to serve customers well. The most important contribution the marketing department can make is arguably to be "exceptionally clever in getting everyone else in the organization to practice marketing."[36]

Singapore Airlines (SIA)

Singapore Airlines is consistently recognized as the world's 'best' airline—it wins so many awards, it has to update its website monthly to keep up to date—in large part due to its stellar efforts at holistic marketing. SIA continually strives to create a 'wow effect' and surpass the expectations of its customers. Famous for pampering passengers, it was the first to launch individual video screens at airplane seats. To improve its food, SIA built the first-of-its-kind US$1 million simulator to mimic the air pressure and humidity found inside a plane. Because taste buds change in the air, SIA found that, among other things, it needed to cut back on spices. SIA places a high emphasis on training through its Transforming Customer Service (TCS) program, which includes staff in five key operational areas: cabin crew, engineering, ground services, flight operations, and sales support. The TCS culture is embedded in all management training, company-wide. TCS also uses a 40-30-30 rule in its holistic approach to people, processes, and products: 40 percent of resources go to training and invigorating staff, 30 percent is spent on reviewing process and procedures, and the last 30 percent on creating new product and service ideas. In 2007, with its innovatively designed Boeing 777-300 ERS and Airbus A380 planes, SIA set new standards of comforts in all classes of service, from eight private minirooms in first class to wider seats, AC power supplies, and USB ports in coach. In business class, SIA offers its customers fully-flat beds, high tech entertainment, and a unique gourmet menu, which make flying with SIA a pleasure that offers you all the comfort needed.[37]

Singapore Airlines adopts a holistic approach to its services, dividing its resources between training staff (employees), reviewing its processes (company), and creating new products and services (customers).

Interactive marketing describes the employees' skill in serving the client. Clients judge service not only by its *technical quality* (was the surgery successful?), but also by its *functional quality* (did the surgeon show concern and inspire confidence?).[38] Teamwork is often key, and delegating authority to frontline employees can allow for greater flexibility and adaptability in service delivery through better problem solving, closer employee cooperation, and more efficient knowledge transfer.[39]

Technology also has great power to make service workers more productive. Many physicians and nurses now carry wireless laptop-like devices in their coat pockets from exam room to exam room. These devices contain all relevant patient information and charts, e-mail correspondence, suggested treatments for certain diagnoses, and billing information. They also allow the physicians to write prescriptions, and they store and automatically process all information entered during the patient visit.

Dubai Smile Dental Center

Dubai Smile Dental Center installed the first automated dental-practice management system, with the support of Dubai's Department of Health and Medical Services (DOHMS) and Global Information Technology (GIT), one of the leading IT system suppliers in the Arab world. With the new dental-practice management system—Dental4Windows—doctors save on paper, time, and money, and communication between doctors and patients is more secure and efficient. The center keeps its patients' information electronically; this information can be shared with other authorized medical practitioners, making the visit to the dentist a smoother and easier process.[40]

Dubai Smile Dental Center uses electronic systems to store information about their patients, which facilitates sharing it with other authorized medical practitioners.

Companies, however, must avoid pushing productivity so hard that they reduce perceived quality. Some methods lead to too much standardization. Service providers must deliver 'high touch' as well as 'high tech.'

Charles Schwab

Charles Schwab, one of the largest discount brokerage houses in the United States, uses the telephone, internet, and wireless devices to create an innovative combination of high-tech and high-touch services. One of the first major brokerage houses to provide online trading, Schwab today services almost 8 million individual and institutional accounts. It has avoided competing on price with low-priced competitors such as Ameritrade.com, and instead has assembled the most comprehensive financial and company information resources to be found online. It offers account information and proprietary research from retail brokers; real-time quotes; an after-hours trading program; the Schwab learning center; live events; online chats with customer-service representatives; a global investing service; and market updates delivered by e-mail. Besides the discount brokerage, the firm offers mutual funds, annuities, bond trading, and now mortgages through its Charles Schwab Bank. Despite a lull in 2004, Schwab fired back to lead its competitors by focusing on three areas: superior service (online, via phone, and in local branch offices), innovative products, and low prices.[41]

The internet lets firms improve their service offerings and strengthen their relationships with customers by allowing for true interactivity, customer-specific and situational personalization, and real-time adjustments of the firm's offerings.[42] But as companies collect, store, and use more information about customers, concerns have arisen about security and privacy.[43] Companies must incorporate the proper safeguards and reassure customers about their efforts.

Managing Service Quality

The service quality of a firm is tested at each service encounter. If service personnel are bored, cannot answer simple questions, or are visiting with each other while customers are waiting, customers will think twice about doing business again with that seller.

Customer Expectations

Customers form service expectations from many sources, such as past experiences, word of mouth, and advertising. In general, customers compare the *perceived service* with the *expected service*.[44] If the perceived service falls below the expected service, customers are disappointed. Successful companies add benefits to their offering that not only *satisfy* customers but surprise and *delight* them. Delighting customers is a matter of exceeding expectations.[45]

Kempinski Hotel Mall of the Emirates
A "magical marriage of sand and snow" brings together the essence of the Gulf desert and the atmosphere of alpine snow at the indoor ski park, Ski Dubai, the first of its kind in the Arab world. It is situated in the Kempinski Hotel Mall of the Emirates, winner of the 2010 World Travel Award's Middle East Leading Leisure Hotel prize. It is not just a five-star hotel: every guest at the Kempinski hotel is considered a star. What sets the Kempinski apart is the way it fulfills the simplest of requests with the greatest service. Every service is tailored to be an experience of luxury, uniqueness, and indulgence.[46]

The service-quality model in △ **Figure 13.4** highlights the main requirements for delivering high service quality.[47] It identifies five gaps that cause unsuccessful delivery:

1. *Gap between consumer expectation and management perception.* Management does not always correctly perceive what customers want. Hospital administrators may think patients want better food, but patients may be more concerned with nurse responsiveness.
2. *Gap between management perception and service-quality specification.* Management might correctly perceive customers' wants but not set a performance standard. Hospital administrators may tell the nurses to give 'fast' service without specifying it in minutes.
3. *Gap between service-quality specifications and service delivery.* Personnel might be poorly trained, or incapable of or unwilling to meet the standard; or they may be held to conflicting standards, such as taking time to listen to customers and serving them fast.
4. *Gap between service delivery and external communications.* Consumer expectations are affected by statements made by company representatives and ads. If a hospital brochure shows a beautiful room, but the patient arrives and finds the room to be cheap and tacky-looking, external communications have distorted the customer's expectations.
5. *Gap between perceived service and expected service.* This gap occurs when the consumer misperceives the service quality. The physician may keep visiting the patient to show care, but the patient may interpret this as an indication that something really is wrong.

|Fig. 13.4| △

Service Quality Model

Sources: A. Parasuraman, Valarie A. Zeithaml, and Leonard L. Berry, "A Conceptual Model of Service Quality and Its Implications for Future Research," *Journal of Marketing*, Autumn 1985, p. 44. Reprinted with permission of the American Marketing Association. The model is more fully discussed or elaborated in Valarie Zeithaml, Mary Jo Bitner, and Dwayne D. Gremler, *Services Marketing: Integrating Customer Focus across the Firm*, 4th edn (New York: McGraw-Hill, 2006).

marketing
marketing
Memo

Assessing E-Service Quality

Academic researchers Zeithaml, Parasuraman, and Malhotra define online service quality as the extent to which a website facilitates efficient and effective shopping, purchasing, and delivery. They identified 11 dimensions of perceived e-service quality: access, ease of navigation, efficiency, flexibility, reliability, personalization, security/privacy, responsiveness, assurance/trust, site aesthetics, and price knowledge. Some of these service-quality dimensions were the same online as offline, but some specific underlying attributes were different. Different dimensions emerged with e-service quality too. Empathy didn't seem to be as important online, unless there were service problems. Core dimensions of regular service quality were efficiency, fulfillment, reliability, and privacy; core dimensions of service recovery were responsiveness, compensation, and real-time access to help.

Another set of academic researchers, Wolfinbarger and Gilly, developed a reduced scale of online service quality with four key dimensions: reliability/fulfillment, website design, security/privacy, and customer service. The researchers interpret their study findings to suggest that the most basic building blocks of a "compelling online experience" are reliability and functionality to provide time savings, easy transactions, good selection, in-depth information, and the "right level" of personalization. Their 14-item scale is displayed here:

Reliability/fulfillment

The product that came was represented accurately by the website.

You get what you ordered from this website.

The product is delivered by the time promised by the company.

Website design

This website provides in-depth information.

The site doesn't waste my time.

It is quick and easy to complete a transaction at this website.

The level of personalization at this site is about right, not too much or too little.

This website has good selection.

Security/privacy

I feel that my privacy is protected at this site.

I feel safe in my transactions with this website.

This website has adequate security transactions.

Customer service

The company is willing and ready to respond to customer needs.

When you have a problem, the website shows a sincere interest in solving it.

Enquiries are answered promptly.

Sources: Mary Wolfinbarger and Mary C. Gilly, "E-TailQ: Dimensionalizing, Measuring, and Predicting E-Tail Quality," *Journal of Retailing*, 79, Autumn 2003, pp. 183–98; Valarie A. Zeithaml, A. Parsu Parasuraman, and Arvind Malhotra, "A Conceptual Framework for Understanding E-Service Quality: Implications for Future Research and Managerial Practice," *Marketing Science Institute Working Paper*, Report No. 00-115, 2000.

Based on this service-quality model, researchers identified the following five determinants of service quality, in order of importance.[48]

1. *Reliability.* The ability to perform the promised service dependably and accurately.
2. *Responsiveness.* The willingness to help customers and to provide prompt service.
3. *Assurance.* The knowledge and courtesy of employees and their ability to convey trust and confidence.
4. *Empathy.* The provision of caring, individualized attention to customers.
5. *Tangibles.* The appearance of physical facilities, equipment, personnel, and communication materials.

Based on these five factors, the researchers developed the 22-item SERVQUAL scale (see **Box 13.3**).[49] They also note there is a *zone of tolerance* or a range where a service dimension would be deemed satisfactory, anchored by the minimum level consumers are willing to accept and the level they believe can and should be delivered. The Marketing Memo: *Assessing E-Service Quality* reviews two models of online service quality. The Marketing Insight: *The Role of Expectations in Service-Quality Perceptions* on page 357 describes important recent research on services marketing.

Best Practices of Service-Quality Management

Various studies have shown that well-managed service companies share the following common practices: a strategic concept, a history of top-management commitment to quality, high standards, self-service technologies, systems for monitoring service performance and customer complaints, and an emphasis on employee satisfaction. Raya, a leading IT solutions and telecommunications provider based in Cairo, provides its clients with tele-service support for all customer enquiries.

BOX 13.3   SERVQUAL Attributes

Reliability

- Providing service as promised
- Dependability in handling customers' service problems
- Performing services right the first time
- Providing services at the promised time
- Maintaining error-free records
- Employees who have the knowledge to answer customer questions

Responsiveness

- Keeping customers informed as to when services will be performed
- Prompt service to customers
- Willingness to help customers
- Readiness to respond to customers' requests

Assurance

- Employees who instill confidence in customers
- Making customers feel safe in their transactions
- Employees who are consistently courteous

Empathy

- Giving customers individual attention
- Employees who deal with customers in a caring fashion
- Having the customer's best interests at heart
- Employees who understand the needs of their customers
- Convenient business hours

Tangibles

- Modern equipment
- Visually appealing facilities
- Employees who have a neat, professional appearance
- Visually appealing materials associated with the service

Source: A. Parasuraman, Valarie A. Zeithaml, and Leonard L. Berry, "A Conceptual Model of Service Quality and Its Implications for Future Research," *Journal of Marketing*, Autumn 1985, pp. 41–50. Reprinted by permission of American Marketing Association.

Raya Contact Center

Raya has signed a contract with Ahli United Bank to implement tele-service support for Ahli United Bank customers enquiring about their loans and accounts. Raya Contact Center will provide "database profiling and validation, general inquiries, complaints handling, and marketing and advertising campaign handling." Raya's Contact Center was the first choice for Ahli United Bank, due to the company's well-known reputation and experience with the banking sector. The contact center will serve as a 'help desk' and a source of information for those enquiring about financial product offerings, and is designed to facilitate the management and monitoring of the service level. These banking best practices will enable Raya to handle a high volume of calls from customers in a timely fashion, and will enrich the service experience for customers, which in turn will result in better customer loyalty and retention.[50]

Raya aims for its contact center to act as a 'help desk' and a source of information about its financial products.

STRATEGIC CONCEPT Top service companies are 'customer-obsessed.' They have a clear sense of their target customers and their needs. They have developed a distinctive strategy for satisfying these needs. At the Four Seasons luxury hotel chain, employees must pass four interviews before being hired. Each hotel also employs a 'guest historian' to track guest preferences.

TOP-MANAGEMENT COMMITMENT Companies such as Marriott, Disney, and Aramex have a thorough commitment to service quality. Their managements look not only at financial performance on a monthly basis, but also at service performance. Ray Kroc of McDonald's insisted on continually measuring each McDonald's outlet on its conformance to QSCV: quality, service, cleanliness, and value. Some companies

Marketing Insight

The Role of Expectations in Service-Quality Perceptions

The service-quality model in Figure 13.5 highlights some of the gaps that cause unsuccessful service delivery. Subsequent research has extended the model to incorporate additional considerations. One *dynamic process model* of service quality was based on the premise that customer perceptions and expectations of service quality change over time, but at any one point they are a function of prior expectations about what *will* and what *should* happen during the service encounter, as well as the *actual* service delivered during the last contact. Tests of the model reveal that the two different types of expectation have opposite effects on perceptions of service quality.

1. ***Increasing*** customer expectations of what the firm *will* deliver can lead to improved perceptions of overall service quality.

2. ***Decreasing*** customer expectations of what the firm *should* deliver can lead to improved perceptions of overall service quality.

Much work has validated the role of expectations in consumers' interpretations and evaluations of the service encounter and the relationship they adopt with a firm over time. Consumers are often forward-looking with respect to their decision to keep or switch from a service relationship. Any marketing activity that affects current or expected future usage can help to solidify a service relationship.

With continuously provided services, such as public utilities, health care, financial services, computing services, insurance, and other professional, membership, or subscription services, customers have been observed to mentally calculate their *payment equity*: the perceived fairness of the level of economic benefits derived from service usage in relationship to the level of economic costs. Payment costs typically consist of some combination of an initial payment such as a membership fee or retainer; a fixed, periodic fee such as a monthly service charge; and a variable fee such as usage-based charges. Payment benefits depend on current payment and usage levels. The perceived fairness of the exchange determines service satisfaction and future usage. In other words, customers ask themselves, "Am I using this service enough, given what I pay for it?"

There can be a dark side to long-term service relationships. For example, with an ad agency, the client may feel that over time, the agency loses objectivity and becomes stale in its thinking or begins to take advantage of the relationship.

Sources: Roland T. Rust and Tuck Siong Chung, "Marketing Models of Service and Relationships," *Marketing Science*, 25, November–December 2006, pp. 560–580; Katherine N. Lemon, Tiffany Barnett White, and Russell S. Winer, "Dynamic Customer Relationship Management: Incorporating Future Considerations into the Service Retention Decision," *Journal of Marketing*, 6, January 2002, pp. 1–14; Ruth N. Bolton and Katherine N. Lemon, "A Dynamic Model of Customers' Usage of Services: Usage as an Antecedent and Consequence of Satisfaction," *Journal of Marketing*, 36, May 1999, pp. 171–186; Kent Grayson and Tim Ambler, "The Dark Side of Long-Term Relationships in Marketing Services," *Journal of Marketing Research*, 36, February 1999, pp. 132–141; William Boulding, Ajay Kalra, Richard Staelin, and Valarie A. Zeithaml, "A Dynamic Model of Service Quality: From Expectations to Behavioral Intentions," *Journal of Marketing Research*, 30, February 1993, pp. 7–27.

insert a reminder along with employees' paychecks: Brought to You by the Customer. Sam Walton of Walmart required the following employee pledge: "I solemnly swear and declare that every customer that comes within 10 feet of me, I will smile, look them in the eye, and greet them, so help me Sam."

HIGH STANDARDS The best service providers set high service-quality standards. Citibank aims to answer phone calls within 10 seconds and customer letters within 2 days. The standards must be set *appropriately* high. A 98 percent accuracy standard may sound good, but it would result in 64,000 lost FedEx packages a day; six misspelled words on each page of a book; 400,000 misfilled prescriptions daily; and unsafe drinking water 8 days a year. We can distinguish between companies offering 'merely good' service and those offering 'breakthrough' service, aimed at being 100 percent defect-free.[51]

A service company can differentiate itself by designing a better and faster delivery system. There are three levels of differentiation.[52] The first is *reliability*: some suppliers are more reliable in their on-time delivery, order completeness, and order-cycle time. The second is *resilience*: some suppliers are better at handling emergencies, product recalls, and answering inquiries. The third is *innovativeness*: some suppliers create better information systems, introduce bar coding and mixed pallets, and in other ways help the customer. The Marketing Insight: *Developing Customer Interface Systems* discusses how service marketers must reengineer their customer interface systems for optimal efficiency and effectiveness.

Marketing Insight

Developing Customer Interface Systems

Marketing academics and consultants Jeffrey Rayport and Bernie Jaworski define a *customer-service interface* as any place at which a company seeks to manage a relationship with a customer, whether through people, technology, or some combination of the two. They believe that to deliver high levels of customer-perceived value, any interface should excel on four dimensions:

- *Physical presence and appearance.* Be on the scene in sufficient numbers and presentable in appearance. At the Four Seasons Hotel, the frontline staff is differentiated on appearance as uniformed, clean-cut, businesslike, courteous, individual, and authentic.

- *Cognition.* Be able to recognize patterns, draw intelligent conclusions, and communicate articulately. At Zara, a high-scale retail store, salespeople are skilled at recognizing and rewarding the store's best customers with appropriate service and attention.

- *Emotion or attitude.* Be respectful and attentive, displaying brand-consistent personality attributes, and be emotionally calibrated with the customer. Southwest Airline's flight crew's sense of humor and positive dispositions enhance passengers' travel experience.

- *Connectedness.* Remain well connected to other resources important to the customer's experience. Four Seasons, Zara, and Southwest Airlines all coordinate communications and activities to provide a holistic, positive experience.

Rayport and Jaworski believe companies are facing a crisis in customer interaction and relationship management. Although many companies serve customers through a broad array of interfaces, from retail sales clerks to websites to voice-response telephone systems, these more often constitute an interface *collection*, not an actual interface *system*, as the whole set does not add up to the sum of its parts in its ability to provide superior service and build strong customer relationships. Rising complexity and costs, and customer dissatisfaction can result. Networked technologies, however, such as websites, kiosks, interactive voice-response units, vending machines, and touch screens let managers successfully introduce machines into front office roles that have long been held by humans. Here are a few examples they note:

- Borders, the now defunct book store, deployed Title Sleuth self-service kiosks to take the burden of title searches off its employees. The 300 machines handled up to 1.2 million customer searches per week, and customers using these machines spent 50 percent more per store visit and generated 20 percent more special-order sales.

- Outdoor gear store REI uses interactive kiosks in its stores to hold information about its 78,000 stock keeping units or SKUs: information which no store clerks could keep in their heads. Kiosk sales are growing at 30 percent a year, building revenues to the equivalent of an additional 2,300-square-meter brick-and-mortar store.

- Rite Aid pharmacy chain is using prescription-dispensing robots and interactive voice-response units to fulfill an anticipated labor shortage: prescriptions filled in the United States are expected to grow by 30 percent over the next 2 years while the number of pharmacists is projected to expand by only 6 percent. Automation of rote tasks lets Rite Aid pharmacists use their time to personally attend to customer's needs, providing much-needed brand differentiation in a commoditized category of the retail sector.

According to Rayport and Jaworski, successfully integrating technology into the workforce requires a comprehensive reengineering of the front office to identify what people do best, what machines do best, and how to deploy them separately and together. Managers can take the following steps in conducting a service interface reengineering project:

1. *Understand the experience customers want.* Do customers seek information, advice, social exchange, affirmation, anonymity, discretion, efficiency, or something else? What interactions and relationships will shape those experiences? What are the implications of these experiences for the firm's own goals and objectives?

2. *Understand the potential of technology.* What is the effectiveness and efficiency of possible technology? What new roles can technology assume?

3. *Match the interface type to the task.* Should the interface be people-dominant, machine-dominant, or a hybrid of the two? What are the associated costs and customer outcomes?

4. *Put work in its right place.* Should services be provided proximally (in stores or on site) or remotely (through network connections to customers or operations off site)?

5. *Optimize performance across the system.* Whereas most customers use multiple channels, is the interface system able to capitalize on the economic potential of each?

Sources: Jeffrey F. Rayport and Bernard J. Jaworski, *Best Face Forward* (Boston: Harvard Business School Press, 2005); Jeffrey F. Rayport, Bernard J. Jaworski, and Ellie J. Kyung, "Best Face Forward," *Journal of Interactive Marketing*, 19, Autumn 2005, pp. 67–80; Jeffrey F. Rayport and Bernard J. Jaworski, "Best Face Forward," *Harvard Business Review*, 82, December 2004, pp. 47–58.

SELF-SERVICE TECHNOLOGIES Consumers value convenience in services.[53] Many person-to-person service interactions are being replaced by self-service technologies (SSTs).[54] To the traditional vending machines we can add ATMs, self-pumping at gas stations, self-checkout at hotels, and a variety of activities on the internet, such as ticket purchasing, investment trading, and customization of products.

Not all SSTs improve service quality, but they can make service transactions more accurate, convenient, and faster. Obviously they can also reduce costs. IBM saved US$2 billion by shifting 99 million service telephone calls online.[55] Every company needs to think about improving its service using SSTs.

Some companies have found that the biggest obstacle is not the technology itself, but convincing customers to use it, especially for the first time. Customers must have a clear sense of their roles in the SST process, must see a clear benefit to SST, and must feel they have the ability to actually use it.[56] Etihad Airways has been successful in getting customers to use its self-service kiosks by employing a number of tactics, such as advertising the advantages of self-service, providing customer reps to facilitate the process, and ensuring as many machines are available as possible. Peter Baumgartner, Etihad Airways' chief commercial officer, said: "The introduction of the new self-service kiosks is another achievement in our pledge to continually enhance the services we offer our customers at all times in their journey."[57]

Hotel Front Desks   After a long journey—from taxi to plane, to taxi, to hotel—the hotel's front desk can sometimes seem like a barrier to the longed-for respite of the hotel room. In order to reduce lines and get guests to their rooms more quickly, many hotels are trying to streamline the process through self-service check-in kiosks in the hotel lobby. Many Hilton Hotels use kiosks in their lobbies; travelers can slide in their credit cards and receive their purple key cards. The kiosk is no replacement for the front desk, but it allows front desk staff to truly serve a concierge function, devoting more time to guests who need attention. Hilton Hotels, then, is using a combination of high tech and high touch to give it an advantage in the fiercely competitive hotel industry. In contrast, Kimpton Hotels, a San Francisco-based chain of boutique hotels, is putting all its efforts into beefing up front desk services, going for high touch rather than high tech. The chain is teaching employees how to better read and respond to guest behavior: to differentiate between the hurried guest and the one who seeks more information, such as parents who want to know all the kid-friendly events and activities in the area. "Guests are looking for an expedient friendly process," said Niki Leondakis, chief operating officer of Kimpton Hotels, "but are also using the desk as a complete resource center for all services."[58]

MONITORING SYSTEMS Top firms audit service performance, both their own and competitors', on a regular basis. They collect *voice of the customer* (VOC) *measurements* to probe customer satisfiers and dissatisfiers. They use comparison shopping, ghost shopping, customer surveys, suggestion and complaint forms, service-audit teams, and letters to the president.

Mystery shopping—the use of undercover shoppers who are paid to report back to the company—is now big business: US$600 million in the United States.[59] Fast-food chains, big-box stores, gas stations, and even large government agencies are using mystery shoppers to pinpoint and fix customer-service problems.

We can judge services on *customer importance* and *company performance*. *Importance-performance analysis* rates the various elements of the service bundle and identifies what actions are required. ▢ **Table 13.1** shows how customers rated 14 service elements or attributes of an automobile dealer's service department on importance and performance. For example, "Job done right the first time" (attribute 1) received a mean importance rating of 3.83 and a mean performance rating of 2.63, indicating that customers felt it was highly important but not performed well. The ratings of the 14 elements are displayed in △ **Figure 13.5** and divided into four sections.

- Quadrant A shows important service elements that are not being performed at the desired levels; they include elements 1, 2, and 9. The dealer should concentrate on improving the service department's performance on these elements.

- Quadrant B shows important service elements that are being performed well; the company needs to maintain the high performance.

TABLE 13.1	Customer Importance and Performance Ratings for an Auto Dealership		
Number Attribute	Attribute Description	Mean Importance Rating[a]	Mean Performance Rating[b]
1	Job done right the first time	3.83	2.63
2	Fast action on complaints	3.63	2.73
3	Prompt warranty work	3.60	3.15
4	Able to do any job needed	3.56	3.00
5	Service available when needed	3.41	3.05
6	Courteous and friendly service	3.41	3.29
7	Car ready when promised	3.38	3.03
8	Perform only necessary work	3.37	3.11
9	Low prices on service	3.29	2.00
10	Clean up after service work	3.27	3.02
11	Convenient to home	2.52	2.25
12	Convenient to work	2.43	2.49
13	Courtesy buses and cars	2.37	2.35
14	Send out maintenance notices	2.05	3.33

[a] Ratings obtained from a four-point scale of extremely important (4), important (3), slightly important (2), and not important (1).
[b] Ratings obtained from a four-point scale of excellent (4), good (3), fair (2), and poor (1). A 'no basis for judgment' category was also provided.

|Fig. 13.5|

Importance-Performance Analysis

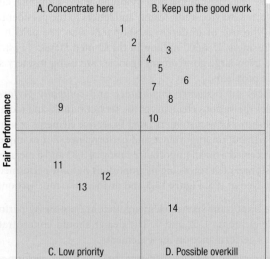

- Quadrant C shows minor service elements that are being delivered in a mediocre way but do not need any attention.
- Quadrant D shows that a minor service element, "Send out maintenance notices," is being performed in an excellent manner.

Perhaps the company should spend less on sending out maintenance notices and use the savings to improve performance on important elements. Management can enhance the analysis by checking on the competitors' performance levels on each element.[60]

SATISFYING CUSTOMER COMPLAINTS Every complaint is a gift if handled well. Companies that encourage disappointed customers to complain—and also empower employees to remedy the situation on the spot—have been shown to achieve higher revenues and greater profits than companies that do not have a systematic approach for addressing service failures.[61] Pizza Hut prints its toll-free number on all pizza boxes. When a customer complains, Pizza Hut sends a voicemail to the store manager, who must call the customer within 48 hours and resolve the complaint. Hyatt Hotels also gets high marks on many of these criteria.

Getting frontline employees to adopt *extra-role behaviors* and to advocate the interests and image of the firm to consumers, as well as take initiative and engage in conscientious behavior in dealing with customers, can be a critical asset in handling complaints.[62] Research has shown that customers evaluate complaint incidents in terms of the outcomes they receive, the procedures used to arrive at those outcomes, and the nature of the interpersonal treatment during the process.[63] Companies also are increasing the quality of their *call centers* and their *customer-service representatives* (CSRs).

Handling phone calls more efficiently can improve service, reduce complaints, and extend customer longevity. Yet more often than not the problem isn't poor quality but that customers are asked to use an automated voice-response system instead of interacting with a customer-service representative. Although some automated voices are actually popular with customers—such as Nihal Saad's voice on Mobinil's voice-response system—most just incite frustration and even rage. One Arab world telecommunications company has implemented different automated systems to deal with specific customer concerns more efficiently.

 Mobinil Since its inception in 1998, Mobinil has managed to maintain its position in Egypt and by 2011 had gained the trust of more than 30 million customers. Among the key factors behind Mobinil's success is its ability to handle customer complaints efficiently. Mobinil has created different automated voice-response systems to deal with specific customer concerns. For example, calling 300 allows the customer to check for new Mobinil offers, promotions, and services, whereas calling 210 provides the customer with information about account balances and payment options. Since some customers favor person-to-person communication over automated voices, Mobinil enables its customers to call 110 to speak to a customer-service representative. Customers can also dial a different number to speak directly to a customer-service representative instead of having to listen to prompts first. In addition to the call centers, all its customers can submit an enquiry or complaint via the Mobinil website.[64]

SATISFYING EMPLOYEES AS WELL AS CUSTOMERS Excellent service companies know that positive employee attitudes will promote stronger customer loyalty. Instilling a strong customer orientation in employees can also increase their job satisfaction and commitment, especially if they're in service settings that allow for a high degree of customer-contact time. Employees thrive in customer-contact positions when they have an internal drive to (1) pamper customers, (2) accurately read customer needs, (3) develop a personal relationship with customers, and (4) deliver quality service to solve customers' problems.[65]

Consistent with this reasoning, Sears, a large department store in the United States, found a high correlation between customer satisfaction, employee satisfaction, and store profitability. In companies such as Hallmark, Southwest Airlines, and Four Seasons Hotels, employees exhibit real company pride. Consider the crucial role of employees of Saudi Aramco, a leading producer of crude oil and natural gas.

Saudi Aramco   Oil company Saudi Aramco has a diverse global workforce of 54,000 employees. Every employee is considered a vital contributor to the company's success in supplying the world's petroleum products. Therefore, every single employee is granted a competitive compensation and benefits package, designed to express Saudi Aramco's appreciation to its employees and encourage them to invest their efforts in maintaining the company's top rank position worldwide. Compensation consists of a base salary, plus benefits designed to incentivize employees to accept and continue expatriate assignments. The benefits include competitive retirement, savings, and insurance plans; a repatriation allowance; educational assistance for employees' to enroll their children in international schools; and generous leave allowances, comprising 38 days annual leave, plus 2 to 4 'travel days', and additional company holidays between 9 and 11 days each year. This extensive package goes some way toward explaining the long service of Saudi Aramco's numerous employees.[66]

Given the importance of positive employee attitudes to customer satisfaction, service companies must attract the best employees they can find. They need to market a career rather than just a job. They must design a sound training program and provide support and rewards for good performance. They can use the intranet, internal newsletters, daily reminders, and employee roundtables to reinforce customer-centered attitudes. Finally, they must audit employee job satisfaction regularly.

Managing Service Brands

Some of the world's strongest brands are services: consider financial service leaders such as Citicorp, American Express, and HSBC, and regional ones such as the National Bank of Kuwait, Arab Bank, and Commercial International Bank. Like any brand, service brands must be skillful at differentiating themselves and developing appropriate brand strategies.

Differentiating Services

Service marketers frequently complain about the difficulty of differentiating their services. The deregulation of several major service industries—communications, transportation, energy, banking—has resulted in intense price competition. To the extent that customers view a service as fairly homogeneous, they care less about the provider than about the price.

Marketers, however, can differentiate their service offerings in many ways, through people and processes that add value. The offering can include innovative features. What the customer expects is called the *primary service package*. Vanguard, the second-largest no-load mutual fund company, has a unique client ownership structure that lowers costs and permits better fund returns. Strongly differentiated from many competitors, the brand grew through word of mouth, PR, and viral marketing.[67]

The provider can add *secondary service features* to the package. In the hotel industry, various chains have introduced such secondary service features as merchandise for sale, free breakfast buffets, and loyalty award programs. Marriott is setting up hotel rooms for high-tech travelers who need accommodation that will support computers and e-mail.

Many companies are using the web to offer secondary service features that were never possible before. Conversely, other service providers, including large stores that sell medicine, are adding a human element to combat competition from online businesses. As in-store pharmacies see competition from low-cost online mail-order drugstores, they are playing up the presence of on-site health care professionals. For instance, Brooks Pharmacy is establishing RX Care Centers in many of its remodeled stores. There are private consulting rooms where pharmacists can speak at length with patients about complicated prescription benefit plans, potentially dangerous drug interactions, and embarrassing subjects like urinary incontinence.[68]

Sometimes the company achieves differentiation through the sheer range of its service offerings and the success of its cross-selling efforts. The major challenge is that most service offerings and innovations are easily copied. Still, the company that regularly introduces innovations will gain a succession of temporary advantages over competitors.

Etihad Airways In order to differentiate its service from other distinguished airlines, Etihad Airways offers its customers a unique rewards system. The Etihad Guest Miles program allows customers to enjoy free flights, experience the warmth of the welcome in Etihad's Pearl business class, or the unparalleled luxury of the Diamond first class. What is also unique about the service is that no limits are placed on when the customer can reward herself by spending her Etihad Guest Miles. As an additional special service, customers who fly business or first class are rewarded with a complimentary stay in their choice of two of Abu Dhabi's finest hotels. The more a customer flies with Etihad, the higher she will rise through the three unique tiers of the Etihad guest program, and the more benefits she will enjoy.[69]

Etihad Airways offers a unique loyalty rewards system and complimentary hotel stays for business and first class passengers.

Creativity and innovation is as vital in services as in any industry. There are always ways to improve the customer experience. When a group of hospitality and travel industry experts convened late in 2006 to share their insights into what the ideal 2025 hotel might look like, their visions suggested a totally transformed service experience. One idea, turning hotels into retail showrooms where guests can try out and buy displayed items, was later adopted by chains such as Hyatt and Kimpton. Some of the other ideas have yet to be implemented and may take more time, but they help point out how achieving service excellence is a never-ending process:[70]

- Kinetic corridors could light up with a blanket of stars and illuminated signs to provide guests with an easy, relaxing entry to their rooms.

- A multipurpose bed could be flipped over to create more work surfaces or rise all the way up to be a ceiling panel.

- A multitask chair could be equipped with reading lights, fold-up tablet tray tables, integrated speakers near the ears, and a muscle massager.

Developing Brand Strategies for Services

Developing brand strategies for a service brand requires special attention to choosing brand elements, establishing image dimensions, and devising the branding strategy.

CHOOSING BRAND ELEMENTS   Because services are intangible, and because customers often make decisions and arrangements about them away from the actual service location itself (at home or at work), brand recall becomes critically important. So an easy-to-remember brand name is critical.

Other brand elements—logos, symbols, characters, and slogans—can also 'pick up the slack' and complement the brand name to build brand awareness and brand image. These brand elements often attempt to make the service and some of its key benefits more tangible, concrete, and real: for example, the 'golden arches' of McDonald's and the 'dynamic nature' of Pepsi.

Because a physical product does not exist, the physical facilities of the service provider—its primary and secondary signage, environmental design and reception area, apparel, collateral material, and so on—are especially important. All aspects of the service-delivery process can be branded, which is why Four Seasons is concerned about the appearance of its front-line employees; why UPS has developed such strong equity with its brown trucks, and why DoubleTree hotels offer warm, fresh-baked cookies as a means of symbolizing care and friendliness.

ESTABLISHING IMAGE DIMENSIONS   Given the human nature of services, it's no surprise that brand personality is an important image dimension for services. Starwood trains its hotel employees and call center operators to convey different experiences for the firm's different hotel chains: Sheraton is positioned as warm, comforting, and casual; Westin is positioned in terms of renewal and is a little more formal; Four Points by Sheraton is designed to be all about honest, uncomplicated comfort.[71]

Cirque du Soleil's branding strategy includes spectacular themed performances by circus players with elaborate costumes, New Age music, and no animals. Each touring production is unique; there are no duplicate casts, protecting the brand from overexposure and easy imitation.

Service firms can also design marketing communication and information programs so that consumers learn more about the brand than the information they get from service encounters alone. In 2000, Mobinil produced its ALO ads, which featured a different advertisement for each of four different regions of Egypt (Upper Egypt, Delta, Cairo, and Alexandria). By catering to the different regions, ALO aimed to inform customers that it was available throughout Egypt.

DEVISING BRANDING STRATEGY Finally, services also must consider developing a brand hierarchy and brand portfolio that permits positioning and targeting of different market segments. Marketers can brand classes of service vertically on the basis of price and quality. Vertical extensions often require subbranding strategies that combine the corporate name with an individual brand name or modifier. In the hotel and airline industries, brand lines and portfolios have been created by brand extension and introductions. Hilton Hotels has a portfolio of brands that includes Hilton Garden Inns to target budget-conscious business travelers and compete with the popular Courtyard by Marriott chain, as well as DoubleTree, Embassy Suites, Homewood Suites, and Hampton Inn. Cirque du Soleil has adopted a very disciplined branding strategy.[72]

 Cirque du Soleil   In its 25-year history, Cirque du Soleil (French for "circus of the sun") has continually broken loose from circus convention. It takes traditional ingredients such as trapeze artists, clowns, muscle men, and contortionists and places them in a nontraditional setting with lavish costumes, New Age music, and spectacular stage designs. And it eliminates other commonly observed elements: there are no animals. Each production is loosely tied together with a theme such as "a tribute to the nomadic soul" (*Varekai*) or "a phantasmagoria of urban life" (*Saltimbanco*). The group has grown from its Quebec street-performance roots to become a half-billion dollar enterprise with 3,000 employees on four continents entertaining audiences of millions annually. Part of the success is a company culture that encourages artistic creativity and innovation and carefully safeguards the brand (see ▬ **Box 13.4**). Each new production is created in-house—roughly one a year—and is unique: there are no duplicate touring companies. In addition to using a varied mix of media and local promotion, an extensive interactive e-mail program to its million-plus-member Cirque Club creates an online community of fans: 20 to 30 percent of all ticket sales for touring shows come from club members. The Cirque du Soleil brand has expanded to encompass a record label, a retail operation, and resident productions in Las Vegas (five in all), Orlando, and Tokyo.

Managing Product-Support Services

No less important than service industries are product-based industries that must provide a service bundle. Manufacturers of equipment—small appliances, office machines, tractors, mainframes, airplanes—all must provide *product-support services*. Product-support service is becoming a major battleground for competitive advantage.

Chapter 12 described how products could be augmented with key service differentiators: ordering ease, delivery, installation, customer training, customer consulting, maintenance, and repair. Some equipment companies, such as Caterpillar Tractor and John Deere, make over 50 percent of their profits from these services. In the global marketplace, companies that make a good product but provide poor local service support are seriously disadvantaged.

Identifying and Satisfying Customer Needs

Customers have three specific worries:[73]

* They worry about reliability and *failure frequency*. A farmer may tolerate a combine harvester that will break down once a year, but not two or three times a year.

BOX 13.4 ▨ Flying High without a Net: Cirque du Soleil's Formula for Creative Success

1. **Cast teams for creative conflict.**

   Cirque officials generally make sure there's a mix of nationalities and viewpoints when they draft a creative team. Then they lock creators in a room with the instructions, "Don't come out till you have something great."

2. **Always shoot for the triple somersault.**

   Cirque's founder, Guy Laliberte, is famous for asking his people to stretch beyond the great to the jawdropping. "It's a commitment to a degree of sophistication and performance that distinguishes Cirque du Soleil productions from their less demanding peers," says coach Boris Verkhovsky.

3. **Recruit the near-great.**

   Elite athletes who just missed the national team generally have the same work ethic, the same tricks, and nearly the same skills as medal winners. The difference: they still have something to prove, and they're rarely prima donnas.

4. **Push the envelope—at the interview.**

   Cirque scouts routinely ask candidates to do something unexpected at their audition: Climb a rope . . . then sing a song when you get to the top ("Happy Birthday" is forbidden). It's a good way to find talent that's multidimensional and comfortable improvising, not to mention a great character test.

5. **Don't be greedy.**

   Cirque limits its show production to one a year. "If we want to have fun creating shows and pushing the boundaries, one show a year is good enough for us. We don't want to jeopardize quality," says Daniel Lamarre, president and CEO of Cirque du Soleil. Besides, "if there's not a creative challenge, we're not going to do a deal, regardless of the financial impact."

6. **Protect creative teams from business pressures.**

   Lamarre isolates his creative teams from the Cirque du Soleil 'machine.' "I want them to eat and breathe their show," he says, "and keeping them away from day-to-day operations is the best thing."

Source: Linda Tischler, "Join the Circus," *Fast Company,* July 2005; 53–58. Reprinted by permission of Fast Company via Copyright Clearance Center.

- They worry about *downtime.* The longer the downtime, the higher the cost. The customer counts on the seller's *service dependability*: the seller's ability to fix the machine quickly, or at least provide a loan as a substitute.[74]
- They worry about *out-of-pocket costs.* How much does the customer have to spend on regular maintenance and repair costs?

A buyer takes all these factors into consideration and tries to estimate the **life-cycle cost**, which is the product's purchase cost plus the discounted cost of maintenance and repair less the discounted salvage value. A one-computer office will need higher product reliability and a faster repair service than an office where other computers are available if one breaks down. An airline needs 100 percent reliability in the air. Where reliability is important, manufacturers or service providers can offer guarantees to promote sales.

life-cycle cost the product's purchase cost plus the discounted cost of maintenance and repair less the discounted salvage value.

To provide the best support, a manufacturer must identify the services customers value most and their relative importance. In the case of expensive equipment, manufacturers offer *facilitating services* such as installation, staff training, maintenance and repair services, and financing. They may also add *value-augmenting services* that extend beyond the functioning and performance of the product itself. Johnson Controls, present in Arab countries such as Egypt, Oman, Qatar, and Saudi Arabia, among others, introduced services that extended beyond its climate control equipment and components business to manage integrated facilities by offering products and services that optimize energy use and improve comfort and security.

A manufacturer can offer, and charge for, product-support services in different ways. One specialty organic-chemical company provides a standard offering plus a basic level of services. If the customer wants additional services, it can pay extra or increase its annual purchases to a higher level, in which case additional services are included. Many companies offer *service contracts* (also called *extended warranties*), in which sellers agree to provide free maintenance and repair services for a specified period of time at a specified contract price.

Product companies must understand their strategic intent and competitive advantage in developing services. Are service units supposed to support or protect existing product businesses or to grow as an independent platform? Are the sources of competitive advantage based on economies of scale or economies of skill?[75] See ■ **Box 13.5** for examples of strategies of different service companies.

Postsale Service Strategy

The quality of customer-service departments varies greatly. At one extreme are departments that simply transfer customer calls to the appropriate person or department for action, with little follow-up. At the other extreme are departments eager to receive customer requests, suggestions, and even complaints and handle them expeditiously. Publications like Business Week have published lists of companies with the best customer service standards in the past—lists which are always changing—which could prove useful to companies.

CUSTOMER-SERVICE EVOLUTION Manufacturers usually start out by running their own parts-and-service departments. They want to stay close to the equipment and know its problems. They also find it expensive and time consuming to train others, and discover that they can make good money running the parts-and-service business, especially if they are the only supplier of the needed parts and can charge a premium price. In fact, many equipment manufacturers price their equipment low and compensate by charging high prices for parts and service.

Over time, manufacturers switch more maintenance and repair service to authorized distributors and dealers. These intermediaries are closer to customers, operate in more locations, and can offer quicker service. Still later, independent service firms emerge and offer a lower price or faster service. A significant percentage of auto-service work is now done outside franchised automobile dealerships by independent garages and chains such as Dubai Cars Clinic in the UAE, or Le Garage in Egypt. Independent service organizations handle mainframes, telecommunications equipment, and a variety of other equipment lines.

BOX 13.5 ■	Service Strategies for Product Companies	
	Strategic Intent	
	Protect or Enhance Product	**Expand Independent Service**
Economies of Scale	Apple's iPod music download and transaction management service (iTunes) Otis Elevator's remote monitoring and diagnostics service Blackberry's messenger system (BBM) Symantec's virus protection and data security services	Cardinal Healthcare's hospital inventory-management services Raya Data Center IBM's data-center-outsourcing services Johnson Controls' integrated facilities-management services
Economies of Skill	Cisco's network integration and maintenance services SAP Systems' integration services UTC's utilities field support services National Petroleum Services Company's machinery and equipment for petroleum companies	Raya trade maintenance services General Electric's aircraft-engine-maintenance services GE Healthcare's hospital equipment-support and diagnostics services for hospital equipment IBM's systems integration services

The left axis label reads: **Source of Competitive Advantage**

Source: Byron G. Auguste, Eric P. Harmon, and Vivek Pandit, "The Right Service Strategies for Product Companies," *The McKinsey Quarterly*, 1, 2006, pp. 41–51. Reprinted by permission of McKinsey Quarterly.

THE CUSTOMER-SERVICE IMPERATIVE Customer-service choices are increasing rapidly, however, and equipment manufacturers increasingly must figure out how to make money on their equipment, independent of service contracts. Some new-car warranties now cover 100,000 miles before servicing. The increase in disposable or never-fail equipment makes customers less inclined to pay 2 to 10 percent of the purchase price every year for a service. A company with several hundred personal computers, printers, and related equipment might find it cheaper to have its own service personnel on site.

Summary

1. A service is any act or performance that one party can offer to another that is essentially intangible and does not result in the ownership of anything. It may or may not be tied to a physical product.

2. Services are intangible, inseparable, variable, and perishable. Each characteristic poses challenges and requires certain strategies. Marketers must find ways to give tangibility to intangibles; to increase the productivity of service providers; to increase and standardize the quality of the service provided; and to match the supply of services with market demand.

3. In the past, service industries lagged behind manufacturing firms in adopting and using marketing concepts and tools, but this situation has now changed. Service marketing must be done holistically: it calls not only for external marketing but also for internal marketing to motivate employees, and interactive marketing to emphasize the importance of both 'high tech' and 'high touch.'

4. Customers' expectations play a critical role in their service experiences and evaluations. Companies must manage service quality by understanding the effects of each service encounter.

5. Top service companies excel at the following practices: a strategic concept, a history of top-management commitment to quality, high standards, self-service technologies, systems for monitoring service performance and customer complaints, and an emphasis on employee satisfaction.

6. To brand a service organization effectively, the company must differentiate its brand through primary and secondary service features and develop appropriate brand strategies. Effective branding programs for services often employ multiple brand elements. They also develop brand hierarchies and portfolios and establish image dimensions to reinforce or complement service offerings.

7. Even product-based companies must provide postpurchase service. To provide the best support, a manufacturer must identify the services customers value most and their relative importance. The service mix includes both presale services (facilitating and value-augmenting services) and postsale services (customer-service departments, repair and maintenance services).

Applications

Marketing Debate

Is Service Marketing Different from Product Marketing?

Some service marketers vehemently maintain that service marketing is fundamentally different from product marketing and that different skills are involved. Some traditional product marketers disagree, saying "good marketing is good marketing."

Take a position: Product and service marketing are fundamentally different *versus* product and service marketing are highly related.

Marketing Discussion

Colleges, universities, and other educational institutions can be classified as service organizations. How can you apply the marketing principles developed in this chapter to your school? Do you have any advice as to how it could become a better service marketer?

Marketing Excellence

>>Emirates Airline

Emirates Airline is one of the top 10 carriers globally in terms of revenue and passenger satisfaction, and has the highest revenue, fleet size, and number of passengers carried of any airline in the region. In 2010 the airline was the largest in the world in terms of scheduled international passenger-kilometers flown and passengers carried. Emirates' mission and core values are committed to the fundamental objective of delivering quality services to customers in a way that far exceeds expectations. Exceeding customers' expectations is harder in the service than the physical goods sector, the difficulties being mainly due to the unique characteristics of services. Emirates Airline managed to create unique customer experience by personalizing service delivery.

Internal marketing is the fundamental principle that led Emirates Airline to realize its tremendous success: the recipient of over 400 international awards, it has expanded its routes to over 111 cities on six continents around the globe, and has 142 modern and technologically advanced wide-body aircraft in service and another 197 aircraft on order to meet the expected future demand. The table below further illustrates the company's progress in the financial year (FY) 2009–2010.

Emirates Airline is convinced that service delivery should embody traits like being cosmopolitan, considerate, personal, thorough, and pioneering. Under the leadership of Sheikh Ahmed bin Saeed Al Makhtoum, critical management decisions are considered through the prism of this commitment to provide world-class customer service while enhancing the knowledge and training of its employees. The Aviation College offers Emirates Airline staff members continuous motivation to learn and upgrade their performance, whether in the classroom, on the job, or through full-scale simulations. Also, it gives Emirates Airline a threefold advantage of:

1. Forging ahead in service quality when other carriers may be cutting back on training programs.
2. Demonstrating to all staff that continuous learning and improvement are essential principles for success.
3. Giving staff an added incentive to continue in serving a world-class airline that is equally committed to employees as "internal customers."

Emirates Airline is growing at a very high rate, which represents a corporate challenge to the organization. Its employees are located in cities and subsidiaries throughout the world. People from different cultures must work together to produce a seamless and positive customer experience. The Aviation College established cultural solidarity among all staff members. The college helps in molding a unified internal corporate brand championship that spans business silos, departmental functions, and geographic locations.

	FY 2008–2009	FY 2009–2010	+/– Year on Year
Revenue	$11.8 billion	$11.8 billion	+0.4%
Net Profit	$187 million	$964 million	+416%
Passengers Carried	22.7 million	27.5 million	+20.8%
Passenger Seat Factor	75.8%	78.1%	+2.3%
Cargo Revenues	$1.9 billion	$1.7 billion	−8.1%
Cargo Carried (tons)	1.4 million	1.6 million	+12.2%

Prices in US$.
Source: www.albawaba.com/business/pr/emirates-skycargo-celebrates-start-new-freighter-service-393971.

Continued on next page >>

Marketing **Excellence**...continued

>>Emirates Airline

Emirates Airline staff members are regularly appraised for performance and potential career development. High-flyers are identified early and given every opportunity to learn and grow. Senior managers are uniquely well developed with frequent rotations among top positions in the company. Also, the college helps Emirates in building a shared understanding of "the big picture" with a commitment to doing what's best for the customers and the business. It helps in building and harmonizing a service culture among the employees. The core principle is that passengers are so important that they should be served not only by the flight hostesses. Hence, the college managed to create the awareness that all departments should zero in on customer needs.

To keep everyone on the same wavelength, the Aviation College created an innovative training program called *Nujoum* (Stars) that helps employees understand the meaning of service in Emirates and what is demanded of each employee to deliver world-class services. Each employee is an important part of service delivery, and has a role to play in personalizing the experience to the passengers and delivering the world best in-flight experience. Nujoum represents a dialogue platform between Emirates and new staff members to keep communication flowing. Additionally, a variety of workshops, simulations, and boot camps are offered to stimulate knowledge sharing on best practices in customer care.

The airline industry is intensely competitive, with every carrier seeking new ways to 'get ahead of the pack.' Emirates' Aviation College offers a great opportunity for introducing new innovations and tracking the progress of competitors closely. It instils in its employees the cultural determination to try things, make them work, and see them through. While excellent staff performance is rewarded with increased pay and position, the most prestigious award of all is reserved for extraordinary acts of truly superior service that makes employees feel like stars.

Questions

1. In your opinion, how does the Aviation College harmonize the Emirates Airline brand?

2. What are the traits that embody the service delivery experience of the Nujoum initiative?

3. Based on your past experience as a customer of other service providers, how should their service delivery have been personalized?

Sources: *The Emirates Group Annual Report 2009–2010*, www.theemiratesgroup.com/english/facts-figures/archive/2009-2010.aspx.

In this chapter, we will address the following questions:

1. How do consumers process and evaluate prices? (pg. 372)

2. How should a company set prices initially for products or services? (pg. 379)

3. How should a company adapt prices to meet varying circumstances and opportunities? (pg. 392)

4. When should a company initiate a price change? (pg. 397)

5. How should a company respond to a competitor's price change? (pg. 399)

Developing Pricing Strategies and Programs

Price is the one element of the marketing mix that produces revenue; the other elements produce costs. Prices are perhaps the easiest element of the marketing program to adjust; product features, channels, and even communications take more time. Price also communicates to the market the company's intended value positioning of its product or brand. A well-designed and marketed product can command a price premium and reap big profits. Consider Gillette.

 Gillette has a tradition of product innovation, beginning with the invention of the safety razor by King C. Gillette in 1901. Subsequent product breakthroughs include the first twin-blade shaving system, Trac II, in 1971; the first razor with a pivoting head, Atra, in 1977; the first razor with spring-mounted twin blades, Sensor, in 1989; and the first triple-blade system, Mach3, in 1998. January 2006 saw the launch of the "best shave on the planet" with the six-bladed Fusion—five blades in the front for regular shaving and one in the back for trimming—in both power and nonpower versions. Gillette conducts exhaustive consumer research in designing its new products and markets aggressively to spread the word. Gillette spent over US$1.2 billion on research and development after the Mach3 was introduced. About 9,000 men tested potential new products and preferred the new Fusion razor by a two-to-one margin over the older Mach3 varieties. To back the introduction, Procter & Gamble, which acquired Gillette in 2005 for $57 billion (a record five times sales), spent $200 million in the United States and over $1 billion worldwide. The payoff? Gillette enjoys enormous market leadership in the razors and blades categories, owning roughly 70 percent of the global market. Gillette also commands sizable price premiums. Refills for the Fusion Power cost $14 for a four-pack, compared to $5.29 for a five-pack of Sensor Excel. All this adds up to significant, sustained profitability for corporate owner P&G.[1]

The Gillette example reveals the power of pricing. Pricing decisions are clearly complex and difficult though, and many marketers neglect their pricing strategies.[2] Holistic marketers must take into account many factors in making pricing decisions: the company, the customers, the competition, and the marketing environment. Pricing decisions must be consistent with the firm's marketing strategy and its target markets and brand positionings.

In this chapter, we provide concepts and tools to facilitate the setting of initial prices and adjusting prices over time and markets. ▽

Understanding Pricing

Nescafé Cappucino was introduced at a lower price than their regular coffee sachets.

Price is not just a number on a tag. Price comes in many forms and performs many functions. Rent, tuition, fares, fees, rates, tolls, retainers, wages, and commissions all may in some way be the price you pay for some good or service. It's also made up of many components. If you buy a new car, the sticker price may be adjusted by rebates and dealer incentives. Some firms allow for payment through multiple forms, such as US$129 plus 25,000 frequent flier miles from an airline loyalty program.[3]

Throughout most of history, prices were set by negotiation between buyers and sellers. Bargaining is still common in the Arab world. Customers negotiate prices on all varieties of products ranging from clothing to cars and houses. Setting one price for all buyers is a relatively modern idea that arose with the development of large-scale retailing at the end of the nineteenth century. F. W. Woolworth, Tiffany and Co., John Wanamaker, and others advertised a 'strictly one-price policy,' because they carried so many items and supervised so many employees.

Traditionally, price has operated as the major determinant of buyer choice. Consumers and purchasing agents have more access to price information and price discounters. Consumers put pressure on retailers to lower their prices. Retailers put pressure on manufacturers to lower their prices. The result is a marketplace characterized by heavy discounting and sales promotion.

A Changing Pricing Environment

Pricing practices have changed significantly in recent years. Many firms are bucking the low-price trend and have been successful in trading consumers up to more expensive products and services by combining unique product formulations with engaging marketing campaigns. Even products in fiercely competitive supermarket categories have been able to enjoy price hikes for the right new offerings. Procter & Gamble launched Crest Pro-Health toothpaste at a 50 percent premium over other premium toothpastes, as well as the Olay Definity mass-market skin care line with a US$25-plus price point that rivaled the lower end of department store brands. Rival Unilever has struck gold with Axe deodorants, which have pushed prices in the category to over $4. Nestlé introduced the Nescafé Cappuccino sachets at US$0.40 per sachet as opposed to the regular Nescafé Coffee sachet for $0.15.[4]

Today the internet is also partially reversing the fixed pricing trend. As one industry observer noted, "We are moving toward a very sophisticated economy. It's kind of an arms race between merchant technology and consumer technology."[5] Here is a short list of how the internet allows sellers to discriminate between buyers and buyers to discriminate between sellers.[6]

Buyers can:

- ***Get instant price comparisons from thousands of vendors.*** Customer can compare the prices offered by various stores by visiting waffar.com. Other international websites such as Price-SCAN.com lure thousands of visitors a day, most of them corporate buyers. Intelligent shopping agents ('bots') take price comparison a step further and seek out products, prices, and reviews from hundreds if not thousands of merchants.

- ***Name their price and have it met.*** At Priceline.com, the customer states the price he wants to pay for an airline ticket, hotel, or rental car, and Priceline checks whether any seller is willing to meet that price. Volume-aggregating sites combine the orders of many customers and press the supplier for a deeper discount.

- ***Get products free.*** Open Source, the free software movement that started with Linux, will erode margins for just about any company creating software. The biggest challenge confronting Microsoft, Oracle, IBM, and virtually every other major software producer is: how do you compete with programs that can be had for free? The Marketing Insight: *Giving It All Away* describes how firms have been successful with low pricing or free offerings.

Sellers can:

- ***Monitor customer behavior and tailor offers to individuals.*** GE Lighting, which gets 55,000 pricing requests a year, has web programs that evaluate 300 factors that go into a pricing quote, such as past sales data and discounts, so it can reduce processing time from up to 30 days to 6 hours.

Marketing Insight

Giving It All Away

Rio Lento is a premier water park in Lebanon offering exiting attractions for children and youth including the Wave Pool, the Kamikaze Slide, and the Party Island. This extraordinary water park has adopted a low entrance fee for visitors, and as a result enjoys high profitability (see ▮ **Box 14.1** on page 374 for guidance on a successful freemium strategy). Its entrance fee is low but visitors are required to pay for almost everything else offered at Rio Lento, including food, parking, and even some rides. Adults are charged around US$17, and children under 9 years old are charged about US$15. If visitors decide to park their car inside the premises, they have to pay extra. And since visitors are not allowed to bring food or drinks inside the park, they have no other choice but to visit the New York Time Café to purchase a snack. In order to generate more money, Rio Lento has introduced three more exciting activities—paintball, bungee jumping, and wall climbing—appealing to children and youth. Again, these are not included in the entrance fee, and so parents end up spending additional money to allow their children to have even more fun at the park. The park also caters for events such as weddings and parties, for a special fee.

While entrance fees to the Rio Lento Park are low, visitors are charged for other things such as parking, food, and some rides.

By charging visitors for almost everything inside the water park, while demanding a low entrance fee, Rio Lento is able to attract visitors from around the world, contributing to the park's high revenue. Also, the fact that Rio Lento hosts celebrations enables it to differentiate itself from other amusement parks in the region, and hence encourage even more customers to visit this outstanding Lebanese attraction site.

Source: See www.riolento.com.

- *Give certain customers access to special prices.* CDWOW, an online vendor of music albums, e-mails certain buyers a special website address with lower prices. Business marketers are already using extranets to get a precise handle on inventory, costs, and demand at any given moment in order to adjust prices instantly.

Both buyers and sellers can:

- *Negotiate prices in online auctions and exchanges.* Want to sell mobile phones, electronics, computers, games and toys, and other items? You can sell them on souq.com.

How Companies Price

Companies do their pricing in a variety of ways. In small companies, prices are often set by the boss. In large companies, pricing is handled by division and product-line managers. And even there, top management sets general pricing objectives and policies, and often approves the prices proposed by lower levels of management. In industries where pricing is a key factor (aerospace, railroads, oil companies), companies will often establish a pricing department to set or assist others in determining appropriate prices. This department reports to the marketing department, finance department, or top management. Others who exert an influence on pricing include sales managers, production managers, finance managers, and accountants.

Executives complain that pricing is a big headache, and one that is getting worse by the day. Many companies do not handle pricing well and throw up their hands with 'strategies' such as this:

BOX 14.1 🔲   Guidelines for a Successful Freemium Strategy

1. **Have a product or service that truly stands out.** Its performance, ease of use, and reliability should be superior to those of current offerings.

2. **Know your up-selling plan from the beginning.** Before you even go into beta, make sure you have at least one paid, add-on premium service up your sleeve. Better yet, have more than one.

3. **Once you've decided that a product will be given away for free, don't change your mind.** "The fundamental 'what's for free' and 'what's for pay' divide needs to be set early," says Adeo Ressi, CEO of Game Trust, a start-up that hosts 45 free games and sells enhancements online. If you make changes, Ressi says, you risk alienating customers accustomed to getting your product for free.

4. **Access to your product should be just one click away.** The fewer time-consuming plug-ins, downloads, and registration forms required, the better. Otherwise people may get bored or frustrated and abort.

5. **Make sure the major bugs have been exterminated.** Your product can be in beta, Rimer says, but not "so much in beta that it doesn't work well."

6. **Harness the collective intelligence of your users.** Måårten Mickos, CEO of MySQL, says customer suggestions can help speed up product improvements or inspire ideas for premium services.

7. **Keep improving the product to give users more reasons to stick with it.** "The reality is that offering a product for free can be far riskier than if you actually charged for your product," says Howard Anderson, a lecturer at the MIT Entrepreneurship Center. "Only one in 10 companies will succeed at pulling this off."

8. **Identify a range of revenue sources.** The Epocrates service, which offers medical professionals both free and premium access to reference material via PDAs, doesn't charge just for the premium information. It also charges fees to pharmaceutical firms for surveys it conducts of Epocrates customers. Similarly, MySQL makes money from customer service as well as from fees charged to firms that redistribute the software.

9. **Timing is everything. Make sure that revenue from your premium service soon covers the cost of your free service.** Otherwise, cut your losses and move on to the next start-up.

Source: Peter J. Howe, "The Next Pinch: Fees to Check Bags," *Boston Globe*, March 8, 2007; Katherine Heires, "Why It Pays to Give Away the Store," *Business 2.0*, October 2006, pp. 36–37; Kerry Capel, "Wal-Mart with Wings," *BusinessWeek*, November 27, 2006, pp.44–45; Matthew Maier, "A Radical Fix for Airlines: Make Flying Free," *Business 2.0*, April 2006, pp. 32–34; Gary Stoller, "Would You Like Some Golf Balls with That Ticket," *USA Today*, October 30, 1996.

"We determine our costs and take our industry's traditional margins." Other common mistakes are not revising price often enough to capitalize on market changes; setting price independently of the rest of the marketing mix rather than as an intrinsic element of market-positioning strategy; and not varying price enough for different product items, market segments, distribution channels, and purchase occasions. General Electric CEO Jeffrey Immelt expresses grief to which many executives can relate.[7]

> We're getting the sales force better trained and equipped with better tools and metrics. A good example is what we're doing to create discipline around pricing. Not long ago, a guy here named Dave McCalpin did an analysis of our pricing in appliances and found out that about US$5 billion of it is discretionary. Given all the decisions that sales reps can make on their own, that's how much is in play. It was the most astounding number I'd ever heard—and that's just in appliances. Extrapolating across our businesses, there may be $50 billion that few people are tracking or accountable for. We would never allow something like that on the cost side. When it comes to the prices we pay, we study them, we map them, we work them. But with the prices we charge, we're too sloppy.

GE is responding by making pricing one of its top three initiatives and instituting a wholesale set of changes:[8]

- A matrix organization dedicated to pricing has been created.
- The CMO, reporting to the CEO, leads the pricing initiative.
- Dedicated pricing managers focus on product pricing, and in each business unit there is generally a VP or director of pricing reporting to the head of marketing.
- Pricing has been added to the GE executive education curriculum and is a mandatory initiative for the Commercial Excellence Council of Top 100 GE executives.
- A Global Pricing Council, made up of pricing leaders from each GE business unit, is looking for best pricing practices across GE and seeding them throughout the organization.
- Within large business units, specialized Industry Pricing Councils cater to unique industry needs.

For any organization, effectively designing and implementing pricing strategies requires a thorough understanding of consumer pricing psychology and a systematic approach to setting, adapting, and changing prices.

Consumer Psychology and Pricing

Many economists assume that consumers are 'price takers' and accept prices at 'face value' or as given. Marketers recognize that consumers often actively process price information, interpreting prices in terms of their knowledge from prior purchasing experience, formal communications (advertising, sales calls, and brochures), informal communications (friends, colleagues, or family members), **point-of-purchase** or online resources, or other factors.[9]

Purchase decisions are based on how consumers perceive prices and what they consider the current actual price to be, *not* the marketer's stated price. Customers may have a lower price threshold below which prices signal inferior or unacceptable quality, as well as an upper price threshold above which prices are prohibitive and seen as not worth the money. The following example helps illustrate the large part consumer psychology plays in determining three different prices for essentially the same item: a simple top.

point-of-purchase the location where a purchase is made, typically thought of in terms of a retail setting.

Dalydress versus Fabulous   Egypt has always been known for its high-quality cotton, so one might expect that the local fashion industry would be a flourishing one. Strangely enough, this is not the case as many Egyptians prefer imported clothes to their local alternatives. Nevertheless, a number of Egyptian designers have successfully managed to penetrate the market by offering fashionable and chic clothes that compete with the imported ones. Among these local brands are Dalydress and Fabulous. Dalydress offers stylish men and women shoppers a wide range of elegant and classic sweaters, tops, shirts, and accessories, and also offers scarves, casual jewelery, and exceptionally stylish handbags. Fabulous has a great selection of basic tops, maxi dresses, lycra skirts, and leggings in every colour. A simple top from Dalydress costs around US$33 whereas basic tops from Fabulous start at around $4. Customers who purchase a top from Dalydress are paying for an item made from silk and cotton, compared to tops from Fabulous, which are made from cotton. Even though a basic top of 100 percent Egyptian cotton indicates that the item is of high quality, sophisticated customers may associate the low prices of Fabulous with lesser quality. On the other hand, the slightly overpriced tops in Dalydress signal to these customers that they are buying the premium quality that is definitely worth the money. This example shows that value is not only translated in terms of quality, but more importantly in the customer's perception of a specific brand.[10]

Understanding how consumers arrive at their perceptions of prices is an important marketing priority. Here we consider three key topics: reference prices, price–quality inferences, and price endings.

REFERENCE PRICES   Research has shown that although consumers may have fairly good knowledge of the range of prices involved, surprisingly few can accurately recall specific prices of

BOX 14.2	Possible Consumer Reference Prices

- 'Fair Price' (what the product should cost)
- Typical Price
- Last Price Paid
- Upper-Bound Price (reservation price or what most consumers would pay)
- Lower-Bound Price (lower threshold price or the least consumers would pay)
- Competitor Prices
- Expected Future Price
- Usual Discounted Price

Source: Adapted from Russell S. Winer, "Behavioral Perspectives on Pricing: Buyers' Subjective Perceptions of Price Revisited," in *Issues in Pricing: Theory and Research*, ed. Timothy Devinney (Lexington, MA: Lexington Books, 1988), pp. 35–57.

reference prices   pricing information a consumer retains in memory which is used to interpret and evaluate a new price.

products.[11] When examining products, however, consumers often employ **reference prices**, comparing an observed price to an internal reference price they remember or to an external frame of reference such as a posted 'regular retail price.'[12]

All types of reference price are possible (see **Box 14.2**), and sellers often attempt to manipulate them. For example, a seller can situate its product among expensive competitors to imply that it belongs in the same class. Department stores will display women's apparel in separate departments differentiated by price; dresses found in the more expensive department are assumed to be of better quality.[13] Marketers also encourage reference-price thinking by stating a high manufacturer's suggested price, or by indicating that the product was priced much higher originally, or by pointing to a competitor's high price.[14]

Consumer Electronics   On JVC's website, the manufacturer's suggested retail price often bears no relationship to what a retailer would charge for the same item. For instance, in the summer of 2011, for the GZ-HM30AUS model of a mini digital video camcorder, JVC suggested a retail price of US$229.95, but Amazon.com was selling it for $189.95. Compared with other consumer items, from clothing to cars to furniture to toothbrushes, the gap between the prices routinely quoted by manufacturer and retailer in consumer electronics is large. "The simplest thing to say is that we have trained the consumer electronics buyer to think he is getting 20% or 30% or 40% off," said Robert Atkins, a vice president at Mercer Management Consulting. A product manager for Olympus America, primarily known for its cameras, defends the practice by saying that the high manufacturer's suggested retail price is a psychological tool, a reference price that makes people see they are getting something of value for less than top price.[15]

High reference prices in the consumer electronics industry have trained consumers to gravitate toward 'sale' prices.

When consumers evoke one or more of these frames of reference, their perceived price can vary from the stated price.[16] Research on reference prices has found that 'unpleasant surprises'—when reference or perceived price is lower than the stated price—can have a greater impact on purchase likelihood than pleasant surprises.[17] Consumer expectations can also play a key role in price response. In the case of internet auction sites, such as eBay, when consumers know similar goods will be available in future auctions, they will bid less in the current auction.[18]

Clever marketers try to frame the price to signal the best value possible. For example, a relatively more expensive item can look less expensive if the price is broken down into smaller units. A US$500 annual membership may look more expensive than "under $50 a month" even if the totals are the same.[19]

Sarah's Bag   Sarah's Bag is a Lebanese line of handcrafted women's fashion accessories. It started out in the year 2000 as a collection of handbags, but soon expanded to include many different types of bags, along with shoes, scarves, belts, and jewelry. What makes this brand unique is that all the bags are made by female prisoners and former inmates, and each piece requires 10–15 days of meticulous hand-working to produce. Founder Sarah Beydoun has proven to be a very smart businesswoman. She sets high prices for the bags; for example, the price of small clutches and evening bags starts at around US$200 and the cheapest bags do not cost less than $65. The fact that the prices are high causes consumers to compare them with the prices of other foreign, highly sophisticated brands. In this way, Sarah's Bag has successfully adopted a reference-pricing strategy by situating her products among expensive competitors and thereby convincing her customers that Sarah's Bag products belong to the same class. In addition, Sarah was able to convert her local brand into a worldwide brand after attracting international celebrities, including the French actress Catherine Deneuve and Queen Rania of Jordan.[20]

PRICE–QUALITY INFERENCES   Many consumers use price as an indicator of quality. Image pricing is especially effective with ego-sensitive products such as perfumes, expensive cars, and Armani T-shirts. A US$100 bottle of perfume might contain $10 worth of scent, but gift givers pay $100 to communicate their high regard for the receiver.

Price and quality perceptions of cars interact.[21] Higher-priced cars are perceived to possess high quality. Higher-quality cars are likewise perceived to be higher priced than they actually are. Box 14.3 shows how consumer perceptions about cars can differ from reality. When alternative information about true quality is available, price becomes a less significant indicator of quality. When this information is not available, price acts as a signal of quality.

BOX 14.3	Consumer Perceptions versus Reality for Cars

Wall Street firm Morgan Stanley used J. D. Power and Associates' 2003 Vehicle Dependability Study, which tracks reliability over 3 years, and CNW Market Research's Perceived Quality Survey to find out which car brands were potentially over- and undervalued.

Overvalued: Brands whose perceived quality exceeds actual quality by percentage

Land Rover	75.3%
Kia	66.6%
Volkswagen	58.3%
Volvo	36.0%
Mercedes	34.2%

Undervalued: Brands whose actual quality exceeds perceived quality by percentage

Mercury	42.3%
Infiniti	34.1%
Buick	29.7%
Lincoln	25.3%
Chrysler	20.8%

Source: David Kiley, "U.S. Automakers Get a Bum Rap," *USA Today*, January 15, 2004, p. B5. Copyright © 2004 USA TODAY. Reprinted with permission.

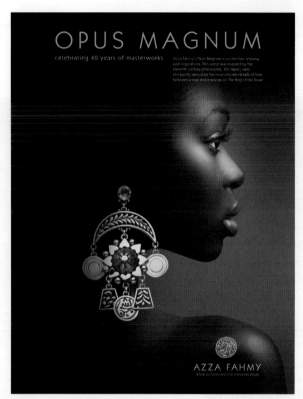

For years, the link between price and quality was what made Azza Fahmy special. The luxury jewelry store was successful in introducing exclusive designer jewelry that justified premium prices.

Some brands adopt exclusivity and scarcity as a means to signify uniqueness and justify premium pricing. Luxury-goods makers of watches, jewelry, perfume, and other products often emphasize exclusivity in their communication messages and channel strategies. For luxury-goods customers who desire uniqueness, demand may actually increase with higher prices, as they may believe that fewer other customers will be able to afford to purchase the product.[22]

Azza Fahmy Azza Fahmy is known internationally as the leading jewelry designer of the Arab world and celebrated as Egypt's first international designer export. The brand is unique in that it draws on culture for its inspiration. Historically, this was its Arabic heritage, before exploring wider, global cultures, nature, and even architecture. Today, Azza Fahmy's contemporary jewelry collections maintain the same design values, one of which is the use of calligraphy that reflects verses and 'sayings', but from international poets. Now, however, there are three core lines. Culture, the first range to be produced 40 years ago, is designed with a combination of silver and gold on one piece in an artistic blend of semi-precious stones, and adorned with the brand's signature calligraphy—which has become one of the company's trademarks. There is also the Exclusive line in gold with precious stones produced in limited edition quantities, and Fashion—in silver, silver & gold and gold—inspired by current fashion trends. The prices start at $250 and do not have a limit especially for commissioned work.

Some consumers who still value jewelry according to its weight in gold or silver perceive Azza Fahmy's products to be overpriced for the Egyptian market. Azza Fahmy competes locally and internationally with other luxury designers, but her USP is a strong heritage which has helped her to convince her customers that she is offering them not only luxury, but craftsmanship, innovative design, great value, and sophistication, featuring new themes every year. Now, when the customer purchases an Azza Fahmy item, it is not only because it is made of silver or gold, but simply because it is an Azza Fahmy item, proof that the Egyptian designer has succeeded in introducing exclusive designer jewelry to the Egyptian market that justifies premium pricing.[23]

PRICE ENDINGS Many sellers believe prices should end in an odd number. Customers see an item priced at US$299 in the $200 rather than the $300 range. Research has shown that consumers tend to process prices in a 'left-to-right' manner rather than by rounding.[24] Price encoding in this fashion is important if there is a mental price break at the higher, rounded price.

Another explanation for the popularity of '9' endings is that they convey the notion of a discount or bargain, suggesting that if a company wants a high-price image, it should avoid the odd-ending tactic.[25] One study even showed that demand was actually increased one-third when the price of a dress *rose* from US$34 to $39 but was unchanged when the price increased from $34 to $44.[26]

Prices that end with 0 and 5 are also common in the marketplace; they are thought to be easier for consumers to process and retrieve from memory.[27] 'Sale' signs next to prices have been shown to spur demand, but only if not overused: total category sales are highest when some, but not all, items in a category have sale signs; past a certain point, sale signs may cause total category sales to fall.[28]

Pricing cues such as sale signs and prices that end in 9 become less effective the more they are employed. They are more influential when consumers' price knowledge is poor, when they purchase the item infrequently or are new to the category, and when product designs vary over time, prices vary seasonally, or quality or sizes vary across stores.[29] Limited availability (for example, "3 days only") also can spur sales among consumers actively shopping for a product.[30]

Setting the Price

A firm must set a price for the first time when it develops a new product, when it introduces its regular product into a new distribution channel or geographical area, and when it enters bids on new contract work. The firm must decide where to position its product on quality and price.

Most markets have three to five price points or tiers. Marriott Hotels is good at developing different brands for different price points: Marriott Vacation Club—Vacation Villas (highest price), Marriott Marquis (high price), Marriott (high-medium price), Renaissance (medium-high price), Courtyard (medium price), Towne Place Suites (medium-low price), and Fairfield Inn (low price). Consumers often rank brands according to these price tiers in a category.[31]

The firm must consider many factors in setting its pricing policy.[32] Let's look in some detail at a six-step procedure: (1) selecting the pricing objective; (2) determining demand; (3) estimating costs; (4) analyzing competitors' costs, prices, and offers; (5) selecting a pricing method; and (6) selecting the final price.

Step 1: Selecting the Pricing Objective

The company first decides where it wants to position its market offering. The clearer a firm's objectives, the easier it is to set price. Five major objectives are: survival, maximum current profit, maximum market share, maximum market skimming, and product-quality leadership.

SURVIVAL Companies pursue *survival* as their major objective if they are plagued with over-capacity, intense competition, or changing consumer wants. As long as prices cover variable costs and some fixed costs, the company stays in business. Survival is a short-run objective; in the long run, the firm must learn how to add value or face extinction.

MAXIMUM CURRENT PROFIT Many companies try to set a price that will *maximize current profits*. They estimate the demand and costs associated with alternative prices and choose the price that produces maximum current profit, cash flow, or rate of return on investment. This strategy assumes that the firm has knowledge of its demand and cost functions; in reality, these are difficult to estimate. In emphasizing current performance, the company may sacrifice long-run performance by ignoring the effects of other marketing-mix variables, competitors' reactions, and legal restraints on price.

MAXIMUM MARKET SHARE Some companies want to *maximize their market share*. They believe that a higher sales volume will lead to lower unit costs and higher long-run profit. They set the lowest price, assuming the market is price sensitive. Etisalat, the UAE-based telecom operator practiced this **market-penetration pricing** for years. Etisalat would lower its prices when it penetrated new markets, and increase its share of the market, which would help lower their costs even further and result in higher profits in the long run.

The following conditions favor adopting a market-penetration pricing strategy: (1) the market is highly price sensitive and a low price stimulates market growth; (2) production and distribution costs fall with accumulated production experience; and (3) a low price discourages actual and potential competition.

market-penetration pricing pricing strategy where prices start low to drive higher sales volume from price-sensitive customers and produce productivity gains.

IKEA IKEA is using market-penetration pricing to get a lock on China's surging market for home furnishings. When the Swedish home furnishings giant opened its first store in Beijing in 2002, shoppers would come in mainly to take advantage of the air-conditioning and the decorating ideas on display. Outside the store, shops were selling copies of IKEA's furniture designs at a fraction of IKEA's prices. The only way for IKEA to lure China's price-sensitive and frugal customers was to drastically slash its prices. By stocking its Chinese stores with Chinese-made products, IKEA has been able to slash prices as low as 70 percent below its own prices outside China. The move has worked. Customers are taking their low-priced goods to the check-out counters in droves, and IKEA is building its largest store in the world—aside from the flagship store in Stockholm—in Beijing. Western brands in China usually price products such as makeup and running shoes 20 to 30 percent higher than in their other markets, both to make up for China's high import taxes and to give their products added cachet. Now, IKEA plans to more than double the number of its stores in China by 2015, and Euromonitor figures show the Swedish retailer has the biggest share of China's home-furnishings market.[33]

market-skimming pricing pricing strategy where prices start high and are slowly lowered over time to maximize profits from less price-sensitive customers.

MAXIMUM MARKET SKIMMING Companies unveiling a new technology favor setting high prices to *maximize market skimming*. Sony is a frequent practitioner of **market-skimming pricing**, in which prices start high and slowly drop over time. When Sony introduced the world's first high-definition television (HDTV) to the Japanese market in 1990, it was priced at US$43,000. So that Sony could 'skim' the maximum amount of revenue from the various segments of the market, the price dropped steadily through the years: a 71-centimeter Sony HDTV cost just over US$6,000 in 1993 and a 101-centimeter Sony HDTV about $1,000 in 2011.

This strategy can be fatal, however, if a worthy competitor decides to price low. When Philips, the Dutch electronics manufacturer, priced its videodisc players to make a profit on each player, Japanese competitors priced low and succeeded in building their market share rapidly, which in turn pushed down their costs substantially.

Market skimming makes sense under the following conditions: (1) a sufficient number of buyers have a high current demand; (2) the unit costs of producing a small volume are not so high that they cancel the advantage of charging what the traffic will bear; (3) the high initial price does not attract more competitors to the market; (4) the high price communicates the image of a superior product.

PRODUCT-QUALITY LEADERSHIP A company might aim to be the *product-quality leader* in the market. Many brands strive to be 'affordable luxuries:' products or services characterized by high levels of perceived quality, taste, and status with a price just high enough not to be out of consumers' reach. Brands such as Cilantro coffee, Pantene shampoo, and BMW cars have been able to position themselves as quality leaders in their categories, combining quality, luxury, and premium prices with an intensely loyal customer base.[34] Choice is a gift shop in Egypt that sells high-quality leather products.

Choice   Choice is a small gift shop that started operations in 1983. It is now one of the largest chains in Egypt, offering premium quality leather products such as women's bags, purses, and jewelry boxes, and men's briefcases, belts, and wallets. In order to keep its customers satisfied, Choice constantly offers the latest fashion to its customers, who look to be stylish. Choice products are unique in that they have a modern touch, while retaining the feel of their Arabic heritage.[35]

OTHER OBJECTIVES Nonprofit and public organizations may have other pricing objectives. A university aims for *partial cost recovery*, knowing that it must rely on private gifts and public grants to cover its remaining costs. A nonprofit hospital may aim for full cost recovery in its pricing. A nonprofit theater company may price its productions to fill the maximum number of theater seats. A social service agency may set a service price geared to client income.

Whatever the specific objective, businesses that use price as a strategic tool will profit more than those that simply let costs or the market determine their pricing. For art museums, which earn only an average of 5 percent of their revenues from admission charges, pricing can send a message that affects their public image and the amount of donations and sponsorships they receive. Following is an example of a museum that has free admissions to attract the public, and covers its costs by charging for exhibitions and catalogs, from gift shop sales, and company sponsorships.

The Museum of Islamic Art (MIA)

The Museum of Islamic Art (MIA) in Qatar was opened to the public in 2008. It holds a multimillion dollar collection of Islamic art: the royal family of Qatar reportedly spent more than US$300 million to find the best artifacts and artworks for the museum. Given the cost of establishing the museum, what should be charged for admission? In fact, MIA general admission is free, so the museum covers its costs in other ways. Admission to temporary exhibitions is charged, and catalogs describing the temporary exhibitions are offered for sale. Items inspired by the MIA treasures are sold in the gift shop, which stocks tableware, stationery, jewelry, posters, ties, and even iPods. MIA has major sponsors, including Q-TEL and the Qatar Financial Center, that provide material and technical support, and whose employees give voluntary support to the museum's educational and cultural outreach programs.[36]

The Museum of Islamic Art in Qatar boasts free general admission and a gift shop featuring items inspired by museum treasures.

Step 2: Determining Demand

Each price will lead to a different level of demand and will therefore have a different impact on a company's marketing objectives. The relationship between price and demand is captured in a demand curve (see △ **Figure 14.1**). In the normal case, the two are inversely related: the higher the price, the lower the demand. In the case of prestige goods, the demand curve sometimes slopes upward. One perfume company raised its price and sold *more* perfume rather than less! Some consumers take the higher price to signify a better product. However, if the price is too high, the level of demand may fall.

PRICE SENSITIVITY The demand curve shows the market's probable purchase quantity at alternative prices. It sums the reactions of many individuals who have different price sensitivities. The first step in estimating demand is to understand what affects price sensitivity. Generally speaking, customers are less price sensitive to low-cost items or items they buy infrequently. They are also less price sensitive when (1) there are few or no substitutes or competitors; (2) they do not readily notice the higher price; (3) they are slow to change their buying habits; (4) they think the higher prices are justified; and (5) price is only a small part of the total cost of obtaining, operating, and servicing the product over its lifetime.

A seller can charge a higher price than competitors and still get the business if it can convince the customer that it offers the lowest *total cost of ownership* (TCO). Marketers often do not realize the value they actually provide but think only in terms of product features. They treat the service elements in a product offering as sales incentives rather than as value-enhancing augmentations for which they can charge. In fact, pricing expert Tom Nagle believes the most common mistake

|Fig. 14.1| △

Inelastic and Elastic Demand

manufacturers have made in recent years has been to offer all sorts of services to differentiate their products without charging for them in any way.[37]

Of course, companies prefer customers who are less price sensitive.   Box 14.4 lists some characteristics associated with decreased price sensitivity. On the other hand, the internet has the potential to *increase* price sensitivity. Research has found that in some established, fairly big-ticket categories such as auto retailing and term insurance, consumers pay lower prices as a result of the internet. Car buyers use the internet to gather information and to use the negotiating clout of an online buying service.[38] But customers must visit multiple sites to realize these savings, and they don't always do so. Targeting only price-sensitive consumers may in fact be 'leaving money on the table.'

ESTIMATING DEMAND CURVES   Most companies make some attempt to measure their demand curves using several different methods.

- *Surveys* can explore how many units consumers would buy at different proposed prices, although there is always the chance they might understate their purchase intentions at higher prices to discourage the company from setting higher prices.

- *Price experiments* can vary the prices of different products in a store or charge different prices for the same product in similar territories to see how the change affects sales. Another approach is to use the internet. An e-business could test the impact of a 5 percent price increase by quoting a higher price to every 40th visitor to compare the purchase response. However, it must do this carefully and not alienate customers.[39]

- *Statistical analysis* of past prices, quantities sold, and other factors can reveal their relationships. The data can be longitudinal (over time) or cross-sectional (from different locations at the same time). Building the appropriate model and fitting the data with the proper statistical techniques calls for considerable skill.

Advances in database management have improved marketers' abilities to optimize pricing. New York-based Duane Reade pharmacy chain uncovered a new strategy by analyzing its data: set the price markup on diapers as a function of a child's age. Making the newborn's sizes more expensive and big-kids pull-ups cheaper boosted the chain's baby care revenue by 27 percent.

In measuring the price–demand relationship, the market researcher must control for various factors that will influence demand.[40] The competitor's response will make a difference. Also, if the company changes other marketing-mix factors besides price, the effect of the price change itself will be hard to isolate.

PRICE ELASTICITY OF DEMAND   Marketers need to know how responsive, or elastic, demand would be to a change in price. Consider the two demand curves in Figure 14.1. In demand

---

BOX 14.4   Factors Leading to Less Price Sensitivity

- The product is more distinctive.
- Buyers are less aware of substitutes.
- Buyers cannot easily compare the quality of substitutes.
- The expenditure is a smaller part of the buyer's total income.
- The expenditure is small compared to the total cost of the end product.
- Part of the cost is borne by another party.
- The product is used in conjunction with assets previously bought.
- The product is assumed to have more quality, prestige, or exclusiveness.
- Buyers cannot store the product.

Source: Adapted from Thomas T. Nagle and Reed K. Holden, *The Strategy and Tactics of Pricing*, 3rd edn (Upper Saddle River, NJ: Prentice Hall, 2001), Chapter 4.

curve (a), a price increase from US$10 to $15 leads to a relatively small decline in demand from 105 to 100. In demand curve (b), the same price increase leads to a substantial drop in demand from 150 to 50. If demand hardly changes with a small change in price, we say the demand is *inelastic*. If demand changes considerably, demand is *elastic*.

The higher the elasticity, the greater the volume growth resulting from a 1 percent price reduction. If demand is elastic, sellers will consider lowering the price. A lower price will produce more total revenue. This makes sense as long as the costs of producing and selling more units do not increase disproportionately.[41]

Price elasticity depends on the magnitude and direction of the contemplated price change. It may be negligible with a small price change and substantial with a large price change. It may differ for a price cut versus a price increase, and there may be a *price indifference band* within which price changes have little or no effect.

Finally, long-run price elasticity may differ from short-run elasticity. Buyers may continue to buy from a current supplier after a price increase, but they may eventually switch suppliers. Here demand is more elastic in the long run than in the short run, or the reverse may happen: buyers may drop a supplier after being notified of a price increase but return later. The distinction between short-run and long-run elasticity means that sellers will not know the total effect of a price change until time passes.

One comprehensive study reviewing a 40-year period of academic research projects that investigated price elasticity yielded a number of interesting findings:[42]

- The average price elasticity across all products, markets, and time periods studied was –2.62.

- Price elasticity magnitudes were higher for durable goods than for other goods, and higher for products in the introduction/growth stages of the product life cycle than in the mature/decline stages.

- Inflation led to substantially higher price elasticities, especially in the short run.

- Promotional price elasticities were higher than actual price elasticities in the short run (although the reverse was true in the long run).

- Price elasticities were higher at the individual item or stock-keeping unit (SKU) level than at the overall brand level.

Step 3: Estimating Costs

Demand sets a ceiling on the price the company can charge for its product. Costs set the floor. The company wants to charge a price that covers its cost of producing, distributing, and selling the product, including a fair return for its effort and risk. Yet, when companies price products to cover their full costs, profitability isn't always the net result.

TYPES OF COST AND LEVELS OF PRODUCTION
A company's costs take two forms, fixed and variable. **Fixed costs** (also known as **overheads**) are costs that do not vary with production level or sales revenue. A company must pay bills each month for rent, heat, interest, salaries, and so on regardless of output.

Variable costs vary directly with the level of production. For example, each hand calculator produced by Texas Instruments incurs the cost of plastic, microprocessor chips, and packaging. These costs tend to be constant per unit produced, but they're called *variable* because their total varies with the number of units produced.

Total costs consist of the sum of the fixed and variable costs for any given level of production. **Average cost** is the cost per unit at that level of production; it equals total costs divided by production. Management wants to charge a price that will at least cover the total production costs at a given level of production.

To price intelligently, management needs to know how its costs vary with different levels of production. Take the case in which a company such as TI has built a fixed-size plant to produce 1,000 hand calculators a day. The cost per unit is high if few units are produced per day. As production approaches 1,000 units per day, the average cost falls because the fixed costs are spread over more units. Short-run average cost (SRAC) *increases* after 1,000 units, however, because the

overheads   see 'fixed costs'.

fixed costs (overhead)   costs that do not vary with production or sales revenue.

variable costs   costs that vary directly with the level of production.

total costs   the sum of the fixed and variable costs for any given level of production.

average cost   the cost per unit at a given level of production; it is equal to total costs divided by production.

**(a) Cost Behavior in
a Fixed-Size Plant**

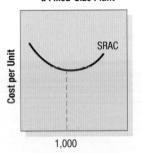

Quantity Produced per Day

**(b) Cost Behavior over
Different-Size Plants**

Quantity Produced per Day

|Fig. 14.2| ◬

Cost per Unit at
Different Levels
of Production per
Period

**activity-based cost (ABC)
accounting** procedures that
can quantify the true profitability of different activities by
identifying their actual costs.

**experience curve (learning
curve)** a decline in the average
cost with accumulated production
experience.

|Fig. 14.3| ◬

Cost per Unit
as a Function
of Accumulated
Production: The
Experience Curve

plant becomes inefficient: workers must line up for machines, getting in each other's way, and machines break down more often (see ◬ **Figure 14.2a**).

If TI believes it can sell 2,000 units per day, it should consider building a larger plant. The plant will use more efficient machinery and work arrangements, and the unit cost of producing 2,000 units per day will be lower than the unit cost of producing 1,000 units per day. This is shown in the long-run average cost (LRAC) curve in Figure 14.2b. In fact, a 3,000-capacity plant would be even more efficient according to Figure 14.2b, but a 4,000-daily production plant would be less so because of increasing diseconomies of scale: there are too many workers to manage, and paperwork slows things down. Figure 14.2b indicates that a 3,000-daily production plant is the optimal size if demand is strong enough to support this level of production.

There are more costs than those associated with manufacturing. To estimate the real profitability of selling to different types of retailer or customer, the manufacturer needs to use **activity-based cost (ABC)** accounting instead of standard cost accounting. This is sometimes known as activity cost. ABC accounting tries to identify the real costs associated with serving each customer. It allocates indirect costs such as clerical costs, office expenses, supplies, and so on to the activities that use them, rather than in some proportion to direct costs. This is sometimes known as activity costs. Both variable and overhead costs are tagged back to each customer.

Companies that fail to measure their costs correctly are also not measuring their profit correctly, and are likely to misallocate their marketing effort. The key to effectively employing ABC is to define and judge 'activities' properly. One proposed time-based solution calculates the cost of one minute of overhead and then decides how much of this cost each activity uses.[43]

ACCUMULATED PRODUCTION Suppose TI runs a plant that produces 3,000 hand calculators per day. As TI gains experience producing hand calculators, its methods improve. Workers learn shortcuts, materials flow more smoothly, and procurement costs fall. The result, as ◬ **Figure 14.3** shows, is that average cost falls with accumulated production experience. Thus the average cost of producing the first 100,000 hand calculators is US$10 per calculator. When the company has produced the first 200,000 calculators, the average cost has fallen to $9. After its accumulated production experience doubles again to 400,000, the average cost is $8. This decline in the average cost with accumulated production experience is called the **experience curve** or *learning curve*.

Now suppose three firms compete in this industry, TI, A, and B. TI is the lowest-cost producer at US$8, having produced 400,000 units in the past. If all three firms sell the calculator for $10, TI makes $2 profit per unit, A makes $1 per unit, and B breaks even. The smart move for TI would be to lower its price to $9. This will drive B out of the market, and even A may consider leaving. TI will pick up the business that would have gone to B (and possibly A). Furthermore, price-sensitive customers will enter the market at the lower price. As production increases beyond 400,000 units, TI's costs will drop still further and faster and will more than restore its profits, even at a price of $9. TI has used this aggressive pricing strategy repeatedly to gain market share and drive others out of the industry.

Experience-curve pricing nevertheless carries major risks. Aggressive pricing might give the product a cheap image. The strategy also assumes that competitors are weak followers. It leads the company into building more plants to meet demand, but a competitor may choose to innovate with a lower-cost technology. The market leader is now stuck with the old technology.

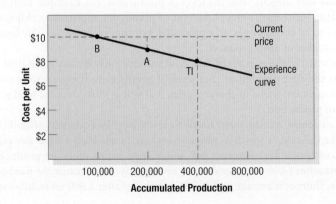

Most experience-curve pricing has focused on manufacturing costs, but all costs can be improved on, including marketing costs. If three firms are each investing a large sum of money in marketing, the firm that has used it the longest might achieve the lowest costs. This firm can charge a little less for its product and still earn the same return, all other costs being equal.[44]

TARGET COSTING Costs change with production scale and experience. They can also change as a result of a concentrated effort by designers, engineers, and purchasing agents to reduce them through **target costing**.[45] Market research establishes a new product's desired functions and the price at which the product will sell, given its appeal and competitors' prices. Deducting the desired profit margin from this price leaves the target cost the marketer must achieve.

The firm must examine each cost element—design, engineering, manufacturing, sales—and consider different ways to bring down costs so the final cost projections are in the target cost range. If this is not possible, it may be necessary to stop developing the product because it cannot sell for the target price and make the target profit. To hit price and margin targets, marketers of the 9Lives® brand of cat food employed target costing to bring their price down to "four cans for a dollar" through a reshaped package and redesigned manufacturing processes. Even with lower prices, profits for the brand doubled.

> **target costing** deducting the desired profit margin from the price at which a product will sell, given its appeal and competitors' prices.

Step 4: Analyzing Competitors' Costs, Prices, and Offers

Within the range of possible prices determined by market demand and company costs, the firm must take competitors' costs, prices, and possible price reactions into account. The firm should first consider the nearest competitor's price. If the firm's offer contains features not offered by the nearest competitor, it should evaluate their worth to the customer and add that value to the competitor's price. If the competitor's offer contains some features not offered by the firm, the firm should subtract their value from its own price. Now the firm can decide whether it can charge more, the same, or less than the competitor.

The introduction of any price or the change of any existing price can provoke a response from customers, competitors, distributors, suppliers, and even government. Competitors are most likely to react when the number of firms are few, the product is homogeneous, and buyers are highly informed. Competitor reactions can be a special problem when these firms have a strong value proposition. For example, the Four Seasons Nile Plaza in Cairo is able to put a premium price on its rate per night, which is sometimes double or three times the price of the Semiramis Intercontinental a few blocks away, because of the better service quality and options.

How can a firm anticipate a competitor's reactions? One way is to assume the competitor reacts in the standard way to a price being set or changed. Another is to assume the competitor treats each price difference or change as a fresh challenge and reacts according to self-interest at the time. Now the company will need to research the competitor's current financial situation, recent sales, customer loyalty, and corporate objectives. If the competitor has a market share objective, it is likely to match price differences or changes.[46] If it has a profit-maximization objective, it may react by increasing the advertising budget or improving product quality.

The problem is complicated because the competitor can put different interpretations on lowered prices or a price cut: that the company is trying to steal the market, that the company is doing poorly and trying to boost its sales, or that the company wants the whole industry to reduce prices to stimulate total demand.

Step 5: Selecting a Pricing Method

Given the customers' demand schedule, the cost function, and competitors' prices, the company is now ready to select a price. △ **Figure 14.4** summarizes the three major considerations in price setting: costs set a floor to the price. Competitors' prices and the price of substitutes provide an orienting point. Customers' assessment of unique features establishes the price ceiling.

Companies select a pricing method that includes one or more of these three considerations. We will examine six price-setting methods: markup pricing, target-return pricing, perceived-value pricing, value pricing, going-rate pricing, and auction-type pricing.

High Price
(No possible demand at this price)
Ceiling price
Customers' assessment of unique product features
Orienting point
Competitors' prices and prices of substitutes
Costs
Floor price
Low Price
(No possible profit at this price)

|Fig. 14.4| △

The Three Cs Model for Price Setting

markup   pricing an item by adding a standard increase to the product's cost.

MARKUP PRICING The most elementary pricing method is to add a standard **markup** to the product's cost. Construction companies submit job bids by estimating the total project cost and adding a standard markup for profit. Lawyers and accountants typically price by adding a standard markup on their time and costs.

Suppose a toaster manufacturer has the following costs and sales expectations:

Variable cost per unit	US$10
Fixed costs	US$300,000
Expected unit sales	50,000

The manufacturer's unit cost is given by:

$$\text{Unit cost} = \text{variable cost} + \frac{\text{fixed cost}}{\text{unit sales}} = \$10 + \frac{\$300,000}{50,000} = \$16$$

Now assume the manufacturer wants to earn a 20 percent markup on sales. The manufacturer's markup price is given by:

$$\text{Markup price} = \frac{\text{unit cost}}{(1 - \text{desired return on sales})} = \frac{\$16}{1 - 0.2} = \$20$$

The manufacturer would charge dealers US$20 per toaster and make a profit of $4 per unit. The dealers in turn will mark up the toaster. If dealers want to earn 50 percent on their selling price, they will mark up the toaster 100 percent to $40. Markups are generally higher on seasonal items (to cover the risk of not selling), specialty items, slower-moving items, items with high storage and handling costs, and demand-inelastic items, such as prescription drugs.

Does the use of standard markups make logical sense? Generally, no. Any pricing method that ignores current demand, perceived value, and competition is not likely to lead to the optimal price. Markup pricing works only if the marked-up price actually brings in the expected level of sales.[47] Consider the markup pricing used by Tunisian Manufacturing Industries.

 Tunisian Manufacturing Industries   Imperfect competition dominated the Tunisian manufacturing market over the period 1975 to 1999. As a result, the existing suppliers of, for example, the food-processing, construction materials, mechanical and electrical goods, chemicals, and textile industries expected to remain easily dominant, and used markup pricing for their products. Some of the Tunisian industries were highly concentrated—that is, dominated by a few large firms—and the markup rate tended to be higher in concentrated industries, such as the chemicals industry, than in less concentrated ones such as textiles and construction materials.

When a competition policy is introduced, as it was in Tunisia, it tends either to have no effect on price-cost margins or its affect only appears after a certain adjustment period. Competition is affected by many things: the number of firms in a market, the degree of concentration, the prevailing regulations, the openness of an economy to international competition, and so on. Markups also seem to be related to the market structure of the particular industry. Rather than being the result of competition policy, the grounds for competition in the manufacturing goods sectors in Tunisia are changing due to increasingly liberalized Tunisian economic policies. For example, the high markup on chemicals went down from 39 to 28 percent over the course of 1991–1999.[48]

Markup pricing remains popular. First, sellers can determine costs much more easily than they can estimate demand. By tying the price to cost, sellers simplify the pricing task. Second, where all firms in the industry use this pricing method, prices tend to be similar and price competition is minimized. Third, many people feel that cost-plus pricing is fairer to both buyers and sellers. Sellers do not take advantage of buyers when the latter's demand becomes acute, and sellers earn a fair return on investment.

TARGET-RETURN PRICING In **target-return pricing**, the firm determines the price that would yield its target rate of return on investment (ROI). General Motors has priced its automobiles to achieve a 15 to 20 percent ROI. Public utilities, which need to make a fair return on investment, can also use this method.

target-return pricing determining the price that would yield the firm's target rate of return on investment (ROI).

Suppose the toaster manufacturer has invested US$1 million in the business and wants to set a price to earn a 20 percent ROI, specifically US$200,000. The target-return price is given by the following formula:

$$\text{Target-return price} = \text{unit cost} + \frac{\text{desired return} \times \text{invested capital}}{\text{unit sales}}$$

$$= \$16 + \frac{.20 \times \$1,000,000}{50,000} = \$20$$

The manufacturer will realize this 20 percent ROI provided its costs and estimated sales turn out to be accurate. But what if sales don't reach 50,000 units? The manufacturer can prepare a break-even chart to learn what would happen at other sales levels (see △ **Figure 14.5**). Fixed costs are US$300,000 regardless of sales volume. Variable costs, not shown in the figure, rise with volume. Total costs equal the sum of fixed costs and variable costs. The total revenue curve starts at zero and rises with each unit sold.

The total revenue and total cost curves cross at 30,000 units. This is the break-even volume. We can verify it by the following formula:

$$\text{Break-even volume} = \frac{\text{fixed cost}}{(\text{price} - \text{variable cost})} = \frac{\$300,000}{\$20 - \$10} = 30,000$$

The manufacturer, of course, is hoping the market will buy 50,000 units at US$20, in which case it earns $200,000 on its $1 million investment, but much depends on price elasticity and competitors' prices. Unfortunately, target-return pricing tends to ignore these considerations. The manufacturer needs to consider different prices and estimate their probable impacts on sales volume and profits. The manufacturer should also search for ways to lower its fixed or variable costs, because lower costs will decrease its required break-even volume.

PERCEIVED-VALUE PRICING An increasing number of companies now base their price on the customer's **perceived value**. Perceived value is made up of several elements, such as the buyer's image of the product performance, the channel deliverables, the warranty quality, customer support, and softer attributes such as the supplier's reputation, trustworthiness, and esteem. Companies must deliver the value promised by their value proposition, and the customer must perceive this value. Firms use the other marketing-mix elements, such as advertising and sales force, to communicate and enhance perceived value in buyers' minds.[49]

perceived value the value promised by the company's value proposition and perceived by the customer.

Fig. 14.5 △

Break-Even Chart for Determining Target-Return Price and Break-Even Volume

Caterpillar uses perceived value to set prices on its construction equipment. It might price its tractor at US$100,000, although a similar competitor's tractor might be priced at $90,000. When a prospective customer asks a Caterpillar dealer why he should pay $10,000 more for the Caterpillar tractor, the dealer answers:

$ 90,000	is the tractor's price if it is only equivalent to the competitor's tractor
$ 7,000	is the price premium for Caterpillar's superior durability
$ 6,000	is the price premium for Caterpillar's superior reliability
$ 5,000	is the price premium for Caterpillar's superior service
$ 2,000	is the price premium for Caterpillar's longer warranty on parts
$110,000	is the normal price to cover Caterpillar's superior value
−$10,000	discount
$100,000	final price

The Caterpillar dealer is able to indicate why Caterpillar's tractor delivers more value than the competitor's. Although the customer is asked to pay a $10,000 premium, he is actually getting $20,000 extra value! He chooses the Caterpillar tractor because he is convinced that its lifetime operating costs will be lower.

Ensuring that customers appreciate the total value of a product or service offering is crucial. For example, Paccar Inc., maker of Kenworth and Peterbilt trucks—one of the leading companies in manufacturing trucks worldwide—is able to command a 10 percent premium by its relentless focus on all aspects of the customer experience to maximize total value. Contract Freighters trucking company, a loyal Paccar customer for 20 years, justified ordering another 700 new trucks in 2006, despite their higher price, because of their higher perceived quality: greater reliability, higher trade-in value, even the superior plush interiors that might attract experienced, more particular, drivers. Paccar bucks the commoditization trend by custom-building its trucks to individual specifications.

Yet even when a company claims that its offering delivers more total value, not all customers will respond positively. There is always a segment of buyers who care only about the price. Other buyers suspect the company is exaggerating its product quality and services. One company installed its software system in one or two plants operated by a customer. The substantial and well-documented cost savings convinced the customer to buy the software for its other plants.

The key to perceived-value pricing is to deliver more value than the competitor and to demonstrate this to prospective buyers. Basically, a company needs to understand the customer's decision-making process. The company can try to determine the value of its offering in several ways: managerial judgments within the company, value of similar products, focus groups, surveys, experimentation, analysis of historical data, and conjoint analysis.[50]

value pricing   winning loyal customers by charging a fairly low price for a high-quality offering.

VALUE PRICING   In recent years, several companies have adopted **value pricing**: they win loyal customers by charging a fairly low price for a high-quality offering. Value pricing is thus not a matter of simply setting lower prices; it is a matter of reengineering the company's operations to become a low-cost producer without sacrificing quality, to attract a large number of value-conscious customers.

Among the best practitioners of value pricing are IKEA, Carrefour, and Al Arabiya Airlines. In the early 1990s, Procter & Gamble created quite a stir when it reduced prices on supermarket staples such as Pampers and Luvs diapers and Tide liquid detergent to value price them. In the past, a brand-loyal family had had to pay what amounted to a US$725 premium over private-label or low-priced items for a year's worth of P&G products. To offer value prices, P&G underwent a major overhaul. It redesigned the way it developed, manufactured, distributed, priced, marketed, and sold products to deliver better value at every point in the supply chain.[51]

everyday low pricing (EDLP)   in retailing, a constant low price with few or no price promotions and special sales.

An important type of value pricing is **everyday low pricing** (EDLP), which takes place at the retail level. A retailer that holds to an EDLP pricing policy charges a constant low price with little or no price promotions and special sales. These constant prices eliminate week-to-week price uncertainty and the 'high-low' pricing of promotion-oriented competitors. In **high-low pricing**,

high-low pricing   charging higher prices on an everyday basis but then running frequent promotions and special sales.

the retailer charges higher prices on an everyday basis but then runs frequent promotions in which prices are temporarily lowered below the EDLP level.[52] The two different pricing strategies have been shown to affect consumer price judgments: deep discounts (EDLP) can lead customers to perceive lower prices over time than frequent, shallow discounts (high-low), even if the actual averages are the same.[53]

In recent years, high-low pricing has given way to EDLP in widely differing arenas, from the Al Masriya car dealership to upscale department stores such as H&M; but the king of EDLP is surely Walmart in the United States, which practically defined the term, and Carrefour in the Arab world. Except for a few sale items every month, Walmart promises everyday low prices on major brands. "It's not a short-term strategy," says one Walmart executive. "You have to be willing to make a commitment to it, and you have to be able to operate with lower ratios of expense than everybody else."

Some retailers have even based their entire marketing strategy around what could be called *extreme* everyday low pricing. Carrefour Egypt has been successful in catering to the needs of price-sensitive consumers by guaranteeing an everyday low price.

Carrefour Egypt Egypt's first hypermarket Carrefour opened at the end of 2002, and has since become the most popular retailer. Carrefour sells a bit of everything, with an emphasis on low prices. Carrefour's low pricing policy was able to appeal to the Egyptian culture which is family-oriented, encouraging families to spend their free time shopping at Carrefour rather than at smaller neighborhood supermarkets. Carrefour targets middle-income families as its customers, setting itself apart from other popular supermarket chains that cater to high-income families, such as Metro and Alpha Market. It offers the best-quality products for the lowest prices, 'value for money' products, and is able to offer and sustain its low prices because of its ability to exert pressure on its suppliers to give it deep price reductions, and to pay opening fees to sell their products in Carrefour. This is because of the company's strong brand and presence in the market and its differentiated product portfolio of over 55,000 different items. All products are available under the same roof, including specialty departments such as fish, bakery, delicatessen, fresh meat, clothing, hardware, and even electronics. Carrefour has achieved this success throughout the region: the chain is known for selling more food than any other French food retailer, and more total goods worldwide, second only to Walmart.[55]

going-rate pricing price based largely on competitors' prices.

The most important reason retailers adopt EDLP is that constant sales and promotions are costly and have eroded consumer confidence in the credibility of everyday shelf prices. Consumers also have less time and patience for time-honored traditions such as watching for supermarket specials and clipping coupons. Yet there is no denying that promotions create excitement and draw shoppers. For this reason, EDLP is not a guarantee of success. As supermarkets face heightened competition from their counterparts and from alternative channels, many find that the key to drawing shoppers is using a combination of high-low and everyday low pricing strategies, with increased advertising and promotions.

GOING-RATE PRICING In **going-rate pricing**, the firm bases its price largely on competitors' prices, charging the same, more, or less than major competitor(s). In oligopolistic industries that sell a commodity such as steel, paper, or fertilizer, all firms normally charge the same price. The smaller firms 'follow the leader,' changing their prices when the market leader's prices change rather than when their own demand or costs change. Some firms may charge a slight premium or slight discount, but they preserve the amount of difference. Thus minor gasoline retailers usually charge a few cents less per liter than the major oil companies, without letting the difference increase or decrease.

Carrefour uses a low pricing policy to appeal to middle-income Egyptian families.

Going-rate pricing is quite popular. Where costs are difficult to measure or competitive response is uncertain, firms feel the going price is a good solution because it is thought to reflect the industry's collective wisdom.

AUCTION-TYPE PRICING Auction-type pricing is growing more popular, especially with the growth of the internet. There are over 2,000 electronic marketplaces selling everything from pigs to used vehicles to cargo to chemicals. One major purpose of auctions is to dispose of excess inventories or used goods. Companies need to be aware of the three major types of auctions and their separate pricing procedures.

- *English auctions (ascending bids)* involve one seller and many buyers. On sites such as Yahoo!, eBay, and souq.com the seller puts up an item and bidders raise the offer price until the top price is reached. The highest bidder gets the item. English auctions are used today for selling antiques, cattle, real estate, and used equipment and vehicles. After seeing eBay and other ticket brokers and middlemen reap millions by charging what the market would bear, Ticketmaster Corp., which has a presence in many countries, has overhauled the way it sells tickets, including running auctions for 30 percent of major music tours for popular artists such as Madonna and Britney Spears and allowing some customers to resell their seats on its website.[55]

- *Dutch auctions (descending bids)* involve one seller and many buyers, or one buyer and many sellers. In the first kind, an auctioneer announces a high price for a product and then slowly decreases the price until a bidder accepts the price. In the other, the buyer announces something he or she wants to buy, and potential sellers compete to get the sale by offering the lowest price. Each seller sees what the last bid is and decides whether to go lower. FreeMarkets .com—later acquired by Ariba—helped Royal Mail Group plc, the United Kingdom's public mail service company, save approximately US$4.0 million in 2003, in part via an auction where 25 airlines bid for its international freight business.[56]

- *Sealed-bid auctions* involve would-be suppliers who can submit only one bid and cannot know the other bids. The U.S. government often uses this method to procure supplies. A supplier will not bid below its cost but cannot bid too high for fear of losing the job. The net effect of these two pulls can be described in terms of the bid's *expected profit*. Using expected profit for setting price makes sense for the seller that makes many bids. The seller who bids only occasionally or who needs a particular contract badly will not find it advantageous to use expected profit. This criterion does not distinguish between a US$1,000 profit with a 0.10 probability and a $125 profit with a 0.80 probability. Yet the firm that wants to keep production going would prefer the second contract to the first.

As more and more firms use online auctions for industrial buying, they need to recognize the possible effects it can have on their suppliers. If the increased savings a firm obtains in an online auction translates into decreased margins for an incumbent supplier, the supplier may feel the firm is opportunistically squeezing out price concessions.[57] Online auctions with a large number of bidders, greater economic stakes, and less visibility in pricing have been shown to result in greater overall satisfaction, more positive future expectations, and fewer perceptions of opportunism.

Step 6: Selecting the Final Price

Pricing methods narrow the range from which the company must select its final price. In selecting that price, the company must consider additional factors, including the impact of other marketing activities, company pricing policies, gain-and-risk-sharing pricing, and the impact of price on other parties.

IMPACT OF OTHER MARKETING ACTIVITIES The final price must take into account the brand's quality and advertising relative to the competition. In a classic study, Farris and Reibstein examined the relationships among relative price, relative quality, and relative advertising for 227 consumer businesses and found the following:

- Brands with average relative quality but high relative advertising budgets were able to charge premium prices. Consumers were willing to pay higher prices for known products than for unknown products.

- Brands with high relative quality and high relative advertising obtained the highest prices. Conversely, brands with low quality and low advertising charged the lowest prices.
- The positive relationship between high prices and high advertising held most strongly in the later stages of the product life cycle for market leaders.[58]

These findings suggest that price is not as important as quality and other benefits in the market offering. One study asked consumers to rate the importance of price and other attributes in using online retailing. Only 19 percent cared about price; far more cared about customer support (65 percent), on-time delivery (58 percent), and product shipping and handling (49 percent).[59]

COMPANY PRICING POLICIES The price must be consistent with company pricing policies. At the same time, companies are not averse to establishing pricing penalties under certain circumstances.[60]

Airlines charge US$150 to those who change their reservations on discount tickets. Banks charge fees for too many withdrawals in a month or for early withdrawal of a certificate of deposit. Dentists, hotels, car rental companies, and other service providers charge penalties for no-shows who miss appointments or reservations. Although these policies are often justifiable, marketers must use them judiciously so as not to unnecessarily alienate customers (see Marketing Insight: *Stealth Price Increases*).

Many companies set up a pricing department to develop policies and establish or approve decisions. The aim is to ensure that salespeople quote prices that are reasonable to customers and profitable to the company.

GAIN-AND-RISK-SHARING PRICING Buyers may resist accepting a seller's proposal because of a high perceived level of risk. The seller has the option of offering to absorb part or all the risk if it does not deliver the full promised value. Baxter Healthcare, a leading

Marketing Insight

Stealth Price Increases

With consumers stubbornly resisting higher prices, companies are trying to figure out how to increase revenue without really raising prices. Increasingly, the solution has been through the addition of fees for what had once been free features. Although some consumers hate charging separately for various extras (such as luggage, meals, and ear phones in airplanes), small additional charges can add up to a substantial source of revenue.

The numbers can be staggering. Fees for consumers who pay bills online, bounce checks, or use automated teller machines bring banks billions of dollars annually. In the United States, penalty fees for late credit card payments more than doubled over a 10-year span—from an average of US$13 in 1995 to as much as $34 in 2005—and credit card companies collected $22.9 billion dollars in total late and over-the-limit penalty fees in 2009. The telecommunications industry in general has been aggressive at adding fees for setup, change-of-service, ser-

vice termination, directory assistance, regulatory assessment, number portability, and cable hookup and equipment, costing consumers billions of dollars. By charging its customers a 5 piaster call set-up fee, Telecom Egypt could bring in as much as almost US$17 million.

This explosion of fees has a number of implications. Given that list prices stay fixed, they may understate inflation. They also make it harder for consumers to compare competitive offerings. Although various citizens' groups have been formed to pressure companies to roll back some of these fees, they don't always get a sympathetic ear from state and local governments, which have been guilty of using their own array of fees, fines, and penalties to raise necessary revenue.

Companies justify the extra fees as the only fair and viable way to cover expenses without losing customers. Many argue that it makes sense to charge a premium for added services that cost more to provide, rather than charging all customers the same amount whether or not they use the extra service. Breaking out charges and fees according to the related services is a way to keep basic costs low. Companies also use fees as a means to weed out unprofitable customers or get them to change their behavior.

Ultimately, the viability of extra fees will be decided in the marketplace, and by the willingness of consumers to vote with their wallets and pay the fees, or vote with their feet and move on.

Sources: Adapted from Kathy Chu, "Credit Card Fees Can Suck You In," *USA Today*, December 15, 2006; Michael Arndt, "Fees! Fees! Fees!" *BusinessWeek*, September 29, 2003, pp. 99–104; "The Price Is Wrong," *The Economist*, May 25, 2002, pp. 59–60.

medical products firm, was able to secure a contract for an information management system from Columbia/HCA, a leading health care provider, by guaranteeing the firm several million dollars in savings over an 8-year period. An increasing number of companies, especially business marketers who promise great savings with their equipment, may have to stand ready to guarantee the promised savings, but also possibly participate in the upside if the gains are much greater than expected.

IMPACT OF PRICE ON OTHER PARTIES Management must also consider the reactions of other parties to the contemplated price.[61] How will distributors and dealers feel about it? If they don't make enough profit, they may not choose to bring the product to market. Will the sales force be willing to sell at that price? How will competitors react? Will suppliers raise their prices when they see the company's price? Will the government intervene and prevent this price from being charged?

Marketers need to know the laws regulating pricing. Legislation in most developed nations states that sellers must set prices without talking to competitors: price-fixing is illegal. Many federal and state statutes in the United States protect consumers against deceptive pricing practices. For example, it is illegal for a company to set artificially high 'regular' prices, then announce a 'sale' at prices close to previous everyday prices.

Adapting the Price

Companies usually do not set a single price, but rather develop a pricing structure that reflects variations in geographical demand and costs, market-segment requirements, purchase timing, order levels, delivery frequency, guarantees, service contracts, and other factors. As a result of discounts, allowances, and promotional support, a company rarely realizes the same profit from each unit of a product that it sells. Here we will examine several price-adaptation strategies: geographical pricing, price discounts and allowances, promotional pricing, and differentiated pricing.

Geographical Pricing (Cash, Countertrade, Barter)

In geographical pricing, the company decides how to price its products to different customers in different locations and countries.

Procter & Gamble   As a nation of 85 million people, Egypt is P&G's largest market in the Arab world. More than 50 percent of the Egyptian population earns less than US$250 per month. Thus, buying a regular large boxed Ariel detergent, which can cost up to $15 or more, is expensive for many Egyptians. So, P&G introduced the small 200-gram Ariel bags, intended for one wash. The price is significantly cheaper than the large boxed one—almost half a dollar per bag—due to the smaller size and cheaper packaging used.[62]

Should the company charge higher prices to distant customers to cover the higher shipping costs, or a lower price to win additional business? How should it account for exchange rates and the strength of different currencies?

Another question is how to get paid. This issue is critical when buyers lack sufficient hard currency to pay for their purchases. Many buyers want to offer other items in payment, a practice known as **countertrade**. Many companies in the Arab market are often forced to engage in countertrade if they want the business. Countertrade may account for 15 to 25 percent of world trade and takes several forms:[63]

countertrade international trade involving the direct or indirect exchange of goods for other goods instead of cash.

- **Barter.** The buyer and seller directly exchange goods, with no money and no third party involved.

- **Compensation deal.** The seller receives some percentage of the payment in cash and the rest in products. A British aircraft manufacturer sold planes to Brazil for 70 percent cash and the rest in coffee.

- **Buyback arrangement.** The seller sells a plant, equipment, or technology to another country and agrees to accept as partial payment products manufactured with the supplied equipment. A United States chemical company built a plant for an Indian company and accepted partial payment in cash and the remainder in chemicals manufactured at the plant.

- **Offset.** The seller receives full payment in cash but agrees to spend a substantial amount of the money in that country within a stated time period. For example, PepsiCo sells its cola syrup to Russia for rubles and agrees to buy Russian kvass—a bread-based nonalcoholic drink—at a certain rate for sale in the United States.

Price Discounts and Allowances

Most companies will adjust their list price and give discounts and allowances for early payment, volume purchases, and off-season buying (see ⬛ **Box 14.5**).[64] Companies must do this carefully or find their profits much lower than planned.[65]

Discount pricing has become the mode of setting prices of a surprising number of companies offering both products and services. Some product categories tend to self-destruct by always being on sale. Salespeople, in particular, are quick to give discounts in order to close a sale. But word can get around fast that the company's list price is 'soft,' and discounting becomes the norm. The discounts undermine the value perceptions of the offerings.

Some companies with overcapacity are tempted to give discounts or even begin to supply a retailer with a store-brand version of their product at a deep discount. Because the store brand is priced lower, however, it may start making inroads on the manufacturer's brand. Manufacturers should stop to consider the implications of supplying products to retailers at a discount, because they may end up losing long-run profits in an effort to meet short-run volume goals.

BOX 14.5 ⬛	Price Discounts and Allowances
Discount	A price reduction to buyers who pay bills promptly. A typical example is "2/10, net 30," which means that payment is due within 30 days and that the buyer can deduct 2% by paying the bill within 10 days.
Quantity Discount	A price reduction to those who buy large volumes. A typical example is "US$10 per unit for fewer than 100 units; $9 per unit for 100 or more units." Quantity discounts must be offered equally to all customers and must not exceed the cost savings to the seller. They can be offered on each order placed or on the number of units ordered over a given period.
Functional Discount	Discount (also called *trade discount*) offered by a manufacturer to trade-channel members if they will perform certain functions, such as selling, storing, and recordkeeping. Manufacturers must offer the same functional discounts within each channel.
Seasonal Discount	A price reduction to those who buy merchandise or services out of season. Hotels, motels, and airlines offer seasonal discounts in slow selling periods.
Allowance	An extra payment designed to gain reseller participation in special programs. *Trade-in allowances* are granted for turning in an old item when buying a new one. *Promotional allowances* reward dealers for participating in advertising and sales support programs.

Kevin Clancy, chairman of Copernicus, a major marketing research and consulting firm in the United States, found that only 15 to 35 percent of buyers in most categories are price sensitive. People with higher incomes and higher product involvement willingly pay more for features, customer service, quality, added convenience, and the brand name. So it can be a mistake for a strong, distinctive brand to plunge into price discounting to respond to low-price attacks.[66] One such distinctive brand is financial information giant Bloomberg LP, which refuses to discount its product.

 Bloomberg LP   Bloomberg LP markets a subscription service that sells reams of financial data, analytic software to leverage the data's usefulness, trading tools, and even news. Users get all this data via a specialized terminal and a color-coded keyboard that pops the desired information onto the screen. The price is US$1,800 a month, or just a little over $1,500 each for multiple setups in the same company, whether two or 2,000. Banking on the perceived worth of its product and strong user loyalty, Bloomberg knows it doesn't need to discount. Nor does it need to unbundle its data. Reuters, a competing service, actually has more terminals installed than Bloomberg, but it doesn't come close to getting as much revenue from each. Bloomberg's revenue, on the other hand, keeps going up. Revenues for 2010 were almost US$7 billion, making up almost a third of the world's global financial data. When Bloomberg needs to raise its rates, it has an equally simple, one-size-fits-all policy; it raises price 5 percent every 2 years (customers enter a 2-year contract when they subscribe).[67]

At the same time, discounting can be a useful tool if a company can gain concessions in return, such as when the customer agrees to sign a longer contract, is willing to order electronically, thus saving the company money, or agrees to buy in truckload quantities.

Sales management needs to monitor the proportion of customers who are receiving discounts, the average discount, and the particular salespeople who are overrelying on discounting. Higher levels of management should conduct a **net price analysis** to arrive at the 'real price' of the offering. The real price is affected not only by discounts, but by many other expenses that reduce the realized price (see Promotional Pricing section): suppose the company's list price is US$3,000. The average discount is $300. The company's promotional spending averages $450 (15 percent of the list price). Co-op advertising money of $150 is given to retailers to back the product. The company's net price is $2,100, not $3,000.

net price analysis   analysis that encompasses company list price, average discount, promotional spending, and co-op advertising to arrive at net price.

Promotional Pricing

Companies can use several pricing techniques to stimulate early purchase:

- *Loss-leader pricing.* Supermarkets and department stores often drop the price on well-known brands to stimulate additional store traffic. This pays if the revenue on the additional sales compensates for the lower margins on the loss-leader items. Manufacturers of loss-leader brands typically object because this practice can dilute the brand image and bring complaints from retailers who charge the list price. Manufacturers have tried to restrain intermediaries from loss-leader pricing through lobbying for retail-price-maintenance laws, but these laws do not exist in many countries today.

- *Special-event pricing.* Sellers will establish special prices in certain seasons to draw in more customers. Every August, there are back-to-school sales.

- *Cash rebates.* Auto companies and other consumer-goods companies offer cash rebates to encourage purchase of the manufacturers' products within a specified time period. Rebates can help clear inventories without cutting the stated list price.

- *Low-interest financing.* Instead of cutting its price, the company can offer customers low-interest financing. Automakers have used no-interest financing to try to attract more customers.

- *Longer payment terms.* Sellers, especially mortgage banks and auto companies, stretch loans over longer periods and thus lower the monthly payments. Consumers often worry less about the cost (the interest rate) of a loan and more about whether they can afford the monthly payment.

- *Warranties and service contracts.* Companies can promote sales by adding a free or low-cost warranty or service contract.

- *Psychological discounting.* This strategy sets an artificially high price and then offers the product at substantial savings; for example, "Was $359, now $299." Trade and Business Bureaus fight illegal discount tactics. Discounts from normal prices are a legitimate form of promotional pricing.

Promotional-pricing strategies are often a zero-sum game. If they work, competitors copy them and they lose their effectiveness. If they don't work, they waste money that could have been put into other marketing tools, such as building up product quality and service or strengthening product image through advertising.

Differentiated Pricing

Companies often adjust their basic price to accommodate differences in customers, products, locations, and so on. BTM creates men's shirts in many different styles, weights, and levels of quality. A men's button-down shirt may cost as little as US$20 or as much as $50.[68]

Price discrimination occurs when a company sells a product or service at two or more prices that do not reflect a proportional difference in costs. In first-degree price discrimination, the seller charges a separate price to each customer depending on the intensity of his or her demand.

> **price discrimination** a company sells a product or service at two or more prices that do not reflect a proportional difference in costs.

Al-Ahly Football Club   The Al-Ahly Football Club has a fan base estimated at 50 million. It has won the Confederation of African Football Champions League several times, and secured a third-place spot in the intercontinental cup. For its 100th anniversary in 2007, Al-Ahly hosted a game against FC Barcelona and paid them US$2 million. They sold 67,500 seats for the game, with ticket prices ranging from $4 to $525, which were snapped up within hours of going on sale. Even for the Egyptian premier league Al-Ahly match tickets are always sold out within days, if not hours. Prices vary depending on the match. For example, if the football match is between Ahly and Zamalek, the prices are very high, reaching up to $200. For other matches, prices can be as low as $5. Thus, they have different prices depending on the popularity of the rival team. Furthermore, their important matches are sold to TV channels for prices that can reach up to $100,000 per match, up from the regular $50,000.[69]

In second-degree price discrimination, the seller charges less to buyers who buy a larger volume. In third-degree price discrimination, the seller charges different amounts to different classes of buyers, as in the following cases:

- *Customer-segment pricing.* Different customer groups pay different prices for the same product or service. For example, museums often charge a lower admission fee to students and senior citizens.

- *Product-form pricing.* Different versions of the product are priced differently, but not proportionately to their costs. Evian prices a 1,350-milliliter bottle of its mineral water at US$2.00. It takes the same water and packages 48 milliliters in a moisturizer spray for $6.00. Through product-form pricing, Evian manages to charge much more for one form of the product than for another.

Variable pricing has come to sports. Al-Ahly Football Club charges different prices for its football games, depending on the popularity of the rival team.

- **Image pricing.** Some companies price the same product at two different levels based on image differences. A perfume manufacturer can put the perfume in one bottle, give it a name and image, and price it at US$10 for 30 milliliters. It can put the same perfume in another bottle with a different name and image and price it at $30 for 30 milliliters.

- **Channel pricing.** Coca-Cola carries a different price depending on whether the consumer purchases it in a fine restaurant, a fast-food restaurant, or a vending machine.

- **Location pricing.** The same product is priced differently at different locations even though the cost of offering it at each location is the same. A theater varies its seat prices according to audience preferences for different locations.

- **Time pricing.** Prices are varied by season, day, or hour. Public utilities vary energy rates to commercial users by time of day and weekend versus weekday. Restaurants charge less to 'early bird' customers, and some hotels charge less on weekends.

yield pricing situation in which companies offer (1) discounted but limited early purchases, (2) higher-priced late purchases, and (3) the lowest rates on unsold inventory just before it expires.

The airline and hospitality industries use yield-management systems and **yield pricing**, by which they offer discounted but limited early purchases, higher-priced late purchases, and the lowest rates on unsold inventory just before it expires.[70] Airlines charge different fares to passengers on the same flight, depending on the seating class; the time of day (morning or night coach); the day of the week (workday or weekend); the season; the person's employer, past business, or status (youth, military, senior citizen); and so on. That's why on a flight from Amman to Riyadh you might have paid US$500 and be sitting across from someone who has paid $1,500. Egypt Air launches 50 flights a day and each flight has between 10 and 20 prices. Egypt Air starts booking flights 1 year in advance, and every flying day is different from every other flying day.[71] At any given moment the market has more than 7 million prices. And in a system that tracks the difference in prices and the price of competitors' offerings, airlines collectively change 75,000 different prices a day! It's a system designed to punish procrastinators by charging them the highest possible prices.

The phenomenon of offering different pricing schedules to different consumers and dynamically adjusting prices is exploding.[72] Many companies are using software packages that provide real-time controlled tests of actual consumer response to different pricing schedules. Constant price variation, however, can be tricky where consumer relationships are concerned. Research shows it tends to work best in situations where there's no bond between the buyer and the seller. One way to make it work is to offer customers a unique bundle of products and services to meet their needs precisely, making it harder for them to make price comparisons.

The tactic most companies favor, however, is to use variable prices as a reward for good behavior rather than as a penalty. For instance, shipping company APL Inc. rewards customers who can better predict how much cargo space they'll need with cheaper rates for booking early. Customers are also getting savvier about how to avoid buyer's remorse from overpaying. They are changing their buying behavior to accommodate the new realities of dynamic pricing, where prices vary frequently by channels, products, customers, and time.

Most consumers are probably not even aware of the degree to which they are the targets of discriminatory pricing. For instance, catalog retailers such as office product superstore Staples routinely send out catalogs that sell identical goods at different prices. Consumers who live in a more free-spending zip code may see only the higher prices.

We've seen that some forms of price discrimination (in which sellers offer different price terms to different people within the same trade group) are illegal. However, price discrimination is legal if the seller can prove that its costs are different when selling different volumes or different qualities of the same product to different retailers. Predatory pricing—selling below cost with the intention of destroying competition—is unlawful in many parts of the world.[73] Even if legal, some differentiated pricing may meet with a hostile reaction. Coca-Cola considered using wireless technology to raise its vending machine soda prices on hot days and lower them on cold days. Customers so disliked the idea that Coke abandoned it.

For price discrimination to work, certain conditions must exist. First, the market must be segmentable and the segments must show different intensities of demand. Second, members in the lower-price segment must not be able to resell the product to the higher-price segment. Third, competitors must not be able to undersell the firm in the higher-price segment. Fourth, the cost of segmenting and policing the market must not exceed the extra revenue derived from price discrimination. Fifth, the practice must not breed customer resentment and ill will. Sixth, of course, the particular form of price discrimination must not be illegal.[74]

Initiating and Responding to Price Changes

Companies often need to cut or raise prices.

Initiating Price Cuts

Several circumstances might lead a firm to cut prices. One is *excess plant capacity*: the firm needs additional business and cannot generate it through increased sales effort, product improvement, or other measures. Companies sometimes initiate price cuts in a drive to dominate the market through lower costs. Either the company starts with lower costs than its competitors, or it initiates price cuts in the hope of gaining market share and lower costs.

Cutting prices to keep customers or beat competitors often encourages customers to demand price concessions, however, and trains salespeople to offer them.[75] A price-cutting strategy can lead to other possible traps:

- *Low-quality trap.* Consumers assume quality is low.

- *Fragile-market-share trap.* A low price buys market share but not market loyalty. The same customers will shift to any lower-priced firm that comes along.

- *Shallow-pockets trap.* Higher-priced competitors match the lower prices but have longer staying power because of deeper cash reserves.

- *Price-war trap.* Competitors respond by lowering their prices even more, triggering a price war.

Customers often question the motivation behind price changes.[76] They may assume the item is about to be replaced by a new model; the item is faulty and is not selling well; the firm is in financial trouble; the price will come down even further; or the quality has been reduced. The firm must monitor these attributions carefully.

Initiating Price Increases

A successful price increase can raise profits considerably. For example, if the company's profit margin is 3 percent of sales, a 1 percent price increase will increase profits by 33 percent if sales volume is unaffected. This situation is illustrated in 🖎 **Table 14.1**. The assumption is that a company charged US$10 and sold 100 units and had costs of $970, leaving a profit of $30, or 3 percent on sales. By raising its price by 10 cents (a 1 percent price increase), it boosted its profits by 33 percent, assuming the same sales volume.

TABLE 14.1 🖎 Profits Before and After a Price Increase		
	Before	**After**
Price	$10	$10.10	(a 1% price increase)
Units sold	100	100	
Revenue	$1,000	$1,010	
Costs	−970	−970	
Profit	$30	$40	(a 33% profit increase)
Prices are in US$.		

A major circumstance provoking price increases is *cost inflation*. Rising costs unmatched by productivity gains squeeze profit margins and lead companies to regular rounds of price increases. Companies often raise their prices by more than the cost increase, in anticipation of further inflation or government price controls, in a practice called *anticipatory pricing*.

Another factor leading to price increases is *overdemand*. When a company cannot supply all its customers, it can raise its prices, ration supplies to customers, or both. The price can be increased in the following ways, each of which has a different impact on buyers.

- *Delayed quotation pricing.* The company does not set a final price until the product is finished or delivered. This pricing is prevalent in industries with long production lead times, such as industrial construction and heavy equipment.

- *Escalator clauses.* The company requires the customer to pay today's price and all or part of any inflation increase that takes place before delivery. An escalator clause bases price increases on some specified price index. Escalator clauses are found in contracts for major industrial projects, such as aircraft construction and bridge building.

- *Unbundling.* The company maintains its price but removes or prices separately one or more elements that were part of the former offer, such as free delivery or installation. Car companies sometimes add antilock brakes and passenger-side airbags as supplementary extras to their vehicles.

- *Reduction of discounts.* The company instructs its sales force not to offer its normal cash and quantity discounts.

Although there is always a chance that a price increase can carry some positive meanings to customers—for example, that the item is 'hot' and represents an unusually good value—consumers generally dislike higher prices. In passing price increases on to customers, the company must avoid looking like a price gouger.[77] Consumer concern and dissatisfaction with high gasoline and prescription drug prices, Coca-Cola's proposed smart vending machines that would raise prices as temperatures rose, and Amazon.com's dynamic pricing experiment whereby prices varied by purchase occasion became front-page news. The more similar the products or offerings from a company, the more likely consumers are to interpret any pricing differences as unfair. Product customization and differentiation and communications that clarify differences are thus critical.[78]

Generally, consumers prefer small price increases on a regular basis to sudden, sharp increases. Their memories are long, and they can turn against companies they perceive as price gougers. Price hikes without corresponding investments in the value of the brand increase vulnerability to lower-priced competition. Consumers may be willing to 'trade down' because they no longer can justify to themselves that the higher-priced brand is worth it.

Several techniques help consumers avoid sticker shock and a hostile reaction when prices rise: one is that a sense of fairness must surround any price increase, and customers must be given advance notice so they can do forward buying or shop around. Sharp price increases need to be explained in understandable terms. Making low-visibility price moves first is also a good technique: eliminating discounts, increasing minimum order sizes, and curtailing production of low-margin products are some examples; and contracts or bids for long-term projects should contain escalator clauses based on such factors as increases in recognized national price indexes.[79]

Given strong consumer resistance to price hikes, marketers go to great lengths to find alternative approaches that will allow them to avoid increasing prices when they otherwise would have done so. Here are a few popular ones.

- Shrinking the amount of product instead of raising the price. (Hershey Foods maintained its chocolate bar price but trimmed its size. Nestlé maintained its size but raised the price.)

- Substituting less-expensive materials or ingredients. (Many chocolate bar companies substituted synthetic chocolate for real chocolate to fight price increases in cocoa.)

- Reducing or removing product features. (Sears—a retailer for appliances that can ship to over 90 countries—engineered down a number of its appliances so they could be priced competitively with those sold in discount stores.)

- Removing or reducing product services, such as installation or free delivery.

- Using less-expensive packaging material or larger package sizes.

- Reducing the number of sizes and models offered.

- Creating new economy brands. (Hyper One—a chain of hypermarket stores in Egypt—introduced around 30 generic items selling at around 40 percent less than national brands.)

Responding to Competitors' Price Changes

How should a firm respond to a price cut initiated by a competitor? In general, the best response varies with the situation. The company must consider the product's stage in the life cycle, its importance in the company's portfolio, the competitor's intentions and resources, the market's price and quality sensitivity, the behavior of costs with volume, and the company's alternative opportunities.

In markets characterized by high product homogeneity, the firm can search for ways to enhance its augmented product. If it cannot find any, it may need to meet the price reduction. If the competitor raises its price in a homogeneous product market, other firms might not match it if the increase will not benefit the industry as a whole. Then the leader will need to roll back the increase.

 Air Arabia   Air Arabia, a leading airline in the Arab world, pioneered e-ticketing services to make air travel more accessible and affordable. The airline is able to under-price conventional carriers such as Etihad Airways' and Emirates Airline's special offer and discount flights. The fares of the three carriers for trips from the UAE to different cities in the region were analyzed (assuming departure on 15 March 2009 and return on 22 March 2009). Taking the lowest fare offered by each carrier, Air Arabia still offered the lowest prices and was on average around 35 percent cheaper than its conventional peers, and in some cases more than 50 percent cheaper. Maintaining these levels of advantage should allow Air Arabia to at least maintain its market share and potentially expand it.[80]

In nonhomogeneous product markets, a firm has more latitude. It needs to consider the following issues: (1) why did the competitor change the price? To steal the market, to utilize excess capacity, to meet changing cost conditions, or to lead an industry-wide price change? (2) Does the competitor plan to make the price change temporary or permanent? (3) What will happen to the company's market share and profits if it does not respond? Are other companies going to respond? (4) What are the competitors' and other firms' responses likely to be to each possible reaction?

Market leaders often face aggressive price cutting by smaller firms trying to build market share. Using price, Fuji has attacked Kodak, Schick has attacked Gillette, and AMD has attacked Intel. Brand leaders also face lower-priced private-label store brands. The brand leader can respond in several ways. The Marketing Memo: *How to Fight Low-Cost Rivals* highlights some possible responses.

An extended analysis of alternatives may not always be feasible when the attack occurs. The company may have to react decisively within hours or days, especially in those industries where price changes occur with some frequency and where it is important to react quickly, such as the meatpacking, lumber, or oil industries. It would make better sense to anticipate possible competitors' price changes and prepare contingent responses.

How to Fight Low-Cost Rivals

London Business School's Nirmalya Kumar spent 5 years studying 50 incumbents and 25 low-cost businesses to better understand the threats posed by disruptive, low-cost competitors. He notes that successful price warriors, such as Germany's Aldi supermarkets and India's Aravind Eye Hospitals are changing the nature of competition all over the world by employing several key tactics, such as focusing on just one or a few consumer segments, delivering the basic product or providing one benefit better than rivals do, and backing low prices with superefficient operations.

Kumar believes ignoring low-cost rivals is a mistake, because they eventually force companies to vacate entire market segments. He doesn't see price wars as the answer either; slashing prices usually lowers profits for incumbents without driving the low-cost entrants out of business. In the race to the bottom, he says, the challengers always come out ahead of the incumbents. Instead, he offers three possible responses that will vary in their success depending on different factors, as outlined in ◢◣ **Figure 14.6**.

The first approach to competing against cut-price players is to differentiate the product or service through various means:

- Design cool products (Apple; Bang & Olufsen).
- Continually innovate (Gillette; 3M).
- Offer a unique product mix (Sharper Image; Whole Foods).
- Brand a community (Harley-Davidson; Red Bull).
- Sell experiences (Four Seasons; Starbucks).

Kumar cautions that three conditions will determine the success of a differentiation response:

1. **Companies must not use differentiation tactics in isolation.** Bang & Olufsen has competed effectively against low-cost electronics manufacturers in part because of its strong design capabilities, but also because the company continually introduces new products, cultivates an upscale brand image, and supports modern-looking retail outlets.

2. **Companies must be able to persuade consumers to pay for added benefits.** Charging a small premium for greater services or benefits, as with Metro Market and Alpha Market, can be a powerful defense.

3. **Companies must first bring costs and benefits in line.** HP's resurgence in the PC industry can be attributed in part to its success in cutting Dell's cost advantage from 20 to 10 percent.

Kumar cautions that unless sizable numbers of consumers demand additional benefits, companies may need to yield some markets to price warriors. For example, British Airways has relinquished some short-haul routes to low-cost rivals easyJet and Ryanair. Kumar also believes strategies that help an incumbent firm coexist with low-cost rivals can work initially, but over the long haul, consumers migrate to low-cost options as they become more familiar with them.

Another approach that many companies have tried in responding to low-cost competitors is to introduce a low-cost venture themselves. Citing the failure of no-frills second carriers such as Continental Lite, Delta's Song, US Airways' MetroJet, and Egypt Air Express, however, Kumar asserts that companies should set up low-cost operations only if (1) the traditional operation will become more competitive as a result and (2) the new business will derive some advantages that it would not have gained as an independent entity.

A dual strategy succeeds only if companies can generate synergies between the existing businesses and the new ventures, as financial service providers HSBC and ING did. The low-cost venture most likely includes a unique brand name or identity, adequate resources, and a willingness to endure some cannibalization between the two businesses.

If there are no synergies between traditional and low-cost businesses, companies should consider two other options: they can switch from selling products to selling solutions, or even convert themselves into low-cost players. In the former approach, Kumar believes that by offering products and services as an integrated package, companies can expand the segment of the market that is willing to pay more for additional benefits. Selling solutions requires managing customers' processes and increasing their revenues or lowering their costs and risks.

And if all else fails, the best solution may be reinvention as a low-cost player. After all, as noted above, Ryanair was an unprofitable, high-cost traditional airline before it completely—and quite successfully—transformed itself into a low-cost carrier.

Source: Nirmalya Kumar, "Strategies to Fight Low-Cost Rivals," *Harvard Business Review*, December 2006, pp. 104–112.

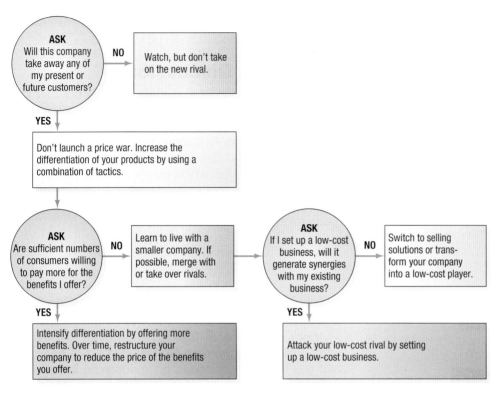

Summary

1. Despite the increased role of nonprice factors in modern marketing, price remains a critical element of the marketing mix. Price is the only element that produces revenue; the others produce costs.

2. In setting pricing policy, a company follows a six-step procedure. It selects its pricing objective. It estimates the demand curve, the probable quantities it will sell at each possible price. It estimates how its costs vary at different levels of output, at different levels of accumulated production experience, and for differentiated marketing offers. It examines competitors' costs, prices, and offers. It selects a pricing method. It selects the final price.

3. Companies do not usually set a single price, but rather a pricing structure that reflects variations in geographical demand and costs, market-segment requirements, purchase timing, order levels, and other factors. Several price-adaptation strategies are available: (1) geographical pricing; (2) price discounts and allowances; (3) promotional pricing; and (4) discriminatory pricing.

4. After developing pricing strategies, firms often face situations in which they need to change prices. A price decrease might be brought about by excess plant capacity, declining market share, a desire to dominate the market through lower costs, or economic recession. A price increase might be brought about by cost inflation or overdemand. Companies must carefully manage customer perceptions in raising prices.

5. Companies must anticipate competitor price changes and prepare contingent responses. A number of responses are possible in terms of maintaining or changing price or quality.

6. The firm facing a competitor's price change must try to understand the competitor's intent and the likely duration of the change. Strategy often depends on whether a firm is producing homogeneous or nonhomogeneous products. A market leader attacked by lower-priced competitors can seek to better differentiate itself, introduce its own low-cost competitor, or transform itself more completely.

Applications

Marketing Debate

Is the Right Price a Fair Price?

Prices are often set to satisfy demand or to reflect the premium that consumers are willing to pay for a product or service. Some critics shudder, however, at the thought of US$2 bottles of water, $150 running shoes, and $500 concert tickets.

Take a position: Prices should reflect the value that consumers are willing to pay *versus* prices should primarily just reflect the cost involved in making a product or service.

Marketing Discussion

Think of the various pricing methods described in this chapter: markup pricing, target-return pricing, perceived-value pricing, value pricing, going-rate pricing, and auction-type pricing. As a consumer, which method do you personally prefer to deal with? Why? If the average price were to stay the same, which would you prefer: (1) for firms to set one price and not deviate or (2) to employ slightly higher prices most of the year, but slightly lower discounted prices or specials for certain occasions?

Marketing Excellence

>>eBay

Pierre Omidayar, a French-Iranian immigrant, created eBay as a way to help his girlfriend sell and trade her Pez candy dispenser collection (Pez is a candy brand that is well known in the United States and also the Arab world). Soon the site grew into a broader auction site where consumers could auction collectibles such as baseball cards and Barbie dolls. The momentum continued, and soon small businesses discovered that eBay was an efficient way to reach consumers and other businesses. Large companies saw it as an opportunity to sell bulk lots of unsold inventory.

By helping buyers get the best price for their items and letting customers decide the price they want to pay, eBay created a pricing revolution. Customers gain control as they choose the price, and the efficiency and wide reach of the site lets sellers make good margins.

eBay generated US$9 billion in consolidated new revenues in 2010. The site has close to 300 million registered users and receives around 50 million unique visitors a month. More than 1 million of its members make their living from the site. Yet, eBay itself doesn't buy any inventory or own the products on its site. It earns its money by collecting a fee for the auction listing, plus a commission that ranges from 1 to 5 percent when the sale is completed. Merchants report profit margins of 40 percent. With eBay's expansion into a whole range of other categories—from boats and cars to travel and tickets, and from health and beauty to home and garden—collectibles now make up only 13 percent of eBay sales.

Consumer trust is a key element of eBay's success. The company tracks and publishes the reputations of both buyers and sellers on the basis of feedback from each transaction. eBay's millions of passionate users have a voice in all major decisions the company makes through its Voice of the Customer program. Every few months, eBay brings in as many as a dozen sellers and buyers and asks them questions about how they work and what else eBay needs to do. At least twice a week the company holds hour-long teleconferences to poll users on almost every new feature or policy. The result is that users (eBay's customers) feel like owners, and they have taken the initiative to expand the company into ever-new territory.

Although eBay began as an auction site, it has evolved to also offer a fixed-price 'buy it now' option to those who don't want to wait for an auction and are willing to pay the price set by the seller. For years, buyers and sellers have used eBay as an informal guide to market value. A consumer or businessperson—or even a company with

Continued on next page >>

Marketing Excellence...continued

>>eBay

a new-product design—who wants to know the 'going price' for anything from a copier to a new DVD player checks on eBay.

Current CEO Meg Whitman believes eBay's acquisitions of PayPal online payment service in 2002 and Skype internet voice and video communication service in 2005 have synergistically expanded the company's auction capabilities and revenue sources: eBay buyers and sellers can talk over Skype (generating ad revenue for eBay); Skype callers can use Paypal to pay for any calls that require payment; and Skype will facilitate the further global expansion of PayPal which is positioning itself as a global giant; part international swap meet and part clearing-house for the world's manufacturers and retailers.

Acquisitions of shopping.com, an online comparison shopping service, rent.com online, an apartment-listing service in 2005, and StubHub online ticket resale service in 2007 provided additional diversification, but eBay has also encountered increased competition from Google and new challenges as it expands globally into tough markets such as China. eBay will need to continue to transform the modern electronic marketplace to achieve lasting success.

Questions

1. How did the concept of eBay evolve?
2. What need did eBay offer its customers?
3. How does eBay generate profits?
4. What are some of eBay's factors of success?
5. How is eBay's business growing?

Sources: Adam Lashinsky, "Building EBay 2.0," *Fortune*, October 16, 2006, pp. 161–164; Matthew Creamer, "A Million Marketers," *Advertising Age*, June 26, 2006, pp. 1, 71; Clive Thompson, "EBay Heads East," *Fast Company*, July–August 2006, pp. 87–89; Betsy Streisand, "Make New Sales, but Keep the Old," *U.S. News & World Report*, February 16, 2004, p. 40; Glen L. Urban, "The Emerging Era of Customer Advocacy," *MIT Sloan Management Review*, Winter 2004, pp. 77–82; Robert D. Hof, "The EBay Economy," *BusinessWeek*, August 25, 2003, pp. 125–128.

PART 6 Delivering Value

Chapter **15** | Designing and Managing Integrated Marketing Channels
Chapter **16** | Managing Retailing, Wholesaling, and Logistics

CHAPTER 15

PepsiCo uses a complex distribution network to make its products conveniently available to ultimate consumers.

In this chapter, we will address the following questions:

Designing and Managing Integrated Marketing Channels

Successful value creation needs successful value delivery. Holistic marketers are increasingly taking a value network view of their businesses. Instead of limiting their focus to their immediate suppliers, distributors, and customers, they are examining the whole supply chain that links raw materials, components, and manufactured goods and shows how they move toward the final consumers. Companies are looking at their suppliers' suppliers upstream and at their distributors' customers downstream. They are looking at customer segments and considering a wide range of different possible means to sell, distribute, and service their offerings.

PepsiCo's worldwide network is divided into three independent sectors: 1) America; 2) Europe; and 3) Asia, the Middle East and Africa. Each sector is headed by a dedicated CEO. In each sector, PepsiCo sells its product range, with snacks and beverages being the two most prominent categories. Snacks are mostly produced and sold via company-owned operations where PepsiCo controls the entire chain from raw material procurement to production, distribution, and marketing. In the beverages sector, PepsiCo operates under two models: company-owned bottling operations (COBOs) and franchise-owned bottling operations (FOBO). While the COBOs are similar to snacks operations, the FOBOs differ in that PepsiCo does not operate any of them. It just sells concentrate to appointed bottlers who, in turn, convert the concentrate into finished goods, which they then distribute. However, PepsiCo retains control over the brand and the advertising. "PepsiCo's Beverage business in Saudi Arabia falls under the FOBO model whereby PepsiCo has entered into franchising agreements with four bottlers in the main regions of Saudi Arabia (West, Central, East, and South)," says Nadim Nakfoor, general manager of PepsiCo's Al-Jumaih Bottling Plant. This contrasts with PepsiCo's main competitor, Coca-Cola, which operates a joint venture across all of Saudi Arabia with just one bottler. Some industry experts believe that in a market as large and a geography as vast as Saudi Arabia, having four bottlers, each focused on its own area and with its own local networks and production facilities, has given a competitive edge to PepsiCo. Moreover, bottlers have created a network with each other and can share best practices and market intelligence, and even support each other with raw materials or spare parts in case of shortages. At times, even finished goods have been exchanged to meet certain market demands.[1]

Companies today must build and manage a continuously evolving and increasingly complex channel system and value network. In this chapter, we consider strategic and tactical issues with integrating marketing channels and developing value networks. We will examine marketing channel issues from the perspective of retailers, wholesalers, and physical distribution agencies in Chapter 16. ▽

Marketing Channels and Value Networks

Most producers do not sell their goods directly to the final users; between them stands a set of intermediaries performing a variety of functions. These intermediaries constitute a marketing channel (also called a trade channel or distribution channel). Formally, **marketing channels** are sets of interdependent organizations involved in the process of making a product or service available for use or consumption. They are the set of pathways a product or service follows after production, culminating in purchase and use by the final end user.[2]

marketing channels sets of interdependent organizations involved in the process of making a product or service available for use or consumption.

Some intermediaries—such as wholesalers and retailers—buy, take title to, and resell the merchandise; they are called *merchants*. Others—brokers, manufacturers' representatives, sales agents—search for customers and may negotiate on the producer's behalf but do not take title to the goods; they are called *agents*. Still others—transportation companies, independent warehouses, banks, advertising agencies—assist in the distribution process but neither take title to goods nor negotiate purchases or sales; they are called *facilitators*.

The Importance of Channels

marketing channel system the particular set of marketing channels employed by a firm.

A **marketing channel system** is the particular set of marketing channels a firm employs, and decisions about it are among the most critical ones management faces. Channel members collectively can earn margins that constitute 30 to 50 percent of the ultimate selling price. In contrast, advertising typically accounts for less than 5 to 7 percent of the final price.[3] Marketing channels also represent a substantial opportunity cost. One of the chief roles of marketing channels is to convert potential buyers into profitable customers. Marketing channels must not just serve markets, they must also make markets.[4]

The channels chosen affect all other marketing decisions. The company's pricing depends on whether it uses mass merchandisers or high-quality boutiques. The firm's sales force and advertising decisions depend on how much training and motivation dealers need. In addition, channel decisions include relatively long-term commitments with other firms as well as a set of policies and procedures. When an automaker signs up independent dealers to sell its automobiles, the automaker cannot buy them out the next day and replace them with company-owned outlets. But at the same time, channel choices themselves depend on the company's marketing strategy with respect to segmentation, targeting, and positioning. Holistic marketers ensure that marketing decisions in all these different areas are made to collectively maximize value.

push strategy when the manufacturer uses its sales force and trade promotion money to induce intermediaries to carry, promote, and sell the product to end users.

pull strategy when the manufacturer uses advertising and promotion to persuade consumers to ask intermediaries for the product, thus inducing the intermediaries to order it.

In managing its intermediaries, the firm must decide how much effort to devote to push versus pull marketing. A **push strategy** uses the manufacturer's sales force, trade promotion money, or other means to induce intermediaries to carry, promote, and sell the product to end users. Push strategy is appropriate where there is low brand loyalty in a category, brand choice is made in the store, the product is an impulse item, and product benefits are well understood. In a **pull strategy** the manufacturer uses advertising, promotion, and other forms of communication to persuade consumers to demand the product from intermediaries, thus inducing the intermediaries to order it. Pull strategy is appropriate when there is high brand loyalty and high involvement in the category, when consumers are able to perceive differences between brands, and when they choose the brand before they go to the store. For example, Intel ran an extremely successful advertising campaign with its Intel Inside.

Intel Inside   While few average PC users are knowledgeable about PC hardware and processors, Intel invested tens of millions of dollars on its Intel Inside campaign, which targeted the ultimate PC user. The campaign created awareness among regular PC users of the importance of what is inside the computer: the chip by which computer processing takes place. Intel's campaign started as a cooperative advertising program, in which Intel contributed to its PC manufacturers' advertising budgets, on condition that they included the Intel Inside logo, and stated in their ads that the PCs contained the Intel chip. Intel would take a percentage of the purchase price of the processors and put it in a co-op fund to support such ads. The company also launched its own print and TV ad campaign for Intel Inside, reminding the user to request a simple feature in their PC: an Intel processor. The Intel Inside program placed thc Intel brand among the top-ten most known brands in the world, in the same league as consumer giants Coca-Cola, Disney, and McDonald's.[5]

In most countries of the world, the practice of advertising prescription drugs to ultimate consumers (patients) is banned by law. Drug companies have thus aimed their ads and communication approaches at physicians, hospitals, and other health care providers. Yet, some countries are loosening up their laws, allowing such advertisements within a very defined set of guidelines, opening the way for pharmaceuticals to reach consumers directly.

Top marketing companies such as Coca-Cola, Intel, and Nike skillfully employ both push and pull strategies. Marketing activities directed towards the channel as part of a push strategy are more effective when accompanied by a well-designed and well-executed pull strategy that activates consumer demand. On the other hand, without at least some consumer interest, it can be very difficult to gain much channel acceptance and support.

Channel Development

A new firm typically starts as a local operation selling in a fairly confined market, using existing intermediaries. The number of such intermediaries is usually limited to a few manufacturers' sales agents, a few wholesalers, several established retailers, a few trucking companies, and a few warehouses. Deciding on the best channels might not be a problem; the problem is often to convince the available intermediaries to handle the firm's line.

If the firm is successful, it might branch into new markets and use different channels in different markets. In smaller markets, the firm might sell directly to retailers; in larger markets, it might sell through distributors. In rural areas, it might work with general-goods merchants; in urban areas, with limited-line merchants. In one part of the country, it might grant exclusive franchises; in another, it might sell through all outlets willing to handle the merchandise. In one country, it might use international sales agents; in another, it might partner with a local firm.

International markets pose distinct challenges. Customers' shopping habits can vary by countries, and many retailers such as Germany's Aldi, the United Kingdom's Tesco, and Spain's Zara have redefined themselves to a certain degree when entering a new market to better tailor their image to local needs and wants. Retailers that have largely stuck to the same selling formula regardless of geography, such as Marks & Spencer and Walmart, have sometimes encountered trouble in entering new markets.[6]

In short, the channel system evolves as a function of local opportunities and conditions, emerging threats and opportunities, company resources and capabilities, and other factors. Consider some of the challenges Dell has encountered in recent years.

 Dell   Dell revolutionized the personal computer category by selling directly to customers via the telephone and later the internet. Customers could custom-design the exact PC they wanted, and rigorous cost cutting allowed for low everyday prices. Sound like a winning formula? It was for almost two decades. But by 2006, the company was encountering problems that led to a steep stock price decline. First, reinvigorated competitors such as HP narrowed the gap in productivity and price. Always focused more on the business market, Dell struggled to sell effectively to the consumer market. A shift in consumer preferences to buying in retail stores didn't help, but self-inflicted damage from an ultra-efficient supply chain model that squeezed costs—and quality—out of customer service was perhaps the most painful. Managers evaluated call center employees primarily on how quickly they finished each call—a recipe for disaster, as scores of customers felt their problems were ignored or not properly handled. A drop in R&D spending that hindered new-product development and led to a lack of differentiation didn't help either. Clearly, Dell had entered a new chapter in its history. A fundamental rethinking of its channel strategy and its marketing approach as a whole would consume the company for the next five years.[7]

Hybrid Channels

hybrid channels use of multiple channels of distribution to reach customers in a defined market.

Today's successful companies are also multiplying the number of 'go-to-market' or **hybrid channels** in any one market area. In contrast to Dell, HP has used its sales force to sell to large accounts, outbound telemarketing to sell to medium-sized accounts, direct mail with an inbound number to sell to small accounts, retailers to sell to still smaller accounts, and the internet to sell specialty items. Staples, a leading office stationery and accessory store, markets through its traditional retail channel, a direct-response internet site, virtual malls, and thousands of links on affiliated sites. Apple markets its wide range of products of PCs, iPads, iPods, iPhones, and other products through a complex network of channels which includes its own Apple stores, its own Apple website, authorized dealers, university and school bookstores, consumer electronic stores, music and entertainment stores, and licensed mobile operators, among others.

Companies that manage hybrid channels must make sure these channels work well together and match each target customer's preferred ways of doing business. Customers expect *channel integration*, characterized by features such as:

- the ability to order a product online and pick it up at a convenient retail location;
- the ability to return an online-ordered product to a nearby store of the retailer;
- the right to receive discounts and promotional offers based on total online and offline purchases.

Understanding Customer Needs

Consumers may choose the channels they prefer based on a number of factors: the price, product assortment, and convenience of a channel option, as well as their own particular shopping goals (economic, social, or experiential).[8] As with products, segmentation exists, and marketers employing different types of channels must be aware that different consumers have different needs during the purchase process.

Researchers Nunes and Cespedes argue that, in many markets, buyers fall into one of four categories.[9]

1. *Habitual shoppers* purchase from the same places in the same manner over time.
2. *High-value deal seekers* know their needs and 'channel surf' a great deal before buying at the lowest possible price.
3. *Variety-loving shoppers* gather information in many channels, take advantage of high-touch services, and then buy in their favorite channel, regardless of price.
4. *High-involvement shoppers* gather information in all channels, make their purchase in a low-cost channel, but take advantage of customer support from a high-touch channel.

One study of 40 grocery and clothing retailers in France, Germany, and the United Kingdom found that retailers in those countries served three types of shopper: (1) *service/quality customers* who cared most about the variety and performance of products in stores as well as the service provided; (2) *price/value customers* who were most concerned about spending their money wisely; and (3) *affinity customers* who primarily sought stores that suited people like themselves or the members of groups they aspired to join. As ▲ **Figure 15.1** shows, customer profiles for these types of retailers differed across the three markets: In France, shoppers placed more importance on service and quality, in the United Kingdom, affinity, and in Germany, price and value.[10] A similar three-tier breakdown of shoppers can be found in the Arab world, with shoppers perhaps placing the most importance on service and quality.

Even the same consumer, though, may choose to use different channels for different functions in making a purchase. For instance, someone may choose to browse through a catalog before visiting a store or take a test drive at a dealer before renting a car online. Consumers may also seek different types of channels depending on the particular types of goods involved. Some consumers are willing to 'trade up' to retailers offering higher-end goods such as TAG Heuer or Montblanc watches, Lanvin ties, or Hermes scarfs; these same consumers are also willing to 'trade down' to discount retailers to buy private-label paper towels, detergent, or ketchup.[11]

Value Networks

A supply chain view of a firm sees markets as destination points and amounts to a linear view of the flow. The company should first think of the target market, however, and then design the supply

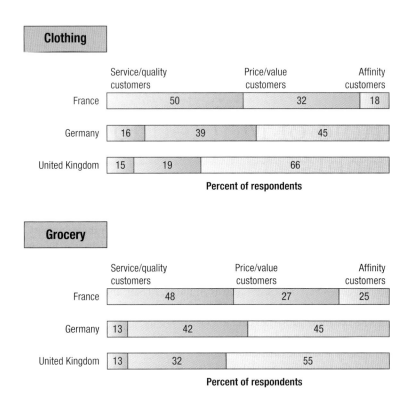

Clothing

	Service/quality customers	Price/value customers	Affinity customers
France	50	32	18
Germany	16	39	45
United Kingdom	15	19	66

Percent of respondents

Grocery

	Service/quality customers	Price/value customers	Affinity customers
France	48	27	25
Germany	13	42	45
United Kingdom	13	32	55

Percent of respondents

Fig. 15.1 △

What Do European Customers Value?

Source: Peter N. Child, Suzanne Heywood, and Michael Kliger, "Do Retail Brands Travel?," *McKinsley Quarterly*, January 2002, pp. 11–13. Reprinted by permission.

chain backward from that point. This view has been called **demand chain planning**. Northwestern's Don Schultz says: "A demand chain management approach doesn't just push things through the system. It emphasizes what solutions consumers are looking for, not what products we are trying to sell them." Schultz has suggested that the traditional marketing 'four Ps' be replaced by a new acronym, SIVA, which stands for solutions, information, value, and access.[12]

An even broader view sees a company at the center of a **value network**: a system of partnerships and alliances that a firm creates to source, augment, and deliver its offerings. A value network includes a firm's suppliers and its suppliers' suppliers, and its immediate customers and their end customers. The value network includes valued relations with others such as university researchers and government approval agencies.

A company needs to orchestrate these parties in order to deliver superior value to the target market. Palm, the famous manufacturer of handheld devices, consists of a whole community of suppliers and assemblers of semiconductor components, plastic cases, LCD displays, and accessories; of offline and online resellers; of 275,000 developers in the Palm Developer Network who have created over 21,000 software programs and 100 hardware add-ons for the Palm operating systems for handheld computers and smartphones.

Demand chain planning yields several insights. First, the company can estimate whether more money is made upstream or downstream, in case it might want to integrate backward or forward. Second, the company is more aware of disturbances anywhere in the supply chain that might cause costs, prices, or supplies to change suddenly. Third, companies can go online with their business partners to carry on faster and more accurate communications, transactions, and payments to reduce costs, speed up information, and increase accuracy. For example, Ford not only manages numerous supply chains but also sponsors or transacts on many business to business (B2B) websites and exchanges as needs arise.

Managing this value network has required companies to make increasing investments in information technology (IT) and software. Firms have introduced supply chain management (SCM) software and invited such software firms as SAP and Oracle to design comprehensive *enterprise resource planning* (ERP) systems to manage cash flow, manufacturing, human resources, purchasing, and other major functions within a unified framework. They hope to break up department bureaucracy and interdepartmental boundaries and carry out core business processes more smoothly and accurately. In most cases, however, companies are still a long way from truly comprehensive ERP systems.

demand chain planning   the process of designing the supply chain based on adopting a target market perspective and working backward.

value network   a system of partnerships and alliances that a firm creates to source, augment, and deliver its offerings.

Marketers, for their part, have traditionally focused on the side of the value network that looks toward the customer, adopting customer relationship management (CRM) software and practices. In the future, they will increasingly participate in and influence their companies' upstream activities and become network managers, not just product and customer managers.

The Role of Marketing Channels

Why would a producer delegate some of the selling job to intermediaries? Delegation means relinquishing some control over how and to whom the products are sold. But producers can often gain in effectiveness and efficiency by using intermediaries. Through their contacts, experience, specialization, and scale of operation, intermediaries make goods widely available and accessible to target markets, usually offering the firm more than it can achieve on its own.[13]

Many producers lack the financial resources and expertise to sell directly on their own. Fast-moving-consumer-goods manufacturers such as Al Rabie, Al Safi, and KDD, and even giants such as Procter & Gamble, would find it impractical to sell directly to the ultimate consumer. For example, Ghandour, the Lebanese pan-Arab confectionary manufacturer, would not find it practical to establish small retail chocolate and confectionary shops throughout the Arab world or to sell by mail order through the internet. Ghandour finds it easier to work through the extensive network of privately owned distribution organizations that serve groceries and supermarkets. Car manufacturers such as Honda or General Motors would be hard-pressed to replace all the tasks done by their networks of thousands of dealers worldwide.

Channel Functions and Flows

A marketing channel performs the work of moving goods from producers to consumers. It overcomes the time, place, and possession gaps that separate goods and services from those who need or want them. Members of the marketing channel perform a number of key functions (see ▥ **Box 15.1**).

Some functions (physical, title, promotion) constitute a *forward flow* of activity from the company to the customer; other functions (ordering and payment) constitute a *backward flow* from customers to the company. Still others (information, negotiation, finance, and risk taking) occur in both directions. Five flows are illustrated in ⚠ **Figure 15.2** for the marketing of forklift trucks. If these flows were superimposed in one diagram, the tremendous complexity of even simple marketing channels would be apparent.

BOX 15.1 ▬   Channel Member Functions

- Gather information about potential and current customers, competitors, and other actors and forces in the marketing environment.
- Develop and disseminate persuasive communications to stimulate purchasing.
- Reach agreements on price and other terms so that transfer of ownership or possession can be effected.
- Place orders with manufacturers.
- Acquire the funds to finance inventories at different levels in the marketing channel.
- Assume risks connected with carrying out channel work.
- Provide for the successive storage and movement of physical products.
- Provide for buyers' payment of their bills through banks and other financial institutions.
- Oversee actual transfer of ownership from one organization or person to another.

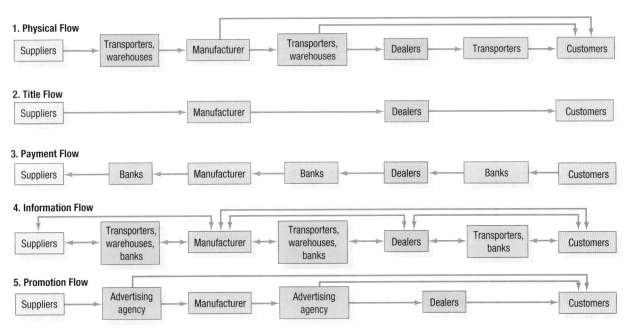

1. Physical Flow

Suppliers → Transporters, warehouses → Manufacturer → Transporters, warehouses → Dealers → Transporters → Customers

2. Title Flow

Suppliers → Manufacturer → Dealers → Customers

3. Payment Flow

Suppliers ← Banks ← Manufacturer ← Banks ← Dealers ← Banks ← Customers

4. Information Flow

Suppliers ↔ Transporters, warehouses, banks ↔ Manufacturer ↔ Transporters, warehouses, banks ↔ Dealers ↔ Transporters, banks ↔ Customers

5. Promotion Flow

Suppliers → Advertising agency → Manufacturer → Advertising agency → Dealers → Customers

|Fig. 15.2| △

Five Marketing Flows in the Marketing Channel for Forklift Trucks

A manufacturer selling a physical product and services might require three channels: a *sales channel*, a *delivery channel*, and a *service channel*. To sell its Bowflex fitness equipment, the Nautilus Group historically has emphasized direct marketing via television infomercials and ads, inbound/outbound call centers, response mailings, and the internet as sales channels; courier service as the delivery channel; and local repair people as the service channel. Reflecting shifting consumer buying habits, Nautilus also sells Bowflex through commercial, retail, and specialty retail channels. Nautilus Fitness Centers now have a presence in a good number of Arab cities including Kuwait City, Manama, Sharjah, Dubai, Beirut, Jeddah, and Muscat.

The question is not *whether* various channel functions need to be performed—they must be—but rather, *who* is to perform them. All channel functions have three things in common: they use up scarce resources; they can often be performed better through specialization; and they can be shifted among channel members. When the manufacturer shifts some functions to intermediaries, the producer's costs and prices are lower, but the intermediary must add a charge to cover its work. If the intermediaries are more efficient than the manufacturer, prices to consumers should be lower. If consumers perform some functions themselves, they should enjoy even lower prices. Changes in channel institutions thus largely reflect the discovery of more efficient ways to combine or separate the economic functions that provide assortments of goods to target customers.

Channel Levels

The producer and the final customer are part of every channel. We will use the number of intermediary levels to designate the length of a channel. △ **Figure 15.3a** illustrates several consumer-goods marketing channels of different lengths.

A **zero-level channel** (also called a **direct marketing channel**) consists of a manufacturer selling directly to the final customer. The major examples are door-to-door sales, mail order, telemarketing, TV selling, internet selling, and manufacturer-owned stores. Live'ly (see the opening vignette in

zero-level channel (direct-marketing channel) a manufacturer selling directly to the final customer.

Nautilus now sells products like Bowflex through commercial, retail, and specialty retail channels.

|Fig. 15.3| ▲

Consumer and Industrial Marketing Channels

Chapter 8) delivers its nutritious food door to door; Etisalat uses the telephone to prospect for new customers or to sell enhanced services to existing customers; Rotana sells music and video collections through TV commercials; Al-Hallab sells Arabic and oriental sweets online; and Apple sells computers and other consumer electronics through its own stores.

A *one-level channel* contains one selling intermediary, such as a retailer. A *two-level channel* contains two intermediaries. In consumer markets, these are typically a wholesaler and a retailer. A *three-level channel* contains three intermediaries. In the meatpacking industry, wholesalers sell to jobbers, who sell to small retailers. In Japan, food distribution may include as many as six levels. From the producer's point of view, obtaining information about end users and exercising control becomes more difficult as the number of channel levels increases.

Figure 15.3b shows channels commonly used in B2B marketing. An industrial-goods manufacturer can use its sales force to sell directly to industrial customers; or it can sell to industrial distributors, who sell to the industrial customers; or it can sell through manufacturer's representatives or its own sales branches directly to industrial customers, or indirectly to industrial customers through industrial distributors. Zero-, one-, and two-level marketing channels are quite common.

Channels normally describe a forward movement of products from source to user, but there are also *reverse-flow channels*. These are important in the following cases: (1) to reuse products or containers (such as refillable chemical containers); (2) to refurbish products (such as circuit boards or computers) for resale; (3) to recycle products (such as paper); and (4) to dispose of products and packaging (waste products). Several intermediaries play a role in reverse-flow channels, including manufacturers' redemption centers, community groups, traditional intermediaries such as soft-drink intermediaries, trash-collection specialists, recycling centers, trash-recycling brokers, and central processing warehousing.[14]

Service Sector Channels

Marketing channels are not limited to the distribution of physical goods. Producers of services and ideas also face the problem of making their output available and accessible to target populations. Schools develop 'education-dissemination systems' and hospitals develop 'health-delivery systems.' These institutions must figure out agencies and locations for reaching a population spread out over an area. If we take private universities in the Arab world as an example, some leading universities choose to confine their presence and educational services in a single geographic location while attempting to attract students from around the Arab world. The American University of Beirut houses around 8,000 students at its only campus in Beirut, Lebanon. About 20 percent of AUB's student body is non-Lebanese, with the bulk coming from neighboring Arab countries Jordan, Palestine, Saudi Arabia, and Kuwait. The Arab Open University, on the other hand, follows a different strategy.

Arab Open University

The Arab Open University (AOU) is a pan-Arab university, headquartered in Kuwait, with seven branches in seven Arab countries: Kuwait, Bahrain, Saudi Arabia, Egypt, Jordan, Lebanon, and Oman. AOU was established under the umbrella of the Arab Gulf Program for Development (formerly known as the Arab Gulf Program for United Nations Development Organizations [AGFUND]). Since then, it has been adopted, in principle, as a private Arab institution of higher education with a special status. As a result of coordination between AOU and the Arab Ministers of Higher Education, nine Arab countries offered to approve the establishment of branches of the AOU, five of which offered certain facilities and privileges for hosting the AOU Headquarters. AOU's programs and degrees have also been accredited by the U.K.'s Open University. Similar to the Open University, AOU promotes an open system of higher education that provides opportunities of studies for professional development and lifelong learning.

Of the two modes of open education, mainly that which requires attendance and that which does not, the open system of learning at AOU represents the former. Unlike distance education, which does not involve face-to-face interaction between students and instructors, the AOU open learning platform involves a tutoring process. To accommodate working students and those commuting from remote areas, tutorials are scheduled at their convenience. AOU now has around 30,000 Arab students across the eight campuses.[15]

The AOU has over 30,000 students, thanks to their wide spread of eight campuses in the Arab world.

Marketing channels also keep changing in 'person' marketing. Besides live and programmed entertainment, entertainers, musicians, and other artists can reach prospective and existing fans online in many ways: via their own websites, social community sites such as MySpace and Facebook, and third-party websites. A large number of contemporary pan-Arab singers and artists (such as Ragheb Alama, Haifa Wehbe, Amr Diab, Latifa, and Mohamed Abdo) have their own websites in addition to official and unofficial fan sites, and their news, updates, and photos are found and exchanged on third-party sites and blogs. Politicians also must choose a mix of channels—mass media, rallies, coffee hours, spot TV ads, direct mail, billboards, faxes, e-mail, blogs, podcasts, websites—to deliver their messages to voters.[16] The whole world witnessed the power of social networking sites Facebook and Twitter as they proved to be excellent venues for communication and exchange during the popular revolutions in Tunisia and Egypt.

As internet and other technologies advance, service industries such as banking, insurance, travel, and stock buying and selling are operating through new channels. Kodak offers its customers four different ways to print their digital photos: minilabs in retail outlets, home printers, online services with the Kodak-owned Ofoto website, and self-service kiosks. Kodak, the world leader with 80,000 kiosks including 2,000 at Walmart, makes money both by selling kiosks and by supplying the units with the chemical and paper used to make the prints.[17]

Channel-Design Decisions

Designing a marketing channel system requires analyzing customer needs, establishing channel objectives, and identifying and evaluating major channel alternatives.

Analyzing Customers' Desired Service Output Levels

In designing the marketing channel, the marketer must understand the service output levels its target customers want. Channels produce five service outputs:

1. *Lot size.* The number of units the channel permits a typical customer to purchase on one occasion. In buying cars for their fleets, car-rental companies (such as Avis, Hertz, and Budget) and taxi and limousine service companies (such as Allo Taxi in Lebanon, National Taxi in the UAE, and TaxisEgypt) prefer a channel from which they can buy large lot sizes; a household wants a channel that permits buying a lot size of one.
2. *Waiting and delivery time.* The average time customers of that channel wait for receipt of the goods. Customers increasingly prefer faster and faster delivery channels.
3. *Spatial convenience.* The degree to which the marketing channel makes it easy for customers to purchase the product. McDonald's, for example, offers greater spatial convenience than Hardee's, because there are more McDonald's restaurants.
4. *Product variety.* The assortment breadth provided by the marketing channel. Normally, customers prefer a greater assortment because more choices increase the chance of finding what they need. Product variety is one of the main reasons behind the success of department stores such as Carrefour and supermarkets such as Spinneys across many Arab countries.
5. *Service backup.* The add-on services (credit, delivery, installation, repairs) provided by the channel. The greater the service backup, the greater the work provided by the channel.[18]

The marketing channel designer knows that providing greater service outputs also means increasing channel costs and raising prices for customers. Different customers have different service needs. The success of discount stores indicates that many consumers are willing to accept smaller service outputs if they can save money.

Establishing Objectives and Constraints

Marketers should state their channel objectives in terms of targeted service output levels. Under competitive conditions, channel institutions should arrange their functional tasks to minimize total channel costs and still provide desired levels of service outputs.[19] Usually, planners can identify several market segments that want different service levels. Effective planning requires determining which market segments to serve and choosing the best channels for each.

Channel objectives vary with product characteristics. Perishable products require more direct marketing. Bulky products, such as building materials, require channels that minimize the shipping distance and the amount of handling. Nonstandard products, such as custom-built machinery and specialized business forms, are sold directly by company sales representatives. Products requiring installation or maintenance services, such as heating and cooling systems, are usually sold and maintained by the company or by franchised dealers. High-unit-value products such as generators and turbines are often sold through a company sales force rather than intermediaries.

A number of other factors affect channel objectives. In entering new markets, for instance, firms often closely observe what other firms from their home market are doing in those markets. American fast-food chains McDonald's and Burger King watch each other's strategic moves as each expands into new markets. French supermarket stores Carrefour, Géant Casino, and Monoprix keep an eye on each other's market expansions and use these as drivers for them to also these enter new markets.

Marketers must adapt their channel objectives to the larger environment. When economic conditions are depressed, producers want to move their goods to market using shorter channels and without services that add to the final price of the goods. Legal regulations and restrictions also affect channel design. Laws of some countries (such as the United States) look unfavorably on channel arrangements that substantially lessen competition or create a monopoly.

Identifying and Evaluating Major Channel Alternatives

Companies can choose from a wide variety of channels for reaching customers, from sales forces to agents, distributors, dealers, direct mail, telemarketing, and the internet. Each channel has unique strengths as well as weaknesses. Sales forces can handle complex products and transactions, but they are expensive. The internet is much less expensive, but it may not be as effective with complex products. Distributors can create sales, but the company loses direct contact with customers. Manufacturers' reps are able to contact customers at a low cost per customer because several clients share the cost, but the selling effort per customer is less intense than if company sales reps did the selling.

The problem is further complicated by the fact that most companies now use a mix of channels. The idea is that each channel reaches a different segment of buyers and delivers the right products at the least cost. When this doesn't happen, there is usually channel conflict and excessive cost.

A channel alternative is described by three elements: the types of available business intermediary, the number of intermediaries needed, and the terms and responsibilities of each channel member.

TYPES OF INTERMEDIARY A firm needs to identify the types of intermediaries available to carry on its channel work. **Box 15.2** lists channel alternatives identified by a consumer electronics company that produces car mobile phone accessories.

Companies should search for innovative marketing channels. In some markets, global chains and franchises may find it necessary to introduce new means to its otherwise standard mode of operation in order to be able to reach out to its customer base. McDonald's, for example, undertakes home delivery in many Arab countries – a customer service option that McDonald's does not practice in many other parts of the world.

McDonald's McDelivery Service in Bahrain

McDonald's launched its McDelivery Service, delivering food to people's doors, in Bahrain in the summer 2007. The service was test-marketed for months before it was fully introduced. With the introduction of McDelivery, McDonald's Bahrain undertook a customer-centric initiative by offering a 24-hour delivery service, 7 days a week, through designated McDonald's outlets. Commenting on the launch of the McDelivery Service, Jamil Badran, operations director at McDonald's Bahrain said: "We are proud to be one of the few countries in the world to offer 24/7 McDelivery Service. At McDonald's we are constantly working towards customizing our products/services to cater to the fast-paced life style of customers. The new service demonstrates our commitment to offering quality, fresh meals at great value and convenience."[20]

Sometimes a company chooses a new or unconventional channel because of the difficulty, cost, or ineffectiveness of working with the dominant channel. The advantage is that the company will encounter less competition during the initial move into this channel. Years ago, after trying to sell its inexpensive Timex watches through regular jewelry stores, the U.S. Time Company placed them instead in fast-growing mass-merchandise outlets, drugstores, and discount stores. This strategy allowed Timex to penetrate the competitive watch market at an unprecedented rate, and eventually ended up selling more watches than any other watch company worldwide.[21]

NUMBER OF INTERMEDIARIES Companies must decide on the number of intermediaries to use at each channel level. Three strategies are available: exclusive distribution, selective distribution, and intensive distribution.

BOX 15.2 Channel Alternatives for a Manufacturer of Car Phone Accessories

- The company could sell its car phone accessories to automobile manufacturers to be installed as original equipment.
- The company could sell its car phone accessories to auto dealers.
- The company could sell its car phone accessories to retail automotive-equipment dealers through a direct sales force or through distributors.
- The company could sell its car phone accessories to car phone specialist dealers through a direct sales force or dealers.
- The company could sell its car phone accessories through mail-order catalogs.
- The company could sell its car phone accessories through mass merchandisers such as Carrefour.

McDonald's Bahrain operates one of the few 24/7 McDelivery services in the world.

Exclusive distribution means severely limiting the number of intermediaries. It's appropriate when the producer wants to maintain control over the service level and outputs offered by the resellers, and it often includes *exclusive dealing* arrangements. By granting exclusive distribution, the producer hopes to obtain more dedicated and knowledgeable selling. Exclusive distribution requires a closer partnership between seller and reseller and is used in the distribution of new automobiles, some major appliances, and some women's apparel brands. Exclusive deals between suppliers and retailers are becoming a mainstay for specialists looking for an edge in a business world that is increasingly driven by price.[22] When the legendary Italian designer label Gucci found its image severely tarnished and negatively affected by overexposure from licensing and discount stores, it decided to end contracts with third-party suppliers, control its distribution, and open its own stores to bring back some of the luster and glory.[23]

exclusive distribution severely limiting the number of intermediaries, in order to maintain control over the service level and outputs offered by resellers.

selective distribution the use of more than a few but less than all of the intermediaries who are willing to carry a particular product.

Selective distribution relies on more than a few but less than all of the intermediaries willing to carry a particular product. It makes sense for established companies and for new companies seeking distributors. The company does not need to worry about too many outlets; it can gain adequate market coverage with more control and less cost than intensive distribution. Beesline is a good example of selective distribution.

Beesline The Beesline range of hypoallergenic cosmetic products was the brainchild of Natural Ltd, a Lebanese company that has gained local, regional, and even international acclaim. Beesline is a cosmetic line based 100 percent on bee products and plant extracts, and formulated with natural ingredients. Beesline products pass stringent lab tests in laboratories and clinics by dermatologists. Beesline has a range of 90 products, sold in select pharmacies and beauty parlors in Lebanon, Saudi Arabia, Bahrain, Oman, and the UAE. It is also available in Natural Ltd's three showrooms in Lebanon.[24]

intensive distribution the manufacturer placing the goods or services in as many outlets as possible.

In **intensive distribution** the manufacturer places the goods or services in as many outlets as possible. This strategy is generally used for items such as snack foods, soft drinks, newspapers, candies and gum, products the consumer seeks to buy frequently or in a variety of locations. Convenience stores such as gas-station-linked stores prosper by selling items that provide just that: location and time convenience.

Manufacturers are constantly tempted to move from exclusive or selective distribution to more intensive distribution to increase coverage and sales. This strategy may help in the short term, but it can hurt long-term performance. Intensive distribution increases product and service availability but may also encourage retailers to compete aggressively. Price wars can then erode profitability, potentially dampening retailer interest in supporting the product and harming brand equity. Some firms avoid intensive distribution and do not want to be sold everywhere.

TERMS AND RESPONSIBILITIES OF CHANNEL MEMBERS Each channel member must be treated respectfully and given the opportunity to be profitable.[25] The main elements in the 'trade-relations mix' are price policies, conditions of sale, territorial rights, and specific services to be performed by each party.

- *Price policy* calls for the producer to establish a price list and schedule of discounts and allowances that intermediaries see as equitable and sufficient.

- **Conditions of sale** refers to payment terms and producer guarantees. Most producers grant cash discounts to distributors for early payment. Producers might also provide distributors a guarantee against defective merchandise or price declines. A guarantee against price declines gives distributors an incentive to buy larger quantities.

- **Distributors' territorial rights** define the distributors' territories and the terms under which the producer will enfranchise other distributors. Distributors normally expect to receive full credit for all sales in their territory, whether or not they did the selling.

- **Mutual services and responsibilities** must be carefully spelled out, especially in franchised and exclusive-agency channels. McDonald's provides franchisees with promotional support, a recordkeeping system, training, and general administrative and technical assistance. In turn, franchisees are expected to satisfy company standards for the physical facilities, cooperate with new promotional programs, furnish requested information, and buy supplies from specified vendors.

Evaluating the Major Alternatives

Each channel alternative needs to be evaluated against economic, control, and adaptive criteria.

ECONOMIC CRITERIA Each channel alternative will produce a different level of sales and costs. △ **Figure 15.4** shows how six different sales channels stack up in terms of the value added per sale and the cost per transaction. For example, in the sale of industrial products costing between US$2,000 and $5,000, the cost per transaction has been estimated at $500 (field sales), $200 (distributors), $50 (telesales), and $10 (internet). In the sale of retail banking services, a Booz Allen Hamilton study shows the average transaction at a full-service branch costs the bank $4.07, a phone transaction costs 54 cents, and an automated teller machine (ATM) transaction 27 cents, but a typical web-based transaction costs only 1 cent.[26]

Firms will try to align customers and channels to maximize demand at the lowest overall cost. Clearly, sellers try to replace high-cost channels with low-cost channels as long as the value added per sale is sufficient. HSBC was one of the first banks in the Arab world to introduce ATM machines. HSBC offered monetary incentives to clients to open ATM accounts, which carried lower service and transaction fees. Not only was HSBC looking to cut down on cost per transaction, but was also able to free its service representatives to attend to higher-return operations and problem situations. Asset manager Vanguard's service representatives set out to train customers to use its websites over the telephone. As a result, Vanguard was able to cut staff in half, an important accomplishment given that a phone call to a rep cost the company US$9 versus cents for a web log-in.[27]

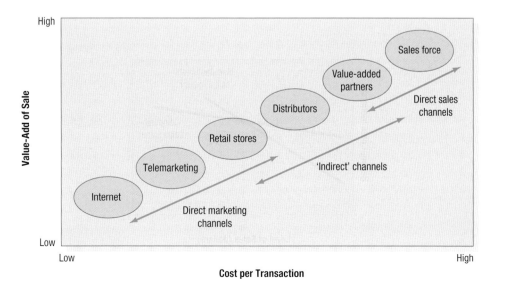

|Fig. 15.4| △

The Value-Adds versus Costs of Different Channels

Source: Oxford Associates, adapted from Dr. Rowland T. Moriarty, Cubex Corp.

As an example of an economic analysis of channel choices, consider the following situation:

> The Arabian Gulf furniture manufacturer based in the Eastern Province of Saudi Arabia wants to sell its line to retailers in Jeddah on the Red Sea. The manufacturer is trying to decide between two alternatives: one calls for hiring 10 new sales representatives who would operate out of a sales office in Jeddah. They would receive a base salary plus commissions. The other alternative would be to use a Jeddah manufacturers' sales agency that has extensive contacts with retailers. The agency has 30 sales representatives who would receive a commission based on their sales.

The first step in the analysis is to estimate how many sales are likely to be generated by a company sales force or a sales agency. On one hand, a company sales force will concentrate on the company's products; will be better trained to sell those products; will be more aggressive because each rep's future depends on the company's success; and will be more successful because many customers prefer to deal directly with the company. On the other hand, the sales agency has 30 representatives, not just 10; it may be just as aggressive as a direct sales force, depending on the commission level; it may be better received by customers as more independent; and it may have extensive contacts and marketplace knowledge. The marketer needs to evaluate all these factors in formulating a demand function for the two different channels.

The next step is to estimate the costs of selling different volumes through each channel. The cost schedules are shown in ▲ **Figure 15.5**. The fixed costs of engaging a sales agency are lower than those of establishing a new company sales office, but costs rise faster through an agency because sales agents get a larger commission than company salespeople.

The final step is comparing sales and costs. As Figure 15.5 shows, there is one sales level (S_B) at which selling costs are the same for the two channels. The sales agency is thus the better channel for any sales volume below S_B, and the company sales branch is better at any volume above S_B. Given this information, it is not surprising that sales agents tend to be used by smaller firms, or by large firms in smaller territories where the volume is low.

CONTROL AND ADAPTIVE CRITERIA Using a sales agency poses a control problem. A sales agency is an independent firm seeking to maximize its profits. Agents may concentrate on the customers who buy the most, not necessarily on those who buy the manufacturer's goods. Furthermore, agents might not master the technical details of the company's product or handle its promotion materials effectively.

To develop a channel, members must make some degree of commitment to each other for a specified period of time. Yet these commitments invariably lead to a decrease in the producer's ability to respond to a changing marketplace. In rapidly changing, volatile, or uncertain product markets, the producer needs channel structures and policies that provide high adaptability.

|Fig. 15.5| ▲

Break-Even Cost Chart for the Choice between a Company Sales Force and a Manufacturer's Sales Agency

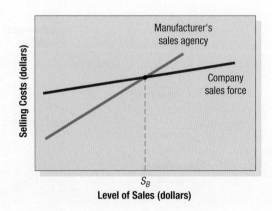

Channel-Management Decisions

After a company has chosen a channel system, it must select, train, motivate, and evaluate individual intermediaries for each channel. It must also modify channel design and arrangements over time.

Selecting Channel Members

To customers, the channels are the company. Consider the negative impression customers would get of Pizza Hut, Mercedes-Benz, or Qatar Airways if one or more of their outlets, dealers, or representative offices consistently appeared dirty, inefficient, or unpleasant.

To facilitate channel member selection, producers should determine what characteristics distinguish the better intermediaries. They should evaluate the number of years in business, other lines carried, growth and profit record, financial strength, cooperativeness, and service reputation. If the intermediaries are sales agents, producers should evaluate the number and character of other lines carried and the size and quality of the sales force. If the intermediaries are department stores that want exclusive distribution, the producer should evaluate locations, future growth potential, and type of clientele.

Training and Motivating Channel Members

A company needs to view its intermediaries in the same way it views its end users. It needs to determine intermediaries' needs and construct a channel positioning such that its channel offering is tailored to provide superior value to these intermediaries. The Marketing Excellence case at the end of this chapter offers an example of a successful Lebanon-based distributor whose success took it into several other Arab countries.

Being able to stimulate channel members to top performance starts with understanding their needs and wants. The company should plan and implement careful training programs, market research programs, and other capability-building programs to improve intermediaries' performance. Microsoft requires third-party service engineers to complete a set of courses and take certification exams. Those who pass are formally recognized as Microsoft Certified Professionals, and they can use this designation to promote their own business. Others use customer surveys rather than exams. The company must constantly communicate its view that the intermediaries are partners in a joint effort to satisfy end users of the product.

Producers vary greatly in their skill in managing distributors. **Channel power** is the ability to alter channel members' behavior so that they take actions they would not have taken otherwise.[28] Manufacturers can draw on the following types of power to elicit cooperation:

channel power   the ability to alter channel members' behavior so that they take actions they would not otherwise have taken.

- *Coercive power.* A manufacturer threatens to withdraw a resource or terminate a relationship if intermediaries fail to cooperate. This power can be effective, but its exercise produces resentment and can generate conflict and lead the intermediaries to organize a counter action.

- *Reward power.* The manufacturer offers intermediaries an extra benefit for performing specific acts or functions. Reward power typically produces better results than coercive power, but it can be overrated. The intermediaries may come to expect a reward every time the manufacturer wants a certain behavior to occur.

- *Legitimate power.* The manufacturer requests a behavior that is warranted under the contract. As long as the intermediaries view the manufacturer as a legitimate leader, legitimate power works.

- *Expert power.* The manufacturer has special knowledge the intermediaries value. Once the intermediaries acquire this expertise, however, expert power weakens. The manufacturer must continue to develop new expertise so that the intermediaries will want to continue cooperating.

- *Referent power.* The manufacturer is so highly respected that intermediaries are proud to be associated with it. Companies such as IBM, Caterpillar, and Hewlett-Packard have high referent power.[29]

Coercive and reward power are objectively observable; legitimate, expert, and referent power are more subjective and depend on the ability and willingness of parties to recognize them.

Most producers see gaining intermediaries' cooperation as a huge challenge.[30] They often use positive motivators, such as higher margins, special deals, premiums, cooperative advertising allowances, display allowances, and sales contests. At times they will apply negative sanctions, such as threatening to reduce margins, slow down delivery, or terminate the relationship. The weakness of this approach is that the producer is using crude, stimulus-response thinking.

More sophisticated companies try to forge a long-term partnership with distributors. The manufacturer clearly communicates what it wants from its distributors in the way of market coverage, inventory levels, marketing development, account solicitation, technical advice and services, and marketing information. The manufacturer seeks distributor agreement with these policies and may introduce a compensation plan for adhering to the policies.

To streamline the supply chain and cut costs, many manufacturers and retailers have adopted *efficient consumer response* (ECR) *practices* to organize their relationships in three areas: (1) *demand-side management* or collaborative practices to stimulate consumer demand by promoting joint marketing and sales activities, (2) *supply-side management* or collaborative practices to optimize supply (with a focus on joint logistics and supply chain activities), and (3) *enablers and integrators*, or collaborative information technology and process improvement tools, to support joint activities that reduce operational problems, allow greater standardization, and so on. Research has shown that although ECR has a positive impact on manufacturers' economic performance and capability development, it may also generate greater perceptions of inequity on the manufacturer's part in that they feel they are inequitably sharing the burdens of ECR adoption and not getting as much as they deserve.[31]

Evaluating Channel Members

Producers must periodically evaluate intermediaries' performance against such standards as sales-quota attainment, average inventory levels, customer delivery time, treatment of damaged and lost goods, and cooperation in promotional and training programs. A producer will occasionally discover that it is paying particular intermediaries too much for what they are actually doing. One manufacturer compensating a distributor for holding inventories found that the inventories were actually held in a public warehouse at its own expense. Producers should set up functional discounts in which they pay specified amounts for the trade channel's performance of each agreed-upon service. Underperformers need to be counseled, retrained, motivated, or terminated.

Modifying Channel Design and Arrangements

A producer must periodically review and modify its channel design and arrangements. It will want to modify them when the distribution channel is not working as planned, consumer buying patterns change, the market expands, new competition arises, innovative distribution channels emerge, and the product moves into later stages in the product life cycle.

No marketing channel will remain effective over the whole product life cycle. Early buyers might be willing to pay for high-value-added channels, but later buyers will switch to lower-cost channels. Small office copiers were first sold by manufacturers' direct sales forces, later through office equipment dealers, still later through mass merchandisers, and now by mail-order firms and internet marketers.

In competitive markets with low entry barriers, the optimal channel structure will inevitably change over time. The change could mean adding or dropping individual channel members, adding or dropping particular market channels, or developing a totally new way to sell goods. Consider Apple.

Apple Stores   When Apple stores were launched in 2001, many critics questioned their prospects and *BusinessWeek* published an article titled, "Sorry Steve, Here's Why Apple Stores Won't Work." Fast-forward 5 years, and Apple was celebrating the launch of its spectacular new Manhattan showcase store. Now with over 300 locations (including in Dubai, its first in the Arab world) and ever-increasing annual sales per square meter, Apple stores are an unqualified success. Opened because of the company's frustration with its poor retail presentation by others, the stores sell Apple products exclusively and target tech-savvy customers with in-store product presentations and workshops; a full line of Apple products, software, and accessories; and a Genius Bar staffed by Apple specialists who provide technical support often free of charge. Although the move upset existing retailers, Apple has worked hard to smooth relationships, in part justifying the decision to add its own stores as a natural evolution of its already existing online sales channel.[32]

To preserve its channel relationships, Apple has justified the opening of hundreds of its own retail stores as a natural extension of its online sales channel. The stores have proven extremely profitable.

Adding or dropping individual channel members requires an incremental analysis. What would the firm's profits look like with and without this intermediary? A producer may drop any intermediary whose sales drop below a certain level. Increasingly more detailed customer shopping information stored in databases, and sophisticated means to analyze that data, can provide guidance into those decisions.[33]

Perhaps the most difficult decision of all is whether to revise the overall channel strategy.[34] Distribution channels clearly become outmoded, and a gap arises between the existing distribution system and the ideal system that would satisfy target customers' needs and desires. For example Avon's door-to-door system for selling cosmetics was modified as more women entered the workforce. In retail banking, despite a belief that technological advances such as ATMs, online banking, and telephone call centers would reduce customers' reliance on their neighborhood branches, banks have found that many people still want high touch over high tech, or at least the choice. Banks are responding by opening more branches and developing more cross-selling and up-selling practices to take advantage of the face-to-face contact that produces results. Arab Bank and NBK not only offer a wide range of technology-backed financial services, but also pride themselves on their vast networks of branches, extending all over the Arab world and beyond.

Arab Bank and NBK offer their customers face-to-face premier service through its vast network of branches, which extend all over the Arab world.

Channel Integration and Systems

Distribution channels don't stand still. New wholesaling and retailing institutions emerge, and new channel systems evolve. We'll look at the recent growth of vertical, horizontal, and multichannel marketing systems; the next section examines how these systems cooperate, conflict, and compete.

Vertical Marketing Systems

One of the most significant recent channel developments is the rise of vertical marketing systems. A **conventional marketing channel** comprises an independent producer, wholesaler(s), and retailer(s). Each is a separate business seeking to maximize its own profits, even if this goal reduces profit for the system as a whole. No channel member has complete or substantial control over other members.

A **vertical marketing system** (**VMS**), by contrast, comprises the producer, wholesaler(s), and retailer(s) acting as a unified system. One channel member, the *channel captain*, owns the others or franchises them or has so much power that they all cooperate. The Marketing Insight: *The Importance of Channel Stewards* provides some perspective on how *channel stewards*, a closely related concept, should work.

conventional marketing channel   an independent producer, wholesaler(s), and retailer(s).

vertical marketing system (VMS)   producer, wholesaler(s), and retailer(s) acting as a unified system.

The Importance of Channel Stewards

Harvard's V. Kasturi Rangan believes that companies should adopt a new approach to going to market: channel stewardship. He defines channel stewardship as the ability of a given participant in a distribution channel—a steward—to create a go-to-market strategy that simultaneously addresses customers' best interests and drives profits for all channel partners. A channel steward might be the maker of the product or service (such as Procter & Gamble or Emirates Airline); the maker of a key component (such as microchip maker Intel); the supplier or assembler (such as Dell); or the distributor (such as Transmed) or retailer (such as Spinneys or Panda). Within a company, Rangan notes the steward-ship function might reside with the CEO, a top manager, or a team of senior managers.

The concept of channel stewardship is meant to appeal to any organization in the distribution channel that wants to bring a disciplined approach to channel strategy. An effective channel steward considers the channel from the customer's point of view. With that view in mind, the steward then advocates for change among all participants, trans-forming disparate entities into partners having a common purpose.

Channel stewardship has two important outcomes. One is to expand value for the steward's customers and increase the size of the market or existing customers' purchases through the channel in the process. A second outcome is to create a more tightly woven, and yet adaptable, channel where valuable members are suitably rewarded and the less valuable members are weeded out.

Rangan outlines three key disciplines of channel management:

1. *Mapping* is undertaken at an industry level to gain a sense of what the key determinants of channel strategy are and how they are evolving. It gives an idea of current best practices and gaps, and it projects what the future requirements might be.

2. *Building and editing* is an assessment of the producer's own chan-nels with a view to identifying any deficits in meeting customers' needs and/or competitive best practices.

3. *Aligning and influencing* closes the gaps and works out a com-pensation package in tune with effort and performance for channel members that add or could add value.

Rangan maintains that the beauty of the channel stewardship disci-pline is that it works at the level of customer needs and not at the level of channel institutions. As a result, channel managers can evolve and change their fulfillment of customer needs without having to change channel struc-ture all at once. An evolutionary approach to channel change, it requires constant monitoring, learning, and adaptation, but all in the best interests of customers, channel partners, and the channel steward. Rangan also notes that a channel steward need not be a huge company or market leader.

Source: V. Kasturi Rangan, *Transforming Your Go-to-Market Strategy: The Three Disciplines of Channel Management* (Boston: Harvard Business School Press, 2006).

Vertical marketing systems (VMSs) arose as a result of strong channel members' attempts to control channel behavior and eliminate the conflict that results when independent members pursue their own objectives. VMSs achieve economies through size, bargaining power, and elimination of duplicated services. Business buyers of complex products and systems have been shown to value the extensive exchange of information they can obtain from a VMS.[35] VMSs are becoming a dominant mode of distribution in many countries of the world. In the U.S. consumer marketplace, it is estimated that VMSs serve between 70 and 80 percent of the total market. There are three types of VMS: corporate, administered, and contractual.

CORPORATE VMS   A *corporate VMS* combines successive stages of production and distribution under single ownership. For example, U.S. retailer Sears obtains over 50 percent of the goods it sells from companies that it partly or wholly owns. National Paints of the UAE and Tinol Paints of Lebanon manufacture paint that they sell through appointed dealers and specialty outlets, but they also own and operate their own showroom retail outlets.

ADMINISTERED VMS   An *administered VMS* coordinates successive stages of production and distribution through the size and power of one of the members. Manufacturers of a dominant brand are able to secure strong trade cooperation and support from resellers. Thus P&G, Gillette, and Americana are able to command high levels of cooperation from their resellers in connection with displays, shelf space, promotions, and price policies.

The most advanced supply-distributor arrangement for administered VMSs relies on **distribution programming**, which builds a planned, professionally managed, vertical marketing system that meets the needs of both manufacturer and distributors. The manufacturer establishes a department within the company called *distributor relations planning*. Its job is to identify distributor needs and build up merchandising programs to help each distributor operate as efficiently as possible. This department and the distributors jointly plan merchandising goals, inventory levels, space and visual merchandising plans, sales-training requirements, and advertising and promotion plans. The aim is to convert the distributors from thinking that they make their money primarily on the buying side (through tough negotiation with the manufacturer) to seeing that they make their money on the selling side (by being part of a sophisticated, vertical marketing system).

distribution programming
building a planned, professionally managed, vertical marketing system that meets the needs of both manufacturer and distributors.

CONTRACTUAL VMS   A *contractual VMS* consists of independent firms at different levels of production and distribution, integrating their programs on a contractual basis to obtain more economies or sales impact than they could achieve alone. Johnston and Lawrence call them "value-adding partnerships" (VAPs).[36] Contractual VMSs now constitute one of the most significant developments in the economy. They are of three types:

1. *Wholesaler-sponsored voluntary chains.* Wholesalers organize voluntary chains of independent retailers to help them standardize their selling practices and achieve buying economies in order to compete with large chain organizations.
2. *Retailer cooperatives.* Retailers take the initiative and organize a new business entity to carry on wholesaling and possibly some production. Members concentrate their purchases through the retailer co-op and plan their advertising jointly. Profits pass back to members in proportion to their purchases. Nonmember retailers can also buy through the co-op but do not share in the profits.
3. *Franchise organizations.* A channel member called a *franchisor* might link several successive stages in the production-distribution process. Franchising has been the fastest-growing retailing development in recent years.

Although the basic idea is an old one, some forms of franchising are quite new. The traditional system is the *manufacturer-sponsored retailer franchise*. Nissan, for example, licenses dealers to sell its cars. The dealers are independent businesspeople who agree to meet specified conditions of sales and services. Another is the *manufacturer-sponsored wholesaler franchise*. Pepsi Cola and Coca-Cola, for example, license bottlers (wholesalers) in various markets that buy their syrup concentrate and then carbonate, bottle, and sell it to retailers in local markets. A newer system is the *service-firm-sponsored retailer franchise*. A service firm organizes a whole system for bringing its service efficiently to consumers. We find examples in the auto-rental business (Hertz, Avis, and Budget), fast-food-service business (McDonald's and Burger King), and hotel business (Holiday Inn). Franchising has particularly gained popularity as an opportunity for fast growth across the

Arab world for a number of outlets, such as restaurants (e.g. Casper & Gambini, Kabab-ji, Zaatar w Zeit, Mo'men, and Kudu). Some franchising is done via a dual distribution system in which firms use both vertical integration (where the franchisor actually owns and runs the units) and market governance (in which the franchisor licenses the units to other franchisees).[37]

THE NEW COMPETITION IN RETAILING Many independent retailers that have not joined VMSs have developed specialty stores that serve special market segments. The result is a polarization in retailing between large vertical marketing organizations and independent specialty stores, which creates a problem for manufacturers. They are strongly tied to independent intermediaries but must eventually realign themselves with the high-growth vertical marketing systems on less attractive terms. Furthermore, vertical marketing systems constantly threaten to bypass large manufacturers and set up their own manufacturing. The new competition in retailing is no longer between independent business units but between whole systems of centrally programmed networks (corporate, administered, and contractual) competing against one another to achieve the best cost economies and customer response.

Horizontal Marketing Systems

horizontal marketing system two or more unrelated companies put together resources or programs to exploit an emerging market opportunity.

Another channel development is the **horizontal marketing system**, in which two or more unrelated companies put together resources or programs to exploit an emerging marketing opportunity. Each company lacks the capital, know-how, production, or marketing resources to venture alone, or it is afraid of the risk. The companies might work with each other on a temporary or permanent basis or create a joint venture company.

HDFC Bank Established in 1977, HDFC (Housing Development Finance Corporation Limited) is India's leading housing finance company. In 1994, HDFC was incorporated as HDFC Bank Limited, and has been providing a vast array of financial and banking services to its clients ever since. HDFC expanded outside India to serve widespread Indian expatriates, particularly across the Arab world, and has a presence in Kuwait, Qatar, Saudi Arabia, Oman, Bahrain, and the UAE. To reach its client base effectively and efficiently, HDFC operates a number of arrangements with local institutions. For example, in Saudi Arabia and Qatar it has arrangements with Arab National Bank and Qatar National Bank, respectively. HDFC has also entered into restricted arrangements with exchange companies to provide easy remittance and transfer services to the huge Indian expatriate base in the Gulf Cooperation Council. For example, HDFC benefits from the massive network of Al-Rostamani, Sharaf, and Al-Ansari exchange companies in the UAE; Modern and Sultan exchanges in Oman; Gulf Exchange in Qatar; Bahrain India International Exchange in Bahrain; and Al Mulla, Al Muzaini, and City exchanges in Kuwait. Such agreements with exchange companies allow clients to tap into HDFC services in numerous locations, including malls, shopping centers, cinema complexes, supermarkets, and cooperatives.[38]

Horizontal marketing systems include HDFC Bank's arrangement with exchange houses throughout several Gulf countries.

Integrating Multichannel Marketing Systems

Most companies today have adopted multichannel marketing. Disney sells its DVDs through five main channels: specialty entertainment stores such as Virgin; Disney Stores; retail stores such as Best Buy; online retailers such as Amazon.com and Disney's own online Disney Stores; and the Disney catalog and other catalog sellers. These varied channels afford Disney maximum market coverage and enable the company to offer its DVDs at a number of price points.[39]

Multichannel marketing occurs when a single firm uses two or more marketing channels to reach one or more customer segments. An **integrated marketing** channel system is one in which the strategies and tactics of selling through one channel reflect the strategies and tactics of selling through other channels. Airline companies nowadays use a multitude of channels to reach out to potential passengers. Whether it is Emirates Airline, Etihad Airways, Qatar Airways, Gulf Air, Egypt Air, Middle East Airlines, or any other, a traveler can get flight schedule information and rates and buy a ticket through the airline's own office, through airline-appointed agents, through a travel agent, through the airline's website, or through an online web portal or intermediary.

By adding more channels, companies can gain three important benefits. The first is increased market coverage. Not only are more customers able to shop for the company's products in more places, but customers who buy in more than one channel are often more profitable than single-channel customers.[40] The second is lower channel cost: selling by phone is cheaper than selling via personal visits to small customers. The third is more customized selling: such as adding a technical sales force to sell more-complex equipment. The gains from adding new channels come at a price, however. New channels typically introduce conflict and problems with control. Two or more channels may end up competing for the same customers. The new channels may be more independent and make cooperation more difficult. The Marketing Memo: *Multichannel Shopping Checklist* offers some concrete advice on channel integration of online and offline channels.

Clearly, companies need to think through their channel architecture. They must determine which channels should perform which functions. △ **Figure 15.6** shows a simple grid to help make channel architecture decisions. The grid consists of major marketing channels (as rows) and the major channel tasks that must be completed (as columns).[41]

Airline companies like Egypt Air use an integrated marketing channel system, including airline offices, agents and websites to reach their customers.

multichannel marketing a single firm uses two or more marketing channels to reach one or more customer segments.

integrated marketing mixing and matching marketing activities to maximize their individual and collective efforts.

---

marketing Memo

Multichannel Shopping Checklist

The e-tailing group, an e-commerce consulting firm, studied the integrated shopping experience in the online/retail returns process of 16 e-tailers. Overall, the study found that 44 percent of in-store returns of merchandise purchased online required a store manager to override the retail system in order to accept the return. In response to this and several other inadequacies revealed by the study, the e-tailing group created a Best of Breed Multichannel Shopping Checklist to help marketers better integrate online and offline channels:

- Train all store associates on processes for online merchandise returns.
- List your company's freephone number on the internet homepage, and be sure your customer-service hours of operation are easily accessible.
- Provide an information center that is easy to navigate and includes contact information, FAQs, guarantees, return policies, and tips for first-time customers.

- Implement a store locator feature that includes store locations, hours, and events.
- Make store pickup for purchases an option and include real-time inventory levels, where applicable.
- Post the store's weekly circular online for a more complete multichannel experience.
- Offer gift certificates that can be redeemed online and offline.
- Send e-mail notifications of the order, shipping, and return credit; include a reminder of the returns process in notifications as well as a link to your store locator.
- Supply all pertinent/compatible information for store return of merchandise on the packing slip or invoice.

Source: Excerpted from Hallie Mummert, "Multichannel Marketers Earn a 'C+' on Returns," *Target Marketing*, October 2003, p. 158.

Marketing Channels and Methods		Demand-Generation Tasks								
		Better communication information	Disseminate communication	Reach price agreements	Pace orders	Acquire funds for inventories	Assume risks	Facilitate product storage & movement	Facilitate payment	Oversee ownership terms
VENDOR	Internet									
	National account management									
	Direct sales									
	Telemarketing									
	Direct mail									
	Retail stores									
	Distributors									
	Dealers and value-added resellers									
	Advertising									

|Fig. 15.6| ▲

The Hybrid Grid

Source: Adapted from Rowland T. Moriarty and Ursula Moran, "Marketing Hybrid Marketing Systems," *Harvard Business Review*, November–December 1990, p. 150.

The grid illustrates why using only one channel is not efficient. Consider using only a direct sales force. A salesperson would have to find leads, qualify them, presell, close the sale, provide service, and manage account growth. It's more efficient for the company to perform the earlier tasks, leaving the salesperson to invest his or her costly time primarily in closing the sale. The company's marketing department would run a preselling campaign informing prospects about the company's products through advertising, direct mail, and telemarketing; generate leads through telemarketing, direct mail, advertising, and trade shows; and qualify leads into hot, warm, and cool. The salesperson comes to the prospect when the prospect is ready to talk business. This multichannel architecture optimizes coverage, customization, and control while minimizing cost and conflict.

Channels should be designed to work together effectively. In recent years, many retailers have seen their website sales increase at the expense of declining catalog sales. Yet, some of these companies chose not to abandon paper catalogs, because they believe that catalogs offer a very effective way to make an emotional appeal and a good lead to convince customers to go online. Catalogs have actually grown in the internet world as more firms use them as branding devices. Victoria's Secret ships 400 million catalogs a year in the United States alone, and catalog and online orders account for nearly 28 percent of its overall revenue, growing at double the rate of sales from its stores.[42] In Lebanon, office supplies specialist stores EZOrder and Malik's offer their wide product range of office stationery, office furniture, and office equipment through their paper catalogs as well as their online catalogs at www.ezorder.com.lb and www.maliks.com, respectively. After its success in Lebanon, EZOrder also ventured into Saudi Arabia, replicating its business model to serve clients across the kingdom.

Companies should use different channels for selling to different-size business customers. A company can use its direct sales force to sell to large customers, telemarketing to sell to midsize customers, and distributors to sell to small customers; but these gains can be compromised by an increased level of conflict over who has account ownership. For example, territory-based sales representatives may want credit for all sales in their territories, regardless of the marketing channel used.

Multichannel marketers also need to decide how much of their product to offer in each of the channels. Some retailers view the intenet as the ideal channel for showing off their entire line of goods, noting that their stores and outlets are limited by space to offering a selection only.[43] Other marketers prefer to limit their online offerings on the theory that customers look to websites and catalogs for a 'best of' array of merchandise and don't want to have to click through dozens of pages.

Conflict, Cooperation, and Competition

No matter how well channels are designed and managed, there will be some conflict, if for no other reason than that the interests of independent business entities do not always coincide. **Channel conflict** is generated when one channel member's actions prevent another channel member from achieving its goal. Software giant Oracle Corp. suffered from channel conflict between its sales force and its vendor partners. Oracle decided to introduce All Partner Territories where all deals except for specific strategic accounts would go through select Oracle partners rather than its sales force.[44]

Channel coordination occurs when channel members are brought together to advance the goals of the channel, as opposed to their own potentially incompatible goals.[45] Here we examine three questions: what types of conflict arise in channels? What causes channel conflict? What can marketers do to resolve conflict situations?

channel conflict when one channel member's actions prevent another channel member from achieving its goal.

channel coordination when channel members are brought together to advance the goals of the channel, as opposed to their own potentially incompatible goals.

Types of Conflict and Competition

Suppose a manufacturer sets up a vertical channel consisting of wholesalers and retailers. The manufacturer hopes for channel cooperation that will produce greater profits for each channel member. Yet vertical, horizontal, and multichannel conflict can occur.

Vertical channel conflict means conflict between different levels within the same channel. Car manufacturers, such as General Motors, sometimes come into conflict with their dealers in trying to enforce policies on service, pricing, and advertising.

Greater retailer consolidation has led to increased price pressure and influence from retailers. For instance, the 10 largest U.S. retailers accounted for 80 percent of the average manufacturer's business in 2005 versus roughly 30 percent a decade earlier.[46] In Dubai, Carrefour, for example, is the principal buyer for many manufacturers, including Sony, Nokia, and Procter & Gamble, and is able to command concessions from its suppliers through reduced prices or quantity discounts.

Horizontal channel conflict is conflict between members at the same level within the channel. Some Pizza Inn franchisees complained about other Pizza Inn franchisees cheating on ingredients, providing poor service, and hurting the overall Pizza Inn image. Some travel agents choose to pass a good part of the commission they get from airline companies to their regular clients, leading to price wars and complaints from other agents.

Multichannel conflict exists when the manufacturer has established two or more channels that sell to the same market. It's likely to be especially intense when the members of one channel get a lower price (based on larger-volume purchases) or work with a lower margin. When Goodyear began selling its popular tire brands through Sears, Walmart, and Discount Tire, it angered its independent dealers. It eventually placated them by offering exclusive tire models that would not be sold in other retail outlets. Other strategies to reduce multichannel conflict are creating and enforcing rules of engagement beforehand (rather than mediating disputes after the fact) and compensating both parties that participate in a sale regardless of which one books the order.[47]

Causes of Channel Conflict

Some causes of channel conflict are easy to resolve, others are not. Conflict may arise from:

- *Goal incompatibility.* For example, the manufacturer may want to achieve rapid market penetration through a low-price policy. Dealers, in contrast, may prefer to work with high margins and pursue short-run profitability.
- *Unclear roles and rights.* A manufacturer may sell personal computers to large accounts through its own sales force, but its licensed dealers may also be trying to sell to large accounts. Territory boundaries and credit for sales often produce conflict.

- *Differences in perception.* The manufacturer may be optimistic about the short-term economic outlook and want dealers to carry higher inventory. Dealers may be pessimistic. In the beverage category, it is not uncommon for disputes to arise between manufacturers and their distributors about the optimal advertising strategy.

- *Intermediaries' dependence on the manufacturer.* The fortunes of exclusive dealers, such as auto dealers, are profoundly affected by the manufacturer's product and pricing decisions. This situation creates a high potential for conflict.

Managing Channel Conflict

As companies add channels to grow sales, they run the risk of creating channel conflict. Some channel conflict can be constructive and lead to better adaptation to a changing environment, but too much conflict is dysfunctional.[48] The challenge is not to eliminate conflict but to manage it better. While the addition of an e-commerce channel can be the cause of conflict between a company and its channel intermediaries, it can also be a source of building further cooperation and trust if managed properly. For instance, the company could develop a tiered dealer model and form strategic supply chain partnerships with influential distributors. The company would deal directly via the intenet with all customers in a respective dealer's territory for sales of supplies. The dealer would act as the distribution point, bill and collect from the customer, earn incremental margins from the online sales of supplies, and remain the local contact for equipment sales. Dealers would be pleased as they pick up a margin on business they never had. But they also pick up collections, freight, transportation, and labor.[49]

There are several mechanisms for effective conflict management (see ▨ **Box 15.3**).[50] One is the adoption of superordinate goals. Channel members come to an agreement on the fundamental goal they are jointly seeking, whether it is survival, market share, high quality, or customer satisfaction. They usually do this when the channel faces an outside threat, such as a more efficient competing channel, an adverse piece of legislation, or a shift in consumer desires.

A useful step is to exchange persons between two or more channel levels. General Motors executives might agree to work for a short time in some dealerships, and some dealership owners might work in GM's dealer policy department. The hope is that the participants will grow to appreciate each other's point of view.

Co-optation is an effort by one organization to win the support of the leaders of another organization by including them in advisory councils, boards of directors, and the like. As long as the initiating organization treats the leaders seriously and listens to their opinions, co-optation can reduce conflict, but the initiating organization may need to compromise its policies and plans to win their support.

When conflict is chronic or acute, however, the parties may need to resort to diplomacy, mediation, or arbitration. *Diplomacy* takes place when each side sends a person or group to meet with its counterpart to resolve the conflict. *Mediation* means resorting to a neutral third party skilled in conciliating the two parties' interests. *Arbitration* occurs when the two parties agree to present their arguments to one or more arbitrators and accept the arbitration decision.

Finally, when none of these methods proves effective, a company or a channel partner may choose to file a lawsuit. Coca-Cola came into conflict with several of its key bottlers when the company

BOX 15.3 ▨	Strategies to Manage Channel Conflict

Adoption of superordinate goals

Exchange of employees

Joint membership in trade associations

Co-optation

Diplomacy, mediation, or arbitration

Legal recourse

decided to distribute Powerade thirst quencher directly to Walmart's regional warehouses. After 60 bottlers complained that the practice would undermine their core direct-store-distribution (DSD) duties and filed a lawsuit, a compromise settlement was reached that allowed for the mutual exploration of new service and distribution systems to supplement the DSD system.[51]

Dilution and Cannibalization

Marketers must also be careful not to dilute their brands through inappropriate channels. This is especially a concern with luxury brands whose images are often built on the basis of exclusivity and personalized service. The images of brands such as Calvin Klein and Tommy Hilfiger took a hit when they sold too many of their products in discount channels. Coach has worked hard to avoid diluting its image.

Coach   Handbag maker Coach's sustained double-digit growth through 2004–2005 was the result of some timely product introductions, but also a well-designed expansion in channels. As it turned out, the fastest-growing segment of Coach's business was factory outlets selling discontinued or older styles at 25 percent discounts. The company manages its channels carefully, however, and seeks to keep discount shoppers separate from more upscale and profitable clientele. Coach maintains full price in its 199 regular stores and doesn't discount. Merchandise that doesn't sell is not reduced in price but instead is sent to factory outlets located at least 95 kilometers away. As evidence of the firm's success in distinguishing the two channels, the average full-price shopper (a 35-year-old, college-educated, and single or newly married working woman) is very different from the average factory outlet shopper (a 45-year-old, college-educated married woman who buys 80 percent of her Coach purchases from outlets).[52]

Coach avoids brand dilution while enjoying multichannel distribution by keeping its full-price store shoppers separate from its discount shoppers, even locating its factory outlets a minimum of 95 kilometers from its retail stores.

To help tap into affluent shoppers who work long hours and have little time to shop, high-end fashion brands such as Dior, Louis Vuitton, and Fendi have unveiled e-commerce sites. These luxury makers also see their websites as a way for customers to research items before walking into a store and a means to help combat fakes sold over the internet. Given the lengths to which these brands go to pamper their customers in their stores (doormen, welcoming refreshments, extravagant design and surroundings) they have had to work hard to provide a high-quality experience online.[53]

Legal and Ethical Issues in Channel Relations

For the most part, companies are legally free to develop whatever channel arrangements suit them. In fact, the law seeks to prevent companies from using exclusionary tactics that might keep competitors from using a channel. Here we briefly consider the legality of certain practices, including exclusive dealing, exclusive territories, tying agreements, and dealers' rights.

Many producers like to develop exclusive channels for their products. A strategy in which the seller allows only certain outlets to carry its products is called *exclusive distribution*. When the seller requires that these dealers not handle competitors' products, this is called *exclusive dealing*. Both parties benefit from exclusive arrangements: the seller obtains more loyal and dependable outlets, and the dealers obtain a steady source of supply of special products and stronger seller support. In some countries, the legality of exclusive arrangements is challenged if they substantially lessen competition or tend to create a monopoly.

Exclusive dealing often includes exclusive territorial agreements. The producer may agree not to sell to other dealers in a given area, or the buyer may agree to sell only in its own territory. The first practice increases dealer enthusiasm and commitment. It is also perfectly legal: a seller has no legal obligation to sell through more outlets than it wishes. The second practice, whereby the producer tries to keep a dealer from selling outside its territory, has become a major legal issue.

Producers of a strong brand sometimes sell it to dealers only if they will take some or all of the rest of the line. This practice is called full-line forcing. Such **tying agreements** are not necessarily illegal.

E-Commerce Marketing Practices

tying agreements agreement in which producers of strong brands sell their products to dealers only if dealers purchase related products or services, such as other products in the brand line.

E-business describes the use of electronic means and platforms to conduct a company's business.[54] **E-commerce** means that the company or site offers to transact or facilitate the selling of products and services online. E-commerce has given rise in turn to e-purchasing and e-marketing. **E-purchasing** means companies decide to purchase goods, services, and information from various online suppliers. Smart e-purchasing has already saved companies millions of dollars. **E-marketing** describes company efforts to inform buyers, communicate, promote, and sell its products and services over the internet.

Online retail sales have exploded, growing in some countries at 30 percent a year. It's easy to see why. Online retailers can predictably provide convenient, informative, and personalized experiences for vastly different types of consumers and businesses. By not having to bear the cost of maintaining retail floor space, staff, and inventory, online retailers can sell low-volume products to niche markets. Online retailers compete among themselves in terms of three key aspects of a transaction: (1) customer interaction with the website, (2) delivery of the product, and (3) ability to address problems when they occur.[55]

We can distinguish between **pure-click** companies, those that have launched a website without any previous existence as a firm, and **brick-and-click** companies, existing companies that have added an online site for information or e-commerce.

e-business the use of electronic means and platforms to conduct a company's business.

e-commerce a company or site offers to transact or facilitate the selling of products and services online.

e-purchasing purchase of goods, services, and information from various online suppliers.

e-marketing company efforts to inform buyers, communicate, promote, and sell its products and services over the internet.

pure-click companies that have launched a website without any previous existence as a firm.

brick-and-click existing companies that have added an online site for information and/ or e-commerce.

Pure-Click Companies

There are several kinds of pure-click company: search engines, internet service providers (ISPs), commerce sites, transaction sites, content sites, and enabler sites. Commerce sites sell all types of products and services, notably books, music, toys, insurance, stocks, clothes, financial services, and so on. Amazon.com is a perfect example. Souq.com (initiated by Maktoob.com) and e-Mall.com.sa (initiated by Saudi Post) are popular broad-based Arab e-commerce sites. AdabWaFan.com is a popular online store for Arabic books, music, films, and software.

Souq.com   Souq.com was established in 2005 and has grown to become the largest e-commerce site in the Arab world, covering Saudi Arabia, the UAE, Jordan, and expanding to new markets. Souq.com is the channel where thousands of buyers and sellers in the region meet on a daily basis to buy and sell products over a trusted platform, which offers both various local payment options and integrated delivery methods catering to the markets that Souq.com serves. Souq.com is considered a pioneer in the field of e-commerce in the Arab world. It offers users a constant safe, easy, and fun place to conduct business. Souq.com started as the first online auction site and quickly evolved into a fully integrated e-commerce site offering fixed price options, online stores, and Souq SafePay. Backed by Maktoob Group's enormous online presence and expertise and a logistics solution by the leading delivery company, Aramex, Souq.com offers a local alternative to eBay.[56]

Companies must set up and operate their e-commerce websites carefully. Customer service is critical. Often, online shoppers select an item for purchase but fail to complete the transaction: the conversion rate of internet shoppers among the top 100 internet retailers is only about 5 percent, much lower than the norm from similar top firms using traditional channels.[57] Worse, only 1.8 percent of visits to online retailers lead to sales, compared with 5 percent of visits to department stores.

Consumer surveys suggest that the most significant inhibitors of online shopping are the absence of pleasurable experiences, social interaction, and personal consultation with a company representative.[58] Firms are responding. For example, some online vendors use live online chat to give potential customers immediate advice about products for sale on their websites.[59] Another benefit of providing live sales assistance is the ability to sell additional items. When a representative is involved in the sale, the average amount per order is typically higher. Online footwear retailer Zappos offers fast turnaround and free returns for a wide selection of shoes and finds that two-thirds of purchases during any one day are from repeat customers.[60] B2B marketers also need to put a human face on their e-commerce presence, and some are doing so by taking advantage of web 2.0 technologies such as virtual environments, blogs, online videos, and click-to-chat.

 Cisco Systems   Cisco is experimenting with a variety of web 2.0 applications such as posting videos of its Human Network campaign on YouTube, holding analyst briefings in the virtual world of Second Life, and especially using click-to-chat. "The single biggest [success] we've achieved in the last month is click-to-chat," said Michael Metz, Cisco's senior director of internet marketing and strategy. When users, who tend to be small-business customers, click on a button in the technical portion of Cisco's website, they are connected to a call center representative who helps them solve their problem. Then Cisco added a more sales-oriented click-to-chat feature. If a user comes back to a product page several times to look at a particular item, a chat box comes up saying, "Can we help you with product X?" So-called proactive chat enabled Cisco to improve its lead conversion rate by 50 percent in just the first 3 months.[61]

To increase the entertainment and information value and the customer satisfaction from web-based shopping experiences, some firms are employing *avatars*, graphical representations of virtual, animated characters that can act as company representatives. Avatars can provide a more interpersonal shopping experience by serving as identification figures, as personal shopping assistants, as website guides, or as conversation partners. Research has shown that avatars can enhance the effectiveness of a web-based sales channel, especially if they are seen as expert or attractive.[62]

Ensuring security and privacy online remains important. Customers must find the website trustworthy, even if it represents an already highly credible offline firm. Investments in website design and processes can help reassure customers sensitive to online risk.[63] Online retailers are also trying new technologies such as blogs, social networks, and mobile marketing to attract new shoppers.

Although the popular press has given the most attention to business-to-consumer (B2C) websites, even more activity is being conducted on business-to-business (B2B) sites. These are changing the supplier–customer relationship in profound ways. Firms are using B2B auction sites, spot exchanges, online product catalogs, barter sites, and other online resources to obtain better prices.

The purpose of B2B sites is to make markets more efficient. In the past, buyers exerted a lot of effort to gather information on worldwide suppliers. With the internet, buyers have easy access to a great deal of information. They can get information from: (1) supplier websites; (2) *infomediaries*, third parties that add value by aggregating information about alternatives; (3) *market makers*, third parties that create markets linking buyers and sellers; and (4) *customer communities*, websites where buyers can swap stories about suppliers' products and services.[64] Ironically, the largest of the B2B market makers is homegrown in China, a country where private businesses had faced decades of opposition and obstacles.

Alibaba   The brainchild of 42-year-old Jack Ma, Alibaba has become the world's largest online B2B marketplace, Asia's most popular online auction site, and now, with its acquisition of Yahoo! China, the 12th most popular website in the world. At its heart are two B2B websites, alibaba.com and china.alibaba. The former is a marketplace for companies around the globe to buy and sell in English, and the latter is a domestic Chinese marketplace. Whereas Alibaba's rivals, such as Commerce One, were founded with the goal of slashing procurement costs, the Chinese powerhouse has a more nationalist agenda: to build markets for China's vast number of small and medium-sized enterprises (SMEs). Alibaba enables them to both trade with each other and link to global supply chains. Of his focus on SMEs, Jack Ma says, "We are interested in catching shrimp, not the whales. When you catch the shrimp, then you will also catch the whales." European importers are particularly drawn to Alibaba's B2B net, in large part because Alibaba has set up a system by which businesses can easily establish trust. When membership in Alibaba's B2B exchange was free, members complained, "I don't trust this guy!" says Jack Ma; so he set up TrustPass, in which users pay Alibaba a fee to hire a third party that verifies them. Users must have five people vouch for them and provide a list of all their certificates/business licenses. Finally, anyone on Alibaba who has done business with a user is encouraged to comment on the firm, in the same way buyers comment on sellers in Amazon.com's or eBay's marketplace. This feature was not very common in the online B2B world, but Alibaba has made it a standard. Businesses are even starting to print "TrustPass" on their business cards, a true sign of Alibaba's B2B credibility.[65]

The net impact of these mechanisms is to make prices more transparent.[66] In the case of undifferentiated products, price pressure will increase. For highly differentiated products, buyers will gain a better picture of the items' true value. Suppliers of superior products will be able to offset price transparency with value transparency; suppliers of undifferentiated products will need to drive down their costs in order to compete.

Brick-and-Click Companies

Many brick-and-mortar companies debated whether to add an online e-commerce channel for fear that selling their products or services online might produce channel conflict with their offline retailers, agents, or their own stores.[67] Most eventually added the internet as a distribution channel after seeing how much business their online competitors were generating.

Yet adding an e-commerce channel creates the threat of a backlash from retailers, brokers, agents, and other intermediaries. The question is how to sell both through intermediaries and online. There are at least three strategies for trying to gain acceptance from intermediaries. One, offer different brands or products on the internet. Two, offer offline partners higher commissions to cushion the negative impact on sales. Three, take orders on the website but have retailers deliver and collect payment. Airline companies have had another challenge to manage in their relationship with travel agencies as airlines ventured heavily into online booking and ticket purchase through their own corporate websites.

M-Commerce

Consumers and businesspeople no longer need to be near a computer to send and receive information. All they need is a mobile phone or personal digital assistant (PDA). While they're on the move, they can connect to the internet to check stock prices, the weather, and sports scores; send and receive e-mail messages; and place online orders. Du, the UAE-based mobile operator, attempted to capitalize on this benefit through its communication and advertising messages as it approached the business market segment with its services. A whole field called *telematics* places wireless internet-connected computers in the dashboards of cars and trucks, and makes more home appliances (such as computers) wireless so they can be used anywhere in or near the home. Many see a big future in what is now called *m-commerce* (m for mobile).[68] A popular application throughout the Arab world is the purchase of downloadable mobile-phone ringtones through text messaging.

Summary

1. Most producers do not sell their goods directly to final users. Between producers and final users stand one or more marketing channels, a host of marketing intermediaries performing a variety of functions.

2. Marketing channel decisions are among the most critical decisions facing management. The company's chosen channel(s) profoundly affect all other marketing decisions.

3. Companies use intermediaries when they lack the financial resources to carry out direct marketing, when direct marketing is not feasible, and when they can earn more by doing so. The most important functions performed by intermediaries are information, promotion, negotiation, ordering, financing, risk taking, physical possession, payment, and title.

4. Manufacturers have many alternatives for reaching a market. They can sell direct or use one-, two-, or three-level channels. Deciding which type(s) of channel to use calls for analyzing customer needs, establishing channel objectives, and identifying and evaluating the major alternatives, including the types and numbers of intermediaries involved in the channel.

5. Effective channel management calls for selecting intermediaries and training and motivating them. The goal is to build a long-term partnership that will be profitable for all channel members.

6. Marketing channels are characterized by continuous and sometimes dramatic change. Three of the most important trends are the growth of vertical marketing systems, horizontal marketing systems, and multichannel marketing systems.

7. All marketing channels have the potential for conflict and competition resulting from such sources as goal incompatibility, poorly defined roles and rights, perceptual differences, and interdependent relationships. Companies can manage conflict by striving for superordinate goals, exchanging people among two or more channel levels, co-opting the support of leaders in different parts of the channel, encouraging joint membership in and between trade associations, employing diplomacy, mediation, or arbitration, or pursuing legal recourse.

8. Channel arrangements are up to the company, but there are certain legal and ethical issues to be considered with regard to practices such as exclusive dealing or territories, tying agreements, and dealers' rights.

9. E-commerce has grown in importance as companies have adopted 'brick-and-click' channel systems. Channel integration must recognize the distinctive strengths of online and offline selling and maximize their joint contributions. An emerging new area is m-commerce and marketing through mobile phones and PDAs.

Applications

Marketing Debate
Does It Matter Where You Are Sold?

Some marketers feel that the image of the particular channel in which they sell their products does not matter: all that matters is that the right customers shop there and the product is displayed in the right way. Others maintain that channel images—such as a retail store—can be critical and must be consistent with the image of the product.

Take a position: Channel images do not greatly affect the brand images of the products they sell *versus* channel images must be consistent with the brand image.

Marketing Discussion

Think of your favorite retailers. How have they integrated their channel system? How would you like their channels to be integrated? Do you use multiple channels from them? Why?

Marketing Excellence

>>Transmed

Transmed

Established in 1946 as a sales and distribution company in Lebanon, Transmed has grown to become one of the largest distribution, bottling, and food service organizations in the region. Transmed's portfolio includes many successful household FMCG principals and brands: Clorox, Mars, P&G, Coca-Cola, McVities, Perfetti, Afia, Sysco, Danone, Americana, Pampa, McCain, Wrigleys, President, and many others.

Transmed's journey throughout its 65-year history has not been a smooth ride. In addition to the increasingly competitive business environment, Transmed had to face a challenging political environment, a 15-year Lebanese civil war, and several conflicts with Israel, including the 2006 war that destroyed most of Transmed's fleet and storage facilities. Yet, during all of this, Transmed has endured and grown stronger because of the company's determination, and its firm and unwavering commitment to be "fully dedicated to the sales and distribution of high quality fast moving consumer goods … that address the needs of local consumers, offering excellent value for money and real consumer satisfaction with significant growth potential."

After asserting itself as a prime distribution company in the Lebanese market with full coverage of the Lebanese territories, Transmed looked beyond Lebanon's border for expansion. In 1975, the company entered the United Arab Emirates (UAE), and quickly followed its entry with rapid expansion to keep up with the growth of the UAE's market. Transmed began operating warehouses to store its dry, chilled, and frozen products in Dubai and Abu Dhabi to ensure that only quality products reached their final destinations.

In 1977, just two years after making its debut in the UAE, Transmed felt confident enough to enter another regional neighbor, Jordan. Transmed's sales team based in the capital, Amman, extends its services to Zarqa, Irbid, Karak, and Aqaba. Transmed has warehouse facilities in Amman and a satellite warehouse in the Aqaba Free Zone. In 1995, Transmed opened offices in Damascus and began operations covering the Syrian market. Their expansion did not stop there; in 2009 they expanded into Sudan, setting up offices and a distribution centre in Khartoum. This African venture was a stepping stone into West Africa, and in 2011 Transmed began operating in Senegal and the Ivory Coast, followed by the opening of its latest business in the newly created South Sudan. "Expanding into new markets has forced us to be agile and flexible, especially when managing our customers. For instance, in the UAE we have a very complicated and dedicated multi-functional team that manages our largest customer, Carrefour. This customer team comprises of dedicated people in sales, customer service, finance, marketing, and logistics working exclusively for Carrefour, whereas in Senegal, we require a totally different skill set to manage the open markets, which are outdoor, overcrowded, dusty and quite chaotic," says Fouad Es-Said, Chairman and CEO of Transmed.

On the manufacturing side, it wasn't until 2001 that the company decided to combine its expertise in sales and distribution with a new venture: bottling. Transmed acquired a majority share in Société Najem pour l'Industrie et le Commerce, the manufacturer of Pampa juice. Using their expertise, the company rebranded and packaged the product and used their sales and distribution channels to successfully take Pampa juice regionally by introducing it to the Syrian and Jordanian markets. After the success of Pampa juice, Coca-Cola took notice and decided to partner with Transmed's subsidiary, 'The Lebanese Beverage Holding Company,' making Transmed the sole official bottler of Coca-Cola in Lebanon. In mid 2004, Transmed further consolidated its beverage business by acquiring Nada and Dynamics mineral water brands with a bottling facility in the Shouf region. This strategic move allowed Transmed to further expand and leverage its distribution reach to new segments such as hotels, restaurants, clubs, beaches, snacks, vending, soda fountains, and fast food outlets. Manufacturing has become a cornestone in Transmed's strategy, and in 2010 they invested in a state-of-the-art ice-cream factory, better known for producing the Cornelli brand. This great success will be the launch pad for further investments in manufacturing and production.

In 2007, Transmed acquired a large share in C-Food International, known as Siblou, a leading seafood brand. Today, Siblou is distributed in 22 markets across the Middle East, Africa, and Europe.

Similar to most businesses in Lebanon and the Arab world, Transmed is family owned and operated. The Es-Said family is the majority shareholder. The company employs 2500 people across all markets with its headquarters in Beirut's Central District. Such an organization "ensures a wide coverage and a deep market penetration by covering all trade channels and directly calling on a

Continued on next page >>

Marketing Excellence...continued

>>Transmed

wide spectrum of different store formats including hyper-markets, supermarkets, self-service stores, groceries, and pharmacies. Coverage also extends to the non-traditional channels including petrol stations, schools, hotels, restaurants, clubs, and other recreational outlets." This structure is replicated to a certain extent in its overseas operations as well, including Syria, Jordan, UAE, Sudan, Senegal, the Ivory Coast, and the newly created South Sudan.

To be able to achieve its mission, Transmed has always sought to set itself apart from its competition. One of its main ingredients in this regard is establishing strong ties with its partners, and always striving to provide them with the highest quality of service even in the most difficult conditions and markets. It is crucial for Transmed to be able to continue delivering the value that it has promised to its loyal customers. Accordingly, Transmed invested highly in its infrastructure and its human resource management and technological processes to stay ahead of its competition. For example, the Supply Chain Lab is an initiative taken by Transmed that aims at collaborating efforts with retailers in the region "to resolve discontinuities and disruptions in the supply chain ... to improve speed, eliminate delays, inventory, cost and resources ... In summary the Supply Chain Lab is the place that assembles the best supply chain tools and concepts to help both retailers and Transmed create the best possible shopper-driven supply chain."

"Challenging [its] work processes and performance measures to improve efficiency, cost effectiveness and profitability" has always been at the core of Transmed's innovation strategy. This strategy combined with Transmed's long-term commitment "to create value for [its] shareholders, business partners, customers, staff and communities" has played an important role in setting it apart from its competition, and has fueled its regional expansion.

Questions

In light of the concepts covered in this chapter, and the knowledge you have accumulated so far in the course, answer the following questions:

1. What benefits does Transmed offer to multinational companies such as P&G, Mars, and Arab regional companies such as Americana?

2. Why do you think Coca-Cola was interested in appointing Transmed as its sole bottling company in Lebanon?

3. How would you categorize Transmed's decision to invest in Siblou's C-Food in terms of the concepts learned under Channel Integration and Systems? How can you categorize the arrangement between Transmed and Coca-Cola?

Sources: www.transmed.com; ae.zawya.com/cm/profile.cfm/cid1003153; Gehad Al-Hadidi, Suzanne Charbaji, and Zeina El-Khoury, *Transmed Case Study*, American University of Beirut, Fall 2010–11; Interview with Fouad Es-Said, Chairman and CEO, Transmed, February 2012.

Zara's nimble retailing model enables it to bring new fashions from drawing board to selling floor in a matter of weeks and to sell most of its merchandise at full price.

In this chapter, we will address the following **questions:**

1. What major types of marketing intermediaries occupy this sector? (pg. 437)

2. What marketing decisions do these marketing intermediaries make? (pg. 442)

3. What are the major trends with marketing intermediaries? (pg. 452)

Managing Retailing, Wholesaling, and Logistics

In the previous chapter, we examined marketing intermediaries from the viewpoint of manufacturers who wanted to build and manage marketing channels. In this chapter, we view these intermediaries—retailers, wholesalers, and logistical organizations—as requiring and forging their own marketing strategies. Intermediaries also strive for marketing excellence and can reap the benefits like any other company.

 Spain's Zara has become Europe's leading apparel retailer in recent years by adopting a different retail model. The firm's strategy is to give customers a wide variety at affordable prices. It can offer 20,000 different items in a year, about triple what Gap would do. Zara distributes all its merchandise, regardless of origin, from Spain, and is willing to experience occasional shortages to preserve an image of exclusivity. Unlike some other retailers, Zara doesn't spend lavish amounts of money on advertising or on deals with designers, and instead invests more in its store locations. Zara places its stores—over 90 percent of which it owns—in heavily trafficked, high-end retail zones. These practices help it to sell more at full price—85 percent of its merchandise—than the industry average of 60 percent. By controlling all aspects of the supply chain, Zara can take an idea and make it a reality on the store floor in about 5 weeks, compared to the months needed by a typical clothing manufacturer. Zara also identified the Arab world as an important market and currently operates stores in Bahrain, Egypt, Jordan, Kuwait, Lebanon, Oman, Qatar, Saudi Arabia, Syria, and the UAE.[1]

While 'fast-forward' retailers such as Zara and Mango have thrived in recent years, others such as former U.S. star Gap have struggled. Many of the more successful intermediaries use strategic planning, advanced information systems, and sophisticated marketing tools. They measure performance more on a return-on-investment basis than on a profit-margin basis. They segment their markets, improve their market targeting and positioning, and aggressively pursue market expansion and diversification strategies. In this chapter, we consider marketing excellence in retailing, wholesaling, and logistics. ▽

Retailing

Retailing includes all the activities in selling goods or services directly to final consumers for personal, non-business use. A **retailer** or *retail store* is any business enterprise whose sales volume comes primarily from retailing.

Any organization selling to final consumers—whether it is a manufacturer, wholesaler, or retailer—is doing retailing. It doesn't matter *how* the goods or services are sold (in person, by mail, telephone, vending machine, or on the internet) or *where* (in a store, on the street, or in the consumer's home).

retailing All activities involved in selling goods or services directly to final consumers for their personal, non-business use.

retailer a business whose sales come primarily from retailing.

Types of Retailers

Consumers today can shop for goods and services at store retailers, nonstore retailers, and retail organizations. Perhaps the best-known type of retailer is the department store. ABC Mall in Lebanon, Dubai Shopping Mall, and the Mall of Arabia in Jeddah all attract millions

BOX 16.1 ▬　　Major Retailer Types

Specialty store: Narrow product line. Mikyajy, Nayomi, Fustany, and Mazaya.

Department store: Several product lines. ABC Lebanon, Alsawani, and Panda in Saudi Arabia.

Supermarket: Large, low-cost, low-margin, high-volume, self-service store designed to meet total needs for food and household products. Al Muntazah, Lulu Supermarket, and Carrefour are a few examples.

Convenience store: Small store in residential area, often open 24/7, limited line of high-turnover convenience products plus takeout. Emarat, On the Run, and 24-Seven are some examples.

Discount store: Standard or specialty merchandise; low-price, low-margin, high-volume stores. Walmart, Kmart, and Al Tawheed wa Al Noor in Egypt.

Off-price retailer: Leftover goods, overruns, and irregular merchandise sold at less than retail. Factory outlets (independent off-price retailers): Filene's Basement and Marshalls. Warehouse clubs: Sam's Club and Costco.

Superstore: Huge selling space, routinely purchased food and household items, plus services (laundry, shoe repair, dry cleaning, check cashing). Category killer (deep assortment in one category): IKEA and Dary in Egypt. Combination store: e.g. combine food items with general merchandize, such as Royal House. Hypermarket (huge stores that combine supermarket, discount, and warehouse retailing): Carrefour and Spinneys.

Catalog showroom: Broad selection of high-markup, fast-moving, brand-name goods sold by catalog at discount. Customers pick up merchandise at the store, but no merchandise is displayed.

of shoppers every year and offer shoppers restaurants, children's playgrounds, coffee shops, supermarkets, and entertainment.

Retail-store types pass through stages of growth and decline that we can think of as the *retail life cycle*.[2] Department stores took 80 years to reach maturity, whereas warehouse retail outlets reached maturity in 10 years. The most important retail-store types are described in ▬ **Box 16.1**.

LEVELS OF SERVICE The *wheel-of-retailing* hypothesis explains one reason that new store types emerge.[3] Conventional retail stores typically increase their services and raise their prices to cover the costs. These higher costs provide an opportunity for new store forms to offer lower prices and less service. New store types meet widely different consumer preferences for service levels and specific services.

Retailers position themselves as offering one of four levels of service:

1. *Self-service*. Self-service is the cornerstone of all discount operations. Many customers are willing to carry out their own locate-compare-select process to save money.
2. *Self-selection*. Customers find their own goods, although they can ask for assistance.
3. *Limited service*. These retailers carry more shopping goods and services such as credit and merchandise-return privileges. Customers need more information and assistance.
4. *Full service*. Salespeople are ready to assist in every phase of the locate-compare–select process. Customers who like to be waited on prefer this type of store. The high staffing cost, along with the higher proportion of specialty goods and slower-moving items and the many services, result in high-cost retailing.

By combining these different service levels with different assortment breadths, we can distinguish the four broad positioning strategies available to retailers. Each of the below retailers represent different breadths of product line and different levels of value added.

1. *Bloomingdale's*. Stores that feature a broad product assortment and high value added pay close attention to store design, product quality, service, and image. Their profit margin is high, and if they have high enough volume, they will be very profitable.

2. *Tiffany*. Stores that feature a narrow product assortment and high value added cultivate an exclusive image and operate on high margin and low volume.
3. *Sunglass Hut*. Stores that feature a narrow line and low value added keep costs and prices low by centralizing buying, merchandising, advertising, and distribution.
4. *Carrefour*. Stores that feature a broad line and low value added focus on keeping prices low and have the image of a place for good buys. High volume makes up for low margin.[4]

Although the overwhelming bulk of goods and services—97 percent—is sold through stores, *nonstore retailing* has been growing much faster than store retailing. Nonstore retailing falls into four major categories: direct selling, direct marketing (which includes telemarketing and internet selling), automatic vending, and buying services.

1. **Direct selling**, also called *multilevel selling* and *network marketing*, is a multibillion-dollar industry, with hundreds of companies selling door-to-door or at home sales parties. "Direct Selling is a multibillion industry, which has not been exploited in this part of the world," says Niusha Ehsan, marketing manager of the Direct Selling Festival in Dubai. "Bearing in mind that 85 percent in the business are women, I think we will have considerable interest from women here, as women enjoy the flexibility of this business."[5] Well-known in one-to-one selling are Avon makeup and Gano Exel in Saudi Arabia and Dubai. Tupperware products are sold one-to-many: a salesperson goes to the home of a host who has invited friends; the salesperson demonstrates the products and takes orders. The multilevel, or network, marketing sales system works by recruiting independent businesspeople who act as distributors. The distributor's compensation includes a percentage of sales made by those he or she recruits, as well as earnings on direct sales to customers. These direct-selling firms, now finding fewer consumers at home, are developing multidistribution strategies.

2. **Direct marketing** has roots in direct-mail and catalog marketing; it includes **telemarketing**, *television direct-response marketing* (Meshop and Citruss TV in the UAE), and *electronic shopping* (Amazon.com). As people become more accustomed to shopping on the internet, they are ordering a greater variety of goods and services from a wider range of websites.

    telemarketing the use of telephone and call centers to attract prospects, sell to existing customers, and provide service by taking orders and answering questions.

3. **Automatic vending** offers a variety of merchandise, including impulse goods such as cigarettes, soft drinks, coffee, candy, newspapers, magazines, and other products such as hosiery, cosmetics, hot food, and paperbacks. Vending machines are found in factories, offices, large retail stores, gasoline stations, hotels, restaurants, and many other places. They offer 24-hour selling, self-service, and merchandise that is always fresh.

4. **Buying service or warehouse clubs** are storeless retailers serving a specific clientele—usually employees of large organizations—who are entitled to buy from a list of retailers that have agreed to give discounts in return for membership.

CORPORATE RETAILING Although many retail stores are independently owned, an increasing number are part of a **corporate retailing** organization. These organizations achieve economies of scale, greater purchasing power, wider brand recognition, and better-trained employees than independent stores can usually gain alone. The major types of corporate retailing—corporate chain stores, voluntary chains, retailer and consumer cooperatives, franchises, and merchandising corporations—are described in **Box 16.2** on page 440.

corporate retailing corporately owned retailing outlets that achieve economies of scale, greater purchasing power, wider brand recognition, and better-trained employees.

To sustain growth, firms are looking overseas and in nontraditional site locations such as airports, sports stadiums, college campuses, hospitals, theme parks, and convention halls. Franchises that offer a unique product or service can usually find customers.

In a franchising system, individual *franchisees* are a tightly knit group of enterprises whose systematic operations are planned, directed, and controlled by the operation's innovator, called a *franchisor*. Franchises are distinguished by three characteristics:

1. The franchisor owns a trade or service mark and licenses it to franchisees in return for royalty payments.
2. The franchisee pays for the right to be part of the system. Start-up costs include rental and lease equipment and fixtures, and usually a regular license fee. McDonald's franchisees may

Corporate chain store: Two or more outlets owned and controlled, employing central buying and merchandising, and selling similar lines of merchandise. For example, Gap.

Voluntary chain: A wholesaler-sponsored group of independent retailers engaged in bulk buying and common merchandising.

Retailer cooperative: Independent retailers using a central buying organization and joint promotion efforts. Abu Dhabi Cooperative Society, Al Ain Cooperative Society, and Union Co-op in the UAE are some examples.

Consumer cooperative: A retail firm owned by its customers. Members contribute money to open their own store, vote on its policies, elect a group to manage it, and receive dividends.

Franchise organization: Contractual association between a franchisor and franchisees, popular in a number of product and service areas. For example, McDonald's, Subway, Pizza Hut, Mo'men, and Cook-Door.

Merchandising conglomerate: A corporation that combines several diversified retailing lines and forms under central ownership, with some integration of distribution and management. For example Azadea Group Lebanon with Zara, along with 35 international franchise concepts ranging from clothing, accessories, food, multimedia, to home furnishings, and recently sports goods.

invest as much as US$1.6 million in total start-up costs and fees. The franchisee then pays McDonald's a certain percentage of sales plus a monthly rent.

3.   The franchisor provides its franchisees with a system for doing business. McDonald's requires franchisees to attend Hamburger University in Oak Brook, Illinois in the United States for 2 weeks to learn how to manage the business. Franchisees must follow certain procedures in buying materials.

Franchising benefits both franchisor and franchisee. Franchisors gain the motivation and hard work of employees who are entrepreneurs rather than 'hired hands,' the franchisees' familiarity with local communities and conditions, and the enormous purchasing power of being a franchisor. Franchisees benefit from buying into a business with a well-known and accepted brand name. They find it easier to borrow money for their business from financial institutions, and they receive support in areas ranging from marketing and advertising to site selection and staffing. Franchisees walk a line between being independent and loyal to the franchisor. Their independence can allow them more flexibility.

The New Retail Environment

In the past, retailers secured customer loyalty by offering convenient locations, special or unique assortments of goods, greater or better services than competitors, and store credit cards. All this has changed. Retail-store assortments have grown more alike as national-brand manufacturers place their branded goods in more and more places. Service differentiation also has eroded. Many department stores have trimmed services, and many discounters have increased theirs. Customers have become smarter shoppers. They don't want to pay more for identical brands, especially when service differences have diminished; nor do they need credit from a particular store, because bank credit cards are almost universally accepted.

Retailers must react to market changes or risk going out of business. In the face of increased competition from discount houses and specialty stores, department stores are waging a come-back war. In addition to locations in the centers of cities, many have branches in suburban shopping centers, where parking is plentiful and family incomes are higher. To better compete, other department stores update merchandise more frequently, remodel their stores, introduce their own brands, and sell through mail-order catalogs, websites, and the phone.[6]

Similarly, supermarkets have opened larger stores, carry a larger number and variety of items, and are upgrading facilities. They've also increased their promotional budgets and moved heavily into private labels. Others have sought to create stronger differentiation.

Panda The United Azizia Panda Company is one of Savola's group companies and it is considered to be one of the biggest Saudi companies in Saudi Arabia. Panda was established in 1979 when its first branch was opened in Riyadh. Since then, the company has been concentrating its effort to expand in order to satisfy customers' needs all around Saudi Arabia and to offer them the best service coupled with competitive prices. Panda directs and controls the work of a chain that consists of 100 supermarkets and hypermarkets inside and outside Saudi Arabia. It expanded into the United Arab Emirates when it opened its HyperPanda in Dubai. Panda has over 130 branches inside and outside Saudi Arabia and around 13,000 employees. In 2008 Panda merged with the Giant stores thus benefiting a larger group of consumers with Panda's services. What distinguishes Panda's stores is the brand. Panda's own-brand sales grew and have become one of the most desirable choices for its customers. These products are characterized by high quality, competitive prices, and wide diversity to satisfy varied customer needs.[7]

Panda distinguishes its brand by having a wide range of high-quality products at competitive prices.

Here are some other retail developments that are changing the way consumers buy and manufacturers and retailers sell.

- **New retail forms and combinations.** Some superstores include bank branches. Bookstores feature coffee shops. Gas stations include food stores. Retailers are also experimenting with limited-time-only stores called 'pop-ups' that let retailers promote brands, reach seasonal shoppers for a few weeks in busy areas and create buzz.[8] Other retailing formats include combination stores which sell food along with general merchandise items to create a single, multipurpose shopping trip for customers.

- **Growth of intertype competition.** Department stores can't worry just about other department stores. Different types of stores—discount stores and catalog showrooms—also compete for the same consumers by carrying the same type of merchandise. The biggest winners are retailers that have helped shoppers to be economically cautious, simplified their increasingly busy and complicated lives, and provided an emotional connection, including supercenters, dollar stores, warehouse clubs, and the internet.[9] Nowadays in Cairo, traditional small kiosks compete with On the Run convenience stores, and small independent grocery stores compete with the French supermarket giant Carrefour.

- **Competition between store-based and nonstore-based retailing.** Consumers now receive sales offers through direct-mail letters and catalogs, and through the television, on computers, and by telephone. These nonstore-based retailers are taking business away from the retail stores. For example, Sinbadmall.com was the first online shopping website in the Arab world. Hellwafashion.com is another website where people can shop online and benefit from discounts. Tamima is a telemarketing retailer in the Middle East which witnessed tremendous success during the mid-1990s and early 2000s.[10]

- **Growth of giant retailers.** Through their superior information systems, logistical systems, and buying power, giant retailers such as Walmart are able to deliver good service and huge volumes of product at appealing prices to masses of consumers. They are crowding out smaller manufacturers that cannot deliver enough quantity, and often dictate to the most powerful manufacturers what to make, how to price and promote, when and how to ship, and even how to improve production and management. Manufacturers need these accounts; otherwise they would lose 10 to 30 percent of the market. Some giant retailers are *category killers* that concentrate on one product category, such as IKEA, Ragab Sons, and Nagy for cosmetics. Others are *supercenters* or combination stores that combine grocery items with a huge selection of nonfood merchandise, such as Spinneys and Royal House.

- **Decline of middle-market retailers.** Today we can characterize the retail market as hourglass or dog-bone shaped: growth seems to be centered at the top (with luxury offerings from retailers such as Nordstrom and Tiffanys) and at the bottom (with discount pricing from retailers such as Target, Al Tawheed wa Al Noor, and Walmart). Opportunities are scarcer in the middle where retailers and others have struggled or gone out of business. Supermarkets, department stores, and drugstores are most at risk or on the edge: fewer consumers have shopped these channels weekly in recent years as newer, more relevant places have come to serve their needs.[11] As discount retailers improve their quality and image, consumers have been willing to trade down. In the Arab world, customers prefer the modern or trendy shopping practices of giant retailers as a sort of entertainment experience.

- **Growing investment in technology.** Retailers are using computers to produce better forecasts, control inventory costs, order electronically from suppliers, send e-mail between stores, and even sell to customers within stores. Some retailers are borrowing technological tactics from other industries, and with great success. Retailers are also adopting checkout scanning systems,[12] electronic funds transfer, electronic data interchange,[13] in-store television, store traffic radar systems,[14] and improved merchandise-handling systems. Some employ goggle-like devices that record what test customers see by projecting an infrared beam onto the wearer's retina. One finding was that many shoppers ignored products at eye level: the optimum location was between their waist and chest level.[15] Retailers are also introducing features to help customers as they shop. Some supermarkets are installing personal shopping 'assistants' on shopping carts that help customers locate items in the store, find out about sales and special offers, and even place a deli order.[16]

Wendy's International Inc.　Drive-through business accounts for a sizable percentage of fast-food sales, but the system is dogged by two major profit killers: (1) employee theft (when late-night drive-through employees give food to their friends and pocket the cash) and (2) slowness. No one wants to sit in a hot car waiting for cold french fries to arrive. Now, Wendy's, McDonald's, and a host of fast-food companies are adopting call center technology to fill orders even faster. When you pull into one of the drive-through lanes at Wendy's store in Burbank, California, the voice that takes your order will be coming from Nashua, New Hampshire, 4,800 kilometers away. It's connected to the computer of a call center employee using internet calling technology, who needs a mere 40 milliseconds to transfer your order to a screen in the drive-through kitchen. Call centers not only free employees to put orders together faster; they also make orders more accurate and more profitable. Call center employees are trained to urge customers to order extras, such as a larger order of fries or a drink with each order. It's a win-win strategy, especially for Wendy's, which differentiates itself on its drive-through speed and has been the industry's speediest server for a straight 7 years. With call center technology, Wendy's expects to complete orders in under 90 seconds.[17]

- **Global profile of major retailers.** Retailers with unique formats and strong brand positioning are increasingly appearing in other countries.[18] United States retailers such as The Limited and Gap have become globally prominent. Walmart operates over 2,700 stores outside of the United States, where it does 20 percent of its business. Among foreign-based global retailers in the United States are Britain's Marks & Spencer, Italy's Benetton, France's Carrefour hypermarkets, and Sweden's IKEA home furnishing stores.

Marketing Decisions

With this new retail environment as a backdrop, we will examine retailers' marketing decisions in the areas of target market, product assortment and procurement, prices, services and store atmosphere, store activities and experiences, communications, and location.

TARGET MARKET Until it defines and profiles the target market, the retailer cannot make consistent decisions about product assortment, store decor, advertising messages and media, price, or service levels. Nayomi was founded to tap into the needs of thousands of fashion-conscious female shoppers in the region. It began as a lingerie concept and has since become a leading brand offering a wide selection of underwear, nightwear, outerwear, bridalwear, fashion, activewear, and more recently beauty products to satisfy Arab women's tastes. Nayomi has a total presence of nearly 126 stores in 32 key cities across Saudi Arabia, the UAE, Qatar, Oman, and Kuwait.[19]

Mistakes in choosing or switching target markets can be costly. When historically mass-market jeweler Zales decided to chase upscale customers, it replaced one-third of its merchandise, dropping inexpensive, low-quality diamond jewelry for high-margin, fashionable 14-karat gold and silver pieces, and also shifted its ad campaign in the process. The move was a disaster. Zales lost many of its traditional customers without winning over the new customers it had hoped to attract.[20]

To better hit their targets, retailers are slicing the market into finer and finer segments and introducing new lines of stores to provide a more relevant set of offerings to exploit niche markets; for example, Aïshti launched Aizone, selling apparel specifically for teenagers.

PRODUCT ASSORTMENT The retailer's product assortment must match the target market's shopping needs, preferences, and shopping expectations. The retailer must decide on product-assortment *breadth* and *depth*. A restaurant can offer a narrow and shallow assortment (small lunch counters), a narrow and deep assortment (delicatessen), a broad and shallow assortment (cafeteria), or a broad and deep assortment (large restaurant).

Product assortment can be especially challenging in fast-moving industries such as technology or fashion.

 Mikyajy Mikyajy is a Saudi Arabian cosmetics retailer, founded in 1999. Mikyajy's success in Saudi Arabia led the company to open 160 stores across the Arab world, achieving expansion through Saudi Arabia, the UAE, Bahrain, Oman, Qatar, Kuwait, and Libya. In *Forbes Arabia*'s list of the top 40 brands in the Arab world, Mikyajy ranked 29th, an outstanding achievement for a 10-year-old brand. Mikyajy has a wide range of products to satisfy the requirements of its customers. The Mikyajy product assortment includes cosmetics, skin care products, and makeup tools. The Mikyajy brand is characterized by creativity, fun, and innovation, and is continually improving its cosmetics and skin care offers.[21]

The real challenge begins after defining the store's product assortment, and that is to develop a product-differentiation strategy. Here are some possibilities:

- *Feature exclusive national brands that are not available at competing retailers.* Saks might get exclusive rights to carry the dresses of a well-known international designer.

- *Feature mostly private-label merchandise.* Benetton and Gap design most of the clothes carried in their stores. Many supermarket and drug chains carry private-label merchandise.

- *Feature blockbuster distinctive merchandise events.* Bloomingdale's will run month-long shows featuring the goods of another country, such as India or China, throughout the store.

- *Feature surprise or ever-changing merchandise.* Off-price apparel retailer T.J. Maxx offers surprise assortments of distress merchandise (goods the owner must sell immediately because it needs cash), overstocks, and closeouts, totaling 10,000 new items each week.

- *Feature the latest or newest merchandise first.* Aizone sells hip clothing and hard-to-find pop culture merchandise to teens.

- *Offer merchandise-customizing services.* Fustany.com will make custom-tailored dresses for customers. Elie Saab Couture and other fashion designers will design specific dresses for customers based on their requests.

- *Offer a highly targeted assortment.* Uaeflowers.com delivers upon customers' requests cakes, chocolates, balloons, and soft toys along with their flowers to enhance the presentation.

It is important to mention that merchandise may vary by geographical market. What can be appealing to the tastes and preferences of consumers in Oman, for example, may not be appealing to Kuwaiti or Bahraini consumers.

PROCUREMENT   After deciding on the product-assortment strategy, the retailer must establish merchandise sources, policies, and practices. In the corporate headquarters of a supermarket chain, specialist buyers (sometimes called *merchandise managers* or *planners*) are responsible for developing brand assortments and listening to salespersons' presentations. In some chains, buyers who are usually responsible for buying orders and work alongside planners have the authority to accept or reject new items. In other chains, they are limited to screening 'obvious rejects' and 'obvious accepts;' they bring other items to the buying committee for approval. Even when an item is accepted by a chain-store buying committee, individual stores in the chain may not carry it, according to geographic differences between locations. About one-third of the items must be stocked, and about two-thirds are stocked at the discretion of each store manager.

Manufacturers face a major challenge trying to get new items onto store shelves. They offer the nation's supermarkets between 150 and 250 new items each week, of which store buyers reject over 70 percent. Manufacturers need to know the acceptance criteria used by buyers, buying committees, and store managers. A. C. Nielsen Company interviewed store managers and found they are most influenced by (in order of importance) strong evidence of consumer acceptance, a well-designed advertising and sales promotion plan, and generous financial incentives to the trade.

Retailers are rapidly improving their skills in demand forecasting, merchandise selection, stock control, space allocation, and display. They use computers to track inventory, compute economic order quantities, order goods, and analyze money spent on vendors and products. Supermarket chains use scanner data to manage their merchandise mix on a store-by-store basis, and soon all stores will probably rely on 'smart tags' to track goods in real time as they move from factories to supermarkets to shopping baskets. For more on the possible uses—and abuses—of this technology, see Marketing Insight: *Making Labels Smarter*.

Marketing Insight

Making Labels Smarter

Radio frequency identification (RFID) systems are made up of 'smart' tags—microchips attached to tiny radio antennas—and electronic readers. The smart tags can be embedded on products or stuck on labels, and when the tag is near a reader, it transmits a unique identifying number to its computer database. The use of RFIDs has been exploding, with an estimated 1.3 billion tags sold in 2006, and an estimated 10.5 million tags will be in use by 2014. Radio-tagging products allow retailers to alert manufacturers before shelves are empty, and consumer-goods manufacturers can further perfect their supply chain so they don't produce or distribute too few or too many goods.

Gillette maintains that retailers and consumer-goods firms lose around US$30 billion a year from being out of stock on crucial items. The firm is using smart tags to let store owners know they need to reorder, as well as to provide alerts if a large decrease on a shelf may be the result of shoplifting. Gillette also is using smart tags to improve logistics and shipping from factories. RFID technology enabled Gillette to get the new Fusion razor on store shelves 11 days faster than its normal turnaround time. Gillette forecasts a 25 percent return on its RFID investment over the next 10 years, through increased sales and productivity savings.

Gillette isn't alone. Coca-Cola is embedding RFID readers in 200,000 of its 1 million vending machines in Japan to allow consumers to buy a Coke using wallet phones with RFID chips. Dutch bookseller Selexyz is tagging every title it stocks after a pilot study showed a 25 percent increase in sales. RFID-tagged books make for easier inventory control, consumer search, and checkout at the register.

The ability to link product IDs with databases containing the life histories and whereabouts of products makes RFID useful for preventing counterfeiting and even ensuring food and drug safety. A food company could program a system to alert plant managers when cases of meat sit unrefrigerated for too long. The U.S. Food and Drug Administration is already pushing for the widespread tagging of medicines to keep counterfeit pharmaceuticals from entering the market. Some retailers are using RFID to prevent stealing.

Sources: Diane Anderson, "RFID Technology Getting Static in New Hampshire," *Brandweek*, January 23, 2006, p. 13; Mary Catherine O'Conner, "Gillette Fuses RFID with Product Launch," *RFID Journal*, March 27, 2006; "The End of Privacy?," *Consumer Reports*, June 2006, pp. 33–40; Erick Schonfeld, "Tagged for Growth," *Business 2.0*, December 2006, pp. 58–61; www.tersosolutions.com/the-cloud-and-rfid-making-deployments-seamless/.

When retailers do study the economics of buying and selling individual products, they typically find that a third of their square footage is tied up in products that don't make an economic profit for them (above the cost of capital). Another third is typically allocated to product categories that break even. The final third of the space creates more than 100 percent of the economic profit. Yet, most retailers are unaware of which third of their products generate the profit.[22]

Stores are using **direct product profitability** (DPP) to measure a product's handling costs (receiving, moving to storage, paperwork, selecting, checking, loading, and space cost) from the time it reaches the warehouse until a customer buys it in the retail store. Users learn to their surprise that the gross margin on a product often bears little relation to the direct product profit. Some high-volume products may have such high handling costs that they are less profitable and deserve less shelf space than low-volume products.

To better differentiate themselves and generate consumer interest, some luxury retailers are making their stores and merchandise more varied.

> **direct product profitability (DDP)** a way of measuring a product's handling costs from the time it reaches the warehouse until a customer buys it in the retail store.

Jumbo Electronics

Jumbo Electronics is a giant distributor of consumer electronics, established in 1974 in the UAE, and now with a retail network of 30 stores. Its wide geographic coverage and deep assortment of stockkeeping units (SKUs) have given Jumbo Electronics a competitive advantage in the market. Carrying the most appealing brand names and a wide variety of electronics has also differentiated Jumbo Electronics from other conventional providers. Jumbo Electronics' progress has appealed to well-known brand names including BlackBerry, Apple, Asus, Compaq, Microsoft, HP, Nokia, and Sony. Sony is one of the international brands aligned with Jumbo Electronics to distribute its products in the Arab world. Other competitors refer to Jumbo's customer service as a benchmark for their internal operations.[23]

PRICES Prices are a key positioning factor and must be decided in relation to the target market, the product-and-service assortment mix, and the competition.[24] All retailers would like high *Turns x Earns* (high volumes and high gross margins), but the two don't usually go together. Most retailers fall into the *high-markup, lower-volume* group (fine specialty stores) or the *low-markup, higher-volume* group (mass merchandisers and discount stores). Within each of these groups are further degrees. Azal, in Bahrain, is Al Tayer Group's first undertaking in the area of multibrand retail for luxury watches, fine jewelry, and accessories. At the other end, 100-Fils Shop in Kuwait and 2-Riyal Shop in Saudi Arabia and other Gulf countries are on the low-price, lower-quality side of retailing.

Retailers must also pay attention to pricing tactics. Most retailers will put low prices on some items to serve as traffic builders or loss leaders or to signal their pricing policies.[25] They will run storewide sales. They will plan markdowns on slower-moving merchandise. Shoe retailers, for example, expect to sell 50 percent of their shoes at the normal markup, 25 percent at a 40 percent markup, and the remaining 25 percent at cost.

As Chapter 14 notes, some retailers have abandoned 'sales pricing' in favor of everyday low pricing (EDLP). EDLP can lead to lower advertising costs, greater pricing stability, a stronger image of fairness and reliability, and higher retail profits. Research has shown that supermarket chains practicing everyday low pricing can be more profitable than those practicing high-low sale pricing, but only in certain circumstances (see Chapter 14).[26]

SERVICES The services mix is a key tool for differentiating one store from another. Retailers must decide on the *services mix* to offer customers:

- Prepurchase services include accepting telephone and mail orders, advertising, window and interior display, fitting rooms, shopping hours, fashion shows, and trade-ins.

Jumbo Electronics is classified as a category killer in the UAE.

- Postpurchase services include shipping and delivery, gift wrapping, adjustments and returns, alterations and tailoring, installations, and engraving.
- Ancillary services include general information, check cashing, parking, restaurants, repairs, interior decorating, credit, rest rooms, and baby-attendant service.

Retailers also need to consider differentiation based on precisely reliable customer service, whether it is face-to-face, across phone lines, or even via a technological innovation. Frontline employees can be a means of differentiating and positioning a retailer's brand. All banks in the Arab world require their employees to be clean-cut, professionally dressed, and to have a passion for helping customers resolve their queries.

Whatever retailers do to enhance customer equity, they must keep women in mind. Although in some parts of the Arab world, women are not the main decision-makers in a household, the female role is increasing and more women are participating in the decision-making process. They are finding every possible way around the system, from ordering online to resisting fake sales or just doing without.[27] And when they do shop, they want well-organized layouts, helpful staff, and speedy checkouts.[28]

STORE ATMOSPHERE *Atmosphere* is another element in the store arsenal. Every store has a look and a physical layout that makes it hard or easy to move around (see Marketing Memo: *Helping Stores to Sell*). Roadster diner, which operates in Lebanon and recently in the UAE, capitalizes on its typical American diner décor.

Here's how Safeway increased profits by thoroughly reinventing the look of its stores:[29]

- *Walls.* Replaced plain old white walls with earthy tones to convey freshness and wholesomeness.
- *Lighting.* Replaced bright glaring lights with warm accent lights that direct attention to products and departments.
- *Signage.* Added big pictures of healthy food, as well as display stations throughout the store to suggest meal ideas for time-starved shoppers.
- *Produce department.* Enlarged organic section, moving it from a case against the wall to wooden crates at the center of the floor, suggesting a farmer's market.
- *Floors.* Installed hardwood floors in perishables department to provide a natural feel.
- *Bakery.* Knocked down walls to show off bread baking in wood-fired oven; added island in center of department that offers custom bread slicing.

Retailers must consider all the senses in shaping the customer's experience. Supermarkets have found that varying the tempo of music affects average time spent in the store and average expenditures. Retailers are adding fragrances to stimulate certain moods.

STORE ACTIVITIES AND EXPERIENCES The growth of e-commerce has forced traditional brick-and-mortar retailers to respond. In addition to their natural advantages, such as products that shoppers can actually see, touch, and test, real-life customer service, and no delivery lag time for small or medium-sized purchases, they also provide a shopping experience as a strong differentiator.[30]

Brick-and-mortar retailers are adopting practices as simple as calling each shopper a 'guest' and as extravagant as building an indoor amusement park. The store atmosphere should match the basic motivations of the shopper: if target consumers are more likely to be in a task-oriented and functional mindset, then a simpler, more restrained in-store environment may be better.[31]

Consistent with this reasoning, some retailers of experiential products are creating in-store entertainment to attract customers who want fun and excitement:

- REI, seller of outdoor gear and clothing products, allows consumers to test climbing equipment on 8-meter or even 20-meter walls in the store and to try Gore-Tex raincoats under a simulated rain shower.[32]
- Victoria's Secret, retailer of lingerie, other women's clothing, and beauty products, works on the concept of 'retail theater:' customers feel they are in a romance novel, with lush music and faint floral scents in the background.
- Bass Pro Shops, a retailer of outdoor sports equipment, features giant aquariums, waterfalls, trout ponds, archery and rifle ranges, putting greens, and classes in everything from ice fishing to conservation: all free.

marketing Memo

Helping Stores To Sell

In the pursuit of higher sales volume, retailers are studying their store environments for ways to improve the shopper experience. Paco Underhill is managing director of the retail consultant Envirosell Inc., whose clients include McDonald's, Starbucks, Estée Lauder, Blockbuster, Citibank, Gap, Burger King, CVS, and Wells Fargo. He offers the following advice for fine-tuning retail space in order to keep shoppers spending:

- *Attract shoppers and keep them in the store.* The amount of time shoppers spend in a store is perhaps the single most important factor in determining how much they will buy. To increase shopping time, give shoppers a sense of community; recognize them in some way, manner, or form; give them ways to deal with their accessories, such as husbands and children; and keep an environment that is both familiar and fresh each time they come in.

- *Honor the 'transition zone.'* On entering a store, people need to slow down and sort out the stimuli, which means they will likely be moving too fast to respond positively to signs, merchandise, or sales clerks in the zone they cross before making that transition. Make sure there are clear sight lines. Create a focal point for information within the store.

- *Don't make them hunt.* Put the most popular products up front to reward busy shoppers and encourage leisurely shoppers to look more. At Staples, ink cartridges are one of the first products shoppers encounter after entering.

- *Make merchandise available to the reach and touch.* It is hard to overemphasize the importance of customers' hands. A store can offer the finest, cheapest, coolest goods, but if the shopper cannot reach or pick them up, much of their appeal can be lost.

- *Note that men do not ask questions.* Men always move faster than women do through a store's aisles. In many settings, it is hard to get them to look at anything they had not intended to buy. Men also do not like asking where things are. If a man cannot find the section he is looking for, he will wheel about once or twice, then leave the store without ever asking for help.

- *Remember, women need space.* A shopper, especially a woman, is far less likely to buy an item if her derriere is brushed, even lightly, by another customer when she is looking at a display. Keeping aisles wide and clear is crucial.

- *Make checkout easy.* Be sure to have the right high-margin goods near cash registers to satisfy impulse shoppers. And people love to buy candy when they check out, so satisfy their sweet tooth.

Some of Paco Underhill's additional words of wisdom for modern retailers include: (1) develop expertise in the mature market; (2) sell both to and through your customer; (3) localize your presence; (4) extend your brand: use your history better; (5) build on the internet-to-phone-to-store connection; (6) find your customers where they are; (7) refine the details of each point of sale; and (8) go undercover as your reality check.

Source: Paco Underhill, *Call of the Mall: The Geography of Shopping* (New York: Simon & Schuster, 2004); Paco Underhill, *Why We Buy: The Science of Shopping* (New York: Simon & Schuster, 1999). See also Kenneth Hein, "Shopping Guru Sees Death of Detergent Aisle," *Brandweek*, March 27, 2006, p. 11; "Monday Keynote: Why They Buy," *Loupe Online*, 15, Autumn 2006; Bob Parks, "5 Rules of Great Design," *Business 2.0*, March 2003, pp. 47–49; Keith Hammonds, "How We Sell," *Fast Company*, November 1999, p. 294; www.envirosell.com.

- The Discovery Zone, a chain of children's play spaces, offers indoor spaces where kids can go wild without breaking anything and stressed-out parents can exchange stories.

COMMUNICATIONS Retailers use a wide range of communication tools to generate traffic and purchases. They place ads, run special sales, issue money-saving coupons, and run frequent-shopper-reward programs, in-store food sampling, and coupons on shelves or at checkout points. They will also work with manufacturers to design point-of-sale materials that reflect the retailer's image as well as that of the manufacturer's brand.[33] Fine stores will place tasteful, full-page ads in magazines such as *Mondanite* or *Layalina* and carefully train salespeople to greet customers, interpret their needs, and handle complaints. Off-price retailers will arrange their merchandise to promote bargains and savings, while conserving on service and sales assistance.

LOCATION DECISION The three keys to retail success are 'location, location, and location.' Department store chains, oil companies, and fast-food franchisers exercise great care in selecting regions of the country in which to open outlets, then particular cities, and then particular sites. Retailers can place their stores in the following locations:

- *Central business districts.* The oldest and most heavily trafficked city areas, often known as 'downtown.'

- *Regional shopping centers.* Large suburban malls containing 40 to 200 stores, typically featuring one or two nationally known anchor stores, and a great number of smaller stores, many under franchise operation.[34]

- *Community shopping centers.* Smaller malls with one anchor store and between 20 and 40 smaller stores.

Lulu in the UAE prefer a site location which is more isolated or freestanding.

- *Shopping strips.* A cluster of stores, usually housed in one long building, serving a neighborhood's needs for groceries, hardware, laundry, shoe repair, and dry cleaning.
- *A location within a larger store.* Certain well-known retailers—McDonald's, Starbucks, Dunkin' Donuts—locate new, smaller units as concession space within larger stores or operations, such as airports, schools, or department stores.
- *Freestanding or isolated areas.* Hyper 1 in Egypt, Lulu and Choithram in the UAE, and Panda in Saudi Arabia prefer this site location in order to use a spacious utility at cheaper prices than planned or crowded shopping zones.

In view of the relationship between high traffic and high rents, retailers must decide on the most advantageous locations for their outlets, using traffic counts, surveys of consumer shopping habits, and analysis of competitive locations.[35] Several models for site location have also been formulated.[36]

Retailers can assess a particular store's sales effectiveness by looking at four indicators: (1) number of people passing by on an average day; (2) percentage who enter the store; (3) percentage who buy; and (4) average amount per sale.

Private Labels

private label brand brands that retailers and wholesalers develop and market.

A **private-label brand** (also called a reseller, store, house, or distributor brand) is a brand that retailers and wholesalers develop. Benetton and The Body Shop carry mostly own-brand merchandise.

Private labels are rapidly gaining ascendance in a way that has many manufacturers of name brands running scared.

Some experts believe though that 50 percent is the natural limit for volume of private labels to carry because (1) consumers prefer certain national brands, and (2) many product categories are not feasible or attractive on a private-label basis.[37]

Role of Private Labels

Why do intermediaries bother to sponsor their own brands? First, they can be more profitable. Intermediaries search for manufacturers with excess capacity that will produce the private label at a low cost. Other costs, such as research and development, advertising, sales promotion, and physical distribution are also much lower, so private labels can be sold at a lower price yet generate a higher profit margin. Second, retailers develop exclusive store brands to differentiate themselves from competitors. Many consumers prefer store brands in certain categories.

Almarai   Almarai, part of the Almarai Group, has been a well-established brand since 1976 and is positively perceived by Saudi Arabians as a seller of high-quality dairy products, serving more than 43,500 loyal customers on a daily basis. Almarai is strong in the market due to their determination to guard their brand name and their emphasis on quality. Raw milk is produced in Saudi Arabia and the UAE, then distributed along with their food manufacturing products through different distribution centers by the Group. Bakery products are traded with international bakeries under the brand name L'usine. Another field in which the Group operates is the poultry sector, under the Alyoum brand. Generally, the distribution process is managed mainly by the Group. In some cases there are distribution agency agreements, such as with Al Kharafi in Kuwait (dairy products) and Khalid in the UAE for foodstuffs. With such a wide network of distributors, the company is witnessing more expansion.[38]

Some retailers have turned to a 'no branding' strategy for certain staple consumer goods and pharmaceuticals. Carrefour, the originator of the French hypermarket, introduced a line of 'no brands' or **generics** in its stores in the early 1970s. However, the chain has again started to carry national brands as well as private ones.

Generics are unbranded, plainly packaged, less expensive versions of common products such as spaghetti, paper towels, and canned peaches. They offer standard or lower quality at a price that may be as much as 20 to 40 percent lower than nationally advertised brands and 10 to 20 percent lower than the retailer's private-label brands. The lower price of generics is made possible by lower-quality ingredients, lower-cost labeling and packaging, and minimal advertising. Generic drugs have become big business.

generics unbranded, plainly packaged, less expensive versions of common products.

The Private-Label Threat

In the confrontation between manufacturers' brands and private labels, retailers have many advantages and increasing market power.[39] Because shelf space is limited, many supermarkets now charge a *slotting fee* for accepting a new brand, to cover the cost of listing and stocking it. Retailers also charge for special display space and in-store advertising space. They typically give more prominent display to their own brands and make sure they are well stocked. Retailers are now building better quality into their store brands and are emphasizing attractive packaging. Some are even advertising aggressively.

The growing power of store brands is not the only factor weakening national brands. Many consumers are more price sensitive. Competing manufacturers and national retailers copy and duplicate the qualities of the best brands. The continuous barrage of coupons and price specials has trained a generation of shoppers to buy on price. The fact that companies have reduced advertising to 30 percent of their total promotion budget has in some cases weakened their brand equity. A steady stream of brand extensions and line extensions has blurred brand identity at times and led to a confusing amount of product proliferation.

To maintain their power, leading brand marketers are investing significantly in R&D to bring out new brands, line extensions, features, and quality improvements to stay a step ahead of the store brands. They are also investing in strong 'pull' advertising programs to maintain high consumer brand recognition and preference and overcome the in-store marketing advantage that private labels can enjoy. Top brand marketers also are seeking ways to partner with major mass distributors in a joint search for logistical economies and competitive strategies that produce savings, such as the strategic alliance between Procter & Gamble and Walmart.

Cutting all unnecessary costs allows national brands to command a price premium, although it can't exceed the value perceptions of consumers.[40] The Marketing Memo: *Competing Against Store Brands* reflects the private-label challenge and what leading brand marketers must do in response.[41]

Wholesaling

Wholesaling includes all the activities in selling goods or services to those who buy for resale or business use. It excludes manufacturers and farmers because they are engaged primarily in production, and it excludes retailers. The major types of wholesaler are described in ▣ **Box 16.3** on page 451.

Wholesalers (also called *distributors*) differ from retailers in a number of ways. First, wholesalers pay less attention to promotion, atmosphere, and location because they are dealing with business customers rather than final consumers. Second, wholesale transactions are usually larger than retail transactions, and wholesalers usually cover a larger trade area than retailers. Third, the government deals with wholesalers and retailers differently in terms of legal regulations and taxes.

Why do manufacturers not sell directly to retailers or final consumers? Why are wholesalers used at all? In general, wholesalers are more efficient in performing one or more of the following functions:

wholesaling includes all the activities in selling goods or services to those who buy for resale or business use.

- *Selling and promoting.* Wholesalers' sales forces help manufacturers reach many small business customers at a relatively low cost. They have more contacts, and buyers often trust them more than they trust a distant manufacturer.

- *Buying and assortment building.* Wholesalers are able to select items and build the assortments their customers need, saving them considerable work.

- *Bulk breaking.* Wholesalers achieve savings for their customers by buying large carload lots and breaking the bulk into smaller units.

marketing Memo

Competing Against Store Brands

Store brands, or private labels, have enjoyed tremendous market success in recent years. Jan-Benedict E. M. Steenkamp and Nirmalya Kumar put forward a series of observations about the proliferation and acceptance of private labels in today's market.

- *Private labels are everywhere.* Store brands are available in a multitude of product categories (be it clothing, books, financial services, or pharmaceuticals), with a very strong presence in more than 95% of consumer packaged-goods product categories.

- *Consumers accept private labels.* Around 75% of consumers accept store brands as a viable alternative to manufacturer brands.

- *Private-label buyers come from all socioeconomic groups.* Even more consumers believe that it is smart to buy store-brands instead of the more expensive manufacturer brands.

- *Private labels are not a recessionary phenomenon.* While consumers might try store-brands during tough economic times, a good number of them come to appreciate the value these lower-priced alternatives deliver and remain loyal to these brands even after the economy improves.

- *Consumer loyalty shifts from manufacturers to retailers.* More and more, consumer loyalty is shifting from being manufacturer-specific to retailer-specific.

- *Profits flow from manufacturers to retailers.* Retailers have capitalized on the above and have translated that into a greater share of the manufacturer–retailer profit pool.

After thorough research, Steenkamp and Kumar propose a number of strategies for manufacturer brands in competing against store brands.

- Select your battle and fight vigorously. Manufacturers should fight off private labels when the manufacturer's brand is a category leader or occupies a niche position. Their brand is of value to consumers, retailers, and shareholders alike.

- Engage in effective partnerships. Partner with retailers through complementing their successful private labels and ensuring a win–win relationship.

- Innovate. Introduce new products to fight off private labels. Incremental new products keep the manufacturer brand fresh. Radical new products draw the brand away from private labels.

- Offer an unbeatable value proposition. Enhance the functional features and quality of the product, as well as its symbolic meaning. When customers are asked to pay a price premium, the perceived benefits should justify the additional premium.

Source: Jan-Benedict E. M. Steenkamp and Nirmalya Kumar, *Private Label Strategy: How to Meet the Store-Brand Challenge* (Boston: Harvard Business School Press, 2007).

- *Warehousing.* Wholesalers hold inventories, thereby reducing inventory costs and risks to suppliers and customers.

- *Transportation.* Wholesalers can often provide quicker delivery to buyers because they are closer to the buyers.

- *Financing.* Wholesalers finance customers by granting credit, and finance suppliers by ordering early and paying bills on time.

- *Risk bearing.* Wholesalers absorb some risk by taking title and bearing the cost of theft, damage, spoilage, and obsolescence.

- *Market information.* Wholesalers supply information to suppliers and customers regarding competitors' activities, new products, price developments, and so on.

- *Management services and counseling.* Wholesalers often help retailers improve their operations by training sales clerks, helping with store layouts and displays, and setting up accounting and inventory-control systems. They may help industrial customers by offering training and technical services.

Trends in Wholesaling

Wholesaler-distributors have faced mounting pressures in recent years from new sources of competition, demanding customers, new technologies, and more direct-buying programs by large industrial, institutional, and retail buyers. Manufacturers' major complaints against wholesalers are: they don't aggressively promote the manufacturer's product line, and they act more like order takers; they don't carry enough inventory and therefore fail to fill customers' orders fast enough; they don't supply the manufacturer with up-to-date market, customer, and competitive information; they don't attract high-caliber managers, bringing down their own costs; and they charge too much for their services.

BOX 16.3 ▨   Major Wholesaler Types

Merchant wholesalers: Independently owned businesses that take title to the merchandise they handle. They are full-service and limited-service jobbers, distributors, mill supply houses.

Full-service wholesalers: Carry stock, maintain a sales force, offer credit, make deliveries, provide management assistance. Wholesale merchants sell primarily to retailers: some carry several merchandise lines, some carry one or two lines, others carry only part of a line. Industrial distributors sell to manufacturers and also provide services such as credit and delivery.

Limited-service wholesalers: Cash and carry wholesalers sell a limited line of fast-moving goods to small retailers for cash. Truck wholesalers sell and deliver a limited line of semi-perishable goods to supermarkets, grocery stores, hospitals, restaurants, and hotels. Drop shippers serve bulk industries such as heavy equipment. They assume title and risk from the time an order is accepted to its delivery. Rack jobbers serve grocery retailers in nonfood items. Delivery people set up displays, price goods, keep inventory records; they retain title to goods and bill retailers only for goods sold to end of year. Producers' cooperatives assemble farm produce to sell in local markets. Mail-order wholesalers send catalogs to retail, industrial, and institutional customers; orders are filled and sent by mail, rail, plane, or truck.

Brokers and agents: Facilitate buying and selling, on commission of 2 to 6 percent of the selling price; limited functions; generally specialize by product line or customer type. Brokers bring buyers and sellers together and assist in negotiation; paid by the party hiring them. Food brokers, real estate brokers, insurance brokers. Agents represent buyers or sellers on a more permanent basis. Most manufacturers' agents are small businesses with a few skilled salespeople: Selling agents have contractual authority to sell a manufacturer's entire output; purchasing agents make purchases for buyers and often receive, inspect, warehouse, and ship merchandise; commission merchants take physical possession of products and negotiate sales.

Manufacturers' and retailers' branches and offices: Wholesaling operations conducted by sellers or buyers themselves rather than through independent wholesalers. Separate branches and offices are dedicated to sales or purchasing. Many retailers set up purchasing offices in major market centers.

Specialized wholesalers: Agricultural assemblers (buy the agricultural output of many farms), petroleum bulk plants and terminals (consolidate the output of many wells), and auction companies (auction cars, equipment, etc., to dealers and other businesses).

Savvy wholesalers have rallied to the challenge and adapted their services to meet their suppliers' and target customers' changing needs. They recognize that they must add value to the channel.

One major drive by wholesalers has been to increase asset productivity by managing inventories and receivables better. They're also reducing operating costs by investing in more advanced materials-handling technology, information systems, and the internet. Finally, they're improving their strategic decisions about target markets, product assortment and services, price, communications, and distribution.

Arrow Electronics   Arrow Electronics is a global provider of products, services, and solutions to the electronic component and computer product industries. It serves as a supply channel partner for more than 900 suppliers and 125,000 original equipment manufacturers, contract manufacturers, and commercial customers through a global network of 310 locations in 51 countries and territories. With huge contract manufacturers buying more parts directly from suppliers, distributors such as Arrow are being squeezed out. To better compete, Arrow has embraced services, providing financing, on-site inventory management, parts-tracking software, and chip programming. Services helped quadruple Arrow's share price in five years, and the company approached $15 billion in sales in 2009.[42]

Narus and Anderson interviewed leading industrial distributors and identified four ways they strengthened their relationships with manufacturers:

1. They sought a clear agreement with their manufacturers about their expected functions in the marketing channel.
2. They gained insight into the manufacturers' requirements by visiting their plants and attending manufacturer association conventions and trade shows.

3. They fulfilled their commitments to the manufacturer by meeting the volume targets, paying bills promptly, and feeding back customer information to their manufacturers.
4. They identified and offered value-added services to help their suppliers.[43]

The wholesaling industry remains vulnerable to one of the most enduring trends: fierce resistance to price increases and the winnowing out of suppliers based on cost and quality. The trend toward vertical integration, in which manufacturers try to control or own their intermediaries, is still strong.

Market Logistics

Physical distribution starts at the factory. Managers choose a set of warehouses (stocking points) and transportation carriers that will deliver the goods to final destinations in the desired time or at the lowest total cost. Physical distribution has now been expanded into the broader concept of **supply chain management** (SCM). Supply chain management starts before physical distribution and means strategically procuring the right inputs (raw materials, components, and capital equipment); converting them efficiently into finished products; and dispatching them to the final destinations. An even broader perspective calls for studying how the company's suppliers themselves obtain their inputs. The supply chain perspective can help a company identify superior suppliers and distributors and help them improve productivity, which ultimately brings down the company's costs.

Market logistics includes planning the infrastructure to meet demand, then implementing and controlling the physical flows of materials and final goods from points of origin to points of use, to meet customer requirements at a profit.

Market logistics planning has four steps:[44]

1. Deciding on the company's value proposition to its customers. (What on-time delivery standard should we offer? What levels should we attain in ordering and billing accuracy?)
2. Deciding on the best channel design and network strategy for reaching the customers. (Should the company serve customers directly or through intermediaries? What products should we source from which manufacturing facilities? How many warehouses should we maintain and where should we locate them?)
3. Developing operational excellence in sales forecasting, warehouse management, transportation management, and materials management.
4. Implementing the solution with the best information systems, equipment, policies, and procedures.

Studying market logistics leads managers to find the most efficient way to deliver value. For example, a software company normally sees its challenge as producing and packaging software disks and manuals, then shipping them to wholesalers, who ship them to retailers, who sell them to customers. Customers bring the software package to the home or office and download the software onto a hard drive. Market logistics would look at two superior delivery systems. The first includes ordering the software to be downloaded directly onto the customer's computer. The second system allows the computer manufacturer to download the software onto its products. Both solutions eliminate the need for printing, packaging, shipping, and stocking millions of disks and manuals. The same solutions are available for distributing music, newspapers, video games, films, and other products that deliver voice, text, data, or images. The newspaper industry, for instance, is rethinking the way it delivers the news to readers who are now becoming accustomed to getting it free over the internet. Here's what one newspaper company is doing to revamp its market logistics.

supply chain management (SCM) procuring the right inputs (raw materials, components, and capital equipment); converting them efficiently into finished products; and dispatching them to the final destinations.

market logistics planning the infrastructure to meet demand, then implementing and controlling the physical flows or materials and final goods from points of origin to points of use, to meet customer requirements at a profit.

The New York Times   When Ameritech executive Martin Nisenholtz came to the New York Times to take over its digital operations, the Times' publisher said to him, "We're not in the ink-on-paper business, we're in the news business. It doesn't matter how we distribute information; what matters is that we can make money out of it." The majority of the Times' readers, who cling to their inky 5-centimeter-thick editions of the Sunday Times, have been slower to agree. But the Times has emerged as one of the most web-savvy newspapers in the United States. The turning point came in 2005, when the company began focusing on building communities rather than pushing information. The *Times* purchased About.com, integrated print and online newsrooms, added blogs, podcasts, and other web 2.0 technologies, and launched the premium service TimesSelect, which allows only paying users to access the work of certain columnists and selected features. Of 513,000 subscribers in June 2006, almost half were paying the web-only rate of US$49.95 a year, contributing $9.5 million to the *Times'* bottom line. And in 2011 the *Times* introduced paid subscriptions to its apps for iPhone and iPad. The biggest challenge is making all these changes appealing to those *Times* subscribers who aren't technologically savvy.[45]

Integrated Logistics Systems

The market-logistics task calls for **integrated logistics systems** (**ILS**), which include materials management, material flow systems, and physical distribution, aided by information technology (IT). Third-party suppliers, such as FedEx Logistics Services, often participate in designing or managing these systems. A dealer, needing a part in an emergency, phones a toll-free number, and the part is flown out the same day and delivered that night at either the airport or the dealer's office, or even at the roadside repair site.

integrated logistics systems (ILS) materials management, material flow systems, and physical distribution, abetted by information technology (IT).

Information systems play a critical role in managing market logistics, especially computers, point-of-sale terminals, uniform product bar codes, satellite tracking, electronic data interchange (EDI), and electronic funds transfer (EFT). These developments have shortened the order-cycle time, reduced clerical labor, reduced the error rate in documents, and provided improved control of operations. They have enabled companies to make a promise such as "the product will be at dock 25 at 10:00 a.m. tomorrow," and control that promise through information.

Market logistics encompass several activities. The first is sales forecasting, on the basis of which the company schedules distribution, production, and inventory levels. Production plans indicate the materials the purchasing department must order. These materials arrive through inbound transportation, enter the receiving area, and are stored in raw-material inventory. Raw materials are converted into finished goods. Finished-goods inventory is the link between customer orders and manufacturing activity. Customers' orders draw down the finished-goods inventory level, and manufacturing activity builds it up. Finished goods flow off the assembly line and pass through packaging, in-plant warehousing, shipping-room processing, outbound transportation, field warehousing, and customer delivery and servicing.

Management has become concerned about the total cost of market logistics, which can amount to as much as 30 to 40 percent of the product's cost. The grocery industry alone thinks it can decrease its annual operating costs by 10 percent, or US$30 billion, by revamping its market logistics. A box of breakfast cereal can take 104 days to get through a network of wholesalers, distributors, brokers, and consolidators from factory to supermarket.

Many experts call market logistics "the last frontier for cost economies," and firms are determined to wring every unnecessary cost out of the system: in 1982, logistics represented 14.5 percent of U.S. GDP; by 2006, the share had dropped to just over 8 percent.[46] Lower market-logistics costs will permit lower prices, yield higher profit margins, or both. Even though the cost of market logistics can be high, a well-planned program can be a potent tool in competitive marketing.

Market-Logistics Objectives

Many companies state their market-logistics objective as "getting the right goods to the right places at the right time for the least cost." Unfortunately, this objective provides little practical guidance. No system can simultaneously maximize customer service and minimize distribution cost. Maximum customer service implies large inventories, premium transportation, and multiple warehouses, all of which raise market-logistics costs.

Nor can a company achieve market-logistics efficiency by asking each market-logistics manager to minimize his or her own logistics costs. Market-logistics costs interact and are often negatively related. For example:

- The traffic manager favors rail shipment over air shipment because rail costs less. However, because the railroads are slower, rail shipment ties up working capital longer, delays customer payment, and might cause customers to buy from competitors who offer faster service.

- The shipping department uses cheap containers to minimize shipping costs. Cheaper containers lead to a higher rate of damaged goods and customer ill will.
- The inventory manager favors low inventories. This increases stock outs, back orders, paperwork, special production runs, and high-cost, fast-freight shipments.

Given that market-logistics activities require strong trade-offs, managers must make decisions on a total-system basis. The starting point is to study what customers require and what competitors are offering. Customers are interested in on-time delivery, supplier willingness to meet emergency needs, careful handling of merchandise, and supplier willingness to take back defective goods and resupply them quickly.

The company must then research the relative importance of these service outputs. For example, service-repair time is very important to buyers of copying equipment. Xerox developed a service delivery standard that "can put a disabled machine anywhere in the continental United States back into operation within three hours after receiving the service request." It then designed a service division of personnel, parts, and locations to deliver on this promise.

The company must also consider competitors' service standards. It will normally want to match or exceed the competitors' service level, but the objective is to maximize profits, not sales. The company must look at the costs of providing higher levels of service. Some companies offer less service and charge a lower price; other companies offer more service and charge a premium price.

The company ultimately must establish some promise it makes to the market. Some companies define standards for each service factor. One appliance manufacturer has established the following service standards: to deliver at least 95 percent of the dealer's orders within 7 days of order receipt, to fill the dealer's orders with 99 percent accuracy, to answer dealer inquiries on order status within 3 hours, and to ensure that damage to merchandise in transit does not exceed 1 percent. Perhaps the king of all logistics is Walmart.

Walmart   Walmart Stores Inc. is the largest retailer in the world, with sales of US$405 billion in 2010, 2 million employees, and 8,400 facilities across 15 countries. Each week, over 200 million customers visit a Walmart store. Sam Walton founded the company in 1962 with a simple goal: offer low prices to everyone. Walmart keeps prices low through their unrivaled logistics. The company effectively and efficiently coordinates more than 85,000 suppliers, manages billions in inventory in its warehouses, and brings that inventory to its retail shelves. Over 100 million items per day must get to the right store at the right time. To accomplish this goal, Walmart developed several IT systems that work together. Using up-to-the-minute sales information based on point-of-sale (POS) scanner data, Walmart's Inventory Management System calculates the rate of sales, factors in seasonal and promotional elements, and automatically places replenishment orders to distribution centers and vendor partners. Suppliers can use its voluminous POS databases to analyze customers' regional buying habits. Walmarts may look the same on the outside, but the company uses its information systems and logistics to customize the offerings inside each store to suit regional demand.[47]

With its network of IT systems customized for each store, Walmart is the 'king of (store) logistics' and the largest retailer in the world.

Given the market-logistics objectives, the company must design a system that will minimize the cost of achieving these objectives. Each possible market-logistics system will lead to the following cost:

$$M = T + FW + VW + S$$

where

> M = total market-logistics cost of proposed system,
>
> T = total freight cost of proposed system,
>
> FW = total fixed warehouse cost of proposed system,
>
> VW = total variable warehouse costs (including inventory) of proposed system,
>
> S = total cost of lost sales due to average delivery delay under proposed system.

Choosing a market-logistics system calls for examining the total cost (M) associated with different proposed systems and selecting the system that minimizes it. If it is hard to measure S, the company should aim to minimize $T + FW + VW$ for a target level of customer service.

Market-Logistics Decisions

The firm must make four major decisions about its market logistics: (1) how should we handle orders (order processing)?, (2) where should we locate our stock (warehousing)?, (3) how much stock should we hold (inventory)?, and (4) how should we ship goods (transportation)?

ORDER PROCESSING Most companies today are trying to shorten the *order-to-payment cycle*; that is, the amount of time between an order's receipt, delivery, and payment. This cycle has many steps, including order transmission by the salesperson, order entry and customer credit check, inventory and production scheduling, order and invoice shipment, and receipt of payment. The longer this cycle takes, the lower the customer's satisfaction and the lower the company's profits. General Electric operates an information system that checks the customer's credit standing upon receipt of an order and determines whether and where the items are in stock. The computer issues an order to ship, bills the customer, updates the inventory records, sends a production order for new stock, and relays the message back to the sales representative that the customer's order is on its way, all in less than 15 seconds.

WAREHOUSING Every company must store finished goods until they are sold, because production and consumption cycles rarely match. The storage function helps to smooth discrepancies between production and quantities desired by the market. The company must decide on the number of inventory stocking locations. Consumer-packaged-goods companies have been reducing their number of stocking locations from 10–15 to about 5–7; and pharmaceutical and medical distributors have cut their stocking locations from 90 to about 45. On the one hand, more stocking locations means that goods can be delivered to customers more quickly, but it also means higher warehousing and inventory costs. To reduce warehousing and inventory duplication costs, the company might centralize its inventory in one place and use fast transportation to fill orders.

Some inventory is kept at or near the plant, and the rest is located in warehouses in other locations. The company might own private warehouses and also rent space in public warehouses. *Storage warehouses* store goods for moderate to long periods of time. *Distribution warehouses* receive goods from various company plants and suppliers and move them out as soon as possible. *Automated warehouses* employ advanced materials-handling systems under the control of a central computer.

Some warehouses are now taking on activities formerly done in the plant. These include assembly, packaging, and constructing promotional displays. Postponing finalization of the offering can achieve savings in costs and finer matching of offerings to demand.

INVENTORY Inventory levels represent a major cost. Salespeople would like their companies to carry enough stock to fill all customer orders immediately. However, this is not cost-effective. Inventory cost increases at an accelerating rate as the customer-service level approaches 100 percent. Management needs to know how much sales and profits would increase as a result of carrying larger inventories and promising faster order fulfillment times, and then make a decision.

Inventory decision making requires knowing when and how much to order. As inventory draws down, management must know at what stock level to place a new order. This stock level is called the *order* (or *reorder*) *point*; it may be called *economic order quantity* (EOQ) as well. An order point of 20 means reordering when the stock falls to 20 units. The order point should balance the risks of stockout against the costs of overstock. The other decision is how much to order. The larger the quantity ordered, the less frequently an order needs to be placed. The company needs to balance order-processing costs and inventory-carrying costs. *Order-processing costs* for a manufacturer consist of *setup costs* and *running costs* (operating costs when production is running) for the item. If setup costs are low, the manufacturer can produce the item often, and the average cost per item is stable and equal to the running costs. If setup costs are high, however, the manufacturer can reduce the average cost per unit by producing a long run and carrying more inventory.

Order-processing costs must be compared with *inventory-carrying costs*. The larger the average stock carried, the higher the inventory-carrying costs. These carrying costs include storage charges, cost of capital, taxes and insurance, and depreciation and obsolescence. Carrying costs might run as high as 30 percent of inventory value. This means that marketing managers who want their companies to carry larger inventories need to show that the larger inventories would produce incremental gross profits to exceed incremental carrying costs.

We can determine the optimal order quantity by observing how order-processing costs and inventory-carrying costs sum up at different order levels. △ **Figure 16.1** shows that the order-processing cost per unit decreases with the number of units ordered because the order costs are spread over more units. Inventory-carrying charges per unit increase with the number of units ordered because each unit remains longer in inventory. The two cost curves are summed vertically into a total-cost curve. The lowest point on the total-cost curve is projected down on the horizontal axis to find the optimal order quantity, Q.[48]

Companies are reducing their inventory costs by treating inventory items differently, positioning them according to risk and opportunity. They distinguish between bottleneck items (high risk, low opportunity), critical items (high risk, high opportunity), commodities (low risk, high opportunity), and nuisance items (low risk, low opportunity).[49] They are also keeping slow-moving items in a central location and carrying fast-moving items in warehouses closer to customers. All these strategies give them more flexibility should anything go wrong, as it often does, be it a dock strike in California, a tsunami in Asia, or an earthquake in Turkey.[50] Flexibility is essential to cope with different environmental changes, such as the political changes occurring in the Arab world, known as the Arab Spring.

The ultimate answer to carrying *near-zero inventory* is to build for order, not for stock. Sony calls it SOMO: "sell one, make one." Dell, for example, gets the customer to order a computer and pay for it in advance. Then Dell uses the customer's money to pay suppliers to ship the necessary components. As long as customers do not need the item immediately, everyone can save money. Some retailers are using eBay to unload excess inventory. By cutting out the traditional liquidator middleman, retailers can make 60 to 80 cents on the dollar as opposed to 10 cents.[51] And some suppliers are snapping up excess inventory to create opportunity.

TRANSPORTATION   Transportation choices will affect product pricing, on-time delivery performance, and the condition of the goods when they arrive, all of which affect customer satisfaction.

In shipping goods to its warehouses, dealers, and customers, the company can choose among five transportation modes: rail, air, truck, waterway, and pipeline. Shippers consider such criteria as speed, frequency, dependability, capability, availability, traceability, and cost. For speed, air, rail, and truck are the prime contenders. If the goal is low cost, then the choice is water or pipeline.

|Fig. 16.1| △

Determining Optimal
Order Quantity

Shippers are increasingly combining two or more transportation modes, thanks to containerization. **Containerization** consists of putting the goods in boxes or trailers that are easy to transfer between two transportation modes. *Piggyback* describes the use of rail and trucks; *fishyback*, water and trucks; *trainship*, water and rail; and *airtruck*, air and trucks. Each coordinated mode offers specific advantages. For example, piggyback is cheaper than trucking alone, yet provides flexibility and convenience.

Shippers can choose from private, contract, and common carriers. If the shipper owns its own truck or air fleet, it becomes a *private carrier*. A *contract carrier* is an independent organization selling transportation services to others on a contract basis. A *common carrier* provides services between predetermined points on a scheduled basis and is available to all shippers at standard rates.

To reduce costly handing at arrival, some firms are putting items into shelf-ready packaging so they don't need to be unpacked from a box and placed on a shelf individually. In Europe, P&G uses a three-tier logistic system to schedule deliveries of fast- and slow-moving goods, bulky items, and small items in the most efficient way.[52]

> **containerization** putting the goods in boxes or trailers that are easy to transfer between two transportation modes.

Organizational Lessons

Market-logistics strategies must be derived from business strategies, rather than solely from cost considerations. The logistics system must be information intensive and establish electronic links among all the significant parties. Finally, the company should set its logistics goals to match or exceed competitors' service standards and should involve members of all relevant teams in the planning process. Getting logistics right can have a big payoff.

 Pepsi Bottling Group   In 2002, Pepsi Bottling Group—Pepsi's largest independent bottler and distributor—was saddled with a creaky supply chain that resulted in many stockouts. It completely overhauled its supply chain, from order taking to truck loading to store deliveries. The new program included technology upgrades, revised work schedules, and a renewed focus on customer service. Warehouse workers, called 'pickers,' began to wear headsets and bar-code scanners on their wrists to create 'certified pallets' with close to 100 percent accuracy. By 2006, stockouts had decreased significantly as a result. As one Pepsi Bottling employee said, "It was almost like when I went to bed I was Fred Flintsone and when I woke up I was George Jetson."[53]

Today's stronger demands for logistical support from large customers will increase suppliers' costs. Customers want more frequent deliveries so they don't have to carry as much inventory. They want shorter order-cycle times, which means that suppliers must carry high in-stock availability. Customers often want direct store delivery rather than shipments to distribution centers. They want mixed pallets rather than separate pallets. They want tighter promised delivery times. They may want custom packaging, price tagging, and display building.

Suppliers can't refuse many of these requests, but at least they can set up different logistical programs with different service levels and customer charges. Smart companies will adjust their offerings to each major customer's requirements. The company's trade group will set up *differentiated distribution* by offering different bundled service programs for different customers.

Summary

1. Retailing includes all the activities involved in selling goods or services directly to final consumers for personal, nonbusiness use. Retailers can be understood in terms of store retailing, nonstore retailing, and retail organizations.

2. Like products, retail-store types pass through stages of growth and decline. As existing stores offer more services to remain competitive, costs and prices go up, which opens the door to new retail forms that offer a mix of merchandise and services at lower prices. The major types

of retail stores are specialty stores, department stores, supermarkets, convenience stores, discount stores, off-price retailers (factory outlets, independent off-price retailers, and warehouse clubs), superstores (combination stores and supermarkets), and catalog showrooms.

3. Although most goods and services are sold through stores, nonstore retailing has been growing. The major types of nonstore retailing are direct selling (one-to-one selling, one-to-many party selling, and multilevel network marketing), direct marketing (which includes e-commerce and internet retailing), automatic vending, and buying services.

4. Although many retail stores are independently owned, an increasing number are falling under some form of corporate retailing. Retail organizations achieve many economies of scale, such as greater purchasing power, wider brand recognition, and better-trained employees. The major types of corporate retailing are corporate chain stores, voluntary chains, retailer cooperatives, consumer cooperatives, franchise organizations, and merchandising conglomerates.

5. Like all marketers, retailers must prepare marketing plans that include decisions on target markets, product assortment and procurement, services and store atmosphere, price, promotion, and place. These decisions must take into account major trends, such as the growth of private labels, new retail forms and combinations, growth of intertype retail competition, competition between store-based and nonstore-based retailing,

growth of giant retailers, decline of middle-market retailers, growing investment in technology, and global presence of major retailers.

6. Wholesaling includes all the activities involved in selling goods or services to those who buy for resale or business use. Wholesalers can perform functions better and more cost-effectively than the manufacturer can. These functions include selling and promoting, buying and assortment building, bulk breaking, warehousing, transportation, financing, risk bearing, dissemination of market information, and provision of management services and consulting.

7. There are four types of wholesalers: merchant wholesalers; brokers and agents; manufacturers' and retailers' sales branches, sales offices, and purchasing offices; and miscellaneous wholesalers such as agricultural assemblers and auction companies.

8. Like retailers, wholesalers must decide on target markets, product assortment and services, price, promotion, and place. The most successful wholesalers are those who adapt their services to meet suppliers' and target customers' needs.

9. Producers of physical products and services must decide on market logistics: the best way to store and move goods and services to market destinations; to coordinate the activities of suppliers, purchasing agents, manufacturers, marketers, channel members, and customers. Major gains in logistical efficiency have come from advances in information technology.

Applications

Marketing Debate

Should National-Brand Manufacturers Also Supply Private-Label Brands?

One controversial move by some marketers of major brands is to supply private-label makers. For example, Ralston-Purina, Borden, ConAgra, and Heinz have all admitted to supplying products—sometimes lower in quality—to be used for private labels. Other marketers, however, criticize this 'if you can't beat them, join them' strategy, maintaining that these actions, if revealed, may create confusion or even reinforce a perception amongst consumers that all brands in a category are essentially the same.

Take a position: Manufacturers should feel free to sell private labels as a source of revenue *versus* national manufacturers should never get involved with private labels.

Marketing Discussion

Think of your favorite stores. What do they do that encourages your loyalty? What do you like about the in-store experience? What further improvements could they make?

Marketing Excellence

>>Carrefour

Carrefour is a French word meaning 'cross-roads.' As the second largest hypermarket after Walmart, Carrefour in Egypt is more than just a big store; it's a big experience. The chain represents a unique experience for Egyptian customers, as well as for other small, independent retailers. Carrefour opened its first store in Egypt on December 17, 2002, and has proved to be very successful, unlike British supermarket Sainsbury's.

Sainsbury's entered the market in 2001 with 2,000 employees and 100 stores in Egypt. However, the company faced many obstacles in the Egyptian market due to a lack of information concerning cultural factors and norms. The company wanted to take advantage of the strong bond between the Egyptian and British governments. It is a strong brand that is successful in Britain, and sought to apply similar strategies in Egypt. But understanding the difference between the home market and the international market is one of the essential factors for a business to operate in a new market, and Sainsbury's did not fully understand customer needs in the market they were approaching. Sainsbury's terminated their business in Egypt 1 year after entering the market, with losses of over US$100 million, according to El-Amir and Burt.

Carrefour is a joint venture company between Majid Al Futtaim and Carrefour France, which offers Egyptians the same quality and variety of products for very reasonable prices that it provides all over the world. The Majid Al Futtaim (MAF) group of companies was founded in 1992 and is regarded as the most dynamic and professional business in the Arab world. It has helped to introduce Carrefour in Oman, Qatar, the UAE, Saudi Arabia, and Egypt, and is still planning to expand in other countries.

Carrefour didn't depend only on the 55,000 brands that their 8,500-square-meter stores carry, but instead counted on its understanding of the Egyptian culture. For example, during Ramadan, the holy fasting month for the Islamic faith, Carrefour broadcast readings from the Qur'an throughout the store. And when the time came for prayer, Carrefour would announce it in the store by broadcasting the *Azan*, called out by the *muezzin* in the mosque. It also provided a small zone in the store where Muslims were able to practice their prayers.

Carrefour Egypt targets mainly average-income people by offering the lowest prices. This strategy created a unique niche market for Carrefour, sidelining the main competitors Metro and Alpha Market. These superstores target the high social classes (who are cash-rich and time-poor) who appreciate shopping quality and convenient locations.

Carrefour deals directly with manufacturers. Multinational companies and other private producers are assigning key account managers to serve Carrefour and other superstores of a similar size. Dealing directly with manufacturers allows Carrefour to completely eliminate all markups, thus obtaining the lowest price lists from producers.

Further, economies of scale allow Carrefour to offer its customers better prices, sometimes even lower than wholesalers. When small independent retailers realized that Carrefour was offering lower prices than wholesalers, some store owners started to buy their merchandize from Carrefour directly. Small stores capitalized on the benefits that were directed originally at Carrefour's customers.

Carrefour management realized that this was creating market leakage, or disintermediation, and established a discriminatory policy by imposing a buying quota to limit transactions by owners of small stores. However, there is no clear-cut way for Carrefour to differentiate between ultimate consumers and business buyers or small retailers.

Questions

1. Suppose you are enlisted by Sainsbury's as a marketing advisor. What kind of recommendations would you make?

2. What are the advantages and disadvantages of Carrefour serving small independent retailers directly?

3. Based on this case, list the pros and cons of marketing disintermediation.

Sources: "Egypt Gets Hyper," *AL-AHRAM Weekly*, 623, January 30–February 5, 2003, http://weekly.ahram.org.eg/2003/623/li1.htm; El-Amir, A. and Burt, S., "Sainsbury's in Egypt: The Strange Case of Dr. Jekyll and Mr. Hyde?," *International Journal of Retail & Distribution Management*, 36, no. 4, pp. 300–322; "Sainsbury's Pulls out of Egypt," *BBC News*, April 9, 2001, http://news.bbc.co.uk/1/hi/business/1268099.stm; Tomlinson, R., "Who's Afraid Of Wal-Mart? Not Carrefour. The world's second-largest retailer is bounding ahead of the Bentonville behemoth in most markets outside North America. But can the French titan hold its lead?," *Fortune*, June 26, 2000, http://money.cnn.com/magazines/fortune/fortune_archive/2000/06/26/282982/index.htm.

CHAPTER 17

Dove (the UniLever brand, focusing on skin products including moisturizing cream) changed their approach to advertising in 2003, with enormous success.

In this chapter, we will address the following questions:

1. **What is the role of marketing communications?** (pg. 462)

2. **How do marketing communications work?** (pg. 462)

3. **What are the major steps in developing effective communications?** (pg. 468)

4. **What is the communications mix and how should it be set?** (pg. 475)

5. **What is an integrated marketing communications program?** (pg. 481)

Designing and Managing Integrated Marketing Communications

Modern marketing calls for more than developing a good product, pricing it attractively, and making it accessible. Companies must also communicate with present and potential stakeholders and the general public. For most, therefore, the question is not whether to communicate but rather what to say, how and when to say it, to whom, and how often. But communications get harder and harder as more and more companies scream to grab an increasingly empowered consumer's divided attention. Consumers themselves are taking a more active role in the communication process and deciding what communications they want to receive and how they want to communicate to others about the products and services they use. To effectively reach and influence target markets, holistic marketers are creatively employing multiple forms of communications.

 Dove has been a Unilever stalwart for decades, backed by traditional advertising touting the brand's benefit of one-quarter moisturizing cream and exhorting women to take the 7-day Dove test to discover its effects. A significant shift in strategy occurred for Dove in 2003 with the launch of the Real Beauty campaign, which celebrated "real women" of all shapes, sizes, ages, and colors. The campaign arose from research revealing that only 2 percent of women worldwide considered themselves beautiful. It featured candid and confident images of curvy, full-bodied women: not traditional models. The ads promoted Dove skin products such as Intensive Firming Cream, Lotion, and Body Wash. The multimedia campaign was thoroughly integrated. Traditional TV and print ads were combined with all forms of new media, such as real-time voting for models on mobile phones and tabulated displays of results on giant billboards. PR was dialed up; paid media was dialed down. The internet was crucial for creating a dialogue with women. A website was launched and supplemented with ad videos. The Dove Evolution video showed a rapid-motion view of an ordinary-looking woman transformed by makeup artists, hairdressers, lighting, and digital retouching to look like a model. When it was uploaded to YouTube by Dove's ad agency Ogilvy & Mather, it was an instant viral hit, drawing 2.5 million views. A subsequent ad, No Age Limit, featuring older women, also aimed for a primarily online audience. Although the campaign sparked much debate, it was credited with boosting Dove sales and share in every country in which it was launched. The Real Beauty campaign received the Grand Effie for the most effective marketing campaign in 2006 from the American Marketing Association.[1]

Done right, marketing communications can have a huge payoff. This chapter describes how communications work and what marketing communications can do for a company. It also addresses how holistic marketers combine and integrate marketing communications. Chapter 18 examines the different forms of mass (non-personal) communications (advertising, sales promotion, events and experiences, and public relations and publicity); Chapter 19 examines the different forms of personal communications (direct and interactive marketing, word-of-mouth marketing, and personal selling). ▽

The Role of Marketing Communications

marketing communications
the means by which firms attempt to inform, persuade, and remind consumers—directly or indirectly   about products and brands that they sell.

Marketing communications are the means by which firms attempt to inform, persuade, and remind consumers—directly or indirectly—about the products and brands they sell. In a sense, marketing communications represent the 'voice' of the company and its brands and are a means by which it can establish a dialogue and build relationships with consumers.

Marketing communications also perform many functions for consumers. They can tell or show consumers how and why a product is used, by what kind of person, and where and when. Consumers can learn about who makes the product and what the company and brand stand for; and they can get an incentive or reward for trial or usage. Marketing communications allow companies to link their brands to other people, places, events, brands, experiences, feelings, and things. They can contribute to brand equity—by establishing the brand in memory and creating a brand image—as well as drive sales and even affect shareholder value.[2]

The Changing Marketing Communication Environment

Although marketing communications can play a number of crucial roles, they must do so in an increasingly tough communication environment. Technology and other factors have profoundly changed the way consumers process communications, and even whether they choose to process them at all. The rapid distribution of powerful broadband internet connections, ad-skipping digital video recorders, multipurpose mobile phones, and portable music and video players have forced marketers to rethink a number of their traditional practices.[3]

These dramatic changes have eroded the effectiveness of the mass media.[4] Before smart phones became the norm, and before social media became so popular around the world, companies relied on regular mail, television, and radio to spread their message and market their products. However, with the success and spread of social media and the internet, more companies in the Arab world are taking advantage of the opportunities it offers. Statistics from March 2010 show that there are roughly 56 million Arab internet users, representing only 17 percent of the 337 million population of the region.[5]

- More people are getting online in the Arab world, and are relying more and more on the internet for their news, videos, social interactions, and more, but only 1 percent of all content online is in Arabic, not offering them much choice.

- Online news consumption is gaining ground with 22 to 34 percent of people using the internet at least as much as print media to read news.

- On average, 70 percent of people in the four main Arab markets researched use social networks in some capacity and about 15 percent use social networking sites at least once a day. Online communities were basically the anchor for the Egyptian and Tunisian political movements which started in January 2011.

- About 6 million internet users in the Middle East—or about 12 percent of the total online population in the region—have access to broadband networks.

- People in the Arab world are spending about 3 hours per day on the internet on average, which is already on par with the amount of time spent on TV.

- About US$56 million, or 1 percent of the total media advertising spend, is online in the Middle East.

- Some 8.3 percent of active Facebook users come from the Middle East and North Africa, representing a 7.9 percent penetration. Users under 25 years of age represent 60 percent of active Facebook users in the region. Fastest growth in user adoption in the region is in the 55+ age group.

- Among the Arab countries, the top seven countries for active Facebook usership are: Egypt (7,100,000), Saudi Arabia (3,800,000), Morocco (3,500,000), the UAE (2,200,000), Tunisia (2,500,000), Lebanon (1,240,000), and Jordan (1,770,000).

It's pretty clear from these statistics that there are a lot of opportunities for Arab companies to tap into social media and introduce their brands and products to the highest number of potential consumers locally and internationally.

The internet is the most powerful tool for creating accurate customer profiles and reaching diversified audiences. Consumers not only have more choices of media to use, they also have a choice about whether and how they want to receive commercial content. What's new is the proliferation of media and entertainment options: from hundreds of cable TV and radio stations and thousands of magazines and webzines to uncountable websites, blogs, video games, and mobile phone screens.

And that's part of the second force taking power out of the 30-second TV ad spot. DVRs allow consumers to eliminate commercials with the push of a fast-forward button. The internet is even more of a threat, with an Arab penetration of 56 million users who can choose whether to view an ad by clicking on an icon. For all these reasons and others, McKinsey projected that by 2010 traditional TV advertising would be one-third as effective as it was in 1990.[6]

However, as some marketers flee traditional media, they still encounter challenges. Commercial clutter is uncontrolled, and it seems the more consumers tune out marketing appeals, the more marketers try to dial them up. Ads in almost every medium and form have been on the rise, and some consumers feel the ads are becoming increasingly invasive.[7]

Marketing Communications, Brand Equity, and Sales

In this new communication environment, although advertising is often a central element of a marketing communications program, it is usually not the only one—or even the most important one—in terms of building brand equity and driving sales. Consider how PepsiCo was among the first international companies to invest heavily in the Arab world, producing a full movie with Arab celebrities to market its products and increase their share value in the Arab world.

 PepsiCo   In 2008, PepsiCo International used a new approach to communicate with their consumers in the Arab world by entering the world of movie entertainment. The company produced a full-length musical feature film entitled *Bahr Al Nujoom*, featuring celebrities Haifa Wehbe, Wael Kfouri, Carole Samaha, Ahmad Al Cherif, and Ruweida Al Mahrouqi. "Pepsi constantly looks at new innovative techniques that give us an edge from a consumer marketing perspective, and *Bahr Al Nojoom* will certainly cause a stir!" said Rima Chammas, regional marketing director of PepsiCo International. "We have simply taken our existing marketing strategies to new levels and given them a creative edge, daring customers to ask for more in generations to come."[8]

Prominent Arab stars such as Amr Diab, Elissa, and Nawal Al Zoughbi joined the Pepsi family in the early 90s. "Associating products with a celebrity that the target consumer likes, enjoys, and identifies with has been successful in the past," Chammas explains. "Of course you need to select the right celebrity, someone who is a good role model for consumers, which is why the celebrities we have chosen for *Bahr Al Nujoom* are all either at the height of their career or just getting started in the business. Together they bring credibility to the project because some of them have been around for a long time, while others are new faces on the Arab music scene, making fans keen to get to know them even better."[9]

MARKETING COMMUNICATIONS MIX The marketing communications mix consists of eight major modes of communication:[10]

1. *Advertising*. Any paid form of nonpersonal presentation and promotion of ideas, goods, or services by an identified sponsor.
2. *Sales promotion*. A variety of short-term incentives to encourage trial or purchase of a product or service.

3. *Events and experiences*. Company-sponsored activities and programs designed to create daily or special brand-related interactions.
4. *Public relations and publicity*. A variety of programs designed to promote or protect a company's image or its individual products.
5. *Direct marketing*. Use of mail, telephone, fax, e-mail, or internet to communicate directly with or solicit response or dialogue from specific customers and prospects.
6. *Interactive marketing*. Online activities and programs designed to engage customers or prospects and directly or indirectly raise awareness, improve image, or elicit sales of products and services.
7. *Word-of-mouth marketing*. People-to-people oral, written, or electronic communications that relate to the merits or experiences of purchasing or using products or services.
8. *Personal selling*. Face-to-face interaction with one or more prospective purchasers for the purpose of making presentations, answering questions, and procuring orders.

Box 17.1 lists numerous communication platforms. Company communication goes beyond those specific platforms. The product's styling and price, the shape and color of the package, the salesperson's manner and dress, the store décor, and the company's stationery all communicate something to buyers. Every *brand contact* delivers an impression that can strengthen or weaken a customer's view of a company.[11]

As ▲ Figure 17.1 shows, marketing communications activities contribute to brand equity and drive sales in many ways: by creating awareness of the brand; linking the right associations to the brand image in consumers' memory; drawing positive brand judgments or feelings; and/or facilitating a stronger consumer–brand connection.

BOX 17.1   Common Communication Platforms

Advertising	Sales Promotion	Events & Experiences	Public Relations & Publicity	Direct & Interactive Marketing	Word-of-Mouth Marketing	Personal Selling
Print and broadcast ads	Contests, games, sweepstakes, lotteries	Sports	Press kits	Catalogs	Person-to-person	Sales presentations
Packaging–outer	Premiums and gifts	Entertainment	Speeches	Mailings	Chat rooms	Sales meetings
Packaging inserts	Sampling	Festivals	Seminars	Telemarketing	Blogs	Incentive programs
Motion pictures	Fairs and trade shows	Arts	Annual reports	Electronic shopping		Samples
Brochures and booklets	Exhibits	Causes	Charitable donations	TV shopping		Fairs and trade shows
Posters and leaflets	Demonstrations	Factory tours	Publications	Fax mail		
Directories	Coupons	Company museums	Community relations	E-mail		
Reprints of ads	Rebates	Street activities	Lobbying	Voice mail		
Billboards	Low-interest financing		Identity media	Blogs		
Display signs	Entertainment		Company magazine	Websites		
Point-of-purchase displays	Trade-in allowances					
Audiovisual material	Continuity programs					
Symbols and logos	Tie-ins					
Videotapes						

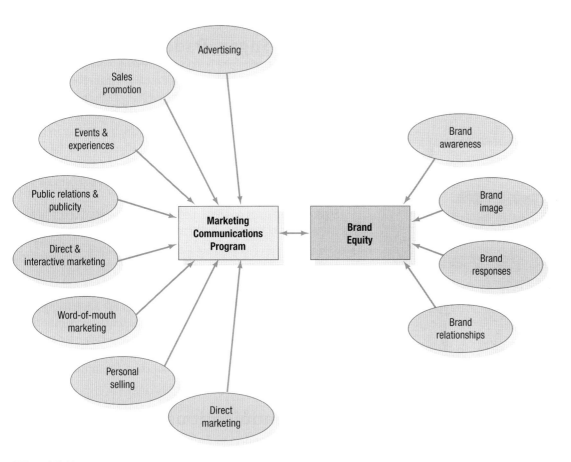

|Fig. 17.1| △

Integrating Marketing Communications to Build Brand Equity

MARKETING COMMUNICATION EFFECTS The manner in which brand associations are formed does not matter. In other words, a consumer who is exposed to Aramex commercials, billboards, or trucks may have an equally strong, favorable, and unique brand association of Aramex with the concepts 'international,' 'shipping,' and 'delivery,' regardless of the mode of delivery.

But these marketing communications activities must be integrated to deliver a consistent message and achieve the strategic positioning. The starting point in planning marketing communications is an audit of all the potential interactions that customers in the target market may have with the company and all its products and services. For example, someone interested in purchasing a new laptop computer might talk to others, see television ads, read articles, look for information on the internet, and look at laptops in a store.

Marketers need to assess which experiences and impressions will have the most influence at each stage of the buying process. This understanding will help them allocate communications money more efficiently and design and implement the right communications programs. Armed with these insights, marketers can judge marketing communications according to its ability to affect experiences and impressions, build brand equity, and drive brand sales. For example, how well does a proposed ad campaign contribute to awareness or to creating, maintaining, or strengthening brand associations? Does a sponsorship cause consumers to have more favorable brand judgments and feelings? To what extent does a promotion encourage consumers to buy more of a product? At what price premium?

From the perspective of building brand equity, marketers should be 'media-neutral' and evaluate *all* the different possible communication options according to effectiveness criteria (how well does it work?) as well as efficiency considerations (how much does it cost?). This broad view of brand-building activities is especially relevant when marketers are considering strategies to improve brand awareness.[12]

Sugar Daddy's opened its first branch in Amman in 2007. The company uses the freshest ingredients to bake treats from scratch. This picture shows its founder, Fadi Jaber.

Sugar Daddy's   Having a passion for baking and being an entrepreneur at heart, Fadi Jaber identified the need for a bakery that offers cakes and cupcakes with a home-made feel, and decided to open the bakery and cafe known as Sugar Daddy's in 2007 in Amman, Jordan. Sugar Daddy's doesn't use any premade cake mixes or frostings; instead, it uses only the freshest ingredients to bake its treats from scratch. The café and bakery has branches in Amman, Beirut, and Dubai, and has opened its latest branch in Abu Dhabi's Al Khalidiyah Mall in a bid to meet the growing demand from customers in the UAE.

Sugar Daddy's relies on social media to spread the word about its business. It has a Facebook profile, a Twitter account, and a Linkedin account, where it can share the latest news about the company with followers and fans.[13]

Anything that causes the consumer to notice and pay attention to the brand—such as sponsorship and out-of-home advertising—can increase brand awareness, at least in terms of brand recognition. To enhance brand recall, however, more intense and elaborate processing may be necessary, so that stronger brand links to the product category or consumer needs are established to improve memory performance.

The Communications Process Models

Marketers should understand the fundamental elements of effective communications. Two models are useful: a macromodel and a micromodel.

MACROMODEL OF THE COMMUNICATIONS PROCESS   ▲ **Figure 17.2** shows a communications macromodel with nine elements. Two represent the major parties in a communication: *sender* and *receiver*. Two represent the major communication tools: *message* and *media*. Four represent major communication functions: *encoding, decoding, response,* and *feedback*. The last element in the system is *noise* (random and competing messages that may interfere with the intended communication).[14]

The model emphasizes the key factors in effective communication. Senders must know what audiences they want to reach and what responses they want to get. They must encode their messages so the target audience can decode them. They must transmit the message through media that reach the target audience and develop feedback channels to monitor the responses. The more the sender's field of experience overlaps that of the receiver, the more effective the message is likely to be. Note that selective attention, distortion, and retention processes—concepts first introduced in Chapter 6—may be operating during communication.

|Fig. 17.2| ▲

Elements in the
Communications
Process

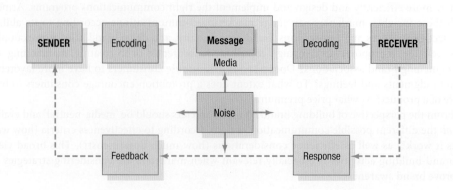

MICROMODEL OF CONSUMER RESPONSES

Micromodels of marketing communications concentrate on consumers' specific responses to communications. △ **Figure 17.3** summarizes four classic *response hierarchy models.*

All these models assume that the buyer passes through a cognitive, affective, and behavioral stage, in that order. This 'learn-feel-do' sequence is appropriate when the audience has high involvement with a product category perceived to have high differentiation, such as an automobile or house. An alternative sequence, 'do-feel-learn,' is relevant when the audience has high involvement but perceives little or no differentiation within the product category, such as an airline ticket or personal computer. A third sequence, 'learn-do-feel,' is relevant when the audience has low involvement and perceives little differentiation within the product category, such as salt or batteries. By choosing the right sequence, the marketer can do a better job of planning communications.[15]

Here we will assume the buyer has high involvement with the product category and perceives high differentiation within it. We will illustrate the *hierarchy-of-effects model* (in the second column of Figure 17.3) in the context of a marketing communications campaign for a small beach resort in Wadi Shab, Oman:

- **Awareness.** If most of the target audience is unaware of the object, the communicator's task is to build awareness. Suppose Wadi Shab seeks tourists from other parts of the Arab world but has no name recognition there. There are 205 million people who may potentially be interested in the Wadi Shab beach resort. The company thinking of building the resort might set the objective of making 30 percent of these potential clients aware of its name within 1 year.

- **Knowledge.** The target audience might have brand awareness but not know much more. Wadi Shab resort may want its target audience to know that it is a private resort offering some water activities along with a spa and restaurants. It needs to learn how many people in the target audience have little, some, or much knowledge about Wadi Shab. If knowledge is weak, Wadi Shab may decide to select brand knowledge as its communications objective.

- **Liking.** If target members know the brand, how do they feel about it? If the audience looks unfavorably on Wadi Shab, the communicator needs to find out why. If the unfavorable view is based on real problems, they will need to fix its problems and then communicate its renewed quality. Good public relations calls for 'good deeds followed by good words.'

- **Preference.** The target audience might like the product but not prefer it to others. In this case, the communicator must try to build consumer preference by comparing quality, value, performance, and other features to likely competitors.

Models

Stages	AIDA Model[a]	Hierarchy-of-Effects Model[b]	Innovation-Adoption Model[c]	Communications Model[d]
Cognitive Stage	Attention	Awareness → Knowledge	Awareness	Exposure ↓ Reception ↓ Cognitive response
Affective Stage	Interest ↓ Desire	Liking ↓ Preference ↓ Conviction	Interest ↓ Evaluation	Attitude ↓ Intention
Behavior Stage	Action	Purchase	Trial ↓ Adoption	Behavior

|Fig. 17.3| △

Response Hierarchy Models

Source: [a]E. K. Strong, *The Psychology of Selling* (New York: McGraw-Hill, 1925), p.9; [b]Robert J. Lavidge and Gary A. Steiner, "A Model for Predictive Measurements of Advertising Effectiveness," *Journal of Marketing,* October 1961, p. 61; [c]Everett M. Rogers, *Diffusion of Innovation* (New York: Free Press, 1962), pp. 79–86; [d]various sources.

- **Conviction.** A target audience might prefer a particular product but not develop a conviction about buying it. The communicator's job is to build conviction and purchase intent among tourists interested in Wadi Shab resort.

- **Purchase.** Finally, some members of the target audience might have conviction but not quite get around to making the purchase. The communicator must lead these consumers to take the final step, perhaps by offering the product at a low price, offering a premium, or letting consumers try it out. Wadi Shab resort might offer discounts on entrance fees, or be part of a package with a major hotel.

To show how fragile the whole communications process is, assume that the probability of *each* of the six steps being successfully accomplished is 50 percent. The laws of probability suggest that the probability of *all* six steps occurring successfully, assuming they are independent events, is $0.5 \times 0.5 \times 0.5 \times 0.5 \times 0.5 \times 0.5$, which equals 1.5625 percent. If the probability of each step occurring was, on average, a more moderate 10 percent, then the joint probability of all six events occurring would be 0.0001 percent; in other words, only 1 in 10,000.

To increase the odds for a successful marketing communications campaign, marketers must attempt to increase the likelihood that *each* step occurs. For example, from an advertising standpoint, the ideal ad campaign would ensure that:

1. The right consumer is exposed to the right message at the right place and at the right time.
2. The ad causes the consumer to pay attention to the ad but does not distract from the intended message.
3. The ad properly reflects the consumer's level of understanding of and behaviors with the product and the brand.
4. The ad correctly positions the brand in terms of desirable and deliverable points-of-difference and points-of-parity.
5. The ad motivates consumers to consider purchase of the brand.
6. The ad creates strong brand associations with all these stored communications effects so that they can have an impact when consumers are considering making a purchase.

Developing Effective Communications

|Fig. 17.4| △

Steps in Developing Effective Communications

△ **Figure 17.4** shows the eight steps in developing effective communications. We begin with the basics: identifying the target audience, determining the objectives, designing the communications, selecting the channels, and establishing the budget.

Identify the Target Audience

The process must start with a clear target audience in mind: potential buyers of the company's products, current users, deciders, or influencers; individuals, groups, particular publics, or the general public. The target audience is a critical influence on the communicator's decisions about what to say, how, when, where, and to whom.

Though we can profile the target audience in terms of any of the market segments identified in Chapter 8, it's often useful to do so in terms of usage and loyalty. Is the target new to the category or a current user? Is the target loyal to the brand, loyal to a competitor, or someone who switches between brands? If a brand user, is he or she a heavy or light user? Communication strategy will differ depending on the answers. We can also conduct *image analysis* to provide further insight, by profiling the target audience in terms of brand knowledge.

Determine the Communications Objectives

As we showed with Wadi Shab resort, marketers can set communications objectives at any level of the hierarchy-of-effects model. Rossiter and Percy identify four possible objectives, as follows:[16]

1. **Category need.** Establishing a product or service category as necessary to remove or satisfy a perceived discrepancy between a current motivational state and a desired emotional state.

A new-to-the-world product such as electric cars would always begin with a communications objective of establishing category need.

2. *Brand awareness*. Ability to identify (recognize or recall) the brand within the category, in sufficient detail to make a purchase. Recognition is easier to achieve than recall. Brand recall is important outside the store; brand recognition is important inside the store. Brand awareness provides a foundation for brand equity.

3. *Brand attitude*. Evaluating the brand with respect to its perceived ability to meet a currently relevant need. Relevant brand needs may be negatively oriented (problem removal, problem avoidance, incomplete satisfaction, or normal depletion) or positively oriented (sensory gratification, intellectual stimulation, or social approval). Household cleaning products often use problem solution; food products, on the other hand, often use sensory-oriented ads emphasizing appetite appeal.

4. *Brand purchase intention*. Self-instructions to purchase the brand or to take purchase-related action. Promotional offers in the form of coupons or two-for-one deals encourage consumers to make a mental commitment to buy a product. But many consumers do not have an expressed category need and may not be in the market when exposed to an ad, so they are unlikely to form buy intentions. For example, in any given week, only about 20 percent of adults may be planning to buy detergent; only 2 percent may be planning to buy a carpet cleaner; and only 0.25 percent may be planning to buy a car.

The most effective communications often can achieve multiple objectives.

Design the Communications

Formulating the communications to achieve the desired response will require solving three problems: what to say (message strategy), how to say it (creative strategy), and who should say it (message source).

MESSAGE STRATEGY In determining message strategy, management searches for appeals, themes, or ideas that will tie into the brand positioning and help to establish points-of-parity or points-of-difference. Some of these may be related directly to product or service performance (the quality, economy, or value of the brand), whereas others may relate to more inessential considerations (the brand as being contemporary, popular, or traditional).

John Maloney saw buyers as expecting one of four types of reward from a product: rational, sensory, social, or ego satisfaction.[17] Buyers might visualize these rewards from results-of-use experience, product-in-use experience, or incidental-to-use experience. Crossing the four types of rewards with the three types of experience generates 12 types of messages. For example, the appeal 'gets clothes cleaner' is a rational-reward promise following results-of-use experience.

CREATIVE STRATEGY Communications effectiveness depends on how a message is being expressed, as well as on the content of the message itself. If a communication is ineffective, it may mean the wrong message was used, or the right one was just poorly expressed. *Creative strategies* are the way marketers translate their messages into a specific communication. We can broadly classify them as either *informational* or **transformational appeals**.[18] These two general categories each encompass several different specific creative approaches.

Informational Appeals An **informational appeal** elaborates on product or service attributes or benefits. Examples in advertising are problem solution ads (Excedrin stops the toughest headache pain), product demonstration ads (Herbalaxa can help you lose weight), product comparison ads (Ariel cleans better than Persil), and testimonials from celebrity endorsers (Vodafone used Egyptian celebrities who indicate their membership in its wireless network; I am Vodafone or Ana Vodafone). Informational appeals assume very rational processing of the communication on the part of the consumer. Logic and reason rule.

Hovland's research at Yale has shed much light on informational appeals and their relationship to such issues as conclusion drawing, one-sided versus two-sided arguments, and order of argument presentation. Some early experiments supported stating conclusions for the audience. Subsequent research, however, indicates that the best ads ask questions and allow readers and viewers to form their own conclusions.[19] Some stimulus ambiguity can lead to a broader market definition and more spontaneous purchases.

transformational appeals
a communication strategy used by marketers that elaborates on a non-product-related benefit or image, to stir up emotions that will motivate a purchase.

informational appeal
a communication strategy ruled by logic and reason used by marketers that elaborates on product or service attributes or benefits.

You would think one-sided presentations that praise a product would be more effective than two-sided arguments that also mention shortcomings. Yet two-sided messages may be more appropriate, especially when negative associations must be overcome. Heinz ran the message "Heinz Ketchup is slow good" and Listerine said "The taste you hate twice a day."[20] Two-sided messages are more effective with more educated audiences and those who are initially opposed.[21]

Finally, the order in which arguments are presented is important.[22] In a one-sided message, presenting the strongest argument first has the advantage of arousing attention and interest. This is important in media where the audience often does not attend to the whole message. With a captive audience, a climactic presentation might be more effective. In the case of a two-sided message, if the audience is initially opposed, the communicator might start with the other side's argument and conclude with his or her strongest argument.[23]

Transformational Appeals A transformational appeal elaborates on a nonproduct-related benefit or image. It might depict what kind of person uses a brand (VW advertised to active, youthful people with its 'Drivers Wanted' campaign) or what kind of experience results from using the brand (for years Pringles advertised 'Once You Pop, the Fun Don't Stop'). Transformational appeals often attempt to stir up emotions that will motivate purchase.

Communicators use negative appeals such as fear, guilt, and shame to get people to do things (brush their teeth, have an annual health checkup) or stop doing things (smoking, overeating). Fear appeals work best when they are not too strong, when source credibility is high, and when the communication promises to relieve, in a believable and efficient way, the fear it arouses. Messages are most persuasive when they are moderately discrepant with what the audience believes. Stating only what the audience already believes at best only reinforces beliefs, and if the messages are too discrepant, audiences will counterargue and disbelieve them.[24]

Communicators also use positive emotional appeals such as humor, love, pride, and joy. Motivational or 'borrowed-interest' devices—such as the presence of cute babies, frisky puppies, popular music, or provocative actors or actresses—are often employed to attract consumer attention and raise their involvement with an ad. Borrowed-interest techniques are thought to be necessary in the tough new media environment characterized by low-involvement consumer processing and much competing ad and programming clutter.

Although these borrowed-interest approaches can attract attention and create more likability of and belief in the sponsor, they may also detract from comprehension, wear out their welcome fast, and overshadow the product.[25] Attention-getting tactics are often *too* effective and distract from brand or product claims. Thus, one challenge in arriving at the best creative strategy is figuring out how to 'break through the clutter' to attract the attention of consumers, but still deliver the intended message.

The magic of advertising is to bring concepts on a piece of paper to life in the minds of the consumer target. In a print ad, the communicator must decide on headline, copy, illustration, and color.[26] For a radio message, the communicator must choose words, voice qualities, and vocalizations. If the message is to be carried on television or in person, all these elements plus body language (nonverbal clues) must be planned. Presenters need to pay attention to facial expressions, gestures, dress, posture, and hairstyle. If the message is carried by the product or its packaging, the communicator must pay attention to color, texture, scent, size, and shape.

MESSAGE SOURCE Many communications do not use a source beyond the company itself. Others use known or unknown people. Messages delivered by attractive or popular sources can achieve higher attention and recall, which is why advertisers often use celebrities as spokespeople. Celebrities are likely to be effective when they are credible or personify a key product attribute.

What *is* important is the spokesperson's credibility. What factors underlie source credibility?

Michelin's use of the Michelin Man brand character in its advertising helps to break through the clutter and reinforce the brand's key safety and trust messages.

The three most often identified are expertise, trustworthiness, and likability.[27] *Expertise* is the specialized knowledge the communicator possesses to back the claim. *Trustworthiness* is related to how objective and honest the source is perceived to be. Friends are trusted more than strangers or salespeople, and people who are not paid to endorse a product are viewed as more trustworthy than people who are paid.[28] *Likability* describes the source's attractiveness. Qualities such as honesty, humor, and spontaneity make a source more likable. Business-to-business marketer Accenture found all these qualities and more in golf pro Tiger Woods.

The most highly credible source would score high on all three dimensions: expertise, trustworthiness, and likability. Pharmaceutical companies want doctors to testify about product benefits because doctors have high credibility. The Marketing Insight: *Celebrity Endorsements as a Strategy* focuses on the use of testimonials.

If a person has a positive attitude toward a source and a message, or a negative attitude toward both, a state of *congruity* is said to exist. What happens if the person holds one attitude toward the source and the opposite one toward the message? Suppose a consumer hears a likable celebrity praise a brand she dislikes. Osgood and Tannenbaum say that attitude change will take place in the

Marketing Insight

Celebrity Endorsements as a Strategy

A well-chosen celebrity can draw attention to a product or brand, as when Al Jawhara chose famous movie stars Omar El Sharif and Yousra to advertise its porcelain. Both movie stars are icons for superior taste and elegance. Their unique style reflected the brand's personality and created the desired perception in the minds of Al Jawhara's customers.

The choice of the celebrity is critical. The celebrity should have high recognition, high positive affect, and high appropriateness to the product. Paris Hilton and Donald Trump have high recognition but negative affect among many groups. Robin Williams has high recognition and high positive affect but might not be appropriate for advertising a World Peace Conference. Tom Hanks and Oprah Winfrey could successfully advertise a large number of products because they have extremely high ratings for familiarity and likability (known as the Q factor in the entertainment industry).

Athletes commonly endorse athletic products, beverages, and apparel. One of the premier athletic endorsers has been cyclist Lance Armstrong, who battled and beat testicular cancer on his way to winning six consecutive Tour de France championships. He has endorsed a number of bicycle and sports products and companies, including Trek, PowerBar, and Nike. Armstrong's improbable 'against all odds' success story also enabled him to win multimillion-dollar endorsement contracts from companies not affiliated with sports, such as Bristol-Myers Squibb pharmaceuticals, Coca-Cola, Subaru, and 24 Hour Fitness.

Using celebrities poses certain risks. The celebrity might hold out for a larger fee at contract renewal time or withdraw. And just like

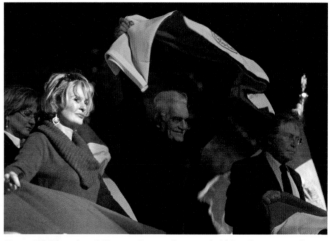

Omar El Sharif and Yousra have advertised Al Jawhara porcelain.

movies and records, celebrity campaigns can sometimes be expensive flops. Pepsi chose to drop star endorsers Britney Spears and Beyoncé Knowles, whose personalities may have been too overpowering for the brand, to focus on promoting occasions that go well with drinking Pepsi.

The celebrity might lose popularity or, even worse, get caught in a scandal or embarrassing situation. After NBA legend Magic Johnson went public with his HIV diagnosis and his extramarital affairs in 1991, his ads were pulled from the air and his endorsement deals were not renewed. And after Tiger Woods admitted having extramarital affairs in 2009, he lost sponsorship deals with brands including AT&T, Accenture, and Gatorade.

Sources: Keith Naughton, "The Soft Sell," *Newsweek*, February 2, 2004, pp. 46–47; Theresa Howard, "Pepsi Takes Some Fizz off Vanilla Rival," *USA Today*, November 16, 2003; Betsy Cummings, "Star Power," *Sales & Marketing Management*, April 2001, pp. 52–59; Bruce Horovitz, "Armstrong Rolls to Market Gold," *USA Today*, May 4, 2000; Irving Rein, Philip Kotler, and Martin Scoller, *The Making and Marketing of Professionals into Celebrities* (Chicago: NTC Business Books, 1997); "Gatorade Cuts Ties with Wood," *ESPN Golf*, February 27, 2010, http://sports.espn.go.com/golf/news/story?id=4950137.

direction of increasing the amount of congruity between the two evaluations.[29] The consumer will end up respecting the celebrity somewhat less or respecting the brand somewhat more. If a person encounters the same celebrity praising other disliked brands, he or she will eventually develop a negative view of the celebrity and maintain negative attitudes toward the brands. The **principle of congruity** implies that communicators can use their good image to reduce some negative feelings toward a brand, but in the process might lose some esteem with the audience.

principle of congruity
psychological mechanism that states that consumers like to see seemingly related objects as being as similar as possible in their favorability.

GLOBAL ADAPTATIONS Multinational companies wrestle with a number of challenges in developing global communications programs: They must decide whether the product is appropriate for a country. They must make sure the market segment they address is both legal and customary. They must decide whether the style of the ad is acceptable, and whether ads should be created at headquarters or locally.[30]

- *Product*. Many products are restricted or forbidden in certain parts of the world. Beer, wine, and spirits cannot be advertised or sold in many Muslim countries, while tobacco products are subject to strict regulation in many countries.

- *Market segment*. U.S. toy makers were surprised to learn that in many countries (Norway and Sweden, for example) no TV ads may be directed at children under 12. Sweden lobbied hard to extend that ban to all European Union member countries in 2001 but failed. To play it safe, McDonald's advertises itself as a family restaurant in Sweden.

- *Style*. Comparative ads, although acceptable and even common in the United States and Canada, are unacceptable in the Arab world. By the same token, a lawyer advertising his services is prohibited in the Arab world, but is totally acceptable in the United States.

- *Local or global*. Today, more and more multinational companies are attempting to build a global brand image by using the same advertising in all markets.

Companies that sell their products to different cultures or in different countries must be prepared to vary their messages.

Select the Communications Channels

Selecting efficient means to carry the message becomes more difficult as channels of communication become more fragmented and cluttered. Think of the challenges in the pharmaceutical industry: a big number of sales representatives 'detail' doctors every day, but only a little over 40 percent of calls result in seeing the doctor, and then for an average of only 2 minutes or less, which makes sales calling extremely expensive. The industry has had to expand its battery of communications channels to include ads in medical journals, direct mail (including audio and videotapes), free samples, and even telemarketing. Pharmaceutical companies sponsor clinical conferences at which they pay physicians to spend a weekend listening to leading colleagues commend certain drugs in the morning, followed by an afternoon of golf or tennis.

Pharmaceuticals use all these channels in the hope of building physician preference for their branded therapeutic agent. They are also using new technologies to reach doctors through handheld devices, online services, and videoconferencing equipment.[31]

Communications channels may be personal and nonpersonal. Within each are many subchannels.

personal communications channels two or more persons communicating directly face-to-face, person-to-audience, over the telephone, or through e-mail.

PERSONAL COMMUNICATIONS CHANNELS **Personal communications channels** let two or more persons communicate face-to-face, person-to-audience, over the telephone, or through e-mail. Instant messaging and independent sites to collect consumer reviews are another channel, one of growing importance in recent years. Personal communication channels derive their effectiveness through individualized presentation and feedback.

We can draw a further distinction between advocate, expert, and social communications channels. *Advocate channels* consist of company salespeople contacting buyers in the target market. *Expert channels* consist of independent experts making statements to target buyers. *Social channels* consist of neighbors, friends, family members, and associates talking to target buyers.[32]

A study by Burson-Marsteller and Roper Starch Worldwide found that one influential person's word of mouth tends to affect the buying attitudes of two other people, on average. That circle of influence, however, jumps to eight online. Considerable consumer-to-consumer communication takes place on the internet on a wide range of subjects. Online visitors also increasingly create product information, not just consume it. They join internet interest groups to share information, so that 'word of web' is joining 'word of mouth' as an important buying influence. Word about good companies travels fast; word about bad companies travels even faster. As one marketer noted, "You don't need to reach 2 million people to let them know about a new product—you just need to reach the right 2,000 people in the right way and they will help you reach 2 million."[33]

Personal influence carries especially great weight in two situations. One occurs when products are expensive, risky, or purchased infrequently. The other arises when products suggest something about the user's status or taste. People often ask others for a recommendation for a doctor, plumber, hotel, lawyer, accountant, architect, insurance agent, interior decorator, or financial consultant. If we have confidence in the recommendation, we normally act on the referral. In such cases, the recommender has potentially benefited the service provider as well as the service seeker. Service providers clearly have a strong interest in building referral sources. Sending the right message to the right consumers can be crucial.

NONPERSONAL COMMUNICATIONS CHANNELS
Nonpersonal channels are communications directed to more than one person and include media, sales promotions, events and experiences, and public relations.

- *Media* consist of print media (newspapers and magazines); broadcast media (radio and television); network media (telephone, cable, satellite, wireless); electronic media (audiotape, videotape, videodisk, CD-ROM, web page); social media (Youtube, Facebook, Twitter); and display media (billboards, signs, posters). Most nonpersonal messages come through paid media.
- *Sales promotions* consist of consumer promotions (such as samples, coupons, and premiums); trade promotions (such as advertising and display allowances); and business and sales-force promotions (contests for sales reps).
- *Events and experiences* include sports, arts, entertainment, and cause events as well as less formal activities that create novel brand interactions with consumers.
- *Public relations* include communications directed internally to employees of the company or externally to consumers, other firms, the government, and media.

Much of the recent growth of nonpersonal channels has taken place through events and experiences. A company can build its brand image by creating or sponsoring events. Emirates Airline sponsors many sporting events, ranging from the FIFA World Cup to Formula One, golf, and tennis tournaments.

Companies are searching for better ways to quantify the benefits of sponsorship and demanding greater accountability from event owners and organizers. They are also creating events designed to surprise the public and create a buzz. Many amount to guerrilla marketing tactics, but if not done properly, they can backfire and have unintended consequences.

The increased use of attention-getting events is a response to the fragmentation of media: consumers can turn to hundreds of cable channels, thousands of magazine titles, and millions of internet pages. Events can create attention, although whether they have a lasting effect on brand awareness, knowledge, or preference will vary considerably, depending on the quality of the product, the event itself, and its execution.

INTEGRATION OF COMMUNICATIONS CHANNELS
Although personal communication is often more effective than mass communication, mass media might be the major means of stimulating personal communication. Mass communications affect personal attitudes and behavior through a two-step process. Ideas often flow from radio, television, and print to opinion leaders, and from these to the less media-involved population groups. This two-step flow has several implications. First, the influence of mass media on public opinion is not as direct, powerful, and automatic as marketers have supposed. It is mediated by opinion leaders, people whose opinions others seek, or who carry their opinions to others. Second, the two-step flow challenges the notion that consumption styles are primarily influenced by a 'trickle-down' or 'trickle-up' effect from mass media. People interact primarily within their own social groups and acquire ideas from opinion leaders in their groups. Third, two-step communication suggests that mass communicators should direct messages specifically to opinion leaders and let them carry the message to others. For example, Mini automobiles developed a clever communication strategy to get people talking and driving.

Mini   The tiny Mini automobile was sold for only 7 years in the United States, during the 1960s, before it was withdrawn due to stiff emission regulations. In March 2002, BMW decided to relaunch a new, modernized Mini Cooper in the United States, targeting hip city dwellers who wanted a cool, fun, small car for under US$20,000. With only $20 million to spend on the introduction, the Mini marketers decided to launch a guerrilla communications campaign featuring nontraditional uses of billboards, posters, print ads, and grassroots efforts, and no TV ads. The Mini was stacked on top of three Ford Excursion SUVs and driven around national auto shows and 21 major cities. The car showed up in other unusual places, such as inside a sports stadium as seats. Text-only billboards proclaimed: "The SUV Backlash Officially Starts Now," "Goliath Lost," and "XXL-XL-L-M-S-MINI." Many communications were linked to a cleverly designed website that provided the necessary product information. The imaginative campaign resulted in a buyer waiting list that was 6 months long in spring 2002. And Mini hasn't stopped innovating. Using radio frequency identification (RFID) technology, it began to deliver custom messages in January 2007 to Mini owners in four cities on digital signs the company calls "talking billboards." Its 2006 'covert' print campaign, which challenged Mini owners to solve various puzzles in ads, won the Grand Prize among the coveted MPA Kelly Awards for excellence and effectiveness in magazine ads, partly because it deepened brand engagement to 21 percent, its highest level ever, and increased online chat 75 percent.[34]

Establish the Total Marketing Communications Budget

One of the most difficult marketing decisions is determining how much to spend on marketing communications or promotion. John Wanamaker, the department store magnate, once said, "I know that half of my advertising is wasted, but I don't know which half."

Industries and companies vary considerably in how much they spend on marketing communications or promotion. Expenditures might be 40 to 45 percent of sales in the cosmetics industry and 5 to 10 percent in the industrial-equipment industry. Within a given industry, there are low- and high-spending companies.

How do companies decide on the promotion budget? We will describe four common methods: the affordable method, the percentage-of-sales method, the competitive-parity method, and the objective-and-task method.

AFFORDABLE METHOD   Many companies set the promotion budget at what they think the company can afford. The affordable method completely ignores the role of promotion as an investment and the immediate impact of promotion on sales volume. It leads to an uncertain annual budget, which makes long-range planning difficult.

PERCENTAGE-OF-SALES METHOD   Many companies set promotion expenditures at a specified percentage of sales (either current or anticipated) or of the sales price. Automobile companies typically budget a fixed percentage for promotion based on the planned car price. Oil companies set the appropriation at a fraction of a cent for each gallon of gasoline sold under their own label.

Supporters of the percentage-of-sales method see a number of advantages. First, promotion expenditures will vary with what the company can afford. This satisfies financial managers, who believe expenses should be closely related to the movement of corporate sales over the business cycle. Second, it encourages management to think of the relationship among promotion cost, selling price, and profit per unit. Third, it encourages stability when competing firms spend approximately the same percentage of their sales on promotion.

In spite of these advantages, the percentage-of-sales method has little to justify it. It views sales as the determiner of promotion rather than as the result. It leads to a budget set by the availability of funds rather than by market opportunities. It discourages experimentation with countercyclical promotion or aggressive spending. Dependence on year-to-year sales fluctuations interferes with long-range planning. There is no logical basis for choosing the specific percentage, except what has been done in the past or what competitors are doing. Finally, it does not encourage building the promotion budget by determining what each product and territory deserves.

COMPETITIVE-PARITY METHOD Some companies set their promotion budget to achieve share-of-voice parity with competitors. There are two supporting arguments. One is that competitors' expenditures represent the collective wisdom of the industry. The other is that maintaining competitive parity prevents promotion wars. Neither argument is valid. There are no grounds for believing that competitors know better. Company reputations, resources, opportunities, and objectives differ so much that promotion budgets are hardly a guide. And there is no evidence that budgets based on competitive parity discourage promotion wars.

OBJECTIVE-AND-TASK METHOD The objective-and-task method calls upon marketers to develop promotion budgets by defining specific objectives, determining the tasks that must be performed to achieve these objectives, and estimating the costs of performing these tasks. The sum of these costs is the proposed promotion budget.

For example, suppose Masafi Juice wants to introduce a new natural energy drink, called Taka, for the casual athlete.[35]

1. **Establish the market share goal**. The company estimates 50 million potential users and sets a target of attracting 8 percent of the market; that is, 4 million users.
2. **Determine the percentage of the market that should be reached by advertising**. The advertiser hopes to reach 80 percent (40 million prospects) with the advertising message.
3. **Determine the percentage of aware prospects that should be persuaded to try the brand**. The advertiser would be pleased if 25 percent of aware prospects (10 million) tried Taka. It estimates that 40 percent of all triers, or 4 million people, will become loyal users. This is the market goal.
4. **Determine the number of advertising impressions per 1 percent trial rate**. The advertiser estimates that 40 advertising impressions (exposures) for every 1 percent of the population will bring about a 25 percent trial rate.
5. **Determine the number of gross rating points that would have to be purchased**. A gross rating point is one exposure to 1 percent of the target population. Because the company wants to achieve 40 exposures to 80 percent of the population, it will want to buy 3,200 gross rating points.
6. **Determine the necessary advertising budget on the basis of the average cost of buying a gross rating point**. To expose 1 percent of the target population to one impression costs an average of US$3,277. Therefore, 3,200 gross rating points will cost $10,486,400 (= $3,277 × 3,200) in the introductory year.

The objective-and-task method has the advantage of requiring management to spell out its assumptions about the relationship among money spent, exposure levels, trial rates, and regular usage.

A major question is how much weight marketing communications should receive in relationship to alternatives such as product improvement, lower prices, or better service. The answer depends on where the company's products are in their life cycles, whether they are commodities or highly differentiable products, whether they are routinely needed or must be 'sold,' and other considerations. Marketing communications budgets tend to be higher when there is low channel support, much change in the marketing program over time, many hard-to-reach customers, more complex customer decision making, differentiated products and non-homogeneous customer needs, and frequent product purchases in small quantities.[36]

In theory, marketers should establish the total communications budget so that the marginal profit from the last communication dollar just equals the marginal profit from the last dollar in the best non-communication use. Implementing this principle, however, is not easy.

Deciding on the Marketing Communications Mix

Companies must allocate the marketing communications budget over the eight major modes of communication: advertising, sales promotion, public relations and publicity, events and experiences, direct marketing, interactive marketing, word-of-mouth marketing, and the sales force. Within the same industry, companies can differ considerably in their media and channel choices. Avon concentrates its promotional funds on personal selling, whereas L'Oreal spends heavily on advertising. Electrolux spent heavily on a door-to-door sales force for years, whereas Hoover has relied more on advertising. Other forms of communication include cinema advertising, direct mail marketing, consumer magazines, local and regional television, radio, and business-to-business magazines. .

Companies are always searching for ways to gain efficiency by replacing one communications tool with others. Many companies are replacing some field sales activity with ads, direct mail, telemarketing, and now social media. One auto dealer dismissed his five salespeople and cut prices, and sales exploded. The substitutability among communications tools explains why marketing functions need to be coordinated.

Characteristics of the Marketing Communications Mix

Each communication tool has its own unique characteristics and costs. We briefly review each of these here and discuss them in more detail in Chapters 18 and 19.

ADVERTISING Advertising reaches geographically dispersed buyers. It can build up a long-term image for a product (Coca-Cola ads) or trigger quick sales (a Panda ad for a weekend sale). Certain forms of advertising such as TV can require a large budget, whereas other forms such as newspaper do not. Just the presence of advertising might have an effect on sales: consumers might believe that a heavily advertised brand must offer 'good value.'[37] Because of the many forms and uses of advertising, it's difficult to make generalizations about it.[38] Yet a few observations are worthwhile:

1. *Pervasiveness*. Advertising permits the seller to repeat a message many times. It also allows the buyer to receive and compare the messages of various competitors. Large-scale advertising says something positive about the seller's size, power, and success.
2. *Amplified expressiveness*. Advertising provides opportunities for dramatizing the company and its products through the artful use of print, sound, and color.
3. *Impersonality*. The audience does not feel obligated to pay attention or respond to advertising. Advertising is a monologue in front of, not a dialogue with, the audience.

SALES PROMOTION Companies use sales promotion tools—coupons, contests, premiums, and the like—to draw a stronger and quicker buyer response, including short-run effects such as highlighting product offers and boosting sagging sales. Sales promotion tools offer three distinctive benefits:

1. *Communication*. They gain attention and may lead the consumer to the product.
2. *Incentive*. They incorporate some concession, inducement, or contribution that gives value to the consumer.
3. *Invitation*. They include a distinct invitation to engage in the transaction now.

PUBLIC RELATIONS AND PUBLICITY Marketers tend to underuse public relations, yet a well-thought-out program coordinated with the other communications-mix elements can be extremely effective, especially if a company needs to challenge consumers' misconceptions.

Scientific Atlanta (SA)   Although Forrester Research predicted that high-definition TV (HDTV) sets would be in 16 million homes by the end of 2005, Scientific Atlanta (SA), now a Cisco company, was disappointed in sales of its digital set-top boxes to digital cable TV operators in the United States. It turns out consumers weren't demanding set-top boxes because they didn't realize one was required to receive HD programs. As a B2B company, Scientific Atlanta had never needed to communicate directly to consumers before, but it saw the need for a public relations blitz, and fast. The campaign started with SA's commissioning a phone survey of HDTV owners. When the survey revealed all the varied reasons that almost 50 percent of those surveyed were not taking advantage of HDTV, SA reported the survey results to *USA Today* and the *New York Times*. When the results were published, the company immediately gained credibility by being associated with the survey, but that was only the first step in what became a multimedia campaign. SA's video news release showed friends gathered in living rooms watching HD programs, while a voice-over explained that in order to experience HDTV, you had to "turn on, hook up, and tune in." It ultimately got a respectable 204 broadcast airings, and SA's public relations efforts resulted in a huge jump in the number of HD set-top boxes it shipped.[39]

The appeal of public relations and publicity is based on three distinctive qualities:

1. **High credibility**. News stories and features are more authentic and credible to readers than ads.
2. **Ability to catch buyers off guard**. Public relations can reach prospects who prefer to avoid salespeople and advertisements.
3. **Dramatization**. Public relations has the potential for dramatizing a company or product.

EVENTS AND EXPERIENCES There are many advantages to events and experiences:

1. **Relevant**. A well-chosen event or experience can be seen as highly relevant because the consumer gets personally involved.
2. **Involving**. Given their live, real-time quality, events and experiences are more actively engaging for consumers.
3. **Implicit**. Events are an indirect 'soft sell.'

DIRECT AND INTERACTIVE MARKETING Direct and interactive marketing takes many forms: over the phone, online, or in person. They share three distinctive characteristics. Direct and interactive marketing messages are:

1. **Customized**. The message can be prepared to appeal to the addressed individual.
2. **Up-to-date**. A message can be prepared very quickly.
3. **Interactive**. The message can be changed depending on the person's response.

WORD-OF-MOUTH MARKETING Word of mouth also takes many forms online or offline. Three noteworthy characteristics are that they are:

1. **Credible**. Because people trust others they know and respect, word of mouth can be highly influential.
2. **Personal**. Word of mouth can be a very intimate dialogue that reflects personal facts, opinions, and experiences.
3. **Timely**. It occurs when people want it to and when they are most interested, and it often follows noteworthy or meaningful events or experiences.

PERSONAL SELLING Personal selling is the most effective tool at later stages of the buying process, particularly in building up buyer preference, conviction, and action. Personal selling has three distinctive qualities:

1. **Personal interaction**. Personal selling creates an immediate and interactive episode between two or more persons. Each party is able to observe the other's reactions.
2. **Cultivation**. Personal selling also permits all kinds of relationships to spring up, ranging from a matter-of-fact selling relationship to a deep personal friendship.
3. **Response**. The buyer may feel under some obligation for having listened to the sales talk.

Factors in Setting the Marketing Communications Mix

Companies must consider several factors in developing their **communications mix**: type of product market, consumer readiness to make a purchase, and stage in the product life cycle. Also important is the company's market rank.

marketing communications mix   advertising, sales promotion, events and experiences, public relations and publicity, direct marketing, and personal selling.

TYPE OF PRODUCT MARKET Communications-mix allocations vary between consumer and business markets. Consumer marketers tend to spend comparatively more on sales promotion and advertising; business marketers tend to spend comparatively more on personal selling. In general, personal selling is used more with complex, expensive, and risky goods and in markets with fewer and larger sellers (hence, business markets).

Although marketers use advertising less than sales calls in business markets, advertising still plays a significant role:

- Advertising can provide an introduction to the company and its products.
- If the product has new features, advertising can explain them.

- Advertising is more economical than sales calls.
- Advertisements offering brochures and carrying the company's phone number are an effective way to generate leads for sales representatives.
- Sales representatives can use copies of the company's ads to legitimize their company and products.
- Advertising can remind customers how to use the product and reassure them about their purchase.

A number of studies have underscored advertising's role in business markets. Advertising combined with personal selling can increase sales over what would have resulted if there had been no advertising. Corporate advertising can improve a company's reputation and improve the sales force's chances of getting a favorable first hearing and early adoption of the product.[40] It can also help to position or reposition a business marketer's products or a particular product line, as it did for General Electric.

GE   Beginning in 2005, GE initiated an integrated marketing campaign that included TV, print, and online advertising as well as events, to highlight GE products and services that help customers manage their environment impact. The campaign was dubbed 'ecomagination' and highlighted GE's solar energy products and hybrid locomotives, fuel cells, and lower-emission aircraft. The ads, developed for the company by BBD&O, revolved around this simple, central concept: although the world's natural resources may be limited, the human imagination is unlimited. In print ads entitled 'Shadows', the shadow of a GE aircraft engine appeared as a giant bird, and the shadow of a GE locomotive as a herd of zebras. Another campaign melded GE 'ecomagination' products with the natural world. The ads, events, and interactive online ads and games all proved extremely successful for GE. There are currently 140 products and solutions in the 'ecomagination' portfolio and these products have generated over US$100 billion in revenues since its inception in 2005.[41]

RENEWABLE ENERGY. WATER DESALINATION. FUEL CONSERVATION.

IT'S NOT A VISION OF THE FUTURE.

IT'S ECOMAGINATION

RIGHT

NOW.

   imagination at work   ecomagination.com

GE's 'ecomagination' campaign was a hit with consumers.

Personal selling can also make a strong contribution in consumer-goods marketing. Some consumer marketers use the sales force mainly to collect weekly orders from dealers and to see that sufficient stock is on the shelf. Yet an effectively trained company sales force can make four important contributions:

1. **Increased stock position**. Sales reps can persuade dealers to take more stock and devote more shelf space to the company's brand.
2. **Enthusiasm building**. Sales reps can build dealer enthusiasm by dramatizing planned advertising and sales promotion backup.
3. **Missionary selling**. Sales reps can sign up more dealers.
4. **Key account management**. Sales reps can take responsibility for growing business with the most important accounts.

BUYER-READINESS STAGE Communication tools vary in cost-effectiveness at different stages of buyer readiness. △ **Figure 17.5** shows the relative cost-effectiveness of three communication tools. Advertising and publicity play the most important roles in the awareness-building stage. Customer comprehension is primarily affected by advertising and personal selling. Customer conviction is influenced mostly by personal selling. Closing the sale is influenced mostly by personal selling and sales promotion. Reordering is also affected mostly by personal selling and sales promotion, and somewhat by reminder advertising.

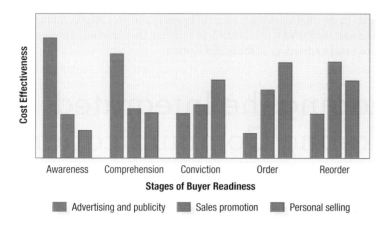

|Fig. 17.5| △

Cost-Effectiveness
of Three Different
Communication Tools
at Different Buyer-
Readiness Stages

PRODUCT LIFE-CYCLE STAGE Communication tools also vary in cost-effectiveness at different stages of the product life cycle. In the introduction stage, advertising, events and experiences, and publicity have the highest cost-effectiveness, followed by personal selling to gain distribution coverage and sales promotion and direct marketing to induce trial. In the growth stage, demand has its own momentum through word of mouth. In the maturity stage, advertising, events and experiences, and personal selling all become more important. In the decline stage, sales promotion continues strong, other communication tools are reduced, and salespeople give the product only minimal attention.

Measuring Communication Results

Senior managers want to know the *outcomes* and *revenues* resulting from their communications investments. Too often, however, their communications directors supply only *outputs* and *expenses*: press clipping counts, numbers of ads placed, media costs. In fairness, the communications directors try to translate outputs into intermediate outputs such as reach and frequency, recall and recognition scores, persuasion changes, and cost-per-thousand calculations. Ultimately, behavior-change measures capture the real payoff.

After implementing the communications plan, the communications director must measure its impact on the target audience. Members of the target audience are asked whether they recognize or recall the message, how many times they saw it, what points they recall, how they felt about the message, and their previous and current attitudes toward the product and the company. The communicator should also collect behavioral measures of audience response, such as how many people bought the product, liked it, and talked to others about it.

△ **Figure 17.6** provides an example of good feedback measurement. We find that 80 percent of the consumers in the total market are aware of brand A, 60 percent have tried it, and only 20 percent who have tried it are satisfied. This indicates that the communications program is effective in creating awareness, but the product fails to meet consumer expectations. In contrast, 40 percent

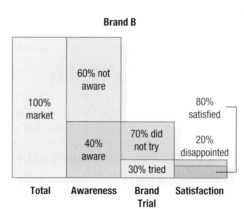

|Fig. 17.6| △

Current Consumer
States for Two Brands

of the consumers in the total market are aware of brand B, and only 30 percent have tried it, but 80 percent of those who have tried it are satisfied. In this case, the communications program needs to be strengthened to take advantage of the brand's power.

Managing the Integrated Marketing Communications Process

integrated marketing communications (IMC)
a concept of marketing communications planning that recognizes the added value of a comprehensive plan.

As defined by the American Association of Advertising Agencies, **integrated marketing communications (IMC)** is a concept of marketing communications planning that recognizes the added value of a comprehensive plan. Such a plan evaluates the strategic roles of a variety of communications disciplines—for example, general advertising, direct response, sales promotion, and public relations—and combines these disciplines to provide clarity, consistency, and maximum impact through the seamless integration of messages.

Unfortunately, many companies still rely on one or two communication tools. This practice persists in spite of the fragmenting of mass markets into a multitude of minimarkets, each requiring its own approach; the proliferation of new types of media; and the growing sophistication of consumers. The wide range of communication tools, messages, and audiences makes it imperative that companies move toward integrated marketing communications.[42] Companies must adopt a '360-degree view' of consumers to fully understand all the different ways that communications can affect consumer behavior in their daily lives.

Media companies and ad agencies are expanding their capabilities to offer multiplatform deals for marketers. For example, newspapers and magazines have been frantically formulating digital strategies, such as adding videos to their homepages, to increase advertising revenue. *Country Living* magazine and HGTV cable channel offer online video segments on their websites with home-decorating themes. These expanded capabilities make it easier for marketers to assemble various media properties in an integrated communication program.

 GMC & ESPN   General Motors Corp's GMC unit worked with Disney's ABC and ESPN units to develop a promotion that prompted more than 1.5 million people to enter a competition called GMC Keys to Victory during *Monday Night Football*. In addition to a large schedule of traditional commercials on ESPN, the promotion included integration of GMC branding and vehicles within the *Monday Night Football* opening sequence. There was a Keys to the Game feature on the *Monday Night Countdown* show and on the episodes of *SportsCenter* that ran just after MNF games. GMC ran a season-long promotion for the competition on ESPN.com, and also ran a large gatefold insert in *ESPN the Magazine*, which included a schedule of the *Monday Night Football* games. As part of the deal, GMC gave away a Sierra pickup weekly for 16 weeks on www.keystovictory.com, linked on both www.GMC.com and www.ESPN.com. GMC markers noted that the ESPN deal hit a broad spectrum of media that reached the youthful male target of the GMC truck brand.[43]

Coordinating Media

Media coordination can occur across and within media types, but marketers should combine personal and non-personal communications channels to achieve maximum impact. Imagine a marketer using a single tool in a 'one-shot' effort to reach and sell to a prospect. An example of a *single-vehicle, single-stage campaign* is a one-time mailing offering a cookware item. A *single-vehicle, multiple-stage campaign* would rely on successive mailings to the same prospect. Magazine publishers, for example, send about four renewal notices to a household before giving up. A more powerful approach is the *multiple-vehicle, multiple-stage campaign*. Consider the sequence in △ **Figure 17.7**.

| New campaign about a new product | → | Paid ad with a response mechanism | → | Direct mail | → | Outbound telemarketing | → | Face-to-face sales call | → | Ongoing communication |

|Fig. 17.7| △

Example of Multiple-Vehicle, Multiple-Stage Communication Campaign

Multiple media deployed within a tightly defined time frame can increase message reach and impact. Research has also shown that promotions can be more effective when combined with advertising.[44] The awareness and attitudes created by advertising campaigns can improve the success of more-direct sales pitches. Many companies are coordinating their online and offline communications activities. Listing internet addresses in ads (especially print ads) and on packages allows people to more fully explore a company's products, find store locations, and get more product or service information. For example, Dannon makes it a priority to drive traffic to its Dannon Yogurt homepage, so the company can benefit from the twin paybacks of (1) forging direct relationships with customers and (2) building a database of its best customers, whose loyalty can be strengthened with more targeted coupon and direct-mail promotional efforts.[45]

Even if consumers don't order online, they can use websites in ways that drive them into stores to buy. Best Buy's website can function as a research tool for consumers, as surveys revealed that 40 percent of its customers looked online first before coming into the store.[46]

Implementing IMC

Integrated marketing communications has been slow to take hold for several reasons.[47] Large companies often employ several different communications specialists who may know comparatively little about the other communication tools. Further complicating matters is that many global companies use a large number of ad agencies located in different countries and serving different divisions, resulting in uncoordinated communications and image diffusion. One company that has managed to coordinate the integrated marketing effort of a number of agencies and internal departments is British Gas.

British Gas   Jane Bednall, head of brand and marketing services at British Gas, holds twice-monthly planning meetings with all the agencies working on various aspects of an integrated marketing campaign: from the ad agency to the PR agency to the company's own internal communications department. One reason Bednall thinks these different factions are truly 'integrated' is that British Gas retains them on a project basis and assigns a budget to a specific business initiative rather than to a media channel. Bringing planners from various disciplines together in an open forum to discuss their views shatters preconceptions, Bednall feels. In British Gas's recent campaign around energy efficiency, the company used this collaborative approach and garnered 1 million responses from people who wanted to learn more about the issue. "We all got behind the single objective and message, starting with advertising, and followed by direct and online marketing. But integration isn't just about marketing communications. It is about everything from PR to the service experience to internal communications," said Bednall. If, in her role as coordinator, Bednall can't coax an agency to be collaborative or if she is forced into a hand-holding role, she makes no bones about finding another agency.[48]

Today, however, a few large agencies have substantially improved their integrated offerings. To facilitate one-stop shopping, major ad agencies have acquired promotion agencies, public relations firms, package-design consultancies, website developers, and direct-mail houses. These agencies are redefining themselves as *communications companies* that assist clients to improve their overall communications effectiveness by offering strategic and practical advice on many

marketing Memo

How Integrated is Your IMC Program?

In assessing the collective impact of an IMC program, the marketer's overriding goal is to create the most effective and efficient communications program possible. The following six criteria can help determine whether communications are truly integrated

- **Coverage.** Coverage is the proportion of the audience reached by each communication option employed, as well as how much overlap exists among communication options. In other words, to what extent do different communication options reach the designated target market and the same or different consumers making up that market?

- **Contribution.** Contribution is the inherent ability of a marketing communication to create the desired response and communication effects from consumers in the absence of exposure to any other communication option. How much does a communication affect consumer processing and build awareness, enhance image, elicit responses, and induce sales?

- **Commonality.** Commonality is the extent to which *common* associations are reinforced across communication options; that is, the extent to which information conveyed by different communication options share meaning. The consistency and cohesiveness of the brand image is important because it determines how easily existing associations and responses can be recalled and how easily additional associations and responses can become linked to the brand in memory.

- **Complementarity.** Communication options are often more effective when used in tandem. Complementarity relates to the extent to which *different* associations and linkages are emphasized across communication options. Different brand associations may be most effectively established by capitalizing on those marketing communication options best suited to eliciting a particular consumer response or establishing a particular type of brand association. As part of their Now What? ad campaign showing people dealing with common, but difficult situations, State Farm has used television to introduce a story line that it continued and embellished on its website.[49]

- **Versatility.** In any integrated communication program, when consumers are exposed to a particular marketing communication, some will have already been exposed to other marketing communications for the brand, and some will not have had any prior exposure. Versatility refers to the extent to which a marketing communication option is robust and 'works' for different groups of consumers. The ability of a marketing communication to work at two levels—effectively communicating to consumers who have or have *not* seen other communications—is critically important.

- **Cost.** Marketers must weigh evaluations of marketing communications on all these criteria against their cost to arrive at the most effective *and* efficient communications program.

Source: Kevin Lane Keller, *Strategic Brand Management*, 3rd edn (Upper Saddle River, NJ: Prentice Hall, 2008).

forms of communication.[50] Many international clients have opted to put a substantial portion of their communications work through one full-service agency. An example is IBM turning all its advertising over to Ogilvy to attain uniform branding. The result is integrated and more-effective marketing communications at a much lower total communications cost.

Integrated marketing communications can produce stronger message consistency and help to build brand equity and create greater sales impact.[51] It forces management to think about every way the customer comes in contact with the company, how the company communicates its positioning, the relative importance of each vehicle, and timing issues. It gives someone the responsibility—where none existed before—to unify the company's brand images and messages as they come through thousands of company activities. IMC should improve the company's ability to reach the right customers with the right messages at the right time and in the right place.[52] The Marketing Memo: *How Integrated Is Your IMC Program?* provides some guidelines.

Summary

1. Modern marketing calls for more than developing a good product, pricing it attractively, and making it accessible to target customers. Companies must also communicate with present and potential stakeholders and with the general public.

2. The marketing communications mix consists of eight major modes of communication: advertising, sales promotion, public relations and publicity, events and experiences, direct marketing, interactive marketing, word-of-mouth marketing, and personal selling.

3. The communications process consists of nine elements: sender, receiver, message, media, encoding, decoding, response, feedback, and noise. To get their messages through, marketers must encode their messages in a way that takes into account how the target audience usually decodes messages. They must also transmit the message through efficient media that reach the target audience and develop feedback channels to monitor response to the message.

4. Developing effective communications involves eight steps: (1) identify the target audience, (2) determine the communications objectives, (3) design the communications, (4) select the communications channels, (5) establish the total communications budget, (6) decide on the communications mix, (7) measure the communications results, and (8) manage the integrated marketing communications process.

5. In identifying the target audience, the marketer needs to close any gap that exists between current public perception and the image sought. Communications objectives may involve category need, brand awareness, brand attitude, or brand purchase intention. Formulating the communication requires solving three problems: what to say (message strategy), how to say it (creative strategy), and who should say it (message source). Communications channels may be personal (advocate, expert, and social channels) or nonpersonal (media, atmospheres, and events). The objective-and-task method of setting the promotion budget, which calls upon marketers to develop their budgets by defining specific objectives, is the most desirable.

6. In deciding on the marketing communications mix, marketers must examine the distinct advantages and costs of each communication tool and the company's market rank. They must also consider the type of product market in which they are selling, how ready consumers are to make a purchase, and the product's stage in the product life cycle. Measuring the effectiveness of the marketing communications mix involves asking members of the target audience whether they recognize or recall the communication, how many times they saw it, what points they recall, how they felt about the communication, and their previous and current attitudes toward the product and the company.

7. Managing and coordinating the entire communications process calls for integrated marketing communications (IMC): marketing communications planning that recognizes the added value of a comprehensive plan that evaluates the strategic roles of a variety of communications disciplines and combines these disciplines to provide clarity, consistency, and maximum impact through the seamless integration of discrete messages.

Applications

Marketing Debate
Has TV Advertising Lost Power?

Long deemed the most successful medium, television advertising has received increased criticism as being too expensive and, even worse, no longer as effective as it once was. Critics maintain that consumers tune out too many ads by zipping and zapping and that it is difficult to make a strong impression. The future, claim some, is with online advertising. Supporters of TV advertising disagree, contending that the multisensory impact of TV is unsurpassed and that no other media option offers the same potential impact.

Take a position: TV advertising has faded in importance *versus* TV advertising is still the most powerful advertising medium.

Marketing Discussion

Pick a brand and go to its website. Locate as many forms of communication as you can find. Conduct an informal communications audit. What do you notice? How consistent are the various methods of communications?

Marketing Excellence

>>Diwan Bookstore

Ten years ago, a group of five friends saw a gap in the market for an inviting bookstore with a multicultural product mix, offering a positive customer service experience. Hind Wassef, Nadia Wassef, and Nihal Schawky decided to make buying a book a memorable encounter. Building from their own life experiences, they set out to share their knowledge with others: the three active managing partners always looked to books in their lives to solve problems or to find knowledge and enrichment.

The first branch of the Diwan Bookstore opened in March 2002 in Cairo's Zamalek area with four employees, the Wassefs having financed 80 percent of the startup capital for Diwan from their personal savings of US$170,000. The store stocked books in Arabic, English, French, and German, including children's books; the shop also sold films and music in both Arabic and English, as well as stationery items, and had a café. Within a decade, nine other branches had opened, distributed all over Cairo, and the company now employs 190 people.

Using its unique logo and branding initiatives, Diwan Bookstores began to communicate value to customers. Diwan Bookstores wanted to introduce people to different cultures and ways of thinking through books, music, and film, and to bridge the gap between East and West. This was achieved through many steps, the first being the choice of name for the bookstore. *Diwan* has multiple meanings in the Arab world. It is a Persian word referring to a collection of poems by a single author or a set of work by an Urdu, Persian, or Turkish poet. It was also used to reflect a governmental body during the former Ottoman Empire; a place where people meet; and a long comfortable mattress. Secondly, the product mix in the stores catered for both Eastern and Western tastes. Third—and most importantly—was the visual element.

Diwan's unique logo merged English and Arabic script and punctuation marks. Their interiors combined scripts, words, and concepts from different cultures.

Diwan Bookstores never used above-the-line advertising to communicate with its customers. As a bookstore they preferred to rely on word of mouth between customers and their below-the-line marketing: the popular Diwan Bag. New designs were used to commemorate anniversaries, new store openings, and other important milestones. The bags were of such high quality and visual appeal that they were constantly being re-used. They became walking billboards for the stores and their carriers were proud of what sporting this bag signified.

In describing the nature of her business, Wassef said, "We are in the business of culture and knowledge: we are dedicated to the production and consumption of culture." Diwan is not a conventional bookstore that merely sells books: "we provide a cultural engagement delivered in a distinctive setting." Positive word-of-mouth messages attracted more customers to experience Diwan. Staying true to their promise of being "more than a bookstore," Diwan's continued events such as book signings, workshops for kids and adults, arts and crafts, and musical events has contributed to building a Diwan community.

In an effort to continue direct lines of communication with Diwan's customers and community, Diwan has embraced social media tools such as Facebook and Twitter. With more than 30,000 friends and followers, Diwan is able to promptly answer questions, raise topics for discussion, and handle any queries that may come up. The art of listening and creating a dialogue with customers necessitates intensive training for customer service staff who deal directly with clients. Diwan has to guarantee that their message is delivered consistently.

Undoubtedly, Diwan has succeeded in communicating the value of its products and its brand to its customers. This decade has seen a rise in prices and a decline in standards of living; yet customers continue to buy and read books. Diwan's expansion along with the birth of its two new spin-off brands—Qirtassiya (stationery) and Diwan Kids (kids' toys)—proves that the ability to communicate the value of a brand results in strong loyalty. Maintaining connections with kids through kids' toys, arts and crafts,

Continued on next page >>

Marketing Excellence...continued

>>Diwan Bookstore

or books is essential to creating a strong brand affiliation from early childhood.

Diwan aspires to continue expanding its presence in other Egyptian governorates prior to entering the international arena. This vision is based on Diwan's commitment to delivering its value to its home market, then replicating its success in Cairo and Alexandria. On August 22, 2011, *TIME magazine* cited Diwan as an Egyptian entrepreneurial dream company, coping well with economic recession and unstable politics. Intelligent branding, outstanding customer service, and the ability to talk and listen to its clients has positioned Diwan as an essential component of people's lives.

Questions

1. What is Diwan's main communication vehicle? Do you think this method is sufficient for communicating and delivering value? Why?

2. Identify and differentiate between the controllable and uncontrollable communication sources for Diwan.

Sources: Diwan Bookstore Company Profile 2010, www.diwanegypt.com/files/profile/diwan_profile.pdf; Michael Schuman, "Seeking Growth After the Arab Spring: Unless it can nurture entrepreneurs and create jobs, the popular movement that toppled the dictators won't make a difference in real lives," *TIME Magazine*, August 22, 2011, pp. 39–42.

Arab telecom companies have seen impressive returns after investing heavily in mass-media advertising.

In this chapter, we will address the following questions:

1. What steps are required in developing an advertising program? (pg. 487)

2. How should sales promotion decisions be made? (pg. 505)

3. What are the guidelines for effective brand-building events and experiences? (pg. 510)

4. How can companies exploit the potential of public relations and publicity? (pg. 513)

Managing Mass Communications: Advertising, Sales Promotions, Events and Experiences, and Public Relations

Although there has been an enormous increase in the use of personal communications by marketers in recent years, due to the rapid penetration of the internet and other factors, the fact remains that mass media, if used correctly, can still dramatically improve the fortunes of a brand or company. Arab telecommunication companies have invested heavily in mass-media advertising and have seen their investments reap excellent returns in terms of communicating a compelling value proposition and brand image, and, eventually, financial returns.

 Telecommunication companies in the Arab world spend hundreds of millions of dollars on advertising annually, making telecommunication one of the top advertising spenders across all product categories. Arab telecom brands are among the top advertised brands, with two of the top five, and four of the top ten brands advertised. According to research conducted by global research house Ipsos MediaCT Middle East and North Africa (MENA), and published in the pan-Arab monthly communications magazine ArabAd, telecommunication brands Zain, Mobily, Saudi Telecom, and Etisalat were among the top 10 advertised brands across all media in the region. These telecommunication companies were among the top spenders across different media channels: television, print (newspapers and magazines), radio, and outdoor.[1]

Marketers are trying to come to grips with how to best use mass media in the new communication environment.[2] In this chapter, we examine the nature and use of four mass-communication tools—advertising, sales promotion, events and experiences, and public relations and publicity. ▽

Developing and Managing an Advertising Program

Advertising is any paid form of nonpersonal presentation and promotion of ideas, goods, or services by an identified sponsor. Ads can be a cost-effective way to disseminate messages, whether to build a brand preference or to educate people. Even in today's challenging media environment, good ads can pay off. Ads publicizing the effectiveness of Olay Definity anti-aging products and Head & Shoulders Intensive Treatment shampoo helped both Procter & Gamble brands enjoy double-digit sales gains in recent years.[3] As mentioned in the opening example, telecommunication companies in the Arab world spend hundreds of millions of dollars on advertising

advertising any paid form of nonpersonal presentation and promotion of ideas, goods, or services by an identified sponsor.

TABLE 18.1	Advertising Media Expenditures in MENA Region: Top 10 Categories 2011
Rank	**Category**
1	Hygiene & Beauty Care
2	Servicing Companies
3	Foods
4	Entertainment & Leisure
5	Non-alcoholic drinks
6	Telecommunication
7	Automotive
8	Media & Publishing & Advertising
9	Banking & Finance
10	Clothing & Accessories

Source: *ArabAd*, 22, no. 2, February 2012.

annually with four out of the top 10 brands advertised being for telecom and mobile operators. Refreshment giants PepsiCo and Coca Cola rank first and third in total media spending. In terms of advertising by sector, hygiene and beauty care led advertising spending across all Arab markets (see 🔲 **Tables 18.1** and **18.2**).

TABLE 18.2	Advertising Media Expenditures in MENA Region: Top 10 Brands 2011	
Rank	**Brand**	**Industry**
1	Pepsi	Soft Drinks
2	Zain	Telecommunications
3	Coca Cola	Soft Drinks
4	Mobily	Telecommunications
5	Chevrolet	Cars
6	Sedar	Home Furnishing
7	Saudi Telecom	Telecommunications
8	Galaxy	Food
9	Etisalat	Telecommunications
10	Dabur	Hygiene and Beauty

Source: *ArabAd*, 22, no. 2, February 2012.

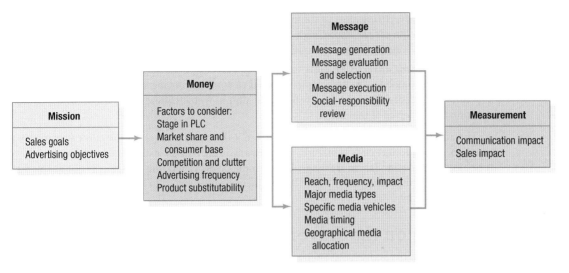

|Fig. 18.1| △

The Five Ms of Advertising

In developing an advertising program, marketing managers must always start by identifying the target market and buyer motives. Then they can make the five major decisions, known as "the five Ms:" *mission*: what are our advertising objectives?; *money*: how much can we spend?; *message*: what message should we send?; *media*: what media should we use?; and *measurement*: how should we evaluate the results? These decisions are summarized in △ **Figure 18.1** and described in the following sections.

Setting the Objectives

The advertising objectives must flow from prior decisions on target market, brand positioning, and the marketing program.

An **advertising goal** (or objective) is a specific communications task and achievement level to be accomplished with a specific audience in a specific period of time.[4] An example for a mobile telephone service company could be:

> To increase among the 10 million mobile users in the age bracket 15–25 the level of awareness of our brand X prepaid phone cards from 75 to 85 percent, the level of conviction that we offer a good service from 35 to 45 percent, and our market share from 25 to 30 percent in 1 year.

Advertising objectives can be classified according to whether their aim is to inform, persuade, remind, or reinforce. These goals correspond to different stages in the *hierarchy-of-effects model* discussed in Chapter 17.

- *Informative advertising* aims to create brand awareness and knowledge of new products or new features of existing products. One of the most memorable ads ever is that of Energizer batteries featuring 'the Energizer Bunny that keeps on going.' The ad was very well received and liked, and created a very strong brand awareness and equity for Energizer. Yet, advertisers have to be careful, as some memorable ads might not necessarily translate into positive brand attitude. An ad campaign might lead to a strong brand awareness but through a memorable ad that people actually hate. Brand awareness cannot come at the expense of brand attitudes.

- *Persuasive advertising* aims to create liking, preference, conviction, and purchase of a product or service. Some persuasive advertising uses comparative advertising, which makes an explicit comparison of the attributes of two or more brands.[5] Comparative advertising works best when it elicits cognitive and affective motivations simultaneously, and when consumers are processing advertising in a detailed, analytical mode.[6] In countries where direct comparative advertising is not allowed by law, as in many Arab countries, some advertisers, convinced by the effectiveness of this method, resort to indirect comparative advertising, whereby the brand name of the competitor is not directly revealed but is alluded to through the shape, color, or other dominant aspect of the package.

advertising goal a specific communication task and achievement level to be accomplished with a specific audience in a specific period of time.

- *Reminder advertising* aims to stimulate repeat purchase of products and services. Expensive, full-page, color ads for PepsiCola or Galaxy chocolate bars in international and local magazines are intended to remind people to purchase the product.
- *Reinforcement advertising* aims to convince current purchasers that they made the right choice. Automobile ads often depict satisfied customers enjoying special features of their new car. A university ad might depict successful alumni who attribute their success to the education they received at that university.

The advertising objective should emerge from a thorough analysis of the current marketing situation. If the product class is mature, the company is the market leader, and brand usage is low, the objective is to stimulate more usage. If the product class is new, the company is not the market leader, but the brand is superior to the leader, then the objective is to convince the market of the brand's superiority.

Deciding on the Advertising Budget

How does a company know it's spending the right amount? Some critics charge that large consumer-packaged-goods firms overspend on advertising as a form of insurance against not spending enough, and industrial companies underestimate the power of company and product image building and so underspend.[7]

Although advertising is treated as a current expense, part of it is really an investment in building brand equity and customer loyalty. When a company spends US$5 million on capital equipment, it may treat the equipment as a 5-year depreciable asset and write off only one-fifth of the cost in the first year. When it spends US$5 million on advertising to launch a new product, it must write off the entire cost in the first year, reducing its reported profit.

FACTORS AFFECTING BUDGET DECISIONS Here are five specific factors to consider when *setting* the advertising budget:[8]

1. *Stage in the product life cycle.* New products typically merit large advertising budgets to build awareness and to gain consumer trial. Established brands usually are supported with lower advertising budgets, measured as a ratio to sales.[9]
2. *Market share and consumer base.* High-market-share brands usually require less advertising expenditure as a percentage of sales to maintain share. To build share by increasing market size requires larger expenditures.
3. *Competition and clutter.* In a market with a large number of competitors and high advertising spending, a brand must advertise more heavily to be heard. Even simple clutter from advertisements not directly competitive to the brand creates a need for heavier advertising.
4. *Advertising frequency.* The number of repetitions needed to put across the brand's message to consumers has an obvious impact on the advertising budget.
5. *Product substitutability.* Brands in less-well-differentiated or commodity-like product classes (soft drinks, banks, and airlines) require heavy advertising to establish a differential image.

In one study of budget allocation, Low and Mohr found that managers allocate less to advertising as brands move to the more mature phase of the product life cycle; when a brand is well-differentiated from the competition; when managers are rewarded on short-term results; as retailers gain more power; and when managers have less experience with the company.[10]

ADVERTISING ELASTICITY The predominant response function for advertising is often concave but can be S-shaped.[11] When consumer response is S-shaped, some positive amount of advertising is necessary to generate any sales impact, but sales increases eventually flatten out.[12]

One classic study found that increasing the TV advertising budget had a measurable effect on sales only half the time. The success rate was higher on new products or line extensions than on established brands, and when there were changes in copy or in media strategy (such as an expanded target market). When advertising was successful in increasing sales, its impact lasted up to 2 years after peak spending. Moreover, the long-term incremental sales generated were approximately double the incremental sales observed in the first year of an advertising spending increase.[13]

Other studies reinforce these conclusions. In a 2004 study of 23 brands, advertising often didn't increase sales for mature brands or categories in decline. A review of academic research found that advertising elasticities were estimated to be higher for new (0.3) than for established products (0.1).[14]

Developing the Advertising Campaign

In designing and evaluating an ad campaign, marketers employ both art and science to develop the *message strategy* or positioning of an ad—*what* the ad attempts to convey about the brand—and its *creative strategy*—*how* the ad expresses the brand claims. Advertisers go through three steps: message generation and evaluation, creative development and execution, and social-responsibility review.

MESSAGE GENERATION AND EVALUATION

For an advertisement to be effective, it is important that it carries a fresh idea and avoids replicating appeals that others use. Many of today's automobile ads have a sameness about them: a car drives at high speed on a curved mountain road or across a desert. The result is that only a weak link forms between the brand and the message. Advertisers are always seeking 'the big idea' that connects with consumers rationally and emotionally, sharply distinguishes the brand from competitors, and is broad and flexible enough to translate to different media, markets, and time periods.[15] Fresh insights are important for avoiding using the same appeals and position as others.

A good ad normally focuses on one or two core selling propositions. As part of refining the brand positioning, the advertiser should conduct market research to determine which appeal works best with its target audience and then prepare a *creative brief*, typically covering one or two pages. This is an elaboration of the *positioning statement* and includes: key message, target audience, communications objectives (to do, to know, to believe), key brand benefits, supports for the brand promise, and media. How many alternative ad themes should the advertiser create before making a choice? The more ads themes explored, the higher the probability of finding an excellent one. Fortunately, the expense of creating rough ads is rapidly falling, thanks to computers. An ad agency's creative department can compose many alternative ads in a short time by drawing from computer files containing still and video images.

CREATIVE DEVELOPMENT AND EXECUTION

The ad's impact depends not only on what it says, but often more important, *how* it says it. Message execution can be decisive. Every advertising medium has advantages and disadvantages. Here we review television, print, and radio advertising media.

Television Ads Television is generally acknowledged as the most powerful advertising medium and reaches a broad spectrum of consumers. The wide reach translates to low cost per exposure. TV advertising has two particularly important strengths. First, it can be an effective means of vividly demonstrating product attributes and persuasively explaining their corresponding consumer benefits. Second, it can dramatically portray user and usage imagery, brand personality, and other intangibles.

Because of the fleeting nature of the ad, however, and the distracting creative elements often found in it, product-related messages and the brand itself can be overlooked. Moreover, the high volume of ads and nonprogramming material on television creates clutter that makes it easy for consumers to ignore or forget ads. And although production and placement are expensive, the major networks' share of the prime-time audience has steadily declined, taking the average effectiveness of any one ad with it. For example, research has shown that the number of viewers who said they paid attention to TV ads dropped significantly in the past decade.

Nevertheless, properly designed and executed TV ads can improve brand equity and affect sales and profits. One of the most consistently successful TV advertisers has been Apple. The 1984 ad introducing the Macintosh personal computer ran only once on U.S. national TV but is one of the best-known ads ever made. In the following years, Apple successfully created awareness and image for a series of products, most recently with its acclaimed iPod ad campaign. A well-done TV commercial can still be a powerful marketing tool.

Garnier   Garnier has regularly partnered with beautiful and inspirational women as spokespeople to promote its beauty products. In the Arab world, Garnier has partnered with Tunisian actress, TV presenter, and magazine columnist Hend Sabry for its Garnier Color Naturals by Nutrisse product. Maya Ghantous, marketing manager at Garnier Middle East, said that, "Hend's personality is the perfect match for Garnier's Take Care Philosophy. Hend has the happy confidence and ease of a woman that takes care of herself, and beneath her beautiful-actress exterior lies a generous and compassionate environmentalist who uses her success to help take care of others, and of the world around her." Hend Sabry is known for her community work. She was recently recognized as an Ambassador against Hunger by the United Nations World Food Program.

In media appearances, Sabry has praised Garnier Color Natural's unique formula, which uses natural olive oil, and its ability to enhance her hair: "It is the only hair color that contains olive oil and nourishes as it colors. Finally, what mothers recommend can now be found in a bottle."[16]

Print Ads   Print media offer a stark contrast to broadcast media. Because readers consume them at their own pace, magazines and newspapers can provide detailed product information and effectively communicate user and usage imagery. At the same time, the static nature of the visual images in print media makes dynamic presentations or demonstrations difficult, and print media can be fairly passive.

The two main print media—magazines and newspapers—share many advantages and disadvantages. Although newspapers are timely and pervasive, magazines are typically more effective at building user and usage imagery. Newspapers are popular for local—especially retailer—advertising. Yet, newspaper readership has been dropping steadily in recent years, including in the Arab word.[17] Although advertisers have some flexibility in designing and placing newspaper ads, poor reproduction quality and short shelf life can diminish the ads' impact.

Format elements such as ad size, color, and illustration also affect a print ad's impact. Larger ads gain more attention, though not necessarily by as much as their difference in cost. Four-color illustrations increase ad effectiveness and ad cost. New electronic eye-movement studies show that consumers can be led through an ad by strategic placement of dominant elements.

Researchers studying print advertisements report that the *picture*, *headline*, and *copy* matter are viewed in that order. The picture must be strong enough to draw attention. The headline must reinforce the picture and lead the person to read the copy. The copy must be engaging and the brand's name sufficiently prominent. Even then, less than 50 percent of the exposed audience will notice even a really outstanding ad. About 30 percent might recall the headline's main point; about 25 percent the advertiser's name; and fewer than 10 percent will read most of the body copy. Ordinary ads don't achieve even these results.

For attracting attention to a print ad, the picture is important, especially if it happens to be a picture of *you*, which is what Unisys, a renowned information technology company, creatively attempted to do.

Unisys   Info-tech company Unisys undertook a radical change in ad direction in 2006. The company bought print ads in *Fortune* magazine, but only in select magazines going to about 20 chief information officers at major corporations such as DHL, Subaru of America, Citigroup, and Northwest Airlines. These executives opened the cover wrap of an actual *Fortune* magazine edition to see their own faces smiling up at them. On the reverse side was a customized letter written by a Unisys manager that spoke to the unique challenges in the executive's industry. Also featured were links to mock news videos mentioning the executive's name and a capsule bio focusing on business achievements. Flattery will get you somewhere, according to Unisys's marketing department. To integrate the ads with other forms of marketing communications, Unisys also strategically placed billboard ads (not featuring photos of the executives) so that the executives would see them on their daily commute and even hired field teams to scope out how these high-ranking men and women got to work or where they stopped for coffee.[18]

Given how consumers process print ads, some clear managerial implications emerge, as summarized in the Marketing Memo: *Print Ad Evaluation Criteria*.

Radio Ads Radio continues to maintain its powerful media presence worldwide. In the Arab world, radio penetration continues to exceed other forms of media such as newspapers and television (in its various forms: national, cable, and satellite).[19] Perhaps radio's main advantage is flexibility: stations are very targeted, ads are relatively inexpensive to produce and place, and short closings allow for quick response. Radio is a particularly effective medium in the morning; it can also let companies achieve a balance between broad and localized market coverage.

The obvious disadvantages of radio are the lack of visual images and the relatively passive nature of the consumer processing that results.[20] Nevertheless, radio ads can be extremely creative. Some see the lack of visual images as a plus because they feel the clever use of music, sound, and other creative devices can tap into the listener's imagination to create powerfully relevant and liked images.

57357 Among the top 10 most advertised brands in Egypt is 57357: not your typical advertised brand. 57357 is the brand of the Children's Cancer Hospital Egypt. The idea of establishing a children cancer hospital started among a group of volunteers in 1995, and their dream was realized in 2007 when the hospital admitted its first patient. The Children's Cancer Hospital Egypt (CCHE) 75357 strives to be one of the best comprehensive pediatric oncology hospitals in the world, an international example of care, and a model of a philanthropic, financially viable organization. It attempts to cure and to improve the quality of life for children with cancer regardless of race, religion, or ability to pay. Big financial obligations accompany this vision and mission, which require donations; as a result, CCHE 57357 embarked on a massive

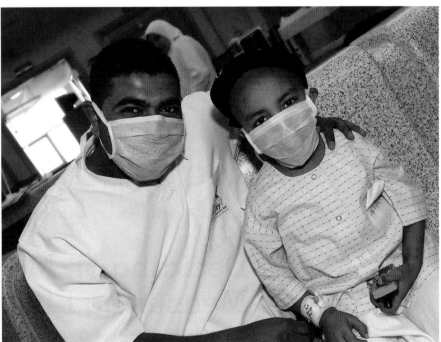

The Children's Cancer Hospital Egypt (CCHE) 75357 strives to be one of the leading pediatric oncology hospitals in the world.

awareness and fundraising campaign utilizing a multitude of media vehicles. CCHE 57357 is now among the top five most advertised brands on Egyptian radio networks, in the same league as telecom operators Etisalat, Mobinil, and Vodafone, and soft drink giant PepsiCo. The 57357 brand awareness even extends beyond the geographic boundaries of Egypt, thanks to satellite television channels which feature 57357 advertising commercials and infomercials.[21]

LEGAL AND SOCIAL ISSUES Advertisers and their agencies must be sure advertising does not overstep social and legal norms. Public policy makers have developed a substantial body of laws and regulations to govern advertising.

More and more countries are passing laws prohibiting advertisers from making false claims, such as stating that a product cures something when it does not. Advertisers should avoid false demonstrations, such as portraying that a single drop of a liquid detergent can clean hundreds of dirty plates. It is illegal in some countries to create ads that have the capacity to deceive, even though no one may actually be deceived. For example, a floor wax advertiser can't say the product gives 6 months' protection unless it does so under typical conditions, and the maker of a diet bread can't say it has fewer calories simply because its slices are thinner. The problem is how to tell the difference between deception and 'puffery:' simple exaggerations that are not meant to be believed and that are permitted by law. The battle between two of the world's most popular sweeteners is an example.

 Splenda versus Equal Splenda's tagline for its artificial sweetener was "Made from sugar, so it tastes like sugar," with "but it's not sugar" in small writing, almost as an afterthought. McNeil Nutritionals, its manufacturer, does begin production of Splenda with pure cane sugar but burns it off in the manufacturing process. However, Merisant, maker of Equal, claimed that Splenda's advertising confuses consumers who are likely to conclude that a product "made from sugar" is healthier than one made from aspartame, Equal's main ingredient. A document used in court and taken from McNeil's own files notes that consumers' perception of Splenda as "not an artificial sweetener" was one of the largest triumphs of the company's marketing campaign, which began in 2003. Splenda became the runaway leader in the sugar-substitute category with 60 percent of the market, leaving roughly 14 percent each to Equal (in the blue packets) and Sweet'N Low (pink packets). So, although McNeil agreed to settle the lawsuit and pay Merisant an undisclosed but "substantial" award (and change its advertising), it may be too late for consumers to change their perception of Splenda as something sugary but not sugar-free.[22]

Sellers in some countries (such as in the United States) are legally obligated to avoid bait-and-switch advertising that attracts buyers under false pretenses. Suppose a seller advertises a sewing machine at US$149. When consumers try to buy the advertised machine, the seller cannot then refuse to sell it, downplay its features, show a faulty one, or promise unreasonable delivery dates in order to switch the buyer to a more expensive machine.[23]

To be socially responsible, advertisers must be careful not to offend the general public as well as any social or ethnic groups, or racial minorities.[24]

Deciding on Media and Measuring Effectiveness

After choosing the message, the advertiser's next task is to choose media to carry it. The steps here are deciding on desired reach, frequency, and impact; choosing among major media types; selecting specific media vehicles; deciding on media timing; and deciding on geographical media allocation. Then the marketer evaluates the results of these decisions.

Deciding on Reach, Frequency, and Impact

Media selection is finding the most cost-effective media to deliver the desired number and type of exposures to the target audience. What do we mean by the desired number of exposures? The advertiser seeks a specified advertising objective and response from the target audience; for example, a target level of product trial. This level depends on, among other things, level of brand awareness. Suppose the rate of product trial increases at a diminishing rate with the level of audience awareness, as shown in △ **Figure 18.2 (a)**. If the advertiser seeks a product trial rate of T^*, it will be necessary to achieve a brand awareness level of A^*.

The next task is to find out how many exposures, E^*, will produce a level of audience awareness of A^*. The effect of exposures on audience awareness depends on the exposures' reach, frequency, and impact:

- **Reach (R).** The number of different persons or households exposed to a particular media schedule at least once during a specified time period.

- **Frequency (F).** The number of times within the specified time period that an average person or household is exposed to the message.

- **Impact (I).** The qualitative value of an exposure through a given medium (thus a food ad in *Soufra Daimeh* would have a higher impact than in *Arabian Business* magazine).

△ **Figure 18.2 (b)** shows the relationship between audience awareness and reach. Audience awareness will be greater, the higher the exposures' reach, frequency, and impact. There are important trade-offs here. Suppose the planner has an advertising budget of US$1,000,000 and the cost per thousand exposures of average quality is $5. This means it can buy 200,000,000 exposures ($1,000,000 ÷ [$5/1,000]). If the advertiser seeks an average exposure frequency of 10, it can reach 20,000,000 people (200,000,000 ÷ 10) with the given budget. But if the advertiser wants higher-quality media costing $10 per thousand exposures, it will be able to reach only 10,000,000 people unless it is willing to lower the desired exposure frequency.

The relationship between reach, frequency, and impact is captured in the following concepts:

- **Total number of exposures (E).** This is the reach times the average frequency; that is, $E = R \times F$; also called the gross rating points (GRP). If a given media schedule reaches 80 percent of homes with an average exposure frequency of 3, the media schedule has a GRP of 240 (80 × 3). If another media schedule has a GRP of 300, it has more weight, but we cannot tell how this weight breaks down into reach and frequency.

- **Weighted number of exposures (WE).** This is the reach times average frequency times average impact, that is $WE = R \times F \times I$.

The media planner should figure out the most cost-effective combination of reach, frequency, and impact. Reach is most important when launching new products, extensions of well-known brands, or infrequently purchased brands; or going after an undefined target market. Frequency is most important where there are strong competitors, a complex story to tell, high consumer resistance, or a frequent-purchase cycle.[25] Many advertisers believe a target audience needs a large

media selection finding the most cost-effective media to deliver the desired number and type of exposures to the target audience.

(a) Relationship between Product Trial Rate and Audience Awareness Level

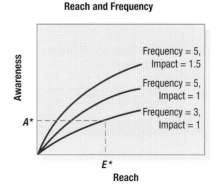

(b) Relationship between Audience Awareness Level and Exposure Reach and Frequency

|Fig. 18.2| △

Relationship among Trial, Awareness, and the Exposure Function number of exposures. Others believe that after people see the same ad a few times, they either act on it, get irritated by it, or stop noticing it.[26]

Another reason for repetition is forgetting. The higher the forgetting rate associated with a brand, product category, or message, the higher the warranted level of repetition. However, advertisers should not coast on a tired ad but insist on fresh executions by their ad agency.[27]

Choosing among Major Media Types

The media planner must know the capacity of the major advertising media types to deliver reach, frequency, and impact. The major advertising media along with their costs, advantages, and limitations are profiled in Table 18.3.

Media planners make their choices by considering the following variables:

- **Target audience media habits.** Radio and television are the most effective media for reaching teens.

TABLE 18.3	Profiles of Major Media Types	
Medium	**Advantages**	**Limitations**
Newspapers	Flexibility; timeliness; good local market coverage; broad acceptance; high believability	Short life; poor reproduction quality; small 'pass-along' audience
Television	Combines sight, sound, and motion; appealing to the senses; high attention; high reach	High absolute cost; high clutter; fleeting exposure; less audience selectivity
Direct mail	Audience selectivity; flexibility; no ad competition within the same medium; personalization	Relatively high cost; 'junk mail' image
Radio	Mass use; high geographic and demographic selectivity; low cost	Audio presentation only; lower attention than television; nonstandardized rate structures; fleeting exposure
Magazines	High geographic and demographic selectivity; credibility and prestige; high-quality reproduction; long life; good pass-along readership	Long ad purchase lead time; some waste circulation; no guarantee of position
Outdoor	Flexibility; high repeat exposure; low cost; low competition	Limited audience selectivity; creative limitations
Yellow Pages	Excellent local coverage; high believability; wide reach; low cost	High competition; long ad purchase lead time; creative limitations
Newsletters	Very high selectivity; full control; interactive opportunities; relatively low-cost	Costs could run away
Brochures	Flexibility; full control; can dramatize messages	Overproduction could lead to runaway costs
Telephone	Many users; opportunity to give a personal touch	Relative high cost unless volunteers are used
Internet	High selectivity; interactive possibilities; relatively low cost	Relatively new media with a low number of users in some countries

- **Product characteristics.** Media types have different potential for demonstration, visualization, explanation, believability, and color. Women's dresses are best shown in color magazines, but high-tech products requiring dynamic presentation such as digital cameras, printers, or mobile phones are best demonstrated on television.

- **Message characteristics**. Timeliness and information content will influence media choice. A message announcing a major sale tomorrow will require radio, TV, or newspaper. A message containing a great deal of technical data might require specialized magazines or mailings.

- **Cost**. Television is very expensive, whereas newspaper advertising is relatively inexpensive. What counts is the cost per thousand exposures.

Given the abundance of media, the planner must first decide how to allocate the budget to the major media types. ⬜ **Tables 18.4** and **18.5** list the breakdown of advertising media expenditures across the MENA region in 2011 by media and market, according to Ipsos MediaCT as published in *ArabAd* magazine. Consumers are increasingly time-starved. Attention is a scarce currency, and advertisers need strong devices to capture people's attention.[28]

Alternative Advertising Options

In recent years, researchers have noticed reduced effectiveness for television due to increased commercial clutter, increased 'zipping and zapping' of commercials, and lower viewing owing to the growth in cable and satellite TV and DVD/VCRs.[29] Furthermore, television advertising costs have risen faster than other media costs. Many marketers are looking for alternative media.[30]

PLACE ADVERTISING **Place advertising**, or out-of-home advertising, is a broad category including many creative and unexpected forms to grab consumers' attention. The rationale is that marketers are better off reaching people where they work, play, and, of course, shop. Some of the options include billboards, public spaces, product placement, and point of purchase.

place advertising (also out-of-home advertising) ads that appear outside of home and where consumers work and play.

Billboards The use of billboards and other forms of outdoor advertising have grown in popularity in the Arab world. Recent statistics show outdoor advertising expenditures to exceed advertising spending on magazine or radio ads (refer to Table 18.4). Billboards have been transformed and now use colorful, digitally produced graphics, backlighting, sounds, movement, and unusual—even three-dimensional—images.[31] Nongovernment organizations (NGOs) have made good use of billboards to bring awareness to issues of social and community good.

TABLE 18.4 ⬜	Advertising Media Expenditures in MENA Region by Media, 2011	
Media	**Amount in millions of USD**	**Amount %**
TV	11510.5	68%
Newspaper	3418.4	20%
Outdoor	934.1	5%
Magazines	706.6	4%
Radio	390.9	2%
Cinema	24.9	0%
Totals	16985.6	100%
Source: *ArabAd*, 22, no. 2, February 2012.		

Country	Amount in millions of USD	Amount %
TABLE 18.5	Advertising Expenditures in MENA Region by Market, 2011	
Pan-Arab	6754.1	40%
Egypt	3290.7	19%
UAE	1726.1	10%
KSA	1442.2	8%
Lebanon	1237.2	7%
Kuwait	902.6	5%
Pan Asian	340.1	2%
Iraq	306.9	2%
Jordan	290.7	2%
Qatar	230.5	1%
Oman	290.7	1%
Bahrain	193.3	1%
Syria	60.9	0%
Total	16985.6	100%

Source: *ArabAd*, 22, no. 2, February 2012.

 Kunhadi   When Hadi was killed in a tragic car accident caused by a reckless driver, his family and friends decided to establish an association to promote youth awareness of road safety. Called Kunhadi, the organization is managed by volunteers. Kunhadi advertisements focus on promoting better understanding by the community of road safety issues and awareness and understanding of the factors contributing to road injuries and deaths (such as speeding, driving while tired, and not wearing a seat belt). Kunhadi places its awareness ads in magazines, on television, and, most importantly, on the roads where such accidents happen. Kunhadi's billboard ads are among the most recalled ads.[32]

Public Spaces Advertisers are placing ads in unconventional places such as movies, airlines, and lounges, as well as classrooms, sports arenas, office and hotel elevators, and other public places. Billboard-type poster ads are showing up everywhere. Transit ads on buses and other forms of mass transportation, and on 'street furniture' such as bus shelters, mass transportation stations, kiosks, and public areas, have grown in popularity in recent years as a valuable way to reach working men and women.

Advertisers can buy space in stadiums and arenas and on garbage cans, bicycle racks, parking meters, airport luggage carousels, elevators, gasoline pumps, airline boarding passes, supermarket bags, and even supermarket produce in the form of tiny labels on apples and bananas. They can even buy space in bathrooms which, according to research studies, office workers visit an average of three to four times a day for roughly four minutes per visit.[33]

Kunhadi effectively uses billboards to create awareness of road safety.

MAKE THE RIGHT CHOICE TAKE A CAB

Advertising at airports has also grown in popularity, with the increase in traffic through airports, the increased time travelers spend at airports, and the dedication of increasingly more space to duty-free shopping areas at airports. Ad agency JCDecaux Airport is world renowned for its work with major airports. It is the number one airport ad agency in the world with 145 airports including Algiers, Sharjah, and Dubai International Airports.

Dubai International Airport & Sorouh In October 2007 Dubai International Airport made the record books with the world's largest advertising banner. The ad for Sorouh Real Estate measured 200 by 100 meters and covered an area of 20,000 square meters, around the size of three football fields. The ad lay flat on the ground along flight paths, where it could be seen from the air by the tens of millions of passengers traveling via Dubai airport. The ad was verified by the *Guinness Book of World Records* and awarded the world record for banner size.

The banner was created to launch Sorouh's Faces campaign, a corporate social responsibility campaign to raise US$1 million for the UAE Red Crescent. The company asked people to send their photos to populate the banner with 1 million photos; in return Sorouh would donate $1 for every photo to the UAE Red Crescent.[34]

PRODUCT PLACEMENT Product placement has expanded from movies to all types of TV shows. Marketers pay fees of US$50,000 to $100,000 and even higher so that their products will make passing appearances in movies and on television. Sometimes placements are the result of a larger network advertising deal, but other times they are the work of small product-placement shops that maintain ties with prop masters, set designers, and production executives.[35]

7-Up soft drink, Aston Martin cars, Visa cards, and Omega watches all initiated major promotional pushes based on product-placement tie-ins with the James Bond film *Die Another Day*.[36] With over US$100 million paid for product-placement rights, some critics called the film 'Buy Another Day.'

Some firms get product placement at no cost by supplying their product to the movie company (Nike does not pay to be in movies but often supplies shoes, jackets, bags, etc.).[37] Firms sometimes just get lucky and are included in shows for plot reasons. FedEx received a great deal of favorable exposure from the movie *Castaway*, starring Tom Hanks as a FedEx employee stranded on an uninhabited island after his FedEx plane crashed over water.[38]

Marketers are finding inventive ways to advertise during real-time television broadcasts. Sports fans are familiar with virtual logos that networks add digitally to the playing field. Invisible to spectators at the event, these ads look just like painted-on logos to home viewers. Ads also appear in best-selling paperback books and movie videotapes. Written material such as annual reports, data sheets, catalogs, and newsletters increasingly carries ads. **Advertorials** are print ads that offer editorial content reflecting favorably on the brand and are difficult to distinguish from newspaper or magazine content. Many companies include advertising inserts in monthly bills. Some companies mail CDs or DVDs to prospects.

advertorials   print ads that offer editorial content that reflects favorably on the brand and resemble newspaper or magazine content.

Academy, The University News Magazine

Academy is a quarterly magazine addressing issues of interest to the growing number of university students in Lebanon. It is distributed for free; the publishers' revenues are primarily made through selling advertising space in the magazine and advertising inserts. The magazine is distributed to university students and faculty in a transparent wrap that also includes product samples. International, regional, and local brand names such as Sunsilk shampoo, Adidas perfume, and HiGeen antibacterial sanitizer have found *Academy* to be a good vehicle, not only to advertise their products but also to distribute product samples.

point-of-purchase (P-O-P)   the location where a purchase is made, typically thought of in terms of a retail setting.

POINT OF PURCHASE   There are many ways to communicate with consumers at the **point of purchase (P-O-P)**. In-store advertising includes ads on shopping carts, cart straps, aisles, and shelves, as well as promotion options such as in-store demonstrations, live sampling, and instant coupon machines. Some supermarkets are selling floor space for company logos and experimenting with talking shelves. P-O-P radio provides FM-style programming and commercial messages to thousands of food stores and drugstores. Programming includes a store-selected music format, consumer tips, and commercials. Some stores have their own close-circuit TV network that airs commercials and long infomercials. Spotmedia is an agency that specializes in innovative in-store digital mediums. Spotmedia's network in Saudi Arabia covers more than 150 stores and 2,000 screens in the highest traffic supermarkets in Saudi Arabia, such as Panda, BinDawood, Farm Supermarket, Al-Raya, Noori, and Danube.[39]

The appeal of point-of-purchase advertising lies in the fact that in many product categories consumers make the bulk of their final brand decisions in the store.

EVALUATING ALTERNATIVE MEDIA   Ads now can appear virtually anywhere consumers have a few spare minutes or even seconds to notice them. The main advantage of nontraditional media is that they can often reach a very precise and captive audience in a cost-effective manner. The message must be simple and direct. In fact, outdoor advertising is often called the '15-second sell.' It's more effective at enhancing brand awareness or brand image than creating new brand associations.

The challenge with nontraditional media is demonstrating its reach and effectiveness through credible, independent research. Unique ad placements designed to break through clutter may also be perceived as invasive and obtrusive, or simply inappropriate and out of place. Negative consumer reaction often results when people see ads in traditionally ad-free spaces, such as in schools, in government buildings, in hospitals, on police cars, and in doctors' waiting rooms.

Not everyone is turned off by the proliferation of advertising. One marketing consultant says, "Kids 18 and under aren't thinking twice about it. Branded merchandise is just the landscape of their lives." Perhaps because of its increased frequency of use, some consumers seem to be less bothered by nontraditional media now than in the past.

Consumers must be favorably affected in some way to justify the marketing expenditures for nontraditional media. Some firms offering ad placement in supermarket checkout lines, fast-food restaurants, physicians' waiting rooms, health clubs, and truck stops have suspended business, in part because of a lack of consumer interest. Nonetheless, there will always be room for creative means of placing the brand in front of consumers. The possibilities are endless: the Marketing Insight: *Playing Games with Brands* describes the emergence of yet another new media trend.

Selecting Specific Media Vehicles

The media planner must search for the most cost-effective vehicles within each chosen media type. The advertiser who decides to buy 30 seconds of advertising on a pan-Arab satellite television can pay around US$1,000 for a new show, between $5,000 and $7,000 for a prime-time show, or more than double that for a hit TV show such as LBCI's *Star Academy* or MBC's *Arabs Got Talent*.[40] These choices are critical; the cost to run an ad few times on television could match the cost to produce it!

In making choices, the planner must rely on measurement services that provide estimates of audience size, composition, and media cost. Audience size has several possible measures:

- **Circulation.** The number of physical units carrying the advertising.
- **Audience.** The number of people exposed to the vehicle (if the vehicle has pass-on readership, then the audience is larger than circulation).
- **Effective audience.** The number of people with target audience characteristics exposed to the vehicle.
- **Effective ad-exposed audience.** The number of people with target audience characteristics who actually saw the ad.

Media planners calculate the cost per thousand persons reached by a vehicle. If a full-page ad in *Nisf el-Dunia* costs US$10,000 and *Nisf el-Dunia*'s estimated readership is 225,000 people, the cost of exposing the ad to 1,000 persons is approximately $44. The same ad in *Hawaa* may cost $5,000 but reach only 75,000 persons, at a cost-per-thousand of $67. The media planner ranks

Playing Games with Brands

Given the explosive popularity of video games with younger consumers, many advertisers have adopted an 'if you can't beat them, join them' attitude. Online games have wide appeal. Today there are millions of teen and adult gamers. Contrary to general perceptions, gamers are not only confined to males. In some countries, women could constitute as much as 40 percent of gamers. Women seem to prefer puzzles and collaborative games, whereas men seem more attracted to competitive or simulation games.

A top-notch 'advergame' can cost between US$100,000 and $500,000 to develop. The game can be played on the sponsor's corporate homepage, on gaming portals, or even at restaurants.

7-Up, McDonald's, and Porsche have all been featured in games. Honda developed a game that allowed players to choose a Honda and zoom around city streets plastered with Honda logos. In the first 3 months, 78,000 people played for an average of 8 minutes. The cost per thousand (CPM) of US$7 compared favorably to a prime-time TV commercial CPM of $11.65. Marketers collect valuable customer data upon registration and often seek permission to send e-mail. On a game sponsored by Ford Escape SUV, 54 percent of players signed up to receive e-mail.

Marketers are also playing starring roles in popular videogames. In the multiplayer videogame *Test Drive Unlimited*, players can take a break from the races to go shopping, where they can encounter at least 10 real-world brands such as Lexus and Hawaiian Airlines. *Tomb Raider*'s Lara Craft tools around with a Jeep Commander. Mainstream marketers such as Apple, Procter & Gamble, Toyota, and Visa are all jumping on board. Spending on in-game advertising and product placement was expected to grow from US$56 million in 2005 to $730 million in 2010, with a typical cost per thousand of $30.

The growing popularity of Second Life and other virtual communities is creating new placement opportunities for marketers. Coca-Cola, IBM, and Toyota are among the first 80 companies that have set up a virtual presence there. The NBA introduced an NBA headquarters in Second Life that included a merchandise store as well as venues and activities sponsored by three existing partners: Cisco Systems, T-Mobile, and Toyota. Getting on board is cheap—it only costs US$1,675 plus $295 a month to occupy an island—and advertisers are thrilled at the opportunity to access the hard-to-reach 18- to 34-year-olds and others that make up the 7.1 million registered users. One online agency executive noted, "If brands go into a space like this, they have to go in with their eyes open about the hazards they might have to deal with."

Sources: "Virtual Worlds Generate Real-Life Benefits for Properties, Sponsors," *IEG Sponsorship* Report, June 11, 2007, pp. 1, 8; Allison Fass, "Sex, Pranks, and Reality," *Forbes*, July 2, 2007, p. 48; Erika Brown, "Game On!" *Forbes*, July 24, 2006, pp. 84–86; David Radd, "Advergaming: You Got It," *BusinessWeek*, October 11, 2006; Stuart Elliott, "Madison's Avenue's Full-Court Pitch to Video Gamers," *New York Times*, October 16, 2005; "Women Get in the Game," www.microsoft.com, January 8, 2004.

each magazine by cost-per-thousand and favors magazines with the lowest cost-per-thousand for reaching target consumers. The magazines themselves often put together a 'reader profile' for their advertisers, summarizing the characteristics of the magazine's readers with respect to age, income, residence, marital status, and leisure activities.

Marketers need to apply several adjustments to the cost-per-thousand measure. First, they should adjust the measure for *audience quality*. For a baby lotion ad, a magazine read by 1 million young mothers has an exposure value of 1 million, if read by 1 million teenagers, it would have an exposure value of almost zero. Second, adjust the exposure value for the *audience-attention probability*. Readers of *Zahrat Al Khaleej* may pay more attention to ads than do readers of *Forbes Arabia*.[41] Third, adjust for the magazine's *editorial quality* (prestige and believability). People are more likely to believe a TV or radio ad and to become more positively disposed toward the brand when the ad is placed within a program they like.[42] Fourth, adjust for the magazine's *ad placement policies and extra services* (such as regional or occupational editions and lead-time requirements).

Media planners are increasingly using more sophisticated measures of effectiveness and employing them in mathematical models to arrive at the best media mix. Many advertising agencies use a computer program to select the initial media and then make further improvements based on subjective factors.[43] MediaSource is a company that provides data and statistics that could prove to be of valuable use in planning and executing media campaigns.

 MediaSource   MediaSource is the leading supplier of media data in the Arab region, offering various services to media professionals. Sold by annual subscription, the company's Mediadisk service provides access to around 1 million media contacts and outlets throughout the world, and is updated every day. Also popular is MediaSource's *Middle East & North Africa Media Guide*, a comprehensive media directory for the region, listing contact details, telephone and fax numbers, postal and e-mail addresses, distribution and circulation data for over 4,500 media outlets across 18 Arab countries, from newspapers to television stations, as well as analysis of the regional media industry. Finally, the company's Lists & Labels service allows subscribers to choose from a selection of popular media lists to access up-to-date contact information for distributing press releases.[44]

Deciding on Media Timing and Allocation

In choosing media, the advertiser faces both a macroscheduling and a microscheduling problem. The *macroscheduling problem* involves scheduling the advertising in relationship to seasons and the business cycle. Suppose 70 percent of a product's sales occur between June and September. The firm can vary its advertising expenditures to follow the seasonal pattern, to oppose the seasonal pattern, or to be constant throughout the year.

The *microscheduling problem* calls for allocating advertising expenditures within a short period to obtain maximum impact. Suppose the firm decides to buy 30 radio spots in the month of September. ▲ **Figure 18.3** shows several possible patterns. The left side shows that advertising messages for the month can be concentrated ('burst' advertising), dispersed continuously throughout the month, or dispersed intermittently. The top side shows that the advertising messages can be beamed with a level, rising, falling, or alternating frequency.

The most effective pattern depends on the communications objectives in relationship to the nature of the product, target customers, distribution channels, and other marketing factors. The timing pattern should consider three factors. *Buyer turnover* expresses the rate at which new buyers enter the market; the higher this rate, the more continuous the advertising should be. *Purchase frequency* is the number of times during the period that the average buyer buys the product; the higher the purchase frequency, the more continuous the advertising should be. The *forgetting rate* is the rate at which the buyer forgets the brand; the higher the forgetting rate, the more continuous the advertising should be.

In launching a new product, the advertiser must choose among continuity, concentration, flighting, and pulsing.

- *Continuity* means exposures appear evenly throughout a given period. Generally, advertisers use continuous advertising in expanding market situations, with frequently purchased items, and in tightly defined buyer categories.

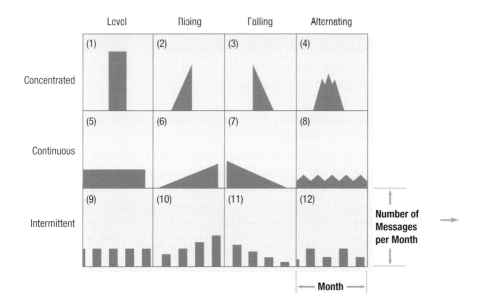

|Fig. 18.3| △

Classification of
Advertising Timing
Patterns

- *Concentration* calls for spending all the advertising dollars in a single period. This makes sense for products with one selling season or related holiday.

- *Flighting* calls for advertising for a period, followed by a period with no advertising, followed by a second period of advertising activity. It is useful when funding is limited, the purchase cycle is relatively infrequent, or items are seasonal.

- *Pulsing* is continuous advertising at low-weight levels reinforced periodically by waves of heavier activity. It draws on the strength of continuous advertising and flights to create a compromise scheduling strategy.[45] Those who favor pulsing believe the audience will learn the message more thoroughly, and at a lower cost to the firm.

Evaluating Advertising Effectiveness

Most advertisers try to measure the communication effect of an ad: that is, its potential effect on awareness, knowledge, or preference. They would also like to measure the ad's sales effect.

COMMUNICATION-EFFECT RESEARCH   **Communication-effect research**, called *copy testing*, seeks to determine whether an ad is communicating effectively. Marketers should perform this test both before an ad is put into media and after it is printed or broadcast.

communication-effect research determining whether an ad is communicating effectively.

There are three major methods of pretesting. The *consumer feedback method* asks consumers questions such as these:

1. What is the main message you get from this ad?
2. What do you think they want you to know, believe, or do?
3. How likely is it that this ad will influence you to undertake the action?
4. What works well in the ad and what works poorly?
5. How does the ad make you feel?
6. Where is the best place to reach you with this message?

Portfolio tests ask consumers to view or listen to a portfolio of advertisements. Consumers are then asked to recall all the ads and their content, aided or unaided by the interviewer. Recall level indicates an ad's ability to stand out and to have its message understood and remembered.

Laboratory tests use equipment to measure physiological reactions—heartbeat, blood pressure, pupil dilation, galvanic skin response, perspiration—to an ad; or consumers may be asked to turn a knob to indicate their moment-to-moment liking or interest while viewing sequenced material.[46] These tests measure attention-getting power but reveal nothing about impact on beliefs, attitudes, or intentions. As we noted in Chapter 4, marketers have begun to explore various neural research methods to study how the brain evaluates different types of ad messages.[47] ▨ **Box 18.1** describes some specific advertising research techniques.

BOX 18.1   Advertising Research Techniques

For Print Ads. Test ads are placed in magazines, which are then circulated to consumers. These consumers are contacted later and interviewed. Recall and recognition tests are used to determine advertising effectiveness.

For Broadcast Ads. *In-home tests*: A video is taken or downloaded into the homes of target consumers, who then view the commercials.

Trailer tests: In a trailer in a shopping center, shoppers are shown the products and given an opportunity to select a series of brands. They then view commercials and are given coupons to be used in the shopping center. Redemption rates indicate commercials' influence on purchase behavior.

Theater tests: Consumers are invited to a theater to view a potential new television series along with some commercials. Before the show begins, consumers indicate preferred brands in different categories; after the viewing, consumers again choose preferred brands. Preference changes measure the commercials' persuasive power.

On-air tests: Respondents are recruited to watch a program on a regular TV channel during the test commercial or are selected based on their having viewed the program. They are asked questions about commercial recall.

Pretest critics maintain that agencies can design ads that test well but may not necessarily perform well in the marketplace. Proponents of ad pretesting maintain that useful diagnostic information can emerge and that pretests should not be used as the sole decision criterion anyway. Widely acknowledged as being one of the best advertisers around, Nike is notorious for doing very little ad pretesting.

Many advertisers use posttests to assess the overall impact of a completed campaign. If a company hoped to increase brand awareness from 20 to 50 percent and succeeded in increasing it to only 30 percent, then the company is not spending enough, its ads are poor, or it has overlooked some other factor.

SALES-EFFECT RESEARCH   What sales are generated by an ad that increases brand awareness by 20 percent and brand preference by 10 percent? The fewer or more controllable other factors such as features and price are, the easier it is to measure advertising's effect on sales. The sales impact is easiest to measure in direct marketing situations and hardest in brand or corporate image-building advertising.

Companies are generally interested in finding out whether they are overspending or underspending on advertising. One approach to answering this question is to work with the formulation shown in △ **Figure 18.4**.

A company's *share of advertising expenditures* produces a *share of voice* (proportion of company advertising of that product to all advertising of that product) that earns a *share of consumers' minds and hearts* and, ultimately, a *share of market*.

Researchers try to measure the sales impact through analyzing historical or experimental data. The *historical approach* involves correlating past sales to past advertising expenditures using advanced statistical techniques.[48] Other researchers use an *experimental design* to measure advertising's sales impact. An example follows.

|Fig. 18.4| △

Formula for Measuring Sales Impact of Advertising

Information Resources Inc.   Information Resources Inc. (IRI) offers a service called BehaviorScan that provides marketers in the United States with data about advertising effectiveness by tracking consumer purchases tied to specific advertising. Consumers in test markets who sign up to be members of IRI's Shoppers Hotline panel agree to have microcomputers record when the TV set is on and to which station it is tuned, and electronic scanners record UPC codes of their household purchases at supermarkets. IRI has the capability to send different commercials to different homes. The company also conducts in-store tests in most chains and in most markets to study the effects of promotions, displays, coupons, store features, and packaging.[49]

A growing number of researchers are striving to measure the sales effect of advertising expenditures instead of settling for communication-effect measures.[50] Millward Brown International has conducted tracking studies for years to help advertisers decide whether their advertising is benefiting their brand.[51] Another research pioneer, Nielsen, has begun tracking commercials electronically.[52]

Sales Promotion

Sales promotion, a key ingredient in marketing campaigns, consists of a collection of incentive tools, mostly short term, designed to stimulate quicker or greater purchase of particular products or services by consumers or the trade.[53]

Whereas advertising offers a reason to buy, sales promotion offers an incentive to buy. Sales promotion includes tools for *consumer promotion* (samples, coupons, cash refund offers, prices off, premiums, prizes, patronage rewards, free trials, warranties, tie-in promotions, cross-promotions, point-of-purchase displays, and demonstrations); *trade promotion* (prices off, advertising and display allowances, and free goods); and *business* and *sales-force promotion* (trade shows and conventions, contests for sales reps, and specialty advertising).

sales promotion a collection of incentive tools, mostly short term, designed to stimulate quicker or greater purchase of particular products or services by consumers or the trade.

Objectives

Sales promotion tools vary in their specific objectives. A free sample stimulates consumer trial, whereas a free management-advisory service aims at cementing a long-term relationship with a retailer.

Sellers use incentive-type promotions to attract new triers, to reward loyal customers, and to increase the repurchase rates of occasional users. Sales promotions often attract brand switchers, who are primarily looking for low price, good value, or premiums. If some of them would not have otherwise tried the brand, promotion can yield long-term increases in market share.[54]

Sales promotions in markets of high brand similarity can produce a high sales response in the short run but little permanent gain in brand preference over the longer term. In markets of high brand dissimilarity, they may be able to alter market share permanently. In addition to brand switching, consumers may engage in stockpiling: purchasing earlier than usual (purchase acceleration) or purchasing extra quantities.[55] But sales may then hit a postpromotion decline.[56]

A number of sales promotion benefits flow to manufacturers and consumers.[57] Manufacturers can adjust to short-term variations in supply and demand and test how high a list price they can charge, because they can always discount it. Promotions induce consumers to try new products and lead to more varied retail formats, such as everyday low pricing and promotional pricing. For retailers, promotions may increase sales of complementary categories (cake mix promotions may drive frosting sales) as well as induce store switching. They promote greater consumer awareness of prices. They help manufacturers sell more than normal at the list price and adapt programs to different consumer segments. Service marketers also employ sales promotions to attract new customers and establish loyalty.

Advertising versus Promotion

A decade ago, the advertising-to-sales-promotion ratio was about 60:40. Today, in many consumer-packaged-goods companies, sales promotion accounts for 75 percent of the combined budget (roughly 50 percent is trade promotion and 25 percent is consumer promotion). Sales promotion expenditures increased as a percentage of budget expenditure annually for almost two decades, although its growth has slowed down in recent years.

Several factors contributed to this rapid growth, particularly in consumer markets.[58] Promotion became more accepted by top management as an effective sales tool; the number of brands increased; competitors used promotions frequently; many brands were seen as similar; consumers became more price oriented; the trade demanded more deals from manufacturers; and advertising efficiency declined.

But the rapid growth of sales promotion created clutter. Very frequent use of money-off coupons deals, and premiums may devalue the product in buyers' minds. So there is risk in putting a well-known brand on promotion over 30 percent of the time.[59] When automobile dealers turn to 0 percent financing, no down payment, and large cash rebates to ignite sales in a soft economy, they typically find it difficult to change consumers' expectations that they are entitled to such discounts when the economy recovers and improves.[60] Dominant brands offer deals less frequently, because most deals subsidize only current users.

Loyal brand buyers tend not to change their buying patterns as a result of competitive promotions. Advertising appears to be more effective at deepening brand loyalty, although added-value promotions can be distinguished from price promotions.[61] Certain types of sales promotions may be able to actually enhance brand image.

American Express   American Express is a leading credit card service provider which competes fiercely with Visa and MasterCard worldwide, with a notable presence in the Arab world. In general, American Express shies away from competing directly with Visa and MasterCard over annual card membership fees or commission charged to retail outlets on credit card purchases. Rather, American Express focuses on the benefits and services rendered through and because of the American Express credit card. One of the benefits offered to cardholders in the Arab world is complementary access to a multitude of airport lounges across the region. Another is accumulation of Membership Reward points on applying for the American Express card and on every use of the card. Through the American Express Selects program, cardholders enjoy thousands of exclusive everyday offers on travel, entertainment, dining, and shopping. Such arrangements between American Express and a number of retail shops, hotels, restaurants, and other venues across the Arab countries are continuously updated on the American Express website, with details about each program and how the cardholder can benefit from such arrangements.[62]

Price promotions may not build permanent total-category volume. One study of more than 1,000 promotions concluded that only 16 percent paid off.[63] Small-share competitors find it advantageous to use sales promotion because they cannot afford to match the market leaders' large advertising budgets; nor can they obtain shelf space without offering trade allowances or stimulate consumer trial without offering incentives. Price competition is often used by a small brand seeking to enlarge its share, but it is less effective for a category leader whose growth lies in expanding the entire category.

The upshot is that many consumer-packaged-goods companies feel they are forced to use more sales promotion than they wish. They blame the heavy use of sales promotion for decreasing brand loyalty, increasing consumer price sensitivity, brand-quality-image dilution, and a focus on short-run marketing planning. One review of promotion effectiveness concluded, "When the strategic disadvantages of promotions are included, that is, losing control to the trade and training consumers to buy only on deal, the case is compelling for a reevaluation of current practices and the incentive systems responsible for this trend."[64]

Major Decisions

In using sales promotion, a company must establish its objectives, select the tools, develop the program, pretest the program, implement and control it, and evaluate the results.

ESTABLISHING OBJECTIVES   Sales promotion objectives derive from broader promotion objectives, which derive from more basic marketing objectives for the product. For consumers, objectives include encouraging purchase of larger-sized units, building trial among nonusers, and attracting switchers away from competitors' brands. Ideally, promotions with consumers would have short-run sales impact as well as long-run brand equity effects. For retailers, objectives include persuading retailers to carry new items and higher levels of inventory, encouraging off-season buying, encouraging stocking of related items, offsetting competitive promotions, building brand loyalty, and gaining entry into new retail outlets. For the sales force, objectives include encouraging support of a new product or model, encouraging more prospecting, and stimulating off-season sales.[65]

SELECTING CONSUMER PROMOTION TOOLS   The promotion planner should take into account the type of market, sales promotion objectives, competitive conditions, and each tool's cost-effectiveness. The main consumer promotion tools are summarized in ▦ **Box 18.2**. *Manufacturer promotions* are, for instance in the auto industry, rebates, gifts to motivate test-drives and purchases, and high-value trade-in credit. *Retailer promotions* include price cuts, feature advertising, retailer coupons, and retailer contests or premiums.[66]

We can also distinguish between sales promotion tools that are *consumer franchise building* and those that are not. The former impart a selling message along with the deal, such as free samples, frequency awards, coupons when they include a selling message, and premiums when they are related to the product. Sales promotion tools that typically are *not* brand building include price-off packs, consumer premiums not related to a product, contests and sweepstakes, consumer refund offers, and trade allowances. Consumer franchise-building promotions offer the best of both worlds: they build brand equity while moving product. The following is an example of an award-winning consumer franchise-building promotion which ran in the United States, but had worldwide media attention.

BOX 18.2 ▦   Major Consumer Promotion Tools

Samples: Offer of a free amount of a product or service delivered door-to-door, sent in the mail, picked up in a store, attached to another product, or featured in an advertising offer.

Coupons: Certificates entitling the bearer to a stated saving on the purchase of a specific product: mailed, enclosed in other products or attached to them, or inserted in magazine and newspaper ads.

Cash Refund Offers (rebates): Provide a price reduction after purchase rather than at the retail shop: consumer sends a specified 'proof of purchase' to the manufacturer who 'refunds' part of the purchase price by mail.

Price Packs (cents-off deals): Offers to consumers of savings off the regular price of a product, flagged on the label or package. A *reduced-price pack* is a single package sold at a reduced price (such as two for the price of one). A *banded pack* is two related products banded together (such as a toothbrush and toothpaste).

Premiums (gifts): Merchandise offered at a relatively low cost or free as an incentive to purchase a particular product. A *with-pack premium* accompanies the product inside or on the package. A *free in-the-mail premium* is mailed to consumers who send in a proof of purchase, such as a box top or UPC code. A *self-liquidating premium* is sold below its normal retail price to consumers who request it.

Frequency Programs: Programs providing rewards related to the consumer's frequency and intensity in purchasing the company's products or services.

Prizes (contests, sweepstakes, games): *Prizes* are offers of the chance to win cash, trips, or merchandise as a result of purchasing something. A *contest* calls for consumers to submit an entry to be examined by a panel of judges who will select the best entries. A *sweepstake* asks consumers to submit their names in a draw. A *game* presents consumers with something every time they buy—bingo numbers, missing letters—which might help them win a prize.

Patronage Awards: Values in cash or in other forms that are proportional to patronage of a certain vendor or group of vendors.

Free Trials: Inviting prospective purchasers to try the product without cost in the hope that they will buy.

Product Warranties: Explicit or implicit promises by sellers that the product will perform as specified or that the seller will fix it or refund the customer's money during a specified period.

Tie-in Promotions: Two or more brands or companies team up on coupons, refunds, and contests to increase pulling power.

Cross-Promotions: Using one brand to advertise another noncompeting brand.

Point-of-Purchase (P-O-P) Displays and Demonstrations: P-O-P displays and demonstrations take place at the point of purchase or sale.

Body by Milk

Although almost every home has milk in the refrigerator, milk consumption by teenagers has been in decline for years. To help teens better understand and appreciate that milk helps them stay lean, toned, and healthy for the "look they want," the Body by Milk promotion from the National Fluid Milk Processor Promotion Board was launched in 2006. Milk mustache ads run in magazines read by teenagers featured four celebrities chosen for their physiques and appeal to teenagers: soccer star David Beckham; New York Yankees baseball player Alex Rodriguez; ice skater Sasha Cohen; and *American Idol* winner Carrie Underwood. The campaign's interactive components included a page on MySpace and banner ads on websites such as Alloy.com, Bolt.com, Facebook, and Gamezone.com. The bodybymilk.com website featured an 'auction' in which visitors could bid each day for merchandise—from companies such as Adidas, the sports apparel maker; Baby Phat, a clothing maker; Fender, the guitar manufacturer; and CCS, which makes skateboards—using barcode or expiration-date data from milk containers. Visitors to the site could also create their own milk mustache ads. The celebrities also appeared in posters that were distributed through school food service directors in more than 100,000 schools, illuminating milk's new message and driving teens to bodybymilk.com for engagement in the Milk Auction. The campaign resulted in much online and offline activity and a change in teen perceptions.[67]

Sales promotion seems most effective combined with advertising. In one study, a price promotion alone produced only a 15 percent increase in sales volume. When combined with feature advertising, sales volume increased 19 percent; when combined with feature advertising and a point-of-purchase display, sales volume increased 24 percent.[68]

Many large companies have a sales promotion manager whose job is to help brand managers choose the right promotional tools. Some, such as Colgate-Palmolive and Hershey Foods, are also going online with their coupons. One million consumers visit www.CoolSavings.com each month for money-saving coupons and offers from name brands, as well as helpful tips and articles, newsletters, free recipes, sweepstakes, free trials, free samples, and more. Makhsoom.com is an Arab website which provides access to daily offers at places to eat, shop, exercise, or relax through online coupons. They have certain focuses, such as products aimed at women (under a 'ladies only' tab on their website) and gifts (under the 'gifts idea' tab). The website was launched in 2010, and is operational in Beirut, Dubai, Abu Dhabi, Doha, Jeddah, Riyadh, and Kuwait City. Makhsoom.com offers daily deals on meals, clothing and apparel, beauty services, and the like by presenting the offer online and noting the original value, the discount, the final price, the number of coupons available, and the time left to purchase the offer.[69]

SELECTING TRADE PROMOTION TOOLS

Manufacturers use a number of trade promotion tools (see ▮ **Box 18.3**).[70] Manufacturers award money to the trade (1) to persuade the retailer or wholesaler to carry the brand; (2) to persuade the retailer or wholesaler to carry more units than the normal amount; (3) to induce retailers to promote the brand by featuring, display, and price reductions; and (4) to stimulate retailers and their sales clerks to push the product.

The growing power of large retailers has increased their ability to demand trade promotion at the expense of consumer promotion and advertising.[71] The company's sales force and its brand managers are often at odds over trade promotion. The sales force says local retailers will not keep the company's products on the shelf unless they receive more trade promotion

Makhsoom.com uses changing daily deals with a limited number of online coupons as its promotional tool.

BOX 18.3 ▒   Major Trade Promotion Tools

Price-Off (off-invoice or off-list): A straight discount off the list price on each case purchased during a stated time period.

Allowance: An amount offered in return for the retailer's agreeing to feature the manufacturer's products in some way. An *advertising allowance* compensates retailers for advertising the manufacturer's product. A *display allowance* compensates them for carrying a special product display.

Free Goods: Offers of extra cases of merchandise to intermediaries who buy a certain quantity or who feature a certain flavor or size.

Source: For more information, see Betsy Spethman, "Trade Promotion Redefined," *Brandweek*, March 13, 1995, pp. 25–32.

money, whereas brand managers want to spend the limited funds on consumer promotion and advertising.

Manufacturers face several challenges in managing trade promotions. First, they often find it difficult to police retailers to make sure they are doing what they agreed to do. Manufacturers are increasingly insisting on proof of performance before paying any allowances. Second, some retailers are doing *forward buying*; that is, buying a greater quantity during the deal period than they can immediately sell. Retailers might respond to a 10 percent-off-case allowance by buying a 12-week or longer supply. The manufacturer must schedule more production than planned and bear the costs of extra work shifts and overtime. Third, some retailers are *diverting*, buying more cases than needed in a region in which the manufacturer offered a deal, and shipping the surplus to their stores in nondeal regions. Manufacturers handle forward buying and diverting by limiting the amount they will sell at a discount, or producing and delivering less than the full order in an effort to smooth production.[72]

All said, many manufacturers feel that trade promotion has become a nightmare. It contains layers of deals, is complex to administer, and often leads to lost revenues.

SELECTING BUSINESS AND SALES-FORCE PROMOTION TOOLS Companies spend billions of dollars on business and sales-force promotion tools (see ▒ **Box 18.4**) to gather business leads, impress and reward customers, and motivate the sales force to greater effort. They typically develop budgets for tools that remain fairly constant from year to year. For many new businesses that want to make a splash to a targeted audience, especially in the business-to-business world, trade shows are an important tool, but the cost per contact might be extremely high compared to other communication options. Gitex, Horeca, and Cityscape attract tens of thousands of attendees every year. Gitex (Gulf Information Technology Exhibition) is an annual consumer computer and electronics trade show; Horeca is a hospitality and food trade show; and Cityscape is an annual real estate investment and development event.

BOX 18.4 ▒   Major Business and Sales-Force Promotion Tools

Trade Shows and Conventions: Industry associations organize annual trade shows and conventions. Business marketers may spend as much as 35 percent of their annual promotion budget on trade shows. Trade show attendance can range from a few hundred people to tens of thousands for large shows. Participating vendors expect several benefits, including generating new sales leads, maintaining customer contacts, introducing new products, meeting new customers, selling more to present customers, and educating customers with publications, videos, and other audiovisual materials.

Sales Contests: A sales contest aims at inducing the sales force or dealers to increase their sales results over a stated period, with prizes (money, trips, gifts, or points) going to those who succeed.

Specialty Advertising: Specialty advertising consists of useful, low-cost items bearing the company's name and address, and sometimes an advertising message that salespeople give to prospects and customers. Common items are ballpoint pens, calendars, key chains, flashlights, tote bags, and memo pads.

DEVELOPING THE PROGRAM In planning sales promotion programs, marketers are increasingly blending several media into a total campaign concept.

In deciding to use a particular incentive, marketers must first determine the *size* of the incentive. A certain minimum is necessary if the promotion is to succeed. Second, the marketing manager must establish *conditions* for participation. Incentives might be offered to everyone or to select groups. Third, the marketer must decide on the *duration* of the promotion. According to one researcher, the optimal frequency is about 3 weeks per quarter, and optimal duration is the length of the average purchase cycle.[73] Fourth, the marketer must choose a *distribution vehicle.* A discount coupon can be distributed in the package, in stores, by mail, in print advertising, or through the web. Fifth, the marketing manager must establish the *timing* of promotion. Finally, the marketer must determine the *total sales promotion budget.* The cost of a particular promotion consists of the administrative cost (printing, mailing, and promoting the deal) and the incentive cost (cost of premium or cents-off, including redemption costs), multiplied by the expected number of units sold. The cost of a coupon deal would recognize that only a fraction of consumers will redeem the coupons.

PRETESTING, IMPLEMENTING, CONTROLLING, AND EVALUATING THE PROGRAM Although most sales promotion programs are designed on the basis of experience, pretests can determine whether the tools are appropriate, the incentive size optimal, and the presentation method efficient. Consumers can be asked to rate or rank different possible deals, or trial tests can be run in limited geographic areas.

Marketing managers must prepare implementation and control plans that cover lead time and sell-in time for each individual promotion. *Lead time* is the time necessary to prepare the program prior to launching it.[74] *Sell-in time* begins with the promotional launch and ends when approximately 95 percent of the deal merchandise is in the hands of consumers.

Manufacturers can evaluate the program using sales data, consumer surveys, and experiments. Sales (scanner) data helps analyze the types of people who took advantage of the promotion, what they bought before the promotion, and how they behaved later toward the brand and other brands. Sales promotions work best when they attract competitors' customers who then switch. *Consumer surveys* can uncover how many recall the promotion, what they thought of it, how many took advantage of it, and how the promotion affected subsequent brand-choice behavior.[75] *Experiments* vary such attributes as incentive value, duration, and distribution media. For example, coupons can be sent to half the households in a consumer panel. Scanner data can track whether the coupons led more people to buy the product and when.

Additional costs beyond the cost of specific promotions include the risk that promotions might decrease long-run brand loyalty. Second, promotions can be more expensive than they appear. Some are inevitably distributed to the wrong consumers. Third are the costs of special production runs, extra sales-force effort, and handling requirements. Finally, certain promotions irritate retailers, who may demand extra trade allowances or refuse to cooperate.[76]

Events and Experiences

According to the IEG Sponsorship Report, global sponsorship expenditures reached around US$44 billion in 2009, an increase of 2.1 percent over 2008 figures despite a weak global economy. North America accounts for about $16.5 billion, with 68 percent of this going to sports; another 10 percent to entertainment tours and attractions; 5 percent to festivals, fairs, and annual events; 5 percent to the arts; 2 percent to associations and membership organizations; and 10 percent to cause marketing.[77]

Daily encounters with brands may also affect consumers' brand attitudes and beliefs. *Atmospheres* are 'packaged environments' that create or reinforce leanings toward product purchase. Law offices decorated with oriental rugs and oak furniture communicate 'stability' and 'success.'[78] A five-star hotel will use elegant chandeliers, marble columns, and other tangible signs of luxury.

Many firms are creating on-site and off-site product and brand experiences. There is Everything Coca-Cola in Las Vegas, M&M World in New York and London, and General Mills Cereal Adventure in the Mall of America in Minnesota.[79] Ferrari World in Abu Dhabi offers the visitors unique experiences at the world's largest indoor amusement park.

Ferrari World In November 2010, Ferrari World Abu Dhabi, the world's largest indoor amusement park, opened in Abu Dhabi. Ferrari World offers its visitors unique experiences inspired by Ferrari and Formula 1 with a number of attractions. These include the Formula Rossa, which reaches a top speed of 240 kilometers per hour; the Junior Grand Prix, which offers visitors the chance to drive a child-sized Ferrari Formula 1 race car; The Pit Wall, an interactive game focusing on strategies created by the technical team and the drivers; and Made in Maranello, a virtual tour of the Ferrari factory in Maranello, Italy. The theme park also features the world's largest Ferrari store, Galleria Ferrari, and a Ferrari boutique that offers personalized souvenirs.[80]

Ferrari World Abu Dhabi offers visitors unique experiences inspired by Ferrari and Formula 1.

Events Objectives

Marketers report a number of reasons to sponsor events:

1. *To identify with a particular target market or lifestyle*. Customers can be targeted geographically, demographically, psychographically, or behaviorally according to events.
2. *To increase awareness of company or product name*. Sponsorship often offers sustained exposure to a brand, a necessary condition to build brand recognition and enhance brand recall.
3. *To create or reinforce perceptions of key brand image associations*. Events themselves have associations that help to create or reinforce brand associations.[81]
4. *To enhance corporate image*. Sponsorship can improve perceptions that the company is likable and prestigious.
5. *To create experiences and evoke feelings*. The feelings engendered by an exciting or rewarding event may indirectly link to the brand.
6. *To express commitment to the community or on social issues*. Cause-related marketing sponsors nonprofit organizations and charities.
7. *To entertain key clients or reward key employees*. Many events include lavish hospitality tents and other special services or activities only for sponsors and their guests. These perks engender goodwill and establish valuable business contacts. From an employee perspective, events can also build participation and morale or be used as an incentive.
8. *To permit merchandising or promotional opportunities*. Many marketers tie in contests or sweepstakes, in-store merchandising, direct response, or other marketing activities with an event.

Despite these potential advantages, the success of an event can still be unpredictable and beyond the control of the sponsor. Although many consumers will credit sponsors for providing the financial assistance to make an event possible, some may resent the commercialization of events.

Major Sponsorship Decisions

Successful sponsorships require choosing the appropriate events; designing the optimal sponsorship program; and measuring the effects of sponsorship.[82]

CHOOSING EVENTS Because of the number of opportunities and their huge cost, many marketers are becoming more selective about choosing sponsorship events.

The event must meet the marketing objectives and communication strategy defined for the brand. The audience must match the target market. The event must have sufficient awareness, possess the desired image, and be capable of creating the desired effects. Consumers must make

Hundreds of millions of dollars are spent annually by businesses on sponsorship of sports clubs.

favorable attributions for the sponsor's engagement. An ideal event is also unique but not encumbered with many sponsors, lends itself to ancillary marketing activities, and reflects or enhances the sponsor's brand or corporate image.[83]

More firms are also using their names to sponsor the arenas, stadiums, and other venues that hold the events.[84] Billions of dollars have been spent over the past few years for naming rights to major sports facilities and for sponsorship of sports clubs. In 2004, Arsenal Football Club and Emirates Airline signed what was at the time a record-breaking deal worth US$159 million for naming rights of the new Arsenal stadium and for the club's shirt sponsorship. Arsenal's stadium in London, England, was to be named the Emirates Stadium until 2021, while the club's shirt will feature the words 'Fly Emirates' until 2014.[85] In another record-breaking deal signed in 2011, Barcelona Football Club signed a 5-year shirt-sponsorship agreement worth $200 million with the Qatar Foundation, a not-for-profit organization concerned primarily with advancing education.[86]

DESIGNING SPONSORSHIP PROGRAMS Many marketers believe it's the marketing program accompanying an event sponsorship that ultimately determines its success. At least two to three times the amount of the sponsorship expenditure should be spent on related marketing activities. Jamba Juice augments its running-race sponsorships with bunches of runners in banana costumes. Any runner who finishes the race before a banana gets free smoothies for a year. Jamba Juice banners are displayed all around and smoothies are sampled by race finishers and onlookers.[87]

Samsung & Asian Cup Qatar 2011   As the official sponsor for the AFC Asian Cup Qatar 2011, Samsung Electronics launched a new mobile application called AFC 2011 Samsung, for Samsung's smart devices, including the Galaxy Tab, Galaxy S, Wave I, and Wave II. The app used content from the AFC's MatchCast, displaying real-time information and statistics from the Player Tracking System, so fans could stay up to date on facts like player pass accuracy and sprint speeds. The mobile application also let users compare player and team performance

"This is the first time that Samsung has introduced a mobile application specifically designed for a sports event," said vice president and head of worldwide sports marketing at Samsung, Gyehyun Kwon. "With the launch of the 'AFC 2011 Samsung' app, we hope to provide a new standard of football viewing experience to football lovers around the world. Samsung will continue to strive to add excitement to sporting events through our core competency, the latest mobile technology." Samsung also ran an online promotion, Be Proud, Support Your Country, on Facebook.[88]

Event creation is a particularly important skill in publicizing fundraising drives for nonprofit organizations. Fundraisers have developed a large repertoire of special events, including anniversary celebrations, art exhibits, auctions, benefit evenings, bingo games, book sales, cake sales, contests, dances, dinners, fairs, fashion shows, parties in unusual places, phonathons, rummage sales, tours, and walkathons. No sooner is one type of event created, such as a walkathon, than competitors spawn new versions, such as readathons, bikeathons, and jogathons.[89]

MEASURING SPONSORSHIP ACTIVITIES As with public relations, measurement of events is difficult. The *supply-side* measurement method focuses on potential exposure to the brand by assessing the extent of media coverage; and the *demand-side* method focuses on reported exposure from consumers.

Supply-side methods approximate the amount of time or space devoted to media coverage of an event; for example, the number of seconds the brand is clearly visible on a television screen or the length of columns in press clippings covering an event that mention the brand. These potential 'impressions' translate into an equivalent value in advertising dollars according to the fees associated with actually advertising in the particular media vehicle. Some industry consultants have estimated that 30 seconds of TV logo exposure during a televised event can be worth 6 percent, 10 percent, or as much as 25 percent of a 30-second TV ad spot.

Although supply-side exposure methods provide quantifiable measures, equating media coverage with advertising exposure ignores the content of the respective communications. The advertiser uses media space and time to communicate a strategically designed message. Media coverage and telecasts only expose the brand and don't necessarily embellish its meaning in any direct way. Although some public relations professionals maintain that positive editorial coverage can be worth five to 10 times the equivalent advertising value, sponsorship rarely provides such favorable treatment.[90]

The demand-side method identifies the effect sponsorship has on consumers' brand knowledge. Marketers can survey event spectators to measure sponsor recall of the event as well as resulting attitudes and intentions toward the sponsor.

Creating Experiences

A large part of local, grassroots marketing is experiential marketing, which not only communicates features and benefits but also connects a product or service with unique and interesting experiences. "The idea is not to sell something, but to demonstrate how a brand can enrich a customer's life."[91] The Marketing Insight: *Experiential Marketing* describes the concept of customer experience management.

Consultants and authors Pine and Gilmore, pioneers on the topic, argue that we are on the threshold of the "experience economy," a new economic era in which all businesses must orchestrate memorable events for their customers.[92] They assert:

- If you charge for stuff, then you are in the *commodity business*.
- If you charge for tangible things, then you are in the *goods business*.
- If you charge for the activities you perform, then you are in the *service business*.
- If you charge for the time customers spend with you, then and only then are you in the *experience* business.

Citing a range of companies from Disney to AOL, they maintain that salable experiences come in four varieties: entertainment, education, aesthetic, and escapist. Consumers seem to appreciate that. One survey showed four of five respondents found participating in a live event was more engaging than all other forms of communication. The vast majority also felt experiential marketing gave them more information than other forms of communication and would make them more likely to tell others about participating in the event and be receptive to other marketing for the brand.[93]

Companies can even create a strong image by inviting prospects and customers to visit their headquarters and factories. Some companies such as Aramco in Saudi Arabia have built corporate museums at their headquarters that display their history and the drama of producing and marketing their products.

Public Relations

Not only must the company relate constructively to customers, suppliers, and dealers, it must also relate to a large number of interested publics. A **public** is any group that has an actual or potential interest in or impact on a company's ability to achieve its objectives. **Public relations (PR)** includes a variety of programs to promote or protect a company's image or individual products.

The wise company takes concrete steps to manage successful relations with its key publics. Most companies have a public relations department that monitors the attitudes of the organization's publics and distributes information and communications to build goodwill. The best PR departments counsel top management to adopt positive programs and eliminate questionable practices so negative publicity doesn't arise in the first place.

public any group that has an actual or potential interest in or impact on a company's ability to achieve its objectives.

public relations (PR) a variety of programs designed to promote or protect a company's image or its individual products.

Marketing Insight

Experiential Marketing

Through several books and papers, Columbia University's Bernd Schmitt has developed the concept of customer experience management (CEM): the process of strategically managing a customer's entire experience with a product or company. According to Schmitt, brands can help to create five different types of experience: sense, feel, think, act, and relate. In each case, Schmitt distinguishes between hard-wired and acquired experiential response levels. He maintains that marketers can provide experiences for customers through a set of experience providers.

1. **Communications.** Advertising, public relations, annual reports, brochures, newsletters, and magalogs (a combination of a magazine and a catalog).

2. **Visual/verbal identity.** Names, logos, signage, and transportation vehicles.

3. **Product presence.** Product design, packaging, and point-of-sale displays.

4. **Co-branding.** Event marketing and sponsorships, alliances and partnerships, licensing, and product placement in movies or TV.

5. **Environments.** Retail and public spaces, trade booths, corporate buildings, office interiors, and factories.

6. **Websites and electronic media.** Corporate sites, product or service sites, CD-ROMs, automated e-mails, online advertising, and intranets.

7. **People.** Salespeople, customer-service representatives, technical support or repair providers, company spokepersons, and CEOs and other executives.

The CEM framework is made up of five basic steps:

1. **Analyzing the experiential world of the customer.** Gaining insights into the sociocultural context of consumers or the business context of business customers.

2. **Building the experiential platform.** Developing a strategy that includes the positioning for the kind of experience the brand stands for ('what'), the value proposition of what relevant experience to deliver ('why'), and the overall implementation theme that will be communicated ('how').

3. **Designing the brand experience.** Implementing their experiential platform in the look and feel of logos and signage, packaging, and retail spaces, in advertising, collaterals, and online.

4. **Structuring the customer interface.** Implementing the experiential platform in the dynamic and interactive interfaces including face-to-face, in stores, during sales visits, at the check-in desk of a hotel, or the e-commerce engine of a website.

5. **Engaging in continuous innovation.** Implementing the experiential platform in new-product development, creative marketing events for customers, and fine-tuning the experience at every point of contact.

Schmitt cites Pret A Manger, the U.K.-based sandwich company, as an example of an attractive brand experience, customer interface, and ongoing innovation: "The Pret A Manger brand is about great tasting, handmade, natural products served by amazing people who are passionate about their work. The sandwiches and stores look appealing and attractive. The company hires only 5 percent of those who apply and only after they have worked for a day in the shop. This process ensures good fit and good teamwork." He also offers Singapore Airlines, Starbucks, and Amazon.com as outstanding providers of customer experiences.

Sources: www.exgroup.com; Bernd Schmitt, *Customer Experience Management: A Revolutionary Approach to Connecting with Your Customers* (New York: John Wiley and Sons, 2003); Bernd Schmitt, David L. Rogers, and Karen Vrotsos, *There's No Business That's Not Show Business: Marketing in an Experience Culture* (Upper Saddle River, NJ: Prentice Hall, 2003); Bernd Schmitt, *Experiential Marketing: How to Get Companies to Sense, Feel, Think, Act, and Relate to Your Company and Brands* (New York: Free Press, 1999); Bernd Schmitt and Alex Simonson, *Marketing Aesthetics: The Strategic Management of Brands, Identity, and Image* (New York: Free Press, 1997).

They perform the following five functions:

1. *Press relations.* Presenting news and information about the organization in the most positive light.
2. *Product publicity.* Sponsoring efforts to publicize specific products.
3. *Corporate communications.* Promoting understanding of the organization through internal and external communications.
4. *Lobbying.* Dealing with legislators and government officials to promote or defeat legislation and regulation.
5. *Counseling.* Advising management about public issues, company positions, and image during good times and bad.

As Marketing Insight: *Managing a Brand Crisis* explains, sometimes PR must spearhead marketing communication efforts to help when a brand gets into trouble.

Marketing Insight

Managing a Brand Crisis

Marketing managers must assume that at some point in time, some kind of brand crisis will arise. Diverse brands such as Firestone tires, Exxon oil, and Toyota have all experienced potentially crippling brand crises. These may be particularly damaging if there are widespread repercussions: (1) a loss in product sales, (2) reduced effectiveness of its marketing activities for the product, (3) increased sensitivity to rival firms' marketing activities, and (4) reduced effectiveness of its marketing activities on the sales of competing, unaffected brands.

In general, the more strongly brand equity and corporate image have been established—especially corporate credibility and trustworthiness—the more likely that the firm can weather the storm. Careful preparation and a well-managed crisis management program, however, are also critical. As Johnson & Johnson's nearly flawless handling of the Tylenol product-tampering incident suggests, the key to managing a crisis is that consumers see the response by the firm as both *swift* and *sincere*. Customers must feel an immediate sense that the company truly cares. Listening is not enough.

The longer it takes a firm to respond, the more likely that consumers can form negative impressions from unfavorable media coverage or word of mouth. Perhaps worse, consumers may find they don't really like the brand after all and permanently switch brands or products. Getting in front of a problem with PR, and then perhaps ads, can help avoid those problems.

Consider Perrier. In 1994, Perrier was forced to halt production worldwide and recall all existing product when benzene, a known carcinogen, was found in excessive quantities in its bottled water. Over the next few weeks, several explanations of the contamination were offered, creating confusion and skepticism. Perhaps even more damaging, the product itself was off the shelves for over 3 months. Despite an expensive relaunch featuring ads and promotions, the brand struggled to regain lost market share, and a full year later found sales less than half what they once had been. Part of the problem was that during the time the product was unavailable, consumers and retailers found satisfactory substitutes. With its key 'purity' association tarnished—the brand had been advertised as "The Earth's First Soft Drink" and "It's Perfect. It's Perrier."—the brand had no other compelling points-of-difference over competitors. The brand never recovered and eventually was taken over by Nestlé SA.

Second, the more sincere the firm's response— public acknowledgment of the impact on consumers and willingness to take whatever steps are necessary to solve the crisis—the less likely that consumers will form negative attributions. When consumers reported finding pieces of glass in some jars of its baby food, Gerber tried to reassure the public that there were no problems in its manufacturing plants but adamantly refused to have products withdrawn from food stores. After market share slumped from 66 percent to 52 percent within a couple of months, one company official admitted, "Not pulling our baby food off the shelf gave the appearance that we aren't a caring company."

Sources: Norman Klein and Stephen A. Greyser, "The Perrier Recall: A Source of Trouble," Harvard Business School Case #9-590-104 and "The Perrier Relaunch," Harvard Business School Case #9-590-130; Harald Van Heerde, Kristiaan Helsen, and Marnik G. Dekimpe, "The Impact of a Product-Harm Crisis on Marketing Effectiveness," *Marketing Science*, 26, March–April 2007, pp. 230–245; Michelle L. Roehm and Alice M. Tybout, "When Will a Brand Scandal Spill Over and How Should Competitors Respond?" *Journal of Marketing Research*, 43, August 2006, pp. 366–373; Jill Klein and Niraj Dawar, "Corporate Social Responsibility and Consumers' Attributions and Brand Evaluations in a Product-Harm Crisis," *International Journal of Research in Marketing*, 21, no. 3, September 2004, pp. 203–217; Rohini Ahluwalia, Robert E. Burnkrant, and H. Rao Unnava, "Consumer Response to Negative Publicity: The Moderating Role of Commitment," *Journal of Marketing Research*, 37, May 2000, pp. 203–214; Niraj Dawar and Madan M. Pillutla, "The Impact of Product-Harm Crises on Brand Equity: The Moderating Role of Consumer Expectations," *Journal of Marketing Research*, 37, May 2000, pp. 215–226; Ronald Alsop, "Enduring Brands Hold Their Allure by Sticking Close to Their Roots," *Wall Street Journal Centennial Edition*, June 23, 1989.

Marketing Public Relations

Many companies are turning to **marketing public relations (MPR)** to support corporate or product promotion and image making. MPR, like financial PR and community PR, serves a special constituency, the marketing department.[94]

The old name for MPR was **publicity**, the task of securing editorial space—as opposed to paid space—in print and broadcast media to promote or 'hype' a product, service, idea, place, person, or organization. MPR goes beyond simple publicity and plays an important role in the following tasks:

- Launching new products.
- Repositioning a mature product.
- Building interest in a product category.
- Influencing specific target groups.
- Defending products that have encountered public problems.
- Building the corporate image in a way that reflects favorably on its products.

marketing public relations (MPR) publicity and other activities that build corporate or product image to facilitate marketing goals.

publicity the task of securing editorial space—as opposed to paid space—in print and broadcast media to promote something.

As the power of mass advertising weakens, marketing managers are turning to MPR to build awareness and brand knowledge for both new and established products. MPR is also effective in reaching local communities and specific groups and can be more cost-effective than advertising. Nevertheless, it must be planned jointly with advertising.[95] Marketing managers need to acquire more skill in using MPR resources.

Clearly, creative public relations can affect public awareness at a fraction of the cost of advertising. The company doesn't pay for media space or time but only for staff to develop and circulate the stories and manage certain events. An interesting story picked up by the media can be worth millions of dollars in equivalent advertising. Some experts say consumers are five times more likely to be influenced by editorial copy than by advertising.

Major Decisions in Marketing PR

In considering when and how to use MPR, management must establish the marketing objectives, choose the PR messages and vehicles, implement the plan carefully, and evaluate the results. The main tools of MPR are described in ▦ **Box 18.5**.[96]

ESTABLISHING OBJECTIVES MPR can build *awareness* by placing stories in the media to bring attention to a product, service, person, organization, or idea. It can build *credibility* by communicating the message in an editorial context. It can help boost sales force and dealer *enthusiasm* with stories about a new product before it is launched. It can hold down *promotion cost* because MPR costs less than direct-mail and media advertising.

Whereas PR practitioners reach their target publics through the mass media, MPR is increasingly borrowing the techniques and technology of direct-response marketing to reach target audience members one-on-one.

CHOOSING MESSAGES AND VEHICLES The Arab world has recently witnessed the establishment of many new private universities and colleges. Suppose a relatively new college wants more visibility. The MPR practitioner will search for stories. Do any faculty members have unusual backgrounds, or are any working on unusual projects? Are any new and unusual courses being taught? Are any interesting events taking place on campus? If there are no interesting stories, the MPR practitioner should propose newsworthy events the college could sponsor. Here the challenge is to create news. PR ideas include hosting major academic conventions, inviting expert or celebrity speakers, and developing news conferences. Each event is an opportunity to develop a multitude of

---

BOX 18.5 ▦   Major Tools in Marketing PR

Publications: Companies rely extensively on published materials to reach and influence their target markets. These include annual reports, brochures, articles, company newsletters and magazines, and audiovisual materials.

Events: Companies can draw attention to new products or other company activities by arranging special events such as news conferences, seminars, outings, trade shows, exhibits, contests and competitions, and anniversaries that will reach the target publics.

Sponsorships: Companies can promote their brands and corporate name by sponsoring sports and cultural events and highly regarded causes.

News: One of the major tasks of PR professionals is to find or create favorable news about the company, its products, and its people and to get the media to accept press releases and attend press conferences.

Speeches: Increasingly, company executives must field questions from the media or give talks at trade associations or sales meetings, and these appearances can build the company's image.

Public Service Activities: Companies can build goodwill by contributing money and time to good causes.

Identity Media: Companies need a visual identity that the public immediately recognizes. The visual identity is carried by company logos, stationery, brochures, signs, business forms, business cards, buildings, uniforms, and dress codes.

stories directed at different audiences. In 2002, the American University in Dubai (AUD) caught the attention of the region and the world when former U.S. President Bill Clinton was the keynote speaker at AUD's fifth commencement ceremony. Very few universities can claim they have made it into so many regional and international headlines only a handful of years after their establishment.

IMPLEMENTING THE PLAN AND EVALUATING RESULTS
MPR's contribution to the bottom line is difficult to measure, because it is used along with other promotional tools.

The easiest measure of MPR effectiveness is the number of *exposures* carried by the media. Publicists supply the client with a clippings book showing all the media that carried news about the product and a summary statement such as the following:

> Media coverage included 3,500 column inches of news and photographs in 350 publications with a combined circulation of 79.4 million; 2,500 minutes of air time on 290 radio stations and an estimated audience of 65 million; and 660 minutes of air time on 160 television stations with an estimated audience of 91 million. If this time and space had been purchased at advertising rates, it would have amounted to $1,047,000.[97]

This measure is not very satisfying because it contains no indication of how many people actually read, heard, or recalled the message and what they thought afterward; nor does it contain information about the net audience reached, because publications overlap in readership. Publicity's goal is reach, not frequency, so it would be more useful to know the number of unduplicated exposures.

A better measure is the *change in product awareness, comprehension, or attitude* resulting from the MPR campaign (after allowing for the effect of other promotional tools). For example, how many people recall hearing the news item? How many told others about it (a measure of word of mouth)? How many changed their minds after hearing it?

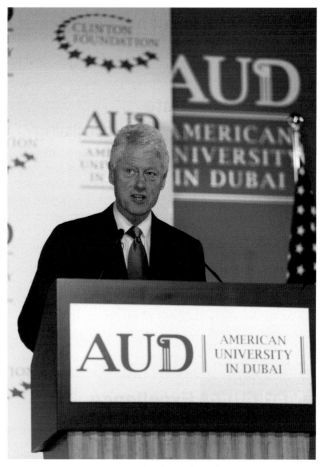

American University in Dubai (AUD) made international headlines when it hosted former President Clinton as commencement keynote speaker.

Summary

---

1. Advertising is any paid form of nonpersonal presentation and promotion of ideas, goods, or services by an identified sponsor. Advertisers include not only business firms but also charitable, nonprofit, and government agencies.

2. Developing an advertising program is a five-step process: (1) set advertising objectives; (2) establish a budget; (3) choose the advertising message and creative strategy; (4) decide on the media; and (5) evaluate communication and sales effects.

3. Sales promotion consists of a diverse collection of incentive tools, mostly short term, designed to stimulate quicker or greater purchase of particular products or services by consumers or the trade. Sales promotion includes tools for consumer promotion, trade promotion, and business and sales-force promotion (trade shows and conventions, contests for sales reps, and specialty advertising). In using sales promotion, a company must

establish its objectives, select the tools, develop the program, pretest the program, implement and control it, and evaluate the results.

4. Events and experiences are a means to become part of special and more personally relevant moments in consumers' lives. Involvement with events can broaden and deepen the relationship of the sponsor with its target market, but only if managed properly.

5. Public relations (PR) involves a variety of programs designed to promote or protect a company's image or its individual products. Many companies today use marketing public relations (MPR) to support the marketing department in corporate or product promotion and image making. MPR can affect public awareness at a fraction of the cost of advertising and is often much more credible. The main tools of PR are publications, events, news, speeches, public service activities, and identity media.

Applications

Marketing Debate

Should Marketers Test Advertising?

Advertising creatives have long lamented ad pretesting. They believe that it inhibits their creative process and results in much sameness in commercials. Marketers, on the other hand, believe that ad pretesting provides necessary checks and balances as to whether an ad campaign is being developed in a way so that it will connect with consumers and be well received in the marketplace.

Take a position: Ad pretesting is often an unnecessary waste of marketing dollars *versus* ad pretesting provides an important diagnostic function for marketers as to the likely success of an ad campaign.

Marketing Discussion

What are some of your favorite TV ads? Why? How effective are the message and creative strategies? How are they building brand equity?

Marketing Excellence

>>Silkor

After graduating from the School of Civil Engineering, University of Southern California, Oscar Tarakjian returned to his hometown Beirut to work as real estate broker. Being an ambitious young entrepreneur, Oscar imported hair removal products from the USA which he bought at US$18 and sold at $155 in Lebanon. Repeating this activity for three months enabled Oscar to earn $50,000, a sizeable profit compared with that obtained from brokering in real estate. Oscar decided to explore the laser hair removal market in Lebanon in anticipation of identifying a business opportunity. He visited hair removal centers and learned that it cost $7,500 for neck and upper back hair removal. Oscar understood that one would need to serve only 20 customers to offset the high cost of the laser machine. In 1997, after conducting careful marketing research, Oscar decided to open Silkor, a hair removal facility, in Beirut. He sold his beloved motorcycle and car and decided to venture his life savings of $20,000 and obtain an equipment loan for $110,000 at a 16 percent interest rate. Silkor was born. Silkor has the connotation of a 'silky body', since Silkor combines the English word 'silk' with the French word 'corps' (meaning body).

Lara, Oscar's sister, an engineering graduate with an Executive MBA from the American University of Beirut (AUB), joined her brother. Like all family-owned start-up entrepreneurs, Oscar, Lara, and their two staff members "did everything; no job was too small; no one was too important. Everyone had to learn all aspects of the business," noted Oscar.

Silkor tried to maintain the standard market prices, and follow a similar 50-50 allocation of fees between Silkor and the dermatologists who conducted the laser operations. Yet, Silkor differentiated itself through offering better customer service to both clients and dermatologists. This included efficient systems for setting up appointments, high level support from nurses to dermatologists, and diligent post-treatment follow-up with customers.

Lara decided to flowchart all tasks the business entailed. She discovered that dermatologists were not ideal to perform the hair removal procedures, which are tedious and time consuming. Doctors felt that laser hair removal operation was beneath their skills; they were late for appointments, rushed the procedures, and con-

Continued on next page >>

Marketing Excellence...continued

>>Silkor

sequently the service and results suffered. Lara noticed that nurses, on the other hand, were more empathic, noting that "they are sweet, patient, know medicine, are really smart, know women, and can talk about sensitive issues comfortably." The service model was subsequently adjusted to rely more and more on nurses, improving the service and lowering the cost at the same time.

Oscar and Lara were creative in their promotional strategies. They hung out in clubs and at parties to promote Silkor by inviting people to their premises. They networked with doctors, raised awareness, and promoted their services. They offered incentives to those who referred customers. Oscar managed to convince media professionals to spread positive word of mouth in return for free laser hair removal. The two young entrepreneurs allocated a relatively small budget for promotional activities. Limited online contests were developed on Silkor's website to attract customers and seek testimonials. In 2002 a major Lebanese TV channel ran a documentary film featuring Silkor's services, earning Silkor wide name recognition and broadening their customer base.

In 2003 the Tarakjians decided to buy new equipment, which allowed them to double their capacity. They also invested more in advertising, recruiting celebrities such as Miss Lebanon, who promoted Silkor on one of the major Lebanese TV stations. In 2004 Silkor expanded by adding a beauty center at the same facility. Success prompted management to open new branches. In 2005 a second branch opened in Kaslik, an upscale northern suburb in Beirut. After a few months a third facility opened in Verdun, another upscale area in Beirut. During the Israeli invasion of Lebanon in 2006, Oscar and Lara decided to expand outside Lebanon, and ventured into Dubai. The Dubai operation replicated the success in Lebanon. Silkor opened a further facility in Abu Dhabi in 2008.

In its very early beginnings, Silkor relied on word-of-mouth, billboards, and PR efforts, especially through documentaries on major TV stations, to create awareness and promote Silkor's services. As it progressed,

Silkor relied more on advertising, with billboards constituting a major portion. A survey conducted in 2009 by Silkor indicated that word of mouth contributed the most in creating awareness and increasing sales volume. Satisfied customers were the real engine that drove Silkor operations. "The Lebanese tend to ask at least 10 friends and relatives when they want to try something new," explained Lara. "In the UAE, it is different: people rely more heavily on the web. Since so many people there are foreigners, the web is their friend and relative."

As Silkor's range of services grew, brand positioning became critical and challenging. Essentially, Silkor was operating at the intersection between three service operators: medical clinics, spas, and beauty institutes; and Silkor was positioned as such. This positioning allowed Silkor to extend its brand offering over a broad range of services. In 2011, Silkor had six facilities in Lebanon, four in the UAE, and one each in Muscat, Qatar, Iraq, and Jordan.

Questions

1. In your opinion, why was word of mouth considered the most effective communication tool for Silkor?

2. What role do you think nurses play in communicating with Silkor customers?

3. Choose a relevant positioning theme for Silkor and explain how you would promote it using the communication media listed in the case and in the chapter.

4. Silkor has ventured into conservative cultures. What challenges does Silkor face in advertising its services? Through information provided in the case, and through additional web search, how did Silkor attempt to tackle such challenges? Comment on the creativity and the success of Silkor's ad campaigns.

Sources: Jessica Jackley, Riad Dimechkie, and Carla Sayegh, "Silkor Laser Medical Center," Case E-353, April 12, 2009, Stanford Graduate School of Business and the Suliman S. Olayan School of Business at the American University of Beirut; www.silkor.com.

In this chapter, we will address
the following questions:

1. How can companies integrate direct marketing for competitive advantage? (pg. 522)

2. How can companies do effective interactive marketing? (pg. 527)

3. How can marketers best take advantage of the power of word of mouth? (pg. 535)

4. What decisions do companies face in designing and managing a sales force? (pg. 541)

5. How can salespeople improve their selling, negotiating, and relationship marketing skills? (pg. 551)

Consumers are now empowered to become as engaged with a marketer's campaign as technology will allow. Some even create their own ads and commercials. Frito-Lay ran a consumer-generated TV ad for its Doritos brand in the most expensive media vehicle around the world: the American Football championship game, the Super Bowl.

Managing Personal Communications: Direct and Interactive Marketing, Word of Mouth, and Personal Selling

Today, marketing communications increasingly occur as a kind of personal dialogue between the company and its customers. Companies must ask not only "How should we reach our customers?" but also "How should our customers reach us?" and even "How can our customers reach each other?" Technological advances allow people and companies to communicate with each other through the internet, fax machines, mobile phones, pagers, and wireless appliances. By increasing communication effectiveness and efficiency, new technologies have encouraged companies to move from mass communication to more targeted, two-way communications. Consumers now play a much more participatory role in the marketing process.

 Newly empowered by the internet, consumers—especially younger ones—are more actively involved with a firm's marketing. When Coke.com was relaunched by Coca-Cola, it went from a typical corporate website, with facts, figures, and annual reports, to an interactive community for consumers to share their creativity. Its MyCoke.com site invites visitors to participate in a virtual world, play games, mix music tracks, read or write blog entries, download screen savers, and more. Knowing that not every online feature will gain an audience right away, Coca-Cola—like other advertisers—has been experimenting to discover which site activities will draw audiences most effectively. A Second Life design contest asked consumers to imagine a vending machine that could dispense the essence of Coca-Cola—entertainment, adventure, or happiness—as well as satisfy curiosities and fulfill virtual wishes. Coke is not alone in getting consumers involved. One of the first major marketers to feature consumer-generated ads was Converse with its award-winning campaign, Brand Democracy, which used films created by consumers in a series of TV and web ads. One of the most popular ads during the 2007 Super Bowl broadcast was a homemade contest winner for Doritos that cost only US$12.79 to make. But not all consumer-generated videos will be winners. When H. J. Heinz ran a Top This TV Challenge inviting the public to create the next commercial for its Heinz Ketchup brand and win $57,000, entrants clearly experimented with previously unfamiliar ad territory. One submission had a teenage boy rubbing ketchup over his face like face cream, another contestant drank ketchup straight from the bottle, and yet another brushed his teeth, washed his hair, and shaved his face with ketchup.[1]

Personalizing communications and creating dialogues by saying and doing the right thing to the right person at the right time is critical for marketing. In this chapter, we consider how companies personalize their marketing communications to have more impact. We begin by evaluating direct and interactive marketing, then move to word-of-mouth marketing, and finish by considering personal selling and the sales force. ▽

Direct Marketing

Direct marketing is the use of consumer-direct channels to reach and deliver goods and services to customers without using marketing middlemen. Direct marketers can use a number of channels to reach individual prospects and customers: direct mail, catalog marketing, telemarketing, interactive TV, kiosks, websites, and mobile devices. They often seek a measurable response, typically a customer order, through **direct-order marketing**.

direct-order marketing
marketing in which direct marketers seek a measurable response, typically a customer order.

Today, many direct marketers build long-term relationships with customers.[2] They send birthday cards, information materials, or small premiums. Airlines, hotels, and other businesses build strong customer relationships through frequency reward programs and club programs.[3]

Direct marketing has been a fast-growing avenue for serving customers, partly in response to the high and increasing costs of reaching business markets through a sales force. Sales produced through traditional direct marketing channels (catalogs, direct mail, and telemarketing) have been growing rapidly, along with direct-mail sales, which include sales to the consumer market, business to business (B2B), and fundraising by charitable institutions.[4]

In the United States, direct marketing has been outpacing retail sales. In 2009, it accounted for almost 54 percent of total advertising spending, when companies spent around US$150 billion on direct marketing per year, accounting for 10.3 percent of GDP. According to the Direct Marketing Association (DMA), these direct marketing expenditures generated around $1.78 trillion in incremental sales. DMA estimates that every $1 spent on direct marketing generates $11.73 return, compared to a return on investment of $5.23 for non-direct marketing expenditures. In 2009, DMA established the Arab Direct Marketing Association (ADMA) in Saudi Arabia, an organization aimed at bringing together different players involved in the field of direct marketing, to provide benefits such as advocacy, reputation management, networking, education, and research.[5]

The Benefits of Direct Marketing

Market demassification has resulted in an ever-increasing number of market niches. Consumers short of time and tired of traffic and parking headaches appreciate toll-free phone numbers, websites available 24 hours a day and 7 days a week, and direct marketers' commitment to customer service. The growth of next-day delivery via courier services provided by companies such as FedEx, UPS, and Aramex has made ordering fast and easy. Aramex's two shopping services have had great customer reception across the Arab world.

Aramex has made shopping from anywhere in the world fast and easy through services such as Shop and Ship, allowing customers to shop from, and deliver to, just about anywhere in the world.

Aramex: Shop and... Shop

Aramex provides the Arab customer with two shopping services: Shop and Ship, and Shop the World. Essentially, these services allow customers to shop from anywhere in the world and ship it to wherever they are: to "buy it over there, and get it over here." Aramex's Shop and Ship service offers the customer a personal mailing address in the United States and the United Kingdom where the customer can receive mail and packages such as internet orders or magazine subscriptions. Aramex then forwards the mailbox contents to the customer's door at competitive rates. At any time, the customer can log into shopandship.com and track the status of an order. Shop the World comes in handy in cases where online stores do not ship to the Arab world, or when the customer doesn't have a credit card, or is not comfortable with making payments online. Instead, the customer requests the desired items from a range of popular fashion catalogs and online retailers, and

Aramex orders it, pays for it, and delivers the goods to the customer. The cost to the customer is simply that of the price of the item, plus shipping, customs, and tax. While the Shop and Ship service is available across all Arab countries, Shop the World is so far available only in Jordan and Egypt.[6]

In addition, many chain stores have dropped slower-moving specialty items, creating an opportunity for direct marketers to promote these items to interested buyers instead.

Sellers benefit as well. Direct marketers can buy a mailing list containing the names of almost any group: left-handed people, overweight people, millionaires. They can customize and personalize messages and build a continuous relationship with each customer. New parents will receive periodic mailings describing new clothes, toys, and other goods as the child grows. Direct marketing can reach prospects at the right moment and be read by more-interested prospects. It lets marketers test alternative media and messages to find the most cost-effective approach. Direct marketing also makes the direct marketer's offer and strategy less visible to competitors. Finally, direct marketers can measure responses to their campaigns to decide which have been the most profitable. One successful direct marketer is Lands' End.

 Lands' End   A direct merchant of traditionally styled, upscale clothing for the family, as well as soft luggage and products for the home, Lands' End sells its offerings through catalogs, on the internet, and, after being acquired by Sears in 2002, in stores. Lands' End was an early adopter of the internet, launching its website in 1995. It offers every Lands' End product and is one of the world's largest apparel websites in sales volume. A leader in developing new ways to enhance shopping experiences, Lands' End lets customers create a 3-D virtual model of themselves and try clothing on by providing critical measurements such as body shape, build, height, weight, and so on. A 'personal wardrobe consultant' is available via text chat or phone to answer questions about clothing preferences. Weekly e-mails with unusual tales and discounts also drive sales. A story of how a customer wore his Lands' End mesh shirt to a preserve for orphaned chimpanzees in the Republic of Ghana led to an increase of 40 percent in sales of the shirt that week.[7]

Direct marketing must be integrated with other communications and channel activities.[8] Citigroup, IBM, Ford, Etisalat, and Emirates Airline have used integrated direct marketing to build profitable relationships with customers over the years. Retailers such as Nieman Marcus, Saks Fifth Avenue, and Bloomingdale's regularly send catalogs to supplement in-store sales. Some direct marketing companies (such as L. L. Bean, Eddie Bauer, and The Sharper Image) made fortunes building their brands in the direct marketing mail-order and phone-order business and then opened retail stores. They cross-promote their stores, catalogs, and websites, for example, by putting their web addresses on their shopping bags.

Successful direct marketers ensure that customers can contact the company with questions and view a customer interaction as an opportunity to up-sell, cross-sell, or just deepen a relationship. These marketers make sure they know enough about each customer to customize and personalize offers and messages and develop a plan for lifetime marketing to each valuable customer, based on knowledge of life events and transitions. They also carefully integrate each element of their campaigns.

We next consider some of the key issues that characterize different direct marketing channels.

Direct Mail

Direct-mail marketing means sending an offer, announcement, reminder, or other item to an individual consumer. Using highly selective mailing lists, direct marketers send out millions of mail pieces each year: letters, flyers, foldouts, and other 'salespeople with wings.' Some direct marketers mail CDs, DVDs, and computer disks to prospects and customers.

Direct mail is a popular medium because it permits target market selectivity, can be personalized, is flexible, and allows early testing and response measurement. Although the cost per thousand people reached is higher than with mass media, the people reached are much better prospects. The success of direct mail, however, has also become its liability; so many marketers are sending out direct-mail pieces that mailboxes are becoming stuffed, leading some consumers to disregard the huge number of solicitations they receive. Some of the biggest users of direct mail have seen their response rates from campaigns drop significantly in recent years.[9]

In constructing an effective direct-mail campaign, direct marketers must decide on their objectives; target markets, and prospects; offer elements; means of testing the campaign; and measures of campaign success.

OBJECTIVES Most direct marketers aim to receive an order from prospects and judge a campaign's success by the response rate. An order-response rate of 2 percent is normally considered good, although this number varies with product category, price, and the nature of the offering. Direct mail can also produce prospect leads, strengthen customer relationships, inform and educate customers, remind customers of offers, and reinforce recent customer purchase decisions.

TARGET MARKETS AND PROSPECTS Most direct marketers apply the R-F-M formula (*recency, frequency, monetary amount*) to select customers according to how much time has passed since their last purchase (*recency*), how many times they have purchased (*frequency*), and how much they have spent since becoming a customer (*monetary amount*). Suppose the company is offering a leather jacket. It might make this offer to the most attractive customers: those who made their last purchase between 30 and 60 days ago, who make three to six purchases a year, and who have spent at least US$100 since becoming customers. Points are established for varying R-F-M levels; the more points, the more attractive the customer.[10]

Marketers also identify prospects on the basis of age, sex, income, education, previous mail-order purchases, and occasions. First-year college students will buy backpacks and laptop computers; newlyweds look for housing, furniture, appliances, and bank loans. Another useful variable is consumer life style or 'passions' such as computers, cooking, and the outdoors.

Companies such as Dun & Bradstreet, Zawya, Middle East and North Africa Financial Network (MENAFN), and AMEInfo.com provide a wealth of data which can be used for B2B direct marketing. Here the prospect is often not an individual but a group or committee of both decision makers and decision influencers. Each member needs to be treated differently, and the timing, frequency, nature, and format of contact must reflect the member's status and role. AMEinfo.com provides a number of useful directories, including a list of directory and mailing-list publishers in a number of Arab countries. The 5 Index offers another useful service in Lebanon.

5 Index   The 5 Index is a business directory database which provides information on businesses in Lebanon. It publishes information on more than 25,000 Lebanese businesses including the headquarters, names of owners, names of key managers, industry classification, year of establishment, turnover, advertising spending, bankers, major suppliers, advertising agency, and the like. This information is updated periodically to ensure its currency. The website offers free basic information on any listed company, and subscribers to the Digital Book service have access to more detailed information. The service allows the subscriber to send e-mail and SMS messages to e-mail addresses and mobile numbers on the 5 Index Digital Book.[11]

A company's best prospects are customers who have bought its products in the past. The direct marketer can also buy lists of names from list brokers, but these lists often have problems, including name duplication, incomplete data, and obsolete addresses. Better lists include overlays of demographic and psychographic information. Direct marketers typically buy and test a sample before buying more names from the same list. They can build their own lists by advertising a free offer and collecting responses.

OFFER ELEMENTS The offer strategy has five elements—the *product*, the *offer*, the *medium*, the *distribution method*, and the *creative strategy*.[12] Fortunately, all can be tested. The direct-mail marketer also must choose five components of the mailing itself: the outside envelope, sales letter, circular, reply form, and reply envelope. Here are some findings:

1. The outside envelope should contain an illustration, preferably in color, or a catchy reason to open it, such as the announcement of a contest, premium, or benefit. A colorful commemorative stamp, a nonstandard shape or size of envelope, and a handwritten address all attract attention.[13]

2. The sales letter, brief and on good-quality paper, should use a personal salutation and start with a headline in bold type. A computer-typed letter usually outperforms a printed letter, and a P.S. increases response rate, as does the signature of someone whose title is important.
3. A colorful circular accompanying the letter usually increases the response rate by more than its cost.
4. Direct mailers should feature a toll-free number and a website where recipients can print coupons.
5. A postage-free reply envelope will dramatically increase the response rate.

Direct mail should be followed up by an e-mail, which is less expensive and less intrusive than a telemarketing call.

TESTING ELEMENTS One of the great advantages of direct marketing is the ability to test, under real marketplace conditions, different elements of an offer strategy, such as products, product features, copy platform, mailer type, envelope, prices, or mailing lists. The following is an example of an informative market test for The Phoenician, a high-end luxury resort.

The Phoenician When research revealed that potential guests would actually welcome communications directly from The Phoenician luxury resort in Arizona, USA, a market test was conducted that increased the emphasis of direct mail and inbound telemarketing (via well-trained reservation agents accessible by phone) with traditional television, newspaper, and magazine image advertising. Specifically, the marketing budget for The Phoenician had been historically allocated as TV (36 percent), newspaper (32 percent), magazine (26 percent), and direct mail (6 percent). The budget was redeployed for the test as TV (32 percent), newspaper (31 percent), magazine (21 percent), and direct mail plus inbound telecontact (15 percent). Adding the combination of integrated direct mail and inbound telecontact yielded a significantly higher conversion rate of prospects, 21 percent versus the historical baseline of 13 percent. Television generated 5 percent of the revenue resulting from the campaign, newspapers 21 percent, magazines 10 percent, and, despite making up only 15 percent of the budget, direct mail plus inbound generated 64 percent of the revenue. The Phoenician concluded that coordinating traditional image advertising and new multichannel direct marketing increased revenue.[14]

Response rates typically understate a campaign's long-term impact. Suppose only 2 percent of the recipients who receive a direct-mail piece advertising Samsonite luggage place an order. A much larger percentage became aware of the product, and some percentage may have formed an intention to buy at a later date (either by mail or at a retail outlet). Furthermore, some may mention Samsonite luggage to others as a result of the direct-mail piece. To better estimate a promotion's impact, some companies measure the impact of direct marketing on awareness, intention to buy, and word of mouth.

MEASURING CAMPAIGN SUCCESS: LIFETIME VALUE By adding up the planned campaign costs, the direct marketer can determine the needed break-even response rate. This rate must be net of returned merchandise and bad debts.

Even when a specific campaign fails to break even in the short run, it can still be profitable in the long run if customer lifetime value is factored in (see Chapter 5) by calculating the average customer longevity, average customer annual expenditure, and average gross margin, minus the average cost of customer acquisition and maintenance (discounted for the opportunity cost of money).[15]

A test of marketing channels for The Phoenician luxury resort in Arizona, USA, showed significantly higher results from boosting the budget for direct mail and inbound telecontact.

Catalog Marketing

In catalog marketing, companies may send full-line merchandise catalogs, specialty consumer catalogs, and business catalogs, usually in print form but also sometimes as CDs, videos, or online. Through their catalogs, Avon sells cosmetics, IKEA sells furniture, EZOrder sells stationery and office supplies, and Get For Less sells a wide range of personal and business electronics and home appliances. Many direct marketers find combining catalogs and websites an effective way to sell. Thousands of small businesses also issue specialty catalogs.

Catalogs are a huge business. In the United States, the internet and catalog retailing industry includes 16,000 companies with combined annual revenue of US$235 billion.[16] The success of a catalog business depends on managing customer lists carefully to avoid duplication or bad debts, controlling inventory carefully, offering quality merchandise so returns are low, and projecting a distinctive image. Some companies add literary or information features, send swatches of materials, operate a special hotline to answer questions, send gifts to their best customers, and donate a percentage of profits to good causes.

Business marketers are making inroads as well. Putting their entire catalog online provides better access to regional and global consumers than ever before, saving printing and mailing costs. Black Box Corporation owes much of its international growth to its customer-service policies, but it doesn't hurt that it also has an award-winning catalog.[17]

 Black Box   Black Box is the world's largest technical services company dedicated to designing, building, and maintaining today's complicated data and voice infrastructure systems. It has 175,000 clients in 141 countries with 173 offices throughout the world, including several Arab countries. Black Box has been recognized as best in its category for 15 years in a row, and in 3 of 4 years it won Catalog of the Year at the Annual Conference for Catalog and Multichannel Merchants. The award recognizes excellence in merchandising, creativity, customer services, and catalog effectiveness. The Black Box catalog, long known as the "Big Book," features 900 pages of data, voice, and networking and communications services and products and is divided into 15 different sections, including comprehensive technical reference information.[18]

Telemarketing

telemarketing the use of telephone and call centers to attract prospects, sell to existing customers, and provide service by taking orders and answering questions.

Telemarketing is the use of the telephone and call centers to attract prospects, sell to existing customers, and provide service by taking orders and answering questions. Telemarketing helps companies increase revenue, reduce selling costs, and improve customer satisfaction. Companies use call centers for *inbound telemarketing*—receiving calls from customers—and *outbound telemarketing*—initiating calls to prospects and customers.

Although telemarketing is a major direct marketing tool, its sometimes intrusive nature led consumer groups in some countries to push their governments to regulate the practice. In the United States, the Federal Trade Commission established a National Do Not Call Registry in 2003, so consumers could indicate they did not want telemarketing calls at home.[19]

Telemarketing is increasing in business-to-business marketing. B2B marketers can use telemarketing to reduce personal selling for contacting their dealers and customers. Some have implemented telemarketing tactics with great success, yielding huge reductions in sales force travel costs (by 50 percent in some documented instances), while still realizing double-digit sales increases at the same time. As it improves with the use of videophones, telemarketing will increasingly replace, though never eliminate, more expensive field sales calls. Effective telemarketing depends on choosing the right telemarketers, training them well, and providing performance incentives.

Other Media for Direct-Response Marketing

Direct marketers use all the major media. Newspapers and magazines carry abundant print ads offering books, clothes, appliances, vacations, and other goods and services that individuals can order via paid or toll-free numbers. Radio ads present offers 24 hours a day. Some companies prepare 30- and 60-minute *infomercials* to combine the sell of television commercials with the draw of information and entertainment. Infomercials promote products that are complicated or technologically advanced, or require a great deal of explanation.[20] Some at-home TV shopping channels are dedicated to selling goods and services on a toll-free number for delivery within 48 hours.

Public and Ethical Issues in Direct Marketing

Direct marketers and their customers usually enjoy mutually rewarding relationships. Occasionally, however, a darker side emerges:

- *Irritation.* Many people don't like the large number of hard-sell, direct marketing solicitations. Especially bothersome are dinnertime or late-night phone calls, poorly trained callers, and computerized calls by auto-dial recorded-message players.
- *Unfairness.* Some direct marketers take advantage of impulsive or less sophisticated buyers or prey on the vulnerable, especially the elderly.[21]
- *Deception and fraud.* Some direct marketers design mailers and write copy intended to mislead. They may exaggerate product size, performance claims, or the purported 'retail price.' There are thousands of complaints each year about fraudulent investment scams or phony charities.
- *Invasion of privacy.* It seems that almost every time consumers order products by mail or telephone, enter sweepstakes, apply for a credit card, or take out a magazine subscription, their names, addresses, and purchasing behavior may be added to several company databases. Critics worry that marketers may know too much about consumers' lives, and that they may use this knowledge to take unfair advantage.

People in the direct marketing industry are addressing these issues. They know that, left unattended, such problems will lead to increasingly negative consumer attitudes, lower response rates, and calls for greater state and federal regulation. In the final analysis, most direct marketers want the same thing consumers want: honest and well-designed marketing offers targeted only to those who appreciate hearing about the offer.

Interactive Marketing

The newest channels for communicating and selling directly to customers are electronic.[22] The internet provides marketers and consumers with opportunities for much greater *interaction* and *individualization.* Few marketing programs are considered complete without some type of prominent online component.

Advantages and Disadvantages of Interactive Marketing

Interactive marketing offers unique benefits.[23] Companies can send tailored messages that engage consumers by reflecting their special interests and behavior. The internet is highly accountable and its effects can be easily traced. Marketers can cut their marketing cost per sale considerably by concentrating on higher-performing ads.[24] Online, advertisers can gauge response instantaneously by noting how many unique visitors, or 'UVs,' click on a page or ad, how long they spend with it, where they go afterwards, and so on.[25]

The web offers the advantage of *contextual placement* and buying ads on sites that are related to the marketer's offerings. Marketers can also place advertising based on keywords from search engines to reach people when they've actually started the buying process. Light consumers of other media, especially television, can be reached online. The web is especially effective at reaching people during the day. Young, high-income, high-education customers' total online media consumption exceeds that of TV.[26]

Using the web also has disadvantages. Consumers can effectively screen out most messages. Marketers may think their ads are more effective than they are if fake clicks are generated by software-powered websites. Advertisers lose some control over what consumers will do with their online messages and activity. Consumers could place a video in undesirable or unseemly places.

But many feel the pros outweigh the cons, and the web is attracting marketers of all kinds. Visa blanketed the web with rich media ads as a major component of its first new brand campaign in 20 years, Life Takes Visa. To reinforce its image as a technology innovator, IBM launched an online campaign for two new B2B platforms, What Makes You Special? and Take Back Control.[27]

To capitalize on advertisers' interest, firms are rushing online services and other support to marketers. Microsoft has invested in a broad range of businesses for placing ads on the web, video games, and mobile phones, and alongside internet search results. The Marketing Excellence case at the end of this chapter, about Yahoo!, describes that company's online efforts and its expansion into the Arab world.

For marketers of automobiles, financial services, personal computers, and telecommunications, marketing activities on the web have become crucial. But others are quickly following. Although beauty pioneer Estée Lauder said she relied on three means of communication to build her multimillion-dollar cosmetics business—"telephone, telegraph, and tell a woman"—she would now have to add the web, which helps to support brands such as its anti-aging treatment, Advanced Night Repair Concentrate.[28] Consumer packaged-goods giants such as Procter & Gamble, General Mills, and Kraft are also significantly increasing their online budgets. PepsiCo spent between 5 and 10 percent of its overall ad budget online in 2006, compared to just 1 percent in 2001, because of its cost-effectiveness.[29] In 2010, PepsiCo made a historic move in redistributing its advertising budget.

PepsiCo   Advertisers rarely sit on the fence when it comes to the Super Bowl, America's most popular sporting event of the year. They can either afford to pay the staggering US$2.5–3 million for the most coveted 30-second television spot or they can't. If they can, the benefits are enormous; revenue from commercials screened during the 2010 game exceeded $210 million. It is for precisely this reason that PepsiCo poured millions of dollars into advertising during the game for 23 consecutive years. Britney Spears, Cindy Crawford, Farrah Fawcett, Oprah Winfrey, and Will Ferrell are just some of the famous faces to have sipped Pepsi during the Super Bowl. At least that was the case until 2010. For the first time in over two decades, the drinks giant decided that instead of parting with the $33 million it had spent during the 2009 game, it would spend the money on its online marketing campaign, the Refresh Project. The Refresh Project gave PepsiCo's readers the opportunity to vote on which health, environment, culture, or education organization deserved to be given up to $250,000 in grants. The new campaign wasn't just about saving money—although it did save them $13 million—it was about reaching an audience of billions across 365 days of the year. "Pepsi's decision was hugely significant," says Elie Khouri, CEO of Omnicom Media Group's Middle East and North Africa operations. "Digital advertising is growing, it's the future and it's what everyone has got their eyes on," he adds.[30]

Marketers must go where the customers are, and increasingly that's online. Customers define the rules of engagement, however, and insulate themselves with the help of agents and intermediaries if they so choose. Customers define what information they need, what offerings they're interested in, and what they're willing to pay.[31] According to Mohamad Mourad, Google's managing director for emerging markets, the average Arab consumer currently spends 29 percent of their media time online, compared to 28 percent watching television. Among the different age segments, Arab youngsters spend much more time online compared to watching television. This is a critical piece of information for marketers as they try to promote their products, communicate their messages, and reach out to their customers, given that two-thirds of the Arab population is under the age of 25.[32]

A 2010 study conducted by MasterCard, covering 15 countries including the UAE, revealed continuous growth in the use of the internet as a medium for consumer shopping, signifying the role that interactive marketing can play in reaching out to this growing pool of shoppers.

Online Shopping in the UAE   In late 2010, MasterCard concluded a survey of 8,500 consumers from 15 markets across the Asia-Pacific, Middle East, and Africa, to gain information about online shopping habits. The survey included one Arab country—the UAE—and revealed some interesting insights. According to the study, the number of people in the UAE who used the internet to make purchases rose to 42 percent in 2010, up from 29 percent in 2009. Online shopping was led by the 25–44 age group, though the 35–44 age group purchased more items, with more frequency, than others. Women were increasingly using the internet to shop, with 40 percent of respondents saying they bought online in 2010, compared to 33 percent in 2009. In addition, 20 percent of the UAE sample said they used mobile devices to shop online, a trend consistent with other countries covered in the survey. Leading the purchases in the UAE were airline tickets, with 74 percent of respondents buying them online, followed by hotel bookings at 66 percent, music concert and performing arts tickets at 60 percent, and cinema tickets at 48 percent. Around 32 percent of those surveyed bought home appliances and electronic products online, while 34 percent bought clothing and accessories.[33]

Online shopping varies significantly across Arab countries. According to the Effective Measures Survey shared at the ArabNet 2011 forum, while online shopping reaches 41 percent across Gulf Cooperation Council countries, it is at 28 percent in the Levant, 21 percent in North Africa, and less than 2 percent in Egypt.[34]

Online advertising was estimated at a little less than 6 percent of global ad spending in 2006. By 2009 it had jumped to around 10 percent to become a US$25 billion business, and reached $26 billion (around a 13 percent share) in 2010. The United Kingdom leads the world in terms of market share of online advertising, accounting for around 23 percent of total advertising expenditures. For the first time ever, U.K. online advertising even overtook television advertising expenditures to reach US$2.8 billion (compared to $2.6 billion for television advertising). In the Arab world, around $56 million was spent on online advertising in 2009, accounting for only a 1 percent share of total advertising spending. However, this figure is expected to grow more than fourfold to $266 million by 2013. Samih Toukan, CEO of Jabbar Internet Group, which owns online businesses such as the e-commerce website Souq.com, estimates that online advertising spending may reach $400 million by 2015. Helping fuel this growth is the proliferation of broadband internet and the emergence of rich media ads that combine animation, video, and sound with interactive features.[35]

Axe   The world's most popular male grooming brand, Axe, has won numerous advertising awards. Much of its success can also be attributed to its edgy online efforts. Winner of *Business 2.0*'s 2003 Sweet Spot Award for Most Innovative Campaign, Unilever's Axe Deodorant body spray was launched in 2002, targeting the 18- to 24-year-old male audience interested in improving their appeal to the opposite sex. The centerpiece of the effort was a set of commercials said to be home videos and playing only on Axe's website (www.theaxeeffect.com). In each, a pretty young woman is instantly attracted by a whiff and scent of Axe deodorant. Banner ads on targeted websites were linked to Axe's website to encourage viewership of the video clips. Four months into the campaign, 1.7 million people had visited the site and one-third reported they had been sent there by friends. Engaging young adult males on their own turf, subsequent online efforts used streaming videos, downloads to mobile phones, blogs, chat rooms, and video games equally successfully. An ad costing US$200,000 featuring men in a small town in Alaska who use Axe to attract women was viewed more than 10 million times. Axe has also used content-integration deals as launch platforms, featuring websites built around TV shows such as the "Gamekillers" special with MTV. A global campaign, Bom Chika Wah Wah, coincided with Axe's ascent to become the leader in what many people had thought was the mature $2.4 billion deodorant category.[36]

Different people have different attitudes and experiences with the web. The Marketing Memo: *Segmenting Tech Users* profiles different groups and their usage of technology. **Box 19.1** on page 530 provides a recent summary of typical daily internet activities.

Segmenting Tech Users

Group Name	Percentage of Adults	What you Need to Know about Them	Key Demographic Facts
Motivated by Mobility (39%)			
Digital Collaborators	8%	With the most tech assets, Digital Collaborators use them to work with and share their creations with others. They are enthusiastic about how ICTs help them connect with others and confident in how to manage digital devices and information.	Mostly male (56%), late 30s, well-educated and well-off
Ambivalent Networkers	7%	Ambivalent Networkers have folded mobile devices into how they run their social lives, whether through texting or social networking tools online. They also rely on ICTs for entertainment. But they also express worries about connectivity; some find that mobile devices are intrusive and many think it is good to take a break from online use.	Primarily male (60%), they are young (late 20s) and ethnically diverse
Media Movers	7%	Media Movers have a wide range of online and mobile habits, and they are bound to find or create an information nugget, such as a digital photo, and pass it on. These social exchanges are central to this group's use of ICTs. Cyberspace, as a path to personal productivity or an outlet for creativity, is less important.	Males (56%) in their mid-30s, many with children and in middle income range
Roving Nodes	9%	Roving Nodes are active managers of their social and work lives using their mobile device. They get the most out of basic applications with their assets such as e-mail or texting and find them great for arranging the logistics of their lives and enhancing personal productivity.	Mostly women (56%) in their late 30s, well educated and well-off
Mobile Newbies	8%	This group rates low on tech assets, but its members really like their mobile phones. Mobile Newbies, many of whom acquired a mobile in the past year, like how the device helps them be more available to others. They would be hard pressed to give up the mobile phone.	Mainly women (55%) about age 50, lower educational and income levels
Stationary Media Majority (61%)			
Desktop Veterans	13%	This group of older, veteran online users is content to use a high-speed connection and a desktop computer to explore the internet and stay in touch with friends, placing their mobile phone and mobile applications in the background.	Mainly men (55%) in mid-40s, well-educated and well-off economically
Drifting Surfers	14%	Many have the requisite tech assets, such as broadband or a mobile phone, but Drifting Surfers are infrequent online users. When they use technology, it is for basic information gathering. It wouldn't bother the typical Drifting Surfer to give up the internet or mobile phone.	Majority women (56%) in their early 40s, middle income and average education levels
Information Encumbered	10%	Most people in this group suffer from information overload and think taking time off from the internet is a good thing. The Information Encumbered are firmly rooted in old media to get information.	Two-thirds men, in their early 50s, average education, lower-middle income
Tech-Indifferent	10%	Members of this group are not heavy internet users and although most have mobile phones, they don't like their intrusiveness. The Indifferent could easily do without modern gadgets and services.	Mainly women (55%) in their late 50s, low-income and education levels
Off the Network	14%	Members of this group have neither mobile phones nor online access, and tend to be older and low-income. But a few have experience with ICTs; some used to have online access and as many as one in five used to have a mobile phone.	Low-income senior women, high share of African Americans

Source: "The Mobile Difference—Tech User Types," Pew Internet & American Life Project, March 31, 2009, www.pewinternet.org/Infographics/The-Mobile-Difference—Tech-User-Types.aspx.

BOX 19.1 — Top Daily Internet Activities

[Percentage of internet users who reported doing the activity 'yesterday.']

Activity	Total Internet users
Send or read e-mail	62
Use a search engine to find information	49
Get news online	43
Use a social networking site	38
Check weather reports and forecasts online	34
Do any banking online	26
Watch a video on a video-sharing site	23
Look for news or information about politics	19
Look for information on Wikipedia	17
Send instant messages	15
Visit a local, state, or federal government website	12
Get financial information online	12
Use online classified ads or sites like Craig's List	11
Look online for info about a job	10
Buy a product online	8
Buy or make a reservation for travel	5
Look for religious or spiritual information online	5
Create or work on your own online journal or blog	4
Rate a product, service, or person	4
Participate in an online auction	4
Download a podcast so you can listen to it or view it later	3
Make a donation to a charity online	1

Source: Pew Internet & American Life Project Surveys, www.pewinternet.org, released 15 December 2010; Table adapted from www.census.gov/compendia/statab/2011/tables/11s1159.xls.

Placing Ads and Promotions Online

A company chooses which forms of interactive marketing will be most cost-effective in achieving communication and sales objectives.

WEBSITES Companies must design websites that embody or express their purpose, history, products, and vision.[37] A key challenge is designing a site that's attractive on first viewing and interesting enough to encourage repeat visits.[38] Rayport and Jaworski propose that effective sites feature seven design elements they call the 7Cs (see Box 19.2):[39] To encourage repeat visits, companies must pay special attention to context and content factors and embrace another 'C:' constant change.[40]

Visitors will judge a site's performance on ease of use and physical attractiveness. Ease of use has three attributes: (1) the site downloads quickly, (2) the first page is easy to understand, and (3) it is easy to navigate to other pages that open quickly. Physical attractiveness is determined by these factors: (1) individual pages are clean and not crammed with content, (2) typefaces and font sizes are very readable, and (3) the site makes good use of color (and sound). Websites must also be sensitive to security and privacy-protection issues.[41]

MICROSITES A **microsite** is a limited area on the web managed and paid for by an external advertiser/company. Microsites are individual web pages or clusters of pages that function as

microsite a limited area on the web managed and paid for by an external advertiser/company.

BOX 19.2 ⬛ Seven Key Design Elements of an Effective Website

- *Context.* Layout and design
- *Content.* Text, pictures, sound, and video the site contains
- *Community.* How the site enables user-to-user communication
- *Customization.* Site's ability to tailor itself to different users or to allow users to personalize the site
- *Communication.* How the site enables site-to-user, user-to-site, or two-way communication
- *Connection.* Degree that the site is linked to other sites
- *Commerce.* Site's capabilities to enable commercial transactions

Source: Jeffrey F. Rayport and Bernard J. Jaworski, *e-commerce* (New York: McGraw-Hill, 2001), p. 116.

---

supplements to a primary site. They're particularly relevant for companies selling low-interest products. People rarely visit an insurance company's website, but the company can create a microsite on used-car sites that offers advice for buyers of used cars and at the same time a good insurance deal. Some microsites have become huge online hits.

Burger King's Obedient Chicken   To compete with McDonald's wholesome, family-friendly image, Burger King adopted a youthful, irreverent personality and menu-driven positioning via its longtime "Have It Your Way" slogan. To promote its TenderCrisp sandwich, ad agency Crispin, Porter & Bogusky created a website featuring an "obedient chicken," an actor dressed in a chicken costume who performed a wide range of weird and crazy actions based on a user's typed commands: dust furniture, play air guitar, or, naturally, lay an egg! The site employed prerecorded footage but looked like an interactive webcam. Within a week of launch, about 54 million people had checked out the chicken for an average of 8 minutes. This program was designed not only to entertain and connect with target market 14- to 25-year-olds, but to help reinforce the brand's customization message and contemporary image. Said one Burger King executive, "We're really trying to do something different and not just give consumers a straight ad over and over."[42]

---

paid-search sponsored search results, where companies pay to have ads for products or services displayed when keywords are entered into a search engine.

pay-per-click ads see 'paid-search'.

SEARCH ADS A hot growth area in interactive marketing is **paid-search** or **pay-per-click ads**, which now account for almost half of all online ad spending.[43] Thirty-five percent of all searches are reportedly for products or services. The search terms serve as a proxy for the consumer's consumption interests and trigger relevant links to product or service offerings alongside search results from Google, MSN, and Yahoo! Advertisers pay only if people click on the links, but marketers believe consumers who have already expressed interest by virtue of the search are prime prospects.

The cost per click depends on how high the link is ranked and the popularity of the keyword. Average click-through is about 2 percent, much more than for comparable online ads.[44] At an average of 35 cents, paid search is a lot cheaper than that in other media (such as telephone directory or Yellow Pages). One Samsung executive estimated it was 50 times cheaper to reach 1,000 people online than on TV, and the company shifted 10 percent of its advertising budget to the internet.[45]

Some believe the internet is moving from the era of search to the era of discovery, thanks to recommender sites and systems that suggest music, movies, websites, or whatever is meaningful to users whether they've heard of it or even ask.

display ads small, rectangular boxes containing text and/or a picture that companies pay to place on relevant websites.

banner ads (internet) small, rectangular boxes containing text and perhaps a picture to support a brand.

DISPLAY ADS Display ads or **banner ads** are small, rectangular boxes containing text and perhaps a picture that companies pay to place on relevant websites. Earlier in the chapter we referred to websites such as Zawya.com, MENAFN.com, and AMEinfo.com. Moody's Analytics (provider of risk management solutions for Arab investors) used a display ad on Zawya.com that display as a rectangular box on Zawya's homepage. A click on that display ad box would open a new window featuring Moody's Analytics website. Forex.com (provider of global foreign exchange secured online trading service) and Dragon Options (an online financial trading platform) posted similar display ads on the AMEinfo.com and MENAFN.com websites, which are frequented by businesses and investors. The larger the audience, the more the placement costs. Some banners are accepted on a barter basis. In the early days of the internet, viewers clicked on 2 to 3 percent of the banner ads they saw, but that percentage quickly plummeted and advertisers began to explore other forms of communication.[46]

Dispay ads still hold great promise compared to popular search ads. Given that internet users spend only 5 percent of their time online actually searching for information, there are many opportunities to reach and influence consumers while they travel the web. But ads need to be more attention getting and influential, better targeted, and more closely tracked.[47]

The emergence of *behavioral targeting* is allowing companies to track the online behavior of target customers to find the best match between ad and prospect. For example, if a person clicks on three websites related to auto insurance, then visits an unrelated site for sports or entertainment, auto insurance ads may show up on that site, in addition to the auto insurance sites. This practice ensures that ads are readily apparent for a potential customer likely to be in the market. Although critics worry about companies knowing too much about customers, Microsoft claims behavioral targeting can increase the likelihood a visitor clicks an ad by as much as 76 percent.[48]

INTERSTITIALS **Interstitials** are advertisements, often with video or animation, that pop up between changes on a website. Ads for Johnson & Johnson's Tylenol headache reliever would pop up on brokers' websites whenever the stock market fell by 100 points or more. Because consumers found pop-up ads intrusive and distracting, many computer users installed software to block these ads.[49]

INTERNET-SPECIFIC ADS AND VIDEOS With user-generated content sites such as YouTube, MySpace Video, and Google Video, consumers and advertisers can upload ads and videos to be shared virally by millions of people.

> **interstitials** advertisements, often with video or animation, that pop up between changes on a website.

BMW Films BMW is positioned as the Ultimate Driving Machine on the basis of its dual benefits of luxury and high performance. Beginning in 2001, it created *The Hire* series, eight short films by famous action movie directors such as John Woo, Guy Ritchie, and Ang Lee and starring actors such as Mickey Rourke and Madonna. Each was less than 10 minutes long and could be downloaded only from a corporate website, www.bmwfilms.com, and viewed on the internet. With a budget of US$3 million per film, the films were cinematic in look, but also designed to showcase the unique qualities of different BMW models. To build traffic to the site, BMW used television spots that mirrored movie trailers. The response was overwhelming. According to BMW's ad agency, 55.1 million people viewed *The Hire* series, and tremendous PR buzz resulted. Many film critics even gave the films rave reviews. And by having visitors register before downloading the films, BMW was able to collect contact information for a large number of potential buyers, many of whom were younger and not necessarily as well represented in BMW's prior marketing efforts.[50]

> **sponsorship** financial support of an event or activity in return for recognition and acknowledgment as the sponsor.

Online videos can be cost-effective—costing US$50,000 to $200,000—and marketers can take more freedom with them. While the marketer usually posts the ad on its own site, it is likely that attractive and entertaining ads find their way to YouTube where they might eventually be seen by literally millions of people.[51]

SPONSORSHIPS Many companies get their name on the internet by sponsoring special content on websites that carry news, financial information, and so on. **Sponsorships** are best placed in well-targeted sites that offer relevant information or service. The sponsor pays for showing the content and in turn receives acknowledgment as the sponsor of that particular service on the site. For example, in 2011, Bank of Sharjah sponsored the online search service of the

BMW's online videos had cinematic production quality and stars to match. The ads showcased various BMW models and won an enthusiastic response from consumers and film critics alike.

online business intelligence platform Zawya.com. Bank of Sharjah's logo was clearly displayed next to the search bar on all of Zawya.com's webpages, which are frequented by nearly 1 million professionals.

A popular vehicle for sponsorship is *podcasts*, digital media files created for playback on portable MP3 players, laptops, or PCs. Sponsors pay roughly US$25 per thousand listeners to run a 15- or 30-second audio ad at the beginning of the podcast. Although these rates are higher than for popular radio shows, because podcasts are able to reach very specific market segments, analysts expect their popularity to grow.[52]

alliances and affiliate programs when one company works with another one and they advertise each other.

ALLIANCES When one internet company works with another, they end up advertising each other through online **alliances and affiliate programs**. Amazon has almost 1 million affiliates that post its banners on their websites. Companies can also undertake guerrilla marketing actions to publicize their site and generate word of mouth. When Yahoo! started its Denmark site, it distributed apples at the country's busiest train station with the message that in the next few hours a trip to New York could be won on the Yahoo! site. It also managed to get the offer mentioned in Danish newspapers. Companies can offer to push content and ads to targeted audiences who agree to receive them and are presumably more interested in the product or product category.

ONLINE COMMUNITIES Many companies sponsor online communities whose members communicate through postings, instant messaging, and chat discussions about special interests related to the company's products and brands. These communities can provide companies with useful, hard-to-get information. When GlaxoSmithKline prepared to launch its first weight-loss drug, Alli, it sponsored a weight-loss community. The firm felt the feedback it gained was more valuable than what it could have received from traditional focus groups. Kraft learned from its online group that members really wanted the ability to control how much they ate, giving rise to 100-calorie bags and US$100 million in sales. A key to success with online communities is to create individual and group activities that help form bonds among community members.[53]

E-MAIL E-mail uses only a fraction of the cost of a 'd-mail,' or direct mail, campaign. Microsoft spent approximately US$70 million a year on paper-driven campaigns. It switched to sending out 20 million pieces of e-mail every month at a significant savings. Consumers are besieged by e-mails though, and many employ spam filters. Following are some important guidelines for productive e-mail campaigns, followed by pioneering e-mail marketers:[54]

- *Give the customer a reason to respond.* Offer powerful incentives for reading e-mail pitches and online ads, such as e-mail trivia games, scavenger hunts, and instant-win sweepstakes.
- *Personalize the content of your e-mails.* IBM's iSource has been distributed directly to customers' office e-mail each week, delivering only 'the news they choose' in announcements and weekly updates. Customers who agree to receive the newsletter select from topics listed on an interest profile.
- *Offer something the customer can't get via direct mail.* Because e-mail campaigns can be carried out quickly, they can offer time-sensitive information. Airline companies send frequent e-mails pitching last-minute cheap airfares. This tactic is practiced by both high-end airlines such as Emirates Airline and by low-cost airlines such as Air Arabia.
- *Make it easy for customers to 'unsubscribe.'* Online customers demand a positive exit experience. According to a Burston-Marsteller and Roper Starch Worldwide study, the top 10 percent of web users who communicate much more often online typically share their views by e-mail with 11 friends when satisfied, but contact 17 friends when dissatisfied.[55]

To increase the effectiveness of e-mails, some researchers are employing 'heat mapping,' by which they can measure what people read on a computer screen by using cameras attached to a computer that track eye movements. One study showed that clickable graphic icons and buttons that linked to more details of a marketing offer increased click-through rates by 60 percent compared to links that used an internet address.[56]

MOBILE MARKETING According to eMarketer, mobile ad spending was estimated to grow from US$2.7 billion in 2007 to over $19 billion in 2011, most of which went into text messages. SMS messaging has the lion's share of mobile marketing with around 6.1 trillion advertising messages sent in 2010. Text message advertising was expected to exceed $14 billion in 2011. But new smart phones make it increasingly easy to blend mobile phones with wireless internet service. With mobile phones' ubiquitous nature and marketers' ability to personalize messages based on demographics, the appeal of mobile marketing is obvious. But some still wonder how consumers will react to ads on the 'third screen.'[57]

Some marketers are testing the waters. Every 2-minute mobile episode of Fox's *Prison Break: Proof of Innocence* starts with a 10-second message that showcases Toyota's new subcompact sedan, Yaris. Unilever ran a campaign on mobile phones for its I Can't Believe It's Not Butter brand that placed small banner ads on sites such as the Weather Channel and asked consumers to click on a link to visit the Kitchen of Love website featuring spokesman Fabio, the international fashion model.[58]

Marketing and advertising experts in the Arab world believe that mobile marketing will witness massive growth, given the high mobile penetrations in several Arab countries and the rapid increase in mobile penetration in others (for example, the UAE has a mobile penetration of more than 200 percent, while that of Saudi Arabia and Egypt, the two most populous Arab countries, record 138 and 80 percent respectively). Ahmed Nassef, vice president and managing director of Yahoo! Middle East, believes that by 2016 more people will connect to the internet via mobile devices than via PCs.[59]

Word of Mouth

Word of mouth has been increasingly taking center stage in terms of importance in generating positive (or sometimes negative) communication messages about a company or a brand. This is particularly true as such messages are seen as coming from independent sources that do not have a stake in promoting this company or that brand. That said, word of mouth is believed to have much more relevance in the Arab world, given the tight family and social networks that characterizes the Arab culture. In addition to the traditional means of word of mouth dissemination, social networks such as mySpace, Facebook, and Twitter have become an important force in both business-to-consumer and business-to-business marketing.[60] Even media giants such as Al Rabiya and Al Jazeera came to realize the key role that social networks play in feeding in breaking news from the Arab streets.

A key aspect of social networks is the number and nature of conversations and communications between different parties. Consumers talk about dozens of brands each day. Although many are media and entertainment products such as movies, TV shows, and publications, there is often mention of food products, travel services, retail stores, and many other types of products as well.[61] And although meganetworks such as MySpace and Facebook offer the most exposure, niche social networks offer a more targeted market that is more likely to spread the brand message.

CaféMom Started in 2006 by parent company CMI Marketing, CaféMom has several thousand members who participate in dozens of different forums for mothers. When the site started a forum for discussing developmentally appropriate play activities, toymaker Playskool sent toy kits to over 2,500 members and encouraged them to share their experiences with each other. "The great thing is you get direct feedback from actual moms," enthuses the director of media at Hasbro, Playskool's parent company. This kind of feedback can be invaluable in the product-development process as well.

Companies are becoming extremely aware of the power of word of mouth. Products and brands as diverse as BlackBerry mobile phones, Hush Puppies shoes, Krispy Kreme doughnuts, Zaatar w Zeit restaurants, and Jazeera Airways, as well as companies such as The Body Shop, Palm, Red Bull, Starbucks, and Amazon.com, were built through strong word of mouth.[62] In some cases, positive word of mouth happens organically with little advertising, but in many cases it is managed and facilitated.[63]

Doubletree Hotels (Hilton) Hilton Hotels' Doubletree hotels figured out how to get customers talking about the chain via an amazingly simple device: a warm cookie. At check-in every guest gets a delicious, freshly baked chocolate chip cookie. Not only does it taste great, it also gives Doubletree a homey, warm reputation. The Doubletree website boasts, "More than 125 million served to grateful guests," and "Synonymous with

Doubletree hospitality, the cookie has played a starring role in differentiating the Doubletree hotel brand from its competition." After all, what else are guests going to discuss with their friends when they return home from a Doubletree hotel? All hotels in the mid-size range provide the same basic amenities, but Doubletree guests can even purchase gift tins of the cookies for delivery anywhere in the world.[64]

Word of mouth can be particularly effective for smaller businesses for whom customers may feel a more personal relationship. Here we consider how word of mouth is formed and travels.

Social Media

Social networks in the form of online virtual communities can be a vital resource for companies. Apple has a large number of discussion groups organized by product lines and also by consumer versus professional use. These groups are customers' primary source of product information after warranties expire. Philip Morris developed a 26-million-plus database of Marlboro smokers, partly from necessity as media options diminished due to laws and regulations restricting tobacco advertising. It is now the primary means of marketing the brand.[65]

With a huge young population which is becoming more tech-savvy by the day, the Arab world is witnessing one of the fastest adoption rates of social media in the world. In only the first 3 months of 2011, the number of Facebook users in the Arab world increased by 30 percent to reach 27.7 million. This built on an already staggering 78 percent increase through 2010. As for Twitter, the number of users reached 1.1 million who tweet at least once every 2 weeks.[66] Several Arab companies are making good use of this medium, including two examples from the banking sector.

BLOM Bank   BLOM Bank is one of the oldest established banks not only in Lebanon, where it is headquartered, but also in the Arab region. BLOM Bank's network covers Lebanon, other Arab countries (Jordan, Syria, the UAE, Qatar, Saudi Arabia, and Egypt), and Europe. BLOM has a Retail Banking Facebook presence. Recently BLOM relied on social media to promote two initiatives. The first was the Let's Help Demine Lebanon initiative, created to market BLOM's Giving credit card, launched in cooperation with the Lebanese Army. A proportion of the annual fee goes to benefit the Lebanese Army's Mine Action Center which is responsible for removing the estimated half a million land mines in southern areas of Lebanon. When cardholders use the Giving card, BLOM makes a donation on their behalf to the demining program. BLOM had three main objectives behind this social media strategy: to raise awareness about the danger of landmines and the importance of the demining project; to promote the Giving card so that people enroll in the program, use the card, and contribute to the cause; and to encourage people to donate directly to the cause, whether they subscribe to the card or not. The Facebook group attracted about 1,500 members. BLOM complemented the social media campaign by also using traditional media, with ads on television, radio, and billboards.

Another social media based initiative of BLOM is Blomshabeb (which means 'BLOM youth'). Blomshabeb is a youth guidance program which provides educational and career guidance to teenagers and college students through a dedicated website blomshabeb.com. The Blomshabeb.com Facebook page launched in autumn 2010, gathered close to 1000 'likers' in the first 6 months. Blomshabeb.com also has a discussion forum, putting youngsters in contact with specialists and mentors from the bank who attempt to answer queries and give guidance.[67]

One social media based initiative of BLOM is Blomshabeb which provides educational and career guidance to teenagers and college students.

AlMashreq Bank   The UAE's AlMashreq Bank, with the help of Socialize, a social media agency, built a social networking strategy for its MashreqMillionaire competition. Simply, contestants shared their dreams and the reasons why they should win a prize of about US$1.4 million on the dedicated Facebook page. Periodically, the dream receiving the most votes was rewarded with a MashreqMillionaire certificate worth about $2,750, and a chance to win the ultimate prize of $1.4 million. In 2 months the bank's Share Your Dreams contest on Facebook attracted almost 18,000 fans. Needless to say, the bank now has a valuable database of potential customers and an effective medium by which it can communicate with them.[68]

Buzz and Viral Marketing

Some marketers highlight two particular forms of word of mouth: buzz and viral marketing.[69] *Buzz marketing* generates excitement, creates publicity, and conveys new relevant brand-related information through unexpected or even outrageous means.[70] **Viral marketing** is another form of word of mouth, or 'word of mouse,' that encourages consumers to pass along company-developed products and services or audio, video, or written information to others online.[71]

Contrary to popular opinion, products don't have to be outrageous or edgy to generate buzz. Companies can help to create buzz; and media or advertising are not always necessary for buzz to occur.[72]

viral marketing   using the internet to create word of mouth effects to support marketing efforts and goals.

 Blendtec   Blendtec used to be known primarily for its commercial blenders and food mills. The company wasn't really known to the general public until it launched a hilarious series of "Will it blend?" online videos to promote some of its commercial products for home use. The videos feature founder and CEO Tom Dickson wearing a white lab coat and pulverizing objects ranging from golf balls to pens, all in a genial but deadpan manner. The genius of the videos (willitblend.com) is that they tie into current events. As soon as the iPhone was launched with huge media fanfare, Blendtec aired a video in which Dickson smiled and said, "I love my iPhone. It does everything. But will it blend?" After the blender crushed the iPhone to bits, Dickson lifted the lid on the small pile of black dust and said simply, "iSmoke." The clip drew more than 3.5 million downloads on YouTube and gained even more momentum by linking to eBay, where viewers bid on the crushed iPhone and a US$400 Blendtec blender to go with it.[73]

Outrageousness is a two-edged sword. The Blendtec website clearly puts its comic videos in the 'don't try this at home' category and another set showing how to grind up vegetables for soup, for instance, in the 'try this at home' category. Kimberly-Clark's popular baby hygiene brand Huggies offer another example that is more traditional in approach and far less outrageous.

Huggies launched a Best Hug contest through a dedicated Facebook page. The competition generated a lot of hype and interest and added to the brand awareness and equity of Huggies.

 Huggies   In autumn 2010, Kimberly-Clark embarked on a web-based campaign in Lebanon to promote its world-renowned Huggies brand of baby diapers and wipes. Through the services of online marketing strategists Eastline Marketing, the company launched a Best Hug contest through a dedicated Facebook page. The campaign invited parents to submit photo entries portraying special parent-baby hugs. The competition ran for two months. It attracted around 1,000 entries, drew around 5,700 'likers,'

and tallied some 31,000 votes. Needless to say, the campaign generated a lot of hype and interest among that market segment and added to the brand awareness and equity of Huggies in the Lebanese market.[74]

Agencies have been created solely to help clients create buzz. P&G has 225,000 teens enlisted in Tremor and 600,000 mothers enrolled in Vocalpoint. Both groups are built on the premise that certain individuals want to learn about products, receive samples and coupons, share their opinions with companies, and, of course, talk up their experiences with others. P&G chooses well-connected people—the Vocalpoint moms have big social networks and generally speak to 25 to 30 other women during the day, compared to an average of 5 for other moms—and their messages carry a strong reason to share product information with a friend.[75]

Buzz and viral marketing both try to create a splash in the marketplace to showcase a brand and its noteworthy features. Some believe that viral and buzz marketing are driven more by the rules of entertainment than the rules of selling. A successful viral campaign has been characterized as "that addictive, self-propagating advertainment that lives on websites, blogs, mobile phones, message boards, and even in real-world stunts…"

 Campfire   A viral campaign for Sega's Beta-7 sports video game, featuring a fictitious gamer playing the game nonstop for 3 months, collected 2.2 million online followers and helped Sega top sales projections by 25 percent. The campaign was created by viral experts Campfire, also responsible for Audi's A3 automobile Art of the Heist promotion. For Audi, Campfire staged a complicated cross-country heist for a new 2006 A3 'stolen' from its Park Avenue showroom. More than 5,000,000 people tracked the heist online and through live events, resulting in 10,000 leads. Campfire designs its online promotions carefully to have multiple layers of 'rabbit holes' (or escape options from the game maze) for people with varying levels of interest: the 'divers' who participate minute-by-minute; the 'dippers' who casually check the message boards once a week, and the 'skimmers' who accidentally read about it while surfing online.[76]

Opinion Leaders

Communication researchers propose a social-structure view of interpersonal communication.[77] They see society as consisting of *cliques*, small groups whose members interact frequently. Clique members are similar, and their closeness facilitates effective communication but also insulates the clique from new ideas. The challenge is to create more openness so that cliques exchange information with others in the society. This openness is helped by people who function as liaisons and connect two or more cliques without belonging to either, and *bridges*, people who belong to one clique and are linked to a person in another.

Best-selling author Malcolm Gladwell claims three factors work to ignite public interest in an idea.[78] According to the first, "the law of the few," three types of people help to spread an idea like an epidemic. First are *Mavens*, people knowledgeable about big and small things. Second are *Connectors*, people who know and communicate with a great number of other people. Third are *Salesmen*, who possess natural persuasive power. Any idea that catches the interest of Mavens, Connectors, and Salesmen is likely to be broadcast far and wide. The second factor is "stickiness." An idea must be expressed so that it motivates people to act. Otherwise, the law of the few will not lead to a self-sustaining epidemic. Finally, the third factor, "the power of context," controls whether those spreading an idea are able to organize groups and communities around it.

One team of viral marketing experts caution that although influencers or 'alphas' start trends, they are often too introspective and socially alienated to spread them. They advise marketers to cultivate 'bees,' hyperdevoted customers who are not just satisfied knowing about the next trend but live to spread the word.[79] Companies can take several steps to stimulate personal influence channels to work on their behalf. The Marketing Memo: *How to Start a Buzz Fire* describes some techniques.

Consumers can resent personal communications if unsolicited. Some word-of-mouth tactics walk a fine line between acceptable and unethical. One controversial tactic, sometimes called *shill marketing* or *stealth marketing*, pays people to anonymously promote a product or service in public places without disclosing their financial relationship to the sponsoring firm. They may pretend they're ordinary consumers who happen to like the product, displaying, demonstrating, or talking it up in the process.

How to Start a Buzz Fire

Although many word-of-mouth effects are beyond marketers' control, certain steps improve the likelihood of starting a positive buzz. ▪ **Box 19.3** displays more dos and don'ts.

- **Identify influential individuals and companies and devote extra effort to them.** In technology, influencers might be large corporate customers, industry analysts and journalists, selected policy makers, and a sampling of early adopters.

- **Supply key people with product samples.** When two pediatricians launched MD Moms to market baby-skin-care products, they gave samples of the product to physicians and mothers, hoping they would mention them on internet message boards and parenting websites. The strategy worked: the company hit year 1 distribution goals by the end of the first month.

- **Work through community influentials.** When Ford introduced the Focus, it handed out cars to DJs and trendy people so they would be seen around town in them. Ford also identified 100 influential young consumers in five key geographic areas and gave them cars to drive around.

- **Develop word-of-mouth referral channels to build business.** Professionals will often encourage clients to recommend their services. Weight loss and nutrition centers such as Live'ly and Diet Center found that word-of-mouth referrals from someone in the program had a huge impact on business.

- **Provide compelling information that customers want to pass along.** Companies shouldn't communicate with customers in terms better suited for a press release. Make it easy and desirable for a customer to borrow elements from an e-mail message or blog. Information should be original and useful. Originality increases the amount of word of mouth, but usefulness determines whether it will be positive or negative.

Sources: Sarit Moldovan, Jacob Goldenberg, and Amitava Chattopadhyay, "What Drives Word of Mouth? The Roles of Product Originality and Usefulness," MSI Report No. 06-111 (Cambridge, MA: Marketing Science Institute, 2006); Karen J. Bannan, "Online Chat Is a Grapevine That Yields Precious Fruit," *New York Times,* December 25, 2006; John Batelle, "The Net of Influence," *Business 2.0,* March 2004, p. 70; Ann Meyer, "Word-of-Mouth Marketing Speaks Well for Small Business," *Chicago Tribune,* July 28, 2003; Malcolm Macalister Hall, "Selling by Stealth," *Business Life,* November 2001, pp. 51–55.

BOX 19.3 ▪ BuzzAgent's Word-of-Mouth Dos and Don'ts

"PAY" WITH FEEDBACK

You don't need to pay cash to get someone to say something about your product—they're already doing it. Find a way to let your customers communicate with you, then listen to them and provide them real support and appreciation. They'll volunteer to help a brand that lets them be part of the process.

INSIST ON OPENNESS

Campaign success—and perhaps your company's reputation—hinges on the openness of your word-of-mouth participants. If you're creating an organized word-of-mouth program, require that your volunteers are above board.

DEMAND HONESTY

If you listen closely, you'll realize that honest opinions influence purchasing decisions more so than questionably positive opinions.

HELP CUSTOMERS TELL STORIES

Consumers place products in the context of their daily lives. If a runner's footwear helps her set a personal best in a marathon, she doesn't exclaim, "Just do it!" Rather, she talks about how the sneakers benefited her stride. In a word-of-mouth campaign for Levi's Dockers, participants described the pride of being dressed sharply at social events. Provide your customers with tools to help them share their real stories more effectively.

DON'T SCRIPT

For years marketers have delivered their messages as taglines that make every product sound perfect. Forcing word-of-mouth participants to repeat these messages is awkward and unnatural. Worse still is asking participants to repeat a marketing script of a perfect opinion that's not their own. Communicate the history, benefits, and unique attributes of your product to those who volunteer to experience and discuss it—and then get out of the way.

Continued on next page>>

BOX 19.3   Continued

DON'T PLAN

Word of mouth is a spontaneous event. It can happen at anytime or anywhere—and yes, it can also not happen, even when you want it to. If you try to force word of mouth to take place when it's not appropriate or comfortable, the result will no longer resemble real word of mouth. The key is to help people become more conscious of their opinions. They'll share them when others are really listening.

DON'T SELL

Odds are your company employs a trained and qualified sales force. Let them do their job . . . and let word-of-mouth volunteers do theirs. No one likes to be forcibly sold a product. We like to learn about the pros and cons and then arrive at our own decision. Your word-of-mouth volunteers are not salespeople. They are siblings, friends, coworkers, and accidental acquaintances.

DON'T IGNORE

Listening to word of mouth about your product can be like a trip to the dentist: it's uncomfortable for a moment, but the benefits last a lifetime. However difficult the feedback may be to hear, it is even more powerful to incorporate. Honest word of mouth provides you with a unique opportunity to use real opinions as an incredible feedback loop; and the more you listen and perfect your product, the better your word of mouth will become.

Source: Dave Balter, "Rules of the Game," *Advertising Age Point,* December 2005, pp.22–23.

Hiring a person to go into a café and loudly order a specific branded drink strikes some as inappropriate.[80] To launch its T681 mobile camera phone, Sony Ericsson hired actors dressed as tourists to approach people at tourist locations and ask to have their photo taken. Handing over the mobile phone was an opportunity to discuss its merits. Although the approach no doubt created positive benefits, some found the deception distasteful.

Blogs

Blogs, regularly updated online journals or diaries, have become an important outlet for word of mouth. They vary widely, some personal for close friends and families, others designed to reach and influence a vast audience. Acccording to blog search leader Technorati, every day over 175,000 new blogs are created and existing blogs are updated with over 1.6 million posts.

One obvious appeal of blogs is bringing together people with common interests. Corporations are creating their own blogs and carefully monitoring those of others.

 Ford Bold Moves   Ford created a Bold Moves website—www.ford-boldmoves.com—in the summer of 2006 to better connect with the car-buying public and convince skeptics that its turnaround plan was gaining traction. The company posted 50 short episodes that brought viewers inside the company. "It's engaging consumers in a conversation," said Mary Lou Quesnell, director of brand DNA for the company's Ford division. "We need to recognize our challenges, and we need to communicate to consumers and our own employees how we're moving forward and to tell our story." In addition to the videos, the website featured opinion pieces both critical and complimentary, links to recent news stories about Ford, and space for public feedback. Ford drove viewers to the new site with a marketing initiative focused on digital media and gauged success by monitoring internet traffic and tracking the online buzz created by the videos.[81]

Blog search engines provide up-to-the-minute analysis of millions of blogs to find out what's on people's minds.[82] Popular blogs on networks Gawker and Weblogs are creating influential opinion leaders. Roughly a third of internet users have read blogs.[83] Although many of these consumers examine product information contained in blogs, they may still see information from corporate websites as more trustworthy.[84]

Some consumers use blogs and videos as a means of retribution and revenge on companies for bad service and faulty products. Dell's customer-service shortcomings were splashed all over the internet through a series of 'Dell Hell' postings. AOL took some heat when a frustrated customer recorded and broadcasted online a service representative's emphatic resistance to canceling his service. Comcast was embarrassed when a video surfaced of one of its technicians sleeping on a customer's couch.[85]

Measuring the Effects of Word of Mouth

Marketers are exploring a range of measures to capture word-of-mouth effects.[86] Research and consulting firm Keller Fay notes that although 80 percent of word of mouth occurs offline, many marketers concentrate on online effects, given the ease of tracking them.

In measuring the viral success of its jackrabbit.intuit.com website designed to support new small business owners, Intuit identified blogs that either picked up stories originally posted by a few influential bloggers given a special preview, or wrote their own stories. Intuit classified each blog according to *velocity* (whether it took a month or happened in a few days), *share of voice* (how much talk occurred in the blogosphere), *voice quality* (what was said and how positive or negative it was), and *sentiment* (how meaningful the comments were).

DuPont suggests possible measures such as campaign scale (how far it reached); speed (how fast it spread); share of voice in that space; share of voice in that speed; whether it achieved positive lift in sentiment; whether the message was understood; whether it was relevant; whether it had sustainability (and was not a one-shot deal); and how far it moved from its source.

Designing the Sales Force

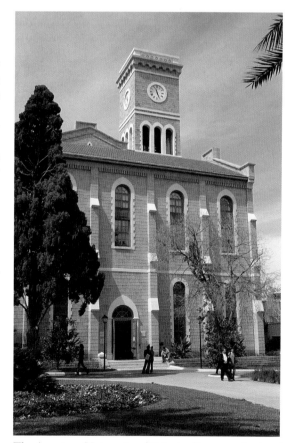

The original and oldest form of direct marketing is the field sales call. Today most industrial companies rely heavily on a professional sales force to locate prospects, develop them into customers, and grow the business, or they hire manufacturers' representatives and agents to carry out the direct-selling task. In addition, many consumer companies, such as Avon cosmetics, use a direct-selling force to expand their presence across the Arab world.

In the United States, firms spend over a trillion dollars annually on sales forces and sales force materials: more than on any other promotional method. Over 10 percent of the total workforce were full time in sales occupations, both non-profit and for profit.[87] For many firms, sales-force performance is critical. Not-for-profit such as universities, hospitals, museums, and NGOs use fundraisers to contact donors and solicit donations. Below is an example from the American University of Beirut.

American University of Beirut The American University of Beirut (AUB) is a private not-for-profit academic institution established in 1866. The university relies on student tuition, hospital billings, and donations to run its operations. Donations, grants, and return on endowment represent around 20 percent of AUB's US$250 million operating budget. In 2002, the university embarked on a 5-year fundraising campaign to raise $140 million to celebrate its 140th anniversary. This was a major leap in fundraising goals. Prior to the Campaign, AUB used to receive around $5 million a year in donations. The $140 million target meant a goal averaging $28 million a year—more than a five-fold increase. To be able to achieve such a target, AUB undertook several internal initiatives. This included investments to expand its Office of Development, the university unit responsible for fundraising. A new Director of Development was

The American University of Beirut relies on professional fundraisers to contact prospect donors for much-needed funds to support its academic and health care services.

recruited with an academic and professional background in marketing. Four dedicated fundraisers were also hired. With a lack of professional fundraisers in the Arab world, the university resorted to hiring professionals with a proven track record in marketing and sales. These fundraisers had to identify and solicit affluent alumni and friends of the university, and to contact them individually through personal and impersonal forms of communication. The university president and members of its Board of Trustees were also involved in such personal solicitations of donations. As the campaign reached its closure in 2007, the university had surpassed the goals of the campaign and raised more than $171 million. This made it not only the most successful fundraising campaign in AUB's history, but also the largest university fundraising campaign ever in the Arab world. It was a record-setting campaign in all aspects, such as total donations, number of donors, individual alumni participation, alumni chapter participation, and trustee participation.[88]

Although no one debates the importance of the sales force in marketing programs, companies are sensitive to the high and rising costs of maintaining one, including salaries, commissions, bonuses, travel expenses, and benefits. Because the average cost of a personal sales call ranges from US$200 to $300, and closing a sale typically requires four calls, the total cost can range from $800 to $1,200.[89] Not surprisingly, companies are trying to increase the productivity of the sales force through better selection, training, supervision, motivation, and compensation.

The term *sales representative* covers six positions, ranging from the least to the most creative types of selling:[90]

1. *Deliverer*. A salesperson whose major task is the delivery of a product (water, fuel, oil).
2. *Order taker*. An inside order taker (standing behind the counter) or outside order taker (calling on the supermarket manager).
3. *Missionary*. A salesperson not expected or permitted to take an order but rather to build goodwill or educate the actual or potential user (the medical 'detailer' representing an ethical pharmaceutical house).
4. *Technician*. A salesperson with a high level of technical knowledge (the engineering salesperson who is primarily a consultant to client companies).
5. *Demand creator*. A salesperson who relies on creative methods for selling tangible products (vacuum cleaners, cleaning brushes, household products) or intangibles (insurance, advertising services, or education).
6. *Solution vendor*. A salesperson whose expertise is solving a customer's problem, often with a system of the company's products and services (for example, computer and communications systems).

Sales personnel serve as the company's personal link to its customers. Fred Hassan, CEO of global pharmaceutical company Schering-Plough, calls salespeople "active representatives of the company [who] can influence people's perception of it through their ability to interact, to customize, and to build relationships with customers." Hassan also offers first-hand experience of the important feedback role the sales force performs:[91]

> The sales reps are usually the first to spot gaps in the product line. There was a case of this recently in our respiratory business. The sales reps had told me that they would like to be able to offer an antibiotic in addition to our antihistamine line. I remembered this request when the opportunity came up to access an antibiotic called Avelox, which is used to treat pneumonia. Licensing Avelox wasn't a very big deal in terms of its bottom-line effect, but its strategic fit was good. It allowed our salespeople to present a much broader range of respiratory products.... If it hadn't been for their input, we would probably have passed on the Avelox opportunity, and Schering-Plough would have struggled longer in respiratory products.

In designing the sales force, the company must consider the development of sales-force objectives, strategy, structure, size, and compensation (see △ **Figure 19.1**).

Sales-Force Objectives and Strategy

The days when all the sales force did was 'sell, sell, and sell' are long gone. Sales reps need to know how to diagnose a customer's problem and propose a solution. They show a customer-prospect how their company can help improve the customer's profitability.

Companies need to define specific sales-force objectives. For example, a company might want its sales representatives to spend 80 percent of their time with current customers and 20 percent

|Fig. 19.1| △

Designing a Sales Force

with prospects, and 85 percent of their time on established products and 15 percent on new products. The specific allocation depends on the kind of products and customers, but regardless of the selling context, salespeople will have one or more of the following specific tasks to perform:

- **Prospecting.** Searching for prospects, or leads.
- **Targeting.** Deciding how to allocate their time among prospects and customers.
- **Communicating.** Communicating information about the company's products and services.
- **Selling.** Approaching, presenting, answering questions, overcoming objections, and closing sales.
- **Servicing.** Providing various services to the customers—consulting on problems, rendering technical assistance, arranging financing, expediting delivery.
- **Information gathering.** Conducting market research and doing intelligence work.
- **Allocating.** Deciding which customers will get scarce products during product shortages.

Because of the expense, most companies are choosing a *leveraged sales force* that focuses reps on selling the company's more complex and customized products to large accounts and uses inside salespeople and web ordering for low-end selling. Tasks such as lead generation, proposal writing, order fulfillment, and postsale support are turned over to others. Salespeople handle fewer accounts and are rewarded for key account growth. This is far different from expecting salespeople to sell to every possible account, the common weakness of geographically based sales forces.[92]

Companies must deploy sales forces strategically so they call on the right customers at the right time in the right way. Today's sales representatives act as 'account managers' who arrange fruitful contact between people in the buying and selling organizations. Selling increasingly calls for teamwork and the support of others, such as *top management*, especially when national accounts or major sales are at stake; *technical people*, who supply information and service before, during, or after product purchase; *customer-service representatives*, who provide installation, maintenance, and other services; and an *office staff*, consisting of sales analysts, order expediters, and assistants.

To maintain a market focus, salespeople should know how to analyze sales data, measure market potential, gather market intelligence, and develop marketing strategies and plans. Sales representatives, especially at the higher levels of sales management, need analytical marketing skills. Marketers believe sales forces are more effective in the long run if they understand and appreciate marketing as well as selling. Too often marketing and sales are in conflict: marketers complain the sales force isn't converting leads, and the sales force complains marketing isn't generating enough leads (see ▇ **Box 19.4**). Improved internal collaboration and communication between these two departments can increase revenues and profits.[93]

Once the company chooses an approach, it can use a direct or a contractual sales force. A **direct (company) sales force** consists of full- or part-time paid employees who work exclusively for the company. Inside sales personnel conduct business from the office using the telephone and receive visits from prospective buyers, and field sales personnel travel and visit customers. A **contractual sales force** consists of manufacturers' reps, sales agents, and brokers, who earn a commission based on sales.

direct (company) sales force full- or part-time paid employees who work exclusively for the company.

contractual sales force manufacturers' reps, sales agents, and brokers, who are paid a commission based on sales.

BOX 19.4 ▇	A Hypothetical (Dysfunctional) Sales-Marketing Exchange

Sales: I need leads, but marketing never sends me any good leads. How am I supposed to get new business with no good leads?

Marketing: We deliver tons of leads and they just sit in the system. Why won't sales call on any of them?

Sales: I have nothing new to sell. What is marketing doing? Why can't they figure out what customers want before they give it to us? Why don't they give me anything that's easy to sell?

Marketing: Why won't sales get out and sell my new programs? How do they expect customers to place orders without sales contacts?

Sales: My people spend too much time on administration and paperwork. I need them out selling.

Marketing: We need information to get new ideas. How long does it take to type in a few words? Don't they know their own customers?

Sales: How am I going to hit my number? Marketing is a waste of time. I'd rather have more sales reps.

Marketing: How am I going to hit my number? Sales won't help and I don't have enough people to do it myself.

Source: based on a talk by Scott Sanderude and Jeff Standish, "Work Together, Win Together: Resolving Misconceptions between Sales and Marketing," talk given at Marketing Science Institute's Marketing, Sales, and Customers conference, December 7, 2005.

Sales-Force Structure

The sales-force strategy has implications for its structure. A company that sells one product line to one end-using industry with customers in many locations would use a territorial structure. A company that sells many products to many types of customers might need a product or market structure. Some companies need a more complex structure. Motorola, for example, manages four types of sales force: (1) a strategic market sales force composed of technical, applications, and quality engineers and service personnel assigned to major accounts; (2) a geographic sales force calling on thousands of customers in different territories; (3) a distributor sales force calling on and coaching Motorola distributors; and (4) an inside sales force doing telemarketing and taking orders via phone and fax.

Established companies need to revise their sales-force structures as market and economic conditions change.

Hewlett-Packard   When Mark Hurd took the helm of a troubled Hewlett-Packard, he made it a priority to do a sales-force makeover. He's now credited with transforming HP's sales culture by radically changing its structure. Before, each salesperson was responsible for selling the entire portfolio of HP's products. Although that allowed reps to cross-sell and up-sell and streamlined things for the client, who dealt with only one rep, it was a nearly impossible task for reps and often kept them mired in administrative tasks. Hurd decentralized the sales force and divided sales between HP's three main divisions: IT for large enterprises, printers and printing, and personal computers (including laptops and handhelds). Customers' fairly linear needs mean HP can still keep things streamlined with one contact salesperson per customer. The salesperson, however, is backed up by a 'virtual' sales team of specialists who deal with specific areas such as storage, software, and servers. This massive transformation couldn't have taken place without intensive sales training. For instance, a rep who sells to large global enterprise accounts is given a thorough understanding of the client industry in order to converse intelligently about it with both general business executives and IT executives.[94]

▲ **Figure 19.2** shows how a company must focus on different aspects of its sales-force structure over the life cycle of the business. SAS, seller of business intelligence software, reorganized its sales force into industry-specific groups such as banks, brokerages, and insurers and saw revenue soar by 14 percent.[95] The Marketing Insight: *Major Account Management* discusses a specialized form of sales-force structure.

|Fig. 19.2| ▲

The Four Factors for a Successful Sales Force

Source: Andris Zoltners, Prabhakant Sinha, and Sally E. Lorimer, "Match Your Sales-Force Structure to Your Business Life Cycle," *Harvard Business Review*, July–August 2006, pp. 81–89.

	BUSINESS LIFE CYCLE STAGE			
	Start-Up	Growth	Maturity	Decline
EMPHASIS				
ROLE OF SALES FORCE AND SELLING PARTNERS	⇨⇨⇨⇨	⇨⇨	⇨	⇨⇨⇨
SIZE OF SALES FORCE	⇨⇨⇨	⇨⇨⇨⇨	⇨⇨	⇨⇨⇨⇨
DEGREE OF SPECIALIZATION	⇨	⇨⇨⇨⇨	⇨⇨⇨	⇨⇨
SALES FORCE RESOURCE ALLOCATION	⇨⇨	⇨	⇨⇨⇨⇨	⇨
UNDERLYING CUSTOMER STRATEGY				
	Create awareness and generate quick product uptake	Penetrate deeper into existing segments and develop new ones	Focus on efficiently serving and retaining existing customers	Emphasize efficiency, protect critical customer relationships, exit unprofitable segments

Major Account Management

Marketers typically single out for attention major accounts (also called key accounts, national accounts, global accounts, or house accounts). These are important customers with multiple divisions in many locations that require uniform pricing and coordinated service for all divisions. A major account manager (MAM) usually reports to the national sales manager and supervises field reps calling on customer plants within their territories. Large accounts are often handled by a strategic account management team with cross-functional personnel to cover all aspects of the relationship. For example, in 1992, Procter & Gamble stationed a strategic account management team to work with Walmart in its headquarters. By 1998, P&G and Walmart had already jointly saved US$30 billion through supply chain improvements. Today, the P&G strategic account management team at Walmart headquarters in the United States consists of approximately 300 staffers, with more stationed at Walmart headquarters in Europe, Asia, and Latin America. In the Arab world, large retailers such as Carrefour, Panda, and Spinneys command the same dedicated major account manager treatment from suppliers.

The average company manages about 75 key accounts. If a company has several such accounts, it's likely to organize a major account management division, in which the average MAM handles nine accounts. Some firms are creating cross-functional strategic account teams that integrate new-product development, technical support, supply chain, marketing activities, and multiple communication channels.

Major account management is growing. As buyer concentration increases through mergers and acquisitions, fewer buyers account for a larger share of a company's sales. Many are centralizing their purchases for certain items, which gives them more bargaining power. Sellers in turn need to devote more attention to these major buyers. And as products become more complex, more groups in the buyer's organization participate in the purchase process. The typical salesperson might not have the skill, authority, or coverage to be effective in selling to the large buyer.

In selecting major accounts, companies look for those that purchase a high volume (especially of more profitable products), purchase centrally, require a high level of service in several geographic locations, may be price sensitive, and may want a long-term partnering relationship. Major account managers act as the single point of contact; develop and grow customer business; understand customer decision processes; identify added-value opportunities; provide competitive intelligence; negotiate sales; and orchestrate customer service.

Favorable pricing based on purchase volume is not enough to retain customer loyalty. Competitors can match or beat a price, or increased costs may necessitate raising prices. Many major accounts look for added value more than a price advantage. They appreciate having a single point of dedicated contact; single billing; special warranties; electronic data interchange (EDI) links; priority shipping; early information releases; customized products; and efficient maintenance, repair, and upgraded service. And there's the value of goodwill. Personal relationships with people who value the major account's business and have a vested interest in the success of that business are compelling reasons for remaining a loyal customer.

Sources: Clare Doyle, Brad McPhee, and Ian Harris, "Marketing, Sales, and Major Account Management: Managing Enterprise Customers as a Portfolio of Opportunities," talk at Marketing Science Institute's *Marketing, Sales, and Customers* conference, December 7, 2005; Sallie Sherman, Joseph Sperry, and Samuel Reese, *The Seven Keys to Managing Strategic Accounts* (New York: McGraw-Hill Trade, 2003); Jack Neff, "Bentonville or Bust," *Advertising Age*, February 24, 2003; Noel Capon, *Key Account Management and Planning: The Comprehensive Handbook for Managing Your Company's Most Important Strategic Asset* (New York: Free Press, 2001). More information can be obtained from NAMA (National Account Management Association); and at www.nasm.com.

Sales-Force Size

Sales representatives are one of the company's most productive and expensive assets. Increasing their number will increase both sales and costs. Once the company establishes the number of customers it wants to reach, it can use a *workload approach* to establish sales-force size. This method has five steps:

1. Group customers into size classes according to annual sales volume.
2. Establish desirable call frequencies (number of calls on an account per year) for each customer class.
3. Multiply the number of accounts in each size class by the corresponding call frequency to arrive at the total workload for the country, in sales calls per year.
4. Determine the average number of calls a sales representative can make per year.
5. Divide the total annual calls required by the average annual calls made by a sales representative, to arrive at the number of sales representatives needed.

Suppose the company estimates that there are 1,000 A accounts and 2,000 B accounts in the nation. A accounts require 36 calls a year, and B accounts require 12 calls a year. The company needs a sales force that can make 60,000 sales calls a year. Suppose the average rep can make 1,000 calls a year. The company would need 60 full-time sales representatives.

Sales-Force Compensation

To attract top-quality sales reps, the company must develop an attractive compensation package. Sales reps want income regularity, extra reward for above-average performance, and fair payment for experience and longevity. Management wants control, economy, and simplicity. Some of these objectives will conflict. No wonder compensation plans exhibit a tremendous variety from industry to industry and even within the same industry.

The company must quantify four components of sales-force compensation—a fixed amount, a variable amount, expense allowances, and benefits. The *fixed amount*, a salary, is intended to satisfy the need for income stability. The *variable amount*, which might be commissions, bonus, or profit sharing, is intended to stimulate and reward effort. *Expense allowances* enable sales reps to meet the expenses involved in travel and entertaining. *Benefits*, such as paid vacations, sickness or accident benefits, pensions, and life insurance, are intended to provide security and job satisfaction.

Fixed compensation is common in jobs with a high ratio of nonselling to selling duties, and jobs where the selling task is technically complex and requires teamwork. Variable compensation works where sales are cyclical or depend on individual initiative. Fixed and variable compensation give rise to three basic types of compensation plans: straight salary, straight commission, and combination salary and commission. One survey revealed that over half of sales reps receive 40 percent or more of their compensation in variable pay.[96]

Straight-salary plans provide sales reps with a secure income, make them more willing to perform nonselling activities, and give them less incentive to overstock customers. From the company's perspective, these plans represent administrative simplicity and lower turnover. Straight-commission plans attract higher performers, provide more motivation, require less supervision, and control selling costs. On the negative side, they emphasize getting the sale over building the relationship. Combination plans feature the benefits of both plans while reducing their disadvantages.

With compensation plans that combine fixed and variable pay, companies may link the variable portion of a salesperson's pay to a wide variety of strategic goals. One recent trend deemphasizes volume measures in favor of factors such as gross profitability, customer satisfaction, and customer retention. Other companies reward reps partly on a sales team's performance, or even on company-wide performance, increasing the likelihood that reps work closely together for the common good.

Managing the Sales Force

Various policies and procedures guide the firm in recruiting, selecting, training, supervising, motivating, and evaluating sales representatives (see ▲ **Figure 19.3**).

Recruiting and Selecting Representatives

At the heart of any successful sales force is a means of selecting effective representatives. One survey revealed that the top 27 percent of the sales force brought in over 52 percent of the sales. Conversely, it's a great waste to hire the wrong people. The average annual turnover rate for all industries is almost 20 percent. Sales-force turnover leads to lost sales, costs of finding and training replacements, and often a strain on existing salespeople to pick up the slack.

Numerous studies have shown little relationship between sales performance on one hand, and background and experience variables, current status, lifestyle, attitude, personality, and skills on the other. More effective predictors have been composite tests and assessment centers that simulate the working environment so applicants are assessed in an environment similar to the one in which they would work.[97]

|Fig. 19.3| ▲

Managing the Sales Force

After management develops its selection criteria, it must recruit. The human resources department seeks applicants by soliciting names from current sales representatives, using employment agencies, placing job ads, and contacting college students. Selection procedures can vary from a single informal interview to prolonged testing and interviewing. Although scores from formal tests are only one information element in a set that includes personal characteristics, references, past employment history, and interviewer reactions, tests have been weighted quite heavily by companies such as IBM and Procter & Gamble. Gillette claims tests have reduced turnover and scores correlated well with the progress of new reps.

Training and Supervising Sales Representatives

Today's customers expect salespeople to have deep product knowledge, to add ideas to improve the customer's operations, and to be efficient and reliable. These demands have required companies to make a much higher investment in sales training.

New reps may spend a few weeks to several months in training. The median training period is 28 weeks in industrial-products companies, 12 in service companies, and 4 in consumer-products companies. Training time varies with the complexity of the selling task and the type of person recruited. For all sales, new hire 'ramp-up' to full effectiveness is taking longer than ever, with 27 percent taking 3–6 months, 38 percent taking 6–12 months, and 28 percent having a 12+ month ramp-up time.

New methods of training are continually emerging, such as the use of audio or videotapes, CDs and CD-ROMs; and programmed learning, distance learning, and films. Some firms are now using role playing and sensitivity or empathy training to help their sales force identify with customers' situations, feelings, and motives.

Altera   Altera makes chips that customers can continually reprogram, offering an alternative to custom designs in the computing, car manufacturing, and consumer electronic industries. Over a 5-year period beginning in 2002, Altera spent nearly US$11 million on empathy training for its sales force using a variety of training methods. The sales force first took the Myers-Briggs type indicator personality test to help form the right sales teams. Next, reps went through a series of exercises to help put themselves in their customers' shoes. One method, 'the hot seat,' asked salespeople to imagine stepping up behind a person and looking at the world through her eyes. An empathy trainer playing the role of the customer would give the salesperson 10 minutes to ask as many questions as he could to uncover what problems the customer faced. The training and other organizational changes to create greater customer intimacy seemed to pay off; Altera was one of the fastest-growing chip companies in 2005.[98]

Companies vary in how closely they supervise sales reps. Reps paid mostly on commission generally receive less supervision. Those who are salaried and must cover definite accounts are likely to receive substantial supervision. With multilevel selling, independent distributors are also in charge of their own sales force selling company products. These independent contractors or reps are paid a commission not only on their own sales but also on the sales of people they recruit and train.[99]

Sales Rep Productivity

How many calls should a company make on a particular account each year? Some research suggests today's sales reps spend too much time selling to smaller, less profitable accounts instead of focusing on larger, more profitable accounts.[100]

NORMS FOR PROSPECT CALLS Companies often specify how much time reps should spend prospecting for new accounts.

Companies set up prospecting standards for a number of reasons. Left to their own devices, many reps will spend most of their time with current customers, who are known quantities. Reps can depend on them for some business, whereas a prospect might never deliver any. Some companies rely on a missionary sales force instead to open new accounts.

USING SALES TIME EFFICIENTLY   The best sales reps manage their time efficiently. *Time-and-duty analysis* helps reps understand how they spend their time and how they might increase their productivity. In the course of a day, sales reps spend time planning, traveling, waiting, selling, and doing administrative tasks (report writing and billing, attending sales meetings, and talking to others in the company about production, delivery, billing, sales performance, and other matters). It's no wonder face-to-face selling time amounts to as little as 29 percent of total working time![101]

Companies constantly try to improve sales-force productivity. To cut costs, reduce time demands on their outside sales force, and take advantage of computer and telecommunications innovations, many have increased the size and responsibilities of their inside sales force.[102]

Inside salespeople are of three types: *Technical support people* provide technical information and answers to customers' questions. *Sales assistants* provide clerical backup for outside salespersons, call ahead to confirm appointments, run credit checks, follow up on deliveries, and answer customers' questions. *Telemarketers* use the phone to find new leads, qualify them, and sell to them. Telemarketers can call up to 50 customers a day, compared to four for an outside salesperson.

The inside sales force frees the outside reps to spend more time selling to major accounts, identifying and converting new major prospects, placing electronic ordering systems in customers' facilities, and obtaining more blanket orders and systems contracts. Inside salespeople spend more time checking inventory, following up orders, and phoning smaller accounts. Outside sales reps are paid largely on an incentive-compensation basis, and inside reps on a salary or salary-plus-bonus pay.

The salesperson today has truly gone electronic. Not only is sales and inventory information transferred much faster, but specific computer-based decision support systems on CDs have been created for sales managers and sales representatives. Using laptop computers, salespeople can access valuable product and customer information. With a few keystrokes, salespeople can prime themselves on backgrounds of clients; call up prewritten sales letters; transmit orders and resolve customer-service issues on the spot during customer calls; and have samples, pamphlets, brochures, and other materials sent to clients.

One of the most valuable electronic tools for the sales rep is the company website, and one of its most useful applications is as a prospecting tool. Company websites can help define the firm's relationships with individual accounts and identify those whose business warrants a personal sales call. They provide an introduction to self-identified potential customers and might even receive the initial order. For more complex transactions, the site provides a way for the buyer to contact the seller. Selling over the internet supports relationship marketing by solving problems that do not require live intervention and thus allows more time to be spent on issues that are best addressed face to face.

Motivating Sales Representatives

The majority of sales representatives require encouragement and special incentives, especially those in the field who encounter a number of daily challenges.[103] Most marketers believe that the higher the salesperson's motivation, the greater the effort and the resulting performance, rewards, and satisfaction: all of which further motivation.

Marketers reinforce intrinsic and extrinsic rewards of all types. One research study measuring the importance of different rewards found the reward with the highest value was pay, followed by promotion, personal growth, and sense of accomplishment.[104] The least valued rewards were liking and respect, security, and recognition. In other words, salespeople are highly motivated by pay and the chance to get ahead and satisfy their intrinsic needs, and less motivated by compliments and security.

Many companies set annual sales quotas, developed from the annual marketing plan, on dollar sales, unit volume, margin, selling effort or activity, or product type. Compensation is often tied to degree of quota fulfillment. The company first prepares a sales forecast that becomes the basis for planning production, workforce size, and financial requirements. Management then establishes quotas for regions and territories, which typically add up to more than the sales forecast to encourage managers and salespeople to perform at their best. Even if they fail to make their quotas, the company nevertheless may reach its sales forecast.

Each area sales manager divides the area's quota among its reps. Sometimes a rep's quotas are set high, to spur extra effort, or more modestly, to build confidence. One general view is that a salesperson's quota should be at least equal to the person's last year's sales, plus some fraction of the difference between territory sales potential and last year's sales. The more favorably the salesperson reacts to pressure, the higher the fraction should be.

Conventional wisdom is that profits are maximized by sales reps focusing on the more important products and more profitable products. Reps are unlikely to achieve their quotas for established products when the company is launching several new products at the same time. The company will need to expand its sales force for new-product launches.

Setting sales quotas can create problems. If the company underestimates and the sales reps easily achieve their quotas, it has overpaid them. If the company overestimates sales potential, the salespeople will find it very hard to reach their quotas and be frustrated or quit. Another downside is that quotas can drive reps to get as much business as possible, often ignoring the service side of the business. The company gains short-term results at the cost of long-term customer satisfaction.

Some companies are dropping quotas.[105] Some judge their sales reps using a number of metrics, such as customer satisfaction, repeat business, and profitable revenues. A good amount of incentive compensation is based on customers' reported satisfaction with service and product. Such close scrutiny of the sales process leads to satisfied customers and repeat business.[106] Even hard-driving Oracle has changed its approach to sales compensation.

Oracle   Finding sales declining and customers complaining, Oracle, the second-largest software company in the world, has been overhauling its sales department and practices in recent years. Its rapidly expanding capabilities, with diverse applications such as human resources, supply chain, and customer relationship management (CRM), made its account management system difficult. One rep could no longer be responsible for selling all Oracle products to certain customers. Reorganization let reps specialize in a few particular products. To tone down the sales force's reputation as overly aggressive, Oracle changed the commission structure from a range of 2–12 percent to a flat 4–6 percent and adopted a set of sales staff guidelines on how to 'play nice' with partners, including channels, independent software vendors (ISVs), resellers, integrators, and value-added resellers (VARs). The six principles instructed sales staff to identify and work with partners in accounts and respect their positions and the value they add in those accounts. The principles were intended to address partner feedback that Oracle can and should be more predictable and reliable.[107]

Evaluating Sales Representatives

We have been describing the *feed-forward* aspects of sales supervision: how management communicates what the sales reps should be doing and motivates them to do it. But good feed-forward requires good *feedback*, which means getting regular information from reps to evaluate performance.

SOURCES OF INFORMATION   The most important source of information about reps is sales reports. Additional information comes through personal observation, salesperson self-reports, customer letters and complaints, customer surveys, and conversations with other sales representatives.

Sales reports are divided between *activity plans* and *write-ups of activity results*. The best example of the former is the salesperson's work plan, which reps submit a week or month in advance to describe intended calls and routing. This report forces sales reps to plan and schedule their activities and inform management of their whereabouts. It provides a basis for comparing their plans and accomplishments or their ability to 'plan their work and work their plan.'

Many companies require representatives to develop an annual territory-marketing plan in which they outline their program for developing new accounts and increasing business from existing accounts. Sales managers study these plans, make suggestions, and use them to develop sales quotas. Sales reps write up completed activities on *call reports*. Sales representatives also submit expense reports, new-business reports, lost-business reports, and reports on local business and economic conditions.

These reports provide raw data from which sales managers can extract key indicators of sales performance: (1) average number of sales calls per salesperson per day, (2) average sales call time per contact, (3) average revenue per sales call, (4) average cost per sales call, (5) entertainment cost per sales call, (6) percentage of orders per hundred sales calls, (7) number of new customers per period, (8) number of lost customers per period, and (9) sales-force cost as a percentage of total sales.

FORMAL EVALUATION The sales force's reports along with other observations supply the raw materials for evaluation. There are several approaches to conducting evaluations. One type of evaluation compares current performance to past performance. An example is shown in ☐ **Table 19.1**.

The sales manager can learn many things about a rep from this table. Total sales increased every year (line 3). This does not necessarily mean he is doing a better job. The product breakdown shows he has been able to push the sales of product B further than the sales of product A (lines 1 and 2). According to his quotas for the two products (lines 4 and 5), his success in increasing product B sales could be at the expense of product A sales. According to gross profits (lines 6 and 7), the company earns more selling A than B. The rep might be pushing the higher-volume, lower-margin product at the expense of the more profitable product. Although the rep increased total sales by US$1,100 between 2010 and 2011 (line 3), the gross profits on total sales actually decreased by $580 (line 8).

Sales expense (line 9) shows a steady increase, although total expense as a percentage of total sales seems to be under control (line 10). The upward trend in total dollar expense does not seem to be explained by any increase in the number of calls (line 11), although it might be related to success in acquiring new customers (line 14). There is a possibility that in prospecting for new customers, this rep is neglecting present customers, as indicated by an upward trend in the annual number of lost customers (line 15).

TABLE 19.1 ☐ Form for Evaluating Sales Representative's Performance

Territory: Middle East and North Africa

Sales Representative: Mohamad Ahmad	2008	2009	2010	2011
1. Net sales product A	$251,300	$253,200	$270,000	$263,100
2. Net sales product B	423,200	439,200	553,900	561,900
3. Net sales total	$674,500	$692,400	$823,900	$825,000
4. Percent of quota product A	95.6	92.0	88.0	84.7
5. Percent of quota product B	120.4	122.3	134.9	130.8
6. Gross profits product A	$50,260	$50,640	$54,000	$52,620
7. Gross profits product B	42,320	43,920	55,390	56,190
8. Gross profits total	92,580	94,560	109,390	108,810
9. Sales expense	$10,200	$11,100	$11,600	$13,200
10. Sales expense to total sales (%)	1.5	1.6	1.4	1.6
11. Number of calls	1,675	1,700	1,680	1,660
12. Cost per call	$6.09	$6.53	$6.90	$7.95
13. Average number of customers	320	24	328	334
14. Number of new customers	13	14	15	20
15. Number of lost customers	8	0	11	14
16. Average sales per customer	$2,108	$2,137	$2,512	$2,470
17. Average gross profit per customer	$289	$292	$334	$326

Prices in US$.

The last two lines show the level and trend in sales and gross profits per customer. These figures become more meaningful when compared with overall company averages. If this rep's average gross profit per customer is lower than the company's average, he could be concentrating on the wrong customers or not spending enough time with each customer. A review of annual number of calls (line 11) shows he might be making fewer annual calls than the average salesperson. If distances in the territory are similar to other territories, the rep might not be putting in a full work-day, be poor at sales planning and routing, or be spending too much time with certain accounts.

Even if effective in producing sales, the rep may not rate high with customers. Success may come because competitors' salespeople are inferior, the rep's product is better, or new customers are always found to replace those who dislike the rep. Managers can capture customer opinion of the salesperson, product, and service by mail questionnaires or telephone calls. Sales reps can analyze the success or failure of a sales call and how they would improve the chances on subsequent calls. Their performance could be related to internal factors (effort, ability, and strategy) and external factors (task and luck).[108]

Principles of Personal Selling

Personal selling is an ancient art. Effective salespeople today, however, have more than instinct; they are trained in methods of analysis and customer management. Companies now spend hundreds of millions of dollars each year to train salespeople and transform them from passive order takers into active order getters. Reps are taught the SPIN method to build long-term relationships with questions such as:[109]

1. **Situation questions**. These ask about facts or explore the buyer's present situation. For example, "What system are you using to invoice your customers?"
2. **Problem questions**. These deal with problems, difficulties, and dissatisfactions the buyer is experiencing. For example, "What parts of the system create errors?"
3. **Implication questions**. These ask about the consequences or effects of a buyer's problems, difficulties, or dissatisfactions. For example, "How does this problem affect your people's productivity?"
4. **Need-payoff questions**. These ask about the value or usefulness of a proposed solution. For example, "How much would you save if our company could help reduce the errors by 80 percent?"

Most sales training programs agree on the major steps involved in any effective sales process. We show these steps in △ **Figure 19.4** and discuss their application to industrial selling next.[110]

|Fig. 19.4| △

Major Steps in
Effective Selling

The Six Steps

PROSPECTING AND QUALIFYING The first step in selling is to identify and qualify prospects. More companies are taking responsibility for finding and qualifying leads so salespeople can use their expensive time doing what they do best: selling. Companies qualify the leads by contacting them by mail or phone to assess their level of interest and financial capacity. 'Hot' prospects are turned over to the field sales force and 'warm' prospects to the telemarketing unit for follow-up. Even then, it takes about four calls on a prospect to consummate a business transaction.

PREAPPROACH The salesperson needs to learn as much as possible about the prospect company (what it needs, who is involved in the purchase decision) and its buyers (personal characteristics and buying styles). The rep should set call objectives: to qualify the prospect, gather information, make an immediate sale. Another task is to choose the best contact approach, whether a personal visit, a phone call, or a letter. Finally, the salesperson should plan an overall sales strategy for the account.

PRESENTATION AND DEMONSTRATION The salesperson tells the product 'story' to the buyer, using a *features, advantages, benefits,* and *value* approach (FABV). Features describe physical characteristics of a market offering, such as chip processing speeds or memory capacity. Advantages describe why the features provide an advantage to the customer. Benefits describe the economic, technical, service, and social benefits delivered by the offering. Value describes the offering's worth (often in monetary terms). Salespeople often spend too much time on product features (a product orientation) and not enough time stressing benefits and value (a customer orientation).

OVERCOMING OBJECTIONS Customers typically pose objections. *Psychological resistance* includes resistance to interference, preference for established supply sources or brands, apathy, reluctance to giving up something, unpleasant associations created by the sales rep, predetermined ideas, dislike of making decisions, and neurotic attitude toward money. *Logical resistance* might be objections to the price, delivery schedule, or product or company characteristics.

To handle these objections, the salesperson maintains a positive approach, asks the buyer to clarify the objection, questions in such a way that the buyer answers his own objection, denies the validity of the objection, or turns it into a reason for buying. Although price is the most frequently negotiated issue, others include contract completion time; quality of goods and services offered; purchase volume; responsibility for financing, risk taking, promotion, and title; and product safety.

Salespeople sometimes give in too easily when customers demand a discount. One company recognized this problem when sales revenues went up 25 percent but profit remained flat. The company decided to retrain its salespeople to 'sell the price,' rather than 'sell through price.' Salespeople were given richer information about each customer's sales history and behavior. They received training to recognize value-adding opportunities rather than price-cutting opportunities. As a result, the company's sales revenues climbed and so did its margins.[111]

CLOSING Closing signs from the buyer include physical actions, statements or comments, and questions. Reps can ask for the order, recapitulate the points of agreement, offer to help write up the order, ask whether the buyer wants A or B, get the buyer to make minor choices such as color or size, or indicate what the buyer will lose by not placing the order now. The salesperson might offer specific inducements to close, such as a special price, an extra quantity, or a token gift.

FOLLOW-UP AND MAINTENANCE Follow-up and maintenance are necessary to ensure customer satisfaction and repeat business. Immediately after closing, the salesperson should cement any necessary details about delivery time, purchase terms, and other matters important to the customer. The salesperson should schedule a follow-up call after delivery to ensure proper installation, instruction, and servicing and to detect any problems, assure the buyer of the salesperson's interest, and reduce any cognitive dissonance. The salesperson should develop a maintenance and growth plan for the account.

Relationship Marketing

The principles of personal selling and negotiation are largely transaction oriented because their purpose is to close a specific sale. But in many cases the company seeks not an immediate sale, but rather a long-term supplier–customer relationship. Today's customers prefer suppliers who can sell and deliver a coordinated set of products and services to many locations; who can quickly solve problems in different locations; and who can work closely with customer teams to improve products and processes.

Salespeople working with key customers must do more than call only when they think customers might be ready to place orders. They should call or visit at other times, take customers to dinner, and make useful suggestions about the business. They should monitor key accounts, know customers' problems, and be ready to serve them in a number of ways. They must be adaptive and respond to different customer needs or situations.[112]

When a relationship management program is properly implemented, the organization will focus as much on managing its customers as on managing its products. At the same time, companies should realize relationship marketing is not effective in all situations. Ultimately, companies must judge which segments and which customers will respond profitably to relationship management.

Summary

1. Direct marketing is an interactive marketing system that uses one or more media to effect a measurable response or transaction at any location. Direct marketing, especially electronic marketing, is showing explosive growth.

2. Direct marketers plan campaigns by deciding on objectives, target markets and prospects, offers, and prices. This is followed by testing and establishing measures to determine the campaign's success.

3. Major channels for direct marketing include face-to-face selling, direct mail, catalog marketing, telemarketing, interactive TV, kiosks, websites, and mobile devices.

4. Interactive marketing provides marketers with opportunities for much greater interaction and individualization through well-designed websites, as well as online ads and promotions and other approaches.

5. Word-of-mouth marketing finds ways to engage customers so that they choose to talk with others about products, services, and brands.

6. Two notable forms of word-of-mouth marketing are buzz marketing, which seeks to get people talking about a brand by ensuring that a product or service or how it is marketed is out of the ordinary, and viral marketing, which encourages people to exchange information related one way or another to a product or service online.

7. Sales personnel serve as a company's link to its customers. The sales rep is the company to many of its customers, and it is the rep who brings back to the company much-needed information about the customer.

8. Designing the sales force requires decisions regarding objectives, strategy, structure, size, and compensation. Objectives may include prospecting, targeting, communicating, selling, servicing, information gathering, and allocating. Determining strategy requires choosing the most effective mix of selling approaches. Choosing the sales-force structure entails dividing territories by geography, product, or market (or some combination of these). Estimating how large the sales force needs to be involves estimating the total workload and how many sales hours (and hence salespeople) will be needed. Compensating the sales force entails determining what types of salaries, commissions, bonuses, expense accounts, and benefits to give, and how much weight customer satisfaction should have in determining total compensation.

9. There are five steps involved in managing the sales force: (1) recruiting and selecting sales representatives; (2) training the representatives in sales techniques and in the company's products, policies, and customer-satisfaction orientation; (3) supervising the sales force and helping reps to use their time efficiently; (4) motivating the sales force and balancing quotas, monetary rewards, and supplementary motivators; and (5) evaluating individual and group sales performance.

10. Effective salespeople are trained in the methods of analysis and customer management, as well as the art of sales professionalism. No approach works best in all circumstances, but most trainers agree that selling is a six-step process: prospecting and qualifying customers, preapproach, presentation and demonstration, overcoming objections, closing, and follow-up and maintenance.

Applications

Marketing Debate
Are Great Salespeople Born or Made?

One debate in sales is about the impact of training versus selection in developing an effective sales force. Some observers maintain the best salespeople are born that way and are effective due to their personalities and interpersonal skills developed over a lifetime. Others contend that application of leading-edge sales techniques can make virtually anyone a sales star.

Take a position: The key to developing an effective sales force is selection *versus* the key to developing an effective sales force is training.

Marketing Discussion

Pick a company and go to its website. How would you evaluate the website? How well does it score on the 7Cs design elements: context, content, community, customization, communication, connection, and commerce?

Marketing Excellence

>>Yahoo!

Yahoo! has grown from a tiny upstart company to a powerful force in internet media. David Filo and Jerry Yang, two computer science Ph.D. students at Stanford University, created a simple search engine in 1994. Using a homemade filing system, the pair cataloged sites on the newly created world wide web and published the directory, called Jerry and David's Guide to the World Wide Web, on the internet. They named their effort Yahoo! after they left school to devote their full attention to the business.

From its start, Yahoo! conveyed a cheeky attitude that came from the top of the corporate ladder, in the personalities of Filo and Yang. The two had conceived of Yahoo! while housed "in trailers full of pizza boxes," and each of their business cards bore the title "Chief Yahoo!" The name even contains a hidden joke: Yahoo is an acronym meaning 'Yet Another Hierarchical Officious Oracle.' Yahoo!'s marketing reflected the company's style as well: in one ad, Eskimos ordered a hot tub online. For years, each ad closed with the tagline "Do You Yahoo!?" and the signature Yahoo! yodel, an audio cue to reinforce brand recall.

Yahoo! has worked hard to be more than just a search engine. The company proudly proclaims it is, "The only place anyone needs to go to find anything, communicate with anyone, or buy anything." Its wide range of web services includes e-mail, news, weather, music, photos, games, shopping, auctions, travel, and more.

Yahoo! sees one of its main advantages over rival Google as its vast array of original content. Yahoo! partners with hundreds of premier content providers to offer a personalization option in My Yahoo!, which enables users to specify their favourite Yahoo! features and content to fit a single page. With a database of information about where its millions of registered users live and what their interests are, Yahoo! can present users with both more relevant search results and more relevant advertising.

August 2011 statistics showed that Yahoo receives more than 65 million unique visitors each day.

Yahoo! continues to expand. Its acquisition of photo-sharing service Flickr in March 2005, social bookmark manager del.icio.us, and online video editing site Jumpcut strengthened the company's capabilities in those areas. In March 2005, it launched its blogging and social network service Yahoo! 360°. Its mobile display advertising platform on the company's Yahoo! Mobile Web service (m.yahoo.com) allows advertisers to reach consumers around the globe on their mobile phones.

In 2009, Yahoo! ventured significantly into the Arab world through its acquisition of Maktoob.com for US$164 million. At the time, Maktoob was the leading Arabic portal with around 16.5 million unique users, or a third of the total users in the Middle East. In less than 2 years Yahoo! grew its users from the region from 30 million to 80 million. Yahoo! started offering Arabic versions of its homepage, search, messenger, mail, news, sports, finance, and other Yahoo! features and services on its Maktoob page. One interesting spinoff is Yahoo! Maktoob Research which houses the Arab world's largest online consumer panel, providing marketing professionals with a valuable venue to tap into the needs and preferences of the Arab consumer. In 2011, Yahoo!'s Middle East website became the company's fifth-most-visited homepage.

A large percentage of Yahoo! revenues comes from advertising, but the company continues to supplement its revenues through subscription sources such as online personal ads, premium e-mail products, and services for small businesses. In 2007, Yahoo! launched a new search advertising system, Panama, to increase the quality of its search results as well the advertising revenue it generates from search. In the Arab world, after the acquisition of Maktoob, Yahoo! ad sales in the first year increased by more than 50 percent, says Ahmed Nassef, vice president and managing director of Yahoo! Middle East. "We are an emerging market so from a revenue standpoint it's small. However, it's one of the fastest growing in the company in terms of revenue growth so we're looking at very strong double-digit growth every year," says Nassef.

Yahoo! attracts a diverse range of advertisers. A long-time fan is PepsiCo, an early sign-up for the mobile service. "We've had exceptional results reaching our consumers on Yahoo! online," said John Vail, director of interactive marketing, PepsiCo's North American operations. "Now we can reach consumers when they're on the move and communicate with them in a way we haven't before."

Continued on next page >>

Marketing Excellence...continued

>>Yahoo!

Questions

1. What are the main benefits that Yahoo! offers to its users?

2. What is the added value that Yahoo! offers to businesses and advertisers?

3. What could be some of the strategic reasons that led Yahoo! to buy Maktoob.com?

4. Visit the Yahoo! Maktoob Research website. What benefits does this service offer to marketing professionals? What service does it offer to its panel members? Evaluate your answers to the above questions: would you consider becoming an Arab Eye panel member? Why, or why not?

Sources: Catherine Holahan, "Yahoo!'s Bid to Think Small," *BusinessWeek*, February 26, 2007, p. 94; Ben Elgin, "Yahoo!'s Boulevard of Broken Dreams," *BusinessWeek*, March 13, 2006, pp. 76–77; Justin Hibbard, "How Yahoo! Gave Itself a Face-Lift," *BusinessWeek*, October 9, 2006, pp. 74–77; Kevin J. Delaney, "As Yahoo! Falters, Executive's Memo Calls for Overhaul," *Wall Street Journal*, November 18, 2006; "Yahoo!'s Personality Crisis," *The Economist*, August 13, 2005, pp. 49–50; Fred Vogelstein, "Yahoo!'s Brilliant Solution," *Fortune*, August 8, 2005, pp. 42–55; http://yahoo.com.hypestat.com; Claire Ferris-Lay, "Let's Get Digital," *arabianbusiness.com*, May 29, 2011, www.arabianbusiness.com/let-s-get-digital-402205.html?page=0; Clint Boulton, "Yahoo to Buy Arab Portal Maktoob.com to Reach the Middle East," *eWeek.com*, August 25, 2009, www.eweek.com/c/a/Search-Engines/Yahoo-to-Buy-Arab-Portal-Maktoobcom-to-Reach-The-Middle-East-435957/.

CHAPTER 20

Mobinil knows the value of new-product development for the world of telecommunications. The company is moving forward using new technology to create mobile services that will meet the demands of a rapidly evolving market.

In this chapter, we will address the following questions:

1. What challenges does a company face in developing new products and services? (pg. 559)

2. What organizational structures and processes do managers use to manage new-product development? (pg. 563)

3. What are the main stages in developing new products and services? (pg. 572)

4. What is the best way to manage the new-product development process? (pg. 578)

5. What factors affect the rate of diffusion and consumer adoption of newly launched products and services? (pg. 583)

Introducing New Market Offerings

Companies need to grow their revenue over time by developing new products and services and expanding into new markets. New-product development shapes the company's future. Improved or replacement products and services can maintain or build sales; new-to-the-world products and services can transform industries and companies and change lives. But the low success rate of new products and services points to the many challenges involved. More and more companies are doing more than just talking about innovation. They are fundamentally changing the way they develop their new products and services. Look what's happening at Mobinil.[1]

 Mobinil, a telecommunication company, started its business in the Egyptian market in 1998, with the vision to put a "mobile in every hand." At that time, many people thought that mobile telephones were only for the affluent segment, but based on R&D, Mobinil proved this was a myth. Mobinil has since launched several mobile plans fitting all Egyptian segments. In 2010, there were 57 million mobile users in Egypt obtaining telecommunication services from three different providers. The Mobinil share was 25 million subscribers, making it the market leader. In 2007, the company took the decision to launch a 3G service, which helped the company to evolve its position from "mobile in every hand" to "internet in every hand."[2]

Firms all over the world are trying to come up with creative ways to develop even better new products and services, faster and more efficiently. Marketers are playing a key role in the development of new products by identifying and evaluating new-product ideas and working with R&D and other areas in every stage of development. This chapter provides a detailed analysis of the new-product development process. Much of the discussion is equally relevant to new products, services, or business models. Chapter 21 considers how marketers can tap into global markets as another source of long-term growth. ▽

New-Product Options

There are a variety of types of new product and ways to create them.[3]

Make or Buy

A company can add new products through acquisition or development. The acquisition route can take three forms. The company can buy other companies, it can acquire patents from other companies, or it can buy a license or franchise from another company.

Cadbury When Kuwaiti food company Americana suggested in the 1980s that Cadbury join them in the Egyptian market, Cadbury signed up for a 35 percent share of the new subsidiary. According to Cadbury's specifications, a factory was established to produce Dairy Milk, Dairy Milk Krisp, and Dairy Milk Hazelnut in 49 gram bars. Cadbury appealed only to the Egyptian higher class, who could afford to buy from refrigerated stores, not kiosks which are widely dispersed to serve the very low income Egyptian segment. Cadbury struggled in Egypt until 1997 when it acquired a strong local market player, Bim-Bim, which became the market leader dominating the kiosk trade. Cadbury utilized the Bim-Bim distribution network and low production facilities to serve the middle and lower Egyptian segments. The acquisition gave Cadbury the missing components of affordability and availability, balancing the Cadbury product range, which made it relevant to the Egyptian market.[4]

Cadbury Egypt launched new economical sizes to be relevant to the Egyptian market.

But firms can successfully make only so many acquisitions. At some point, there becomes a pressing need for *organic growth*: the development of new products from within the company. When Praxair, in Danbury, Connecticut in the United States, set an ambitious goal of US$200 million per year of double-digit new annual sales growth, it achieved that goal only through a healthy dose of organic growth and a large number of smaller but significant $5 million projects.[5]

For product development, the company can create new products in its own laboratories, or it can contract with independent researchers or new-product development firms to develop specific new products or provide new technology.[6] Many firms such as Samsung, GE, Diwan Bookstore, Farm Frits, El Rashidi El Mizan Confectionary, and others have engaged new-product consulting boutiques to provide fresh insights and different points of view.

Types of New Product

New products range from new-to-the-world products that create an entirely new market at one end, to minor improvements or revisions of existing product at the other. Most new-product activity is devoted to improving existing products. At Sony, over 80 percent of new-product activity is modifying and improving existing products. Some of the most successful new consumer products in recent years have been brand extensions of existing products: Tide with Febreze and Tide Coldwater; Crest ProHealth Rinse and Crest Whitestrips Premium Plus; and Gillette Venus Vibrance.

In many categories, it is becoming increasingly difficult to identify blockbuster products that will transform a market; but continuous innovation to better satisfy consumer needs can force competitors to play catch-up.[7] Continually launching new products as brand extensions into related product categories can also broaden the brand meaning. Nike started as a running-shoe manufacturer but now competes in the sports market with all types of athletic shoes, clothing, and equipment. Mo'men, an Egyptian fast food restaurant, opened its first outlet in Heliopolis in 1988 and moved from selling oriental sandwiches to a wide variety of westernized fast-food meals to appeal to the modern Egyptian lifestyle. Now Mo'men is competing on the same level against established food chains such as KFC and McDonald's.[8] Product innovation and effective marketing programs have allowed these firms to expand their market footprint.

Fewer than 10 to 15 percent of all new products are truly innovative and new to the world.[9] These products incur the greatest cost and risk because they are new to both the company and the marketplace.[10] Radical innovations can hurt the company's bottom line in the short run, but the good news is that success can create a greater sustainable competitive advantage than more ordinary products. Companies typically must create a strong R&D and marketing partnership to pull off a radical innovation.[11] Few reliable techniques exist for estimating demand for these innovations. Focus groups will provide some perspectives on customer interest and need, but marketers may need to use a probe-and-learn approach based on observation and feedback of early users' experiences and other means.[12]

Many high-tech firms strive for radical innovation.[13] High tech covers a wide range of industries: telecommunications, computers, consumer electronics, biotech, and software. High-tech marketers face a number of challenges in launching their products: high technological uncertainty; high market uncertainty; high competitive volatility; high investment costs; short product life cycles; and difficulty in finding funding sources for risky projects.[14]

Challenges in New-Product Development

New-product introductions have accelerated in recent years. In many industries, such as retailing, consumer goods, electronics, autos, and others, the time it takes to bring a product to market has been cut in half.[15] Luxury leather-goods maker Louis Vuitton implemented a new factory format dubbed Pégase so that it could ship fresh collections to its boutiques every 6 weeks—more than twice as frequently as in the past—giving customers more new looks to choose from.[16]

The Innovation Imperative

In an economy of rapid change, continuous innovation is a necessity. Highly innovative firms are able to identify and quickly seize new market opportunities. ▭ **Table 20.1** lists the 2011 rankings of the top 25 globally innovative firms on the basis of a *Fast Company* online survey. Innovative firms create a positive attitude toward innovation and risk taking, routinize the innovation process, practice teamwork, and allow their people to experiment and even fail.

The Cleopatra Industrial Group The Cleopatra Industrial Group is a world leader in the production of ceramics; it produces 100 million square meters every year. The company was founded in 1982 and has 20,000 employees working in diversified production plants. In order to distinguish the company products and to cover an unmet customer need, the Cleopatra Group utilized its technological production resources to launch porcelain stoneware products in the Egyptian market. The porcelain is a regular ceramic but gives the impression of being a marble. This new innovation differentiated Cleopatra products and appealed to the moderate-income segment that value marble but couldn't afford it.[17]

Companies that fail to develop new products put themselves at risk. Their existing products are vulnerable to changing customer needs and tastes, new technologies, shortened product life cycles, and increased domestic and foreign competition. New technologies are especially threatening. Kodak has worked hard to develop a new business model and product-development processes that work well in a digital photography world. Its new goal is to do for photos what Apple does for music, by helping people to organize and manage their personal libraries of images.

TABLE 20.1	The World's Top 25 Most Innovative Companies				
2011 Rank	**2010 Rank**	**Company Name**	**HQ City**	**HQ Country**	**HQ Continent**
1	03	Apple	Cupertino, CA	USA	North America
2	50	Twitter	San Francisco, CA	USA	North America
3	01	Facebook	Menlo Park, CA	USA	North America
4	–	Nissan	Yokohama	Japan	Asia
5	–	Groupon	Chicago, IL	USA	North America
6	04	Google	Mountain View, CA	USA	North America
7	–	Dawning Information Industry	Beijing	China	Asia
8	12	Netflix	Los Gatos, CA	USA	North America
9	–	Zynga	San Francisco, CA	USA	North America
10	–	Epocrates	San Mateo, CA	USA	North America
11	–	Trader Joe's	Monrovia, CA	USA	North America
12	–	Arm	Cambridge	UK	Europe
13	–	Burberry	London	UK	Europe
14	–	Kosaka Smelting and Refining	Kosaka	Japan	Asia
15	–	Foursquare	New York, NY	USA	North America
16	–	ESPN	Bristol, CT	USA	North America
17	–	Turner Sports	Atlanta, GA	USA	North America
18	05	Huawei	Shenzhen	China	Asia
19	14	Intel	Santa Clara, CA	USA	North America
20	–	Syncardia	Tucson, AZ	USA	North America
21	–	Donorscho	New York, NY	USA	North America
22	–	eBay	San Jose, CA	USA	North America
23	13	Nike	Washington County, OR	USA	North America
24	–	LinkedIn	Mountain View, CA	USA	North America
25	–	Wieden+Kennedy	Portland, OR	USA	North America

Source: "The World's Fifty Most Innovative Companies," *Fast Company*, www.fastcompany.com/most-innovative-companies/2011.

New-Product Success

Most established companies focus on *incremental innovation*. Incremental innovation can allow companies to enter new markets by tweaking products for new customers, use variations on a core product to stay one step ahead of the market, and create interim solutions for industry-wide problems. Southwest Airlines has made some notable incremental innovations.

Southwest Airlines

An airline known for resisting traditions, Southwest used incremental innovations to offset the impact of an important competitor innovation: frequent flier miles. Begun by American Airlines more than 20 years ago to boost customer loyalty, frequent flier rewards programs were soon rolled out by all the major airlines. Southwest, however, decided to tie its rewards to the number of flights taken rather than miles flown. The airline offers mainly short flights for business travelers who often fly the same route over and over. The program was a big hit with this target market.[18]

Newer companies create *disruptive technologies* that are cheaper and more likely to alter the competitive space. Established companies can be slow to react or invest in these disruptive technologies because they threaten their investment. Then they suddenly find themselves facing formidable new competitors, and many fail.[19] To avoid this trap, firms must carefully monitor the preferences of both customers and noncustomers over time and uncover evolving, difficult-to-articulate customer needs.[20] What else can a company do to develop successful new products? In a study of industrial products, new-product specialists Cooper and Kleinschmidt found that the number-one success factor is a unique, superior product. Such products succeed 98 percent of the time, compared to products with a moderate advantage (58 percent success) or minimal advantage (18 percent success). Another key factor is a well-defined product concept. The company carefully defines and assesses the target market, product requirements, and benefits before proceeding. Other success factors are technological and marketing synergy, quality of execution in all stages, and market attractiveness.[21]

Cooper and Kleinschmidt also found that domestic products designed solely for the domestic market tend to show a high failure rate, low market share, and low growth. In contrast, products designed for the world market—or at least to include neighboring countries—achieve significantly more profits, both at home and abroad. Yet only 17 percent of the products in their study were designed with an international orientation.[22] The implication is that companies should adopt an international focus in designing and developing new products.

New product ideas are not limited to large companies only. On the contrary, small entrepreneurs have their own very successful new ideas as well as new marketing themes and value propositions.

Catwalk Cow

"We've Just Made Dessert Guilt Free!" says Catwalk Cow. The Sharjah-based company offers healthy dessert alternatives to consumers, and recently launched its fat-free Chewy Fudge Brownie Mix into the UAE market. This is an excellent example of female entrepreneurs in the Arab world; the company was founded and is managed by a U.S.-educated Palestinian-American woman. Catwalk Cow's success in the UAE depended on health and fitness concerns. This orientation is relevant nowadays, as an increasing demand for healthy food has been created by educated and empowered customers. Catwalk Cow offers tasty, fat-free chocolate desserts that satisfy the urge for a rich chocolate treat.[23]

Catwalk Cow has found success in the UAE with its fat-free Chewy Fudge Brownie Mix, which offers flavor satisfaction, but cares for customers' health as well.

New-Product Failure

New-product development can be quite risky. New products continue to fail at a disturbing rate. Recent studies put the rate at 50 percent and potentially as high as 95 percent in the United States and 90 percent in Europe.[24]

New products can fail for many reasons: ignored or misinterpreted market research; overestimates of market size; high development costs; poor design; incorrect positioning, ineffective advertising, or wrong price; insufficient distribution support; and competitors who fight back hard. Some additional factors hindering new-product development are:

- *Shortage of important ideas in certain areas.* There may be few ways left to improve some basic products (such as steel or detergents).

- *Fragmented markets.* Companies must aim their new products at smaller market segments, and this can mean lower sales and profits for each product.

- *Social and governmental constraints.* New products must satisfy consumer safety and environmental concerns.

- *Cost of development.* A company typically must generate many ideas to find just one worthy of development and often faces high R&D, manufacturing, and marketing costs.

- *Capital shortages.* Some companies with good ideas cannot raise the funds needed to research and launch them.

- *Shorter required development time.* Companies must learn how to compress development time by using new techniques, strategic partners, early concept tests, and advanced marketing planning.

- *Shorter product life cycles.* When a new product is successful, rivals are quick to copy it. Sony used to enjoy a 3-year lead on its new products. Now Matsushita will copy the product within 6 months, barely leaving time for Sony to recoup its investment.

Box 20.1 summarizes causes of new-product failure.

But failure comes with the territory, and truly innovative firms accept it as part of what's needed to be successful. Silicon Valley California marketing expert Seth Godin maintains: "It is not just OK to fail; it's imperative to fail."[25] Many web companies are the result of failed business ventures and experience numerous failed initiatives as they evolve their services.

BOX 20.1   Causes of New-Product Failure

1. **Market/marketing failure**
   - Small size of the potential market
   - No clear product differentiation
   - Poor positioning
   - Misunderstanding of customer needs

2. **Financial failure**
   - Low return on investment

3. **Timing failure**
   - Late in the market
   - 'Too' early: market not yet developed

4. **Technical failure**
   - Product did not work
   - Bad design

5. **Organizational failure**
   - Poor fit with the organizational culture
   - Lack of organizational support

6. **Environmental failure**
   - Government regulations
   - Macroeconomic factors

Source: Dipak Jain, "Managing New-Product Development for Strategic Competitive Advantage," Table 6.1 in Chapter 6 in *Kellogg on Marketing*, ed. Dawn Iacobucci (New York: John Wiley, 2001), p. 131.

Dogster.com, a social network site for dog lovers, emerged after the spectacular fall of Pets.com. Like.com, a site for people seeking look-alike clothes, fared better than a service for searching for similar-looking photos; and even Google found that a Google Answers service for people seeking specialized information failed.[26]

Initial product failure is not always the end of the road for an idea. Recognizing that 90 percent of experimental drugs fail, Eli Lilly has established a corporate culture that looks at failure as an inevitable part of discovery, and its scientists are encouraged to look for new uses for compounds that fail at any stage in a human clinical trial. Evista was a failed contraceptive that became a US$1 billion-a-year drug for osteoporosis. Strattera was unsuccessful as an antidepressant but became a top seller for attention deficit/hyperactivity disorder. One promising cardiovascular drug in development started as an asthma project.[27]

Organizational Arrangements

Many companies today use *customer-driven engineering* to design new products. This strategy attaches high importance to incorporating customer preferences in the final design.

Xerox   Xerox traditionally developed new products as many firms did in the past: come up with an idea, develop a sample, and get some consumer feedback. When Xerox researchers first came up with the idea for a dual-engine commercial printer, they decided to first go straight to the consumer to collect feedback before even developing any prototypes. Lucky they did. Although the Xerox team thought customers would want a second engine for special purposes, the fact that the second engine would be a back-up if the main engine failed turned out to be the biggest draw. As one customer said, "If you're down, you're dead." In introducing the dual-engine Nuvera 288 Digital Perfecting System in April 2007, Xerox Chief Technology Officer Sophie V. Vandebroek cited "customer-led innovation" as an important driver. Xerox now believes in brainstorming, or "dreaming with the customer," by combining company experts who know technology with customers who know the "pain points" and what the most valuable product features can be. In addition, scientists and engineers are encouraged to meet face to face with customers, in some cases working on-site for a few weeks to see how customers interact with products.[28]

Box 20.2 shows how three other companies instituted internal changes to try to develop more successful new products and growth initiatives.

New-product development requires senior management to define business domains, product categories, and specific criteria. General Motors has a hefty US$400 million benchmark it must apply to new car models; that is what it costs to get a new vehicle into production.[29] One company established the following acceptance criteria:

- The product can be introduced within 5 years.
- The product has a market potential of at least US$50 million and a 15 percent growth rate.
- The product can provide at least 30 percent return on sales and 40 percent on investment.
- The product can achieve technical or market leadership.

Xerox's popular new dual-engine printer was a response to customers' feedback on the value of a commercial printer with a back-up engine.

BOX 20.2 📁 Three Innovation Models

- It has been proven that either formal or informal cross-functional product innovation teams facilitate idea generation and create new product concepts. Almarai Innovation Management (AIM) was established in 2008 as an initiative to increase the number of new product introductions as well as to foster continuous product development. The AIM team focused on product development efficiency through smooth productive coordination [30]

- In 1996 Shell authorized a team of its employees to allocate US$20 million to rule-breaking ideas originating anywhere in the company. Any employee can make a 10-minute pitch followed by a 15-minute question-and-answer session. Greenlight ideas get an average of US$100,000 and up to $600,000. Four teams out of 12 received 6-month funding for next-stage development. Of Shell's five largest growth initiatives in 1999, four started this way.

- Samsung Electronics established the Value Innovation Program (VIP) Center in 1998. Core cross-functional team members come together to discuss their strategic projects. In 2003, the center completed 80 projects. Samsung runs an annual Value Innovation conference, and awards are given for the best cases.

Budgeting for New-Product Development

Senior management must decide how much to budget for new-product development. R&D outcomes are so uncertain that it is difficult to use normal investment criteria. Some companies solve this problem by financing as many projects as possible, hoping to achieve a few winners. Other companies apply a conventional percentage-of-sales figure or spend what the competition spends. Still other companies decide how many successful new products they need and work backward to estimate the required investment.

📁 **Table 20.2** shows how a company might calculate the cost of new-product development. The new-products manager at a large consumer packaged-goods company reviewed the results of 64 ideas. Only one in four, or 16, passed the screening stage. It cost US$1,000 to review each idea at this stage. Half these ideas, or eight, survived the concept-testing stage, at a cost of $20,000 each. Half of these, or four, survived the product-development stage, at a cost of $200,000 each. Half

---

TABLE 20.2 📁 Finding One Successful New Product (starting with 64 new ideas)

Stage	Number of Ideas	Pass Ratio	Cost per Product Idea	Total Cost
Idea screening	64	1:4	$1,000	$64,000
Concept testing	16	1:2	20,000	320,000
Product development	8	1:2	200,000	1,600,000
Test marketing	4	1:2	500,000	2,000,000
National launch	2	1:2	5,000,000	10,000,000
			$5,721,000	$13,984,000

Costs in US$.

of these, or two, did well in the test market, at a cost of $500,000 each. When the two ideas were launched, at a cost of $5 million each, only one was highly successful. Thus, this one successful idea cost the company $5,721,000 to develop.

In the process, 63 other ideas fell by the wayside. The total cost for developing one successful new product from the 64 ideas was $13,984,000. Unless the company can improve the pass ratios and reduce the costs at each stage, it will need to budget nearly $14 million for each successful new idea it hopes to find.

Hit rates vary. Inventor Sir James Dyson claims he made 5,127 prototypes of his bagless, transparent vacuum cleaner before finally getting it right, eventually resulting in the best-selling vacuum cleaner by revenue in the United States. He doesn't lament his failures though: "If you want to discover something that other people haven't, you need to do things the wrong way…swatching why that fails can take you on a completely different path."[31]

Organizing New-Product Development

Companies handle the organizational aspect of new-product development in several ways.[32] Many companies assign responsibility for new-product ideas to *product managers*. But product managers are often so busy managing existing lines that they give little thought to new products other than line extensions. They also lack the specific skills and knowledge needed to develop and critique new products. Kraft and Johnson & Johnson have employed *new-product managers* who report to category managers. Some companies have a *high-level management committee* charged with reviewing and approving proposals. Large companies often establish a *new-product department* headed by a manager who has considerable authority and access to top management. The department's major responsibilities include generating and screening new ideas, working with the R&D department, and carrying out field testing and commercialization.

Adobe Systems Inc. A developer of software solutions for graphic designers and publishers, Adobe established a task force in 2004 to identify all the obstacles company innovators faced in trying to develop new products. The team found the corporate hierarchy resisted ideas needing a new sales channel, new business model, or even new packaging, and the company had grown so large that ideas originating in branch offices were not getting a fair shake. The company then established a New Business Initiatives Group that holds quarterly Adobe Idea Champion Showcases. About 20 product managers and other employees (except top executives who are barred from the proceedings) watch as potential employee-entrepreneurs give brief presentations and question-and-answer sessions. The ideas are examined by Adobe entrepreneurs-in-residence, but even one that's discontinued can still get a hearing on the company's brainstorming site. Since the new initiative was formed, the event has become extremely popular within Adobe: a stylish way for good ideas to come to the fore.[33]

3M, Dow, and General Mills have assigned new-product development work to **venture teams**, cross-functional groups charged with developing a specific product or business. These 'intrapreneurs' are relieved of their other duties and given a budget, time frame, and informal workplaces where new products can be developed.

Cross-functional teams can collaborate and use concurrent new-product development to push new products to market.[34] Concurrent product development resembles a football match, with team members passing the new product back and forth as they head toward the goal. Using this system, the Allen-Bradley Corporation (a maker of industrial controls) was able to develop a new electrical control device in just two years, as opposed to six under its old system. Cross-functional teams help ensure that engineers are not driven to create a 'better mousetrap' when potential customers don't need or want one.

venture team a cross-functional group charged with developing a specific product or business.

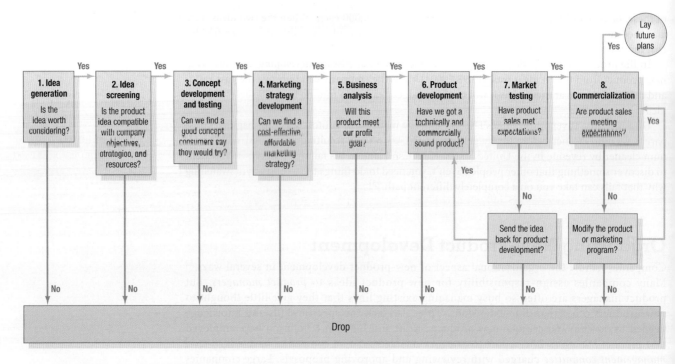

|Fig. 20.1|

The New-Product Development Decision Tree

Many top companies use the *stage-gate system* to manage the innovation process.[35] They divide the process into stages, at the end of each being a gate or checkpoint. The project leader, working with a cross-functional team, must bring a set of known deliverables to each gate before the project can pass to the next stage. To move from the business plan stage into product development requires a convincing market research study of consumer needs and interest, a competitive analysis, and a technical appraisal. Senior managers review the criteria at each gate to make one of four decisions: *go*, *kill*, *hold*, or *recycle*. Stage-gate systems make the innovation process visible to all involved and clarify the project leader's and team's responsibilities at each stage.[36]

The stages in the new-product development process are shown in △ **Figure 20.1**. Many firms have parallel sets of projects working through the process, each at a different stage.[37] A large number of initial new-product ideas and concepts are winnowed down to a few high-potential products that are ultimately launched. But the process is not always linear. Many firms use a *spiral development process* that recognizes the value of returning to an earlier stage to make improvements before moving forward.[38]

Managing the Development Process: Ideas

The new-product development process starts with the search for ideas. Some marketing experts believe the greatest opportunities and highest leverage with new products are found by uncovering the best possible set of unmet customer needs or technological innovation.[39]

Idea Generation

New-product ideas can come from interacting with various groups and using creativity-generating techniques[40] (see Marketing Memo: *Ten Ways to Find Great New-Product Ideas*).

Ten Ways to Find Great New-Product Ideas

1. Run informal sessions where groups of customers meet with company engineers and designers to discuss problems and needs and brainstorm potential solutions.

2. Allow time off for technical people to work on their own pet projects. 3M has allowed 15 percent time off; Rohm & Haas 10 percent.

3. Make a customer brainstorming session a standard feature of plant tours.

4. Survey your customers: find out what they like and dislike in your and competitors' products.

5. Undertake research with off-the-street customers, as Hewlett-Packard does.

6. Use a group of customers in one room, focusing on identifying problems, and a group of your technical people in the next room, listening and brainstorming solutions. Immediately test proposed solutions with the group of customers.

7. Set up a keyword search that routinely scans trade publications in multiple countries for new-product announcements.

8. Treat trade shows as intelligence missions, where you view all that is new in your industry under one roof.

9. Have your technical and marketing people visit your suppliers' labs and spend time with their technical people: find out what's new.

10. Set up an idea vault, and make it open and easily accessed. Allow employees to review the ideas and add constructively to them.

Source: Adapted from Robert Cooper, *Product Leadership: Creating and Launching Superior New Products* (New York: Perseus Books, 1998).

INTERACTING WITH OTHERS Encouraged by the *open innovation* movement, many firms are increasingly going outside the company to tap external sources of new ideas,[41] including customers, employees, scientists, engineers, channel members, marketing agencies, top management, and even competitors. The Marketing Insight: *P&G's New Connect-and-Develop Approach to Innovation* describes how that company has become more externally focused in its new-product development.

Customer needs and wants are the logical place to start the search.[42] One-on-one interviews and focus-group discussions can explore product needs and reactions. Griffin and Hauser suggest that conducting 10 to 20 in-depth experiential interviews per market segment often uncovers the vast majority of customer needs.[43] But many additional approaches can be profitable (see Marketing Memo: *Seven Ways to Draw New Ideas from Your Customers* on page 569).

The traditional company-centric approach to product innovation is giving way to a world in which companies co-create products with consumers.[44] Companies are increasingly turning to 'crowd-sourcing' to generate new ideas or, as we saw in the previous chapter, to create consumer-generated marketing campaigns. Crowd-sourcing means inviting the internet community to help create content or software, often with prize money or a moment of glory involved. This strategy has helped create new products and companies such as the open-source encyclopedia Wikipedia, the hugely popular video website YouTube, which was purchased by Google, and iStockphoto, a 'microstock' company.

iStockphoto The stock photography industry once consisted of large companies such as Getty and Corbis that licensed their high-end photos and images to ad agencies and other customers for hundreds or thousands of dollars per photo. Then Calgary, Canada, photographer Bruce Livingstone began giving his photos away online. Once users began trading photos via the site, Livingstone decided to sell the images for a small fee and offer photographers 40 percent royalties. iStockphoto has been enormously successful, both as a company and as a tool for freelance photographers like Lisa Gagne; in 2006, Gagne became the first iStockphoto photographer to sell over 500,000 images, and she now makes a six-figure sum yearly. Getty recently decided to purchase the company for US$50 million rather than compete with it.[45]

Besides producing new and better ideas, co-creation can help customers feel closer to and more favorably towards the company, and to tell others of their involvement through favorable word of mouth.[46]

Marketing Insight

P&G's New Connect-and-Develop Approach to Innovation

From fiscal years 2000 to 2004, Procter & Gamble's corporate profits jumped by almost 70 percent, to US$9.8 billion, and revenues increased by almost 30 percent, to $51 billion. Helping fuel that growth were successful new products such as Swiffer (a sweeper for hard floor surfaces), Mr. Clean Magic Eraser (a soft cleaning pad that removes dirt and stains), and Actonel (a prescription medication for osteoporosis). In January 2005, P&G acquired Gillette for $54 billion. But to a large degree P&G's growth in recent years has been driven by what CEO A. G. Lafley calls "the core"—core markets, categories, brands, technologies, and capabilities—and innovation has been at the heart of that.

To more effectively develop its core, P&G adopted a 'connect-and-develop' model that emphasizes the pursuit of more externally sourced innovation. Twenty-five percent of new products and technologies come from outside the company; Lafley wants to raise that to 50 percent, so "half would come out of P&G labs and half would come through P&G labs, from the outside."

P&G collaborates with organizations and individuals around the world, systematically searching for proven technologies, packages, and products it can improve, scale up, and market, either on its own or in partnership with other companies. It has forged strong relationships with external designers, distributing product development around the world to increase what P&G calls 'consumer sensing,' and even bringing John Osher, who invented the successful Crest SpinBrush electric rotating toothbrush, inside the company for a period to help make it more innovative.

To focus its idea search, P&G identifies the top 10 customer needs, closely related products that could leverage or benefit from existing brand equity, and technology 'game boards' that map the flow of technology adoption across different product categories. With these sources as boundaries, P&G may consult government and private labs, as well as academic and other research institutions; suppliers, retailers, competitors, and development and trade partners; Venture Capital firms; and individual entrepreneurs. P&G uses online networks to reach thousands of experts worldwide.

All these connections have helped to produce 100 new products in 2 years. For example, new ink-jet technology for printing edible images on cakes invented by a professor in Bologna, Italy, was used to create Pringles potato chips with jokes and pictures printed on them. The product was developed 2 to 3 years faster than usual at a fraction of the cost and resulted in double-digit growth for the Pringles brand. P&G has identified three core requirements for a successful connect-and-develop strategy:

1. Never assume that 'ready-to-go' ideas found outside are truly ready to go. There will always be development work to do, including risky scale-up.

2. Don't underestimate the internal resources required. You'll need a full-time, senior executive to run any connect-and-develop initiative.

3. Never launch without a mandate from the CEO. Connect and develop cannot succeed if it's restricted to R&D. It must be a top-down, company-wide strategy.

The connect-and-develop model certainly seems to be working for P&G. Forty-five percent of initiatives in the product-development portfolio have key elements that were discovered externally. Through connect and develop—along with improvements in other aspects of innovation related to product cost, design, and marketing—R&D productivity has increased by nearly 60 percent. The innovation success rate has more than doubled, and the cost of innovation has fallen. R&D investment as a percentage of sales is down from 4.8 percent in 2000 to 3.4 percent today. Since 2000, P&G's share price has doubled, and the company now has a portfolio of 22 billion-dollar brands.

Sources: Steve Hamm, "Speed Demons," *BusinessWeek*, March 27, 2006, pp. 69–76; Larry Huston and Nabil Sakkab, "Connect and Develop: Inside Procter & Gamble's New Model for Innovation," *Harvard Business Review*, March 2006, pp. 58–66; Geoff Colvin, "Lafley and Immelt: In Search of Billions," *Fortune*, December 11, 2006, pp. 70–72; Rajat Gupta and Jim Wendler, "Leading Change: An Interview with the CEO of P&G," *McKinsey Quarterly*, July 2005.

Lead users can be a good source of input when they innovate products without the consent or even the knowledge of the companies that produce them. Mountain bikes developed as a result of youngsters taking their bikes up to the top of a mountain and riding down. When the bikes broke, the youngsters began building more durable bikes and adding things such as motorcycle brakes, improved suspension, and accessories. The youngsters, not the companies, developed these innovations. Some companies, particularly those that want to appeal to hip young consumers, bring the lead users into their product-design process.

Technical companies can learn a great deal by studying customers who make the most advanced use of the company's products and who recognize the need for improvements before other customers do.[47] Microsoft studied 13- to 24-year-olds—the Net Gen—and developed its 'threedegrees' software product to satisfy their instant messaging needs.[48]

marketing Memo

Seven Ways to Draw New Ideas from Your Customers

1. **Observe how your customers are using your product.** Abou Ghaly Motors in Egypt, the official agent for Chrysler, Subaru, Jeep, Dodge, and Speranza, has salespeople and market researchers who regularly contact their customers to ensure maximum satisfaction. The company is always aiming to improve the services offered to customers through seven state-of-the-art service centers in the country.

2. **Ask your customers about their problems with your products.** Procter & Gamble, recognizing consumers were frustrated that potato chips would break and were difficult to save after opening the bag, designed Pringles to be uniform in size and encased in a tennis-ball-type can so consumers could open the can, consume a few unbroken chips, and close it again.

3. **Ask your customers about their dream products.** Ask your customers what they want your product to do, even if the ideal sounds impossible. One 70-year-old camera user told Minolta he would like the camera to make his subjects look better and not show their wrinkles and aging. In response, Minolta produced a camera with two lenses, one of which was for rendering softer images of the subjects.

4. **Use a customer advisory board to comment on your company's ideas.** Levi Strauss uses youth panels to discuss lifestyles, habits, values, and brand engagements; Cisco runs Customer Forums to improve its offerings; and Harley-Davidson solicits product ideas from its 1 million Harley Owners Group (H.O.G.) members.

5. **Use websites for new ideas.** Companies can use specialized search engines such as Technorati and Day Pop to find blogs and postings relevant to their businesses. P&G's site has 'We're Listening' and 'Share Your Thoughts' sections and advisory feedback sessions to gain advice and feedback from customers.

6. **Form a brand community of enthusiasts who discuss your product.** Harley-Davidson and Apple have strong brand enthusiasts and advocates; Sony engaged in collaborative dialogues with consumers to codevelop its PlayStation 2. Lego draws on kids and influential adult enthusiasts for feedback on new-product concepts in early stages of development.

7. **Encourage or challenge your customers to change or improve your product.** Salesforce.com wants its users to develop and share new software applications using simple programming tools. International Flavors & Fragrances gives a toolkit to its customers to modify specific flavors, which IFF then manufactures; LSI Logic Corporation also provides customers with do-it-yourself toolkits so that customers can design their own specialized chips; and BMW posted a toolkit on its website to let customers develop ideas using telematics and in-car online services.

Source: From an unpublished paper, Philip Kotler, "Drawing New Ideas from Your Customers," 2007.

Not everyone, however, believes a customer focus helps to create better new products. As Henry Ford famously said, "If I'd asked people what they wanted, they would have said a faster horse." Or as Bill Mitchell, the one-time head of GM car design in the 1960s said: "Frank Lloyd Wright did not go around ringing doorbells asking people what kind of houses they wanted! There is not one good-looking car I designed that market research had anything to do with." And some still caution that being overly focused on consumers who may not really know what they want, or what could be possible, can result in short-sighted product development and miss real potential breakthroughs.[49]

Employees throughout the company can be a source of ideas for improving production, products, and services. Toyota claims its employees submit 2 million ideas annually (about 35 suggestions per employee), over 85 percent of which are implemented. Kodak, Milliken, and other firms give monetary, holiday, or recognition awards to employees who submit the best ideas. BankDhofar in Oman promotes staff ideas through its Afkar programme, which recognizes innovative ideas by employees that can enhance BankDhofar's products and customer service.[50] Nokia inducts engineers with at least 10 patents into its 'Club 10,' recognizing them each year in a formal awards ceremony hosted by CEO Jorma Ollila.[51]

A company can motivate its employees to submit new ideas to an *ideas manager* whose name and phone number are widely circulated. Internal brainstorming sessions also can be quite effective, if they are conducted correctly. The Marketing Memo: *How to Run a Successful Brainstorming Session* provides some brainstorming guidelines.

Companies can find good ideas by researching the products and services of competitors and other companies. They can find out what customers like and dislike about competitors' products. They can buy their competitors' products, take them apart, and build better ones. Company sales representatives and intermediaries are a particularly good source of ideas. These groups have first-hand exposure to customers and are often the first to learn about competitive developments. Electronic retailer Best Buy actually checks with venture capitalists to find out what start-ups are working on.

marketing Memo

How to Run a Successful Brainstorming Session

Group brainstorming sessions have much upside, but also downside. If done incorrectly, they are a painful waste of time that can frustrate and antagonize participants; if done correctly, they can create insights, ideas, and solutions that would have been impossible without everyone's participation. To ensure success, experts recommend the following guidelines:

1. There should be a trained facilitator to guide the session.
2. Participants must feel that they can express themselves freely.
3. Participants must see themselves as collaborators working towards a common goal.
4. Rules need to be set up and followed, so conversations don't get off track.

5. Participants must be given proper background preparation and materials so that they can get into the task quickly.
6. Individual sessions before and after the brainstorming workshop can be useful to think and learn about the topic ahead of time as well as reflect afterwards on what happened.
7. Brainstorming sessions must lead to a clear plan of action and implementation, so the ideas that materialize can provide tangible value.
8. Brainstorming sessions can do more than just generate ideas—they can help build teams and leave participants better informed and energized.

Sources: Linda Tischler, "Be Creative: You Have 30 Seconds," *Fast Company*, May 2007, pp. 47–50; Michael Myser, "When Brainstorming Goes Bad," *Business 2.0*, October 2006, p. 76; Robert I. Sutton, "Eight Rules to Brilliant Brainstorming," *BusinessWeek IN Inside Innovation*, September 2006, pp. 17–21.

Top management can be another major source of ideas. Some company leaders, such as former CEO Andy Grove of Intel, take personal responsibility for technological innovation in their companies. New-product ideas can come from inventors, patent attorneys, university and commercial laboratories, industrial consultants, advertising agencies, marketing research firms, and industrial publications. However, although ideas can flow from many sources, their chances of receiving serious attention often depend on someone in the organization taking the role of product champion.

CREATIVITY TECHNIQUES The following list is a sampling of techniques for stimulating creativity in individuals and groups.[52]

- *Attribute listing.* List the attributes of an object, such as a screwdriver. Then modify each attribute, such as replacing the wooden handle with plastic, providing torque power, adding different screw heads, and so on.

- *Forced relationships.* List several ideas and consider each in relation to each other idea. In designing new office furniture, for example, consider a desk, bookcase, and filing cabinet as separate ideas. Then imagine a desk with a built-in bookcase or a desk with built-in files or a bookcase with built-in files.

- *Morphological analysis.* Start with a problem, such as 'getting something from one place to another via a powered vehicle.' Now think of dimensions, such as the type of platform (cart, chair, sling, bed), the medium (air, water, oil, rails), and the power source (compressed air, electric motor, magnetic fields). By listing every possible combination, you can generate many new solutions.

- *Reverse assumption analysis.* List all the normal assumptions about an entity and then reverse them. Instead of assuming that a restaurant has menus, charges for food, and serves food, reverse each assumption. The new restaurant may decide to serve only what the chef bought that morning and cooked; may provide some food and charge only for how long the person sits at the table; and may design an exotic atmosphere and rent out the space to people who bring their own food and beverages.

- *New contexts.* Take familiar processes, such as people-helping services, and put them into a new context. Imagine helping dogs and cats instead of people with day care service, stress reduction, psychotherapy, animal funerals, and so on. As another example, instead of sending hotel guests to the front desk to check in, greet them at curbside and use a wireless device to register them.

- *Mind mapping.* Start with a thought, such as a car, write it on a piece of paper, then think of the next thought that comes up (say Mercedes), link it to car, then think of the next association (Germany), and do this with all associations that come up with each new word. Perhaps a whole new idea will materialize.

Increasingly, new-product ideas arise from *lateral marketing* that combines two product concepts or ideas to create a new offering. Here are some successful examples:

- Gas station stores = gas stations + food
- Cyber cafés = cafeteria + internet
- Cereal bars = cereal + snacking
- Kinder Surprise = candy + toy
- Sony MP3 Player = audio + portable

Idea Screening

In screening ideas, the company must avoid two types of error. A *DROP-error* occurs when the company dismisses a good idea. It is extremely easy to find fault with other people's ideas (△ **Figure 20.2**). Some companies shudder when they look back at ideas they dismissed or breathe sighs of relief when they realize how close they came to dropping what eventually became a huge success. This was the case with the hit television show *Friends*.

 Friends The NBC situation comedy *Friends* enjoyed a 10-year run from 1994 to 2004 as a perennial ratings powerhouse. But the show almost didn't see the light of day. According to an internal NBC research report, the pilot episode was described as "not very entertaining, clever, or original" and was given a failing grade, scoring 41 out of 100. Ironically, the pilot for an earlier hit sitcom, *Seinfeld*, was also rated "weak," although the pilot for the medical drama *ER* scored a healthy 91. Courtney Cox's Monica was the *Friends* character who scored best with test audiences, but characters portrayed by Lisa Kudrow and Matthew Perry were deemed to have marginal appeal, and the Rachel, Ross, and Joey characters scored even lower. Adults 35 and over in the sample found the characters as a whole, "smug, superficial, and self-absorbed."[53]

A *GO-error* occurs when the company permits a poor idea to move into development and commercialization. An *absolute product failure* loses money; its sales do not cover variable costs. A *partial product failure* loses money, but its sales cover all its variable costs and some of its fixed costs. A *relative product failure* yields a profit lower than the company's target rate of return.

The purpose of screening is to drop poor ideas as early as possible. The rationale is that product-development costs rise substantially with each successive development stage. Most companies require new-product ideas to be described on a standard form for a new-product committee's review. The

"I've got a great idea!"

"It won't work here."

"We've tried it before."

"This isn't the right time."

"It can't be done."

"It's not the way we do things."

"We've done all right without it."

"It will cost too much."

"Let's discuss it at our next meeting."

|Fig. 20.2| △

Forces Fighting New Ideas

Source: With permission of Jerold Panas, Young & Partners Inc.

An idea that almost didn't get off the storyboard was the pilot for *Friends*, one of the longest-running hit comedies on television. The test episode was deemed "not very entertaining, clever, or original." Dismissing an idea that later proves to be successful is called a DROP-error.

TABLE 20.3	Product–Idea Rating Device		
Product Success Requirements	**Relative Weight (a)**	**Product Score (b)**	**Product Rating (c = a × b)**
Unique or superior product	0.40	0.8	0.32
High performance-to-cost ratio	0.30	0.6	0.18
High marketing dollar support	0.20	0.7	0.14
Lack of strong competition	0.10	0.5	0.05
Total	1.00		0.69[a]

[a]Rating scale: 0.00–0.30 poor; 0.31–0.60 fair; 0.61–0.80 good. Minimum acceptance rate: 0.61

description states the product idea, the target market, and the competition and roughly estimates market size, product price, development time and costs, manufacturing costs, and rate of return.

The executive committee then reviews each idea against a set of criteria. Does the product meet a need? Would it offer superior value? Can it be distinctively advertised? Does the company have the necessary know-how and capital? Will the new product deliver the expected sales volume, sales growth, and profit? Consumer input may be necessary to tap into marketplace realities.[54]

Management can rate the surviving ideas using a weighted-index method like that in Table 20.3. The first column lists factors required for successful product launches, and the second column assigns importance weights. The third column scores the product idea on a scale from 0 to 1.0, with 1.0 the highest score. The final step multiplies each factor's importance by the product score to obtain an overall rating. In this example, the product idea scores 0.69, which places it in the 'good idea' level. The purpose of this basic rating device is to promote systematic evaluation and discussion. It is not supposed to make the decision for management.

As the idea moves through development, the company will need to constantly revise its estimate of the product's overall probability of success, using the following formula:

$$\begin{array}{c} \text{Overall} \\ \text{probability} \\ \text{of success} \end{array} = \begin{array}{c} \text{Probability} \\ \text{of technical} \\ \text{completion} \end{array} \times \begin{array}{c} \text{Probability of} \\ \text{commercialization} \\ \text{given technical} \\ \text{completion} \end{array} \times \begin{array}{c} \text{Probability of} \\ \text{economic} \\ \text{success given} \\ \text{commercialization} \end{array}$$

For example, if the three probabilities are estimated as 0.50, 0.65, and 0.74, respectively, the overall probability of success is 0.24. The company then must judge whether this probability is high enough to warrant continued development.

Managing the Development Process: Concept to Strategy

Attractive ideas must be refined into testable product concepts. A *product idea* is a possible product the company might offer to the market. A *product concept* is an elaborated version of the idea expressed in consumer terms.

Concept Development and Testing

CONCEPT DEVELOPMENT Let us illustrate concept development with the following situation: a large food-processing company gets the idea of producing a powder to add to milk to increase its nutritional value and taste. This is a product *idea*, but consumers don't buy product ideas; they buy product *concepts*.

A product idea can be turned into several concepts. The first question is: who will use this product? The powder can be aimed at infants, children, teenagers, young or middle-aged adults, or older adults. Second, what primary benefit should this product provide? Taste, nutrition, refreshment, energy? Third, when will people consume this drink? Breakfast, midmorning, lunch, midafternoon, dinner, late evening? By answering these questions, a company can form several concepts:

- **Concept 1.** An instant breakfast drink for adults who want a quick nutritious breakfast without preparation.

- **Concept 2.** A tasty snack for children to drink as a midday refreshment.

- **Concept 3.** A health supplement for older adults to drink in the late evening before they go to bed.

Each concept represents a *category concept* that defines the product's competition. An instant breakfast drink would compete against eggs, breakfast cereals, coffee and pastry, and other breakfast alternatives. A tasty snack drink would compete against soft drinks, fruit juices, sports drinks, and other thirst quenchers.

Suppose the instant-breakfast-drink concept looks best. The next task is to show where this powdered product would stand in relationship to other breakfast products. *Perceptual maps* are a visual way to display consumer perceptions and preferences. They provide quantitative portrayals of market situations and how consumers see different products, services, and brands along various dimensions. By overlaying consumer preferences with brand perceptions, marketers can reveal 'holes' or 'openings' that suggest unmet consumer needs.

△ **Figure 20.3a** uses the two dimensions of cost and preparation time to create a *product-positioning map* for the breakfast drink. An instant breakfast drink offers low cost and quick preparation. Its nearest competitor is cold cereal or breakfast bars; its most distant competitor is eggs. These contrasts can help communicate and promote the concept to the market.

Next, the product concept becomes a *brand concept*. Figure 20.3b is a *brand-positioning map*, a perceptual map showing the current positions of three existing brands of instant breakfast drinks (A–C), as seen by consumers. It can also be useful to overlay consumer preferences on to the map in terms of their current or desired preferences. Figure 20.3b also shows that there are four segments of consumers whose preferences are clustered around the points displayed on the map.

The brand-positioning map helps the company to decide how much to charge and how calorific to make its drink. Three segments (1–3) are well served by existing brands (A–C). The company would not want to position itself next to one of those existing brands, unless that brand is weak or inferior or market demand is high enough to be shared. As it turns out, the new brand would be distinctive in the medium-price, medium-calorie market or in the high-price, high-calorie market. There is also a segment of consumers (4) clustered fairly near the medium-price, medium-calorie market, suggesting that it may offer the greatest opportunity.

CONCEPT TESTING Concept testing means presenting the product concept, symbolically or physically, to target consumers and getting their reactions. The more the tested concepts resemble the final product or experience, the more dependable concept testing is. Concept testing of prototypes can help avoid costly mistakes, but it may be especially challenging with radically different, new-to-the-world products.[55]

In the past, creating physical prototypes was costly and time consuming, but today firms can use *rapid prototyping* to design products on a computer, and then produce rough models of each to show potential consumers for their reactions. Companies are also using *virtual reality* to test product concepts. Virtual reality programs use computers and sensory devices (such as gloves or goggles) to simulate reality.

Concept testing presents consumers with an elaborated version of the concept. Here is the elaboration of concept 1 in our milk example:

Our product is a powdered mixture added to milk to make an instant breakfast that gives the person all the day's needed nutrition along with good taste and high convenience. The product comes in three flavors (chocolate, vanilla, and strawberry) and individual packets, six to a box, at US$2.49 a box.

After receiving this information, researchers measure product dimensions by having consumers respond to the following types of questions:

1. **Communicability and believability.** Are the benefits clear to you and believable? If the scores are low, the concept must be refined or revised.

(a) Product-Positioning Map (Breakfast Market)

(b) Brand-Positioning Map (Instant Breakfast Market)

|Fig. 20.3| △

Product and Brand Positioning

2. **Need level**. Do you see this product solving a problem or filling a need for you? The stronger the need, the higher the expected consumer interest.
3. **Gap level**. Do other products currently meet this need and satisfy you? The greater the gap, the higher the expected consumer interest. Marketers can multiply the need level by the gap level to produce a *need-gap score*. A high score means the consumer sees the product as filling a strong need not satisfied by available alternatives.
4. **Perceived value**. Is the price reasonable in relationship to value? The higher the perceived value, the higher the expected consumer interest.
5. **Purchase intention**. Would you (definitely, probably, probably not, definitely not) buy the product? Consumers who answered the first three questions positively should answer 'Definitely' here.
6. **User targets, purchase occasions, purchasing frequency**. Who would use this product, when, and how often?

Respondents' answers indicate whether the concept has a broad and strong consumer appeal, what products it competes against, and which consumers are the best targets. The need-gap levels and purchase-intention levels can be checked against norms for the product category to see whether the concept appears to be a winner, a long shot, or a loser. One food manufacturer rejects any concept that draws a definitely-would-buy score of lower than 40 percent.

CONJOINT ANALYSIS   We measure consumer preferences for alternative product concepts with **conjoint analysis**, a method for deriving the utility values that consumers attach to varying levels of a product's attributes.[56] Conjoint analysis has become one of the most popular concept-development and testing tools. For example, Marriott used it to design its Courtyard hotel concept.[57]

With conjoint analysis, respondents see different theoretical offers formed by combining varying levels of the attributes, then rank the various offers. Management can identify the most appealing offer and its estimated market share and profit. Green and Wind have illustrated this approach in connection with developing a new spot-removing, carpet-cleaning agent for home use.[58] Suppose the new-product marketer is considering five design elements:

- Three package designs (A, B, C—see ▲ **Figure 20.4**)
- Three brand names (K2R, Glory, Bissell)
- Three prices (US$1.19, $1.39, $1.59)
- A possible certification by the relevant authority seal (yes, no)
- A possible money-back guarantee (yes, no)

Although the researcher can form 108 possible product concepts ($3 \times 3 \times 3 \times 2 \times 2$), it would be too much to ask consumers to rank 108 concepts. A sample of, say, 18 contrasting product concepts is feasible, and consumers would rank them from most to least preferred.

The marketer now uses a statistical program to derive the consumer's utility functions for each of the five attributes (see ▲ **Figure 20.5**). Utility ranges between zero and one; the higher the utility, the stronger the consumer's preference for that level of the attribute. Looking at packaging, we see that package B is the most favored, followed by C and then A (A hardly has any utility). The preferred names are Bissell, K2R, and Glory, in that order. The consumer's utility varies inversely with price. A certification by a relevant authority is preferred, but it does not add that much utility and may not be worth the effort to obtain it. A money-back guarantee is strongly preferred.

The consumer's most desired offer is package design B, brand name Bissell, priced at US$1.19, with a *Good Housekeeping* seal and a money-back guarantee. We can also determine the relative importance of each attribute to this consumer: the difference between the highest and lowest utility level for that attribute. The greater the difference, the more important the attribute. Clearly, this consumer sees price and package design as the most important attributes, followed by money-back guarantee, brand name, and a certification by a relevant authority.

Preference data from a sufficient sample of target consumers helps us estimate the market share any specific offer is likely to achieve, given any assumptions about competitive response. Still, the company may not launch the market offer that promises to gain the greatest market share, because

conjoint analysis   a method for deriving the utility values that consumers attach to varying levels of a product's attributes.

|Fig. 20.4| ▲

Samples for Conjoint Analysis

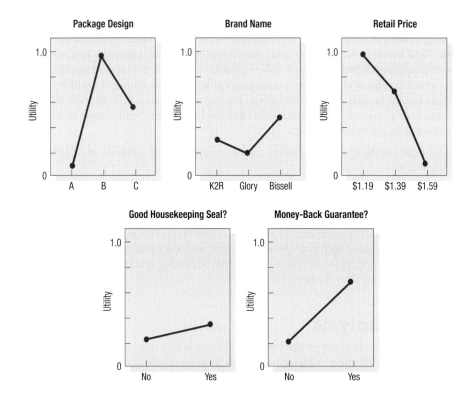

|Fig. 20.5| △

Utility Functions
Based on Conjoint
Analysis

of cost considerations. The most customer-appealing offer is not always the most profitable offer to make.

Under some conditions, researchers will collect the data not with a full-profile description of each offer, but by presenting two factors at a time. For example, respondents may see a table with three price levels and three package types and indicate which of the nine combinations they would like most, second-best, and so on. A further table consists of trade-offs between two other variables. The trade-off approach may be easier to use when there are many variables and possible offers. However, it is less realistic in that respondents are focusing on only two variables at a time. Adaptive conjoint analysis (ACA) is a 'hybrid' data-collection technique that combines self-explicated importance ratings with pairwise trade-off tasks.

Marketing Strategy Development

Following a successful concept test, the new-product manager will develop a preliminary three-part strategy plan for introducing the new product into the market. The first part describes the target market's size, structure, and behavior; the planned product positioning; and the sales, market share, and profit goals sought in the first few years:

> The target market for the instant breakfast drink is families with children who are receptive to a new, convenient, nutritious, and inexpensive form of breakfast. The company's brand will be positioned at the higher-price, higher-quality end of the instant-breakfast-drink category. The company will aim initially to sell 500,000 cases or 10 percent of the market, with a loss in the first year not exceeding US$1.3 million. The second year will aim for 700,000 cases or 14 percent of the market, with a planned profit of $2.2 million.

The second part outlines the planned price, distribution strategy, and marketing budget for the first year:

> The product will be offered in chocolate, vanilla, and strawberry, in individual packets of six to a box, at a retail price of US$2.49 a box. There will be 48 boxes per case, and the case price to distributors will be $24. For the first 2 months, dealers will be offered one case free for every four cases bought, plus cooperative-advertising allowances. Free samples will be

distributed door-to-door. Coupons for 20 cents off will appear in newspapers. The total sales promotional budget will be $2.9 million. An advertising budget of $6 million will be split 50:50 between national and local. Two-thirds will go into television and one-third into newspapers. Advertising copy will emphasize the benefit concepts of nutrition and convenience. The advertising-execution concept will revolve around a small boy who drinks instant breakfast and grows strong. During the first year, $100,000 will be spent on marketing research to buy store audits and consumer-panel information to monitor market reaction and buying rates.

The third part of the marketing strategy plan describes the long-run sales and profit goals and marketing-mix strategy over time:

The company intends to win a 25 percent market share and realize an after-tax return on investment of 12 percent. To achieve this return, product quality will start high and be improved over time through technical research. Price will initially be set at a high level and lowered gradually to expand the market and meet competition. The total promotion budget will be boosted each year about 20 percent, with the initial advertising–sales promotion split of 65:35 evolving eventually to 50:50. Marketing research will be reduced to US$60,000 per year after the first year.

Business Analysis

After management develops the product concept and marketing strategy, it can evaluate the proposal's business attractiveness. Management needs to prepare sales, cost, and profit projections to determine whether they satisfy company objectives. If they do, the concept can move to the development stage. As new information comes in, the business analysis will undergo revision and expansion.

ESTIMATING TOTAL SALES Total estimated sales are the sum of estimated first-time sales, replacement sales, and repeat sales. Sales-estimation methods depend on whether the product is purchased once (such as an engagement ring or retirement home), infrequently, or often. For one-time products, sales rise at the beginning, peak, and approach zero as the number of potential buyers is exhausted (see ▲ **Figure 20.6a**). If new buyers keep entering the market, the curve will not go down to zero.

Infrequently purchased products—such as automobiles, toasters, and industrial equipment—exhibit replacement cycles dictated by physical wear or obsolescence associated with changing styles, features, and performance. Sales forecasting for this product category calls for estimating first-time sales and replacement sales separately (see Figure 20.6b).

Frequently purchased products, such as consumer and industrial nondurables, have product life-cycle sales resembling Figure 20.6c. The number of first-time buyers initially increases and then decreases as fewer buyers are left (assuming a fixed population). Repeat purchases occur soon, providing the product satisfies some buyers. The sales curve eventually falls to a plateau representing a level of steady repeat-purchase volume; by this time, the product is no longer a new product.

In estimating sales, the manager's first task is to estimate first-time purchases of the new product in each period. To estimate replacement sales, management researches the product's *survival-age distribution*; that is, the number of units that fail in year one, two, three, and so on. The low end of the distribution indicates when the first replacement sales will take place. Because replacement sales are difficult to estimate before the product is in use, some manufacturers base the decision to launch a new product solely on the estimate of first-time sales.

For a frequently purchased new product, the seller estimates repeat sales as well as first-time sales. A high rate of repeat purchasing means customers are satisfied; sales are likely to stay high even after all first-time purchases take place. The seller should note the percentage of repeat purchases in each repeat-purchase class: those who re-buy once, twice, three times, and so on. Some products and brands are bought a few times and dropped.[59]

ESTIMATING COSTS AND PROFITS Costs are estimated by the R&D, manufacturing, marketing, and finance departments. ▱ **Table 20.4** illustrates a 5-year projection of sales, costs, and profits for the instant breakfast drink.

(a) One-Time Purchased Product

(b) Infrequently Purchased Product

(c) Frequently Purchased Product

|Fig. 20.6| ▲

Product Life-Cycle Sales for Three Types of Products

TABLE 20.4	Projected Five-Year Cash Flow Statement (in thousands of US dollars)					
	Year 0	**Year 1**	**Year 2**	**Year 3**	**Year 4**	**Year 5**
1. Sales revenue	$0	$11,889	$15,381	$19,654	$28,253	$32,491
2. Cost of goods sold	0	3,981	5,150	6,581	9,461	10,880
3. Gross margin	0	7,908	10,231	13,073	18,792	21,611
4. Development costs	−3,500	0	0	0	0	0
5. Marketing costs	0	8,000	6,460	8,255	11,866	13,646
6. Allocated overhead	0	1,189	1,538	1,965	2,825	3,249
7. Gross contribution	−3,500	−1,281	2,233	2,853	4,101	4,716
8. Supplementary contribution	0	0	0	0	0	0
9. Net contribution	−3,500	−1,281	2,233	2,853	4,101	4,716
10. Discounted contribution (15%)	−3,500	−1,113	1,691	1,877	2,343	2,346
11. Cumulative discounted cash flow	−3,500	−4,613	−2,922	−1,045	1,298	3,644

Row 1 shows projected sales revenue over the 5-year period. The company expects to sell US$11,889,000 (approximately 500,000 cases at $24 per case) in the first year. Behind this projection is a set of assumptions about the rate of market growth, the company's market share, and the factory-realized price. Row 2 shows the cost of goods sold, which hovers around 33 percent of sales revenue. We find this cost by estimating the average cost of labor, ingredients, and packaging per case. Row 3 shows the expected gross margin, the difference between sales revenue and cost of goods sold.

Row 4 shows anticipated development costs of $3.5 million, including product-development cost, marketing research costs, and manufacturing development costs. Row 5 shows the estimated marketing costs over the five-year period to cover advertising, sales promotion, and marketing research and an amount allocated for sales-force coverage and marketing administration. Row 6 shows the allocated overhead to this new product to cover its share of the cost of executive salaries, heat, light, and so on.

Row 7, the gross contribution, is gross margin minus the preceding three costs. Row 8, supplementary contribution, lists any change in income to other company products caused by the new-product introduction. *Dragalong income* is additional income to them, and *cannibalized income* is reduced income.[60] Table 20.4 assumes no supplementary contributions. Row 9 shows net contribution, which in this case is the same as gross contribution. Row 10 shows discounted contribution; that is, the present value of each future contribution discounted at 15 percent per annum. For example, the company will not receive $4,716,000 until the fifth year. This amount is worth only $2,346,000 today if the company can earn 15 percent on its money through other investments.[61]

Finally, row 11 shows the cumulative discounted cash flow, the accumulation of the annual contributions in row 10. Two things are of central interest. First is the maximum investment exposure, the highest loss the project can create. The company will be in a maximum loss position of $4,613,000 in year 1. The second is the payback period, the time when the company recovers all its investment, including the built-in return of 15 percent. The payback period here is about three and a half years. Management must decide whether to risk a maximum investment loss of $4.6 million and a possible payback period of three and a half years.

Companies use other financial measures to evaluate the merit of a new-product proposal. The simplest is **breakeven analysis**, which estimates how many units the company must sell (or how

breakeven analysis a means by which management estimates how many units of the product the company would have to sell to break even with the given price and cost structure.

many years it will take) to break even with the given price and cost structure. If management believes sales could easily reach the break-even number, it is likely to move the project into product development.

A more complex method of estimating profit is **risk analysis**. Here we obtain three estimates (optimistic, pessimistic, and most likely) for each uncertain variable affecting profitability, under an assumed marketing environment and marketing strategy for the planning period. The computer simulates possible outcomes and computes a distribution showing the range of possible rates of returns and their probabilities.[62]

risk analysis   a method by which possible rates of returns and their probabilities are calculated by obtaining estimates for uncertain variables affecting profitability.

Managing the Development Process: Development to Commercialization

Up to now, the product has existed only as a word description, a drawing, or a prototype. The next step represents a jump in investment that dwarfs the costs incurred so far. The company will determine whether the product idea can translate into a technically and commercially feasible product. If not, the accumulated project cost will be lost, except for any useful information gained in the process.

Product Development

The job of translating target customer requirements into a working prototype is helped by a set of methods known as *quality function deployment* (QFD). The methodology takes the list of desired *customer attributes* (CAs) generated by market research and turns them into a list of *engineering attributes* (EAs) that engineers can use. For example, customers of a proposed truck may want a certain acceleration rate (CA). Engineers can turn this into the required horsepower and other engineering equivalents (EAs). The methodology measures the trade-offs and costs of meeting customer requirements. A major contribution of QFD is improved communication between marketers, engineers, and manufacturing people.[63]

PHYSICAL PROTOTYPES   The R&D department will develop one or more physical versions of the product concept. Its goal is to find a prototype that embodies the key attributes described in the product-concept statement, that performs safely under normal use and conditions, and that the firm can produce within budgeted manufacturing costs. In the past, developing and manufacturing a successful prototype could take days, weeks, months, or even years. The web now permits more rapid prototyping and more flexible development processes.[64] Sophisticated virtual-reality technology is also speeding the process. By designing and testing product designs through simulation, for example, companies achieve the flexibility to respond to new information and to resolve uncertainties by quickly exploring alternatives.

 Boeing   Boeing designed its 777 aircraft on a totally digital basis. Engineers, designers, and more than 500 suppliers designed the aircraft on a special computer network without ever making a blueprint on paper. Project partners were connected by an extranet enabling them to communicate, share ideas, and work on the design at a distance. A computer-generated 'human' could climb inside the three-dimensional design on-screen to show how difficult maintenance access would be for a live mechanic. Such computer modeling allowed engineers to spot design errors that otherwise would have remained undiscovered until a person began to work on a physical prototype. Avoiding the time and cost of building physical prototypes reduced development time and scrappage and rework by 60 to 90 percent.[65]

Lab scientists must not only design the product's functional characteristics, but also communicate its psychological aspects and brand image through physical cues. How will consumers react to different colors, sizes, and weights? In the case of a mouthwash, for example, a yellow color could support an 'antiseptic' claim, a red color could support a 'refreshing' claim, and a green or blue color could support a 'cool' claim. Marketers need to supply lab people with information about what attributes consumers seek and how consumers judge whether these attributes are present.

CUSTOMER TESTS When the prototypes are ready, they must be put through exact functional tests and customer tests before they enter the marketplace. *Alpha testing* is testing the product within the firm to see how it performs in different applications. After refining the prototype further, the company moves to *beta testing* with customers.[66]

How do designers and product engineers make something 'everyday' such as toothpaste or an iron, interesting? In-home placement tests help.

Consumer testing can take several forms, from bringing consumers into a laboratory to giving them samples to use in their homes. Procter & Gamble has on-site labs such as a diaper-testing center where dozens of mothers bring their babies to be studied. To develop its Cover Girl Outlast all-day lip color, P&G invited 500 women to come to its labs each morning to apply the lipstick, record their activities, and return 8 hours later so it could measure remaining lip color, resulting in a product that came with a tube of glossy moisturizer that women can reapply on top of their color without having to look in a mirror. In-home placement tests are common for products ranging from ice cream flavors to new appliances. When DuPont developed its new synthetic carpeting, it installed free carpeting in several homes in exchange for the homeowners' willingness to report their likes and dislikes about the product.

How do we measure customer preferences? The *rank-order* method asks the consumer to rank the options. The *paired-comparison* method presents pairs of options and asks the consumer which one is preferred in each pair. The *monadic-rating* method asks the consumer to rate each product on a scale so marketers can derive the individual's preference order and levels.

Market Testing

After management is satisfied with functional and psychological performance, the product is ready to be dressed up with a brand name and packaging and put into a market test. In a genuine setting, marketers can learn how large the market is and how consumers and dealers react to handling, using, and repurchasing the product.

Not all companies undertake market testing. A company officer at Revlon Inc. stated: "In our field—primarily higher-priced cosmetics not geared for mass distribution—it would be unnecessary for us to market test. When we develop a new product, say an improved liquid makeup, we know it's going to sell because we're familiar with the field. And we've got 1,500 demonstrators in department stores to promote it." Many companies, however, believe market testing can yield valuable information about buyers, dealers, marketing program effectiveness, and market potential. The main issues are: How much market testing should be done, and what kind(s)?

The amount of market testing is influenced by the investment cost and risk on the one hand, and the time pressure and research cost on the other. High-investment/high-risk products, where the chance of failure is high, must be market tested; the cost of the market tests will be an insignificant percentage of total project cost. High-risk products—those that create new-product categories (first instant breakfast drink) or have novel features (first gum-strengthening toothpaste)—warrant more market testing than modified products (another toothpaste brand).

The amount of market testing may be severely reduced if the company is under great time pressure because the season is just starting, or because competitors are about to launch their brands. The company may prefer the risk of a product failure to the risk of losing distribution or market penetration on a highly successful product.

CONSUMER-GOODS MARKET TESTING Consumer-products tests seek to estimate four variables: *trial*, *first repeat*, *adoption*, and *purchase frequency.* The company hopes to find all these variables at high levels. Many consumers may try the product but few re-buy it; or it might achieve high permanent adoption but low purchase frequency (like gourmet frozen foods).

Here are four major methods of consumer-goods market testing, from least to most costly.

Sales-Wave Research In *sales-wave research,* consumers who initially try the product at no cost are reoffered it, or a competitor's product, at slightly reduced prices. The offer may be made as many as five times (sales waves), while the company notes how many customers selected that product again and their reported level of satisfaction. Sales-wave research can also expose consumers to one or more advertising concepts to measure the impact of that advertising on repeat purchase.

Sales-wave research can be implemented quickly, conducted with a fair amount of security, and carried out without final packaging and advertising. However, it does not indicate trial rates the product would achieve with different sales promotion incentives, because the consumers are preselected to try the product; nor does it indicate the brand's power to gain distribution and favorable shelf position.

Simulated Test Marketing Simulated test marketing calls for finding 30 to 40 qualified shoppers and questioning them about brand familiarity and preferences in a specific product category. These consumers attend a brief screening of both well-known and new TV commercials or print ads. One ad advertises the new product but is not singled out for attention. Consumers receive a small amount of money and are invited into a store where they may buy any items. The company notes how many consumers buy the new brand and competing brands. This provides a measure of the ad's relative effectiveness against competing ads in stimulating trial. Consumers are asked the reasons for their purchases or non-purchases. Those who did not buy the new brand are given a free sample. Some weeks later, they are interviewed by phone to determine product attitudes, usage, satisfaction, and repurchase intention and are offered an opportunity to repurchase any products.

This method gives fairly accurate results on advertising effectiveness and trial rates (and repeat rates if extended) in a much shorter time and at a fraction of the cost of using real test markets. The results are incorporated into new-product forecasting models to project ultimate sales levels. Marketing research firms have reported surprisingly accurate predictions of sales levels of products that are subsequently launched in the market.[67] In a world where media and channels have become highly fragmented, however, it will become increasingly harder for simulated test marketing to truly simulate market conditions with only traditional approaches.

Controlled Test Marketing In controlled test marketing, a research firm manages a panel of stores that will carry new products for a fee. The company with the new product specifies the number of stores and geographic locations it wants to test. The research firm delivers the product to the participating stores and controls shelf position; number of facings, displays, and point-of-purchase promotions; and pricing. Electronic scanners measure sales at the checkout. The company can also evaluate the impact of local advertising and promotions.

Controlled test marketing allows the company to test the impact of in-store factors and limited advertising on buying behavior. A sample of consumers can be interviewed later to give their impressions of the product. The company does not have to use its own sales force, give trade allowances, or 'buy' distribution. However, controlled test marketing provides no information on how to sell the trade on carrying the new product. This technique also exposes the product and its features to competitors' investigations.

Test Markets The ultimate way to test a new consumer product is to put it into full-blown test markets. The company chooses a few representative cities, and the sales force tries to sell the trade on carrying the product and giving it good shelf exposure. The company puts on a full advertising and promotion campaign similar to the one it would use in national marketing. Test marketing also measures the impact of alternative marketing plans by varying the marketing program in different cities: a full-scale test can cost over US$1 million, depending on the number of test cities, the test duration, and the amount of data the company wants to collect.

Management faces several decisions:

1. *How many test cities?* Most tests use two to six cities. The greater the possible loss, the greater the number of contending marketing strategies, the greater the regional differences, and the greater the chance of test-market interference by competitors, the more cities management should test.

2. **Which cities?** Each company must develop selection criteria such as having good media coverage, cooperative chain stores, and average competitive activity. How representative the city is of other markets must also be considered.
3. **Length of test?** Market tests last anywhere from a few months to a year. The longer the average repurchase period, the longer the test period.
4. **What information to collect?** Warehouse shipment data will show gross inventory buying but will not indicate weekly sales at the retail level. Store audits will show retail sales and competitors' market shares but will not reveal buyer characteristics. Consumer panels will indicate which people are buying which brands and their loyalty and switching rates. Buyer surveys will yield in-depth information about consumer attitudes, usage, and satisfaction.
5. **What action to take?** If the test markets show high trial and repurchase rates, the marketer should launch the product nationally; if a high trial rate and low repurchase rate, redesign or drop the product; if a low trial rate and high repurchase rate, develop marketing communications to convince more people to try it. If trial and repurchase rates are both low, abandon the product. Many managers find it difficult to kill a project that created much effort and attention even if they should, resulting in an unfortunate (and typically unsuccessful) escalation of commitment.[68]

In spite of its benefits, many companies today skip test marketing and rely on faster and more economical testing methods. General Mills prefers to launch new products in perhaps 25 percent of the United States, an area too large for rivals to disrupt. Managers review retail scanner data, which tell them within days how the product is doing and what corrective fine-tuning to do. Colgate-Palmolive often launches a new product in a set of small 'lead countries' and keeps rolling it out if it proves successful.

BUSINESS-GOODS MARKET TESTING Business goods can also benefit from market testing. Expensive industrial goods and new technologies will normally undergo alpha testing (within the company) and beta testing (with outside customers). During beta testing, the company's technical people observe how test customers use the product, a practice that often exposes unanticipated problems of safety and servicing and alerts the company to customer training and servicing requirements. The company can also observe how much value the equipment adds to the customer's operation as a clue to subsequent pricing.

The company will ask test customers to express their purchase intention and other reactions after the test. Companies must interpret beta test results carefully, because only a small number of test customers are used, they are not randomly drawn, and tests are somewhat customized to each site. Another risk is that test customers who are unimpressed with the product may leak unfavorable reports about it.

A second common test method for business goods is to introduce the new product at trade shows. The company can observe how much interest buyers show in the new product, how they react to various features and terms, and how many express purchase intentions or place orders.

New industrial products can be tested in distributor and dealer display rooms, where they may stand next to the manufacturer's other products and possibly competitors' products. This method yields preference and pricing information in the product's normal selling atmosphere. The disadvantages are that the customers might want to place early orders that cannot be filled, and those customers who come in might not represent the target market.

Industrial manufacturers come close to using full test marketing when they give a limited supply of the product to the sales force to sell in a limited number of areas that receive promotional support and printed catalog sheets.

Commercialization

If the company goes ahead with commercialization, it will face its largest costs to date.[69] It will need to contract for manufacture or build or rent a full-scale manufacturing facility. Another major cost is marketing. To introduce a major new consumer packaged good into the national market can cost from US$25 million to as much as $100 million in advertising, promotion, and other communications in the first year. In the introduction of new food products, marketing expenditures typically represent 57 percent of sales during the first year. Most new-product campaigns rely on a sequenced mix of market communication tools.

WHEN (TIMING) In commercializing a new product, market-entry timing is critical. Suppose a company has almost completed the development work on its new product and learns that a competitor is nearing the end of its development work. The company faces three choices:

1. **First entry**. The first firm entering a market usually enjoys the 'first mover advantages' of locking up key distributors and customers and gaining leadership. But if the product is rushed to market before it is thoroughly debugged, the first entry can backfire.
2. **Parallel entry**. The firm might time its entry to coincide with the competitor's entry. The market may pay more attention when two companies are advertising the new product.[70]
3. **Late entry**. The firm might delay its launch until after the competitor has entered. The competitor will have borne the cost of educating the market, and its product may reveal faults the late entrant can avoid. The late entrant can also learn the size of the market.

The timing decision requires additional considerations.[71] If a new product replaces an older product, the company might delay the introduction until the old product's stock is drawn down. If the product is seasonal, it might be delayed until the right season arrives; often a product waits for a 'killer application' to occur. Complicating new-product launches, many companies are encountering competitive 'design-arounds:' rivals are imitating inventions but making their own versions just different enough to avoid patent infringement and the need to pay royalties.

WHERE (GEOGRAPHIC STRATEGY) The company must decide whether to launch the new product in a single locality, a region, several regions, the national market, or the international market. Most will develop a planned market rollout over time. Company size is an important factor here. Small companies will select an attractive city and put on a blitz campaign, entering other cities one at a time. Large companies will introduce their product into a whole region and then move to the next region. Companies with national distribution networks, such as auto companies, will launch their new models in the national market.

Most companies design new products to sell primarily in the domestic market. If the product does well, the company considers exporting to neighboring countries or the world market, redesigning if necessary. In choosing rollout markets, the major criteria are market potential, the company's local reputation, the cost of filling the pipeline, the cost of communication media, the influence of the area on other areas, and competitive penetration.

The presence of strong competitors will influence rollout strategy. Suppose McDonald's wants to launch a new chain of fast-food 'McPizza' pizza parlors. Historically, Pizza Hut, Domino's, Papa John's, and Little Caesar's have been strongly entrenched in the Arab world, with an opportunity to compete in the Maghreb countries and the newly established state of South Sudan (which is likely to host many expatriates accustomed to these well-known brands). In this case, McDonald's would need to carefully select a geographic rollout strategy that balances consumer, competitive, and company considerations.

With the web connecting far-flung parts of the globe, competition is more likely to cross national borders. Companies are increasingly rolling out new products simultaneously across the globe, rather than nationally or even regionally. However, masterminding a global launch poses challenges, and a sequential rollout across countries may still be the best option.[72]

TO WHOM (TARGET-MARKET PROSPECTS) Within the rollout markets, the company must target its initial distribution and promotion to the best prospect groups. The company will have profiled these, and ideally they should be early adopters, heavy users, and opinion leaders who can be reached at low cost.[73] Few groups have all these characteristics. The company should rate the various prospect groups on these characteristics and target the best group. The aim is to generate strong sales as soon as possible to attract further prospects.

HOW (INTRODUCTORY MARKET STRATEGY) The company must develop an action plan for introducing the new product into the rollout markets. Because new-product launches often take longer and cost more money than expected, many potentially successful offerings suffer from underfunding. It's important to allocate sufficient time and resources—but also not to overspend—as the new product gains traction in the marketplace.[74]

A master of new-product introductions, Apple Computer staged a massive marketing blitz in 1998 to launch the iMac, its reentry into the computer PC business after a hiatus of 14 years. After that, Apple struck gold several times again, with subsequent launches of the iPod, iPhone, and iPad.

To coordinate the many activities involved in launching a new product, management can use network-planning techniques such as **critical path scheduling (CPS)**. This calls for developing a master chart showing the simultaneous and sequential activities that must take place to launch the product. By estimating how much time each activity takes, the planners estimate completion time for the entire project. Any delay in any activity on the critical path—the shortest route to completion—will cause the project to be delayed. If the launch must be completed earlier, the planner searches for ways to reduce time along the critical path.[75]

critical path scheduling (CPS) a network-planning technique that uses a master chart to show simultaneous and sequential activities that must take place to launch a product.

The Consumer-Adoption Process

Adoption is an individual's decision to become a regular user of a product. The *consumer-adoption process* is followed by the *consumer-loyalty process*, which is the concern of the established producer. Years ago, new-product marketers used a *mass-market approach* to launch products, which had two main drawbacks: it called for heavy marketing expenditures, and it wasted many exposures. These drawbacks led to a second approach, *heavy-user target marketing*. This approach makes sense, provided that heavy users are identifiable and are early adopters. However, even within the heavy-user group, many heavy users are loyal to existing brands. New-product marketers now aim at early adopters and use the theory of innovation diffusion and consumer adoption to identify them.

Stages in the Adoption Process

An **innovation** is any good, service, or idea that someone *perceives* as new, no matter how long its history. Innovations take time to spread. Everett Rogers defines the **innovation diffusion process** as "the spread of a new idea from its source of invention or creation to its ultimate users or adopters."[76] The consumer-adoption process is a series of mental steps through which an individual passes from first hearing about an innovation to final adoption.[77]

Adopters of new products move through five stages:

1. **Awareness**. The consumer becomes aware of the innovation but lacks information about it.
2. **Interest**. The consumer is stimulated to seek information about the innovation.
3. **Evaluation**. The consumer considers whether to try the innovation.
4. **Trial**. The consumer tries the innovation to improve his or her estimate of its value.
5. **Adoption**. The consumer decides to make full and regular use of the innovation.

The new-product marketer should facilitate movement through these stages. A portable electric-dishwasher manufacturer might discover that many consumers are stuck in the interest stage; they do not buy because of their uncertainty and the large investment cost.[78] But these same consumers would be willing to use an electric dishwasher on a trial basis for a small monthly fee. The manufacturer should consider offering a trial-use plan with an option to buy.

innovation any good, service, or idea that is perceived by someone as new.

innovation diffusion process the spread of a new idea from its source of invention or creation to its ultimate users or adopters.

Factors Influencing the Adoption Process

Marketers recognize the following characteristics of the adoption process: differences in individual readiness to try new products; the effect of personal influence; differing rates of adoption; and differences in organizations' readiness to try new products. Some researchers are focusing on use-diffusion processes as a complement to adoption process models, to see how consumers actually use new products.[79]

READINESS TO TRY NEW PRODUCTS AND PERSONAL INFLUENCE Everett
Rogers defines a person's level of innovativeness as "the degree to which an individual is relatively earlier in adopting new ideas than the other members of his social system." In each product area, there are pioneers and early adopters. Some people are the first to adopt new clothing fashions or new appliances; some doctors are the first to prescribe new medicines; some farmers are the first to

adopt new farming methods.[80] People fall into adopter categories. After a slow start, an increasing number of people adopt the innovation, the number reaches a peak, and then it diminishes as fewer non-adopters remain. So, around 2½ percent of people are innovators, 13½ percent are early adopters, 34 percent are known as the 'early majority,' another 34 percent as the 'late majority,' and the final 16 percent are 'laggards.' The five adopter groups differ in their value orientations and their motives for adopting or resisting the new product.[81]

- *Innovators* are technology enthusiasts; they are venturesome and enjoy tinkering with new products and mastering their intricacies. In return for low prices, they are happy to conduct alpha and beta testing and report on early weaknesses.
- *Early adopters* are opinion leaders who carefully search for new technologies that might give them a dramatic competitive advantage. They are less price sensitive and willing to adopt the product if given personalized solutions and good service support.
- *Early majority* are deliberate pragmatists who adopt the new technology when its benefits are proven and a lot of adoption has already taken place. They make up the mainstream market.
- *Late majority* are skeptical conservatives who are risk averse, technology shy, and price sensitive.
- *Laggards* are tradition-bound and resist the innovation until they find that the status quo is no longer defensible.

Each group must be approached with a different type of marketing if the firm wants to move its innovation through the full product life cycle.[82]

personal influence the effect one person has on another's attitude or purchase probability.

Personal influence is the effect one person has on another's attitude or purchase probability. Its significance is greater in some situations and for some individuals than others, and it is more important in the evaluation stage than the other stages. It has more influence on late adopters than early adopters and is more important in risky situations.

Companies often target innovators and early adopters with product rollouts. For Vespa scooters, Piaggio hired models to go around cafés and clubs in trendy Los Angeles areas to talk up the brand.[83] When Nike entered the skateboarding market, it recognized that an anti-establishment, anti-big-company bias among the target market could present a sizable challenge. To gain teen skaters it sold exclusively to independent shops, advertised nowhere but skate magazines, and gained sponsorships from well-admired pro riders by engaging them in product design.[84]

CHARACTERISTICS OF THE INNOVATION Some products catch on immediately (rollerblades), whereas others take a long time to gain acceptance (diesel engine autos). Five characteristics influence the rate of adoption of an innovation. We will consider them in relation to the adoption of personal video recorders (PVRs) for home use, as exemplified by TiVo.[85]

The first characteristic is *relative advantage*: the degree to which the innovation appears superior to existing products. The greater the perceived relative advantage of using a PVR, say, for easily recording favorite shows, pausing live TV, or skipping commercials, the more quickly it will be adopted. The second is *compatibility*: the degree to which the innovation matches the values and experiences of the individuals. PVRs, for example, are highly compatible with the preferences of avid television watchers. Third is *complexity*: the degree to which the innovation is difficult to understand or use. PVRs are somewhat complex and will therefore take a slightly longer time to penetrate into home use. Fourth is *divisibility*: the degree to which the innovation can be tried on a limited basis. This provides a sizable challenge for PVRs: sampling can only occur in a retail store or perhaps a friend's house. Fifth is *communicability*: the degree to which the benefits of use are observable or describable to others. The fact that PVRs have some clear advantages can help create interest and curiosity.

Other characteristics that influence the rate of adoption are cost, risk and uncertainty, scientific credibility, and social approval. The new-product marketer must research all these factors and give the key ones maximum attention in designing the new product and marketing program.[86]

ORGANIZATIONS' READINESS TO ADOPT INNOVATIONS The creator of a new teaching method would want to identify innovative schools. The producer of a new piece of medical equipment would want to identify innovative hospitals. Adoption is associated with variables in the organization's environment (community progressiveness, community income), the organization itself (size, profits, pressure to change), and the administrators (education level, age, sophistication). Other forces come into play in trying to get a product adopted into organizations that receive the bulk of their funding from the government, such as public schools. A controversial or innovative product can be ruined by negative public opinion.

Summary

1. Once a company has segmented the market, chosen its target customer groups and identified their needs, and determined its desired market positioning, it is ready to develop and launch appropriate new products and services. Marketing should participate with other departments in every stage of new-product development.

2. Successful new-product development requires the company to establish an effective organization for managing the development process. Companies can choose to use product managers, new-product managers, new-product committees, new product department ments, or new-product venture teams. Increasingly, companies are adopting cross-functional teams, connecting to individuals and organizations outside the company, and developing multiple product concepts.

3. Eight stages take place in the new-product development process: idea generation, screening, con-

cept development and testing, marketing strategy development, business analysis, product development, market testing, and commercialization. At each stage, the company must determine whether the idea should be dropped or moved to the next stage.

4. The consumer-adoption process is the process by which customers learn about new products, try them, and adopt or reject them. Today many marketers are targeting heavy users and early adopters of new products, because both groups can be reached by specific media and tend to be opinion leaders. The consumer-adoption process is influenced by many factors beyond the marketer's control, including consumers' and organizations' willingness to try new products, personal influences, and the characteristics of the new product or innovation.

Applications

Marketing Debate
Who Should You Target with New Products?

Some new-product experts maintain that getting close to customers through intensive research is the only way to develop successful new products. Other experts disagree and maintain that customers can't possibly provide useful feedback on what they don't know and can't provide insights that will lead to breakthrough products.

Take a position: Consumer research is critical to new-product development *versus* consumer research may not be all that helpful in new-product development.

Marketing Discussion

Think about the last new product you bought. How do you think its success will be affected by the five characteristics of an innovation: relative advantage, compatibility, complexity, divisibility, and communicability?

Marketing Excellence

>>Apple iPod

In a few short years, the iPod MP3 music player became a cultural phenomenon, and these days they are very common. The iPod exemplified Apple's innovative design skills and looked, felt, and operated like no other. With the launch of the iTunes music store, a dynamic duo of legally downloadable music and a cutting-edge portable music player caused iPod sales to skyrocket. To the delight of Apple (and the chagrin of competitor Sony), the iPod has become 'the Walkman of the 21st century.'

Beyond spurring sales, the iPod has been central in changing the way people listen to and use music. The shuffle feature of iPods helped people make connections between different genres of music. According to musician John Mayer, "People feel they're walking through musicology" when they use their iPods, leading them to listen to more music, and with more passion." Podcasting enables users to replace radio broadcasts and listen to DJ sets without commercial interruption. The new video, photo, and phone features have the potential to change how people interact with those media as well.

Apple reached this impressive state of market domination through a combination of shrewd product innovation and clever marketing. It defined a broad access point for its target market: music lovers who wanted their music, whenever and wherever. The marketing effort was designed to appeal to Mac fans as well as people who had not used Apple products in the past. This broader access required a shift in Apple's channel strategies. Adding 'mass electronic' retailers such as Max Electronics (Emax) to Apple's existing channels and company stores resulted in an increase of outlets from 4,000 to 21,000.

Besides this enhanced 'push' effort, Apple also developed memorable, creative 'pull' advertising that helped drive the popularity of the iPod. The Silhouettes campaign ran all over the world with a message simple enough to work across cultures, portraying the iPod as cool, but not so cool as to be beyond the reach of anyone

Continued on next page >>

Marketing Excellence...continued

>>Apple iPod

who enjoyed music. Television commercials featured people in silhouette listening to iPods and dancing in front of neon backgrounds. Similar images populated print ads, billboards, and posters. Ad text told the story of iPod's capabilities in a simple, appealing way, such as "iPod. Welcome to the digital music revolution. 10,000 songs in your pocket. Mac or PC."

Apple's campaign also flooded a handful of big cities such as Dubai and Shanghai with iPod billboards, bus posters, print ads, and TV commercials that were intended to spread the message that 'iPod is everywhere." The brand enjoyed exceedingly strong PR, buzz, and word of mouth. Apple has continually updated the iPod and released new versions, spawning an 'iPod economy' of third-party accessories and add-ons. Even though some analysts thought sales might slow, consumers have continued to snap up the music players. By January 2011, more than 304 million iPods had been sold worldwide and the iPod contributed one-third of Apple's corporate revenue. A halo effect from iPod was thought to help explain Apple's increase in market share in retail computers of more than 3 percentage points in recent years.

Questions

1. Discuss the product concept of the Apple iPod.

2. Analyze to what extent the iPod is spreading as an international product.

3. Think about your own experiences of personal music devices. Compare a Sony Walkman with an iPod.

4. Imagine if the iPod was not yet released in the Arab world. In which cities would you start selling the product, and why?

Sources: TerrilYue Jones, "How Long Can the iPod Stay on Top?," *Los Angeles Times*, March 5, 2006; Beth Snyder Bulik, "Grab an Apple and a Bag of Chips," *Advertising Age*, May 23, 2005; Jay Parsons, "A Is for Apple on iPod," *Dallas Morning News*, October 6, 2005; Peter Burrows, "Rock On, iPod," *BusinessWeek*, June 7, 2004, pp. 130–131; Jay Lyman, "Mini iPod Moving Quickly, Apple Says," *TechNewsWorld*, February 26, 2004; Steven Levy, "iPod Nation," *Newsweek*, July 25, 2004; www.apple.com; www.effie.org; "Apple Computer: iPod Silhouettes," New York Marketing Association; John Mayer quote from Steven Levy, "iPod Nation," *Newsweek*, July 25, 2004.

Nokia's global view motivates its broad product lines that appeal to all kinds of customers and price ranges all over the world.

In this chapter, we will address the following **questions:**

1. What factors should a company review before deciding to go abroad? (pg. 590)

2. How can companies evaluate and select specific foreign markets to enter? (pg. 591)

3. What are the major ways of entering a foreign market? (pg. 597)

4. To what extent must the company adapt its products and marketing program to each foreign country? (pg. 600)

5. How should the company manage and organize its international activities? (pg. 612)

Tapping Into Global Markets

With faster communication, transportation, and financial flows, the world is rapidly shrinking. Products and services developed in one country are finding enthusiastic acceptance in others. An Egyptian businessman may wear an Italian suit to meet an American friend at an Asian restaurant, who later returns home to watch a Turkish series on a Korean TV set. More and more countries are becoming increasingly multicultural. Companies need to be able to cross boundaries within and outside their country. Consider the international success of Nokia.

 Nokia has made a remarkable transformation from an obscure Finnish conglomerate into the world's largest maker of mobile phones. Part of Nokia's success is due to the broad view it takes of its business, selling a wide range of products to consumers of all kinds all over the world. Nokia also takes a broad perspective on competition, viewing Apple, Sony, and Canon as threats as much as traditional rivals Motorola and Samsung. To sustain its market leadership, Nokia launched a range of handsets, the N-series, with advanced features such as music playing, video recording, and e-mail. But Nokia wants to be a leader in all global markets, so it can't afford to sell just high-end products. With the bulk of industry growth coming from developing markets, Nokia has made sure its cheapest handsets are appealing—and profitable—in markets such as China, India, Latin America, and Egypt. Along with a US$750 handset with built-in global-positioning receivers, it also sells basic models that cost just $45. Although Nokia has struggled a little in North America—in part because many networks there use a different wireless standard (CDMA) than in Europe (GSM)—Nokia remains a major player in the mobile handset business in the Arab world and internationally, and its global footprint is still impressive. Of the 1.4 billion mobile phones sold worldwide in 2010, 453 million were made by Nokia.[1]

Although opportunities to enter and compete in international markets are significant, the risks can also be high. Companies selling in global industries, however, have no choice but to internationalize their operations. In this chapter, we review the major decisions in expanding into global markets. ▽

Competing on a Global Basis

Two hundred giant corporations, most larger than many national economies, together have sales that exceed a quarter of the world's economic activity. Altria, including its main subsidiary Philip Morris, is about the same size as the economy of New Zealand and operates in over 160 countries. Exports accounted for over one-quarter of U.S. GDP growth in 2010.[2]

Many companies have conducted international marketing for decades: firms such as Nestlé, Shell, Bayer, and Toshiba have been familiar around the world for years. But global competition is intensifying as new firms make their mark on the international stage.

Domestic companies that never thought about foreign competitors suddenly find them in their backyards. Newspapers report on the success of Japanese, German, and Korean car imports in the Arab market, and the loss of textile and shoe markets to imports from developing countries in Eastern Europe and Asia. Some of the foreign brands that have succeeded in Arab markets include Nestlé, Lipton, Four Seasons, Bvlgari, Sony, Mercedes, and Tommy Hilfiger. This puts pressure on local brands to compete with the foreign brands. In fact, foreign brands tend to have a stronger presence in the Arab region than their local counterparts.

global industry   an industry in which the strategic positions of competitors in major geographic or national markets are fundamentally affected by their overall global positions.

global firm   a firm that operates in more than one country and captures R&D, production, logistical, marketing, and financial advantages in its costs and reputation that are not available to purely domestic competitors.

Although some Arab businesses may want to eliminate foreign competition through protective legislation, the better way to compete is to continuously improve products at home and expand into foreign markets. In a **global industry**, competitors' strategic positions in major geographic or national markets are affected by their overall global positions.[3] A **global firm** operates in more than one country and captures R&D, production, logistical, marketing, and financial advantages not available to purely domestic competitors.

Global firms plan, operate, and coordinate their activities on a worldwide basis. Otis Elevator uses door systems from France, small geared parts from Spain, electronics from Germany, and motor drives from Japan; systems integration happens in the United States. One successful global company is SABIC, which has established joint venture partnerships with major international companies.

 SABIC   SABIC, the Saudi Basic Industries Corporation, represents one of the world's leading manufacturers of chemicals, fertilizers, plastics, and metals and is the largest and most profitable corporation in the region. SABIC's success results from its focus on three main goals: investing in local partnerships, applying the best research and technology programs, and, above all, implementing an ambitious global growth strategy. The corporation's global approach enabled it to improve its position from being the world's 301st largest corporation in 2006 to 227th in 2007. By 2011, SABIC had moved up again to 210 on the *Fortune* Global 500 ranking, with revenues of US$40.5 billion, profits of $5.7 billion, and assets standing at $84.7 billion. Many of SABIC's partnerships have been established with major international corporations such as Dow Chemical, Exxon, and Mitsubishi, but it has also developed sound partnerships with three major Bahraini groups, creating ALBA, GARMCO, and GPIC. In order to maintain is prominent position in the market, SABIC invests large amounts of money in training and technology. It currently employs 30,000 people in Saudi Arabia and has 60 major manufacturing and compounding plants in more than 40 countries. By establishing strong partnerships with different countries around the world, SABIC has successfully managed to acquire new resources, expand its knowledge concerning the best ways to conduct its business, and—most importantly—expand its customer base.[4]

Small and medium-sized firms can practice global nichemanship: designing a profitable niche product. The Poilane Bakery sells 15,000 loaves of old-style bread each day in Paris—2.5 percent of all bread sold in that city—via company-owned delivery trucks. But each day, Poilane-branded bread is also shipped via FedEx to loyal customers in roughly 20 countries around the world.[5]

Service businesses increasingly fuel the world economy, and, in turn, a globalizing economy fuels the service industry. The world market for services is growing at double the rate of world merchandise trade. Although some countries have erected entry barriers or regulations, the World Trade Organization, consisting of 150 countries, continues to press for more free trade in international services and other areas.[6]

Large firms in accounting, advertising, banking, communications, construction, insurance, law, management consulting, and retailing are pursuing global expansion. Emirates Airline, Carrefour, American Express, Citigroup, Hilton, and BMW are all known worldwide. Isis organic food, produced by SEKEM, depends mainly on the foreign market as its source of revenue. It has a small market in Egypt and sells its products to 17 countries in Europe. For global service firms, diversity has become a business imperative, but it has become true for all firms too. As one former Colgate executive says, "The speed of global business is accelerating diversity. All business processes cut across country borders now, with virtual teams in North America, Latin America, and Asia."[7]

For a company of any size or any type to go global, it must make a series of decisions (see △ **Figure 21.1**). We'll examine each of these decisions here.

Deciding whether to go abroad

↓

Deciding which markets to enter

↓

Deciding how to enter the market

↓

Deciding on the marketing program

↓

Deciding on the marketing organization

|Fig. 21.1| △

Major Decisions in International Marketing

Deciding Whether to Go Abroad

Most companies would prefer to remain domestic if their domestic market were large enough. Managers would not need to learn other languages and laws, deal with volatile currencies, face political and legal uncertainties, or redesign their products to suit different customer needs and expectations. Business would be easier and safer. Yet several factors draw companies into the international arena:

- Some international markets present higher profit opportunities than the domestic market.
- The company needs a larger customer base to achieve economies of scale.
- The company wants to reduce its dependence on any one market.
- The company decides to counterattack global competitors in their home markets.
- Customers are going abroad and require international service.

Before making a decision to go abroad, the company must be aware of and weigh several risks:

- The company might not understand foreign preferences and could fail to offer a competitively attractive product.
- The company might not understand the foreign country's business culture.
- The company might underestimate foreign regulations and incur unexpected costs.
- The company might lack managers with international experience.
- The foreign country might change its commercial laws, devalue its currency, or undergo a political revolution and expropriate foreign property.

Some companies don't act until events thrust them into the international arena. The *internationalization process* typically has four stages:[8]

1. No regular export activities.
2. Export via independent representatives (agents).
3. Establishment of one or more sales subsidiaries.
4. Establishment of production facilities abroad.

The first task is to move from stage 1 to stage 2. Most firms work with an independent agent and enter a nearby or similar country. Later, the firm establishes an export department to manage its agent relationships. Still later, it replaces agents with its own sales subsidiaries in its larger export markets. This increases investment and risk, but also earning potential.

To manage subsidiaries, the company replaces the export department with an international department. If markets are large and stable, or the host country requires local production, the company will locate production facilities in those markets. By this time, it's operating as a multinational and is optimizing its global sourcing, financing, manufacturing, and marketing. According to some researchers, top management begins to pay more attention to global opportunities when over 15 percent of revenues comes from international markets.[9]

Deciding Which Markets to Enter

In deciding to go abroad, the company needs to define its marketing objectives and policies. What proportion of international to total sales will it seek? Most companies start small when they venture abroad. Some plan to stay small; others have bigger plans.

How Many Markets to Enter

The company must decide how many countries to enter and how fast to expand. Typical entry strategies are the *waterfall* approach, gradually entering countries in sequence, and the *sprinkler* approach, entering many countries simultaneously. Increasingly, firms—especially technology-intensive firms—are born *global* and market to the entire world from the outset.[10]

Matsushita, BMW, General Electric, Benetton, and The Body Shop followed the waterfall approach. It allows firms to carefully plan expansion and is less likely to strain human and financial resources. When first-mover advantage is crucial and a high degree of competitive intensity prevails, such as when Microsoft introduces a new version of Windows software, the sprinkler approach is better. The main risk is the substantial resources needed and the difficulty of planning entry strategies into many diverse markets.

The company must also decide on the countries to consider. Their attractiveness is influenced by the product and by geography, income and population, and political climate.

Developed versus Developing Markets

One of the sharpest distinctions in global marketing is between developed and developing or less mature markets such as Brazil, Russia, India, China, and South Africa.[11] The unmet needs of the emerging or developing world represent huge potential markets for food, clothing, shelter, consumer electronics, appliances, and many other goods. Market leaders rely on developing markets to fuel their growth. Unilever and Colgate have generated 40 percent of their business in developing markets.[10]

Developed nations and the prosperous parts of developing nations account for about 20 percent of the world's population. Can marketers serve the other 80 percent, which has much less purchasing power and living conditions ranging from mild deprivation to severe deficiency?[13] This imbalance is likely to get worse, as more than 90 percent of future population growth is projected to occur in the less developed countries.

Successfully entering developing markets requires a special set of skills and plans. Consider how the following companies pioneered ways to serve these 'invisible' consumers:[14]

- Grameen-Phone marketed mobile phones to 35,000 villages in Bangladesh by hiring village women as agents who leased phone time to other villagers, one call at a time.
- Colgate-Palmolive rolled into Indian villages with video vans that showed the benefits of toothbrushing.
- Fiat developed a 'third-world car,' the Palio, to sell in developing nations. The car is produced in Brazil, India, Turkey, South Africa, China, Morocco, Egypt, and other countries.
- Corporacion GEO builds low-income housing in Mexico. The two-bedroom homes are modular and can be expanded. The company has moved into Chile.

These marketers capitalize on the potential of developing markets by changing their conventional marketing practices.[15] Selling in developing areas can't be 'business as usual.' Economic and cultural differences abound; a marketing infrastructure may barely exist; and local competition can be surprisingly stiff.[16] In China, PC maker Lenovo, mobile-phone provider TCL, and appliance manufacturer Haier have thrived despite strong foreign competition. Besides their sharp grasp of Chinese tastes, these companies have vast distribution networks, especially in rural areas. Competition is also growing from other developing markets. China has been exporting cars to Africa, Southeast Asia, and the Middle East. Tata of India, Cemex of Mexico, and Petronas of Malaysia have emerged from developing markets to become strong multinationals selling in many countries.[17]

Eighty percent of consumers in emerging markets buy their products from tiny bodegas, stalls, kiosks, and small stores not much bigger than a closet, which Procter & Gamble calls 'high-frequency stores.' Smaller packaging and lower sales prices are often critical when incomes and housing spaces are limited. Unilever's 4-cent sachets of detergent and shampoo have been a big hit in rural India, where 70 percent of the country's population still lives. When Coca-Cola moved to a smaller, 200 ml bottle in India, selling it for 10 to 12 cents in small shops, bus-stop stalls, and roadside eateries, sales jumped.[18] A Western image can also be helpful, as Coca-Cola discovered in China. Part of its success against local cola brand Jianlibao was due to its symbolic values of modernity and affluence.[19]

Recognizing that its cost structure made it difficult to compete effectively in developing markets, Procter & Gamble devised cheaper, clever ways to make the right kinds of products to suit consumer demand. It now uses contract manufacturers in certain markets and gained eight market-share points in Russia for Always feminine protection pads by responding to consumer wishes for a thicker pad.[20] In Mexico, Cemex received kudos for helping to actually improve housing in poor areas by introducing a pay-as-you-go system for buying building supplies.[21]

Danone   In Bangladesh, French food giant Danone partnered with Muhammed Yunus' Nobel-Prize-winning microcredit organization, Grameen Bank, to make and sell low-cost, nutritionally fortified yogurts under the brand name Shoktidoi. The joint venture will provide income to thousands of local farmers who supply the milk (and who raise cows by borrowing small amounts of money from Grameen) and to villagers who distribute the yogurt. At 8 cents per 80-gram pot, Shoktidoi is not likely to net profits for Danone right now, but the firm is confident tangible returns will match the intangible returns of feeding the poor. In Bangladesh, Danone has created a laboratory in which it is able to develop new food products for malnourished children in very poor countries, but it could also churn out new products there for mature and richer markets, all at low cost.[22]

The challenge is to think creatively about how marketing can fulfill the dreams of most of the world's population for a better standard of living. Many companies are betting they can do that. The Marketing Insight: *Spotlight on Key Developing Markets* highlights some important developments in the five key emerging market areas often called BRICS for short: Brazil, Russia, India, China, and South Africa.

Regional economic integration—the creation of trading agreements between blocs of countries—has intensified in recent years. This means companies are more likely to enter entire regions at the same time. Certain countries have formed free-trade zones or economic communities: groups of nations organized to work toward common goals in the regulation of international trade.

THE EUROPEAN UNION Formed in 1957, the European Union set out to create a single European market by reducing barriers to the free flow of products, services, finances, and labor among member countries, and by developing trade policies with nonmember nations. Today, it's one of the world's largest single markets, with 27 member countries, a common currency—the euro—and more than 502.5 million consumers, accounting for 23 percent of the world's exports.[23] Companies that plan to create 'pan-European' marketing campaigns should proceed with caution, however. Even as the EU standardizes its general trade regulations and currency, creating an economic community will not create a homogeneous market. Companies marketing in Europe face 14 different languages, 2,000 years of historical and cultural differences, and a daunting mass of local rules. Please note, that as this book went to press in 2012, there were some questions in the media about how long this currency was going to last.

Spotlight on Key Developing Markets

Brazil

The vast majority of people in Latin America have little to spend. According to the World Bank, 25 percent live on less than US$2 a day, and many millions more earn only a few hundred dollars a month. In Brazil, the region's biggest market and 12th-largest economy in the world, low-income groups make up 87 percent of the population, but earn only 53 percent of the income. Marketers in the region are finding innovative ways to sell products and services to these poor and low-income residents.

Nestlé Brazil saw sales of Bono cookies jump 40 percent after it shrank the package from 200 grams to 140 grams and lowered the price. Recognizing that illiteracy is a problem, Unilever launched a brand of soap in northeast Brazil with the simple name Ala. Brazilian firms that have succeeded internationally include aircraft manufacturer Embraer, national airline Varig, and sandal maker Havaianas. The world famous Rio Carnival and world-champion national football team have helped create an image of fun and physical fitness for Brazil.

Brazil has already experienced some 'go-go' growth years in the 1960s and 1970s, when it was the world's second-fastest-growing large economy. It also differs from other emerging markets in being a full-blown democracy, unlike Russia and China, and it has no serious disputes with neighbors, unlike India. But Brazil's growth in recent years has been slower, and a number of obstacles exist that are popularly called *custo Brasil* ('the cost of Brazil'). For example, the cost of transporting products eats up nearly 13 percent of Brazil's GDP, five percentage points more than in the United States. Most observers see Brazil's economic, social, and political transformation as still a work in process.

Russia

Russia has seen a recent rise in foreign investment and, importantly, not just in its traditionally strong markets in natural resources such as oil and gas. Swedish retailer IKEA, U.S. bank Citibank, and more than a dozen carmakers have ramped up operations in Russia. Their target is Russia's growing middle class, which expanded from 8 million in 2000 to 60 million in 2010 and now accounts for over one-third of the population. The mood in the country has become more upbeat too: the share of Russians who think life is 'not bad' has risen to 25 percent in 2010 from just 7 percent in 1999. Salaries are rising fast, savings are comparatively low, and consumer credit is increasingly available even for small purchases.

But not everyone has participated in this increased prosperity. The average Russian earns US$700 a month, just 20 percent of the U.S. average, and only a third own cars. Many elderly people feel they have been left behind, as do those who live far from Moscow, the capital. Concerns about the business climate remain. Although the economy

Continued on next page >>

Marketing Insight...continued
Spotlight on Key Developing Markets

has produced 7 percent annual growth in GDP, the Organization for Economic Cooperation & Development (OECD) cautions that economic reforms have been stagnant and ranks Russia as one of the most corrupt countries in the world. Many feel the government under Vladimir Putin has been unpredictable and sometimes difficult to work with.

Motorola's recent experience in Russia is instructive. In 2006, 167,500 Motorola handsets were seized on arrival at Moscow airport, alleged to be smuggled and counterfeit; to violate a Russian patent; and to be a danger to public health. Around 50,000 were supposedly destroyed by the interior ministry, though some were later said to have turned up on the black market. Eventually most of the handsets were returned, but perhaps more telling was Motorola's reaction. With Russia being the company's third-biggest handset market in the world (behind the United States and China), Motorola takes a fairly sanguine attitude towards the ups and downs inherent in doing business there and plans to stay the course.

India

India's recent growth rate has been as explosive as its neighbor China's. Reforms in the early 1990s that significantly lowered barriers to trade and liberalized capital markets have brought booming investment and consumption. But it's not all about demand. With its large numbers of low-cost, high-IQ, English-speaking employees, India is snapping up programming and call center jobs in a wave of outsourcing that shows no signs of stopping. Outsourcing witnessed a striking 8.1 percent growth in 2008. It is expected that by 2012 Indian outsourcers will earn US$220–280 billion. IT services and back-office work in India employ 6 million people and account for 7 percent of India's GDP.

Although India's ascent inevitably means lost jobs in other markets for white-collar workers, it also means a larger market for U.S. and Western goods, and pain for traditional Indian families. Along with training in U.S. accents and geography, India's legions of call center employees are absorbing new ideas about family, material possessions, and romance and are questioning conservative traditions. They want to watch Hollywood movies, listen to Western music, chat on mobile phones, buy on credit rather than save, and eat in restaurants or cafés. They're being targeted relentlessly by companies that have waited to see India develop a Western-style consumer class.

India still struggles with poor infrastructure and highly restrictive labor laws. Its retail channel structure, although improving, still lags. The quality of public services—education, health, provision of water—is also often lacking. But all these obstacles have not prevented global firms with strong Indian roots such as Mittal, Reliance, Tata, WiPro, and Infosys from achieving varying degrees of international success.

China

China's 1.3 billion people have marketers scrambling to gain a foothold there, and competition has been heating up between domestic and international firms. Initial gains in the Chinese market didn't necessarily spell long-term success for many international firms. After investing to establish the markets, foreign pioneers in television sets and motorcycles saw domestic Chinese firms emerge as rivals. In 1995, virtually all mobile phones in China were made by global giants Nokia, Motorola, and Ericsson. Within 10 years, their market share had dropped to 60 percent. China's 2001 entry into the World Trade Organization has eased manufacturing and investment rules and modernized retail and logistics industries. Greater competition in pricing, products, and channels has resulted.

Selling in China means going beyond the big cities to the 700 million potential consumers who live in small villages, towns, and cities in the rural interior. About half of potential PC buyers live outside major cities; only one-third of overall retail revenues come from China's 24 largest cities. Rural consumers can be challenging though, as they have lower incomes, are less sophisticated buyers, and often cling to local cultural and buying habits.

Luxury cars, however, are the fastest-growing segment of the auto market thanks to China's growing ranks of millionaires and booming stock market and economy. China's emerging middle class consists of more active and more discerning consumers who demand higher-quality products. Despite their high population, the Chinese consumers spent just 12 percent of what U.S. consumers did in 2010.

South Africa

One of the toughest places in the world to do business is Africa. According to the World Bank, of the 35 least business-friendly countries, 27 are in sub-Saharan Africa. Sierra Leone imposes harsh taxes; in the Democratic Republic of Congo, registering a business takes 155 days and costs almost five times the average Congolese's annual income of $120; and in Angola, enforcing a contract takes over 1,000 days. To avoid all the government red tape and restrictions, 42 percent of the region's economy is informal, the highest proportion in the world. Bad roads, if there are roads at all, a lack of reliable electricity, and volatile currency fluctuations add to the logistical and financial challenges. War, famine, AIDS, and disaster are even more significant human difficulties.

But some successful businesses are emerging, especially in banking, retailing, and mobile telephones, and many are using South Africa as a launch pad. Although many Africans are poor, they will still pay for what they need. Mobile phone operator Celtel invested in rural services by introducing the Me2U service, by which callers could send airtime credit to other mobile phones. Because most Africans don't have bank accounts, it's become a convenient and cheap way to transfer money, even substituting for cash in some villages. South Africa's MTN, the largest mobile phone company in the region, built its own microwave transmission backbone and power supplies in Nigeria, and the first solar pay phone in Lake Victoria, Uganda. South Africa's Net 1 has built a customer base of 3.6 million accounts by issuing free smart cards to indigent people who have no bank accounts or credit cards, taking tiny percentages of their transactions for revenue.

Continued on next page >>

Marketing Insight...continued
Spotlight on Key Developing Markets

The payoff for companies willing to deal with the complications and risk associated with doing business in Africa is often large margins and a lack of competition. SABMiller, the world's second-largest brewer, enjoys its best operating margins (over 42 percent) in Africa. Local knowledge is key, and South African companies are well placed to take advantage of opportunities. Finding a local partner can help in terms of expertise and contacts. SABMiller's African operations are joint ventures with locals, some of them government.

Sources: *Brazil*: Antonio Regalado, "Marketers Pursue the Shallow Pocketed," *Wall Street Journal*, January 26, 2007; "Land of Promise," *The Economist*, April 12, 2007; Melissa Campanelli, "Marketing to Latin America? Think Brazil," *DMNEWS*, June 20, 2006. *Russia*: "Dancing with the Bear," *The Economist*, February 3, 2007, pp. 63–64; Jason Bush, "Russia: How Long Can the Fun Last?" *BusinessWeek*, December 18, 2006, pp. 50–51. *India*: "India on Fire," *The Economist*, February 3, 2007, pp. 69–71; Joanna Slater, "Call of the West," *Wall Street Journal*, January 2, 2004; Manjeet Kripalani and Pete Engardio, "The Rise of India," *BusinessWeek*, December 8, 2003, pp. 66–76. *China*: Dexter Roberts, "Cadillac Floors It in China," *BusinessWeek*, June 4, 2007, p. 52; Bruce Einhorn, "Grudge Match in China," *BusinessWeek*, April 2, 2007, pp. 42–43; Russell Flannery, "Watch Your Back," *Forbes*, April 23, 2007, pp. 104–105; Dexter Roberts, "Cautious Consumers," *BusinessWeek*, April 30, 2007, pp. 32–34; Seung Ho Park and Wilfried R. Vanhonacker, "The Challenge for Multinational Corporations in China: Think Local, Act Global," *MIT Sloan Management Review*, May 31, 2007; Dexter Roberts, "Scrambling to Bring Crest to the Masses," *BusinessWeek*, June 25, 2007, pp. 72–73. *South Africa*: Helen Coster, "Great Expectations," *Forbes*, February 12, 2007, pp. 56–58; "The Flicker of a Brighter Future," *The Economist*, September 9, 2006, pp. 60–62; "Going Global," *The Economist*, July 15, 2006, pp. 59–60.

NAFTA In January 1994, the North American Free Trade Agreement (NAFTA) unified the United States, Mexico, and Canada in a single market of 360 million people who produce and consume US$6.7 trillion worth of goods and services annually. Over a 15-year period, NAFTA eliminated all trade barriers and investment restrictions among the three countries. Before NAFTA, tariffs on U.S. products entering Mexico averaged 13 percent, whereas U.S. tariffs on Mexican goods averaged 6 percent. In terms of combined GDP, NAFTA represents the world's largest free-trade area, linking 450 million people who produce $17 trillion worth of goods and services.[24]

MERCOSUR Other free-trade areas are forming in Latin America. MERCOSUR (or MERCOSUL) links Brazil, Argentina, Paraguay, and Uruguay to promote free-trade and the fluid movement of goods, peoples, and currency. Bolivia, Chile, Columbia, Ecuador, and Peru are associate members, and Venezuela signed a membership agreement in 2006. NAFTA will likely eventually merge with this and other arrangements to form an all-Americas free-trade zone. Chile and Mexico have already formed a successful free-trade zone.

APEC Twenty-one countries, as well as the NAFTA members, Japan, and China, are working to create a pan-Pacific free-trade area under the auspices of the Asia-Pacific Economic Cooperation (APEC) forum. Heads of government of APEC members meet at an annual summit to discuss regional economy, cooperation, trade, and investment.

GCC The Gulf Cooperation Council, established in 1981, includes the six countries that lie on the Arabian Gulf: Kuwait, Saudi Arabia, Qatar, Bahrain, the UAE, and Oman. The GCC is an advanced example of subregional integration within the Middle East and Africa (MENA) region. It has evolved over the past three decades from free trade in goods to include cross-national labor and capital mobility, and also the opening of many sectors within each economy to all members of the GCC.

ARAB MAGHREB UNION The Arab Maghreb Union is a trade agreement formed for economic and political reasons in countries in North Africa: Morocco, Algeria, Tunisia, Libya, and Mauritania. Formally developed in 1989, their aim is to cooperate in trade and business to enrich the economies of the union. They plan to establish the Maghreb common market and adopt common customs legislation, common financial legislation, and some form of integrated economic planning.

SEAN Ten countries make up the Association of Southeast Asian Nations: Brunei Darussalam, Cambodia, Indonesia, Laos, Malaysia, Myanmar, Philippines, Singapore, Thailand, and Vietnam. The region is an attractive market of over 550 million people and the member countries are aiming to work together to enhance its area as a major production and export center.

Active attempts at regional economic integration are underway in the Caribbean and parts of Africa.

Evaluating Potential Markets

Although the world is becoming flatter, there is still some 'roundedness.' However much nations and regions integrate their trading policies and standards, each nation still has unique features. Its readiness for different products and services, and its attractiveness as a market, depend on its economic, political-legal, and cultural environments.

Suppose a company has assembled a list of potential markets to enter. How does it choose among them? Many companies prefer to sell to neighboring countries because they understand these countries better and can control their costs more effectively. It's not surprising that the one of the largest export markets for many Arab countries are Saudi Arabia and the UAE, or that Saudi companies first sold to their GCC neighbors.

At other times, *psychic proximity* determines choices. Many U.S. firms prefer to sell in Canada, England, and Australia—rather than in larger markets such as Germany and France—because they feel more comfortable with the language, laws, and culture. Companies should be careful, however, in choosing markets according to cultural distance. Besides overlooking potentially better markets, firms may perform superficial analysis of some very real differences among countries and adopt predictable marketing actions that put them at a disadvantage.[25]

It often makes sense to operate in fewer countries, with a deeper commitment and penetration in each. In general, a company prefers to enter countries (1) that rank high on market attractiveness, (2) that are low in market risk, and (3) in which it possesses a competitive advantage. Here is how Bechtel Corporation, the construction giant, goes about evaluating overseas markets.

 Bechtel Corporation   Bechtel provides premier technical, management, and related services to develop, manage, engineer, build, and operate installations for customers in nearly 60 countries worldwide. Before it ventures into new markets, Bechtel starts with a detailed strategic market analysis. It looks at its markets and tries to determine where it should be in four or five years' time. A management team does a cost-benefit analysis that factors in the position of competitors, infrastructure, regulatory and trade barriers, and the tax situation (both corporate and individual). Ideally, the new market should be a country with an untapped need for its products or services, a skilled labor pool capable of manufacturing the product, and a welcoming environment (governmental and physical).

Are there countries that meet Bechtel's requirements? Bechtel is able to penetrate many of the markets in the Arab world due to the high demand for building infrastructure and mega engineering projects. For example, Bechtel managed the Jubail project, one of the biggest civil engineering projects in modern times. The project basically involved building a city from the ground up, requiring lots of resources and logistical planning on a very large scale. Bechtel was also involved in managing Jubail II, a US$3.8 billion expansion of the city's industrial and residential zones.

Bechtel has a strong presence in the Arabian Gulf region; for example, building Saudi Arabia's first commercial ports and airports, in addition to the first oil refinery and pipeline for exporting oil. It helped put out many of the oil wells that were set alight in the Gulf War and in cleaning up areas that were hurt by the oil spills, and was also responsible for building a petrochemical plant, which was suspended in 1991 because of the Gulf War.[26]

Here is how Cilantro, Egypt's famous Western-style cafe, went about evaluating overseas markets.

 Cilantro Café   In 2000, Cilantro Café opened in Egypt when the Western coffee culture was just beginning to grow in the country. In less than a decade, Cilantro has successfully managed to open 60 branches in Egypt. According to Nadine Beshir, the general manager of the parent company (Delicious Inc.), Cilantro has reached a point where a further domestic expansion of its branches in some areas will actually harm existing outlets. Reduced emphasis on Cilantro's domestic expansion encouraged the company to focus on international growth. After examining the different markets abroad, the company decided to open new Cilantro branches in London, Jordan, and Saudi Arabia. According to Beshir, the decision to open in London was based on two main factors. First of all, real estate prices were falling and the company realized that Cilantro was well suited to satisfy the needs of British tea and coffee lovers. Moreover, Beshir explains that Cilantro's move to franchise in Jordan and Saudi Arabia, rather than open its own branches, was driven by local conditions. The company realized that in the Gulf and Middle Eastern countries, it is better to move in with a partner that knows the country, the locals, the locations, and the trends. While opening without a local partner, which is the case in London, gives the parent company more control over the different Cilantro branches abroad, it undoubtedly requires additional effort and resources. Relying on franchises, however, facilitates Cilantro's expansion more than if the chain had taken all overseas efforts on its own. Cilantro is planning to continue its expansion in its three overseas markets. Currently, London has two Cilantro branches and two or three more branches are expected to open soon. In addition, the company is considering opening one more branch in Jordan and in Saudi Arabia. Cilantro's success overseas has encouraged the parent company to look into more new markets abroad, such as Bahrain, Algeria, France, and the United States, where there are a number of interested franchisees.[27]

London met Cilantro's criteria for overseas investment; property prices were falling, and there is a huge British market demand for tea and coffee.

Deciding How to Enter the Market

Once a company decides to target a particular country, it must determine the best mode of entry. Its broad choices are *indirect exporting, direct exporting, licensing, joint ventures,* and *direct investment.* These five market-entry strategies are shown in △ **Figure 21.2**. Each succeeding strategy entails more commitment, risk, control, and profit potential.

Indirect and Direct Exporting

The normal way to get involved in an international market is through export. Companies typically start with *indirect exporting*: that is, they work through independent intermediaries. *Domestic-based export merchants* buy the manufacturer's products and then sell them abroad. *Domestic-based export agents* seek and negotiate foreign purchases for a commission. Included in this group are trading companies. *Cooperative organizations* carry on exporting activities on behalf of several producers—often of primary products such as fruits or nuts—and are partly under their administrative control. *Export-management companies* agree to manage a company's export activities for a fee.

Indirect export has two advantages. First, there is less investment: the firm doesn't have to develop an export department, an overseas sales force, or a set of international contacts. Second, there's less risk: because international marketing intermediaries bring know-how and services to the relationship, the seller will make fewer mistakes.

Companies eventually may decide to handle their own exports.[28] The investment and risk are somewhat greater, but so is the potential return. A company can carry on direct exporting in several ways:

- **Domestic-based export department or division.** This might evolve from a purely service function into a self-contained export department operating as its own profit center.

- **Overseas sales branch or subsidiary.** The sales branch handles sales and distribution and perhaps warehousing and promotion as well. It often serves as a display and customer-service center.

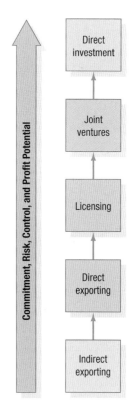

|Fig. 21.2| △

Five Modes of Entry into Foreign Markets

Source: Fred R. David, "How Companies Define Their Mission," *Long Range Planning.*

- *Traveling export sales representatives.* Home-based sales representatives travel abroad to find business.
- *Foreign-based distributors or agents.* These distributors and agents can hold limited or exclusive rights to represent the company in that country.

Many companies use direct or indirect exporting as a way to 'test the waters' before building a plant and manufacturing a product overseas. Here's an example of one of the fastest-growing organizations in Saudi Arabia, which engages in indirect exporting.

 Al Faisaliah Group   Al Faisaliah Group (AFG) is a major diversified organization located in Saudi Arabia and operating across the Arab world. The company has businesses in various economic sectors, including foods and beverages. Among the major Al Faisaliah companies in this sector are the Al Safi Dairy and Al Safi Danone. By engaging in indirect exporting through an intermediary firm called Al Yasra Foods, the Al Safi Dairy and Al Safi Danone are able to access well-established expert and trade contacts in Kuwait and Iraq, while still retaining considerable control over the exporting process. Al Yasra Foods therefore enables the Al Faisaliah companies to penetrate different markets without having to encounter the complexities and risks of direct exporting. Al Yasra Foods' various distribution centers in Iraq and Kuwait have over 1,500 employees and a fleet strength of about 400 vehicles, which have undoubtedly contributed to the firm's success in providing maximum coverage of all trade channels.[29]

Using a Global Web Strategy

With the web, it's now not even necessary to attend international trade shows to show your wares abroad: electronic communication via the internet is extending the reach of companies large and small, allowing them to attract new customers outside their home countries, support existing customers who live abroad, source from international suppliers, and build global brand awareness.

These companies adapt their websites to provide country-specific content and services to their best potential international markets, ideally in the local language. The number of internet users is rising quickly as access costs decline, local-language content increases, and infrastructure improves. After going online, upscale retailer and cataloger The Sharper Image found that more than 25 percent of its online business came from overseas customers.[30]

The internet has become an effective means of conducting market research and offering customers a secure process for ordering and paying for products across time zones. Finding free information about trade and exporting has never been easier. Here are some places to start a search:

www.amcham.org.eg	American Chamber of Commerce in Egypt
www.mci.gov.sa	Ministry of Commerce and Industry in Saudi Arabia
www.jocc.org.jo	Jordan Chamber of Commerce
www.fcciuae.ae	Federation of UAE Chambers of Commerce & Industry

Licensing

Licensing is a simple way to engage in international marketing. The licensor issues a license to a foreign company to use a manufacturing process, trademark, patent, trade secret, or other item of value for a fee or royalty. The licensor gains entry at little risk; the licensee gains production expertise or a well-known product or brand name.

Licensing has potential disadvantages. The licensor has less control over the licensee than it does over its own production and sales facilities. If the licensee is very successful, the firm has given up profits, and if and when the contract ends, the company might find it has created a competitor. To prevent this, the licensor usually supplies some proprietary product ingredients or components (as Coca-Cola does). But the best strategy is to lead in innovation so the licensee will continue to depend on the licensor.

There are variations on a licensing arrangement. Companies such as Hyatt and Marriott sell *management contracts* to owners of foreign hotels to manage these businesses for a fee. The management firm may have the option to purchase some share in the managed company within a stated period.

In *contract manufacturing*, the firm hires local manufacturers to produce the product. When Sears opened department stores in Mexico and Spain, it found qualified local manufacturers to produce many of its products. Contract manufacturing gives the company less control over the manufacturing process and risks loss of potential profits on manufacturing. However, it offers a chance to start faster, with the opportunity to form a partnership or buy out the local manufacturer later.

Finally, a company can enter a foreign market through *franchising*, a more complete form of licensing. The franchisor offers a complete brand concept and operating system. In return, the franchisee invests in and pays certain fees to the franchisor. McDonald's, KFC, and Avis have entered scores of countries by franchising their retail concepts and making sure their marketing is culturally relevant.

KFC Corporation   KFC is the world's largest fast-food chicken chain, owning or franchising 11,000 outlets in 80 countries and territories—60 percent of them outside the United States—and serving 8 million customers daily. KFC had a number of obstacles to overcome when it entered the Japanese market. The Japanese saw fast food as artificial, made by mechanical means, and unhealthy. To build trust in the KFC brand, advertising showed scenes depicting Colonel Sanders' beginnings in Kentucky that conveyed Southern hospitality, old American tradition, and authentic home cooking. The campaign was hugely successful, and in less than 8 years KFC expanded its presence from 400 locations to more than 1,000. KFC is China's largest, oldest, most popular, and fastest-growing quick-service restaurant chain, with over 1,800 locations. It has set up its own supply and distribution system in China, allowing it to expand quickly into ever-smaller cities. The company has also tailored its menu to local tastes with items such as the Dragon Twister, a sandwich stuffed with chicken strips, Peking duck sauce, cucumbers, and scallions. KFC even has a Chinese mascot, a kid-friendly character named Chicky, which the company boasts has become "the Ronald McDonald of China."[31]

Joint Ventures

Historically, foreign investors have often joined with local investors to create a **joint venture** company in which they share ownership and control. For instance:[32]

> **joint venture** a company in which multiple investors share ownership and control.

- Al Marai Co. entered into a joint venture with PepsiCo to invest in dairy and juice processors in Southeast Asia, Africa, and the Middle East.

- Coca-Cola and Nestlé joined forces to develop the international market for 'ready-to-drink' tea and coffee, which currently they sell in significant amounts in Japan.

- Procter & Gamble formed a joint venture with its Italian archrival Fater to market diapers in the United Kingdom and Italy.

- Whirlpool took a 53 percent stake in the Dutch electronics group Philips' white-goods business to leapfrog into the European market.

A joint venture may be necessary or desirable for economic or political reasons. The foreign firm might lack the financial, physical, or managerial resources to undertake the venture alone; or the foreign government might require joint ownership as a condition for entry. Joint ownership has certain drawbacks. The partners might disagree over investment, marketing, or other policies. One might want to reinvest earnings for growth, and the other to declare more dividends. Joint ownership can also prevent a multinational company from carrying out specific manufacturing and marketing policies on a worldwide basis.

KFC has tailored its approach, its menu, and even its mascot to appeal to Chinese tastes and has become China's fastest-growing and most popular fast-food chain. But it still retains some of its iconic imagery.

Direct Investment

The ultimate form of foreign involvement is direct ownership of foreign-based assembly or manufacturing facilities. The foreign company can buy part or full interest in a local company or build its own facilities. General Motors has invested billions of dollars in auto manufacturers around the world, such as Shangai GM, Fiat Auto Holdings, Isuzu, Daewoo, Suzuki, Saab, Fuji Heavy Industries, Jinbei GM Automotive Co., and AvtoVAZ.[33]

If the market appears large enough, foreign production facilities offer distinct advantages. First, the firm secures cost economics in the form of cheaper labor or raw materials, foreign-government investment incentives, and freight savings. Second, the firm strengthens its image in the host country because it creates jobs. Third, the firm develops a deeper relationship with government, customers, local suppliers, and distributors, enabling it to better adapt its products to the local environment. Fourth, the firm retains full control over its investment and therefore can develop manufacturing and marketing policies that serve its long-term international objectives. Fifth, the firm assures itself access to the market in case the host country insists locally purchased goods have domestic content.

The main disadvantage of direct investment is that the firm exposes a large investment to risks such as blocked or devalued currencies, worsening markets, or expropriation. It can be expensive to reduce or close down operations, because the host country might require substantial severance pay to employees.

Deciding on the Marketing Program

International companies must decide how much to adapt their marketing strategy to local conditions.[34] At one extreme are companies that use a globally *standardized marketing mix* worldwide. Standardization of the product, communication, and distribution channels promises the lowest costs. ▇ **Box 21.1** summarizes some pros and cons of standardizing the marketing program. At the other extreme is an *adapted marketing mix*, where the producer, consistent with the marketing concept, holds that consumer needs vary and tailors marketing programs to each target group.

The development of the web, the rapid spread of cable and satellite TV around the world, and the global linking of telecommunications networks have led to a convergence of life styles.

BOX 21.1 ▇   Global Marketing Pros and Cons

Advantages

Economies of scale in production and distribution

Lower marketing costs

Power and scope

Consistency in brand image

Ability to leverage good ideas quickly and efficiently

Uniformity of marketing practices

Disadvantages

Ignores differences in consumer needs, wants, and usage patterns for products

Ignores differences in consumer response to marketing-mix elements

Ignores differences in brand and product development and the competitive environment

Ignores differences in the legal environment

Ignores differences in marketing institutions

Ignores differences in administrative procedures

Increasingly common needs and wants have created global markets for standardized products, particularly among the young middle class. Consider Red Bull.

Red Bull A billion-dollar brand in less than 15 years, Red Bull has gained 70 percent of the worldwide energy drink market by skillfully connecting with global youth. Founded in Austria by Dietrich Mateschitz, Red Bull was introduced into its first foreign market, Hungary, in 1992, and is now sold in over 100 countries. Red Bull consists of the amino acid taurine, B-complex vitamins, caffeine, and carbohydrates. The drink was sold originally in only one size—the silver 250-milliliter can—and received little traditional advertising support beyond animated television commercials with the tagline "Red Bull Gives You Wings." Red Bull built buzz about the product through its 'seeding program:' the company microtargets 'in' shops, clubs, and stores, gradually moves to convenience stores and restaurants, and finally enters supermarkets. It targets opinion leaders by making Red Bull available at sports competitions, in limos before award shows, and at exclusive after-parties. Red Bull also built its cool image through sponsorship of extreme sports such as its X-Fighters events, and unique grassroots efforts. In cities throughout the world, for example, the company sponsors an annual Flugtag where contestants build flying machines that they launch off ramps into water, true to the brand's slogan!³⁵

Red Bull relies on many nontraditional marketing activities to expand worldwide from its European base. The annual Flugtag contest is just one. Here a competitor is seen flying his camel machine in the Dubai Creek as part of the Flying Day Red Bull Flugtag competition there. Flying machines were launched from a 6-meter-high runway using only human power.

Although many companies have tried to launch their version of a world product, most products require at least some adaptation. Toyota's Corolla will exhibit some differences in styling. Even Coca-Cola is sweeter or less carbonated in certain countries. Rather than assuming it can introduce its domestic product 'as is' in another country, the company should review the following elements and determine which add more revenue than cost:

- Product features
- Labeling
- Colors
- Materials
- Sales promotion
- Advertising media
- Brand name
- Packaging
- Advertising execution
- Prices
- Advertising themes

Consumer behavior can dramatically differ across markets. One of the highest per-capita consumers of carbonated soft drinks is the United States, at 204 liters; Italy is among the lowest. But Italy is one of the highest per-capita drinkers of bottled water, with 203 liters, whereas the United Kingdom uses only 23 liters. When it comes to beer, Ireland and the Czech Republic lead the pack, with 157 and 131 liters per capita, respectively, and France is among the lowest at 36 liters.³⁶

Cultural differences can be pronounced across countries. Hofstede identifies four cultural dimensions that differentiate countries:³⁷

1. ***Individualism versus collectivism.*** In collectivist societies, such as Japan and the Arab countries, the self-worth of an individual is rooted more in the social system than in individual achievement.
2. ***High versus low power distance.*** High power-distance cultures tend to be less egalitarian.
3. ***Masculine versus feminine.*** This dimension measures how much the culture is dominated by assertive males versus nurturing females.
4. ***Weak versus strong uncertainty avoidance.*** Uncertainty avoidance indicates how risk-tolerant or risk-averse people are.

Besides demand-side differences, supply-side differences can prevail. Flexible manufacturing techniques make it easier to produce many different product versions, tailored to particular countries.

Most brands are adapted to some extent to reflect significant differences in consumer behavior, brand development, competitive forces, and the legal or political environment.[38] Even global brands undergo some changes in product features, packaging, channels, pricing, or communications in different global markets[39] (see the Marketing Memo: *The Ten Commandments of Global Branding*). Firms must make sure their message is relevant to consumers in every market.

Orascom Telecom Holding   Orascom Telecom Holding (OTH) is part of the Orascom group of companies, which represents leading international telecommunications companies with operations across the Arab world, in Algeria (OTA), Egypt (Mobinil), and the UAE (du), as well as Bangladesh (Banglalink), Canada (Wind Mobile), and Pakistan (Mobilink). In order to cater for the unique needs of its customers in these diverse countries, Orascom Telecom has successfully modified its service features and offers according to the characteristic consumer behavior, needs, and expectations as well as the political and legal environment of each country. For example, Mobinil in Egypt offers three different services to satisfy the needs of customers belonging to distinct social classes: Star is a postpaid service designed for Egyptians belonging to the upper class, who are interested in exclusive offers; Alo is a prepaid service that offers students and low-income groups a variety of packages, all at a relatively low price per minute; and Mobinil Business caters for the needs of small or large companies by offering a wide array of business buckets. Orascom Telecom in Algeria, called Djezzy, also provides its customers with different packages, each catering to the different demands of the various Algerian socioeconomic groups. Orascom Telecom's efficient adaptation to different global markets explains why it is considered one of the leading mobile telecommunications networks in the world.[40]

---

marketing Memo

The Ten Commandments of Global Branding

For many companies, global branding has been both a blessing and a curse. A global branding program can lower marketing costs, realize greater economies of scale in production, and provide a long-term source of growth. If not designed and implemented properly, however, it may ignore important differences in consumer behavior and/or the competitive environment in the individual countries. These suggestions can help a company retain the advantages of global branding while minimizing potential disadvantages:

1. *Understand similarities and differences in the global branding landscape*. International markets can vary in terms of brand development, consumer behavior, competitive activity, legal restrictions, and so on.

2. *Do not take shortcuts in brand building*. Build a brand in new markets from the 'bottom up,' both strategically (building awareness before brand image) and tactically (creating sources of brand equity in new markets).

3. *Establish a marketing infrastructure*. A company must either build marketing infrastructure 'from scratch' or adapt to existing infrastructure in other countries.

4. *Embrace integrated marketing communications*. A company must often use many forms of communication in overseas markets, not just advertising.

5. *Establish brand partnerships*. Most global brands have marketing partners in their international markets that help companies achieve advantages in distribution, profitability, and added value.

6. *Balance standardization and customization*. Some elements of a marketing program can be standardized (packaging, brand name); others typically require greater customization (distribution channels).

7. *Balance global and local control*. Companies must balance global and local control within the organization and distribute decision making between global and local managers.

8. *Establish operable guidelines*. Brand definition and guidelines must be established, communicated, and properly enforced so marketers everywhere know what they are expected to do and not do. The goal is to set rules for how the brand should be positioned and marketed.

9. *Implement a global brand-equity measurement system*. A global brand-equity system is a set of research procedures designed to provide timely, accurate, and actionable information for marketers so they can make the best possible short-run tactical decisions and long-run strategic decisions.

10. *Leverage brand elements*. Proper design and implementation of brand elements (brand name and trademarked brand identifiers) can be an invaluable source of brand equity worldwide.

Source: Adapted from Kevin Lane Keller and Sanjay Sood, "The Ten Commandments of Global Branding," *Asian Journal of Marketing*, 8, no. 2, 2001, pp. 97–108.

	Product		
	Do Not Change Product	Adapt Product	Develop New Product
Do Not Change Communications	Straight extension	Product adaptation	Product invention
Adapt Communications	Communication adaptation	Dual adaptation	

|Fig. 21.3| △

Five International Product and Communication Strategies

Warren Keegan has distinguished five adaptation strategies of product and communications to a foreign market (see △ **Figure 21.3**).[41]

Product

Some types of product travel better across borders than others: food and beverage marketers must contend with widely varying tastes.[42]

Straight extension introduces the product in the foreign market without any change. It's been successful with cameras, consumer electronics, and many machine tools. In other cases, it has been a disaster. General Foods introduced its standard powdered Jell-O in the British market only to find that British consumers prefer the solid wafer or cake form. Campbell Soup Company lost an estimated US$30 million in introducing condensed soups in England; consumers saw expensive small-sized cans and didn't realize water needed to be added. Straight extension is tempting because it requires no additional R&D expense, manufacturing retooling, or promotional modification; but it can be costly in the long run.

Product adaptation alters the product to meet local conditions or preferences. There are several levels of adaptation.

- A company can produce a *regional version* of its product, such as a Western European version. Finnish mobile phone superstar Nokia customized its 6100 series phone for every major market. Developers built in rudimentary voice recognition for Asia, where keyboards are a problem, and raised the ring volume so the phone could be heard on crowded Asian streets.

- A company can produce a *country version* of its product. In Japan, Mister Donut's coffee cup is smaller and lighter to fit the hand of the average Japanese consumer; even the doughnuts are a little smaller. Kraft blends different coffees for the British (who drink their coffee with milk), the French (who drink their coffee black), and Latin Americans (who want a chicory taste).

- A company can produce a *city version* of its product; for instance, bread with more wheat in Cairo.

- A company can produce different *retailer versions* of its product, such as one coffee brew for the Migros chain store and another for the Cooperative chain store, both in Switzerland.

Some companies have learned the importance of adapting the hard way. When Walt Disney launched the Euro Disney theme park outside Paris in 1992, it was harshly criticized as an example of U.S. cultural imperialism. A number of local French customs and values, such as serving wine with meals, were ignored. As one Euro Disney executive noted, "When we first launched, there was the belief that it was enough to be Disney. Now we realize our guests need to be welcomed on the basis of their own culture and travel habits." Renamed Disneyland Paris, the theme park eventually has become Europe's biggest tourist attraction—even more popular than the Eiffel Tower—by making a number of changes and adding more local touches.[43]

Product invention consists of creating something new. It can take two forms:

- **Backward invention** is reintroducing earlier product forms that are well adapted to a foreign country's needs. The National Cash Register Company reintroduced its crank-operated cash register at half the price of a modern cash register and sold substantial numbers in Latin America and Africa.

straight extension introducing a product in a foreign market without any change in the product.

product adaptation altering the product to meet local conditions or preferences.

product invention creating something new via product development or other means.

backward invention reintroducing earlier product forms that can be well adapted to a foreign country's needs.

Bertelsmann   In Ukraine, where the average person makes US$8,000 a year and bookstores are few and far between, the old-fashioned book club is enjoying huge popularity. German book-publishing giant Bertelsmann has seen a decline in its Book-of-the-Month and Literary Guild units in both the United States and Europe. In Ukraine, however, those clubs are seeing profit margins triple the 4 percent global average. Bertelsmann has been astute at marketing its 'old' media to 20- to 30-year-old consumers there, and the clubs draw a younger following than in the United States. They recruit hot young Ukrainian authors and serve as their exclusive distributor, a masterstroke in a country with only 300 bookstores. The publisher also keeps prices low because its main competition in Ukraine is the open-air book market, where books sell very cheaply. Its Family Leisure book club titles go for under $5, for instance. To keep costs down, Bertelsmann delivers books to post offices where customers pick them up.[44]

forward invention   creating a new product to meet a need in another country.

- **Forward invention** is creating a new product to meet a need in another country. Less developed countries need low-cost, high-protein foods. Companies such as Quaker Oats, Swift, and Monsanto have researched these countries' nutrition needs, formulated new foods, and developed advertising campaigns to gain product trial and acceptance.

  Product invention is a costly strategy, but the payoffs can be great, particularly if a company can parlay a product innovation into other countries. Sometimes the innovation even works at home.

McDonald's McArabia   McDonald's introduced the McArabia for the Arab consumer. There are two versions of the McArabia: grilled chicken and grilled kofta. Both versions are served with lettuce, tomatoes, onions, and garlic mayonnaise, and the sandwich is wrapped in the Arabic style pita bread. The McArabia is available at all McDonald's outlets in the Arab region and is especially popular in Morocco, the UAE, and Saudi Arabia.[45]

When they launch products and services globally, marketers may need to change certain brand elements. When Clairol introduced the Mist Stick, a hair curling iron, in Germany, it found that *mist* is slang for manure. Brand slogans or ad taglines sometimes need to be changed too.[46]

Box 21.2 lists some other famous blunders in this area.

BOX 21.2   Blunders in International Marketing
• Hallmark cards failed when they were introduced in France. The French dislike syrupy sentiment and prefer writing their own cards.
• Philips began to earn a profit in Japan only after it reduced the size of its coffeemakers to fit into smaller Japanese kitchens and its shavers to fit smaller Japanese hands.
• Coca-Cola withdrew its 2-liter bottle in Spain after discovering that few Spaniards owned refrigerators with large enough compartments to accommodate it.
• General Foods' Tang initially failed in France because it was positioned as a substitute for orange juice at breakfast. The French drink little orange juice and almost none at breakfast.
• Kellogg's Pop-Tarts failed in Britain because the percentage of British homes with toasters was significantly lower than in the United States, and the product was too sweet for British tastes.
• Procter & Gamble's Crest toothpaste initially failed in Mexico when it used the U.S. campaign. Mexicans did not care as much for the decay-prevention benefit, nor did scientifically oriented advertising appeal to them.
• General Foods squandered millions trying to introduce packaged cake mixes to Japanese consumers. The company failed to note that only 3 percent of Japanese homes were equipped with ovens.
• S.C. Johnson's wax floor polish initially failed in Japan. The wax made the floors too slippery, and Johnson had overlooked the fact that Japanese people do not wear shoes in their homes.

Communications

Companies can run the same marketing communications programs they use in the home market or change them for each local market, a process called **communication adaptation**. If it adapts both the product and the communications, the company engages in **dual adaptation**.

Consider the message. The company can use one message everywhere, varying only the language, name, and perhaps colors to avoid taboos in some countries. [47]Purple is associated with death in Burma and some Latin American nations; white is a mourning color in India; and green is associated with disease in Malaysia.[48]

The second possibility is to use the same creative theme globally but adapt the specific execution to appropriate local markets. Apple Computer's 'Mac vs. PC,' which was voted the best U.S. ad campaign of 2006 by *Adweek* magazine, features two actors bantering. One is hip looking (Apple), the other nerdy looking (PC). Apple dubbed the ads for Spain, France, Germany, and Italy but chose to reshoot and rescript for the United Kingdom and Japan, two important markets with unique advertising and comedy cultures. The UK ads followed a similar formula but tweaked the jokes to reflect British humor; the Japanese ads avoided direct comparisons and were more subtle in tone.[49]

communication adaptation changing marketing communications programs for each local market.

dual adaptation adapting both the product and the communications to the local market.

Unilever Unilever is a British-Dutch multinational corporation that produces a wide variety of nutritionally balanced foods, ice creams, soaps, shampoos, and everyday household care products. Since Unilever is a global company it must continuously modify its advertisement message, copy, or content in order to best meet the demands of the individual global markets. For example, its soap Lux is advertised differently across different countries. Its foamy characteristic is stressed in the ads in Europe where Lux is sold as a liquid soap, but in other countries, like China, Taiwan, India, the Philippines, and those in the Middle East, Lux is advertised as a traditional soap. Hence, the benefits of Lux are emphasized differently in each global market. In addition, advertisements shown in Egypt differ from those shown in Saudi Arabia, Kuwait, Dubai, and other Gulf markets. While ads shown in Egypt do not include veiled women, those shown in Saudi Arabia must only show women in veils. Ads aiming for the Kuwaiti, Dubai, and other Gulf markets, on the other hand, tend to mix things up a bit, going for the stylish, attractive, but conservative style that is increasingly becoming a trend among elites in the region. This creates a challenge for Unilever when it advertises shampoos in Saudi Arabia and other Gulf countries. Since the focus has to be on the person's hair, the ad shows the hair of a woman from the back and another veiled woman from the front elaborating on the benefits of the advertised shampoo. The fact that Unilever has successfully managed to undergo communication adaptation enabled it to attract diverse customers to its products and thus maintain a leading position in the global market.[50]

The third approach consists of developing a global pool of ads, from which each country selects the most appropriate. Coca-Cola and Goodyear have used this approach. Finally, some companies allow their country managers to create country-specific ads; within guidelines, of course. The challenge is to make sure the message is as compelling and effective as in the home market.

Chinese officials objected to Nike television commercials featuring James battling animated characters, prompting the company to focus on adapting its powerful "Just Do It" message instead.

Nike China's state-owned media actively enforce rules on what communications can and cannot say. In 2004, Nike ran afoul of those rules with its Chamber of Fear commercial, which was banned for "insulting national pride." It showed the NBA star LeBron James fighting a Kung-Fu character, two women in Chinese dress, and a pair of dragons (considered sacred symbols). The Chinese interpretation of the ad was that LeBron was trying to defeat Chinese culture. The State Administration for Radio, Film, and Television said the ad "violates regulations that mandate all advertisement in China should uphold national dignity and interest and respect the motherland's culture." Censorship aside,

Nike has recently decided its Chinese ad campaigns need to focus less on U.S. or even Chinese athletes with 'you should...' or 'try this...' messages intended for China's younger generation, which is rapidly creating its own style. Instead, Nike is trying to get its "Just Do It" tagline across by saluting unknown Chinese youngsters who have surmounted obstacles to play basketball, to skateboard, or to cycle. In addition to being able to watch the gritty ads featuring genuinely moving stories of kids, internet-connected Chinese tweens and teens can send their personal stories to the Nike website. So instead of insulting national pride, Nike is tapping into the vast store of 'personal pride' of China's newest generation of consumers.[51]

The use of media also requires international adaptation because media availability varies from country to country. Norway, Belgium, and France don't allow cigarettes and alcohol to be advertised on TV. Austria and Italy regulate TV advertising to children. Saudi Arabia does not want advertisers to use women in ads. India has taxed advertising. Magazines vary in availability and effectiveness; they play a major role in Italy and a minor one in Austria.

In developing markets, high mobile phone penetration makes mobile marketing attractive. A pioneer in China, Coca-Cola China created a national campaign asking Beijing residents to send text messages guessing the high temperature in the city every day for just over a month, for a chance to win a one-year supply of Coke products. The campaign attracted more than 4 million messages over the course of 35 days.[52]

Personal selling tactics may need to change too. The indirect subtle approach (characterized by knowing more personal and family information) may not work as well in the United States or Europe where a more direct, obvious approach (let's get down to business or what's in it for me) can be more effective.[53] With younger, more international employees, however, such cultural differences may be less pronounced.

Price

Multinationals face several pricing problems when selling abroad. They must deal with price escalation, transfer prices, dumping charges, and gray markets.

Microsoft   When Microsoft entered China, the company made its first big blunder by trying to sell its Windows operating system at the same high price it commands in the developed world, while pirated copies were available at rock bottom prices. Microsoft spent the next 10 years trying to crack down on piracy in China, suing companies for using its software illegally and always losing in court. The Chinese government grew ever more mistrustful of Microsoft—even suspecting the United States was spying via the software—and put open-source Linux operating systems on all workers' PCs. So how did Microsoft become so respected in China that CEO Bill Gates is now a celebrity? For one thing, by doing a complete turnaround and tolerating piracy. "It's easier for our software to compete with Linux when there's piracy than when there's not," says Gates. Yet, the best move Microsoft made was to collaborate with the Chinese government and open a research center in Beijing, which today lures the country's top computer scientists. Rather than being known as a company that comes to China to sue people, it's regarded as a company with long-term vision.[54]

price escalation   an increase in the price of a product due to added costs of selling it in different countries.

When companies sell their goods abroad, they face a **price escalation** problem. A Gucci handbag may sell for US$120 in Italy and $240 in Dubai. Why? Gucci must add the cost of transportation, tariffs, importer margin, wholesaler margin, and retailer margin to its factory price. Depending on these added costs, as well as the currency-fluctuation risk, the product might sell for two to five times as much in another country to make the same profit for the manufacturer. Companies have three choices for setting prices in different countries:

1. ***Set a uniform price everywhere.*** Coca-Cola might want to charge 75 cents for Coke everywhere in the world, but then it would earn quite different profit rates in different countries. Also, this strategy would make the price too high in poor countries and not high enough in rich countries.

2. **Set a market-based price in each country.** Here Coca-Cola would charge what each country could afford, but this strategy ignores differences in the actual cost from country to country. Also, it could lead to a situation in which intermediaries in low-price countries reship their Coca-Cola to high-price countries.

3. **Set a cost-based price in each country.** Here Coca-Cola would use a standard markup of its costs everywhere, but this strategy might price Coca-Cola out of the market in countries where its costs are high.

A different problem arises when one unit charges another unit in the same company a **transfer price** for goods it ships to its foreign subsidiaries. If the company charges a subsidiary too high a price, it may end up paying higher tariff duties, although it may pay lower income taxes in the foreign country. If the company charges too low a price to its subsidiary, it can be accused of **dumping**, charging either less than its costs or less than it charges at home in order to enter or win a market. Stelco, a Canadian steelmaker, successfully fought dumping of steel products by steelmakers in Brazil, Finland, India, Indonesia, Thailand, and Ukraine. A Canadian tribunal found that cut-price steel imports from these countries caused "material injury to Canadian producers, including Stelco."[55]

When Egypt's Custom Authority finds evidence of dumping, it can levy a dumping tariff on the guilty company. Various governments are watching for abuses and often force companies to charge the **arm's-length price**, the price charged by other competitors for the same or a similar product.

Many multinationals are plagued by the gray market problem. The **gray market** consists of branded products diverted from normal or authorized distribution channels in the country of product origin or across international borders. Dealers in the low-price country find ways to sell some of their products in higher-price countries, thus earning more. Often a company finds some enterprising distributors buying more than they can sell in their own country and reshipping the goods to another country to take advantage of price differences. The Marketing Insight: *Unauthorized Sales: Dealing with the Gray Market and Counterfeit Products* describes some issues with gray markets, as well as product fakes.

transfer price the price a company charges another unit in the company for goods it ships to foreign subsidiaries.

dumping situation in which a company charges either less than its costs or less than it charges in its home market, in order to enter or win a market.

arm's-length price the price charged by other competitors for the same or a similar product.

gray market branded products diverted from normal or authorized distribution channels in the country of product origin or across international borders.

Marketing Insight

Unauthorized Sales: Dealing with the Gray Market and Counterfeit Products

One of the downsides of globalization is that someone, somewhere, could be making money from your products and services without your authorization or even knowledge. Two particularly thorny problems exist with gray markets and counterfeits.

The Gray Market

Research suggests that gray market activity—sales of genuine trademarked products through distribution channels unauthorized by the manufacturer or brand owner—accounts for over US$40 billion in revenue each year. Gray markets create a 'free-riding problem' and make legitimate distributors' investments in supporting a manufacturer's product less productive. Gray markets also make a selective distribution system more intensive. Gray markets harm distributor relations, tarnish the manufacturer's brand equity, and undermine the integrity of the distribution channel.

Multinationals try to prevent gray markets by policing the distributors, by raising their prices to lower-cost distributors, or by altering the product characteristics or service warranties for different countries. 3Com successfully sued several companies in Canada (for a total of US$10 million) that provided written and oral misrepresentations to get deep discounts on 3Com networking equipment. The equipment, worth millions of dollars, was to be sold to a U.S. education software company and sent to China and Australia, but instead ended up back in the United States.

One research study found that gray market activity was most effectively deterred when the penalties were severe, when manufacturers were able to detect violations or mete out punishments in a timely fashion, or both.

Counterfeit Products

With the latest technology available everywhere, it's no surprise that fakes and imitations have become a major problem. Counterfeiting, estimated to cost businesses US$600 billion a year, is expected to

Continued on next page >>

Marketing Insight...continued
Unauthorized Sales: Dealing with the Gray Market and Counterfeit Products

increase to $1.5 trillion by 2012. The Chinese have been prime offenders. In the United States, 88 percent of all goods seized by customs in a recent year originated in China (81 percent), Hong Kong (6 percent), or Taiwan (1 percent). This percentage is also high for many countries in the Arab region, including the UAE, Jordan, and Iraq.

Fakes take a big bite of the profits of luxury brands such as Hermès, LVMH Moët Hennessy Louis Vuitton, and Tiffany, but faulty counterfeits can literally kill people. Mobile phones with counterfeit batteries, fake brake pads made of compressed grass trimmings, and counterfeit airline parts pose safety risks to consumers. Virtually every product is vulnerable. As one anti-counterfeit consultant observed, "If you can make it, they can fake it." Defending against counterfeiters is difficult; some observers estimate that a new security system can be just months old before counterfeiters start nibbling at sales again.

The web has been especially problematic. One estimate put web sales of counterfeit goods from watches to pharmacueticals at US$150 billion in 2010; up from $84 billion in 2006. eBay has come under heavy criticism from some manufacturers. Based on a survey of thousands of items, LVMH estimated 90 percent of Louis Vuitton and Christian Dior items listed on eBay were fakes, prompting the firm to sue.

Manufacturers are fighting back online with web-crawling software that detects fraud and automatically sends warnings to apparent violaters without the need for any human intervention. Acushnet, maker of Titleist golf clubs and balls, shut down 75 auctions of counterfeit gear in one day with just one mouse click. Web-crawling technology searches for counterfeit storefronts and sales by detecting domain names similar to legitimate brands and unauthorized websites that plaster brand trademarks and logos all over their homepages. It also checks for keywords such as 'cheap,' 'discount,' 'authentic,' and 'factory variants,' as well as colors that products were never made in and prices that are far too low.

Dealing with counterfeits is a never-ending struggle, and firms are trying all kinds of tacks online and off-line to fight back. To combat piracy in China, Disney developed a Disney Magical Journey rewards program. Consumers had to peel red hologram-covered stickers off legitimate Disney products, attach them to a form with some personal details, and mail them in to enter a contest for free Disney DVDs, television sets, and a trip to Hong Kong Disneyland. In addition to raising awareness of legitimate products and developing a database of Disney-friendly Chinese consumers, the promotion helped clean up some of Disney's channels as consumers would call to alert the company to retailers that, perhaps even unknowingly, were selling product fakes.

Sources: *Gray Markets*: www.agmaglobal.org; David Blanchard, "Just in Time—How to Fix a Leaky Supply Chain," *IndustryWeek*, May 1, 2007; Kersi D. Antia, Mark E. Bergen, Shantanu Dutta, and Robert J. Fisher, "How Does Enforcement Deter Gray Market Incidence?" *Journal of Marketing*, 70, January 2006, pp. 92–106; Matthew B. Myers and David A. Griffith, "Strategies for Combating Gray Market Activity," *Business Horizons*, 42, November–December 1999, pp. 2–8. *Counterfeiting*: Deborah Kong, "Smart Tech Fights Fakes," *Business 2.0*, March 2007, p. 30; Eric Shine, "Faking Out the Fakers," *BusinessWeek*, June 4, 2007, pp. 76–80; Geoffrey A. Fowler, "Disney Tries New Antipiracy Tack," *Wall Street Journal*, May 31, 2006; Carol Matlack, "Fed Up with Fakes," *BusinessWeek*, October 9, 2006, pp. 56–57.

When companies sell their wares over the internet, price becomes transparent, and price differentiation between countries declines: consider an online training course. Whereas the price of a classroom-delivered day of training can vary significantly from the United States to France to Thailand, the price of an online-delivered day of training would be similar.

Another new global pricing challenge is that countries with overcapacity, cheap currencies, and the need to export aggressively have pushed prices down and devalued their currencies. For multinational firms this poses challenges: sluggish demand and reluctance to pay higher prices make selling in these emerging markets difficult. Instead of lowering prices and taking a loss, some multinationals have found more lucrative and creative means of coping.[56]

 General Electric Company   Rather than striving for larger market share, GE's power systems unit focused on winning a larger percentage of each customer's expenditures. The unit asked its top 100 customers what services were most critical and how GE could provide or improve them. The answers prompted the company to cut response time for replacing old or damaged parts from 12 weeks to 6. It began advising customers on the nuances of doing business in Europe and Asia and providing maintenance staff for occasional equipment upgrades. By adding value and helping customers reduce costs and become more efficient, GE avoided a move to commodity pricing and generated bigger margins and record revenues.[57]

Distribution Channels

Too many manufacturers think their job is done once the product leaves the factory. They should instead note how the product moves within a foreign country and take a whole-channel view of distributing products to final users. **Figure 21.4** shows three links between seller and ultimate buyer. In the first, *seller's international marketing headquarters*, the export department or international division makes decisions about channels and other marketing activities. The second link, *channels between nations*, gets the products to the borders of the foreign nation. Decisions made in this link include the types of intermediaries (agents, trading companies), type of transportation (air, sea), and financing and risk management. The third link, *channels within foreign nations*, gets products from their entry point to final buyers and users.

Distribution channels within countries vary considerably. To sell consumer products in Japan, companies must work through one of the most complicated distribution systems in the world. They sell to a general wholesaler, who sells to a product wholesaler, who sells to a product-specialty wholesaler, who sells to a regional wholesaler, who sells to a local wholesaler, who finally sells to retailers. All these distribution levels can make the consumer's price double or triple the importer's price. Taking these same consumer products to tropical Africa, the company might sell to an import wholesaler, who sells to several jobbers, who sell to petty traders (mostly women) working in local markets.

Another difference is the size and character of retail units abroad. Large-scale retail chains dominate the U.S. scene, but much foreign retailing is in the hands of small, independent retailers. In India, millions of retailers operate tiny shops or sell in open markets. Their markups are high, but the real price comes down through haggling. Incomes are low, and people shop daily for small amounts, limited to whatever they can carry home on foot or by bicycle. Most homes lack storage space and refrigeration. Packaging costs are kept low in order to keep prices low. In India, people often buy one cigarette at a time. Breaking bulk remains an important function of intermediaries and helps perpetuate the long channels of distribution, which are a major obstacle to the expansion of large-scale retailing in developing countries.

When multinationals first enter a country, they prefer to work with local distributors who have good local knowledge, but friction often arises later.[58] The multinational complains that the local distributor doesn't invest in business growth, doesn't follow company policy, and doesn't share enough information. The local distributor complains of insufficient corporate support, impossible goals, and confusing policies. The multinational must choose the right distributors, invest in them, and set up performance goals to which they can agree.[59]

Some companies choose to invest in infrastructure to ensure they benefit from the right channels. Peruvian cola company Kola Real has been able to compete with Coca-Cola and Pepsi-Cola in Mexico by setting up its own distribution network of 600 leased lorries, 24 distribution centers, and 800 salespeople. Many retailers are trying to make inroads into global markets. France's Carrefour, Germany's Metro, and the United Kingdom's Tesco have all established global positions. But some of the world's most successful retailers have had mixed success meeting the challenges of going abroad.

|Fig. 21.4| △

Whole-Channel Concept for International Marketing

 Jawad Express In 1960, Jawad opened its first store, thereby introducing the concept of the supermarket to Bahrain. The group's first supermarket gained immediate popularity in Bahrain and became famous for offering high-quality products as well as a friendly service. Recently the Jawad corporation introduced a smaller version of the Jawad supermarket, called Jawad Express, that offers the same quality of products but in a much smaller quantity and variety. The objective behind opening Jawad Express was to offer premium quality and service to customers who have a fast-paced in-and-out shopping concept. Jawad Express became so successful that the company started to open new branches in strategic locations across Bahrain, targeting the business and working community. Due to the fact that Jawad Express sells a small quantity and variety of products, it is able to control the quality of its products and services and also simplify shipping processes. This explains why Jawad Express has become so successful that it constitutes a threat to the popular mini markets found everywhere in Bahrain.[60]

Walmart   The world's largest retailer, Walmart generates 20 percent of its total sales from international operations. Although this is the fastest-growing segment of its business, it has had mixed success globally. When it first went overseas in the early 1990s, Walmart tried to bring a little Americana wherever it went: in football-crazed Brazil, it pushed golf clubs; in blazing hot Mexico, it promoted ice skates; in staid Germany, it instructed its cashiers to smile, prompting suspicions they were flirting. Walmart's tried-and-true formula of low prices, tight inventory control, and big selection doesn't always pay off in markets where consumers have different shopping habits, discount competitors are already entrenched, and employees and suppliers are less subservient. After struggling for years, Walmart withdrew from Germany and South Korea. In some countries, such as Mexico or England with its Asda subsidiary, the traditional formula of 'cheap, steep, and deep' has worked well. But Walmart has learned to adapt in those markets where more challenges exist. After realizing its suburban supercenter concept would not be the answer in Brazil, it purchased chains with an assortment of formats to better satisfy the diverse domestic market, and it has also made inroads in the enormous Chinese market.[61]

Country-of-Origin Effects

In an increasingly connected, highly competitive global marketplace, government officials and marketers are concerned with how attitudes and beliefs about their country affect consumer and business decision making. *Country-of-origin perceptions* are the mental associations and beliefs triggered by a country. Government officials want to strengthen their country's image to help domestic marketers who export, and to attract foreign firms and investors. Marketers want to use positive country-of-origin perceptions to sell their products and services.

Building Country Images

Governments now recognize that the images of their cities and countries affect more than tourism and have important value in commerce. Attracting foreign business can improve the local economy, provide jobs, and improve infrastructure. City officials in Kobe, Japan, were able to entice multinationals Procter & Gamble, Nestlé, and Eli Lilly to locate their Japanese headquarters in the city through traditional marketing techniques, with careful targeting and positioning.[62] Across the globe, after seeing its name being used to help sell everything from pizza to perfume to window blinds, the city of Venice made it a priority to capitalize on its image. City officials developed a trademark that could be licensed to product marketers.[63] Hong Kong officials also developed a symbol—a stylized dragon—to represent their city's core brand values.[64]

Countries all over the world are being marketed like any other brand.[65] New Zealand has developed concerted marketing programs to both sell its products outside the country, via its New Zealand Way program, and to attract tourists by showing the dramatic landscapes featured in *The Lord of the Rings* film trilogy. Both efforts reinforce the image of New Zealand as fresh and pure. But not all films can help the image of a country. Although Kazakhstan has a story to tell given its huge size, rich natural resources, and rapid modernization, British comedian Sacha Baron Cohen's mock documentary *Borat* portrayed the country in an entirely different way, sometimes crude and vulgar.[66]

Attitudes toward country of origin can change over time. Before World War II, Japan had a poor quality image. The success of Sony and its Trinitron TV sets and Japanese automakers Honda and Toyota helped change people's opinions. A strong company that emerges as a global player can do wonders for the image of a country. Relying partly on the global success of Nokia, Finland launched a campaign to enhance its image as a center of high-tech innovation.[67] The Marketing Insight: *The Ups and Downs of Brand America* describes some of the issues that arose due to the anti-U.S. sentiment after the commencement of the Iraq war in 2003.

The spectacular landscapes of New Zealand were brought to millions of viewers through the hugely successful *Lord of the Rings* film trilogy, shot there in its entirety. Marketing for a new surge of tourism to New Zealand has carefully played on the films' popularity.

Marketing Insight

The Ups and Downs of Brand America

One concern for global marketers is how political issues about their domestic country can spill over to influence consumers' perceptions of their products and services in overseas markets. As the United States found itself at odds with other countries in recent years over various issues, including the war in Iraq, marketers wondered how that might influence the effectiveness of their marketing programs.

Initially, the answer appeared to be little. As one protester against the U.S. policy on North Korea observed, "Calling for political independence is one thing, and liking American brands is another. I like IBM, Dell, Microsoft, Starbucks, and Coke." Many consumers seemed willing to separate politics and products. U.S. technology was widely admired and young people all over the world continued to embrace U.S. youth culture. Perhaps the most compelling example of the power of U.S. brands overseas is the fact that McDonald's most successful market in Europe has been France, a country often dismissive of U.S. politics and culture.

Part of the explanation for this mental compartmentalization may be the way global U.S. brands have been built and marketed over the years. Many successfully tapped into universal consumer values and needs, such as Nike with athletic performance, MTV with youth culture, and Coca-Cola with youthful optimism. These firms hire thousands of employees abroad and make sure their products and marketing activities are consistent with local sensibilities.

Many brands have gone to great lengths to weave themselves into the cultural fabric of their foreign markets. One Coca-Cola executive tells of a young child visiting the United States from Japan who commented to her parents on seeing a Coca-Cola vending machine: "Look, they have Coca-Cola too!" As far as she was concerned, Coca-Cola was a Japanese brand.

Although some U.S. brands such as McDonald's, Coca-Cola, Microsoft, and Yahoo! did sustain some tarnishing of their images as time and the war ground on, the resilience of U.S. brands surprised many observers. One mid-2006 study of brand preferences in emerging markets found that even if the United States was not necessarily always that popular, its brands were. In Saudi Arabia, Kraft packaged cheese, Lay's potato chips, and McDonald's restaurants were all viewed as top brands in their categories. Overall, the study found that 70 percent of consumers in developing countries, ranging from Argentina to the UAE, felt local products weren't as good as international brands. As one marketer said of the study, "Regardless of all the problems we have as a country, we are still looked to as the consumer capital of the world."

Sources: Kenneth Hein, "Emerging Markets Still Like U.S. Brands," *Brandweek*, April 16, 2007, p. 4; Parija Bhatnagar, "U.S. Brands Losing Luster," *CNN/Money*, May 21, 2004; "Burgers and Fries a la Francaise," *The Economist*, April 17, 2004, pp. 60–61; Janet Guyon, "Brand America," *Fortune*, October 27, 2003, pp. 179–182; Richard Tompkins, "As Hostility towards America Grows, Will the World Lose Its Appetite for Coca-Cola, McDonald's, and Nike?" *Financial Times*, March 27, 2003, p. 13; Gerry Kermouch and Diane Brady, "Brands in an Age of Anti-Americanism," *BusinessWeek*, August 4, 2003, pp. 69–78.

Consumer Perceptions of Country of Origin

Global marketers know that buyers hold distinct attitudes and beliefs about brands or products from different countries.[68] These country-of-origin perceptions can affect consumer decision making directly and indirectly. The perceptions may be included as an attribute in decision making or influence other attributes in the process (such as 'if it's French, it must be stylish'). The mere fact that a brand is perceived as successful on a global stage may lend credibility and respect.[69] Several studies have found the following:[70]

- People are often ethnocentric and favorably predisposed to their own country's products, unless they come from a less developed country.

- The more favorable a country's image, the more prominently the 'Made in…' label should be displayed.

- The impact of country of origin varies with the type of product. Consumers want to know where a car was made, but not the lubricating oil.

- Certain countries enjoy a reputation for certain goods: Japan for automobiles and consumer electronics; the United States for high-tech innovations, soft drinks, toys, cigarettes, and jeans; France for perfume and luxury goods.

- Sometimes country-of-origin perception can encompass an entire country's products. In one study, Chinese consumers in Hong Kong perceived U.S. products as prestigious, Japanese products as innovative, and Chinese products as cheap.

Marketers must look at country-of-origin perceptions from both a domestic and a foreign perspective. In the domestic market, these perceptions may stir consumers' patriotic notions or remind them of their past. As international trade grows, consumers may view certain brands as symbolically important in their own cultural heritage and identity. Patriotic appeals have been the basis of marketing strategies all over the world, but they can lack uniqueness and even be overused. For example, after the 25th of January revolution in Egypt, many Egyptian brands used pro-Egyptian themes in their advertising. This was found in products such as tissue paper boxes, clothes, and women's accessories, among others.

In some cases, consumers don't know where brands come from, because the brand has become intertwined with multiple countries or the country of origin is not widely known. In surveys, consumers routinely guess that Heineken is German and Nokia is Japanese (they are Dutch and Finnish, respectively). Few consumers know Häagen-Dazs and Estée Lauder originated in the United States.

With so much outsourcing and foreign manufacturing, it's hard to know what the actual country of origin really is anyway. The Ideal Zanussi brand of refrigerators which is manufactured Egypt has many components that are imported from Italy. Most components of cars assembled in Egypt come from Germany and Japan. Foreign auto makers continue to invest in Egypt, investing mainly in plants and suppliers for the industry. But what makes a product more 'Egyptian:' having a higher percentage of Egyptian components or creating more jobs in Egypt? The two measures may not lead to the same conclusion.[71]

Companies can target niches to establish a footing in new markets. China's leading maker of refrigerators, washing machines, and air conditioners, Haier, is building a beachhead in the United States with U.S. college students who loyally buy its minifridges at Walmart and elsewhere.[72] Haier's long-term plans are to introduce innovative products in other areas, such as flat-screen TV sets and wine-cooling cabinets.

As they make progress, companies can start to build local roots to increase relevance, as Toyota has done.

 Toyota   Toyota is known for its long history in the Arab region. It has strong presence in GCC countries, especially in Saudi Arabia. Abdel Latif Jameel (ALJ) Co. is the agent for Toyota in Saudi Arabia, the largest market for Toyota in the Arab world, and ALJ is the largest independent distributor of Toyota vehicles in the world. Recently, ALJ became the agent for Toyota in Turkey. Because Saudi Arabia and the GCC are important markets for Toyota, it produces specially configured cars to cope with the high temperatures in the GCC region. They are referred to as Gulf Configured Cars, and they have more powerful air-conditioning systems than the regular ones.[73]

Deciding on the Marketing Organization

Companies manage their international marketing activities in three ways: through export departments, international divisions, or a global organization.

Export Department

A firm normally gets into international marketing by simply shipping out its goods. If its international sales expand, the company organizes an export department, consisting of a sales manager and a few assistants. As sales increase, the export department expands to include various marketing services so the company can go after business more aggressively. If the firm moves into joint ventures or direct investment, the export department will no longer be adequate to manage international operations.

International Division

Many companies engage in several international markets and ventures. Sooner or later they create international divisions to handle all their international activity. The international division is headed by a division president who sets goals and budgets and is responsible for the company's international growth.

The international division's corporate staff consists of functional specialists who provide services to various operating units. Operating units can be organized in several ways. First, they can be *geographical organizations*. Reporting to the international-division president might be regional vice presidents for North America, Latin America, Europe, Africa, the Middle East, and the Far East. Reporting to the regional vice presidents are country managers responsible for a sales force, sales branches, distributors, and licensees in the respective countries. The operating units may be *world product groups*, each with an international vice president responsible for worldwide sales of each product group. The vice presidents may draw on corporate-staff area specialists for expertise on different geographical areas. Finally, operating units may be *international subsidiaries*, each headed by a president. The various subsidiary presidents report to the president of the international division.

Global Organization

Several firms have become truly global organizations. Their top corporate management and staff plan worldwide manufacturing facilities, marketing policies, financial flows, and logistical systems. The global operating units report directly to the chief executive or executive committee, not to the head of an international division. The firm trains its executives in worldwide operations, recruits management from many countries, purchases components and supplies where it can obtain them at least cost, and makes investments where anticipated returns are greatest.

These companies face several organizational complexities. For example, when the firm is pricing a company's mainframe computers to a large banking system in Germany, how much influence should the headquarter's product manager have? And the company's market manager for the banking sector? And the company's German country manager?

Different circumstances will dictate different approaches.[74] When forces for 'global integration' (capital-intensive production, homogeneous demand) are strong and forces for 'national responsiveness' (local standards and barriers, strong local preferences) are weak, a global strategy that treats the world as a single market can make sense (for example, with consumer electronics). When the reverse is true, then a multinational strategy that treats the world as a portfolio of national opportunities can be more appropriate (such as for food or cleaning products).

When both forces prevail to some extent, a 'glocal' strategy that standardizes certain elements and localizes other elements can be the way to go (for instance, with telecommunications). As this is often the case, many firms seek a blend of centralized global control from corporate headquarters with input from local and regional marketers. Finding that balance can be tricky, though. Coca-Cola's "think local, act local" philosophy, which decentralized much of the power and responsibility for designing marketing programs and activities, fell apart because many local managers lacked the necessary skills or discipline to do the job. Decidedly un-Coke-like ads appeared—such as skinny-dippers streaking down a beach in Italy—and sales stalled. The pendulum swung back, and Coke executives in their United States headquarters in Atlanta, Georgia, began to play a stronger strategic role again.[75]

Summary

1. Despite the many challenges in the international arena (shifting borders, unstable governments, foreign-exchange problems, corruption, and technological pirating), companies selling in global industries need to internationalize their operations. Companies cannot simply stay domestic and expect to maintain their markets.

2. In deciding to go abroad, a company needs to define its international marketing objectives and policies. The company must determine whether to market in a few countries or many countries. It must decide which countries to consider. In general, the candidate countries should be rated on three criteria: market attractiveness, risk, and competitive advantage. Developing countries offer a unique set of opportunities and risks.

3. Once a company decides on a particular country, it must determine the best mode of entry. Its broad choices are indirect exporting, direct exporting, licensing, joint ventures, and direct investment. Each succeeding strategy involves more commitment, risk, control, and profit potential.

4. In deciding on the marketing program, a company must decide how much to adapt its marketing program. At the product level, firms can pursue a strategy of straight extension, product adaptation, or product invention. At the

communication level, firms may choose communication adaptation or dual adaptation. At the price level, firms may encounter price escalation, dumping, gray markets, and discounted counterfeit products. At the distribution level, firms need to take a whole-channel view of the challenge of distributing products to the final users. In creating all elements of the marketing program, firms must be aware of the cultural, social, political, technological, environmental, and legal limitations they face in other countries.

5. Country-of-origin perceptions can affect consumers and businesses alike. Managing those perceptions in the most advantageous way possible is an important marketing priority.

6. Depending on the level of international involvement, companies manage their international marketing activity in three ways: through export departments, international divisions, or a global organization.

Applications

Marketing Debate

Is the World Coming Closer Together?

Many social commentators maintain that youth and teens are becoming more and more alike across countries as time goes on. Others, although not disputing this fact, point out that differences between cultures at even younger ages by far exceed the similarities.

Take a position: People are becoming more and more similar *versus* the differences between people of different cultures far outweigh their similarities.

Marketing Discussion

Think of some of your favorite brands. Do you know where they come from? Where and how they are made or provided? Do you think knowing these answers would affect your perceptions of quality or satisfaction?

Marketing Excellence

>>Samsung

Korean consumer electronics giant Samsung has made a remarkable transformation, from a provider of value-priced commodity products that original equipment manufacturers sold under their own brands, to a global marketer of premium-priced Samsung-branded consumer electronics such as flat-screen TVs, digital cameras, and mobile phones. Its high-end mobile phones have been a growth engine, and Samsung has released a steady stream of innovations, popularizing the PDA phone and the first mobile phone with an MP3 player.

Samsung used to stress volume and market domination rather than profitability. Yet during the Asian financial crisis of the late 1990s, when other Korean *chaebols* collapsed beneath a mountain of debt, Samsung took a different tack. It cut costs and reemphasized product quality and manufacturing flexibility, which allowed its consumer electronics to go from project phase to store shelves within 6 months. It also refocused on innovation, using technological leapfrogging to produce best-selling mobile handsets for Asia, Europe, and the United States.

Samsung's success has been driven by well-designed, path-breaking products, but also by an upgrade in its brand image. In 2010, it spent around US$600 million on marketing, sponsoring the Olympics, and the 2010 Africa Cup of Nations, and running a global ad campaign themed Imagine. Samsung views its brand message as 'technology,' 'design,' and 'sensation.' With increasing digital convergence, it's been able to introduce a wide range of electronic products under its strong brand umbrella. The company planned to invest $22.6 billion in R&D in 2010, the largest ever annual investment

Continued on next page>>

Marketing Excellence...continued

>>Samsung

in R&D for a company. Also, it continues to increase its number of researchers to help develop more innovative products.

Its greatest sign of success, though, may be that longtime market leader Sony has been courting Samsung for joint ventures, partnering on a US$2 billion state-of-the-art LCD factory in South Korea and agreeing to share 24,000 basic patents covering a range of components and production processes. Perhaps this is not surprising, given that in 2005, for the first time, brand valuation experts Interband valued the Samsung brand as worth more than the Sony brand. To maintain its market leadership, however, Samsung cannot rest on its laurels and must continue to successfully expand via new products and new markets.

Samsung continues to grow significantly in the Middle East and North Africa region. In 2010, Samsung achieved sales of US$4.4 billion, the highest record ever reached, representing a 34 percent growth rate. "Despite the economic turmoil in the recent years, Samsung Electronics grew dramatically and it is expected that the regional economy continues improving and competition to be fierce in 2011," said Kyung Tae Bae, president and CEO of Samsung Electronics MENA HQ. "Samsung will continue to look for opportunities to become stronger and more flexible as we compete for market leadership across product categories. Our goals are ambitious as we seek to become an ultra-premium and iconic brand that is preferred throughout the MENA region."

Mr Bae identified the three main pillars of Samsung's "Smarter Life" philosophy as being smart design, smart experiences, and smart connections. The smart design refers to the creative designs that add value to the consumer. The smart experiences are the variety of applications and solutions offered over a range of platforms on clear and dynamic screens. The smart connections are the ability of Samsung devices to connect with one another, enabling sharing of content and enhancing the value-added to users.

Questions

1. What was Samsung's strategy during the Asian financial crisis?

2. How did Samsung emerge as a global brand?

3. How did Sony, a longtime market leader, react to Samsung's growth and success?

4. What are the main pillars of Samsung's "Smarter Life" philosophy?

Sources: Moon Ihlwan, "Samsung Is Having a Sony Moment," *BusinessWeek*, July 30, 2007, p. 38; Martin Fackler, "Raising the Bar at Samsung," *New York Times*, April 25, 2006; "Brand New," *The Economist*, January 15, 2005, pp. 10–11; Patricia O'Connell, "Samsung's Goal: Be Like BMW," *BusinessWeek*, August 1, 2005; Heidi Brown and Justin Doeble, "Samsung's Next Act," *Forbes*, July 26, 2004; John Quelch and Anna Harrington, "Samsung Electronics Company: Global Marketing Operations," Harvard Business School Case 9-504-051; "Samsung Electronics Celebrates its Continuous Growing Success in the Middle East and North Africa," www.albawaba.com/samsung-electronics-celebrates-it%E2%80%99s-continuous-growing-success-middle-east-and-north-africa.

Emirates Airline's commitment to holistic marketing has paid off in terms of concrete results that help the environment by using fewer resources and producing less waste and less pollution. This makes it one of the most efficient airlines worldwide.

In this chapter, we will address the following questions:

1. What are important trends in marketing practices? (pg. 618)

2. What are the keys to effective internal marketing? (pg. 618)

3. How can companies be responsible social marketers? (pg. 626)

4. How can a company improve its marketing skills? (pg. 637)

5. What tools are available to help companies monitor and improve their marketing activities? (pg. 638)

Managing a Holistic Marketing Organization for the Long Run

Healthy long-term growth for a brand requires that the marketing organization be managed properly. Holistic marketers must engage in a host of carefully planned, interconnected marketing activities and satisfy an increasingly broader set of constituents.[1] They must also consider a wider range of effects of their actions. Corporate social responsibility and sustainability have become a priority as organizations grapple with the short-term and long-term effects of their marketing. Some firms have embraced this new vision of corporate enlightenment and made it the very core of what they do. Consider Emirates Airline.

 Emirates Airline began in 1985 with two leased aircraft. Over the years, Emirates has grown from a regional carrier to a truly international airline, known for its unique customer service. It continues to be one of the fastest-growing airlines in the world, with some of the highest orders for aircraft in the aviation industry, the latest being ten of Boeing's new 747-8F models in a deal worth US$3.3 billion. This growth has been coupled with the need to use fewer resources and create less waste and pollution. The billions of dollars that were invested in purchasing the latest aircraft means that Emirates operates one of the newest and most efficient fleets in the world. An Emirates Airline flight from Dubai to San Francisco International Airport, covering around 13,000 kilometers, is known as the "longest green air flight in the world."

The airline spent months planning for the flight in order to maximize fuel savings and minimize greenhouse gas emissions. Prior to take off, the aircraft is washed to reduce air friction, unnecessary weight is removed from inside the plane, auxiliary power from the airport terminal is used, rather than power from the jet engine, and a tug vehicle is used to take the plane to the runway. These efforts brought about a reduction in flight time from 16 hours to just above 15 hours, reduced fuel consumption by 6 percent, and saved 18,000 kilograms of greenhouse gas emissions. Emirates extended its commitment to the environment through its involvement with the Dubai Desert Conservation Reserve to help preserve the natural and cultural heritage of the Dubai desert, and its involvement with the National Park, an area that is home to 30 species native to the Arabian Peninsula.[2]

Other brands such as Qatar Airways, Southwest Airlines, Japan Airlines, and British Airways have embraced similar philosophies and practices. Successful holistic marketing requires effective relationship marketing, integrated marketing, internal marketing, and performance marketing. Preceding chapters addressed the first two topics and the strategy and tactics of marketing.[3] In this chapter, we consider the latter two topics and how to conduct marketing responsibly. In our discussion, we look at how firms organize, implement, evaluate, and control marketing activities. We also discuss the increased importance of social responsibility. We begin by examining changes in how companies conduct marketing today. ▽

Trends in Marketing Practices

Chapters 1 and 3 describe some important changes in the marketing macroenvironment, such as globalization, deregulation, technological advances, customer empowerment, and market fragmentation. In response to this rapidly changing environment, companies have restructured their business and marketing practices in many ways.

- *Reengineering.* Appointing teams to manage customer value building processes and break down walls between departments.
- *Outsourcing.* Buying more goods and services from outside domestic or foreign vendors.
- *Benchmarking.* Studying 'best-practice companies' to improve performance.
- *Supplier partnering.* Partnering with fewer but better value-adding suppliers.
- *Customer partnering.* Working more closely with customers to add value to their operations.
- *Merging.* Acquiring or merging with firms in the same or complementary industries to gain economies of scale and scope.
- *Globalizing.* Increasing efforts to 'think global' and 'act local.'
- *Flattening.* Reducing the number of organizational levels to get closer to the customer.
- *Focusing.* Determining the most profitable businesses and customers and focusing on them.
- *Accelerating.* Designing the organization and setting up processes to respond more quickly to changes in the environment.
- *Empowering.* Encouraging and empowering personnel to produce more ideas and take more initiative.

The role of marketing in the organization is also changing.[4] Traditionally, marketers have played the roles of middlemen, charged with understanding customer needs and transmitting the voice of the customer to various functional areas in the organization. But in a networked enterprise, every functional area can interact directly with customers. Marketing no longer has sole ownership of customer interactions; rather, marketing needs to integrate all the customer-facing processes so customers see a single face and hear a single voice when they interact with the firm.

Internal Marketing

Internal marketing requires that everyone in the organization buys into the concepts and goals of marketing and engages in choosing, providing, and communicating customer value. Over the years, marketing has evolved from work done by the sales department into a complex group of activities spread through the organization.[5]

 Selections Antique Store   Selections is a small store in Alexandria, Egypt, the second largest city after Cairo. Despite the store's small size, many people prefer to go there than buy at any other store, partly because it has a strategic location where it is easy to park (a big issue in Egypt) but most importantly because of the sales staff. The manager, Mrs. Fattheya El Soury, says internal marketing is one of the main reasons for this. Her staff know the objectives of the store and are well-educated about the products. Every 6 months, because the antiques market changes rapidly, a 3-day 'orientation' takes place during which her staff learn how it feels to be the customer and what kind of experience should be delivered. As Mrs. El Soury explains, it is not all about the external marketing and advertising; sometimes it has to come from within to reflect on the outside. Sales improve as customers become more loyal over the years. Even though it is considered small in size, it has higher customer satisfaction than other similar or even larger stores.[6]

A company can have an excellent marketing department, however, and fail at marketing. Much depends on how other company departments view customers. If they point to the marketing department and say, "They do the marketing," the company has not implemented effective marketing. Only when all employees realize their job is to create, serve, and satisfy customers does the company become an effective marketer.[7] The Marketing Memo: *Characteristics of Company Departments that are Truly Driven* presents a tool that evaluates which company departments are customer driven.[8]

Let's look at how marketing departments are being organized, how they can work effectively with other departments, and how firms can foster a creative marketing culture within the entire organization.

marketing Memo

Characteristics of Company Departments that are Truly Customer Driven

R&D	___	They spend time meeting customers and listening to their problems.
	___	They welcome the involvement of marketing, manufacturing, and other departments on each new project.
	___	They benchmark competitors' products and seek 'best-of-class' solutions.
	___	They solicit customer reactions and suggestions as the project progresses.
	___	They continuously improve and refine the product on the basis of market feedback.
Purchasing	___	They proactively search for the best suppliers rather than choose only from those who solicit their business.
	___	They build long-term relations with fewer but more reliable high-quality suppliers.
	___	They do not compromise quality for price savings.
Manufacturing	___	They invite customers to visit and tour their plants.
	___	They visit customer factories to see how customers use the company's products.
	___	They willingly work overtime when it is important to meet promised delivery schedules.
	___	They continuously search for ways to produce goods faster and/or at lower costs.
	___	They continuously improve product quality, aiming for zero defects.
	___	They meet customer requirements for 'customization' where this can be done profitably.
Marketing	___	They study customer needs and wants in well-defined market segments.
	___	They allocate marketing effort in relation to the long-run profit potential of the targeted segments.
	___	They develop winning offerings for each target segment.
	___	They measure company image and customer satisfaction on a continuous basis.
	___	They continuously gather and evaluate ideas for new products, product improvements, and services to meet customers' needs.
	___	They influence all company departments and employees to be customer centered in their thinking and practice.
Sales	___	They have specialized knowledge of the customer's industry.
	___	They strive to give the customer 'the best solution.'
	___	They make only promises they can keep.
	___	They feed back customers' needs and ideas to those in charge of product development.
	___	They serve the same customers for a long period of time.
Logistics	___	They set a high standard for service delivery time and they meet this standard consistently.
	___	They operate a knowledgeable and friendly customer-service department that can answer questions, handle complaints, and resolve problems in a satisfactory and timely manner.
Accounting	___	They prepare periodic 'profitability' reports by product, market segment, geographic areas (regions, sales territories), order sizes, and individual customers.
	___	They prepare invoices tailored to customer needs and answer customer queries courteously and quickly.
Finance	___	They understand and support marketing expenditures (e.g. image advertising) that represent marketing investments that produce long-term customer preference and loyalty.
	___	They tailor the financial package to the customers' financial requirements.
	___	They make quick decisions on customer creditworthiness.
Public Relations	___	They disseminate favorable news about the company and they 'damage control' unfavorable news.
	___	They act as an internal customer and public advocate for better company policies and practices.
Other Customer-Contact Personnel	___	They are competent, courteous, cheerful, credible, reliable, and responsive.

Organizing the Marketing Department

Modern marketing departments can be organized in a number of different, sometimes overlapping ways:[9] functionally, geographically, by product or brand, by market, or in a matrix.

FUNCTIONAL ORGANIZATION The most common form of marketing organization consists of functional specialists reporting to a marketing vice president, who coordinates their activities. **Figure 22.1** shows five specialists. Additional specialists might include a customer service manager, a marketing planning manager, a market logistics manager, a direct marketing manager, and a digital marketing manager.

The main advantage of a functional marketing organization is its administrative simplicity. It can be quite a challenge to develop smooth working relationships, however, within the marketing department.[10] This form can also lose its effectiveness as the number of products and markets increases. A functional organization often leads to inadequate planning for specific products and markets. Then, each functional group competes with others for budget and status. The marketing vice president constantly weighs the claims of competing functional specialists and faces a difficult coordination problem.

GEOGRAPHIC ORGANIZATION A company selling in a national market often organizes its sales force (and sometimes other functions, including marketing) along geographic lines. The national sales manager may supervise four regional sales managers, who each supervise six zone managers, who in turn supervise eight district sales managers, who each supervise 10 salespeople.

Several companies are now adding *area market specialists* (regional or local marketing managers) to support the sales efforts in high-volume markets. One such market might be Dubai, where roughly 70 percent of the households are expatriate. A Dubai specialist would know the customer and trade makeup, help marketing managers at headquarters adjust their marketing mix for Dubai, and prepare local annual and long-range plans for selling all the company's products there.

Companies that have shifted to a greater regional marketing emphasis are McDonald's, which now spends about 50 percent of its total advertising budget regionally; American Airlines, which realized that the travel needs of Chicagoans and Southwesterners are very different in the winter months; and Toyota in Kuwait, who imported small-sized engines for Egyptian expatriates who want to go back home with their cars and pay lower import tariffs. Some companies must develop different marketing programs in different parts of the country because their brand development varies so much.

 Vitrac   Vitrac was founded in 1981 in Egypt as a producer of fruit jam. As the jam gained a reputation as the best in Egypt, Hero Group, the parent company, decided to extend into other product lines such as juices, food, and beverages. After testing different ingredients and bottling methods, Hero decided to enter the market with fruit juice in a carton. The juice was relatively sweet compared to other competing brands, and the product was not successful in major cities such as Cairo and Alexandria. Then, when the product was introduced into rural areas, the customers found the taste very appealing but the carton-based packaging was not well received, particularly because it is not acceptable for men to drink from a straw. Thus, Vitrac decided to package the drink in a glass bottle. The drink was successful and remains one of the biggest selling brands in rural Egypt.[11]

|Fig. 22.1|

Functional
Organization

PRODUCT- OR BRAND-MANAGEMENT ORGANIZATION

Companies producing a variety of products and brands often establish a product- (or brand-) management organization. The product-management organization does not replace the functional organization, but serves as another layer of management. A product manager supervises product category managers, who in turn supervise specific product and brand managers.

A product-management organization makes sense if the company's products are quite different, or if the sheer number of products is beyond the ability of a functional organization to handle. Kraft has used a product-management organization in its Post division, with separate product category managers in charge of cereals, pet food, and beverages. Within the cereal-product group, Kraft has had separate subcategory managers for nutritional cereals, children's presweetened cereals, family cereals, and miscellaneous cereals.

Kraft has category managers for its different types of cereals: nutritional, presweetened, family, and so on.

Product and brand management is sometimes characterized as a **hub-and-spoke system**. The brand or product manager is figuratively at the center, with spokes emanating out to various departments (see △ **Figure 22.2**). Some tasks that product or brand managers may perform include:

- Developing a long-range and competitive strategy for the product.

- Preparing an annual marketing plan and sales forecast.

- Working with advertising and merchandising agencies to develop copy, programs, and campaigns.

- Increasing support of the product among the sales force and distributors.

- Gathering continuous intelligence on the product's performance, customer and dealer attitudes, and new problems and opportunities.

- Initiating product improvements to meet changing market needs.

hub-and-spoke system
a term used to describe product and brand management, where the brand or product manager is figuratively at the center, with spokes emanating out to various departments.

The product-management organization lets the product manager concentrate on developing a cost-effective marketing mix and react more quickly to new products in the marketplace; it also gives the company's smaller brands a product advocate. However, this organization has disadvantages too:

- Product and brand managers may lack enough authority to carry out their responsibilities.

- Product and brand managers become experts in their product area but rarely achieve functional expertise.

- The product-management system often turns out to be costly. One person is appointed to manage each major product or brand, and soon more are appointed to manage even minor products and brands.

- Brand managers normally manage a brand for only a short time. Short-term involvement leads to short-term planning and fails to build long-term strengths.

- The fragmentation of markets makes it harder to develop a national strategy. Brand managers must please regional and local sales groups, transferring power from marketing to sales.

- Product and brand managers focus the company on building market share rather than the customer relationship.

A second alternative in a product-management organization is *product teams*. There are three types of structure: vertical product team, triangular product team, and the horizontal product team (see △ **Figure 22.3**).

|Fig. 22.2| ▲

The Product
Manager's
Interactions

(a) Vertical Product Team

(b) Triangular Product Team

(c) Horizontal Product Team

PM = product manager
AP = associate product manager
PA = product assistant
R = market researcher
C = communication specialist
S = sales manager
D = distribution specialist
F = finance/accounting specialist
E = engineer

|Fig. 22.3| ▲

Three Types of
Product Team

The triangular and horizontal product-team approaches let each major brand be run by a **brand-asset management team (BAMT)** consisting of key representatives from functions that affect the brand's performance. The company is made of several BAMTs that periodically report to a BAMT directors committee, which itself reports to a chief branding officer. This is quite different from the way brands have traditionally been handled.

A third alternative for product-management organization is to eliminate product manager positions for minor products and assign two or more products to each remaining manager. This is feasible where two or more products appeal to a similar set of needs. A cosmetics company doesn't need product managers for each product because cosmetics serve one major need: beauty. A toiletries company needs different managers for headache remedies, toothpaste, soap, and shampoo, because these products differ in use and appeal.

A fourth alternative is to introduce *category management*, in which a company focuses on product categories to manage its brands. Procter & Gamble, pioneers of the brand-management system, and several other top firms made a significant shift to category management.[12]

P&G cites a number of advantages. By fostering internal competition among brand managers, the traditional brand-management system created strong incentives to excel, but also much internal competition for resources and a lack of coordination. The new scheme was designed to ensure that all categories would be able to receive adequate resources.

Another rationale for category management is the increasing power of the trade. Because the retail trade has tended to think of profitability in terms of product categories, P&G felt it only made sense to deal along similar lines. Retailers and regional grocery chains such as Carrefour and Dominick's respectively have embraced category management as a means to define a particular product category's strategic role within the store and address logistics, the role of private-label products, and the trade-offs between product variety and inefficient duplication.[13]

Category management is not a panacea. It is still a product-driven system. Colgate has moved from brand management (Colgate toothpaste) to category management (toothpaste category) to a new stage called 'customer-need management' (mouth care). This last step finally focuses the organization on a basic customer need.[14]

MARKET-MANAGEMENT ORGANIZATION Many companies sell to different markets. Canon sells color printers to consumer, business, and government markets. The Maghreb Steel Company sells to the construction, road, and farming industries.[15] When customers fall into different user groups with distinct buying preferences and practices, a **market-management organization** is desirable. Market managers supervise several market-development managers, market specialists, or industry specialists and draw on functional services as needed. Market managers of important markets might even have functional specialists reporting to them.

Market managers are staff (not line) people, with duties similar to those of product managers. They develop long-range and annual plans for their markets. Their performance is judged by their market's growth and profitability. This system shares many advantages and disadvantages of product-management systems. Its strongest advantage is organizing marketing activity to meet the needs of distinct customer groups rather than focusing on marketing functions, regions, or products. Many companies are reorganizing along market lines and becoming **market-centered organizations**. Xerox has converted from geographic selling to selling by industry, as have IBM and Hewlett-Packard.

In a **customer-management organization**, companies can organize themselves to understand and deal with individual customers rather than with the mass market or even market segments.[16] When a close relationship is advantageous, such as when customers have diverse and complex requirements and buy an integrated bundle of products and services, customer-management organizations should prevail. IBM's Global Services and General Electric's Power Systems are organized in this fashion because of their need to interact closely with customers. One study showed that companies organized by customer groups reported much higher accountability for the overall quality of relationships and employees' freedom to take actions to satisfy individual customers.[17]

MATRIX-MANAGEMENT ORGANIZATION

Companies that produce many products for many markets may adopt a matrix organization. Some provide the context in which a matrix can thrive: flat, lean team organizations focused around business processes that cut horizontally across functions.[18] DuPont was a pioneer in developing the matrix structure (see △ **Figure 22.4**).

DuPont Before it was spun off, DuPont's textile fibers department consisted of separate product managers for rayon, acetate, nylon, orlon, and dacron; and separate market managers for menswear, women's wear, home furnishings, and industrial markets. The product managers planned sales and profits for their respective fibers. They asked market managers to estimate how much of their fiber they could sell in each market at a proposed price. Market managers, however, were generally more interested in meeting their market's needs than pushing a particular fiber. In preparing their market plans, they asked each product manager about the fiber's planned prices and availabilities. The final sales forecast of the market managers and the product managers should have added up to the same grand total.

Companies like DuPont can go one step further and view the market managers as the main marketers, and their product managers as suppliers. The menswear market manager, for example, would be empowered to buy textile fibers from DuPont's product managers or, if DuPont's price is too high, from outside suppliers, forcing DuPont product managers to become more efficient. If a DuPont product manager couldn't match the 'arm's-length pricing' levels of competitive suppliers, then perhaps DuPont should not produce that fiber.

|Fig. 22.4| △

Product/Market-Management Matrix System

brand-asset management team (BAMT) a team that runs each major brand, consisting of key representatives from functions that affect a brand's performance.

market-management organization a marketing department organization where marketing managers supervise market or industry specialists; used when customers fall into different user groups with distinct buying preferences and behaviors.

market-centered organization a marketing department organized along specific market segments.

customer-management organization companies organized to understand and deal with individual customers rather than with the mass market or even market segments.

A matrix organization seems desirable in a multiproduct, multimarket company. The problem is that it's costly and often creates conflicts. There's the cost of supporting all the managers, and questions about where authority and responsibility for marketing activities should reside: at headquarters or in the division?[19] Some corporate marketing groups assist top management with overall opportunity evaluation, provide divisions with consulting assistance on request, help divisions that have little or no marketing, and promote the marketing concept throughout the company.

Relations with Other Departments

Under the marketing concept, all departments need to 'think customer' and work together to satisfy customer needs and expectations. The marketing department must drive this point home. The marketing vice president, or CMO, has two tasks: (1) to coordinate the company's internal marketing activities and (2) to coordinate marketing with finance, operations, and other company functions to serve the customer.

Yet, there is little agreement on how much influence and authority marketing should have over other departments. Departments define company problems and goals from their viewpoint, so conflicts of interest and communications problems are unavoidable. Typically, the marketing vice president must work through persuasion rather than authority.

To develop a balanced orientation in which marketing and other functions jointly determine what is in the company's best interests, companies can provide joint seminars to understand each others' viewpoints, joint committees and liaison personnel, personnel exchange programs, and analytical methods to determine the most profitable course of action.[20]

Many companies now focus on key processes rather than departments, because departmental organization can be a barrier to the smooth performance of fundamental business processes. They appoint process leaders, who manage cross-disciplinary teams that include marketing and sales people. As a result, marketing personnel may have a solid-line responsibility to their teams and a dotted-line responsibility to the marketing department.

 Arab Bank   Responding to customer demands is a key factor that the Arab Bank has emphasized since it started operations in 1930. The ability to respond to customer demands is reflected in the bank's organizational structure and the various initiatives it has implemented. As Abdel Hamid Shoman, chairman and CEO of the Arab Bank, says, "[we] realized that we must ensure our front line staff is focused on providing the right service to our customers. This is why we are pushing forward and changing the look of our branches, a move which is being well received in the market." The Arab Bank made major changes in its internal operating procedures, which moved administrative, non-customer-related activities to the central operations unit. This enabled the branch staff to focus on providing world-class service to clients. It also helped to ensure that the bank's strategy and planning reaches each branch, to guarantee a consistent customer experience throughout all the possible channels through which customers deal with the Arab Bank.[21]

Building a Creative Marketing Organization

Many companies realize they're not yet really market and customer driven: they are product and sales driven. General Motors, Shell, Misr Petroleum, and the National Bank of Egypt are attempting to transform into truly market-driven companies. This requires:

1. Developing a company-wide passion for customers.
2. Organizing around customer segments instead of products.
3. Understanding customers through qualitative and quantitative research.

The task is not easy, but the payoffs can be considerable.[22] It won't happen as a result of the CEO making speeches and urging every employee to 'think customer.' See the Marketing Insight: *The Marketing CEO* for actions a CEO can take to improve marketing capabilities.

Marketing Insight

The Marketing CEO

What steps can a CEO take to create a market- and customer-focused company?

1. *Convince senior management of the need to become customer focused.* The CEO personally exemplifies strong customer commitment and rewards those in the organization who do likewise. For example, Medhat Khalil, CEO of Raya, visits stores and asks customers about their experiences there; former CEOs Jack Welch of GE and Lou Gerstner of IBM are said to have spent 100 days a year visiting customers, in spite of their many strategic, financial, and administrative burdens; current Starbucks CEO Jim Donald visits 10–20 stores a week to go to the back of the counter and talk to store partners (employees) and customers.

2. *Appoint a senior marketing officer and marketing task force.* The marketing task force should include the CEO; the vice presidents of sales, R&D, purchasing, manufacturing, finance, and human resources; and other key individuals.

3. *Get outside help and guidance.* Consulting firms have considerable experience in helping companies move toward a marketing orientation.

4. *Change the company's reward measurement and system.* As long as purchasing and manufacturing are rewarded for keeping costs low, they will resist accepting some costs required to serve customers better. As long as finance focuses on short-term profit, it will oppose major investments designed to build satisfied, loyal customers.

5. *Hire strong marketing talent.* The company needs a strong marketing vice president who not only manages the marketing department but also gains respect from and influence with the other vice presidents. A multidivisional company will benefit from establishing a strong corporate marketing department.

6. *Develop strong in-house marketing training programs.* The company should design well-crafted marketing training programs for corporate management, divisional general managers, marketing and sales personnel, manufacturing personnel, R&D personnel, and others. Emirates, GE, and PepsiCo run these programs.

7. *Install a modern marketing planning system.* The planning format will require managers to think about the marketing environment, opportunities, competitive trends, and other forces. These managers then prepare strategies and sales-and-profit forecasts for specific products and segments and are accountable for performance.

8. *Establish an annual marketing excellence recognition program.* Business units that believe they've developed exemplary marketing plans should submit a description of their plans and results. Winning teams should be rewarded at a special ceremony and the plans disseminated to the other business units as 'models of marketing thinking.' Accenture and Starbucks follow this strategy.

9. *Shift from a department focus to a process-outcome focus.* After defining the fundamental business processes that determine its success, the company should appoint process leaders and cross-disciplinary teams to reengineer and implement these processes.

10. *Empower the employees.* Progressive companies encourage and reward their employees for coming up with new ideas and empower them to settle customer complaints to save the customer's business. IBM, for example, lets its frontline employees spend up to US$5,000 to solve a customer problem on the spot.

Although it's necessary to be customer oriented, it's not enough. The organization must also be creative. Companies today copy each others' advantages and strategies with increasing speed. Differentiation gets harder to achieve, let alone maintain, and margins fall when firms become more alike. The only answer is to build a capability in strategic innovation and imagination (see Marketing Memo: *Fueling Strategic Innovation*). This capability comes from assembling tools, processes, skills, and measures that let the firm generate more and better new ideas than its competitors.[23] Companies must watch trends and be ready to capitalize on them. Motorola was 18 months late in moving from analog to digital mobile phones, giving Nokia and Ericsson a big lead. Barnes & Noble was late to recognize online ordering of books and music, allowing Amazon.com to gain a head start. Nestlé was late seeing the trend toward coffeehouses such as Starbucks. Coca-Cola was slow to pick up beverage trends toward fruit-flavored drinks such as Snapple, energy drinks such as Gatorade, and designer water brands. Coca-Cola has recently introduced Arwa Fruits, a fruit-flavored sparkling water, in Bahrain.[24] Market leaders tend to miss trends when they are risk averse, obsessed about protecting their existing markets and physical resources, and more interested in efficiency than innovation.[25]

marketing Memo

Fueling Strategic Innovation

Professor Stephen Brown of Ulster University in Ireland has challenged a number of fundamental assumptions underlying the marketing concept. He thinks marketers make too much of researching and satisfying consumers, and they risk losing marketing imagination and significant consumer impact. How can companies build a capability for strategic innovation? Here are some approaches he advocates:

- Hire marketers who are unusually creative to counterbalance the majority who do marketing by the textbook. These people may be unconventional, rule breaking, risk taking, and even more argumentative, but their ideas will at least present a challenge.

- Train your employees in the use of creativity techniques, for groups (brainstorming, synectics) and individuals (visualization, attribute listing, forced relationships, morphological analysis, mind mapping).

- Note trends such as longer working hours, single parenting, and new life styles, and tease out their implications for your firm.

- List unmet customer needs and imagine new offerings or solutions: how to help people lose weight, stop smoking, relieve stress, or meet others.

- Run a 'best idea' competition once a month. Give a cash reward, extra vacation time, or travel awards to those who come up with the best ideas.

- Have senior managers take small sets of employees out to lunch or dinner once a week to discuss ideas for improving the business. Go to new settings, such as a wrestling match, a drug rehabilitation center, or a poor neighborhood.

- Set up groups of employees to critique the company's and competitors' products and services. Let them critique the company's cherished beliefs and consider turning them upside down.

- Occasionally hire creative resources from outside the firm. Many large advertising agencies, such as Leo Burnett, run a creativity service for clients.

Sources: For more on Brown's views, see Stephen Brown, *Marketing: The Retro Revolution* (Thousand Oaks, CA: Sage, 2001). For more on creativity, see Pat Fallon and Fred Senn, *Juicing the Orange: How to Turn Creativity into a Powerful Business Advantage* (Boston: Harvard Business School Press, 2006); Bob Schmetterer, *Leap: A Revolution in Creative Business Strategy* (Hoboken, NJ: John Wiley & Sons, 2003); Jean-Marie Dru, *Beyond Disruption: Changing the Rules in the Marketplace* (Hoboken, NJ: John Wiley & Sons, 2002); Michael Michalko, *Cracking Creativity: The Secrets of Creative Genius* (Berkeley, CA: Ten Speed Press, 1998); James M. Higgins, *101 Creative Problem-Solving Techniques* (New York: New Management Publishing, 1994); and all the books by Edward DeBono.

Socially Responsible Marketing

Effective internal marketing must be matched by a strong sense of ethics, values, and social responsibility.[26] A number of forces are driving companies to practice a higher level of corporate social responsibility: rising customer expectations, evolving employee goals and ambitions, tighter government legislation and pressure, developing investor interest in social criteria, relentless media scrutiny, and changing business procurement practices.[27] The commercial success of Al Gore's 2006 documentary, *An Inconvenient Truth*, shows how the general public has become more concerned about environmental issues.

Virtually all firms have decided to take a more active, strategic role with corporate responsibility. As Aramex CEO Fadi Ghandour said, "By adopting sustainability reporting we are sending a clear message to our stakeholders: community development is a strategic responsibility for which we will hold ourselves accountable. Respecting our environmental surroundings is a principle that is deeply ingrained in our corporate culture, and our ambitious goals in that area are a reflection of how seriously we take the issue."[28] Similarly, CEO of Qatar Airways, Akbar Al Baker, says: "An integral part of being an industry leader is to help lead the charge towards environmental sustainability

The CEO of Qatar Airways believes in the charge towards environmental sustainability.

and corporate social responsibility. We take our responsibility in protecting the environment seri-ously, and are confident in our abilities to play an integral role."[29] Even banana-producer Chiquita, which once had a poor reputation for exploiting farmworkers, contaminating water, and destroying rainforest, has improved workers' conditions; significantly reduced pesticide use; reduced erosion and chemical runoff; and even implemented a major recycling program on its farms.[30]

There were not always these beliefs in the value of social responsibility. In 1776, Adam Smith proclaimed, "I have never known much good done by those who profess to trade for the public good." Legendary economist Milton Friedman famously declared social initiatives "fundamentally subversive" because he felt they undermined the profit-seeking purpose of public companies and wasted shareholders' money. Some critics worry that important business investment in areas such as R&D could suffer as a result of a focus on social responsibility.[31]

But these critics are in the minority. Many now believe that satisfying customers, employees, and other stakeholders and achieving business success are closely tied to the adoption and implementa-tion of high standards of business and marketing conduct. Firms are finding that one benefit of being seen as a socially responsible company is the ability to attract employees, especially younger people who want to work for companies they feel good about. The most admired—and increasingly most successful—companies in the world abide by a code of serving people's interests, not only their own.

Firms of Endearment
Researchers Sisodia, Wolfe, and Sheth believe humanistic companies make great companies. They define "firms of endearment" as those that have a culture of caring and serve the interests of their stakeholders. Stakeholders are defined in terms of the acronym SPICE: Society, Partners, Investors, Customers, and Employees. Firms of endearment create a love affair with stakeholders. Their senior managers run an open-door policy, are passionate about customers, and their compensation is mod-est. They pay more to their employees, relate more closely to a smaller group of excellent suppliers, and give back to the communities in which they work. The researchers assert that firms of endearment actually spend less on marketing as a percentage yet earn greater profits. It appears that the customers who love the company do most of the marketing. The authors see the 21st-century marketing paradigm as creating value for all stakeholders and becoming a beloved firm.

Box 22.1 on page 628 displays firms receiving top marks as firms of endearment from a sample of thousands of customers, employees, and suppliers.[32] But many smaller firms excel too. El Abd, a well-known sweet shop in Cairo, is always crowded with customers who want to buy their fresh sweets and bakery products. El Abd not only focuses on delivering fresh sweets at reasonable prices, but also provides meals for Muslims who are fasting in the holy month of Ramadan. This makes El Abd more popular with Egyptians. Zain is a good example of a company that aligns its corporate social responsibility strategy with the strategic goals of the organization. Its involvement with funding schools and universities in Sudan shows how effective philanthropy can be when it is aligned with a company's mission.

Zain
Zain, established in 1983 in Kuwait, is one of the leading wireless ser-vice providers in the Arab region, with a presence across the Arab world. 2010 was a major year of change for Zain as it sold its 15 operations in Africa. This change also required a change in its corporate social responsibility initiatives, and Zain decided to focus more on knowledge and education. Beyond the importance of education as a driver of development and growth, education will ultimately enable Zain to get better-educated people to work for the company. In Sudan, Zain supports more than 14 schools by providing financial assistance for the construction of theaters, and providing computers, school uniforms, lab coats and equipment, notebooks, and many other items. These activities help increase the awareness of Zain and improve its image in the public's eyes.[33]

Companies are increasingly working with public interest groups to avoid perceptions of 'green-washing:' insincere, phony efforts to appear more environmentally sensitive than they really are. Alliances with environmentalists can achieve more satisfying solutions that both address public

BOX 22.1	Top Firms of Endearment		
Best Buy	BMW	CarMax	Caterpillar
Commerce Bank	Container Store	Costco	eBay
Google	Harley Davidson	Honda	IDEO
IKEA	JetBlue	Johnson & Johnson	Jordan's Furniture
L.L.Bean	New Balance	Patagonia	Progressive Insurance
REI	Southwest	Starbucks	Timberland
Toyota	Trader Joe's	UPS	Wegmans
Whole Foods			

Source: Raj Sisodia, David B. Wolfe, and Jag Sheth, *Firms of Endearment: How World-Class Companies Profit from Passion and Purpose* (Upper Saddle River, NJ: Wharton School Publishing, 2007).

concerns and increase the firm's image and profits. DuPont once viewed Greenpeace as an enemy; the firm now uses Greenpeace's former head as a consultant. Greenpeace has also worked with McDonald's, Cargill, and others to stop farmers cutting down the Amazon rainforest to grow soybeans. When Greenpeace exposed Coca-Cola on the eve of the 2000 Sydney Olympics for using a potent greenhouse gas in its nearly 10 million coolers and vending machines, Coke, along with PepsiCo, Unilever, and McDonald's, invested US$30 million in a less damaging system that now displays a "technology approved by Greenpeace" banner.[34]

Firms are fundamentally changing the way they conduct their business, sometimes even where they work. In 2006, US$2 billion software maker Adobe Systems became the first company to receive a platinum award from the U.S. Green Building Council, making the firm's San Jose headquarters the greenest corporate site on record. By retrofitting its building with automatic faucets, waterless urinals, timed outages, energy-saver compact fluorescent lights, weather-controlled irrigation systems, and motion sensors, Adobe reduced electricity use by 35 percent and gas consumption by 41 percent over a 5-year period, while still increasing its head count by 80 percent.[35]

Corporate Social Responsibility

Raising the level of socially responsible marketing calls for making a three-pronged attack that relies on proper legal, ethical, and social responsibility behavior.

LEGAL BEHAVIOR Organizations must ensure every employee knows and observes relevant laws. For example, it's illegal for salespeople to lie to consumers or mislead them about the advantages of buying a product. Salespeople's statements legally must match advertising claims. Salespeople may not offer bribes to purchasing agents or others influencing a B2B sale. They may not obtain or use competitors' technical or trade secrets through bribery or industrial espionage. Finally, they must not disparage competitors or their products by suggesting things that are not true. Managers must make sure every sales representative knows the law and acts accordingly.[36]

ETHICAL BEHAVIOR Business practices come under attack because business situations routinely pose tough ethical dilemmas: It's not easy to draw a clear line between normal marketing practice and unethical behavior. Some issues sharply divide critics. Though Kraft chose to stop advertising some of its less healthy products such as Oreos and Chips Ahoy! on television programs targeted to children aged 6 to 11, some watch groups felt that was not enough.[37]

At the same time, certain business practices are clearly unethical or illegal. These include bribery, theft of trade secrets, false and deceptive advertising, exclusive dealing and tying agreements, quality or safety defects, false warranties, inaccurate labeling, price-fixing or undue discrimination, and barriers to entry and predatory competition.

Companies must adopt and disseminate a written code of ethics, build a company tradition of ethical behavior, and hold people fully responsible for observing ethical and legal guidelines.[38] Companies that don't perform ethically or well are at greater risk of being exposed, thanks to the internet. In the past, a disgruntled customer might bad-mouth a firm to 12 other people; today he or she can reach thousands. Microsoft, for example, has attracted scores of anti-Microsoft sites, including Hate

BOX 22.2 ▦ Top-Rated Companies for Social Responsibility

1. Johnson & Johnson
2. The Walt Disney Company
3. Kraft Foods Inc.
4. Microsoft
5. PepsiCo.
6. Apple
7. Hershey Company
8. SC Johnson
9. Kellogg's
10. Google

Source: "The 2010 Corporate Social Responsibility Index, Who Made the Top 10?," http://inspiredeconomist.com/2010/10/12/the-2010-corporate-social-responsibility-index-who-made-the-top-10/.

Microsoft and Boycott Microsoft. The general distrust of companies among global consumers is evident with the increase in the number of people who have unfavorable opinions about corporations.

SOCIAL RESPONSIBILITY BEHAVIOR Individual marketers must practice a 'social conscience' in specific dealings with customers and stakeholders. Increasingly, people want information about a company's record on social and environmental responsibility to help decide which companies to buy from, invest in, and work for.[39] ▦ **Box 22.2** lists companies receiving high marks for social responsibility.

Deciding how to communicate corporate social responsibility can be difficult. Once a firm touts an environmental initiative, it can become a target for criticism. When Levi's launched its Eco organic jeans line, it added organic cotton to its products quietly for several years until it reached 100 percent, because it feared drawing attention to the fact that according to USDA and EPA data, a third of a kilogram of chemicals is used to grow a kilogram of the regular, nonorganic cotton in the United States used in some of its other jeans lines. Many well-intentioned product or marketing initiatives attract unforeseen negative consequences. Palm oil was hailed as a renewable fuel for food companies looking to find a solution to a trans-fat ban, until its use was linked to the potential extinction of the orangutan and the sun bear.[40]

Corporate philanthropy also can pose problems.[41] ExxonMobil, BP, Starbucks, and Citibank donate tens of million of dollars each year to charities. Yet good deeds can be overlooked—even resented—if the company is seen as exploitive or fails to live up to a 'good guys' image.[42] Philip Morris Company's US$250 million ad campaign touting its charitable activities was met with skepticism because of its negative corporate image.

SUSTAINABILITY *Sustainability*—the importance of meeting humanity's needs without harming future generations—has risen to the top of many corporate agendas. Major corporations now outline in great detail how they are trying to improve the long-term impact of their actions on communities and the environment. As one sustainability consultant put it, "There is a triple bottom line—people, planet, and profit—and the people part of the equation must come first. Sustainability means more than being eco-friendly, it also means you are in it for the long haul."[43]

Many CEOs believe embracing sustainability can avoid the negative consequences of environmental disasters, political protests, and human rights or workplace abuses. Often a target of environmental criticism in the past, DuPont has moved through two phases of sustainability in the past 15 years: first, drastically reducing the emission of greenhouse gases, release of carcinogens, and discharge of hazardous wastes; and second, embracing sustainability as a strategic goal via the introduction of alternative biofuels and energy-saving materials such as its new bio-PDO fiber.[44]

Investors are even demanding more concrete information about what firms are doing to achieve sustainability. Sustainability ratings exist, although there is little agreement about what the appropriate metrics might be.[45]

Innovest   Founded in 1995, Innovest studies firms on 120 different factors, such as energy use, health and safety records, litigation, employee practices, regulatory history, and management systems for dealing with supplier problems. It uses these measures to assign 2,200 listed companies grades ranging from AAA to CCC, much like a bond rating. Companies scoring well include Nokia Corp. and Ericsson, which excel at tailoring products for developing nations, and banks such as HSBC Holdings and ABN-AMRO, which study the environmental impact of projects they help finance. Although Hewlett-Packard and Dell both rate AAA, Apple gets a middling BBB rating on the grounds of weaker oversight of offshore factories and lack of a "clear environmental business strategy."

Some feel companies that score well on sustainability factors typically exhibit high levels of management quality in that "they tend to be more strategically nimble and better equipped to compete in the complex, high-velocity, global environment."[46]

Many companies in diverse industries beyond edible food products are embracing organic offerings that avoid the use of chemicals and pesticides to stress ecological preservation. Apparel and other nonfood items make up the second-fastest growth category of the US$3.5 billion organic product industry. Organic cotton grown by farmers who fight boll weevils with ladybugs, weed their crops by hand, and use manure for fertilizer has become a hot product at retail. Sustainability is becoming more mainstream, and consumers are increasingly willing to pay more to support the environment.[47]

Socially Responsible Business Models

The future holds a wealth of opportunities.[48] Technological advances in solar energy, online networks, cable and satellite television, biotechnology, and telecommunications promise to change the world as we know it. At the same time, forces in the socioeconomic, cultural, and natural environments will impose new limits on marketing and business practices. Companies that innovate solutions and values in a socially responsible way are the most likely to succeed.[49]

Many companies and institutions, such as The Body Shop, Raya, and the Arab African International Bank (AAIB), are giving social responsibility a more prominent role. The AAIB organizes a national university competition on a yearly basis, which gives students from ten different public and private universities in Egypt the opportunity to develop an innovative financial product or service, whereby they conduct a presentation and submit a project report addressing the research, feasibility study, and marketing plan associated with their idea. The AAIB provides a comprehensive training program covering various areas such as banking, marketing, and feasibility as well as report writing and presentation skills for personal development. Students also receive assistance as they develop their projects. Volunteerism is one of the key principles of the AAIB Award, with senior bank executives as well as market leaders providing full guidance to the students and conducting the final evaluation of the projects. The top three teams receive a cash prize in addition to an internship at AAIB.[50]

Corporate philanthropy as a whole is on the rise, increasing to total around US$15 billion in cash and in-kind support in 2009. Most corporate support in the Arab world goes to sustainable development projects such as microfinance projects, illiteracy, and skills development. This is in addition to support given to health services, education, and overall public support. More firms are coming to the belief that corporate social responsibility in the form of cash donations, in-kind contributions, cause marketing, and employee volunteerism programs is not just the "right thing" but also the "smart thing-" to do.[51] The Marketing Insight: *New Views on Corporate Social Responsibility* offers two high-profile perspectives on how to make progress in that area.

cause-related marketing
that links a firm's contributions to a designated cause to customers' direct or indirect engagement in revenue-producing transactions with the firm.

AAIB's sponsorship of students leads to the top three teams receiving a cash prize.

Cause-Related Marketing

Many firms blend corporate social responsibility initiatives with marketing activities.[52] **Cause-related marketing** links the firm's contributions to a designated cause to customers' engaging directly or indirectly in revenue-producing transactions with

New Views on Corporate Social Responsibility

Two of management's most renowned thinkers have turned their attention to corporate social responsibility, offering some unique perspectives that builds on their past management research and thinking.

Michael Porter

Harvard's Michael Porter and Mark Kramer, managing director of FSG Social Impact Advisors, believe good corporate citizenship can be a source of opportunity, innovation, and competitive advantage, as long as firms evaluate it using the same frameworks and concepts that guide their core business strategies. They feel corporate social responsibility must mesh with a firm's strengths, capabilities, and positioning. They assert that strategic corporate social responsibility results when firms (1) transform value chain activities to benefit society while reinforcing strategy and (2) engage in strategic philanthropy that leverages capabilities to improve salient areas of competitive context.

According to the authors, firms should select causes that intersect their particular businesses to create shared value for the firm and society. For example, Toyota addressed public concerns about auto emissions by creating a competitively strong and environmentally friendly hybrid vehicle, Prius; Mexican construction company Urbi prospered by using novel financing approaches to build housing for disadvantaged buyers; and French banking giant Crédit Agricole differentiated itself through specialized environmentally friendly financial products.

Porter and Kramer note that, "By providing jobs, investing capital, purchasing goods, and doing business every day, corporations have a profound and positive influence on society. The most important thing a corporation can do for society, and for any community, is contribute to a prosperous economy." Although companies can address hundreds of social issues, only a handful offer the opportunity to build focused, proactive, and integrated social initiatives that link with core business strategies to make a real difference to society and create a competitive advantage in the marketplace.

Clayton Christensen

Harvard's Clayton Christensen, along with his research colleagues, advocates catalytic innovations to address social sector problems. Like Christensen's disruptive innovations—which challenge industry incumbents by offering simpler, good enough alternatives to an underserved group of customers—catalytic innovations offer good enough solutions to inadequately addressed social problems. Catalytic innovators share five qualities:

1. They create systemic social change through scaling and replication.

2. They meet a need that is either overserved (because the existing solution is more complex than many people require) or not served at all.

3. They offer simpler, less costly products and services that may have a lower level of performance, but that users consider to be good enough.

4. They generate resources, such as donations, grants, volunteer manpower, or intellectual capital, in ways that are initially unattractive to competitors.

5. They are often ignored, disparaged, or even encouraged by existing players for whom the business model is unprofitable or otherwise unattractive and who therefore avoid or retreat from the market segment.

As support for their approach, the authors note how community colleges have dramatically changed the shape of higher education in the United States by providing a low-cost alternative of choice for 44 percent of the nation's undergraduates. The Minneapolis-based MinuteClinic provides affordable walk-in diagnosis and treatment for common health problems, as well as vaccinations, via 87 clinics located in CVS stores in 10 U.S. states.

To find organizations that are creating a catalytic innovation for investment or other purposes, Christensen and his colleagues offer some guidelines:

1. *Look for signs of disruption in the process*. Although not necessarily easily observed, preexisting catalytic innovators may already be present in a market.

2. *Identify specific catalytic innovations*. Apply the five criteria listed.

3. *Assess the business model*. Determine whether the organization can effectively introduce the innovation and scale it up and sustain it.

Sources: Michael F. Porter and Mark R. Kramer, "Strategy & Society," *Harvard Business Review*, December 2006, pp. 78–82; Clayton M. Christensen, Heiner Baumann, Rudy Ruggles, and Thomas M. Stadtler, "Disruption Innovation for Social Change," *Harvard Business Review*, December 2006, pp. 94–101. See also, Richard Steckel, Elizabeth Ford, Casey Hilliard, and Traci Sanders, *Cold Cash for Warm Hearts: 101 Best Social Marketing Initiatives* (Homewood, IL: High Tide Press, 2004).

---

the firm.[53] Cause marketing is part of *corporate societal marketing* (CSM), which Drumwright and Murphy define as marketing efforts "that have at least one noneconomic objective related to social welfare and use the resources of the company and/or of its partners."[54] They also include other activities such as traditional and strategic philanthropy and volunteerism as part of CSM.

Tesco, a leading UK retailer, has created a Computers for Schools program: customers receive vouchers for every 10 pounds (US$16) spent, which they can donate to the school of their choice; the school exchanges the vouchers for new computer equipment. Dawn, the top dishwashing liquid in the United States, introduced a campaign highlighting the fact that the product's grease-cleaning power had an unusual side benefit: it could clean birds caught in oil spills. A website launched in 2006, www.DawnSavesWildlife.com, drew 130,000 people who formed virtual groups to encourage friends and others to stop gas and oil leaks from their cars into the environment.[55] British Airways has a particularly successful and highly visible program.

British Airways   British Airways partnered with UNICEF and developed a cause-marketing campaign called Change for Good. Passengers on British Airways flights are encouraged to donate leftover foreign currency from their travels. The scheme is simple: passengers deposit their surplus currency in envelopes provided by British Airways, which collects the deposits and donates them directly to UNICEF. British Airways advertises its program during an in-flight video, on the backs of seat cards, and with in-flight announcements. The company also developed a television ad that featured a child thanking British Airways for its contribution to UNICEF. Because Change for Good can be directly targeted to passengers and can produce immediate results, it does not require extensive advertising or promotion and is highly cost-efficient. Since 1994, it has distributed almost US$45 million around the world.[56]

CAUSE-MARKETING BENEFITS AND COSTS   A successful cause-marketing program can improve social welfare; create differentiated brand positioning; build strong consumer bonds; enhance the company's public image with government officials and other decision makers; create a reservoir of goodwill; boost internal morale and galvanize employees; drive sales; and increase the market value of the firm.[57]

Consumers may develop a strong, unique bond with the firm that transcends normal marketplace transactions.[58] Specifically, cause marketing can (1) build brand awareness, (2) enhance brand image, (3) establish brand credibility, (4) evoke brand feelings, (5) create a sense of brand community, and (6) elicit brand engagement.[59] Cause marketing has a particular interested audience in civic-minded 13- to 25-year-old millennial consumers. The results of a survey administered to that group of consumers found that 89 percent of the 13 to 25 year olds say that they are likely to switch to brands (given equal price and quality) to support a cause, 75 percent feel companies should join in the effort to make a difference in the world, and 74 percent are more likely to pay attention to messages of companies deeply committed to a cause.[60]

The danger, however, is that a cause-related marketing program could backfire if cynical consumers question the link between the product and the cause and see the firm as self-serving and exploitive.[61]

Cadbury Schweppes PLC   Cadbury's Sports for Schools promotion offered sports and fitness equipment for schools in exchange for tokens. The problem was, the public and media saw a perverse incentive for children to eat more chocolate, a product associated with obesity. As Britain's Food Commission, a nongovernmental organization, said, "Cadbury wants children to eat two million kilograms of fat: to get fit." The commission estimated that to generate the 90 tokens to purchase a US$8 netball would require spending $61 on Cadbury products and consuming more than 20,000 calories and over 1,000 grams of fat. The product and the cause seemed to be at war. Cadbury Schweppes quickly discontinued the token program, but it continued its Get Active campaign offering teachers tips for sporty games in conjunction with the Youth Sport Trust and sponsoring events such as Get Active Day with British sports stars. Putting a positive spin on the bad press, a Cadbury spokesperson insisted, "The ensuing debate was very welcome. We have been trying to promote Get Active for 2 months. I don't think there can be anyone in the country who hasn't heard of it this week."[62]

Nike's alliance with the Lance Armstrong Foundation for cancer research sold over 70 million yellow LIVESTRONG bracelets for US$1, but, deliberately, the famed Nike swoosh logo was nowhere to be seen.[63] One of the more interesting cause programs in recent years is the Project Red campaign.[64]

(RED) 2006 saw the highly publicized launch of (RED), championed by U2 singer and activist Bono and Bobby Shriver, Chairman of DATA. (RED) was created to raise awareness and money for The Global Fund by teaming with some of the world's most iconic branded products— American Express cards, Motorola phones, Converse sneakers, Gap T-shirts, Apple iPods, and Emporio Armani sunglasses—to produce (PRODUCT) RED-branded products. Up to 50 percent of the profits from the sale of (PRODUCT) RED products are given to The Global Fund to help women and children affected by HIV/AIDS in Africa. The parentheses or brackets in the logo were designed to signify "the embrace:" each company that becomes (RED) places its logo in this embrace and is then "elevated to the power of red." Although some critics felt the project was overmarketed, in the first 18 months of its existence, (RED) contributed more than US$36 million to The Global Fund, more than seven times the amount businesses had contributed since it was founded in 2002.

The brainchild of U2's Bono and Bobby Shriver, chairman of DATA, (RED) was a highly publicized effort to raise money for AIDS relief in Africa through partnerships with iconic brands such as Apple, Motorola, American Express, and Gap. Bono and talk-show host Oprah Winfrey are shown here shopping at the Red launch in Chicago.

The knowledge, skills, resources, and experiences of a top firm may even be more important to a nonprofit or community group than funding. Nonprofits must be clear about what their goals are, communicate clearly what they hope to accomplish, and have an organizational structure in place to work with different firms. Developing a long-term relationship with a firm can take a long time. As one consultant noted, "What's often a problem between corporations and nonprofits is different expectations and different understanding about the amount of time everything will take."[65]

Firms must make a number of decisions in designing and implementing a cause-marketing program, such as how many and which cause(s) to choose and how to brand the cause program.

CHOOSING A CAUSE Some experts believe the positive impact of cause-related marketing is reduced by sporadic involvement with numerous causes. For example, Cathy Chizauskas, Gillette's director of civic affairs, states: "When you're spreading out your giving in fifty-dollar to one-thousand-dollar increments, no one knows what you are doing....It doesn't make much of a splash."[66]

Many companies choose to focus on one or a few main causes to simplify execution and maximize impact. One such focused marketer is McDonald's. Ronald McDonald Houses in more than 27 countries offer more than 6,000 rooms each night to families needing support while their child is in the hospital. The Ronald McDonald House program has provided a "home away from home" for nearly 10 million family members since its beginning in 1974.

Limiting support to a single cause, however, may limit the pool of consumers or other stakeholders who can transfer positive feelings from the cause to the firm. In addition, many popular causes already have numerous corporate sponsors. Over 300 companies, including Telecom Egypt, Commercial International Bank (CIB), Ford, Lee Jeans, Polo Ralph Lauren, Yoplait, BMW, and American Express, have associated themselves with breast cancer as a cause.[67] As a consequence, the brand may find itself 'lost in the shuffle,' overlooked in a sea of symbolic pink ribbons.

Opportunities may be greater with 'orphan causes:' diseases that afflict fewer than 200,000 people.[68] Another option is overlooked diseases, such as pancreatic cancer, which is the fourth-deadliest form of cancer behind skin, lung, and breast, yet has received little or no corporate support. Even major killers such as prostate cancer for men and heart disease for women have been relatively neglected compared to breast cancer, but a number of firms have begun to fill the void. Recent years have seen a dozen new sponsors such as Gillette and Grolsch beer join longtime supporters Safeway and Major League Baseball in the fight against prostate cancer. The American Heart Association launched a marketing program, Go Red for Women, with a Red Dress symbol to heighten awareness and attract interest from corporations and others to a disease that kills roughly 12 times more women than breast cancer each year.[69]

Most firms choose causes that fit their corporate or brand image and matter to their employees and shareholders. LensCrafters' Give the Gift of Sight program is a family of charitable vision care programs that provides free vision screenings, eye exams, and glasses to more than 3 million needy people in North America and developing countries around the world. All stores are empowered to deliver free glasses in their communities. In addition, Give the Gift of Sight sponsors two traveling Vision Vans targeting children in North America as well as monthly 2-week optical missions overseas. The Marketing Memo: *Making A Difference* on page 635 provides some tips from a top cause-marketing firm.

Social Marketing

social marketing   marketing done by a nonprofit or government organization to further a cause, such as "say no to drugs."

Cause-related marketing supports a cause. **Social marketing** by nonprofit or government organizations furthers a cause, such as 'say no to drugs' or 'exercise more and eat better.'[70]

Social marketing goes back many years. In the 1950s, India started family planning campaigns. In the 1970s, Sweden ran social marketing campaigns to turn the country into a nation of nonsmokers and nondrinkers, the Australian government ran Wear Your Seat Belt campaigns, and the Canadian government launched campaigns to Say No to Drugs, Stop Smoking, and Exercise for Health. In the 1980s, the World Bank, World Health Organization, and U.S. Centers for Disease Control and Prevention started to use the term and promote interest in social marketing. Some notable global social marketing successes include these:

- Oral rehydration therapy in Honduras significantly decreased deaths from diarrhea in small children under the age of five.

- Population Communication Services created and promoted two extremely popular songs in Latin America, 'Stop' and 'When We Are Together', to help young women "say no."

- The National Heart, Lung, and Blood Institute successfully raised awareness about cholesterol and high blood pressure, which helped to significantly reduce deaths.

A number of different types of organization conduct social marketing in the Arab region. Government agencies include Ministries of Health, consumer protection agencies, Ministries of Transportation, and the Ministries of the Environment. Literally hundreds of nonprofit organizations conduct social marketing, including the Foundation for Middle East Peace, the King Hussein Cancer Center, Masr El Kheir, and the Food Bank.

PepsiCo Jordan   Pepsi is known for its worldwide campaigns featuring famous sports players, and it plays out that idea in its social responsibility activities too. PepsiCo Jordan sponsors the Zaha football tournament for children aged 7–13 years, and in 2011 sponsored this tournament at the Zaha Cultural Center football field for the fifth time. A total of 32 teams from a different schools and clubs joined in the tournament, organized with the support of the Zaha Center Interactive Program, with the aim of creating a better future for children and developing their personalities. These children gain physical, mental, and psychological benefits by engaging in sports, thus contributing to social development. The company sponsors similar football tournaments for young children in other countries in the Arab world.[71]

Choosing the right goal or objective for a social marketing program is critical. Should a family-planning campaign focus on abstinence or birth control? Should a campaign to fight air pollution focus on ride sharing or mass transit?

marketing Memo

Making a Difference

One of the most accomplished cause-marketing consulting firms, Boston's Cone Communications, offers perspectives on the current state of cause marketing and how it should best be practiced:

> With new vigor, consumers, customers, employees, investors, and communities are closely watching how companies behave in relation to them and to society. Influential groups such as Business for Social Responsibility, Dow Jones Sustainability Index, *Fortune* magazine, and others are judging companies based on a complex series of global standards. Business practices such as governance, philanthropy, sourcing, the environment, employee relations, and community relations have moved from behind the scenes to center stage. For executives today, appropriately defining, executing, and communicating corporate social responsibility (CSR) has never been more important.

To help execute and communicate CSR more effectively, Cone offers the following considerations:

- *Define CSR for your company.* Make sure that your senior executives are all talking about the same thing. CSR includes a broad range of complex internal and external business practices. Although they are vital components of the CSR mix, corporate philanthropy and community relations alone don't define CSR.

- *Build a diverse team.* The development and execution of CSR strategies require a collaborative, concerted team effort. Create a decision-making task force that integrates and brings together a range of expertise and resources, including marketing, public affairs, community relations, legal, human resources, manufacturing, and others. Put a formal process in place to approach CSR strategy development, ongoing implementation, and continuous improvement.

- *Analyze your current CSR-related activities and revamp them if necessary.* Do your due diligence at the outset to understand CSR gaps and risks specific to your company. Research industry examples and cull best practices from leading case studies. Make sure to consider global trends, as Europe is advanced compared to many other nations.

- *Forge and strengthen NGO relationships.* The more than 300,000 nongovernmental organizations (NGOs) around the world are a powerful force on corporate policies and behavior, serving as both advocates and loud critics. Forge sincere partnerships with organizations that can offer you independent, unbiased insight into and evaluation of your CSR activities, provide expertise on social issues and developing global markets, and offer access to key influentials.

- *Develop a cause-branding initiative.* Create a public face for your citizenship activities through a signature cause-branding initiative that integrates philanthropy, community relations, marketing, and human resources assets. ConAgra Foods' Feeding Children Better program, for example, is a multiyear initiative created to feed millions of hungry children through innovative partnerships, grant making, employee volunteerism, and education and awareness. This program recently earned ConAgra Foods the U.S. Chamber of Commerce's Corporate Citizenship Award.

- *Walk your talk.* Critics often assert that companies exploit CSR as a PR smokescreen to conceal or divert attention from corporate misdeeds and blemishes. Before introducing any new CSR initiative or drawing attention to good corporate behavior, make sure that your company is addressing stakeholder expectations of CSR at the most basic level.

- *Don't be silent.* Not only do the public expect businesses to behave socially, the majority want companies to tell them how they are doing so. An overwhelming majority also say they prefer to find out about CSR activities from a third-party source, particularly the media.

- *Beware.* Greater public awareness for your corporate citizenship record can be double-edged. Claims of socially responsible behavior, even sincere ones, often invite public scrutiny. Be prepared. Even if your company is not ready to proactively communicate about your CSR activities, be ready to respond to public inquiries immediately. Don't let the threat of public scrutiny keep you mute, though. More often than not, silence regarding CSR issues is translated as indifference, or worse, inaction.

Sources: Anish K. Verrghese, "Partnerships and Cause Related Marketing: Building Brands for the Future," http://www.brandchannel.com/papers-review.asp?sp-id=583. See also, Carol L. Cone, Mark A. Feldman, and Alison T. DaSilva, "Cause and Effects," *Harvard Business Review*, July 2003, pp. 95–101.

Social marketing campaigns may have objectives related to changing people's cognition, values, actions, or behaviors. The following examples illustrate the range of possible objectives.

Cognitive campaigns

- Explain the nutritional value of different foods.
- Explain the importance of conservation.

Action campaigns

- Attract people for mass immunization.
- Motivate people to vote 'yes' on a certain issue.
- Motivate people to donate blood.
- Motivate women to take a pap test.

Behavioral campaigns

- Demotivate cigarette smoking.
- Demotivate usage of hard drugs.
- wise consumption of energy and water.
- motivate to go and vote.

Value campaigns

- change attitudes about having children and family size.
- change attitudes of narrow-minded people.

Social marketing uses a number of different tactics to achieve its goals.[72] The planning process follows many of the same steps as for traditional products and services (see Box 22.3). Some key success factors in developing and implementing a social marketing program include:

- Study the literature and previous campaigns.
- Choose target markets that are most ready to respond.
- Promote a single, doable behavior in clear, simple terms.
- Explain the benefits in compelling terms.
- Make it easy to adopt the behavior.
- Develop attention-grabbing messages and media.
- Consider an education-entertainment approach.

Vodafone Egypt launched its Knowledge is the Power of Everyone campaign to eradicate illiteracy in Egypt. Their campaign shows how they want to be involved in solving broader problems for Egyptian society as a whole.

BOX 22.3 💬 **Social Marketing Planning Process**

Where Are We?
- Determine program focus.
- Identify campaign purpose.
- Conduct an analysis of strengths, weaknesses, opportunities, and threats (SWOT).
- Review past and similar efforts.

Where Do We Want to Go?
- Select target audiences.
- Set objectives and goals.
- Analyze target audiences and the competition.

How Will We Get There?
- Product: design the market offering.
- Price: manage costs of behavior change.
- Distribution: make the product available.
- Communications: create messages and choose media.

How Will We Stay on Course?
- Develop a plan for evaluation and monitoring.
- Establish budgets and find funding sources.
- Complete an implementation plan.

Vodafone Egypt Vodafone decided tackle a very important problem: illiteracy in Egypt. They started a nationwide initiative called Knowledge is the Power of Everyone in cooperation with UNESCO, Life Makers, and the General Authority for Adult Education. Vodafone's goal is to eradicate illiteracy in 17 million Egyptians over the next 5 years, which has become the nation's goal. The Vodafone Egypt Foundation for Community Development gave support at a critical time for Egypt. In 2009, the number of illiterate people in the Arab world was around 70 million, which, according to the Arab League Educational, Cultural and Scientific Organization (ALECSO), accounts for around 35 percent of the population. The Arab world rates the highest in global illiteracy, with Egypt ranking first. This affects Egypt badly and hinders its further development. The Vodafone Egypt Foundation introduced a marketing campaign across Egypt with the goal of supporting literacy for all Egyptians.[73]

Social marketing programs are complex; they take time and may require phased programs or actions. For example, recall the steps in discouraging smoking: cancer reports, labeling of cigarettes, banning cigarette advertising, education about secondary smoke effects, no smoking in closed areas, no smoking on planes, and raising taxes on cigarettes to pay for antismoking campaigns.

Social marketing organizations should evaluate program success in terms of objectives. Criteria might include incidence of adoption, speed of adoption, continuance of adoption, low cost per unit of adoption, and absence of counterproductive consequences.

Marketing Implementation

Box 22.4 summarizes the characteristics of a great marketing company, great not for 'what it is,' but for 'what it does.' **Marketing implementation** is the process that turns marketing plans into action assignments and ensures they accomplish the plan's stated objectives.[74]

A brilliant strategic marketing plan counts for little if not implemented properly. Strategy addresses the what and why of marketing activities; implementation addresses the who, where, when, and how. They are closely related: one layer of strategy implies certain tactical implementation assignments at a lower level. For example, top management's strategic decision to 'harvest' a product must be translated into specific actions and assignments.

Companies today are striving to make their marketing operations more efficient and their return on marketing investment more measurable (see Chapter 4). Marketing costs can amount to 20 to 40 percent of a company's total operating budget. Marketers need better templates for

marketing implementation
the process that turns marketing plans into action assignments and ensures that such assignments are executed in a manner that accomplishes the plan's stated objectives.

BOX 22.4	Characteristics of a Great Marketing Company

- The company selects target markets in which it enjoys superior advantages and exits or avoids markets where it is intrinsically weak.
- Virtually all the company's employees and departments are customer and market minded.
- There is a good working relationship between marketing, R&D, and manufacturing.
- There is a good working relationship between marketing, sales, and customer service.
- The company has installed incentives designed to lead to the right behaviors.
- The company continuously builds and tracks customer satisfaction and loyalty.
- The company manages a value delivery system in partnership with strong suppliers and distributors.
- The company is skilled in building its brand name(s) and image.
- The company is flexible in meeting customers' varying requirements.

marketing processes, better management of marketing assets, and better allocation of marketing resources. Certain repetitive processes can be automated under such names as *marketing resource management* (MRM), *marketing investment management* (MIM), *enterprise marketing management* (EMM), and *marketing automation systems* (MAS).[75]

Marketing resource management (MRM) software provides a set of web-based applications that automate and integrate such activities as project management, campaign management, budget management, asset management, brand management, customer relationship management, and knowledge management. The knowledge management component consists of process templates, how-to wizards, and best practices.

Software packages are web hosted and available to users with passwords. They add up to what some have called *desktop marketing* and give marketers whatever information and decision structures they need on computer dashboards. MRM software lets marketers improve spending and investment decisions, bring new products to market more quickly, and reduce decision time and costs.

BinSina Pharmacy In 2009, BinSina, a leading retail pharmacy chain in the UAE, teamed up with an innovative health care research and consultancy group, Acorn Research FZ LLC, to develop an nationwide research tool enabling health care and pharmaceutical companies to access up-to-date market and customer information. This web-based marketing resource management system (MRS) will use the most up-to-date field research and benchmark surveying techniques with touch-screen survey devices to capture feedback from visitors to BinSina Pharmacy. BinSina serves 5 million customers in its pharmacies each year and up to 14,000 customers a day; thus it is an excellent environment in which to collect customer feedback. The marketing department of BinSina Pharmacy sees this use of state-of-the-art technology as a major step toward improving pharmaceutical and health care services in the Middle East.[76]

Evaluation and Control

In spite of the need to monitor and control marketing activities, many companies have inadequate control procedures. ▢ **Table 22.1** lists four types of marketing control that are needed: annual-plan control, profitability control, efficiency control, and strategic control. We consider each.

Annual-Plan Control

Annual-plan control ensures the company achieves the sales, profits, and other goals established in its annual plan. At its heart is management by objectives. There are four steps (see △ **Figure 22.5**). First, management sets monthly or quarterly goals. Second, management monitors its performance in the marketplace. Third, management determines the causes of serious performance deviations. Fourth, management takes corrective action to close gaps between goals and performance.

This control model applies to all levels of the organization. Top management sets annual sales and profit goals; each product manager, regional district manager, sales manager, and sales rep is committed to attaining specified levels of sales and costs. Each period, top management reviews and interprets the results.

Marketers today have better marketing metrics for measuring the performance of marketing plans (see ▢ **Box 22.5** for some sample ones).[77] They can use four tools to check on plan performance: sales analysis, market share analysis, marketing expense-to-sales analysis, and financial analysis.

SALES ANALYSIS **Sales analysis** measures and evaluates actual sales in relationship to goals. Two specific tools make it work.

Sales-variance analysis measures the relative contribution of different factors to a gap in sales performance. Suppose the annual plan called for selling 4,000 pens in the first quarter at US$1 per pen, for total revenue of $4,000. At quarter's end, only 3,000 pens were sold at $0.80 per pen, for

|Fig. 22.5| △

The Control Process

sales analysis measuring and evaluating actual sales in relation to goals.

sales-variance analysis a measure of the relative contribution of different factors to a gap in sales performance.

TABLE 22.1	Types of Marketing Control		
Type of Control	**Prime Responsibility**	**Purpose of Control**	**Approaches**
I. Annual-Plan Control	Top management Middle management	To examine whether the planned results are being achieved	• Sales analysis • Market share analysis • Sales-to-expense ratios • Financial analysis • Market-based scorecard analysis
2. Profitability Control	Marketing controller	To examine where the company is making and losing money	Profitability by: • product • territory • customer • segment • trade channel • order size
3. Efficiency Control	Line and staff management Marketing controller	To evaluate and improve the spending efficiency and impact of marketing expenditures	Efficiency of: • sales force • advertising • sales promotion • distribution
4. Strategic Control	Top management Marketing auditor	To examine whether the company is pursuing its best opportunities with respect to markets, products, and channels	• Marketing effectiveness rating instrument • Marketing audit • Marketing excellence review • Company ethical and social responsibility review

total revenue of $2,400. How much of the sales performance gap is due to the price decline, and how much to the volume decline? This calculation answers the question:

Variance due to price decline = ($1.00 − $.80) (3,000) =	$600	37.5%
Variance due to volume decline = ($1.00) (4,000 − 3,000)=	$1,000	62.5%
	$1,600	100.0%

Almost two-thirds of the variance is due to failure to achieve the volume target. The company should look closely at why it failed to achieve expected sales volume.

Microsales analysis looks at specific products, territories, and so forth that failed to produce expected sales. Suppose the company sells in three territories, and expected sales were 1,500 units, 500 units, and 2,000 units, respectively. Actual volumes were 1,400 units, 525 units, and 1,075 units, respectively. Thus territory 1 showed a 7 percent shortfall in terms of expected sales; territory 2, a 5 percent improvement over expectations; and territory 3, a 46 percent shortfall! Territory 3 is causing most of the trouble. Maybe territory 3's sales rep is underperforming; a major competitor has entered this territory; or business is in a recession there.

microsales analysis examination of specific products and territories that fail to produce expected sales.

MARKET SHARE ANALYSIS Company sales don't reveal how well the company is performing relative to competitors. For this purpose, management needs to track its market share in one of three ways.

BOX 22.5 ▭   Marketing Metrics

Sales Metrics
- Sales growth
- Market share
- Sales from new products

Customer Readiness to Buy Metrics
- Awareness
- Preference
- Purchase intention
- Trial rate
- Repurchase rate

Customer Metrics
- Customer complaints
- Customer satisfaction
- Number of promoters to detractors
- Customer-acquisition costs
- New-customer gains
- Customer losses
- Customer churn
- Retention rate
- Customer lifetime value
- Customer equity
- Customer profitability
- Return on customer

Distribution Metrics
- Number of outlets
- Share in shops handling
- Weighted distribution
- Distribution gains
- Average stocks volume (value)
- Stocks cover in days
- Out of stock frequency
- Share of shelf
- Average sales per point of sale

Communication Metrics
- Spontaneous (unaided) brand awareness
- Top-of-mind brand awareness
- Prompted (aided) brand awareness
- Spontaneous (unaided) advertising awareness
- Prompted (aided) advertising awareness
- Effective reach
- Effective frequency
- Gross rating points (GRP)
- Response rate

---

overall market share   the company's sales expressed as a percentage of total market sales.

served market share   a company's sales expressed as a percentage of the total sales to its served market.

served market   all the buyers who are able and willing to buy a company's product.

relative market share   market share in relation to a company's largest competitor.

Overall market share expresses the company's sales as a percentage of total market sales. **Served market share** is sales as a percentage of the total sales to the market. The **served market** is all the buyers able and willing to buy the product, and served market share is always larger than overall market share. A company could capture 100 percent of its served market and yet have a relatively small share of the total market. **Relative market share** is market share in relationship to the largest competitor. A relative market share over 100 percent indicates a market leader. A relative market share of exactly 100 percent means the company is tied for the lead. A rise in relative market share means a company is gaining on its leading competitor.

Conclusions from market share analysis, however, are subject to certain qualifications:

- *The assumption that outside forces affect all companies in the same way is often not true.* The U.S. Surgeon General's Report on the harmful consequences of cigarette smoking caused total cigarette sales to falter, but not equally for all companies.

- *The assumption that a company's performance should be judged against the average performance of all companies is not always valid.* A company's performance is best judged against that of its closest competitors.

- *If a new firm enters the industry, every existing firm's market share might fall.* A decline in market share might not mean the company is performing any worse than other companies. Share loss depends on the degree to which the new firm hits the company's specific markets.

- *Sometimes a market share decline is deliberately engineered to improve profits.* For example, management might drop unprofitable customers or products.

- *Market share can fluctuate for many minor reasons.* For example, it can be affected by whether a large sale occurs on the last day of the month or at the beginning of the next month. Not all shifts in market share have marketing significance.[78]

A useful way to analyze market-share movements is in terms of four components:

$$\text{Overall market share} = \text{Customer penetration} \times \text{Customer loyalty} \times \text{Customer selectivity} \times \text{Price selectivity}$$

where:

Customer penetration = Percentage of all customers who buy from the company.

Customer loyalty = Purchases from the company by its customers as a percentage of their total purchases from all suppliers of the same products.

Customer selectivity = Size of the average customer purchase from the company as a percentage of the size of the average customer purchase from an average company.

Price selectivity = Average price charged by the company as a percentage of the average price charged by all companies.

Now suppose the company's dollar market share falls during the period. The overall market share equation provides four possible explanations: the company lost some customers (lower customer penetration); existing customers are buying less from the company (lower customer loyalty); the company's remaining customers are smaller in size (lower customer selectivity); or the company's price has slipped relative to competition (lower price selectivity).

MARKETING EXPENSE-TO-SALES ANALYSIS

Annual-plan control requires making sure the company isn't overspending to achieve sales goals. The key ratio to watch is *marketing expense-to-sales*. In one company, this ratio was 30 percent and consisted of five component expense-to-sales ratios: sales force-to-sales (15 percent); advertising-to-sales (5 percent); sales promotion-to-sales (6 percent); marketing research-to-sales (1 percent); and sales administration-to-sales (3 percent).

Fluctuations outside normal range are cause for concern. Management needs to monitor period-to-period fluctuations in each ratio on a *control chart* (see △ **Figure 22.6**). This chart shows that the advertising expense-to-sales ratio normally fluctuates between 8 percent and 12 percent, say 99 out of 100 times. In the 15th period, however, the ratio exceeded the upper control limit. One of two hypotheses can explain: (1) the company still has good expense control, and this situation represents a rare chance event; or (2) the company has lost control over this expense and should find the cause. If there is no investigation, the risk is that some real change might have occurred, and the company will fall behind. An investigation may also uncover nothing and be a waste of time and effort.

Managers should watch the behavior of successive observations even within the upper and lower control limits. Note in Figure 22.6 that the level of the expense-to-sales ratio rose steadily from the 9th period onward. The probability of encountering six successive increases in what should be independent events is only 1 in 64.[79] This unusual pattern should have led to an investigation sometime before the 15th observation.

|Fig. 22.6| △

The Control-Chart Model

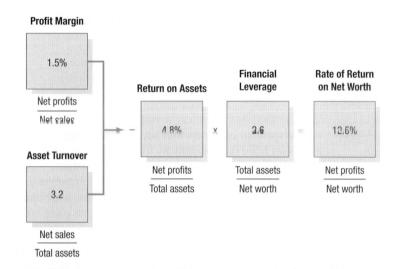

Profit Margin

1.5%

Net profits
Net sales

Asset Turnover

3.2

Net sales
Total assets

Return on Assets

4.8%

Net profits
Total assets

Financial Leverage

2.6

Total assets
Net worth

Rate of Return on Net Worth

12.5%

Net profits
Net worth

|Fig. 22.7| ▲

Financial Model of Return on Net Worth

FINANCIAL ANALYSIS Marketers should analyze the expense-to-sales ratios in an over-all financial framework to determine how and where the company is making its money. They can, and are increasingly, using financial analysis to find profitable strategies beyond building sales.

Management uses financial analysis to identify factors that affect the company's *rate of return on net worth*.[80] The main factors are shown in ▲ **Figure 22.7**, along with illustrative numbers for a large chain-store retailer. The retailer is earning a 12.5 percent return on net worth. The return on net worth is the product of two ratios, the company's *return on assets* and its *financial leverage*. To improve its return on net worth, the company must increase its ratio of net profits to assets, or increase the ratio of assets to net worth. The company should analyze the composition of its assets (cash, accounts receivable, inventory, and plant and equipment) and see whether it can improve its asset management.

The return on assets is the product of two ratios, the *profit margin* and the *asset turn-over*. The profit margin in Figure 22.7 seems low, whereas the asset turnover is more normal for retailing. The marketing executive can seek to improve performance in two ways: (1) increase the profit margin by increasing sales or cutting costs; and (2) increase the asset turnover by increasing sales or reducing assets (inventory, receivables) held against a given level of sales.[81]

Profitability Control

Companies can benefit from deeper financial analysis and should measure the profitability of their products, territories, customer groups, segments, trade channels, and order sizes. This information can help management determine whether to expand, reduce, or eliminate any products or marketing activities.

MARKETING PROFITABILITY ANALYSIS We will illustrate the steps in marketing profitability analysis with the following example: the marketing vice president of a women's clothing company wants to determine the profitability of selling through three types of retail chan-nels: company stores, department stores, and online stores. The company's profit-and-loss statement is shown in ▬ **Box 22.6**.

Step 1: Identifying Functional Expenses Assume the expenses listed in Box 22.6 are incurred to sell the product, advertise it, pack and deliver it, and bill and col-lect for it. The first task is to measure how much of each expense was incurred in each activity.

BOX 22.6 ▬ A Simplified Profit-and-Loss Statement		
Sales		$60,000
Cost of goods sold		39,000
Gross margin		$21,000
Expenses		
Salaries	$ 9,300	
Rent	3,000	
Supplies	3,500	
	$15,800	
Net profit		$5,200
Amounts in US$.		

TABLE 22.2	Mapping Natural Expenses into Functional Expenses				
Natural Accounts	Total	Selling	Advertising	Packing and Delivery	Billing and Collecting
Salaries	$9,300	$5,100	$1,200	$1,400	$1,600
Rent	3,000	—	400	2,000	600
Supplies	3,500	400	1,500	1,400	200
	$15,800	$5,500	$3,100	$4,800	$2,400

Amounts in US$.

Suppose most of the salary expense went to sales representatives and the rest to an advertising manager, packing and delivery help, and an office accountant. Let the breakdown of the US$9,300 be $5,100, $1,200, $1,400, and $1,600, respectively.   Table 22.2 shows the allocation of the salary expense to these four activities.

Table 22.2 also shows the rent account of $3,000 allocated to the four activities. Because the sales reps work away from the office, none of the building's rent expense is assigned to selling. Most of the expenses for floor space and rented equipment are for packing and delivery. The supplies account covers promotional materials, packing materials, fuel purchases for delivery, and home office stationery. The $3,500 in this account is reassigned to functional uses of the supplies.

Step 2: Assigning Functional Expenses to Marketing Entities The next task is to measure how much functional expense was associated with selling through each type of channel. Consider the selling effort, indicated by the number of sales in each channel. This number is in the selling column of   Table 22.3. Altogether, 275 sales calls were made during the period. Because the total selling expense amounted to US$5,500 (see Table 22.3), the selling expense averaged $20 per call.

We can allocate advertising expense according to the number of ads addressed to different channels. Because there were 100 ads altogether, the average ad cost $31.

The packing and delivery expense is allocated according to the number of orders placed by each type of channel. This same basis was used for allocating billing and collection expense.

Step 3: Preparing a Profit-and-Loss Statement for Each Marketing Entity We can now prepare a profit-and-loss statement for each type of channel (see   Table 22.4). Because company stores accounted for half of total sales (US$30,000 out of $60,000), charge this channel with half the cost of goods sold ($19,500 of $39,000). This leaves a gross margin from company stores of $10,500. From this we deduct the proportions of functional expenses company stores consumed. According to Table 22.3, company stores received 200 of 275 total sales calls.

TABLE 22.3	Bases for Allocating Functional Expenses to Channels			
Channel Type	Selling	Advertising	Packing and Delivery	Billing and Collecting
Company stores	200	50	50	50
Department stores	65	20	21	21
Online stores	10	30	9	9
	275	100	80	80
Functional expense	$5,500	$3,100	$4,800	$2,400
÷ No. of Units				
	275	100	80	80
Equals	$20	$31	$60	$30

Amounts in US$.

TABLE 22.4 Profit-and-Loss Statements for Channels				
	Company Stores	**Department Stores**	**Online Stores**	**Whole Company**
Sales	$30,000	$10,000	$20,000	$60,000
Cost of goods sold	19,500	6,600	13,000	39,000
Gross margin	$10,500	$3,500	$7,000	$21,000
Selling expenses ($20 per call)	$4,000	$1,300	$200	$5,500
Advertising ($31 per advertisement)	1,550	620	930	3,100
Packing and delivery ($60 per order)	3,000	1,260	540	4,800
Billing ($30 per order)	1,500	630	270	2,400
Total expenses	$10,050	$3,810	$1,940	$15,800
Net profit or loss	$450	$(310)	$5,060	$5,200
Amounts in US$.				

At an imputed value of $20 a call, company stores must bear a $4,000 selling expense. Table 22.3 also shows company stores were the target of 50 ads. At $31 an ad, the company stores are charged with $1,550 of advertising. The same reasoning applies in computing the share of the other functional expenses. The result is that company stores gave rise to $10,050 of the total expenses. Subtracting this from gross margin, we find the profit of selling through company stores is only $450.

Repeat this analysis for the other channels. The company is losing money in selling through department store shops and makes virtually all its profits through online stores. Notice that gross sales is not a reliable indicator of the net profits for each channel.

DETERMINING CORRECTIVE ACTION It would be naive to conclude that the company should drop department stores and possibly company stores so that it can concentrate on online stores. We need to answer the following questions first:

- To what extent do buyers buy on the basis of type of retail outlet versus brand?
- What are the trends with respect to the importance of these three channels?
- How good are the company marketing strategies directed at the three channels?

On the basis of the answers, marketing management can evaluate five alternatives:

1. Establish a special charge for handling smaller orders.
2. Give more promotional aid to company stores and online stores.
3. Reduce the number of sales calls and the amount of advertising going to department store shops and company stores.
4. Do not abandon any channel entirely, but only the weakest retail units in each channel.
5. Do nothing.

In general, marketing profitability analysis indicates the relative profitability of different channels, products, territories, or other marketing entities. It does not prove that the best course of action is to drop the unprofitable marketing entities, nor does it capture the likely profit improvement if these marginal marketing entities were dropped.

DIRECT VERSUS FULL COSTING Like all information tools, marketing profitability analysis can lead or mislead marketing executives, depending on how well they understand its methods and limitations. The women's clothing company showed some randomness in its choice of bases for allocating the functional expenses to its marketing entities. It used 'number of sales calls' to allocate selling expenses, generating less recordkeeping and computation, when in principle 'number of sales working hours' is a more accurate indicator of cost.

Far more serious is another judgmental element affecting profitability analysis: whether to allocate full costs or only direct and traceable costs in evaluating a marketing entity's performance. The women's clothing company sidestepped this problem by assuming only simple costs that fit in with marketing activities, but we cannot avoid the question in real-world analyses of profitability. We distinguish three types of costs:

1. *Direct costs*. We can assign direct costs directly to the proper marketing entities. Sales commissions are a direct cost in a profitability analysis of sales territories, sales representatives, or customers. Advertising expenditures are a direct cost in a profitability analysis of products to the extent that each advertisement promotes only one product. Other direct costs for specific purposes are sales-force salaries and traveling expenses.
2. *Traceable common costs*. We can assign traceable common costs only indirectly, but on a plausible basis, to the marketing entities. In the example, we analyzed rent this way.
3. *Nontraceable common costs*. Common costs whose allocation to the marketing entities is highly arbitrary are nontraceable common costs. To allocate 'corporate image' expenditures equally to all products would be arbitrary, because all products don't benefit equally. To allocate them proportionately to the sales of the various products would be arbitrary, because relative product sales reflect many factors besides corporate image making. Other examples are top management salaries, taxes, interest, and other overheads.

No one disputes the inclusion of direct costs in marketing cost analysis. There is some controversy about including traceable common costs, which lump together costs that would and would not change with the scale of marketing activity. If the women's clothing company drops department store shops, it would probably continue to pay the same rent. In this event, its profits would not rise immediately by the amount of the present loss in selling to department store shops (US$310).

The major controversy is about whether to allocate the nontraceable common costs to the marketing entities. Such allocation is called the *full-cost approach*, and its advocates argue that all costs must ultimately be imputed in order to determine true profitability. However, this argument confuses the use of accounting for financial reporting with its use for managerial decision making. Full costing has three major weaknesses:

1. The relative profitability of different marketing entities can shift radically when we replace one arbitrary way to allocate nontraceable common costs with another.
2. The randomness demoralizes managers, who feel their performance is judged adversely.
3. The inclusion of nontraceable common costs could weaken efforts at real cost control.

Operating management is most effective in controlling direct costs and traceable common costs. Arbitrary assignments of nontraceable common costs can lead managers to spend their time fighting cost allocations instead of managing controllable costs well.

Companies show growing interest in using marketing profitability analysis, or its broader version, activity-based cost accounting (ABC), to quantify the true profitability of different activities.[82] Managers can then reduce the resources required to perform various activities, make the resources more productive, acquire them at lower cost, or raise prices on products that consume heavy amounts of support resources. The contribution of ABC is to refocus management's attention away from using only labor or material standard costs to allocate full cost, and toward capturing the actual costs of supporting individual products, customers, and other entities.

Efficiency Control

Suppose a profitability analysis reveals the company is earning poor profits in certain products, territories, or markets. Are there more efficient ways to manage the sales force, advertising, sales promotion, and distribution in connection with these marketing entities?

Some companies have established a *marketing controller* position to work out of the controller's office but specialize in improving marketing efficiency. At companies such as Etisalat, Procter &

Gamble, and Nestlé, sophisticated financial analysis of marketing expenditures and results is performed. They examine adherence to profit plans, help prepare brand managers' budgets, measure the efficiency of promotions, analyze media production costs, evaluate customer and geographic profitability, and educate marketing personnel on the financial implications of marketing decisions.[83] They can examine the efficiency of the channel, sales force, advertising, or any other form of marketing communication.

For example, in assessing channel efficiency, management needs to search for distribution economies in inventory control, warehouse locations, and transportation modes. It should track such measures as:

- Logistics costs as a percentage of sales.
- Percentage of orders filled correctly.
- Percentage of on-time deliveries.
- Number of billing errors.

Management should strive to reduce inventory while at the same time speeding up the order-to-delivery cycle. Dell Computer shows how to do both simultaneously.

 Dell   A customer-customized computer ordered from Dell's website at 9:00 a.m. on Wednesday can be on the delivery truck by 9:00 p.m. Thursday. In that short period, Dell electronically orders the computer components from its suppliers' warehouses. Equally impressive, Dell gets paid electronically within 24 hours, whereas Compaq, supplying its computers to retailers, receives payment days later.

Strategic Control

Each company should periodically reassess its strategic approach to the marketplace with a good marketing audit. Companies can also perform marketing excellence reviews and ethical/social responsibility reviews.

THE MARKETING AUDIT   Many corporations lose half their customers in 5 years, half their employees in 4 years, and half their investors in less than 1 year. Clearly, this points to some weaknesses. Companies that discover weaknesses should undertake a thorough study known as a marketing audit.[84] A **marketing audit** is a comprehensive, systematic, independent, and periodic examination of a company's or business unit's marketing environment, objectives, strategies, and activities, with a view to determining problem areas and opportunities and recommending a plan of action to improve the company's marketing performance.

Let's examine the marketing audit's four characteristics:

1. *Comprehensive*. The marketing audit covers all the major marketing activities of a business, not just a few trouble spots. It would be called a functional audit if it covered only the sales force, pricing, or some other marketing activity. Although functional audits are useful, they sometimes mislead management. Excessive sales-force turnover, for example, could be a symptom not of poor sales-force training or compensation but of weak company products and promotion. A comprehensive marketing audit usually is more effective in locating the real source of problems.
2. *Systematic*. The marketing audit is an orderly examination of the organization's macro- and micromarketing environments, marketing objectives and strategies, marketing systems, and specific activities. The audit indicates the most-needed improvements, incorporating them into a corrective-action plan with short- and long-run steps to improve overall effectiveness.
3. *Independent*. Marketers can conduct a marketing audit in six ways: self-audit, audit from across, audit from above, company auditing office, company task-force audit, and outsider audit. Self-audits, in which managers use a checklist to rate their own operations, lack objectivity and independence.[85] The 3M Company has made good use of a corporate auditing office, which provides marketing audit services to divisions on request.[86] Generally speaking, however, the best audits come from outside consultants who have the necessary objectivity, broad experience in a number of industries, some familiarity with the industry being audited, and undivided time and attention.
4. *Periodic*. Typically, firms initiate marketing audits only after sales have turned down, sales-force morale has fallen, and other problems have occurred. Companies are thrown into a crisis

marketing audit   a comprehensive, systematic, independent, and periodic examination of a company's or business unit's marketing environment, objectives, strategies, and activities.

partly because they failed to review their marketing operations during good times. A periodic marketing audit can benefit companies in good health as well as those in trouble.

A marketing audit starts with a meeting between the company officer(s) and the marketing auditor(s) to work out an agreement on the audit's objectives, coverage, depth, data sources, report format, and time frame. It includes a detailed plan of who is to be interviewed, the questions to be asked, and where and when to minimize time and cost. The cardinal rule in marketing auditing is: don't rely solely on company managers for data and opinions. Ask customers, dealers, and other outside groups. Many companies don't really know how their customers and dealers see them, nor do they fully understand customer needs.

The marketing audit examines six major components of the company's marketing situation. Box 22.7 lists the major questions.

BOX 22.7 ▦ Components of a Marketing Audit

Part I. Marketing Environment Audit

Macroenvironment

A. Demographic	What major demographic developments and trends pose opportunities or threats to this company? What actions has the company taken in response to these developments and trends?
B. Economic	What major developments in income, prices, savings, and credit will affect the company? What actions has the company been taking in response to these developments and trends?
C. Environmental	What is the outlook for the cost and availability of natural resources and energy needed by the company? What concerns have been expressed about the company's role in pollution and conservation, and what steps has the company taken?
D. Technological	What major changes are occurring in product and process technology? What is the company's position in these technologies? What major generic substitutes might replace this product?
E. Political	What changes in laws and regulations might affect marketing strategy and tactics? What is happening in the areas of pollution control, equal employment opportunity, product safety, advertising, price control, and so forth, that affects marketing strategy?
F. Cultural	What is the public's attitude toward business and toward the company's products? What changes in customer lifestyles and values might affect the company?

Task Environment

A. Markets	What is happening to market size, growth, geographical distribution, and profits? What are the major market segments?
B. Customers	What are the customers' needs and buying processes? How do customers and prospects rate the company and its competitors on reputation, product quality, service, sales force, and price? How do different customer segments make their buying decisions?
C. Competitors	Who are the major competitors? What are their objectives, strategies, strengths, weaknesses, sizes, and market shares? What trends will affect future competition and substitutes for the company's products?
D. Distribution and Dealers	What are the main trade channels for bringing products to customers? What are the efficiency levels and growth potentials of the different trade channels?
E. Suppliers	What is the outlook for the availability of key resources used in production? What trends are occurring among suppliers?
F. Facilitators and Marketing Firms	What is the cost and availability outlook for transportation services, warehousing facilities, and financial resources? How effective are the company's advertising agencies and marketing research firms?
G. Publics	Which publics represent particular opportunities or problems for the company? What steps has the company taken to deal effectively with each public?

Part II. Marketing Strategy Audit

A. Business Mission	Is the business mission clearly stated in market-oriented terms? Is it feasible?
B. Marketing Objectives and Goals	Are the company and marketing objectives and goals stated clearly enough to guide marketing planning and performance measurement? Are the marketing objectives appropriate, given the company's competitive position, resources, and opportunities?

Continued on next page>>

BOX 22.7 ▩ Components of a Marketing Audit ...continued

C. Strategy	Has the management articulated a clear marketing strategy for achieving its marketing objectives? Is the strategy convincing? Is the strategy appropriate to the stage of the product life cycle, competitors' strategies, and the state of the economy? Is the company using the best basis for market segmentation? Does it have clear criteria for rating the segments and choosing the best ones? Has it developed accurate profiles of each target segment? Has the company developed an effective positioning and marketing mix for each target segment? Are marketing resources allocated optimally to the major elements of the marketing mix? Are enough resources or too many resources budgeted to accomplish the marketing objectives?

Part III. Marketing Organization Audit

A. Formal Structure	Does the marketing vice president have adequate authority and responsibility for company activities that affect customers' satisfaction? Are the marketing activities optimally structured along functional, product, segment, end user, and geographic lines?
B. Functional Efficiency	Are there good communication and working relations between marketing and sales? Is the product-management system working effectively? Are product managers able to plan profits or only sales volume? Are there any groups in marketing that need more training, motivation, supervision, or evaluation?
C. Interface Efficiency	Are there any problems between marketing and manufacturing, R&D, purchasing, finance, accounting, and/or legal that need attention?

Part IV. Marketing Systems Audit

A. Marketing Information System	Is the marketing intelligence system producing accurate, sufficient, and timely information about marketplace developments with respect to customers, prospects, distributors and dealers, competitors, suppliers, and various publics? Are company decision makers asking for enough marketing research, and are they using the results? Is the company employing the best methods for market measurement and sales forecasting?
B. Marketing Planning System	Is the marketing planning system well conceived and effectively used? Do marketers have decision support systems available? Does the planning system result in acceptable sales targets and quotas?
C. Marketing Control System	Are the control procedures adequate to ensure that the annual-plan objectives are being achieved? Does management periodically analyze the profitability of products, markets, territories, and channels of distribution? Are marketing costs and productivity periodically examined?
D. New-Product Development System	Is the company well organized to gather, generate, and screen new-product ideas? Does the company do adequate concept research and business analysis before investing in new ideas? Does the company carry out adequate product and market testing before launching new products?

Part V. Marketing Productivity Audit

A. Profitability Analysis	What is the profitability of the company's different products, markets, territories, and channels of distribution? Should the company enter, expand, contract, or withdraw from any business segments?
B. Cost-Effectiveness Analysis	Do any marketing activities seem to have excessive costs? Can cost-reducing steps be taken?

Part VI. Marketing Function Audits

A. Products	What are the company's product-line objectives? Are they sound? Is the current product line meeting the objectives? Should the product line be stretched or contracted upward, downward, or both ways? Which products should be phased out? Which products should be added? What are the buyers' knowledge and attitudes toward the company's and competitors' product quality, features, styling, brand names, and so on? What areas of product and brand strategy need improvement?
B. Price	What are the company's pricing objectives, policies, strategies, and procedures? To what extent are prices set on cost, demand, and competitive criteria? Do the customers see the company's prices as being in line with the value of its offer? What does management know about the price elasticity of demand, experience-curve effects, and competitors' prices and pricing policies? To what extent are price policies compatible with the needs of distributors and dealers, suppliers, and government regulation?
C. Distribution	What are the company's distribution objectives and strategies? Is there adequate market coverage and service? How effective are distributors, dealers, manufacturers' representatives, brokers, agents, and others? Should the company consider changing its distribution channels?

Continued on next page>>

BOX 22.7	Components of a Marketing Audit ...continued
D. Marketing Communications	What are the organization's advertising objectives? Are they sound? Is the right amount being spent on advertising? Are the ad themes and copy effective? What do customers and the public think about the advertising? Are the advertising media well chosen? Is the internal advertising staff adequate? Is the sales promotion budget adequate? Is there effective and sufficient use of sales promotion tools such as samples, coupons, displays, and sales contests? Is the public relations staff competent and creative? Is the company making enough use of direct, online, and database marketing?
E. Sales Force	What are the sales force's objectives? Is the sales force large enough to accomplish the company's objectives? Is the sales force organized along the proper principles of specialization (territory, market, product)? Are there enough (or too many) sales managers to guide the field sales representatives? Do the sales compensation level and structure provide adequate incentive and reward? Does the sales force show high morale, ability, and effort? Are the procedures adequate for setting quotas and evaluating performance? How does the company's sales force compare to competitors' sales forces?

BOX 22.8	The Marketing Excellence Review: Best Practices	
Poor	**Good**	**Excellent**
Product driven	Market driven	Market driving
Mass-market oriented	Segment oriented	Niche oriented and customer oriented
Product offer	Augmented product offer	Customer solutions offer
Average product quality	Better than average	Legendary
Average service quality	Better than average	Legendary
End-product oriented	Core-product oriented	Core-competency oriented
Function oriented	Process oriented	Outcome oriented
Reacting to competitors	Benchmarking competitors	Leapfrogging competitors
Supplier exploitation	Supplier preference	Supplier partnership
Dealer exploitation	Dealer support	Dealer partnership
Price driven	Quality driven	Value driven
Average speed	Better than average	Legendary
Hierarchy	Network	Teamwork
Vertically integrated	Flattened organization	Strategic alliances
Stockholder driven	Stakeholder driven	Societally driven

THE MARKETING EXCELLENCE REVIEW The three columns in ▬ **Box 22.8** distinguish among poor, good, and excellent business and marketing practices. Management can place a checkmark to indicate its perception of where the business stands. The profile that results from this marketing excellence review exposes weaknesses and strengths, highlighting where the company might make changes to become a truly outstanding player in the marketplace.

The Future of Marketing

Top management recognizes that past marketing has been highly wasteful and demands more accountability. The Marketing Memo: *Major Marketing Weaknesses* summarizes companies' major deficiencies in marketing, and how to find and correct them.

Going forward, marketing must be 'holistic' and less departmental. Marketers must achieve larger influence in the company if they are to be the main architects of business strategy. They must continuously create new ideas if the company is to prosper in a hypercompetitive economy. They must strive for customer insight and treat customers differently but appropriately. Marketers must build their brands through performance, more than through promotion. Marketers must go electronic and win through building superior information and communication systems.

Major Marketing Weaknesses

A number of 'deadly sins' signal that the marketing program is in trouble. Here are 10 deadly sins, the signs, and some solutions.

Deadly Sin: The company is not sufficiently market focused and customer driven.

Signs: There is evidence of poor identification of market segments, poor prioritization of market segments, no market segment managers, employees who think it is the job of marketing and sales to serve customers, no training program to create a customer culture, and no incentives to treat the customer especially well.

Solutions: Use more advanced segmentation techniques, prioritize segments, specialize the sales force, develop a clear hierarchy of company values, foster more 'customer consciousness' in employees and company agents, and make it easy for customers to reach the company and respond quickly to any communication.

Deadly Sin: The company does not fully understand its target customers.

Signs: The latest study of customers is 3 years old; customers are not buying your product like they once did; competitors' products are selling better; and there is a high level of customer returns and complaints.

Solutions: Do more sophisticated consumer research, use more analytical techniques, establish customer and dealer panels, use customer relationship software, and do datamining.

Deadly Sin: The company needs to better define and monitor its competitors.

Signs: The company focuses on near competitors, misses distant competitors and disruptive technologies, and has no system for gathering and distributing competitive intelligence.

Solutions: Establish an office for competitive intelligence, hire competitors' people, watch for technology that might affect the company, and prepare offerings like those of competitors.

Deadly Sin: The company does not properly manage relationships with stakeholders.

Signs: Employees, dealers, and investors are not happy; and good suppliers do not come.

Solutions: Move from zero-sum thinking to positive-sum thinking; and do a better job of managing employees, supplier relations, distributors, dealers, and investors.

Deadly Sin: The company is not good at finding new opportunities.

Signs: The company has not identified any exciting new opportunities for years, and the new ideas the company has launched have largely failed.
Solutions: Set up a system for stimulating the flow of new ideas.

Deadly Sin: The company's marketing planning process is deficient.

Signs. The marketing plan format does not have the right components, there is no way to estimate the financial implications of different strategies, and there is no contingency planning.
Solutions: Establish a standard format including situational analysis, SWOT, major issues, objectives, strategy, tactics, budgets, and controls; ask marketers what changes they would make if they were given 20 percent more or less budget; and run an annual marketing awards program with prizes for best plans and performance.

Deadly Sin: Product and service policies need tightening.

Signs: There are too many products and many are losing money; the company is giving away too many services; and the company is poor at cross-selling products and services.
Solutions: Establish a system to track weak products and fix or drop them; offer and price services at different levels; and improve processes for cross-selling and up-selling.

Deadly Sin: The company's brand-building and communications skills are weak.

Signs: The target market does not know much about the company; the brand is not seen as distinctive; the company allocates its budget to the same marketing tools in about the same proportion each year; and there is little evaluation of the return-on-investment (ROI) impact of promotions.
Solutions: Improve brand-building strategies and measurement of results; shift money into effective marketing instruments; and require marketers to estimate the ROI impact in advance of funding requests.

Deadly Sin: The company is not organized for effective and efficient marketing.

Signs: Staff lacks 21st-century marketing skills, and there are bad vibes between marketing/sales and other departments.
Solutions: Appoint a strong leader and build new skills in the marketing department, and improve relationships between marketing and other departments.

Deadly Sin: The company has not made maximum use of technology.

Signs: There is evidence of minimal use of the internet, an outdated sales automation system, no market automation, no decision-support models, and no marketing dashboards.
Solutions: Use the internet more, improve the sales automation system, apply market automation to routine decisions, and develop formal marketing decision models and marketing dashboards.

Source: Philip Kotler, *Ten Deadly Marketing Sins: Signs and Solutions* (Hoboken, NJ: John Wiley & Sons, 2004).

In these ways, modern marketing will continue to evolve and confront new challenges and opportunities. As a result, the coming years will see:

- The demise of the marketing department and the rise of holistic marketing.
- The demise of free-spending marketing and the rise of ROI marketing.
- The demise of marketing intuition and the rise of marketing science.
- The demise of manual marketing and the rise of automated marketing.
- The demise of mass marketing and the rise of precision marketing.

To accomplish these changes and become truly holistic, marketers need a new set of skills and competencies in areas such as:

- Customer relationship management (CRM).
- Partner relationship management (PRM).
- Database marketing and datamining.
- Contact center management and telemarketing.
- Public relations marketing (including event and sponsorship marketing).
- Brand-building and brand-asset management.
- Experiential marketing.
- Integrated marketing communications.
- Profitability analysis by segment, customer, and channel.

It is an exciting time for marketing. In the relentless pursuit of marketing superiority and dominance, new rules and practices are emerging. The benefits of successful 21st-century marketing are many, but will only come with hard work, insight, and inspiration. The words of 19th-century U.S. author Ralph Waldo Emerson may never have been more true, "This time like all times is a good one, if we but know what to do with it."

Summary

1. The modern marketing department has evolved through the years from a simple sales department to an organizational structure where marketing personnel work mainly on cross-disciplinary teams.

2. Modern marketing departments can be organized in a number of ways. Some companies are organized by functional specialization, whereas others focus on geography and regionalization. Still others emphasize product and brand management or market-segment management. Some companies establish a matrix organization consisting of both product and market managers. Finally, some companies have strong corporate marketing, others have limited corporate marketing, and still others place marketing only in the divisions.

3. Effective modern marketing organizations are marked by a strong cooperation and customer focus among the company's departments: marketing, R&D, engineering, purchasing, manufacturing, operations, finance, accounting, and credit.

4. Companies must practice social responsibility through their legal, ethical, and social words and actions. Cause marketing can be a means for companies to productively link social responsibility to consumer marketing programs. Social marketing is done by a nonprofit or government organization to directly address a social problem or cause.

5. A brilliant strategic marketing plan counts for little if it is not implemented properly. Implementing marketing plans calls for skills in recognizing and diagnosing a problem, assessing the company level where the problem exists, and evaluating results.

6. The marketing department must monitor and control marketing activities continuously. Marketing plan control involves analysis to ensure that the company achieves the sales, profits, and other goals established in its annual plan. The main tools are sales analysis, market share analysis, marketing expense-to-sales analysis, and financial analysis of the marketing plan. Profitability control seeks to measure and control the profitability of various products, territories, customer groups, trade channels, and order sizes. An important part of controlling for profitability is assigning costs and generating profit-and-loss statements. Efficiency control focuses on finding ways to increase the efficiency of the sales force, advertising, sales promotion, and distribution.

Strategic control entails a periodic reassessment of the company and its strategic approach to the marketplace using marketing effectiveness and marketing excellence reviews as well as the marketing audit as tools.

7. Achieving marketing excellence in the future will require new challenges and oppportunities. The resulting marketing imperatives will require a new set of skills and competencies.

Applications

Marketing Debate

Is Marketing Management an Art or a Science?

Some marketing observers maintain that good marketing is something that is more than anything an art and does not lend itself to rigorous analysis and deliberation. Others strongly disagree and contend that marketing management is a highly disciplined enterprise that shares much in common with other business disciplines.

Take a position: Marketing management is largely an artistic exercise and therefore highly subjective *versus* marketing management is largely a scientific exercise with well-established guidelines and criteria.

Marketing Discussion

How does cause or corporate societal marketing affect your personal consumer behavior? Do you ever buy or not buy any products or services from a company because of its environmental policies or programs? Why or why not?

Marketing Excellence

>>Oriental Weavers

There is no doubt that Oriental Weavers is the largest producer of machine-made rugs and carpets worldwide. Surprisingly, during the Egyptian revolution that took place in January 2011, Oriental Weavers' sales jumped 6 percent compared to the same period the year before. In the first quarter of 2011, Oriental Weavers' global sales volume reached US$161 million compared to $152 million in 2010. It can't be said that this sales achievement is due only to overseas operations, given that the Egyptian local market provided $57 million. Strong export performance, efficient utilization in factories, solid and positive organizational culture, and a well-established local market share are the fundamental reasons for Oriental Weavers' stability and progression even in bad market situations.

As Mohamed Farid Khamis, the Egyptian entrepreneur who established Oriental Weavers in 1980, said, "Sound financial management, low cost and high quality production, efficient logistics and distribution, flexible production and a globally diverse revenue base, allowed expanding market share in any climate."

Globally, Oriental Weavers is committed to all stakeholders, defined as employees, customers, and partners. This commitment is mutual, as employees, customers, and esteemed partners continued their faith in the company. Their continuous support has crowned the company over the past decade with international recognition and many awards. The tremendous success of Oriental Weavers is directly correlated to the company's internal marketing and corporate social responsibility, which are embedded in two fundamental principles: human rights and environmental protection.

All human rights best practices applied by the company far exceed the domestic requirements for both management and labor. Oriental Weavers takes care to ensure that all suppliers and service providers are committed to the same International Standards of Human Rights. To monitor fair and transparent management practices, the

Continued on next page >>

>>Oriental Weavers

company established a joint committee composed of both management and union representatives to enact any productive insights made by employees, as well as to ensure comfortable and safe working conditions. Within the same context, a board has been put in place to consider and grant additional financial assistance to employees who encounter adverse conditions. The board is representative of all company departments to ensure interaction across various levels and to eliminate missing opportunities by taking immediate corrective measures if needed.

Oriental Weavers has very strict child labor policies, and makes it clear to all partners that the company will not conduct business with any entity that uses child labor, either directly or indirectly, in the making of its products. To ensure this policy is enacted overseas, Oriental Weavers established a committee to monitor its foreign handmade production lines managed by other manufacturers. The committee members are sent on random checking missions to foreign manufacturers to confirm that no child labor is being used. Violators of this policy have their contract terminated immediately.

Oriental Weavers' production process is also compliant with international environmental standards. This is achieved through consistent improvement in production processes. The company works to minimize its water, air, noise, and solid waste emissions into the environment. Procurement and use of raw materials is carried out to specific operational standards. European firms such as IKEA and Marks & Spencer require Oriental Weavers to comply with EU environmental and occupational health and safety standards, while U.S. firms such as Home Depot require compliance with U.S. Environmental Protection Agency measures. Oriental Weavers has extended these environmental standards to its domestic and international suppliers of raw materials. Oriental

Weavers' industrial safety and environment department has 85 employees. Members are responsible for ensuring operational compliance with international standards as well as all standards enforced by the Egyptian Environmental Affairs Agency (EAA). Frequent monitoring reports are sent to the EAA to maintain Oriental Weavers' operating license for all production facilities.

The company's success is based on continuous innovation, research and development, a strong and positive internal culture, and customer orientation. The quality of its production within international environmental standards and its alignment with human rights practices has solidified Oriental Weavers' position globally as the largest producer of printed and tufted rugs. Lately, Oriental Weavers has established a division to enable incorporation of customers' ideas into its rugs and carpets. This reflects the company's clear understanding that good marketing and management practices should be accompanied by a market-driven demand approach.

Questions

1. Marketing is a set of activities done inside and outside of the organization. Based on your analysis, do you think that Oriental Weavers' approach is in line with this vision? Why?

2. Marketing is too important to be left to marketers alone. Comment on this statement within the context of Oriental Weavers' operations.

3. Discuss how Oriental Weavers is able to deliver holistic customer value in the long run.

Sources: Oriental Weavers Carpets, 2011, "Oriental Weavers Carpets First Quarter 2011 Results," http://phx.corporate-ir.net/External.File?item=UGFyZW50SUQ9OTc 3MDZ8Q2hpbGRGRJRD0tMXxUeXBlPTM=&t=1; "Social Responsibility," www .orientalweavers.com/en/SOCIAL%20RESPONSIBILITY/default.aspx.

Credits

Figures

Figure 2.1 from *Competitive Advantage: Creating and Sustaining Superior Performance*, Free Press (Michael E. Porter), adapted with the permission of Free Press, a Division of Simon & Schuster, Inc., copyright © 1985, 1998 by Michael E. Porter. All rights reserved; Figure 2.2 from "Formulating a Market Renewal Strategy", *Marketing Moves (Part 1)*, Fig. 1-1, p.29, (Kotler, D. C., and Maesincee, S., 2002), Harvard Business School Press, copyright © 2002 by President and Fellows of Harvard College. All rights reserved; Figure 2.5 adapted from "Strategies for Diversification", *Harvard Business Review* (Ansoff, I.), September–October 1957, copyright © 1957 by the President and Fellows of Harvard College. All rights reserved; Figure 2.8 from 'Break-Even Analysis', www.mplans.com, copyright © Palo Alto Software, Inc.; Figure 4.3 adapted from *Marketing by the Dashboard Light – How to Get More Insight, Foresight, and Accountability from Your Marketing Investments* (Patrick LaPointe, 2005), copyright © 2005, Patrick LaPointe. Reproduced with permission; Figure 5.5 from *Customer Loyalty: How to Earn It, How to Keep It,* John Wiley and Sons (Griffin, J., 2002), p.36, copyright © 2002, John Wiley and Sons; Figure 6.2 from *Motivation and Personality, 3rd edition*, Prentice Hall (Maslow, A.H., and Frager, R.D., Fadiman, J. (eds), 1987); and Figure 8.4 adapted from *Defining the Business: The Starting Point of Strategic Planning*, Prentice Hall (Abell, D.F., 1980), pp.192–196, copyright © 1980. Printed and electronically reproduced by permission of Pearson Education, Inc., Upper Saddle River, New Jersey; Figure 9.2 from BrandDynamics™ Pyramid. Reprinted by permission of MillwardBrown Optimor; Figure 9.5 from *Strategic Brand Management, 3rd edition*, Prentice Hall (Keller, K.L., 2008), copyright © 2008. Printed and electronically reproduced by permission of Pearson Education, Inc., Upper Saddle River, New Jersey; Figure 12.4 from "Industrial Product Policy: Managing the Existing Product Line", *Marketing Science Institute Report No. 77–110*, (Benson P. Shapiro), copyright © 2003. Reprinted by permission of Marketing Science Institute and Benson P. Shapiro; Figure 13.2 from *Services Marketing: Integrating Customer Focus across the Firm, 4th edition*, McGraw-Hill (Zeithaml, V., Bitner, M.J., and Gremler, D.D., 2006), copyright © McGraw-Hill; Figure 13.3 from "Root Causes of Customer Failure", *MIT Sloan Management Review,* 1 April 2006, pp.30–38 (Tax, S., Colgate, M., and Bowen, D.), copyright © 2006 from MIT Sloan Management Review/Massachusetts Institute of Technology. All rights reserved. Distributed by Tribune Media Services; Figure 13.5 from "A Conceptual Model of Service Quality and Its Implications for Future Research", *Journal of Marketing,* Fall 1985, p.44, (Parasuraman, A., Zeithaml, V.A., and Berry, L.L.), copyright © American Marketing Association. Permission conveyed through Copyright Clearance Center; Figure 14.6 from "Strategies to Fight Low-Cost Rivals", *Harvard Business Review*, pp.104–112, (Kumar, N., 2006), copyright © 2006 by the Harvard Business School Publishing Corporation. All rights reserved; Figure 15.4 'The Value-Adds versus Costs of Different Channels' adapted from Oxford Associates, Dr. Rowland T. Moriarty, Cubex Corporation. Reproduced with kind permission; Figure 15.6 adapted from "Marketing Hybrid Marketing Systems" *Harvard Business Review*, p.150 (Moriarty, R.T., and Moran, U.), November–December 1990, copyright © 1990 by President and Fellows of Harvard College. All rights reserved; and Figure 19.2 from "Match Your Sales-Force Structure to Your Business Life Cycle", *Harvard Business Review*, pp.81–89, (Zoltners, A., Sinha, P., and Lorimer, S.E. 2006), copyright © 2006 by the Harvard Business School Publishing Corporation. All rights reserved.

Photographs

(Key: b-bottom; c-centre; l-left; r-right; t-top)

Alamy Images: Adams Picture Library t / a apl 98, allOver photography 201, Ange 327, Bon Appetit 64, 65, Peter Bowater 69, ClyntGarnham Business 151, dbimages 300, epaeuropeanpressphoto agency b.v. 556, 557, Eddie Gerald 8b, 214, Jeff Greenberg 105, Marc F. Henning 454, Jack Hobhouse 184, Barry Iverson 35, Andre Jenny 340, 341, Justin Kasezfivez 179, Kevpix 25, 74, ArkadiusKozera 460, 461, Le Desk 381, MARKA 332, Iain Masterton 218, mediablitzimages (uk) Limited 372, Megapress 75, 605, Antony Nettle 616, 617, B. O'Kane 2, 3, 124, 125, 389, davidpearson 459, philipus 511, Photo Japan 338, Realimage 579, Jochen Tack 416, Tom Tracy Photography 404, 405, travelstock44 421t, vario images GmbH & Co.KG 204, Web Pix 277, World Pictures 448; **Alan J.Norris:** 597; **American University of Beirut:** 541; **Arab African International Bank:** 630; **Art Directors and TRIP Photo Library:** Helene Rogers 115, 138, 162, 262, 470; **aviation-images.com:** Mark Wagner 320, 363, 632; **Camera Press Ltd:** Lutz Jaekel / Bilderberg 7, Jurgen Tap / Hochzwei / Gamma 182, Richard Wayman 90, 91; **Catwalk Cow:** 561; **Children's Cancer Hospital 57357, Egypt:** 493; **Christian Short Photography, photographersdirect.com:** 152, 153; **Copyright (c) H. J. Heinz Company:** 17; **Corbis:** Georgina Bowater 78, NameerGalal / Demotix 395, Ali Haider / epa 32, 33, 315, Daniel Karmann / dpa 13, Mike Kemp / In Pictures 402, Stephanie Kuykendal / dpa 352, Bernd Weissbrod / dpa 318, WWD / Condé Nast 258; **Courtesy of Aramex International:** 288, 289; **Courtesy of the Xerox Corporation:** 563; **Crepaway Corporation:** 267; **David Gabis Photography, photographersdirect.com:** 30, 353; **Diwan:** 485; **FotoLibra:** Nicola Beykirch 297, 445, Philip Carr 209, Louis Champion 230, SYLVIE DE LEU 88, James W Fowler 554, Rawya A. Al Malik 522; **Getty Images:** AFP / Nasser Younes 208, AFP / Yasser Al-Zayyat 87, Bloomberg 8t, 376, 614, Cover 436, 437, Michael Crabtree 46, India Today Group 424, KavehKazemi 588, 589, Dan Kitwood 70, New York Daily News 211, Richard Nowitz / National Geographic 652, Sean Gallup , Justin Sullivan 45, 251, HaiderYousuf 517; **Glow Images:** JuergenStumpe / LOOKfoto 80; **Image courtesy of The Advertising Archives:** 129, 586; **ISIS Organic:** 264, 265; **Joie De Vivre Hotels:** 130; **Kinepolis Antwerp(Kinepolis Group):** 292; **Kunhadi:** 499; **Maatouk Factories SAL:** 123; **Nautilus, Inc:** 411; **Obegi Consumer Products, Huggies, OgilvyAction, Beirut, Eastline Marketing,**

Beirut: 537; **Olson Zaltman Associates:** 103; **OttmarBierwagen:** 180, 181, 373; **Panda Stores:** 441; **Press Association Images:** AP Photo / Kamran Jebreili 486, 487, Huang jiexian / AP 599, LANDOV 421b, Wilfredo Lee / AP 92, Nick Potts / PA Wire 512, RICK BOWMER / AP 269, DON RYAN / AP 370, 371, Paul Sakuma / AP 520, 521, M. Spencer Green / AP 633, JON SUPER / AP 368, Tom Uhlman / AP 227, Weng lei / AP 429; **Raya Group:** 312, 313, 356; **Reuters:** Stringer 601, AsmaaWaguih 146, 471; **Rex Features:** Mario Beauregard 364, PAUL COOPER 86, Richard Jones 621, Steve Meddle 558, NBCUPHOTOBANK 571; **Roadster Diner:** 272; **Salem Alforaih Photography, photographersdirect.com:** 44; **Silkor Holding:** 518; **Stephen Faust, photographersdirect.com:** 299; **Sugar Daddy's Bakery:** Simon Milne-Day 466; **SuperStock:** Richard Cummins 525, OleksiyMaksymenko / age fotostock 6; **The Kobal Collection:** NEW LINE / SAUL ZAENTZ / WING NUT 610; **Reproduced with kind permission of Unilever PLC and group companies:** 329; **Zawya:** 194

All other images © Pearson Education

Logos

Logo on page 234 from Almarai, almarai.com. Reproduced with permission. Logo on page 434 from Transmed, www.transmed.com. Reproduced with permission.

Screenshot/Adverts

Screenshot on page 11 from AutoMarket, www.automarket.com.lb. Reproduced with permission; Advert on page 160 from NAS Trends. Reproduced with permission; Advert on page 198 from 'Ford Customized Fleet Solutions'. Granted with permission by Al Tayer Motors LLC; Advert on page 285 from BEE, http://www.bee.com.eg. Reproduced with permission; Advert on page 310 from Damas, www.damasjewel.com. Reproduced with permission; Advert on page 346 from Mashaweer, www.mashaweeronline.com. Reproduced with permission; Photograph and logo on page 356 from Raya Contact Center, www.rayacorp.com. Reproduced with permission; Advert on page 378 from Azza Fahmy. Reproduced with permission; Advert on page 413 from Arab Open University, www.arabou.edu.kw. Reproduced with permission; Advert on page 425 from Egypt Air, www.egyptair.com. Reproduced with kind permission; Store photograph on page 441 from Panda. Reproduced with permission; Advert on page 479 from GE ecomangination www.ge.com/company/advertising/ads_eco.html, courtesy of GE; Screenshot on page 508 from Mahksoom, www.Makhsoom.com Reproduced with permission; Screenshot on page 533 from BMW, www.bmwusa.com. Reproduced with permission of BMW of North America, LLC; and Screenshot on page 538, Blom Shabeb, www.blombank.com, Reproduced with permission of Blom Bank SAL.

Tables

Table 2.2 from "The 12 Different Ways for Companies to Innovate", *MIT Sloan Management Review,* 1 April 2006, p.76, (Sawhney, M., Wolcott, R.C., and Arroniz, I.), copyright © 2006 from MIT Sloan Management Review/Massachusetts Institute of Technology. All rights reserved. Distributed by Tribune Media Services; Table 2.3 Historical Data; Table 2.4 Break-Even Analysis; Table 2.5 Sales Forecast; Table 2.6 Marketing Expense Budget www.mplans.com, copyright © Palo Alto Software, Inc.; Table 3.1 Data from League of Arab States and UDNP 2008,

IMF and CIA World Factbook. From *UNDP Arab Knowledge Report 2009.* Reproduced with permission; Table 3.2 from "Internet penetration in the Arab countries", 2011, www.internetworldstats.com, copyright © 2000 - 2012, Miniwatts Marketing Group. All rights reserved; Table 4.6 from "What does marketing success look like?", *Marketing Management*, Vol 10 (1), pp.12–18, (Ambler, T., 2001), copyright © American Marketing Association. Reproduced by permission of AMA and the author; Table 5.4 from "Avoid the Four Perils of CRM", *Harvard Business Review*, p.106 (Rigby, D.K., Reichheld, F.F., and Schefter, P., 2002), copyright © 2002 by the Harvard Business School Publishing Corporation. All rights reserved; Table 6.1 from LOHAS Market Segments, www.lohas.com. Reproduced with permission; Table 8.2 adapted from *Market-Based Management, 4th edition*, Prentice Hall, (Best, R.J., 2005) copyright © 2005. Printed and electronically reproduced by permission of Pearson Education, Inc., Upper Saddle River, New Jersey; Table 9.1 from "The Top 40 Arab Brands" Forbes, www.forbes.com. Reprinted by permission of Forbes Media LLC, copyright © 2011; Table 9.2 from "The World's Most Valuable Brands", *Forbes*, 28 July 2010, (Badenhausen, K.). Reprinted by permission of Forbes Media LLC, copyright © 2011; Table 11.3 from "Defensive Marketing: How a Strong Incumbent Can Protect Its Position", *Harvard Business Review*, p.156 (Roberts, J.H., 2005), copyright © 2005 by the Harvard Business School Publishing Corporation. All rights reserved; Tables 18.1, 18.2, 18.4 from "Advertising Media Expenditures in MENA Region – Top 10 Categories 2010" and Table 18.5 "Advertising Expenditures in MENA Region by Market 2010", *ArabAd*, Vol 21 (2), February 2011, copyright © ArabAd; and Table 20.1 from "The World's Fifty Most Innovative Companies," Fast Company, 2011, www.fastcompany.com, copyright © 2011 from Fast Company Magazine/Mansueto Ventures Ltd. LLC. All rights reserved. Distributed by Tribune Media Services.

Text

Extract on page 5 from American Marketing Association 2007. Reproduced by permission of The AMA; Extract on page 11 adapted from "mashreq 'Opens the Way' with the latest mortgage solutions", 28 May 2007, mashreq Press Release, source: www.ameinfo.com; Box 1.1 on page 12 from "The Fall and Rise of the CMO", *strategy+business,* (Gail McGovern and John A. Quelch, 2004), Winter 2004, published by Booz & Company Inc. copyright © 2004. All rights reserved. www.strategy-business.com; Text on page 20 adapted from *Ten Deadly Marketing Sins: Signs and Solutions*, John Wiley & Sons, Inc., (Kotler, P., 2004), copyright © 2004, John Wiley and Sons; Box 1.2 in page 23 from *Kotler on Marketing*, The Free Press, (Philip Kotler, 1999). Reprinted with permission of The Free Press, a Division of Simon & Schuster, Inc., copyright © 1999 by Philip Kotler. All rights reserved; Extract on page 25 adapted from "The Arab world's first defensive driving Academy opens at Jeddah Raceway", 11 November 2008. Safra Defensive Driving Academy (SDDA) Press Release, source: www.ameinfo.com; Box 2.2 on page 40 Orbit Mission Statement, www.orbit-iq.com. Reproduced with permission; Mission Statement on page 40 from St. Jude Medical, Inc. Reproduced with permission; Box 2.3 on page 41 Google's Mission Statement and Philosophy, www.google.com. Reproduced with permission; Extract on pages 46–47 from "Insight", *BusinessWeek*, p.32, June 2006 (DevPatnaik), Reproduced by permission by Jump Associates; Extract on page 56

Appendix

OASIS MARKETING PLAN AND EXERCISES

The Marketing Plan: An Introduction

As a marketer, you'll need a good marketing plan to provide direction and focus for your brand, product, or company. With a detailed plan, any business will be better prepared to launch an innovative new product or increase sales to current customers. Nonprofit organizations also use marketing plans to guide their fundraising and outreach efforts. Even government agencies put together marketing plans for initiatives such as building public awareness of proper nutrition and stimulating area tourism.

The Purpose and Content of a Marketing Plan

A marketing plan has a more limited scope than a business plan, which offers a broad overview of the entire organization's mission, objectives, strategy, and resource allocation. The marketing plan documents how the organization's strategic objectives will be achieved through specific marketing strategies and tactics, with the customer as the starting point. It is also linked to the plans of other organizational departments. Suppose a marketing plan calls for selling 200,000 units annually. The production department must gear up to make that many units, finance must arrange funding to cover the expenses, human resources must be ready to hire and train staff, and so on. Without the appropriate level of organizational support and resources, no marketing plan can succeed.

Although the exact length and layout varies from company to company, a marketing plan usually contains the sections described in Chapter 2. Smaller businesses may create shorter or less formal marketing plans, whereas corporations generally require highly structured marketing plans. To guide implementation effectively, every part of the plan must be described in considerable detail. Sometimes a company will post its marketing plan on an internal website so managers and employees in different locations can consult specific sections and collaborate on additions or changes.

The Role of Research

To develop innovative products, successful strategies, and action programs, marketers need up-to-date information about the environment, the competition, and the selected market segments. Often, analysis of internal data is the starting point for assessing the current marketing situation, supplemented by marketing intelligence and research investigating the overall market, the competition, key issues, threats, and opportunities. As the plan is put into effect, marketers use research to measure progress toward objectives and to identify areas for improvement if results fall short of projections.

Finally, marketing research helps marketers learn more about their customers' requirements, expectations, perceptions, satisfaction, and loyalty. This deeper understanding provides a foundation for building competitive advantage through well-informed segmenting, targeting, and positioning decisions. Thus, the marketing plan should outline what marketing research will be conducted and when, as well as how the findings will be applied.

The Role of Relationships

Although the marketing plan shows how the company will establish and maintain profitable customer relationships, it also affects both internal and external relationships. First, it influences how marketing personnel work with each other and with other departments to deliver value and satisfy customers. Second, it affects how the company works with suppliers, distributors, and partners to achieve the plan's objectives. Third, it influences the company's dealings with other stakeholders, including government regulators, the media, and the community at large. All these relationships are important to the organization's success and must be considered when developing a marketing plan.

From Marketing Plan to Marketing Action

Most companies create yearly marketing plans, although some plans cover a longer period. Marketers start planning well in advance of the implementation date to allow time for marketing research, analysis, management review, and coordination between departments. Then, after each action program begins, marketers monitor ongoing results, investigate any deviation from the projected outcome, and take corrective steps as needed. Some marketers also prepare contingency plans for implementation if certain conditions emerge. Because of inevitable and sometimes unpredictable environmental changes, marketers must be ready to update and adapt marketing plans at any time.

For effective implementation and control, the marketing plan should define how progress toward objectives will be measured. Managers typically use budgets, schedules, and marketing metrics for monitoring and evaluating results. With budgets, they can compare planned expenditures with actual expenditures for a given period. Schedules allow management to see when tasks were supposed to be completed and when they were actually completed. Marketing metrics track the actual outcomes of marketing programs to see whether the company is moving toward its objectives.

Sample Marketing Plan for Oasis

This section takes you inside the sample marketing plan for Oasis,[A] a hypothetical start-up company formed by a group of Arab entrepreneurs with diverse educational backgrounds (telecommunication, computer engineering, computer science, finance, and marketing) who have accumulated professional and technical experience and expertise in leading multinational companies. Although they come from different Arab countries, the core members of this group came to know each other several years ago through the friendship they developed in university. The company's first product is the Oasis 1000, a multimedia, mobile/wi-fi-enabled personal digital assistant (PDA), also known as a handheld computer. Oasis will be competing with Palm, Hewlett-Packard, Motorola, Apple, and other well-established rivals in a crowded, fast-changing marketplace where smart phones and many other electronics devices have PDA functionality as well as entertainment capabilities. The annotations explain more about what each section of the plan should contain.

1.0 Executive Summary

This section summarizes market opportunities, marketing strategy, and marketing and financial objectives for senior managers who will read and approve the marketing plan.

Oasis is preparing to launch a new multimedia, dual-mode PDA product, the Oasis 1000, in a mature market. We can compete with both PDAs and smart phones because our product offers a unique combination of advanced features and functionality at a value-added price. Oasis 1000 will be offering full English as well as Arabic language functionality to suit the spectrum of language use and proficiency across the Arab world (Arab as well as non-Arab users). We are targeting specific segments in the consumer and business markets, taking advantage of the growing interest in a single device with communication, organization, and entertainment benefits.

The primary marketing objective is to achieve a first-year market share of 3 percent with unit sales of 240,000 in Egypt, the Levant, and the Arabian Gulf regions. The primary financial objectives are to achieve first-year sales revenues of US$60 million, keep first-year losses to less than $10 million, and break even early in the second year. Oasis plans to expand into the Arab Maghreb states toward the end of the second year.

2.0 Situation Analysis

Oasis is about to enter the now mature PDA market. Multifunction mobile phones, e-mail devices, and wireless communication devices are increasingly popular for both personal and professional use, with more than 5 million PDAs and 22 million smart phones sold worldwide each year. Competition is increasingly intense even as technology evolves, industry consolidation continues, and pricing pressures squeeze profitability. Palm, a PDA pioneer, is one of several key players having difficulty adapting to the smart-phone challenge. To gain market share in this dynamic environment, Oasis must carefully target specific segments with valued features and plan for a next-generation product to keep brand momentum going.

The situation analysis describes the market, the company's capability to serve targeted segments, and the competition.

2.1 MARKET SUMMARY Oasis's market consists of consumers and business users who prefer to use a single device for communication, information storage and exchange, organization, and entertainment on the go. Specific segments being targeted during the first year include professionals, corporations, students, entrepreneurs, and medical users. △ **Exhibit A.1** shows how the Oasis 1000 addresses the needs of targeted consumer and business segments.

Market summary includes size, needs, growth, and trends. Describing the targeted segments in detail provides context for marketing strategies and programs discussed later in the plan.

PDA purchasers can choose between models based on several different operating systems, including systems from Palm, Microsoft, and Symbian, plus Linux variations. Oasis licenses a Linux-based system because it is somewhat less vulnerable to attack by hackers and viruses. Storage capacity (hard drive or flash drive) is an expected feature for PDAs, so Oasis is equipping its first product with an ultra-fast 20-gigabyte drive that can be supplemented by extra storage.

Targeted Segment	Customer Need	Corresponding Feature/Benefit
Professionals (consumer market)	• Stay in touch while on the go	• Wireless e-mail to conveniently send and receive messages from anywhere; mobile phone capability for voice communication from anywhere
	• Record information while on the go	• Voice recognition for no-hands recording
	• Operate, use and communicate in Arabic	• Full Arabic language functionality
Students (consumer market)	• Perform many functions without carrying multiple gadgets	• Compatible with numerous applications and peripherals for convenient, cost-effective functionality
	• Express style and individuality	• Case wardrobe of different colors and patterns allows users to make a fashion statement
	• Operate, use, and communicate in Arabic	• Full Arabic language functionality
Corporate Users (business market)	• Input and access critical data on the go	• Compatible with widely available software
	• Use for proprietary tasks	• Customizable to fit diverse corporate tasks and networks
	• Operate, use, and communicate in Arabic	• Full Arabic language functionality
Entrepreneurs (business market)	• Organize and access contacts, schedule details	• No-hands, wireless access to calendar and address book to easily check appointments and connect with contacts
	• Operate, use, and communicate in Arabic	• Full Arabic language functionality
Medical Users (business market)	• Update, access, and exchange medical records	• No-hands, wireless recording and exchange of information to reduce paperwork and increase productivity
	• Operate, use, and communicate in Arabic	• Full Arabic language functionality
Government Users (government market)	• Input and access critical data on the go	• Compatible with widely available software
	• Operate, use, and communicate in Arabic (the official language)	• Full Arabic language functionality

|Exh. A.1| △

Needs and Corresponding Features/Benefits of the Oasis PDA

Technology costs are decreasing even as capabilities are increasing, which makes value-priced models more appealing to consumers and to business users with older PDAs who want to trade up to new, high-end multifunction units.

2.2 STRENGTHS, WEAKNESSES, OPPORTUNITIES, AND THREATS ANALYSIS
Oasis has several powerful strengths on which to build, but our major weakness is lack of brand awareness and image. The major opportunity is demand for multifunctional communication, organization, and entertainment devices that deliver a number of valued benefits. We also face the threat of ever higher competition and downward pricing pressure.

Strengths Oasis can build on three important strengths:

1. *Innovative product*. The Oasis 1000 offers a combination of features that would otherwise require customers to carry multiple devices, such as speedy, hands-free dual-mode mobile/wi-fi telecommunications capabilities, and digital video/music/TV program storage/playback. In addition, the full Arabic language functionality is a unique feature of Oasis 1000. Preliminary research shows potentially very good reception among Arab users.
2. *Security*. Our PDA uses a Linux-based operating system that is less vulnerable to hackers and other security threats that can result in stolen or corrupted data.
3. *Pricing*. Our product is priced lower than competing multifunction PDAs—none of which offer the same bundle of features—which gives us an edge with price-conscious customers.

Weaknesses By waiting to enter the PDA market until considerable consolidation of competitors has occurred, Oasis has learned from the successes and mistakes of others. Nonetheless, we have three main weaknesses:

1. *Lack of brand awareness*. Oasis has no established brand or image, whereas Palm, Apple, and others have strong brand recognition. We will address this issue with aggressive promotion.
2. *Heavier and thicker unit*. The Oasis 1000 is slightly heavier and thicker than most competing models because it incorporates many multimedia features and offers far more storage capacity than the average PDA. To counteract this weakness, we will emphasize our product's benefits and value-added pricing, two compelling competitive strengths.
3. *Possible negative country-of-origin effect*. As a technology product put forward by an Arab company, it might carry certain negative perceptions associated with the country of origin. The Arab world is little known for its technological innovations.

Opportunities Oasis can take advantage of three major market opportunities:

1. *Increasing demand for multimedia devices with communication functions*. The market for multimedia, multifunction devices is growing much faster than the market for single-use devices. Growth is accelerating as dual-mode capabilities become mainstream, giving customers the flexibility to make phone calls over mobile or internet connections. PDAs and smart phones are already commonplace in public, work, and educational settings; in fact, users who bought entry-level models are now trading up.
2. *Lower technology costs*. Better technology is now available at a lower cost than ever before. Thus, Oasis can incorporate advanced features at a value-added price that allows for reasonable profits.
3. *Demographic and economic growth in the Arab world*. The Arab world leads the world regions in terms of population growth. It has a substantial youth segment, a segment that is a prime prospect to embrace technological telecommunication innovations. It is also a region which was least affected by the world economic downturn, fueled primarily by the population growth and high oil prices.

Threats We face three main threats at the introduction of the Oasis 1000:

1. *Increased competition*. More companies are offering devices with some but not all of the features and benefits provided by the Oasis PDA. Therefore, Oasis's marketing communications must stress our clear differentiation and value-added pricing.

Strengths are internal capabilities that can help the company reach its objectives.

Weaknesses are internal elements that may interfere with the company's ability to achieve its objectives.

Opportunities are areas of buyer need or potential interest in which the company might perform profitably.

Threats are challenges posed by an unfavorable trend or development that could lead to lower sales and profits.

2. **Downward pressure on pricing**. Increased competition and market share strategies are pushing PDA prices down. Still, our objective of seeking a 10 percent profit on second-year sales of the original model is realistic, given the lower margins in the PDA market.

3. **Compressed product life cycle**. PDAs have reached the maturity stage of their life cycle more quickly than earlier technology products. Because of this compressed life cycle, we plan to introduce a media-oriented second product during the year following the Oasis 1000's launch. We also plan to expand into the Arab Maghreb countries.

2.3 COMPETITION

The emergence of new multifunction smart phones, including the Apple iPhone, has increased competitive pressure. Dell has already left the PDA market; the remaining competitors are continually adding features and sharpening price points. Competition from specialized devices for text and e-mail messaging, such as BlackBerry devices, is another major factor. Key competitors:

This section identifies key competitors, describes their market positions, and provides an overview of their strategies.

- **Palm.** As the PDA market leader, with a 34 percent share, Palm has excellent distribution in multiple channels and alliances with a number of U.S. and European telecommunications carriers. However, Palm's smart-phone share is well below that of Nokia and other handset marketers. Palm products use either the proprietary Palm operating system or Windows.

- **Hewlett-Packard.** HP holds 22 percent of the PDA market and targets business segments with its numerous iPAQ Pocket PC devices. Some of its PDAs can send documents to Bluetooth-equipped printers and prevent data loss if batteries run down. For extra security, one model allows access by fingerprint match as well as by password. HP enjoys widespread distribution and offers a full line of PDAs at various price points.

- **Motorola.** Motorola sold 100 million of its RAZR clamshell phones worldwide in 3 years and now offers the RAZR2, smaller and lighter than earlier models and with two operating system options. The Motorola Q targets professionals and business users with PDA and e-mail functions, a tiny keyboard, Bluetooth connections, multimedia capabilities, and more.

- **Apple.** The iPhone, a smart phone with a 3.5-inch color screen, has been designed with entertainment enthusiasts in mind. It's well equipped for music, video, and web access, plus calendar and contact management functions. Apple initially partnered only with the AT&T network and cut the product's price to US$399 just 2 months after introduction to speed market penetration. Its iPod Touch media player has iPhone styling without phone functionality.

- **RIM.** Research in Motion makes the lightweight BlackBerry wireless phone/PDA products that are popular among corporate users. RIM's continuous innovation and solid customer service support strengthen its competitive standing as it introduces more smart phones and PDAs.

- **Samsung.** Value, style, function: Samsung is a powerful competitor, offering a variety of smart phones and ultra mobile PCs for consumer and business segments. Some of its smart phones are available for specific telecommunications carriers and some are 'unlocked,' ready for any compatible telecommunications network.

Despite strong competition, Oasis can carve out a definite image and gain recognition among targeted segments. Our voice-recognition system for hands-off operation is a critical point of differentiation for competitive advantage. Our second product will have PDA functions but will be more media-oriented to appeal to segments where we will have strong brand recognition. △ **Exhibit A.2** shows a sample of competitive products and prices.

2.4 PRODUCT OFFERINGS

The Oasis PDA 1000 offers the following standard features:

This section summarizes the main features of the company's various products.

- Full English and Arabic language functionality.
- Voice recognition for hands-free operation.
- Organization functions, including calendar (world and Hijri calendars), address book, synchronization.
- Built-in dual mobile phone/internet phone and push-to-talk instant calling.
- Digital music/video/television recording, wireless downloading, and instant playback.
- Wireless web and e-mail, text messaging, instant messaging.

Competitor	Model	Features	Price (US$)
PalmOne	Tungsten C	PDA functions, wireless capabilities, color screen, tiny keyboard, wireless capabilities	$499
PalmOne	M130	PDA functions, color screen, expandable functionality	$199
Handspring	Treo 270	PDA and mobile phone functions, color screen, tiny keyboard, speakerphone capabilities, no expansion slot	$499
Samsung	i500	PDA functions, mobile phone functions, MP3 player, color screen, video capabilities	$599
Garmin	iQue 3600	PDA functions, global positioning system technology, voice recorder, expansion slot, MP3 player	$589
Dell	Axim X5	PDA functions, color screen, e-mail capable, voice recorder, speaker, expandable	$199
Sony	Clie PEG-NX73V	PDA functions, digital camera, tiny keyboard, games, presentation software, MP3 player, voice recorder	$499

|Exh. A.2| △

Selected PDA Products and Pricing

- 7.7-centimeter color screen for easy viewing.
- Ultra-fast 20-gigabyte drive and expansion slots.
- Five megapixel camera with flash and photo editing/sharing tools.

First-year sales revenues are projected to be US$60 million, based on sales of 240,000 of the Oasis 1000 model at a wholesale price of $250 each. Our second-year product will be the Oasis All Media 2000, stressing multimedia communication, networking, and entertainment functions with PDA capabilities as secondary features. The Oasis All Media 2000 will include Oasis 1000 features plus:

- Built-in media beaming to share music, video, and television files with other devices.
- Webcam for instant video capture and uploading to popular video websites.
- Voice-command access to popular social networking websites.
- Integrated eight megapixel camera, flash, and photo editing/sharing tools.

Distribution explains each channel for the company's products and mentions new developments and trends.

2.5 DISTRIBUTION Oasis-branded products will be distributed through a network of well-established retailers across the Arab world. Among the most important channel partners being contacted are:

- Office supply superstores.
- Computer stores.
- Electronics specialty stores.
- Online retailers.

These channels will help conveniently place Oasis products in stores, in catalogs, and online.

As mentioned, distribution will initially be restricted to Arab countries in Egypt, the Levant, and the Gulf, with appropriate sales promotion support. Later, we plan to expand into the Arab Maghreb countries and beyond (such as Euro-Mediterranean countries).

3.0 Marketing Strategy

Objectives should be defined in specific terms so management can measure progress and take corrective action to stay on track.

3.1 OBJECTIVES We have set aggressive but achievable objectives for the first and second years of market entry.

- *First-year objectives.* We are aiming for a 3-percent share of the Egypt, Levant, and Arab Gulf PDA market through a unit sales volume of 240,000.

- *Second-year objectives.* We aim to achieve breakeven on the Oasis 1000, launch our second model, and expand into the remaining Arab countries (and possibly Euro-Med countries).

3.2 TARGET MARKETS

Oasis's strategy is based on a positioning of product differentiation. Our primary consumer target for the Oasis 1000 is middle- to upper-income professionals who need one device to coordinate their busy schedules, stay in touch with family and colleagues, and be entertained on the go. Our secondary consumer target is high school, college, and graduate students who want a multimedia, dual-mode device. This segment can be described demographically by age (16–30) and education status. Our Oasis All Media 2000 will be aimed at teens and twentysomethings who want a device with features to support social networking and heavier entertainment media consumption.

The primary business target for the Oasis 1000 is mid- to large-sized corporations that want to help their managers and employees stay in touch and input or access critical data while out of the office. This segment consists of companies with more than US$25 million in annual sales and more than 50 employees. A secondary target is entrepreneurs and small-business owners. We will also target medical users who want to update or access patients' medical records.

In addition to the consumer and business markets, we anticipate that government agencies would also be interested in Oasis products, particularly for its full Arabic language functionality. This functionality would allow government officials of various agencies and units (particularly those whose jobs are in the field, such as police and security officials, customs officials, and health inspectors) to communicate and exchange data on a real-time basis in the official government language: Arabic.

Each of the marketing-mix strategies conveys Oasis's differentiation for these target market segments.

> All marketing strategies start with segmentation, targeting, and positioning.

3.3 POSITIONING

Using product differentiation, we are positioning the Oasis PDA as the most versatile, convenient, value-added model for personal and professional use. Our marketing will focus on the hands-free operation of multiple communication, entertainment, and information capabilities, all in full dual English–Arabic functionality, differentiating the Oasis 1000.

> Positioning identifies the brand, benefits, points of difference, and parity for the product or line.

3.4 STRATEGIES

Product The Oasis 1000, including all the features described in the earlier product review section, will be sold with a 1-year warranty. We will introduce the Oasis All Media 2000 during the following year, after we have established our Oasis brand. The brand and logo (Oasis's distinctive green palm tree) will be displayed on our products and packaging as well as in all marketing campaigns.

> Product strategy includes decisions about product mix and lines, brands, packaging and labeling, and warranties.

Pricing The Oasis 1000 will be introduced at US$250 wholesale/$350 estimated retail price per unit. We expect to lower the price of this model when we expand the product line by launching the Oasis All Media 2000, to be priced at $350 wholesale per unit. These prices reflect a strategy of (1) attracting desirable channel partners and (2) taking share from established competitors.

> Pricing strategy covers decisions about setting initial prices and adapting prices in response to opportunities and competitive challenges.

Distribution Our channel strategy is to use selective distribution, marketing Oasis PDAs through well-known stores and online retailers. During the first year, we will add channel partners until we have coverage in all major Arab markets and the product is included in the major electronics catalogs and websites. We will also investigate distribution through mobile-phone outlets maintained by major Arab carriers. In support of channel partners, we will provide demonstration products, detailed specification handouts, and full-color photos and displays featuring the product. Finally, we plan to arrange special payment terms for retailers that place volume orders.

> Distribution strategy includes selection and management of channel relationships to deliver value to customers.

Marketing Communications By integrating all messages in all media, we will reinforce the brand name and the main points of product differentiation. Research about media consumption patterns will help our advertising agency choose appropriate media and timing to reach prospects before and during product introduction. Thereafter, advertising will appear on a pulsing basis to maintain brand awareness and communicate various differentiation messages. The agency will also coordinate public relations efforts to build the Oasis brand and support the differentiation message.

> Marketing communications strategy covers all efforts to communicate to target audiences and channel members.

To generate buzz, we will host a user-generated video contest on our website. To attract, retain, and motivate channel partners for a push strategy, we will use trade sales promotions and personal selling. Until the Oasis brand has been established, our communications will encourage purchases through channel partners rather than from our website.

The marketing mix includes tactics and programs that support product, pricing, distribution, and marketing communications strategy.

3.5 MARKETING MIX

The Oasis 1000 will be introduced in February. Here are summaries of action programs we will use during the first 6 months to achieve our stated objectives.

Action programs should coordinate with the resources and activities of other departments that contribute to customer value for each product.

- *January.* We will launch a US$200,000 trade sales promotion campaign and participate in major industry trade shows to educate dealers and generate channel support for the product launch in February. Also, we will create buzz by providing samples to selected product reviewers, opinion leaders, influential bloggers, and celebrities. Our training staff will work with retail sales personnel at major chains to explain the Oasis 1000's features, benefits, and advantages.

- *February.* We will start an integrated print/radio/internet campaign targeting professionals and consumers. The campaign will show how many functions the Oasis PDA can perform and emphasize the convenience of a single, powerful handheld device. This multimedia campaign will be supported by point-of-sale signage as well as online-only ads and video tours.

- *March.* As the multimedia advertising campaign continues, we will add consumer sales promotions such as a contest in which consumers post videos to our website, showing how they use the Oasis in creative and unusual ways. We will also distribute new point-of-purchase displays to support our retailers.

- *April.* We will hold a trade sales contest offering prizes for the salesperson and retail organization that sells the most Oasis PDAs during the 4-week period.

- *May.* We plan to roll out a new advertising campaign this month across the Arab countries in which we operate. The radio ads will feature celebrity voices telling their Oasis PDAs to perform functions such as initiating a phone call, sending an e-mail, playing a song or video, and so on. The stylized print and online ads will feature avatars of these celebrities holding their Oasis PDAs. We plan to reprise this theme for next year's product launch.

- *June.* Our radio campaign will add a new voice-over tag line promoting the Oasis 1000 as a graduation gift. We will exhibit at the electronics trade show and provide retailers with new competitive comparison handouts as a sales aid. In addition, we will analyze the results of customer satisfaction research for use in future campaigns and product development efforts.

This section shows how marketing research will support the development, implementation, and evaluation of marketing strategies and programs.

3.6 MARKETING RESEARCH

Using research, we will identify specific features and benefits our target market segments value. Feedback from market tests, surveys, and focus groups will help us develop and fine-tune the Oasis All Media 2000. We are also measuring and analyzing customers' attitudes toward competing brands and products. Brand awareness research will help us determine the effectiveness and efficiency of our messages and media. Finally, we will use customer satisfaction studies to gauge market reaction.

4.0 Financials

Financials include budgets and forecasts to plan for marketing expenditures, scheduling, and operations.

Total first-year sales revenue for the Oasis 1000 is projected at US$60 million, with an average wholesale price of $250 per unit and variable cost per unit of $150 for a unit sales volume of 240,000. We anticipate a first-year loss of up to $10 million. Breakeven calculations indicate that the Oasis 1000 will become profitable after the sales volume exceeds 267,500 during the product's second year. Our breakeven analysis assumes per-unit wholesale revenue of $250 per unit, variable costs of $150 per unit, and estimated first-year fixed costs of $26,750,000. With these assumptions, the breakeven calculation is:

$$\frac{26{,}750{,}000}{\$250\text{-}\$150} = 267{,}500 \text{ units}$$

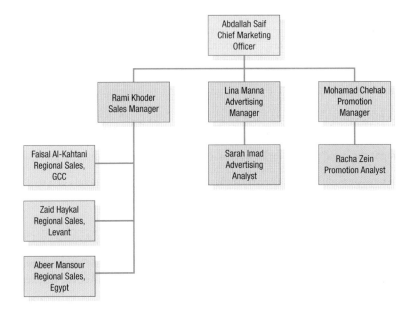

5.0 Controls

Controls are being established to cover implementation and the organization of our marketing activities.

5.1 IMPLEMENTATION We are planning tight control measures to closely monitor quality and customer service satisfaction. This will enable us to react very quickly to correct any problems that may occur. Other early warning signals that will be monitored for signs of deviation from the plan include monthly sales (by segment and channel) and monthly expenses.

Controls help management measure results and identify any problems or performance variations that need corrective action.

5.2 MARKETING ORGANIZATION Oasis's chief marketing officer, Abdallah Saif, holds overall responsibility for all of the company's marketing activities. △ **Exhibit A.3** above shows the structure of the eight-person marketing organization. Oasis has hired Arab marketing experts to handle its sales campaigns, trade and consumer sales promotions, and public relations efforts.

The marketing department may be organized by function, as in this sample, or by geography, product, customer, or some combination of these.

Oasis Marketing Plan Chapter Assignments

Chapter 2

As an assistant to Abdallah Saif, Oasis's chief marketing officer, you've been assigned to draft a mission statement for top management's review. This should cover the competitive spheres within which the firm will operate and your recommendation of an appropriate generic competitive strategy. Using your knowledge of marketing, the information you have about Oasis, and library or internet resources, answer the following questions.

- What should Oasis's mission be?
- In what competitive spheres (industry, products and applications, competence, market-segment, vertical, and geographic) should Oasis operate?
- Which of Porter's generic competitive strategies would you recommend Oasis follow in formulating overall strategy?

As your instructor directs, enter your answers and supporting information in a written marketing plan or use *Marketing Plan Pro* software to document your ideas.

Chapter 3

Abdallah Saif asks you to scan Oasis's external environment for early warning signals of new opportunities and emerging threats that could affect the success of the Oasis 1000 PDA. Using internet or library sources (or both), locate information to answer three questions about key areas of the macroenvironment.

- What demographic changes are likely to affect Oasis's targeted segments?
- What economic trends might influence buyer behavior in Oasis's targeted segments?
- How might the rapid pace of technological change/alter Oasis's competitive situation?

Enter your answers about Oasis's environment in the appropriate sections of a written marketing plan or use the *Marketing Plan Pro* software to record your comments.

Chapter 4

Your next task is to consider how marketing research can help Oasis support its marketing strategy. Abdallah Saif also asks you how Oasis can measure results after the marketing plan is implemented. He wants you to answer the following three questions.

- What surveys, focus groups, observation, behavioral data, or experiments will Oasis need to support its marketing strategy? Be specific about the questions or issues that Oasis needs to resolve using marketing research.
- Where can you find suitable secondary data about total demand for PDAs over the next 2 years? Identify at least two sources (online or offline), describe what you plan to draw from each source, and indicate how the data would be useful for Oasis's marketing planning.
- Recommend three specific marketing metrics for Oasis to apply in determining marketing effectiveness and efficiency.

Enter this information in the marketing plan you've been writing or use the *Marketing Plan Pro* software to document your responses.

Chapter 5

With this in mind, you've been assigned to analyze the following specific issues as you continue working on Oasis's marketing plan.

- How (and how often) should Oasis monitor customer satisfaction?
- Would you recommend that Oasis use the Net Promoter method? Explain your reasoning.
- Which customer touch points should Oasis pay particularly close attention to, and why?

Consider your answers in the context of Oasis's current situation and the objectives it has set. Then enter your latest decisions in the written marketing plan or using *Marketing Plan Pro* software.

Chapter 6

You're responsible for researching and analyzing the consumer market for Oasis's PDA product. Look again at the data you've already entered about the company's current situation and macroenvironment, especially the market being targeted. Now answer these questions about the market and buyer behavior.

- What cultural, social, and personal factors are likely to most influence consumer purchasing of PDAs? What research tools would help you better understand the effect on buyer attitudes and behavior?

- Which aspects of consumer behavior should Oasis's marketing plan emphasize and why?
- What marketing activities should Oasis plan to coincide with each stage of the consumer buying process?

After you've analyzed these aspects of consumer behavior, consider the implications for Oasis's marketing efforts to support the launch of its PDA. Finally, document your findings and conclusions in a written marketing plan or with *Marketing Plan Pro*.

Chapter 7

You've been learning more about the business market for Oasis's PDA. Abdallah Saif has defined this market as mid- to large-sized corporations that want their employees to stay in touch and be able to input or access data from any location. Respond to the following three questions based on your knowledge of Oasis's current situation and business-to-business marketing.

- What types of businesses appear to fit Saif's market definition? How can you research the number of employees and find other data about these types of businesses?
- What type of purchase would an Oasis PDA represent for these businesses? Who would participate in and influence this type of purchase?
- Would demand for PDAs among corporate buyers tend to be inelastic? What are the implications for Oasis's marketing plan?

Your answers to these questions will affect how Oasis plans marketing activities for the business segments to be targeted. Take a few minutes to note your ideas in a written marketing plan or using *Marketing Plan Pro*.

Chapter 8

Identifying suitable market segments and selecting targets are critical to the success of any marketing plan. As Abdallah Saif's assistant, you're responsible for market segmentation and targeting. Look back at the market information, buyer behavior data, and competitive details you previously gathered as you answer the following questions.

- Which variables should Oasis use to segment its consumer and business markets?
- How can Oasis evaluate the attractiveness of each identified segment? Should Oasis market to one consumer segment and one business segment or target more than one in each market? Why?
- Should Oasis pursue full market coverage, market specialization, product specialization, selective specialization, or single-segment concentration? Why?

Next, consider how your decisions about segmentation and targeting will affect Oasis's marketing efforts. Depending on your instructor's directions, summarize your conclusions in a written marketing plan or use *Marketing Plan Pro*.

Chapter 9

Oasis is a new brand with no prior brand associations, which presents a number of marketing opportunities and challenges. Abdallah Saif has given you responsibility for making recommendations about three brand equity issues that are important to Oasis's marketing plan.

- What brand elements would be most useful for differentiating the Oasis brand from competing brands?
- How can Oasis sum up its brand promise for the new PDA?
- Should Oasis add a brand for its second product or retain the Oasis name?

Be sure your brand ideas are appropriate in light of what you've learned about your targeted segments and the competition. Then add this information to your written marketing plan or the plan you've been developing with *Marketing Plan Pro* software.

Chapter 10

As before, you're working with Abdallah Saif and his team on Oasis's marketing plan for launching a new PDA. Now you're focusing on Oasis's positioning and product life-cycle strategies by answering three specific questions.

- In a sentence or two, what is an appropriate positioning statement for the Oasis 1000 PDA?
- Knowing the stage of Oasis's PDA in the product life cycle, what are the implications for pricing, promotion, and distribution?
- In which stage of its evolution does the PDA market appear to be? What does this mean for Oasis's marketing plans?

Document your ideas in a written marketing plan or in *Marketing Plan Pro*. Note any additional research you may need to determine how to proceed after the Oasis 1000 has been launched.

Chapter 11

Oasis is a new entrant in an established industry characterized by competitors with relatively high brand identity and strong market positions. Use research and your knowledge of how to deal with competitors to consider three issues that will affect the company's ability to successfully introduce its first product:

- What factors will you use to determine Oasis's strategic group?
- Should Oasis select a class of competitor to attack on the basis of strength versus weakness, closeness versus distance, or good versus bad? Why is this appropriate in the PDA market?
- As a start-up company, what competitive strategy would be most effective as Oasis introduces its first product?

Take time to analyze how Oasis's competitive strategy will affect its marketing strategy and tactics. Now summarize your ideas in a written marketing plan or using *Marketing Plan Pro* software.

Chapter 12

Introducing a new product entails a variety of decisions about product strategy, including differentiation, ingredient branding, packaging, labeling, warranty, and guarantee. Your next task is to answer the following questions about Oasis's product strategy.

- Which aspect of product differentiation would be most valuable in setting Oasis apart from its competitors, and why?
- Should Oasis use ingredient branding to tout the Linux-based operating system that it says makes its PDA more secure than PDAs based on some other operating systems?
- How can Oasis use packaging and labeling to support its brand image and help its channel partners sell the PDA product more effectively?

Once you've answered these questions, incorporate your ideas into the marketing plan you've been writing or document them using the *Marketing Plan Pro* software.

Chapter 13

Abdallah Saif has asked you to work with Rami Khoder, Oasis Sales Manager, and his team on planning customer support services for Oasis's new PDA product. Review what you know about your target market and its needs; also think about what Oasis's competitors are offering. Then respond to these three questions about designing and managing services.

- What support services are buyers of PDA products likely to want and need?
- How can Oasis manage gaps between perceived service and expected service to satisfy customers?
- What postsale service arrangements must Oasis make and how would you expect these to affect customer satisfaction?

Consider how your service strategy will support Oasis's overall marketing efforts. Summarize your recommendations in a written marketing plan or use *Marketing Plan Pro* to document your ideas.

Chapter 14

You're in charge of pricing Oasis's product for its launch early next year. Review the strengths, weaknesses, opportunities, and threats (SWOT) analysis you previously prepared as well as Oasis's competitive environment, targeting strategy, and product positioning. Now continue working on your marketing plan by responding to the following questions.

- What should Oasis's primary pricing objective be? Explain your reasoning.
- Are PDA customers likely to be price sensitive? What are the implications for your pricing decisions?
- What price adaptations (such as discounts, allowances, and promotional pricing) should Oasis include in its marketing plan?

Make notes about your answers to these questions and then document the information in a written marketing plan or use *Marketing Plan Pro* software, depending on your instructor's directions.

Chapter 15

At Oasis, you have been asked to develop a marketing channel system for the new Oasis 1000 PDA. Based on what you know about designing and managing integrated marketing channels, answer the three questions that follow.

- Do you agree with Abdallah Saif's decision to use a push strategy for the new product? Explain your reasoning.
- How many channel levels are appropriate for Oasis's targeted consumer and business segments?
- In determining the number of channel members, should you use exclusive, selective, or intensive distribution? Why?

Be sure your marketing channel ideas support the product positioning and are consistent with the goals that have been set. Record your recommendations in a written marketing plan or use *Marketing Plan Pro*.

Chapter 16

At this point, you need to make more specific decisions about managing the marketing intermediaries for Oasis's first product. Formulate your ideas by answering the following questions.

- What types of retailers would be most appropriate for distributing Oasis's PDA? What are the advantages and disadvantages of selling through these types of retailers?
- What role should wholesalers play in Oasis's distribution strategy? Why?
- What market-logistics issues must Oasis consider for the launch of its first PDA?

Summarize your decisions about retailing, wholesaling, and logistics in the marketing plan you've been writing or in the *Marketing Plan Pro* software.

Chapter 17

Abdallah Saif has assigned you to work with Lina Manna and Mohamad Chehab to plan integrated marketing communications for Oasis's new product introduction. Review the data, decisions, and strategies you previously documented in your marketing plan before you answer the next three questions.

- What communications objectives are appropriate for Oasis's initial campaign?
- How can Oasis use personal communications channels to influence its target audience?
- Which communication tools would you recommend using after Oasis's initial product has been in the market for 6 months? Why?

Confirm that your marketing communications plans make sense in light of Oasis's overall marketing efforts. Now, as your instructor directs, summarize your thoughts in a written marketing plan or in the *Marketing Plan Pro* software.

Chapter 18

Mass communications will play a key role in Oasis's product introduction. After reviewing your earlier decisions and thinking about the current situation (especially your competitive circumstances), respond to the following questions to continue planning Oasis's marketing communications strategy.

- Once Oasis begins to use consumer advertising, what goals would be appropriate?
- Should Oasis continue consumer and trade sales promotion after the new product has been in the market for 6 months? Explain your reasoning.
- Abdallah Saif wants you to recommend an event sponsorship possibility that would be appropriate for the new product campaign. What type of event would you suggest and what objectives would you set for the sponsorship?

Record your ideas about mass communications in the marketing plan you've been writing or use *Marketing Plan Pro*.

Chapter 19

Oasis needs a strategy for managing personal communications during its new product launch. This is the time to look at interactive marketing, word-of-mouth, and personal selling. Answer these three questions as you consider Oasis's personal communications strategy.

- Which forms of interactive marketing are appropriate for Oasis, given its objectives, mass communications arrangements, and channel decisions?
- How should Oasis use word-of-mouth to generate brand awareness and encourage potential buyers to visit retailers to see the new PDA in person?
- Does Oasis need a direct sales force or can it sell through agents and other outside representatives?

Look back at earlier decisions and ideas before you document your comments about personal communications in your written marketing plan or using *Marketing Plan Pro* software.

Chapter 20

Knowing that the PDA market isn't growing as quickly as the market for multimedia, multifunction communication devices, Abdallah Saif wants you to look ahead at how Oasis can develop new products outside the PDA market. Review the competitive situation and the market situation before you continue working on the Oasis marketing plan.

- List three new-product ideas that build on Oasis's strengths and the needs of its various target segments. What criteria should Oasis use to screen these ideas?
- Develop the most promising idea into a product concept and explain how Oasis can test this concept. What particular dimensions must be tested?
- Assume that the most promising idea tests well. Now develop a marketing strategy for introducing it, including: a description of the target market; the product positioning; the estimated sales, profit, and market share goals for the first year; your channel strategy; and the marketing budget you recommend for this new product introduction. If possible, estimate Oasis's costs and conduct a breakeven analysis.

Document all the details of your new-product development ideas in the written marketing plan or use *Marketing Plan Pro* software.

Chapter 21

As Abdallah Saif's assistant, you're researching how to market the Oasis 1000 PDA product in the Arab Maghreb countries, and possibly the European countries of the Mediterranean basin, within a year. You've been asked to answer the following questions about Oasis's use of global marketing.

- As a start-up company, should Oasis use indirect or direct exporting, licensing, joint ventures, or direct investment to enter the Arab Maghreb market next year? And to enter other markets in the Mediterranean basin? Explain your answers.
- If Oasis starts marketing its PDA in other countries, which of the international product strategies is most appropriate? Why?
- Oasis is an Arab technology and telecommunication company. Its PDAs have components from Europe (Germany, Sweden, and Finland) and the Far East (China, Korea, Indonesia, Malaysia, and Taiwan). Oasis's PDAs will be assembled in Turkey through a contractual arrangement with a local Turkish factory (Technik). How are country-of-origin perceptions likely to affect your marketing recommendations?

Think about how these global marketing issues fit into Oasis's overall marketing strategy. Now document your ideas in the marketing plan you've been writing or using *Marketing Plan Pro*.

Chapter 22

With the rest of the marketing plan in place, you're ready to make recommendations about how to manage Oasis's marketing activities. Here are some specific questions Abdallah Saif wants you to consider.

- How can Oasis drive customer-focused marketing and strategic innovation throughout the organization?
- What role should social responsibility play in Oasis's marketing?
- How can Oasis evaluate its marketing? Suggest several specific steps the company should take.

To complete your marketing plan, enter your answers to these questions in the written marketing plan or in *Marketing Plan Pro* software. Finally, draft the executive summary of the plan's highlights.

Endnotes

Chapter 1

1. See www.a-arabiata.com.
2. The Conference Board, "The CEO Challenge 2006 – Top Ten Challenges," Research Report R-1380-05-RR, 2006.
3. "New Xerox Printer Offers Businesses of All Size High-impact Color Printing at Low Cost," www.ameinfo.com/175046.html.
4. "Xerox Hosts Its Annual Partner Conference in Dubai Reflecting the Growing Importance of the MEA Region," www.ameinfo.com/180467.html.
5. Peter Drucker, *Management: Tasks, Responsibilities, Practices* (New York: Harper and Row, 1973), pp. 64–65.
6. S. Pearlstein, "Davos Shows Us the Instability of a Tri-partite Global Economy," *Washington Post*, January 29, 2011, www.washingtonpost.com/wp-dyn/content/article/2011/01/29/AR2011012903424.html.
7. Irving J. Rein, Philip Kotler, and Martin Stoller, *High Visibility* (Chicago: NTC Publishers, 1998).
8. Philip Kotler, Irving J. Rein, and Donald H. Haider, *Marketing Places: Attracting Investment, Industry, and Tourism to Cities, States, and Nations* (New York: Free Press, 1993); and Philip Kotler, Christer Asplund, Irving Rein, and Donald H. Haider, *Marketing Places in Europe: Attracting Investment, Industry and Tourism to Cities, States and Nations* (London: Financial Times Prentice-Hall, 1999).
9. See www.hsbcamanah.com.
10. Carl Shapiro and Hal R. Varian, "Versioning: The Smart Way to Sell Information," *Harvard Business Review*, November–December 1998, pp. 106–114.
11. John R. Brandt, "Dare to Be Different," *Chief Executive*, May 2003, pp. 34–38.
12. Jeffrey Rayport and John Sviokla, "Managing in the Marketspace," *Harvard Business Review*, November–December 1994, pp. 141–150. Also see their "Exploring the Virtual Value Chain," *Harvard Business Review*, November–December 1995, pp. 75–85.
13. Constantine von Hoffman, "Armed With Intelligence," *Brandweek*, May 29, 2006, pp. 17–20.
14. Lara Lynn Golden, "Mashreq 'Opens the Way' with the Latest Mortgage Solutions," *AMEinfo.com*, May 28, 2007, www.ameinfo.com/121622.html.
15. Richard Rawlinson, "Beyond Brand Management," *Strategy+Business*, Summer 2006.
16. Gail McGovern and John A. Quelch, "The Fall and Rise of the CMO," *Strategy+Business*, Winter 2004.
17. Adam Lashinsky, "Shoutout in Gadget Land," *Fortune*, November 10, 2003, pp. 77–86.
18. "2005 Marketing Receptivity Survey," Yankelovich Partners, Inc., April 18, 2005; Deborah J. Webb, Lois A. Mohr, Katherine E. Harris, "A Re-examination of Socially Responsible Consumption and Its Measurement," *Journal of Business Research*, 61, 2008, pp. 91–98.
19. "MAC Cosmetics Dubai," Dubai FAQs, www.dubaifaqs.net/mac-cosmetics-dubai.html.
20. Danielle Sacks, "MAC Cosmetics Inc.," *Fast Company*, September 2006, p. 62.
21. David Kiley, "Advertisers, Start Your Engines," *BusinessWeek*, March 6, 2006, p. 26.
22. Anya Kamenetz, "The Network Unbound," *Fast Company*, June 2006, pp. 69–73.
23. Bruce Einhorn, "Mad as Hell in China's Blogosphere," *BusinessWeek*, August 14, 2006, p. 39.
24. Laura Mazur, "Personal Touch is Now Crucial to Growing Profits," *Marketing*, November 27, 2003, p. 18.
25. Kenneth Hein, "Marketers Map Out Their GPS Ad Plans," *Brandweek*, April 24, 2006, p. 4.
26. Suzanne Vranica, "Marketers Aim New Ads at Video iPod Users," *Wall Street Journal*, January 31, 2006; Li Yuan and Brian Steinberg, "Sales Call: More Ads Hit Cellphone Screens," *Wall Street Journal*, February 2, 2006, p. B3.
27. Bruce Horovitz, "In Trend Toward Vanity Food, It's Getting Personal," *USA Today*, August 9, 2006.
28. Stanley Holmes, "Into the Wild Blog Yonder," *BusinessWeek*, May 22, 2006, pp. 84–85.
29. "Aramex CEO Takes Care of His Customers on Twitter," blog post, http://kermittheblog.net/aramex-ceo-takes-care-of-his-customers-on-twitter.
30. Gerry Khermouch, "Breaking into the Name Game," *BusinessWeek*, April 7, 2003, p. 54; Anonymous, "China's Challenge," *Marketing Week*, October 2, 2003, pp. 22–24.
31. Bruce I. Newman, ed., *Handbook of Political Marketing* (Thousand Oaks, CA: Sage Publications, 1999); and Bruce I. Newman, *The Mass Marketing of Politics* (Thousand Oaks, CA: Sage Publications, 1999).
32. John B. McKitterick, "What Is the Marketing Management Concept?," In Frank M. Bass ed., *The Frontiers of Marketing Thought and Action* (Chicago: American Marketing Association, 1957), pp. 71–82; Fred J. Borch, "The Marketing Philosophy as a Way of Business Life," *The Marketing Concept: Its Meaning to Management* (Marketing Series, no. 99) (New York: American Management Association, 1957), pp. 3–5; Robert J. Keith, "The Marketing Revolution," *Journal of Marketing*, January 1960, pp. 35–38.
33. Levitt, "Marketing Myopia," *Harvard Business Review*, July–August 1960, p. 50.
34. Ajay K. Kohli and Bernard J. Jaworski, "Market Orientation: The Construct, Research Propositions, and Managerial Implications," *Journal of Marketing*, April 1990, pp. 1–18; John C. Narver and Stanley F. Slater, "The Effect of a Market Orientation on Business Profitability," *Journal of Marketing*, October 1990, pp. 20–35; Rohit Deshpande and John U. Farley, "Measuring Market Orientation: Generalization and Synthesis," *Journal of Market-Focused Management*, 2, 1998, pp. 213–232.
35. John C. Narver, Stanley F. Slater, and Douglas L. MacLachlan, "Responsive and Proactive Market

Orientation and New-Product Success," *Journal of Product Innovation Management*, 21, no. 5, September 2004, pp. 334–347. See also, Ken Matsuno and John T. Mentzer, "The Effects of Strategy Type on the Market Orientation–Performance Relationship," *Journal of Marketing*, October 2000, pp. 1–16.

36. Evert Gummesson, *Total Relationship Marketing* (Boston: Butterworth-Heinemann, 1999); Regis McKenna, *Relationship Marketing* (Reading, MA: Addison-Wesley, 1991); Martin Christopher, Adrian Payne, and David Ballantyne, *Relationship Marketing: Bringing Quality*, *Customer Service*, *and Marketing Together* (Oxford, Butterworth-Heinemann, 1991).

37. James C. Anderson, Hakan Hakansson, and Jan Johanson, "Dyadic Business Relationships within a Business Network Context," *Journal of Marketing*, October 15, 1994, pp. 1–15.

38. "National Bank of Kuwait Enhances Customer Experience Through Online Initiative," case study, www.microsoft .com/middleeast/press/casestudy/nbk.mspx.

39. Neil H. Borden, "The Concept of the Marketing Mix," *Journal of Advertising Research*, 4, June, pp. 2–7. For another framework, see George S. Day, "The Capabilities of Market-Driven Organizations," *Journal of Marketing*, 58, no. 4, October 1994, pp. 37–52.

40. E. Jerome McCarthy and William D. Perreault, *Basic Marketing: A Global-Managerial Approach*, 14th edn (Homewood, IL: McGraw-Hill Irwin, 2002).

41. Chekitan S. Dev and Don E. Schultz, "A Customer-Focused Approach Can Bring the Current Marketing Mix into the 21st Century," *Marketing Management*, 14, January/February 2005.

42. Christian Homburg, John P. Workman Jr., and Harley Krohmen, "Marketings Influence Within the Firm," *Journal of Marketing*, January 1999, pp. 1–15.

43. Samar Farah, "Future Tense," Editorial, *CMO Magazine*, May 2005.

44. "Etisalat Signs Strategic MOU with Health Authority-Abu Dhabi (HAAD) to Jointly Develop Innovative m-Health and e-Health Services," 2011, www.etisalat.ae/index.jsp ?lang=en&type=content&currentid=10c8e15c0b56a010 VgnVCM1000000a0a0a0a_____&contentid=aa59ad405f5 a0310VgnVCM1000000c24a8c0RCRD&parentid=fa588 00d1f52a010VgnVCM1000000a0a0a0a)_.

45. Eman Hassan, "The Arab World's First Defensive Driving Academy Opens at Jeddah Raceway," *AMEinfo.com*, November 11, 2008, www.ameinfo.com/175260.html.

46. Hamish Pringle and Marjorie Thompson, *Brand Soul: How Cause-Related Marketing Builds Brands* (New York: John Wiley & Sons, 1999); Richard Earle, *The Art of Cause Marketing* (Lincolnwood, IL: NTC, 2000).

47. Jeffrey Hollender and Stephen Fenichell, *What Matters Most* (Basic Books, 2004), p. 168.

48. Jonathan Glancey, "The Private World of the Walkman," *The Guardian*, October 11, 1999.

49. Joann Muller, "Ford: Why It's Worse Than You Think," *BusinessWeek*, June 25, 2001; Ford *1999 Annual Report*;

Greg Keenan, "Six Degrees of Perfection," *The Globe and Mail*, December 20, 2000.

50. "Social Media Expert Calls for More Native Arabic Content on the Web, Which Is Now "Just 1.4%," *AMEinfo. com*, June 27, 2010, www.ameinfo.com/232671.html.

Chapter 2

1. See www.emirates.com.

2. Nirmalya Kumar, *Marketing As Strategy: The CEO's Agenda for Driving Growth and Innovation* (Boston: Harvard Business School Press, 2004).

3. Frederick E. Webster Jr., "The Future Role of Marketing in the Organization," in *Reflections on the Futures of Marketing*, ed. Donald R. Lehmann and Katherine Jocz (Cambridge, MA: Marketing Science Institute, 1997), pp. 39–66.

4. Michael E. Porter, *Competitive Advantage: Creating and Sustaining Superior Performance* (New York: Free Press, 1985).

5. Robert Hiebeler, Thomas B. Kelly, and Charles Ketteman, *Best Practices: Building Your Business with Customer-Focused Solutions* (New York: Simon and Schuster, 1998).

6. "About Us: TE Data," www.tedata.net/eg/en/About-Us/ About-Corporate.

7. Michael Hammer and James Champy, *Reengineering the Corporation: A Manifesto for Business Revolution* (New York: Harper Business, 1993).

8. Ibid.; Jon R. Katzenbach and Douglas K. Smith, *The Wisdom of Teams: Creating the High-Performance Organization* (Boston: Harvard Business School Press, 1993).

9. C. K. Prahalad and Gary Hamel, "The Core Competence of the Corporation," *Harvard Business Review*, May–June 1990, pp. 79–91.

10. George S. Day, "The Capabilities of Market-Driven Organizations," *Journal of Marketing*, October 1994, p. 38.

11. George S. Day and Paul J. H. Schoemaker, *Peripheral Vision: Detecting the Weak Signals That Will Make or Break Your Company* (Cambridge, MA: Harvard Business School Press, 2006).

12. "Kodak Plans to Cut Up to 5,000 More Jobs," *Bloomberg News*, February 8, 2007; Leon Lazaroff, "Kodak's Big Picture Focusing on Image Change," *Chicago Tribune*, January 29, 2006.

13. Pew Internet and American Life Project Survey, November–December 2000.

14. Kasuaki Ushikubo, "A Method of Structure Analysis for Developing Product Concepts and Its Applications," *European Research*, 14, no. 4, 1986, pp. 174–175.

15. Yoram J. Wind and Vijay Mahajan with Robert E. Gunther, *Convergence Marketing: Strategies for Reaching the New Hybrid Consumer* (Upper Saddle River, NJ: Prentice Hall PTR, 2002).

16. Peter Drucker, *Management: Tasks*, *Responsibilities and Practices* (New York: Harper and Row, 1973), Chapter 7.

17. Ralph A. Oliva, "Nowhere to Hide," *Marketing Management*, July/August 2001, pp. 44–46.

18. Rima Ali Al Mashni, "90% of Companies Re-Focusing on Core Competencies: Ernst and Young," *AMEinfo.com*, October 21, 2009, www.ameinfo.com/213266.html.

19. Pew Internet and American Life Project Survey, November–December 2000.

20. Google company website, www.google.com/about/corporate/company/index.html

21. Jeffrey F. Rayport and Bernard J. Jaworski, *e-commerce* (New York: McGraw-Hill, 2001), p. 116.

22. This section is based on Chapter 16 of Robert M. Grant's, *Contemporary Strategy Analysis*, 5th edn (Malden, MA: Blackwell Publishing, 2005).

23. The same matrix can be expanded into nine cells by adding modified products and modified markets. See S. J. Johnson and Conrad Jones, "How to Organize for New Products," *Harvard Business Review*, May–June 1957, pp. 49–62.

24. http://www.londonstockexchange.com/companies-and-advisors/news-events/capital-markets-events/past-capital-markets-days/saudi-arabia/almarai.pdf

25. "The Consumer-Centric Marketer as Guru of Exponential Growth: Kelly Styring," *KNOW*, Spring/Summer 2006; www._knowledgenetworks._com.

26. Jena McGregor, "The World's Most Innovative Companies," *BusinessWeek*, April 24, 2006, pp. 63–74.

27. E. Jerome McCarthy, *Basic Marketing: A Managerial Approach*, 12th edn (Homewood, IL: Irwin, 1996).

28. DevPatnaik, "Insight," *BusinessWeek* (June 2006): 32.

29. Paul J. H. Shoemaker, "Scenario Plannning: A Tool for Strategic Thinking," *Sloan Management Review*, Winter 1995, pp. 25–40.

30. Philip Kotler, *Kotler on Marketing* (New York: Free Press, 1999).

31. Ibid.

32. Information from company website, www.orientory.com/egynet.

33. Dominic Dodd and Ken Favaro, "Managing the Right Tension," *Harvard Business Review*, December 2006, pp. 62–74.

34. Ram Charan and Noel M. Tichy, *Every Business Is a Growth Business: How Your Company Can Prosper Year after Year* (New York: Times Business, Random House, 1998).

35. Michael E. Porter, *Competitive Strategy: Techniques for Analyzing Industries and Competitors* (New York: Free Press, 1980), Chapter 2.

36. "Company Details: Ghadeer Mineral Water, Nestlé Waters in Jordan," www.bayt.com/en/company/?xid=70449 and http://www.epha.eg.net/pdf/n5-6-2008/9-Magda-bottled%20water_Final2.pdf.

37. Michael E. Porter, "What Is Strategy?," *Harvard Business Review*, November–December 1996, pp. 61–78.

38. For some readings on strategic alliances, see John R. Harbison and Peter Pekar, *Smart Alliances: A Practical Guide to Repeatable Success* (San Francisco, CA: Jossey-Bass, 1998); Peter Lorange and Johan Roos, *Strategic Alliances: Formation, Implementation and Evolution* (Cambridge, MA: Blackwell, 1992); Jordan D. Lewis, *Partnerships for Profit: Structuring and Managing Strategic Alliances* (New York: Free Press, 1990).

39. Robin Cooper and Robert S. Kalpan, "Profit Priorities from Activity-Based Costing," *Harvard Business Review*, May–June 1991, pp. 130–135.

40. See Robert S. Kaplan and David P. Norton, *The Balanced Scorecard: Translating Strategy into Action* (Boston: Harvard Business School Press, 1996) as a tool for monitoring stakeholder satisfaction.

41. Thomas J. Peters and Robert H. Waterman Jr., *In Search of Excellence: Lessons from America's Best-Run Companies* (New York: Harper and Row, 1982), pp. 9–12.

42. John P. Kotter and James L. Heskett, *Corporate Culture and Performance* (New York: Free Press, 1992); Stanley M. Davis, *Managing Corporate Culture* (Cambridge, MA: Ballinger, 1984); Terrence E. Deal and Allan A. Kennedy, *Corporate Cultures: The Rites and Rituals of Corporate Life* (Reading, MA: Addison-Wesley, 1982); "Corporate Culture," *BusinessWeek*, October 27, 1980, pp. 148–160.

43. Nitin Nohria, William Joyce, and Bruce Roberson, "What Really Works," *Harvard Business Review* 81, no. 7, 2003, pp. 42–53.

44. Marian Burk Wood, *The Marketing Plan: A Handbook* (Upper Saddle River, NJ: Prentice Hall, 2003).

45. Donald R. Lehmann and Russell S. Winer, *Product Management*, 3rd edn (Boston: McGraw-Hill/Irwin, 2001).

Chapter 3

1. All quotes come from the following source: "A Rich Inheritance," reported by Hani Bathiche, Nour Nasser, and Soha Yammine, ed. Hugh MacLeod, *Lebanon Opportunities*, May 2010, pp. 68–87.

2. "The World's Largest Consumers," http://factoidz.com/the-worlds-largest-consumers.

3. A. Mukund, "Cisco Systems – The Supply Chain Story," ICFAI Center for Management Research, 2003, www.icmrindia.org.

4. Charles Babcock, "Data, Data Everywhere," *InformationWeek*, January 9, 2006.

5. Charles Fishman, "The Wal-Mart You Don't Know," *Fast Company*, December 2003, pp. 68–80.

6. Mara Der Hovanesian, "Wells Fargo," *BusinessWeek*, November 24, 2004, p. 96.

7. Sara Steindorf, "Shoppers Spy on Those Who Serve," *Christian Science Monitor*, May 28, 2002; Edward F. McQuarrie, *Customer Visits: Building a Better Market Focus*, 2nd edn (Newbury Park, CA: Sage Press, 1998).

8. Julie Forster, "You Deserve a Better Break Today," *BusinessWeek*, September 30, 2002, p. 42.

9. Shirley S. Wang, "Heath Care Taps 'Mystery Shoppers'," *Wall Street Journal*, August 10, 2006.

10. "The National Bank of Abu Dhabi Strengthen Their Strategy of Putting Customers First by Implementing the First Real-Time Mystery Shopping Program in the UAE," February 21, 2005, www.ameinfo.com/news/Detailed/54375.html.

11. American Productivity & Quality Center, "User-Driven Competitive Intelligence: Crafting the Value Proposition," December 3–4, 2002.

12. Data based on Apple press releases.

13. See www.badfads.com for examples of fads and collectibles through the years.

14. "Profiting from Consumer Mega-Trends in the UAE and Saudi Arabia: Health," *Data Monitor*, September 2009, www.reportlinker.com/p0151778/Profiting-From-Consumer-Mega-Trends-in-the-UAE-and-Saudi-Arabia-Health.html.

15. John Naisbitt and Patricia Aburdene, *Megatrends 2000* (New York: Avon Books, 1990).

16. Steve Chazin, "The True Power of Great Marketing," *Marketing Apple*, March 14, 2010, www.marketingapple.com/marketing-apple/2010/03/the-true-power-of-great-marketing.html.

17. Philip Lam, "iPad Pre-Orders Hits 120,000 Units on First Day?," March 15, 2010, www.ipadinsider.com/ipad-pre-orders-hits-120000-units-on-first-day/.

18. See www.information-international.com.

19. Roy Greenslade, "Facebook Beats Newspapers in Arab World," *Guardian*, May 27, 2010, www.guardian.co.uk/media/greenslade/2010/may/27/facebook-newspapers.

20. World POPClock, U.S. Census Bureau, www.census.gov, May 2010.

21. Although over 15 years old, this breakdown provides useful perspective. See Donella H. Meadows, Dennis L. Meadows, and Jorgen Randers, *Beyond Limits* (White River Junction, VT: Chelsea Green, 1993) for some commentary.

22. "Unlocking the Employment Potential in the Middle East and North Africa," World Bank, 2004.

23. "Survey: Forever Young," *The Economist*, March 27, 2004, pp. 53–54.

24. "Unlocking the Employment Potential in the Middle East and North Africa," World Bank, 2004.

25. Ibid.

26. Jacquelyn Lynn, "Tapping the Riches of Bilingual Markets," *Management Review*, March 1995, pp. 56–61; Mark R. Forehand and Rohit Deshpandé, "What We See Makes Us Who We Are: Priming Ethnic Self-Awareness and Advertising Response," *Journal of Marketing Research*, August 2001, pp. 336–348.

27. "Magda Sami [a profile]," www.ashoka-arab.org/egypt/magda-sami.html.

28. *World Factbook*, Central Intelligence Agency www.cia.gov/library/publications/the-world-factbook/.

29. "Unlocking the Employment Potential in the Middle East and North Africa," World Bank, 2004.

30. Michelle Conlin, "Unmarried America," *BusinessWeek*, October 20, 2003, pp. 106–116; James Morrow, "A Place for One," *American Demographics*, November 2003, pp. 25–30.

31. "Unlocking the Employment Potential in the Middle East and North Africa," World Bank, 2004.

32. "Family Businesses and Private Equity," supplement, *Euromoney*, June 2005, pp. 10–11.

33. Stuart G. Makings, *Family Business Governance in the Middle East: the Challenges facing Continuity of Business in the Middle East* (Oxford: Oxford University Press, 2009).

34. Pamela Paul, "Corporate Responsibility," *American Demographics*, May 2002, pp. 24–25.

35. Stephen Baker, "Wiser about the Web," *BusinessWeek*, March 27, 2006, pp. 53–57.

36. "Clearing House Suit Chronology," *Associated Press*, January 26, 2001; Paul Wenske, "You Too Could Lose $19,000!" *Kansas City Star*, October 31, 1999.

37. Laura Zinn, "Teens: Here Comes the Biggest Wave Yet," *BusinessWeek*, April 11, 2004, pp. 76–86.

38. Clay Chandler, "Full Speed Ahead," *Fortune*, February 7, 2005, pp. 78–84; "What You Can Learn from Toyota," *Business 2.0*, January–February 2005, pp. 67–72; Keith Naughton, "Red, White, and Bold," *Newsweek*, April 25, 2005, pp. 34–36; Omar Obeidat, "Local Demand for Hybrid Cars on the Rise," *The Jordan Times*, July 27, 2011, www.jordantimes.com/?news=22586.

39. Rebecca Gardyn, "Eco-Friend or Foe," *American Demographics*, October 2003, pp. 12–13. See also Rebecca Gardyn, "Being Green," *American Demographics*, September 2002, pp. 10–11.

40. Subhabrata Bobby Banerjee, Easwar S. Iyer, and Rajiv K. Kashyap, "Corporate Environmentalism: Antecedents and Influence of Industry Type," *Journal of Marketing,* 67, April 2003, pp. 106–122.

41. "Internet Usage in the Middle East," Bayt.com; www.bayt.com.

42. *UNDP Arab Knowledge Report 2009,* www.mbrfoundation.ae/English/Documents/AKR-2009-En/AKR-English.pdf.

43. Ibid.

44. Nicholas Carlson, "Facebook Reached 150 Million Users 84 Years Faster Than The Telephone," *Business Insider*, February 20, 2009, www.businessinsider.com/facebook-reached-150-million-users-84-years-faster-than-the-telephone-2009-2.

45. See Dorothy Cohen, *Legal Issues on Marketing Decision Making* (Cincinnati: South-Western, 1995).

46. Rebecca Gardyn, "Swap Meet," *American Demographics*, July 2001, pp. 51–55.

47. Pamela Paul, "Mixed Signals," *American Demographics*, July 2001, pp. 45–49.

48. *Bloomberg Business Week*, Arab Edition, May 2010; see also www.agilitylogistics.com.

Chapter 4

1. Robert Hartley, "Cola Wars: Coca-Cola versus Pepsi," in *Marketing Mistakes and Successes* (Hoboken, NJ: Wiley, 2005).

2. See Robert Schieffer, *Ten Key Customer Insights: Unlocking the Mind of the Market* (Mason, OH: Thomson, 2005) for a comprehensive, in-depth discussion of how to generate customer insights to drive business results.

3. www.esomar.org/uploads/industry/reports/global-market-research-2011/ESOMAR-GMR-2011_Preview.pdf.

4. Melanie Haiken, "Tuned In to CrowdCasting," *Business 2.0*, November 2006, pp. 66–68.

5. "Would You Fly in Chattering Class?," *The Economist*, September 9, 2006, p. 63.

6. For some background information on in-flight internet services, see "Boeing In-Flight Internet Plan Goes Airborne," *The Associated Press*, April 18, 2004; John Blau, "In-Flight Internet Service Ready for Takeoff," *IDG News Service*, June 14, 2002; "In-Flight Dogfight," *Business2.Com*, January 9, 2001, pp. 84–91.

7. For a discussion of the decision-theory approach to the value of research, see Donald R. Lehmann, Sunil Gupta, and Joel Steckel, *Market Research* (Reading, MA: Addison-Wesley, 1997).

8. "Market Research Products," www.infopro.com.lb.

9. Linda Tischler, "Every Move You Make," *Fast Company*, April 2004, pp. 73–75; Allison Stein Wellner, "Look Who's Watching," *Continental*, April 2003, pp. 39–41.

10. For a detailed review of relevant academic work, see Eric J. Arnould and Amber Epp, "Deep Engagement with Consumer Experience," in *Handbook of Marketing Research*, ed. Rajiv Grover and Marco Vriens (Thousand Oaks, CA: Sage Publications, 2006). For a range of academic discussions, see the following special issue, "Can Ethnography Uncover Richer Consumer Insights?," *Journal of Advertising Research*, 46, September 2006. For some practical tips, see Richard Durante and Michael Feehan, "Leverage Ethnography to Improve Strategic Decision Making," *Marketing Research*, Winter 2005.

11. Eric J. Arnould and Linda L. Price, "Market-Oriented Ethnography Revisited," *Journal of Advertising Research*, 46, September 2006, pp. 251–262; Eric J. Arnould and Melanie Wallendorf, "Market-Oriented Ethnography: Interpretation Building and Marketing Strategy Formulation," *Journal of Marketing Research*, 31, November 1994, pp. 484–504.

12. "Case Study: Bank of America," Inside Innovation, *BusinessWeek*, June 19, 2006; Spencer E. Ante, "Inprogress," *IN*, June 2006, pp. 28–29.

13. Spencer E. Ante, "The Science of Desire," *BusinessWeek*, June 5, 2006, pp. 98–106.

14. "Qualitative and Online Safari," *TNS Consumer*, www.tnsglobal.com/pginnovation/qualitative.html.

15. See www.arabian-echo.com.

16. Eric Pfanner, "Agencies Look beyond Focus Groups to Spot Trends," *New York Times*, January 2, 2006.

17. Eric Schellhorn, "A Tsunami of Surveys Washes over Consumers," *The Christian Science Monitor*, October 2, 2006, p. 13.

18. Louise Witt, "Inside Intent," *American Demographics*, March 2004, pp. 34–39; Andy Raskin, "A Face Any Business Can Trust," *Business 2.0*, December 2003, pp. 58–60; Gerald Zaltman, "Rethinking Market Research: Putting People Back In," *Journal of Marketing Research*, 34, November 1997, pp. 424–437; Wally Wood, "The Race to Replace Memory," *Marketing and Media Decisions*, July 1986, pp. 166–167; Roger D. Blackwell, James S. Hensel, Michael B. Phillips, and Brian Sternthal, *Laboratory Equipment for Marketing Research* (Dubuque, IA: Kendall/Hunt, 1970).

19. Stephen Baker, "Wiser about the Web," *BusinessWeek*, March 27, 2006, pp. 54–62.

20. Kate Maddox, "The ROI of Research," *B to B*, pp. 25, 28.

21. Bradley Johnson, "Forget Phone and Mail: Online's the Best Place to Administer Surveys," *Advertising Age*, July 17, 2006, p. 23.

22. Deborah L. Vence, "In an Instant: More Researchers Use IM for Fast, Reliable Results," *Marketing News*, March 1, 2006, p. 53–55.

23. Catherine Arnold, "Global Perspective: Synovate Exec Discusses Future of International Research," *Marketing News*, May 15, 2004, p. 43; Michael Erard, "For Technology, No Small World after All," *New York Times*, May 6, 2004; Deborah L. Vence, "Global Consistency: Leave It to the Experts," *Marketing News*, April 28, 2003, p. 37.

24. ESOMAR Market Research Directory, http://directory.esomar.org/countries.php.

25. Michael Fielding, "Global Insights: Synovate's Chedore Discusses MR Trends," *Marketing News*, May 15, 2006, pp. 41–42.

26. Kevin J. Clancy and Peter C. Krieg, *Counterintuitive Marketing: How Great Results Come from Uncommon Sense* (New York: The Free Press, 2000).

27. See "Special Issue on Managerial Decision Making," *Marketing Science*, 18, no. 3, 1999, for some contemporary perspectives. See also John D. C. Little, "Decision Support Systems for Marketing Managers," *Journal of Marketing*, Summer 1979, pp. 11.

28. Leonard M. Lodish, "CALLPLAN: An Interactive Salesman's Call Planning System," *Management Science*, December 1971, pp. 25–40.

29. Rajiv Grover and Marco Vriens, "Trusted Advisor: How It Helps Lay the Foundation for Insight," in *Handbook of Marketing Research* (Thousand Oaks, CA: Sage Publications, 2006), pp. 3–17; Christine Moorman, Gerald Zaltman, and Rohit Deshpandé, "Relationships between Providers and Users of Market Research: The Dynamics of Trust within and between Organizations," *Journal of Marketing Research*, 29, August 1992, pp. 314–328.

30. Robert Shaw and David Merrick, *Marketing Payback: Is Your Marketing Profitable* (London: FT Prentice Hall, 2005).

31. John McManus, "Stumbling into Intelligence," *American Demographics*, April 2004, pp. 22–25.

32. Lisa Sanders, "Measuring ROI Eludes Half of Top Marketers," *Marketing News*, July 7, 2006, p. 4.

33. Tim Ambler, *Marketing and the Bottom Line: The New Metrics of Corporate Wealth* (London: FT Prentice Hall, 2000).

34. Paul Farris, Neil T. Bendle, Phillip E. Pfeifer, and David J. Reibstein, *Marketing Metrics: 50+ Metrics Every Executive Should Master* (Upper Saddle River, NJ: Pearson Education, 2006); John Davis, *Magic Numbers for Consumer Marketing: Key Measures to Evaluate Marketing Success* (Singapore: John Wiley & Sons, 2005).

35. Bob Donath, "Employ Marketing Metrics with a Track Record," *Marketing News*, September 15, 2003, p. 12.

36. Ambler, *Marketing and the Bottom Line*.

37. Kusum L. Ailawadi, Donald R. Lehmann, and Scott A. Neslin, "Revenue Premium as an Outcome Measure of Brand Equity," *Journal of Marketing*, 67, October 2003, pp. 1–17.

38. Ambler, *Marketing and the Bottom Line*.

39. Gerard J. Tellis, "Modeling Marketing Mix," in *Handbook of Marketing Research*, ed. Rajiv Grover and Marco Vriens (Thousand Oaks, CA: Sage Publications, 2006).

40. Jack Neff, "P&G, Clorox Rediscover Modeling," *Advertising Age*, March 29, 2004, p. 10.

41. Laura Q. Hughes, "Econometrics Take Root," *Advertising Age*, August 5, 2002, p. S-4.

42. David J. Reibstein, "Connect the Dots," *CMO Magazine*, May 2005.

43. Jeff Zabin, "Marketing Dashboards: The Visual Display of Marketing Data," *Chief Marketer*, June 26, 2006, http://chiefmarketer.com/marketing_dashboards_06262006/?cid=dashboard.

44. Robert S. Kaplan and David P. Norton, *The Balanced Scorecard* (Boston: Harvard Business School Press, 1996).

45. Spencer Ante, "Giving the Boss the Big Picture," *BusinessWeek*, February 13, 2006, pp. 48–50.

46. For a good discussion and illustration, see Roger J. Best, *Market-Based Management*, 4th edn (Upper Saddle River, NJ: Prentice Hall, 2005).

47. Patrick Lapointe, "Marketing by the Dashboard Light: How to get More Insight, Foresight and Accountability from your Marketing Investments," (Michigan: Association of National Advertisers, 2005).

48. For further discussion, see Gary L. Lilien, Philip Kotler, and K. Sridhar Moorthy, *Marketing Models* (Upper Saddle River, NJ: Prentice Hall, 1992).

49. Stanley F. Slater and Eric M. Olson, "Mix and Match," *Marketing Management*, July–August 2006, pp. 32–37; Brian Sternthal and Alice M. Tybout, "Segmentation and Targeting," in *Kellogg on Marketing*, ed. Dawn Iacobucci (New York: John Wiley & Sons, 2001), pp. 3–30.

50. Bayt.com, *Middle East Consumer Confidence Index Report March 2010*, www.bayt.com.

51. For an excellent overview of market forecasting, see Scott Armstrong, ed., *Principles of Forecasting: A Handbook for Researchers and Practitioners* (Norwell, MA: Kluwer Academic Publishers, 2001); also see Roger J. Best, "An Experiment in Delphi Estimation in Marketing Decision Making," *Journal of Marketing Research*, November 1974, pp. 447–452; Norman Dalkey and Olaf Helmer, "An Experimental Application of the Delphi Method to the Use of Experts," *Management Science*, April 1963, pp. 458–467.

Chapter 5

1. www.ritzcarlton.com; www.brandkeys.com.

2. Robert Schieffer, *Ten Key Consumer Insights* (Mason, OH: Thomson, 2005).

3. Don Peppers and Martha Rogers, "Customers Don't Grow on Trees," *Fast Company*, July 2005, pp. 25–26.

4. Hammude, Faisal (2010), "Why Middle East Companies are not Developing Great Customer Service," *PR Log*, www.prlog.org/10908735-why-middle-east-companies-are-not-developing-great-customer-service.html.

5. For discussion of some of the issues involved, see Glen Urban, *Don't Just Relate—Advocate* (Upper Saddle River, NJ: Pearson Education Wharton School Publishing, 2005).

6. See Glen L. Urban and John R. Hauser, "'Listening In' to Find and Explore New Combinations of Customer Needs," *Journal of Marketing*, 68, April 2004, pp. 72–87.

7. Oliver Ryan, "Putting Your Customer to Work," *Fortune,* March 20, 2006, p. 30.

8. Deborah L. Vence, "Shopping Portal Moves Customer Surveys Online; Metrics Soar," *AMA Marketing News,* June 15, 2006, p. 9.

9. "Dubai Government Excellence Program Measures Customer Satisfaction," www.ameinfo.com/155305.html.

10. Glen L. Urban, "The Emerging Era of Customer Advocacy," *Sloan Management Review*, 45(2), 2004, pp. 77–82.

11. "HP Dell Lead PC Shipment as Tablets Cannibalization Begins," www.onlinemarketing-trends.com/2011/07/hp-dell-lead-netbooks-marketshare-as.html.

12. Steven Burke, "Dell's vs. HP's Value," *CRN,* May 15, 2006, p. 46; David Kirkpatrick, "Dell in the Penalty Box," *Fortune*, 154, no. 6, September 18, 2006, p. 70+.

13. Irwin P. Levin and Richard D. Johnson, "Estimating Price–Quality Tradeoffs Using Comparative Judgments," *Journal of Consumer Research*, June 11, 1984, pp. 593–600. Customer-perceived value can be measured as a difference or as a ratio. If total customer value is US$20,000 and total customer cost is $16,000, then the customer-perceived value is $4,000 (measured as a difference) or 1.25 (measured as a ratio). Ratios that are used to compare offers are often called *value–price ratios*.

14. For more on customer-perceived value, see David C. Swaddling and Charles Miller, *Customer Power* (Dublin, OH: The Wellington Press, 2001).

15. Richard L. Oliver, "Whence Consumer Loyalty?," *Journal of Marketing*, 63 (Special Issue), 1999, pp. 33–44.

16. Brand Keys Customer Loyalty Leaders 2010, www.brand-keys.com/awards/leaders.cfm.

17. Michael J. Lanning, *Delivering Profitable Value* (Oxford, UK: Capstone, 1998).

18. Vikas Mittal, Eugene W. Anderson, Akin Sayrak, and Pandu Tadilamalla, "Dual Emphasis and the Long-Term Financial Impact of Customer Satisfaction," *Marketing Science*, 24, Autumn 2005, pp. 544–555.

19. "Abu Dhabi International Airport named Best Airport in Middle East," June 2011, www.globaltransportforum.com/index.php/news/abu-dhabi-international-airport-named-best-airport-in-middle-east.

20. Michael Tsiros, Vikas Mittal, and William T. Ross Jr., "The Role of Attributions in Customer Satisfaction: A Reexamination," *Journal of Consumer Research*, 31, September 2004, pp. 476–483.

21. For a succinct review, see Richard L. Oliver, "Customer Satisfaction Research," in *Handbook of Marketing Research,* ed. Rajiv Grover and Marco Vriens (Thousand Oaks, CA: Sage Publications, 2006), pp. 569–587.

22. For some provocative analysis and discussion, see Praveen K. Kopalle and Donald R. Lehmann, "Setting Quality Expectations When Entering a Market: What Should the Promise Be?," *Marketing Science*, 25, January–February 2006, pp. 8–24; and Susan Fournier and David Glenmick, "Rediscovering Satisfaction," *Journal of Marketing*, October 1999, pp. 5–23.

23. Jennifer Aaker, Susan Fournier, and S. Adam Brasel, "When Good Brands Do Bad," *Journal of Consumer Research*, 31, June 2004, pp. 1–16; Pankaj Aggrawal, "The Effects of Brand Relationship Norms on Consumer Attitudes and Behavior," *Journal of Consumer Research*, 31, June 2004, pp. 87–101.

24. For in-depth discussion, see Michael D. Johnson and Anders Gustafsson, *Improving Customer Satisfaction, Loyalty, and Profit* (San Francisco: Josey-Bass, 2000).

25. For an interesting analysis of the effects of different types of expectations, see William Boulding, Ajay Kalra, and Richard Staelin, "The Quality Double Whammy," *Marketing Science*, 18, no. 4, April 1999, pp. 463–484.

26. Alice Z. Cuneo, "Magazines as Muses: Hotelier Finds Inspiration in Titles such as Wired," *Advertising Age*, November 6, 2006, p. 10.

27. As quoted in Neal Templin, "Boutique-Hotel Group Thrives on Quirks," *Wall Street Journal*, March 18, 1999.

28. As quoted in Clifford Carlsen, "Joie de Vivre Resorts to New Hospitality Strategy," *San Francisco Business Times*, June 18, 1999.

29. Neil A. Morgan, Eugene W. Anderson, and Vikas Mittal, "Understanding Firms' Customer Satisfaction Information Usage," *Journal of Marketing*, 69, July 2005, pp. 131–151.

30. "The Mystery Shopper," *Jordan Business*, www.jordan-business.net/magazine/index.php?option=com_content&task=view&id=273&Itemid=40.

31. Although for moderating factors, see Kathleen Seiders, Glenn B. Voss, Dhruv Grewal, and Andrea L. Godfrey, "Do Satisfied Customers Buy More? Examining Moderating Influences in a Retailing Context," *Journal of Marketing*, 69, October 2005, pp. 26–43.

32. See, for example, Christian Homburg, Nicole Koschate, and Wayne D. Hoyer, "Do Satisfied Customers Really Pay More? A Study of the Relationship between Customer Satisfaction and Willingness to Pay," *Journal of Marketing*, 69, April 2005, pp. 84–96.

33. Claes Fornell, Sunil Mithas, Forrest V. Morgeson III, and M. S. Krishnan, "Customer Satisfaction and Stock Prices: High Returns, Low Risk," *Journal of Marketing*, 70, January 2006, pp. 3–14. See also, Thomas S. Gruca and Lopo L. Rego, "Customer Satisfaction, Cash Flow, and Shareholder Value," *Journal of Marketing*, 69, July 2005, pp. 115–130; Eugene W. Anderson, Claes Fornell, and Sanal K. Mazvancheryl, "Customer Satisfaction and Shareholder Value," *Journal of Marketing*, 68, October 2004, pp. 172–185.

34. Thomas O. Jones and W. Earl Sasser Jr., "Why Satisfied Customers Defect," *Harvard Business Review*, November–December 1995, pp. 88–99.

35. Companies should also note that managers and salespeople can manipulate customer satisfaction ratings. They can be especially nice to customers just before the survey. They can also try to exclude unhappy customers. Another danger is that if customers know the company will go out of its way to please them, some may express high dissatisfaction in order to receive more concessions.

36. Anne Chen, "Customer Feedback Key for Theme Park: Inquisite Lets Visitors Sound Off," *eWeek*, December 15, 2003, p. 58.

37. James C. Ward and Amy L. Ostrom, "Complaining to the Masses: The Role of Protest Framing in Customer-Created Complaint Sites," *Journal of Consumer Research*, 33, September 2006, pp. 220–230; Kim Hart, "Angry Customers Use Web to Shame Firms," *Washington Post*, July 5, 2006.

38. "Le Pacha 1901 Wins Best Restaurant in Egypt Excellence Award," http://lepacha.com/news.php/.

39. Eugene W. Anderson and Claes Fornell, "Foundations of the American Customer Satisfaction Index," *Total Quality Management*, 11, no. 7, September 2000, pp. S869–S882; Claes Fornell, Michael D. Johnson, Eugene W. Anderson, Jaaesung Cha, and Barbara Everitt Bryant, "The American Customer Satisfaction Index: Nature, Purpose, and Findings," *Journal of Marketing*, October 1996, pp. 7–18.

40. Technical Assistance Research Programs (Tarp), *U.S. Office of Consumer Affairs Study on Complaint Handling in America*, 1986.

41. Stephen S. Tax and Stephen W. Brown, "Recovering and Learning from Service Failure," *Sloan Management Review*, 40, no. 1, Autumn 1998, pp. 75–88; Ruth Bolton and Tina M. Bronkhorst, "The Relationship between Customer Complaints to the Firm and Subsequent Exit Behavior," in *Advances in Consumer Research*, vol. 22 (Provo, UT: Association for Consumer Research, 1995), pp. unknown; Roland T. Rust, Bala Subramanian, and Mark Wells, "Making Complaints a Management Tool," *Marketing Management*, 1, no. 3, March 1992, pp. 40–45; Karl Albrecht and Ron Zemke, *Service America!* (Homewood, IL: Dow Jones-Irwin, 1985), pp. 6–7.

42. Christian Homburg and Andreas Fürst, "How Organizational Complaint Handling Drives Customer Loyalty: An Analysis of the Mechanistic and the Organic Approach," *Journal of Marketing*, 69, July 2005, pp. 95–114.

43. Philip Kotler, *Kotler on Marketing* (New York: The Free Press, 1999), pp. 21–22.

44. Cyndee Miller, "U.S. Firms Lag in Meeting Global Quality Standards," *Marketing News*, February 15, 1993.

45. Roland R. Rust, Anthony J. Zahorik, and Timothy L. Keiningham, "Return on Quality (ROQ): Making

Service Quality Financially Accountable," *Journal of Marketing*, 59, no. 2, April 1995, pp. 58–70; "Quality: The U.S. Drives to Catch Up," *BusinessWeek*, November 1, 1982, pp. 66–80.

46. Robert D. Buzzell and Bradley T. Gale, *The PIMS Principles: Linking Strategy to Performance* (New York: The Free Press, 1987), Chapter 6 (PIMS stands for Profit Impact of Market Strategy).

47. Brian Hindo, "Satisfaction Not Guaranteed," *BusinessWeek*, June 19, 2006, pp. 32–36.

48. Lerzan Aksoy, Timothy L. Keiningham, and Terry G. Vavra, "Nearly Everything You Know about Loyalty Is Wrong," *Marketing News*, October 1, 2005, p. 20–21; Timothy L. Keiningham, Terry G. Vavra, Lerzan Aksoy, and Henri Wallard, *Loyalty Myths* (Hoboken, NJ: John Wiley & Sons, 2005).

49. Werner J. Reinartz and V. Kumar, "The Impact of Customer Relationship Characteristics on Profitable Lifetime Duration," *Journal of Marketing*, 67, January 2003, pp. 77–99; Werner J. Reinartz and V. Kumar, "On the Profitability of Long-Life Customers in a Noncontractual Setting: An Empirical Investigation and Implications for Marketing," *Journal of Marketing*, 64, October 2000, pp. 17–35.

50. Rakesh Niraj, Mahendra Gupta, and Chakravarthi Narasimhan, "Customer Profitability in a Supply Chain," *Journal of Marketing*, July 2001, pp. 1–16.

51. Thomas M. Petro, "Profitability: The Fifth 'P' of Marketing," *Bank Marketing*, September 1990, pp. 48–52; "Who Are Your Best Customers?," *Bank Marketing*, October 1990, pp. 48–52.

52. Michael D. Johnson, and Fred Selnes, "Diversifying Your Customer Portfolio," *MIT Sloan Management Review*, 46, no. 3, Spring 2005, pp. 11–14.

53. Michael D. Johnson, and Fred Selnes, "Customer Portfolio Management," *Journal of Marketing*, 68, no. 2, April 2004, pp. 1–17.

54. Ravi Dhar and Rashi Glazer, "Hedging Customers," *Harvard Business Review*, May 2003, pp. 86–92.

55. V. Kumar, "Customer Lifetime Value," in *Handbook of Marketing Research*, ed. Rajiv Grover and Marco Vriens (Thousand Oaks, CA: Sage Publications, 2006), pp. 602–627; Sunil Gupta, Donald R. Lehmann, and Jennifer Ames Stuart, "Valuing Customers," *Journal of Marketing Research*, 61, February 2004, pp. 7–18; Rajkumar Venkatesan and V. Kumar, "A Customer Lifetime Value Framework for Customer Selection and Resource Allocation Strategy," *Journal of Marketing*, 68, October 2004, pp. 106–125.

56. V. Kumar, "Profitable Relationships," *Marketing Research*, 18, Autumn 2006, pp. 41–46.

57. For some recent analysis and discussion, see Michael Haenlein, Andreas M. Kaplan, and Detlef Schoder, "Valuing the Real Option of Abandoning Unprofitable Customers When Calculating Customer Lifetime Value," *Journal of Marketing*, 70, July 2006, pp. 5–20; Teck-Hua Ho, Young-Hoon Park, and Yong-Pin Zhou, "Incorporating Satisfaction into Customer Value Analysis: Optimal Investment in Lifetime Value," *Marketing Science*, 25, May–June 2006, pp. 260–277; and Peter S. Fader, Bruce G. S. Hardie, and Ka Lok Lee, "RFM and CLV: Using Iso-Value Curves for Customer Base Analysis," *Journal of Marketing Research*, 62, November 2005, pp. 415–430.

58. Nicole E. Coviello, Roderick J. Brodie, Peter J. Danaher, and Wesley J. Johnston, "How Firms Relate to Their Markets: An Empirical Examination of Contemporary Marketing Practices," *Journal of Marketing*, 66, July 2002, pp. 33–46.

59. For an up-to-date view of academic perspectives, see the articles contained in the Special Section on Customer Relationship Management, *Journal of Marketing*, 69, October 2005. For a study of the processes involved, see Werner Reinartz, Manfred Kraft, and Wayne D. Hoyer, "The Customer Relationship Management Process: Its Measurement and Impact on Performance," *Journal of Marketing Research*, 61, August 2004, pp. 293–305.

60. Nora A. Aufreiter, David Elzinga, and Jonathan W. Gordon, "Better Branding," *The McKinsey Quarterly*, 4, 2003, pp. 29–39.

61. Eric Krell, "The 6 Most Overlooked Customer Touch Points," *Customer Relationship Management*, 9, no. 1, January 2005, p. 40+.

62. Michael J. Lanning, *Delivering Profitable Value* (Oxford, UK: Capstone, 1998).

63. Microsoft Dynamics Customer Solution Case Study, "Egyptian Beverages Company Transforms Customer Service with CRM and Retail Solution," July 2006.

64. Ibid.

65. Don Peppers and Martha Rogers, *One-to-One B2B: Customer Development Strategies for the Business-To-Business World* (New York: Doubleday, 2001); Peppers and Rogers, *The One-to-One Future: Building Relationships One Customer at a Time*; Peppers and Rogers, *The One-to-One Manager: Real-World Lessons in Customer Relationship Management* (New York: Doubleday, 1999); Don Peppers, Martha Rogers, and Bob Dorf, *The One-to-One Fieldbook: The Complete Toolkit for Implementing a One-to-One Marketing Program* (New York: Bantam, 1999); Peppers and Rogers, *Enterprise One to One: Tools for Competing in the Interactive Age* (New York: Currency, 1997).

66. Katherine O'Brien, "Differentiation Begins with Customer Knowledge," *American Printer*, July 2003, p. 8.

67. Tom Ostenon, *Customer Share Marketing* (Upper Saddle River, NJ: Prentice-Hall, 2002); Alan W. H. Grant and Leonard A. Schlesinger, "Realize Your Customer's Full Profit Potential," *Harvard Business Review*, September–October 1995, pp. 59–72.

68. See www.cbq.com.qa.

69. Michael Lewis, "Customer Acquisition Promotions and Customer Asset Value," *Journal of Marketing Research*, 63, May 2006, pp. 195–203.

70. Werner Reinartz, Jacquelyn S. Thomas, and V. Kumar, "Balancing Acquisition and Retention Resources to Maximize Customer Profitability," *Journal of Marketing*, 69, January 2005, pp. 63–79.

71. Frederick F. Reichheld, "Learning from Customer Detections," *Harvard Business Review*, March–April 1996, pp. 56–69.

72. Frederick F. Reichheld, *Loyalty Rules* (Boston: Harvard Business School Press, 2001); Reichheld, *The Loyalty Effect* (Boston: Harvard Business School Press, 1996).

73. Leonard L. Berry and A. Parasuraman, *Marketing Services: Computing through Quality* (New York: The Free Press, 1991), pp. 136–142. For an academic examination in a business-to-business context, see Robert W. Palmatier, Srinath Gopalakrishna, and Mark B. Houston, "Returns on Business-to-Business Relationship Marketing Investments: Strategies for Leveraging Profits," *Marketing Science*, 25, September–October 2006, pp. 477–493.

74. "Customer & Partner Experience," www.microsoft.com/about/en/xm/ImportedContent/about/cpe/en/us/egypt.aspx.

75. Reichheld, "Learning from Customer Defections," pp. 56–69.

76. Jim Edwards, "Broken Promises," *Brandweek*, May 22, 2006, pp. 23–28.

77. Utpal M. Dholakia, "How Consumer Self-Determination Influences Relational Marketing Outcomes: Evidence from Longitudinal Field Studies," *Journal of Marketing Research*, 43, February 2006, pp. 109–120.

78. Allison Enright, "Serve Them Right," *Marketing News*, May 1, 2006, pp. 21–22.

79. For a review, see Grahame R. Dowling and Mark Uncles, "Do Customer Loyalty Programs Really Work?," *Sloan Management Review*, 38, no. 4, Summer 1997, pp. 71–82.

80. Thomas Lee, "Retailers Look for a Hook," *St. Louis Post-Dispatch*, December 4, 2004.

81. Theresa Howard, "Hershey's, eBay Team to Reward Customers," *USA Today*, April 21, 2006; Angelo Fernando, "Why Punish, When You Can Reward?," *Communication World*, 23, no. 5, September–October 2006, pp. 14+.

82. Adam Lashinsky, "The Decade of Steve Jobs," *Fortune*, November 23, 2009, pp. 93–100; Apple, www.apple.com; Peter Burrows, "Apple Vs. Google," *Bloomberg BusinessWeek*, January 25, 2010, pp. 28–34.

83. www.hog.com.

84. James H. Donnelly Jr, Leonard L. Berry, and Thomas W. Thompson, *Marketing Financial Services: A Strategic Vision* (Homewood, IL: Dow Jones–Irwin, 1985), p. 113.

85. "EFG-Hermes launches Hermes Online Trading," www.efg-hermes.com/English/NewsDetails.aspx?NID=77&h=h1.

86. Susan Stellin, "For Many Online Companies, Customer Service Is Hardly a Priority," *New York Times*, February 19, 2001; Michelle Johnson, "Getting Ready for the Onslaught," *Boston Globe*, November 4, 1999.

87. Kerry Capell, "BBC: Step Right into the Telly," *BusinessWeek*, July 24, 2006, p. 52; http://backstage.bbc.co.uk.

88. Michael Totty, "E-Commerce (A Special Report): Business Solutions," *Wall Street Journal*, October 20, 2003.

89. Jeffrey Pfeffer, "The Face of Your Business," *Business 2.0*, December 2002–January 2003, p. 58.

90. Jacquelyn S. Thomas, Robert C. Blattberg, and Edward J. Fox, "Recapturing Lost Customers," *Journal of Marketing Research*, 61, February 2004, pp. 31–45.

91. Werner Reinartz and V. Kumar, "The Impact of Customer Relationship Characteristics on Profitable Lifetime Duration," *Journal of Marketing*, 67, no. 1, January 2003, pp. 77–99; Reinartz and Kumar, "The Mismanagement of Customer Loyalty," *Harvard Business Review*, July 2002, pp. 86–97.

92. V. Kumar, Rajkumar Venkatesan, and Werner Reinartz, "Knowing What to Sell, When, and to Whom," *Harvard Business Review*, March 2006, pp. 131–137.

93. See www.reachgulfbusiness.com/middle_east/bahrain/.

94. Christopher R. Stephens and R. Sukumar, "An Introduction to Data Mining," in *Handbook of Marketing Research*, ed. Rajiv Grover and Marco Vriens (Thousand Oaks, CA: Sage Publications, 2006), pp. 455–486; Pang-Ning Tan, Michael Steinbach, and Vipin Kumar, *Introduction to Data Mining* (Upper Saddle River, NJ: Addison Wesley, 2005); Michael J. A. Berry and Gordon S. Linoff, *Data Mining Techniques: For Marketing, Sales, and Customer Relationship Management*, 2nd edn (Hoboken, NJ: Wiley Computer, 2004); James Lattin, Doug Carroll, and Paul Green, *Analyzing Multivariate Data* (Florence, KY: Thomson Brooks/Cole, 2003).

95. Werner Reinartz and V. Kumar, "The Mismanagement of Customer Loyalty," *Harvard Business Review*, July 2002, pp. 86–94; Susan M. Fournier, Susan Dobscha, and David Glen Mick, "Preventing the Premature Death of Relationship Marketing," *Harvard Business Review*, January–February 1998, pp. 42–51.

96. Jon Swartz, "eBay Faithful Expect Loyalty in Return," *USA Today*, July 1, 2002.

97. George S. Day, "Creating a Superior Customer-Relating Capability," *Sloan Management Review*, 44, no. 3, Spring 2003, pp. 77–82.

98. Darrell K. Rigby, Frederick F. Reichheld, and Phil Schefter, "Avoid the Four Perils of CRM," *Harvard Business Review*, February 2002, pp. 101–109.

99. George S. Day, "Creating a Superior Customer-Relating Capability," *Sloan Management Review*, 44, no. 3, Spring 2003, pp. 77–82; George S. Day, "Creating a Superior Customer-Relating Capability," in *MSI Report No. 03–101* (Cambridge, MA: Marketing Science Institute, 2003); "Why Some Companies Succeed at CRM (and Many Fail)," *Knowledge at Wharton*, http://knowledge.wharton.upenn.edu.

Chapter 6

1. "Survey Results: Middle East is Ready For Mobile Ads," *MobiAD News*, November 2, 2007, www.mobiadnews .com/?p=1301; "KSA Cellular Market Most Competitive in Region," *The Saudi Gazette*, www.saudigazette .com.sa/index.cfm?method–home.regcon&conten tID=20110707104675.

2. Stanford University's Itamar Simonson is gratefully acknowledged. For an academic overview of the field of consumer research, see Itamar Simonson, Ziv Carmon, Ravi Dhar, Aimee Drolet, and Stephen M Nowlis, "Consumer Research: In Search of Identity," *Annual Review of Psychology*, 52, 2001, pp. 249–275.

3. Amy Glass, "UAE Tops Arab Consumer Spending," 2008, www.arabianbusiness.com/uae-tops-arab-consumer-spending-122297.html.

4. Ibid.

5. Sonya A. Grier, Anne Brumbaugh, and Corliss G. Thornton, "Crossover Dreams: Consumer Responses to Ethnic-Oriented Products," *Journal of Marketing*, 70, April 2006, pp. 35–51.

6. "Countries and Their Cultures," www.everyculture.com.

7. Leon G. Schiffman and Leslie Lazar Kanuk, *Consumer Behavior*, 9th edn (Upper Saddle River, NJ: Prentice Hall, 2006).

8. See www.virginmegastore.me.

9. See www.virgin.com/company/virgin-megastore.

10. Elizabeth S. Moore, William L. Wilkie, and Richard J. Lutz, "Passing the Torch: Intergenerational Influences as a Source of Brand Equity," *Journal of Marketing*, April 2002, pp. 17–37; Robert Boutilier, "Pulling the Family's Strings," *American Demographics*, August 1993, pp. 44–48; David J. Burns, "Husband-Wife Innovative Consumer Decision Making: Exploring the Effect of Family Power," *Psychology & Marketing*, May–June 1992, pp. 175–189; Rosann L. Spiro, "Persuasion in Family Decision Making," *Journal of Consumer Research*, March 1983, pp. 393–402. For cross-cultural comparisons of husband–wife buying roles, see John B. Ford, Michael S. LaTour, and Tony L. Henthorne, "Perception of Marital Roles in Purchase-Decision Processes: A Cross-Cultural Study," *Journal of the Academy of Marketing Science*, Spring 1995, pp. 120–131.

11. Kay M. Palan and Robert E. Wilkes, "Adolescent-Parent Interaction in Family Decision Making," *Journal of Consumer Research*, 24, no. 2, March 1997, pp. 159–169; Sharon E. Beatty and Salil Talpade, "Adolescent Influence in Family Decision Making: A Replication with Extension," *Journal of Consumer Research*, 21, September 1994, pp. 332–341.

12. Chenting Su, Edward F. Fern, and Keying Ye, "A Temporal Dynamic Model of Spousal Family Purchase-Decision Behavior," *Journal of Marketing Research*, 40, August 2003, pp. 268–281.

13. Anonymous, "Retailers Learn that Electronics Shopping Isn't Just a Guy Thing," *Wall Street Journal*, January 15, 2004.

14. "Saudi Lingerie Shops asked to Hire only Women: No Gender-Mixing and Men are now Allowed into Lingerie Shops," July 2011, www.emirates247.com/ news/region/saudi-lingerie-shops-asked-to-hire-only-women-2011-07-12-1.407169.

15. Hillary Chura, "Failing to Connect: Marketing Messages for Women Fall Short," *Advertising Age*, September 23, 2002, pp. 13–14.

16. Jennifer Bayot, "The Teenage Market; Young, Hip, and Looking for a Bargain," *New York Times*, December 1, 2003.

17. "Global Car Purchase Survey Asks–Do Kids Drive Their Parents?," May 2004, www.synovate.com/news/ article/2004/05/global-car-purchase-survey-asks-do-kids-drive-their-parents.html#/.

18. Jennifer Saranow, "'This Is the Car We Want, Mommy'; Car Makers Direct More Ads at Kids (and Their Parents); A 5-Year-Old's Toy Hummer," *The Wall Street Journal*, November 9, 2006.

19. Susan Linn, *Consuming Kids: The Hostile Takeover of Childhood* (New York: The New Press, 2004).

20. Richard Abbott, "Why Targeting Kids Isn't Childs Play," 2006, www.arabianbusiness.com/492475.

21. See www.stoointernational.com/default.asp.

22. Deborah Roedder John, "Consumer Socialization of Children: A Retrospective Look at Twenty-Five Years of Research," *Journal of Consumer Research*, December 1999; Lan Nguyen Chaplin and Deborah Roedder John, "The Development of Self-Brand Connections in Children and Adolescents," *Journal of Consumer Research*, June 2005.

23. "Masafi Launches Special Modhesh Co-branded labels in 500ml Bottles," www.ameinfo.com/235816.html.

24. Yahya El Haddad, "Major Trends Affecting Families in the Gulf Countries," May 2003, www.un.org/esa/socdev/ family/Publications/mtelhaddad.pdf.

25. Rex Y. Du and Wagner A. Kamakura, "Household Life Cycles and Lifestyles in the United States," *Journal of Marketing Research*, 48, February 2006, pp. 121–132; Lawrence Lepisto, "A Life Span Perspective of Consumer Behavior," in *Advances in Consumer Research*, vol. 12, ed. Elizabeth Hirshman and Morris Holbrook (Provo, UT: Association for Consumer Research, 1985), p. 47. Also see Gail Sheehy, *New Passages: Mapping Your Life across Time* (New York: Random House, 1995).

26. See Frederick Herzberg, *Work and the Nature of Man* (Cleveland: William Collins, 1966); Henk Thierry and Agnes M. Koopman-Iwerna, "Motivation and Satisfaction," in *Handbook of Work and Organizational Psychology*, ed. P. J. Drenth (New York: John Wiley, 1984), pp. 141–142.

27. Harold H. Kassarjian and Mary Jane Sheffet, "Personality and Consumer Behavior: An Update," in *Perspectives in Consumer Behavior*, ed. Harold H. Kassarjian and Thomas S. Robertson (Glenview, IL: Scott, Foresman, 1981), pp. 160–180.

28. Jennifer Aaker, "Dimensions of Measuring Brand Personality," *Journal of Marketing Research*, 34, August 1997, pp. 347–356.

29. "Levi's to Tap into Arab Spring to Sell Jeans," *Hurriyet Daily News*, July 7, 2011, www.hurriyetdailynews.com/n.php?n=levi821/s-to-tap-into-arab-spring-to-sell-jeans-2011-07-07.

30. Jennifer L. Aaker, Veronica Benet-Martinez, and Jordi Garolera, "Consumption Symbols as Carriers of Culture: A Study of Japanese and Spanish Brand Personality Constructs," *Journal of Personality and Social Psychology*, 81, no. 3, March 2001, pp. 492–508.

31. Yongjun Sung and Spencer F. Tinkham, "Brand Personality Structures in the United States and Korea: Common and Culture-Specific Factors," *Journal of Consumer Psychology*, 15, no. 4, December 2005, pp. 334–350.

32. M. Joseph Sirgy, "Self Concept in Consumer Behavior: A Critical Review," *Journal of Consumer Research*, 9, December 1982, pp. 287–300.

33. Timothy R. Graeff, "Consumption Situations and the Effects of Brand Image on Consumers' Brand Evaluations," *Psychology & Marketing*, 14, no. 1, January 1997, pp. 49–70; Timothy R. Graeff, "Image Congruence Effects on Product Evaluations: The Role of Self-Monitoring and Public/Private Consumption," *Psychology & Marketing*, 13, no. 5, August 1996, pp. 481–499.

34. Jennifer L. Aaker, "The Malleable Self: The Role of Self-Expression in Persuasion," *Journal of Marketing Research*, 36, no. 1, February 1999, pp. 45–57.

35. Anonymous, "16m. Young High-Earning Consumers Are Targets of High-End Lifestyle Products," *News India—Times*, 37, no. 31, August 4, 2006, p. 16.

36. Amy Cortese, "They Care about the World (and They Shop Too)," *New York Times*, July 20, 2003.

37. Anthony Banco and Wendy Zellner, "Is Wal-Mart Too Powerful?," *BusinessWeek*, October 6, 2003, p. 100.

38. Toby Weber, "All Three? Gee," *Wireless Review*, May 2003, pp. 12–14.

39. See www.indomie.com.

40. For a review of current academic research on consumer behavior, see "Consumer Psychology: Categorization, Inferences, Affect, and Persuasion," *Annual Review of Psychology*, 57, 2006, pp. 453–495. To learn more about how consumer behavior theory can be applied to policy decisions, see "Special Issue on Helping Consumers Help Themselves: Improving the Quality of Judgments and Choices," *Journal of Public Policy & Marketing*, 25, no. 1, Spring 2006.

41. Thomas J. Reynolds and Jonathan Gutman, "Laddering Theory, Method, Analysis, and Interpretation," *Journal of Advertising Research*, February–March 1988, pp. 11–34.

42. Ernest Dichter, *Handbook of Consumer Motivations* (New York: McGraw-Hill, 1964).

43. Jan Callebaut *et al.*, *The Naked Consumer: The Secret of Motivational Research in Global Marketing* (Antwerp, Belgium: Censydiam Institute, 1994).

44. Melanie Wells, "Mind Games," *Forbes*, September 1, 2003, p. 70.

45. Abraham Maslow, *Motivation and Personality* (New York: Harper and Row, 1954), pp. 80–106.

46. See Frederick Herzberg, *Work and the Nature of Man* (Cleveland: William Collins, 1966); Thierry and Koopman-Iwerma, "Motivation and Satisfaction," pp. 141–142.

47. Bernard Berelson and Gary A. Steiner, *Human Behavior: An Inventory of Scientific Findings* (New York: Harcourt Brace Jovanovich, 1964), p. 88.

48. J. Edward Russo, Margaret G. Meloy, and Victoria Husted Medvec, "The Distortion of Product Information during Brand Choice," *Journal of Marketing Research*, 35, November 1998, pp. 438–452.

49. Leslie de Chernatony and Simon Knox, "How an Appreciation of Consumer Behavior Can Help in Product Testing," *Journal of Market Research Society*, July 1990, pp. 333. See also, Chris Janiszewski and Stiju M. J. Osselar, "A Connectionist Model of Brand–Quality Association," *Journal of Marketing Research*, August 2000, pp. 331–351.

50. Florida's Chris Janiszewski has developed a fascinating research program looking at preconscious processing effects. See Chris Janiszewski, "Preattentive Mere Exposure Effects," *Journal of Consumer Research*, 20, December 1993, pp. 376–392, as well as some of his earlier and subsequent research. For more perspectives, see also John A. Bargh and Tanya L. Chartrand, "The Unbearable Automaticity Of Being," *American Psychologist*, 54, 1999, pp. 462–479 and the research programs of both authors. For lively academic debate, see the Research Dialogue section of the July 2005 issue of the *Journal of Consumer Psychology*.

51. See Timothy E. Moore, "Subliminal Advertising: What You See Is What You Get," *Journal of Marketing*, 46, Spring 1982, pp. 38–47 for an early classic; and Andrew B. Aylesworth, Ronald C. Goodstein, and Ajay Kalra, "Effect of Archetypal Embeds on Feelings: An Indirect Route to Affecting Attitudes?," *Journal of Advertising*, 28, no. 3, Autumn 1999, pp. 73–81 for a more current treatment.

52. Robert S. Wyer Jr. and Thomas K. Srull, "Person Memory and Judgment," *Psychological Review*, 96, no. 1, January 1989, pp. 58–83; John R. Anderson, *The Architecture of Cognition* (Cambridge, MA: Harvard University Press, 1983).

53. "Chipsy Max," *Adweek Talent Gallery*, from http://talent.adweek.com/gallery/Chipsy-MAX/846344.

54. For additional discussion, see John G. Lynch Jr. and Thomas K. Srull, "Memory and Attentional Factors in Consumer Choice: Concepts and Research Methods," *Journal of Consumer Research*, 9, June 1982, pp. 18–36; and Joseph W. Alba, J. Wesley Hutchinson, and John G. Lynch Jr., "Memory and Decision Making," in *Handbook of Consumer Theory and Research*, ed. Harold H. Kassarjian and Thomas S. Robertson (Englewood Cliffs, NJ: Prentice Hall, 1992), pp. 1–49.

55. Robert S. Lockhart, Fergus I. M. Craik, and Larry Jacoby, "Depth of Processing, Recognition, and Recall," in *Recall and Recognition*, ed. John Brown (New York: John Wiley & Sons, 1976); Fergus I. M. Craik and Endel Tulving, "Depth of Processing and the Retention of Words in Episodic Memory," *Journal of Experimental Psychology*, 104, no. 3, September 1975, pp. 268–294; Fergus I. M. Craik and Robert S. Lockhart, "Levels of Processing: A Framework for Memory Research," *Journal of Verbal Learning and Verbal Behavior*, 11, 1972, pp. 671–684.

56. Leonard M. Lodish, Magid Abraham, Stuart Kalmenson, Jeanne Livelsberger, Beth Lubetkin, Bruce Richardson, and Mary Ellen Stevens, "How T.V. Advertising Works: A Meta-Analysis of 389 Real World Split Cable T.V. Advertising Experiments," *Journal of Marketing Research*, 32, May 1995, pp. 125–139.

57. Elizabeth F. Loftus and Gregory R. Loftus, "On the Permanence of Stored Information in the Human Brain," *American Psychologist*, 35, May 1980, pp. 409–420.

58. Kathryn A. Braun, "Postexperience Advertising Effects on Consumer Memory," *Journal of Consumer Research*, 25, March 1999, pp. 319–332.

59. For a comprehensive review of the academic literature on decision making, see J. Edward Russo and Kurt A. Carlson, "Individual Decision Making," in *Handbook of Marketing*, ed. Bart Weitz and Robin Wensley (London: Sage Publications, 2002), pp. 372–408.

60. Benson Shapiro, V. Kasturi Rangan, and John Sviokla, "Staple Yourself to an Order," *Harvard Business Review*, July–August 1992, pp. 113–122. See also Carrie M. Heilman, Douglas Bowman, and Gordon P. Wright, "The Evolution of Brand Preferences and Choice Behaviors of Consumers New to a Market," *Journal of Marketing Research*, May 2000, pp. 139–155.

61. Alison Stein Wellner, "Research on a Shoestring," *American Demographics*, April 2001, pp. 38–39.

62. Marketing scholars have developed several models of the consumer buying process. See Mary Frances Luce, James R. Bettman, and John W. Payne, *Emotional Decisions: Tradeoff Difficulty and Coping in Consumer Choice* (Chicago: University of Chicago Press, 2001); James F. Engel, Roger D. Blackwell, and Paul W. Miniard, *Consumer Behavior*, 8th ed. (Fort Worth, TX: Dryden, 1994); John A. Howard and Jagdish N. Sheth, *The Theory of Buyer Behavior* (New York: Wiley, 1969).

63. William P. Putsis Jr. and Narasimhan Srinivasan, "Buying or Just Browsing? The Duration of Purchase Deliberation," *Journal of Marketing Research*, August 1994, pp. 393–402.

64. Chem L. Narayana and Rom J. Markin, "Consumer Behavior and Product Performance: An Alternative Conceptualization," *Journal of Marketing*, October 1975, pp. 1–6. See also Lee G. Cooper and Akihiro Inoue, "Building Market Structures from Consumer Preferences," *Journal of Marketing Research*, 33, no. 3, August 1996, pp. 293–306; Wayne S. DeSarbo and Kamel Jedidi, "The Spatial Representation of Heterogeneous Consideration

Sets," *Marketing Science*, 14, no. 3, pt. 2, Summer 1995, pp. 326–342.

65. For a market-structure study of the hierarchy of attributes in the coffee market, see Dipak Jain, Frank M. Bass, and Yu-Min Chen, "Estimation of Latent Class Models with Heterogeneous Choice Probabilities: An Application to Market Structuring," *Journal of Marketing Research*, February 1990, pp. 94–101. For an application of means-end chain analysis to global markets, see Frenkel Ter Hofstede, Jan-Benedict E. M. Steenkamp, and Michel Wedel, "International Market Segmentation Based on Consumer–Product Relations," *Journal of Marketing Research*, February 1999, pp. 1–17.

66. Virginia Postrel, "The Lessons of the Grocery Shelf Also Have Something to Say about Affirmative Action," *New York Times*, January 30, 2003.

67. David Krech, Richard S. Crutchfield, and Egerton L. Ballachey, *Individual in Society* (New York: McGraw-Hill, 1962), Chapter 2.

68. "First White Cheese in Tetra Classic Aseptic 65ml Packages in the World," 2009, www.tetrapak.com/about_tetra_pak/cases/pages/whitecheese_tca.aspx.

69. See Leigh McAlister, "Choosing Multiple Items from a Product Class," *Journal of Consumer Research*, December 1979, pp. 213–224; Paul E. Green and Yoram Wind, *Multiattribute Decisions in Marketing: A Measurement Approach* (Hinsdale, IL: Dryden, 1973), Chapter 2; Richard J. Lutz, "The Role of Attitude Theory in Marketing," in *Perspectives in Consumer Behavior*, ed. Kassarjian and Robertson, pp. 317–339.

70. This expectancy-value model was originally developed by Martin Fishbein, "Attitudes and Prediction of Behavior," in *Readings in Attitude Theory and Measurement*, ed. Martin Fishbein (New York: John Wiley, 1967), pp. 477–492. For a critical review, see Paul W. Miniard and Joel B. Cohen, "An Examination of the Fishbein-Ajzen Behavioral-Intentions Model's Concepts and Measures," *Journal of Experimental Social Psychology*, May 1981, pp. 309–339.

71. Michael R. Solomon, *Consumer Behavior: Buying, Having, and Being*, 7th edn (Upper Saddle River, NJ: Prentice Hall, 2007).

72. James R. Bettman, Eric J. Johnson, and John W. Payne, "Consumer Decision Making," in *Handbook of Consumer Theory and Research*, ed. Kassarjian and Robertson, pp. 50–84.

73. Jagdish N. Sheth, "An Investigation of Relationships among Evaluative Beliefs, Affect, Behavioral Intention, and Behavior," in *Consumer Behavior: Theory and Application*, ed. John U. Farley, John A. Howard, and L. Winston Ring (Boston: Allyn & Bacon, 1974), pp. 89–114.

74. Fishbein, "Attitudes and Prediction of Behavior."

75. Margaret C. Campbell and Ronald C. Goodstein, "The Moderating Effect of Perceived Risk on Consumers' Evaluations of Product Incongruity: Preference for the Norm," *Journal of Consumer Research*, 28, December 2001, pp. 439–449; Grahame R. Dowling, "Perceived Risk," in *The Elgar Companion to Consumer Research*

and Economic Psychology, ed. Peter E. Earl and Simon Kemp (Cheltenham, UK: Edward Elgar, 1999), pp. 419–424; Grahame R. Dowling, "Perceived Risk: The Concept and Its Measurement," Psychology and Marketing, 3, Autumn 1986, pp. 193–210; James R. Bettman, "Perceived Risk and Its Components: A Model and Empirical Test," Journal of Marketing Research, 10, May 1973, pp. 184–190; Raymond A. Bauer, "Consumer Behavior as Risk Taking," in Risk Taking and Information Handling in Consumer Behavior, ed. Donald F. Cox (Boston: Division of Research, Harvard Business School, 1967).

76. Richard L. Oliver, "Customer Satisfaction Research," in Handbook of Marketing Research, ed. Rajiv Grover and Marco Vriens (Thousand Oaks, CA: Sage Publications, 2006), pp. 569–587.

77. Ralph L. Day, "Modeling Choices among Alternative Responses to Dissatisfaction," Advances in Consumer Research, 11, 1984, pp. 496–499. Also see Philip Kotler and Murali K. Mantrala, "Flawed Products: Consumer Responses and Marketer Strategies," Journal of Consumer Marketing, Summer 1985, pp. 27–36.

78. Albert O. Hirschman, Exit, Voice, and Loyalty (Cambridge, MA: Harvard University Press, 1970).

79. John D. Cripps, "Heuristics and Biases in Timing the Replacement of Durable Products," Journal of Consumer Research, 21, September 1994, pp. 304–318.

80. Richard E. Petty, Communication and Persuasion: Central and Peripheral Routes to Attitude Change (New York: Springer-Verlag, 1986); Richard E. Petty and John T. Cacioppo, Attitudes and Persuasion: Classic and Contemporary Approaches (New York: McGraw-Hill, 1981).

81. Herbert E. Krugman, "The Impact of Television Advertising: Learning without Involvement," Public Opinion Quarterly, Autumn 1965, pp. 349–356.

82. Frank R. Kardes, Consumer Behavior and Managerial Decision Making, 2nd edn (Upper Saddle River, NJ: Prentice Hall, 2003).

83. For a detailed review of the practical significance of consumer decision making, see Itamar Simonson, "Get Close to Your Customers by Understanding How They Make Their Choices," California Management Review, 35, Summer 1993, pp. 78–79.

84. See www.unvamagazine.com/keys-to-success/four-common-mistakes-of-managers/

85. See Richard Thaler, "Mental Accounting and Consumer Choice," Marketing Science, 4, no. 3, Summer 1985, pp. 199–214 for a seminal piece; and Richard Thaler, "Mental Accounting Matters," Journal of Behavioral Decision Making, 12, no. 3, September 1999, pp. 183–206 for more contemporary perspectives.

86. Gary L. Gastineau and Mark P. Kritzman, Dictionary of Financial Risk Management, 3rd edn (New York: John Wiley & Sons, 1999).

87. Example adapted from Daniel Kahneman and Amos Tversky, "Prospect Theory: An Analysis of Decision under Risk," Econometrica, 47, March 1979, pp. 263–291.

88. Richard Thaler, "Mental Accounting Matters," Journal of Behavioral Decision Making, 12, 1999, pp. 183–206.

89. Harper W. Boyd Jr. and Sidney Levy, "New Dimensions in Consumer Analysis," Harvard Business Review, November–December 1963, pp. 129–140.

90. Sandra Vandermerwe, Customer Capitalism: Increasing Returns in New Market Spaces (London: Nicholas Brealey Publishing 1999) Chapter 11

91. Patricia B. Seybold, "Get Inside the Lives of Your Customers," Harvard Business Review, May 2001, pp. 81–89.

Chapter 7

1. Information from Aramex website, www.aramex.com.

2. For a comprehensive review of the topic, see James C. Anderson and James A. Narus, Business Market Management: Understanding, Creating, and Delivering Value, 2nd edn (Upper Saddle River, NJ: Prentice Hall, 2004). Comments on a draft of this chapter from Northwestern University's Jim Anderson and University of Wisconsin's Jan Heide are gratefully acknowledged.

3. Frederick E. Webster Jr. and Yoram Wind, Organizational Buying Behavior (Upper Saddle River, NJ: Prentice Hall, 1972), p. 2. For a review of recent academic literature on the topic, see Håkan Håkansson and Ivan Snehota, "Marketing in Business Markets," in Handbook of Marketing, ed. Bart Weitz and Robin Wensley (London: Sage Publications, 2002), pp. 513–526.

4. Bob Donath, "Customer Knowledge Takes Priority in Study," Marketing News, December 15, 2005, p. 7.

5. Jennifer Gilbert, "Small but Mighty," Sales & Marketing Management, January 2004, pp. 30–35.

6. Kate Maddox, "BMA Conference Showcases Innovation," B to B, June 12, 2006, p. 3.

7. Michael Collins, "Breaking into the Big Leagues," American Demographics, January 1996, pp. 24.

8. Patrick J. Robinson, Charles W. Faris, and Yoram Wind, Industrial Buying and Creative Marketing (Boston: Allyn & Bacon, 1967).

9. Michele D. Bunn, "Taxonomy of Buying Decision Approaches," Journal of Marketing, 57, January 1993, pp. 38–56; Daniel H. McQuiston, "Novelty, Complexity, and Importance as Causal Determinants of Industrial Buyer Behavior," Journal of Marketing, April 1989, pp. 66–79; Peter Doyle, Arch G. Woodside, and Paul Mitchell, "Organizational Buying in New Task and Rebuy Situations," Industrial Marketing Management, February 1979, pp. 7–11.

10. Urban B. Ozanne and Gilbert A. Churchill Jr., "Five Dimensions of the Industrial Adoption Process," Journal of Marketing Research, August 1971, pp. 322–328.

11. Personal interview, author with Annelie Moukaddem (Rapid Impact Compaction Contracting LLC,) September 2010.

12. To learn more about how business-to-business firms can improve their branding, see Philip Kotler and Waldemar Pfoertsch, *B2B Brand Management* (Berlin: Springer, 2006).

13. See www.ricsa.net; Sylvester Haskins, "New Technology Negates Traditional Soil Compaction Methods," *Engineering News*, February 15, 2008, www.engineering-news.co.za/article/new-technology-negates-traditional-soil-compaction-methods-2008-02-15. To learn more about how business-to-business firms can improve their branding, see Philip Kotler and Waldemar Pfoertsch, *B2B Brand Management* (Berlin: Springer, 2006).

14. See www.saudioger.com. To learn more about how business-to-business firms can improve their branding, see Philip Kotler and Waldemar Pfoertsch, *B2B Brand Management* (Berlin: Springer, 2006).

15. Jeffrey E. Lewin and Naveen Donthu, "The Influence of Purchase Situation on Buying Center Structure and Involvement: A Select Meta-Analysis of Organizational Buying Behavior Research," *Journal of Business Research*, 58, October 2005, pp. 1381–1390; R. Venkatesh and Ajay K. Kohli, "Influence Strategies in Buying Centers," *Journal of Marketing*, 59, October 1995, pp. 71–82.

16. Donald W. Jackson Jr., Janet E. Keith, and Richard K. Burdick, "Purchasing Agents' Perceptions of Industrial Buying Center Influence: A Situational Approach," *Journal of Marketing*, Autumn 1984, pp. 75–83.

17. Webster and Wind, *Organizational Buying Behavior*, p. 6.

18. James C. Anderson and James A. Narus, *Business Market Management: Understanding, Creating, and Delivering Value*, 2nd edn (Upper Saddle River, NJ: Prentice Hall, 2004); Frederick E. Webster Jr. and Yoram Wind, "A General Model for Understanding Organizational Buying Behavior," *Journal of Marketing*, 36, April 1972, pp. 12–19; Webster and Wind, *Organizational Buying Behavior*.

19. Allison Enright, "It Takes a Committee to Buy into B-to-B," *Marketing News*, February 15, 2006, pp. 12–13.

20. David Welch, "Renault-Nissan: Say Hello to Bo," *BusinessWeek*, July 31, 2006, p. 56.

21. Frederick E. Webster Jr. and Kevin Lane Keller, "A Roadmap for Branding in Industrial Markets," *Journal of Brand Management*, 11, May 2004, pp. 388–402.

22. Scott Ward and Frederick E. Webster Jr., "Organizational Buying Behavior" in *Handbook of Consumer Behavior*, ed. Tom Robertson and Hal Kassarjian (Upper Saddle River, NJ: Prentice Hall, 1991), Chapter 12, pp. 419–458.

23. Bob Donath, "Emotions Play Key Role in Biz Brand Appeal," *Marketing News*, June 1, 2006, p. 7.

24. Michael Krauss, "Warriors of the Heart," *Marketing News*, February 1, 2006, p. 7.

25. Webster and Wind, *Organizational Buying Behavior*, p. 6.

26. Source: personal interview with Bilal Itani, Director of Karl Storz operations in Middle East. To learn more about how business-to-business firms can improve their branding, see Philip Kotler and Waldemar Pfoertsch, *B2B Brand Management* (Berlin: Springer, 2006).

27. James C. Anderson, James A. Narus, and Wouter van Rossum, "Customer Value Proposition in Business Markets," *Harvard Business Review*, March 2006, pp. 2–10; James C. Anderson, "From Understanding to Managing Customer Value in Business Markets," in *Rethinking Marketing: New Marketing Tools*, ed. H. Håkansson, D. Harrison, and A. Waluszewski (London: John Wiley & Sons, 2004), pp. 137–159.

28. Wayne Forrest, "McDonald's Applies SRM Strategy to Global Technology Buy," *Purchasing*, 135, no. 12, September 7, 2006, p. 16.

29. Tim Minahan, "OEM Buying Survey—Part 2: Buyers Get New Roles but Keep Old Tasks," *Purchasing*, July 16, 1998, pp. 208–209.

30. Robinson, Faris, and Wind, *Industrial Buying and Creative Marketing*.

31. Rajdeep Grewal, James M. Comer, and Raj Mehta, "An Investigation into the Antecedents of Organizational Participation in Business-to-Business Electronic Markets," *Journal of Marketing*, 65, July 2001, pp. 17–33.

32. Knowledge@Wharton, "Open Sesame? Or Could the Doors Slam Shut for Alibaba.com?," July 27, 2005; Julia Angwin, "Top Online Chemical Exchange Is Unlikely Success Story," *Wall Street Journal*, January 8, 2004; Olga Kharif, "B2B, Take 2," *BusinessWeek*, November 25, 2003; George S. Day, Adam J. Fein, and Gregg Ruppersberger, "Shakeouts in Digital Markets: Lessons from B2B Exchanges," *California Management Review*, 45, no. 2, Winter 2003, pp. 131–151.

33. See www.tejari.com; "Forrester Report Places Tejari in 8th Spot in the World among Global eSourcing Vendors," *Reuters*, January 11, 2009, www.reuters.com/article/2009/01/11/idUS50838+11-Jan-2009+BW20090111; Brid-Aine Conway, "Zain Jordan Goes to Market," *ArabianBusiness.com*, December 11, 2007, www.arabianbusiness.com/zain-jordan-goes-market-195122.html; "Message from the CEO," *Tejari.com*, www.tejari.com/pages/en-US/MessagefromtheCEO.aspx.

34. Brian J. Carroll, *Lead Generation for the Complex Sale* (New York: McGraw-Hill, 2006).

35. See www.zawya.com.

36. Daniel J. Flint, Robert B. Woodruff, and Sarah Fisher Gardial, "Exploring the Phenomenon of Customers' Desired Value Change in a Business-to-Business Context," *Journal of Marketing*, 66, October 2002, pp. 102–117.

37. Ruth N. Bolton and Matthew B. Myers, "Price-Based Global Market Segmentation for Services," *Journal of Marketing*, 67, July 2003, pp. 108–128.

38. Wolfgang Ulaga and Andreas Eggert, "Value-Based Differentiation in Business Relationships: Gaining and Sustaining Key Supplier Status," *Journal of Marketing*, 70, January 2006, pp. 119–136.

39. Christopher Palmeri, "Serving Two (Station) Masters," *BusinessWeek*, July 24, 2006, p. 46.

40. David Kiley, "Small Print Jobs for Peanuts," *BusinessWeek*, July 17, 2006, p. 58.

41. Nirmalya Kumar, *Marketing as Strategy: Understanding the CEO's Agenda for Driving Growth and Innovation* (Boston: Harvard Business School Press, 2004).

42. Kumar, *Marketing as Strategy.*

43. For foundational material, see Lloyd M. Rinehart, James A. Eckert, Robert B. Handfield, Thomas J. Page Jr., and Thomas Atkin, "An Assessment of Buyer–Seller Relationships," *Journal of Business Logistics*, 25, no. 1, 2004, pp. 25–62; F. Robert Dwyer, Paul Schurr, and Sejo Oh, "Developing Buyer–Supplier Relationships," *Journal of Marketing*, 51, April 1987, pp. 11–28; and Barbara Bund Jackson, *Winning & Keeping Industrial Customers: The Dynamics of Customer Relations* (Lexington, MA: D. C. Heath, 1985).

44. Arnt Buvik and George John, "When Does Vertical Coordination Improve Industrial Purchasing Relationships?," *Journal of Marketing*, 64, October 2000, pp. 52–64.

45. Das Narayandas and V. Kasturi Rangan, "Building and Sustaining Buyer–Seller Relationships in Mature Industrial Markets," *Journal of Marketing*, 68, July 2004, pp. 63–77.

46. Robert W. Palmatier, Rajiv P. Dant, Dhruv Grewal, and Kenneth R. Evans, "Factors Influencing the Effectiveness of Relationship Marketing: A Meta-Analysis," *Journal of Marketing*, 70, October 2006, pp. 136–153; Jean L. Johnson, Ravipreet S. Sohli, and Rajdeep Grewal, "The Role of Relational Knowledge Stores in Interfirm Partnering," *Journal of Marketing*, 68, July 2004, pp. 21–36; Fred Selnes and James Sallis, "Promoting Relationship Learning," *Journal of Marketing*, 67, July 2003, pp. 80–95; Patricia M. Doney and Joseph P. Cannon, "An Examination of the Nature of Trust in Buyer–Seller Relationships," *Journal of Marketing*, 61, April 1997, pp. 35–51; Shankar Ganesan, "Determinants of Long-Term Orientation in Buyer–Seller Relationships," *Journal of Marketing*, 58, April 1994, pp. 1–19.

47. William W. Keep, Stanley C. Hollander, and Roger Dickinson, "Forces Impinging on Long-Term Business-to-Business Relationships in the United States: An Historical Perspective," *Journal of Marketing*, 62, April 1998, pp. 31–45.

48. Joseph P. Cannon and William D. Perreault Jr., "Buyer–Seller Relationships in Business Markets," *Journal of Marketing Research*, 36, November 1999, pp. 439–460.

49. Jan B. Heide and Kenneth H. Wahne, "Friends, Businesspeople, and Relationship Roles: A Conceptual Framework and Research Agenda," *Journal of Marketing*, 70, July 2006, pp. 90–103.

50. Cannon and Perreault, "Buyer–Seller Relationships in Business Markets," pp. 439–460.

51. Thomas G. Noordewier, George John, and John R. Nevin, "Performance Outcomes of Purchasing Arrangements in Industrial Buyer–Vendor Arrangements," *Journal of Marketing*, 54, October 1990, pp. 80–93; Buvik and John, "When Does Vertical Coordination Improve Industrial Purchasing Relationships?," pp. 52–64.

52. Akesel I. Rokkan, Jan B. Heide, and Kenneth H. Wathne, "Specific Investment in Marketing Relationships: Expropriation and Bonding Effects," *Journal of Marketing Research*, 40, May 2003, pp. 210–224.

53. Kenneth H. Wathne and Jan B. Heide, "Relationship Governance in a Supply Chain Network," *Journal of Marketing*, 68, January 2004, pp. 73–89; Douglas Bowman and Das Narayandas, "Linking Customer Management Effort to Customer Profitability in Business Markets," *Journal of Marketing Research*, 61, November 2004, pp. 433–447; Mrinal Ghosh and George John, "Governance Value Analysis and Marketing Strategy," *Journal of Marketing*, 63, Special Issue, 1999, pp. 131–145.

54. Sandy Jap, "Pie Expansion Effects: Collaboration Processes in Buyer–Seller Relationships," *Journal of Marketing Research*, 36, November 1999, pp. 461–475.

55. Kenneth H. Wathne and Jan B. Heide, "Opportunism in Interfirm Relationships: Forms, Outcomes, and Solutions," *Journal of Marketing*, 64, October 2000, pp. 36–51.

56. Mary Walton, "When Your Partner Fails You," *Fortune*, May 26, 1997, pp. 151–154.

57. Mark B. Houston and Shane A. Johnson, "Buyer–Supplier Contracts versus Joint Ventures: Determinants and Consequences of Transaction Structure," *Journal of Marketing Research*, 37, February 2000, pp. 1–15.

58. Rokkan, Heide, and Wathne, "Specific Investment in Marketing Relationships: Expropriation and Bonding Effects," pp. 210–224.

59. Siba Sami Ammari, "Aramex joins Dubai Customs and Emirates Airline for e-Freight Initiative," *AMEinfo.com*, May 15, 2010, www.ameinfo.com/232565.html.

60. Matthew Swibel and Janet Novack, "The Scariest Customer," *Forbes*, November 10, 2003, pp. 96–97.

61. Source: interview conducted with the owner for this book.

62. Laura M. Litvan, "Selling to Uncle Sam: New, Easier Rules," *Nation's Business*, March 1995, pp. 46–48.

63. Ellen Messmer, "Feds Do E-Commerce the Hard Way," *Network World*, April 13, 1998, pp. 31–32.

Chapter 8

1. See www.lively.ae, and company brochures.

2. James C. Anderson and James A. Narus, "Capturing the Value of Supplementary Services," *Harvard Business Review*, January–February 1995, pp. 75–83.

3. Tevfik Dalgic and Maarten Leeuw, "Niche Marketing Revisited: Concept, Applications, and Some European Cases," *European Journal of Marketing*, 28, no. 4, April 1994, pp. 39–55.

4. Peter Feuilherade, "Social Networking Surges in the Middle East," *suite101*, May 26, 2010, www.suite101.com/content/social-networking-surges-in-middle-east-a241274; "Arab Facebook Users Reach 32 Million in August," *Egypt.com News*, September 19, 2011, http://news.egypt.com/english/permalink/46486.html.

5. Robert Blattberg and John Deighton, "Interactive Marketing: Exploiting the Age of Addressibility," *Sloan Management Review*, 33, no. 1, Autumn 1991, pp. 5–14.

6. Dale Buss, "Brands in the Hood," *Point*, December 2005, p. 1924.

7. Don Peppers and Martha Rogers, *One-to-One B2B: Customer Development Strategies for the Business-To-Business World* (New York: Doubleday, 2001); Mark Rechtin, "Aston Martin Woos Customers One by One," *Automotive News*, March 28, 2005.

8. Anderson and Narus, "Capturing the Value of Supplementary Services," pp. 75–83.

9. Itamar Simonson, "Determinants of Customers' Responses to Customized Offers: Conceptual Framework and Research Propositions," *Journal of Marketing*, 69, January 2005, pp. 32–45.

10. See www.stuckonyou.biz/uae.

11. Joann Muller, "Kmart con Salsa: Will It Be Enough?," *BusinessWeek*, September 9, 2002.

12. Becky Ebenkamp, "Urban America Redefined," *Brandweek*, October 6, 2003, pp. 12–13.

13. See www.claritas.com.

14. Art Weinstein, *Handbook of Market Segmentation: Strategic Targeting for Business and Technology Firms*, 3rd edn (Binghamton, NY: Haworth Press, 2004); Michael J. Weiss, *The Clustered World* (Boston: Little, Brown & Co., 2000).

15. Michael J. Weiss, "To Be about to Be," *American Demographics*, September 2003, pp. 29–36.

16. Gina Chon, "Car Makers Talk 'Bout G-G-Generations," *Wall Street Journal*, May 9, 2006.

17. Jim Rendon, "Rear Window," *Business 2.0*, August 2003, pp. 72.

18. Tom Lowry, "Young Man, Your Couch Is Calling," *BusinessWeek*, July 28, 2003, pp. 68–69.

19. Jessica Hopper, "The Dove Campaign: Conforming or Transforming?," *National NOW Times*, 38, no. 3, Autumn 2006, pp. 16+.

20. Borzou Daragahi, "Plastic Surgery Loans Popular in Lebanon", *Los Angeles Times*, February 8, 2008, www.azcentral.com/arizonarepublic/news/articles/0208leb-cosmetic0208.html.

21. Marti Barletta, "Who's Really Buying That Car? Ask Her," *Brandweek*, September 4, 2006, p. 20; Robert Craven, Kiki Maurey, and John Davis, "What Women Really Want," *Critical Eye*, 15, July 2006, pp. 50–53.

22. Aixa Pascual, "Lowe's Is Sprucing Up Its House," *BusinessWeek*, June 3, 2002, pp. 56–57; Pamela Sebastian Ridge, "Tool Sellers Tap Their Feminine Side," *Wall Street Journal*, June 16, 2002.

23. Ian Zack, "Out of the Tube," *Forbes*, November 26, 2001, p. 200.

24. Gregory L. White and Shirley Leung, "Middle Market Shrinks as Americans Migrate toward the Higher End," *Wall Street Journal*, March 29, 2002.

25. Linda Tischler, "The Price Is Right," *Fast Company*, November 2003, pp. 83–91.

26. Christopher Noxon, "Toyification Nation," *Brandweek*, October 9, 2006; Rod O'Connor, "Adulthood: Are We There Yet? If You're Still Watching Cartoons or Playing Kickball, Then You, Kiddo, Just Might Be a 'Rejuvenile'," *Chicago Tribune*, August 6, 2006.

27. Andrew E. Serwer, "42,496 Secrets Bared," *Fortune*, January 24, 1994, pp. 13–14; Kenneth Labich, "Class in America," *Fortune*, February 7, 1994, pp. 114–126.

28. See www.strategicbusinessinsights.com/vals/.

29. Paula Haddad, *Psychographic Segmentation of the Lebanese Population*, MBA project (American University of Beirut, 2002).

30. "The Arab As Consumer – 20/20 Woman," TNS, www.tnsglobal.com/research/key-insight-reports/5EF7E785DA1B48DAA244EB8AF12266B9.aspx.

31. Pam Danziger, "Getting More for V-Day," *Brandweek*, February 9, 2004, p. 19.

32. This classification was adapted from George H. Brown, "Brand Loyalty: Fact or Fiction?," *Advertising Age*, June 1952–January 1953, a series. See also Peter E. Rossi, Robert E. McCulloch, and Greg M. Allenby, "The Value of Purchase History Data in Target Marketing," *Marketing Science*, 15, no. 4, Autumn 1996, pp. 321–340.

33. Chip Walker, "How Strong Is Your Brand," *Marketing Tools*, January–February 1995, pp. 46–53.

34. See www.conversionmodel.com.

35. Daniel Yankelovich and David Meer, "Rediscovering Market Segmentation," *Harvard Business Review*, February 2006, pp. 122-131.

36. For a review of many of the methodological issues in developing segmentation schemes, see William R. Dillon and Soumen Mukherjee, "A Guide to the Design and Execution of Segmentation Studies," in *Handbook of Marketing Research*, ed. Rajiv Grover and Marco Vriens (Thousand Oaks, CA: Sage, 2006); and Michael Wedel and Wagner A. Kamakura, *Market Segmentation: Conceptual and Methodological Foundations* (Boston: Kluwer, 1997).

37. Wendell R. Smith, "Product Differentiation and Market Segmentation as Alternative Marketing Strategies," *Journal of Marketing*, July 1956, pp. 4.

38. See www.esteelauder.com.

39. Christopher Hosford, "A Transformative Experience," *Sales and Marketing Management*, 158, no. 5, June 2006, pp. 32–36.

40. Bart Macchiette and Roy Abhijit, "Sensitive Groups and Social Issues," *Journal of Consumer Marketing*, 11, no. 4, Autumn 1994, pp. 55–64.

Chapter 9

1. Saied Tarek. Interview by author, Cairo, August 16, 2011; My Diamond Company profile (2010), www.my-diamond.org.

2. For foundational work on branding, see Jean-Noel Kapferer, *Strategic Brand Management*, 2nd edn (New York: Free Press, 2005); David A. Aaker and Erich Joachimsthaler, *Brand Leadership* (New York: Free Press, 2000); David A. Aaker, *Building Strong Brands* (New York: Free Press, 1996); David A. Aaker, *Managing Brand Equity* (New York: Free Press, 1991).

3. Interbrand Group, *World's Greatest Brands: An International Review* (New York: John Wiley, 1992). See also Karl Moore and Susan E. Reid, "The Birth of a Brand," Working paper, Desautels Faculty of Management, McGill University, 2006.

4. Rajneesh Suri and Kent B. Monroe, "The Effects of Time Pressure on Consumers' Judgments of Prices and Products," *Journal of Consumer Research*, 30, June 2003, pp. 92–104.

5. Rita Clifton and John Simmons, eds, *The Economist on Branding* (New York: Bloomberg Press, 2004); Rik Riezebos, *Brand Management: A Theoretical and Practical Approach* (Harlow: Pearson Education, 2003); and Paul Temporal, *Advanced Brand Management: From Vision to Valuation* (Singapore: John Wiley & Sons, 2002).

6. Constance E. Bagley, *Managers and the Legal Environment: Strategies for the 21st Century*, 3rd edn (Cincinnati, OH: Southwestern College/West Publishing, 2005). For a marketing academic point of view of some important legal issues, see Judith Zaichkowsky, *The Psychology behind Trademark Infringement and Counterfeiting* (Mahwah, NJ: LEA Publishing, 2006) and Maureen Morrin and Jacob Jacoby, "Trademark Dilution: Empirical Measures for an Elusive Concept," *Journal of Public Policy & Marketing*, 19, no. 2, May 2000, pp. 265–276.

7. Tulin Erdem, "Brand Equity as a Signaling Phenomenon," *Journal of Consumer Psychology*, 7, no. 2, 1998, pp. 131–157.

8. Scott Davis, *Brand Asset Management: Driving Profitable Growth through Your Brands* (San Francisco: Jossey-Bass, 2000); Mary W. Sullivan, "How Brand Names Affect the Demand for Twin Automobiles," *Journal of Marketing Research*, 35, May 1998, pp. 154–165; D. C. Bello and M. B. Holbrook, "Does an Absence of Brand Equity Generalize across Product Classes?" *Journal of Business Research*, 34, October 1996, pp. 125–131; Adrian J. Slywotzky and Benson P. Shapiro, "Leveraging to Beat the Odds: The New Marketing Mindset," *Harvard Business Review*, September–October 1993, pp. 97–107.

9. The power of branding is not without its critics, however; some of whom reject the commercialism associated with branding activities. See Naomi Klein, *No Logo: Taking Aim at the Brand Bullies* (New York: Picador, 2000).

10. "Company Portrait: DHL," www.dhl.com/en/about_us/company_portrait.html.

11. http://www.ide.go.jp/English/Data/Africa_file/Company/egypt06.html.

12. Natalie Mizik and Robert Jacobson, "Talk about Brand Strategy," *Harvard Business Review*, October 2005, pp. 1; Baruch Lev, *Intangibles: Management, Measurement, and Reporting* (Washington, DC: Brookings Institute, 2001).

13. For an academic discussion of how consumers become so strongly attached to people as brands, see Matthew Thomson, "Human Brands: Investigating Antecedents to Consumers' Stronger Attachments to Celebrities," *Journal of Marketing*, 70, July 2006, pp. 104–119. For some practical branding tips from the world of rock and roll, see Roger Blackwell and Tina Stephan, *Brands That Rock* (Hoboken, NJ: John Wiley & Sons, 2004), and from the world of sports, see Irving Rein, Philip Kotler, and Ben Shields, *The Elusive Fan: Reinventing Sports in a Crowded Marketplace* (New York: McGraw-Hill, 2006).

14. Other approaches are based on economic principles of signaling, e.g. Tulin Erdem, "Brand Equity as a Signaling Phenomenon," *Journal of Consumer Psychology*, 7, no. 2, 1998, pp. 131–157; or more of a sociological, anthropological, or biological perspective, e.g. Grant McCracken, *Culture and Consumption II: Markets, Meaning, and Brand Management*, (Bloomington: Indiana University Press, 2005); or Susan Fournier, "Consumers and Their Brands: Developing Relationship Theory in Consumer Research," *Journal of Consumer Research*, 24, September 1998, pp. 343–373.

15. Kevin Lane Keller, *Strategic Brand Management*, 3rd edn (Upper Saddle River, NJ: Prentice Hall, 2008); David A. Aaker and Erich Joachimsthaler, *Brand Leadership* (New York: Free Press, 2000); David A. Aaker, *Building Strong Brands* (New York: Free Press, 1996); David A. Aaker, *Managing Brand Equity* (New York: Free Press, 1991).

16. Jennifer L. Aaker, "Dimensions of Brand Personality," *Journal of Marketing Research*, August 1997, pp. 347–356; Jean-Noel Kapferer, *Strategic Brand Management: New Approaches to Creating and Evaluating Brand Equity* (London: Kogan Page, 1992), p. 38; Davis, *Brand Asset Management*. For an overview of academic research on branding, see Kevin Lane Keller, "Branding and Brand Equity," in *Handbook of Marketing*, ed. Bart Weitz and Robin Wensley (London: Sage Publications, 2002), pp. 151–178.

17. Keller, *Strategic Brand Management*.

18. Theodore Levitt, "Marketing Success through Differentiation—of Anything," *Harvard Business Review*, January–February 1980, pp. 83–91.

19. Kusum Ailawadi, Donald R. Lehmann, and Scott Neslin, "Revenue Premium as an Outcome Measure of Brand Equity," *Journal of Marketing*, 67, October 2003, pp. 1–17.

20. Alice Z. Cuneo, "Apple Transcends as Lifestyle Brand," *Advertising Age*, June 15, 2003, pp. S2, S6.

21. Jon Miller and David Muir, *The Business of Brands* (Chichester: John Wiley & Sons, 2004).

22. Douglas Holt, *How Brands Become Icons: The Principle of Cultural Branding* (Cambridge, MA: Harvard Business School Press, 2004); Douglas Holt, "Branding as Cultural Activism," zibs.com; Douglas Holt, "What Becomes an Icon Most," *Harvard Business Review*, 81, March 2003, pp. 43–49.

23. Stuart Elliott, "Letting Consumers Control Marketing: Priceless," *New York Times*, October 9, 2006; Elizabeth Holmes, "On MySpace, Millions of Users Make 'Friends' with Ads," *Wall Street Journal*, August 7, 2006, Vol. CCXLVIII, no. 31, p. B1.

24. David A. Aaker and Erich Joachimsthaler, *Brand Leadership* (New York: Free Press, 2000).

25. David A. Aaker, *Building Strong Brands* (New York: Free Press, 1996).

26. Kevin Lane Keller, "Building Customer-Based Brand Equity: A Blueprint for Creating Strong Brands," *Marketing Management*, 10, July–August 2001, pp. 15–19.

27. For some academic insights, see Matthew Thomson, Deborah J. MacInnis, and C. W. Park, "The Ties That Bind: Measuring the Strength of Consumers' Emotional Attachments to Brands," *Journal of Consumer Psychology*, 15, no. 1, 2005, pp. 77–91; and Jennifer Edson Escalas, "Narrative Processing: Building Consumer Connections to Brands," *Journal of Consumer Psychology*, 14, no. 1 & 2, 1996, pp. 168–179. For some managerial guidelines, see Kevin Roberts, *Lovemarks: The Future beyond Brands* (New York: Powerhouse Books, 2004); and Douglas Atkins, *The Culting of Brands* (New York: Penguin Books, 2004).

28. Paul Rittenberg and Maura Clancey, "Testing the Value of Media Engagement for Advertising Effectiveness," at www.knowledgenetworks.com, Spring–Summer 2006, pp. 35–42.

29. www.aishti.com

30. Alina Wheeler, *Designing Brand Identity* (Hoboken, NJ: John Wiley & Sons, 2003).

31. Pat Fallon and Fred Senn, *Juicing the Orange: How to Turn Creativity into a Powerful Business Advantage* (Cambridge, MA: Harvard Business School Press, 2006).

32. http://tna.tareknour.com/news.aspx

33. John R. Doyle and Paul A. Bottomly, "Dressed for the Occasion: Font-Product Congruity in the Perception of Logotype," *Journal of Consumer Psychology*, 16, no. 2, 2006, pp. 112–123; Kevin Lane Keller, Susan Heckler, and Michael J. Houston, "The Effects of Brand Name Suggestiveness on Advertising Recall," *Journal of Marketing*, 62, January 1998, pp. 48–57. For an in-depth examination of how brand names get developed, see Alex Frankel, *Wordcraft: The Art of Turning Little Words into Big Business* (New York: Crown Publishers, 2004).

34. Don Schultz and Heidi Schultz, *IMC: The Next Generation* (New York: McGraw-Hill, 2003); Don E. Schultz, Stanley I. Tannenbaum, and Robert F. Lauterborn, *Integrated Marketing Communications* (Lincolnwood, IL: NTC Business Books, 1993).

35. Mohanbir Sawhney, "Don't Harmonize, Synchronize," *Harvard Business Review*, July–August 2001, pp. 101–108.

36. David C. Court, John E. Forsyth, Greg C. Kelly, and Mark A. Loch, "The New Rules of Branding: Building Strong Brands Faster," *McKinsey White Paper Fall 1999*; Scott Bedbury, *A New Brand World* (New York: Viking Press, 2002).

37. Christopher Locke, Rick Levine, Doc Searls, and David Weinberger, *The Cluetrain Manifesto: The End of Business as Usual* (Cambridge, MA: Perseus Press, 2000).

38. Seth Godin, *Permission Marketing: Turning Strangers into Friends, and Friends into Customers* (New York: Simon & Schuster, 1999). See also Susan Fournier, Susan Dobscha, and David Mick, "Preventing the Premature Death of Relationship Marketing," *Harvard Business Review*, January–February 1998, pp. 42–51.

39. Dawn Iacobucci and Bobby Calder, eds, *Kellogg on Integrated Marketing* (New York: John Wiley & Sons, 2003).

40. Michael Dunn and Scott Davis, "Building Brands from the Inside," *Marketing Management*, May–June 2003, pp. 32–37; Scott Davis and Michael Dunn, *Building the Brand-Driven Business* (New York: John Wiley & Sons, 2002).

41. Stan Maklan and Simon Knox, *Competing on Value* (Upper Saddle River, NJ: Financial Times, Prentice Hall, 2000).

42. Coeli Carr, "Seeking to Attract Top Prospects, Employers Brush Up on Brands," *New York Times*, September 10, 2006.

43. Sherrie Bossung and Mark Pocharski, "Building a Communication Strategy: Marketing the Brand to Employees," presentation at Marketing Science Institute Conference, *Brand Orchestration*, Orlando, Florida, USA, December 4, 2003.

44. The principles and examples from this passage are based on Colin Mitchell, "Selling the Brand Inside," *Harvard Business Review*, January 2002, pp. 99–105. For an in-depth discussion of how two organizations, QuikTrip and Wawa, have developed stellar internal branding programs, see Neeli Bendapudi and Venkat Bendapudi, "Creating the Living Brand," *Harvard Business Review*, May 2005, pp. 124–132.

45. Rima Ali Al Mashni, "Global Brands Group Signs FIFA Official Store Agreement in the Middle East," *AMEinfo. com*, February 22, 2010, www.ameinfo.com/ 224684.html.

46. Deborah Roeddder John, Barbara Loken, Kyeong-Heui Kim, and Alokparna Basu Monga, "Brand Concept Maps: A Methodology for Identifying Brand Association Networks," *Journal of Marketing Research*, 43, November 2006, pp. 549–563.

47. In terms of related empirical insights, see Manoj K. Agrawal and Vithala Rao "An Empirical Comparison of Consumer-Based Measures of Brand Equity," *Marketing Letters*, 7, no. 3, July 1996, pp. 237–247; and Walfried Lassar, Banwari Mittal, and Arun Sharma, "Measuring Customer-Based Brand Equity," *Journal of Consumer Marketing*, 12, no. 4, 1995, pp. 11–19.

48. For the latest and more detailed information, see http:// www.interbrand.com/en/best-global-brands/Best-Global-Brands-2011.aspx.

49. Mark Sherrington, *Added Value: The Alchemy of Brand-Led Growth* (Hampshire, UK: Palgrave Macmillan, 2003).

50. For an up-to-date discussion of what factors determine long-term branding success, see Allen P. Adamson, *Brand Simple* (New York: Palgrave Macmillan, 2006).

51. David Kiley, "To Boost Sales, Volvo Returns to Its Roots: Safety," *USA Today*, August 26, 2002.

52. Natalie Mizik and Robert Jacobson, "Trading Off between Value Creation and Value Appropriation: The Financial Implications of Shifts in Strategic Emphasis," *Journal of Marketing*, 67, January 2003, pp. 63–76.

53. Mark Speece, "Marketer's Malady: Fear of Change," *Brandweek*, August 19, 2002, p. 34.

54. Joseph Weber, "Harley Just Keeps on Cruisin'," *BusinessWeek*, November 6, 2006, pp. 71–72.

55. Keith Naughton, "Fixing Cadillac," *Newsweek*, May 28, 2001, pp. 36–37.

56. Peter Farquhar, "Managing Brand Equity," *Marketing Research*, 1, September 1989, pp. 24–33.

57. Steven M. Shugan, "Branded Variants," 1989 AMA Educators' Proceedings (Chicago: American Marketing Association, 1989), pp. 33–38; also M. Bergen, S. Dutta, and S. M. Shugan, "Branded Variants: A Retail Perspective," *Journal of Marketing Research*, 33, February 1996, pp. 9–21.

58. Adam Bass, "Licensed Extension: Stretching to Communicate," *Journal of Brand Management*, 12, September 2004, pp. 31–38. Also see Aaker, *Building Strong Brands*.

59. Jean Halliday, "Troubled Automakers' Golden Goose," *AutoWeek*, August 14, 2006; Becky Ebenkamp, "The Creative License," *Brandweek*, June 9, 2003, pp. 36–40.

60. For comprehensive corporate branding guidelines, see James R. Gregory, *The Best of Branding: Best Practices in Corporate Branding* (New York: McGraw-Hill, 2004). For some international perspectives, see *The Expressive Organization: Linking Identity, Reputation, and Corporate Brand*, ed. Majken Schultz, Mary Jo Hatch, and Mogens Holten Larsen (Oxford: Oxford University Press, 2000); and *Corporate Branding: Purpose, People, and Process*, ed. Majken Schultz, Yun Mi Antorini, and Fabian F. Csaba (Denmark: Copenhagen Business School Press, 2005).

61. Guido Berens, Cees B. M. van Riel, and Gerrit H. van Bruggen, "Corporate Associations and Consumer Product Responses: The Moderating Role of Corporate Brand Dominance," *Journal of Marketing*, 69, July 2005, pp. 35–48; Zeynep Gürhan-Canli and Rajeev Batra, "When Corporate Image Affects Product Evaluations: The Moderating Role of Perceived Risk," *Journal of Marketing Research*, 41, May 2004, pp. 197–205; Kevin Lane Keller and David A. Aaker, "Corporate-Level Marketing: The Impact of Credibility on a Company's Brand Extensions," *Corporate Reputation Review*, 1, August 1998, pp. 356–378; Thomas J. Brown and Peter Dacin, "The Company and the Product: Corporate Associations and Consumer Product Responses," *Journal of Marketing*, 61, January 1997, pp. 68–84.

62. Vithala R. Rao, Manoj K. Agarwal, and Denise Dalhoff, "How Is Manifest Branding Strategy Related to the Intangible Value of a Corporation?" *Journal of Marketing*, 68, October 2004, pp. 126–141. For an examination of the financial impact of brand portfolio decisions, see Neil A. Morgan and Lopo L. Rego, "The Marketing and Financial Performance Consequences of Firms' Brand Portfolio Strategy," Working paper, Kelley School of Business, Indiana University, 2006.

63. www.ameinfo.com/6187.html.

64. David A. Aaker and Erich Joachimsthaler, *Brand Leadership* (New York: Free Press, 2000).

65. Source of interview with Mr. Gerald Lawless from http://www.breakingtravelnews.com/news/article/jumeirah-group-reports-record-festive-season-in-dubai/

66. Byung-Do Kim and Mary W. Sullivan, "The Effect of Parent Brand Experience on Line Extension Trial and Repeat Purchase," *Marketing Letters*, 9, April 1998, pp. 181–193.

67. John Milewicz and Paul Herbig, "Evaluating the Brand Extension Decision Using a Model of Reputation Building," *Journal of Product & Brand Management*, 3, no. 1, January 1994, pp. 39–47; Kevin Lane Keller and David A. Aaker, "The Effects of Sequential Introduction of Brand Extensions," *Journal of Marketing Research*, 29, February 1992, pp. 35–50.

68. Valarie A. Taylor and William O. Bearden, "Ad Spending on Brand Extensions: Does Similarity Matter?" *Journal of Brand Management*, 11, September 2003, pp. 63–74; Sheri Bridges, Kevin Lane Keller, and Sanjay Sood, "Communication Strategies for Brand Extensions: Enhancing Perceived Fit by Establishing Explanatory Links," *Journal of Advertising*, 29, Winter 2000, pp. 1–11; Daniel C. Smith, "Brand Extension and Advertising Efficiency: What Can and Cannot Be Expected," *Journal of Advertising Research*, November–December 1992, pp. 11–20; Daniel C. Smith and C. Whan Park, "The Effects of Brand Extensions on Market Share and Advertising Efficiency," *Journal of Marketing Research*, 29, August 1992, pp. 296–313.

69. Bruce Meyer, "Rubber Firms Extend Brands to Gain Customers' Revenue," *B to B*, 90, no. 12, October 10, 2005, p. 6.

70. Subramanian Balachander and Sanjoy Ghose, "Reciprocal Spillover Effects: A Strategic Benefit of Brand Extensions," *Journal of Marketing*, 67, no. 1, January 2003, pp. 4–13.

71. Bharat N. Anand and Ron Shachar, "Brands as Beacons: A New Source of Loyalty to Multiproduct Firms," *Journal of Marketing Research*, 41, May 2004, pp. 135–150.

72. See http://www.huawei.com/en/static/hw-072377.pdf.

73. Kevin Lane Keller and David A. Aaker, "The Effects of Sequential Introduction of Brand Extensions," *Journal of Marketing Research*, 29, February 1992, pp. 35–50. For consumer processing implications, see Huifung Mao and H. Shanker Krishnan, "Effects of Prototype and Exemplar Fit on Brand Extension Evaluations: A Two-Process Contingency Model," *Journal of Consumer Research*, 33, June 2006, pp. 41–49.

74. Maureen Morrin, "The Impact of Brand Extensions on Parent Brand Memory Structures and Retrieval Processes," *Journal of Marketing Research*, 36, no. 4, November 1999, pp. 517–525; John A. Quelch and David Kenny, "Extend Profits, Not Product Lines," *Harvard Business Review*, September–October 1994, pp. 153–160; Perspectives from the Editors, "The Logic of Product-Line Extensions," *Harvard Business Review*, November–December 1994, pp. 53–62.

75. Al Ries and Jack Trout, *Positioning: The Battle for Your Mind*, 20th anniversary edition (New York: McGraw-Hill, 2000).

76. David A. Aaker, *Brand Portfolio Strategy: Creating Relevance, Differentiation, Energy, Leverage, and Clarity* (New York: Free Press, 2004).

77. "Lego's Turnaround: Picking Up the Pieces," *The Economist*, October 28, 2006, p. 76.

78. Mary W. Sullivan, "Measuring Image Spillovers in Umbrella-Branded Products," *Journal of Business*, 63, no. 3, July 1990, pp. 309–329.

79. Deborah Roedder John, Barbara Loken, and Christopher Joiner, "The Negative Impact of Extensions: Can Flagship Products Be Diluted," *Journal of Marketing*, January 1998, pp. 19–32; Susan M. Broniarcyzk and Joseph W. Alba, "The Importance of the Brand in Brand Extension," *Journal of Marketing Research*, May 1994, pp. 214–228 (this entire issue of *JMR* is devoted to brands and brand equity); Barbara Loken and Deborah Roedder John, "Diluting Brand Beliefs: When Do Brand Extensions Have a Negative Impact?" *Journal of Marketing*, July 1993, pp. 71–84. See also, Chris Pullig, Carolyn Simmons, and Richard G. Netemeyer, "Brand Dilution: When Do New Brands Hurt Existing Brands?" *Journal of Marketing*, 70, April 2006, pp. 52–66; R. Ahluwalia and Z. Gürhan-Canli, "The Effects of Extensions on the Family Brand Name: An Accessibility-Diagnosticity Perspective," *Journal of Consumer Research*, 27, December 2000, pp. 371–381; Z. Gürhan-Canli and M. Durairaj, "The Effects of Extensions on Brand Name Dilution and Enhancement," *Journal of Marketing Research*, 35, November 1998, pp. 464–473; S. J. Milberg, C. W. Park, and M. S. McCarthy, "Managing Negative Feedback Effects Associated with Brand Extensions: The Impact of Alternative Branding Strategies," *Journal of Consumer Psychology*, 6, 1997, pp. 119–140.

80. See also, Franziska Völckner and Henrik Sattler, "Drivers of Brand Extension Success," *Journal of Marketing*, 70, April 2006, pp. 1–17.

81. Andrea Rothman, "France's Bic Bets U.S. Consumers Will Go for Perfume on the Cheap," *Wall Street Journal*, January 12, 1989.

82. David A. Aaker, *Brand Portfolio Strategy: Creating Relevance, Differentiation, Energy, Leverage, and Clarity.*

83. Jack Trout, *Differentiate or Die: Survival in Our Era of Killer Competition* (New York: John Wiley, 2000).

84. Nirmalya Kumar, "Kill a Brand, Keep a Customer," *Harvard Business Review*, December 2003, pp. 87–95.

85. For a methodological approach for assessing the extent and nature of cannibalization, see Charlotte H. Mason and George R. Milne, "An Approach for Identifying Cannibalization within Product Line Extensions and MultiBrand Strategies," *Journal of Business Research*, 31, October–November 1994, pp. 163–170.

86. Roland T. Rust, Valerie A. Zeithaml, and Katherine A. Lemon, "Measuring Customer Equity and Calculating Marketing ROI," in *Handbook of Marketing Research*, ed. Rajiv Grover and Marco Vriens (Thousand Oaks, CA: Sage Publications, 2006), pp. 588–601; Roland T. Rust, Valerie A. Zeithaml, and Katherine A. Lemon, *Driving Customer Equity* (New York: Free Press, 2000).

87. Robert C. Blattberg and John Deighton, "Manage Marketing by the Customer Equity Test," *Harvard Business Review*, July–August 1996, pp. 136–144.

88. Robert C. Blattberg and Jacquelyn S. Thomas, "Valuing, Analyzing, and Managing the Marketing Function Using Customer Equity Principles," in *Kellogg on Marketing*, ed. Dawn Iacobucci (New York: John Wiley & Sons, 2002); Robert C. Blattberg, Gary Getz, and Jacquelyn S. Thomas, *Customer Equity: Building and Managing Relationships as Valuable Assets* (Boston: Harvard Business School Press, 2001).

89. Much of this section is based on: Robert Leone, Vithala Rao, Kevin Lane Keller, Man Luo, Leigh McAlister, and Rajendra Srivatstava, "Linking Brand Equity to Customer Equity," *Journal of Service Research*, 9, November 2006, pp. 125–138. This special issue is devoted to customer equity and has a number of thought-provoking articles.

90. Niraj Dawar, "What Are Brands Good For?" *MIT Sloan Management Review*, Autumn 2004, pp. 31–37.

Chapter 10

1. "SEKEM Report on Sustainable Development," 2009, www.sekem.com/Files/PDFs/SEKEM%20%20 Report%20on%20Sustainable%20Development%20 2009.pdf.

2. Al Ries and Jack Trout, *Positioning: The Battle for Your Mind*, 20th anniversary edition (New York: McGraw-Hill, 2000).

3. See www.crepaway.com.

4. Kevin Lane Keller, Brian Stenthal, and Alice Tybout, "Three Questions You Need to Ask about Your Brand," *Harvard Business Review*, 80, September 2002, pp. 80–89.

5. Thomas A. Brunner and Michaela Wänke, "The Reduced and Enhanced Impact of Shared Features on Individual Brand Evaluations," *Journal of Consumer Psychology*, 16, April 2006, pp. 101–111.

6. Janet Bigham Bernstel, "A New Blend of Bank," *ABA Bank Marketing*, 38, no. 2, March 2006, pp. 14+; Pat Allen, "How Umpqua Sustains and Builds on Its 'Pretty Cool' Status," *BAI Online Banking Strategies*, November–December 2006, www.bai.org/bankingstrategies/2006-nov-dec/UmpquaSustains/print.asp.

7. See http://menewswire.blogspot.com/2012/01/dubai-media-city-receives-student.html

8. Keith Naughton, "Ford's 'Perfect Storm'," *Newsweek*, September 17, 2001, pp. 48–50.

9. Susan M. Broniarczyk and Andrew D. Gershoff, "The Reciprocal Effects of Brand Equity and Trivial Attributes," *Journal of Marketing Research*, 40, May 2003, pp. 161–175; Gregory S. Carpenter, Rashi Glazer, and Kent Nakamoto, "Meaningful Brands from Meaningless Differentiation: The Dependence on Irrelevant Attributes," *Journal of Marketing Research*, 31, August 1994, pp. 339–350.

10. Michael Applebaum, "Comfy to Cool: A Brand Swivel," *Brandweek*, May 2, 2005, pp. 18–19.

11. Dale Buss, "Sweet Success," *Brandweek*, May 12, 2003, pp. 22–23.

12. "History," Roadster Diner website, www.roadsterdiner.com/index.php'?option=com_content&view=article&id=28&Itemid-80.

13. "Cravia Launches UAE's Second Roadster Diner," *AME Info*, April 28, 2009, www.ameinfo.com/194375.html.

14. Michael E. Porter, *Competitive Strategy: Techniques for Analyzing Industries and Competitors* (New York: Free Press, 1980).

15. Patrick Barwise, *Simply Better: Winning and Keeping Customers by Delivering What Matters Most* (Cambridge, MA: Harvard Business School Press, 2004).

16. Some authors distinguished additional stages. Wasson suggested a stage of competitive turbulence between growth and maturity. See Chester R. Wasson, *Dynamic Competitive Strategy and Product Life Cycles* (Austin, TX: Austin Press, 1978). Maturity describes a stage of sales growth slowdown and saturation, a stage of flat sales after sales have peaked.

17. John E. Swan and David R. Rink, "Fitting Market Strategy to Varying Product Life Cycles," *Business Horizons*, January–February 1982, pp. 72–76; Gerald J. Tellis and C. Merle Crawford, "An Evolutionary Approach to Product Growth Theory," *Journal of Marketing*, Autumn 1981, pp. 125–134.

18. William E. Cox Jr., "Product Life Cycles as Marketing Models," *Journal of Business*, October 1967, pp. 375–384.

19. Jordan P. Yale, "The Strategy of Nylon's Growth," *Modern Textiles Magazine*, February 1964, p. 32. Also see Theodore Levitt, "Exploit the Product Life Cycle," *Harvard Business Review*, November–December 1965, pp. 81–94.

20. Chester R. Wasson, "How Predictable Are Fashion and Other Product Life Cycles?" *Journal of Marketing*, July 1968, pp. 36–43.

21. Wasson, "How Predictable Are Fashion and Other Product Life Cycles?"

22. William H. Reynolds, "Cars and Clothing: Understanding Fashion Trends," *Journal of Marketing*, July 1968, pp. 44–49.

23. Robert D. Buzzell, "Competitive Behavior and Product Life Cycles," in *New Ideas for Successful Marketing*, ed. John S. Wright and Jack Goldstucker (Chicago: American Marketing Association, 1956), p. 51.

24. Rajesh J. Chandy, Gerard J. Tellis, Deborah J. MacInnis, and Pattana Thaivanich, "What to Say When: Advertising Appeals in Evolving Markets," *Journal of Marketing Research*, 38, November 2001, pp. 399–414.

25. As reported in Joseph T. Vesey, "The New Competitors: They Think in Terms of Speed to Market," *Academy of Management Executive*, 5, no. 2, May 1991, pp. 23–33; and Brian Dumaine, "How Managers Can Succeed through Speed," *Fortune*, February 13, 1989, pp. 54–59.

26. Glen L. Urban et al, "Market Share Rewards to Pioneering Brands: An Empirical Analysis and Strategic Implications," *Management Science*, June 1986, pp. 645–659; William T. Robinson and Claes Fornell, "Sources of Market Pioneer Advantages In Consumer Goods Industries," *Journal of Marketing Research*, August 1985, pp. 305–317.

27. Gregory S. Carpenter and Kent Nakamoto, "Consumer Preference Formation and Pioneering Advantage," *Journal of Marketing Research*, August 1989, pp. 285–298.

28. William T. Robinson and Sungwook Min, "Is the First to Market the First to Fail? Empirical Evidence for Industrial Goods Businesses," *Journal of Marketing Research*, 39, February 2002, pp. 120–128.

29. Frank R. Kardes, Gurumurthy Kalyanaram, Murali Chankdrashekaran, and Ronald J. Dornoff, "Brand Retrieval, Consideration Set Composition, Consumer Choice, and the Pioneering Advantage," *Journal of Consumer Research*, June 1993, pp. 62–75. See also Frank H. Alpert and Michael A. Kamins, "Pioneer Brand Advantage and Consumer Behavior: A Conceptual Framework and Propositional Inventory," *Journal of the Academy of Marketing Science*, Summer 1994, pp. 244–253.

30. Thomas S. Robertson and Hubert Gatignon, "How Innovators Thwart New Entrants into Their Market," *Planning Review*, September–October 1991, pp. 4–11, 48; Douglas Bowman and Hubert Gatignon, "Order of Entry as a Moderator of the Effect of Marketing Mix on Market Share," *Marketing Science*, 15, no. 3, Summer 1996, pp. 222–242.

31. Venkatesh Shankar, Gregory S. Carpenter, and Lakshman Krishnamurthi, "Late Mover Advantage: How Innovative Late Entrants Outsell Pioneers," *Journal of Marketing Research*, 35, February 1998, pp. 54–70.

32. Mark Ritson, "It Sometimes Pays to Come Second," *Marketing*, October 25, 2006, p. 23; Richard Waters, "Wikipedia Founder Plans Rival 'Citizendium' Aims to Introduce Order to Chaos of Web Encyclopedias; Editors Will Control the Posting of Articles," *Financial Times*, October 17, 2006, p. 19.

33. Steven P. Schnaars, *Managing Imitation Strategies* (New York: Free Press, 1994). See also Jin K. Han, Namwoon Kim, and Hony-Bom Kin, "Entry Barriers: A Dull-, One-, or Two-Edged Sword for Incumbents? Unraveling the Paradox from a Contingency Perspective," *Journal of Marketing*, January 2001, pp. 1–14.

34. Victor Kegan, "Second Sight: Second Movers Take All," *The Guardian*, October 10, 2002.

35. Peter N. Golder, "Historical Method in Marketing Research with New Evidence on Long-Term Market Share Stability," *Journal of Marketing Research*, 37, May 2000, pp. 156–172; Peter N. Golder and Gerald J. Tellis, "Pioneer Advantage: Marketing Logic or Marketing Legend?" *Journal of Marketing Research*, May 1992, pp. 34–46. See also Shi Zhang and Arthur B. Markman,

"Overcoming the Early Advantage: The Role of Alignable and Nonalignable Differences," *Journal of Marketing Research*, November 1998, pp. 1–15.

36. Gerald Tellis and Peter Golder, *Will and Vision: How Latecomers Can Grow to Dominate Markets* (New York: McGraw-Hill, 2001); Rajesh K. Chandy and Gerald J. Tellis, "The Incumbent's Curse? Incumbency, Size, and Radical Product Innovation," *Journal of Marketing Research*, July 2000, pp. 1–17.

37. Sungwook Min, Manohar U. Kalwani, and William T. Robinson, "Market Pioneer and Early Follower Survival Risks: A Contingency Analysis of Really New versus Incrementally New Product-Markets," *Journal of Marketing*, 70, January 2006, pp. 15–35. See also Raji Srinivasan, Gary L. Lilien, and Arvind Rangaswamy, "First In, First Out? The Effects of Network Externalities on Pioneer Survival," *Journal of Marketing*, 68, January 2004, pp. 41–58.

38. Trond Riiber Knudsen, "Escaping the Middle-Market Trap: An Interview with CEO of Electrolux," *McKinsey Quarterly*, December 2006, pp. 72–79.

39. Stephanie Thompson, "Coffee Brands Think outside of the Can," *Advertising Age*, July 28, 2003, p. 26.

40. Brian Wansink and Michael L. Ray, "Advertising Strategies to Increase Usage Frequency," *Journal of Marketing*, January 1996, pp. 31–46. Also see Brian Wansink, "Expansion Advertising," in *How Advertising Works*, ed. John Philip Jones (Thousand Oaks, CA: Sage Publications), pp. 95–103.

41. Stephen M. Nowlis and Itamar Simonson, "The Effect of New Product Features on Brand Choice," *Journal of Marketing Research*, February 1996, pp. 36–46.

42. Allen J. McGrath, "Growth Strategies with a '90s Twist," *Across the Board*, March 1995, pp. 43–46.

43. Rajan Varadarajan, Mark P. DeFanti, and Paul S. Busch, "Brand Portfolio, Corporate Image, and Reputation: Managing Brand Deletions," *Journal of the Academy of Marketing Science*, 34, Spring 2006, pp. 195–205; Stephen J. Carlotti Jr., Mary Ellen Coe, and Jesko Perrey, "Making Brand Portfolios Work," *McKinsey Quarterly*, 4, 2004, pp. 24–36; Nirmalya Kumar, "Kill a Brand, Keep a Customer," *Harvard Business Review*, 81, December 2003, pp. 86–95; George J. Avlonitis, "Product Elimination Decision Making: Does Formality Matter," *Journal of Marketing*, Winter 1985, pp. 41–52; Philip Kotler, "Phasing Out Weak Products," *Harvard Business Review*, March–April 1965, pp. 107–118.

44. Kathryn Rudie Harrigan, "The Effect of Exit Barriers upon Strategic Flexibility," *Strategic Management Journal*, 1, February 1980, pp. 165–176.

45. Laurence P. Feldman and Albert L. Page, "Harvesting: The Misunderstood Market Exit Strategy," *Journal of Business Strategy*, Spring 1985, pp. 79–85; Philip Kotler, "Harvesting Strategies for Weak Products," *Business Horizons*, August 1978, pp. 15–22.

46. Peter N. Golder and Gerard J. Tellis, "Growing, Growing, Gone: Cascades, Diffusion, and Turning Points in the Product Life Cycle," *Marketing Science*, 23, Spring 2004, pp. 207–218.

47. Youngme Moon, "Break Free from the Product Life Cycle," *Harvard Business Review*, May 2005, pp. 87–94.

48. Hubert Gatignon and David Soberman, "Competitive Response and Market Evolution," in *Handbook of Marketing*, ed. Barton A. Weitz and Robin Wensley (London, UK: Sage Publications, 2002), pp. 126–147; Robert D. Buzzell, "Market Functions and Market Evolution," *Journal of Marketing*, 63, Special Issue 1999, pp. 61–63.

49. For a discussion of the evolution of the minivan market between 1982 and 1998, see Jose Antonio Rosa, Joseph F. Porac, Jelena Runser-Spanjol, and Michael S. Saxon, "Sociocognitive Dynamics in a Product Market," *Journal of Marketing*, 63, Special Issue 1999, pp. 64–77.

50. Daniel Fisher, "Six Feet Under," *Forbes*, July 7, 2003, pp. 66–68.

Chapter 11

1. Information from Aramex company website, www.aramex.com.

2. For a detailed academic treatment of a number of issues on competition, see the Special Issue on Competitive Responsiveness, *Marketing Science*, 24, Winter 2005.

3. Michael E. Porter, *Competitive Strategy* (New York: Free Press, 1980), pp. 22–23.

4. See www.etisalat.com.

5. See www.cleopatraceramics.com/welcome.do.

6. Allan D. Shocker, "Determining the Structure of Product-Markets: Practices, Issues, and Suggestions," in *Handbook of Marketing*, ed. Barton A. Weitz and Robin Wensley (London: Sage, 2002), pp. 106–25. See also, Bruce H. Clark and David B. Montgomery, "Managerial Identification of Competitors," *Journal of Marketing*, 63, July 1999, pp. 67–83.

7. "What Business Are You In? Classic Advice from Theodore Levitt," *Harvard Business Review*, October 2006, pp. 127–137. See also Theodore Levitt's seminal article, "Marketing Myopia," *Harvard Business Review*, July–August 1960, pp. 45–56.

8. Jeffrey F. Rayport and Bernard J. Jaworski, *e-Commerce* (New York: McGraw-Hill, 2001), p. 53.

9. Richard A. D'Aveni, "Competitive Pressure Systems: Mapping and Managing Multimarket Contact," *MIT Sloan Management Review*, Autumn 2002, pp. 39–49.

10. Porter, *Competitive Strategy*, Chapter 7.

11. For discussion of some of the long-term implications of marketing activities, see Koen Pauwels, "How Dynamic Consumer Response, Competitor Response, Company Support, and Company Inertia Shape Long-Term Marketing Effectiveness," *Marketing Science*, 23, Autumn 2004, pp. 596–610; Koen Pauwels, Dominique M. Hanssens, and S. Siddarth, "The Long-Term Effects

of Price Promotions on Category Incidence, Brand Choice, and Purchase Quantity," *Journal of Marketing Research*, 34, November 2002, pp. 421–439; and Marnik Dekimpe and Dominique Hanssens, "Sustained Spending and Persistent Response: A New Look at Long-term Marketing Profitability," *Journal of Marketing Research*, 36, November 1999, pp. 397–412.

12. Rajendra S. Sisodia, David B. Wolfe, and Jagdish N. Sheth, *Firms of Endearment: How World-Class Companies Benefit Profit from Passion & Purpose* (Upper Saddle River, NJ: Wharton School Publishing, 2007).

13. For an academic treatment of benchmarking, see Douglas W. Vorhies and Neil A. Morgan, "Benchmarking Marketing Capabilities for Sustained Competitive Advantage," *Journal of Marketing*, 69, no. 1, January 2005, pp. 80–94.

14. Porter, *Competitive Strategy*, Chapter 7.

15. These taxonomies and the Telstra example come from the writings of Australian marketing academic John H. Roberts: John H. Roberts, "Defensive Marketing: How a Strong Incumbent Can Protect Its Position," *Harvard Business Review*, November 2005, pp. 150–157; John Roberts, Charlie Nelson, and Pamela Morrison, "Defending the Beachhead: Telstra vs. Optus," *Business Strategy Review*, 12, Spring 2001, pp. 19–24.

16. See www.mobinil.com; www.estisalat.com; www.zain.com.

17. Sarah Buxbury, "Gap Sept. Same Store Sales Down 4%; Other Retailers Strong," *San Francisco Business Times*, October 6, 2011, www.bizjournals.com/sanfrancisco/news/2011/10/06/gap-same-store-sales-down-4-september.html.

18. Michael Barbaro and Hillary Chura, "The Gap Is in Need of a Niche," *New York Times*, January 27, 2007 p. C1 Copyright ©2007 The New York Times. Reprinted by permission.

19. Zachs Investment Research, "Gap Coming to Egypt, Morocco," www.dailymarkets.com/stock/2011/06/30/gap-coming-to-egypt-morocco/.

20. Financial Statements for Starbucks, http://investing.businessweek.com/research/stocks/financials/financials.asp?ticker=SBUX:US; "Company Information," www.starbucks.com/about-us/company-information.

21. Brian Wansink, "Can Package Size Accelerate Usage Volume?," *Journal of Marketing*, 60, July 1996, pp. 1–14. See also Priya Raghubir and Eric A. Greenleaf, "Ratios in Proportion: What Should the Shape of the Package Be?," *Journal of Marketing*, 70, April 2006, pp. 95–107; and Valerie Folkes and Shashi Matta, "The Effect of Package Shape on Consumers' Judgments of Product Volume: Attention as a Mental Contaminant," *Journal of Consumer Research*, 31, September 2004, pp. 390–401.

22. John D. Cripps, "Heuristics and Biases in Timing the Replacement of Durable Products," *Journal of Consumer Research*, 21, September 1994, pp. 304–318.

23. "Business Bubbles," *The Economist*, October 12, 2002.

24. George Stalk Jr and Rob Lachanauer, "Hardball: Five Killer Strategies for Trouncing the Competition," *Harvard Business Review*, 82, April 2004, pp. 62–71; Richard D'Aveni, "The Empire Strikes Back: Counterrevolutionary Strategies for Industry Leaders," *Harvard Business Review*, November 2002, pp. 66–74.

25. Robert D. Hof, "There's Not Enough 'Me' in MySpace," *BusinessWeek*, December 4, 2006, p. 40; Patricia Sellers, "MySpace Cowboys," *Fortune*, September 4, 2006, pp. 66–74; Aaron Pressman, "MySpace for Baby Boomers, *BusinessWeek*, October 16, 2006, pp. 120–122.

26. Information from www.airarabia.com; "Air Arabia announces second quarter 2010 net profit of AED 50 million," *Albawaba*, www.albawaba.com/business/air-arabia-announces-second-quarter-2010-net-profit-aed-50-million.

27. See www.tareknour.com.

28. Jonathan Glancey, "The Private World of the Walkman," *Guardian*, October 11, 1999.

29. These six defense strategies, as well as the five attack strategies, are taken from Philip Kotler and Ravi Singh, "Marketing Warfare in the 1980s," *Journal of Business Strategy*, Winter 1981, pp. 30–41.

30. Porter, *Competitive Strategy*, Chapter 4; Jaideep Prabhu and David W. Stewart, "Signaling Strategies in Competitive Interaction: Building Reputations and Hiding the Truth," *Journal of Marketing Research*, 38, February 2001, pp. 62–72.

31. Roger J. Calantone and Kim E. Schatzel, "Strategic Foretelling: Communication-Based Antecedents of a Firm's Propensity to Preannounce," *Journal of Marketing*, 64, January 2000, pp. 17–30; Jehoshua Eliashberg and Thomas S. Robertson, "New Product Preannouncing Behavior: A Market Signaling Study," *Journal of Marketing Research*, 25, August 1988, pp. 282–292.

32. Thomas S. Robertson, Jehoshua Eliashberg, and Talia Rymon, "New-Product Announcement Signals and Incumbent Reactions," *Journal of Marketing*, 59, July 1995, pp. 1–15.

33. Yuhong Wu, Sridhar Balasubramanian, and Vijay Mahajan, "When Is a Preannounced New Product Likely to Be Delayed?" *Journal of Marketing*, 68, April 2004, pp. 101–113; Barry L. Bayus, Sanjay Jain, and Ambar G. Rao, "Truth or Consequences: An Analysis of Vaporware and New-Product Announcements," *Journal of Marketing Research*, 38, February 2001, pp. 3–13.

34. Kevin Kelleher, "Why FedEx Is Gaining Ground," *Business 2.0*, October 2003, pp. 56–57; Charles Haddad, "FedEx: Gaining on Ground," *BusinessWeek*, December 16, 2002, pp. 126–128.

35. J. Scott Armstrong and Kesten C. Green, "Competitor-Oriented Objectives: The Myth of Market Share," *International Journal of Business*, 12, no. 1, Winter 2007, pp. 115–134; Stuart E. Jackson, *Where Value Hides: A New Way to Uncover Profitable Growth for Your Business* (New York: John Wiley & Sons, 2006).

36. Nirmalya Kumar, *Marketing as Strategy* (Cambridge, MA: Harvard Business School Press, 2004); Philip Kotler and Paul N. Bloom, "Strategies for High-Market-Share

Companies," *Harvard Business Review*, November–December 1975, pp. 63–72.

37. Robert D. Buzzell and Frederick D. Wiersema, "Successful Share-Building Strategies," *Harvard Business Review*, January–February 1981, pp. 135–144.

38. Robert J. Dolan, "Models of Competition: A Review of Theory and Empirical Evidence," in *Review of Marketing*, ed. Ben M. Enis and Kenneth J. Roering (Chicago: American Marketing Association, 1981), pp. 224–234.

39. Linda Hellofs and Robert Jacobson, "Market Share and Customer's Perceptions of Quality: When Can Firms Grow Their Way to Higher versus Lower Quality?" *Journal of Marketing*, 63, January 1999, pp. 16–25.

40. Jon Birger, "Second-Mover Advantage," *Fortune*, March 20, 2006, pp. 20–21.

41. Venkatesh Shankar, Gregory Carpenter, and Lakshman Krishnamurthi, "Late-Mover Advantage: How Innovative Late Entrants Outsell Pioneers," *Journal of Marketing Research*, 35, February 1998, pp. 54–70; Gregory S. Carpenter and Kent Nakamoto, "The Impact of Consumer Preference Formation on Marketing Objectives and Competitive Second-Mover Strategies," *Journal of Consumer Psychology*, 5, no. 4, 1996, pp. 325–358; Gregory S. Carpenter and Kent Nakamoto, "Competitive Strategies for Late Entry into a Market with a Dominant Brand," *Management Science*, October 1990, pp. 1268–1278.

42. Megan Johnston, "The Ketchup Strategy," *Forbes*, November 13, 2006, p. 185.

43. Michael V. Copeland, "These Boots Really Were Made for Walking," *Business 2.0*, October 2004, pp. 72–74.

44. Katrina Booker, "The Pepsi Machine," *Fortune*, February 6, 2006, pp. 68–72.

45. Jonathan Last, "Setting the Stage for Another Flop?," *philly.com*, June 4, 2006; Eryn Brown, "Sony's Big Bazooka," *Fortune*, December 30, 2002, pp. 111–114.

46. Suzanne Smalley and Raja Mishra, "Froth, Fear, and Fury," *Boston Globe*, February 1, 2007.

47. Theodore Levitt, "Innovative Imitation," *Harvard Business Review*, September–October 1966, p. 63. Also see Steven P. Schnaars, *Managing Imitation Strategies: How Later Entrants Seize Markets from Pioneers* (New York: Free Press, 1994).

48. See www.eipico.com.eg/Eipico.html.

49. See www.meed.com.

50. Jayne O'Donnell, "Family Rolling to Success on Tire Rack," *USA Today*, December 8, 2003.

51. Mark Morrison, "This Wildcatter Feels Right at Home in Gabon," *BusinessWeek*, June 5, 2006, p. 63.

52. Reported in E. R. Linneman and L. J. Stanton, *Making Niche Marketing Work* (New York: McGraw-Hill, 1991).

53. See www.apgglass.com.

54. Sana Fashion Store in Dubai Directory, www.datadubai.com/United_Arab_Emirates/Dubai/Shopping/Online_Stores/402719-1662.html.

55. Robert Spector, *Amazon.com: Get Big Fast* (New York: HarperBusiness, 2000), p. 151.

Chapter 12

1. Based on interview with Amina Khalil, Senior Marketing Manager, Raya Trade.

2. This discussion is adapted from Theodore Levitt, "Marketing Success through Differentiation: Of Anything," *Harvard Business Review*, January–February 1980, pp. 83–91. The first level, core benefit, has been added to Levitt's discussion.

3. Harper W. Boyd Jr. and Sidney Levy, "New Dimensions in Consumer Analysis," *Harvard Business Review*, November–December 1963, pp. 129–140.

4. See www.corporateinformation.com/Company-Snapshot.aspx?cusip=C682Q0E00; www.saudipaper.com/en/Organization.html.

5. For some definitions, see Peter D. Bennett, ed., *Dictionary of Marketing Terms* (Chicago: American Marketing Association, 1995). Also see Patrick E. Murphy and Ben M. Enis, "Classifying Products Strategically," *Journal of Marketing*, July 1986, pp. 24–42.

6. Some of these bases are discussed in David A. Garvin, "Competing on the Eight Dimensions of Quality," *Harvard Business Review*, November–December 1987, pp. 101–109.

7. Paul Kedrosky, "Simple Minds," *Business 2.0*, April 2006, p. 38; Debora Viana Thompson, Rebecca W. Hamilton, and Roland Rust, "Feature Fatigue: When Product Capabilities Become Too Much of a Good Thing," *Journal of Marketing Research*, 42, November 2005, pp. 431–442.

8. James H. Gilmore and B. Joseph Pine, *Markets of One: Creating Customer-Unique Value through Mass Customization* (Boston: Harvard Business School Press, 2000).

9. Paul Grimaldi, "Consumers Design Products Their Way," *Knight Ridder Tribune Business News*, November 25, 2006; Michael A. Prospero, *Fast Company*, September 2005, p. 35.

10. Gail Edmondson, "Mercedes Gets Back up to Speed," *BusinessWeek*, November 13, 2006, pp. 46–47.

11. Bernd Schmitt and Alex Simonson, *Marketing Aesthetics: The Strategic Management of Brand, Identity, and Image* (New York: Free Press, 1997).

12. Bruce Nussbaum, "The Power of Design," *BusinessWeek*, May 17, 2004, pp. 88–94; "Masters of Design," *Fast Company*, June 2004, pp. 61–75. Also see Philip Kotler, "Design: A Powerful but Neglected Strategic Tool," *Journal of Business Strategy*, Autumn 1984, pp. 16–21.

13. See www.nodust-eg.com/?pg=home.

14. See www.topdesignmag.com/awesome-package-design-concepts-made-by-students/.

15. Stanley Reed, "Rolls Royce at Your Service," *BusinessWeek*, November 15, 2005, pp. 92–93.

16. For a comprehensive discussion of Cemex, see Adrian J. Slywotzky and David J. Morrison, *How Digital Is Your Business* (New York: Crown Business, 2000), Chapter 5.

17. "Hydra Properties Launches in-House Bilingual Call Centre," March 2010, AME Info, www.ameinfo.com/225564.html.

18. Linda Knapp, "A Sick Computer?" *Seattle Times*, January 28, 2001.

19. Bruce Einhorn and Tim Culpan, "Acer: Past Dell, and Chasing HP," *Bloomberg Businessweek*, February 25, 2010, www.businessweek.com/magazine/content/10_10/b4169050062005.htm; Ralph Jennings, "Acer Reports Record Revenue, Profit in 2010," *PCWorld Business Center*, January 26, 2011, www.pcworld.com/businesscenter/article/217750/acer_reports_record_revenue_profit_in_2010.html; Anne Birte Stensgaard, "Acer's 'Pick and Drop' Named Best in the Region," *AMEinfo.com*, July 1, 2007, www.ameinfo.com/125189.html; Stuart Wilson, "Acer Lauds MEA Service Levels," *Channel EMEA*, April 19, 2010, www.channelemea.com/spip.php?article2514.

20. Leslie Earnest and Adrian G. Uribarri, "Costco Halts Liberal Electronics Return Policy; Refunds Were Costing the Warehouse Store Chain 'Tens of Millions of Dollars' a Year," *Los Angeles Times*, February 28, 2007, p. C1. Reprinted by permission.

21. This section is based on a comprehensive treatment of product returns, James Stock and Thomas Speh, "Managing Product Returns for Competitive Advantage," *MIT Sloan Management Review*, Autumn 2006, pp. 57–62.

22. Robert Bordley, "Determining the Appropriate Depth and Breadth of a Firm's Product Portfolio," *Journal of Marketing Research*, 40, February 2003, pp. 39–53; Peter Boatwright and Joseph C. Nunes, "Reducing Assortment: An Attribute-Based Approach," *Journal of Marketing*, 65, July 2001, pp. 50–63.

23. Adapted from a Hamilton Consultants White Paper, December 1, 2000.

24. This illustration is found in Benson P. Shapiro, *Industrial Product Policy: Managing the Existing Product Line* (Cambridge, MA: Marketing Science Institute, 1977), pp. 3–5, 98–101.

25. "Brand Challenge," *The Economist*, April 6, 2002, p. 68.

26. Simon Gilham, "Brand Identity Design," www.simongilham.co.uk/gilham_myfolio_200906.pdf.

27. Amna Kirmani, Sanjay Sood, and Sheri Bridges, "The Ownership Effect in Consumer Responses to Brand-Line Stretches," *Journal of Marketing*, 63, January 1999, pp. 88–101; T. Randall, K. Ulrich, and D. Reibstein, "Brand Equity and Vertical Product-Line Extent," *Marketing Science*, 17, Autumn 1998, pp. 356–379; David A. Aaker, "Should You Take Your Brand to Where the Action Is?" *Harvard Business Review*, September–October 1997, pp. 135–143.

28. See www.rotana.com/index.php; www.centrobyrotana.com/.

29. France Leclerc, Christopher K. Hsee, and Joseph C. Nunes, "Narrow Focusing: Why the Relative Position of a Good in Its Category Matters More Than It Should," *Marketing Science*, 24, Spring 2005, pp. 194–205.

30. "Hamil Al Musk, by Zahras Perfumes," http://zahras.com/Perfume/Hamil%20Al%20Musk%20-%20by%20Zahras%20Perfumes.pdf; see also www.hamilalmusk.com/.

31. Steuart Henderson Britt, "How Weber's Law Can Be Applied to Marketing," *Business Horizons*, February 1975, pp. 21–29.

32. Stanley Holmes, "All the Rage Since Reagan," *BusinessWeek*, July 25, 2005, p. 68.

33. Nirmalya Kumar, "Kill a Brand, Keep a Customer," *Harvard Business Review*, December 2003, pp. 86–95; Brad Stone, "Back to Basics," *Newsweek*, August 4, 2003, pp. 42–44.

34. Laurens M. Sloot, Dennis Fok, and Peter Verhoef, "The Short- and Long-Term Impact of an Assortment Reduction on Category Sales," *Journal of Marketing Research*, 43, November 2006, pp. 536–548.

35. Patricia O'Connell, "A Chat with Unilever's Niall FitzGerald," *BusinessWeek Online*, August 2, 2001; John Willman, "Leaner, Cleaner, and Healthier Is the Stated Aim," *Financial Times*, February 23, 2000; "Unilever's Goal: 'Power Brands'," *Advertising Age*, January 3, 2000.

36. "Personal Care Brands: Good Morning," www.unileverme.com/brands/personalcarebrands/goodmorning.aspx.

37. George Rädler, Jan Kubes, and Bohdan Wojnar, "Skoda Auto: From 'No-Class' to World-Class in One Decade," *Critical EYE*, 15, July 2006; Scott D. Upham, "Beneath the Brand," *Automotive Manufacturing & Production*, June 2001.

38. "About Vodafone," www.vodafone.com.qa/go/en/aboutus/aboutvodafone.

39. See www.vodafone.com.qa/.

40. See Gerald J. Tellis, "Beyond the Many Faces of Price: An Integration of Pricing Strategies," *Journal of Marketing*, October 1986, p. 155; see also Dilip Soman and John T. Gourville, "Transaction Decoupling: How Price Bundling Affects the Decision to Consume," *Journal of Marketing Research*, 38, February 2001, pp. 30–44.

41. Adapted from George Wuebker, "Bundles Effectiveness Often Undermined," *Marketing News*, March 18, 2002, pp. 9–12. See also Stefan Stremersch and Gerard J. Tellis, "Strategic Bundling of Products and Prices," *Journal of Marketing* 66, January 2002, pp. 55–72.

42. Akshay R. Rao, Lu Qu, and Robert W. Ruekert, "Signaling Unobservable Quality through a Brand Ally," *Journal of Marketing Research*, 36, no. 2, May 1999, pp. 258–268; Akshay R. Rao and Robert W. Ruekert, "Brand Alliances as Signals of Product Quality," *Sloan Management Review*, Autumn 1994, pp. 87–97.

43. Bernard L. Simonin and Julie A. Ruth, "Is a Company Known by the Company It Keeps? Assessing the Spillover Effects of Brand Alliances on Consumer Brand Attitudes," *Journal of Marketing Research*, February 1998, pp. 30–42; see also C. W. Park, S. Y. Jun, and A. D. Shocker, "Composite Branding Alliances: An Investigation of Extension and Feedback Effects," *Journal of Marketing Research*, 33, November 1996, pp. 453–466.

44. Park, Jun, and Shocker, "Composite Branding Alliances: An Investigation of Extension and Feedback Effects;" Lance Leuthesser, Chiranjier Kohli, and Rajneesh Suri, "2 + 2 = 5? A Framework for Using Co-Branding to Leverage a Brand," *Journal of Brand Management*, 2, no. 1, September 2003, pp. 35–47.

45. Based in part on a talk by Nancy Bailey, "Using Licensing to Build the Brand," Brand Masters conference, December 7, 2000.

46. "Our Products," *Moroccan Oil*, www.moroccanoil.com/en/our-products.html; "About Us," *Argan Oil and More*, www.arganoilandmore.com//aboutus.asp.

47. Kalpesh Kaushik Desai and Kevin Lane Keller, "The Effects of Brand Expansions and Ingredient Branding Strategies on Host Brand Extendibility," *Journal of Marketing*, 66, January 2002, pp. 73–93; D. C. Denison, "Ingredient Branding Puts Big Names in the Mix," *Boston Globe*, May 26, 2002.

48. See www.dupont.com.

49. Seth Goldin, "In Praise of Purple Cows," *Fast Company*, February 2003, pp. 74–85.

50. Susan B. Bassin, "Value-Added Packaging Cuts Through Store Clutter," *Marketing News*, September 26, 1988, p. 21.

51. Karen Springen, "Nancy's Still Nice," *Newsweek*, February 16, 2004, p. 9; Judith Rosen, "Classics Strategies; Classics Sale," *Publishers Weekly*, October 6, 2003, pp. 16–18.

52. Susanna Hamner, "Packaging That Pays," *Business 2.0*, July 2006, pp. 68–69.

53. Mya Frazier, "How Can Your Package Stand Out? Eye Tracking Looks Hard for Answers," *Advertising Age*, October 16, 2006, p. 14.

54. Kate Fitzgerald, "Packaging Is the Capper," *Advertising Age*, May 5, 2003, p. 22.

55. "Brand Watch," *Food and Drug Corporation*, www.fdc.com.lb/special/specialOffer.asp; Darine Sabbagh, "Kazouza 1941 Mystery Uncovered!" *The Identity Chef*, October 12, 2009, http://theidentitychef.com/2009/10/12/kazouza-1941-mystery-uncovered/.

56. "Labeling and Marking Requirements in Egypt," www.globaltrade.net/international-trade-import-exports/f/business/text/Egypt/Legal-and-Compliance-Marketing-Regulations-Labeling-and-Marking-Requirements-in-Egypt.html?folderId=4025.

57. John C. Kozup, Elizabeth H. Creyer, and Scot Burton, "Making Healthful Food Choices: The Influence of Health Claims and Nutrition Information on Consumers' Evaluations of Packaged Food Products and Restaurant Menu Items," *Journal of Marketing*, 67, April 2003, pp. 19–34; Siva K. Balasubramanian and Catherine Cole, "Consumers' Search and Use of Nutrition Information: The Challenge and Promise of the Nutrition Labeling and Education Act," *Journal of Marketing*, 66, July 2002, pp. 112–127.

58. "Company Profile," www.elarabygroup.com/CompanyProfile.aspx; www.toshiba.co.jp/about/ir/en/finance/ar/ar2011/tar2011e.pdf.

59. Barbara Ettore, "Phenomenal Promises Mean Business," *Management Review*, March 1994, pp. 18–23; "More Firms Pledge Guaranteed Service," *Wall Street Journal*, July 17, 1991; see also Sridhar Moorthy and Kannan Srinivasan, "Signaling Quality with a Money-Back Guarantee: The Role of Transaction Costs," *Marketing Science*, 14, no. 4, Autumn 1995, pp. 442–446; Christopher W. L. Hart, *Extraordinary Guarantees* (New York: Amacom, 1993).

60. "Jaguar Extended Warranty," www.jaguar.com/me/en/#/owner_support/servicemaintenance/warranty/extended_warranty.

61. "Toyota Recalls Another 2.3 Million Vehicles Because of Sticking Accelerator Pedals," *Auto Arabia*, www.autoarabia.org/articles/576/Toyota%20recalls%20another%202.3%20million%20vehicles%20because%20of%20sticking%20.

Chapter 13

1. Leonard L. Berry, *On Great Service: A Framework for Action* (New York: Free Press, 2006); Leonard L. Berry, *Discovering the Soul of Service: The Nine Drivers of Sustainable Business Success* (New York: Free Press, 1999); Fred Wiersema, ed., *Customer Service: Extraordinary Results at Southwest Airlines, Charles Schwab, Lands' End, American Express, Staples, and USAA* (New York: HarperBusiness, 1998).

2. Leonard L. Berry and Kent D. Seltman, "Building a Strong Services Brand: Lessons from Mayo Clinic," *Business Horizons*, 50, May 2007, pp. 199–209; Leonard L. Berry, "Leadership Lessons from Mayo Clinic," *Organizational Dynamics*, 33, August 2004, pp. 228–242; Leonard L. Berry and Neeli Bendapudi, "Clueing in Customers," *Harvard Business Review*, February 2003, pp. 100–106; John La Forgia, Kent Seltman, and Scott Swanson, "Mayo Clinic: Sustaining a Legacy Brand and Leveraging Its Equity in the 21st-Century Market," Presentation at the Marketing Science Institute's Conference on Brand Orchestration, Orlando, FL, December 4–5, 2003.

3. Jena McGregor, "Customer Service Champs," *BusinessWeek*, March 5, 2007, pp. 52–64; Mohanbir Sawhney, Sridhar Balasubramanian, and Vish V. Krishnan, "Creating Growth with Services," *MIT Sloan Management Review*, Winter 2004, pp. 34–43.

4. "Lebanese Agency Receives Nomination, Honorable Mention at 15th Annual Webby Awards," www.zawya.com/story.cfm/sidZAWYA20110419092105/Lebanese_Agency_Receives_Nomination_Honorable_Mention_at_15th_Annual_Webby_Awards; www.beirutterraces.com/.

5. Further classifications of services are described in Christopher H. Lovelock, *Services Marketing*, 3rd edn (Upper Saddle River, NJ: Prentice Hall, 1996). Also see John E. Bateson, *Managing Services Marketing: Text and Readings*, 3rd edn (Hinsdale, IL: Dryden, 1995).

6. Valarie A. Zeithaml, "How Consumer Evaluation Processes Differ between Goods and Services," in

Marketing of Services, ed. J. Donnelly and W. R. George (Chicago: American Marketing Association, 1981), pp. 186–190.

7. Amy Ostrom and Dawn Iacobucci, "Consumer Trade-Offs and the Evaluation of Services," *Journal of Marketing*, January 1995, pp. 17–28.

8. For discussion of how the blurring of the line distinguishing products and services changes the meaning of this taxonomy, see Christopher Lovelock and Evert Gummesson, "Whither Services Marketing? In Search of a New Paradigm and Fresh Perspectives," *Journal of Service Research*, 7, August 2004, pp. 20–41; and Stephen L. Vargo and Robert F. Lusch, "Evolving to a New Dominant Logic for Marketing," *Journal of Marketing*, 68, January 2004, pp. 1–17.

9. Theodore Levitt, "Marketing Intangible Products and Product Intangibles," *Harvard Business Review*, May–June 1981, pp. 94–102; Leonard L. Berry, "Services Marketing Is Different," *Business*, May–June 1980, pp. 24–30.

10. B. H. Booms and M. J. Bitner, "Marketing Strategies and Organizational Structures for Service Firms," in *Marketing of Services*, ed. J. Donnelly and W. R. George (Chicago: American Marketing Association, 1981), pp. 47–51.

11. Lewis P. Carbone and Stephan H. Haeckel, "Engineering Customer Experiences," *Marketing Management*, 3, Winter 1994, p. 17.

12. Interview with Sherif El Atroush, Managing Director of Grand Royal; http://grandroyal-alex.com/.

13. Personal interview with Ahmed Kordy, www.mashaweeronline.com.

14. Gila E. Fruchter and Eitan Gerstner, "Selling with 'Satisfaction Guaranteed'," *Journal of Service Research*, 1, no. 4, May 1999, pp. 313–323. See also Rebecca J. Slotegraaf and J. Jeffrey Inman, "Longitudinal Shifts in the Drivers of Satisfaction with Product Quality: The Role of Attribute Resolvability," *Journal of Marketing Research*, 41, August 2004, pp. 269–280.

15. For a similar list, see Leonard L. Berry and A. Parasuraman, *Marketing Services: Competing through Quality* (New York: Free Press, 1991), p. 16.

16. The material in this paragraph is based in part on Valarie Zeithaml, Mary Jo Bitner, and Dwayne D. Gremler, *Services Marketing: Integrating Customer Focus across the Firm*, 4th edn (New York: McGraw-Hill, 2006), Chapter 9.

17. G. Lynn Shostack, "Service Positioning through Structural Change," *Journal of Marketing*, January 1987, pp. 34–43.

18. Vikas Mittal, Wagner A. Kamakura, and Rahul Govind, "Geographical Patterns in Customer Service and Satisfaction: An Empirical Investigation," *Journal of Marketing*, 68, July 2004, pp. 48–62.

19. Jeffrey F. Rayport, Bernard J. Jaworski, and Ellie J. Kyung, "Best Face Forward: Improving Companies' Service Interface with Customers," *Journal of Interactive Marketing*, 19, Autumn 2005, pp. 67–80; Asim Ansari and Carl F. Mela, "E-Customization," *Journal of Marketing Research*, 40, May 2003, pp. 131–145.

20. W. Earl Sasser, "Match Supply and Demand in Service Industries," *Harvard Business Review*, November–December 1976, pp. 133–140.

21. Steven M. Shugan and Jinhong Xie, "Advance Selling for Services," *California Management Review*, 46, no. 3, Spring 2004, pp. 37–54; Eyal Biyalogorsky and Eitan Gerstner, "Contingent Pricing to Reduce Price Risks," *Marketing Science*, 23, no. 1, Winter 2003, pp. 146–155; Steven M. Shugan and Jinhong Xie, "Advance Pricing of Services and Other Implications of Separating Purchase and Consumption," *Journal of Service Research*, 2, no. 3, February 2000, pp. 227–239.

22. Seth Godin, "If It's Broke, Fix It," *Fast Company*, October 2003, p. 131.

23. Diane Brady, "Why Service Stinks," *BusinessWeek*, October 23, 2000, pp. 119–128.

24. Based on an interview with Amina Khalil, senior marketing manager, Raya Trade.

25. Hannah Clark, "Customer Service Hell," *Forbes*, March 30, 2006.

26. Clark, "Customer Service Hell."

27. See www.mobinil.com; www.cibeg.com.

28. Michelle Slatella, "Toll-Free Apology Soothes Savage Beast," *New York Times*, February 12, 2004; Jane Spencer, "Cases of Customer Rage Mount as Bad Service Prompts Venting," *Wall Street Journal*, September 17, 2003; Judi Ketteler, "Grumbling Groundswell," *Cincinnati Business Courier*, September 8, 2003; Richard Halicks, "You Can Count on Customer Disservice," *Atlanta Journal Constitution*, June 29, 2003; Bruce Horovitz, "Whatever Happened to Customer Service?" *USA Today*, September 26, 2003.

29. See www.vodafone.com.eg.

30. David Lazarus, "JetBlue Response Praised," *San Francisco Chronicle*, February 25, 2007, B1. Reprinted by permission.

31. Stephen S. Tax, Mark Colgate, and David Bowen, "How to Prevent Your Customers from Failing," *MIT Sloan Management Review*, Spring 2006, pp. 30–38; Mei Xue and Patrick T. Harker, "Customer Efficiency: Concept and Its Impact on E-Business Management," *Journal of Service Research*, 4, no. 4, May 2002, pp. 253–267; Matthew L. Meuter, Amy L. Ostrom, Robert I. Roundtree, and Mary Jo Bitner, "Self-Service Technologies: Understanding Customer Satisfaction with Technology-Based Service Encounters," *Journal of Marketing*, 64, no. 3, July 2000, pp. 50–64.

32. Valarie Zeithaml, Mary Jo Bitner, and Dwayne D. Gremler, *Services Marketing: Integrating Customer Focus across the Firm*, 4th edn (New York: McGraw-Hill, 2006).

33. Tax, Colgate, and Bowen, "How to Prevent Your Customers from Failing."

34. Susan M. Keaveney, "Customer Switching Behavior in Service Industries: An Exploratory Study," *Journal of Marketing*, April 1995, pp. 71–82. See also Jaishankar Ganesh, Mark J. Arnold, and Kristy E. Reynolds, "Understanding the Customer Base of Service Providers:

An Examination of the Differences between Switchers and Stayers," *Journal of Marketing*, 64, July 2000, pp. 65–87; Michael D. Hartline and O. C. Ferrell, "The Management of Customer-Contact Service Employees: An Empirical Investigation," *Journal of Marketing*, October 1996, pp. 52–70; Linda L. Price, Eric J. Arnould, and Patrick Tierney, "Going to Extremes: Managing Service Encounters and Assessing Provider Performance," *Journal of Marketing*, April 1995, pp. 83–97; Lois A. Mohr, Mary Jo Bitner, and Bernard H. Booms, "Critical Service Encounters: The Employee's Viewpoint," *Journal of Marketing*, October 1994, pp. 95–106.

35. Christian Gronroos, "A Service-Quality Model and Its Marketing Implications," *European Journal of Marketing*, 18, no. 4, 1984, pp. 36–44.

36. Leonard Berry, "Big Ideas in Services Marketing," *Journal of Consumer Marketing*, Spring 1986, pp. 47–51. See also Jagdip Singh, "Performance Productivity and Quality of Frontline Employees in Service Organizations," *Journal of Marketing*, 64, April 2000, pp. 15–34; John R. Hauser, Duncan I. Simester, and Birger Wernerfelt, "Internal Customers and Internal Suppliers," *Journal of Marketing Research*, August 1996, pp. 268–280; Walter E. Greene, Gary D. Walls, and Larry J. Schrest, "Internal Marketing: The Key to External Marketing Success," *Journal of Services Marketing*, 8, no. 4, 1994, pp. 5–13.

37. Justin Doebele, "The Engineer," *Forbes*, January 9, 2006, pp. 122–124; Stanley Holmes, "Creature Comforts at 30,000 Feet," *BusinessWeek*, December 18, 2006, p. 138; Anonymous, "What Makes Singapore a Service Champion?" *Strategic Direction*, April 2003, pp. 26–28; Erin Schulte, "Singapore Airlines Sets Lofty Standard for Business Class," *Town & Country Travel*, March 4, 2008, www.townandcountrytravelmag.com/travel-tips/expert-advice/singapore-airlines-business-class.

38. Christian Gronroos, "A Service-Quality Model," pp. 38–39; Michael D. Hartline, James G. Maxham III, and Daryl O. McKee, "Corridors of Influence in the Dissemination of Customer-Oriented Strategy to Customer-Contact Service Employees," *Journal of Marketing*, April 2000, pp. 35–50.

39. Ad de Jong, Ko de Ruyter, and Jos Lemmink, "Antecedents and Consequences of the Service Climate in Boundary-Spanning Self-Managing Service Teams," *Journal of Marketing*, 68, April 2004, pp. 18–35; Michael D. Hartline and O. C. Ferrell, "The Management of Customer-Contact Service Employees: An Empirical Investigation," *Journal of Marketing*, 60, October 1996, pp. 52–70.

40. "First dental practice management system of Middle East goes online in Dubai's DOHMS," www.ameinfo.com/181322.html; http://dubaismile.com/index.htm.

41. John Batelle, "Charles Schwab, Back from the Brink," *Business 2.0*, March 2006; "Q&A with Becky Saeger, CMO, Charles Schwab," *ANA Marketing Musings*, September 11, 2006; Betsy Morris, "Charles Schwab's Big Challenge," *Fortune*, May 30, 2005.

42. Roland T. Rust and Katherine N. Lemon, "E-Service and the Consumer," *International Journal of Electronic Commerce*, 5, no. 3, Spring 2001, pp. 83–99. See also Balaji Padmanabhan and Alexander Tuzhilin, "On the Use of Optimization for Data Mining: Theoretical Interactions and ECRM opportunities," *Management Science*, 49, no. 10, October 2003, pp. 1327–1343; B. P. S. Murthi and Sumit Sarkar, "The Role of the Management Sciences in Research on Personalization," *Management Science*, 49, no. 10, October 2003, pp. 1344–1362.

43. Roland T. Rust, P. K. Kannan, and Na Peng, "The Customer Economics of Internet Privacy," *Journal of the Academy of Marketing Science* 30, no. 4, 2002, pp. 455–464.

44. Glenn B. Voss, A. Parasuraman, and Dhruv Grewal, "The Role of Price, Performance, and Expectations in Determining Satisfaction in Service Exchanges," *Journal of Marketing*, 62, October 1998, pp. 46–61.

45. Roland T. Rust and Richard L. Oliver, "Should We Delight the Customer?" *Journal of the Academy of Marketing Science*, 28, no. 1, Fall 2002, pp. 86–94.

46. Haitham Assem, "Kempinski Hotel Mall of the Emirates, in a class of its own," www.kempinski.com/en/dubai/Press%20Room/Pages/HotelBackground.aspx; "Hotels," www.malloftheemirates.com/en/Hotels/Kempinski/.

47. A. Parasuraman, Valarie A. Zeithaml, and Leonard L. Berry, "A Conceptual Model of Service Quality and Its Implications for Future Research," *Journal of Marketing*, Autumn 1985, pp. 41–50. See also Michael K. Brady and J. Joseph Cronin Jr., "Some New Thoughts on Conceptualizing Perceived Service Quality," *Journal of Marketing*, 65, July 2001, pp. 34–49; Susan J. Devlin and H. K. Dong, "Service Quality from the Customers' Perspective," *Marketing Research*, Winter 1994, pp. 4–13.

48. Leonard L. Berry and A. Parasuraman, *Marketing Services: Competing through Quality* (New York: Free Press, 1991), p. 16.

49. Parasuraman, Zeithaml, and Berry, "A Conceptual Model of Service Quality and Its Implications for Future Research," pp. 41–50.

50. Raya Contact Center Implements Banking Best Practices for Ahli United Bank (Egypt), www.rayacorp.com/ShowPage.aspx?PID=950.

51. James L. Heskett, W. Earl Sasser Jr., and Christopher W. L. Hart, *Service Breakthroughs* (New York: Free Press, 1990).

52. William C. Copacino, *Supply Chain Management* (Boca Raton, FL: St. Lucie Press, 1997).

53. Leonard L. Berry, Kathleen Seiders, and Dhruv Grewal, "Understanding Service Convenience," *Journal of Marketing*, 66, July 2002, pp. 1–17.

54. Mary Jo Bitner, "Self-Service Technologies: What Do Customers Expect?" *Marketing Management*, Spring 2001, pp. 10–11; Matthew L. Meuter, Amy L. Ostrom, Robert J. Roundtree, and Mary Jo Bitner, "Self-Service Technologies: Understanding Customer Satisfaction with Technology-Based Service Encounters," *Journal of Marketing*, 64, July 2000, pp. 50–64.

55. Peter Burrows, "The Era of Efficiency," *BusinessWeek*, June 18, 2001, pp. 94–98.

56. Matthew L. Meuter, Mary Jo Bitner, Amy L. Ostrom, and Stephen W. Brown, "Choosing among Alternative Service Delivery Modes: An Investigation of Customer Trial of Self-Service Technologies," *Journal of Marketing*, 69, April 2005, pp. 61–83.

57. See www.etihadairways.com/sites/Etihad/tr/en/aboutetihad/mediacenter/newslisting/newsdetails/Pages/Etihad-launches-self-service-kiosks-at-home-base.aspx?fromNewsListing=false.

58. Michelle Higgins, "Go Directly to Your Room Key! Pass the Desk!" *New York Times*, August 20, 2006, pp. 5–6. Copyright © 2006 The New York Times. Reprinted by permission.

59. "Mystery Shopping Company Offers Paid Opportunities for Fliers Looking to Beat the Boredom at the Airport," PRWEB, August 23, 2011, www.prweb.com/releases/2011/8/prweb8738926.htm.

60. John A. Martilla and John C. James, "Importance-Performance Analysis," *Journal of Marketing*, January 1977, pp. 77–79.

61. Jeffrey G. Blodgett and Ronald D. Anderson, "A Bayesian Network Model of the Customer Complaint Process," *Journal of Service Research*, 2, no. 4, May 2000, pp. 321–38; Stephen S. Tax and Stephen W. Brown, "Recovering and Learning from Service Failures," *Sloan Management Review*, Autumn 1998, pp. 75–88; Claes Fornell and Birger Wernerfelt, "A Model for Customer Complaint Management," *Marketing Science*, 7, Summer 1988, pp. 271–86.

62. James G. Maxham III and Richard G. Netemeyer, "Firms Reap What They Sow: The Effects of Shared Values and Perceived Organizational Justice on Customers' Evaluations of Complaint Handling," *Journal of Marketing*, 67, January 2003, pp. 46–62; Singh, "Performance Productivity and Quality of Frontline Employees in Service Organizations," pp. 15–34; Barry J. Rabin and James S. Boles, "Employee Behavior in a Service Environment: A Model and Test of Potential Differences between Men and Women," *Journal of Marketing*, 62, April 1998, pp. 77–91.

63. Tax, Brown, and Chandrashekaran, "Customer Evaluations of Service Complaint Experiences: Implications for Relationship Marketing," pp. 60–76; Tax and Brown, "Recovering and Learning from Service Failures," pp. 75–88.

64. "Directory," www.mobinil.com/Support/Directory.aspx; "Contact Us," www.mobinil.com/Support/ContactUs.aspx; "Mobinil," http://egyptwww.com/en/more.php?mode=view_item&sub=1607&item=1140.

65. D. Todd Donovan, Tom J. Brown, and John C. Mowen, "Internal Benefits of Service Worker Customer Orientation: Job Satisfaction, Commitment, and Organizational Citizenship Behaviors," *Journal of Marketing*, 68, January 2004, pp. 128–146.

66. "Saudi Aramco Employment Opportunities," www.jobsataramco.com/Home/Default.aspx; "Compensation and Benefits," www.jobsataramco.com/compensation.aspx.

67. Amy Barrett, "Vanguard Gets Personal," *BusinessWeek*, October 3, 2005, pp. 115–118; Carolyn Marconi and Donna MacFarland, "Growth by Marketing under the Radar," Presentation made at Marketing Science Institute Board of Trustees Meeting: Pathways to Growth, Tucson, AZ, November 7, 2002.

68. Christopher Rowland, "The Pharmacists in Chains Promote Personal Touch to Keep Edge Over Mail-Order Firms," *Boston Globe*, December 10, 2003.

69. "Our History," www.etihadairways.com/sites/etihad/global/en/aboutetihad/etihadstory/pages/etihadhistory.aspx; "How to Earn," www.etihadairways.com/sites/etihad/global/en/guestrecognition/visitor/yourmiles/HowToEarn/pages/howtoearn.aspx; "Free Stopovers in Abu Dhabi," www.etihadairways.com/sites/Etihad/global/en/home/Pages/Abu-Dhabi-Break.aspx.

70. Susanna Hamner, "Checking In at the Hotel of Tomorrow," *Business 2.0*, November 2006, pp. 38–40.

71. Mike Beirne and Javier Benito, "Starwood Uses Personnel to Personalize Marketing," *Brandweek*, April 24, 2006, p. 9.

72. Linda Tischler, "Join the Circus," *Fast Company*, July 2005, pp. 53–58; "Cirque du Soliel," *America's Greatest Brands*, 3, 2004; Geoff Keighley, "The Phantasmagoria Factory," *Business 2.0*, February 2004, pp. 102; Robin D. Rusch, "Cirque du Soleil—Contorts," *brandchannel.com*, December 1, 2003.

73. Mark Vandenbosch and Niraj Dawar, "Beyond Better Products: Capturing Value in Customer Interactions," *MIT Sloan Management Review*, 43, Summer 2002, pp. 35–42; Milind M. Lele and Uday S. Karmarkar, "Good Product Support Is Smart Marketing," *Harvard Business Review*, 61, November–December 1983, pp. 124–132.

74. For recent research on the effects of delays in service on service evaluations, see Michael K. Hui and David K. Tse, "What to Tell Consumers in Waits of Different Lengths: An Integrative Model of Service Evaluation," *Journal of Marketing*, April 1996, pp. 81–90; Shirley Taylor, "Waiting for Service: The Relationship between Delays and Evaluations of Service," *Journal of Marketing*, April 1994, pp. 56–69.

75. Byron G. Auguste, Eric P. Harmon, and Vivek Pandit, "The Right Service Strategies for Product Companies," *McKinsey Quarterly*, 1, 2006, pp. 41–51.

Chapter 14

1. Dan Beucke, "A Blade Too Far," *BusinessWeek*, August 14, 2006; Jenn Abelson, "And Then There Were Five," *Boston Globe*, September 15, 2005; Jack Neff, "Six-Blade Blitz," *Advertising Age*, September 19, 2005, pp. 3, 53; Editorial, "Gillette Spends Smart on Fusion," *Advertising Age*, September 26, 2005, p. 24.

2. "The Price Is Wrong," *The Economist*, May 25, 2002.

3. Xavier Dreze and Joseph C. Nunes, "Using Combined-Currency Prices to Lower Consumers' Perceived Cost,"

Journal of Marketing Research, 41, February 2004, pp. 59–72.

4. Jack Neff, "Moving to Margins in a New Marketing Age," *Advertising Age*, July 24, 2006, pp. 1, 21; Nescafé retail prices from Carrefour Egypt.

5. Michael Menduno, "Priced to Perfection," *Business 2.0*, March 6, 2001, pp. 40–42.

6. Paul Markillie, "A Perfect Market: A Survey of E-Commerce," *The Economist*, May 15, 2004, pp. 3–20; David Kirpatrick, "How the Open-Source World Plans to Smack Down Microsoft, and Oracle, and …," *Fortune*, February 23, 2004, pp. 92–100; Faith Keenan, "The Price Is Really Right," *BusinessWeek*, March 31, 2003, pp. 61–67; Michael Menduno, "Priced to Perfection," *Business 2.0*, March 6, 2001, pp. 40–42; Amy E. Cortese, "Good-Bye to Fixed Pricing?" *BusinessWeek*, May 4, 1998, pp. 71–84. For a discussion of some of the academic issues involved, see Florian Zettelmeyer, "Expanding to the Internet: Pricing and Communication Strategies When Firms Compete on Multiple Channels," *Journal of Marketing Research*, 37, August 2000, pp. 292–308; John G. Lynch Jr. and Dan Ariely, "Wine Online: Search Costs Affect Competition on Price, Quality, and Distribution," *Marketing Science*, Winter 2000, pp. 83–103; Rajiv Lal and Miklos Sarvary, "When and How Is the Internet Likely to Decrease Price Competition?" *Marketing Science*, 18, no. 4, Autumn 1999, pp. 485–503.

7. "Growth as a Process," Interview with Jeffrey Immelt, *Harvard Business Review*, June 2006.

8. "Pricing Benchmarks for the Future: How General Electric Does It," (White paper), Simon-Kucher Partners, March 6, 2007.

9. For a thorough, up-to-date review of pricing research, see Chezy Ofir and Russell S. Winer, "Pricing: Economic and Behavioral Models," in *Handbook of Marketing*, ed. Bart Weitz and Robin Wensley (London: Sage Publications, 2002).

10. "Egyptian Clothing Guide: Top Local Brands," *Cairo 360*, September 10, 2010, www.cairo360.com/article/shopping/1046/egyptian-clothing-guide-top-local-brands/.

11. Peter R. Dickson and Alan G. Sawyer, "The Price Knowledge and Search of Supermarket Shoppers," *Journal of Marketing*, July 1990, pp. 42–53. For a methodological qualification, however, see Hooman Estalami, Alfred Holden, and Donald R. Lehmann, "Macro-Economic Determinants of Consumer Price Knowledge: A Meta-Analysis of Four Decades of Research," *International Journal of Research in Marketing*, 18, December 2001, pp. 341–355.

12. For a comprehensive review, see Tridib Mazumdar, S. P. Raj, and Indrajit Sinha, "Reference Price Research: Review and Propositions," *Journal of Marketing*, 69, October 2005, pp. 84–102. For a different point of view, see Chris Janiszewski and Donald R. Lichtenstein, "A Range Theory Account of Price Perception," *Journal of Consumer Research*, March 1999, pp. 353–368.

13. For a discussion of how 'incidental' prices outside the category can serve as contextual reference prices, see Joseph C. Nunes and Peter Boatwright, "Incidental Prices and Their Effect on Willingness to Pay," *Journal of Marketing Research*, 41, November 2004, pp. 457–466.

14. K. N. Rajendran and Gerard J. Tellis, "Contextual and Temporal Components of Reference Price," *Journal of Marketing*, January 1994, pp. 22–34; Gurumurthy Kalyanaram and Russell S. Winer, "Empirical Generalizations from Reference-Price Research," *Marketing Science*, 14, no. 3, Summer 1995, pp. G161–G169.

15. Robert Strauss, "Prices You Just Can't Believe," *New York Times*, January 17, 2002.

16. Gurumurthy Kalyanaram and Russell S. Winer, "Empirical Generalizations from Reference-Price Research," *Marketing Science*, 14, no. 3, Summer 1995, pp. 161–169.

17. Glenn E. Mayhew and Russell S. Winer, "An Empirical Analysis of Internal and External Reference-Price Effects Using Scanner Data," *Journal of Consumer Research*, June 1992, pp. 62–70.

18. Robert Ziethammer, "Forward-Looking Buying in Online Auctions," *Journal of Marketing Research*, 43, August 2006, pp. 462–476.

19. John T. Gourville, "Pennies-a-Day: The Effect of Temporal Reframing on Transaction Evaluation," *Journal of Consumer Research*, March 1998, pp. 395–408.

20. "Sarah's Bag," www.khanoum.com/istore/home.php?cat=9&sort=orderby&sort_direction=0&page=1; "Sarah's Bag: Lebanon's Fashionable Bags and Accessories," *Rabih Dagher* blog, April 26, 2009, www.rabihdagher.com/blog/2009/04/sarahs-bag-lebanons-fashionable-bags-and-accessories/.

21. Gary M. Erickson and Johny K. Johansson, "The Role of Price in Multi-Attribute Product-Evaluations," *Journal of Consumer Research*, September 1985, pp. 195–199.

22. Wilfred Amaldoss and Sanjay Jain, "Pricing of Conspicuous Goods: A Competitive Analysis of Social Effects," *Journal of Marketing Research*, 42, February 2005; Angela Chao and Juliet B. Schor, "Empirical Tests of Status Consumption: Evidence from Women's Cosmetics," *Journal of Economic Psychology*, 19, no. 1, January 1998, pp. 107–131.

23. Rigel Celeste, "Azza Fahmy Egyptian Jewelry," May 13, 2008, www.luxist.com/2008/05/13/azza-fahmy-egyptian-jewelry/; "Azza Fahmy," www.azzafahmy.com/collection.php?cPath=21&osCsid=vqdaioa9tfq8nr71k80u9pll05; Sarah El Khodary, "The Jewelry of Azza Fahmy," www.touregypt.net/featurestories/fahmy.htm.

24. Mark Stiving and Russell S. Winer, "An Empirical Analysis of Price Endings with Scanner Data," *Journal of Consumer Research*, June 1997, pp. 57–68.

25. Eric T. Anderson and Duncan Simester, "Effects of $19 Price Endings on Retail Sales: Evidence from Field Experiments," *Quantitative Marketing and Economics*, 1, no. 1, March 2003, pp. 93–110.

26. Eric Anderson and Duncan Simester, "Mind Your Pricing Cues," *Harvard Business Review*, September 2003, pp. 96–103.

27. Robert M. Schindler and Patrick N. Kirby, "Patterns of Rightmost Digits Used in Advertised Prices: Implications for Nine-Ending Effects," *Journal of Consumer Research*, September 1997, pp. 192–201.

28. Anderson and Simester, "Mind Your Pricing Cues," pp. 96–103.

29. Ibid.

30. Daniel J. Howard and Roger A. Kerin, "Broadening the Scope of Reference-Price Advertising Research: A Field Study of Consumer Shopping Involvement," *Journal of Marketing*, 70, October 2006, pp. 185–204.

31. Robert C. Blattberg and Kenneth Wisniewski, "Price-Induced Patterns of Competition," *Marketing Science*, 8, Autumn 1989, pp. 291–309.

32. Shantanu Dutta, Mark J. Zbaracki, and Mark Bergen, "Pricing Process as a Capability: A Resource-Based Perspective," *Strategic Management Journal*, 24, no. 7, July 2003, pp. 615–630.

33. Mei Fong, "IKEA Hits Home in China: The Swedish Design Giant, Unlike Other Retailers, Slashes Prices for the Chinese," *Wall Street Journal*, March 3, 2006, p. B1. Reprinted by permission of Dow Jones via Copyright Clearance Center; Michael Wei, "In Ikea's China Stores, Loitering Is Encouraged," *BusinessWeek*, www.business-week.com/magazine/content/10_45/b4202022164114 .htm, October 28, 2010.

34. Michael Silverstein and Neil Fiske, *Trading Up: The New American Luxury* (New York: Portfolio, 2003).

35. "About Us," www.choice.com.eg/showpage.aspx?ID=7.

36. Huda, "Museum of Islamic Arts—Doha, Qatar," http:// islam.about.com/od/islamart/p/mia.htm; Anne-Birte Stensgaard, "Museum of Islamic Art Receives a Donation of a Valuable Islamic Book," *AMEinfo.com*, August 17, 2008, www.ameinfo.com/166262.html; "Press," www.mia.org.qa/english/index.html#others /pressroom.

37. Timothy Aeppel, "Seeking Perfect Prices, CEO Tears Up the Rules," *Wall Street Journal*, March 27, 2007.

38. Florian Zettelmeyer, Fiona Scott Morton, and Jorge Silva-Risso, "How the Internet Lowers Prices: Evidence from Matched Survey and Automobile Transaction Data," *Journal of Marketing Research*, 43, May 2006, pp. 168–181; Jeffrey R. Brown and Austan Goolsbee, "Does the Internet Make Markets More Competitive? Evidence from the Life Insurance Industry," *Journal of Political Economy*, 110, no. 5, October 2002, pp. 481–507.

39. Walter Baker, Mike Marn, and Craig Zawada, "Price Smarter on the Net," *Harvard Business Review*, February 2001, pp. 122–127.

40. Thomas T. Nagle and Reed K. Holden, *The Strategy and Tactics of Pricing*, 3rd edn (Upper Saddle River, NJ: Prentice Hall, 2002).

41. For a summary of elasticity studies, see Dominique M. Hanssens, Leonard J. Parsons, and Randall L. Schultz, *Market Response Models: Econometric and Time Series Analysis* (Boston: Kluwer, 1990), pp. 187–191.

42. Tammo H. A. Bijmolt, Harald J. Van Heerde, and Rik G. M. Pieters, "New Empirical Generalizations on the Determinants of Price Elasticity," *Journal of Marketing Research*, 42, May 2005, pp. 141–156.

43. "Easier Than ABC," *The Economist*, October 25, 2003, p. 56.

44. William W. Alberts, "The Experience Curve Doctrine Reconsidered," *Journal of Marketing*, July 1989, pp. 36–49.

45. Michael Sivy, "Japan's Smart Secret Weapon," *Fortune*, August 12, 1991, p. 75.

46. Kusum L. Ailawadi, Donald R. Lehmann, and Scott A. Neslin, "Market Response to a Major Policy Change in the Marketing Mix: Learning from Procter & Gamble's Value Pricing Strategy," *Journal of Marketing*, 65, January 2001, pp. 44–61.

47. Timothy Aeppel, "Seeking Perfect Prices, CEO Tears Up the Rules," *Wall Street Journal*, March 27, 2007.

48. Riadh Ben Jelili, "Markup Pricing in Tunisian Manufacturing Industries," *Economic Research Forum*, 2002, www.erf.org.eg/cms.php?id=publication_details& publication_id=805.

49. Tung-Zong Chang and Albert R. Wildt, "Price, Product Information, and Purchase Intention: An Empirical Study," *Journal of the Academy of Marketing Science*, Winter 1994, pp. 16–27. See also G. Dean Kortge and Patrick A. Okonkwo, "Perceived Value Approach to Pricing," *Industrial Marketing Management*, May 1993, pp. 133–140.

50. James C. Anderson, Dipak C. Jain, and Pradeep K. Chintagunta, "Customer Value Assessment in Business Markets: A State-of-Practice Study," *Journal of Business-to-Business Marketing*, 1, no. 1, Spring 1993, pp. 3–29.

51. Bill Saporito, "Behind the Tumult at P&G," *Fortune*, March 7, 1994, pp. 74–82. For empirical analysis of its effects, see Kusim L. Ailawadi, Donald R. Lehmann, and Scott A. Neslin, "Market Response to a Major Policy Change in the Marketing Mix: Learning from Procter & Gamble's Value Pricing Strategy," *Journal of Marketing*, 65, January 2001, pp. 44–61.

52. Stephen J. Hoch, Xavier Dreze, and Mary J. Purk, "EDLP, Hi-Lo, and Margin Arithmetic," *Journal of Marketing*, October 1994, pp. 16–27; Rajiv Lal and R. Rao, "Supermarket Competition: The Case of Everyday Low Pricing," *Marketing Science*, 16, no. 1, Winter 1997, pp. 60–80.

53. Joseph W. Alba, Carl F. Mela, Terence A. Shimp, and Joel E. Urbany, "The Effect of Discount Frequency and Depth on Consumer Price Judgments," *Journal of Consumer Research*, September 1999, pp. 99–114.

54. Hannah Rashdan, "Egypt Gets Hyper," *Al-Ahram Weekly On-line*, http://weekly.ahram.org.eg/2003/623/li1.htm; "About Us," www.carrefour.com.eg/aboutus.aspx.

55. Ethan Smith and Sara Silver, "To Protect Its Box-Office Turf, Ticketmaster Plays Rivals' Tune," *Wall Street Journal*, September 12, 2006.

56. "Royal Mail Drives Major Cost Savings through Free Markets," Free Markets press release, December 15, 2003.

57. Sandy D. Jap, "The Impact of Online Reverse Auction Design on Buyer-Supplier Relationships," *Journal of Marketing*, 71, January 2007, pp. 146–159; Sandy D. Jap, "An Exploratory Study of the Introduction of Online Reverse Auctions," *Journal of Marketing*, 67, July 2003, pp. 96–107.

58. Paul W. Farris and David J. Reibstein, "How Prices, Expenditures, and Profits Are Linked," *Harvard Business Review*, November–December 1979, pp. 173–184. See also Makoto Abe, "Price and Advertising Strategy of a National Brand against Its Private-Label Clone: A Signaling Game Approach," *Journal of Business Research*, July 1995, pp. 241–250.

59. J. P. Morgan Report, "E-Tailing and the Five Cs," March 2000.

60. Eugene H. Fram and Michael S. McCarthy, "The True Price of Penalties," *Marketing Management*, October 1999, pp. 49–56.

61. Joel E. Urbany, "Justifying Profitable Pricing," *Journal of Product and Brand Management*, 10, no. 3, 2001, pp. 141–157; Charles Fishman, "The Wal-Mart You Don't Know," *Fast Company*, December 2003, pp. 68–80.

62. "No Paradise," *The Economist*, July 15, 2010, www.economist.com/node/16564152.

63. P. N. Agarwala, *Countertrade: A Global Perspective* (New Delhi: Vikas, 1991); Michael Rowe, *Countertrade* (London: Euromoney Books, 1989); Christopher M. Korth, ed., *International Countertrade* (New York: Quorum Books, 1987).

64. For an interesting discussion of a quantity surcharge, see David E. Sprott, Kenneth C. Manning, and Anthony Miyazaki, "Grocery Price Settings and Quantity Surcharges," *Journal of Marketing*, 67, July 2003, pp. 34–46.

65. Michael V. Marn and Robert L. Rosiello, "Managing Price, Gaining Profit," *Harvard Business Review*, September–October 1992, pp. 84–94. See also Kusum L. Ailawadi, Scott A. Neslin, and Karen Gedenk, "Pursuing the Value-Conscious Consumer: Store Brands versus National-Brand Promotions," *Journal of Marketing*, 65, January 2001, pp. 71–89; Gerard J. Tellis, "Tackling the Retailer Decision Maze: Which Brands to Discount, How Much, When, and Why?" *Marketing Science*, 14, no. 3, pt 2, Summer 1995, pp. 271–299.

66. Kevin J. Clancy, "At What Profit Price?" *Brandweek*, June 23, 1997.

67. Carol J. Loomis, "The Bloomberg," *Fortune*, April 16, 2007, pp. 60–70; www.albawaba.com/business/pr/emirates-skycargo-celebrates-start-new-freighter-service-393971.

68. Jay E. Klompmaker, William H. Rogers, and Anthony E. Nygren, "Value, Not Volume," *Marketing Management*, May–June 2003, pp. 45–48; www.bishara.com.eg/brand/btm.

69. "Egypt's Al-Ahly Marks 100 Years," *Al Jazeera*, April 23, 2007, http://english.aljazeera.net/sport/2007/04/2008526105912700751.html.

70. Ramarao Deesiraju and Steven M. Shugan, "Strategic Service Pricing and Yield Management," *Journal of Marketing*, 63, January 1999, pp. 44–56; Robert E.

Weigand, "Yield Management: Filling Buckets, Papering the House," *Business Horizons*, September–October 1999, pp. 55–64.

71. "Egyptair Flights to Lagos," www.edreams.com/offers/flights/airline/MS/egyptair/LOS/lagos/;%20; www.egyptair.com.

72. Charles Fishman, "Which Price Is Right?" *Fast Company*, March 2003, pp. 92–102; Bob Tedeschi, "E-Commerce Report," *New York Times*, September 2, 2002; Faith Keenan, "The Price Is Really Right," *BusinessWeek*, March 31, 2003, pp. 62–67; Peter Coy, "The Power of Smart Pricing," *BusinessWeek*, April 10, 2000, pp. 160–164. For a review of recent and seminal work linking pricing decisions with operational insights, see Moritz Fleischmann, Joseph M. Hall, and David F. Pyke, "Research Brief: Smart Pricing," *MIT Sloan Management Review*, Winter 2004, pp. 9–13.

73. Mike France, "Does Predatory Pricing Make Microsoft a Predator?" *BusinessWeek*, November 23, 1998, pp. 130–132. Also see Joseph P. Guiltinan and Gregory T. Gundlack, "Aggressive and Predatory Pricing: A Framework for Analysis," *Journal of Advertising*, July 1996, pp. 87–102.

74. For more information on specific types of price discrimination that are illegal, see Henry Cheesman, *Business Law*, 6th edn (Upper Saddle River, NJ: Prentice Hall, 2007).

75. Bob Donath, "Dispel Major Myths about Pricing," *Marketing News*, February 3, 2003, p. 10.

76. For a classic review, see Kent B. Monroe, "Buyers' Subjective Perceptions of Price," *Journal of Marketing Research*, February 1973, pp. 70–80. See also Z. John Zhang, Fred Feinberg, and Aradhna Krishna, "Do We Care What Others Get? A Behaviorist Approach to Targeted Promotions," *Journal of Marketing Research*, 39, August 2002, pp. 277–291.

77. Margaret C. Campbell, "Perceptions of Pricing Unfairness: Antecedents and Consequences," *Journal of Marketing Research*, 36, May 1999, pp. 187–199.

78. Lan Xia, Kent B. Monroe, and Jennifer L. Cox, "The Price Is Unfair! A Conceptual Framework of Price Fairness Perceptions," *Journal of Marketing*, 68, October 2004, pp. 1–15.

79. Eric Mitchell, "How Not to Raise Prices," *Small Business Reports*, November 1990, pp. 64–67.

80. Nadeen El Ajou, "Air Arabia Launches New Website," *AMEinfo.com*, November 10, 2009, www.ameinfo.com/215506.html; "EFG Hermes report on Air Arabia," www.middleeastevents.com/site/pres_dtls.asp?pid=5767.

Chapter 15

1. Interview with Nadim Nakfoor, general manager of PepsiCo's Al-Jumaih bottling plant, Saudi Arabia.

2. Anne T. Coughlan, Erin Anderson, Louis W. Stern, and Adel I. El-Ansary, *Marketing Channels*, 6th edn (Upper Saddle River, NJ: Prentice Hall, 2001).

3. Louis W. Stern and Barton A. Weitz, "The Revolution in Distribution: Challenges and Opportunities," *Long Range Planning*, 30, no. 6, December 1997, pp. 823–829.

4. For an insightful summary of academic research, see Erin Anderson and Anne T. Coughlan, "Channel Management: Structure, Governance, and Relationship Management," in *Handbook of Marketing*, ed. Bart Weitz and Robin Wensley (London: Sage, 2001), pp. 223–47. See also, Gary L. Frazier, "Organizing and Managing Channels of Distribution," *Journal of the Academy of Marketing Sciences* 27, no. 2, Spring 1999, pp. 226–240.

5. See www.intel.com/pressroom/intel_inside.htm.

6. Peter Child, Suzanne Heywood, and Michael Kilger, "Do Retail Brands Travel?" *McKinsey Quarterly*, January 2002, pp. 11–13.

7. Russ Mitchell, "Can Dell Save Dell?" *Condé Nast Portfolio*, July 2008, pp. 84–90; Cliff Edwards, "Dell's Do-Over," *BusinessWeek*, October 26, 2009, pp. 37–40; Christopher Helman, "The Second Coming," *Forbes*, December 10, 2007, pp. 79–86; David Whitford, "Uh… Maybe I Should Drive," *Fortune,* April 30, 2007, pp. 125–28; Louise Lee, "It's Dell vs. the Dell Way," *BusinessWeek,* March 6, 2006, pp. 61–62; David Kirkpatrick, "Dell in the Penalty Box," *Fortune,* September 18, 2006, pp. 70–78; Nanette Byrnes, Peter Burrows, and Louise Lee, "Dark Days at Dell," *BusinessWeek,* September 4, 2006, pp. 27–30; Elizabeth Corcoran, "A Bad Spell for Dell," *Forbes,* June 19, 2006, pp. 44–46.

8. Asim Ansari, Carl F. Mela, and Scott A. Neslin, "Customer Channel Migration," *Journal of Marketing Research*, 45, February 2008, pp. 60–76; Jacquelyn S. Thomas and Ursula Y. Sullivan, "Managing Marketing Communications," *Journal of Marketing*, 69, October 2005, pp. 239–251; Sridhar Balasubramanian, Rajagopal Raghunathan, and Vijay Mahajan, "Consumers in a Multichannel Environment: Product Utility, Process Utility, and Channel Choice," *Journal of Interactive Marketing*, 19, no. 2, Spring 2005, pp. 12–30; Edward J. Fox, Alan L. Montgomery, and Leonard M. Lodish, "Consumer Shopping and Spending across Retail Formats," *The Journal of Business*, 77, no. 2, April 2004, pp. S25–S60.

9. Paul F. Nunes and Frank V. Cespedes, "The Customer Has Escaped," *Harvard Business Review*, November 2003, pp. 96–105.

10. Peter Child, Suzanne Heywood, and Michael Kilger, "Do Retail Brands Travel?" *McKinsey Quarterly*, January 2002, pp. 11–13.

11. John Helyar, "The Only Company Wal-Mart Fears," *Fortune*, November 24, 2003, pp. 158–66. See also, Michael Silverstein and Neil Fiske, *Trading Up: The New American Luxury* (New York: Portfolio, 2003).

12. Chekitan S. Dev and Don E. Schultz, "In the Mix: A Customer-Focused Approach Can Bring the Current Marketing Mix into the 21st Century," *Marketing Management*, 14, January–February 2005.

13. Coughlan, Anderson, Stern, and El-Ansary, *Marketing Channels*, pp. 5–6.

14. For additional information on backward channels, see Marianne Jahre, "Household Waste Collection as a Reverse Channel: A Theoretical Perspective," *International Journal of Physical Distribution and Logistics*, 25, no. 2, 1995, pp. 39–55; Terrance L. Pohlen and M. Theodore Farris II, "Reverse Logistics in Plastics Recycling," *International Journal of Physical Distribution and Logistics*, 22, no. 7, 1992, pp. 35–37.

15. See www.aou.edu.kw; www.aou.edu.lb.

16. Irving Rein, Philip Kotler, and Martin Stoller, *High Visibility* (New York: Dodd, Mead, 1987).

17. William M. Bulkeley, "Kodak Revamps Wal-Mart Kiosks," *Wall Street Journal*, September 6, 2006; Faith Keenan, "Big Yellow's Digital Dilemma," *BusinessWeek*, March 24, 2003, pp. 80–81.

18. Coughlan, Anderson, Stern, and El-Ansary, *Marketing Channels*.

19. Louis P. Bucklin, *A Theory of Distribution Channel Structure* (Berkeley: Institute of Business and Economic Research, University of California, 1966).

20. "McDonald's Launches McDelivery Service in Bahrain," August 2, 2007, www.ameinfo.com/128200.html.

21. Youngme Moon, "The Birth of the Swatch," Harvard Business School Publishing.

22. "Exclusives Becoming a Common Practice," *DSN Retailing Today*, February 9, 2004, pp. 38, 44.

23. "Trouser Suit," *The Economist*, November 24, 2001, p. 56.

24. See www.natural-ltd.com/beesline.

25. For more on relationship marketing and the governance of marketing channels, see Jan B. Heide, "Interorganizational Governance in Marketing Channels," *Journal of Marketing*, January 1994, pp. 71–85.

26. Robert K. Heady, "Online Bank Offers Best Rates," *South Florida Sun-Sentinel*, November 22, 2004.

27. Duff McDonald, "Customer, Support Thyself," *Business 2.0*, April 2004, pp. 56.

28. Anderson and Coughlan, "Channel Management: Structure, Governance, and Relationship Management," pp. 223–247.

29. These bases of power were identified in John R. P. French and Bertram Raven, "The Bases of Social Power," in *Studies in Social Power*, ed. Dorwin Cartwright (Ann Arbor: University of Michigan Press, 1959), pp. 150–167.

30. Bert Rosenbloom, *Marketing Channels: A Management View*, 5th edn (Hinsdale, IL: Dryden, 1995).

31. Daniel Corsten and Nirmalya Kumar, "Do Suppliers Benefit from Collaborative Relationships with Large Retailers? An Empirical Investigation of Efficient Consumer Response Adoption," *Journal of Marketing*, 69, July 2005, pp. 80–94.

32. Jerry Useem, "Simply Irresistible," *Fortune*, March 19, 2007, pp. 107–112; Nick Wingfield, "How Apple's Store Strategy Beat the Odds," *Wall Street Journal*, May 17, 2006; Tobi Elkin, "Apple Gambles with Retail Plan," *Advertising Age*, June 24, 2001.

33. Thomas H. Davenport and Jeanne G. Harris, *Competing on Analytics: The New Science of Winning* (Boston: Harvard Business School Press, 2007).

34. Junhong Chu, Pradeep K. Chintagunta, and Naufel J. Vilcassim, "Assessing the Economic Value of Distribution Channels: An Application to the Personal Computer Industry," *Journal of Marketing Research*, 44, February 2007, pp. 29–41.

35. Stefan Wuyts, Stefan Stremersch, Christophe Van Den Bulte, and Philip Hans Franses, "Vertical Marketing Systems for Complex Products: A Triadic Perspective," *Journal of Marketing Research*, 41, November 2004, pp. 479–487.

36. Russell Johnston and Paul R. Lawrence, "Beyond Vertical Integration: The Rise of the Value-Adding Partnership," *Harvard Business Review*, July–August 1988, pp. 94–101. See also Arnt Bovik and George John, "When Does Vertical Coordination Improve Industrial Purchasing Relationships," *Journal of Marketing*, 64, October 2000, pp. 52–64; Judy A. Siguaw, Penny M. Simpson, and Thomas L. Baker, "Effects of Supplier Market Orientation on Distributor Market Orientation and the Channel Relationship: The Distribution Perspective," *Journal of Marketing*, July 1998, pp. 99–111; Narakesari Narayandas and Manohar U. Kalwani, "Long-Term Manufacturer–Supplier Relationships: Do They Pay Off for Supplier Firms?" *Journal of Marketing*, January 1995, pp. 1–16.

37. Raji Srinivasan, "Dual Distribution and Intangible Firm Value: Franchising in Restaurant Chains," *Journal of Marketing*, 70, July 2006, pp. 120–135.

38. See www.hdfcbank.com.

39. See www.disney.com/; Edward Helmore, "Media: Why House of Mouse Is Haunted by Failures," *Observer*, February 11, 2001, p. 10.

40. Rajkumar Venkatesan, V. Kumar, and Nalini Ravishanker, "Multichannel Shopping: Causes and Consequences," *Journal of Marketing*, 71, April 2007, pp. 114–132.

41. Based on Rowland T. Moriarty and Ursula Moran, "Marketing Hybrid Marketing Systems," *Harvard Business Review*, November–December 1990, pp. 146–155.

42. Louise Lee, "Catalogs, Catalogs, Everywhere," *BusinessWeek*, December 4, 2006, pp. 32–34.

43. Susan Casey, "Eminence Green," *Fortune*, April 2, 2007, pp. 64–70.

44. Barbara Darow, "Oracle's New Partner Path," *CRN*, August 21, 2006, p. 4.

45. Coughlan and Stern, "Marketing Channel Design and Management," pp. 247–269.

46. Matthew Boyle, "Brand Killers," *Fortune*, August 11, 2003, pp. 51–56; for an opposing view, see Anthony J. Dukes, Esther Gal-Or, and Kannan Srinivasan, "Channel Bargaining with Retailer Asymmetry," *Journal of Marketing Research*, 43, February 2006, pp. 84–97.

47. Alberto Sa Vinhas and Erin Anderson, "How Potential Conflict Drives Channel Structure: Concurrent (Direct and Indirect) Channels," *Journal of Marketing Research*, 42, November 2005, pp. 507–515.

48. For an example of when conflict can be viewed as helpful, see Anil Arya and Brian Mittendorf, "Benefits of Channel Discord in the Sale of Durable Goods," *Marketing Science*, 25, January–February 2006, pp. 91–96; and Nirmalya Kumar, "Living with Channel Conflict," *CMO Magazine*, October 2004.

49. Fareena Sultan and Andrew J. Rohm, "The Evolving Role of the Internet in Marketing Strategy: An Exploratory Study," *Journal of Interactive Marketing*, Spring 2004, pp. 6–19.

50. This section draws on Coughlan, Anderson, Stern, and El-Ansary, *Marketing Channels*, Chapter 6. See also Jonathan D. Hibbard, Nirmalya Kumar, and Louis W. Stern, "Examining the Impact of Destructive Acts in Marketing Channel Relationships," *Journal of Marketing Research*, 38, February 2001, pp. 45–61; Kersi D. Antia and Gary L. Frazier, "The Severity of Contract Enforcement in Interfirm Channel Relationships," *Journal of Marketing*, 65, October 2001, pp. 67–81; James R. Brown, Chekitan S. Dev, and Dong-Jin Lee, "Managing Marketing Channel Opportunism: The Efficiency of Alternative Governance Mechanisms," *Journal of Marketing*, 64, April 2001, pp. 51–65.

51. Andrew Kaplan, "All Together Now?" *Beverage World*, March 2007, pp. 14–16.

52. Allison Fass, "Trading Up," *Forbes*, January 29, 2007, pp. 48–49; Diane Brady, "Coach's Split Personality," *BusinessWeek*, November 7, 2005, pp. 60–62.

53. Christina Passriello, "Fashionably Late? Designer Brands Are Starting to Embrace E-Commerce," *Wall Street Journal*, May 19, 2006.

54. William G. Zikmund and William J. Stanton, "Recycling Solid Wastes: A Channels-of-Distribution Problem," *Journal of Marketing*, July 1971, p. 34.

55. Joel C. Collier and Carol C. Bienstock, "How Do Customers Judge Quality in an E-Tailer," *MIT Sloan Management Review*, Autumn 2006, pp. 35–40.

56. See www.souq.com; "Saudi Post Launches a Domestic eCommerce Website—eMall," *arapost.com*, January 19, 2011, www.arapost.com/showthread.php?t=22702&page=1.

57. Nielsen/NetRatings, "Online Retail Report Card," press release, April 7, 2005.

58. Alexis K. J. Barlow, Noreen Q. Siddiqui, and Mike Mannion, "Development in Information and Communication Technologies for Retail Marketing Channels," *International Journal of Retail and Distribution Management*, 32, March 2004, pp. 157–163; G&J Electronic Media Services, *7th Wave of the GfK-Online-Monitor* (Hamburg: GfK Press, 2001).

59. Heather Green, "Lessons of the Cyber Survivors," *BusinessWeek*, April 22, 2002, p. 42.

60. Sidra Durst, "Shoe In," *Business 2.0*, December 2006, p. 54.

61. Kate Maddox, "Online Marketing Summit Probes New Technologies," *B to B*, 92, no. 3, March 12, 2007, pp. 3, 39. Reprinted by permission.

62. Martin Holzwarth, Chris Janiszewski, and Marcus M. Newmann, "The Influence of Avatars on Online Consumer

Shopping Behavior," *Journal of Marketing*, 70, October 2006, pp. 19–36.

63. Ann E. Schlosser, Tiffany Barnett White, and Susan M. Lloyd, "Converting Web Site Visitors into Buyers: How Web Site Investment Increases Consumer Trusting Beliefs and Online Purchase Intentions," *Journal of Marketing*, 70, April 2006, pp. 133–148.

64. Ronald Abler, John S. Adams, and Peter Gould, *Spatial Organizations: The Geographer's View of the World* (Upper Saddle River, NJ: Prentice Hall, 1971), pp. 531–532.

65. "China's Pied Piper," *The Economist*, September 23, 2006, p. 80; www.alibaba.com.

66. For an in-depth academic examination, see John G. Lynch Jr. and Dan Ariely, "Wine Online: Search Costs and Competition on Price, Quality, and Distribution," *Marketing Science*, 19, Winter 2000, pp. 83–103.

67. Described in *Inside 1-to-1*, Peppers and Rogers Group newsletter, May 14, 2001.

68. Marc Weingarten, "The Medium Is the Instant Message," *Business 2.0*, February 2002, pp. 98–99; Douglas Lamont, *Conquering the Wireless World: The Age of M-Commerce* (New York: Wiley, 2001).

Chapter 16

1. Kerry Capell, "Fashion Conquistador," *BusinessWeek*, September 4, 2006, pp. 38–39; Rachel Tipaldy, "Zara: Taking the Lead in Fast-Fashion," *BusinessWeek*, April 4, 2006; Kasra Ferdows, Michael A. Lewis, and Jose A. D. Machuca, "Zara's Secret for Fast Fashion," *Harvard Business School Working Knowledge*, February 21, 2005; Vivian Manning-Schaffel, "Zara-Zesty," *brandchannel.com*, August 23, 2004.

2. William R. Davidson, Albert D. Bates, and Stephen J. Bass, "Retail Life Cycle," *Harvard Business Review*, November–December 1976, pp. 89–96.

3. Stanley C. Hollander, "The Wheel of Retailing," *Journal of Marketing*, July 1960, pp. 37–42.

4. William T. Gregor and Eileen M. Friars, *Money Merchandising; Retail Revolution in Consumer Financial Service* (Cambridge, MA: The MAC Group, 1982).

5. "First Direct Selling Conference in Dubai," *AME Info*, www.ameinfo.com/153992.html, April 21 2008.

6. Amy Merrick, Jeffrey Trachtenberg, and Ann Zimmerman, "Department Stores Fight to Preserve Role That May Be Outdated," *Wall Street Journal*, March 12, 2002; Ann Zimmerman, "Dillard's Counts on House Brands to Recapture Reputation," *Wall Street Journal*, March 2001.

7. See www.panda.com.sa

8. Theresa Howard, "Retail Stores Pop Up for Limited Time Only," *USA Today*, May 28, 2004.

9. Wendy Liebmann, "Consumers Push Back," *Brandweek*, February 23, 2004, pp. 19–20.

10. See www.geogtv.com/cindex.php?option=tvchannel&task=list&chid=3580

11. Liebmann, "Consumers Push Back," pp. 19–20.

12. Catherine Yang, "Maybe They Should Call Them Scammers," *BusinessWeek*, January 16, 1995, pp. 32–33; Ronald C. Goodstein, "UPC Scanner Pricing Systems: Are They Accurate?" *Journal of Marketing*, April 1994, pp. 20–30.

13. For a listing of the key factors involved in success with an EDI system, see R. P. Vlosky, D. T. Wilson, and P. M. Smith, "Electronic Data Interchange Implementation Strategies: A Case Study," *Journal of Business & Industrial Marketing* nited Arab Emirates 9, no. 4, 1994, pp. 5–18.

14. "Business Bulletin: Shopper Scanner," *Wall Street Journal*, February 18, 1995.

15. Michael Freedman, "The Eyes Have It," *Forbes*, September 4, 2006, p. 70.

16. Matthew Boyle, "IBM Goes Shopping," *Fortune*, 15 27, 2006, pp. 77–78.

17. Jenn Abelson, "Miles Away, 'I'll Have a Burger,'" *Knight Ridder Tribune Business News*, November 5, 2006, p. 1.

18. For further discussion of retail trends, see Anne T. Coughlan, Erin Anderson, Louis W. Stern, and Adel I. El-Ansary, *Marketing Channels*, 6th edn (Upper Saddle River, NJ: Prentice Hall, 2001).

19. See www.nayomi.com.sa/corporate/more-about-the-group.html

20. Ann Zimmerman and Kris Hudson, "Chasing Upscale Customers Tarnishes Mass-Market Jeweler," *Wall Street Journal*, June 26, 2006; Kris Hudson, "Signet Sparkles with Jewelry Strategy," *Wall Street Journal*, June 26, 2006.

21. *Mikyajy*, www.mikyajy.com/eng/22k_Brand.html.

22. Uta Werner, John McDermott, and Greg Rotz, "Retailers at the Crossroads: How to Develop Profitable New Growth Strategies," *Journal of Business Strategy*, 25, no. 2, 2004, pp. 10–17.

23. *Jumbo Electronics*, www.jumbocorp.com/corporate.asp.

24. Venkatesh Shankar and Ruth N. Bolton, "An Empirical Analysis of Determinants of Retailer Pricing Strategy," *Marketing Science*, 23, Winter 2004, pp. 28–49.

25. Duncan Simester, "Signaling Price Image Using Advertised Prices," *Marketing Science*, 14, Summer 1995, pp. 166–188; see also, Jiwoong Shin, "The Role of Selling Costs in Signaling Price Image," *Journal of Marketing Research*, 42, August 2005, pp. 305–312.

26. Frank Feather, *The Future Consumer* (Toronto: Warwick Publishing, 1994), p. 171. Also see David R. Bell and James M. Lattin, "Shopping Behavior and Consumer Preference for Retail Price Format: Why 'Large Basket' Shoppers Prefer EDLP," *Marketing Science*, 17, Spring 1998, pp. 66–68; Stephen J. Hoch, Xavier Dreeze, and Mary E. Purk, "EDLP, Hi-Lo, and Margin Arithmetic," *Journal of Marketing*, October 1994, pp. 1–15.

27. Constance L. Hays, "Retailers Seeking to Lure Customers with Service," *New York Times*, December 1, 2003.

28. Amy Gillentine, "Marketing Groups Ignore Women at Their Own Peril," *Colorado Springs Business Journal*, January 20, 2006; Mary Lou Quinlan, "Women Aren't Buying It," *Brandweek*, June 2, 2003, pp. 20–22.

29. Justin Hibbard, "Put Your Money Where Your Mouth Is," *BusinessWeek*, September 18, 2006, pp. 61–63.

30. "Reinventing the Store," *The Economist*, November 22, 2003, pp. 65–68; Moira Cotlier, "Census Releases First E-Commerce Report," *Catalog Age*, May 1, 2001; Associated Press, "Online Sales Boomed at End of 2000," *Star-Tribune of Twin Cities*, February 17, 2001; Kenneth T. Rosen and Amanda L. Howard, "E-Tail: Gold Rush or Fool's Gold?" *California Management Review*, April 1, 2000, pp. 72–100.

31. Velitchka D. Kaltcheva and Barton Weitz, "When Should a Retailer Create an Exciting Store Environment?" *Journal of Marketing*, 70, January 2006, pp. 107–118.

32. For more discussion, see Philip Kotler, "Atmospherics as a Marketing Tool," *Journal of Retailing*, Winter 1973–1974, pp. 48–64. Also see B. Joseph Pine II and James H. Gilmore, *The Experience Economy* (Boston: Harvard Business School Press, 1999).

33. Jeff Cioletti, "Super Marketing," *Beverage World*, November 2006, pp. 60–61.

34. Carol Tice, "Anchors Away: Department Stores Lose Role at Malls," *Puget Sound Business Journal*, February 13, 2004, p. 1.

35. R. L. Davies and D. S. Rogers, eds, *Store Location and Store Assessment Research* (New York: John Wiley, 1984).

36. Sara L. McLafferty, *Location Strategies for Retail and Service Firms* (Lexington, MA: Lexington Books, 1987).

37. Kusum Ailawadi and Bari Harlam, "An Empirical Analysis of the Determinants of Retail Margins: The Role of Store-Brand Share," *Journal of Marketing*, 68, January 2004, pp. 147–165.

38. *Almarai*, www.almarai.com/main.html#/en/Home.

39. Michael Felding, "No Longer Plain, Simple," *Marketing News*, May 15, 2006, pp. 11–13; Rob Walker, "Shelf Improvement," *New York Times*, May 7, 2006.

40. James A. Narus and James C. Anderson, "Contributing as a Distributor to Partnerships with Manufacturers," *Business Horizons*, September–October 1987. Also see James D. Hlavecek and Tommy J. McCuistion, "Industrial Distributors—When, Who, and How," *Harvard Business Review*, March–April 1983, pp. 96–101.

41. Nirmalya Kumar and Jan-Benedict E. M. Steenkamp, *Private Label Strategy: How to Meet the Store-Brand Challenge* (Boston: Harvard Business School Press, 2007).

42. Brett Nelson, "Stuck in the Middle," *Forbes*, August 15, 2005, p. 88; "Arrow Investor Fact Sheet 2009," Arrow, www.arrow.com.

43. Narus and Anderson, "Contributing as a Distributor to Partnerships with Manufacturers." Also see Hlavecek and McCuistion, "Industrial Distributors—When, Who, and How," pp. 96–101.

44. William C. Copacino, *Supply Chain Management* (Boca Raton, FL: St. Lucie Press, 1997).

45. John Heilemann, "All the News That's Fit for Bits," *Business 2.0*, 7, no. 8, September 2006, p. 40.

46. "Cargo Cults," *The Economist: A Survey of Logistics*, June 17, 2006, pp. 9–14.

47. Anthony Bianco, "Wal-Mart's Midlife Crisis," *BusinessWeek*, April 30, 2007, pp. 46–56; Matthew Maier, "How to Beat Wal-Mart," *Business 2.0*, May 2005; Jerry Useem, "Should We Admire Wal-Mart?" *Fortune*, March 8, 2004, pp. 118–21; www.walmart.com.

48. The optimal order quantity is given by the formula $Q^*=2DS/IC$, where D=annual demand, S=cost to place one order, and I=annual carrying cost per unit. Known as the economic-order quantity formula, it assumes a constant ordering cost, a constant cost of carrying an additional unit in inventory, a known demand, and no quantity discounts. For further reading on this subject, see Richard J. Tersine, *Principles of Inventory and Materials Management*, 4th edn (Upper Saddle River, NJ: Prentice Hall, 1994).

49. Copacino, *Supply Chain Management*, pp. 122–123.

50. "Shining Examples," *The Economist: A Survey of Logistics*, June 17, 2006, pp. 4–6.

51. Renee DeGross, "Retailers Try eBay Overstocks, Returns for Sale Online," *Atlanta Journal-Constitution*, April 10, 2004.

52. "Manufacturing Complexity," *The Economist: A Survey of Logistics*, June 17, 2006, pp. 6–9.

53. Chad Terhune, "Pepsi's Supply Chain Fix," *Wall Street Journal*, June 6, 2006.

Chapter 17

1. Randall Rothenberg, "Dove Effort Gives Packaged-Goods Marketers Lessons for the Future," *Advertising Age*, March 5, 2007; Theresa Howard, "Ad Campaign Tells Women to Celebrate Who They Are," *USA Today*, July 8, 2005; Jack Neff, "In Dove Ads, Normal Is the New Beautiful," *Advertising Age*, September 27, 2004; www.campaignforrealbeauty.com.

2. Xueming Luo and Naveen Donthu, "Marketing's Credibility: A Longitudinal Investigation of Marketing Communication Productivity and Shareholder Value," *Journal of Marketing*, 70, October 2006, pp. 70–91.

3. David Kiley, "Hey Advertisers, TiVo Is Your Friend," *BusinessWeek*, October 17, 2005, pp. 97–98; Linda Kaplan Thaler and Robin Koval with Delia Marshall, *Bang! Getting Your Message Heard in a Noisy World* (New York: Currency, 2003).

4. Anthony Bianco, "The Vanishing Mass Market," *BusinessWeek*, July 12, 2004, pp. 60–68; Susan Thea Posnock, "It Can Control Madison Avenue," *American Demographics*, February 2004, pp. 28–33; Jennifer Pendleton, "Multi TASKERS," *Advertising Age*, March 29, 2004, pp. S1, S8; Christopher Reynolds, "Game Over," *American Demographics*, February 2004, pp. 34–38; Noreen O'Leary, "The 30-Second Spot Is Dead, Long Live the 30-Second Spot," *Adweek*, November 17, 2003, pp. 12–21; Hank Kim, "Madison Ave. Melds Pitches and Content," *Advertising Age*, October 7, 2002, pp. 1, 14.

5. Data from www.startuparabia.com, cited at www.mediazbiz.com/2010/03/05/social-media-in-the-middle-east.

6. Louise Story, "Viewers Fast-Forwarding Past Ads? Not Always," *New York Times*, February 16, 2007; Abbey Klaassen, "Major Turnoff: McKinsey Slams TV Selling Power," *Advertising Age*, August 7, 2006, pp. 1, 33. See also, Ron Briggs and Greg Stuart, *What Sticks: Why Most Advertising Fails and How to Guarantee Yours Succeeds* (New York: Kaplan Business, 2006).

7. Louise Story, "Anywhere the Eye Can See, It's Likely to See an Ad," *New York Times*, January 15, 2007; Laura Petrecca, "Product Placement–You Can't Escape It," *USA Today*, October 11, 2006.

8. "Pepsi Changes the Face of Marketing in the Middle East," *AME Info*, February 7, 2008, www.ameinfo.com/146040. html.

9. Ibid.

10. Some of these definitions are adapted from Peter D. Bennett, ed., *Dictionary of Marketing Terms* (Chicago: American Marketing Association, 1995).

11. Tom Duncan and Sandra Moriarty, "How Integrated Marketing Communication's 'Touch Points' Can Operationalize the Service-Dominant Logic," in *The Service-Dominant Logic of Marketing: Dialog, Debate, and Directions*, ed. Robert F. Lusch and Stephen L. Vargo (Armonk, NY: M.E. Sharpe, 2006); Tom Duncan, *Principles of Advertising and IMC*, 2nd edn (New York, NY: McGraw-Hill/Irwin, 2005).

12. Joseph W. Alba and J. Wesley Hutchinson, "Dimensions of Consumer Expertise," *Journal of Consumer Research*, 13, March 1987, pp. 411–453.

13. See www.sugardaddysbakery.com

14. For an alternate communications model developed specifically for advertising communications, see Barbara B. Stern, "A Revised Communication Model for Advertising: Multiple Dimensions of the Source, the Message, and the Recipient," *Journal of Advertising*, June 1994, pp. 5–15. For some additional perspectives, see Tom Duncan and Sandra E. Morarity, "A Communication-Based Marketing Model for Managing Relationships," *Journal of Marketing*, April 1998, pp. 1–13.

15. Demetrios Vakratsas and Tim Ambler, "How Advertising Works: What Do We Really Know?" *Journal of Marketing* 63, no. 1, January 1999, pp. 26–43.

16. This section is based on the excellent text, John R. Rossiter and Larry Percy, *Advertising and Promotion Management*, 2nd edn (New York: McGraw-Hill, 1997).

17. James F. Engel, Roger D. Blackwell, and Paul W. Minard, *Consumer Behavior*, 9th edn (Fort Worth, TX: Dryden, 2001).

18. Rossiter and Percy, *Advertising and Promotion Management*.

19. Engel, Blackwell, and Minard, *Consumer Behavior*.

20. Ayn E. Crowley and Wayne D. Hoyer, "An Integrative Framework for Understanding Two-Sided Persuasion," *Journal of Consumer Research*, March 1994, pp. 561–574.

21. C. I. Hovland, A. A. Lumsdaine, and F. D. Sheffield, *Experiments on Mass Communication*, vol. 3 (Princeton, NJ: Princeton University Press, 1948), Chapter 8; Crowley

and Hoyer, "An Integrative Framework for Understanding Two-Sided Persuasion." For an alternative viewpoint, see George E. Belch, "The Effects of Message Modality on One- and Two-Sided Advertising Messages," in *Advances in Consumer Research*, ed. Richard P. Bagozzi and Alice M. Tybout (Ann Arbor, MI: Association for Consumer Research, 1983), pp. 21–26.

22. Curtis P. Haugtvedt and Duane T. Wegener, "Message Order Effects in Persuasion: An Attitude Strength Perspective," *Journal of Consumer Research*, June 1994, pp. 205–218; H. Rao Unnava, Robert E. Burnkrant, and Sunil Erevelles, "Effects of Presentation Order and Communication Modality on Recall and Attitude," *Journal of Consumer Research*, December 1994, pp. 481–490.

23. Brian Sternthal and C. Samuel Craig, *Consumer Behavior: An Information Processing Perspective* (Upper Saddle River, NJ: Prentice-Hall, 1982), pp. 282–284.

24. Michael R. Solomon, *Consumer Behavior*, 7th edn (Upper Saddle River, NJ: Prentice Hall, 2007).

25. Some recent research on humor in advertising, for example, includes: Haseeb Shabbir and Des Thwaites, "The Use of Humor to Mask Deceptive Advertising: It's No Laughing Matter," *Journal of Advertising*, 36, Summer 2007, pp. 75–85; Thomas W. Cline and James J. Kellaris, "The Influence of Humor Strength and Humor Message Relatedness on Ad Memorability: A Dual Process Model," *Journal of Advertising*, 36, Spring 2007, pp. 55–67; H. Shanker Krishnan and Dipankar Chakravarti, "A Process Analysis of the Effects of Humorous Advertising Executions on Brand Claims Memory," *Journal of Consumer Psychology*, 13, no. 3, 2003, pp. 230–245.

26. Rik Pieters and Michel Wedel, "Attention Capture and Transfer in Advertising: Brand, Pictorial, and Text-Size Effects," *Journal of Marketing*, 68, April 2004, pp. 36–50.

27. Herbert C. Kelman and Carl I. Hovland, "Reinstatement of the Communication in Delayed Measurement of Opinion Change," *Journal of Abnormal and Social Psychology*, 48, July 1953, pp. 327–335.

28. David J. Moore, John C. Mowen, and Richard Reardon, "Multiple Sources in Advertising Appeals: When Product Endorsers Are Paid by the Advertising Sponsor," *Journal of the Academy of Marketing Science*, Summer 1994, pp. 234–243.

29. C. E. Osgood and P. H. Tannenbaum, "The Principles of Congruity in the Prediction of Attitude Change," *Psychological Review*, 62, January 1955, pp. 42–55.

30. "EU to Try Again on Tobacco Advertising Ban," *Associated Press*, May 9, 2001; Richard C. Morais, "Mobile Mayhem," *Forbes*, July, 6 1998, p. 138; "Working in Harmony," *Soap Perfumery & Cosmetics*, July 1, 1998, p. 27; Rodger Harrabin, "A Commercial Break for Parents," *Independent*, September 8, 1998, p. 19; Naveen Donthu, "A Cross-Country Investigation of Recall of and Attitude toward Comparative Advertising," *Journal of Advertising*, 27, June 1998, p. 111.

31. "Rebirth of a Salesman," *The Economist*, April 14, 2001.

32. Michael Kiely, "Word-of-Mouth Marketing," *Marketing*, September 1993, p. 6. See also Aric Rindfleisch and Christine Moorman, "The Acquisition and Utilization of Information in New Product Alliances: A Strength-of-Ties Perspective," *Journal of Marketing*, April 2001, pp. 1–18.

33. Ian Mount, "Marketing," *Business 2.0*, August–September 2001, p. 84.

34. Steve Miller, "Mini Making Big Claims about Mileage in New Push," *Brandweek*, June 4, 2007, p. 7; Barnaby Feder, "Billboards That Know You by Name," *New York Times*, January 29, 2007; www.kellyawardsgallery.org/; Burt Helm, "For Your Eyes Only," *BusinessWeek*, July 31, 2006, pp. 66–67; Warren Berger, "Dare-Devils," *Business 2.0*, April 2004, pp. 111–116; Karen Lundegaard, "BMW 'Mini' Campaign: Odd to the Max," *Wall Street Journal*, February 28, 2002; John Gaffney, "Most Innovative Campaign," *Business 2.0*, May 2002, pp. 98–99.

35. Adapted from G. Maxwell Ule, "A Media Plan for 'Sputnik' Cigarettes," *How to Plan Media Strategy* (American Association of Advertising Agencies, 1957 Regional Convention), pp. 41–52.

36. Thomas C. Kinnear, Kenneth L. Bernhardt, and Kathleen A. Krentler, *Principles of Marketing*, 6th edn (New York: HarperCollins College Div., 1995).

37. K. Sridhar Moorthy and Scott A. Hawkins, "Advertising Repetition and Quality Perceptions," *Journal of Business Research*, 58, March 2005, pp. 354–360; Amna Kirmani and Akshay R. Rao, "No Pain, No Gain: A Critical Review of the Literature on Signaling Unobservable Product Quality," *Journal of Marketing*, 64, April 2000, pp. 66–79; Amna Kirmani, "The Effect of Perceived Advertising Costs on Brand Perceptions," *Journal of Consumer Research*, 17, September 17, 1990, pp. 160–71; Amna Kirmani and Peter Wright, "Money Talks: Perceived Advertising Expense and Expected Product Quality," *Journal of Consumer Research*, 16, December 1989, pp. 344–353.

38. Demetrios Vakratsas and Tim Ambler, "How Advertising Works: What Do We Really Know?" *Journal of Marketing*, 63, no. 1, January 1999, pp. 26–43.

39. Chris Daniels, "B-to-B Creaks Comms Barrier," *PRweek*, 10, no. 22, June 4, 2007.

40. T. Levitt, *Industrial Purchasing Behaviour: A Study of Communication Effects* (Boston: Harvard Business School, 1965).

41. Kate Maddox, "Integrated Marketing Success Stories," *B to B*, 91, no. 10, August 14, 2006.

42. Prasad A. Naik and Kalyan Raman, "Understanding the Impact of Synergy in Multimedia Communications," *Journal of Marketing Research*, 40, November 2003, pp. 375–388. See also Prasad A. Naik, Kalyan Raman, and Russell S. Winer, "Planning Marketing-Mix Strategies in the Presence of Interaction Effects," *Marketing Science*, 24, January 2005, pp. 25–34.

43. Janet Stilson, "Wide-Ranging Deals Help ESPN Score with Marketers," *Advertising Age*, March 12, 2007, p. S-2.

44. Scott Neslin, *Sales Promotion*, MSI Relevant Knowledge Series (Cambridge, MA: Marketing Science Institute, 2002).

45. Gerry Khermouch, "The Top 5 Rules of the Ad Game," *BusinessWeek*, January 20, 2003, pp. 72–73.

46. Maria Puente, "Online Experience Is Now a Much Better Fit," *USA Today*, December 4, 2002.

47. "A White Paper on the Status, Scope, and Future of IMC," eds. Tom Duncan and Frank Mulhern.

48. Suzy Bashford, "Collaboration Is Imperative," *Marketing*, December 13, 2006, p. 4.

49. Deborah L. Vance, "Better Coverage," *Marketing News*, January 15, 2007, pp. 13–14; Barry Janoff, "State Farm Asks, 'Now What?'" *Brandweek*, August 8, 2006.

50. Ellen Neuborne, "Ads That Actually Sell Stuff," *Business 2.0*, June 2004, p. 78.

51. Sreedhar Madhavaram, Vishag Badrinarayanan, and Robert E. McDonald, "Integrated Marketing Communication (IMC) and Brand Identity as Critical Components of Brand Equity Strategy," *Journal of Advertising*, 34, Winter 2005, pp. 69–80; Mike Reid, Sandra Luxton, and Felix Mavondo, "The Relationship between Integrated Marketing Communication, Market Orientation, and Brand Orientation," *Journal of Advertising*, 34, Winter 2005, pp. 11–23.

52. Don E. Schultz and Heidi Schultz, *IMC, The Next Generation: Five Steps for Delivering Value and Measuring Financial Returns* (New York: McGraw-Hill, 2003); Don E. Shultz, Stanley I. Tannenbaum, and Robert F. Lauterborn, *Integrated Marketing Communications: Putting It Together and Making It Work* (Lincolnwood, IL: NTC Business Books, 1992).

Chapter 18

1. Elie Aoun, "2010's Regional Annual Growth Figures," *ArabAd*, 21, No. 2, February 2011, pp. 6–31.

2. Paul F. Nunes and Jeffrey Merrihue, "The Continuing Power of Mass Advertising," *Sloan Management Review*, Winter 2007, pp. 63–69.

3. Jack Neff, "'Broken' Ad Model Holds Big Advantages for P&G," *Advertising Age*, March 5, 2007.

4. Russell H. Colley, *Defining Advertising Goals for Measured Advertising Results* (New York: Association of National Advertisers, 1961).

5. William L. Wilkie and Paul W. Farris, "Comparison Advertising: Problem and Potential," *Journal of Marketing*, October 1975, pp. 7–15.

6. "Responses to Comparative Advertising," *Journal of Consumer Research*, 32, March 2006, pp. 530–540; Dhruv Grewal, Sukumar Kavanoor, and James Barnes, "Comparative versus Noncomparative Advertising: A Meta-Analysis," *Journal of Marketing*, October 1997, pp. 1–15; Randall L. Rose, Paul W. Miniard, Michael J. Barone, Kenneth C. Manning, and Brian D. Till, "When Persuasion Goes Undetected: The Case of Comparative Advertising," *Journal of Marketing Research*, August 1993, pp. 315–330.

7. For a good discussion, see David A. Aaker and James M. Carman, "Are You Overadvertising?" *Journal of*

Advertising Research, August–September 1982, pp. 57–70.

8. Donald E. Schultz, Dennis Martin, and William P. Brown, *Strategic Advertising Campaigns* (Chicago: Crain Books, 1984), pp. 192–197.

9. Rajesh Chandy, Gerard J. Tellis, Debbie MacInnis, and Pattana Thaivanich, "What to Say When: Advertising Appeals In Evolving Markets," *Journal of Marketing Research*, 38, no. 4, November 2001; Gerard J. Tellis, Rajesh Chandy, and Pattana Thaivanich, "Decomposing the Effects of Direct Advertising: Which Brand Works, When, Where, and How Long?" *Journal of Marketing Research*, 37, February 2000, pp. 32–46.

10. See George S. Low and Jakki J. Mohr, "Brand Managers' Perceptions of the Marketing Communications Budget Allocation Process" (Cambridge, MA: Marketing Science Institute, Report No. 98–105, March 1998); and their "The Advertising Sales Promotion Trade-Off: Theory and Practice" (Cambridge, MA: Marketing Science Institute, Report No. 92–127, October 1992). Also see Gabriel J. Beihal and Daniel A. Sheinen, "Managing the Brand in a Corporate Advertising Environment: A Decision-Making Framework for Brand Managers," *Journal of Advertising*, 17, June 22, 1998, p. 99.

11. For an excellent review, see Greg Allenby and Dominique Hanssens, "Advertising Response," Marketing Science Institute, *Special Report*, No. 05-200, 2005.

12. Demetrios Vakratsas, Fred M. Feinberg, Frank M. Bass, and Gurumurthy Kalyanaram, "The Shape of Advertising Response Functions Revisited: A Model of Dynamic Probabilistic Thresholds," *Marketing Science*, 23, no. 1, Winter 2004, pp. 109–119.

13. Leonard M. Lodish, Magid Abraham, Stuart Kalmenson, Jeanne Livelsberger, Beth Lubetkin, Bruce Richardson, and Mary Ellen Stevens, "How T.V. Advertising Works: A Meta-Analysis of 389 Real-World Split Cable T.V. Advertising Experiments," *Journal of Marketing Research*, 32, May 1995, pp. 125–139.

14. Greg Allenby and Dominique Hanssens, "Advertising Response," Marketing Science Institute, *Special Report*, No. 05-200, 2005; Jack Neff, "TV Doesn't Sell Package Goods," *Advertising Age*, May 24, 2004, pp. 1, 30.

15. Cleve Langton, "Searching for the Holy Global Ad Grail," *Brandweek*, June 5, 2006, p. 16.

16. See www.hend-sabry.com/website/Garnier-HendSabry. pdf; "WFP Appoints Tunisian Film Star Hend Sabry Ambassador Against Hunger," January 12, 2010, www .wfp.org/news/news-release/wfp-appoints-tunisian-film-star-hend-sabry-ambassador-against-hunger.

17. See www.allfacebook.com/more-arabs-use-facebook-than-read-newspapers-2010-05.

18. Brian Steinberg, "Unisys Pitch Finds the I in Niche: Key Executives Are Targeted with *Fortune* 'Cover Shots,' Billboards on Commutes," *Wall Street Journal*, October 24, 2006, p. B4. Reprinted by permission of Dow Jones via Copyright Clearance Center.

19. "Statistics on Arab Media," *Arab Reform Bulletin*, December 2004, Carnegie Endowment for International Peace, www.carnegieendowment.org/files/New_Chart.pdf.

20. David Ogilvy, *Ogilvy on Advertising* (New York: Vintage Books, 1983).

21. Elie Aoun, "2010's Regional Annual Growth Figures," *ArabAd*, 21, No. 2, Feb 2011, pp. 6–31.

22. James P. Miller, "Bitter Sweets Fight Ended," *Chicago Tribune*, May 12, 2007; Avery Johnson, "How Sweet It Isn't: Maker of Equal Says Ads for J&J's Splenda Misled; Chemistry Lesson for Jurors," *Wall Street Journal*, April 6, 2007.

23. For further reading, see Dorothy Cohen, *Legal Issues in Marketing Decision Making* (Cincinnati, OH: South-Western, 1995).

24. Kim Bartel Sheehan, *Controversies in Contemporary Advertising* (Thousand Oaks, CA: Sage, 2003).

25. Schultz et al., *Strategic Advertising Campaigns*, p. 340.

26. Herbert E. Krugman, "What Makes Advertising Effective?" *Harvard Business Review*, March–April 1975, p. 98.

27. Prashant Malaviya, "The Moderating Influence of Advertising Context on Ad Repetition Effects: The Role of Amount and Type of Elaboration," *Journal of Consumer Research*, 34, June 2007, pp. 32–40.

28. Thomas H. Davenport and John C. Beck, *The Attention Economy: Understanding the New Currency of Business* (Boston: Harvard Business School Press, 2000).

29. Susan Thea Posnock, "It Can Control Madison Avenue," *American Demographics*, February 2004, pp. 29–33.

30. James Betzold, "Jaded Riders Are Ever-Tougher Sell," *Advertising Age*, July 9, 2001; Michael McCarthy, "Ads Are Here, There, Everywhere," *USA Today*, June 19, 2001; Michael McCarthy, "Critics Target 'Omnipresent' Ads," *USA Today*, April 16, 2001; Kipp Cheng, "Captivating Audiences," *Brandweek*, November 29, 1999.

31. Sam Jaffe, "Easy Riders," *American Demographics*, March 2004, pp. 20–23.

32. Information from www.kunhadi.org.

33. Jeff Pelline, "New Commercial Twist in Corporate Restrooms," *San Francisco Chronicle*, October 6, 1986.

34. Lynne Roberts, "Dubai Makes Record Books with World's Largest Ad," *Arabian Business*, www.arabianbusiness. com/dubai-makes-world-record-with-world-s-biggest-ad-53517.html; "Sorouh Faces Campaign Receives Strong Global Support," *AME Info*, November 14, 2007, www.ameinfo.com/138426.html.

35. Brian Steinberg and Suzanne Vranica, "Prime-Time TV's New Guest Stars: Products," *Wall Street Journal*, January 13, 2004.

36. Jane Weaver, "A License to Shill," *MSNBC News*, November 17, 2002.

37. John Lippman and Rick Brooks, "Hot Holiday Flick Pairs FedEx, Hanks," *Wall Street Journal*, December 11, 2000;

Joanne Lipman, "Product Placement Can Be Free Lunch," *Wall Street Journal*, November 25, 1991.

38. Warren Berger, "That's Advertainment," *Business 2.0*, March 2003, pp. 91–95.

39. Elie Aoun, "2010's Regional Annual Growth Figures," *ArabAd*, 21, no. 2, February 2011, pp. 6–31.

40. Anne-Birte Stensgaard, "Arab Satellite TV Ad Rates Skyrocket during Reality TV Programs, and Can Be up to 130 Percent of Regular Prime Time Rates," *AMEinfo.com*, May 14, 2004 (updated May 1, 2007), www.ameinfo.com /56444.html.

41. For more on other media context effects, see Michael A. Kamins, Lawrence J. Marks, and Deborah Skinner, "Television Commercial Evaluation in the Context of Program-Induced Mood: Congruency versus Consistency Effects," *Journal of Advertising*, June 1991, pp. 1–14; see also Jing Wang and Bobby J. Calder, "Media Transportation and Advertising," *Journal of Consumer Research*, 33, September 2006, pp. 151–162.

42. Kenneth R. Lord, Myung-Soo Lee, and Paul L. Sauer, "Program Context Antecedents of Attitude toward Radio Commercials," *Journal of the Academy of Marketing Science*, Winter 1994, pp. 3–15; Kenneth R. Lord and Robert E. Burnkrant, "Attention versus Distraction: The Interactive Effect of Program Involvement and Attentional Devices on Commercial Processing," *Journal of Advertising*, March 1993, pp. 47–60.

43. Roland T. Rust, *Advertising Media Models: A Practical Guide* (Lexington, MA: Lexington Books, 1986).

44. Information from www.middleeastmediaguide.com.

45. Hani I. Mesak, "An Aggregate Advertising Pulsing Model with Wearout Effects," *Marketing Science*, Summer 1992, pp. 310–326; Fred M. Feinberg, "Pulsing Policies for Aggregate Advertising Models," *Marketing Science*, Summer 1992, pp. 221–234.

46. Josephine L. C. M. Woltman Elpers, Michel Wedel, and Rik G. M. Pieters, "Why Do Consumers Stop Viewing Television Commercials? Two Experiments on the Influence of Moment-to-Moment Entertainment and Information Value," *Journal of Marketing Research*, 40, November 2003, pp. 437–453.

47. See, for example, Antonio G. Chessa and Jaap M. J. Murre, "A Neurocognitive Model of Advertisement Content and Brand-Name Recall," *Marketing Science*, 26, January–February 2007, pp. 130–141.

48. David B. Montgomery and Alvin J. Silk, "Estimating Dynamic Effects of Market Communications Expenditures," *Management Science*, June 1972, pp. 485–501; Kristian S. Palda, *The Measurement of Cumulative Advertising Effect* (Upper Saddle River, NJ: Prentice Hall, 1964), p. 87.

49. See www.infores.com; Lodish et al., "How T.V. Advertising Works."

50. Gerard J. Tellis, Rajesh K. Chandy, and Pattana Thaivanich, "Which Ad Works, When, Where, and How Often? Modeling the Effects of Direct Television Advertising," *Journal of Marketing Research*, 37, February

2000, pp. 32–46; Ajay Kalra and Ronald C. Goodstein, "The Impact of Advertising Positioning Strategies on Consumer Price Sensitivity," *Journal of Marketing Research*, May 1998, pp. 210–224; Anil Kaul and Dick R. Wittink, "Empirical Generalizations about the Impact of Advertising on Price Sensitivity and Price," *Marketing Science*, 14, no. 3, pt. 1, Summer 1995, pp. G151–G160; David Walker and Tony M. Dubitsky, "Why Liking Matters," *Journal of Advertising Research*, May–June 1994, pp. 9–18; Abhilasha Mehta, "How Advertising Response Modeling (ARM) Can Increase Ad Effectiveness," *Journal of Advertising Research*, May–June 1994, pp. 62–74; John Deighton, Caroline Henderson, and Scott Neslin, "The Effects of Advertising on Brand Switching and Repeat Purchasing," *Journal of Marketing Research*, February 1994, pp. 28–43; Karin Holstius, "Sales Response to Advertising," *International Journal of Advertising*, 9, no. 1, September 1990, pp. 38–56.

51. Nigel Hollis, "The Future of Tracking Studies," *Admap*, October 2004, pp. 151–153.

52. Laura Petrecca and Theresa Howard, "Nielsen Wants to Track Who Watches Commercials," *USA Today*, July 11, 2006.

53. From, Robert C. Blattberg and Scott A. Neslin, *Sales Promotion: Concepts, Methods, and Strategies* (Upper Saddle River, NJ: Prentice Hall, 1990). This text provides the most comprehensive and analytical treatment of sales promotion to date. An extremely up-to-date and comprehensive review of academic work on sales promotions can be found in Scott Neslin, "Sales Promotion," in *Handbook of Marketing*, ed. Bart Weitz and Robin Wensley (London: Sage, 2002), pp. 310–338.

54. Kusum Ailawadi, Karen Gedenk, and Scott A. Neslin, "Heterogeneity and Purchase Event Feedback in Choice Models: An Empirical Analysis with Implications for Model Building," *International Journal of Research in Marketing* 16, September 1999, pp. 177–198. See also Kusum L. Ailawadi, Karen Gedenk, Christian Lutzky, and Scott A. Neslin, "Decomposition of the Sales Impact of Promotion-Induced Stockpiling," *Journal of Marketing Research*, 44, August 2007; Eric T. Anderson and Duncan Simester, "The Long-Run Effects of Promotion Depth on New versus Established Customers: Three Field Studies," *Marketing Science* 23, no. 1, Winter 2004, pp. 4–20; Luc Wathieu, A. V. Muthukrishnan, and Bart J. Bronnenberg. "The Asymmetric Effect of Discount Retraction on Subsequent Choice," *Journal of Consumer Research*, 31, December 2004, pp. 652–665; Praveen Kopalle, Carl F. Mela, and Lawrence Marsh, "The Dynamic Effect of Discounting on Sales: Empirical Analysis and Normative Pricing Implications," *Marketing Science*, 18, Summer 1999, pp. 317–332.

55. Carl Mela, Kamel Jedidi, and Douglas Bowman, "The Long-Term Impact of Promotions on Consumer Stockpiling," *Journal of Marketing Research*, 35, no. 2, May 1998, pp. 250–262.

56. Harald J. Van Heerde, Sachin Gupta, and Dick Wittink, "Is 75% of the Sales Promotion Bump Due to Brand Switching? No, Only 33% Is," *Journal of Marketing*

Research, 40, November 2003, pp. 481–491; Harald J. Van Heerde, Peter S. H. Leeflang, and Dick R. Wittink, "The Estimation of Pre- and Postpromotion Dips with Store-Level Scanner Data," *Journal of Marketing Research*, 37, no. 3, August 2000, pp. 383–395.

57. Paul W. Farris and John A. Quelch, "In Defense of Price Promotion," *Sloan Management Review*, Autumn 1997, pp. 63–69.

58. Roger A. Strang, "Sales Promotion: Fast Growth, Faulty Management," *Harvard Business Review*, July–August 1976, pp. 116–119.

59. For a good summary of the research on whether promotion erodes the consumer franchise of leading brands, see Blattberg and Neslin, *Sales Promotion*.

60. AutoVIBES, *AutoBeat Daily*, March 3, 2004; Karen Lundegaard and Sholnn Freeman, "Detroit's Challenge: Weaning Buyers from Years of Deals," *Wall Street Journal*, January 6, 2004.

61. Robert George Brown, "Sales Response to Promotions and Advertising," *Journal of Advertising Research*, August 1974, pp. 36–37. Also see Kamel Jedidi, Carl F. Mela, and Sunil Gupta, "Managing Advertising and Promotion for Long-Run Profitability," *Marketing Science*, 18, no. 1, Winter 1999, pp. 1–22; Carl F. Mela, Sunil Gupta, and Donald R. Lehmann, "The Long-Term Impact of Promotion and Advertising on Consumer Brand Choice," *Journal of Marketing Research*, May 1997, pp. 248–261; Purushottam Papatla and Lakshman Krishnamurti, "Measuring the Dynamic Effects of Promotions on Brand Choice," *Journal of Marketing Research*, February 1996, pp. 20–35.

62. See www.americanexpress.com.sa.

63. Magid M. Abraham and Leonard M. Lodish, "Getting the Most out of Advertising and Promotion," *Harvard Business Review*, May–June 1990, pp. 50–60. See also Shuba Srinivasan, Koen Pauwels, Dominique Hanssens, and Marnik Dekimpe, "Do Promotions Benefit Manufacturers, Retailers, or Both?" *Management Science*, 50, no. 5, May 2004, pp. 617–629.

64. Lodish et al., "How T.V. Advertising Works."

65. For a model for setting sales promotions objectives, see David B. Jones, "Setting Promotional Goals: A Communications Relationship Model," *Journal of Consumer Marketing*, 11, no. 1, 1994, pp. 38–49.

66. Kusum L. Ailawadi, Bari A. Harlam, Jacques Cesar, and David Trounce, "Promotion Profitability for a Retailer: The Role of Promotion, Brand, Category, and Store Characteristics," *Journal of Marketing Research*, 43, November 2006, pp. 518–536.

67. See www.pmalink.org/awards/; Jane L. Levere, "Body by Milk: More Than Just a White Mustache," *New York Times*, August 30, 2006.

68. See, John C. Totten and Martin P. Block, *Analyzing Sales Promotion: Text and Cases*, 2nd edn (Chicago: Dartnell, 1994), pp. 69–70.

69. See www.makhsoom.com.

70. Miguel Gomez, Vithala Rao, and Edward McLaughlin, "Empirical Analysis of Budget and Allocation of Trade Promotions in the U.S. Supermarket Industry," *Journal of Marketing Research*, 44, August 2007; Norris Bruce, Preyas S. Desai, and Richard Staelin, "The Better They Are, the More They Give: Trade Promotions of Consumer Durables," *Journal of Marketing Research*, 42, February 2005, pp. 54–66.

71. Kusum L. Ailawadi and Bari Harlam, "An Empirical Analysis of the Determinants of Retail Margins: The Role of Store Brand Share," *Journal of Marketing*, 68, January 2004, pp. 147–166; Kusum L. Ailawadi, "The Retail Power-Performance Conundrum: What Have We Learned?" *Journal of Retailing*, 77, no. 3, Autumn 2001, pp. 299–318; Paul W. Farris and Kusum L. Ailawadi, "Retail Power: Monster or Mouse?" *Journal of Retailing*, Winter 1992, pp. 351–369; Koen Pauwels, "How Retailer and Competitor Decisions Drive the Long-Term Effectiveness of Manufacturer Promotions for Fast Moving Consumer Goods," *Journal of Retailing*, 83, March 2007, pp. 297–308.

72. Rajiv Lal, J. Little, and J. M. Vilas-Boas, "A Theory of Forward Buying, Merchandising, and Trade Deals," *Marketing Science*, 15, no. 1, Winter 1996, pp. 21–37; "Retailers Buy Far in Advance to Exploit Trade Promotions," *Wall Street Journal*, October 9, 1986.

73. Arthur Stern, "Measuring the Effectiveness of Package-Goods Promotion Strategies," paper presented to the Association of National Advertisers, Glen Cove, New York, February 1978.

74. Kurt H. Schaffir and H. George Trenten, *Marketing Information Systems* (New York: Amacom, 1973), p. 81.

75. Joe A. Dodson, Alice M. Tybout, and Brian Sternthal, "Impact of Deals and Deal Retraction on Brand Switching," *Journal of Marketing Research*, February 1978, pp. 72–81.

76. Books on sales promotion include Totten and Block, *Analyzing Sales Promotion: Text and Cases;* Don E. Schultz, William A. Robinson, and Lisa A. Petrison, *Sales Promotion Essentials*, 2nd edn (Lincolnwood, IL: NTC Business Books, 1994); John Wilmshurst, *Below-the-Line Promotion* (Oxford, England: Butterworth/Heinemann, 1993); Blattberg and Neslin, *Sales Promotion: Concepts, Methods, and Strategies.* For an expert systems approach to sales promotion, see John W. Keon and Judy Bayer, "An Expert Approach to Sales Promotion Management," *Journal of Advertising Research*, June–July 1986, pp. 19–26.

77. *IEG Sponsorship Report*, 28, No. 24, December 21, 2009; www.marketingpower.com/ResourceLibrary/Documents/Content%20Partner%20Documents/IEG/2010/sponsorship_spending_recedes_for_first_time.pdf.

78. Philip Kotler, "Atmospherics as a Marketing Tool," *Journal of Retailing*, Winter 1973–1974, pp. 48–64.

79. Kathleen Kerwin, "When the Factory Is a Theme Park," *BusinessWeek*, May 3, 2004, p. 94; Vanessa O'Connell, "'You-Are-There' Advertising," *Wall Street Journal*, August 5, 2002.

80. See www.ferrariworldabudhabi.com/; http://en.wikipedia.org/wiki/Ferrari_World; "Ferrari World, Another Success in the UAE," *WEXAX*, http://wexax.com/article/ferrari-world-uae/.

81. Bettina Cornwell, Michael S. Humphreys, Angela M. Maguire, Clinton S. Weeks, and Cassandra Tellegen, "Sponsorship-Linked Marketing: The Role of Articulation in Memory," *Journal of Consumer Research*, 33, December 2006, pp. 312–321.

82. The Association of National Advertisers has a useful source: *Event Marketing: A Management Guide*, which is available at www.ana.net/bookstore.

83. Cornwell et al., "Sponsorship-Linked Marketing."

84. Constantine von Hoffman, "Buying Up the Bleachers," *Brandweek*, February 19, 2007, pp. 18–21.

85. Owen Gibson, "Arsenal-Emirates Deal Worth BP100 Million," October 5, 2004, www.guardian.co.uk/media/2004/oct/05/business.marketingandpr.

86. "Barcelona and Qatar Foundation Agree BP125 Million Deal," December 10, 2010, http://news.bbc.co.uk/sport2/hi/football/europe/9276343.stm.

87. Kelley Gates, "Wild in the Streets," *Brand Marketing*, February 2001, p. 54.

88. "Samsung Launches AFC Asian Cup Qatar 2011 Mobile Application," January 10, 2011, www.ameinfo.com/253314.html.

89. Dwight W. Catherwood and Richard L. Van Kirk, *The Complete Guide to Special Event Management* (New York: John Wiley, 1992).

90. William L. Shankin and John Kuzma, "Buying That Sporting Image," *Marketing Management*, Spring 1992, p. 65.

91. Peter Post, "Beyond Brand: The Power of Experience Branding," *ANA/ Advertiser*, October–November 2000.

92. B. Joseph Pine and James H. Gilmore, *The Experience Economy: Work Is Theatre and Every Business a Stage* (Cambridge, MA: Harvard University Press, 1999).

93. "2006 Experiential Marketing Study," www.jackmorton.com.

94. For an excellent account, see Thomas L. Harris, *The Marketer's Guide to Public Relations* (New York: John Wiley, 1991). Also see Harris, *Value-Added Public Relations* (Chicago: NTC Business Books, 1998).

95. "Do We Have a Story for You!" *The Economist*, January 21, 2006, pp. 57–58; Al Ries and Laura Ries, *The Fall of Advertising and the Rise of PR* (New York: HarperCollins, 2002).

96. For further reading see P. Rajan Varadarajan and Anil Menon, "Cause-Related Marketing: A Co-Alignment of Marketing Strategy and Corporate Philanthropy," *Journal of Marketing*, July 1988, pp. 58–74.

97. Arthur M. Merims, "Marketing's Stepchild: Product Publicity," *Harvard Business Review*, November–December 1972, pp. 111–112. Also see Katherine D. Paine, "There Is a Method for Measuring PR," *Marketing News*, November 6, 1987, p. 5.

Chapter 19

1. Louise Story, "The High Price of Creating Free Ads," *New York Times*, May 26, 2007; Laura Petrecca, "Madison Avenue Wants You! (or at Least Your Videos)," *USA Today*, June 21, 2007; Eric Pfanner, "Leave It to the Professionals? Hey, Let Consumers Make Their Own Ads," *New York Times*, August 4, 2006; Kenneth Hein, "Coke's Web Formula Is a Work in Progress," *Brandweek*, September 4, 2006, p. 9.

2. The terms *direct-order marketing* and *direct-relationship marketing* were suggested as subsets of direct marketing by Stan Rapp and Tom Collins in *The Great Marketing Turnaround* (Upper Saddle River, NJ: Prentice Hall, 1990).

3. Ran Kivetz and Itamar Simonson, "The Idiosyncratic Fit Heuristic: Effort Advantage as a Determinant of Consumer Response to Loyalty Programs," *Journal of Marketing Research*, 40, November 2003, pp. 454–467; Ran Kivetz and Itamar Simonson, "Earning the Right to Indulge: Effort as a Determinant of Customer Preferences toward Frequency Program Rewards," *Journal of Marketing Research*, 39, May 2002, pp. 155–170.

4. Michael McCarthy, "Direct Marketing Gets Cannes Do Spirit," *USA Today*, June 17, 2002.

5. "DMA's 2006 'Power of Direct Marketing' Reports," *Direct Marketing Association*, June 5, 2007; "Direct Marketing's Growth Rate to Cushion Cooling U.S. Economy," *Direct Marketing Association*, October 17, 2006; Carol Krol, "Direct Hits It Big," *B to B*, October 10, 2005, pp. 29–31; www.the-dma.org/aboutdma/whatis-thedma.shtml; "Direct Marketing Association Announces Opening of Arab Direct Marketing Association ADMA," www.the-dma.org/cgi/disppressrelease?article=1302; http://the-adma.org/html/company.html; "DMA's Power of Direct Marketing Report Finds DM Ad Expenditures Climb to Over 54% of All Advertising Expenditures," October 19, 2009, www.the-dma.org/cgi/dispannouncements?article=1335.

6. See www.aramex.com; see also www.shopandship.com.

7. "Lands' End Shines a Beacon on Its Brand," *BusinessWeek*, November 9, 2005; Amy Merrick, "Sears Orders Fashion Makeover from the Lands' End Catalog," *Wall Street Journal*, January 28, 2004; Chana R. Schoenberger, "Web? What Web?" *Forbes*, June 10, 2002, p. 132; Amy Merrick, "Keep It Fresh," *Wall Street Journal*, December 10, 2001.

8. Stan Rapp and Thomas L. Collins, *Maximarketing* (New York: McGraw-Hill, 1987).

9. "On the Mat," *The Economist*," November 26, 2005, p. 78.

10. Bob Stone, *Successful Direct Marketing Methods*, 6th edn (Lincolnwood, IL: NTC Business Books, 1996). Also see David Shepard Associates, *The New Direct Marketing*, 2nd edn (Chicago: Irwin, 1995); Amiya K. Basu, Atasi Basu, and Rajeev Batra, "Modeling the Response Pattern to Direct Marketing Campaigns," *Journal of Marketing Research*, May 1995, pp. 204–212.

11. See www.5index.com.

12. Edward L. Nash, *Direct Marketing: Strategy, Planning, Execution*, 4th edn (New York: McGraw-Hill, 2000).

13. Rachel McLaughlin, "Get the Envelope Opened!" *Target Marketing*, September 1998, pp. 37–39.

14. "Case Study: The Phoenician Utilizes IDM," *Relationship Marketing Insights Newsletter*, Issue #5, 2006.

15. The *average customer longevity (N)* is related to the *customer retention rate (CR)*. Suppose the company retains 80% of its customers each year. Then the average customer longevity is given by: $N = 1/(1 2 CR) = 1/.2 = 5$.

16. "Industry Overview: Internet and Catalog Retailers," *Hoovers*, www.hoovers.com, accessed August 22, 2010.

17. Cacilie Rohwedder, "U.S. Mail-Order Firms Shake Up Europe: Better Service, Specialized Catalogs Find Eager Shoppers," *Wall Street Journal*, January 6, 1998; Kathleen Kiley, "B-to-B Marketers High on Overseas Sales," *Catalog Age*, January 1, 1997, p. 8.

18. See www.blackbox.com; see alsowww.multichannelmerchant.com.

19. See www.ftc.gov/donotcall/.

20. Jim Edwards, "The Art of the Infomercial," *Brandweek*, September 3, 2001, pp. 14–19.

21. Charles Duhigg, "Telemarketing Thieves Sharpen Their Focus on the Elderly," *New York Times*, May 20, 2007.

22. Tony Case, "Growing Up," *Interactive Quarterly*, April 19, 2004, pp. 32–34.

23. David L. Smith and Karen McFee, "Media Mix 101: Online Media for Traditional Marketers," accessed September 2003, at http://advantage.msn.com/_articles/_MediaMix101_2._asp.

24. Kenneth Hein, "Industry Turns Page on Page View Stats," *Brandweek*, June 4, 2007, p. 6; Paul C. Judge, "Will Online Ads Ever Click?" *Fast Company*, March 2001, pp. 181–192.

25. Emily Steel, "Advertising's Brave New World," *Wall Street Journal*, May 25, 2007; Johnnie L. Roberts, "How to Count Eyeballs," *Newsweek*, November 27, 2006, p. 42.

26. Online Publisher's Association, "OPA Media Consumption Study," January 2002.

27. Michael Applebaum, "A Matter of Timing," *Brandweek IQ*, July 10, 2006, pp. 22–24.

28. Ellen Byron, "Estée Lauder Tests Web-Ad Waters," *Wall Street Journal*, September 19, 2006.

29. Kevin J. Delaney, "Once-Wary Industry Giants Embrace Internet Advertising," *Wall Street Journal*, April 17, 2006.

30. Whole case from Claire Ferris-Lay, "Let's Get Digital," *arabianbusiness.com*, May 29, 2011, www.arabianbusiness.com/let-s-get-digital-402205.html?page=0.

31. Asim Ansari and Carl F. Mela, "E-Customization," *Journal of Marketing Research*, 40, no. 2, May 2003, pp. 131–145.

32. Claire Ferris-Lay, "Let's Get Digital."

33. Karen Leigh, "Online Shopping Surges in the UAE, Survey Shows," *Arabian Business*, March 16, 2011, http://new.arabianbusiness.com/online-shopping-surges-in-uae-survey-shows-387619.html; "Eight in Ten Respondents in Asia/Pacific, Middle East and Africa are Satisfied with Online Shopping: MasterCard Survey," www.mastercard.com/hk/personal/en/wce/pdf/100225_Online%20Shopping_HK%20Fina_eng.pdf, accessed March 20, 2011.

34. "Arab Consumers and Online Buying," *MarketingHub.me*, http://marketinghub.bayt.com/articles/arab-consumers-and-online-buying, April 14, 2011.

35. Daniel Michaels and J. Lynn Lunsford, "Ad-Sales Woes Likely to Continue," *Wall Street Journal*, December 4, 2006; Jack Neff, "Axe Cuts Past Competitors, Claims Market Lead," *Advertising Age*, May 14, 2006; Byron Acohido, "Rich Media Enriching PC Ads," *USA Today*, February 25, 2004. "Online Advertising Overtakes TV Expenditure, United Kingdom," http://blog.inpageads.com/index.php/2009/10/online-advertising-overtakes-tv-expenditure-united-kingdom/; "Online Advertising Expenditure Forecast 2009–2010," www.clickz.com/clickz/stats/1708807/online-advertising-expenditure-forecast-2009-2010; "Middle East Internet Ad Spend to Hit 4.5%," www.ameinfo.com/223549.html, February 9, 2010; Alaa Shahine and Massoud Derhally, "Online Advertising Spending Surges in the Middle East," *Bloomberg BusinessWeek*, June 3, 2010, www.businessweek.com/magazine/content/10_24/b4182021808328.htm.

36. Catherine Holahan, "Raising the Bar on Viral Web Ads," *BusinessWeek*, July 23, 2006; Robert Berner, "How Unilever Scored with Young Guys," *BusinessWeek*, May 23, 2005; Thomas Mucha, "Spray Here. Get Girl," *Business 2.0*, June 2003.

37. Philip Kotler, *According to Kotler* (New York: American Management Association, 2005).

38. Peter J. Danaher, Guy W. Mullarkey, and Skander Essegaier, "Factors Affecting Web Site Visit Duration: A Cross-Domain Analysis," *Journal of Marketing Research*, 43, May 2006, pp. 182–194.

39. Jeffrey F. Rayport and Bernard J. Jaworski, *e-commerce* (New York: McGraw-Hill, 2001), p. 116.

40. Bob Tedeschi, "E-Commerce Report," *New York Times*, June 24, 2002.

41. Jan-Benedict E. M. Steenkamp and Inge Geyskens, "How Country Characteristics Affect the Perceived Value of Web Sites," *Journal of Marketing*, 70, July 2006, pp. 136–150.

42. Allison Fass, "A Kingdom Seeks Magic," *Forbes*, October 16, 2006, pp. 68–70; David Kiley, "The Craziest Ad Guys in America," *BusinessWeek*, May 22, 2006, pp. 72–80; www.subservientchicken.com.

43. See *eMarketer*, www.emarketer.com, May 2010.

44. Ned Desmond, "Google's Next Runaway Success," *Business 2.0*, November 2002, pp. 73.

45. Heather Green, "Online Ads Take Off Again," *BusinessWeek*, May 5, 2003, p. 75.

46. Puneet Manchanda, Jean-Pierre Dubé, Khim Yong Goh, and Pradeep K. Chintagunta, "The Effects of Banner Advertising on Internet Purchasing," *Journal of Marketing Research*, 43, February 2006, pp. 98–108; "Pay per Sale," *The Economist*, October 1, 2005, p. 62.

47. Paul Sloan, "The Quest for the Perfect Online Ad," *Business 2.0*, March 2007, pp. 88–93; Catherine Holahan, "The Promise of Online Display Ads," *BusinessWeek*, May 1, 2007.

48. Jessica Mintz, "Microsoft Adds Behavioral Targeting," *Associated Press*, December 28, 2006.

49. Stephen Baker, "Pop-Up Ads Had Better Start Pleasing," *BusinessWeek*, December 8, 2003, p. 40.

50. Youngme Moon, "BMW Films," Harvard Business School Case #9-5-2-046.

51. Brian Morrissey, "Clients Try to Manipulate 'Unpredictable' Viral Buzz," *Adweek*, March 22, 2007; Devin Leonard, "Viral Ads: It's an Epidemic," *Fortune*, October 2, 2006, pp. 61–62.

52. Heather Green, "Searching for the Pod of Gold," *BusinessWeek*, November 14, 2005, pp. 88–90.

53. Heather Green, "It Takes a Web Village," *BusinessWeek*, September 4, 2006, p. 66; Paul Dwyer, "Measuring the Value of Word of Mouth and Its Impact in Consumer Communities," MSI Report No. 06-118, Marketing Science Institute, Cambridge, MA.

54. Seth Godin, *Permission Marketing: Turning Strangers into Friends and Friends into Customers* (New York: Simon & Schuster, 1999).

55. Chana R. Schoenberger, "Web? What Web?," *Forbes*, June 10, 2002, p. 132.

56. Suzanne Vranica, "Marketers Give E-Mail Another Look," *Wall Street Journal*, July 17, 2006.

57. Erina Lin, "SFN Report: Global Mobile Ad Spending to Reach $19.1 Billion in 2012," *sfnblog.com*, August 27, 2009, www.sfnblog.com/industry_trends/2009/08/sfn_report_global_mobile_ad_spending_to.php.

58. Brooks Barnes, "Toyota Aims Young, Sponsors Fox Spinoff for Cell Phone Screens," *Wall Street Journal*, April 24, 2006; Matt Richtel, "Verizon to Allow Ads on Its Mobile Phones," *New York Times*, December 26, 2006.

59. Claire Ferris-Lay, "Let's Get Digital."

60. For a thorough review of relevant academic literature, see Christophe Van Den Bulte and Stefan Wuyts, *Social Networks and Marketing*, Marketing Science Institute Relevant Knowledge Series, Cambridge, MA, 2007.

61. Louise Story, "What We Talk About When We Talk About Brands," *New York Times*, November 24, 2006.

62. Elizabeth Wellington, "Freebies and Chitchat Are Hot Marketing Tools," *Philadelphia Inquirer*, December 31, 2003; Bob Sperber, "Krispy Kreme Word-of-Mouth Tactics Continue to Go against the Grain," *Brandweek*, October 21, 2002, p. 9.

63. Renée Dye, "The Buzz on Buzz," *Harvard Business Review*, November–December 2000, pp. 139–146.

64. Chip Heath, "Give 'Em Something to Talk About," *Fast Company*, 116, June 2007, pp. 58+.

65. See http://discussions.apple.com/index.jspa; http://socialize.morningstar.com/newsocialize/asp/coverpage.asp?pgid=hetabdi; www.fool.com/; Nanette Byrnes, "Leader of the Packs," *BusinessWeek*, October 31, 2005; www.quickbooksgroup.com.

66. "Facebook Users in Arab World Increase 30%," *gulfnews.com*, June 9, 2011, http://gulfnews.com/business/media-marketing/facebook-users-in-arab-world-increase-30-1.819233; Claire Ferris-Lay, "Let's Get Digital"; www.mashreqbank.com/about-us/news/news_30032011.asp.

67. See www.blombank.com; www.blomretail.com/Retail/BLOM-MasterCard-Giving-Cards; "BLOM Bank Launches BLOM MasterCard Giving Affinity Credit Card," May 25, 2010, www.ameinfo.com/233570.html; www.facebook.com/home.php#!/group.php?gid=130857820262230&v=info; www.blomshabeb.com; www.facebook.com/group.php?gid=146369138740235.

68. Claire Ferris-Lay, "Let's Get Digital"; "MashreqMillionaire Launches 'Share Your Dreams' Competition on Facebook," March 30, 2011, www.mashreqbank.com/about-us/news/news_30032011.asp.

69. Dave Balter and John Butman, "Clutter Cutter," *Marketing Management*, July–August 2006, pp. 49–50.

70. Emanuel Rosen, *The Anatomy of Buzz* (New York: Currency, 2000).

71. George Silverman, *The Secrets of Word-of-Mouth Marketing* (New York: Amacom, 2001); Emanuel Rosen, *The Anatomy of Buzz* (New York: Currency, 2000), Chapter 12; "Viral Marketing," *Sales & Marketing Automation*, November 1999, pp. 12–14.

72. Renée Dye, "The Buzz on Buzz," *Harvard Business Review*, November–December 2000, pp. 139.

73. See www.willitblend.com; www.blendtec.com; Jon Fine, "Ready to Get Weird, Advertisers?" *BusinessWeek*, January 8, 2007, p. 24; Paul Gillin, "Podcasting, Blogs Cause Major Boost," *B to B*, 92, no. 5, May 2007, pp. 32.

74. See www.huggies.com.lb; see also www.facebook.com/huggieslebanon.

75. Robert Berner, "I Sold It through the Grapevine," *BusinessWeek*, May 29, 2006, pp. 32–34.

76. Danielle Sacks, "Down the Rabbit Hole," *Fast Company*, November 2006, pp. 86–93; "Fast Talk," *Fast Company*, September 2006, pp. 21–24.

77. Jacqueline Johnson Brown, Peter M. Reingen, and Everett M. Rogers, *Diffusion of Innovations*, 4th edn (New York: Free Press, 1995); J. Johnson Brown and Peter Reingen, "Social Ties and Word-of-Mouth Referral Behavior," *Journal of Consumer Research*, 14, no. 3, December 1987, pp. 350–362; Peter H. Riengen and Jerome B. Kernan, "Analysis of Referral Networks in Marketing: Methods and Illustration," *Journal of Marketing Research*, November 1986, pp. 37–78.

78. Malcolm Gladwell, *The Tipping Point: How Little Things Can Make a Big Difference* (Boston: Little, Brown & Company, 2000).

79. Douglas Atkin, *The Culting of Brands: When Customers Become True Believers* (New York: Penguin, 2004); Marian Salzman, Ira Matathia, and Ann O'Reilly, *Buzz: Harness*

the Power of Influence and Create Demand (New York: John Wiley, 2003).

80. Dave Balter and John Butman, "Clutter Cutter," *Marketing Management*, July–August 2006, pp. 49–50; "Is There a Reliable Way to Measure Word-of-Mouth Marketing?" *Marketing NPV* 3, no. 3, 2006, pp. 3–9.

81. David Kiley, "Ford on the Web, Warts and All," *BusinessWeek*, October 30, 2006, pp. 68–71; Jonathan Fahey, "Candid Camera," *Forbes*, November 13, 2006, pp. 124–126.

82. Stephen Baker, "Looking for a Blog in a Haystack," *BusinessWeek*, July 25, 2006, p. 38.

83. Pew Internet & American Life Project, July 2006; www.pewinternet.org/.

84. Todd Wasserman, "Report: Consumers Don't Trust Blogs," *Brandweek*, September 4, 2006, p. 10; For an academic discussion of chat rooms, recommendation sites, and customer review sections online, see Dina Mayzlin, "Promotional Chat on the Internet," *Marketing Science*, 25, March–April 2006, pp. 155–163; and Judith Chevalier and Dina Mayzlin, "The Effect of Word of Mouth on Sales: Online Book Reviews," *Journal of Marketing Research*, 43, August 2006, pp. 345–354.

85. Kim Hart, "Angry Customers Use Web to Shame Firms," *Washington Post*, July 5, 2006.

86. This section is based on an excellent summary, "Is There a Reliable Way to Measure Word-of-Mouth Marketing?" *Marketing NPV* 3, no. 3, 2006, pp. 3–9, www.marketingnpv.com.

87. "Employment by Major Occupational Group, 2008 and Projected 2018," www.bls.gov/emp/ep_table_101.pdf.

88. "The Campaign for Excellence," www.aub.edu.lb/development/campaign_report/Pages/index.aspx.

89. Bill Keenan, "Cost-per-Call Data Deserve Scrutiny," *Industry Week*, January 10, 2000.

90. Adapted from Robert N. McMurry, "The Mystique of Super-Salesmanship," *Harvard Business Review*, March–April 1961, pp. 114. Also see William C. Moncrief III, "Selling Activity and Sales Position Taxonomies for Industrial Sales Forces," *Journal of Marketing Research*, August 1986, pp. 261–270.

91. Thomas A. Stewart and David Champion, "Leading Change from the Top Line," *Harvard Business Review*, July–August 2006, pp. 90–97.

92. Lawrence G. Friedman and Timothy R. Furey, *The Channel Advantage: Going to Marketing with Multiple Sales Channels* (Oxford, UK: Butterworth-Heinemann, 1999).

93. Philip Kotler, Neil Rackham, and Suj Krishnaswamy, "Ending the War between Sales & Marketing," *Harvard Business Review*, July–August 2006, pp. 68–78; Timothy M. Smith, Srinath Gopalakrishna, and Rubikar Chaterjee, "A Three-Stage Model of Integrated Marketing Communications at the Marketing-Sales Interface," *Journal of Marketing Research*, 43, November 2006, pp. 546–579.

94. Christopher Hosford, "Rebooting Hewlett-Packard," *Sales and Marketing Management*, 158, no. 6, July–August 2006, pp. 32+.

95. Michael Copeland, "Hits and Misses," *Business 2.0*, April 2004, pp. 142.

96. "Sales Performance Benchmarks," *Go-to-Market Strategies*, June 5, 2007.

97. Sonke Albers, "Sales-Force Management: Compensation, Motivation, Selection, and Training," in *Handbook of Marketing*, ed. Bart Weitz and Robin Wensley (London: Sage, 2002), pp. 248–266.

98. Cliff Edwards, "Death of a Pushy Salesman," *BusinessWeek*, July 3, 2006, pp. 108–109.

99. Nanette Byrnes, "Avon Calling: Lots of New Reps," *BusinessWeek*, June 2, 2003, pp. 53–54.

100. Michael R. W. Bommer, Brian F. O'Neil, and Beheruz N. Sethna, "A Methodology for Optimizing Selling Time of Salespersons," *Journal of Marketing Theory and Practice*, Spring 1994, pp. 61–75. See also, Lissan Joseph, "On the Optimality of Delegating Pricing Authority to the Sales Force," *Journal of Marketing*, 65, January 2001, pp. 62–70.

101. Dartnell Corporation, 30th Sales-Force Compensation Survey. Other breakdowns show that 12.7% is spent in service calls, 16% in administrative tasks, 25.1% in telephone selling, and 17.4% in waiting/traveling.

102. James A. Narus and James C. Anderson, "Industrial Distributor Selling: The Roles of the Outside and Inside Sales Forces," *Industrial Marketing Management*, 15, no. 1, February 1986, pp. 55–62.

103. Willem Verbeke and Richard P. Bagozzi, "Sales-Call Anxiety: Exploring What It Means When Fear Rules a Sales Encounter," *Journal of Marketing*, 64, July 2000, pp. 88–101.

104. Gilbert A. Churchill Jr., Neil M. Ford, Orville C. Walker Jr., Mark W. Johnston, and John F. Tanner, *Sales-Force Management*, 6th edn (Homewood, IL: Irwin, 1998). Also see Eric G. Harris, John C. Mowen, and Tom J. Brown, "Reexamining Salesperson Goal Orientations: Personality Influencers, Customer Orientation, and Work Satisfaction," *Journal of the Academy of Marketing Science*, 33, no. 1, Winter 2005, pp. 19–35; Manfred Krafft, "An Empirical Investigation of the Antecedents of Sales-Force Control Systems," *Journal of Marketing*, 63, July 1999, pp. 120–134; Wujin Chu, Eitan Gerstner, and James D. Hess, "Costs and Benefits of Hard Sell," *Journal of Marketing Research*, February 1995, pp. 97–102; Murali K. Mantrala, Prabhakant Sinha, and Andris A. Zoltners, "Structuring a Multiproduct Sales Quota-Bonus Plan for a Heterogeneous Sales Force: A Practical Model-Based Approach," *Marketing Science*, 13, no. 2, Spring 1994, pp. 121–144; Jhinuk Chowdhury, "The Motivational Impact of Sales Quotas on Effort," *Journal of Marketing Research*, February 1993, pp. 28–41.

105. Eilene Zimmerman, "Quota Busters," *Sales & Marketing Management*, January 2001, pp. 59–63.

106. Peter Burrows, "The Era of Efficiency," *BusinessWeek*, June 18, 2001, p. 92; Melanie Warner, "Confessions of a Control Freak," *Fortune*, September 4, 2000, p. 30.

107. Lisa Vaas, "Oracle Teaches Its Sales Force to Play Nice," *eWeek*, July 28, 2004; Lisa Vaas, "Oracle's Sales Force Reorg Finally Bears Fruit," *eWeek*, December 17, 2003; Ian Mount, "Out of Control," *Business 2.0*, August 2002, pp. 38–44.

108. Philip M. Posdakoff and Scott B. MacKenzie, "Organizational Citizenship Behaviors and Sales-Unit Effectiveness," *Journal of Marketing Research*, August 1994, pp. 351–363. See also Andrea L. Dixon, Rosann L. Spiro, and Magbul Jamil, "Successful and Unsuccessful Sales Calls: Measuring Salesperson Attributions and Behavioral Intentions," *Journal of Marketing*, 65, July 2001, pp. 64–78; Willem Verbeke and Richard P. Bagozzi, "Sales-Call Anxiety: Exploring What It Means When Fear Rules a Sales Encounter," *Journal of Marketing*, 64, July 2000, pp. 88–101.

109. Neil Rackham, *SPIN Selling* (New York: McGraw-Hill, 1988). Also see his *The SPIN Selling Fieldbook* (New York: McGraw-Hill, 1996); James Lardner, "Selling Salesmanship," *Business 2.0*, December 2002–January 2003, pp. 66; Sharon Drew Morgen, *Selling with Integrity: Reinventing Sales through Collaboration*, *Respect*, *and Serving* (New York: Berkeley Books, 1999); Neil Rackham and John De Vincentis, *Rethinking the Sales Force* (New York: McGraw-Hill, 1996).

110. George R. Franke and Jeong-Eun Park, "Salesperson Adaptive Selling Behavior and Customer Orientation: A Meta-Analysis," *Journal of Marketing Research*, 43, November 2006, pp. 693–702; Richard G. McFarland, Goutam N. Challagalla, and Tasadduq A. Shervani, "Influence Tactics for Effective Adaptive Selling," *Journal of Marketing*, 70, October 2006, pp. 103–117.

111. Joel E. Urbany, "Justifying Profitable Pricing," Working Paper Series, Marketing Science Institute, Report No. 00-117, 2000, pp. 17–18.

112. George R. Franke and Jeong-Eun Park, "Salesperson Adaptive Selling Behavior and Customer Orientation: A Meta-Analysis," *Journal of Marketing Research*, 43, November 2006, pp. 693–702; Richard G. McFarland, Goutam N. Challagalla, and Tasadduq A. Shervani, "Influence Tactics for Effective Adaptive Selling," *Journal of Marketing*, 70, October 2006, pp. 103–117.

Chapter 20

1. Michael Arndt, "3M's Rising Star," *BusinessWeek*, April 12, 2004, pp. 62–74; Mark Tatge, "Prescription for Growth," *Forbes*, February 17, 2003, pp. 65–66; Michael Arndt, "3M: A Lab for Growth?" *BusinessWeek*, January 21, 2002, pp. 50–51.

2. "Mobinil: From Mobile in Every Hand to Internet in Every Hand," 2010, http://teletimesinternational.com/interview/884/mobinil-from-mobile-in-every-hand-to-internet-in-every-hand.

3. For some scholarly reviews, see Ely Dahan and John R. Hauser, "Product Development: Managing a Dispersed Process," in *Handbook of Marketing*, ed. Bart Weitz and Robin Wensley (London: Sage, 2002), pp. 179–222; Dipak Jain, "Managing New-Product Development for Strategic Competitive Advantage," Chapter 6 in *Kellogg on Marketing*, ed. Dawn Iacobucci (New York: John Wiley, 2001), pp. 130–148; Jerry Wind and Vijay Mahajan, "Issues and Opportunities in New-Product Development: An Introduction to the Special Issue," *Journal of Marketing Research*, 34, February 1997, pp. 1–12.

4. J. Bradley, *Cadbury's Purple Reign: The Story Behind Chocolate's Best-Loved Brand* (Chichester: John Wiley & Sons Ltd, 2008).

5. Scott Sanderude, "Growth from Harvesting the Sky: The $200 Million Challenge," talk at Marketing Science Institute Conference: New Frontiers for Growth, Boston, MA, April 2005.

6. Stephen J. Carson, "When to Give Up Control of Outsourced New-Product Development," *Journal of Marketing*, 71, January 2007, pp. 49–66.

7. "Don't Laugh at Gilded Butterflies," *The Economist*, April 24, 2004, pp. 71–73. For some academic discussion of the effects of new-product introductions on markets, see Harald J. Van Heerde, Carl F. Mela, and Puneet Manchanda, "The Dynamic Effect of Innovation on Market Structure," *Journal of Marketing Research*, 41, May 2004, pp. 166–183.

8. http://www.momen-group.com/sitefiles/sitefiles_pdf/presentation.pdf; http://www.momen-group.com/en/spage/page/21.

9. See http://multimedia.3m.com/mws/medi awebserver?77777XxamfIVO&Wwo_Pw5_W7HYxTHfxajYv7HYv7H777777--

10. Sungwook Min, Manohar U. Kalwani, and William T. Robinson, "Market Pioneer and Early Follower Survival Risks: A Contingency Analysis of Really New versus Incrementally New Product-Markets," *Journal of Marketing*, 70, January 2006, pp. 15–33; C. Page Moreau, Arthur B. Markman, and Donald R. Lehmann, "'What Is It?' Category Flexibility and Consumers' Response to Really New Products," *Journal of Consumer Research*, 27, March 2001, pp. 489–498.

11. Stefan Wuyts, Shantanu Dutta, and Stefan Stremersch, "Portfolios of Interfirm Agreements in Technology-Intensive Markets: Consequences for Innovation and Profitability," *Journal of Marketing*, 68, April 2004, pp. 88–100; AricRindfleisch and Christine Moorman, "The Acquisition and Utilization of Information in New-Product Alliance: A Strength-of-Ties Perspective," *Journal of Marketing*, 65, April 2001, pp. 1–18.

12. Steve Hoeffler, "Measuring Preferences for Really New Products," *Journal of Marketing Research*, 40, November 2003, pp. 406–420; Glen Urban, Bruce Weinberg, and John R. Hauser, "Premarket Forecasting of Really New Products," *Journal of Marketing*, 60, January 1996, pp. 47–60.

13. AshishSood and Gerard J. Tellis, "Technological Evolution and Radical Innovation," *Journal of Marketing*, 69, July 2005, pp. 152–168.

14. For more discussion, see Jakki Mohr, *Marketing of High-Technology Products and Innovations*, 2nd edn (Upper Saddle River, NJ: Prentice Hall, 2005).

15. Steve Hamm, "Speed Demons," *BusinessWeek*, March 27, 2006, pp. 69–76.

16. Christina Passariello, "Brand New Bag: Louis Vuitton Tries Modern Methods on Factory Lines," *Wall Street Journal*, October 9, 2006.

17. *The Cleopatra Industrial Group*, 2011, www.groupcleopatra.com/home.html.

18. Rajan Varadarajan, "Business Insight, A Special Report; Think Small: Every Company Wants to Hit It Big with Market-Shattering Innovations; But the Little Changes, Too, Can Make a Huge Difference," *Wall Street Journal*, March 3, 2007.

19. Clayton M. Christensen, *The Innovator's Dilemma: When New Technologies Cause Great Firms to Fail* (Boston: Harvard University Press, 1997).

20. Dahan and Hauser, "Product Development: Managing a Dispersed Process."

21. Robert G. Cooper and Elko J. Kleinschmidt, *New Products: The Key Factors in Success* (Chicago: American Marketing Association, 1990).

22. Cooper and Kleinschmidt, *New Products*, pp. 35–38.

23. Catwalk Cow, 2011, www.catwalkcow.com.

24. Susumu Ogama and Frank T. Piller, "Reducing the Risks of New-Product Development," *MIT Sloan Management Review*, Winter 2006, pp. 65–71; A. C. Nielsen, "New-Product Introduction—Successful Innovation/Failure: Fragile Boundary," A. C. Nielsen BASES and Ernst & Young Global Client Consulting, June 24, 1999; Deloitte and Touche, "Vision in Manufacturing Study," Deloitte Consulting and Kenan-Flagler Business School, March 6, 1998.

25. Hamm, "Speed Demons."

26. Tom McNichol, "A Start-Up's Best Friend? Failure," *Business 2.0*, March 2007, pp. 39–41.

27. Thomas N. Burton, "By Learning from Failures Lilly Keeps Drug Pipelines Full," *Wall Street Journal*, April 21, 2004.

28. Nanette Byrnes, "Xerox's New Design Team Customers," *BusinessWeek*, May 7, 2007, p. 72.

29. David Welch, "Can Stodgy GM Turn Stylish?" *BusinessWeek*, November 11, 2002, pp. 111–12.

30. "Almarai Enhances Innovation Management Focus with Sopheon's Accolade System," www.ameinfo.com/249152.html.

31. Chuck Salter, "Failure Doesn't Suck," *Fast Company*, May 2007, p. 44.

32. Doug Ayers, Robert Dahlstrom, and Steven J. Skinner, "An Exploratory Investigation of Organizational Antecedents to New-Product Success," *Journal of Marketing Research*, February 1997, pp. 107–116; David S. Hopkins, *Options in New-Product Organization* (New York: Conference Board, 1974).

33. Danielle Sacks, Chuck Salter, Alan Deutschman, and Scott Kirsner, "Innovation Scouts," *Fast Company*, May 2007, pp. 90+.

34. Rajesh Sethi, Daniel C. Smith, and C. Whan Park, "Cross-Functional Product Development Teams, Creativity, and the Innovativeness of New Consumer Products," *Journal of Marketing Research*, 38, February 2001, pp. 73–85.

35. Robert G. Cooper, "Stage-Gate Systems: A New Tool for Managing New Products," *Business Horizons*, May–June 1990, pp. 44–54. See also, Robert G. Cooper, "The NewProd System: The Industry Experience," *Journal of Product Innovation Management*, 9, June 1992, pp. 113–127.

36. Robert G. Cooper, *Product Leadership: Creating and Launching Superior New Products* (New York: Perseus Books, 1998).

37. Dahan and Hauser, "Product Development: Managing a Dispersed Process."

38. Another alternative approach to the funnel process advocates "rocketing." See David Nichols, *Return on Ideas* (West Sussex, England: Wiley, 2007).

39. John Hauser, Gerard J. Tellis, and Abbie Griffin, "Research on Innovation: A Review and Agenda for Marketing Science," *Marketing Science*, 25, November–December 2006, pp. 687–717.

40. Byron Acohido, "Microsoft Cultures Creativity in Unique Lab," *USA Today*, July 11, 2007; Erich Joachimsthaler, *Hidden in Plain Sight: How to Find and Execute Your Company's Next Big Growth Strategy* (Boston: Harvard Business School Press, 2007); SubinIm and John P. Workman Jr., "Market Orientation, Creativity, and New-Product Performance in High-Technology Firms," *Journal of Marketing*, 68, April 2004, pp. 114–32.

41. Henry Chesbrough, *Open Business Models: How to Thrive in the New-Innovation Landscape* (Boston: Harvard University Press, 2006); Eric Von Hippel, *Democratizing Innovation* (Cambridge, MA: MIT Press, 2005); Burt Helm, "Inside a White-Hot Idea Factory," *BusinessWeek*, January 15, 2005, pp. 72–73; C. K. Prahalad and Venkat Ramaswamy, *The Future of Competition: Cocreating Unique Value with Customers* (Boston: Harvard University Press, 2004); Henry Chesbrough, *Open Innovation: The New Imperative for Creating and Profiting from Technology* (Boston: Harvard University Press, 2003).

42. Bruce Horovitz, "Marketers Zooming in on Your Daily Routines," *USA Today*, April 30, 2007; Ashwin W. Joshi and Sanjay Sharma, "Customer Knowledge Development: Antecedents and Impact on New-Product Performance," *Journal of Marketing*, 68, October 2004, pp. 47–59.

43. Abbie J. Griffin and John Hauser, "The Voice of the Customer," *Marketing Science*, Winter 1993, pp. 1–27.

44. Peter C. Honebein and Roy F. Cammarano, "Customers at Work," *Marketing Management*, January–February 2006, pp. 26–31; Peter C. Honebein and Roy F. Cammarano, *Creating Do-It-Yourself Customers: How Great Customer Experiences Build Great Companies* (Mason, OH: Texere Southwestern Educational Publishing, 2005).

45. Robert Levine, "You Ought to Be in Pictures," *Business 2.0*, 8, no. 3, April 2007, pp. 90; Kim Peterson, "Microstock Photography Represents a New Business

Model," *Knight Ridder Tribune Business News*, May 28, 2007, p. 1; "World's Most Successful 'Crowdsourcing' Stock Photographer Reaches Half a Million Images Sold on iStockphoto," *Business Wire*, June 5, 2007.

46. Patricia Seybold, *Outside Innovation: How Your Customers Will Codesign Your Company's Future* (New York: Collins, 2006).

47. Eric von Hippel, "Lead Users: A Source of Novel Product Concepts," *Management Science*, July 1986, pp. 791–805. Also see *The Sources of Innovation* (New York: Oxford University Press, 1988); and "Learning from Lead Users," in *Marketing in an Electronic Age*, ed. Robert D. Buzzell (Cambridge, MA: Harvard Business School Press, 1985), pp. 308–317.

48. Steven Levy, "Microsoft Gets a Clue from Its Kiddie Corps," *Newsweek*, February 24, 2003, pp. 56–57.

49. Kevin Zheng Zhou, Chi Kin (Bennett) Yim, and David K. Tse, "The Effects of Strategic Orientations on Technology- and Market-Based Breakthrough Innovations," *Journal of Marketing*, 69, April 2005, pp. 42–60; Michael Treacy, "Ignore the Consumer," *Advertising Age Point*, September 2005, pp. 15–19.

50. "BankDhofar Rewards Outstanding Employee Ideas," www.smartoman.com/finance-a-economy/banking/2536-bankdhofar-rewards-outstanding-employee-ideas.

51. "The World's Fifty Most Innovative Companies," Special Report, *BusinessWeek*, May 9, 2007.

52. Darren W. Dahl and Page Moreau, "The Influence and Value of Analogical Thinking during New-Product Ideation," *Journal of Marketing Research*, 39, February 2002, pp. 47–60; Michael Michalko, *Cracking Creativity: The Secrets of Creative Genius* (Berkeley, CA: Ten Speed Press, 1998); James M. Higgins, *101 Creative Problem-Solving Techniques* (New York: New Management, 1994).

53. See http://wiki.answers.com/Q/The_program-test-repart-for-what-NBC-show-found-the-characters-smug-superficial-and-self-absorbed-adding-that-this-group-did-not-really-care-about-each-other-the-way-real-friends-would.

54. Olivier Toubia and Laurent Florès, "Adaptive Idea Screening Using Consumers," *Marketing Science*, 26, May–June 2007, pp. 342–360; Melanie Wells, "Have It Your Way," *Forbes*, February 14, 2005.

55. Steve Hoeffler, "Measuring Preferences for Really New Products," *Journal of Marketing Research*, 40, November 2003, pp. 406–420; Dahl and Moreau, "The Influence and Value of Analogical Thinking during New-Product Ideation"; Michelle L. Roehm and Brian Sternthal, "The Moderating Effect of Knowledge and Resources on the Persuasive Impact of Analogies," *Journal of Consumer Research*, 28, September 2001, pp. 257–272; Darren W. Dahl, Amitava Chattopadhyay, and Gerald J. Gorn, "The Use of Visual Mental Imagery in New-Product Design," *Journal of Marketing Research*, 36, February 1999, pp. 18–28; Jennifer Gregan-Paxton and Deborah Roedder John, "Consumer Learning by Analogy: A Model of Internal Knowledge Transfer," *Journal of Consumer Research*, 24, December 1997, pp. 266–284.

56. For additional information, also see David Bakken and Curtis L. Frazier, "Conjoint Analysis: Understanding Consumer Decision Making," in *The Handbook of Marketing Research*, ed. Rajiv Grover and Marco Vriens (Thousand Oaks, CA: Sage, 2006); Vithala R. Rao and John R. Hauser, "Conjoint Analysis, Related Modeling, and Application," in *Market Research and Modeling: Progress and Prospects: A Tribute to Paul Green*, ed. Yoram Wind and Paul E. Green (New York: Springer, 2004), pp. 141–168; Jordan J. Louviere, David A. Hensher, and Joffre D. Swait, *Stated Choice Models: Analysis and Applications* (New York: Cambridge University Press, 2000); Paul E. Green and V. Srinivasan, "Conjoint Analysis in Marketing: New Developments with Implications for Research and Practice," *Journal of Marketing*, October 1990, pp. 3–19; www.sawtoothsoftware.com.

57. Jerry Wind, Paul Green, Douglas Shifflet, and Marsha Scarbrough, "Courtyard by Marriott: Designing a Hotel Facility with Consumer-Based Marketing Models," *Interfaces*, 19, January–February 1989, pp. 25–47. For another interesting application, see Paul E. Green, Abba M. Krieger, and Terry Vavra, "Evaluating EZ-Pass: Using Conjoint Analysis to Assess Consumer Response to a New Tollway Technology," *Marketing Research*, Summer 1999, pp. 5–16.

58. The full-profile example was taken from Paul E. Green and Yoram Wind, "New Ways to Measure Consumers' Judgments," *Harvard Business Review*, July–August 1975, pp. 107–117.

59. Peter N. Golder and Gerald J. Tellis, "Will It Ever Fly? Modeling the Takeoff of Really New Consumer Durables," *Marketing Science*, 16, no. 3, Summer 1997, pp. 256–270; Glen L. Urban, Bruce D. Weinberg, and John R. Hauser, "Premarket Forecasting of Really New Products," *Journal of Marketing*, January 1996, pp. 47–60; Robert Blattberg and John Golany, "Tracker: An Early Test-Market Forecasting and Diagnostic Model for New-Product Planning," *Journal of Marketing Research*, May 1978, pp. 192–202.

60. Roger A. Kerin, Michael G. Harvey, and James T. Rothe, "Cannibalism and New-Product Development," *Business Horizons*, October 1978, pp. 25–31.

61. The present value (V) of a future sum (I) to be received t years from today and discounted at the interest rate (r) is given by $V = I_t/(1 + r)t$. Thus US\$4,716,000/(1.15)^5 = \$2,345,000.

62. David B. Hertz, "Risk Analysis in Capital Investment," *Harvard Business Review*, January–February 1964, pp. 96–106.

63. John Hauser, "House of Quality," *Harvard Business Review*, May–June 1988, pp. 63–73. Customer-driven engineering is also called 'quality function deployment.' See Lawrence R. Guinta and Nancy C. Praizler, *The QFD Book: The Team Approach to Solving Problems and Satisfying Customers through Quality Function Deployment* (New York: AMACOM, 1993); and V. Srinivasan, William S. Lovejoy, and David Beach, "Integrated Product Design for Marketability and Manufacturing," *Journal of Marketing Research*, February 1997, pp. 154–163.

64. Tom Peters, *The Circle of Innovation* (New York: Alfred A. Knopf, 1997), p. 96. For more general discussion, see also, Rajesh Sethi, "New-Product Quality and Product-Development Teams," *Journal of Marketing*, April 2000, pp. 1–14; Christine Moorman and Anne S. Miner, "The Convergence of Planning and Execution Improvisation in New-Product Development," *Journal of Marketing*, July 1998, pp. 1–20; and Ravinchoarnath MacChavan and Rajiv Graver, "From Embedded Knowledge to Embodied Knowledge: New-Product Development as Knowledge Management," *Journal of Marketing*, October 1998, pp. 1–12.

65. Marco Iansiti and Alan MacCormack, "Developing Products on Internet Time," *Harvard Business Review*, September–October 1997, pp. 108–117; Srikant Datar, C. Clark Jordan, and Kannan Srinivasan, "Advantages of Time-Based New-Product Development in a Fast-Cycle Industry," *Journal of Marketing Research*, February 1997, pp. 36–49; Christopher D. Ittner and David F. Larcker, "Product-Development Cycle Time and Organizational Performance," *Journal of Marketing Research*, February 1997, pp. 13–23.

66. Peters, *The Circle of Innovation*, p. 96. For more general discussion, see also Sethi, "New Product Quality and Product Development Teams," pp. 1–14; Moorman and Miner, "The Convergence of Planning and Execution Improvisation in New-Product Development," pp. 1–20; and MacChavan and Graver, "From Embedded Knowledge to Embodied Knowledge," pp. 1–12.

67. Kevin J. Clancy, Peter C. Krieg, and Marianne McGarry Wolf, *Marketing New Products Successfully: Using Simulated Test Marketing Methodology* (New York: Lexington Books, 2005); Glen L. Urban, John R. Hauser, and Roberta A. Chicos, "Information Acceleration: Validation and Lessons from the Field," *Journal of Marketing Research*, February 1997, pp. 143–153; V. Mahajan and Jerry Wind, "New Product Models: Practice, Shortcomings, and Desired Improvements," *Journal of Product Innovation Management*, 9, June 1992, pp. 129–139.

68. Eyal Biyalogorsky, William Boulding, and Richard Staelin, "Stuck in the Past: Why Managers Persist with New-Product Failures," *Journal of Marketing*, 70, April 2006, pp. 108–121.

69. Rajesh Chandy, Brigette Hopstaken, Om Narasimhan, and Jaideep Prabhu, "From Invention to Innovation: Conversion Ability in Product Development," *Journal of Marketing Research*, 43, August 2006, pp. 494–508.

70. RemcoPrins and Peter C. Verhoef, "Marketing Communication Drivers of Adoption Timing of a New E-Service among Existing Customers," *Journal of Marketing*, 71, April 2007, pp. 169–183.

71. For further discussion, see Yuhong Wu, Sridhar Balasubramanian, and Vijay Mahajan, "When Is a Preannounced New Product Likely to Be Delayed?" *Journal of Marketing*, 68, April 2004, pp. 101–113; RajiSrinivasan, Gary L. Lilien, and Arvind Rangaswamy, "First in First out? The Effects of Network Externalities on Pioneer Survival," *Journal of Marketing*, 68, January 2004, pp. 41–58; Barry L. Bayus, Sanjay Jain, and Ambar Rao, "Consequences: An Analysis of Truth or Vaporware and New-Product Announcements," *Journal of Marketing Research*, February 2001, pp. 3–13; Thomas S. Robertson, Jehoshua Eliashberg, and Talia Rymon, "New-Product Announcement Signals and Incumbent Reactions," *Journal of Marketing*, July 1995, pp. 1–15; Frank H. Alport and Michael A. Kamins, "Pioneer Brand Advantages and Consumer Behavior: A Conceptual Framework and Propositional Inventory," *Journal of the Academy of Marketing Science*, Summer 1994, pp. 244–336; Robert J. Thomas, "Timing: The Key to Market Entry," *Journal of Consumer Marketing*, Summer 1985, pp. 77–87.

72. Katrijn Gielens and Jan-Benedict E. M. Steenkamp, "What Drives New-Product Success? An Investigation across Products and Countries," Marketing Science Institute Working Paper 04-108, Cambridge, MA; Katrijn Gielens and Jan-Benedict E. M. Steenkamp, "Drivers of Consumer Acceptance of New Packaged Goods: An Investigation across Products and Countries," *International Journal of Research in Marketing*, 24, June 2007, pp. 97–111; Marc Fischer, Venkatesh Shankar, and Michael Clement, "Can a Late Mover Use International Market Entry Strategy to Challenge the Pioneer?" Marketing Science Institute Working Paper 05-118, Cambridge, MA; Venkatesh Shankar, Gregory S. Carpenter, and Lakshman Krishnamukthi, "Late Mover Advantages: How Innovative Late Entrants Outsell Pioneers," *Journal of Marketing Research*, 35, February 1998, pp. 54–70.

73. Philip Kotler and Gerald Zaltman, "Targeting Prospects for a New Product," *Journal of Advertising Research*, February 1976, pp. 7–20.

74. Mark Leslie and Charles A. Holloway, "The Sales Learning Curve," *Harvard Business Review*, July–August 2006, pp. 114–123.

75. For details, see Keith G. Lockyer, *Critical Path Analysis and Other Project Network Techniques* (London: Pitman, 1984). Also see Arvind Rangaswamy and Gary L. Lilien, "Software Tools for New-Product Development," *Journal of Marketing Research*, February 1997, pp. 177–184.

76. The following discussion leans heavily on Everett M. Rogers, *Diffusion of Innovations* (New York: Free Press, 1962). Also see his third edition, published in 1983.

77. C. Page Moreau, Donald R. Lehmann, and Arthur B. Markman, "Entrenched Knowledge Structures and Consumer Response to New Products," *Journal of Marketing Research*, 38, February 2001, pp. 14–29.

78. John T. Gourville, "Eager Sellers & Stony Buyers," *Harvard Business Review*, June 2006, pp. 99–106.

79. Chuan-Fong Shih and Alladi Venkatesh, "Beyond Adoption: Development and Application of a Use-Diffusion Model," *Journal of Marketing*, 68, January 2004, pp. 59–72.

80. Michal Herzenstein, Steven S. Posavac, and J. Joskon Brakuz, "Adoption of New and Really New Products: The

Effects of Self-Regulation Systems and Risk Salience," *Journal of Marketing Research*, 44, May 2007, pp. 251–260; Christophe Van den Bulte and Yogesh V. Joshi, "New-Product Diffusion with Influentials and Imitators," *Marketing Science*, 26, May–June 2007, pp. 400–421; Steve Hoeffler, "Measuring Preferences for Really New Products," *Journal of Marketing Research*, 40, November 2003, pp. 406–420.

81. Rogers, *Diffusion of Innovations*, (New York: Free Press, 1983), p. 192; Geoffrey A. Moore, *Crossing the Chasm: Marketing and Selling High-Tech Products to Mainstream Customers* (New York: HarperBusiness, 1999).

82. A. Parasuraman and Charles L. Colby, *Techno-Ready Marketing* (New York: Free Press, 2001); Jakki Mohr, *Marketing of High-Technology Products and Innovations* (Upper Saddle River, NJ: Prentice Hall, 2001).

83. Malcolm Macalister Hall, "Selling by Stealth," *Business Life*, November 2001, pp. 51–55.

84. Jordan Robertson, "How Nike Got Street Cred," *Business 2.0*, May 2004, pp. 43–46.

85. Cliff Edwards, "Will Souping Up TiVo Save It?" *BusinessWeek*, May 17, 2004, pp. 63–64; Cliff Edwards, "Is TiVo's Signal Still Fading?"*BusinessWeek*, September 10, 2001, pp. 72–74.

86. Fareena Sultan, John U. Farley, and Donald R. Lehman, "Reflection on 'A Meta-Analysis of Applications of Diffusion Models,'" *Journal of Marketing Research*, May 1996, pp. 247–249; Vijay Mahajan, Eitan Muller, and Frank M. Bass, "Diffusion of New Products: Empirical Generalizations and Managerial Uses," *Marketing Science*, 14, no. 3, part 2, Summer 1995, pp. G79–G89; Minhi Hahn, Sehoon Park, and Andris A. Zoltners, "Analysis of New-Product Diffusion Using a Four-Segment Trial-Repeat Model," *Marketing Science*, 13, no. 3, Summer 1994, pp. 224–247; Hubert Gatignon and Thomas S. Robertson, "A Propositional Inventory for New Diffusion Research," *Journal of Consumer Research*, March 1985, pp. 849–867.

Chapter 21

1. Jack Ewing, "Nokia: Lesson Learned, Reward Reaped," *BusinessWeek*, July 30, 2007, p. 32; "Face Value," *The Economist*, May 27, 2006, p. 64. *Global Mobile Statistics 2011*, http://mobithinking.com/mobile-marketing-tools/latest-mobile-stats.

2. See www.ita.doc.gov.

3. Michael E. Porter, *Competitive Strategy* (New York: Free Press, 1980), p. 275.

4. "Global 500 2011," *Fortune*, http://money.cnn.com/magazines/fortune/global500/2011/snapshots/6316.html; SABIC website, www.sabic.com/corporate/en/default.aspx; Roger Harrison, "SABIC Climbing up the Growth Ladder," *Arab News*, http://archive.arabnews.com, October 5, 2009.

5. Ron Lieber, "Give Us This Day Our Global Bread," *Fast Company*, March 2001, p. 158.

6. Charles P. Wallace, "Charge!" *Fortune*, September 28, 1998, pp. 189–196; www.wto.org.

7. Edward Iwata, "Companies Find Gold inside Melting Pot," *USA Today*, July 9, 2007.

8. Jan Johanson and Finn Wiedersheim-Paul, "The Internationalization of the Firm," *Journal of Management Studies*, October 1975, pp. 305–322.

9. Michael R. Czinkota and Ilkka A. Ronkainen, *International Marketing*, 5th edn (New York: Harcourt Brace Jovanovich, 1999).

10. For a timely and thorough review of academic research on global marketing, see Johny K. Johansson, "Global Marketing: Research on Foreign Entry, Local Marketing, Global Management," in *Handbook of Marketing*, ed. Bart Weitz and Robin Wensley (London: Sage, 2002), pp. 457–483. Also see Johny K. Johansson, *Global Marketing*, 2nd edn (New York: McGraw-Hill, 2003). For some global marketing research issues, see Susan Douglas and Samuel R. Craig, *International Marketing Research*, 2nd edn (Upper Saddle River, NJ: Prentice Hall, 2000).

11. According to the CIA World Factbook (www.cia.gov/library/publications/the-world-factbook/index.html), there are 34 developed countries: Andorra, Australia, Austria, Belgium, Bermuda, Canada, Denmark, Faroe Islands, Finland, France, Germany, Greece, Holy See, Iceland, Ireland, Israel, Italy, Japan, Liechtenstein, Luxembourg, Malta, Mexico Monaco, Netherlands, New Zealand, Norway, Portugal, San Marino, South Africa, Spain, Sweden, Switzerland, Turkey, United Kingdom, and United States. They note that DCs are similar to the new International Monetary Fund (IMF) term "advanced economies" that adds Hong Kong, South Korea, Singapore, and Taiwan but drops Malta, Mexico, South Africa, and Turkey.

12. Jack Neff, "Submerged," *Advertising Age*, March 4, 2002, p. 14.

13. See www.populationmedia.org/issues/population/population-and-poverty.

14. Adapted from Vijay Mahajan, Marcos V. Pratini De Moraes, and Jerry Wind, "The Invisible Global Market," *Marketing Management*, Winter 2000, pp. 31–35. See also Tarun Khanna and Krishna G. Palepu, "Emerging Giants: Building World-Class Companies in Developing Countries," *Harvard Business Review*, October 2006, pp. 60–69.

15. C. K. Prahalad, *The Fortune at the Bottom of the Pyramid: Eradicating Poverty through Profits* (Upper Saddle River, NJ: Wharton School Publishing, 2005); Niraj Dawar and Amitava Chattopadhyay, "Rethinking Marketing Programs for Emerging Markets," *Long Range Planning*, 35, October 2002.

16. Bart J. Bronnenberg, Jean-Pierre Dubé, and Sanjay Dhar, "Consumer Packaged Goods in the United States: National Brands, Local Branding," *Journal of Marketing Research*, 44, February 2007, pp. 4–13; Bart J. Bronnenberg, Jean-Pierre Dubé, and Sanjay Dhar, "National Brands, Local Branding: Conclusions and Future Research Opportunities," *Journal of Marketing Research*, 44, February 2007, pp. 26–28; Bart J. Bronnenberg, Jean-Pierre Dubé, and Sanjay Dhar,

"Market Structure and the Geographic Distribution of Brand Shares in Consumer Package Goods Industries," (Working paper) UCLA Graduate School of Management.

17. Bruce Einhorn, "Grudge Match in China," *BusinessWeek*, April 2, 2007, pp. 42–43; Russell Flannery, "Watch Your Back," *Forbes*, April 23, 2007, pp. 104–105; Steve Hamm and Dexter Roberts, "China's First Global Capitalist," *BusinessWeek*, December 11, 2006, pp. 52–57; "The Fast and the Furious," *The Economist*, November 25, 2006, pp. 63–64.

18. Manjeet Kripalani, "Finally, Coke Gets It Right," *BusinessWeek*, February 10, 2003, p. 47; Manjeet Kripalani, "Battling for Pennies in India's Villages," *BusinessWeek*, June 10, 2002, p. 22.

19. Ellen Byron, "P&G's Global Target: Shelves of Tiny Stores," *Wall Street Journal*, July 16, 2007; "Not So Fizzy," *The Economist*, February 23, 2002, pp. 66–67; Rajeev Batra, Venkatram Ramaswamy, Dana L. Alden, Jan-Benedict E. M. Steenkamp, and S. Ramachander, "Effects of Brand Local and Nonlocal Origin on Consumer Attitudes in Developing Countries," *Journal of Consumer Psychology*, 9, no. 2, 2000, pp. 83–95.

20. Patricia Sellers, "P&G: Teaching an Old Dog New Tricks," *Fortune*, May 31, 2004, pp. 167–180.

21. Antonio Regalado, "Marketers Pursue the Shallow-Pocketed," *Wall Street Journal*, January 26, 2007.

22. Paul Betts, "Danone's Taste for Microfinance Pays Dividends," *Financial Times*, March 30, 2007, p. 24; "The Bottom of the Pyramid Is Where the Real Gold Is Hidden," *Marketing Week*, February 8, 2007, p. 18; Adam Jones, "Danone and Yunus Extend Partnership," *Financial Times*, December 19, 2006, p. 19.

23. "Population grows in 20 EU member states," *Eurostat*, European Commission, 28, July 2011, http://epp.eurostat.ec.europa.eu/portal/page/portal/population/introduction.

24. Information from The Office of the United States Trade Representative, "North American Free Trade Agreement," www.ustr.gov/trade-agreements/free-trade-agreements/north-american-free-trade-agreement-nafta.

25. Johny K. Johansson, "Global Marketing: Research on Foreign Entry, Local Marketing, Global Management," in *Handbook of Marketing*, ed. Bart Weitz and Robin Wensley (London: Sage, 2002), pp. 457–483.

26. "Jubail Industrial City," www.bechtel.com/jubail_industrial_city.html; "Bechtel's Long Game in the Gulf," *BBC News*, April 22, 2003, http://news.bbc.co.uk/2/hi/business/2930457.stm.

27. See www.cilantro-cafe.com; Louis Wasser, "Exporting Success,"*Business Monthly*, www.amcham.org.eg/resources_publications/publications/business_monthly/issue.asp?sec=5&im=3&iy=2009; "Cilantro's Parent Company Delicious Branches Out," *Daily News Egypt*, September 2, 2009, www.thedailynewsegypt.com/cilantros-parent-company-delicious-branches-out.html; "Cilantro Café," http://middleeastarab.com/eg/dir/cilantro-cafe.html; Book Koh, "Review: Cilantro Cafe Brings Refreshing New Concept," *The London Insider*, February 28, 2010, www.london-insider.co.uk/2010/02/review-cilantro-cafe-piccadilly-refreshing-new-concept/; Heba Fateen Bizzari, "Cilantro, 'Appetite for Life'," www.touregypt.net/featurestories/cilantro.htm.

28. For an academic review, see Leonidas C. Leonidou, Constantine S. Katsikeas, and Nigel F. Piercy, "Identifying Managerial Influences on Exporting: Past Research and Future Directions," *Journal of International Marketing*, 6, no. 2, Summer 1998, pp. 74–102.

29. "Business Sectors: Food and Beverage," www.alfaisaliah.com/index.asp?id=124; Mena Report, "Al-Safi Danone Brand Launched in Kuwait," *Al Bawaba Business*, October 8, 2002, www1.albawaba.com/business/al-safi-danone-brand-launched-kuwait; "About Us," www.yasrafood.com/en/aboutus.asp.

30. Brandon Mitchener, "E-Commerce: Border Crossings," *Wall Street Journal*, November 22, 1999.

31. Michael Arndt and Dexter Roberts, "A Finger-Lickin' Good Time in China," *BusinessWeek*, October 30, 2006, p. 50; "Cola down Mexico Way," *The Economist*, October 11, 2003, pp. 69–70.

32. Laura Mazur and Annik Hogg, *The Marketing Challenge* (Wokingham, England: Addison-Wesley, 1993), pp. 42–44; Jan Willem Karel, "Brand Strategy Positions Products Worldwide," *Journal of Business Strategy*, 12, no. 3, May–June 1991, pp. 16–19.

33. Joann Muller, "Global Motors," *Forbes*, January 12, 2004, pp. 62–68.

34. "Burgers and Fries a la Francaise," *The Economist*, April 17, 2004, pp. 60–61; Johny K. Johansson, "Global Marketing: Research on Foreign Entry, Local Marketing, Global Management," in *Handbook of Marketing*, ed. Bart Weitz and Robin Wensley (London: Sage, 2002), pp. 457–483; Shaoming Zou and S. Tamer Cavusgil, "The GMS: A Broad Conceptualization of Global Marketing Strategy and Its Effect on Firm Performance," *Journal of Marketing*, 66, October 2002, pp. 40–56; "What Makes a Company Great?" *Fortune*, October 26, 1998, pp. 218–226; Bernard Wysocki Jr., "The Global Mall: In Developing Nations, Many Youths Splurge, Mainly on U.S. Goods," *Wall Street Journal*, June 26,1997; David M. Szymanski, Sundar G. Bharadwaj, and P. Rajan Varadarajan, "Standardization versus Adaptation of International Marketing Strategy: An Empirical Investigation," *Journal of Marketing*, October 1993, pp. 1–17; Theodore Levitt, "The Globalization of Markets," *Harvard Business Review*, May–June 1983, pp. 92–102.

35. Kevin Lane Keller, "Red Bull: Managing a High-Growth Brand," in *Best Practice Cases in Branding*, 3rd edn (Upper Saddle River, NJ: Prentice Hall, 2008).

36. See www.beverageworld.com; www.beveragemarketing.com.

37. Geert Hofstede, *Culture's Consequences* (Beverley Hills, CA: Sage, 1980).

38. For some recent treatments of branding in Asia in particular, see S. Ramesh Kumar, *Marketing & Branding: The Indian Scenario* (Delhi: Pearson Education, 2007); Martin Roll, *Asian Brand Strategy: How Asia Builds Strong Brands* (New York: Palgrave MacMillan, 2006); Paul Temporal, *Branding in Asia: The Creation, Development, and Management of Asian Brands for the Global Market* (Singapore: John Wiley & Sons, 2001).

39. Pankaj Ghemawat, "Globalization: The Strategy of Differences," *Harvard Business School Working Knowledge*, November 10, 2003; Pankaj Ghemawat, "The Forgotten Strategy," *Harvard Business Review*, 81, November 2003, pp. 76–84.

40. "Mobinil," www.orascomtelecom.com/Subsidiaries/details.aspx?id=100; "Welcome to Star," www.mobinil.com/Star/SavingPlans.aspx; www.dijezzygsm.com "Choose Your Voice Plan," www.windmobile.ca/en/Pages/voice-plans.aspx.

41. Walter J. Keegan and Mark C. Green, *Global Marketing*, 4th edn (Upper Saddle River, NJ: Prentice Hall, 2005); Warren J. Keegan, *Global Marketing Management*, 7th edn (Upper Saddle River, NJ: Prentice Hall, 2002).

42. Arundhati Parmar, "Dependent Variables: Sound Global Strategies Rely on Certain Factors," *Marketing News*, September 16, 2002, p. 4.

43. Paulo Prada and Bruce Orwall, "A Certain 'Je Ne Sais Quoi' at Disney's New Park," *Wall Street Journal*, March 12, 2003.

44. Jack Ewing, "Where the Book Business Is Humming," *BusinessWeek*, May 14, 2007, p. 50.

45. Alkhereiji, Mohammed, "McDonald's Launches McArabia," Arab News, 2003, http://archive.arabnews.com/?page=1&section=0&article=23313&d=5&m=3&y=2003.

46. Mark Lasswell, "Lost in Translation," *Business 2.0*, August 2004, pp. 68–70; Richard P. Carpenter and the *Globe* Staff, "What They Meant to Say Was…," *Boston Globe*, August 2, 1998.

47. For an interesting distinction based on the concept of global consumer culture positioning, see Dana L. Alden, Jan-Benedict E. M. Steenkamp, and Rajeev Batra, "Brand Positioning through Advertising in Asia, North America, and Europe: The Role of Global Consumer Culture," *Journal of Marketing*, 63, January 1999, pp. 75–87.

48. Thomas J. Madden, Kelly Hewett, and Martin S. Roth, "Managing Images in Different Cultures: A Cross-National Study of Color Meanings and Preferences," *Journal of International Marketing*, 8, no. 4, Winter 2000, pp. 90–107; Zeynep Gürhan-Canli and Durairaj Maheswaran, "Cultural Variations in Country-of-Origin Effects," *Journal of Marketing Research*, 37, August 2000, pp. 309–317.

49. Geoffrey Fowler, Brian Steinberg, and Aaron O. Patrick, "Globalizing Apple's Ads," *Wall Street Journal*, March 1, 2007.

50. "Introduction to Unilever," www.unilever.com/aboutus/introductiontounilever/; CITT Rescinds Hot Rolled Steel Plane Orders, http://steelnews.com/Ipsco/tabid/36/cat/76/Doc/4526/Default.aspx; Sharon Otterman, "Does the Veiled Look Sell? Egyptian Advertisers Grapple with the Hijab," *Arab Media & Society*, 2, Summer 2007, www.arabmediasociety.com/index.php?article=205&p=0.

51. Noreen O'Leary, "Bright Lights, Big Challenge," *Adweek*, January 15, 2007, p. 22; Normandy Madden, "Nike Drops Its American Idols," *Advertising Age*, March 20, 2006, p. 12.

52. Loretta Chao, "Cell Phone Ads Are Easier Pitch in China Interactive Campaigns," *Wall Street Journal*, January 4, 2007.

53. John L. Graham, Alma T. Mintu, and Waymond Rogers, "Explorations of Negotiations Behaviors in Ten Foreign Cultures Using a Model Developed in the United States," *Management Science*, 40, January 1994, pp. 72–95.

54. David Kirkpatrick, "How Microsoft Conquered China," *Fortune*, 156, no. 2, July 23, 2007, pp. 78–84.

55. Tony Van Alphen, "Some U.S. Makers Dumping Steel in Canada," *Toronto Star*, May 2, 2001.

56. Ram Charan, "The Rules Have Changed," *Fortune*, March 16, 1998, pp. 159–162.

57. See www.ge.com.

58. David Arnold, "Seven Rules of International Distribution," *Harvard Business Review*, November–December 2000, pp. 131–137.

59. Arnold, "Seven Rules of International Distribution."

60. "Jawad Supermarkets," www.jawad.com/jawadsupermarkets.html; "Supermarkets and Food Shopping in Bahrain," www.whattodoyanee.com/food-shopping-in-bahrain.html.

61. Geraldo Samor, Cecilie Rohwedder, and Ann Zimmerman, "Innocents Abroad," *Wall Street Journal*, May 10, 2006; Mark Landler and Michael Barbaro, "Wal-Mart's Overseas Push Can Be Lost in Translation," *International Herald Tribune*, August 2, 2006; "Heading for the Exit," *The Economist*, August 5, 2006, p. 52; Keith Naughton, "The Great Wal-Mart of China," *Newsweek*, October 30, 2006, pp. 50–52; "Trouble at Till," *The Economist*, November 4, 2006, p. 18.

62. "From Head & Shoulders to Kobe," *The Economist*, March 27, 2004, p. 64.

63. Alessandra Galloni, "Venice: Gondoliers, Lagoons, Moonlight—and Meatballs?" *Wall Street Journal*, August 9, 2002.

64. "A Dragon with Core Values," *The Economist*, March 30, 2002.

65. "The Shock of Old," *The Economist*, July 13, 2002, p. 49.

66. "From Fantasy Worlds to Food," *Economist*, November 11, 2006, p. 73; "A New Sort of Beauty Contest," *The Economist*, November 11, 2006, p. 68.

67. Jim Rendon, "When Nations Need a Little Marketing," *New York Times*, November 23, 2003.

68. Zeynep Gurhan-Canli and Durairaj Maheswaran, "Cultural Variations in Country-of-Origin Effects," *Journal of Marketing Research*, 37, August 2000, pp. 309–317.

69. Douglas B. Holt, John A. Quelch, and Earl L. Taylor, "How Global Brands Compete," *Harvard Business Review*, 82, September 2004, pp. 68–75; Jan-Benedict E. M. Steenkamp, Rajeev Batra, and Dana L. Alden, "How Perceived Brand Globalness Creates Brand Value," *Journal of International Business Studies*, 34, no. 1, January 2003, pp. 53–65.

70. Gürhan-Canli and Maheswaran "Cultural Variations in Country-of-Origin Effects"; Johny K. Johansson, "Global Marketing: Research on Foreign Entry, Local Marketing, Global Management," in *Handbook of Marketing*, ed. Barton A. Weitz and Robin Wensley (London: Sage, 2002), pp. 457–483; "Old Wine in New Bottles," *The Economist*, February 21, 1998, p. 45; Johny K. Johansson, "Determinants and Effects of the Use of 'Made in' Labels," *International Marketing Review (UK)*, 6, no. 1, January 1989, pp. 47–58; Warren J. Bilkey and Erik Nes, "Country-of-Origin Effects on Product Evaluations," *Journal of International Business Studies*, Spring–Summer 1982, pp. 89–99.

71. Jathon Sapsford and Norihiko Shirouzo, "Mom, Apple Pie and…Toyota?," *Wall Street Journal*, May 11, 2006.

72. "Haier's Purpose," *The Economist*, March 20, 2004, p. 72; Gerry Kermouch, "Breaking into the Name Game," *BusinessWeek*, April 7, 2003, p. 54.

73. See www.alj.com.

74. Christopher A. Bartlett and Sumantra Ghoshal, *Managing across Borders* (Cambridge, MA: Harvard Business School Press, 1989).

75. Betsy McKay, "Coke Hunts for Talent to Re-Establish Its Marketing Might," *Wall Street Journal*, March 6, 2002.

Chapter 22

1. Keith Fox, Katherine Jocz, and Bernard Jaworski, "A Common Language," *Marketing Management*, May–June 2003, pp. 14–17.

2. Information from www.emirates.com; "Emirates Airline Completes Low-Tech 'Green Flight'," *Environmental Leader*, December 18, 2008, www.environmentalleader.com/2008/12/18/emirates-airline-completes-low-tech-green-flight; Adam Stern, 'Longest Green Flight in the World,' *The TerraPass Footprint*, December 16, 2008, www.terrapass.com; additional information from www.theemiratesgroup.com/english/our-vision-values/responsibility.aspx.

3. For additional updates on the latest academic thinking on marketing strategy and tactics, see *Kellogg on Integrated Marketing*, ed. Dawn Iacobucci and Bobby Calder (New York: Wiley, 2003); and *Kellogg on Marketing*, ed. Dawn Iacobucci (New York: Wiley, 2001).

4. Frederick E. Webster Jr., Alan J. Malter, and Shankar Ganesan, "Can Marketing Regain Its Seat at the Table?," Marketing Science Institute Report No. 03-113 (Cambridge, MA: Marketing Science Institute, 2003).

5. For a broad historical treatment of marketing thought, see D. G. Brian Jones and Eric H. Shaw, "A History of Marketing Thought," in *Handbook of Marketing*, ed. Barton A. Weitz and Robin Wensley (London: Sage, 2002), pp. 39–65.

6. Interview with the general manager, Mrs. Fattheya El Soury.

7. Hamish Pringle and William Gordon, *Beyond Manners: How to Create the Self Confident Organisation to Live the Brand* (West Sussex, England: John Wiley & Sons, 2001); Frederick E. Webster Jr., "The Changing Role of Marketing in the Corporation," *Journal of Marketing*, October 1992, pp. 1–17. Also see John P. Workman Jr., Christian Homburg, and Kjell Gruner, "Marketing Organization: An Integrative Framework of Dimensions and Determinants," *Journal of Marketing*, July 1998, pp. 21–41; Ravi S. Achrol, "Evolution of the Marketing Organization: New Forms for Turbulent Environment," *Journal of Marketing*, October 1991, pp. 77–93. For some contemporary perspectives, see Special Issue 1999 of *Journal of Marketing Fundamental Issues and Directions for Marketing*.

8. For an excellent account of how to convert a company into a market-driven organization, see George Day, *The Market-Driven Organization: Aligning Culture, Capabilities, and Configuration to the Market* (New York: Free Press, 1989).

9. Frederick E. Webster Jr., "The Role of Marketing and the Firm," in *Handbook of Marketing*, ed. Barton A. Weitz and Robin Wensley (London: Sage, 2002), pp. 39–65.

10. Frank V. Cespedes, *Managing Marketing Linkages: Text, Cases, and Readings* (Upper Saddle River, NJ: Prentice Hall, 1996); Frank V. Cespedes, *Concurrent Marketing: Integrating Product, Sales, and Service* (Boston: Harvard Business School Press, 1995).

11. "About Us: Hero Vitrac," www.tradeegypt.com/Vitrac/?company=y.

12. Laurie Freeman, "P&G Widens Power Base: Adds Category Managers," *Advertising Age*; Michael J. Zenor, "The Profit Benefits of Category Management," *Journal of Marketing Research*, 31, May 1994, pp. 202–213; Gerry Khermouch, "Brands Overboard," *Brandweek*, August 22, 1994, pp. 25–39; Zachary Schiller, "The Marketing Revolution at Procter & Gamble," *BusinessWeek*, July 25, 1988, pp. 72–76.

13. "Carrefour in Middle East Adopts Category Management and Supplier Negotiation from Soft Solutions," www.freshplaza.com/news_detail.asp?id=28856#SlideFrame_1.

14. For further reading, see Robert Dewar and Don Shultz, "The Product Manager, an Idea Whose Time Has Gone," *Marketing Communications*, May 1998, pp. 28–35; George S. Low and Ronald A. Fullerton, "Brands, Brand Management, and the Brand Manager System: A Critical Historical Evaluation," *Journal of Marketing Research*, May 1994, pp. 173–190; Michael J. Zanor, "The Profit Benefits of Category Management," *Journal of Marketing Research*, May 1994, pp. 202–213.

15. "Background: Maghreb Steel," uk.maghrebsteel.ma/about/background.

16. Larry Selden and Geoffrey Colvin, *Angel Customers & Demon Customers* (New York: Portfolio [Penguin], 2003).

17. For an in-depth discussion of issues around implementing a customer-based organization on which much of this paragraph is based, see George S. Day, "Aligning the Organization with the Market," *MIT Sloan Management Review*, Autumn 2006, pp. 41–49.

18. Richard E. Anderson, "Matrix Redux," *Business Horizons*, November–December 1994, pp. 6–10.

19. Frederick E. Webster Jr., "The Role of Marketing and the Firm," in *Handbook of Marketing*, ed. Barton A. Weitz and Robin Wensley (London: Sage, 2002), pp. 39–65.

20. Benson P. Shapiro, "Can Marketing and Manufacturing Coexist?" *Harvard Business Review*, September–October 1977, pp. 104–114. Also see Robert W. Ruekert and Orville C. Walker Jr., "Marketing's Interaction with Other Functional Units: A Conceptual Framework with Other Empirical Evidence," *Journal of Marketing*, January 1987, pp. 1–19.

21. "Banking on Success, Business Management," www.busmanagementme.com/article/Banking-on-success/.

22. Erik Brynjolfsson and Lorin Hitt, "The Customer Counts," *InformationWeek*, September 9, 1996.

23. Gary Hamel, *Leading the Revolution* (Boston: Harvard Business School Press, 2000).

24. "Arwa Launches Flavored Sparkling Water 'Arwa Fruits' in Bahrain," www.ameinfo.com/230700.html.

25. Jagdish N. Sheth, *The Self-Destructive Habits of Good Companies…And How to Break Them* (Upper Saddle River, NJ: Wharton School Publishing, 2007).

26. William L. Wilkie and Elizabeth S. Moore, "Marketing's Relationship to Society," in *Handbook of Marketing*, ed. Barton A. Weitz and Robin Wensley (London: Sage, 2002), pp. 1–38.

27. "Special Report: Corporate Social Responsibility," *The Economist*, December 14, 2002, pp. 62–63.

28. "Aramex Leads the Way in Corporate Social Responsibility through Sustainability Reporting," www.aramex.com/news/item.aspx?ID=935f8506-f24c-469e-8c24-d1ed0312b3fb.

29. "Taking Social Responsibility and the Environment Seriously," www.qatarairways.com/global/en/csr.html.

30. Jennifer Alsever, "Chiquita Cleans Up Its Act, *Business 2.0*, August 2006, pp. 56–58.

31. Brian Grow, "The Debate over Doing Good," *BusinessWeek*, August 15, 2005, pp. 76–78.

32. Raj Sisodia, David B. Wolfe, and Jag Sheth, *Firms of Endearment: How World-Class Companies Profit from Passion and Purpose* (Upper Saddle River, NJ: Wharton School Publishing, 2007).

33. "Introduction: Ahead & Growing," www.zain.com/muse/obj/lang.default/portal.view/content/About%20us/Overview; "2010 CSR Highlights—Sudan," www.zain.com/muse/obj/lang.default/portal.view/content/Social%20Responsibility/Sudan.

34. John Carey, "Hugging the Tree Huggers," *BusinessWeek*, March 12, 2007, pp. 66–68.

35. Jeff Nachtigal, "It's Easy and Cheap Being Green," *Fortune*, October 16, 2006, p. 53.

36. For further reading, see Dorothy Cohen, *Legal Issues in Marketing Decision Making* (Cincinnati, OH: South-Western College Publishing, 1995).

37. Sarah Ellison, "Kraft Limits on Kids' Ads May Cheese Off Rivals," *Wall Street Journal*, January 13, 2005.

38. Shelby D. Hunt and Scott Vitell, "The General Theory of Marketing Ethics: A Retrospective and Revision," in *Ethics in Marketing*, ed. John Quelch and Craig Smith (Chicago: Irwin, 1992).

39. Majken Schultz, Yun Mi Antorini, and Fabian F. Csaba, *Corporate Branding: Purpose, People, and Process* (Køge, Denmark: Copenhagen Business School Press, 2005); Ronald J. Alsop, *The 18 Immutable Laws of Corporate Reputation: Creating, Protecting, and Repairing Your Most Valuable Asset* (New York: Free Press, 2004); Marc Gunther, "Tree Huggers, Soy Lovers, and Profits," *Fortune*, June 23, 2003, pp. 98–104; Ronald J. Alsop, "Perils of Corporate Philanthropy," *Wall Street Journal*, January 16, 2002.

40. Mya Frazier, "Going Green? Plant Deep Roots," *Advertising Age*, April 30, 2007, pp. 1, 54–55.

41. Michael E. Porter and Mark R. Kramer, "The Competitive Advantage of Corporate Philanthropy," *Harvard Business Review*, December 2002, pp. 5–16.

42. Dwane Hal Deane, "Associating the Corporation with a Charitable Event through Sponsorship: Measuring the Effects on Corporate Community Relations," *Journal of Advertising*, Winter 2002, pp. 77–87.

43. Sandra O'Loughlin, "The Wearin' o' the Green," *Brandweek*, April 23, 2007, pp. 26–27. For a critical response, see also, John R. Ehrenfield, "Feeding the Beast," *Fast Company*, December 2006–January 2007, pp. 42–43.

44. Nicholas Varchaver, "Chemical Reaction," *Fortune*, April 2, 2007, pp. 53–58.

45. Pete Engardio, "Beyond the Green Corporation," *BusinessWeek*, January 29, 2007, pp. 50-64.

46. Engardio, "Beyond the Green Corporation."

47. Kenneth Hein, "The World on a Platter," *Brandweek*, April 23, 2007, pp. 27–28; Megan Johnston, "Hard Sell for a Soft Fabric," *Forbes*, October 30, 2006, pp. 73–80.

48. See, Philip Kotler and Nancy Lee, *Corporate Social Responsibility: Doing the Most Good for Your Company and Your Cause* (New York: John Wiley, 2005).

49. Lynn Upshaw, *Truth: The New Rules for Marketing in a Skeptical World* (New York: Amacon, 2007); Cheryl Dahle, "A More Powerful Path," *Fast Company*, December 2006–January 2007, pp. 68–81.

50. Dalia Abdel Kader, marketing director, Arab African International Bank, www.aaibaward.com.

51. Robert Berner, "Smarter Corporate Giving," *BusinessWeek*, November 28, 2005, pp. 68–76; Craig N. Smith, "Corporate Social Responsibility: Whether or How?" *California Management Review*, 45, no. 4, Summer 2003, pp. 52–76.

52. Larry Chiagouris and Ipshita Ray, "Saving the World with Cause-Related Marketing," *Marketing Management*, July–August 2007, pp. 48–51; Hamish Pringle and Marjorie Thompson, *Brand Spirit: How Cause-Related Marketing Builds Brands* (New York: John Wiley & Sons, 1999); Sue Adkins, *Cause-Related Marketing: Who Cares Wins* (Oxford, England: Butterworth-Heineman, 1999); "Marketing, Corporate Social Initiatives, and the Bottom Line," Marketing Science Institute Conference Summary, MSI Report No. 01-106, 2001.

53. Rajan Varadarajan and Anil Menon, "Cause-Related Marketing: A Co-Alignment of Marketing Strategy and Corporate Philanthropy," *Journal of Marketing*, 52, July 1988, pp. 58–74.

54. Minette Drumwright and Patrick E. Murphy, "Corporate Societal Marketing," in *Handbook of Marketing and Society*, ed. Paul N. Bloom and Gregory T. Gundlach (Thousand Oaks, CA: Sage, 2001), pp. 162–183. See also, Minette Drumwright, "Company Advertising with a Social Dimension: The Role of Noneconomic Criteria," *Journal of Marketing*, 60, October 1996, pp. 71–87.

55. Jack Neff and Stephanie Thompson, "Eco-Marketing Has Staying Power This Time Around," *Advertising Age*, April 30, 2007, p. 55.

56. See www.britishairways.com.

57. Xueming Luo and C. B. Bhattacharya, "Corporate Social Responsibility, Customer Satisfaction, and Market Value," *Journal of Marketing*, 70, October 2006, pp. 1–18; Pat Auger, Paul Burke, Timothy Devinney, and Jordan J. Louviere, "What Will Consumers Pay for Social Product Features?" *Journal of Business Ethics*, 42, February 2003, pp. 281–304.

58. Dennis B. Arnett, Steve D. German, and Shelby D. Hunt, "The Identity Salience Model of Relationship Marketing Success: The Case of Nonprofit Marketing," *Journal of Marketing*, 67, April 2003, pp. 89–105; C. B. Bhattacharya and Sankar Sen, "Consumer-Company Identification: A Framework for Understanding Consumers' Relationships with Companies," *Journal of Marketing*, 67, April 2003, pp. 76–88; Sankar Sen and C. B. Bhattacharya, "Does Doing Good Always Lead to Doing Better? Consumer Reactions to Corporate Social Responsibility," *Journal of Marketing Research*, 38, no. 2, May 2001, pp. 225–244.

59. Paul N. Bloom, Steve Hoeffler, Kevin Lane Keller, and Carlos E. Basurto, "How Social-Cause Marketing Affects Consumer Perceptions," *MIT Sloan Management Review*, Winter 2006, pp. 49–55; Carolyn J. Simmons and Karen L. Becker-Olsen, "Achieving Marketing Objectives through Social Sponsorships," *Journal of Marketing*, 70, October 2006, pp. 154–169; Guido Berens, Cees B. M. van Riel, and Gerrit H. van Bruggen, "Corporate Associations and Consumer Product Responses: The Moderating Role of Corporate Brand Dominance," *Journal of Marketing*, 69, July 2005, pp. 35–48; Donald R. Lichtenstein, Minette E. Drumwright, and Bridgette M. Braig, "The Effect of Social Responsibility on Customer Donations to Corporate-Supported Nonprofits," *Journal of Marketing*, 68, October 2004, pp. 16–32; Stephen Hoeffler and Kevin Lane Keller, "Building Brand Equity through Corporate Societal Marketing," *Journal of Public Policy and Marketing*, 21, no. 1, Spring 2002, pp. 78–89. See also, Special Issue: Corporate Responsibility, *Journal of Brand Management*, 10, nos. 4–5, May 2003).

60. "Insights Survey of 1,800 13-25 years-olds" *Businessweek*, November 6, 2006, p. 13.

61. Mark R. Forehand and Sonya Grier, "When Is Honesty the Best Policy? The Effect of Stated Company Intent on Consumer Skepticism," *Journal of Consumer Psychology*, 13, no. 3, 2003, pp. 349–356; Dwane Hal Dean, "Associating the Corporation with a Charitable Event through Sponsorship: Measuring the Effects on Corporate Community Relations," *Journal of Advertising*, 31, no. 4, Winter 2002, pp. 77–87.

62. N. Craig Smith, "Out of Left Field," *Business Strategy Review*, 18, no. 2, Summer 2007, pp. 55–59; Adam Jones, "Choc Horror over Cadbury Tokens," *Financial Times*, May 3, 2003, p. 14.

63. Lauren Gard, "We're Good Guys, Buy from Us," *BusinessWeek*, November 22, 2004, pp. 72–74.

64. Mya Frazier, "Costly Red Campaign Reaps Meager $18 Million," *Advertising Age*, March 5, 2007; Viewpoint: Bobby Shriver, "CEO: Red's Raised Lots of Green," *Advertising Age*, March 12, 2007; Michelle Conlin, "Shop (in the Name of Love)," *BusinessWeek*, October 2, 2006, p. 9.

65. Todd Cohen, "Corporations Aim for Strategic Engagement," *Philanthropy Journal*, September 20, 2006; John A. Quelch and Nathalie Laidler-Kylander, *The New Global Brands: Managing Non-Governmental Organizations in the 21st Century* (Cincinnati, OH: South-Western College Publishing, 2005).

66. Alsop, *The 18 Immutable Laws of Corporate Reputation: Creating, Protecting, and Repairing Your Most Valuable Asset*, p. 125.

67. Susan Orenstein, "The Selling of Breast Cancer," *Business 2.0*, February 2003, pp. 88–94; H. Meyer, "When the Cause Is Just," *Journal of Business Strategy*, November–December 1999, pp. 27–31.

68. Christine Bittar, "Seeking Cause and Effect," *Brandweek*, November 11, 2002, pp. 18–24.

69. Paula Andruss, "'Think Pink' Awareness Much Higher Than Threat," *Marketing News*, February 15, 2006, pp. 14–16; Jessi Hempel, "Selling a Cause, Better Make It Pop," *BusinessWeek*, February 13, 2006, p. 75; Elizabeth Woyke, "Prostate Cancer's Higher Profile," *BusinessWeek*, October 9, 2006, p. 14.

70. Philip Kotler, Ned Roberto, and Nancy Lee, *Social Marketing: Improving the Quality of Life* (Thousand Oaks, CA: Sage, 2002); Michael L. Rothschild, "Carrots, Sticks, and Promises: A Conceptual Framework for the Management of Public Health and Social Issue Behaviors," *Journal of Marketing*, 63, October 1999, pp. 24–37.

71. "PepsiCo Jordan Sponsors 5th Zaha Football Tournament for Children," *Al Bawaba News*, April 11, 2011, www1.albawaba.com/pepsico-jordan-sponsors-5th-zaha-football-tournament-children.

72. See Rothschild, "Carrots, Sticks, and Promises: A Conceptual Framework for the Management of Public Health and Social Issue Behaviors," pp. 24–37.

73. See www.ameinfo.com/259539.html.

74. For more on developing and implementing marketing plans, see H. W. Goetsch, *Developing, Implementing, and Managing an Effective Marketing Plan* (Chicago: NTC Business Books, 1993). See also Thomas V. Bonoma, *The Marketing Edge: Making Strategies Work* (New York: Free Press, 1985). Much of this section is based on Bonoma's work.

75. C. Marcus, "Marketing Resource Management: Key Components," *Gartner Research Note*, August 22, 2001.

76. Randitha, "BinSina Pharmacy Teams up with Acom Research to Provide Healthcare Intelligence Solutions," *Press Release*, September 28, 2009, http://pressrelease.smartoman.com/?p=845.

77. For other examples, see Paul W. Farris, Neil T. Bendle, Phillip E. Pfeifer, and David J. Reibstein, *Marketing Metrics: 50+ Metrics Every Executive Should Master* (Upper Saddle River, NJ: Wharton School Publishing, 2006); Marion Debruyne and Katrina Hubbard, "Marketing Metrics," working paper series, Conference Summary, Marketing Science Institute, Report No. 00-119, 2000.

78. Alfred R. Oxenfeldt, "How to Use Market-Share Measurement," *Harvard Business Review*, January–February 1969, pp. 59–68.

79. There is a one-half chance that a successive observation will be higher or lower. Therefore, the probability of finding six successively higher values is given by (1/2) to the sixth, or 1/64.

80. Alternatively, companies need to focus on factors affecting shareholder value. The goal of marketing planning is to increase shareholder value, which is the present value of the future income stream created by the company's present actions. Rate-of-return analysis usually focuses on only one year's results. See, Alfred Rapport, *Creating Shareholder Value*, rev. edn (New York: Free Press, 1997).

81. For additional reading on financial analysis, see Peter L. Mullins, *Measuring Customer and Product-Line Profitability* (Washington, DC: Distribution Research and Education Foundation, 1984).

82. Robin Cooper and Robert S. Kaplan, "Profit Priorities from Activity-Based Costing," *Harvard Business Review*, May–June 1991, pp. 130–135.

83. Sam R. Goodman, *Increasing Corporate Profitability* (New York: Ronald Press, 1982), chapter 1. Also see Bernard J. Jaworski, Vlasis Stathakopoulos, and H. Shanker Krishnan, "Control Combinations in Marketing: Conceptual Framework and Empirical Evidence," *Journal of Marketing*, January 1993, pp. 57–69.

84. Philip Kotler, William Gregor, and William Rodgers, "The Marketing Audit Comes of Age," *Sloan Management Review*, Winter 1989, pp. 49–62. Frederick Reichheld, *The Loyalty Effect* (Boston: Harvard Business School Press, 1996) discusses attrition of the figures.

85. Useful checklists for a marketing self-audit can be found in Aubrey Wilson, *Aubrey Wilson's Marketing Audit Checklists* (London: McGraw-Hill, 1982); Mike Wilson, *The Management of Marketing* (Westmead, England: Gower Publishing, 1980). A marketing audit software program is described in Ben M. Enis and Stephen J. Garfein, "The Computer-Driven Marketing Audit," *Journal of Management Inquiry*, December 1992, pp. 306–318.

86. Kotler, Gregor, and Rodgers, "The Marketing Audit Comes of Age," pp. 49–62.

Appendix A

A. Background information and market data adapted from Sascha Segan, "Motorola RAZR2: The RAZR2 Cuts Four Ways," *PC Magazine*, October 2, 2007, pp. 32–33; Walter S. Mossberg, "Apple's iPod Touch Is a Beauty of a Player Short on Battery Life," *Wall Street Journal*, September 20, 2007, p. B1; "Roam If You Want To," *PC World*, September 2007, p. 134; Sascha Segam, "Exclusive: One RAZR2, Four Ways to Cut It," *PC Magazine Online*, August 13, 2007, www.pcmag.com; "Apple Unlikely to Budge Anytime Soon on iPhone Pricing," *InformationWeek*, July 26, 2007; "Smartphones Get Smarter, Thanks in Part to the iPhone," *InformationWeek*, July 21, 2007; "Nine Alternatives to Apple's iPhone," *InformationWeek*, June 28, 2007; "Hospital Uses PDA App for Patient Transport," *Health Data Management*, June 2007, p. 14; Jessica E. Vascellaro and Pui-Wing Tam, "RIM's New Gear Fuels Profit Surge; Palm Sputters," *Wall Street Journal*, June 29, 2007, p. B4; "Smart Phones Force Dell from Handhelds," *MicroScope*, April 23, 2007; "2005 PDA Shipments Set Record," *Business Communications Review*, April 2006, p. 6; "Smartphone Market Grows Fast Despite Challenges," *Appliance*, March 2006, p. 16.

Glossary

A

activity-based cost (ABC) accounting | التكلفة على أساس النشاط
Procedures that can quantify the true profitability of different activities by identifying their actual costs.

advertising | الإعلان
Any paid form of nonpersonal presentation and promotion of ideas, goods, or services by an identified sponsor.

advertising goal | الهدف الإعلاني
A specific communication task and achievement level to be accomplished with a specific audience in a specific period of time.

advertorials | مقالات إعلانية
Print ads that offer editorial content that reflects favorably on the brand and resemble newspaper or magazine content.

alliances and affiliate programs | التحالفات وبرامج الشركات التابعة
When one company works with another one and they advertise each other.

anchoring and adjustment heuristic | السعر الاسترشادي والمعدل
When consumers arrive at an initial judgment and then make adjustments of their first impressions based on additional information.

arm's-length price | سعر غير تفضيلي
The price charged by other competitors for the same or a similar product.

aspirational groups | مجموعات يطمح إليها
Groups a person hopes or would like to join.

associative network memory model | نموذج ذاكرة الشبكة المرتبطة
A conceptual representation that views memory as consisting of a set of nodes and interconnecting links, where nodes represent stored information or concepts and links represent the strength of association between this information or concepts.

attitude | الاتجاه
A person's enduring favorable or unfavorable evaluation, emotional feeling, and action tendencies toward some object or idea.

augmented product | المنتج المعزّز
A product that includes features that go beyond consumer expectations and differentiate the product from competitors.

availability heuristic | التوفر التقريبي
When consumers base their predictions on the quickness and ease with which a particular example of an outcome comes to mind.

available market | السوق المتاح
The set of consumers who have interest, income, and access to a particular offer.

average cost | متوسط التكلفة
The cost per unit at a given level of production; it is equal to total costs divided by production.

B

backward invention | منتج موائم لاحتياجات السوق
Reintroducing earlier product forms that can be well adapted to a foreign country's needs.

banner ads (internet) | شعارات إعلانية (الإنترنت)
Small, rectangular boxes containing text and perhaps a picture to support a brand.

basic product | المنتج الأساسي
What specifically the actual product is.

brand | علامة تجارية
A name, term, sign, symbol, or design, or a combination of them, intended to identify the goods or services of one seller or group of sellers and to differentiate them from those of competitors.

brand associations | التداعيات المرتبطة بالعلامة التجارية
All brand-related thoughts, feelings, perceptions, images, experiences, beliefs, attitudes, and so on that become linked to a brand.

brand audit | تدقيق العلامة التجارية
A consumer-focused exercise that involves a series of procedures to assess the health of the brand, uncover its sources of brand equity, and suggest ways to improve and leverage its equity.

brand awareness | الوعي بالعلامة التجارية
Consumers' ability to identify the brand under different conditions, as reflected by their brand recognition or recall performance.

brand contact | معلومات العلامة التجارية
Any information-bearing experience a customer or prospect has with the brand, the product category, or the market that relates to the marketer's product or service.

brand development index (BDI) | مؤشر قوة العلامة التجارية
The index of brand sales to category sales.

brand dilution | إضعاف العلامة التجارية
When consumers no longer associate a brand with a specific product or highly similar products, and start thinking less favorably about the brand.

brand elements | عناصر العلامة التجارية
Those trademarkable devices that serve to identify and differentiate the brand such as a brand name, logo, or character.

brand equity | قيمة العلامة التجارية
The added value endowed to products and services.

brand extension | توسيع نطاق العلامة التجارية
A company's use of an established brand to introduce a new product.

brand image | الصورة العامة للعلامة التجارية
The set of beliefs, ideas, and impressions a person holds regarding a company or product.

brand knowledge | المعرفة المرتبطة بالعلامة التجارية
All the thoughts, feelings, images, experiences, beliefs, and so on that become associated with the brand.

brand line | خط إنتاج العلامة التجارية
All products, original as well as line and category extensions, sold under a particular brand name.

brand mix | تشكيلة العلامات التجارية عند بائع
The set of all brand lines that a particular seller makes available to buyers.

brand personality | الصفات المرتبطة بالعلامة التجارية
The specific mix of human traits that may be attributed to a particular brand.

brand portfolio | مجموعة العلامات التجارية وخطوط الإنتاج
The set of all brands and brand lines a particular firm offers for sale to buyers in a particular category.

brand promise | وعد العلامة التجارية
The marketer's vision of what the brand must be and do for consumers.

brand tracking studies | دراسات تتبع العلامة التجارية
Studies that collect quantitative data from consumers on a routine basis over time to provide marketers with consistent, baseline information about how their brands and marketing programs are performing on key dimensions.

brand valuation | تقييم العلامة التجارية
An estimate of the total financial value of the brand.

brand value chain | سلسلة القيمة للعلامة التجارية
A structured approach to assessing the sources and outcomes of brand equity and the manner in which marketing activities create brand value.

brand-asset management team (BAMT) | فريق إدارة أصول العلامة التجارية
A team that runs each major brand, consisting of key representatives from functions that affect a brand's performance.

branded entertainment | أنشطة ترفيهية تدعم العلامة التجارية
Using sports, music, arts, or other entertainment activities to build brand equity.

branded variants | منتج له مواصفات خاصة
Specific brand lines uniquely supplied to different retailers or distribution channels.

branding | التمييز بالعلامة التجارية
Endowing products and services with the power of a brand.

branding strategy | استراتيجية التمييز التجاري
The number and nature of common and distinctive brand elements applied to the different products sold by the firm.

breakeven analysis | تحليل نقطة التعادل
A means by which management estimates how many units of the product the company would have to sell to break even with the given price and cost structure.

brick-and-click | التجارة متعددة القنوات
Existing companies that have added an online site for information and/or e-commerce.

business database | قاعدة بيانات الأعمال
Complete information about business customers' past purchases; past volumes, prices, and profits.

business market | سوق الأعمال
All the organizations that acquire goods and services used in the production of other products or services that are sold, rented, or supplied to others.

C

capital items | السلع الرأسمالية
Long-lasting goods that facilitate developing or managing the finished product.

captive products | المنتجات المساندة
Products that are necessary to the use of other products, such as razor blades or film.

category extension | توسيع فئة المنتجات
Using the parent brand to brand a new product outside the product category currently served by the parent brand.

category membership | فئة المنتجات
The products or sets of products with which a brand competes and which function as close substitutes.

cause-related marketing | التسويق المرتبط بالمصلحة المشتركة
Marketing that links a firm's contributions to a designated cause to customers' direct or indirect engagement in revenue-producing transactions with the firm.

channel advantage | ميزة قناة التوزيع
When a company successfully switches its customers to lower-cost channels, while assuming no loss of sales or deterioration in service quality.

channel conflict | الصراع بين القنوات التسويقية
When one channel member's actions prevent another channel member from achieving its goal.

channel coordination | تنسيق قنوات التوزيع
When channel members are brought together to advance the goals of the channel, as opposed to their own potentially incompatible goals.

channel power | قدرة قناة التوزيع
The ability to alter channel members' behavior so that they take actions they would not have taken otherwise.

club membership programs | البرامج المرتبطة بالعضوية لنادي
Membership to certain clubs that can be open to everyone who purchases a product or service, or they can be limited to an affinity group or those willing to pay a fee.

clustered preferences | أولويات متجمعة
A market preference segment that occurs when natural market segments emerge from groups of consumers with shared preferences.

co-branding | العلامة التجارية المشتركة
When two or more well-known brands are combined into a joint product or marketed together in some fashion.

communication adaptation | مواءمة الإعلانات التجارية
Changing marketing communications programs for each local market.

communication-effect research | بحث تأثير الإعلانات التجارية
Determining whether an ad is communicating effectively.

company demand | حجم الطلب على الشركة
The company's estimated share of market demand at alternative levels of company marketing effort in a given time period.

company sales forecast | التنبؤ بمبيعات الشركة
The expected level of company sales based on a chosen marketing plan and an assumed marketing environment.

company sales potential | المبيعات المتوقعة للشركة
Sales limit approached by company demand as company marketing effort increases relative to that of competitors.

competitive advantage | الميزة التنافسية
A company's ability to perform in one or more ways that competitors cannot or will not match.

conformance quality | نوعية التوافق
The degree to which all the produced units are identical and meet the promised specifications.

conjoint analysis | تحليل الاقتران
A method for deriving the utility values that consumers attach to varying levels of a product's attributes.

conjunctive heuristic | المستوى الحاسم
The consumer sets a minimum acceptable cutoff level for each attribute and chooses the first alternative that meets the minimum standard for all attributes.

consumer behaviour | سلوك المستهلك
The study of how individuals, groups, and organizations select, buy, use, and dispose of goods, services, ideas, or experiences to satisfy their needs and wants.

consumer involvement | مشاركة العميل
The level of engagement and active processing undertaken by the consumer in responding to a marketing stimulus.

consumerist movement | حركة حماية المستهلك
An organized movement of citizens and government to strengthen the rights and powers of buyers in relation to sellers.

consumption system | نظام الاستهلاك
The way the user performs the tasks of getting and using products and related services.

containerization | شحن البضائع في حاويات
Putting the goods in boxes or trailers that are easy to transfer between two transportation modes.

content-target advertising | الإعلان المستهدف للمحتوى
Links ads not to keywords but to the contents of Web pages.

contractual sales force | الموظفون المتعاقدون للمبيعات
Manufacturers' reps, sales agents, and brokers, who are paid a commission based on sales.

convenience goods | بضائع استهلاكية
Goods the consumer purchases frequently, immediately, and with a minimum of effort.

conventional marketing channel | قناة تسويق تقليدية
An independent producer, wholesaler(s), and retailer(s).

core benefit | الفائدة الفعلية
The service or benefit the customer is really buying.

core competency | الصفة التنافسيّة المميزة
Attribute that (1) is a source of competitive advantage in that it makes a significant contribution to perceived customer benefits, (2) has applications in a wide variety of markets, (3) is difficult for competitors to imitate.

core values | القيم الأساسية
The belief systems that underlie consumer attitudes and behavior, and that determine people's choices and desires over the long term.

corporate culture | ثقافة الشركة
The shared experiences, stories, beliefs, and norms that characterize an organization.

corporate retailing | منافذ الشركة للبيع بالتجزئة
Corporately owned retailing outlets that achieve economies of scale, greater purchasing power, wider brand recognition, and better-trained employees.

countertrade | التجارة عن طريق تبادل السلع بدلا من المال (المقايضة)
International trade involving the direct or indirect exchange of goods for other goods instead of cash.

critical path scheduling (CPS) | جدولة المسار الحرج
A network-planning technique that uses a master chart to show simultaneous and sequential activities that must take place to launch a product.

cues | المحفّزات
Stimuli that determine when, where, and how a person responds.

culture | ثقافة
The fundamental determinant of a person's wants and behavior.

customer churn | ارتداد العميل
High customer defection.

customer consulting | تقديم المشورة للعميل
Data, information systems, and advice services that the seller offers to buyers.

customer database | قاعدة بيانات العملاء
An organized collection of comprehensive information about individual customers or prospects that is current, accessible, and actionable for marketing purposes.

customer equity | قيمة العميل
The total combined customer lifetime values of all of the company's customers.

customer lifetime value (CLV) | القيمة الدائمة للعملاء
The net present value of the stream of future profits expected over the customer's lifetime purchases.

customer mailing list | القائمة البريدية للعملاء
A set of names, addresses, and telephone numbers.

customer perceived value (CPV) | القيمة المدركة للعميل
The difference between the prospective customer's evaluation of all the benefits and all the costs of an offering and the perceived alternatives.

customer profitability analysis (CPA) | تحليل ربحية العميل
A means of assessing and ranking customer profitability through accounting techniques such as Activity-Based Costing (ABC).

customer relationship management (CRM) | إدارة علاقات المستهلكين
Managing detailed information about individual customers and carefully managing customer 'touch points' in order to maximize customer loyalty.

customer training | تدريب العميل
Training the customer's employees to use the vendor's equipment properly and efficiently.

customer-based brand equity |
قيمة العلامة التجارية بناء على استجابة المستهلك
The differential effect that brand knowledge has on a consumer response to the marketing of that brand.

customer-management organization | منظمة إدارة العملاء
Companies organized to understand and deal with individual customers rather than with the mass market or even market segments.

customer-performance scorecard | بطاقة تقييم الأداء وفقاً للعملاء
How well the company is doing year after year on particular customer-based measures.

customer-value analysis | التحليل القيمي للعميل
Report of the company's strengths and weaknesses relative to various competitors.

customer-value hierarchy | تدرج القيمة للمنتج
Five product levels that must be addressed by marketers in planning a market offering.

customerization | توظيف جميع العوامل الممكنة لخدمة الزبون
The combination of operationally driven mass customization with customized marketing in a way that empowers consumers to design the product and service offering of their choice.

D

data warehouse | مستودع البيانات
A collection of current data captured, organized, and stored in a company's contact center.

database marketing | تسويق قاعدة البيانات
The process of building, maintaining, and using customer databases and other databases for the purpose of contacting, transacting, and building customer relationships.

datamining | تنقيب في البيانات
The extracting of useful information about individuals, trends, and segments fom the mass of data.

delivery | التسليم
How well the product or service is delivered to the customer.

demand chain planning | تخطيط سلسلة الطلب
The process of designing the supply chain based on adopting a target market perspective and working backward.

design | التصميم
The totality of features that affect how a product looks, feels, and functions in terms of customer requirements.

diffused preferences | أولويات متضاربة
A market preference segment that occurs when consumer preferences vary greatly.

direct (company) sales force | موظفو المبيعات المباشرون (للشركة)
Full- or part-time paid employees who work exclusively for the company.

direct marketing | التسويق المباشر
The use of consumer-direct (CD) channels to reach and deliver goods and services to customers without using marketing middlemen.

direct product profitability (DDP) | الربحية المباشرة للمنتج
A way of measuring a product's handling costs from the time it reaches the warehouse until a customer buys it in the retail store.

direct-order marketing | التسويق بالأمر المباشر
Marketing in which direct marketers seek a measurable response, typically a customer order.

discrimination | التمييز
The process of recognizing differences in sets of similar stimuli and adjusting responses accordingly.

display ads | إعلانات في صفحات الإنترنت
Small, rectangular boxes containing text and/or a picture that companies pay to place on relevant websites.

dissociative groups | المجموعات المرفوضة
Those groups whose values or behavior an individual rejects.

distribution programming | برمجة التوزيع
Building a planned, professionally managed, vertical marketing system that meets the needs of both manufacturer and distributors.

dual adaptation | المواءمة المزدوجة
Adapting both the product and the communications to the local market.

dumping | إغراق السوق بالبضائع
Situation in which a company charges either less than its costs or less than it charges in its home market, in order to enter or win a market.

durability | التحملية
A measure of a product's expected operating life under natural or stressful conditions.

E

e-business | إدارة الأعمال إلكترونياً
The use of electronic means and platforms to conduct a company's business.

e-commerce | التجارة الإلكترونية
A company or site offers to transact or facilitate the selling of products and services online.

e-marketing | التسويق الإلكتروني
Company efforts to inform buyers, communicate, promote, and sell its products and services over the internet.

e-purchasing | الشراء الإلكتروني
Purchase of goods, services, and information from various online suppliers.

elimination-by-aspects heuristic | الاستبعاد بمقارنة الميزات
The consumer compares brands on an attribute selected probabilistically, and brands are eliminated if they do not meet minimum acceptable cutoff levels.

environmental threat | تهديد بيئي
A challenge posed by an unfavorable trend or development that would lead to lower sales or profit.

everyday low pricing (EDLP) | التسعير المخفض المستدام
In retailing, a constant low price with few or no price promotions and special sales.

exchange | التبادل
The process of obtaining a desired product from someone by offering something in return.

exclusive distribution | التوزيع الحصري
Severely limiting the number of intermediaries, in order to maintain control over the service level and outputs offered by resellers.

expectancy-value model | نموذج قيمة التوقع
Consumers evaluate products and services by combining their brand beliefs—positive and negative—according to their weighted importance.

expected product | المنتج المتوقع
A set of attributes and conditions buyers normally expect when they purchase this product.

experience curve (learning curve) | منحنى الخبرة (منحنى التعلم)
A decline in the average cost with accumulated production experience.

experimental research | البحث التجريبي
Gathering primary data by selecting matched groups of subjects, giving them different treatments, controlling related factors, and checking for differences in group responses.

F

fad | صرعة
A craze that is unpredictable, short-lived, and without social, economic, and political significance.

family brand | عائلة العلامة التجارية
A parent brand that is already associated with multiple products through brand extensions.

family of orientation | العائلة الأصلية (الوالدان والأشقاء)
Parents and siblings.

family of procreation | العائلة بالإنجاب (الزوجة والأطفال)
Spouse and children.

features | الميزات
Things that enhance the basic function of a product.

fixed costs (overhead) | (تكاليف أساسية) التكاليف الثابتة
Costs that do not vary with production or sales revenue.

flexible market offering | عرض السوق المرن
(1) A naked solution containing the product and service elements that all segment members value, and (2) discretionary options that some segment members value.

focus group | فئة (مجموعة) تمثيلية
A gathering of six to ten people who are carefully selected based on certain demographic, psychographic, or other considerations and brought together to discuss various topics of interest.

forecasting | التنبؤ
The art of anticipating what buyers are likely to do under a given set of conditions.

form | الشكل
The size, shape, or physical structure of a product.

forward invention | ابتكار منتج جديد
Creating a new product to meet a need in another country.

frequency program (FP) | برامج التكرار
Program designed to provide rewards to customers who buy frequently and in substantial amounts.

G

generics | منتجات بدون علامة تجارية
Unbranded, plainly packaged, less expensive versions of common products.

goal formulation | صياغة الأهداف
The process of developing specific goals for the planning period.

global firm | شركة عالمية
A firm that operates in more than one country and captures R&D, production, logistical, marketing, and financial advantages in its costs and reputation that are not available to purely domestic competitors.

global industry | صناعة عالمية
An industry in which the strategic positions of competitors in major geographic or national markets are fundamentally affected by their overall global positions.

going-rate pricing | التسعير على أساس السعر الجاري
Price based largely on competitors' prices.

gray market | السوق الرمادية
Branded products diverted from normal or authorized distribution channels in the country of product origin or across international borders.

H

hedonic bias | النزعة التلذذية
The view that people have a general tendency to attribute success to themselves and failure to external causes.

heuristics | المنهج التجريبي
Rules of thumb or mental shortcuts in the decision process.

high-low pricing | تسعير بأعلى الأسعار مع تقديم تخفيضات متكررة
Charging higher prices on an everyday basis but then running frequent promotions and special sales.

holistic marketing | التسويق الشمولي
A concept based on the development, design, and implementation of marketing programs, processes, and activities that recognizes their breadth and interdependencies.

homogeneous preferences | أولويات متشابهة
A market preference segment that occurs when all consumers have roughly the same preference and the market shows no natural segments.

horizontal marketing system | نظام التسويق الأفقي
Two or more unrelated companies put together resources or programs to exploit an emerging market opportunity.

hub-and-spoke system | نظام المحور والفروع
A term used to describe product and brand management, where the brand or product manager is figuratively at the center, with spokes emanating out to various departments.

hybrid channels | قنوات توزيع هجينة
Use of multiple channels of distribution to reach customers in a defined market.

I

image | تصور
The set of beliefs, ideas, and impressions a person holds regarding an object.

industry | صناعة
A group of firms that offer a product or class of products that are close substitutes for one another.

informational appeal | الجذب الإعلامي
A communication strategy ruled by logic and reason used by marketers that elaborates on product or service attributes or benefits.

ingredient branding | وسم المكون بالعلامة التجارية
A special case of co-branding that involves creating brand equity for materials, components, or parts that are necessarily contained within other branded products.

innovation | ابتكار
Any good, service, or idea that is perceived by someone as new.

innovation diffusion process | عملية انتشار المبتكرات
The spread of a new idea from its source of invention or creation to its ultimate users or adopters.

installation | التركيب
The work done to make a product operational in its planned location.

institutional market | السوق المؤسسي
Schools, hospitals, nursing homes, prisons, and other institutions that must provide goods and services to people in their care.

integrated logistics systems (ILS) | نظم اللوجستيات المتكاملة
Materials management, material flow systems, and physical distribution, abetted by information technology (IT).

integrated marketing | التسويق المتكامل
Mixing and matching marketing activities to maximize their individual and collective efforts.

integrated marketing communications (IMC) |
اتصالات التسويق المتكامل
A concept of marketing communications planning that recognizes the added value of a comprehensive plan.

intensive distribution | التوزيع المكثف
The manufacturer placing the goods or services in as many outlets as possible.

internal branding | الترويج داخل الشركة
Activities and processes that help to inform and inspire employees.

interstitials | صفحات الإعلان البينية
Advertisements, often with video or animation, that pop up between changes on a website.

J

joint venture | شركة محاصة
A company in which multiple investors share ownership and control.

L

learning | التعلم
Changes in an individual's behavior arising from experience.

lexicographic heuristic | الاختيار على أساس ميزات العلامة التجارية
A consumer chooses the best brand on the basis of its perceived most important attribute.

licensed product | منتج مرخص
One whose brand name has been licensed to other manufacturers who actually make the product.

life-cycle cost | تكلفة دورة حياة المنتج
The product's purchase cost plus the discounted cost of maintenance and repair less the discounted salvage value.

life stage | مرحلة الحياة
Stages of life that define a person's major concern, such as going through a divorce or deciding to buy a new home.

life style | نمط الحياة
A person's pattern of living in the world as expressed in activities, interests, and opinions.

line extension | توسيع خط الإنتاج
The parent brand is used to brand a new product that targets a new market segment within a product category currently served by the parent brand.

line stretching | تمديد خط الإنتاج
A company lengthens its product line beyond its current range.

long-term memory (LTM) | ذاكرة طويلة المدى
A permanent repository of information.

loyalty | الولاء
A commitment to rebuy or re-patronize a preferred product or service.

M

maintenance and repair | الصيانة والإصلاح
The service program for helping customers keep purchased products in good working order.

market | السوق
The set of all actual and potential buyers of a product or service.

market demand | طلب السوق
The total volume of a product that would be bought by a defined customer group in a defined geographical area in a defined time period in a defined marketing environment under a defined marketing program.

market forecast | التنبؤ بالسوق
The market demand corresponding to the level of industry marketing expenditure.

market logistics | لوجستيات السوق
Planning the infrastructure to meet demand, then implementing and controlling the physical flows or materials and final goods from points of origin to points of use, to meet customer requirements at a profit.

market opportunity analysis (MOA) | تحليل فرص السوق
System used to determine the attractiveness and probability of success.

market partitioning | تقسيم السوق
The process of investigating the hierarchy of attributes consumers examine in choosing a brand, if they use phased decision strategies.

market penetration index | مؤشر اختراق السوق
A comparison of the current level of market demand to the potential demand level.

market potential | طاقة السوق
The upper limit to market demand whereby increased marketing expenditures would not be expected to stimulate further demand.

market share | حصة السوق
The share of the market controlled by a particular brand, product or company.

market-buildup method | طريقة تراكم السوق
Identifying all the potential buyers in each market and estimating their potential purchases.

market-centred organization | منظمة قائمة على السوق
A marketing department organized along specific market segments.

market-management organization | منظمة إدارة السوق
A marketing department organization where marketing managers supervise market or industry specialists, used when customers fall into different user groups with distinct buying preferences and behaviors.

market-penetration pricing | التسعير على أساس اختراق السوق
Pricing strategy where prices start low to drive higher sales volume from price-sensitive customers and produce productivity gains.

market-skimming pricing | التسعير على أساس كشط السوق
Pricing strategy where prices start high and are slowly lowered over time to maximize profits from less price-sensitive customers.

marketer | المُسَوِّق
Someone who seeks a response (attention, a purchase, a vote, a donation) from another party, called the prospect.

marketing | التسويق
The process of planning and executing the conception, pricing, promotion, and distribution of ideas, goods, and services to create exchanges that satisfy individual and organizational goals.

marketing audit | تدقيق التسويق
A comprehensive, systematic, independent, and periodic examination of a company's or business unit's marketing environment, objectives, strategies, and activities.

marketing channel system | نظام قنوات التسويق
The particular set of marketing channels employed by a firm.

marketing channels | قنوات التسويق
Sets of interdependent organizations involved in the process of making a product or service available for use or consumption.

marketing communications | الاتصالات التسويقية
The means by which firms attempt to inform, persuade, and remind consumers—directly or indirectly—about products and brands that they sell.

marketing communications mix | مزيج الاتصالات التسويقية
Advertising, sales promotion, events and experiences, public relations and publicity, direct marketing, and personal selling.

marketing decision support system (MDSS) | نظام دعم قرار التسويق
A coordinated collection of data, systems, tools, and techniques with supporting software and hardware by which an organization gathers and interprets relevant information from business and the environment and turns it into a basis for marketing action

marketing implementation | التنفيذ التسويقي
The process that turns marketing plans into action assignments and ensures that such assignments are executed in a manner that accomplishes the plan's stated objectives.

marketing information system (MIS) | نظام المعلومات التسويقية
People, equipment, and procedures to gather, sort, analyze, evaluate, and distribute information to marketing decision makers.

marketing insights | المعرفة التسويقية
Diagnostic information that shows how and why we observe certain effects in the marketplace.

marketing intelligence system | نظام الاستخبارات التسويقية
A set of procedures and sources managers use to obtain everyday information about developments in the marketing environment.

marketing management | إدارة التسويق
The art and science of choosing target markets and getting, keeping, and growing customers through creating, delivering, and communicating superior customer value.

marketing metrics | معايير التسويق
The set of measures that helps firms to quantify, compare, and interpret their marketing performance.

marketing network | شبكة التسويق
The company and its supporting stakeholders, with whom it has built mutually profitable business relationships.

marketing opportunity | الفرصة التسويقية
An area of buyer need and interest in which there is a high probability that a company can profitably satisfy that need.

marketing plan | الخطة التسويقية
Written document that summarizes what the marketer has learned about the marketplace, indicates how the firm plans to reach its marketing objectives, and helps direct and coordinate the marketing effort.

marketing public relations (MPR) | العلاقات التسويقية العامة
Publicity and other activities that build corporate or product image to facilitate marketing goals.

marketing research | بحث تسويقي
The systematic design, collection, analysis, and reporting of data and findings relevant to a specific marketing situation facing the company.

markup | رفع السعر
Pricing an item by adding a standard increase to the product's cost.

mass customization | التخصيص الشامل
The ability of a company to meet each customer's requirements and to prepare on a mass basis individually designed products, services, programs, and communications.

mass marketing | التسويق الشامل
Mass production, mass distribution, and mass promotion of one product for all buyers.

materials and parts | المواد والأجزاء
Goods that enter the manufacturer's product completely.

media selection | اختيار وسائل الإعلام
Finding the most cost-effective media to deliver the desired number and type of exposures to the target audience.

megamarketing | التسويق الشمولي
The strategic coordination of economic, psychological, political, and public relations skills to gain the cooperation of a number of parties in order to enter or operate in a given market.

megatrends | الاتجاهات الاستهلاكية
Large social, economic, political, and technological changes that are slow to form, and once in place, have an influence for seven to ten years or longer.

membership groups | مجموعات العضوية
Groups having a direct influence on a person.

memory encoding | ترميز الذاكرة
How and where information gets into memory.

memory retrieval | استعادة الذاكرة
How and from where information is recalled from of memory.

mental accounting | المحاسبة الذهنيّة
The manner by which consumers code, categorize, and evaluate financial outcomes of choices.

microsales analysis | تحليل المبيعات الصغيرة
Examination of specific products and territories that fail to produce expected sales.

microsite | موقع مصغّر
A limited area on the Web managed and paid for by an external advertiser/company.

mission statement | بيان الأهداف
A statement of purpose that an organisation develops to share with managers, employees, and (in many cases) customers.

mixed bundling | بيع المنتجات فردياً أو في حزم
The seller offers goods both individually and in bundles.

motive (drive) | حافز (دافع)
A need that is sufficiently pressing to direct the person to seek satisfaction of the need.

multichannel marketing | التسويق متعدد القنوات
A single firm uses two or more marketing channels to reach one or more customer segments.

multitasking | أداء عدة مهام في نفس الوقت
Doing two or more things at the same time.

N

net price analysis | تحليل السعر الصافي
Analysis that encompasses company list price, average discount, promotional spending, and co-op advertising to arrive at net price.

noncompensatory models | نماذج غير قابلة للتعويض
When consumers do not simultaneously consider all positive and negative attributes in making a decision.

O

opinion leader | رائد الرأي
The person in informal, product-related communications who offers advice or information about a specific product or product category.

ordering ease | سهولة الطلب
How easy it is for the customer to place an order with the company.

organization | المنظمة
A company's structures, policies, and corporate culture.

organizational buying | الشراء المؤسسي
The decision-making process by which formal organizations establish the need for purchased products and services and identify, evaluate, and choose among alternative brands and suppliers.

overall market share | حصة السوق الشاملة
The company's sales expressed as a percentage of total market sales.

overheads | المصروفات العامة
See 'fixed costs'.

P

packaging | التعبئة والتغليف
The activities of designing and producing the container or wrapper for a product.

paid-search | البحث المدفوع مقدماً
Sponsored search results, where companies pay to have ads for products or services displayed when keywords are entered into a search engine.

pay per click ads | إعلانات الدفع بالنقر
See 'paid-search'.

parent brand | العلامة التجارية الأم
An existing brand that gives birth to a brand extension.

partner relationship management (PRM) | إدارة علاقات الشريك
Activities the firm undertakes to build mutually satisfying long-term relations with key partners such as suppliers, distributors, ad agencies, and marketing research suppliers.

penetrated market | السوق المخترق
The set of consumers who are buying a company's product.

perceived value | القيمة المدركة
The value promised by the company's value proposition and perceived by the customer.

perception | الإدراك
The process by which an individual selects, organizes, and interprets information to create a meaningful picture of the world.

performance quality | جودة الأداء
The level at which the product's primary characteristics operate.

personal communications channels | قنوات الاتصالات الشخصية
Two or more persons communicating directly face-to-face, person-to-audience, over the telephone, or through e-mail.

personal influence | التأثير الشخصي
The effect one person has on another's attitude or purchase probability.

personality | الشخصية
A set of distinguishing human psychological traits that lead to relatively consistent responses to environmental stimuli.

place advertising (also out-of-home advertising) | إعلان خارجي (أيضاً إعلان خارج المنزل)
Ads that appear outside of home and where consumers work and play.

point-of-purchase (P-O-P) | نقطة الشراء
The location where a purchase is made, typically thought of in terms of a retail setting.

points-of-difference (PODs) | نقاط الاختلاف
Attributes or benefits consumers strongly associate with a brand, positively evaluate, and believe they could not find to the same extent with a competitive brand.

points-of-parity (POPs) | نقاط التكافؤ
Associations that are not necessarily unique to the brand but may in fact be shared with other brands.

positioning | التمركز
Arranging for a product to occupy a clear, distinctive, and desirable place relative to competing products in the minds of target consumers.

potential market | السوق المرتقب
The set of consumers who profess a sufficient level of interest in a market offer.

potential product | منتج مرتقب
All the possible augmentations and transformations the product or offering might undergo in the future.

price discrimination | التمييز بين الأسعار
A company sells a product or service at two or more prices that do not reflect a proportional difference in costs.

price escalation | تصاعد الأسعار
An increase in the price of a product due to added costs of selling it in different countries.

primary groups | المجموعات الأولية
Groups with which a person interacts continuously and informally, such as family, friends, neighbors, and co-workers.

principle of congruity | مبدأ التطابق
Psychological mechanism that states that consumers like to see seemingly related objects as being as similar as possible in their favorability.

private label brand | علامة تجارية خاصة
Brands that retailers and wholesalers develop and market.

product | المنتج
Anything that can be offered to a market for attention, acquisition, use, or consumption that might satisfy a want or need.

product adaptation | مواءمة المنتج
Altering the product to meet local conditions or preferences.

product assortment | تشكيلة المنتج
The set of all products and items a particular seller offers for sale.

product invention | ابتكار المنتج
Creating something new via product development or other means.

product mix | تشكيلة المنتج
See 'product assortment'.

product penetration percentage | النسبة المئوية لاختراق المنتج
The percentage of ownership or use of a product or service in a population.

product system | نظام المنتج
A group of diverse but related items that function in a compatible manner.

product-mix pricing | تسعير تشكيلة المنتجات
Price-setting when a product is part of a product mix.

profitable customer | العميل المربح
A person, household, or company that over time yields a revenue stream that exceeds by an acceptable amount the company's cost stream of attracting, selling, and servicing that customer.

prospect | التوقع
A third party that a marketer seeks a response—a purchase, a vote, a donation—from.

prospect theory | نظرية التوقع
When consumers frame decision alternatives in terms of gains and losses according to a value function.

psychographics | السكوغرافية
The science of using psychology and demographics to better understand consumers.

public | الجمهور
Any group that has an actual or potential interest in or impact on a company's ability to achieve its objectives.

public relations (PR) | العلاقات العامة
A variety of programs designed to promote or protect a company's image or its individual products.

publicity | الدعاية
The task of securing editorial space—as opposed to paid space—in print and broadcast media to promote something.

pull strategy | استراتيجية السحب
When the manufacturer uses advertising and promotion to persuade consumers to ask intermediaries for the product, thus inducing the intermediaries to order it.

purchase probability scale | ميزان احتمالية الشراء
A scale to measure the probability of a buyer making a particular purchase.

pure bundling | المنتجات في حزم فقط
A firm only offers its products as a bundle.

pure-click | شركات موجودة على الإنترنت فقط
Companies that have launched a website without any previous existence as a firm.

push strategy | استراتيجية الدفع
When the manufacturer uses its sales force and trade promotion money to induce intermediaries to carry, promote, and sell the product to end users.

Q

quality | الجودة
The totality of features and characteristics of a product or service that bear on its ability to satisfy stated or implied needs.

questionnaire | استبيان
A set of questions presented to a respondent, for the purposes of a survey or statistical study.

R

reference groups | مجموعات مرجعية
All the groups that have a direct or indirect influence on a person's attitudes or behavior.

reference prices | أسعار مرجعية
Pricing information a consumer retains in memory which is used to interpret and evaluate a new price.

relational equity | القيمة الارتباطية
The cumulative value of the firm's network of relationships with its customers, partners, suppliers, employees, and investors.

relationship marketing | التسويق القائم على العلاقات
Building mutually satisfying long-term relationships with key parties, in order to earn and retain their business.

relative market share | حصة السوق النسبية
Market share in relation to a company's largest competitor.

reliability | الاعتمادية
A measure of the probability that a product will not malfunction or fail within a specified time period.

repairability | قابلية إصلاح المنتج
A measure of the ease of fixing a product when it malfunctions or fails.

representativeness heuristic | التقييم التمثيلي
When consumers base their predictions on how representative or similar an outcome is to other examples.

retailer | بائع التجزئة
A business whose sales come primarily from retailing.

retailing | البيع بالتجزئة
All activities involved in selling goods or services directly to final consumers for their personal, non-business use.

risk analysis | تحليل المخاطر
A method by which possible rates of returns and their probabilities are calculated by obtaining estimates for uncertain variables affecting profitability.

role | الدور
The activities someone or something is expected to perform.

S

sales analysis | تحليل المبيعات
Measuring and evaluating actual sales in relation to goals.

sales budget | موازنة المبيعات
A conservative estimate of the expected volume of sales, used for making current purchasing, production, and cash flow decisions.

sales promotion | ترويج المبيعات
A collection of incentive tools, mostly short term, designed to stimulate quicker or greater purchase of particular products or services by consumers or the trade.

sales quota | حصة من المبيعات
The sales goal set for a product line, company division, or sales representative.

sales-variance analysis | تحليل انحراف المبيعات
A measure of the relative contribution of different factors to a gap in sales performance.

satisfaction | رضاء
A person's feelings of pleasure or disappointment resulting from comparing a product's perceived performance or outcome in relation to his or her expectations.

scenario analysis | تحليل السيناريو
Developing plausible representations of a firm's possible future that make different assumptions about forces driving the market and include different uncertainties.

search-related ads | الإعلانات المرتبطة بالبحث
Ads in which search terms are used as a proxy for the consumer's consumption interests and relevant links to product or service offerings are listed alongside the search results.

secondary groups | المجموعات الثانوية
Groups which tend to be more formal and require less interaction than primary groups, such as religious, professional, and trade-union groups.

selective attention | الاهتمام الانتقائي
The mental process of screening out certain stimuli while noticing others.

selective distortion | التشويه الانتقائي
The tendency to interpret product information in a way that fits consumer perceptions.

selective distribution | توزيع انتقائي
The use of more than a few but less than all of the intermediaries who are willing to carry a particular product.

selective retention | الحفظ الانتقائي
The tendency to recall good points about a product that one likes and forget good points about competing products.

served market | السوق المستهدف
All the buyers who are able and willing to buy a company's product.

served market share | حصة السوق المستهدف
A company's sales expressed as a percentage of the total sales to its served market.

service | الخدمة
Any act or performance that one party can offer to another that is essentially intangible and does not result in the ownership of anything.

share penetration index | مؤشر اختراق الحصة السوقية
A comparison of a company's current market share to its potential market share.

shopping goods | سلع التسوق
Goods that the consumer, in the process of selection and purchase, characteristically compares on such bases as suitability, quality, price, and style.

short-term memory (STM) | ذاكرة قصيرة المدى
A temporary repository of information.

social class | الطبقات الاجتماعية
Homogeneous and enduring divisions in a society, which are hierarchically ordered and whose members share similar values, interests, and behavior.

social marketing | التسويق الاجتماعي
Marketing done by a nonprofit or government organization to further a cause, such as "say no to drugs."

social status | المنزلة الاجتماعية
One's position within his or her own hierarchy or culture.

specialty goods | سلع فريدة / مميزة
Goods that have unique characteristics or brand identification for which a sufficient number of buyers are willing to make a special purchasing effort.

sponsorship | الرعاية
Financial support of an event or activity in return for recognition and acknowledgment as the sponsor.

stakeholder-performance scorecard | بطاقة تقييم أداء أصحاب المصلحة
A measure to track the satisfaction of various constituencies who have a critical interest in and impact on the company's performance.

straight extension | طرح مباشر للمنتج دون تعديل
Introducing a product in a foreign market without any change in the product.

strategic brand management | إدارة استراتيجية للعلامات التجارية
The design and implementation of marketing activities and programs to build, measure, and manage brands to maximize their value.

strategic business unit (SBU) | وحدات أعمال استراتيجية
A single business or collection of related businesses that can be planned separately from the rest of the company, with its own set of competitors and a manager who is responsible for strategic planning and profit performance.

strategic group | مجموعة استراتيجية
Firms pursuing the same strategy directed to the same target market.

strategic marketing plan | خطة تسويق استراتيجية
Lays out the target markets and the value proposition that will be offered, based on analysis of the best market opportunities.

strategy | استراتيجية
A company's game plan for achieving its goals.

sub-brand | علامة تجارية فرعية
A new brand combined with an existing brand.

subculture | ثقافة فرعية
Subdivisions of a culture that provide more specific identification and socialization, such as nationalities, religions, racial groups, and geographical regions.

subliminal perception | الرسائل اللاشعورية
Receiving and processing subconscious messages that affect behavior.

supersegment | تجزئة استثمارية متشابهة
A set of segments sharing some exploitable similarity.

supplies and business services | خدمات الإمدادات والأعمال
Short-term goods and services that facilitate developing or managing the finished product.

supply chain | سلسلة الإمداد
See 'value-delivery network'.

supply chain management (SCM) | إدارة سلسلة الإمداد
Procuring the right inputs (raw materials, components, and capital equipment); converting them efficiently into finished products; and dispatching them to the final destinations.

T

tactical marketing plan | خطة التسويق التكتيكية
Marketing tactics, including product features, promotion, merchandising, pricing, sales channels, and service.

target costing | التكلفة المستهدفة
Deducting the desired profit margin from the price at which a product will sell, given its appeal and competitors' prices.

target market | السوق المستهدف
The part of the qualified available market the company decides to pursue.

target-return pricing | تسعير العائد المستهدف
Determining the price that would yield the firm's target rate of return on investment (ROI).

telemarketing | التسويق عبر الهاتف
The use of telephone and call centers to attract prospects, sell to existing customers, and provide service by taking orders and answering questions.

total costs | التكاليف الإجمالية
The sum of the fixed and variable costs for any given level of production.

total customer cost | تكلفة العميل الإجمالية
The bundle of costs customers expect to incur in evaluating, obtaining, using, and disposing of the given market offering, including monetary, time, energy, and psychological costs.

total customer value | القمية الإجمالية للعميل
The perceived monetary value of the bundle of economic, functional, and psychological benefits customers expect from a given market offering.

total market potential | إجمالي مبيعات السوق المتوقعة
The maximum amount of sales that might be available to all the firms in a given industry, during a given period, under a given level of industry marketing effort and environmental conditions.

total quality management (TQM) | إدارة الجودة الشاملة
An organizationwide approach to continuously improving the quality of all the organization's processes, products, and services.

tracking studies | دراسات تتبعية
Collecting information from consumers on a routine basis over time.

transaction | معاملة تجارية
A trade of values between two or more parties: A gives X to B and receives Y in return.

transfer price | سعر النقل
The price a company charges another unit in the company for goods it ships to foreign subsidiaries.

transformational appeal | الجذب التحولي
A communication strategy used by marketers that elaborates on a non-product-related benefit or image, to stir up emotions that will motivate a purchase.

trend | اتجاه عام
A direction or sequence of events that has some momentum and durability.

two-part pricing | تسعير ثنائي
A fixed fee plus a variable usage fee.

tying agreements | اتفاقات الشراء المرتبط
Agreement in which producers of strong brands sell their products to dealers only if dealers purchase related products or services, such as other products in the brand line.

U

unsought goods | السلع غير المطلوبة
Those the consumer does not know about or does not normally think of buying, such as smoke detectors.

V

value | القيمة
The sum of the perceived tangible and intangible benefits and costs to customers.

value chain | سلسلة الإمدادات؛ سلسلة الأنشطة المضيفة للقيمة
The series of departments that carry out value-creating activities to design, produce, market, deliver, and support a firm's products.

value network | شبكة القيمة
A system of partnerships and alliances that a firm creates to source, augment, and deliver its offerings.

value pricing | تسعير القيمة
Winning loyal customers by charging a fairly low price for a high-quality offering.

value proposition | ستترى القيمة
The whole cluster of benefits the company promises to deliver.

value-delivery network | شبكة التسليم القائمة على القيمة
A company's supply chain and how it partners with specific suppliers and distributors to make products and bring them to markets.

value-delivery system | نظام التسليم القائم على القيمة
All the expectancies the customer will have on the way to obtaining and using the offering.

variable costs | تكاليف متغيرة
Costs that vary directly with the level of production.

venture team | فريق متعدد المهام
A cross-functional group charged with developing a specific product or business.

vertical integration | التكامل الرأسي
Situation in which manufacturers try to control or own their suppliers, distributors, or other intermediaries.

vertical marketing system (VMS) | نظام التسويق الرأسي
Producer, wholesaler(s), and retailer(s) acting as a unified system.

viral marketing | التسويق عبر التداول الإلكتروني
Using the Internet to create word of mouth effects to support marketing efforts and goals.

W

warranties | الضمانات
Formal statements of expected product performance by the manufacturer.

wholesaling | البيع بالجملة
Includes all the activities in selling goods or services to those who buy for resale or business use.

Y

yield pricing | تسعير العائد
Situation in which companies offer (1) discounted but limited early purchases, (2) higher-priced late purchases, and (3) the lowest rates on unsold inventory just before it expires.

Z

zero-level channel (direct-marketing channel) | قناة توزيع مباشر (قناة تسويق مباشر)
A manufacturer selling directly to the final customer.

Index

P

S